GREAT BOOKS OF THE WESTERN WORLD

28. GILBERT
    GALILEO
    HARVEY
29. CERVANTES
30. FRANCIS BACON
31. DESCARTES
    SPINOZA
32. MILTON
33. PASCAL
34. NEWTON
    HUYGENS
35. LOCKE
    BERKELEY
    HUME
36. SWIFT
    STERNE
37. FIELDING
38. MONTESQUIEU
    ROUSSEAU
39. ADAM SMITH
40. GIBBON I
41. GIBBON II
42. KANT
43. AMERICAN STATE PAPERS
    THE FEDERALIST
    J. S. MILL
44. BOSWELL
45. LAVOISIER
    FOURIER
    FARADAY
46. HEGEL
47. GOETHE
48. MELVILLE
49. DARWIN
50. MARX
    ENGELS
51. TOLSTOY
52. DOSTOEVSKY
53. WILLIAM JAMES
54. FREUD

GREAT BOOKS OF THE WESTERN WORLD

ROBERT MAYNARD HUTCHINS, *EDITOR IN CHIEF*

42.

KANT

The Critique of Pure Reason

The Critique of Practical Reason

AND OTHER ETHICAL TREATISES

The Critique of Judgement

BY IMMANUEL KANT

William Benton, *Publisher*

ENCYCLOPÆDIA BRITANNICA, INC.

CHICAGO · LONDON · TORONTO · GENEVA

The Critique of Practical Reason, Fundamental Principles of the Metaphysic of Morals, and *Preface and Introduction to the Metaphysical Elements of Ethics, With a Note on Conscience,* are reprinted from *Kant's Critique of Practical Reason and Other Works on the Theory of Ethics,* published by LONGMANS, GREEN & Co., New York and London, by permission of the Executors of the translator, Thomas Kingsmill Abbott.

General Introduction to the Metaphysic of Morals and *The Science of Right,* translated by W. Hastie, are reprinted by arrangement with T. & T. CLARK, Edinburgh.

The Critique of Judgement, translated by James Creed Meredith, is reprinted by arrangement with OXFORD UNIVERSITY PRESS.

THE UNIVERSITY OF CHICAGO

The Great Books
is published with the editorial advice of the faculties of The University of Chicago

BIOGRAPHICAL NOTE

Immanuel Kant, 1724–1804

Kant was born at Königsberg in East Prussia on April 22, 1724. His father, a saddler in the city, was descended from a Scottish immigrant; his mother was German. Both parents were devoted followers of the Pietist branch of the Lutheran Church, and it was largely through the influence of their pastor that Kant, who was the fourth of eleven children but the eldest surviving son, obtained an education.

In his eighth year Kant entered the Collegium Fredericianum, which his pastor directed. It was a "Latin School," and during the eight and a half years that he was there, Kant acquired a love for the Latin classics, especially for Lucretius. In 1740 he enrolled in the University of Königsberg as a theological student. Though he attended courses in theology, and even preached on one or two occasions, he was principally attracted to mathematics and physics. Given access to the library of his professor in these subjects, he read Newton and Leibniz and in 1744 started his first book, dealing with the problem of kinetic forces. By that time he had decided to pursue an academic career, but on failing to obtain the post of under-tutor in one of the schools attached to the university, he was compelled for financial reasons to withdraw and seek a position as a family tutor.

During the nine years that Kant was a tutor (1746-1755), he was employed by three different families. In this position he was introduced to the influential society of the city, acquired social grace, and made his farthest travels from his native city, which took him to Arnsdorf, about sixty miles from Königsberg. In 1755, aided by a relative, he was able to complete his degree at the university and assume the role of *Privat-docent,* or lecturer. The three dissertations he presented for this post dealt respectively with fire, the first principles of metaphysical knowledge, and "the advantages to natural philosophy of a metaphysic connected with geometry." With the opening of the winter term he began his lectures. At first he restricted himself to mathematics and physics, and that year and the next he published several scientific works, dealing with the different races of men, the nature of winds, the causes of earthquakes, and the general theory of the heavens. But he soon branched into other subjects, including logic, metaphysics, and moral philosophy. He even lectured on fireworks and fortifications, and gave every summer for thirty years a popular course on physical geography. Kant enjoyed great success as a lecturer; his style, which differed markedly from that of his books, was humorous and vivid, enlivened by many examples drawn from his wide reading in English and French literature, and in books of travel and geography, as well as in science and philosophy.

During his fifteen years as a *Privat-docent,* Kant's fame as writer and lecturer steadily increased. Though he failed twice to obtain a professorship at Königsberg, he continued to refuse appointments elsewhere. The only academic preferment he received during this lengthy probation was the post of under-librarian, which he was given in 1766. Finally in 1770 he obtained the chair of logic and metaphysics. In later years he served six times as dean of the philosophical faculty and twice as rector.

Kant's inaugural dissertation as professor, *On the Form and Principles of the Sensible and Intelligible World,* indicated the direction of his philosophical interests. In submitting it to a friend that same year, he wrote: "For about a year I flatter myself that I have attained that conception which I have no fear that I shall ever change, though I may expand it, by means of which all kinds of metaphysical questions can be tested according to sure and easy criteria, and by means of which it can be decided with certainty how far their solution is possible." But it was not until 1781 that the *Critique of Pure Reason* appeared, although he declared that the actual writing took but four or five months. In the same letter he also noted his intention to investigate "pure moral philosophy" and to systematize his metaphysics of morals, which was first accomplished in 1785 with the publication of the *Fundamental Principles of the Metaphysic of Morals.* The *Critique of Practical Reason* was brought out in 1788 and the *Critique of Judgement* two years later.

The "critical philosophy" was soon being taught in every important German-speaking university, and young men flocked to Königsberg as a shrine of philosophy. In some cases the Prussian Government even undertook the expense of their support. Kant came to be consulted as an oracle on all kinds of questions, including such subjects as the lawfulness of vaccination. Such homage did not interrupt Kant's regular habits. Scarcely five feet tall, with a deformed chest, and suffering from weak health, he maintained throughout his life a severe regimen. It was arranged with such regularity that people set their clocks according to his daily walk along the street named for him the Philosopher's Walk. Until old age prevented him, he is said to have missed this regular appearance only on the occasion when Rousseau's *Emile* so engrossed him that for several days he stayed at home.

As early as 1789 Kant's health began to decline seriously. He still had many literary projects, but found it impossible to write more than a few hours a day. In 1792 with the appearance of his work, *On Religion Within the Limits of Reason Alone,* he became involved in a dispute with the Prussian authorities on the right to express religious opinions, and at the request of the government he remained silent for some years on the subject. In 1795 he published his treatise on *Perpetual Peace.* In 1797, after a career of forty-two years, he delivered his last lecture and retired from the university. The following year, by way of asserting his right to resume theological discussions, he wrote on the conflict of the faculties in the university. This proved to be Kant's last book; the large work, at which he labored until his death, on the connection between physics and metaphysics was found to be only a repetition of his already published works. After a gradual decline, which was painful to himself and his friends, he died February 12, 1804.

GENERAL CONTENTS

GENERAL CONTENTS

CONTENTS

CRITIQUE OF PURE REASON

II. TRANSCENDENTAL DOCTRINE OF METHOD

PREFACE TO THE FIRST EDITION, 1781

HUMAN reason, in one sphere of its cognition, is called upon to consider questions, which it cannot decline, as they are presented by its own nature, but which it cannot answer, as they transcend every faculty of the mind.

It falls into this difficulty without any fault of its own. It begins with principles, which cannot be dispensed with in the field of experience, and the truth and sufficiency of which are, at the same time, insured by experience. With these principles it rises, in obedience to the laws of its own nature, to ever higher and more remote conditions. But it quickly discovers that, in this way, its labours must remain ever incomplete, because new questions never cease to present themselves; and thus it finds itself compelled to have recourse to principles which transcend the region of experience, while they are regarded by common sense without distrust. It thus falls into confusion and contradictions, from which it conjectures the presence of latent errors, which, however, it is unable to discover, because the principles it employs, transcending the limits of experience, cannot be tested by that criterion. The arena of these endless contests is called *Metaphysic.*

Time was, when she was the *queen* of all the sciences; and, if we take the will for the deed, she certainly deserves, so far as regards the high importance of her object-matter, this title of honour. Now, it is the fashion of the time to heap contempt and scorn upon her; and the matron mourns, forlorn and forsaken, like Hecuba:

Modo maxima rerum,
Tot generis, natisque potens . . .
Nunc trahor exul, inops.[1]

At first, her government, under the administration of the *dogmatists,* was an absolute *despotism.* But, as the legislative continued to show traces of the ancient barbaric rule, her empire gradually broke up, and intestine wars introduced the reign of *anarchy;* while the *sceptics,* like nomadic tribes, who hate a permanent habitation and settled mode of living, attacked from time to time those who had organized themselves into civil communities. But their number was, very happily, small; and thus they could not entirely put a stop to the exertions of those who persisted in raising new edifices, although on no settled or uniform plan. In recent times the hope dawned upon us of seeing those disputes settled, and the legitimacy of her claims established by a kind of *physiology* of the human understanding—that of the celebrated Locke. But it was found that—although it was affirmed that this so-called queen could not refer her descent to any higher source than that of common experience, a circumstance which necessarily brought suspicion on her claims—as this *genealogy* was incorrect, she persisted in the advancement of her claims to sovereignty. Thus metaphysics necessarily fell back into the antiquated and rotten constitution of *dogmatism,* and again became obnoxious to the contempt from which efforts had been made to save it. At present, as all methods, according to the general persuasion, have been tried in vain, there reigns nought but weariness and complete *indifferentism*—the mother of chaos and night in the scientific world, but at the same time the source of, or at least the prelude to, the re-creation and reinstallation of a science, when it has fallen into confusion, obscurity, and disuse from ill-directed effort.

For it is in reality vain to profess *indifference* in regard to such inquiries, the object of which cannot be indifferent to humanity. Besides, these pretended *indifferentists,* however much they may try to disguise themselves by the assumption of a popular style and by changes on the language of the schools, unavoidably fall into metaphysical declarations and propositions, which they profess to regard with so much contempt. At the same time, this indifference, which has arisen in the world of science, and which relates to that kind of knowledge which we should wish to see destroyed the last, is a phenomenon that well deserves our attention and reflection. It is plainly not the effect of the levity, but of the matured *judgement*[2] of the age,

[1] Ovid, *Metamorphoses.* [xiii, 508-510. "But late on the pinnacle of fame, strong in my many sons . . . now exiled, penniless."]

[2] We very often hear complaints of the shallowness of the present age, and of the decay of profound science. But I do not think that those which rest upon a secure foundation, such as mathematics, physical science, etc., in the least deserve this reproach, but that they rather maintain their ancient fame, and in the latter case, in-

which refuses to be any longer entertained with illusory knowledge. It is, in fact, a call to reason, again to undertake the most laborious of all tasks—that of self-examination—and to establish a tribunal, which may secure it in its well-grounded claims, while it pronounces against all baseless assumptions and pretensions, not in an arbitrary manner, but according to its own eternal and unchangeable laws. This tribunal is nothing less than the *critical investigation of pure reason.*

I do not mean by this a criticism of books and systems, but a critical inquiry into the faculty of reason, with reference to the cognitions to which it strives to attain *without the aid of experience;* in other words, the solution of the question regarding the possibility or impossibility of metaphysics, and the determination of the origin, as well as of the extent and limits of this science. All this must be done on the basis of principles.

This path—the only one now remaining—has been entered upon by me; and I flatter myself that I have, in this way, discovered the cause of—and consequently the mode of removing—all the errors which have hitherto set reason at variance with itself, in the sphere of non-empirical thought. I have not returned an evasive answer to the questions of reason, by alleging the inability and limitation of the faculties of the mind; I have, on the contrary, examined them completely in the light of principles, and, after having discovered the cause of the doubts and contradictions into which reason fell, have solved them to its perfect satisfaction. It is true, these questions have not been solved as dogmatism, in its vain fancies and desires, had expected; for it can only be satisfied by the exercise of magical arts, and of these I have no knowledge. But neither do these come within the compass of our mental powers; and it was the duty of philosophy to destroy the illusions which had their origin in misconceptions, whatever darling hopes and valued expectations may be ruined by its explanations. My chief aim in this work has been thoroughness; and I make bold to say that there is not a single metaphysical problem that does not find its solution, or at least the key to its solution, here. Pure reason is a perfect unity; and therefore, if the principle presented by it prove to be insufficient for the solution of even a single one of those questions to which the very nature of reason gives birth, we must reject it, as we could not be perfectly certain of its sufficiency in the case of the others.

While I say this, I think I see upon the countenance of the reader signs of dissatisfaction mingled with contempt, when he hears declarations which sound so boastful and extravagant; and yet they are beyond comparison more moderate than those advanced by the commonest author of the commonest philosophical programme, in which the dogmatist professes to demonstrate the simple nature of the soul, or the necessity of a primal being. Such a dogmatist promises to extend human knowledge beyond the limits of possible experience; while I humbly confess that this is completely beyond my power. Instead of any such attempt, I confine myself to the examination of reason alone and its pure thought; and I do not need to seek far for the sum-total of its cognition, because it has its seat in my own mind. Besides, common logic presents me with a complete and systematic catalogue of all the simple operations of reason; and it is my task to answer the question how far reason can go, without the material presented and the aid furnished by experience.

So much for the completeness and thoroughness necessary in the execution of the present task. The aims set before us are not arbitrarily proposed, but are imposed upon us by the nature of cognition itself.

The above remarks relate to the *matter* of our critical inquiry. As regards the *form,* there are two indispensable conditions, which any one who undertakes so difficult a task as that of a critique of pure reason, is bound to fulfil. These conditions are *certitude* and *clearness.*

As regards *certitude,* I have fully convinced myself that, in this sphere of thought, *opinion* is perfectly inadmissible, and that everything which bears the least semblance of an hypothesis must be excluded, as of no value in such discussions. For it is a necessary condition of every cognition that is to be established upon *a priori* grounds that it shall be held to be absolutely necessary; much more is this the case with an attempt to determine all pure *a priori* cognition, and to furnish the standard—and consequently an example—of all apodeictic (philosophical)

---

deed, far surpass it. The same would be the case with the other kinds of cognition, if their principles were but firmly established. In the absence of this security, indifference, doubt, and finally, severe criticism are rather signs of a profound habit of thought. Our age is the age of criticism, to which everything must be subjected. The sacredness of religion, and the authority of legislation, are by many regarded as grounds of exemption from the examination of this tribunal. But, if they are exempted, they become the subjects of just suspicion, and cannot lay claim to sincere respect, which reason accords only to that which has stood the test of a free and public examination.

certitude. Whether I have succeeded in what I professed to do, it is for the reader to determine; it is the author's business merely to adduce grounds and reasons, without determining what influence these ought to have on the mind of his judges. But, lest anything he may have said may become the innocent cause of doubt in their minds, or tend to weaken the effect which his arguments might otherwise produce—he may be allowed to point out those passages which may occasion mistrust or difficulty, although these do not concern the main purpose of the present work. He does this solely with the view of removing from the mind of the reader any doubts which might affect his judgement of the work as a whole, and in regard to its ultimate aim.

I know no investigations more necessary for a full insight into the nature of the faculty which we call *understanding,* and at the same time for the determination of the rules and limits of its use, than those undertaken in the second chapter of the "Transcendental Analytic," under the title of *"Deduction of the Pure Conceptions of the Understanding"*; and they have also cost me by far the greatest labour—labour which, I hope, will not remain uncompensated. The view there taken, which goes somewhat deeply into the subject, has two sides. The one relates to the objects of the pure understanding, and is intended to demonstrate and to render comprehensible the objective validity of its *a priori* conceptions; and it forms for this reason an essential part of the *Critique.* The other considers the pure understanding itself, its possibility and its powers of cognition—that is, from a subjective point of view; and, although this exposition is of great importance, it does not belong essentially to the main purpose of the work, because the grand question is what and how much can reason and understanding, apart from experience, cognize, and not, how is the *faculty of thought* itself possible? As the latter is an inquiry into the cause of a given effect, and has thus in it some semblance of an hypothesis (although, as I shall show on another occasion, this is really not the fact), it would seem that, in the present instance, I had allowed myself to enounce a mere *opinion,* and that the reader must therefore be at liberty to hold a different *opinion.* But I beg to remind him that, if my subjective deduction does not produce in his mind the conviction of its certitude at which I aimed, the objective deduction, with which alone the present work is properly concerned, is in every respect satisfactory.

As regards *clearness,* the reader has a right to demand, in the first place, *discursive* or logical clearness, that is, on the basis of conceptions, and, secondly, *intuitive* or aesthetic clearness, by means of intuitions, that is, by examples or other modes of illustration *in concreto.* I have done what I could for the first kind of intelligibility. This was essential to my purpose; and it thus became the accidental cause of my inability to do complete justice to the second requirement. I have been almost always at a loss, during the progress of this work, how to settle this question. Examples and illustrations always appeared to me necessary, and, in the first sketch of the *Critique,* naturally fell into their proper places. But I very soon became aware of the magnitude of my task, and the numerous problems with which I should be engaged; and, as I perceived that this critical investigation would, even if delivered in the driest *scholastic* manner, be far from being brief, I found it unadvisable to enlarge it still more with examples and explanations, which are necessary only from a *popular* point of view. I was induced to take this course from the consideration also that the present work is not intended for popular use, that those devoted to science do not require such helps, although they are always acceptable, and that they would have materially interfered with my present purpose. Abbé Terrasson remarks with great justice that, if we estimate the size of a work, not from the number of its pages, but from the time which we require to make ourselves master of it, it may be said of many a book *that it would be much shorter, if it were not so short.* On the other hand, as regards the comprehensibility of a system of speculative cognition, connected under a single principle, we may say with equal justice: many a book would have been much clearer, if it had not been intended to be so very clear. For explanations and examples, and other helps to intelligibility, aid us in the comprehension of *parts,* but they distract the attention, dissipate the mental power of the reader, and stand in the way of his forming a clear conception of the *whole;* as he cannot attain soon enough to a survey of the system, and the colouring and embellishments bestowed upon it prevent his observing its articulation or organization—which is the most important consideration with him, when he comes to judge of its unity and stability.

The reader must naturally have a strong inducement to co-operate with the present author, if he has formed the intention of erecting a complete and solid edifice of metaphysical science, according to the plan now laid before him. Metaphysics, as here represented, is the only science which admits of completion—and with little labour, if it is united, in a short time; so that nothing will be left to future generations except the task of illustrating and applying it *didactically*. For this science is nothing more than the *inventory* of all that is given us by *pure reason*, systematically arranged. Nothing can escape our notice; for what reason produces from itself cannot lie concealed, but must be brought to the light by reason itself, so soon as we have discovered the common principle of the ideas we seek. The perfect unity of this kind of cognitions, which are based upon pure conceptions, and uninfluenced by any empirical element, or any *peculiar* intuition leading to determinate experience, renders this completeness not only practicable, but also necessary.

Tecum habita, et nôris quam sit tibi curta supellex.[1]

[1] Persius. [*Satirae* iv. 52. "Dwell with yourself, and you will know how short your household stuff is."]

Such a system of pure speculative reason I hope to be able to publish under the title of *Metaphysic of Nature*. The content of this work (which will not be half so long) will be very much richer than that of the present *Critique*, which has to discover the sources of this cognition and expose the conditions of its possibility, and at the same time to clear and level a fit foundation for the scientific edifice. In the present work, I look for the patient hearing and the impartiality of a *judge;* in the other, for the good-will and assistance of a *co-labourer*. For, however complete the list of *principles* for this system may be in the *Critique*, the correctness of the system requires that no *deduced* conceptions should be absent. These cannot be presented *a priori*, but must be gradually discovered; and, while the *synthesis* of conceptions has been fully exhausted in the *Critique*, it is necessary that, in the proposed work, the same should be the case with their *analysis*. But this will be rather an amusement than a labour.

PREFACE TO THE SECOND EDITION, 1787

WHETHER the treatment of that portion of our knowledge which lies within the province of pure reason advances with that undeviating certainty which characterizes the progress of *science,* we shall be at no loss to determine. If we find those who are engaged in metaphysical pursuits, unable to come to an understanding as to the method which they ought to follow; if we find them, after the most elaborate preparations, invariably brought to a stand before the goal is reached, and compelled to retrace their steps and strike into fresh paths, we may then feel quite sure that they are far from having attained to the certainty of scientific progress and may rather be said to be merely groping about in the dark. In these circumstances we shall render an important service to reason if we succeed in simply indicating the path along which it must travel, in order to arrive at any results—even if it should be found necessary to abandon many of those aims which, without reflection, have been proposed for its attainment.

That *logic* has advanced in this sure course, even from the earliest times, is apparent from the fact that, since Aristotle, it has been unable to advance a step and, thus, to all appearance has reached its completion. For, if some of the moderns have thought to enlarge its domain by introducing *psychological* discussions on the mental faculties, such as imagination and wit, *metaphysical* discussions on the origin of knowledge and the different kinds of certitude, according to the difference of the objects (idealism, scepticism, and so on), or *anthropological* discussions on prejudices, their causes and remedies: this attempt, on the part of these authors, only shows their ignorance of the peculiar nature of logical science. We do not enlarge but disfigure the sciences when we lose sight of their respective limits and allow them to run into one another. Now logic is enclosed within limits which admit of perfectly clear definition; it is a science which has for its object nothing but the exposition and proof of the *formal* laws of all thought, whether it be *a priori* or empirical, whatever be its origin or its object, and whatever the difficulties—natural or accidental—which it encounters in the human mind.

The early success of logic must be attributed exclusively to the narrowness of its field, in which abstraction may, or rather must, be made of all the objects of cognition with their characteristic distinctions, and in which the understanding has only to deal with itself and with its own forms. It is, obviously, a much more difficult task for reason to strike into the sure path of science, where it has to deal not simply with itself, but with objects external to itself. Hence, logic is properly only a *propaedeutic*—forms, as it were, the vestibule of the sciences; and while it is necessary to enable us to form a correct judgement with regard to the various branches of knowledge, still the acquisition of real, substantive knowledge is to be sought only in the sciences properly so called, that is, in the objective sciences.

Now these sciences, if they can be termed *rational* at all, must contain elements of *a priori* cognition, and this cognition may stand in a twofold relation to its object. Either it may have to *determine* the conception of the object —which must be supplied extraneously, or it may have to *establish its reality*. The former is *theoretical,* the latter *practical,* rational cognition. In both, the *pure* or *a priori* element must be treated first, and must be carefully distinguished from that which is supplied from other sources. Any other method can only lead to irremediable confusion.

Mathematics and *physics* are the two theoretical sciences which have to determine their objects *a priori*. The former is purely *a priori,* the latter is partially so, but is also dependent on other sources of cognition.

In the earliest times of which history affords us any record, *mathematics* had already entered on the sure course of science, among that wonderful nation, the Greeks. Still it is not to be supposed that it was as easy for this science to strike into, or rather to construct for itself, that royal road, as it was for logic, in which reason has only to deal with itself. On the contrary, I believe that it must have remained long—chiefly among the Egyptians—in the stage of blind groping after its true aims and destination, and that it was revolutionized by the happy idea of one man, who struck out and determined for all time the path which this science must follow, and which admits of an indefinite advancement. The history of this intellectual revolution—much more important in its results than the discovery of the passage round the celebrated Cape of Good Hope—and of its author, has not been preserved. But Diogenes Laertius, in naming the supposed discoverer of some of the simplest elements of geometrical demonstration—elements which, according to the ordinary opinion, do not even require to be proved—makes it apparent that the change introduced by the first indication of this new path, must have seemed of the utmost importance to the mathematicians of that age, and it has thus been secured against the chance of oblivion. A new light must have flashed on the mind of the first man (*Thales,* or whatever may have been his name) who demonstrated the properties of the *isosceles* triangle. For he found that it was not sufficient to meditate on the figure, as it lay before his eyes, or the conception of it, as it existed in his mind, and thus endeavour to get at the knowledge of its properties, but that it was necessary to produce these properties, as it were, by a positive *a priori construction;* and that, in order to arrive with certainty at *a priori* cognition, he must not attribute to the object any other properties than those which necessarily followed from that which he had himself, in accordance with his conception, placed in the object.

A much longer period elapsed before *physics* entered on the highway of science. For it is only about a century and a half since the wise Bacon gave a new direction to physical studies, or rather—as others were already on the right track—imparted fresh vigour to the pursuit of this new direction. Here, too, as in the case of mathematics, we find evidence of a rapid intellectual revolution. In the remarks which follow I shall confine myself to the *empirical* side of natural science.

When Galilei experimented with balls of a definite weight on the inclined plane, when Torricelli caused the air to sustain a weight which he had calculated beforehand to be equal to that of a definite column of water, or when Stahl, at a later period, converted metals into lime, and reconverted lime into metal, by the addition and subtraction of certain elements;[1] a light broke upon all natural philosophers. They learned that reason only perceives that which it produces after its own design; that it must not be content to follow, as it were, in the leading-strings of nature, but must proceed in advance with principles of judgement according to unvarying laws, and compel nature to reply to its questions. For accidental observations, made according to no preconceived plan, cannot be united under a necessary law. But it is this that reason seeks for and requires. It is only the principles of reason which can give to concordant phenomena the validity of laws, and it is only when experiment is directed by these rational principles that it can have any real utility. Reason must approach nature with the view, indeed, of receiving information from it, not, however, in the character of a pupil, who listens to all that his master chooses to tell him, but in that of a judge, who compels the witnesses to reply to those questions which he himself thinks fit to propose. To this single idea must the revolution be ascribed, by which, after groping in the dark for so many centuries, natural science was at length conducted into the path of certain progress.

We come now to *metaphysics,* a purely speculative science, which occupies a completely isolated position and is entirely independent of the teachings of experience. It deals with mere conceptions—not, like mathematics, with conceptions applied to intuition—and in it, reason is the pupil of itself alone. It is the oldest of the sciences, and would still survive, even if all the rest were swallowed up in the abyss of an all-destroying barbarism. But it has not yet had the good fortune to attain to the sure scientific method. This will be apparent, if we apply the tests which we proposed at the outset. We find that reason perpetually comes to a stand, when it attempts to gain *a priori* the perception even of those laws which the most common experience confirms. We find it compelled to retrace its steps in innumerable instances, and to abandon the path on which it had entered, because this does not lead to the desired result. We find, too, that those who are engaged in metaphysical pursuits are far from being able to agree among themselves, but that, on the contrary, this science appears to furnish an arena specially adapted for the display of skill or the exercise of strength in mock-contests—a field in which no combatant ever yet succeeded in gaining an inch of ground, in which, at least, no victory was ever yet crowned with permanent possession.

This leads us to inquire why it is that, in metaphysics, the sure path of science has not hitherto been found. Shall we suppose that it is impossi-

[1] I do not here follow with exactness the history of the experimental method, of which, indeed, the first steps are involved in some obscurity.

ble to discover it? Why then should nature have visited our reason with restless aspirations after it, as if it were one of our weightiest concerns? Nay, more, how little cause should we have to place confidence in our reason, if it abandons us in a matter about which, most of all, we desire to know the truth—and not only so, but even allures us to the pursuit of vain phantoms, only to betray us in the end? Or, if the path has only hitherto been missed, what indications do we possess to guide us in a renewed investigation, and to enable us to hope for greater success than has fallen to the lot of our predecessors?

It appears to me that the examples of mathematics and natural philosophy, which, as we have seen, were brought into their present condition by a sudden revolution, are sufficiently remarkable to fix our attention on the essential circumstances of the change which has proved so advantageous to them, and to induce us to make the experiment of imitating them, so far as the analogy which, as rational sciences, they bear to metaphysics may permit. It has hitherto been assumed that our cognition must conform to the objects; but all attempts to ascertain anything about these objects *a priori,* by means of conceptions, and thus to extend the range of our knowledge, have been rendered abortive by this assumption. Let us then make the experiment whether we may not be more successful in metaphysics, if we assume that the objects must conform to our cognition. This appears, at all events, to accord better with the *possibility* of our gaining the end we have in view, that is to say, of arriving at the cognition of objects *a priori,* of determining something with respect to these objects, before they are given to us. We here propose to do just what Copernicus did in attempting to explain the celestial movements. When he found that he could make no progress by assuming that all the heavenly bodies revolved round the spectator, he reversed the process, and tried the experiment of assuming that the spectator revolved, while the stars remained at rest. We may make the same experiment with regard to the intuition of objects. If the intuition must conform to the nature of the objects, I do not see how we can know anything of them *a priori.* If, on the other hand, the object conforms to the nature of our faculty of intuition, I can then easily conceive the possibility of such an *a priori* knowledge. Now as I cannot rest in the mere intuitions, but —if they are to become cognitions—must refer them, as *representations,* to something, as *object,* and must determine the latter by means of the former, here again there are two courses open to me. *Either,* first, I may assume that the conceptions, by which I effect this determination, conform to the object—and in this case I am reduced to the same perplexity as before; *or* secondly, I may assume that the objects, or, which is the same thing, that *experience,* in which alone as given objects they are cognized, conform to my conceptions—and then I am at no loss how to proceed. For experience itself is a mode of cognition which requires understanding. Before objects are given to me, that is, *a priori,* I must presuppose in myself laws of the understanding which are expressed in conceptions *a priori.* To these conceptions, then, all the objects of experience must necessarily conform. Now there are objects which reason *thinks,* and that necessarily, but which cannot be given in experience, or, at least, cannot be given *so* as reason thinks them. The attempt to think these objects will hereafter furnish an excellent test of the new method of thought which we have adopted, and which is based on the principle that we only cognize in things *a priori* that which we ourselves place in them.[1]

This attempt succeeds as well as we could desire, and promises to metaphysics, in its first part—that is, where it is occupied with conceptions *a priori,* of which the corresponding objects may be given in experience—the certain course of science. For by this new method we are enabled perfectly to explain the possibility of *a priori* cognition, and, what is more, to demonstrate satisfactorily the laws which lie *a priori* at the foundation of nature, as the sum of the objects of experience—neither of which was possible according to the procedure hitherto fol-

[1] This method, accordingly, which we have borrowed from the natural philosopher, consists in seeking for the elements of pure reason in that *which admits of confirmation or refutation by experiment.* Now the propositions of pure reason, especially when they transcend the limits of possible experience, do not admit of our making any experiment with their *objects,* as in natural science. Hence, with regard to those *conceptions* and *principles* which we assume *a priori,* our only course will be to view them from two different sides. We must regard one and the same conception, *on the one hand,* in relation to experience as an object of the senses and of the understanding, *on the other hand,* in relation to reason, isolated and transcending the limits of experience, as an object of mere thought. Now if we find that, when we regard things from this double point of view, the result is in harmony with the principle of pure reason, but that, when we regard them from a single point of view, reason is involved in self-contradiction, then the experiment will establish the correctness of this distinction.

lowed. But from this deduction of the faculty of *a priori* cognition in the first part of metaphysics, we derive a surprising result, and one which, to all appearance, militates against the great end of metaphysics, as treated in the second part. For we come to the conclusion that our faculty of cognition is unable to transcend the limits of possible experience; and yet this is precisely the most essential object of this science. The estimate of our rational cognition *a priori* at which we arrive is that it has only to do with phenomena, and that things in themselves, while possessing a real existence, lie beyond its sphere. Here we are enabled to put the justice of this estimate to the test. For that which of necessity impels us to transcend the limits of experience and of all phenomena is the *unconditioned,* which reason absolutely requires in things as they are in themselves, in order to complete the series of conditions. Now, if it appears that when, on the one hand, we assume that our cognition conforms to its objects as things in themselves, *the unconditioned cannot be thought without contradiction,* and that when, on the other hand, we assume that our representation of things as they are given to us, does not conform to these things as they are in themselves, but that these objects, as phenomena, conform to our mode of representation, *the contradiction disappears:* we shall then be convinced of the truth of that which we began by assuming for the sake of experiment; we may look upon it as established that the unconditioned does not lie in things as we know them, or as they are given to us, but in things as they are in themselves, beyond the range of our cognition.[1]

But, after we have thus denied the power of speculative reason to make any progress in the sphere of the supersensible, it still remains for our consideration whether data do not exist in *practical* cognition which may enable us to determine the transcendent conception of the unconditioned, to rise beyond the limits of all possible experience from a *practical* point of view, and thus to satisfy the great ends of metaphysics. Speculative reason has thus, at least, made room for such an extension of our knowledge; and, if it must leave this space vacant, still it does not rob us of the liberty to fill it up, if we can, by means of practical data—nay, it even challenges us to make the attempt.[2]

This attempt to introduce a complete revolution in the procedure of metaphysics, after the *example* of the geometricians and natural philosophers, constitutes the aim of the *Critique of Pure Speculative Reason.* It is a treatise on the method to be followed, not a system of the science itself. But, at the same time, it marks out and defines both the external boundaries and the internal structure of this science. For pure speculative reason has this peculiarity, that, in choosing the various objects of thought, it is able to define the limits of its own faculties, and even to give a complete enumeration of the possible modes of proposing problems to itself, and thus to sketch out the entire system of metaphysics. For, on the one hand, in cognition *a priori,* nothing must be attributed to the objects but what the thinking subject derives from itself; and, on the other hand, reason is, in regard to the principles of cognition, a perfectly distinct, independent unity, in which, as in an organized body, every member exists for the sake of the others, and all for the sake of each, so that no principle can be viewed, with safety, in one relationship, unless it is, at the same time, viewed in relation to the total use of pure reason. Hence, too, metaphysics has this singular advantage—an advantage which falls to the lot of no other science which has to do with *objects*—that, if once it is conducted into the sure path of science, by means of this criticism, it can then take in the whole sphere of its cognitions, and can thus complete its work, and leave it for the use of posterity, as a capital which can never receive fresh accessions. For metaphysics has to deal only with principles and with the limitations of its own employment as determined by these principles. To this perfection it is, therefore, bound, as the fundamental science, to attain, and to it the maxim may justly be applied:

[1] This experiment of pure reason has a great similarity to that of the *chemists,* which they term the experiment of *reduction,* or, more usually, the *synthetic* process. The *analysis* of the metaphysician separates pure cognition *a priori* into two heterogeneous elements, viz., the cognition of things as phenomena, and of things in themselves. *Dialectic* combines these again into harmony with the necessary rational idea of the unconditioned, and finds that this harmony never results except through the above distinction, which is, therefore, concluded to be just.

[2] So the central laws of the movements of the heavenly bodies established the truth of that which Copernicus, at first, assumed only as a hypothesis, and, at the same time, brought to light that invisible force (Newtonian attraction) which holds the universe together. The latter would have remained forever undiscovered, if Copernicus had not ventured on the experiment—contrary to the senses, but still just—of looking for the observed movements not in the heavenly bodies, but in the spectator. In this Preface I treat the new metaphysical method as a hypothesis with the view of rendering apparent the first attempts at such a change of method, which are always hypothetical. But in the *Critique* itself it will be demonstrated, not hypothetically, but apodeictically, from the nature of our representations of space and time, and from the elementary conceptions of the understanding.

Nil actum reputans, si quid superesset agendum.[1]

But, it will be asked, what kind of a treasure is this that we propose to bequeath to posterity? What is the real value of this system of metaphysics, purified by criticism, and thereby reduced to a permanent condition? A cursory view of the present work will lead to the supposition that its use is merely *negative,* that it only serves to warn us against venturing, with speculative reason, beyond the limits of experience. This is, in fact, its primary use. But this, at once, assumes a *positive* value, when we observe that the principles with which speculative reason endeavours to transcend its limits lead inevitably, not to the *extension,* but to the *contraction* of the use of reason, inasmuch as they threaten to extend the limits of sensibility, which is their proper sphere, over the entire realm of thought and, thus, to supplant the pure (practical) use of reason. So far, then, as this criticism is occupied in confining speculative reason within its proper bounds, it is only negative; but, inasmuch as it thereby, at the same time, removes an obstacle which impedes and even threatens to destroy the use of practical reason, it possesses a positive and very important value. In order to admit this, we have only to be convinced that there is an absolutely necessary use of pure reason—the moral use—in which it inevitably transcends the limits of sensibility, without the aid of speculation, requiring only to be insured against the effects of a speculation which would involve it in contradiction with itself. To deny the positive advantage of the service which this criticism renders us would be as absurd as to maintain that the system of police is productive of no positive benefit, since its main business is to prevent the violence which citizen has to apprehend from citizen, that so each may pursue his vocation in peace and security. That space and time are only forms of sensible intuition, and hence are only conditions of the existence of things as phenomena; that, moreover, we have no conceptions of the understanding, and, consequently, no elements for the cognition of things, except in so far as a corresponding intuition can be given to these conceptions; that, accordingly, we can have no cognition of an object, as a thing in itself, but only as an object of sensible intuition, that is, as phenomenon—all this is proved in the analytical part of the *Critique;* and from this the limitation of all possible speculative cognition to the mere objects of *experience,* follows as a necessary result. At the same time, it must be carefully borne in mind that, while we surrender the power of *cognizing,* we still reserve the power of *thinking* objects, as things in themselves.[2] For, otherwise, we should require to affirm the existence of an appearance, without something that appears—which would be absurd. Now let us suppose, for a moment, that we had not undertaken this criticism and, accordingly, had not drawn the necessary distinction between things as objects of experience and things as they are in themselves. The principle of causality, and, by consequence, the mechanism of nature as determined by causality, would then have absolute validity in relation to all things as efficient causes. I should then be unable to assert, with regard to one and the same being, e.g., the human soul, that its will is *free,* and yet, at the same time, subject to natural necessity, that is, *not free,* without falling into a palpable contradiction, for in both propositions I should take the soul in *the same signification,* as a thing in general, as a thing in itself—as, without previous criticism, I could not but take it. Suppose now, on the other hand, that we *have* undertaken this criticism, and have learnt that an object may be taken in *two senses,* first, as a phenomenon, secondly, as a thing in itself; and that, according to the deduction of the conceptions of the understanding, the principle of causality has reference only to things in the first sense. We then see how it does not involve any contradiction to assert, on the one hand, that the will, in the phenomenal sphere—in visible action—is necessarily obedient to the law of nature, and, in so far, *not free;* and, on the other hand, that, as belonging to a thing in itself, it is not subject to that law, and, accordingly, is *free.* Now, it is true that I cannot, by means of speculative reason, and still less by empirical observation, *cognize* my soul as a thing in itself and consequently, cannot cognize liberty as the property of a being to which I ascribe effects in the world of sense. For, to do so, I must cognize this being as existing, and yet not in time, which —since I cannot support my conception by any

[1] ["He considered nothing done, so long as anything remained to be done."]

[2] In order to *cognize* an object, I must be able to prove its possibility, either from its reality as attested by experience, or *a priori,* by means of reason. But I can *think* what I please, provided only I do not contradict myself; that is, provided my conception is a possible thought, though I may be unable to answer for the existence of a corresponding object in the sum of possibilities. But something more is required before I can attribute to such a conception objective validity, that is real possibility—the other possibility being merely logical. We are not, however, confined to theoretical sources of cognition for the means of satisfying this additional requirement, but may derive them from practical sources.

intuition—is impossible. At the same time, while I cannot *cognize,* I can quite well *think* freedom, that is to say, my representation of it involves at least no contradiction, if we bear in mind the critical distinction of the two modes of representation (the sensible and the intellectual) and the consequent limitation of the conceptions of the pure understanding and of the principles which flow from them. Suppose now that morality necessarily presupposed liberty, in the strictest sense, as a property of our will; suppose that reason contained certain practical, original principles *a priori,* which were absolutely impossible without this presupposition; and suppose, at the same time, that speculative reason had proved that liberty was incapable of being thought at all. It would then follow that the moral presupposition must give way to the speculative affirmation, the opposite of which involves an obvious contradiction, and that *liberty* and, with it, morality must yield to the *mechanism of nature;* for the negation of morality involves no contradiction, except on the presupposition of liberty. Now morality does not require the speculative cognition of liberty; it is enough that I can think it, that its conception involves no contradiction, that it does not interfere with the mechanism of nature. But even this requirement we could not satisfy, if we had not learnt the twofold sense in which things may be taken; and it is only in this way that the doctrine of morality and the doctrine of nature are confined within their proper limits. For this result, then, we are indebted to a criticism which warns us of our unavoidable ignorance with regard to things in themselves, and establishes the necessary limitation of our theoretical *cognition* to mere phenomena.

The positive value of the critical principles of pure reason in relation to the conception of *God* and of the *simple nature* of the *soul,* admits of a similar exemplification; but on this point I shall not dwell. I cannot even make the assumption—as the practical interests of morality require—of God, freedom, and immortality, if I do not deprive speculative reason of its pretensions to transcendent insight. For to arrive at these, it must make use of principles which, in fact, extend only to the objects of possible experience, and which cannot be applied to objects beyond this sphere without converting them into phenomena, and thus rendering the *practical extension* of pure reason impossible. I must, therefore, abolish *knowledge,* to make room for *belief.* The dogmatism of metaphysics, that is, the presumption that it is possible to advance in metaphysics without previous criticism, is the true source of the unbelief (always dogmatic) which militates against morality.

Thus, while it may be no very difficult task to bequeath a legacy to posterity, in the shape of a system of metaphysics constructed in accordance with the *Critique of Pure Reason,* still the value of such a bequest is not to be depreciated. It will render an important service to reason, by substituting the certainty of scientific method for that random groping after results without the guidance of principles, which has hitherto characterized the pursuit of metaphysical studies. It will render an important service to the inquiring mind of youth, by leading the student to apply his powers to the cultivation of genuine science, instead of wasting them, as at present, on speculations which can never lead to any result, or on the idle attempt to invent new ideas and opinions. But, above all, it will confer an inestimable benefit on morality and religion, by showing that all the objections urged against them may be silenced for ever by the *Sacratic* method, that is to say, by proving the ignorance of the objector. For, as the world has never been, and, no doubt, never will be without a system of metaphysics of one kind or another, it is the highest and weightiest concern of philosophy to render it powerless for harm, by closing up the sources of error.

This important change in the field of the sciences, this loss of its fancied possessions, to which speculative reason must submit, does not prove in any way detrimental to the general interests of humanity. The advantages which the world has derived from the teachings of pure reason are not at all impaired. The loss falls, in its whole extent, on the *monopoly of the schools,* but does not in the slightest degree touch the *interests of mankind.* I appeal to the most obstinate dogmatist, whether the proof of the continued existence of the soul after death, derived from the simplicity of its substance; of the freedom of the will in opposition to the general mechanism of nature, drawn from the subtle but impotent distinction of subjective and objective practical necessity; or of the existence of God, deduced from the conception of an *ens realissimum*—the contingency of the changeable, and the necessity of a prime mover, has ever been able to pass beyond the limits of the schools, to penetrate the public mind, or to exercise the slightest influence on its convictions. It must be admitted that this has not been the case and that, owing to the unfitness of the common understanding for such subtle speculations, it can never be expected to take place. On the contrary, it is plain that *the hope of a future life* arises from the feeling, which exists in the breast of every man, that the temporal is inadequate to meet and satisfy the demands of his nature. In like manner, it cannot be doubted that the clear exhibition of duties in opposition to all the claims of inclination, gives rise to the consciousness of *freedom,* and that the glorious order, beauty, and providential care, everywhere displayed in nature, give rise to the belief in a wise and great Author of the Universe. Such is the genesis of these general convictions of mankind, so far as they depend on rational grounds; and this public property not only remains undisturbed, but is even raised to greater importance, by the doctrine that the schools have no right to arrogate to themselves a more profound insight into a matter of general human concernment than that to which the great mass of men, ever held by us in the highest estimation, can without difficulty attain, and that the schools should, therefore, confine themselves to the elaboration of these universally comprehensible and, from a moral point of view, amply satisfactory proofs. The change, therefore, affects only the arrogant pretensions of the schools, which would gladly retain, in their own exclusive possession, the key to the truths which they impart to the public.

Quod mecum nescit, solus vult scire videri.

At the same time it does not deprive the speculative philosopher of his just title to be the sole depositor of a science which benefits the public without its knowledge—I mean, the *Critique of Pure Reason.* This can never become popular and, indeed, has no occasion to be so; for fine-spun arguments in favour of useful truths make just as little impression on the public mind as the equally subtle objections brought against these truths. On the other hand, since both inevitably force themselves on every man who rises to the height of speculation, it becomes the manifest duty of the schools to enter upon a thorough investigation of the rights of speculative reason and, thus, to prevent the scandal which metaphysical controversies are sure, sooner or later, to cause even to the masses. It is only by criticism that metaphysicians (and, as such, theologians too) can be saved from these controversies and from the consequent perversion of their doctrines. Criticism alone can strike a blow at the root of materialism, fatalism, atheism, free-thinking, fanaticism, and superstition, which are universally injurious—as well as of idealism and scepticism, which are dangerous to the schools, but can scarcely pass over to the public. If governments think proper to interfere with the affairs of the learned, it would be more consistent with a wise regard for the interests of science, as well as for those of society, to favour a criticism of this kind, by which alone the labours of reason can be established on a firm basis, than to support the ridiculous despotism of the schools, which raise a loud cry of danger to the public over the destruction of cobwebs, of which the public has never taken any notice, and the loss of which, therefore, it can never feel.

This critical science is not opposed to the *dogmatic procedure* of reason in pure cognition; for pure cognition must always be dogmatic, that is, must rest on strict demonstration from sure principles *a priori*—but to *dogmatism,* that is, to the presumption that it is possible to make any progress with a pure cognition, derived from (philosophical) conceptions, according to the principles which reason has long been in the habit of employing—without first inquiring in what way and by what right reason has come into the possession of these principles. Dogmatism is thus the dogmatic procedure of pure reason *without previous criticism of its own powers,* and in opposing this procedure, we must not be supposed to lend any countenance to that loquacious shallowness which arrogates to itself the name of popularity, nor yet to scepticism, which makes short work with the whole science of metaphysics. On the contrary, our criticism is the necessary preparation for a thoroughly scientific system of metaphysics which must perform its task entirely *a priori,* to the complete satisfaction of speculative reason, and must, therefore, be treated, not popularly, but scholastically. In carrying out the plan which the *Critique* prescribes, that is, in the future system of metaphysics, we must have recourse to the strict method of the celebrated Wolf, the greatest of all dogmatic philosophers. He was the first to point out the necessity of establishing fixed principles, of clearly defining our conceptions, and of subjecting our demonstrations to the most severe scrutiny, instead of rashly jumping at conclusions. The example which he set served to awaken that spirit of profound and thorough investigation which is not yet extinct in Germany. He would have been peculiarly well fitted to give a truly scientific character to metaphysical studies, had it occurred to him to prepare the field by a criticism of the *organum*, that is, of pure reason itself. That he failed to perceive the necessity of such a procedure must be ascribed to the dogmatic mode of thought which characterized his age, and on this point the philosophers of his time, as well as of all previous times, have nothing to reproach each other with. Those who reject at once the method of Wolf, and of the *Critique of Pure Reason*, can have no other aim but to shake off the fetters of *science*, to change labour into sport, certainty into opinion, and philosophy into philodoxy.

In this *second edition*, I have endeavoured, as far as possible, to remove the difficulties and obscurity which, without fault of mine perhaps, have given rise to many misconceptions even among acute thinkers. In the propositions themselves, and in the demonstrations by which they are supported, as well as in the form and the entire plan of the work, I have found nothing to alter; which must be attributed partly to the long examination to which I had subjected the whole before offering it to the public and partly to the nature of the case. For pure speculative reason is an organic structure in which there is nothing isolated or independent, but every single part is essential to all the rest; and hence, the slightest imperfection, whether defect or positive error, could not fail to betray itself in use. I venture, further, to hope, that this system will maintain the same unalterable character for the future. I am led to entertain this confidence, not by vanity, but by the evidence which the equality of the result affords, when we proceed, first, from the simplest elements up to the complete whole of pure reason, and, then, backwards from the whole to each individual part. We find that the attempt to make the slightest alteration, in any part, leads inevitably to contradictions, not merely in this system, but in human reason itself. At the same time, there is still much room for improvement in the *exposition* of the doctrines contained in this work. In the present edition, I have endeavoured to remove misapprehensions of the aesthetical part, especially with regard to the conception of *time;* to clear away the obscurity which has been found in the deduction of the conceptions of the understanding; to supply the supposed want of sufficient evidence in the demonstration of the principles of the pure understanding; and, lastly, to obviate the misunderstanding of the paralogisms which immediately precede the rational psychology. Beyond this point—the end of the second main division of the "Transcendental Dialectic"—I have not extended my alterations,[1] partly from want of time, and partly because I am not aware that any portion of the remainder has given rise to misconceptions among intelligent and impartial critics, whom I

[1] The only addition, properly so called—and that only in the method of proof—which I have made in the present edition, consists of a new refutation of psychological *idealism*, and a strict demonstration—the only one possible, as I believe—of the objective reality of external intuition. However harmless idealism may be considered—although in reality it is not so—in regard to the essential ends of metaphysics, it must still remain a scandal to philosophy and to the general human reason to be obliged to assume, as an article of mere belief, the existence of things external to ourselves (from which, yet, we derive the whole material of cognition even for the internal sense), and not to be able to oppose a satisfactory proof to any one who may call it in question. As there is some obscurity of expression in the demonstration as it stands in the text, I propose to alter the passage in question as follows: "But this permanent cannot be an intuition in me. For all the determining grounds of my existence which can be found in me are representations and, as such, do themselves require a permanent, distinct from them, which may determine my existence in relation to their changes, that is, my existence in time, wherein they change." It may, probably, be urged in opposition to this proof that, after all, I am only conscious immediately of that which is in me, that is, of my *representation* of external things, and that, consequently, it must always remain uncertain whether anything corresponding to this representation does or does not exist externally to me. But I am conscious, through internal *experience*, of my *existence in time* (consequently, also, of the determinability of the former in the latter), and that is more than the simple consciousness of my representation. It is, in fact, the same as the *empirical consciousness of my existence*, which can only be determined in relation to something, which, while connected with my existence, is *external to me*. This consciousness of my existence in time is, therefore, identical with the consciousness of a relation to something external to me, and it is, therefore, experience, not fiction, sense, not imagination, which inseparably connects the external with my internal sense. For the external sense is, in itself, the relation of intuition to something real, external to me; and the reality of this something, as opposed to the mere imagination of it, rests solely on its inseparable connection with internal experience as the condition of its possibility. If with the *intellectual consciousness* of my existence, in the representation: *I am*, which accompanies all my judgements, and all the operations of my understanding, I could, at the same time, connect a determination of my existence by *intellectual intuition*, then the consciousness of a relation to something external to me would not be necessary. But the internal intuition in which alone my existence can be determined, though preceded by that purely intellectual consciousness, is itself sensible and attached to the condition of time. Hence this determination of my existence, and consequently my internal experience itself, must depend on something permanent which is not in me, which can be, therefore, only in something external to me, to which I must look upon myself as being related. Thus the reality of the external sense is necessarily connected with that of the internal, in order to the possibility of experience in general; that is, I am just as certainly conscious that there are things external to me related to my sense as I am that I myself exist as determined in time. But in order to ascertain to what given intuitions objects, external to me, really correspond, in other words, what intuitions belong to the external sense and not to imagination, I must have recourse, in every particular case, to those rules according to which experience in general (even internal experience) is distinguished from imagination, and which are always based on the proposition

do not here mention with that praise which is their due, but who will find that their suggestions have been attended to in the work itself.

In attempting to render the exposition of my views as intelligible as possible, I have been compelled to leave out or abridge various passages which were not essential to the completeness of the work, but which many readers might consider useful in other respects, and might be unwilling to miss. This trifling loss, which could not be avoided without swelling the book beyond due limits, may be supplied, at the pleasure of the reader, by a comparison with the first edition, and will, I hope, be more than compensated for by the greater clearness of the exposition as it now stands.

I have observed, with pleasure and thankfulness, in the pages of various reviews and treatises, that the spirit of profound and thorough investigation is not extinct in Germany, though it may have been overborne and silenced for a time by the fashionable tone of a licence in thinking, which gives itself the airs of genius, and that the difficulties which beset the paths of criticism have not prevented energetic and acute thinkers from making themselves masters of the science of pure reason to which these paths conduct—a science which is not popular, but scholastic in its character, and which alone can hope for a lasting existence or possess an abiding value. To these deserving men, who so happily combine profundity of view with a talent for lucid exposition—a talent which I myself am not conscious of possessing—I leave the task of removing any obscurity which may still adhere to the statement of my doctrines. For, in this case, the danger is not that of being refuted, but of being misunderstood. For my own part, I must henceforward abstain from controversy, although I shall carefully attend to all suggestions, whether from friends or adversaries, which may be of use in the future elaboration of the system of this propaedeutic. As, during these labours, I have advanced pretty far in years—this month I reach my sixty-fourth year—it will be necessary for me to economize time, if I am to carry out my plan of elaborating the metaphysics of nature as well as of morals, in confirmation of the correctness of the principles established in this *Critique of Pure Reason*, both speculative and practical; and I must, therefore, leave the task of clearing up the obscurities of the present work—inevitable, perhaps, at the outset—as well as the defence of the whole, to those deserving men who have made my system their own. A philosophical system cannot come forward armed at all points like a mathematical treatise, and hence it may be quite possible to take objection to particular passages, while the organic structure of the system, considered as a unity, has no danger to apprehend. But few possess the ability, and still fewer the inclination, to take a comprehensive view of a new system. By confining the view to particular passages, taking these out of their connection and comparing them with one another, it is easy to pick out apparent contradictions, especially in a work written with any freedom of style. These contradictions place the work in an unfavourable light in the eyes of those who rely on the judgement of others, but are easily reconciled by those who have mastered the idea of the whole. If a theory possesses stability in itself, the action and reaction which seemed at first to threaten its existence serve only, in the course of time, to smooth down any superficial roughness or inequality, and—if men of insight, impartiality, and truly popular gifts, turn their attention to it—to secure to it, in a short time, the requisite elegance also.

Königsberg, *April* 1787.

---

that there really is an external experience. We may add the remark that the representation of something *permanent* in existence, is not the same thing as the *permanent representation;* for a representation may be very variable and changing—as all our representations, even that of matter, are—and yet refer to something permanent, which must, therefore, be distinct from all my representations and external to me, the existence of which is necessarily included in the determination of my own existence, and with it constitutes *one* experience—an experience which would not even be possible internally, if it were not also at the same time, in part, external. To the question *How?* we are no more able to reply, than we are, in general, to think the stationary in time, the coexistence of which with the variable, produces the conception of change.

INTRODUCTION

I. *Of the difference between Pure and Empirical Knowledge*

That all our knowledge begins with experience there can be no doubt. For how is it possible that the faculty of cognition should be awakened into exercise otherwise than by means of objects which affect our senses, and partly of themselves produce representations, partly rouse our powers of understanding into activity, to compare, to connect, or to separate these, and so to convert the raw material of our sensuous impressions into a knowledge of objects, which is called experience? In respect of time, therefore, no knowledge of ours is antecedent to experience, but begins with it.

But, though all our knowledge begins with experience, it by no means follows that all arises out of experience. For, on the contrary, it is quite possible that our empirical knowledge is a compound of that which we receive through impressions, and that which the faculty of cognition supplies from itself (sensuous impressions giving merely the *occasion*), an addition which we cannot distinguish from the original element given by sense, till long practice has made us attentive to, and skilful in separating it. It is, therefore, a question which requires close investigation, and not to be answered at first sight, whether there exists a knowledge altogether independent of experience, and even of all sensuous impressions? Knowledge of this kind is called *a priori,* in contradistinction to empirical knowledge, which has its sources *a posteriori,* that is, in experience.

But the expression, *"a priori,"* is not as yet definite enough adequately to indicate the whole meaning of the question above started. For, in speaking of knowledge which has its sources in experience, we are wont to say, that this or that may be known *a priori,* because we do not derive this knowledge immediately from experience, but from a general rule, which, however, we have itself borrowed from experience. Thus, if a man undermined his house, we say, "he might know *a priori* that it would have fallen;" that is, he needed not to have waited for the experience that it did actually fall. But still, *a priori,* he could not know even this much. For, that bodies are heavy, and, consequently, that they fall when their supports are taken away, must have been known to him previously, by means of experience.

By the term "knowledge *a priori,*" therefore, we shall in the sequel understand, not such as is independent of this or that kind of experience, but such as is absolutely so of *all* experience. Opposed to this is empirical knowledge, or that which is possible only *a posteriori,* that is, through experience. Knowledge *a priori* is either pure or impure. Pure knowledge *a priori* is that with which no empirical element is mixed up. For example, the proposition, "Every change has a cause," is a proposition *a priori,* but impure, because change is a conception which can only be derived from experience.

II. *The Human Intellect, even in an Unphilosophical State, is in Possession of Certain Cognitions "a priori"*

The question now is as to a *criterion,* by which we may securely distinguish a pure from an empirical cognition. Experience no doubt teaches us that this or that object is constituted in such and such a manner, but not that it could not possibly exist otherwise. Now, in the first place, if we have a proposition which contains the idea of necessity in its very conception, it is a judgement *a priori;* if, moreover, it is not derived from any other proposition, unless from one equally involving the idea of necessity, it is absolutely *a priori.* Secondly, an empirical judgement never exhibits strict and absolute, but only assumed and comparative universality (by induction); therefore, the most we can say is—so far as we have hitherto observed, there is no exception to this or that rule. If, on the other hand, a judgement carries with it strict and absolute universality, that is, admits of no possible exception, it is not derived from experience, but is valid absolutely *a priori.*

Empirical universality is, therefore, only an arbitrary extension of validity, from that which may be predicated of a proposition valid in most cases, to that which is asserted of a proposition which holds good in all; as, for example, in the affirmation, "All bodies are heavy." When, on the contrary, strict universality characterizes a judgement, it necessarily indicates another peculiar source of knowledge, namely, a faculty of cognition *a priori*. Necessity and strict universality, therefore, are infallible tests for distinguishing pure from empirical knowledge, and are inseparably connected with each other. But as in the use of these criteria the empirical limitation is sometimes more easily detected than the contingency of the judgement, or the unlimited universality which we attach to a judgement is often a more convincing proof than its necessity, it may be advisable to use the criteria separately, each being by itself infallible.

Now, that in the sphere of human cognition we have judgements which are necessary, and in the strictest sense universal, consequently pure *a priori*, it will be an easy matter to show. If we desire an example from the sciences, we need only take any proposition in mathematics. If we cast our eyes upon the commonest operations of the understanding, the proposition, "Every change must have a cause," will amply serve our purpose. In the latter case, indeed, the conception of a cause so plainly involves the conception of a necessity of connection with an effect, and of a strict universality of the law, that the very notion of a cause would entirely disappear, were we to derive it, like Hume, from a frequent association of what happens with that which precedes, and the habit thence originating of connecting representations—the necessity inherent in the judgement being therefore merely subjective. Besides, without seeking for such examples of principles existing *a priori* in cognition, we might easily show that such principles are the indispensable basis of the possibility of experience itself, and consequently prove their existence *a priori*. For whence could our experience itself acquire certainty, if all the rules on which it depends were themselves empirical, and consequently fortuitous? No one, therefore, can admit the validity of the use of such rules as first principles. But, for the present, we may content ourselves with having established the fact, that we do possess and exercise a faculty of pure *a priori* cognition; and, secondly, with having pointed out the proper tests of such cognition, namely, universality and necessity.

Not only in judgements, however, but even in conceptions, is an *a priori* origin manifest. For example, if we take away by degrees from our conceptions of a body all that can be referred to mere sensuous experience—colour, hardness or softness, weight, even impenetrability—the body will then vanish; but the space which it occupied still remains, and this it is utterly impossible to annihilate in thought. Again, if we take away, in like manner, from our empirical conception of any object, corporeal or incorporeal, all properties which mere experience has taught us to connect with it, still we cannot think away those through which we cogitate it as substance, or adhering to substance, although our conception of substance is more determined than that of an object. Compelled, therefore, by that necessity with which the conception of substance forces itself upon us, we must confess that it has its seat in our faculty of cognition *a priori*.

III. *Philosophy stands in need of a Science which shall Determine the Possibility, Principles, and Extent of Human Knowledge "a priori"*

Of far more importance than all that has been above said, is the consideration that certain of our cognitions rise completely above the sphere of all possible experience, and by means of conceptions, to which there exists in the whole extent of experience no corresponding object, seem to extend the range of our judgements beyond its bounds. And just in this transcendental or supersensible sphere, where experience affords us neither instruction nor guidance, lie the investigations of *reason*, which, on account of their importance, we consider far preferable to, and as having a far more elevated aim than, all that the understanding can achieve within the sphere of sensuous phenomena. So high a value do we set upon these investigations, that even at the risk of error, we persist in following them out, and permit neither doubt nor disregard nor indifference to restrain us from the pursuit. These unavoidable problems of mere pure reason are *God, freedom* (of will), and *immortality*. The science which, with all its preliminaries, has for its especial object the solution of these problems is named *metaphysics*—a science which is at the very outset dogmatical, that is, it confidently takes upon itself the execution of this task without any previous investigation of the ability or inability of reason for such an undertaking.

Now the safe ground of experience being thus abandoned, it seems nevertheless natural that we should hesitate to erect a building with the cognitions we possess, without knowing whence they come, and on the strength of principles, the origin of which is undiscovered. Instead of thus trying to build without a foundation, it is rather to be expected that we should long ago have put the question, how the understanding can arrive at these *a priori* cognitions, and what is the extent, validity, and worth which they may possess? We say, "This is natural enough," meaning by the word *natural,* that which is consistent with a just and reasonable way of thinking; but if we understand by the term, that which usually happens, nothing indeed could be more natural and more comprehensible than that this investigation should be left long unattempted. For one part of our pure knowledge, the science of mathematics, has been long firmly established, and thus leads us to form flattering expectations with regard to others, though these may be of quite a different nature. Besides, when we get beyond the bounds of experience, we are of course safe from opposition in that quarter; and the charm of widening the range of our knowledge is so great that, unless we are brought to a standstill by some evident contradiction, we hurry on undoubtingly in our course. This, however, may be avoided, if we are sufficiently cautious in the construction of our fictions, which are not the less fictions on that account.

Mathematical science affords us a brilliant example, how far, independently of all experience, we may carry our *a priori* knowledge. It is true that the mathematician occupies himself with objects and cognitions only in so far as they can be represented by means of intuition. But this circumstance is easily overlooked, because the said intuition can itself be given *a priori,* and therefore is hardly to be distinguished from a mere pure conception. Deceived by such a proof of the power of reason, we can perceive no limits to the extension of our knowledge. The light dove cleaving in free flight the thin air, whose resistance it feels, might imagine that her movements would be far more free and rapid in airless space. Just in the same way did Plato, abandoning the world of sense because of the narrow limits it sets to the understanding, venture upon the wings of ideas beyond it, into the void space of pure intellect. He did not reflect that he made no real progress by all his efforts; for he met with no resistance which might serve him for a support, as it were, whereon to rest, and on which he might apply his powers, in order to let the intellect acquire momentum for its progress. It is, indeed, the common fate of human reason in speculation, to finish the imposing edifice of thought as rapidly as possible, and then for the first time to begin to examine whether the foundation is a solid one or no. Arrived at this point, all sorts of excuses are sought after, in order to console us for its want of stability, or rather, indeed, to enable us to dispense altogether with so late and dangerous an investigation. But what frees us during the process of building from all apprehension or suspicion, and flatters us into the belief of its solidity, is this. A great part, perhaps the greatest part, of the business of our reason consists in the analysation of the conceptions which we already possess of objects. By this means we gain a multitude of cognitions, which although really nothing more than elucidations or explanations of that which (though in a confused manner) was already thought in our conceptions, are, at least in respect of their form, prized as new introspections; whilst, so far as regards their matter or content, we have really made no addition to our conceptions, but only disinvolved them. But as this process does furnish a real *a priori* knowledge, which has a sure progress and useful results, reason, deceived by this, slips in, without being itself aware of it, assertions of a quite different kind; in which, to given conceptions it adds others, *a priori* indeed, but entirely foreign to them, without our knowing how it arrives at these, and, indeed, without such a question ever suggesting itself. I shall therefore at once proceed to examine the difference between these two modes of knowledge.

IV. *Of the Difference Between Analytical and Synthetical Judgements*

In all judgements wherein the relation of a subject to the predicate is cogitated (I mention affirmative judgements only here; the application to negative will be very easy), this relation is possible in two different ways. Either the predicate B belongs to the subject A, as somewhat which is contained (though covertly) in the conception A; or the predicate B lies completely out of the conception A, although it stands in connection with it. In the first instance, I term the judgement *analytical,* in the second, *synthetical.* Analytical judgements (affirmative) are therefore those in which the connection of the predicate with the subject is cogitated through identity; those in which this connection is cogitated without identity, are called synthetical judgements. The former may be called *explicative,* the latter *augmentative* judgements; because the former add in the predicate nothing to the conception of the subject, but only analyse it into its constituent conceptions, which were thought already in the subject, although in a confused manner; the latter add to our conceptions of the subject a predicate which was not contained in it, and which no analysis could ever have discovered therein. For example, when I say, "All bodies are extended," this is an analytical judgement. For I need not go beyond the conception of *body* in order to find extension connected with it, but merely analyse the conception, that is, become conscious of the manifold properties which I think in that conception, in order to discover this predicate in it: it is therefore an analytical judgement. On the other hand, when I say, "All bodies are heavy," the predicate is something totally different from that which I think in the mere conception of a body. By the addition of such a predicate, therefore, it becomes a synthetical judgement.

Judgements of experience, as such, are always synthetical. For it would be absurd to think of grounding an analytical judgement on experience, because in forming such a judgement I need not go out of the sphere of my conceptions, and therefore recourse to the testimony of experience is quite unnecessary. That "bodies are extended" is not an empirical judgement, but a proposition which stands firm *a priori.* For before addressing myself to experience, I already have in my conception all the requisite conditions for the judgement, and I have only to extract the predicate from the conception, according to the principle of contradiction, and thereby at the same time become conscious of the necessity of the judgement, a necessity which I could never learn from experience. On the other hand, though at first I do not at all include the predicate of weight in my conception of body in general, that conception still indicates an object of experience, a part of the totality of experience, to which I can still add other parts; and this I do when I recognize by observation that bodies are heavy. I can cognize beforehand by analysis the conception of body through the characteristics of extension, impenetrability, shape, etc., all which are cogitated in this conception. But now I extend my knowledge, and looking back on experience from which I had derived this conception of body, I find weight at all times connected with the above characteristics, and therefore I synthetically add to my conceptions this as a predicate, and say, "All bodies are heavy." Thus it is experience upon which rests the possibility of the synthesis of the predicate of weight with the conception of body, because both conceptions, although the one is not contained in the other, still belong to one another (only contingently, however), as parts of a whole, namely, of experience, which is itself a synthesis of intuitions.

But to synthetical judgements *a priori,* such aid is entirely wanting. If I go out of and beyond the conception A, in order to recognize another B as connected with it, what foundation have I to rest on, whereby to render the synthesis possible? I have here no longer the advantage of looking out in the sphere of experience for what I want. Let us take, for example, the proposition, "Everything that happens has a cause." In the conception of *"something that happens,"* I indeed think an existence which a certain time antecedes, and from this I can derive analytical judgements. But the conception of a cause lies quite out of the above conception, and indicates something entirely different from "that which happens," and is consequently not contained in that conception. How then am I able to assert concerning the general conception—"that which happens"—something entirely different from that conception, and to recognize the conception of cause although not contained in it, yet as belonging to it, and even necessarily? what is here the unknown=X, upon which the understanding rests when it believes it has found, out of the conception A a foreign predicate B, which it nevertheless considers to be connected with it? It cannot be experience, because the principle adduced annexes the two representations, cause and effect, to the representation existence, not only with universality, which experience cannot give, but also with the expression of necessity, therefore completely *a priori* and from pure conceptions. Upon such synthetical, that is augmentative propositions, depends the whole aim of our speculative knowledge *a priori;* for although analytical judgements are indeed highly important and necessary, they are so, only to arrive at that clearness of conceptions which is requisite for a sure and extended synthesis, and this alone is a real acquisition.

V. *In all Theoretical Sciences of Reason, Synthetical Judgements "a priori" are contained as Principles*

1. Mathematical judgements are always synthetical. Hitherto this fact, though incontestably true and very important in its consequences, seems to have escaped the analysts of the human mind, nay, to be in complete opposition to all their conjectures. For as it was found that mathematical conclusions all proceed according to the principle of contradiction (which the nature of every apodeictic certainty re-

quires), people became persuaded that the fundamental principles of the science also were recognized and admitted in the same way. But the notion is fallacious; for although a synthetical proposition can certainly be discerned by means of the principle of contradiction, this is possible only when another synthetical proposition precedes, from which the latter is deduced, but never of itself.

Before all, be it observed, that proper mathematical propositions are always judgements *a priori,* and not empirical, because they carry along with them the conception of necessity, which cannot be given by experience. If this be demurred to, it matters not; I will then limit my assertion to *pure* mathematics, the very conception of which implies that it consists of knowledge altogether non-empirical and *a priori.*

We might, indeed, at first suppose that the proposition $7+5=12$ is a merely analytical proposition, following (according to the principle of contradiction) from the conception of a sum of seven and five. But if we regard it more narrowly, we find that our conception of the sum of seven and five contains nothing more than the uniting of both sums into one, whereby it cannot at all be cogitated what this single number is which embraces both. The conception of twelve is by no means obtained by merely cogitating the union of seven and five; and we may analyse our conception of such a possible sum as long as we will, still we shall never discover in it the notion of twelve. We must go beyond these conceptions, and have recourse to an intuition which corresponds to one of the two—our five fingers, for example, or like Segner in his *Arithmetic* five points, and so by degrees, add the units contained in the five given in the intuition, to the conception of seven. For I first take the number 7, and, for the conception of 5 calling in the aid of the fingers of my hand as objects of intuition, I add the units, which I before took together to make up the number 5, gradually now by means of the material image my hand, to the number 7, and by this process, I at length see the number 12 arise. That 7 should be added to 5, I have certainly cogitated in my conception of a sum $=7+5$, but not that this sum was equal to 12. Arithmetical propositions are therefore always synthetical, of which we may become more clearly convinced by trying large numbers. For it will thus become quite evident that, turn and twist our conceptions as we may, it is impossible, without having recourse to intuition, to arrive at the sum total or product by means of the mere analysis of our conceptions. Just as little is any principle of pure geometry analytical. "A straight line between two points is the shortest," is a synthetical proposition. For my conception of *straight* contains no notion of *quantity,* but is merely *qualitative.* The conception of the *shortest* is therefore wholly an addition, and by no analysis can it be extracted from our conception of a straight line. Intuition must therefore here lend its aid, by means of which, and thus only, our synthesis is possible.

Some few principles preposited by geometricians are, indeed, really analytical, and depend on the principle of contradiction. They serve, however, like identical propositions, as links in the chain of method, not as principles—for example, $a=a$, the whole is equal to itself, or $(a+b) > a$, the whole is greater than its part. And yet even these principles themselves, though they derive their validity from pure conceptions, are only admitted in mathematics because they can be presented in intuition. What causes us here commonly to believe that the predicate of such apodeictic judgements is already contained in our conception, and that the judgement is therefore analytical, is merely the equivocal nature of the expression. We must join in thought a certain predicate to a given conception, and this necessity cleaves already to the conception. But the question is, not what we must join in thought to the given conception, but what we really think therein, though only obscurely, and then it becomes manifest that the predicate pertains to these conceptions, necessarily indeed, yet not as thought in the conception itself, but by virtue of an intuition, which must be added to the conception.

2. The science of *natural philosophy* (physics) contains in itself synthetical judgements *a priori,* as principles. I shall adduce two propositions. For instance, the proposition, "In all changes of the material world, the quantity of matter remains unchanged"; or, that, "In all communication of motion, action and reaction must always be equal." In both of these, not only is the necessity, and therefore their origin *a priori* clear, but also that they are synthetical propositions. For in the conception of matter, I do not cogitate its permanency, but merely its presence in space, which it fills. I therefore really go out of and beyond the conception of matter, in order to think on to it something *a priori,* which I did not think in it. The proposition is therefore not analytical, but synthetical, and nevertheless conceived *a priori;* and so it

is with regard to the other propositions of the pure part of natural philosophy.

3. As to *metaphysics,* even if we look upon it merely as an attempted science, yet, from the nature of human reason, an indispensable one, we find that it must contain synthetical propositions *a priori.* It is not merely the duty of metaphysics to dissect, and thereby analytically to illustrate the conceptions which we form *a priori* of things; but we seek to widen the range of our *a priori* knowledge. For this purpose, we must avail ourselves of such principles as add something to the original conception—something not identical with, nor contained in it, and by means of synthetical judgements *a priori,* leave far behind us the limits of experience; for example, in the proposition, "the world must have a beginning," and such like. Thus metaphysics, according to the proper aim of the science, consists merely of synthetical propositions *a priori.*

VI. *The Universal Problem of Pure Reason*

It is extremely advantageous to be able to bring a number of investigations under the formula of a single problem. For in this manner, we not only facilitate our own labour, inasmuch as we define it clearly to ourselves, but also render it more easy for others to decide whether we have done justice to our undertaking. The proper problem of pure reason, then, is contained in the question: "How are synthetical judgements *a priori* possible?"

That metaphysical science has hitherto remained in so vacillating a state of uncertainty and contradiction, is only to be attributed to the fact that this great problem, and perhaps even the difference between analytical and synthetical judgements, did not sooner suggest itself to philosophers. Upon the solution of this problem, or upon sufficient proof of the impossibility of synthetical knowledge *a priori,* depends the existence or downfall of the science of metaphysics. Among philosophers, David Hume came the nearest of all to this problem; yet it never acquired in his mind sufficient precision, nor did he regard the question in its universality. On the contrary, he stopped short at the synthetical proposition of the connection of an effect with its cause (*principium causalitatis*), insisting that such proposition *a priori* was impossible. According to his conclusions, then, all that we term metaphysical science is a mere delusion, arising from the fancied insight of reason into that which is in truth borrowed from experience, and to which habit has given the appearance of necessity. Against this assertion, destructive to all pure philosophy, he would have been guarded, had he had our problem before his eyes in its universality. For he would then have perceived that, according to his own argument, there likewise could not be any pure mathematical science, which assuredly cannot exist without synthetical propositions *a priori*—an absurdity from which his good understanding must have saved him.

In the solution of the above problem is at the same time comprehended the possibility of the use of pure reason in the foundation and construction of all sciences which contain theoretical knowledge *a priori* of objects, that is to say, the answer to the following questions:

How is pure mathematical science possible?

How is pure natural science possible?

Respecting these sciences, as they do certainly exist, it may with propriety be asked, *how* they are possible?—for that they must be possible is shown by the fact of their really existing.[1] But as to metaphysics, the miserable progress it has hitherto made, and the fact that of no one system yet brought forward, as far as regards its true aim, can it be said that this science really exists, leaves any one at liberty to doubt with reason the very possibility of its existence.

Yet, in a certain sense, this kind of knowledge must unquestionably be looked upon as *given*; in other words, metaphysics must be considered as really existing, if not as a science, nevertheless as a natural disposition of the human mind (*metaphysica naturalis*). For human reason, without any instigations imputable to the mere vanity of great knowledge, unceasingly progresses, urged on by its own feeling of need, towards such questions as cannot be answered by any empirical application of reason, or principles derived therefrom; and so there has ever really existed in every man some system of metaphysics. It will always exist, so soon as reason awakes to the exercise of its power of speculation. And now the question arises: "How is metaphysics, as a natural disposition, possible?" In other words, how, from the nature of universal human reason, do those questions

[1] As to the existence of pure natural science, or physics, perhaps many may still express doubts. But we have only to look at the different propositions which are commonly treated of at the commencement of proper (empirical) physical science—those, for example, relating to the permanence of the same quantity of matter, the *vis inertiae,* the equality of action and reaction, etc.—to be soon convinced that they form a science of pure physics (*physica pura,* or *rationalis*), which well deserves to be separately exposed as a special science, in its whole extent, whether that be great or confined.

arise which pure reason proposes to itself, and which it is impelled by its own feeling of need to answer as well as it can?

But as in all the attempts hitherto made to answer the questions which reason is prompted by its very nature to propose to itself, for example, whether the world had a beginning, or has existed from eternity, it has always met with unavoidable contradictions, we must not rest satisfied with the mere natural disposition of the mind to metaphysics, that is, with the existence of the faculty of pure reason, whence, indeed, some sort of metaphysical system always arises; but it must be possible to arrive at certainty in regard to the question whether we know or do not know the things of which metaphysics treats. We must be able to arrive at a decision on the subjects of its questions, or on the ability or inability of reason to form any judgement respecting them; and therefore either to extend with confidence the bounds of our pure reason, or to set strictly defined and safe limits to its action. This last question, which arises out of the above universal problem, would properly run thus: "How is metaphysics possible as a science?"

Thus, the critique of reason leads at last, naturally and necessarily, to science; and, on the other hand, the dogmatical use of reason without criticism leads to groundless assertions, against which others equally specious can always be set, thus ending unavoidably in scepticism.

Besides, this science cannot be of great and formidable prolixity, because it has not to do with objects of reason, the variety of which is inexhaustible, but merely with Reason herself and her problems; problems which arise out of her own bosom, and are not proposed to her by the nature of outward things, but by her own nature. And when once Reason has previously become able completely to understand her own power in regard to objects which she meets with in experience, it will be easy to determine securely the extent and limits of her attempted application to objects beyond the confines of experience.

We may and must, therefore, regard the attempts hitherto made to establish metaphysical science dogmatically as non-existent. For what of analysis, that is, mere dissection of conceptions, is contained in one or other, is not the aim of, but only a preparation for metaphysics proper, which has for its object the extension, by means of synthesis, of our *a priori* knowledge. And for this purpose, mere analysis is of course useless, because it only shows what is contained in these conceptions, but not how we arrive, *a priori*, at them; and this it is her duty to show, in order to be able afterwards to determine their valid use in regard to all objects of experience, to all knowledge in general. But little self-denial, indeed, is needed to give up these pretensions, seeing the undeniable, and in the dogmatic mode of procedure, inevitable contradictions of Reason with herself, have long since ruined the reputation of every system of metaphysics that has appeared up to this time. It will require more firmness to remain undeterred by difficulty from within, and opposition from without, from endeavouring, by a method quite opposed to all those hitherto followed, to further the growth and fruitfulness of a science indispensable to human reason—a science from which every branch it has borne may be cut away, but whose roots remain indestructible.

VII. *Idea and Division of a Particular Science, under the Name of a Critique of Pure Reason*

From all that has been said, there results the idea of a particular science, which may be called the *Critique of Pure Reason.* For reason is the faculty which furnishes us with the principles of knowledge *a priori.* Hence, pure reason is the faculty which contains the principles of cognizing anything absolutely *a priori.* An organon of pure reason would be a compendium of those principles according to which alone all pure cognitions *a priori* can be obtained. The completely extended application of such an organon would afford us a system of pure reason. As this, however, is demanding a great deal, and it is yet doubtful whether any extension of our knowledge be here possible, or, if so, in what cases; we can regard a science of the mere criticism of pure reason, its sources and limits, as the *propaedeutic* to a system of pure reason. Such a science must not be called a *doctrine,* but only a *critique of pure reason;* and its use, in regard to speculation, would be only negative, not to enlarge the bounds of, but to purify, our reason, and to shield it against error—which alone is no little gain. I apply the term *transcendental* to all knowledge which is not so much occupied with objects as with the mode of our cognition of these objects, so far as this mode of cognition is possible *a priori.* A system of such conceptions would be called *transcendental philosophy.* But this, again, is still beyond the bounds of our present essay. For as such a science must contain a complete exposition not only of our synthetical *a priori,* but of our analytical *a priori* knowledge, it is of too wide a range for our present purpose, because we do not require to carry our analysis any farther than is necessary to understand, in their full extent, the principles of synthesis *a priori,* with which alone we have to do. This investigation, which we cannot properly call a doctrine, but only a transcendental critique, because it aims not at the enlargement, but at the correction and guidance, of our knowledge, and is to serve as a touchstone of the worth or worthlessness of all knowledge *a priori,* is the sole object of our present essay. Such a critique is consequently, as far as possible, a preparation for an organon; and if this new organon should be found to fail, at least for a canon of pure reason, according to which the complete system of the philosophy of pure reason, whether it extend or limit the bounds of that reason, might one day be set forth both analytically and synthetically. For that this is possible, nay, that such a system is not of so great extent as to preclude the hope of its ever being completed, is evident. For we have not here to do with the nature of outward objects, which is infinite, but solely with the mind, which judges of the nature of objects, and, again, with the mind only in respect of its cognition *a priori.* And the object of our investigations, as it is not to be sought without, but, altogether within, ourselves, cannot remain concealed, and in all probability is limited enough to be completely surveyed and fairly estimated, according to its worth or worthlessness. Still less let the reader here expect a critique of books and systems of pure reason; our present object is exclusively a critique of the faculty of pure reason itself. Only when we make this critique our foundation, do we possess a pure touchstone for estimating the philosophical value of ancient and modern writings on this subject; and without this criterion, the incompetent historian or judge decides upon and corrects the groundless assertions of others with his own, which have themselves just as little foundation.

Transcendental philosophy is the idea of a science, for which the *Critique of Pure Reason* must sketch the whole plan architectonically, that is, from principles, with a full guarantee for the validity and stability of all the parts which enter into the building. It is the system of all the principles of pure reason. If this *Critique* itself does not assume the title of transcendental philosophy, it is only because, to be a complete system, it ought to contain a full analysis of all human knowledge *a priori.* Our critique must, indeed, lay before us a complete enumeration of all the radical conceptions which constitute the said pure knowledge. But from the complete analysis of these conceptions themselves, as also from a complete investigation of those derived from them, it abstains with reason; partly because it would be deviating from the end in view to occupy itself with this analysis, since this process is not attended with the difficulty and insecurity to be found in the synthesis, to which our critique is entirely devoted, and partly because it would be inconsistent with the unity of our plan to burden this essay with the vindication of the completeness of such an analysis and deduction, with which, after all, we have at present nothing to do. This completeness of the analysis of these radical conceptions, as well as of the deduction from the conceptions *a priori* which may be given by the analysis, we can, however, easily attain, provided only that we are in possession of all these radical conceptions, which are to serve as principles of the synthesis, and that in respect of this main purpose nothing is wanting.

To the *Critique of Pure Reason,* therefore, belongs all that constitutes transcendental philosophy; and it is the complete idea of transcendental philosophy, but still not the science itself; because it only proceeds so far with the analysis as is necessary to the power of judging completely of our synthetical knowledge *a priori.*

The principal thing we must attend to, in the division of the parts of a science like this, is that no conceptions must enter it which contain aught empirical; in other words, that the knowledge *a priori* must be completely pure. Hence, although the highest principles and fundamental conceptions of morality are certainly cognitions *a priori,* yet they do not belong to transcendental philosophy; because, though they certainly do not lay the conceptions of pain, pleasure, desires, inclinations, etc. (which are all of empirical origin), at the foundation of its precepts, yet still into the conception of duty—as an obstacle to be overcome, or as an incitement which should not be made into a motive—these empirical conceptions must necessarily enter, in the construction of a system of pure morality. Transcendental philosophy is consequently a philosophy of the pure and merely speculative reason. For all that is practical, so far as it contains motives, relates to feelings, and these belong to empirical sources of cognition.

If we wish to divide this science from the universal point of view of a science in general, it ought to comprehend, first, a *Doctrine of the Elements,* and, secondly, a *Doctrine of the Method* of pure reason. Each of these main divisions will have its subdivisions, the separate reasons for which we cannot here particularize. Only so much seems necessary, by way of introduction of premonition, that there are two sources of human knowledge (which probably spring from a common, but to us unknown root), namely, sense and understanding. By the former, objects are *given* to us; by the latter, *thought.* So far as the faculty of sense may contain representations *a priori,* which form the conditions under which objects are given, in so far it belongs to transcendental philosophy. The transcendental doctrine of sense must form the first part of our science of elements, because the conditions under which alone the objects of human knowledge are given must precede those under which they are thought.

I
TRANSCENDENTAL DOCTRINE OF ELEMENTS

FIRST PART. *TRANSCENDENTAL AESTHETIC*

§ 1. *Introductory*

In whatsoever mode, or by whatsoever means, our knowledge may relate to objects, it is at least quite clear that the only manner in which it immediately relates to them is by means of an intuition. To this as the indispensable groundwork, all thought points. But an intuition can take place only in so far as the object is given to us. This, again, is only possible, to man at least, on condition that the object affect the mind in a certain manner. The capacity for receiving representations (receptivity) through the mode in which we are affected by objects, is called *sensibility*. By means of sensibility, therefore, objects are given to us, and it alone furnishes us with intuitions; by the understanding they are *thought*, and from it arise conceptions. But all thought must directly, or indirectly, by means of certain signs, relate ultimately to intuitions; consequently, with us, to sensibility, because in no other way can an object be given to us.

The effect of an object upon the faculty of representation, so far as we are affected by the said object, is sensation. That sort of intuition which relates to an object by means of sensation is called an empirical intuition. The undetermined object of an empirical intuition is called *phenomenon*. That which in the phenomenon corresponds to the sensation, I term its *matter*; but that which effects that the content of the phenomenon can be arranged under certain relations, I call its *form*. But that in which our sensations are merely arranged, and by which they are susceptible of assuming a certain form, cannot be itself sensation. It is, then, the matter of all phenomena that is given to us *a posteriori*; the form must lie ready *a priori* for them in the mind, and consequently can be regarded separately from all sensation.

I call all representations *pure*, in the transcendental meaning of the word, wherein nothing is met with that belongs to sensation. And accordingly we find existing in the mind *a priori*, the pure form of sensuous intuitions in general, in which all the manifold content of the phenomenal world is arranged and viewed under certain relations. This pure form of sensibility I shall call *pure intuition*. Thus, if I take away from our representation of a body all that the understanding thinks as belonging to it, as substance, force, divisibility, etc., and also whatever belongs to sensation, as impenetrability, hardness, colour, etc.; yet there is still something left us from this empirical intuition, namely, extension and shape. These belong to pure intuition, which exists *a priori* in the mind, as a mere form of sensibility, and without any real object of the senses or any sensation.

The science of all the principles of sensibility *a priori*, I call *transcendental aesthetic*.[1] There must, then, be such a science forming the first part of the transcendental doctrine of elements, in contradistinction to that part which contains the principles of pure thought, and which is called *transcendental logic*.

In the science of transcendental aesthetic accordingly, we shall first isolate sensibility or the sensuous faculty, by separating from it all that

[1] The Germans are the only people who at present use this word to indicate what others call the critique of taste. At the foundation of this term lies the disappointed hope, which the eminent analyst, Baumgarten, conceived, of subjecting the criticism of the beautiful to principles of reason, and so of elevating its rules into a science. But his endeavours were vain. For the said rules or criteria are, in respect to their chief sources, merely empirical, consequently never can serve as determinate laws *a priori*, by which our judgement in matters of taste is to be directed. It is rather our judgement which forms the proper test as to the correctness of the principles. On this account it is advisable to give up the use of the term as designating the critique of taste, and to apply it solely to that doctrine, which is true science—the science of the laws of sensibility—and thus come nearer to the language and the sense of the ancients in their well-known division of the objects of cognition into αιοθητα και νοητα, or to share it with speculative philosophy, and employ it partly in a transcendental, partly in a psychological signification.

is annexed to its perceptions by the conceptions of understanding, so that nothing be left but empirical intuition. In the next place we shall take away from this intuition all that belongs to sensation, so that nothing may remain but pure intuition, and the mere form of phenomena, which is all that the sensibility can afford *a priori*. From this investigation it will be found that there are two pure forms of sensuous intuition, as principles of knowledge *a priori*, namely, space and time. To the consideration of these we shall now proceed.

Section I. Of Space

§ 2. *Metaphysical Exposition of this Conception*

By means of the external sense (a property of the mind), we represent to ourselves objects as without us, and these all in space. Therein alone are their shape, dimensions, and relations to each other determined or determinable. The internal sense, by means of which the mind contemplates itself or its internal state, gives, indeed, no intuition of the soul as an object; yet there is nevertheless a determinate form, under which alone the contemplation of our internal state is possible, so that all which relates to the inward determinations of the mind is represented in relations of time. Of time we cannot have any external intuition, any more than we can have an internal intuition of space. What then are time and space? Are they real existences? Or, are they merely relations or determinations of things, such, however, as would equally belong to these things in themselves, though they should never become objects of intuition; or, are they such as belong only to the form of intuition, and consequently to the subjective constitution of the mind, without which these predicates of time and space could not be attached to any object? In order to become informed on these points, we shall first give an exposition of the conception of space. By exposition, I mean the clear, though not detailed, representation of that which belongs to a conception; and an exposition is metaphysical when it contains that which represents the conception as given *a priori*.

1. Space is not a conception which has been derived from outward experiences. For, in order that certain sensations may relate to something without me (that is, to something which occupies a different part of space from that in which I am); in like manner, in order that I may represent them not merely as without, of, and near to each other, but also in separate places, the representation of space must already exist as a foundation. Consequently, the representation of space cannot be borrowed from the relations of external phenomena through experience; but, on the contrary, this external experience is itself only possible through the said antecedent representation.

2. Space then is a necessary representation *a priori*, which serves for the foundation of all external intuitions. We never can imagine or make a representation to ourselves of the non-existence of space, though we may easily enough think that no objects are found in it. It must, therefore, be considered as the condition of the possibility of phenomena, and by no means as a determination dependent on them, and is a representation *a priori*, which necessarily supplies the basis for external phenomena.

3. Space is no discursive, or as we say, general conception of the relations of things, but a pure intuition. For, in the first place, we can only represent to ourselves one space, and, when we talk of divers spaces, we mean only parts of one and the same space. Moreover, these parts cannot antecede this one all-embracing space, as the component parts from which the aggregate can be made up, but can be cogitated only as existing in it. Space is essentially one, and multiplicity in it, consequently the general notion of spaces, of this or that space, depends solely upon limitations. Hence it follows that an *a priori* intuition (which is not empirical) lies at the root of all our conceptions of space. Thus, moreover, the principles of geometry—for example, that "in a triangle, two sides together are greater than the third," are never deduced from general conceptions of line and triangle, but from intuition, and this *a priori*, with apodeictic certainty.

4. Space is represented as an infinite given quantity. Now every conception must indeed be considered as a representation which is contained in an infinite multitude of different possible representations, which, therefore, comprises these under itself; but no conception, as such, can be so conceived, as if it contained within itself an infinite multitude of representations. Nevertheless, space is so conceived of, for all parts of space are equally capable of being produced to infinity. Consequently, the original representation of space is an intuition *a priori*, and not a conception.

§ 3. *Transcendental Exposition of the Conception of Space*

By a transcendental exposition, I mean the explanation of a conception, as a principle, whence can be discerned the possibility of other synthetical *a priori* cognitions. For this purpose, it is requisite, firstly, that such cognitions do really flow from the given conception; and, secondly, that the said cognitions are only possible under the presupposition of a given mode of explaining this conception.

Geometry is a science which determines the properties of space synthetically, and yet *a priori*. What, then, must be our representation of space, in order that such a cognition of it may be possible? It must be originally intuition, for from a mere conception, no propositions can be deduced which go out beyond the conception, and yet this happens in geometry. (Introd. V.) But this intuition must be found in the mind *a priori,* that is, before any perception of objects, consequently must be pure, not empirical, intuition. For geometrical principles are always apodeictic, that is, united with the consciousness of their necessity, as: "Space has only three dimensions." But propositions of this kind cannot be empirical judgements, nor conclusions from them. (Introd. II.) Now, how can an external intuition anterior to objects themselves, and in which our conception of objects can be determined *a priori,* exist in the human mind? Obviously not otherwise than in so far as it has its seat in the subject only, as the *formal* capacity of the subject's being affected by objects, and thereby of obtaining immediate representation, that is, intuition; consequently, only as the *form of the external sense* in general.

Thus it is only by means of our explanation that the possibility of geometry, as a synthetical science *a priori,* becomes comprehensible. Every mode of explanation which does not show us this possibility, although in appearance it may be similar to ours, can with the utmost certainty be distinguished from it by these marks.

§ 4. *Conclusions from the foregoing Conceptions*

(*a*) Space does not represent any property of objects as things in themselves, nor does it represent them in their relations to each other; in other words, space does not represent to us any determination of objects such as attaches to the objects themselves, and would remain, even though all subjective conditions of the intuition were abstracted. For neither absolute nor relative determinations of objects can be intuited prior to the existence of the things to which they belong, and therefore not *a priori.*

(*b*) Space is nothing else than the form of all phenomena of the external sense, that is, the subjective condition of the sensibility, under which alone external intuition is possible. Now, because the receptivity or capacity of the subject to be affected by objects necessarily antecedes all intuitions of these objects, it is easily understood how the form of all phenomena can be given in the mind previous to all actual perceptions, therefore *a priori,* and how it, as a pure intuition, in which all objects must be determined, can contain principles of the relations of these objects prior to all experience.

It is therefore from the human point of view only that we can speak of space, extended objects, etc. If we depart from the subjective condition, under which alone we can obtain external intuition, or, in other words, by means of which we are affected by objects, the representation of space has no meaning whatsoever. This predicate is only applicable to things in so far as they appear to us, that is, are objects of sensibility. The constant form of this receptivity, which we call sensibility, is a necessary condition of all relations in which objects can be intuited as existing without us, and when abstraction of these objects is made, is a pure intuition, to which we give the name of space. It is clear that we cannot make the special conditions of sensibility into conditions of the possibility of things, but only of the possibility of their existence as far as they are phenomena. And so we may correctly say that space contains all which can appear to us externally, but not all things considered as things in themselves, be they intuited or not, or by whatsoever subject one will. As to the intuitions of other thinking beings, we cannot judge whether they are or are not bound by the same conditions which limit our own intuition, and which for us are universally valid. If we join the limitation of a judgement to the conception of the subject, then the judgement will possess unconditioned validity. For example, the proposition, "All objects are beside each other in space," is valid only under the limitation that these things are taken as objects of our sensuous intuition. But if I join the condition to the conception and say, "All things, as external phenomena, are beside each other in space," then the rule is valid universally, and without any limitation. Our expositions, consequently, teach the *reality* (i.e., the objective validity) of space in regard of all which can be presented to us externally as object, and at the same time also the *ideality* of space in regard to objects when they are considered by means of reason as things in themselves, that is, without reference to the constitution of our sensibility. We maintain, therefore, the *empirical reality* of space in regard to all possible external experience, although we must admit its *transcendental ideality*; in other words, that it is nothing, so soon as we withdraw the condition upon which the possibility of all experience depends and look upon space as something that belongs to things in themselves.

But, with the exception of space, there is no representation, subjective and referring to something external to us, which could be called objective *a priori.* For there are no other subjective representations from which we can deduce synthetical propositions *a priori,* as we can from the intuition of space. (See § 3.) Therefore, to speak accurately, no ideality whatever belongs to these, although they agree in this respect with the representation of space, that they belong merely to the subjective nature of the mode of sensuous perception; such a mode, for example, as that of sight, of hearing, and of feeling, by means of the sensations of colour, sound, and heat, but which, because they are only sensations and not intuitions, do not of themselves give us the cognition of any object, least of all, an *a priori* cognition. My purpose, in the above remark, is merely this: to guard any one against illustrating the asserted ideality of space by examples quite insufficient, for example, by colour, taste, etc.; for these must be contemplated not as properties of things, but only as changes in the subject, changes which may be different in different men. For, in such a case, that which is originally a mere phenomenon, a rose, for example, is taken by the empirical understanding for a thing in itself, though to every different eye, in respect of its colour, it may appear different. On the contrary, the transcendental conception of phenomena in space is a critical admonition, that, in general, nothing which is intuited in space is a thing in itself, and that space is not a form which belongs as a property to things; but that objects are quite unknown to us in themselves, and what we call outward objects, are nothing else but mere representations of our sensibility, whose form is space, but whose real correlate, the thing in itself, is not known by means of these representations, nor ever can be, but respecting which, in experience, no inquiry is ever made.

SECTION II. Of Time

§ 5. *Metaphysical Exposition of this Conception*

1. TIME is not an empirical conception. For neither coexistence nor succession would be perceived by us, if the representation of time did not exist as a foundation *a priori.* Without this presupposition we could not represent to ourselves that things exist together at one and the same time, or at different times, that is, contemporaneously, or in succession.

2. Time is a necessary representation, lying at the foundation of all our intuitions. With regard to phenomena in general, we cannot think away time from them, and represent them to ourselves as out of and unconnected with time, but we can quite well represent to ourselves time void of phenomena. Time is therefore given *a priori.* In it alone is all reality of phenomena possible. These may all be annihilated in thought, but time itself, as the universal condition of their possibility, cannot be so annulled.

3. On this necessity *a priori* is also founded the possibility of apodeictic principles of the relations of time, or axioms of time in general, such as: "Time has only one dimension," "Different times are not coexistent but successive" (as different spaces are not successive but coexistent). These principles cannot be derived from experience, for it would give neither strict universality, nor apodeictic certainty. We should only be able to say, "so common experience teaches us," but not "it must be so." They are valid as rules, through which, in general, experience is possible; and they instruct us respecting experience, and not by means of it.

4. Time is not a discursive, or as it is called, general conception, but a pure form of the sensuous intuition. Different times are merely parts of one and the same time. But the representation which can only be given by a single object is an intuition. Besides, the proposition that different times cannot be coexistent could not be derived from a general conception. For this proposition is synthetical, and therefore cannot spring out of conceptions alone. It is therefore contained immediately in the intuition and representation of time.

5. The infinity of time signifies nothing more than that every determined quantity of time is possible only through limitations of one time lying at the foundation. Consequently, the original representation, time, must be given as unlimited. But as the determinate representation of the parts of time and of every quantity of an object can only be obtained by limitation, the *complete* representation of time must not be furnished by means of conceptions, for these contain only partial representations. Conceptions, on the contrary, must have immediate intuition for their basis.

§ 6. *Transcendental Exposition of the Conception of Time*

I may here refer to what is said above (§ 5, 3), where, for the sake of brevity, I have placed under the head of metaphysical exposition, that which is properly transcendental. Here I shall add that the conception of change, and with it the conception of motion, as change of place, is possible only through and in the representation of time; that if this representation were not an intuition (internal) *a priori,* no conception, of whatever kind, could render comprehensible the possibility of change, in other words, of a conjunction of contradictorily opposed predicates in one and the same object, for example, the presence of a thing in a place and the non-presence of the same thing in the same place. It is only in time that it is possible to meet with two contradictorily opposed determinations in one thing, that is, after each other. Thus our conception of time explains the possibility of so much synthetical knowledge *a priori,* as is exhibited in the general doctrine of motion, which is not a little fruitful.

§ 7. *Conclusions from the above Conceptions*

(*a*) Time is not something which subsists of itself, or which inheres in things as an objective determination, and therefore remains, when abstraction is made of the subjective conditions of the intuition of things. For in the former case, it would be something real, yet without presenting to any power of perception any real object. In the latter case, as an order or determination inherent in things themselves, it could not be antecedent to things, as their condition, nor discerned or intuited by means of synthetical propositions *a priori.* But all this is quite possible when we regard time as merely the subjective condition under which all our intuitions take place. For in that case, this form of the inward intuition can be represented prior to the objects, and consequently *a priori.*

(*b*) Time is nothing else than the form of the internal sense, that is, of the intuitions of self and of our internal state. For time cannot be any determination of outward phenomena. It has to do neither with shape nor position; on the contrary, it determines the relation of representations in our internal state. And precisely because this internal intuition presents to us no shape or form, we endeavour to supply this want by analogies, and represent the course of time by a line progressing to infinity, the content of which constitutes a series which is only of one dimension; and we conclude from the properties of this line as to all the properties of time, with this single exception, that the parts of the line are coexistent, whilst those of time are successive. From this it is clear also that the representation of time is itself an intuition, because all its relations can be expressed in an external intuition.

(*c*) Time is the formal condition *a priori* of all phenomena whatsoever. Space, as the pure form of external intuition, is limited as a condition *a priori* to external phenomena alone. On the other hand, because all representations, whether they have or have not external things for their objects, still in themselves, as determinations of the mind, belong to our internal state; and because this internal state is subject to the formal condition of the internal intuition, that is, to time—time is a condition *a priori* of all phenomena whatsoever—the *immediate* condition of all internal, and thereby the *mediate* condition of all external phenomena. If I can say *a priori,* "All outward phenomena are in space, and determined *a priori* according to the relations of space," I can also, from the principle of the internal sense, affirm universally, "All phenomena in general, that is, all objects of the senses, are in time and stand necessarily in relations of time."

If we abstract our internal intuition of ourselves and all external intuitions, possible only by virtue of this internal intuition and presented to us by our faculty of representation, and consequently take objects as they are in themselves, then time is nothing. It is only of objective validity in regard to phenomena, because these are things which we regard as objects of our senses. It is no longer objective, if we make abstraction of the sensuousness of our intuition, in other words, of that mode of representation which is peculiar to us, and speak of things in general. Time is therefore merely a subjective condition of our (human) intuition (which is always sensuous, that is, so far as we are affected by objects), and in itself, independently of the mind or subject, is nothing. Nevertheless, in respect of all phenomena, consequently of all things which come within the sphere of our experience, it is necessarily objective. We cannot say, "All things are in time," because in this conception of things in general, we abstract and make no mention of any sort of intuition of things. But this is the proper condition under which time belongs to our representation of objects. If we add the condition to the conception, and say, "All things, as phenomena, that is, objects of sensuous intuition, are in time," then the proposition has its sound objective validity and universality *a priori*.

What we have now set forth teaches, therefore, the empirical reality of time; that is, its objective validity in reference to all objects which can ever be presented to our senses. And as our intuition is always sensuous, no object ever can be presented to us in experience, which does not come under the conditions of time. On the other hand, we deny to time all claim to absolute reality; that is, we deny that it, without having regard to the form of our sensuous intuition, absolutely inheres in things as a condition or property. Such properties as belong to objects as things in themselves never can be presented to us through the medium of the senses. Herein consists, therefore, the transcendental ideality of time, according to which, if we abstract the subjective conditions of sensuous intuition, it is nothing, and cannot be reckoned as subsisting or inhering in objects as things in themselves, independently of its relation to our intuition. This ideality, like that of space, is not to be proved or illustrated by fallacious analogies with sensations, for this reason—that in such arguments or illustrations, we make the presupposition that the phenomenon, in which such and such predicates inhere, has objective reality, while in this case we can only find such an objective reality as is itself empirical, that is, regards the object as a mere phenomenon. In reference to this subject, see the remark in Section I (pages 25-26).

§ 8. *Elucidation*

Against this theory, which grants empirical reality to time, but denies to it absolute and transcendental reality, I have heard from intelligent men an objection so unanimously urged that I conclude that it must naturally present itself to every reader to whom these considerations are novel. It runs thus: "Changes are real" (this the continual change in our own representations demonstrates, even though the existence of all external phenomena, together with their changes, is denied). Now, changes are only possible in time, and therefore time must be something real. But there is no difficulty in answering this. I grant the whole argument. Time, no doubt, is something real, that is, it is the real form of our internal intuition. It therefore has subjective reality, in reference to our internal experience, that is, I have really the representation of time and of my determinations therein. Time, therefore, is not to be regarded as an object, but as the mode of representation of myself as an object. But if I could intuite myself, or be intuited by another being, without this condition of sensibility, then those very determinations which we now represent to ourselves as changes, would present to us a knowledge in which the representation of time, and consequently of change, would not appear. The empirical reality of time, therefore, remains, as the condition of all our experience. But absolute reality, according to what has been said above, cannot be granted it. Time is nothing but the form of our internal intuition.[1] If we take away from it the special condition of our sensibility, the conception of time also vanishes; and it inheres not in the objects themselves, but solely in the subject (or mind) which intuites them.

But the reason why this objection is so unanimously brought against our doctrine of time, and that too by disputants who cannot start any intelligible arguments against the doctrine of the ideality of space, is this—they have no hope of demonstrating apodeictically the absolute reality of space, because the doctrine of idealism is against them, according to which the reality of external objects is not capable of any strict proof. On the other hand, the reality of the object of our internal sense (that is, myself and my internal state) is clear immediately through consciousness. The former—external objects in space—might be a mere delusion, but the latter—the object of my internal perception—is undeniably real. They do not, however, reflect that both, without question of their reality as representations, belong only to the genus phenomenon, which has always two aspects, the one, the object considered as a thing in itself, without regard to the mode of intuiting it, and the nature of which remains for this very reason problematical, the other, the form of our intuition of the object, which must be sought not in the object as a thing in itself, but in the subject to which it appears—which form of intuition nevertheless belongs really and necessarily to the phenomenal object.

Time and space are, therefore, two sources of knowledge, from which, *a priori*, various synthetical cognitions can be drawn. Of this we find a striking example in the cognitions of space and its relations, which form the foundation of pure mathematics. They are the two pure forms

[1] I can indeed say "my representations follow one another, or are successive"; but this means only that we are conscious of them as in a succession, that is, according to the form of the internal sense. Time, therefore, is not a thing in itself, nor is it any objective determination pertaining to, or inherent in things.

of all intuitions, and thereby make synthetical propositions *a priori* possible. But these sources of knowledge being merely conditions of our sensibility, do therefore, and as such, strictly determine their own range and purpose, in that they do not and cannot present objects as things in themselves, but are applicable to them solely in so far as they are considered as sensuous phenomena. The sphere of phenomena is the only sphere of their validity, and if we venture out of this, no further objective use can be made of them. For the rest, this formal reality of time and space leaves the validity of our empirical knowledge unshaken; for our certainty in that respect is equally firm, whether these forms necessarily inhere in the things themselves, or only in our intuitions of them. On the other hand, those who maintain the absolute reality of time and space, whether as essentially subsisting, or only inhering, as modifications, in things, must find themselves at utter variance with the principles of experience itself. For, if they decide for the first view, and make space and time into substances, this being the side taken by mathematical natural philosophers, they must admit two self-subsisting nonentities, infinite and eternal, which exist (yet without there being anything real) for the purpose of containing in themselves everything that is real. If they adopt the second view of inherence, which is preferred by some metaphysical natural philosophers, and regard space and time as relations (contiguity in space or succession in time), abstracted from experience, though represented confusedly in this state of separation, they find themselves in that case necessitated to deny the validity of mathematical doctrines *a priori* in reference to real things (for example, in space)—at all events their apodeictic certainty. For such certainty cannot be found in an *a posteriori* proposition; and the conceptions *a priori* of space and time are, according to this opinion, mere creations of the imagination, having their source really in experience, inasmuch as, out of relations abstracted from experience, imagination has made up something which contains, indeed, general statements of these relations, yet of which no application can be made without the restrictions attached thereto by nature. The former of these parties gains this advantage, that they keep the sphere of phenomena free for mathematical science. On the other hand, these very conditions (space and time) embarrass them greatly, when the understanding endeavours to pass the limits of that sphere. The latter has, indeed, this advantage, that the representations of space and time do not come in their way when they wish to judge of objects, not as phenomena, but merely in their relation to the understanding. Devoid, however, of a true and objectively valid *a priori* intuition, they can neither furnish any basis for the possibility of mathematical cognitions *a priori*, nor bring the propositions of experience into necessary accordance with those of mathematics. In our theory of the true nature of these two original forms of the sensibility, both difficulties are surmounted.

In conclusion, that transcendental aesthetic cannot contain any more than these two elements—space and time, is sufficiently obvious from the fact that all other conceptions appertaining to sensibility, even that of motion, which unites in itself both elements, presuppose something empirical. Motion, for example, presupposes the perception of something movable. But space considered in itself contains nothing movable, consequently motion must be something which is found in space only through experience—in other words, is an empirical datum. In like manner, transcendental aesthetic cannot number the conception of change among its data *a priori*; for time itself does not change, but only something which is in time. To acquire the conception of change, therefore, the perception of some existing object and of the succession of its determinations, in one word, experience, is necessary.

§ 9. *General Remarks on Transcendental Aesthetic*

I. In order to prevent any misunderstanding, it will be requisite, in the first place, to recapitulate, as clearly as possible, what our opinion is with respect to the fundamental nature of our sensuous cognition in general. We have intended, then, to say that all our intuition is nothing but the representation of phenomena; that the things which we intuite, are not in themselves the same as our representations of them in intuition, nor are their relations in themselves so constituted as they appear to us; and that if we take away the subject, or even only the subjective constitution of our senses in general, then not only the nature and relations of objects in space and time, but even space and time themselves disappear; and that these, as phenomena, cannot exist in themselves, but only in us. What may be the nature of objects considered as things in themselves and without reference to the receptivity of our sensibility is quite unknown to us. We know nothing more than our own mode of perceiving them, which is peculiar to us, and which, though not of necessity pertaining to every animated being, is so to the whole human race. With this alone we have to do. Space and time are the pure forms thereof; sensation the matter. The former alone can we cognize *a priori,* that is, antecedent to all actual perception; and for this reason such cognition is called *pure* intuition. The latter is that in our cognition which is called cognition *a posteriori,* that is, *empirical* intuition. The former appertain absolutely and necessarily to our sensibility, of whatsoever kind our sensations may be; the latter may be of very diversified character. Supposing that we should carry our empirical intuition even to the very highest degree of clearness, we should not thereby advance one step nearer to a knowledge of the constitution of objects as things in themselves. For we could only, at best, arrive at a complete cognition of our own mode of intuition, that is, of our sensibility, and this always under the conditions originally attaching to the subject, namely, the conditions of space and time; while the question: "What are objects considered as things in themselves?" remains unanswerable even after the most thorough examination of the phenomenal world.

To say, then, that all our sensibility is nothing but the confused representation of things containing exclusively that which belongs to them as things in themselves, and this under an accumulation of characteristic marks and partial representations which we cannot distinguish in consciousness, is a falsification of the conception of sensibility and phenomenization, which renders our whole doctrine thereof empty and useless. The difference between a confused and a clear representation is merely logical and has nothing to do with content. No doubt the conception of *right,* as employed by a sound understanding, contains all that the most subtle investigation could unfold from it, although, in the ordinary practical use of the word, we are not conscious of the manifold representations comprised in the conception. But we cannot for this reason assert that the ordinary conception is a sensuous one, containing a mere phenomenon, for *right* cannot appear as a phenomenon; but the conception of it lies in the understanding, and represents a property (the moral property) of actions, which belongs to them in themselves. On the other hand, the representation in intuition of a body contains nothing which could belong to an object considered as a thing in itself, but merely the phenomenon or appearance of something, and the mode in which we are affected by that appearance; and this receptivity of our faculty of cognition is called sensibility, and remains *toto caelo* different from the cognition of an object in itself, even though we should examine the content of the phenomenon to the very bottom.

It must be admitted that the Leibnitz-Wolfian philosophy has assigned an entirely erroneous point of view to all investigations into the nature and origin of our cognitions, inasmuch as it regards the distinction between the sensuous and the intellectual as merely logical, whereas it is plainly transcendental, and concerns not merely the clearness or obscurity, but the content and origin of both. For the faculty of sensibility not only does not present us with an indistinct and confused cognition of objects as things in themselves, but, in fact, gives us no knowledge of these at all. On the contrary, so soon as we abstract in thought our own subjective nature, the object represented, with the properties ascribed to it by sensuous intuition, entirely disappears, because it was only this subjective nature that determined the form of the object as a phenomenon.

In phenomena, we commonly, indeed, distinguish that which essentially belongs to the intuition of them, and is valid for the sensuous faculty of every human being, from that which belongs to the same intuition accidentally, as valid not for the sensuous faculty in general, but for a particular state or organization of this or that sense. Accordingly, we are accustomed to say that the former is a cognition which represents the object itself, whilst the latter presents only a particular appearance or phenomenon thereof. This distinction, however, is only empirical. If we stop here (as is usual), and do not regard the empirical intuition as itself a mere phenomenon (as we ought to do), in which nothing that can appertain to a thing in itself is to be found, our transcendental distinction is lost, and we believe that we cognize objects as things in themselves, although in the whole range of the sensuous world, investigate the nature of its objects as profoundly as we may, we have to do with nothing but phenomena. Thus, we call the rainbow a mere appearance of phenomenon in a sunny shower, and the rain, the reality or thing in itself; and this is right enough, if we understand the latter conception in a merely physical sense, that is, as that which in universal experience, and under whatever conditions of sensuous perception, is known in intuition to be so and so determined, and not otherwise. But if we consider this empirical datum generally, and inquire, without reference to its accordance with all our senses, whether there can be discovered in it aught which represents an object as a thing in itself (the raindrops of course are not such, for they are, as phenomena, empirical objects), the question of the relation of the representation to the object is transcendental; and not only are the raindrops mere phenomena, but even their circular form, nay, the space itself through which they fall, is nothing in itself, but both are mere modifications or fundamental dispositions of our sensuous intuition, whilst the transcendental object remains for us utterly unknown.

The second important concern of our aesthetic is that it does not obtain favour merely as a plausible hypothesis, but possess as undoubted a character of certainty as can be demanded of any theory which is to serve for an organon. In order fully to convince the reader of this certainty, we shall select a case which will serve to make its validity apparent, and also to illustrate what has been said in § 3.

Suppose, then, that space and time are in themselves objective, and conditions of the possibility of objects as things in themselves. In the first place, it is evident that both present us with very many apodeictic and synthetic propositions *a priori,* but especially space—and for this reason we shall prefer it for investigation at present. As the propositions of geometry are cognized synthetically *a priori,* and with apodeictic certainty, I inquire: Whence do you obtain propositions of this kind, and on what basis does the understanding rest, in order to arrive at such absolutely necessary and universally valid truths?

There is no other way than through intuitions or conceptions, as such; and these are given either *a priori* or *a posteriori.* The latter, namely, empirical conceptions, together with the empirical intuition on which they are founded, cannot afford any synthetical proposition, except such as is itself also empirical, that is, a proposition of experience. But an empirical proposition cannot possess the qualities of necessity and absolute universality, which, nevertheless, are the characteristics of all geometrical propositions. As to the first and only means to arrive at such cognitions, namely, through mere conceptions or intuitions *a priori,* it is quite clear that from mere conceptions no synthetical cognitions, but only analytical ones, can be obtained. Take, for example, the proposition: "Two straight lines cannot enclose a space, and with these alone no figure is possible," and try to deduce it from the conception of a straight line and the number two; or take the proposition: "It is possible to construct a figure with three straight lines," and endeavour, in like manner, to deduce it from the mere conception of a straight line and the number three. All your endeavours are in vain, and you find yourself forced to have recourse to intuition, as, in fact, geometry always does. You therefore give yourself an object in intuition. But of what kind is this intuition? Is it a pure *a priori,* or is it an empirical intuition? If the latter, then neither an universally valid, much less an apodeictic proposition can arise from it, for experience never can give us any such proposition. You must, therefore, give yourself an object *a priori* in intuition, and upon that ground your synthetical proposition. Now if there did not exist within you a faculty of intuition *a priori;* if this subjective condition were not in respect to its form also the universal condition *a priori* under which alone the object of this external intuition is itself possible; if the object (that is, the triangle) were something in itself, without relation to you the subject; how could you affirm that that which lies necessarily in your subjective conditions in order to construct a triangle, must also necessarily belong to the triangle in itself? For to your conceptions of three lines, you could not add anything new (that is, the figure); which, therefore, must necessarily be found in the object, because the object is given before your cognition, and not by means of it. If, therefore, space (and time also) were not a mere form of your intuition, which contains conditions *a priori,* under which alone things can become external objects for you, and without which subjective conditions the objects are in themselves nothing, you could not construct any synthetical proposition whatsoever regarding external objects. It is therefore not merely possible or probable, but indubitably certain, that space and time, as the necessary conditions of all our external and internal experience, are merely subjective conditions of all our intuitions, in relation to which all objects are therefore mere phenomena, and not things in themselves, presented to us in this particular manner. And for this reason, in respect to the form of phenomena, much may be said *a priori,* whilst of the thing in itself, which may lie at the foundation of these phenomena, it is impossible to say anything.

II. In confirmation of this theory of the ideality of the external as well as internal sense, consequently of all objects of sense, as mere phenomena, we may especially remark that all in our cognition that belongs to intuition contains nothing more than mere relations. (The feelings of pain and pleasure, and the will, which are not cognitions, are excepted.) The relations, to wit, of place in an intuition (extension), change of place (motion), and laws according to which this change is determined (moving forces). That, however, which is present in this or that place, or any operation going on, or result taking place in the things themselves, with the exception of change of place, is not given to us by intuition. Now by means of mere relations, a thing cannot be known in itself; and it may therefore be fairly concluded, that, as through the external sense nothing but mere representations of relations are given us, the said external sense in its representation can contain only the relation of the object to the subject, but not the essential nature of the object as a thing in itself.

The same is the case with the internal intuition, not only because, in the internal intuition, the representation of the external senses constitutes the material with which the mind is occupied; but because time, in which we place, and which itself antecedes the consciousness of, these representations in experience, and which, as the formal condition of the mode according to which objects are placed in the mind, lies at the foundation of them, contains relations of the successive, the coexistent, and of that which always must be coexistent with succession, the permanent. Now that which, as representation, can antecede every exercise of thought (of an object), is intuition; and when it contains nothing but relations, it is the form of the intuition, which, as it presents us with no representation, except in so far as something is placed in the mind, can be nothing else than the mode in which the mind is affected by its own activity, to wit—its presenting to itself representations, consequently the mode in which the mind is affected by itself; that is, it can be nothing but an internal sense in respect to its form. Everything that is represented through the medium of sense is so far phenomenal; consequently, we must either refuse altogether to admit an internal sense, or the subject, which is the object of that sense, could only be represented by it as phenomenon, and not as it would judge of itself, if its intuition were pure spontaneous activity, that is, were intellectual. The difficulty here lies wholly in the question: How can the subject have an internal intuition of itself? But this difficulty is common to every theory. The consciousness of self (apperception) is the simple representation of the "ego"; and if by means of that representation alone, all the manifold representations in the subject were spontaneously given, then our internal intuition would be intellectual. This consciousness in man requires an internal perception of the manifold representations which are previously given in the subject; and the manner in which these representations are given in the mind without spontaneity, must, on account of this difference (the want of spontaneity), be called sensibility. If the faculty of self-consciousness is to apprehend what lies in the mind, it must affect that and can in this way alone produce an intuition of self. But the form of this intuition, which lies in the original constitution of the mind, determines, in the representation of time, the manner in which the manifold representations are to combine themselves in the mind; since the subject intuites itself, not as it would represent itself immediately and spontaneously, but according to the manner in which the mind is internally affected, consequently, as it appears, and not as it is.

III. When we say that the intuition of external objects, and also the self-intuition of the subject, represent both, objects and subject, in space and time, as they affect our senses, that is, as they appear—this is by no means equivalent to asserting that these objects are mere illusory appearances. For when we speak of things as phenomena, the objects, nay, even the properties which we ascribe to them, are looked upon as really given; only that, in so far as this or that property depends upon the mode of intuition of the subject, in the relation of the given object to the subject, the object as phenomenon is to be distinguished from the object as a thing in itself. Thus I do not say that bodies seem or appear to be external to me, or that my soul seems merely to be given in my self-consciousness, although I maintain that the properties of space and time, in conformity to which I set both, as the condition of their existence, abide in my mode of intuition, and not in the objects in themselves. It would be my own fault, if out of that which I should reckon as phenomenon, I made mere illusory appearance.[1] But this will not happen, because of our principle of

[1] The predicates of the phenomenon can be affixed to the object itself in relation to our sensuous faculty; for example, the red colour or the perfume to the rose. But (illusory) appearance never can be attributed as a predicate to an object, for this very reason, that it attributes to this object in itself that which belongs to it only in relation to our sensuous faculty, or to the subject in general, e.g., the two handles which were formerly ascribed to Saturn. That which is never to be found in

the ideality of all sensuous intuitions. On the contrary, if we ascribe objective reality to these forms of representation, it becomes impossible to avoid changing everything into mere appearance. For if we regard space and time as properties, which must be found in objects as things in themselves, as *sine quibus non* of the possibility of their existence, and reflect on the absurdities in which we then find ourselves involved, inasmuch as we are compelled to admit the existence of two infinite things, which are nevertheless not substances, nor anything really inhering in substances, nay, to admit that they are the necessary conditions of the existence of all things, and moreover, that they must continue to exist, although all existing things were annihilated—we cannot blame the good Berkeley for degrading bodies to mere illusory appearances. Nay, even our own existence, which would in this case depend upon the self-existent reality of such a mere nonentity as time, would necessarily be changed with it into mere appearance—an absurdity which no one has as yet been guilty of.

IV. In natural theology, where we think of an object—God—which never can be an object of intuition to us, and even to himself can never be an object of sensuous intuition, we carefully avoid attributing to his intuition the conditions of space and time—and intuition all his cognition must be, and not thought, which always includes limitation. But with what right can we do this if we make them forms of objects as things in themselves, and such, moreover, as would continue to exist as *a priori* conditions of the existence of things, even though the things themselves were annihilated? For as conditions of all existence in general, space and time must be conditions of the existence of the Supreme Being also. But if we do not thus make them objective forms of all things, there is no other way left than to make them subjective forms of our mode of intuition—external and internal; which is called sensuous, because it is not primitive, that is, is not such as gives in itself the existence of the object of the intuition (a mode of intuition which, so far as we can judge, can belong only to the Creator), but is dependent on the existence of the object, is possible, therefore, only on condition that the representative faculty of the subject is affected by the object.

It is, moreover, not necessary that we should limit the mode of intuition in space and time to the sensuous faculty of man. It may well be that all finite thinking beings must necessarily in this respect agree with man (though as to this we cannot decide), but sensibility does not on account of this universality cease to be sensibility, for this very reason, that it is a deduced (*intuitus derivativus*), and not an original (*intuitus originarius*), consequently not an intellectual intuition, and this intuition, as such, for reasons above mentioned, seems to belong solely to the Supreme Being, but never to a being dependent, *quoad* its existence, as well as its intuition (which its existence determines and limits relatively to given objects). This latter remark, however, must be taken only as an illustration, and not as any proof of the truth of our aesthetical theory.

§ 10. *Conclusion of the Transcendental Aesthetic*

We have now completely before us one part of the solution of the grand general problem of transcendental philosophy, namely, the question: "How are synthetical propositions *a priori* possible?" That is to say, we have shown that we are in possession of pure *a priori* intuitions, namely, space and time, in which we find, when in a judgement *a priori* we pass out beyond the given conception, something which is not discoverable in that conception, but is certainly found *a priori* in the intuition which corresponds to the conception, and can be united synthetically with it. But the judgements which these pure intuitions enable us to make, never reach farther than to objects of the senses, and are valid only for objects of possible experience.

the object itself, but always in the relation of the object to the subject, and which moreover is inseparable from our representation of the object, we denominate *phenomenon*. Thus the predicates of space and time are rightly attributed to objects of the senses as such, and in this there is no illusion. On the contrary, if I ascribe redness of the rose as a thing in itself, or to Saturn his handles, or extension to all external objects, considered as things in themselves, without regarding the determinate relation of these objects to the subject, and without limiting my judgement to that relation—then, and then only, arises illusion.

SECOND PART. *TRANSCENDENTAL LOGIC*

INTRODUCTION. Idea of a Transcendental Logic

I. *Of Logic in general*

OUR knowledge springs from two main sources in the mind, the first of which is the faculty or power of receiving representations (receptivity for impressions); the second is the power of cognizing by means of these representations (spontaneity in the production of conceptions). Through the first an object is given to us; through the second, it is, in relation to the representation (which is a mere determination of the mind), thought. Intuition and conceptions constitute, therefore, the elements of all our knowledge, so that neither conceptions without an intuition in some way corresponding to them, nor intuition without conceptions, can afford us a cognition. Both are either pure or empirical. They are empirical, when sensation (which presupposes the actual presence of the object) is contained in them; and pure, when no sensation is mixed with the representation. Sensations we may call the matter of sensuous cognition. Pure intuition consequently contains merely the form under which something is intuited, and pure conception only the form of the thought of an object. Only pure intuitions and pure conceptions are possible *a priori;* the empirical only *a posteriori.*

We apply the term *sensibility* to the receptivity of the mind for impressions, in so far as it is in some way affected; and, on the other hand, we call the faculty of spontaneously producing representations, or the spontaneity of cognition, *understanding*. Our nature is so constituted that intuition with us never can be other than sensuous, that is, it contains only the mode in which we are affected by objects. On the other hand, the faculty of thinking the object of sensuous intuition is the understanding. Neither of these faculties has a preference over the other. Without the sensuous faculty no object would be given to us, and without the understanding no object would be thought. Thoughts without content are void; intuitions without conceptions, blind. Hence it is as necessary for the mind to make its conceptions sensuous (that is, to join to them the object in intuition), as to make its intuitions intelligible (that is, to bring them under conceptions). Neither of these faculties can exchange its proper function. Understanding cannot intuite, and the sensuous faculty cannot think. In no other way than from the united operation of both, can knowledge arise. But no one ought, on this account, to overlook the difference of the elements contributed by each; we have rather great reason carefully to separate and distinguish them. We therefore distinguish the science of the laws of sensibility, that is, aesthetic, from the science of the laws of the understanding, that is, logic.

Now, logic in its turn may be considered as twofold—namely, as logic of the general, or of the particular use of the understanding. The first contains the absolutely necessary laws of thought, without which no use whatsoever of the understanding is possible, and gives laws therefore to the understanding, without regard to the difference of objects on which it may be employed. The logic of the particular use of the understanding contains the laws of correct thinking upon a particular class of objects. The former may be called elemental logic—the latter, the organon of this or that particular science. The latter is for the most part employed in the schools, as a propaedeutic to the sciences, although, indeed, according to the course of human reason, it is the last thing we arrive at, when the science has been already matured, and needs only the finishing touches towards its correction and completion; for our knowledge of the objects of our attempted science must be tolerably extensive and complete before we can indicate the laws by which a science of these objects can be established.

General logic is again either pure or applied. In the former, we abstract all the empirical conditions under which the understanding is exercised; for example, the influence of the senses, the play of the fantasy or imagination, the laws of the memory, the force of habit, of inclination, etc., consequently also, the sources of prejudice—in a word, we abstract all causes from which particular cognitions arise, because these causes regard the understanding under certain circumstances of its application, and, to the knowledge of them experience is required. Pure general logic has to do, therefore, merely with pure *a priori* principles, and is a canon of understanding and reason, but only in respect of the formal part of their use, be the content what it may, empirical or transcendental. General logic is called applied, when it is directed to the laws of the use of the understanding, under the subjective empirical conditions which psychology teaches us. It has therefore empirical principles, although, at the same time, it is in so far general, that it applies to the exercise of the understanding, without regard to the difference of objects. On this account, moreover, it is neither a canon of the understanding in general, nor an organon of a particular science, but merely a cathartic of the human understanding.

In general logic, therefore, that part which constitutes pure logic must be carefully distinguished from that which constitutes applied (though still general) logic. The former alone is properly science, although short and dry, as the methodical exposition of an elemental doctrine of the understanding ought to be. In this, therefore, logicians must always bear in mind two rules:

1. As general logic, it makes abstraction of all content of the cognition of the understanding, and of the difference of objects, and has to do with nothing but the mere form of thought.

2. As pure logic, it has no empirical principles, and consequently draws nothing (contrary to the common persuasion) from psychology, which therefore has no influence on the canon of the understanding. It is a demonstrated doctrine, and everything in it must be certain completely *a priori*.

What I called applied logic (contrary to the common acceptation of this term, according to which it should contain certain exercises for the scholar, for which pure logic gives the rules), is a representation of the understanding, and of the rules of its necessary employment *in concreto,* that is to say, under the accidental conditions of the subject, which may either hinder or promote this employment, and which are all given only empirically. Thus applied logic treats of attention, its impediments and consequences, of the origin of error, of the state of doubt, hesitation, conviction, etc., and to it is related pure general logic in the same way that pure morality, which contains only the necessary moral laws of a free will, is related to practical ethics, which considers these laws under all the impediments of feelings, inclinations, and passions to which men are more or less subjected, and which never can furnish us with a true and demonstrated science, because it, as well as applied logic, requires empirical and psychological principles.

II. *Of Transcendental Logic*

General logic, as we have seen, makes abstraction of all content of cognition, that is, of all relation of cognition to its object, and regards only the logical form in the relation of cognitions to each other, that is, the form of thought in general. But as we have both pure and empirical intuitions (as transcendental aesthetic proves), in like manner a distinction might be drawn between pure and empirical thought (of objects). In this case, there would exist a kind of logic, in which we should not make abstraction of all content of cognition; for that logic which should comprise merely the laws of pure thought (of an object), would of course exclude all those cognitions which were of empirical content. This kind of logic would also examine the origin of our cognitions of objects, so far as that origin cannot be ascribed to the objects themselves; while, on the contrary, general logic has nothing to do with the origin of our cognitions, but contemplates our representations, be they given primitively *a priori* in ourselves, or be they only of empirical origin, solely according to the laws which the understanding observes in employing them in the process of thought, in relation to each other. Consequently, general logic treats of the form of the understanding only, which can be applied to representations, from whatever source they may have arisen.

And here I shall make a remark, which the reader must bear well in mind in the course of the following considerations, to wit, that not every cognition *a priori,* but only those through which we cognize that and how certain representations (intuitions or conceptions) are applied or are possible only *a priori;* that is to say, the *a priori* possibility of cognition and the *a priori* use of it are transcendental. Therefore neither is space, nor any *a priori* geometrical determination of space, a transcendental representation, but only the knowledge that such a representation is not of empirical origin, and the possibility of its relating to objects of experience, although itself *a priori,* can be called transcendental. So also, the application of space to objects in general would be transcendental; but if it be limited to objects of sense, it is empirical. Thus, the distinction of the transcendental and empirical belongs only to the critique of cognitions, and does not concern the relation of these to their object.

Accordingly, in the expectation that there may perhaps be conceptions which relate *a priori* to objects, not as pure or sensuous intuitions, but merely as acts of pure thought (which are therefore conceptions, but neither of empirical nor aesthetical origin)—in this expectation, I say, we form to ourselves, by anticipation, the idea of a science of pure understanding and rational cognition, by means of which we may cogitate objects entirely *a priori*. A science of this kind, which should determine the origin, the extent, and the objective validity of such cognitions, must be called *transcendental logic,* because it has not, like general logic, to do with the laws of understanding and reason in relation to empirical as well as pure rational cognitions without distinction, but concerns itself with these only in an *a priori* relation to objects.

III. *Of the Division of General Logic into Analytic and Dialectic*

The old question with which people sought to push logicians into a corner, so that they must either have recourse to pitiful sophisms or confess their ignorance, and consequently the vanity of their whole art, is this: "What is truth?" The definition of the word *truth,* to wit, "the accordance of the cognition with its object," is presupposed in the question; but we desire to be told, in the answer to it, what is the universal and secure criterion of the truth of every cognition.

To know what questions we may reasonably propose is in itself a strong evidence of sagacity and intelligence. For if a question be in itself absurd and unsusceptible of a rational answer, it is attended with the danger—not to mention the shame that falls upon the person who proposes it—of seducing the unguarded listener into making absurd answers, and we are presented with the ridiculous spectacle of one (as the ancients said) "milking the he-goat, and the other holding a sieve."

If truth consists in the accordance of a cognition with its object, this object must be, *ipso facto,* distinguished from all others; for a cognition is false if it does not accord with the object to which it relates, although it contains something which may be affirmed of other objects. Now an universal criterion of truth would be that which is valid for all cognitions, without distinction of their objects. But it is evident that since, in the case of such a criterion, we make abstraction of all the content of a cognition (that is, of all relation to its object), and truth relates precisely to this content, it must be utterly absurd to ask for a mark of the truth of this content of cognition; and that, accordingly, a sufficient, and at the same time universal, test of truth cannot possibly be found. As we have already termed the content of a cognition its *matter,* we shall say: "Of the truth of our cognitions in respect of their matter, no universal test can be demanded, because such a demand is self-contradictory."

On the other hand, with regard to our cognition in respect of its mere form (excluding all content), it is equally manifest that logic, in so far as it exhibits the universal and necessary laws of the understanding, must in these very laws present us with criteria of truth. Whatever contradicts these rules is false, because thereby the understanding is made to contradict its own universal laws of thought; that is, to contradict itself. These criteria, however, apply solely to the form of truth, that is, of thought in general, and in so far they are perfectly accurate, yet not sufficient. For although a cognition may be perfectly accurate as to logical form, that is, not self-contradictory, it is notwithstanding quite possible that it may not stand in agreement with its object. Consequently, the merely logical criterion of truth, namely, the accordance of a cognition with the universal and formal laws of understanding and reason, is nothing more than the *conditio sine qua non,* or negative condition of all truth. Farther than this logic cannot go, and the error which depends not on the form, but on the content of the cognition, it has no test to discover.

General logic, then, resolves the whole formal business of understanding and reason into its elements, and exhibits them as principles of all logical judging of our cognitions. This part of logic may, therefore, be called *analytic,* and is at least the negative test of truth, because all cognitions must first of all be estimated and tried according to these laws before we proceed to investigate them in respect of their content, in order to discover whether they contain positive truth in regard to their object. Because, however, the mere form of a cognition, accurately as it may accord with logical laws, is insufficient to supply us with material (objective) truth, no one, by means of logic alone, can venture to predicate anything of or decide concerning objects, unless he has obtained, independently of logic, well-grounded information about them, in order afterwards to examine, according to logical laws, into the use and connection, in a cohering whole, of that information, or, what is still better, merely to test it by them. Notwithstanding, there lies so seductive a charm in the possession of a specious art like this—an art which gives to all our cognitions the form of the understanding, although with respect to the content thereof we may be sadly deficient—that general logic, which is merely a canon of judgement, has been employed as an organon for the actual production, or rather for the semblance of production, of objective assertions, and has thus been grossly misapplied. Now general logic, in its assumed character of organon, is called *dialectic.*

Different as are the significations in which the ancients used this term for a science or an art, we may safely infer, from their actual employment of it, that with them it was nothing else than a logic of illusion—a sophistical art for giving ignorance, nay, even intentional sophistries, the colouring of truth, in which the thoroughness of procedure which logic requires was imitated, and their topic employed to cloak the empty pretensions. Now it may be taken as a safe and useful warning, that general logic, considered as an organon, must always be a logic of illusion, that is, be dialectical, for, as it teaches us nothing whatever respecting the content of our cognitions, but merely the formal conditions of their accordance with the understanding, which do not relate to and are quite indifferent in respect of objects, any attempt to employ it as an instrument (organon) in order to extend and enlarge the range of our knowledge must end in mere prating; any one being able to maintain or oppose, with some appearance of truth, any single assertion whatever.

Such instruction is quite unbecoming the dignity of philosophy. For these reasons we have chosen to denominate this part of logic *dialectic,* in the sense of a critique of dialectical illusion, and we wish the term to be so understood in this place.

IV. *Of the Division of Transcendental Logic into Transcendental Analytic and Dialectic*

In transcendental logic we isolate the understanding (as in transcendental aesthetic the sensibility) and select from our cognition merely that part of thought which has its origin in the understanding alone. The exercise of this pure cognition, however, depends upon this as its condition, that objects to which it may be applied be given to us in intuition, for without intuition the whole of our cognition is without objects, and is therefore quite void. That part of transcendental logic, then, which treats of the elements of pure cognition of the understanding, and of the principles without which no object at all can be thought, is transcendental analytic, and at the same time a logic of truth. For no cognition can contradict it, without losing at the same time all content, that is, losing all reference to an object, and therefore all truth. But because we are very easily seduced into employing these pure cognitions and principles of the understanding by themselves, and that even beyond the boundaries of experience, which yet is the only source whence we can obtain matter (objects) on which those pure conceptions may be employed—understanding runs the risk of making, by means of empty sophisms, a material and objective use of the mere formal principles of the pure understanding, and of passing judgements on objects without distinction—objects which are not given to us, nay, perhaps cannot be given to us in any way. Now, as it ought properly to be only a canon for judging of the empirical use of the understanding, this kind of logic is misused when we seek to employ it as an organon of the universal and unlimited exercise of the understanding, and attempt with the pure understanding alone to judge synthetically, affirm, and determine respecting objects in general. In this case the exercise of the pure understanding becomes dialectical. The second part of our transcendental logic must therefore be a critique of dialectical illusion, and this critique we shall term *transcendental dialectic*—not meaning it as an art of producing dogmatically such illusion (an art which is unfortunately too current among the practitioners of metaphysical juggling), but as a critique of understanding and reason in regard to their hyperphysical use. This critique will expose the groundless nature of the pretensions of these two faculties, and invalidate their claims to the discovery and enlargement of our cognitions merely by means of transcendental principles, and show that the proper employment of these faculties is to test the judgements made by the pure understanding, and to guard it from sophistical delusion.

Transcendental Logic. First Division

Transcendental Analytic

§ 1

Transcendental analytic is the dissection of the whole of our *a priori* knowledge into the elements of the pure cognition of the understanding. In order to effect our purpose, it is necessary: (1) That the conceptions be pure and not empirical; (2) That they belong not to intuition and sensibility, but to thought and understanding; (3) That they be elementary conceptions, and as such, quite different from deduced or compound conceptions; (4) That our table of these elementary conceptions be complete, and fill up the whole sphere of the pure understanding. Now this completeness of a science cannot be accepted with confidence on the guarantee of a mere estimate of its existence in an aggregate formed only by means of repeated experiments and attempts. The completeness which we require is possible only by means of an idea of the totality of the *a priori* cognition of the understanding, and through the thereby determined division of the conceptions which form the said whole; consequently, only by means of their connection in a system. Pure understanding distinguishes itself not merely from everything empirical, but also completely from all sensibility. It is a unity self-subsistent, self-sufficient, and not to be enlarged by any additions from without. Hence the sum of its cognition constitutes a system to be determined by and comprised under an idea; and the completeness and articulation of this system can at the same time serve as a test of the correctness and genuineness of all the parts of cognition that belong to it. The whole of this part of transcendental logic consists of two books, of which the one contains the conceptions, and the other the principles of pure understanding.

BOOK I

Analytic of Conceptions. § 2

By the term *Analytic of Conceptions,* I do not understand the analysis of these, or the usual process in philosophical investigations of dissecting the conceptions which present themselves, according to their content, and so making them clear; but I mean the hitherto little attempted dissection of the faculty of understanding itself, in order to investigate the possibility of conceptions *a priori,* by looking for them in the understanding alone, as their birthplace, and analysing the pure use of this faculty. For this is the proper duty of a transcendental philosophy; what remains is the logical treatment of the conceptions in philosophy in general. We shall therefore follow up the pure conceptions even to their germs and beginnings in the human understanding, in which they lie, until they are developed on occasions presented by experience, and, freed by the same understanding from the empirical conditions attaching to them, are set forth in their unalloyed purity.

Chapter I. *Of the Transcendental Clue to the Discovery of all Pure Conceptions of the Understanding*

Introductory. § 3

When we call into play a faculty of cognition, different conceptions manifest themselves according to the different circumstances, and make known this faculty, and assemble themselves into a more or less extensive collection, according to the time or penetration that has been applied to the consideration of them. Where this process, conducted as it is mechanically, so to speak, will end, cannot be determined with certainty. Besides, the conceptions which we discover in this haphazard manner present themselves by no means in order and systematic unity, but are at last coupled together only according to resemblances to each other, and arranged in series, according to the quantity of their content, from the simpler to the more complex—series which are anything but systematic, though not altogether without a certain kind of method in their construction.

Transcendental philosophy has the advantage, and moreover the duty, of searching for its conceptions according to a principle; because these conceptions spring pure and unmixed out of the understanding as an absolute unity, and therefore must be connected with each other according to one conception or idea. A connection of this kind, however, furnishes us with a ready prepared rule, by which its proper place may be assigned to every pure conception of the understanding, and the completeness of the system of all be determined *a priori*—both which would otherwise have been dependent on mere choice or chance.

SECTION I. *Of the Logical Use of the Understanding in general.* § 4

The understanding was defined above only negatively, as a non-sensuous faculty of cognition. Now, independently of sensibility, we cannot possibly have any intuition; consequently, the understanding is no faculty of intuition. But besides intuition there is no other mode of cognition, except through conceptions; consequently, the cognition of every, at least of every human, understanding is a cognition through conceptions—not intuitive, but discursive. All intuitions, as sensuous, depend on affections; conceptions, therefore, upon functions. By the word *function* I understand the unity of the act of arranging diverse representations under one common representation. Conceptions, then, are based on the spontaneity of thought, as sensuous intuitions are on the receptivity of impressions. Now, the understanding cannot make any other use of these conceptions than to judge by means of them. As no representation, except an intuition, relates immediately to its object, a conception never relates immediately to an object, but only to some other representation thereof, be that an intuition or itself a conception. A judgement, therefore, is the mediate cognition of an object, consequently the representation of a representation of it. In every judgement there is a conception which applies to, and is valid for many other conceptions, and which among these comprehends also a given representation, this last being immediately connected with an object. For example, in the judgement—"All bodies are divisible," our conception of *divisible* applies to various other conceptions; among these, however, it is here particularly applied to the conception of body, and this conception of body relates to certain phenomena which occur to us. These objects, therefore, are mediately represented by the conception of divisibility. All judgements, accordingly, are functions of unity in our representations, inasmuch as, instead of an immediate, a higher representation, which comprises this and various others, is used for our cognition of the object, and thereby many possible cognitions are collected into one. But we can reduce all acts of the understanding to judgements, so that *understanding* may be represented as the *faculty of judging*. For it is, according to what has been said above, a faculty of thought. Now thought is cognition by means of conceptions. But conceptions, as predicates of possible judgements, relate to some representation of a yet undetermined object. Thus the conception of *body* indicates something—for example, metal—which can be cognized by means of that conception. It is therefore a conception, for the reason alone that other representations are contained under it, by means of which it can relate to objects. It is therefore the predicate to a possible judgement; for example: "Every metal is a body." All the functions of the understanding therefore can be discovered, when we can completely exhibit the functions of unity in judgements. And that this may be effected very easily, the following section will show.

SECTION II. *Of the Logical Function of the Understanding in Judgements.* § 5

If we abstract all the content of a judgement, and consider only the intellectual form thereof, we find that the function of thought in a judgement can be brought under four heads, of which each contains three momenta. These may be conveniently represented in the following table:

1
Quantity of judgements
Universal
Particular
Singular

2
Quality
Affirmative
Negative
Infinite

3
Relation
Categorical
Hypothetical
Disjunctive

4
Modality
Problematical
Assertorical
Apodeictical

As this division appears to differ in some, though not essential points, from the usual technique of logicians, the following observations, for the prevention of otherwise possible misunderstanding, will not be without their use.

1. Logicians say, with justice, that in the use of judgements in syllogisms, singular judgements may be treated like universal ones. For, precisely because a singular judgement has no extent at all, its predicate cannot refer to a part of that which is contained in the conception of the subject and be excluded from the rest. The predicate is valid for the whole conception just as if it were a general conception, and had extent, to the whole of which the predicate applied. On the

other hand, let us compare a singular with a general judgement, merely as a cognition, in regard to quantity. The singular judgement relates to the general one, as unity to infinity, and is therefore in itself essentially different. Thus, if we estimate a singular judgement (*judicium singulare*) not merely according to its intrinsic validity as a judgement, but also as a cognition generally, according to its quantity in comparison with that of other cognitions, it is then entirely different from a general judgement (*judicium commune*), and in a complete table of the momenta of thought deserves a separate place—though, indeed, this would not be necessary in a logic limited merely to the consideration of the use of judgements in reference to each other.

2. In like manner, in transcendental logic, infinite must be distinguished from affirmative judgements, although in general logic they are rightly enough classed under affirmative. General logic abstracts all content of the predicate (though it be negative), and only considers whether the said predicate be affirmed or denied of the subject. But transcendental logic considers also the worth or content of this logical affirmation — an affirmation by means of a merely negative predicate, and inquires how much the sum total of our cognition gains by this affirmation. For example, if I say of the soul, "It is not mortal"—by this negative judgement I should at least ward off error. Now, by the proposition, "The soul is not mortal," I have, in respect of the logical form, really affirmed, inasmuch as I thereby place the soul in the unlimited sphere of immortal beings. Now, because of the whole sphere of possible existences, the mortal occupies one part, and the immortal the other, neither more nor less is affirmed by the proposition than that the soul is one among the infinite multitude of things which remain over, when I take away the whole mortal part. But by this proceeding we accomplish only this much, that the infinite sphere of all possible existences is in so far limited that the mortal is excluded from it, and the soul is placed in the remaining part of the extent of this sphere. But this part remains, notwithstanding this exception, infinite, and more and more parts may be taken away from the whole sphere, without in the slightest degree thereby augmenting or affirmatively determining our conception of the soul. These judgements, therefore, infinite in respect of their logical extent, are, in respect of the content of their cognition, merely limitative; and are consequently entitled to a place in our transcendental table of all the momenta of thought in judgements, because the function of the understanding exercised by them may perhaps be of importance in the field of its pure *a priori* cognition.

3. All relations of thought in judgements are those (*a*) of the predicate to the subject; (*b*) of the principle to its consequence; (*c*) of the divided cognition and all the members of the division to each other. In the first of these three classes, we consider only two conceptions; in the second, two judgements; in the third, several judgements in relation to each other. The hypothetical proposition, "If perfect justice exists, the obstinately wicked are punished," contains properly the relation to each other of two propositions, namely, "Perfect justice exists," and "The obstinately wicked are punished." Whether these propositions are in themselves true is a question not here decided. Nothing is cogitated by means of this judgement except a certain consequence. Finally, the disjunctive judgement contains a relation of two or more propositions to each other—a relation not of consequence, but of logical opposition, in so far as the sphere of the one proposition excludes that of the other. But it contains at the same time a relation of community, in so far as all the propositions taken together fill up the sphere of the cognition. The disjunctive judgement contains, therefore, the relation of the parts of the whole sphere of a cognition, since the sphere of each part is a complemental part of the sphere of the other, each contributing to form the sum total of the divided cognition. Take, for example, the proposition, "The world exists either through blind chance, or through internal necessity, or through an external cause." Each of these propositions embraces a part of the sphere of our possible cognition as to the existence of a world; all of them taken together, the whole sphere. To take the cognition out of one of these spheres, is equivalent to placing it in one of the others; and, on the other hand, to place it in one sphere is equivalent to taking it out of the rest. There is, therefore, in a disjunctive judgement a certain community of cognitions, which consists in this, that they mutually exclude each other, yet thereby determine, as a whole, the true cognition, inasmuch as, taken together, they make up the complete content of a particular given cognition. And this is all that I find necessary, for the sake of what follows, to remark in this place.

4. The modality of judgements is a quite pe-

culiar function, with this distinguishing characteristic, that it contributes nothing to the content of a judgement (for besides quantity, quality, and relation, there is nothing more that constitutes the content of a judgement), but concerns itself only with the value of the copula in relation to thought in general. Problematical judgements are those in which the affirmation or negation is accepted as merely possible (*ad libitum*). In the assertorical, we regard the proposition as real (true); in the apodeictical, we look on it as *necessary*.[1] Thus the two judgements (*antecedens et consequens*), the relation of which constitutes a hypothetical judgement, likewise those (the members of the division) in whose reciprocity the disjunctive consists, are only problematical. In the example above given, the proposition, "There exists perfect justice," is not stated assertorically, but as an *ad libitum* judgement, which someone may choose to adopt, and the consequence alone is assertorical. Hence such judgements may be obviously false, and yet, taken problematically, be conditions of our cognition of the truth. Thus the proposition, "The world exists only by blind chance," is in the disjunctive judgement of problematical import only: that is to say, one may accept it for the moment, and it helps us (like the indication of the wrong road among all the roads that one can take) to find out the true proposition. The problematical proposition is, therefore, that which expresses only logical possibility (which is not objective); that is, it expresses a free choice to admit the validity of such a proposition—a merely arbitrary reception of it into the understanding. The assertorical speaks of logical reality or truth; as, for example, in a hypothetical syllogism, the *antecedens* presents itself in a problematical form in the *major*, in an assertorical form in the *minor*, and it shows that the proposition is in harmony with the laws of the understanding. The apodeictical proposition cogitates the assertorical as determined by these very laws of the understanding, consequently as affirming *a priori*, and in this manner it expresses logical necessity. Now because all is here gradually incorporated with the understanding—inasmuch as in the first place we judge problematically; then accept assertorically our judgement as true; lastly, affirm it as inseparably united with the understanding, that is, as necessary and apodeictical—we may safely reckon these three functions of modality as so many momenta of thought.

[1] Just as if thought were in the first instance a function of the *understanding;* in the second, of *judgement;* in the third, of reason. A remark which will be explained in the sequel.

SECTION III. *Of the Pure Conceptions of the Understanding, or Categories.* § 6

General logic, as has been repeatedly said, makes abstraction of all content of cognition, and expects to receive representations from some other quarter, in order, by means of analysis, to convert them into conceptions. On the contrary, transcendental logic has lying before it the manifold content of *a priori* sensibility, which transcendental aesthetic presents to it in order to give matter to the pure conceptions of the understanding, without which transcendental logic would have no content, and be therefore utterly void. Now space and time contain an infinite diversity of determinations of pure *a priori* intuition, but are nevertheless the condition of the mind's receptivity, under which alone it can obtain representations of objects, and which, consequently, must always affect the conception of these objects. But the spontaneity of thought requires that this diversity be examined after a certain manner, received into the mind, and connected, in order afterwards to form a cognition out of it. This process I call synthesis.

By the word *synthesis,* in its most general signification, I understand the process of joining different representations to each other and of comprehending their diversity in one cognition. This synthesis is pure when the diversity is not given empirically but *a priori* (as that in space and time). Our representations must be given previously to any analysis of them; and no conceptions can arise, *quoad* their content, analytically. But the synthesis of a diversity (be it given *a priori* or empirically) is the first requisite for the production of a cognition, which in its beginning, indeed, may be crude and confused, and therefore in need of analysis—still, synthesis is that by which alone the elements of our cognitions are collected and united into a certain content, consequently it is the first thing on which we must fix our attention, if we wish to investigate the origin of our knowledge.

Synthesis, generally speaking, is, as we shall afterwards see, the mere operation of the imagination—a blind but indispensable function of the soul, without which we should have no cognition whatever, but of the working of which we are seldom even conscious. But to reduce this synthesis to conceptions is a function of the understanding, by means of which we attain to cognition, in the proper meaning of the term.

Pure synthesis, represented generally, gives us the pure conception of the understanding. But by this pure synthesis, I mean that which rests upon a basis of *a priori* synthetical unity. Thus, our numeration (and this is more observable in large numbers) is a synthesis according to conceptions, because it takes place according to a common basis of unity (for example, the decade). By means of this conception, therefore, the unity in the synthesis of the manifold becomes necessary.

By means of analysis different representations are brought under one conception—an operation of which general logic treats. On the other hand, the duty of transcendental logic is to reduce to conceptions, not representations, but the pure synthesis of representations. The first thing which must be given to us for the sake of the *a priori* cognition of all objects, is the diversity of the pure intuition; the synthesis of this diversity by means of the imagination is the second; but this gives, as yet, no cognition. The conceptions which give unity to this pure synthesis, and which consist solely in the representation of this necessary synthetical unity, furnish the third requisite for the cognition of an object, and these conceptions are given by the understanding.

The same function which gives unity to the different representation in a judgement, gives also unity to the mere synthesis of different representations in an intuition; and this unity we call the pure conception of the understanding. Thus, the same understanding, and by the same operations, whereby in conceptions, by means of analytical unity, it produced the logical form of a judgement, introduces, by means of the synthetical unity of the manifold in intuition, a transcendental content into its representations, on which account they are called pure conceptions of the understanding, and they apply *a priori* to objects, a result not within the power of general logic.

In this manner, there arise exactly so many pure conceptions of the understanding, applying *a priori* to objects of intuition in general, as there are logical functions in all possible judgements. For there is no other function or faculty existing in the understanding besides those enumerated in that table. These conceptions we shall, with Aristotle, call categories, our purpose being originally identical with his, notwithstanding the great difference in the execution.

TABLE OF THE CATEGORIES

1
Of Quantity
Unity
Plurality
Totality

2
Of Quality
Reality
Negation
Limitation

3
Of Relation
Of Inherence and Subsistence (*substantia et accidens*)
Of Causality and Dependence (cause and effect)
Of Community (reciprocity between the agent and patient)

4
Of Modality
Possibility—Impossibility
Existence—Non-existence
Necessity—Contingence

This, then, is a catalogue of all the originally pure conceptions of the synthesis which the understanding contains *a priori*, and these conceptions alone entitle it to be called a pure understanding; inasmuch as only by them it can render the manifold of intuition conceivable, in other words, think an object of intuition. This division is made systematically from a common principle, namely the faculty of judgement (which is just the same as the power of thought), and has not arisen rhapsodically from a search at haphazard after pure conceptions, respecting the full number of which we never could be certain, inasmuch as we employ induction alone in our search, without considering that in this way we can never understand wherefore precisely these conceptions, and none others, abide in the pure understanding. It was a design worthy of an acute thinker like Aristotle, to search for these fundamental conceptions. Destitute, however, of any guiding principle, he picked them up just as they occurred to him, and at first hunted out ten, which he called *categories* (*predicaments*). Afterwards he believed that he had discovered five others, which were added under the name of *post predicaments*. But his catalogue still remained defective. Besides, there are to be found among them some of the modes of pure sensibility (*quando, ubi, situs,* also *prius, simul*), and likewise an empirical conception (*motus*)—which can by no means belong to this genealogical register of the pure understanding. Moreover, there are deduced conceptions (*actio, passio*) enumerated among the original conceptions, and, of the latter, some are entirely wanting.

With regard to these, it is to be remarked, that the categories, as the true primitive conceptions of the pure understanding, have also their pure deduced conceptions, which, in a complete system of transcendental philosophy, must by no means be passed over; though in a merely critical essay we must be contented with the simple mention of the fact.

Let it be allowed me to call these pure, but deduced conceptions of the understanding, the *predicables* of the pure understanding, in contradistinction to predicaments. If we are in possession of the original and primitive, the deduced and subsidiary conceptions can easily be added, and the genealogical tree of the understanding completely delineated. As my present aim is not to set forth a complete system, but merely the principles of one, I reserve this task for another time. It may be easily executed by any one who will refer to the ontological manuals, and subordinate to the category of causality, for example, the predicables of force, action, passion; to that of community, those of presence and resistance; to the categories of modality, those of origination, extinction, change; and so with the rest. The categories combined with the modes of pure sensibility, or with one another, afford a great number of deduced *a priori* conceptions; a complete enumeration of which would be a useful and not unpleasant, but in this place a perfectly dispensable, occupation.

I purposely omit the definitions of the categories in this treatise. I shall analyse these conceptions only so far as is necessary for the doctrine of method, which is to form a part of this critique. In a system of pure reason, definitions of them would be with justice demanded of me, but to give them here would only hide from our view the main aim of our investigation, at the same time raising doubts and objections, the consideration of which, without injustice to our main purpose, may be very well postponed till another opportunity. Meanwhile, it ought to be sufficiently clear, from the little we have already said on this subject, that the formation of a complete vocabulary of pure conceptions, accompanied by all the requisite explanations, is not only a possible, but an easy undertaking. The compartments already exist; it is only necessary to fill them up; and a systematic topic like the present, indicates with perfect precision the proper place to which each conception belongs, while it readily points out any that have not yet been filled up.

§ 7

Our table of the categories suggests considerations of some importance, which may perhaps have significant results in regard to the scientific form of all rational cognitions. For, that this table is useful in the theoretical part of philosophy, nay, indispensable for the sketching of the complete plan of a science, so far as that science rests upon conceptions *a priori*, and for dividing it mathematically, according to fixed principles, is most manifest from the fact that it contains all the elementary conceptions of the understanding, nay, even the form of a system of these in the understanding itself, and consequently indicates all the momenta, and also the internal arrangement of a projected speculative science, as I have elsewhere shown.[1] Here follow some of these observations.

I. This table, which contains four classes of conceptions of the understanding, may, in the first instance, be divided into two classes, the first of which relates to objects of intuition—pure as well as empirical; the second, to the existence of these objects, either in relation to one another, or to the understanding.

The former of these classes of categories I would entitle the *mathematical*, and the latter the *dynamical* categories. The former, as we see, has no correlates; these are only to be found in the second class. This difference must have a ground in the nature of the human understanding.

II. The number of the categories in each class is always the same, namely, three—a fact which also demands some consideration, because in all other cases division *a priori* through conceptions is necessarily dichotomy. It is to be added, that the third category in each triad always arises from the combination of the second with the first.

Thus totality is nothing else but plurality contemplated as unity; limitation is merely reality conjoined with negation; community is the causality of a substance, reciprocally determining, and determined by other substances; and finally, necessity is nothing but existence, which is given through the possibility itself. Let it not be supposed, however, that the third category is merely a deduced, and not a primitive conception of the pure understanding. For the conjunction of the first and second, in order to produce the third conception, requires a particular function of the understanding, which is by no

[1] In the *Metaphysical Principles of Natural Science.*

means identical with those which are exercised in the first and second. Thus, the conception of a number (which belongs to the category of totality) is not always possible, where the conceptions of multitude and unity exist (for example, in the representation of the infinite). Or, if I conjoin the conception of a cause with that of a substance, it does not follow that the conception of *influence,* that is, how one substance can be the cause of something in another substance, will be understood from that. Thus it is evident that a particular act of the understanding is here necessary; and so in the other instances.

III. With respect to one category, namely, that of community, which is found in the third class, it is not so easy as with the others to detect its accordance with the form of the disjunctive judgement which corresponds to it in the table of the logical functions.

In order to assure ourselves of this accordance, we must observe that in every disjunctive judgement, the sphere of the judgement (that is, the complex of all that is contained in it) is represented as a whole divided into parts; and, since one part cannot be contained in the other, they are cogitated as co-ordinated with, not subordinated to each other, so that they do not determine each other unilaterally, as in a linear series, but reciprocally, as in an aggregate—(if one member of the division is posited, all the rest are excluded; and conversely).

Now a like connection is cogitated in a whole of things; for one thing is not subordinated, as effect, to another as cause of its existence, but, on the contrary, is co-ordinated contemporaneously and reciprocally, as a cause in relation to the determination of the others (for example, in a body—the parts of which mutually attract and repel each other). And this is an entirely different kind of connection from that which we find in the mere relation of the cause to the effect (the principle to the consequence), for in such a connection the consequence does not in its turn determine the principle, and therefore does not constitute, with the latter, a whole—just as the Creator does not with the world make up a whole. The process of understanding by which it represents to itself the sphere of a divided conception, is employed also when we think of a thing as divisible; and in the same manner as the members of the division in the former exclude one another, and yet are connected in one sphere, so the understanding represents to itself the parts of the latter, as having — each of them — an existence (as substances), independently of the others, and yet as united in one whole.

§ 8

In the transcendental philosophy of the ancients there exists one more leading division, which contains pure conceptions of the understanding, and which, although not numbered among the categories, ought, according to them, as conceptions *a priori,* to be valid of objects. But in this case they would augment the number of the categories; which cannot be. These are set forth in the proposition, so renowned among the schoolmen—"*Quodlibet ens est* UNUM, VERUM, BONUM." Now, though the inferences from this principle were mere tautological propositions, and though it is allowed only by courtesy to retain a place in modern metaphysics, yet a thought which maintained itself for such a length of time, however empty it seems to be, deserves an investigation of its origin, and justifies the conjecture that it must be grounded in some law of the understanding, which, as is often the case, has only been erroneously interpreted. These pretended transcendental predicates are, in fact, nothing but logical requisites and criteria of all cognition of objects, and they employ, as the basis for this cognition, the categories of quantity, namely, unity, plurality, and totality. But these, which must be taken as material conditions, that is, as belonging to the possibility of things themselves, they employed merely in a formal signification, as belonging to the logical requisites of all cognition, and yet most unguardedly changed these criteria of thought into properties of objects, as things in themselves. Now, in every cognition of an object, there is *unity* of conception, which may be called *qualitative unity,* so far as by this term we understand only the unity in our connection of the manifold; for example, unity of the theme in a play, an oration, or a story. Secondly, there is *truth* in respect of the deductions from it. The more true deductions we have from a given conception, the more criteria of its objective reality. This we might call the *qualitative plurality* of characteristic marks, which belong to a conception as to a common foundation, but are not cogitated as a quantity in it. Thirdly, there is *perfection*—which consists in this, that the plurality falls back upon the unity of the conception, and accords completely with that conception and with no other. This we may denominate *qualitative completeness.* Hence it is evident that these logical criteria of the possibility of cognition are merely the three categories of quantity modified and transformed to suit an unauthorized manner of applying them. That is to say, the three categories, in which the unity in the production of the quantum must be homogeneous throughout, are transformed solely with a view to the connection of heterogeneous parts of cognition in one act of consciousness, by means of the quality of the cognition, which is the principle of that connection. Thus the criterion of the possibility of a conception (not of its object) is the definition of it, in which the unity of the conception, the truth of all that may be immediately deduced from it, and finally, the completeness of what has been thus deduced, constitute the requisites for the reproduction of the whole conception. Thus also, the criterion or test of an hypothesis is the intelligibility of the received principle of explanation, or its unity (without help from any subsidiary hypothesis)—the truth of our deductions from it (consistency with each other and with experience)—and lastly, the completeness of the principle of the explanation of these deductions, which refer to neither more nor less than what was admitted in the hypothesis, restoring analytically and *a posteriori*, what was cogitated synthetically and *a priori*. By the conceptions, therefore, of unity, truth, and perfection, we have made no addition to the transcendental table of the categories, which is complete without them. We have, on the contrary, merely employed the three categories of quantity, setting aside their application to objects of experience, as general logical laws of the consistency of cognition with itself.

CHAPTER II. *Of the Deduction of the Pure Conceptions of the Understanding*

SECTION I. *Of the Principles of a Transcendental Deduction in general.* § 9

TEACHERS of jurisprudence, when speaking of rights and claims, distinguish in a cause the question of right (*quid juris*) from the question of fact (*quid facti*), and while they demand proof of both, they give to the proof of the former, which goes to establish right or claim in law, the name of *deduction*. Now we make use of a great number of empirical conceptions, without opposition from any one; and consider ourselves, even without any attempt at deduction, justified in attaching to them a sense, and a supposititious signification, because we have always experience at hand to demonstrate their objective reality. There exist also, however, usurped conceptions, such as *fortune, fate,* which circulate with almost universal indulgence, and yet are occasionally challenged by the question, "*quid juris?*" In such cases, we have great difficulty in discovering any deduction for these terms, inasmuch as we cannot produce any manifest ground of right, either from experience or from reason, on which the claim to employ them can be founded.

Among the many conceptions, which make up the very variegated web of human cognition, some are destined for pure use *a priori,* independent of all experience; and their title to be so employed always requires a deduction, inasmuch as, to justify such use of them, proofs from experience are not sufficient; but it is necessary to know how these conceptions can apply to objects without being derived from experience. I term, therefore, an examination of the manner in which conceptions can apply *a priori* to objects, the *transcendental deduction* of conceptions, and I distinguish it from the *empirical* deduction, which indicates the mode in which a conception is obtained through experience and reflection thereon; consequently, does not concern itself with the right, but only with the fact of our obtaining conceptions in such and such a manner. We have already seen that we are in possession of two perfectly different kinds of conceptions, which nevertheless agree with each other in this, that they both apply to objects completely *a priori.* These are the conceptions of space and time as forms of sensibility, and the categories as pure conceptions of the understanding. To attempt an empirical deduction of either of these classes would be labour in vain, because the distinguishing characteristic of their nature consists in this, that they apply to their objects, without having borrowed anything from experience towards the representation of them. Consequently, if a deduction of these conceptions is necessary, it must always be transcendental.

Meanwhile, with respect to these conceptions, as with respect to all our cognition, we certainly may discover in experience, if not the principle of their possibility, yet the occasioning causes of their production. It will be found that the impressions of sense give the first occasion for bringing into action the whole faculty of cognition, and for the production of experience, which contains two very dissimilar elements, namely, a matter for cognition, given by the senses, and a certain form for the arrangement of this matter, arising out of the inner fountain of pure intuition and thought; and these, on occasion given by sensuous impressions, are called into exercise and produce conceptions. Such an investigation into the first efforts of our faculty of cognition to mount from particular perceptions to general conceptions is undoubtedly of great utility; and we have to thank the celebrated Locke for having first opened the way for this inquiry. But a deduction of the pure *a priori* conceptions of course never can be made in this way, seeing that, in regard to their future employment, which must be entirely independent of experience, they must have a far different certificate of birth to show from that of a descent from experience. This attempted physiological derivation, which cannot properly be called deduction, because it relates merely to a *quaestio facti,* I shall entitle an explanation of the *possession* of a pure cognition. It is therefore manifest that there can only be a transcendental deduction of these conceptions and by no means an empirical one; also, that all attempts at an empirical deduction, in regard to pure *a priori* conceptions, are vain, and can only be made by one who does not understand the altogether peculiar nature of these cognitions.

But although it is admitted that the only possible deduction of pure *a priori* cognition is a transcendental deduction, it is not, for that reason, perfectly manifest that such a deduction is absolutely necessary. We have already traced to their sources the conceptions of space and time, by means of a transcendental deduction, and we have explained and determined their objective validity *a priori.* Geometry, nevertheless, advances steadily and securely in the province of pure *a priori* cognitions, without needing to ask from philosophy any certificate as to the pure and legitimate origin of its fundamental conception of space. But the use of the conception in this science extends only to the external world of sense, the pure form of the intuition of which is space; and in *this* world, therefore, all geometrical cognition, because it is founded upon *a priori* intuition, possesses immediate evidence, and the objects of this cognition are given *a priori* (as regards their form) in intuition by and through the cognition itself. With the pure conceptions of understanding, on the contrary, commences the absolute necessity of seeking a transcendental deduction, not only of these conceptions themselves, but likewise of space, because, inasmuch as they make affirmations concerning objects not by means of the predicates of intuition and sensibility, but of pure thought *a priori,* they apply to objects without any of the conditions of sensibility. Besides, not being founded on experience, they are not presented with any object in *a priori* intuition upon which, antecedently to experience, they might base their synthesis. Hence results, not only doubt as to the objective validity and proper limits of their use, but that even our conception of space is rendered equivocal; inasmuch as we are very ready with the aid of the categories, to carry the use of this conception beyond the conditions of sensuous intuition—and, for this reason, we have already found a transcendental deduction of it needful. The reader, then, must be quite convinced of the absolute necessity of a transcendental deduction, before taking a single step in the field of pure reason; because otherwise he goes to work blindly, and after he has wondered about in all directions, returns to the state of utter ignorance from which he started. He ought, moreover, clearly to recognize beforehand the unavoidable difficulties in his undertaking, so that he may not afterwards complain of the obscurity in which the subject itself is deeply involved, or become too soon impatient of the obstacles in his path; because we have a choice of only two things—either at once to give up all pretensions to knowledge beyond the limits of possible experience, or to bring this critical investigation to completion.

We have been able, with very little trouble, to make it comprehensible how the conceptions of space and time, although *a priori* cognitions, must necessarily apply to external objects, and render a synthetical cognition of these possible, independently of all experience. For inasmuch as only by means of such pure form of sensibility an object can appear to us, that is, be an object of empirical intuition, space and time are pure intuitions, which contain *a priori* the condition of the possibility of objects as phenomena, and an *a priori* synthesis in these intuitions possesses objective validity.

On the other hand, the categories of the understanding do not represent the conditions under which objects are given to us in intuition; objects can consequently appear to us without necessarily connecting themselves with these, and consequently without any necessity binding on the understanding to contain *a priori* the conditions of these objects. Thus we find ourselves involved in a difficulty which did not present itself in the sphere of sensibility, that is to say, we cannot discover *how the subjective conditions of thought can have objective validity,* in other words, can become conditions of the possibility of all cognition of objects; for phenomena may certainly be given to us in intuition without any help from the functions of the understanding. Let us take, for example, the conception of *cause,* which indicates a peculiar kind of synthesis, namely, that with something, A, something entirely different, B, is connected according to a law. It is not *a priori* manifest why phenomena should contain anything of this kind (we are of course debarred from appealing for proof to experience, for the objective validity of this conception must be demonstrated *a priori*), and it hence remains doubtful *a priori,* whether such a conception be not quite void and without any corresponding object among phenomena. For that objects of sensuous intuition must correspond to the formal conditions of sensibility existing *a priori* in the mind is quite evident, from the fact that without these they could not be objects for us; but that they must also correspond to the conditions which understanding requires for the synthetical unity of thought is an assertion, the grounds for which are not so easily to be discovered. For phenomena might be so constituted as not to correspond to the conditions of the unity of thought; and all things might lie in such confusion that, for example, nothing could be met with in the sphere of phenomena to suggest a law of synthesis, and so correspond to the conception of cause and effect; so that this conception would be quite void, null, and without significance. Phenomena would nevertheless continue to present objects to our intuition; for mere intuition does not in any respect stand in need of the functions of thought.

If we thought to free ourselves from the labour of these investigations by saying: "Experience is constantly offering us examples of the relation of cause and effect in phenomena, and presents us with abundant opportunity of abstracting the conception of cause, and so at the same time of corroborating the objective validity of this conception"; we should in this case be overlooking the fact, that the conception of cause cannot arise in this way at all; that, on the contrary, it must either have an *a priori* basis in the understanding, or be rejected as a mere chimera. For this conception demands that something, A, should be of such a nature that something else, B, should follow from it necessarily, and according to an absolutely universal law. We may certainly collect from phenomena a law, according to which this or that *usually* happens, but the element of necessity is not to be found in it. Hence it is evident that to the synthesis of cause and effect belongs a dignity, which is utterly wanting in any empirical synthesis; for it is no mere mechanical synthesis, by means of addition, but a dynamical one; that is to say, the effect is not to be cogitated as merely annexed to the cause, but as posited by and through the cause, and resulting from it. The strict universality of this law never can be a characteristic of empirical laws, which obtain through induction only a comparative universality, that is, an extended range of practical application. But the pure conceptions of the understanding would entirely lose all their peculiar character, if we treated them merely as the productions of experience.

Transition to the Transcendental Deduction of the Categories. § 10

There are only two possible ways in which synthetical representation and its objects can coincide with and relate necessarily to each other, and, as it were, meet together. Either the object alone makes the representation possible, or the representation alone makes the object possible. In the former case, the relation between them is only empirical, and an *a priori* representation is impossible. And this is the case with phenomena, as regards that in them which is referable to mere sensation. In the latter case—although representation alone (for of its causality, by means of the will, we do not here speak) does not produce the object as to its existence, it must nevertheless be *a priori* determinative in regard to the object, if it is only by means of the representation that we can cognize anything as an object. Now there are only two conditions of the possibility of a cognition of objects; firstly, *intuition,* by means of which the object, though only as phenomenon, is given; secondly, *conception,* by means of which the object which corresponds to this intuition is thought. But it is evident from what has been said on aesthetic that the first condition, under which alone objects can be intuited, must in fact exist, as a formal basis for them, *a priori* in the mind. With this formal condition of sensibility, therefore, all phenomena necessarily correspond, because it is only through it that they can be phenomena at all; that is, can be empirically intuited and given. Now the question is whether there do not exist, *a priori* in the mind, conceptions of understanding also, as conditions under which alone something, if not intuited, is yet thought as object. If this question be answered in the affirmative, it follows that all empirical cognition of objects is necessarily conformable to such conceptions, since, if they are not presupposed, it is impossible that anything can be an object of experience. Now all experience contains, besides the intuition of the senses through which an object is given, a *conception* also of an object that is given in intuition. Accordingly, conceptions of objects in general must lie as *a priori* conditions at the foundation of all empirical cognition; and consequently, the objective validity of the categories, as *a priori* conceptions, will rest upon *this,* that experience (as far as regards the form of thought) is possible only by their means. For in that case they apply necessarily and *a priori* to objects of experience, because only through them can an object of experience be thought.

The whole aim of the transcendental deduction of all *a priori* conceptions is to show that these conceptions are *a priori* conditions of the possibility of all experience. Conceptions which afford us the objective foundation of the possibility of experience are for that very reason necessary. But the analysis of the experiences in which they are met with is not deduction, but only an illustration of them, because from experience they could never derive the attribute of necessity. Without their original applicability and relation to all possible experience, in which all objects of cognition present themselves, the relation of the categories to objects, of whatever nature, would be quite incomprehensible.

The celebrated Locke, for want of due reflection on these points, and because he met with pure conceptions of the understanding in experience, sought also to deduce them from experience, and yet proceeded so inconsequently as to attempt, with their aid, to arrive at cognitions which lie far beyond the limits of all experience. David Hume perceived that, to render this possible, it was necessary that the conceptions should have an *a priori* origin. But as he could not explain how it was possible that conceptions which are not connected with each other in the understanding must nevertheless be thought as necessarily connected in the object —and it never occurred to him that the understanding itself might, perhaps, by means of these conceptions, be the author of the experience in which its objects were presented to it—he was forced to drive these conceptions from experience, that is, from a subjective necessity arising from repeated association of experiences erroneously considered to be objective—in one word, from *habit.* But he proceeded with perfect consequence and declared it to be impossible, with such conceptions and the principles arising from them, to overstep the limits of experience. The empirical derivation, however, which both of these philosophers attributed to these conceptions, cannot possibly be reconciled with the fact that we do possess scientific *a priori* cognitions, namely, those of pure mathematics and general physics.

The former of these two celebrated men opened a wide door to extravagance—(for if reason has once undoubted right on its side, it will not allow itself to be confined to set limits, by vague recommendations of moderation); the latter gave himself up entirely to scepticism—a natural consequence, after having discovered, as he thought, that the faculty of cognition was not trustworthy. We now intend to make a trial whether it be not possible safely to conduct reason between these two rocks, to assign her determinate limits, and yet leave open for her the entire sphere of her legitimate activity.

I shall merely premise an explanation of what the categories are. They are conceptions of an object in general, by means of which its intuition is contemplated as determined in relation to one of the logical functions of judgement. The following will make this plain. The function of the categorical judgement is that of the relation of subject to predicate; for example, in the proposition: "All bodies are divisible." But in regard to the merely logical use of the understanding, it still remains undetermined to which of these two conceptions belongs the function of subject and to which that of predicate. For we could also say: "Some divisible is a body." But the category of substance, when the conception of a body is brought under it, determines that; and its empirical intuition in experience must be contemplated always as subject and never as mere predicate. And so with all the other categories.

SECTION II. *Transcendental Deduction of the pure Conceptions of the Understanding.* § 11

Of the Possibility of a Conjunction of the manifold representations given by Sense.

The manifold content in our representations can be given in an intuition which is merely sensuous—in other words, is nothing but susceptibility; and the form of this intuition can exist *a priori* in our faculty of representation, without being anything else but the mode in which the subject is affected. But the conjunction (*conjunctio*) of a manifold in intuition never can be given us by the senses; it cannot therefore be contained in the pure form of sensuous intuition, for it is a spontaneous act of the faculty of representation. And as we must, to distinguish it from sensibility, entitle this faculty *understanding;* so all conjunction—whether conscious or unconscious, be it of the manifold in intuition, sensuous or non-sensuous, or of several conceptions—is an act of the understanding. To this act we shall give the general appellation of *synthesis,* thereby to indicate, at the same time, that we cannot represent anything as conjoined in the object without having previously conjoined it ourselves. Of all mental notions, that of conjunction is the only one which cannot be given through objects, but can be originated only by the subject itself, because it is an act of its purely spontaneous activity. The reader will easily enough perceive that the possibility of conjunction must be grounded in the very nature of this act, and that it must be equally valid for all conjunction, and that analysis, which appears to be its contrary, must, nevertheless, always presuppose it; for where the understanding has not previously conjoined, it cannot dissect or analyse, because only as conjoined by it, must that which is to be analysed have been given to our faculty of representation.

But the conception of conjunction includes, besides the conception of the manifold and of the synthesis of it, that of the unity of it also. Conjunction is the representation of the synthetical unity of the manifold.[1] This idea of unity, therefore, cannot arise out of that of conjunction; much rather does that idea, by combining itself with the representation of the manifold, render the conception of conjunction possible. This unity, which *a priori* precedes all conceptions of conjunction, is not the category of unity (§ 6); for all the categories are based upon logical functions of judgement, and in these functions we already have conjunction, and consequently unity of given conceptions. It is therefore evident that the category of unity presupposes conjunction. We must therefore look still higher for this unity (as qualitative, § 8), in that, namely, which contains the ground of the unity of diverse conceptions in judgements, the ground, consequently, of the possibility of the existence of the understanding, even in regard to its logical use.

[1] Whether the representations are in themselves identical, and consequently whether one can be thought analytically by means of and through the other, is a question which we need not at present consider. Our *consciousness* of the one, when we speak of the manifold, is always distinguishable from our consciousness of the other; and it is only respecting the synthesis of this (possible) consciousness that we here treat.

Of the Originally Synthetical Unity of Apperception. § 12

The "I think" must accompany all my representations, for otherwise something would be represented in me which could not be thought; in other words, the representation would either be impossible, or at least be, in relation to me, nothing. That representation which can be given previously to all thought is called intuition. All the diversity or manifold content of intuition, has, therefore, a necessary relation to the "I think," in the subject in which this diversity is found. But this representation, "I think," is an act of *spontaneity;* that is to say, it cannot be regarded as belonging to mere sensibility. I call it pure apperception, in order to distinguish it from empirical; or primitive apperception, because it is self-consciousness which, whilst it gives birth to the representation "I think," must necessarily be capable of accompanying all our representations. It is in all acts of consciousness one and the same, and unaccompanied by it, no representation can exist *for me.* The unity of this apperception I call the transcendental unity of self-consciousness, in order to indicate the possibility of *a priori* cognition arising from it. For the manifold representations which are given in an intuition would not all of them be my representations, if they did not all belong to one self-consciousness, that is, as my representations (even although I am not conscious of them as such), they must conform to the condition under which alone they can exist together in a common self-consciousness, because otherwise they would not all without exception belong to me. From this primitive conjunction follow many important results.

For example, this universal identity of the apperception of the manifold given in intuition contains a synthesis of representations and is possible only by means of the consciousness of this synthesis. For the empirical consciousness which accompanies different representations is in itself fragmentary and disunited, and without relation to the identity of the subject. This relation, then, does not exist because I accompany every representation with consciousness, but because I join one representation to another, and am conscious of the synthesis of them. Consequently, only because I can connect a variety of given representations in one consciousness, is it possible that I can represent to myself the identity of consciousness in these representations; in other words, the analytical unity of apperception is possible only under the presupposition of a synthetical unity.[1] The thought, "These representations given in intuition belong all of them to me," is accordingly just the same as, "I unite them in one self-consciousness, or can at least so unite them"; and although this thought is not itself the consciousness of the synthesis of representations, it presupposes the possibility of it; that is to say, for the reason alone that I can comprehend the variety of my representations in one consciousness, do I call them my representations, for otherwise I must have as many-coloured and various a self as are the representations of which I am conscious. Synthetical unity of the manifold in intuitions, as given *a priori,* is therefore the foundation of the identity of apperception itself, which antecedes *a priori* all determinate thought. But the conjunction of representations into a conception is not to be found in objects themselves, nor can it be, as it were, borrowed from them and taken up into the understanding by perception, but it is on the contrary an operation of the understanding itself, which is nothing more than the faculty of conjoining *a priori* and of bringing the variety of given representations under the unity of apperception. This principle is the highest in all human cognition.

This fundamental principle of the necessary unity of apperception is indeed an identical, and therefore analytical, proposition; but it nevertheless explains the necessity for a synthesis of the manifold given in an intuition, without which the identity of self-consciousness would be incogitable. For the ego, as a simple representation, presents us with no manifold content; only in intuition, which is quite different from the representation ego, can it be given us, and by means of conjunction it is cogitated in one self-consciousness. An understanding, in which all the manifold should be given by means of consciousness itself, would be intuitive; our understanding can only think and must look for its intuition to sense. I am, therefore, conscious of my identical self, in relation to all the variety of representations given to me in an intuition, because I call all of them my representations. In other words, I am conscious myself of a necessary *a priori* synthesis of my representations, which is called the original synthetical unity of apperception, under which rank all the representations presented to me, but that only by means of a synthesis.

The Principle of the Synthetical Unity of Apperception is the highest Principle of all exercise of the Understanding. § 13

The supreme principle of the possibility of all intuition in relation to sensibility was, according to our transcendental aesthetic, that all the manifold in intuition be subject to the formal conditions of space and time. The supreme principle of the possibility of it in relation to the understanding is that all the manifold in it be subject to conditions of the originally synthetical unity or apperception.[2] To the former of these two principles are subject all the various representations of intuition, in so far as they are given to us; to the latter, in so far as they must be capable of conjunction in one consciousness; for without this nothing can be thought or cognized, because the given representations would not have in common the act of the apperception "I think" and therefore could not be connected in one self-consciousness.

Understanding is, to speak generally, *the faculty of cognitions.* These consist in the determined relation of given representation to an object. But an object is that, in the conception of which the manifold in a given intuition is united. Now all union of representations requires unity of consciousness in the synthesis of them. Consequently, it is the unity of consciousness alone that constitutes the possibility of representations relating to an object, and therefore of their objective validity, and of their

[1] All general conceptions—as such—depend, for their existence, on the analytical unity of consciousness. For example, when I think of *red* in general, I thereby think to myself a property which (as a characteristic mark) can be discovered somewhere, or can be united with other representations; consequently, it is only by means of a forethought possible synthetical unity that I can think to myself the analytical. A representation which is cogitated as common to *different* representations, is regarded as belonging to such as, besides this common representation, contain something *different;* consequently it must be previously thought in synthetical unity with other although only possible representations, before I can think in it the analytical unity of consciousness which makes it a *conceptas communis.* And thus the synthetical unity of apperception is the highest point with which we must connect every operation of the understanding, even the whole of logic, and after it our transcendental philosophy; indeed, this faculty is the understanding itself.

[2] Space and time, and all portions thereof, are *intuitions;* consequently are, with a manifold for their content, single representations. (See the *Transcendental Aesthetic.*) Consequently, they are not pure conceptions, by means of which the same consciousness is found in a great number of representations; but, on the contrary, they are many representations contained in one, the consciousness of which is, so to speak, compounded. The unity of consciousness is nevertheless *synthetical* and, therefore, primitive. From this peculiar character of consciousness follow many important consequences. (See §21.)

becoming cognitions, and consequently, the possibility of the existence of the understanding itself.

The first pure cognition of understanding, then, upon which is founded all its other exercise, and which is at the same time perfectly independent of all conditions of mere sensuous intuition, is the principle of the original synthetical unity of apperception. Thus the mere form of external sensuous intuition, namely, space, affords us, *per se,* no cognition; it merely contributes the manifold in *a priori* intuition to a possible cognition. But, in order to cognize something in space (for example, a line), I must draw it, and thus produce synthetically a determined conjunction of the given manifold, so that the unity of this act is at the same time the unity of consciousness (in the conception of a line), and by this means alone is an object (a determinate space) cognized. The synthetical unity of consciousness is, therefore, an objective condition of all cognition, which I do not merely require in order to cognize an object, but to which every intuition must necessarily be subject, in order to become an object for me; because in any other way, and without this synthesis, the manifold in intuition could not be united in one consciousness.

This proposition is, as already said, itself analytical, although it constitutes the synthetical unity, the condition of all thought; for it states nothing more than that all my representations in any given intuition must be subject to the condition which alone enables me to connect them, as my representation with the identical self, and so to unite them synthetically in one apperception, by means of the general expression, "I think."

But this principle is not to be regarded as a principle for every possible understanding, but only for the understanding by means of whose pure apperception in the thought *I* am, no manifold content is given. The understanding or mind which contained the manifold in intuition, in and through the act itself of its own self-consciousness, in other words, an understanding by and in the representation of which the objects of the representation should at the same time exist, would not require a special act of synthesis of the manifold as the condition of the unity of its consciousness, an act of which the human understanding, which thinks only and cannot intuite, has absolute need. But this principle is the first *principle* of all the operations of our understanding, so that we cannot form the least conception of any other possible understanding, either of one such as should be itself intuition, or possess a sensuous intuition, but with forms different from those of space and time.

What Objective Unity of Self-consciousness is. § 14

It is by means of the transcendental unity of apperception that all the manifold given in an intuition is united into a conception of the object. On this account it is called objective, and must be distinguished from the *subjective unity* of consciousness, which is a *determination of the internal sense,* by means of which the said manifold in intuition is given empirically to be so united. Whether I can be *empirically* conscious of the manifold as coexistent or as successive, depends upon circumstances, or empirical conditions. Hence the empirical unity of consciousness by means of association of representations, itself relates to a phenomenal world and is wholly contingent. On the contrary, the pure form of intuition in time, merely as an intuition, which contains a given manifold, is subject to the original unity of consciousness, and that solely by means of the necessary relation of the manifold in intuition to the "I think," consequently by means of the pure synthesis of the understanding, which lies *a priori* at the foundation of all empirical synthesis. The transcendental unity of apperception is alone objectively valid; the empirical which we do not consider in this essay, and which is merely a unity deduced from the former under given conditions *in concreto,* possesses only subjective validity. One person connects the notion conveyed in a word with one thing, another with another thing; and the unity of consciousness in that which is empirical, is, in relation to that which is given by experience, not necessarily and universally valid.

The Logical Form of all Judgements consists in the Objective Unity of Apperception of the Conceptions contained therein. § 15

I could never satisfy myself with the definition which logicians give of a judgement. It is, according to them, the representation of a relation between two conceptions. I shall not dwell here on the faultiness of this definition, in that it suits only for categorical and not for hypothetical or disjunctive judgements, these latter containing a relation not of conceptions but of judgements themselves—a blunder from which many evil results have followed.[1] It is more important for our present purpose to observe, that this definition does not determine in what the said relation consists.

But if I investigate more closely the relation of given cognitions in every judgement, and distinguish it, as belonging to the understanding, from the relation which is produced according to laws of the reproductive imagination (which has only subjective validity), I find that judgement is nothing but the mode of bringing given cognitions under the objective unit of apperception. This is plain from our use of the term of relation *is* in judgements, in order to distinguish the objective unity of given representations from the subjective unity. For this term indicates the relation of these representations to the original apperception, and also their *necessary unity,* even although the judgement is empirical, therefore contingent, as in the judgement: "All bodies are heavy." I do not mean by this, that these representations do *necessarily* belong to each other in empirical intuition, but that by means of the *necessary unity* of appreciation they belong to each other in the synthesis of intuitions, that is to say, they belong to each other according to principles of the objective determination of all our representations, in so far as cognition can arise from them, these principles being all deduced from the main principle of the transcendental unity of apperception. In this way alone can there arise from this relation a *judgement,* that is, a relation which has objective validity, and is perfectly distinct from that relation of the very same representations which has only subjective validity—a relation, to wit, which is produced according to laws of association. According to these laws, I could only say: "When I hold in my hand or carry a body, I feel an impression of weight"; but I could not say: "It, the body, is heavy"; for this is tantamount to saying both these representations are conjoined in the object, that is, without distinction as to the condition of the subject, and do not merely stand together in my perception, however frequently the perceptive act may be repeated.

[1] The tedious doctrine of the four syllogistic figures concerns only categorical syllogisms; and although it is nothing more than an artifice by surreptitiously introducing immediate conclusions (*consequentiae immediatae*) among the premises of a pure syllogism, to give rise to an appearance of more modes of drawing a conclusion than that in the first figure, the artifice would not have had much success, had not its authors succeeded in bringing categorical judgements into exclusive respect, as those to which all others must be referred—a doctrine, however, which, according to §5, is utterly false.

All Sensuous Intuitions are subject to the Categories, as Conditions under which alone the manifold Content of them can be united in one Consciousness. § 16

The manifold content given in a sensuous intuition comes necessarily under the original synthetical unity of apperception, because thereby alone is the *unity* of intuition possible (§ 13). But that act of the understanding, by which the manifold content of given representations (whether intuitions or conceptions) is brought under one apperception, is the logical function of judgements (§ 15). All the manifold, therefore, in so far as it is given in one empirical intuition, is *determined* in relation to one of the logical functions of judgement, by means of which it is brought into union in one consciousness. Now the categories are nothing else than these functions of judgement, so far as the manifold in a given intuition is determined in relation to them (§ 9). Consequently, the manifold in a given intuition is necessarily subject to the categories of the understanding.

Observation. § 17

The manifold in an intuition, which I call mine, is represented by means of the synthesis of the understanding, as belonging to the necessary unity of self-consciousness, and this takes place by means of the category.[2] The category indicates accordingly that the empirical consciousness of a given manifold in an intuition is subject to a pure self-consciousness *a priori,* in the same manner as an empirical intuition is subject to a pure sensuous intuition, which is also *a priori.* In the above proposition, then, lies the beginning of a deduction of the pure conceptions of the understanding. Now, as the categories have their origin in the understanding alone, independently of sensibility, I must in my deduction make abstraction of the mode in which the manifold of an empirical intuition is given, in order to fix my attention exclusively on the unity which is brought by the understanding into the intuition by means of the category. In what follows (§ 22), it will be shown, from the mode in which the empirical intuition is given in the faculty of sensibility, that the unity which belongs to it is no other than that which the category (according to § 16) imposes on the manifold in a given intuition, and thus,

[2] The proof of this rests on the represented *unity of intuition,* by means of which an object is given, and which always includes in itself a synthesis of the manifold to be intuited, and also the relation of this latter to unity of apperception.

its *a priori* validity in regard to all objects of sense being established, the purpose of our deduction will be fully attained.

But there is one thing in the above demonstration of which I could not make abstraction, namely, that the manifold to be intuited must be given previously to the synthesis of the understanding, and independently of it. How this takes place remains here undetermined. For if I cogitate an understanding which was itself intuitive (as, for example, a divine understanding which should not represent given objects, but by whose representation the objects themselves should be given or produced), the categories would possess no significance in relation to such a faculty of cognition. They are merely rules for an understanding, whose whole power consists in thought, that is, in the act of submitting the synthesis of the manifold which is presented to it in intuition from a very different quarter, to the unity of apperception; a faculty, therefore, which cognizes nothing *per se,* but only connects and arranges the material of cognition, the intuition, namely, which must be presented to it by means of the object. But to show reasons for this peculiar character of our understandings, that it produces unity of apperception *a priori* only by means of categories, and a certain kind and number thereof, is as impossible as to explain why we are endowed with precisely so many functions of judgement and no more, or why time and space are the only forms of our intuition.

In Cognition, its Application to Objects of Experience is the only legitimate use of the Category. § 18

To think an object and to cognize an object are by no means the same thing. In cognition there are two elements: firstly, the conception, whereby an object is cogitated (the category); and, secondly, the intuition, whereby the object is given. For supposing that to the conception a corresponding intuition could not be given, it would still be a thought as regards its form, but without any object, and no cognition of anything would be possible by means of it, inasmuch as, so far as I knew, there existed and could exist nothing to which my thought could be applied. Now all intuition possible to us is sensuous; consequently, our thought of an object by means of a pure conception of the understanding, can become cognition for us only in so far as this conception is applied to objects of the senses. Sensuous intuition is either pure intuition (space and time) or empirical intuition—of that which is immediately represented in space and time by means of sensation as real. Through the determination of pure intuition we obtain *a priori* cognitions of objects, as in mathematics, but only as regards their form as phenomena; whether there can exist things which must be intuited in this form is not thereby established. All mathematical conceptions, therefore, are not *per se* cognition, except in so far as we presuppose that there exist things which can only be represented conformably to the form of our pure sensuous intuition. But things in space and time are given only in so far as they are perceptions (representations accompanied with sensation), therefore only by empirical representation. Consequently the pure conceptions of the understanding, even when they are applied to intuitions *a priori* (as in mathematics), produce cognition only in so far as these (and therefore the conceptions of the understanding by means of them) can be applied to empirical intuitions. Consequently the categories do not, even by means of pure intuition afford us any cognition of things; they can only do so in so far as they can be applied to empirical intuition. That is to say, the categories serve only to render empirical cognition possible. But this is what we call experience. Consequently, in cognition, their application to objects of experience is the only legitimate use of the categories.

§ 19

The foregoing proposition is of the utmost importance, for it determines the limits of the exercise of the pure conceptions of the understanding in regard to objects, just as transcendental aesthetic determined the limits of the exercise of the pure form of our sensuous intuition. Space and time, as conditions of the possibility of the presentation of objects to us, are valid no further than for objects of sense, consequently, only for experience. Beyond these limits they represent to us nothing, for they belong only to sense, and have no reality apart from it. The pure conceptions of the understanding are free from this limitation, and extend to objects of intuition in general, be the intuition like or unlike to ours, provided only it be sensuous, and not intellectual. But this extension of conceptions beyond the range of our intuition is of no advantage; for they are then mere empty conceptions of objects, as to the possibility or impossibility of the existence of which they furnish us with no means of discovery. They are mere forms of thought, without objective reality, because we have no intuition to which the synthetical unity of apperception, which alone the categories contain, could be applied, for the purpose of determining an object. Our sensuous and empirical intuition can alone give them significance and meaning.

If, then, we suppose an object of a non-sensuous intuition to be given, we can in that case represent it by all those predicates which are implied in the presupposition that nothing *appertaining to sensuous intuition belongs to it*; for example, that it is not extended, or in space; that its duration is not time; that in it no change (the effect of the determinations in time) is to be met with, and so on. But it is no proper knowledge if I merely indicate what the intuition of the object *is not,* without being able to say what is contained in it, for I have not shown the possibility of an object to which my pure conception of understanding could be applicable, because I have not been able to furnish any intuition corresponding to it, but am only able to say that our intuition is not valid for it. But the most important point is this, that to a *something* of this kind not one category can be found applicable. Take, for example, the conception of substance, that is, something that can exist as subject, but never as mere predicate; in regard to this conception I am quite ignorant whether there can really be anything to correspond to such a determination of thought, if empirical intuition did not afford me the occasion for its application. But of this more in the sequel.

Of the Application of the Categories to Objects of the Senses in general. § 20

The pure conceptions of the understanding apply to objects of intuition in general, through the understanding alone, whether the intuition be our own or some other, provided only it be sensuous, but are, for this very reason, mere forms of thought, by means of which alone no determined object can be cognized. The synthesis or conjunction of the manifold in these conceptions relates, we have said, only to the unity of apperception, and is for this reason the ground of the possibility of *a priori* cognition, in so far as this cognition is dependent on the understanding. This synthesis is, therefore, not merely transcendental, but also purely intellectual. But because a certain form of sensuous intuition exists in the mind *a priori* which rests on the receptivity of the representative faculty (sensibility), the understanding, as a spontaneity, is able to determine the internal sense by means of the diversity of given representations, conformably to the synthetical unity of apperception, and thus to cogitate the synthetical unity of the apperception of the manifold of sensuous intuition *a priori,* as the condition to which must necessarily be submitted all objects of human intuition. And in this manner the categories as mere forms of thought receive objective reality, that is, application to objects which are given to us in intuition, but that only as phenomena, for it is only of phenomena that we are capable of *a priori* intuition.

This synthesis of the manifold of sensuous intuition, which is possible and necessary *a priori,* may be called figurative (*synthesis speciosa*), in contradistinction to that which is cogitated in the mere category in regard to the manifold of an intuition in general, and is called connection or conjunction of the understanding (*synthesis intellectualis*). Both are transcendental, not merely because they themselves precede *a priori* all experience, but also because they form the basis for the possibility of other cognition *a priori.*

But the figurative synthesis, when it has relation only to the originally synthetical unity of apperception, that is to the transcendental unity cogitated in the categories, must, to be distinguished from the purely intellectual conjunction, be entitled the *transcendental synthesis of imagination. Imagination* is the faculty of representing an object even without its presence in intuition. Now, as all our intuition is sensuous, imagination, by reason of the subjective condition under which alone it can give a corresponding intuition to the conceptions of the understanding, belongs to sensibility. But in so far as the synthesis of the imagination is an act of spontaneity, which is determinative, and not, like sense, merely determinable, and which is consequently able to determine sense *a priori,* according to its form, conformably to the unity of apperception, in so far is the imagination a faculty of determining sensibility *a priori,* and its synthesis of intuitions according to the categories must be the transcendental synthesis of the imagination. It is an operation of the understanding on sensibility, and the first application of the understanding to objects of possible intuition, and at the same time the basis for the exercise of the other functions of that faculty. As figurative, it is distinguished from the merely intellectual synthesis, which is produced by the understanding alone, without the aid of imagination. Now, in so far as imagination is spontaneity, I sometimes call it also the *productive* imagination, and distinguish it from the *reproductive,* the synthesis of which is subject entirely to empirical laws, those of association, namely, and which, therefore, contributes nothing to the explanation of the possibility of *a priori* cognition, and for this reason belongs not to transcendental philosophy, but to psychology.

We have now arrived at the proper place for explaining the paradox which must have struck every one in our exposition of the internal sense (§ 6), namely—how this sense represents us to our own consciousness, only as we appear to ourselves, not as we are in ourselves, because, to wit, we intuite ourselves only as we are inwardly affected. Now this appears to be contradictory, inasmuch as we thus stand in a passive relation to ourselves; and therefore in the systems of psychology, the internal sense is commonly held to be one with the faculty of apperception, while we, on the contrary, carefully distinguish them.

That which determines the internal sense is the understanding, and its original power of conjoining the manifold of intuition, that is, of bringing this under an apperception (upon which rests the possibility of the understanding itself). Now, as the human understanding is not in itself a faculty of intuition, and is unable to exercise such a power, in order to conjoin, as it were, the manifold of its own intuition, the synthesis of understanding is, considered *per se,* nothing but the unity of action, of which, as such, it is self-conscious, even apart from sensibility, by which, moreover, it is able to determine our internal sense in respect of the manifold which may be presented to it according to the form of sensuous intuition. Thus, under the name of a transcendental synthesis of imagination, the understanding exercises an activity upon the passive subject, whose faculty it is; and so we are right in saying that the internal sense is affected thereby. Apperception and its synthetical unity are by no means one and the same with the internal sense. The former, as the source of all our synthetical conjunction, applies, under the name of the categories, to the manifold of intuition in general, prior to all sensuous intuition of objects. The internal sense, on the contrary, contains merely the form of intuition, but without any synthetical conjunction of the manifold therein, and consequently does not contain any determined intuition, which is possible only through consciousness of the determination of the manifold by the transcendental act of the imagination (synthetical influence of the understanding on the internal sense), which I have named figurative synthesis.

This we can indeed always perceive in ourselves. We cannot cogitate a geometrical line without *drawing* it in thought, nor a circle without *describing* it, nor represent the three dimensions of space without drawing three lines from the same point perpendicular to one another. We cannot even cogitate time, unless, in drawing a straight line (which is to serve as the external figurative representation of time), we fix our attention on the act of the synthesis of the manifold, whereby we determine successively the internal sense, and thus attend also to the succession of this determination. Motion as an act of the subject (not as a determination of an object),[1] consequently the synthesis of the manifold in space, if we make abstraction of space and attend merely to the act by which we determine the internal sense according to its form, is that which produces the conception of succession. The understanding, therefore, does by no means *find* in the internal sense any such synthesis of the manifold, but *produces* it, in that it affects this sense. At the same time, how "*I* who think" is distinct from the "*I*" which intuites itself (other modes of intuition being cogitable as at least possible), and yet one and the same with this latter as the same subject; how, therefore, I am able to say: "I, as an intelligence and *thinking* subject, cognize myself as an object *thought,* so far as I am, moreover, given to myself in intuition—only, like other phenomena, not as I am in myself, and as considered by the understanding, but merely as I appear"—is a question that has in it neither more nor less difficulty than the question—"How can I be an object to myself?" or this—"How I can be an object of my own intuition and internal perceptions?" But that such must be the fact, if we admit that space is merely a pure form of the phenomena of external sense, can be clearly proved by the consideration that we cannot represent time, which is not an object of external intuition, in any other way than under the image of a line, which we draw in thought, a mode of representation without

1 Motion of an *object* in space does not belong to a pure science, consequently not to geometry; because, that a thing is movable cannot be known *a priori,* but only from experience. But motion, considered as the *description* of a space, is a pure act of the successive synthesis of the manifold in external intuition by means of productive imagination, and belongs not only to geometry, but even to transcendental philosophy.

which we could not cognize the unity of its dimension, and also that we are necessitated to take our determination of periods of time, or of points of time, for all our internal perceptions from the changes which we perceive in outward things. It follows that we must arrange the determinations of the internal sense, as phenomena in time, exactly in the same manner as we arrange those of the external senses in space. And consequently, if we grant, respecting this latter, that by means of them we know objects only in so far as we are affected externally, we must also confess, with regard to the internal sense, that by means of it we intuite ourselves only as we are internally affected by ourselves; in other words, as regards internal intuition, we cognize our own subject only as phenomenon, and not as it is in itself.[1]

§ 21

On the other hand, in the transcendental synthesis of the manifold content of representations, consequently in the synthetical unity of apperception, I am conscious of myself, not as I appear to myself, nor as I am in myself, but only that "I am." This representation is a *thought,* not an *intuition.* Now, as in order to cognize ourselves, in addition to the act of thinking, which subjects the manifold of every possible intuition to the unity of apperception, there is necessary a determinate mode of intuition, whereby this manifold is given; although my own existence is certainly not mere phenomenon (much less mere illusion), the determination of my existence[2] can only take place conformably to the form of the internal sense, according to the particular mode in which the manifold which I conjoin is given in internal intuition, and I have therefore no knowledge of myself as I am, but merely as I appear to myself. The consciousness of self is thus very far from a knowledge of self, in which I do not use the categories, whereby I cogitate an object, by means of the conjunction of the manifold in one apperception. In the same way as I require, for the sake of the cognition of an object distinct from myself, not only the thought of an object in general (in the category), but also an intuition by which to determine that general conception, in the same way do I require, in order to the cognition of myself, not only the consciousness of myself or the thought that I think myself, but in addition an intuition of the manifold in myself, by which to determine this thought. It is true that I exist as an intelligence which is conscious only of its faculty of conjunction or synthesis, but subjected in relation to the manifold which this intelligence has to conjoin to a limitative conjunction called the internal sense. My intelligence (that is, I) can render that conjunction or synthesis perceptible only according to the relations of time, which are quite beyond the proper sphere of the conceptions of the understanding and consequently cognize itself in respect to an intuition (which cannot possibly be intellectual, nor given by the understanding), only as it appears to itself, and not as it would cognize itself, if its intuition were intellectual.

Transcendental Deduction of the universally possible employment in experience of the Pure Conceptions of the Understanding. § 22

In the metaphysical deduction, the *a priori* origin of the categories was proved by their complete accordance with the general logical functions of thought; in the *transcendental* deduction was exhibited the possibility of the categories as *a priori* cognitions of objects of an intuition in general (§§ 16 and 17). At present we are about to explain the possibility of cognizing, *a priori,* by means of the categories, all objects which can possibly be presented to our senses, not, indeed, according to the form of their intuition, but according to the laws of their conjunction or synthesis, and thus, as it were, of prescribing laws to nature and even of rendering nature possible. For if the categories

[1] I do not see why so much difficulty should be found in admitting that our internal sense is affected by ourselves. Every act of attention exemplifies it. In such an act the understanding determines the internal sense by the synthetical conjunction which it cogitates, conformably to the internal intuition which corresponds to the manifold in the synthesis of the understanding. How much the mind is usually affected thereby every one will be able to perceive in himself.

[2] The "I think" expresses the act of determining my own existence. My existence is thus already given by the act of consciousness; but the mode in which I must determine my existence, that is, the mode in which I must place the manifold belonging to my existence, is not thereby given. For this purpose intuition of self is required, and this intuition possesses a form given *a priori,* namely, time, which is sensuous, and belongs to our receptivity of the determinable. Now, as I do not possess another intuition of self which gives the *determining* in me (of the spontaneity of which I am conscious), prior to the act of *determination,* in the same manner as time gives the determinable, it is clear that I am unable to determine my own existence as that of a spontaneous being, but I am only able to represent to myself the spontaneity of my thought, that is, of my determination, and my existence remains ever determinable in a purely sensuous manner, that is to say, like the existence of a phenomenon. But it is because of this spontaneity that I call myself an *intelligence.*

were inadequate to this task, it would not be evident to us why everything that is presented to our senses must be subject to those laws which have an *a priori* origin in the understanding itself.

I premise that by the term *synthesis of apprehension* I understand the combination of the manifold in an empirical intuition, whereby perception, that is, empirical consciousness of the intuition (as phenomenon), is possible.

We have *a priori* forms of the external and internal sensuous intuition in the representations of space and time, and to these must the synthesis of apprehension of the manifold in a phenomenon be always comformable, because the synthesis itself can only take place according to these forms. But space and time are not merely forms of sensuous intuition, but *intuitions* themselves (which contain a manifold), and therefore contain *a priori* the determination of the *unity* of this manifold.[1] (See the *Transcendent Aesthetic.*) Therefore is *unity of the synthesis* of the manifold without or within us, consequently also a conjunction to which all that is to be represented as determined in space or time must correspond, given *a priori* along with (not in) these intuitions, as the condition of the synthesis of all apprehension of them. But this synthetical unity can be no other than that of the conjunction of the manifold of a given intuition in general, in a primitive act of consciousness, according to the categories, but applied to our sensuous intuition. Consequently all synthesis, whereby alone is even perception possible, is subject to the categories. And, as experience is cognition by means of conjoined perceptions, the categories are conditions of the possibility of experience and are therefore valid *a priori* for all objects of experience.

When, then, for example, I make the empirical intuition of a house by apprehension of the manifold contained therein into a perception, the *necessary unity* of space and of my external sensuous intuition lies at the foundation of this act, and I, as it were, draw the form of the house conformably to this synthetical unity of the manifold in space. But this very synthetical unity remains, even when I abstract the form of space, and has its seat in the understanding, and is in fact the category of the synthesis of the homogeneous in an intuition; that is to say, the category of *quantity,* to which the aforesaid synthesis of apprehension, that is, the perception, must be completely conformable.[2]

To take another example, when I perceive the freezing of water, I apprehend two states (fluidity and solidity), which, as such, stand toward each other mutually in a relation of time. But in the time, which I place as an internal intuition, at the foundation of this phenomenon, I represent to myself synthetical *unity* of the manifold, without which the aforesaid relation could not be given in an intuition as *determined* (in regard to the succession of time). Now this synthetical unity, as the *a priori* condition under which I conjoin the manifold of an intuition, is, if I make abstraction of the permanent form of my internal intuition (that is to say, of time), the category of *cause,* by means of which, when applied to my sensibility, *I determine everything that occurs according to relations of time.* Consequently apprehension in such an event, and the event itself, as far as regards the possibility of its perception, stands under the conception of the relation of cause and effect: and so in all other cases.

Categories are conceptions which prescribe laws *a priori to* phenomena, consequently to nature as the complex of all phenomena (*natura materialiter spectata*). And now the question arises—inasmuch as these categories are not derived from nature, and do not regulate themselves according to her as their model (for in that case they would be empirical)—how it is conceivable that nature must regulate herself according to them, in other words, how the categories can determine *a priori* the synthesis of the manifold of nature, and yet not derive their

[1] Space represented as an *object* (as geometry really requires it to be) contains more than the mere form of the intuition; namely, a combination of the manifold given according to the form of sensibility into a representation that can be intuited; so that the *form of the intuition* gives us merely the manifold, but the *formal intuition* gives unity of representation. In the aesthetic, I regarded this unity as belonging entirely to sensibility, for the purpose of indicating that it antecedes all conceptions, although it presupposes a synthesis which does not belong to sense, through which alone, however, all our conceptions of space and time are possible. For as by means of this unity alone (the understanding determining the sensibility) space and time are given as intuitions, it follows that the unity of this intuition *a priori* belongs to space and time, and not to the conception of the understanding (§20).

[2] In this manner it is proved, that the synthesis of apprehension, which is empirical, must necessarily be conformable to the synthesis of apperception, which is intellectual, and contained *a priori* in the category. It is one and the same spontaneity which at one time, under the name of imagination, at another under that of understanding, produces conjunction in the manifold of intuition.

origin from her. The following is the solution of this enigma.

It is not in the least more difficult to conceive how the laws of the phenomena of nature must harmonize with the understanding and with its *a priori* form—that is, its faculty of conjoining the manifold—than it is to understand how the phenomena themselves must correspond with the *a priori* form of our sensuous intuition. For laws do not exist in the phenomena any more than the phenomena exist as things in themselves. Laws do not exist except by relation to the subject in which the phenomena inhere, in so far as it possesses understanding, just as phenomena have no existence except by relation to the same existing subject in so far as it has senses. To things as things in themselves, conformability to law must necessarily belong independently of an understanding to cognize them. But phenomena are only representations of things which are utterly unknown in respect to what they are in themselves. But as mere representations, they stand under no law of conjunction except that which the conjoining faculty prescribes. Now that which conjoins the manifold of sensuous intuition is imagination, a mental act to which understanding contributes unity of intellectual synthesis, and sensibility, manifoldness of apprehension. Now as all possible perception depends on the synthesis of apprehension, and this empirical synthesis itself on the transcendental, consequently on the categories, it is evident that all possible perceptions, and therefore everything that can attain to empirical consciousness, that is, all phenomena of nature, must, as regards their conjunction, be subject to the categories. And nature (considered merely as nature in general) is dependent on them as the original ground of her necessary conformability to law (as *natura formaliter spectata*). But the pure faculty (of the understanding) of prescribing laws *a priori* to phenomena by means of mere categories, is not competent to enounce other or more laws than those on which a *nature* in general, as a conformability to law of phenomena of space and time, depends. Particular laws, inasmuch as they concern empirically determined phenomena, cannot be entirely deduced from pure laws, although they all stand under them. Experience must be superadded in order to know these particular laws; but in regard to experience in general, and everything that can be cognized as an object thereof, these *a priori* laws are our only rule and guide.

Result of this Deduction of the Conceptions of the Understanding. § 23

We cannot think any object except by means of the categories; we cannot cognize any thought except by means of intuitions corresponding to these conceptions. Now all our intuitions are sensuous, and our cognition, in so far as the object of it is given, is empirical. But empirical cognition is experience; consequently no *a priori cognition* is possible for us, except of objects of possible *experience.*[1]

But this cognition, which is limited to objects of experience, is not for that reason derived entirely from experience, but—and this is asserted of the pure intuitions and the pure conceptions of the understanding—there are, unquestionably, elements of cognition, which exist in the mind *a priori.* Now there are only two ways in which a necessary harmony of experience with the conceptions of its objects can be cogitated. Either experience makes these conceptions possible, or the conceptions make experience possible. The former of these statements will not hold good with respect to the categories (nor in regard to pure sensuous intuition), for they are *a priori* conceptions, and therefore independent of experience. The assertion of an empirical origin would attribute to them a sort of *generatio aequivoca.* Consequently, nothing remains but to adopt the second alternative (which presents us with a system, as it were, of the *epigenesis* of pure reason), namely, that on the part of the understanding the categories do contain the grounds of the possibility of all experience. But with respect to the questions how they make experience possible, and what are the principles of the possibility thereof with which they present us in their application to phenomena, the following section on the transcendental exercise of the faculty of judgement will inform the reader.

It is quite possible that someone may propose a species of *preformation-system* of pure

[1] Lest my readers should stumble at this assertion, and the conclusions that may be too rashly drawn from it, I must remind them that the categories in the *act of thought* are by no means limited by the conditions of our sensuous intuition, but have an unbounded sphere of action. It is only the cognition of the object of thought, the determining of the object, which requires intuition. In the absence of intuition, our thought of an object may still have true and useful consequences in regard to the exercise of reason by the subject. But as this exercise of reason is not always directed on the determination of the object, in other words, on cognition thereof, but also on the determination of the subject and its volition, I do not intend to treat of it in this place.

reason—a middle way between the two—to wit, that the categories are neither innate and first *a priori* principles of cognition, nor derived from experience, but are merely subjective aptitudes for thought implanted in us contemporaneously with our existence, which were so ordered and disposed by our Creator, that their exercise perfectly harmonizes with the laws of nature which regulate experience. Now, not to mention that with such an hypothesis it is impossible to say at what point we must stop in the employment of predetermined aptitudes, the fact that the categories would in this case entirely lose that character of *necessity* which is essentially involved in the very conception of them, is a conclusive objection to it. The conception of cause, for example, which expresses the necessity of an effect under a presupposed condition, would be false, if it rested only upon such an arbitrary subjective necessity of uniting certain empirical representations according to such a rule of relation. I could not then say —"The effect is connected with its cause in the object (that is, necessarily)," but only, "I am so constituted that I can think this representation as so connected, and not otherwise." Now this is just what the sceptic wants. For in this case, all our knowledge, depending on the supposed objective validity of our judgement, is nothing but mere illusion; nor would there be wanting people who would deny any such subjective necessity in respect to themselves, though they must feel it. At all events, we could not dispute with any one on that which merely depends on the manner in which his subject is organized.

Short view of the above Deduction

The foregoing deduction is an exposition of the pure conceptions of the understanding (and with them of all theoretical *a priori* cognition), as principles of the possibility of experience, but of experience as the *determination* of all phenomena in space and time *in general*—of experience, finally, from the principle of the *original* synthetical unity of apperception, as the form of the understanding in relation to time and space as original forms of sensibility.

I consider the division by paragraphs to be necessary only up to this point, because we had to treat of the elementary conceptions. As we now proceed to the exposition of the employment of these, I shall not designate the chapters in this manner any further.

BOOK II

Analytic of Principles

General logic is constructed upon a plan which coincides exactly with the division of the higher faculties of cognition. These are, *understanding, judgement, and reason.* This science, accordingly, treats in its analytic of *conceptions, judgements,* and *conclusions* in exact correspondence with the functions and order of those mental powers which we include generally under the generic denomination of understanding.

As this merely formal logic makes abstraction of all content of cognition, whether pure or empirical, and occupies itself with the mere form of thought (discursive cognition), it must contain in its analytic a canon for reason. For the form of reason has its law, which, without taking into consideration the particular nature of the cognition about which it is employed, can be discovered *a priori,* by the simple analysis of the action of reason into its momenta.

Transcendental logic, limited as it is to a determinate content, that of pure *a priori* cognitions, to wit, cannot imitate general logic in this division. For it is evident that the *transcendental employment of reason* is not objectively valid, and therefore does not belong to the *logic of truth* (that is, to analytic), but as a *logic of illusion,* occupies a particular department in the scholastic system under the name of transcendental *dialectic.*

Understanding and judgement accordingly possess in transcendental logic a canon of objectively valid, and therefore true exercise, and are comprehended in the analytical department of that logic. But reason, in her endeavours to arrive by *a priori* means at some true statement concerning objects and to extend cognition beyond the bounds of possible experience, is altogether dialectic, and her illusory assertions cannot be constructed into a canon such as an analytic ought to contain.

Accordingly, the analytic of principles will be merely a canon for the *faculty of judgement,* for the instruction of this faculty in its application to phenomena of the pure conceptions of the understanding, which contain the necessary condition for the establishment of *a priori* laws. On this account, although the subject of the following chapters is the especial principles of *understanding,* I shall make use of the term *Doctrine of the faculty of judgement,* in order to define more particularly my present purpose.

Introduction. Of the Transcendental Faculty of Judgement in General

If understanding in general be defined as the faculty of laws or rules, the faculty of judgement may be termed the faculty of *subsumption* under these rules; that is, of distinguishing whether this or that does or does not stand under a given rule (*casus datae legis*). General logic contains no directions or precepts for the faculty of judgement, nor can it contain any such. For as *it makes abstraction of all content of cognition,* no duty is left for it, except that of exposing analytically the mere form of cognition in conceptions, judgements, and conclusions, and of thereby establishing formal rules for all exercise of the understanding. Now if this logic wished to give some general direction how we should subsume under these rules, that is, how we should distinguish whether this or that did or did not stand under them, this again could not be done otherwise than by means of a rule. But this rule, precisely because it is a rule, requires for itself direction from the faculty of judgement. Thus, it is evident that the understanding is capable of being instructed by rules, but that the judgement is a peculiar talent, which does not, and cannot require tuition, but only exercise. This faculty is therefore the specific quality of the so-called mother wit, the want of which no scholastic discipline can compensate.

For although education may furnish, and, as it were, engraft upon a limited understanding rules borrowed from other minds, yet the power of employing these rules correctly must belong to the pupil himself; and no rule which we can prescribe to him with this purpose is, in the absence or deficiency of this gift of nature, secure from misuse.[1] A physician therefore, a judge or a statesman, may have in his head many admirable pathological, juridical, or political rules, in a degree that may enable him to be a profound teacher in his particular science, and yet in the application of these rules he may very possibly blunder—either because he is wanting in natural judgement (though not in understanding) and, whilst he can comprehend the general *in abstracto,* cannot distinguish whether a particular case *in concreto* ought to rank under the former; or because his faculty of judgement has not been sufficiently exercised by examples and real practice. Indeed, the grand and only use of examples, is to sharpen the judgement. For as regards the correctness and precision of the insight of the understanding, examples are commonly injurious rather than otherwise, because, as *casus in terminis,* they seldom adequately fulfil the conditions of the rule. Besides, they often weaken the power of our understanding to apprehend rules or laws in their universality, independently of particular circumstances of experience; and hence, accustom us to employ them more as formulae than as principles. Examples are thus the go-cart of the judgement, which he who is naturally deficient in that faculty cannot afford to dispense with.

But although general logic cannot give directions to the faculty of judgement, the case is very different as regards transcendental logic, insomuch that it appears to be the especial duty of the latter to secure and direct, by means of determinate rules, the faculty of judgement in the employment of the pure understanding. For, as a doctrine, that is, as an endeavour to enlarge the sphere of the understanding in regard to pure *a priori* cognitions, philosophy is worse than useless, since from all the attempts hitherto made, little or no ground has been gained. But, as a critique, in order to guard against the mistakes of the faculty of judgement (*lapsus judicii*) in the employment of the few pure conceptions of the understanding which we possess, although its use is in this case purely negative, philosophy is called upon to apply all its acuteness and penetration.

But transcendental philosophy has this peculiarity, that besides indicating the rule, or rather the general condition for rules, which is given in the pure conception of the understanding, it can, at the same time, indicate *a priori* the case to which the rule must be applied. The cause of the superiority which, in this respect, transcendental philosophy possesses above all other sciences except mathematics, lies in this: it treats of conceptions which must relate *a priori* to their objects, whose objective validity consequently cannot be demonstrated *a posteriori,* and is, at the same time, under the obligation of presenting in general but sufficient tests, the conditions under which objects can be given in harmony with those conceptions; otherwise they would be mere logical forms, with-

[1] Deficiency in judgement is properly that which is called stupidity; and for such a failing we know no remedy. A dull or narrow-minded person, to whom nothing is wanting but a proper degree of understanding, may be improved by tuition, even so far as to deserve the epithet of *learned*. But as such persons frequently labour under a deficiency in the faculty of judgement, it is not uncommon to find men extremely learned who in the application of their science betray to a lamentable degree this irremediable want.

out content, and not pure conceptions of the understanding.

Our transcendental doctrine of the faculty of judgement will contain two chapters. The first will treat of the sensuous condition under which alone pure conceptions of the understanding can be employed—that is, of the *schematism* of the pure understanding. The second will treat of those synthetical judgements which are derived *a priori* from pure conceptions of the understanding under those conditions, and which lie *a priori* at the foundation of all other cognitions, that is to say, it will treat of the principles of the pure understanding.

Transcendental Doctrine of the Faculty of Judgement Or, Analytic of Principles

Chapter I. *Of the Schematism of the Pure Conceptions of the Understanding*

In all subsumptions of an object under a conception, the representation of the object must be homogeneous with the conception; in other words, the conception must contain that which is represented in the object to be subsumed under it. For this is the meaning of the expression: "An object is contained under a conception." Thus the empirical conception of a *plate* is homogeneous with the pure geometrical conception of a *circle,* inasmuch as the roundness which is cogitated in the former is intuited in the latter.

But pure conceptions of the understanding, when compared with empirical intuitions, or even with sensuous intuitions in general, are quite heterogeneous, and never can be discovered in any intuition. How then is the *subsumption* of the latter under the former, and consequently the application of the categories to phenomena, possible?—For it is impossible to say, for example: "Causality can be intuited through the senses and is contained in the phenomenon." —This natural and important question forms the real cause of the necessity of a transcendental doctrine of the faculty of judgement, with the purpose, to wit, of showing how pure conceptions of the understanding can be applied to phenomena. In all other sciences, where the conceptions by which the object is thought in the general are not so different and heterogeneous from those which represent the object *in concreto*—as it is given, it is quite unnecessary to institute any special inquiries concerning the application of the former to the latter.

Now it is quite clear that there must be some third thing, which on the one side is homogeneous with the category, and with the phenomenon on the other, and so makes the application of the former to the latter possible. This mediating representation must be pure (without any empirical content), and yet must on the one side be *intellectual,* on the other *sensuous.* Such a representation is the *transcendental schema.*

The conception of the understanding contains pure synthetical unity of the manifold in general. Time, as the formal condition of the manifold of the internal sense, consequently of the conjunction of all representations, contains *a priori* a manifold in the pure intuition. Now a transcendental determination of time is so far homogeneous with the *category,* which constitutes the unity thereof, that it is universal and rests upon a rule *a priori.* On the other hand, it is so far homogeneous with the *phenomenon,* inasmuch as time is contained in every empirical representation of the manifold. Thus an application of the category to phenomena becomes possible, by means of the transcendental determination of time, which, as the schema of the conceptions of the understanding, mediates the subsumption of the latter under the former.

After what has been proved in our deduction of the categories, no one, it is to be hoped, can hesitate as to the proper decision of the question, whether the employment of these pure conceptions of the understanding ought to be merely empirical or also transcendental; in other words, whether the categories, as conditions of a possible experience, relate *a priori* solely to phenomena, or whether, as conditions of the possibility of things in general, their application can be extended to objects as things in themselves. For we have there seen that conceptions are quite impossible, and utterly without signification, unless either to them, or at least to the elements of which they consist, an object be given; and that, consequently, they cannot possibly apply to objects as things in themselves without regard to the question whether and how these may be given to us; and, further, that the only manner in which objects can be given to us is by means of the modification of our sensibility; and, finally, that pure *a priori* conceptions, in addition to the function of the understanding in the category, must contain *a priori* formal conditions of sensibility (of the internal sense, namely), which again contain the general condition under which alone the category can be applied to any object. This formal and pure condition of sensibility, to which the conception of the understanding is restricted in its employment, we shall name the *schema* of the conception of the understanding, and the procedure of the understanding with these schemata we shall call the *schematism* of the pure understanding.

The schema is, in itself, always a mere product of the imagination. But, as the synthesis of imagination has for its aim no single intuition, but merely unity in the determination of sensibility, the schema is clearly distinguishable from the image. Thus, if I place five points one after another . . . . . this is an image of the number five. On the other hand, if I only think a number in general, which may be either five or a hundred, this thought is rather the representation of a method of representing in an image a sum (e.g., a thousand) in conformity with a conception, than the image itself, an image which I should find some little difficulty in reviewing, and comparing with the conception. Now this representation of a general procedure of the imagination to present its image to a conception, I call the schema of this conception.

In truth, it is not images of objects, but schemata, which lie at the foundation of our pure sensuous conceptions. No image could ever be adequate to our conception of a triangle in general. For the generalness of the conception it never could attain to, as this includes under itself all triangles, whether right-angled, acute-angled, etc., whilst the image would always be limited to a single part of this sphere. The schema of the triangle can exist nowhere else than in thought, and it indicates a rule of the synthesis of the imagination in regard to pure figures in space. Still less is an object of experience, or an image of the object, ever adequate to the empirical conception. On the contrary, the conception always relates immediately to the schema of the imagination, as a rule for the determination of our intuition, in conformity with a certain general conception. The conception of a dog indicates a rule, according to which my imagination can delineate the figure of a four-footed animal in general, without being limited to any particular individual form which experience presents to me, or indeed to any possible image that I can represent to myself *in concreto*. This schematism of our understanding in regard to phenomena and their mere form, is an art, hidden in the depths of the human soul, whose true modes of action we shall only with difficulty discover and unveil. Thus much only can we say: "The *image* is a product of the empirical faculty of the productive imagination—the *schema* of sensuous conceptions (of figures in space, for example) is a product, and, as it were, a monogram of the pure imagination *a priori*, whereby and according to which images first become possible, which, however, can be connected with the conception only mediately by means of the schema which they indicate, and are in themselves never fully adequate to it." On the other hand, the schema of a pure conception of the understanding is something that cannot be reduced into any image—it is nothing else than the pure synthesis expressed by the category, conformably to a rule of unity according to conceptions. It is a transcendental product of the imagination, a product which concerns the determination of the internal sense, according to conditions of its form (time) in respect to all representations, in so far as these representations must be conjoined *a priori* in one conception, conformably to the unity of apperception.

Without entering upon a dry and tedious analysis of the essential requisites of transcendental schemata of the pure conceptions of the understanding, we shall rather proceed at once to give an explanation of them according to the order of the categories, and in connection therewith.

For the external sense the pure image of all quantities (*quantorum*) is space; the pure image of all objects of sense in general, is time. But the pure *schema* of *quantity* (*quantitatis*) as a conception of the understanding, is *number*, a representation which comprehends the successive addition of one to one (homogeneous quantities). Thus, number is nothing else than the unity of the synthesis of the manifold in a homogeneous intuition, by means of my generating time itself in my apprehension of the intuition.

Reality, in the pure conception of the understanding, is that which corresponds to a sensation in general; that, consequently, the conception of which indicates a being (in time). Negation is that the conception of which represents a not-being (in time). The opposition of these two consists therefore in the difference of one and the same time, as a time filled or a time empty. Now as time is only the form of intuition, consequently of objects as phenomena, that which in objects corresponds to sensation is the transcendental matter of all objects as things in themselves (*Sachheit*, reality). Now every sensation has a degree or quantity by which it can fill time, that is to say, the internal sense in respect of the representation of an object, more or less, until it vanishes into nothing (= o = *negatio*). Thus there is a relation and connection between reality and negation, or rather a transition from the former to the latter, which makes every reality representable to us as a quantum; and the schema of a reality as the quantity of something in so far as it fills time, is exactly this continuous and uniform generation of the reality in time, as we descend in time from the sensation which has a certain degree, down to the vanishing thereof, or gradually ascend from negation to the quantity thereof.

The schema of substance is the permanence of the real in time; that is, the representation of it as a substratum of the empirical determination of time; a substratum which therefore remains, whilst all else changes. (Time passes not, but in it passes the existence of the changeable. To time, therefore, which is itself unchangeable and permanent, corresponds that which in the phenomenon is unchangeable in existence, that is, substance, and it is only by it that the succession and coexistence of phenomena can be determined in regard to time.)

The schema of cause and of the causality of a thing is the real which, when posited, is always followed by something else. It consists, therefore, in the succession of the manifold, in so far as that succession is subjected to a rule.

The schema of community (reciprocity of action and reaction), or the reciprocal causality of substances in respect of their accidents, is the coexistence of the determinations of the one with those of the other, according to a general rule.

The schema of possibility is the accordance of the synthesis of different representations with the conditions of time in general (as, for example, opposites cannot exist together at the same time in the same thing, but only after each other), and is therefore the determination of the representation of a thing at *any* time.

The schema of reality is existence in a determined time.

The schema of necessity is the existence of an object in all time.

It is clear, from all this, that the schema of the category of quantity contains and represents the generation (synthesis) of time itself, in the successive apprehension of an object; the schema of quality the synthesis of sensation with the representation of time, or the filling up of time; the schema of relation the relation of perceptions to each other in all time (that is, according to a rule of the determination of time): and finally, the schema of modality and its categories, time itself, as the correlative of the determination of an object—whether it does belong to time, and how. The schemata, therefore, are nothing but *a priori determinations of time* according to rules, and these, in regard to all possible objects, following the arrangement of the categories, relate to *the series in time, the content in time, the order in time,* and finally, *to the complex or totality in time.*

Hence it is apparent that the schematism of the understanding, by means of the transcendental synthesis of the imagination, amounts to nothing else than the unity of the manifold of intuition in the internal sense, and thus indirectly to the unity of apperception, as a function corresponding to the internal sense (a receptivity). Thus, the schemata of the pure conceptions of the understanding are the true and only conditions whereby our understanding receives an application to objects, and consequently *significance.* Finally, therefore, the categories are only capable of empirical use, inasmuch as they serve merely to subject phenomena to the universal rules of synthesis, by means of an *a priori* necessary unity (on account of the necessary union of all consciousness in one original apperception); and so to render them susceptible of a complete connection in one experience. But within this whole of possible experience lie all our cognitions, and in the universal relation to this experience consists transcendental truth, which antecedes all empirical truth, and renders the latter possible.

It is, however, evident at first sight, that although the schemata of sensibility are the sole agents in realizing the categories, they do, nevertheless, also restrict them, that is, they limit the categories by conditions which lie beyond the sphere of understanding—namely, in sensibility. Hence the schema is properly only the phenomenon, or the sensuous conception of an object in harmony with the category. (*Numerus est quantitas phaenomenon—sensatio realitas phaenomenon; constans et perdurabile rerum substantia phaenomenon—aeternitas, necessitas, phaenomena,* etc.) Now, if we remove a restrictive condition, we thereby amplify, it appears, the formerly limited conception. In this way, the categories in their pure signification, free from all conditions of sensibility, ought to be valid of things *as they are,* and not, as the schemata represent them, merely as they appear; and consequently the categories must have a significance far more extended, and wholly independent of all schemata. In truth, there does always remain to the pure conceptions of the understanding, after abstracting every sensuous condition, a value and significance, which is, however, merely logical. But in this case, no object is given them, and therefore they have no meaning sufficient to afford us a conception of an object. The notion of substance, for example, if we leave out the sensuous determination of permanence, would mean nothing more than a something which can be cogitated as subject, without the possibility of becoming a predicate to anything else. Of this representation I can make nothing, inasmuch as it does not indicate to me what determinations the thing possesses which must thus be valid as *premier* subject. Consequently, the categories, without schemata are merely functions of the understanding for the production of conceptions, but do not represent any object. This significance they derive from sensibility, which at the same time realizes the understanding and restricts it.

Chapter II. *System of all Principles of the Pure Understanding*

In the foregoing chapter we have merely considered the general conditions under which alone the transcendental faculty of judgement is justified in using the pure conceptions of the understanding for synthetical judgements. Our duty at present is to exhibit in systematic connection those judgements which the understanding really produces *a priori.* For this purpose, our table of the categories will certainly afford us the natural and safe guidance. For it is precisely the categories whose application to possible experience must constitute all pure *a priori* cognition of the understanding; and the relation of which to sensibility will, on that very account, present us with a complete and systematic catalogue of all the transcendental principles of the use of the understanding.

Principles *a priori* are so called, not merely because they contain in themselves the grounds of other judgements, but also because they themselves are not grounded in higher and more general cognitions. This peculiarity, however, does not raise them altogether above the need of a proof. For although there could be found no higher cognition, and therefore no objective proof, and although such a principle rather serves as the foundation for all cognition of the object, this by no means hinders us from drawing a proof from the subjective sources of the possibility of the cognition of an object. Such a proof is necessary, moreover, because without it the principle might be liable to the imputation of being a mere gratuitous assertion.

In the second place, we shall limit our investigations to those principles which relate to the categories. For as to the principles of transcendental aesthetic, according to which space and time are the conditions of the possibility of things as phenomena, as also the restriction of these principles, namely, that they cannot be applied to objects as things in themselves—these, of course, do not fall within the scope of our present inquiry. In like manner, the principles of mathematical science form no part of this system, because they are all drawn from intuition, and not from the pure conception of the understanding. The possibility of these principles, however, will necessarily be considered here, inasmuch as they are synthetical judgements *a priori,* not indeed for the purpose of proving their accuracy and apodeictic certainty, which is unnecessary, but merely to render conceivable and deduce the possibility of such evident *a priori* cognitions.

But we shall have also to speak of the principle of analytical judgements, in opposition to synthetical judgements, which is the proper subject of our inquiries, because this very opposition will free the theory of the latter from all ambiguity, and place it clearly before our eyes in its true nature.

System of the Principles of the Pure Understanding

Section I. *Of the Supreme Principle of all Analytical Judgements*

Whatever may be the content of our cognition, and in whatever manner our cognition may be related to its object, the universal, although only negative conditions of all our judgements is that they do not contradict themselves; otherwise these judgements are in themselves (even without respect to the object) nothing. But although there may exist no contraditions in our judgement, it may nevertheless connect conceptions in such a manner that they do not correspond to the object, or without any grounds either *a priori* or *a posteriori* for arriving at such a judgement, and thus, without being self-contradictory, a judgement may nevertheless be either false or groundless.

Now, the proposition: "No subject can have a predicate that contradicts it," is called the *principle of contradiction,* and is a universal but purely negative criterion of all truth. But it belongs to logic alone, because it is valid of cognitions, merely as cognitions and without respect to their content, and declares that the contradiction entirely nullifies them. We can also, however, make a positive use of this principle, that is, not merely to banish falsehood and error (in so far as it rests upon contradiction), but also for the cognition of truth. For *if the judgement is analytical,* be it affirmative or negative, its truth must always be recognizable by means of the principle of contradiction. For the contrary of that which lies and is cogitated as conception in the cognition of the object will be always properly negatived, but the conception itself must always be affirmed of the object, inasmuch as the contrary thereof would be in contradiction to the object.

We must therefore hold the *principle of contradiction* to be the universal and fully sufficient *principle of all analytical cognition.* But as a sufficient criterion of truth, it has no further utility or authority. For the fact that no cognition can be at variance with this principle without nullifying itself, constitutes this principle the *sine qua non,* but not the determining ground of the truth of our cognition. As our business at present is properly with the synthetical part of our knowledge only, we shall always be on our guard not to transgress this inviolable principle; but at the same time not to expect from it any direct assistance in the establishment of the truth of any synthetical proposition.

There exists, however, a formula of this celebrated principle—a principle merely formal and entirely without content—which contains a synthesis that has been inadvertently and quite unnecessarily mixed up with it. It is this: "It is impossible for a thing to be and not to be at the same time." Not to mention the superfluousness of the addition of the word *impossible* to indicate the apodeictic certainty, which ought to be self-evident from the proposition itself, the proposition is affected by the condition of time, and as it were says: "A thing=*A,* which is something=*B*, cannot at the same time be *non-B.*" But both, *B* as well as *non-B,* may quite well exist in succession. For example, a man who is young cannot at the same time be old; but the same man can very well be at one time young, and at another not young, that is, old. Now the principle of contradiction as a merely logical proposition must not by any means limit its application merely to relations of time, and consequently a formula like the preceding is quite foreign to its true purpose. The misunderstanding arises in this way. We first of all separate a predicate of a thing from the conception of the thing, and afterwards connect with this predicate its opposite, and hence do not establish any contradiction with the subject, but only with its predicate, which has been conjoined with the subject synthetically—a contradiction, moreover, which obtains only when the first and second predicate are affirmed in the same time. If I say: "A man who is ignorant is not learned," the condition "at the same time" must be added, for he who is at one time ignorant, may at another be learned. But if I say: "No ignorant man is a learned man," the proposition is analytical, because the characteristic *ignorance* is now a constituent part of the conception of the subject; and in this case the negative proposition is evident immediately from the proposition of contradiction, without the necessity of adding the condition "the the same time." This is the reason why I have altered the formula of this principle—an alteration which shows very clearly the nature of an analytical proposition.

SECTION II. *Of the Supreme Principle of all Synthetical Judgements*

The explanation of the possibility of synthetical judgements is a task with which general logic has nothing to do; indeed she needs not even be acquainted with its name. But in transcendental logic it is the most important matter to be dealt with—indeed the only one, if the question is of the possibility of synthetical judgements *a priori,* the conditions and extent of their validity. For when this question is fully decided, it can reach its aim with perfect ease, the determination, to wit, of the extent and limits of the pure understanding.

In an analytical judgement I do not go beyond the given conception, in order to arrive at some decision respecting it. If the judgement is affirmative, I predicate of the conception only that which was already cogitated in it; if negative, I merely exclude from the conception its contrary. But in synthetical judgements, I must go beyond the given conception, in order to cogitate, in relation with it, something quite different from that which was cogitated in it, a relation which is consequently never one either of identity or contradiction, and by means of which the truth or error of the judgement cannot be discerned merely from the judgement itself.

Granted, then, that we must go out beyond a given conception, in order to compare it synthetically with another, a third thing is necessary, in which alone the synthesis of two conceptions can originate. Now what is this *tertium quid* that is to be the medium of all synthetical judgements? It is only a complex in which all our representations are contained, the internal sense to wit, and its form *a priori,* time.

The synthesis of our representations rests upon the imagination; their synthetical unity (which is requisite to a judgement), upon the unity of apperception. In this, therefore, is to be sought the possibility of synthetical judgements, and as all three contain the sources of *a priori* representations, the possibility of pure synthetical judgements also; nay, they are necessary upon these grounds, if we are to possess a knowledge of objects, which rests solely upon the synthesis of representations.

If a cognition is to have objective reality, that is, to relate to an object, and possess sense and meaning in respect to it, it is necessary that the object be given in some way or another. Without this, our conceptions are empty, and we may indeed have thought by means of them, but by such thinking we have not, in fact, cognized anything, we have merely played with representation. To give an object, if this expression be understood in the sense of "to present" the object, not mediately but immediately in intuition, means nothing else than to apply the representation of it to experience, be that experience real or only possible. Space and time themselves, pure as these conceptions are from all that is empirical, and certain as it is that they are represented fully *a priori* in the mind, would be completely without objective validity, and without sense and significance, if their necessary use in the objects of experience were not shown. Nay, the representation of them is a mere schema, that always relates to the reproductive imagination, which calls up the objects of experience, without which they have no meaning. And so it is with all conceptions without distinction.

The *possibility of experience* is, then, that which gives objective reality to all our *a priori* cognitions. Now experience depends upon the synthetical unity of phenomena, that is, upon a synthesis according to conceptions of the object of phenomena in general, a synthesis without which experience never could become knowledge, but would be merely a rhapsody of perceptions, never fitting together into any connected text, according to rules of a thoroughly united (possible) consciousness, and therefore never subjected to the transcendental and necessary unity of apperception. Experience has therefore for a foundation, *a priori* principles of its form, that is to say, general rules of unity in the synthesis of phenomena, the objective reality of which rules, as necessary conditions—even of the possibility of experience—can always be shown in experience. But apart from this relation, *a priori* synthetical propositions are absolutely impossible, because they have no third term, that is, no pure object, in which the synthetical unity can exhibit the objective reality of its conceptions.

Although, then, respecting space, or the forms which productive imagination describes therein, we do cognize much *a priori* in synthetical judgements, and are really in no need of experience for this purpose, such knowledge would nevertheless amount to nothing but a busy trifling with a mere chimera, were not space to be considered as the condition of the phenomena which constitute the material of external experience. Hence those pure synthetical judgements do relate, though but mediately, to possible experience, or rather to the possibility of experience, and upon that alone is founded the objective validity of their synthesis.

While then, on the one hand, experience, as empirical synthesis, is the only possible mode of cognition which gives reality to all other synthesis; on the other hand, this latter synthesis, as cognition *a priori,* possesses truth, that is, accordance with its object, only in so far as it contains nothing more than what is necessary to the synthetical unity of experience.

Accordingly, the supreme principle of all synthetical judgements is: "Every object is subject to the necessary conditions of the synthetical unity of the manifold of intuition in a possible experience."

A priori synthetical judgements are possible when we apply the formal conditions of the *a priori* intuition, the synthesis of the imagination, and the necessary unity of that synthesis in a transcendental apperception, to a possible cognition of experience, and say: "The conditions of the *possibility of experience* in general are at the same time conditions of the *possibility* of the *objects* of *experience,* and have, for that reason, objective validity in an *a priori* synthetical judgement."

SECTION III. *Systematic Representation of all Synthetical Principles of the Pure Understanding*

That principles exist at all is to be ascribed solely to the pure understanding, which is not only the faculty of rules in regard to that which happens, but is even the source of principles according to which everything that can be presented to us as an object is necessarily subject to rules, because without such rules we never could attain to cognition of an object. Even the laws of nature, if they are contemplated as principles of the empirical use of the understanding, possess also a characteristic of necessity, and we may therefore at least expect them to be determined upon grounds which are valid *a priori* and antecedent to all experience. But all laws of nature, without distinction, are subject to higher principles of the understanding, inasmuch as the former are merely applications of the latter to particular cases of experience. These higher principles alone therefore give the conception, which contains the necessary condition, and, as it were, the exponent of a rule; experience, on the other hand, gives the case which comes under the rule.

There is no danger of our mistaking merely empirical principles for principles of the pure understanding, or conversely; for the character of necessity, according to conceptions which distinguish the latter, and the absence of this in every empirical proposition, how extensively valid soever it may be, is a perfect safeguard against confounding them. There are, however, pure principles *a priori*, which nevertheless I should not ascribe to the pure understanding—for this reason, that they are not derived from pure conceptions, but (although by the mediation of the understanding) from pure intuitions. But understanding is the faculty of conceptions. Such principles mathematical science possesses, but their application to experience, consequently their objective validity, nay the possibility of such *a priori* synthetical cognitions (the deduction thereof) rests entirely upon the pure understanding.

On this account, I shall not reckon among my principles those of mathematics; though I shall include those upon the possibility and objective validity *a priori*, of principles of the mathematical science, which, consequently, are to be looked upon as the principle of these, and which proceed from conceptions to intuition, and not from intuition to conceptions.

In the application of the pure conceptions of the understanding to possible experience, the employment of their synthesis is either *mathematical* or *dynamical*, for it is directed partly on the *intuition* alone, partly on the *existence* of a phenomenon. But the *a priori* conditions of intuition are in relation to a possible experience absolutely necessary, those of the existence of objects of a possible empirical intuition are in themselves contingent. Hence the principles of the mathematical use of the categories will possess a character of absolute necessity, that is, will be apodeictic; those, on the other hand, of the dynamical use, the character of an *a priori* necessity indeed, but only under the condition of empirical thought in an experience, therefore only mediately and indirectly. Consequently they will not possess that immediate evidence which is peculiar to the former, although their application to experience does not, for that reason, lose its truth and certitude. But of this point we shall be better able to judge at the conclusion of this system of principles.

The table of the categories is naturally our guide to the table of principles, because these are nothing else than rules for the objective employment of the former. Accordingly, all principles of the pure understanding are:

1
Axioms
of Intuition

2
Anticipations
of Perception

3
Analogies
of Experience

4
Postulates of
Empirical Thought
in general

These appellations I have chosen advisedly, in order that we might not lose sight of the distinctions in respect of the evidence and the employment of these principles. It will, however, soon appear that—a fact which concerns both the evidence of these principles, and the *a priori* determination of phenomena—according to the categories of *quantity* and *quality* (if we attend merely to the form of these), the principles of these categories are distinguishable from those of the two others, inasmuch as the former are possessed of an intuitive, but the latter of a merely discursive, though in both instances a complete, certitude. I shall therefore call the former *mathematical*, and the latter *dynamical* principles.[1] It must be observed,

[1] All *combination* (*conjunctio*) is either *composition* (*compositio*) or *connection* (*nexus*). The former is the synthesis of a manifold, the parts of which do not necessarily belong to each other. For example, the two triangles into which a square is divided by a diagonal, do not necessarily belong to each other, and of this kind is the synthesis of the *homogeneous* in everything that can be *mathematically* considered. This synthesis can be divided into those of *aggregation* and *coalition*,

however, that by these terms I mean just as little in the one case the principles of mathematics as those of general (physical) dynamics in the other. I have here in view merely the principles of the pure understanding, in their application to the internal sense (without distinction of the representations given therein), by means of which the sciences of mathematics and dynamics become possible. Accordingly, I have named these principles rather with reference to their application than their content; and I shall now proceed to consider them in the order in which they stand in the table.

1. Axioms of Intuition

The principle of these is: *All Intuitions are Extensive Quantities.*

PROOF

All phenomena contain, as regards their form, an intuition in space and time, which lies *a priori* at the foundation of all without exception. Phenomena, therefore, cannot be apprehended, that is, received into empirical consciousness otherwise than through the synthesis of a manifold, through which the representations of a determinate space or time are generated; that is to say, through the composition of the homogeneous and the consciousness of the synthetical unity of this manifold (homogeneous). Now the consciousness of a homogeneous manifold in intuition, in so far as thereby the representation of an object is rendered possible, is the conception of a quantity (*quanti*). Consequently, even the perception of an object as phenomenon is possible only through the same synthetical unity of the manifold of the given sensuous intuition, through which the unity of the composition of the homogeneous manifold in the conception of a *quantity* is cogitated; that is to say, all phenomena are quantities, and *extensive* quantities, because as intuitions in space or time they must be represented by means of the same synthesis through which space and time themselves are determined.

the former of which is applied to *extensive,* the latter to *intensive* quantities. The second sort of combination (*nexus*) is the synthesis of a manifold, in so far as its parts do belong necessarily to each other; for example, the accident to a substance, or the effect to the cause. Consequently it is a synthesis of that which though *heterogeneous,* is represented as connected *a priori.* This combination—not an arbitrary one—I entitle *dynamical* because it concerns the connection of the *existence* of the manifold. This, again, may be divided into the *physical* synthesis, of the phenomena divided among each other, and the *metaphysical* synthesis, or the connection of phenomena *a priori* in the faculty of cognition.

An extensive quantity I call that wherein the representation of the parts renders possible (and therefore necessarily antecedes) the representation of the whole. I cannot represent to myself any line, however small, without drawing it in thought, that is, without generating from a point all its parts one after another, and in this way alone producing this intuition. Precisely the same is the case with every, even the smallest, portion of time. I cogitate therein only the successive progress from one moment to another, and hence, by means of the different portions of time and the addition of them, a determinate quantity of time is produced. As the pure intuition in all phenomena is either time or space, so is every phenomenon in its character of intuition an extensive quantity, inasmuch as it can only be cognized in our apprehension by successive synthesis (from part to part). All phenomena are, accordingly, to be considered as aggregates, that is, as a collection of previously given parts; which is not the case with every sort of quantities, but only with those which are represented and apprehended by us as extensive.

On this successive synthesis of the productive imagination, in the generation of figures, is founded the mathematics of extension, or geometry, with its axioms, which express the conditions of sensuous intuition *a priori,* under which alone the schema of a pure conception of external intuition can exist; for example, "between two points only one straight line is possible," "two straight lines cannot enclose a space," etc. These are the axioms which properly relate only to quantities (*quanta*) as such.

But, as regards the quantity of a thing (*quantitas*), that is to say, the answer to the question: "How large is this or that object?" although, in respect to this question, we have various propositions synthetical and immediately certain (*indemonstrabilia*); we have, in the proper sense of the term, no axioms. For example, the propositions: "If equals be added to equals, the wholes are equal"; "If equals be taken from equals, the remainders are equal"; are analytical, because I am immediately conscious of the identity of the production of the one quantity with the production of the other; whereas axioms must be *a priori* synthetical propositions. On the other hand, the self-evident propositions as to the relation of numbers, are certainly synthetical but not universal, like those of geometry, and for this reason cannot be called axioms, but numerical formulae. That $7+5=12$ is not an analytical proposition. For neither in the representation of seven, nor of five, nor of the composition of the two numbers, do I cogitate the number twelve. (Whether I cogitate the number in the *addition* of both, is not at present the question; for in the case of an analytical proposition, the only point is whether I really cogitate the predicate in the representation of the subject.) But although the proposition is synthetical, it is nevertheless only a singular proposition. In so far as regard is here had merely to the synthesis of the homogeneous (the units), it cannot take place except in one manner, although our *use* of these numbers is afterwards general. If I say: "A triangle can be constructed with three lines, any two of which taken together are greater than the third," I exercise merely the pure function of the productive imagination, which may draw the lines longer or shorter and construct the angles at its pleasure. On the contrary, the number seven is possible only in one manner, and so is likewise the number twelve, which results from the synthesis of seven and five. Such propositions, then, cannot be termed axioms (for in that case we should have an infinity of these), but numerical formulae.

This transcendental principle of the mathematics of phenomena greatly enlarges our *a priori* cognition. For it is by this principle alone that pure mathematics is rendered applicable in all its precision to objects of experience, and without it the validity of this application would not be so self-evident; on the contrary, contradictions and confusions have often arisen on this very point. Phenomena are not things in themselves. Empirical intuition is possible only through pure intuition (of space and time); consequently, what geometry affirms of the latter, is indisputably valid of the former. All evasions, such as the statement that objects of sense do not conform to the rules of construction in space (for example, to the rule of the infinite divisibility of lines or angles), must fall to the ground. For, if these objections hold good, we deny to space, and with it to all mathematics, objective validity, and no longer know wherefore, and how far, mathematics can be applied to phenomena. The synthesis of spaces and times as the essential form of all intuition, is that which renders possible the apprehension of a phenomenon, and therefore every external experience, consequently all cognition of the objects of experience; and whatever mathematics in its pure use proves of the former, must necessarily hold good of the latter. All objections are but the chicaneries of an ill-instructed reason, which erroneously thinks to liberate the objects of sense from the formal conditions of our sensibility, and represents these, although mere phenomena, as things in themselves, presented as such to our understanding. But in this case, no *a priori* synthetical cognition of them could be possible, consequently not through pure conceptions of space and the science which determines these conceptions, that is to say, geometry, would itself be impossible.

2. Anticipations of Perception

The principle of these is: *In all phenomena the Real, that which is an object of sensation, has Intensive Quantity, that is, has a Degree.*

PROOF

Perception is empirical consciousness, that is to say, a consciousness which contains an element of sensation. Phenomena as objects of perception are not pure, that is, merely formal intuitions, like space and time, for they cannot be perceived in themselves. They contain, then, over and above the intuition, the materials for an object (through which is represented something existing in space or time), that is to say, they contain the real of sensation, as a representation merely subjective, which gives us merely the consciousness that the subject is affected, and which we refer to some external object. Now, a gradual transition from empirical consciousness to pure consciousness is possible, inasmuch as the real in this consciousness entirely vanishes, and there remains a merely formal consciousness (*a priori*) of the manifold in time and space; consequently there is possible a synthesis also of the production of the quantity of a sensation from its commencement, that is, from the pure intuition $= 0$ onwards up to a certain quantity of the sensation. Now as sensation in itself is not an objective representation, and in it is to be found neither the intuition of space nor of time, it cannot possess any extensive quantity, and yet there does belong to it a quantity (and that by means of its apprehension, in which empirical consciousness can within a certain time rise from nothing $= 0$ up to its given amount), consequently an *intensive quantity*. And thus we must ascribe intensive quantity, that is, a degree of influence on sense to all objects of perception, in so far as this perception contains sensation.

All cognition, by means of which I am enabled to cognize and determine *a priori* what belongs to empirical cognition, may be called an *anticipation;* and without doubt this is the sense in which Epicurus employed his expression προληψις. But as there is in phenomena something which is never cognized *a priori,* which on this account constitutes the proper difference between pure and empirical cognition, that is to say, sensation (as the matter of perception), it follows, that sensation is just that element in cognition which cannot be at all anticipated. On the other hand, we might very well term the pure determinations in space and time, as well in regard to figure as to quantity, *anticipations of phenomena,* because they represent *a priori* that which may always be given *a posteriori* in experience. But suppose that in every sensation, as sensation in general, without any particular sensation being thought of, there existed something which could be cognized *a priori,* this would deserve to be called anticipation in a special sense—special, because it may seem surprising to forestall experience, in that which concerns the matter of experience, and which we can only derive from itself. Yet such really is the case here.

Apprehension, by means of sensation alone, fills only one moment, that is, if I do not take into consideration a succession of many sensations. As that in the phenomenon, the apprehension of which is not a successive synthesis advancing from parts to an entire representation, sensation has therefore no extensive quantity; the want of sensation in a moment of time would represent it as empty, consequently = 0. That which in the empirical intuition corresponds to sensation is reality (*realitas phaenomenon*); that which corresponds to the absence of it, negation = 0. Now every sensation is capable of a diminution, so that it can decrease, and thus gradually disappear. Therefore, between reality in a phenomenon and negation, there exists a continuous concatenation of many possible intermediate sensations, the difference of which from each other is always smaller than that between the given sensation and zero, or complete negation. That is to say, the real in a phenomenon has always a quantity, which however is not discoverable in apprehension, inasmuch as apprehension take place by means of mere sensation in one instant, and not by the successive synthesis of many sensations, and therefore does not progress from parts to the whole. Consequently, it has a quantity, but not an extensive quantity.

Now that quantity which is apprehended only as unity, and in which plurality can be represented only by approximation to negation = 0, I term *intensive quantity.* Consequently, reality in a phenomenon has intensive quantity, that is, a degree. If we consider this reality as cause (be it of sensation or of another reality in the phenomenon, for example, a change), we call the degree of reality in its character of cause a momentum, for example, the momentum of weight; and for this reason, that the degree only indicates that quantity the apprehension of which is not successive, but instantaneous. This, however, I touch upon only in passing, for with causality I have at present nothing to do.

Accordingly, every sensation, consequently every reality in phenomena, however small it may be, has a degree, that is, an intensive quantity, which may always be lessened, and between reality and negation there exists a continuous connection of possible realities, and possible smaller perceptions. Every colour—for example, red—has a degree, which, be it ever so small, is never the smallest, and so is it always with heat, the momentum of weight, etc.

This property of quantities, according to which no part of them is the smallest possible (no part simple), is called their continuity. Space and time are *quanta continua,* because no part of them can be given, without enclosing it within boundaries (points and moments), consequently, this given part is itself a space or a time. Space, therefore, consists only of spaces, and time of times. Points and moments are only boundaries, that is, the mere places or positions of their limitation. But places always presuppose intuitions which are to limit or determine them; and we cannot conceive either space or time composed of constituent parts which are given before space or time. Such quantities may also be called *flowing,* because the synthesis (of the productive imagination) in the production of these quantities is a progression in time, the continuity of which we are accustomed to indicate by the expression *flowing.*

All phenomena, then, are continuous quantities, in respect both to intuition and mere perception (sensation, and with it reality). In the former case they are extensive quantities; in the latter, intensive. When the synthesis of the manifold of a phenomenon is interrupted, there results merely an aggregate of several phenomena, and not properly a phenomenon as a quantity, which is not produced by the mere continuation of the productive synthesis of a certain kind, but by the repetition of a synthesis always ceasing. For example, if I call thirteen dollars a sum or quantity of money, I employ the term quite correctly, inasmuch as I understand by thirteen dollars the value of a mark in standard silver, which is, to be sure, a continuous quantity, in which no part is the smallest, but every part might constitute a piece of money, which would contain material for still smaller pieces. If, however, by the words thirteen dollars I understand so many coins (be their value in silver what it may), it would be quite erroneous to use the expression a quantity of dollars; on the contrary, I must call them aggregate, that is, a number of coins. And as in every number we must have unity as the foundation, so a phenomenon taken as unity is a quantity, and as such always a continuous quantity (*quantum continuum*).

Now, seeing all phenomena, whether considered as extensive or intensive, are continuous quantities, the proposition: "All change (transition of a thing from one state into another) is continuous," might be proved here easily, and with mathematical evidence, were it not that the causality of a change lies entirely beyond the bounds of a transcendental philosophy, and presupposes empirical principles. For of the possibility of a cause which changes the condition of things, that is, which determines them to the contrary to a certain given state, the understanding gives us *a priori* no knowledge; not merely because it has no insight into the possibility of it (for such insight is absent in several *a priori* cognitions), but because the notion of change concerns only certain determinations of phenomena, which experience alone can acquaint us with, while their cause lies in the unchangeable. But seeing that we have nothing which we could here employ but the pure fundamental conceptions of all possible experience, among which of course nothing empirical can be admitted, we dare not, without injuring the unity of our system, anticipate general physical science, which is built upon certain fundamental experiences.

Nevertheless, we are in no want of proofs of the great influence which the principle above developed exercises in the anticipation of perceptions, and even in supplying the want of them, so far as to shield us against the false conclusions which otherwise we might rashly draw.

If all reality in perception has a degree, between which and negation there is an endless sequence of ever smaller degrees, and if, nevertheless, every sense must have a determinate degree of receptivity for sensations; no perception, and consequently no experience is possible, which can prove, either immediately or mediately, an entire absence of all reality in a phenomenon; in other words, it is impossible ever to draw from experience a proof of the existence of empty space or of empty time. For in the first place, an entire absence of reality in a sensuous intuition cannot of course be an object of perception; secondly, such absence cannot be deduced from the contemplation of any single phenomenon, and the difference of the degrees in its reality; nor ought it ever to be admitted in explanation of any phenomenon. For if even the complete intuition of a determinate space or time is thoroughly real, that is, if no part thereof is empty, yet because every reality has its degree, which, with the extensive quantity of the phenomenon unchanged, can diminish through endless gradations down to nothing (the void), there must be infinitely graduated degrees, with which space or time is filled, and the intensive quantity in different phenomena may be smaller or greater, although the extensive quantity of the intuition remains equal and unaltered.

We shall give an example of this. Almost all natural philosophers, remarking a great difference in the quantity of the matter of different kinds in bodies with the same volume (partly on account of the momentum of gravity or weight, partly on account of the momentum of resistance to other bodies in motion), conclude unanimously that this volume (extensive quantity of the phenomenon) must be void in all bodies, although in different proportion. But who would suspect that these for the most part mathematical and mechanical inquirers into nature should ground this conclusion solely on a metaphysical hypothesis—a sort of hypothesis which they profess to disparage and avoid? Yet this they do, in assuming that the real in space (I must not here call it impenetrability or weight, because these are empirical conceptions) is always identical, and can only be distinguished according to its extensive quantity, that is, multiplicity. Now to this presupposition, for which they can have no ground in experience, and which consequently is merely metaphysical, I oppose a transcendental demonstration, which it is true will not explain the difference in the filling up of spaces, but which nevertheless completely does away with the supposed necessity of the above-mentioned presupposition that we cannot explain the said difference otherwise than by the hypothesis of empty spaces. This demonstration, moreover, has the merit of setting the understanding at liberty to conceive this distinction in a different manner, if the explanation of the fact requires any such hypothesis. For we perceive that although two equal spaces may be completely filled by matters altogether different, so that in neither of them is there left a single point wherein matter is not present, nevertheless, every reality has its degree (of resistance or of weight), which, without diminution of the extensive quantity, can become less and less *ad infinitum,* before it passes into nothingness and disappears. Thus an expansion which fills a space—for example, caloric, or any other reality in the phenomenal world—can decrease in its degrees to infinity, yet without leaving the smallest part of the space empty; on the contrary, filling it with those lesser degrees as completely as another phenomenon could with greater. My intention here is by no means to maintain that this is really the case with the difference of matters, in regard to their specific gravity; I wish only to prove, from a principle of the pure understanding, that the nature of our perceptions makes such a mode of explanation possible, and that it is erroneous to regard the real in a phenomenon as equal *quoad* its degree, and different only *quoad* its aggregation and extensive quantity, and this, too, on the pretended authority of an *a priori* principle of the understanding.

Nevertheless, this principle of the anticipation of perception must somewhat startle an inquirer whom initiation into transcendental philosophy has rendered cautious. We must naturally entertain some doubt whether or not the understanding can enounce any such synthetical proposition as that respecting the degree of all reality in phenomena, and consequently the possibility of the internal difference of sensation itself—abstraction being made of its empirical quality. Thus it is a question not unworthy of solution: "How the understanding can pronounce synthetically and *a priori* respecting phenomena, and thus anticipate these, even in that which is peculiarly and merely empirical, that, namely, which concerns sensation itself?"

The quality of sensation is in all cases merely empirical, and cannot be represented *a priori* (for example, colours, taste, etc.). But the real —that which corresponds to sensation—in opposition to negation=0, only represents something the conception of which in itself contains a being (*ein seyn*), and signifies nothing but the synthesis in an empirical consciousness. That is to say, the empirical consciousness in the internal sense can be raised from 0 to every higher degree, so that the very same extensive quantity of intuition, an illuminated surface, for example, excites as great a sensation as an aggregate of many other surfaces less illuminated. We can therefore make complete abstraction of the extensive quantity of a phenomenon, and represent to ourselves in the mere sensation in a certain momentum, a synthesis of homogeneous ascension from 0 up to the given empirical consciousness. All sensations therefore as such are given only *a posteriori,* but this property thereof, namely, that they have a degree, can be known *a priori.* It is worthy of remark, that in respect to quantities in general, we can cognize *a priori* only a single quality, namely, continuity; but in respect to all quality (the real in phenomena), we cannot cognize *a priori* anything more than the intensive quantity thereof, namely, that they have a degree. All else is left to experience.

3. Analogies of Experience

The principle of these is: *Experience is possible only through the representation of a necessary connection of perceptions.*

PROOF

Experience is an empirical cognition; that is to say, a cognition which determines an object by means of perceptions. It is therefore a synthesis of perceptions, a synthesis which is not itself contained in perception, but which contains the synthetical unity of the manifold of perception in a consciousness; and this unity constitutes the essential of our cognition of *objects* of the senses, that is, of experience (not merely of intuition or sensation). Now in experience our perceptions come together contingently, so that no character of necessity in their connection appears, or can appear from the perceptions themselves, because apprehension is only a placing together of the manifold of empirical intuition, and no representation of a necessity in the connected existence of the phenomena which apprehension brings together, is to be discovered therein. But as experience is a cognition of objects by means of perceptions, it follows that the relation of the existence of the manifold must be represented in experience not as it is put together in time, but as it is objectively in time. And as time itself cannot be perceived, the determination of the existence of objects in time can only take place by means of their connection in time in general, consequently only by means of *a priori* connecting conceptions. Now as these conceptions always possess the character of necessity, experience is possible only by means of a representation of the necessary connection of perception.

The three *modi* of time are *permanence, succession,* and *coexistence.* Accordingly, there are three rules of all relations of time in phenomena, according to which the existence of every phenomenon is determined in respect of the unity of all time, and these antecede all experience and render it possible.

The general principle of all three analogies rests on the necessary *unity* of apperception in relation to all possible empirical consciousness (perception) *at every time,* consequently, as this unity lies *a priori* at the foundation of all mental operations, the principle rests on the synthetical unity of all phenomena according to their relation in time. For the original apperception relates to our internal sense (the complex of all representations), and indeed relates *a priori* to its form, that is to say, the relation of the manifold empirical consciousness in time. Now this manifold must be combined in original apperception according to relations of time —a necessity imposed by the *a priori* transcendental unity of apperception, to which is subjected all that can belong to my (i. e., my own) cognition, and therefore all that can become an object for me. This synthetical and *a priori* determined unity in relation of perceptions in time is therefore the rule: "All empirical determinations of time must be subject to rules of the general determination of time"; and the analogies of experience, of which we are now about to treat, must be rules of this nature.

These principles have this peculiarity, that they do not concern phenomena, and the synthesis of the empirical intuition thereof, but merely the *existence* of phenomena and their *relation* to each other in regard to this existence. Now the mode in which we apprehend a thing in a phenomenon can be determined *a priori* in such a manner that the rule of its synthesis can give, that is to say, can produce this *a priori* intuition in every empirical example. But the existence of phenomena cannot be known *a priori,* and although we could arrive by this path at a conclusion of the fact of some existence, we could not cognize that existence determinately, that is to say, we should be incapable of anticipating in what respect the empirical intuition of it would be distinguishable from that of others.

The two principles above mentioned, which I called mathematical, in consideration of the fact of their authorizing the application of mathematic phenomena, relate to these phenomena only in regard to their possibility, and instruct us how phenomena, as far as regards their intuition or the real in their perception, can be generated according to the rules of a mathematical synthesis. Consequently, numerical quantities, and with them the determination of a phenomenon as a quantity, can be employed in the one case as well as in the other. Thus, for example, out of 200,000 illuminations by the moon, I might compose and give *a priori,* that is construct, the degree of our sensations of the sunlight. We may therefore entitle these two principles constitutive.

The case is very different with those principles whose province it is to subject the existence of phenomena to rules *a priori.* For as existence does not admit of being constructed, it is clear that they must only concern the relations of existence and be merely *regulative* principles. In this case, therefore, neither axioms nor anticipations are to be thought of. Thus, if a perception is given us, in a certain relation of time to other (although undetermined) perceptions, we cannot then say *a priori, what* and *how great* (in quantity) the other perception necessarily connected with the former is, but only *how* it is connected, *quoad* its existence, in this given modus of time. Analogies in philosophy mean something very different from that which they represent in mathematics. In the latter they are formulae, which enounce the equality of two relations of quantity, and are always *constitutive,* so that if two terms of the proportion are given, the third is also given, that is, can be constructed by the aid of these formulae. But in philosophy, analogy is not the equality of two *quantitative* but of two *qualitative* relations. In this case, from three given terms, I can give *a priori* and cognize the *relation* to a fourth member, but not this fourth term itself, although I certainly possess a rule to guide me in the search for this fourth term in experience, and a mark to assist me in discovering it. An analogy of experience is therefore only a rule according to which unity of experience must arise out of perceptions in respect to objects (phenomena) not as a *constitutive,* but merely as a *regulative* principle. The same holds good also of the postulates of empirical thought in general, which relate to the synthesis of mere intuition (which concerns the form of phenomena), the synthesis of perception (which concerns the matter of phenomena), and the synthesis of experience (which concerns the relation of these perceptions). For they are only regulative principles, and clearly distinguishable from the mathematical, which are constitutive, not indeed in regard to the certainty which both possess *a priori*, but in the mode of evidence thereof, consequently also in the manner of demonstration.

But what has been observed of all synthetical propositions, and must be particularly remarked in this place, is this, that these analogies possess significance and validity, not as principles of the transcendental, but only as principles of the empirical use of the understanding, and their truth can therefore be proved only as such, and that consequently the phenomena must not be subjoined directly under the categories, but only under their schemata. For if the objects to which those principles must be applied were things in themselves, it would be quite impossible to cognize aught concerning them synthetically *a priori*. But they are nothing but phenomena; a complete knowledge of which—a knowledge to which all principles *a priori* must at last relate—is the only possible experience. It follows that these principles can have nothing else for their aim than the conditions of the unity of empirical cognition in the synthesis of phenomena. But this synthesis is cogitated only in the schema of the pure conception of the understanding, of whose unity, as that of a synthesis in general, the category contains the function unrestricted by any sensuous condition. These principles will therefore authorize us to connect phenomena according to an analogy, with the logical and universal unity of conceptions, and consequently to employ the categories in the principles themselves; but in the application of them to experience, we shall use only their schemata, as the key to their proper application, instead of the categories, or rather the latter as restricting conditions, under the title of "formulae" of the former.

A. First Analogy

Principle of the Permanence of Substance

In all changes of phenomena, substance is permanent, and the quantum thereof in nature is neither increased nor diminished.

PROOF

All phenomena exist in time, wherein alone as substratum, that is, as the permanent form of the internal intuition, coexistence and succession can be represented. Consequently time, in which all changes of phenomena must be cogitated, remains and changes not, because it is that in which succession and coexistence can be represented only as determinations thereof. Now, time in itself cannot be an object of perception. It follows that in objects of perception, that is, in phenomena, there must be found a substratum which represents time in general, and in which all change or coexistence can be perceived by means of the relation of phenomena to it. But the substratum of all reality, that is, of all that pertains to the existence of things, is substance; all that pertains to existence can be cogitated only as a determination of substance. Consequently, the permanent, in relation to which alone can all relations of time in phenomena be determined, is substance in the world of phenomena, that is, the real in phenomena, that which, as the substratum of all change, remains ever the same. Accordingly, as this cannot change in existence, its quantity in nature can neither be increased nor diminished.

Our *apprehension* of the manifold in a phenomenon is always successive, is consequently always changing. By it alone we could, therefore, never determine whether this manifold, as an object of experience, is coexistent or successive, unless it had for a foundation something *fixed* and *permanent,* of the existence of which all succession and coexistence are nothing but so many modes (*modi* of time). Only in the permanent, then, are relations of time possible (for simultaneity and succession are the only relations in time); that is to say, the permanent is the *substratum* of our empirical representation of time itself, in which alone all determination of time is possible. Permanence is, in fact, just another expression for time, as the abiding correlate of all existence of phenomena, and of all change, and of all coexistence. For change does not affect time itself, but only the phenomena in time (just as coexistence cannot be regarded as a *modus* of time itself, seeing that in time no parts are coexistent, but all successive). If we were to attribute succession to time itself, we should be obliged to cogitate another time, in which this succession would be possible. It is only by means of the permanent that existence in different parts of the successive series of time receives a *quantity,* which we entitle *duration.* For in mere succession, existence is perpetually vanishing and recommencing, and therefore never has even the least quantity. Without the permanent, then, no relation in time is possible. Now, time in itself is not an object of perception; consequently the permanent in phenomena must be regarded as the substratum of all determination of time, and consequently also as the condition of the possibility of all synthetical unity of perceptions, that is, of experience; and all existence and all change in time can only be regarded as a mode in the existence of that which abides unchangeably. Therefore, in all phenomena, the permanent is the object *in itself,* that is, the substance (phenomenon); but all that changes or can change belongs only to the mode of the existence of this substance or substances, consequently to its determinations.

I find that in all ages not only the philosopher, but even the common understanding, has preposited this permanence as a substratum of all change in phenomena; indeed, I am compelled to believe that they will always accept this as an indubitable fact. Only the philosopher expresses himself in a more precise and definite manner, when he says: "In all changes in the world, the *substance* remains, and the *accidents* alone are changeable." But of this decidedly synthetical proposition, I nowhere meet with even an attempt at proof; nay, it very rarely has the good fortune to stand, as it deserves to do, at the head of the pure and entirely *a priori* laws of nature. In truth, the statement that substance is permanent, is tautological. For this very permanence is the ground on which we apply the category of substance to the phenomenon; and we should have been obliged to prove that in all phenomena there is something permanent, of the existence of which the changeable is nothing but a determination. But because a proof of this nature cannot be dogmatical, that is, cannot be drawn from conceptions, inasmuch as it concerns a synthetical proposition *a priori,* and as philosophers never reflected that such propositions are valid only in relation to possible experience, and therefore cannot be proved except by means of a deduction of the possibility of experience, it is no wonder that while it has served as the foundation of all experience (for we feel the need of it in empirical cognition), it has never been supported by proof.

A philosopher was asked: "What is the weight of smoke?" He answered: "Subtract from the weight of the burnt wood the weight of the remaining ashes, and you will have the weight of the smoke." Thus he presumed it to be incontrovertible that even in fire the matter (substance) does not perish, but that only the form of it undergoes a change. In like manner was the saying: "From nothing comes nothing," only another inference from the principle of permanence, or rather of the ever-abiding existence of the true subject in phenomena. For if that in the phenomenon which we call substance is to be the proper substratum of all determination of time, it follows that all existence in past as well as in future time, must be determinable by means of it alone. Hence we are entitled to apply the term substance to a phenomenon, only because we suppose its existence in all time, a notion which the word permanence does not fully express, as it seems rather to be referable to future time. However, the internal necessity perpetually to be, is inseparably connected with the necessity always to have been, and so the expression may stand as it is. *"Gigni de nihilo nihil; in nihilum nil posse reverti,"*[1] are two propositions which the ancients never parted, and which people nowadays sometimes mistakenly disjoin, because they imagine that the propositions apply to objects as things in themselves, and that the former might be inimical to the dependence (even in respect of its substance also) of the world upon a supreme cause. But this apprehension is entirely needless, for the question in this case is only of phenomena in the sphere of experience, the unity of which never could be possible, if we admitted the possibility that new things (in respect of their substance) should arise. For in that case, we should lose altogether that which alone can represent the unity of time, to wit, the identity of the substratum, as that through which alone all change possesses complete and thorough unity. This permanence is, however, nothing but the manner in which we represent to ourselves the existence of things in the phenomenal world.

The determinations of a substance, which are only particular modes of its existence, are called *accidents.* They are always real, because they concern the existence of substance (negations are only determinations, which express the non-existence of something in the substance). Now, if to this real in the substance we ascribe a particular existence (for example, to motion as an accident of matter), this existence is called *inherence,* in contradistinction to the existence of substance, which we call *subsistence.* But hence arise many misconceptions, and it would be a more accurate and just mode of expression to designate the accident only as the mode in which the existence of a substance is positively determined. Meanwhile, by reason of the conditions of the logical exercise of our understand-

[1] [Persius, *Satirae,* iii.83–84. "Nothing can be produced from nothing; nothing can be returned into nothing."]

ing, it is impossible to avoid separating, as it were, that which in the existence of a substance is subject to change, whilst the substance remains, and regarding it in relation to that which is properly permanent and radical. On this account, this category of substance stands under the title of relation, rather because it is the condition thereof than because it contains in itself any relation.

Now, upon this notion of permanence rests the proper notion of the conception *change.* Origin and extinction are not changes of that which originates or becomes extinct. Change is but a mode of existence, which follows on another mode of existence of the same object; hence all that changes is permanent, and only the condition thereof changes. Now since this mutation affects only determinations, which can have a beginning or an end, we may say, employing an expression which seems somewhat paradoxical: "Only the *permanent* (substance) is subject to change; the mutable suffers no change, but rather *alternation,* that is, when certain determinations cease, others begin."

Change, then, cannot be perceived by us except in substances, and origin or extinction in an absolute sense, that does not concern merely a determination of the permanent, cannot be a possible perception, for it is this very notion of the permanent which renders possible the representation of a transition from one state into another, and from non-being to being, which, consequently, can be empirically cognized only as alternating determinations of that which is permanent. Grant that a thing absolutely begins to be; we must then have a point of time in which it was not. But how and by what can we fix and determine this point of time, unless by that which already exists? For a void time—preceding—is not an object of perception; but if we connect this beginning with objects which existed previously, and which continue to exist till the object in question begins to be, then the latter can only be a determination of the former as the permanent. The same holds good of the notion of extinction, for this presupposes the empirical representation of a time, in which a phenomenon no longer exists.

Substances (in the world of phenomena) are the substratum of all determinations of time. The beginning of some, and the ceasing to be of other substances, would utterly do away with the only condition of the empirical unity of time; and in that case phenomena would relate to two different times, in which, side by side, existence would pass; which is absurd. For there is only *one* time in which all different times must be placed, not as coexistent, but as successive.

Accordingly, permanence is a necessary condition under which alone phenomena, as things or objects, are determinable in a possible experience. But as regards the empirical criterion of this necessary permanence, and with it of the substantiality of phenomena, we shall find sufficient opportunity to speak in the sequel.

B. Second Analogy

Principle of the Succession of Time According to the Law of Causality

All changes take place according to the law of the connection of Cause and Effect.

PROOF

(That all phenomena in the succession of time are only changes, that is, a successive being and non-being of the determinations of substance, which is permanent; consequently that a being of substance itself which follows on the non-being thereof, or a non-being of substance which follows on the being thereof, in other words, that the origin or extinction of substance itself, is impossible—all this has been fully established in treating of the foregoing principle. This principle might have been expressed as follows: "All alteration (succession) of phenomena is merely change"; for the changes of substance are not origin or extinction, because the conception of change presupposes the same subject as existing with two opposite determinations, and consequently as permanent. After this premonition, we shall proceed to the proof.)

I perceive that phenomena succeed one another, that is to say, a state of things exists at one time, the opposite of which existed in a former state. In this case, then, I really connect together two perceptions in time. Now connection is not an operation of mere sense and intuition, but is the product of a synthetical faculty of imagination, which determines the internal sense in respect of a relation of time. But imagination can connect these two states in two ways, so that either the one or the other may antecede in time; for time in itself cannot be an object of perception, and what in an object precedes and what follows cannot be empirically determined in relation to it. I am only conscious, then, that my imagination places one state before, and the other after; not that the one state antecedes the other in the object.

In other words, the objective relation of the successive phenomena remains quite undetermined by means of mere perception. Now in order that this relation may be cognized as determined, the relation between the two states must be so cogitated that it is thereby determined as necessary, which of them must be placed before and which after, and not conversely. But the conception which carries with it a necessity of synthetical unity, can be none other than a pure conception of the understanding which does not lie in mere perception; and in this case it is the conception of "the relation of cause and effect," the former of which determines the latter in time, as its necessary consequence, and not as something which might possibly antecede (or which might in some cases not be perceived to follow). It follows that it is only because we subject the sequence of phenomena, and consequently all change, to the law of causality, that experience itself, that is, empirical cognition of phenomena, becomes possible; and consequently, that phenomena themselves, as objects of experience, are possible only by virtue of this law.

Our apprehension of the manifold of phenomena is always successive. The representations of parts succeed one another. Whether they succeed one another in the object also, is a second point for reflection, which was not contained in the former. Now we may certainly give the name of object to everything, even to every representation, so far as we are conscious thereof; but what this word may mean in the case of phenomena, not merely in so far as they (as representations) are objects, but only in so far as they indicate an object, is a question requiring deeper consideration. In so far as they, regarded merely as representations, are at the same time objects of consciousness, they are not to be distinguished from apprehension, that is, reception into the synthesis of imagination, and we must therefore say: "The manifold of phenomena is always produced successively in the mind." If phenomena were things in themselves, no man would be able to conjecture from the succession of our representations how this manifold is connected in the object; for we have to do only with our representations. How things may be in themselves, without regard to the representations through which they affect us, is utterly beyond the sphere of our cognition. Now although phenomena are not things in themselves, and are nevertheless the only thing given to us to be cognized, it is my duty to show what sort of connection in time belongs to the manifold in phenomena themselves, while the representation of this manifold in apprehension is always successive. For example, the apprehension of the manifold in the phenomenon of a house which stands before me, is successive. Now comes the question whether the manifold of this house is in itself successive —which no one will be at all willing to grant. But, so soon as I raise my conception of an object to the transcendental signification thereof, I find that the house is not a thing in itself, but only a phenomenon, that is, a representation, the transcendental object of which remains utterly unknown. What then am I to understand by the question: "How can the manifold be connected in the phenomenon itself—not considered as a thing in itself, but merely as a phenomenon?" Here that which lies in my successive apprehension is regarded as representation, whilst the phenomenon which is given me, notwithstanding that it is nothing more than a complex of these representations, is regarded as the object thereof, with which my conception, drawn from the representations of apprehension, must harmonize. It is very soon seen that, as accordance of the cognition with its object constitutes truth, the question now before us can only relate to the formal conditions of empirical truth; and that the phenomenon, in opposition to the representations of apprehension, can only be distinguished therefrom as the object of them, if it is subject to a rule which distinguishes it from every other apprehension, and which renders necessary a mode of connection of the manifold. That in the phenomenon which contains the condition of this necessary rule of apprehension, is the object.

Let us now proceed to our task. That something happens, that is to say, that something or some state exists which before was not, cannot be empirically perceived, unless a phenomenon precedes, which does not contain in itself this state. For a reality which should follow upon a void time, in other words, a beginning, which no state of things precedes, can just as little be apprehended as the void time itself. Every apprehension of an event is therefore a perception which follows upon another perception. But as this is the case with all synthesis of apprehension, as I have shown above in the example of a house, my apprehension of an event is not yet sufficiently distinguished from other apprehensions. But I remark also that if in a phenomenon which contains an occurrence, I call the antecedent state of my perception, A, and the following state, B, the perception B can only follow A in apprehension, and the perception A cannot follow B, but only precede it. For example, I see a ship float down the stream of a river. My perception of its place lower down follows upon my perception of its place higher up the course of the river, and it is impossible that, in the apprehension of this phenomenon, the vessel should be perceived first below and afterwards higher up the stream. Here, therefore, the order in the sequence of perceptions in apprehension is determined; and by this order apprehension is regulated. In the former example, my perceptions in the apprehension of a house might begin at the roof and end at the foundation, or vice versa; or I might apprehend the manifold in this empirical intuition, by going from left to right, and from right to left. Accordingly, in the series of these perceptions, there was no determined order, which necessitated my beginning at a certain point, in order empirically to connect the manifold. But this rule is always to be met with in the perception of that which happens, and it makes the order of the successive perceptions in the apprehension of such a phenomenon *necessary*.

I must, therefore, in the present case, deduce the *subjective sequence* of apprehension from the *objective sequence* of phenomena, for otherwise the former is quite undetermined, and one phenomenon is not distinguishable from another. The former alone proves nothing as to the connection of the manifold in an object, for it is quite arbitrary. The latter must consist in the order of the manifold in a phenomenon, according to which order the apprehension of one thing (that which happens) follows that of another thing (which precedes), in conformity with a rule. In this way alone can I be authorized to say of the phenomenon itself, and not merely of my own apprehension, that a certain order or sequence is to be found therein. That is, in other words, I cannot arrange my apprehension otherwise than in this order.

In conformity with this rule, then, it is necessary that in that which antecedes an event there be found the condition of a rule, according to which in this event follows always and necessarily; but I cannot reverse this and go back from the event, and determine (by apprehension) that which antecedes it. For no phenomenon goes back from the succeeding point of time to the preceding point, although it does certainly relate to a preceding point of time; from a given time, on the other hand, there is always a necessary progression to the determined succeeding time. Therefore, because there certainly is something that follows, I must of necessity connect it with something else, which antecedes, and upon which it follows, in conformity with a rule, that is necessarily, so that the event, as conditioned, affords certain indication of a condition, and this condition determines the event.

Let us suppose that nothing precedes an event, upon which this event must follow in conformity with a rule. All sequence of perception would then exist only in apprehension, that is to say, would be merely subjective, and it could not thereby be objectively determined what thing ought to precede, and what ought to follow in perception. In such a case, we should have nothing but a play of representations, which would possess no application to any object. That is to say, it would not be possible through perception to distinguish one phenomenon from another, as regards relations of time; because the succession in the act of apprehension would always be of the same sort, and therefore there would be nothing in the phenomenon to determine the succession, and to render a certain sequence objectively necessary. And, in this case, I cannot say that two states in a phenomenon follow one upon the other, but only that one apprehension follows upon another. But this is merely subjective, and does not determine an object, and consequently cannot be held to be cognition of an object—not even in the phenomenal world.

Accordingly, when we know in experience that something happens, we always presuppose that something precedes, whereupon it follows in conformity with a rule. For otherwise I could not say of the object that it follows; because the mere succession in my apprehension, if it be not determined by a rule in relation to something preceding, does not authorize succession in the object. Only, therefore, in reference to a rule, according to which phenomena are determined in their sequence, that is, as they happen, by the preceding state, can I make my subjective synthesis (of apprehension) objective, and it is only under this presupposition that even the experience of an event is possible.

No doubt it appears as if this were in thorough contradition to all the notions which people have hitherto entertained in regard to the procedure of the human understanding. According to these opinions, it is by means of the perception and comparison of similar consequences following upon certain antecedent phenomena that the understanding is led to the discovery of a rule, according to which certain events always follow certain phenomena, and it is only by this process that we attain to the conception of cause. Upon such a basis, it is clear that this conception must be merely empirical, and the rule which it furnishes us with —"Everything that happens must have a cause" —would be just as contingent as experience itself. The universality and necessity of the rule or law would be perfectly spurious attributes of it. Indeed, it could not possess universal validity, inasmuch as it would not in this case be *a priori,* but founded on deduction. But the same is the case with this law as with other pure *a priori* representations (e.g., space and time), which we can draw in perfect clearness and completeness from experience, only because we had already placed them therein, and by that means, and by that alone, had rendered experience possible. Indeed, the logical clearness of this representation of a rule, determining the series of events, is possible only when we have made use thereof in experience. Nevertheless, the recognition of this rule, as a condition of the synthetical unity of phenomena in time, was the ground of experience itself and consequently preceded it *a priori.*

It is now our duty to show by an example that we never, even in experience, attribute to an object the notion of succession or effect (of an event—that is, the happening of something that did not exist before), and distinguish it from the subjective succession of apprehension, unless when a rule lies at the foundation, which compels us to observe this order of perception in preference to any other, and that, indeed, it is this necessity which first renders possible the representation of a succession in the object.

We have representations within us, of which also we can be conscious. But, however widely extended, however accurate and thoroughgoing this consciousness may be, these representations are still nothing more than representations, that is, internal determinations of the mind in this or that relation of time. Now how happens it that to these representations we should set an object, or that, in addition to their subjective reality, as modifications, we should still further attribute to them a certain unknown objective reality? It is clear that objective significancy cannot consist in a relation to another representation (of that which we desire to term object), for in that case the question again arises: "How does this other representation go out of itself, and obtain objective significancy over and above the subjective, which is proper to it, as a determination of a state of mind?" If we try to discover what sort of new property the *relation to an object* gives to our subjective representations, and what new importance they thereby receive, we shall find that this relation has no other effect than that of rendering necessary the connection of our representations in a certain manner, and of subjecting them to a rule; and that conversely, it is only because a certain order is necessary in the relations of time of our representations, that objective significancy is ascribed to them.

In the synthesis of phenomena, the manifold of our representations is always successive. Now hereby is not represented an object, for by means of this succession, which is common to all apprehension, no one thing is distinguished from another. But so soon as I perceive or assume that in this succession there is a relation to a state antecedent, from which the representation follows in accordance with a rule, so soon do I represent something as an event, or as a thing that happens; in other words, I cognize an object to which I must assign a certain determinate position in time, which cannot be altered, because of the preceding state in the object. When, therefore, I perceive that something happens, there is contained in this representation, in the first place, the fact, that something antecedes; because it is only in relation to this that the phenomenon obtains its proper relation of time, in other words, exists after an antecedent time, in which it did not exist. But it can receive its determined place in time only by the presupposition that something existed in the foregoing state, upon which it follows inevitably and always, that is, in conformity with a rule. From all this it is evident that, in the first place, I cannot reverse the order of succession, and make that which happens precede that upon which it follows; and that, in the second place, if the antecedent state be posited, a certain determinate event inevitably and necessarily follows. Hence it follows that there exists a certain order in our representations, whereby the present gives a sure indication of some previously existing state, as a correlate, though still undetermined, of the existing event which is given—a correlate which itself relates to the event as its consequence, conditions it, and connects it necessarily with itself in the series of time.

If then it be admitted as a necessary law of sensibility, and consequently a formal condition of all perception, that the preceding necessarily determines the succeeding time (inasmuch as I cannot arrive at the succeeding except through the preceding), it must likewise be an indispensable law of empirical representation of the series of time that the phenomena of the past determine all phenomena in the succeeding time, and that the latter, as events, cannot take place, except in so far as the former determine their existence in time, that is to say, establish it according to a rule. For it is of course only in phenomena that we can empirically cognize this continuity in the connection of times.

For all experience and for the possibility of experience, understanding is indispensable, and the first step which it takes in this sphere is not to render the representation of objects clear, but to render the representation of an object in general, possible. It does this by applying the order of time to phenomena, and their existence. In other words, it assigns to each phenomenon, as a consequence, a place in relation to preceding phenomena, determined *a priori* in time, without which it could not harmonize with time itself, which determines a place *a priori* to all its parts. This determination of place cannot be derived from the relation of phenomena to absolute time (for it is not an object of perception); but, on the contrary, phenomena must reciprocally determine the places in time of one another, and render these necessary in the order of time. In other words, whatever follows or happens, must follow in conformity with a universal rule upon that which was contained in the foregoing state. Hence arises a series of phenomena, which, by means of the understanding, produces and renders necessary exactly the same order and continuous connection in the series of our possible perceptions, as is found *a priori* in the form of internal intuition (time), in which all our perceptions must have place.

That something happens, then, is a perception which belongs to a possible experience, which becomes real only because I look upon the phenomenon as determined in regard to its place in time, consequently as an object, which can always be found by means of a rule in the connected series of my perceptions. But this rule of the determination of a thing according to succession in time is as follows: "In what precedes may be found the condition, under which an event always (that is, necessarily) follows." From all this it is obvious that the principle of cause and effect is the principle of possible experience, that is, of objective cognition of phenomena, in regard to their relations in the succession of time.

The proof of this fundamental proposition rests entirely on the following momenta of argument. To all empirical cognition belongs the synthesis of the manifold by the imagination, a synthesis which is always successive, that is, in which the representations therein always follow one another. But the order of succession in imagination is not determined, and the series of successive representations may be taken retrogressively as well as progressively. But if this synthesis is a synthesis of apprehension (of the manifold of a given phenomenon), then the order is determined in the object, or, to speak more accurately, there is therein an order of successive synthesis which determines an object, and according to which something necessarily precedes, and when this is posited, something else necessarily follows. If, then, my perception is to contain the cognition of an event, that is, of something which really happens, it must be an empirical judgement, wherein we think that the succession is determined; that is, it presupposes another phenomenon, upon which this event follows necessarily, or in conformity with a rule. If, on the contrary, when I posited the antecedent, the event did not necessarily follow, I should be obliged to consider it merely as a subjective play of my imagination, and if in this I represented to myself anything as objective, I must look upon it as a mere dream. Thus, the relation of phenomena (as possible perceptions), according to which that which happens is, as to its existence, necessarily determined in time by something which antecedes, in conformity with a rule—in other words, the relation of cause and effect—is the condition of the objective validity of our empirical judgements in regard to the sequence of perceptions, consequently of their empirical truth, and therefore of experience. The principle of the relation of causality in the succession of phenomena is therefore valid for all objects of experience, because it is itself the ground of the possibility of experience.

Here, however, a difficulty arises, which must be resolved. The principle of the connection of causality among phenomena is limited in our formula to the succession thereof, although in practice we find that the principle applies also when the phenomena exist together in the same time, and that cause and effect may be simultaneous. For example, there is heat in a room, which does not exist in the open air. I look about for the cause, and find it to be the fire. Now the fire as the cause is simultaneous with its effect, the heat of the room. In this case, then, there is no succession as regards time, between cause and effect, but they are simultaneous; and still the law holds good. The greater part of operating causes in nature are simultaneous with their effects, and the succession in time of the latter is produced only because the cause cannot achieve the total of its effect in one moment. But at the moment when the effect *first* arises, it is always simultaneous with the causality of its cause, because, if the cause had but a moment before ceased to be, the effect could not have arisen. Here it must be specially remembered that we must consider the *order* of time and not the *lapse* thereof. The relation remains, even though no time has elapsed. The time between the causality of the cause and its immediate effect may entirely vanish, and the cause and effect be thus simultaneous, but the relation of the one to the other remains always determinable according to time. If, for example, I consider a leaden ball, which lies upon a cushion and makes a hollow in it, as a cause, then it is simultaneous with the effect. But I distinguish the two through the relation of time of the dynamical connection of both. For if I lay the ball upon the cushion, then the hollow follows upon the before smooth surface; but supposing the cushion has, from some cause or another, a hollow, there does not thereupon follow a leaden ball.

Thus, the law of succession of time is in all instances the only empirical criterion of effect in relation to the causality of the antecedent cause. The glass is the cause of the rising of the water above its horizontal surface, although the two phenomena are contemporaneous. For, as soon as I draw some water with the glass from a larger vessel, an effect follows thereupon, namely, the change of the horizontal state which the water had in the large vessel into a concave, which it assumes in the glass.

This conception of causality leads us to the conception of action; that of action, to the conception of force; and through it, to the conception of substance. As I do not wish this critical essay, the sole purpose of which is to treat of the sources of our synthetical cognition *a priori*, to be crowded with analyses which merely explain, but do not enlarge the sphere of our conceptions, I reserve the detailed explanation of the above conceptions for a future system of pure reason. Such an analysis, indeed, executed with great particularity, may already be found in well-known works on this subject. But I cannot at present refrain from making a few remarks on the empirical criterion of a substance, in so far as it seems to be more evident and more easily recognized through the conception of action than through that of the permanence of a phenomenon.

Where action (consequently activity and force) exists, substance also must exist, and in it alone must be sought the seat of that fruitful source of phenomena. Very well. But if we are called upon to explain what we mean by substance, and wish to avoid the vice of reasoning in a circle, the answer is by no means so easy. How shall we conclude immediately from the action to the *permanence* of that which acts, this being nevertheless an essential and peculiar criterion of substance (phenomenon)? But after what has been said above, the solution of this question becomes easy enough, although by the common mode of procedure—merely analysing our conceptions—it would be quite impossible. The conception of action indicates the relation of the subject of causality to the effect. Now because all effect consists in that which happens, therefore in the changeable, the last subject thereof is the *permanent*, as the substratum of all that changes, that is, substance. For according to the principle of causality, actions are always the first ground of all change in phenomena and, consequently, cannot be a property of a subject which itself changes, because if this were the case, other actions and another subject would be necessary to determine this change. From all this it results that action alone, as an empirical criterion, is a sufficient proof of the presence of substantiality, without any necessity on my part of endeavouring to discover the permanence of substance by a comparison. Besides, by this mode of induction we could not attain to the completeness which the magnitude and strict universality of the conception requires. For that the primary subject of the causality of all arising and passing away, all origin and extinction, cannot itself (in the sphere of phenomena) arise and pass away, is a sound and safe conclusion, a conclusion which leads us to the conception of empirical necessity and permanence in existence, and consequently to the conception of a substance as phenomenon.

When something happens, the mere fact of the occurrence, without regard to that which occurs, is an object requiring investigation. The transition from the non-being of a state into the existence of it, supposing that this state contains no quality which previously existed in the phenomenon, is a fact of itself demanding inquiry. Such an event, as has been shown in No. A, does not concern substance (for substance does not thus originate), but its condition or state. It is therefore only change, and not origin from nothing. If this origin be regarded as the effect of a foreign cause, it is termed creation, which cannot be admitted as an event among phenomena, because the very possibility of it would annihilate the unity of experience. If, however, I regard all things not as phenomena, but as things in themselves and objects of understanding alone, they, although substances, may be considered as dependent, in respect of their existence, on a foreign cause. But this would require a very different meaning in the words, a meaning which could not apply to phenomena as objects of possible experience.

How a thing can be changed, how it is possible that upon one state existing in one point of time, an opposite state should follow in another point of time—of this we have not the smallest conception *a priori.* There is requisite for this the knowledge of real powers, which can only be given empirically; for example, knowledge of moving forces, or, in other words, of certain successive phenomena (as movements) which indicate the presence of such forces. But the form of every change, the condition under which alone it can take place as the coming into existence of another state (be the content of the change, that is, the state which is changed, what it may), and consequently the succession of the states themselves can very well be considered *a priori,* in relation to the law of causality and the conditions of time.[1]

When a substance passes from one state, *a,* into another state, *b,* the point of time in which the latter exists is different from, and subsequent to that in which the former existed. In like manner, the second state, as reality (in the phenomenon), differs from the first, in which the reality of the second did not exist, as *b* from zero. That is to say, if the state, *b,* differs from the state, *a,* only in respect to quantity, the change is a coming into existence of *b—a,* which in the former state did not exist, and in relation to which that state is = o.

Now the question arises how a thing passes from one state = *a,* into another state = *b.* Between two moments there is always a certain time, and between two states existing in these moments there is always a difference having a certain quantity (for all parts of phenomena are in their turn quantities). Consequently, every transition from one state into another is always effected in a time contained between two moments, of which the first determines the state which the thing leaves, and the second determines the state into which the thing passes. Both moments, then, are limitations of the time of a change, consequently of the intermediate state between both, and as such they belong to the total of the change. Now every change has a cause, which evidences its causality in the whole time during which the change takes place. The cause, therefore, does not produce the change all at once or in one moment, but in a time, so that, as the time gradually increases from the commencing instant, *a,* to its completion at *b,* in like manner also, the quantity of the reality (*b—a*) is generated through the lesser degrees which are contained between the first and last. All change is therefore possible only through a continuous action of the causality, which, in so far as it is uniform, we call a momentum. The change does not consist of these momenta, but is generated or produced by them as their effect.

Such is the law of the continuity of all change, the ground of which is that neither time itself nor any phenomenon in time consists of parts which are the smallest possible, but that, notwithstanding, the state of a thing passes in the process of a change through all these parts, as elements, to its second state. There is no smallest degree of reality in a phenomenon, just as there is no smallest degree in the quantity of time; and so the new state of reality grows up out of the former state, through all the infinite degrees thereof, the differences of which one from another, taken all together, are less than the difference between o and *a.*

It is not our business to inquire here into the utility of this principle in the investigation of nature. But how such a proposition, which appears so greatly to extend our knowledge of nature, is possible completely *a priori,* is indeed a question which deserves investigation, although the first view seems to demonstrate the truth and reality of the principle, and the question, how it is possible, may be considered superfluous. For there are so many groundless pretensions to the enlargement of our knowledge by pure reason that we must take it as a general rule to be mistrustful of all such, and without a thoroughgoing and radical deduction, to believe

[1] It must be remarked that I do not speak of the change of certain relations, but of the change of the state. Thus, when a body moves in a uniform manner, it does not change its state (of motion); but only when its motion increases or decreases.

nothing of the sort even on the clearest dogmatical evidence.

Every addition to our empirical knowledge, and every advance made in the exercise of our perception, is nothing more than an extension of the determination of the internal sense, that is to say, a progression in time, be objects themselves what they may, phenomena, or pure intuitions. This progression in time determines everything, and is itself determined by nothing else. That is to say, the parts of the progression exist only in time, and by means of the synthesis thereof, and are not given antecedently to it. For this reason, every transition in perception to anything which follows upon another in time, is a determination of time by means of the production of this perception. And as this determination of time is, always and in all its parts, a quantity, the perception produced is to be considered as a quantity which proceeds through all its degrees—no one of which is the smallest possible—from zero up to its determined degree. From this we perceive the possibility of cognizing *a priori* a law of changes—a law, however, which concerns their form merely. We merely anticipate our own apprehension, the formal condition of which, inasmuch as it is itself to be found in the mind antecedently to all given phenomena, must certainly be capable of being cognized *a priori*.

Thus, as time contains the sensuous condition *a priori* of the possibility of a continuous progression of that which exists to that which follows it, the understanding, by virtue of the unity of apperception, contains the condition *a priori* of the possibility of a continuous determination of the position in time of all phenomena, and this by means of the series of causes and effects, the former of which necessitate the sequence of the latter, and thereby render universally and for all time, and by consequence, objectively, valid the empirical cognition of the relations of time.

C. Third Analogy

Principle of Coexistence, According to the Law of Reciprocity or Community

All substances, in so far as they can be perceived in space at the same time, exist in a state of complete reciprocity of action.

PROOF

Things are coexistent, when in empirical intuition the perception of the one can follow upon the perception of the other, and vice versa—which cannot occur in the succession of phenomena, as we have shown in the explanation of the second principle. Thus I can perceive the moon and then the earth, or conversely, first the earth and then the moon; and for the reason that my perceptions of these objects can reciprocally follow each other, I say, they exist contemporaneously. Now coexistence is the existence of the manifold in the same time. But time itself is not an object of perception; and therefore we cannot conclude from the fact that things are placed in the same time, the other fact, that the perception of these things can follow each other reciprocally. The synthesis of the imagination in apprehension would only present to us each of these perceptions as present in the subject when the other is not present, and contrariwise; but would not show that the objects are coexistent, that is to say, that, if the one exists, the other also exists in the same time, and that this is necessarily so, in order that the perceptions may be capable of following each other reciprocally. It follows that a conception of the understanding or category of the reciprocal sequence of the determinations of phenomena (existing, as they do, apart from each other, and yet contemporaneously), is requisite to justify us in saying that the reciprocal succession of perceptions has its foundation in the object, and to enable us to represent coexistence as objective. But that relation of substances in which the one contains determinations the ground of which is in the other substance, is the relation of influence. And, when this influence is reciprocal, it is the relation of community or reciprocity. Consequently the coexistence of substances in space cannot be cognized in experience otherwise than under the precondition of their reciprocal action. This is therefore the condition of the possibility of things themselves as objects of experience.

Things are coexistent, in so far as they exist in one and the same time. But how can we know that they exist in one and the same time? Only by observing that the order in the synthesis of apprehension of the manifold is arbitrary and a matter of indifference, that is to say, that it can proceed from A, through B, C, D, to E, or contrariwise from E to A. For if they were successive in time (and in the order, let us suppose, which begins with A), it is quite impossible for the apprehension in perception to begin with E and go backwards to A, inasmuch as A belongs to past time and, therefore, cannot be an object of apprehension.

Let us assume that in a number of substances

considered as phenomena each is completely isolated, that is, that no one acts upon another. Then I say that the *coexistence* of these cannot be an object of possible perception and that the existence of one cannot, by any mode of empirical synthesis, lead us to the existence of another. For we imagine them in this case to be separated by a completely void space, and thus perception, which proceeds from the one to the other in time, would indeed determine their existence by means of a following perception, but would be quite unable to distinguish whether the one phenomenon follows objectively upon the first, or is coexistent with it.

Besides the mere fact of existence, then, there must be something by means of which A determines the position of B in time and, conversely, B the position of A; because only under this condition can substances be empirically represented as existing contemporaneously. Now that alone determines the position of another thing in time which is the cause of it or of its determinations. Consequently every substance (inasmuch as it can have succession predicated of it only in respect of its determinations) must contain the causality of certain determinations in another substance, and at the same time the effects of the causality of the other in itself. That is to say, substances must stand (mediately or immediately) in dynamical community with each other, if coexistence is to be cognized in any possible experience. But, in regard to objects of experience, that is absolutely necessary without which the experience of these objects would itself be impossible. Consequently it is absolutely necessary that all substances in the world of phenomena, in so far as they are coexistent, stand in a relation of complete community of reciprocal action to each other.

The word community has in our language[1] two meanings, and contains the two notions conveyed in the Latin *communio* and *commercium*. We employ it in this place in the latter sense—that of a dynamical community, without which even the community of place (*communio spatii*) could not be empirically cognized. In our experiences it is easy to observe that it is only the continuous influences in all parts of space that can conduct our senses from one object to another; that the light which plays between our eyes and the heavenly bodies produces a mediating community between them and us, and thereby evidences their coexistence with us; that we cannot empirically change our position (perceive this change), unless the existence of matter throughout the whole of space rendered possible the perception of the positions we occupy; and that this perception can prove the contemporaneous existence of these places only through their reciprocal influence, and thereby also the coexistence of even the most remote objects—although in this case the proof is only mediate. Without community, every perception (of a phenomenon in space) is separated from every other and isolated, and the chain of empirical representations, that is, of experience, must, with the appearance of a new object, begin entirely *de novo,* without the least connection with preceding representations, and without standing towards these even in the relation of time. My intention here is by no means to combat the notion of empty space; for it may exist where our perceptions cannot exist, inasmuch as they cannot reach thereto, and where, therefore, no empirical perception of coexistence takes place. But in this case it is not an object of possible experience.

1 German.

The following remarks may be useful in the way of explanation. In the mind, all phenomena, as contents of a possible experience, must exist in community (*communio*) of apperception or consciousness, and in so far as it is requisite that objects be represented as coexistent and connected, in so far must they reciprocally determine the position in time of each other and thereby constitute a whole. If this subjective community is to rest upon an objective basis, or to be applied to substances as phenomena, the perception of one substance must render possible the perception of another, and conversely. For otherwise succession, which is always found in perceptions as apprehensions, would be predicated of external objects, and their representation of their coexistence be thus impossible. But this is a reciprocal influence, that is to say, a real community (*commercium*) of substances, without which therefore the empirical relation of coexistence would be a notion beyond the reach of our minds. By virtue of this *commercium,* phenomena, in so far as they are apart from, and nevertheless in connection with each other, constitute a *compositum reale.* Such *composita* are possible in many different ways. The three dynamical relations then, from which all others spring, are those of inherence, consequence, and composition.

These, then, are the three analogies of experience. They are nothing more than principles of the determination of the existence of phenomena in time, according to the three *modi* of this determination; to wit, the relation to time itself as a quantity (the quantity of existence, that is, duration), the relation in time as a series or succession, finally, the relation in time as the complex of all existence (simultaneity). This unity of determination in regard to time is thoroughly dynamical; that is to say, time is not considered as that in which experience determines immediately to every existence its position; for this is impossible, inasmuch as absolute time is not an object of perception, by means of which phenomena can be connected with each other. On the contrary, the rule of the understanding, through which alone the existence of phenomena can receive synthetical unity as regards relations of time, determines for every phenomenon its position in time, and consequently *a priori,* and with validity for all and every time.

By nature, in the empirical sense of the word, we understand the totality of phenomena connected, in respect of their existence, according to necessary rules, that is, laws. There are therefore certain laws (which are moreover *a priori*) which make nature possible; and all empirical laws can exist only by means of experience, and by virtue of those primitive laws through which experience itself becomes possible. The purpose of the analogies is therefore to represent to us the unity of nature in the connection of all phenomena under certain exponents, the only business of which is to express the relation of time (in so far as it contains all existence in itself) to the unity of apperception, which can exist in synthesis only according to rules. The combined expression of all is this: "All phenomena exist in one nature, and must so exist, inasmuch as without this *a priori* unity, no unity of experience, and consequently no determination of objects in experience, is possible."

As regards the mode of proof which we have employed in treating of these transcendental laws of nature, and the peculiar character of it, we must make one remark, which will at the same time be important as a guide in every other attempt to demonstrate the truth of intellectual and likewise synthetical propositions *a priori.* Had we endeavoured to prove these analogies dogmatically, that is, from conceptions; that is to say, had we employed this method in attempting to show that everything which exists, exists only in that which is permanent—that every thing or event presupposes the existence of something in a preceding state, upon which it follows in conformity with a rule—lastly, that in the manifold, which is coexistent, the states coexist in connection with each other according to a rule—all our labour would have been utterly in vain. For more conceptions of things, analyse them as we may, cannot enable us to conclude from the existence of one object to the existence of another. What other course was left for us to pursue? This only, to demonstrate the possibility of experience as a cognition in which at last all objects must be capable of being presented to us, if the representation of them is to possess any objective reality. Now in this third, this mediating term, the essential form of which consists in the synthetical unity of the apperception of all phenomena, we found *a priori* conditions of the universal and necessary determination as to time of all existences in the world of phenomena, without which the empirical determination thereof as to time would itself be impossible, and we also discovered rules of synthetical unity *a priori,* by means of which we could anticipate experience. For want of this method, and from the fancy that it was possible to discover a dogmatical proof of the synthetical propositions which are requisite in the empirical employment of the understanding, has it happened that a proof of the principle of sufficient reason has been so often attempted, and always in vain. The other two analogies nobody has ever thought of, although they have always been silently employed by the mind,[1] because the guiding thread furnished by the categories was wanting, the guide which alone can enable us to discover every hiatus, both in the system of conceptions and of principles.

4. The Postulates of Empirical Thought

1. That which agrees with the formal conditions (intuition and conception) of experience, is *possible.*

2. That which coheres with the material conditions of experience (sensation), is *real.*

3. That whose coherence with the real is de-

[1] The unity of the universe, in which all phenomena must be connected, is evidently a mere consequence of the tacitly admitted principle of the community of all substances which are coexistent. For were substances isolated, they could not as parts constitute a whole, and were their connection (reciprocal action of the manifold) not necessary from the very fact of coexistence, we could not conclude from the fact of the latter as a merely ideal relation to the former as a real one. We have, however, shown in its place that community is the proper ground of the possibility of an empirical cognition of coexistence, and that we may therefore properly reason from the latter to the former as its condition.

termined according to universal conditions of experience is (exists) necessary.

Explanation

The categories of modality possess this peculiarity, that they do not in the least determine the object, or enlarge the conception to which they are annexed as predicates, but only express its relation to the faculty of cognition. Though my conception of a thing is in itself complete, I am still entitled to ask whether the object of it is merely possible, or whether it is also real, or, if the latter, whether it is also necessary. But hereby the object itself is not more definitely determined in thought, but the question is only in what relation it, including all its determinations, stands to the understanding and its employment in experience, to the empirical faculty of judgement, and to the reason of its application to experience.

For this very reason, too, the categories of modality are nothing more than explanations of the conceptions of possibility, reality, and necessity, as employed in experience, and at the same time, restrictions of all the categories to empirical use alone, not authorizing the transcendental employment of them. For if they are to have something more than a merely logical significance, and to be something more than a mere analytical expression of the form of *thought,* and to have a relation to *things* and their possibility, reality, or necessity, they must concern possible experience and its synthetical unity, in which alone objects of cognition can be given.

The postulate of the possibility of things requires also, that the conception of the things agree with the formal conditions of our experience in general. But this, that is to say, the objective form of experience, contains all the kinds of synthesis which are requisite for the cognition of objects. A conception which contains a synthesis must be regarded as empty and without reference to an object, if its synthesis does not belong to experience—either as borrowed from it, and in this case it is called an *empirical conception,* or such as is the ground and *a priori* condition of experience (its form), and in this case it is a *pure conception,* a conception which nevertheless belongs to experience, inasmuch as its object can be found in this alone. For where shall we find the criterion or character of the possibility of an object which is cogitated by means of an *a priori* synthetical conception, if not in the synthesis which constitutes the form of empirical cognition of objects? That in such a conception no contradiction exists is indeed a necessary logical condition, but very far from being sufficient to establish the objective reality of the conception, that is, the possibility of such an object as is thought in the conception. Thus, in the conception of a figure which is contained within two straight lines, there is no contradiction, for the conceptions of two straight lines and of their junction contain no negation of a figure. The impossibility in such a case does not rest upon the conception in itself, but upon the construction of it in space, that is to say, upon the conditions of space and its determinations. But these have themselves objective reality, that is, they apply to possible things, because they contain *a priori* the form of experience in general.

And now we shall proceed to point out the extensive utility and influence of this postulate of possibility. When I represent to myself a thing that is permanent, so that everything in it which changes belongs merely to its state or condition, from such a conception alone I never can cognize that such a thing is possible. Or, if I represent to myself something which is so constituted that, when it is posited, something else follows always and infallibly, my thought contains no self-contradiction; but whether such a property as causality is to be found in any possible thing, my thought alone affords no means of judging. Finally, I can represent to myself different things (substances) which are so constituted that the state or condition of one causes a change in the state of the other, and reciprocally; but whether such a relation is a property of things cannot be perceived from these conceptions, which contain a merely arbitrary synthesis. Only from the fact, therefore, that these conceptions express *a priori* the relations of perceptions in every experience, do we know that they possess objective reality, that is, transcendental truth; and that independent of experience, though not independent of all relation to the form of an experience in general and its synthetical unity, in which alone objects can be empirically cognized.

But when we fashion to ourselves new conceptions of substances, forces, action, and reaction, from the material presented to us by perception, without following the example of experience in their connection, we create mere chimeras, of the possibility of which we cannot discover any criterion, because we have not taken experience for our instructress, though we have borrowed the conceptions from her. Such fictitious conceptions derive their character of possibility not, like the categories, *a priori,* as conceptions on which all experience depends, but only, *a posteriori,* as conceptions given by means of experience itself, and their possibility must either be cognized *a posteriori* and empirically, or it cannot be cognized at all. A substance which is permanently present in space, yet without filling it (like that *tertium quid* between matter and the thinking subject which some have tried to introduce into metaphysics), or a peculiar fundamental power of the mind of intuiting the future by anticipation (instead of merely inferring from past and present events), or, finally, a power of the mind to place itself in community of thought with other men, however distant they may be—these are conceptions the possibility of which has no ground to rest upon. For they are not based upon experience and its known laws; and, without experience, they are a merely arbitrary conjunction of thoughts, which, though containing no internal contradiction, has no claim to objective reality, neither, consequently, to the possibility of such an object as is thought in these conceptions. As far as concerns reality, it is self-evident that we cannot cogitate such a possibility *in concreto* without the aid of experience; because reality is concerned only with sensation, as the matter of experience, and not with the form of thought, with which we can no doubt indulge in shaping fancies.

But I pass by everything which derives its possibility from reality in experience, and I purpose treating here merely of the possibility of things by means of *a priori* conceptions. I maintain, then, that the possibility of things is not derived from such conceptions *per se,* but only when considered as formal and objective conditions of an experience in general.

It seems, indeed, as if the possibility of a triangle could be cognized from the conception of it alone (which is certainly independent of experience); for we can certainly give to the conception a corresponding object completely *a priori,* that is to say, we can construct it. But as a triangle is only the form of an object, it must remain a mere product of the imagination, and the possibility of the existence of an object corresponding to it must remain doubtful, unless we can discover some other ground, unless we know that the figure can be cogitated under the conditions upon which all objects of experience rest. Now, the facts that space is a formal condition *a priori* of external experience, that the formative synthesis, by which we construct a triangle in imagination, is the very same as that we employ in the apprehension of a phenomenon for the purpose of making an empirical conception of it, are what alone connect the notion of the possibility of such a thing with the conception of it. In the same manner, the possibility of continuous quantities, indeed of quantities in general, for the conceptions of them are without exception synthetical, is never evident from the conceptions in themselves, but only when they are considered as the formal conditions of the determination of objects in experience. And where, indeed, should we look for objects to correspond to our conceptions, if not in experience, by which alone objects are presented to us? It is, however, true that without antecedent experience we can cognize and characterize the possibility of things, relatively to the formal conditions, under which something is determined in experience as an object, consequently, completely *a priori.* But still this is possible only in relation to experience and within its limits.

The postulate concerning the cognition of the *reality* of things requires *perception,* consequently conscious sensation, not indeed immediately, that is, of the object itself, whose existence is to be cognized, but still that the object have some connection with a real perception, in accordance with the analogies of experience, which exhibit all kinds of real connection in experience.

From the *mere conception* of a thing it is impossible to conclude its existence. For, let the conception be ever so complete, and containing a statement of all the determinations of the thing, the existence of it has nothing to do with all this, but only with the question whether such a thing is given, so that the perception of it can in every case precede the conception. For the fact that the conception of it precedes the perception, merely indicates the possibility of its existence; it is perception which presents matter to the conception, that is the sole criterion of reality. Prior to the perception of the thing, however, and therefore comparatively *a priori,* we are able to cognize its existence, provided it stands in connection with some perceptions according to the principles of the empirical conjunction of these, that is, in conformity with the analogies of perception. For, in this case, the existence of the supposed thing is connected with our perception in a possible experience, and we are able, with the guidance of these analogies, to reason in the series of possible perceptions from a thing which we do really perceive to the thing we do not perceive.

Thus, we cognize the existence of a magnetic matter penetrating all bodies from the perception of the attraction of the steel-filings by the magnet, although the constitution of our organs renders an immediate perception of this matter impossible for us. For, according to the laws of sensibility and the connected context of our perceptions, we should in an experience come also on an immediate empirical intuition of this matter, if our senses were more acute—but this obtuseness has no influence upon and cannot alter the *form* of possible experience in general. Our knowledge of the existence of things reaches as far as our perceptions, and what may be inferred from them according to empirical laws, extend. If we do not set out from experience, or do not proceed according to the laws of the empirical connection of phenomena, our pretensions to discover the existence of a thing which we do not immediately perceive are vain. *Idealism*, however, brings forward powerful objections to these rules for proving existence mediately. This is, therefore, the proper place for its refutation.

REFUTATION OF IDEALISM

Idealism—I mean *material* idealism—is the theory which declares the existence of objects in space without us to be either (1) doubtful and indemonstrable, or (2) false and impossible. The first is the *problematical* idealism of Descartes, who admits the undoubted certainty of only one empirical assertion (*assertio*), to wit, "I am." The second is the *dogmatical* idealism of Berkeley, who maintains that space, together with all the objects of which it is the inseparable condition, is a thing which is in itself impossible, and that consequently the objects in space are mere products of the imagination. The dogmatical theory of idealism is unavoidable, if we regard space as a property of things in themselves; for in that case it is, with all to which it serves as condition, a nonentity. But the foundation for this kind of idealism we have already destroyed in the transcendental aesthetic. Problematical idealism, which makes no such assertion, but only alleges our incapacity to prove the existence of anything besides ourselves by means of immediate experience, is a theory rational and evidencing a thorough and philosophical mode of thinking, for it observes the rule not to form a decisive judgement before sufficient proof be shown. The desired proof must therefore demonstrate that we have *experience* of external things, and not mere *fancies*. For this purpose, we must prove, that our internal and, to Descartes, indubitable experience is itself possible only under the previous assumption of external experience.

THEOREM

The simple but empirically determined consciousness of my own existence proves the existence of external objects in space.

PROOF

I am conscious of my own existence as determined in time. All determination in regard to time presupposes the existence of *something permanent* in perception. But this permanent something cannot be something in me, for the very reason that my existence in time is itself determined by this permanent something. It follows that the perception of this permanent existence is possible only through a *thing* without me and not through the mere *representation* of a thing without me. Consequently, the determination of my existence in time is possible only through the existence of real things external to me. Now, consciousness in time is necessarily connected with the consciousness of the possibility of this determination in time. Hence it follows that consciousness in time is necessarily connected also with the existence of things without me, inasmuch as the existence of these things is the condition of determination in time. That is to say, the consciousness of my own existence is at the same time an immediate consciousness of the existence of other things without me.

Remark I. The reader will observe, that in the foregoing proof the game which idealism plays is retorted upon itself, and with more justice. It assumed that the only immediate experience is internal and that from this we can only *infer* the existence of external things. But, as always happens, when we reason from given effects to *determined* causes, idealism has reasoned with too much haste and uncertainty, for it is quite possible that the cause of our representations may lie in ourselves, and that we ascribe it falsely to external things. But our proof shows that external experience is properly immediate,[1] that only by virtue of it—not,

[1] The *immediate* consciousness of the existence of external things is, in the preceding theorem, not presupposed, but proved, by the possibility of this consciousness understood by us or not. The question as to the possibility of it would stand thus: "Have we an internal sense, but no external sense, and is our belief in external perception a mere delusion?" But it is evident that, in order merely to fancy to ourselves anything *as* external, that is, to present it to the sense in intuition we must already possess an external sense, and must there-

indeed, the consciousness of our own existence, but certainly the determination of our existence in time, that is, internal experience—is possible. It is true, that the representation "I am," which is the expression of the consciousness which can accompany all my thoughts, is that which immediately includes the existence of a subject. But in this representation we cannot find any knowledge of the subject, and therefore also no empirical knowledge, that is, experience. For experience contains, in addition to the thought of something existing, intuition, and in this case it must be internal intuition, that is, time, in relation to which the subject must be determined. But the existence of external things is absolutely requisite for this purpose, so that it follows that internal experience is itself possible only mediately and through external experience.

Remark II. Now with this view all empirical use of our faculty of cognition in the determination of time is in perfect accordance. Its truth is supported by the fact that it is possible to perceive a determination of time only by means of a change in external relations (motion) to the permanent in space (for example, we become aware of the sun's motion by observing the changes of his relation to the objects of this earth). But this is not all. We find that we possess nothing permanent that can correspond and be submitted to the conception of a substance as intuition, except *matter*. This idea of permanence is not itself derived from external experience, but is an *a priori* necessary condition of all determination of time, consequently also of the internal sense in reference to our own existence, and that through the existence of external things. In the representation "I," the consciousness of myself is not an intuition, but a merely intellectual representation produced by the spontaneous activity of a thinking subject. It follows, that this "I" has not any predicate of intuition, which, in its character of permanence, could serve as correlate to the determination of time in the internal sense—in the same way as impenetrability is the correlate of matter as an empirical intuition.

Remark III. From the fact that the existence of external things is a necessary condition of the possibility of a determined consciousness of ourselves, it does not follow that every intuitive representation of external things involves the existence of these things, for their representations may very well be the mere products of the imagination (in dreams as well as in madness); though, indeed, these are themselves created by the reproduction of previous external perceptions, which, as has been shown, are possible only through the reality of external objects. The sole aim of our remarks has, however, been to prove that internal experience in general is possible only through external experience in general. Whether this or that supposed experience be purely imaginary must be discovered from its particular determinations and by comparing these with the criteria of all real experience.

Finally, as regards the third postulate, it applies to material necessity in existence, and not to merely formal and logical necessity in the connection of conceptions. Now as we cannot cognize completely *a priori* the existence of any object of sense, though we can do so comparatively *a priori,* that is, relatively to some other previously given existence—a cognition, however, which can only be of such an existence as must be contained in the complex of experience, of which the previously given perception is a part—the necessity of existence can never be cognized from conceptions, but always, on the contrary, from its connection with that which is an object of perception. But the only existence cognized, under the condition of other given phenomena, as necessary, is the existence of effects from given causes in conformity with the laws of causality. It is consequently not the necessity of the existence of things (as substances), but the necessity of the state of things that we cognize, and that not immediately, but by means of the existence of other states given in perception, according to empirical laws of causality. Hence it follows that the criterion of necessity is to be found only in the law of possible experience—that everything which happens is determined *a priori* in the phenomenon by its cause. Thus we cognize only the necessity of *effects* in nature, the causes of which are given us. Moreover, the criterion of necessity in existence possesses no application beyond the field of possible experience, and even in this it is not valid of the existence of things as substances, because these can never be considered as empirical effects, or as something that happens and has a beginning. Necessity, therefore, regards only the relations of phenomena according to the dynamical law of causality, and the possi-

by distinguish immediately the mere receptivity of an external intuition from the spontaneity which characterizes every act of imagination. For merely to imagine also an external sense, would annihilate the faculty of intuition itself which is to be determined by the imagination.

bility grounded thereon, of reasoning from some given existence (of a cause) *a priori* to another existence (of an effect). "Everything that happens is hypothetically necessary," is a principle which subjects the changes that take place in the world to a law, that is, to a rule of necessary existence, without which nature herself could not possibly exist. Hence the proposition, "Nothing happens by blind chance (*in mundo non datur casus*)," is an *a priori* law of nature. The case is the same with the proposition, "Necessity in nature is not blind," that is, it is conditioned, consequently intelligible necessity (*non datur fatum*). Both laws subject the play of change to "a nature of things (as phenomena)," or, which is the same thing, to the unity of the understanding, and through the understanding alone can changes belong to an experience, as the synthetical unity of phenomena. Both belong to the class of dynamical principles. The former is properly a consequence of the principle of causality—one of the analogies of experience. The latter belongs to the principles of modality, which to the determination of causality adds the conception of necessity, which is itself, however, subject to a rule of the understanding. The principle of continuity forbids any *leap* in the series of phenomena regarded as changes (*in mundo non datur saltus*); and likewise, in the complex of all empirical intuitions in space, any break or hiatus between two phenomena (*non datur hiatus*)—for we can so express the principle, that experience can admit nothing which proves the existence of a vacuum, or which even admits it as a part of an empirical synthesis. For, as regards a vacuum or void, which we may cogitate as out and beyond the field of possible experience (the world), such a question cannot come before the tribunal of mere understanding, which decides only upon questions that concern the employment of given phenomena for the construction of empirical cognition. It is rather a problem for ideal reason, which passes beyond the sphere of a possible experience and aims at forming a judgement of that which surrounds and circumscribes it, and the proper place for the consideration of it is the transcendental dialectic. These four propositions, *"In mundo non datur hiatus, non datur saltus, non datur casus, non datur fatum,"* as well as all principles of transcendental origin, we could very easily exhibit in their proper order, that is, in conformity with the order of the categories, and assign to each its proper place. But the already practised reader will do this for himself, or discover the clue to such an arrangement. But the combined result of all is simply this, to admit into the empirical synthesis nothing which might cause a break in or be foreign to the understanding and the continuous connection of all phenomena, that is, the unity of the conceptions of the understanding. For in the understanding alone is the unity of experience, in which all perceptions must have their assigned place, possible.

Whether the field of possibility be greater than that of reality, and whether the field of the latter be itself greater than that of necessity, are interesting enough questions, and quite capable of synthentic solution, questions, however, which come under the jurisdiction of reason alone. For they are tantamount to asking whether all things as phenomena do without exception belong to the complex and connected whole of a single experience, of which every given perception is a part which therefore cannot be conjoined with any other phenomena—or, whether my perceptions can belong to more than one possible experience? The understanding gives to experience, according to the subjective and formal conditions, of sensibility as well as of apperception, the rules which alone make this experience possible. Other forms of intuition besides those of space and time, other forms of understanding besides the discursive forms of thought, or of cognition by means of conceptions, we can neither imagine nor make intelligible to ourselves; and even if we could, they would still not belong to experience, which is the only mode of cognition by which objects are presented to us. Whether other perceptions besides those which belong to the total of our possible experience, and consequently whether some other sphere of matter exists, the understanding has no power to decide, its proper occupation being with the synthesis of that which is given. Moreover, the poverty of the usual arguments which go to prove the existence of a vast sphere of possibility, of which all that is real (every object of experience) is but a small part, is very remarkable. "All real is possible"; from this follows naturally, according to the logical laws of conversion, the particular proposition: "Some possible is real." Now this seems to be equivalent to: "Much is possible that is not real." No doubt it does seem as if we ought to consider the sum of the possible to be greater than that of the real, from the fact that something must be added to the former to constitute the latter. But this notion of adding to the possible is absurd. For that which is not in the sum of the possible, and consequently requires to be added to it, is manifestly impossible. In addition to accordance with the formal conditions of experience, the understanding requires a connection with some perception; but that which is connected with this perception is real, even although it is not immediately perceived. But that another series of phenomena, in complete coherence with that which is given in perception, consequently more than one all-embracing experience is possible, is an inference which cannot be concluded from the data given us by experience, and still less without any data at all. That which is possible only under conditions which are themselves merely possible, is not possible *in any respect*. And yet we can find no more certain ground on which to base the discussion of the question whether the sphere of possibility is wider than that of experience.

I have merely mentioned these questions, that in treating of the conception of the understanding, there might be no omission of anything that, in the common opinion, belongs to them. In reality, however, the notion of absolute possibility (possibility which is valid in every respect) is not a mere conception of the understanding, which can be employed empirically, but belongs to reason alone, which passes the bounds of all empirical use of the understanding. We have, therefore, contented ourselves with a merely critical remark, leaving the subject to be explained in the sequel.

Before concluding this fourth section, and at the same time the system of all principles of the pure understanding, it seems proper to mention the reasons which induced me to term the principles of modality postulates. This expression I do not here use in the sense which some more recent philosophers, contrary to its meaning with mathematicians, to whom the word properly belongs, attach to it—that of a proposition, namely, immediately certain, requiring neither deduction nor proof. For if, in the case of synthetical propositions, however evident they may be, we accord to them without deduction, and merely on the strength of their own pretensions, unqualified belief, all critique of the understanding is entirely lost; and, as there is no want of bold pretensions, which the common belief (though for the philosopher this is no credential) does not reject, the understanding lies exposed to every delusion and conceit, without the power of refusing its assent to those assertions, which, though illegitimate, demand acceptance as veritable axioms. When, therefore, to the conception of a thing an *a priori* determination is synthetically added, such a proposition must obtain, if not a proof, at least a deduction of the legitimacy of its assertion.

The principles of modality are, however, not objectively synthetical, for the predicates of possibility, reality, and necessity do not in the least augment the conception of that of which they are affirmed, inasmuch as they contribute nothing to the representation of the object. But as they are, nevertheless, always synthetical, they are so merely subjectively. That is to say, they have a reflective power, and apply to the conception of a thing, of which, in other respects, they affirm nothing, the faculty of cognition in which the conception originates and has its seat. So that if the conception merely agree with the formal conditions of experience, its object is called possible; if it is in connection with perception, and determined thereby, the object is real; if it is determined according to conceptions by means of the connection of perceptions, the object is called necessary. The principles of modality therefore predicate of a conception nothing more than the procedure of the faculty of cognition which generated it. Now a postulate in mathematics is a practical proposition which contains nothing but the synthesis by which we present an object to ourselves, and produce the conception of it, for example—"With a given line, to describe a circle upon a plane, from a given point"; and such a proposition does not admit of proof, because the procedure, which it requires, is exactly that by which alone it is possible to generate the conception of such a figure. With the same right, accordingly, can we postulate the principles of modality, because they do not augment[1] the conception of a thing, but merely indicate the manner in which it is connected with the faculty of cognition.

GENERAL REMARK ON THE SYSTEM OF PRINCIPLES

It is very remarkable that we cannot perceive the possibility of a thing from the category alone, but must always have an intuition, by which to make evident the objective reality of the pure conception of the understanding. Take, for example, the categories of relation. How (1) a thing can exist only as a *subject*, and not

[1] When I think the *reality* of a thing, I do really think more than the possibility, but not *in the thing;* for that can never contain more in reality than was contained in its complete possibility. But while the notion of possibility is merely the notion of a position of a thing in relation to the understanding (its empirical use), reality is the conjunction of the thing with perception.

as a mere determination of other things, that is, can be *substance;* or how (2), because something exists, some other thing must exist, consequently how a thing can be a cause; or how (3), when several things exist, from the fact that one of these things exists, some consequence to the others follows, and reciprocally, and in this way a community of substances can be possible—are questions whose solution cannot be obtained from mere conceptions. The very same is the case with the other categories; for example, how a thing can be of the same sort with many others, that is, can be a quantity, and so on. So long as we have not intuition we cannot know whether we do really think an object by the categories, and where an object can anywhere be found to cohere with them, and thus the truth is established, that the categories are not in themselves *cognitions,* but mere *forms of thought* for the construction of cognitions from given intuitions. For the same reason is it true that from categories alone no synthetical proposition can be made. For example: "In every existence there is substance," that is, something that can exist only as a subject and not as mere predicate; or, "Everything is a quantity"—to construct propositions such as these, we require something to enable us to go out beyond the given conception and connect another with it. For the same reason the attempt to prove a synthetical proposition by means of mere conceptions, for example: "Everything that exists contingently has a cause," has never succeeded. We could never get further than proving that, without this relation to conceptions, we could *not conceive* the existence of the contingent, that is, could not *a priori* through the understanding cognize the existence of such a thing; but it does not hence follow that this is also the condition of the possibility of the thing itself that is said to be contingent. If, accordingly, we look back to our proof of the principle of causality, we shall find that we were able to prove it as valid only of objects of possible experience, and, indeed, only as itself the principle of the possibility of experience, consequently of the *cognition* of an object given in *empirical intuition,* and not from mere conceptions. That, however, the proposition: "Everything that is contingent must have a cause," is evident to every one merely from conceptions, is not to be denied. But in this case the conception of the contingent is cogitated as involving not the category of modality (as that the non-existence of which can be *conceived*), but that of relation (as that which can exist only as the consequence of something else), and so it is really an identical proposition: "That which can exist only as a consequence, has a cause." In fact, when we have to give examples of contingent existence, we always refer to *changes,* and not merely to the possibility of *conceiving the opposite.*[1] But change is an event, which, as such, is possible only through a cause, and considered *per se* its non-existence is therefore possible, and we become cognizant of its contingency from the fact that it can exist only as the effect of a cause. Hence, if a thing is assumed to be contingent, it is an analytical proposition to say, it has a cause.

But it is still more remarkable that, to understand the possibility of things according to the categories and thus to demonstrate the *objective reality* of the latter, we require not merely intuitions, but *external intuitions.* If, for example, we take the pure conceptions of relation, we find that (1) for the purpose of presenting to the conception of *substance* something *permanent* in intuition corresponding thereto, and thus of demonstrating the objective reality of this conception, we require an intuition (of matter) in *space,* because space alone is permanent and determines things as such, while time, and with it all that is in the internal sense, is in a state of continual flow; (2) in order to represent *change* as the intuition corresponding to the conception of causality, we require the representation of motion as change in space; in fact, it is through it alone that changes, the possibility of which no pure understanding can perceive, are capable of being intuited. Change is the connection of determinations contradictorily opposed to each other in the existence of one and the same thing. Now, how it is possible that out of a given state one quite opposite to it in the same thing should follow, reason without an example can not only not conceive, but cannot even make intelligible without intuition; and this intuition is the mo-

[1] We can easily conceive the non-existence of matter; but the ancients did not thence infer its contingency. But even the alternation of the existence and non-existence of a given state in a thing, in which all change consists, by no means proves the contingency of that state—the ground of proof being the reality of its opposite. For example, a body is in a state of rest after motion, but we cannot infer the contingency of the motion from the fact that the former is the opposite of the latter. For this opposite is merely a logical and not a real opposite to the other. If we wish to demonstrate the contingency of the motion, what we ought to prove is that, *instead* of the motion which took place in the preceding point of time, it was possible for the body to have been *then* in rest, not, that it is *afterwards* in rest; for, in this case, both opposites are perfectly consistent with each other.

tion of a point in space; the existence of which in different spaces (as a consequence of opposite determinations) alone makes the intuition of change possible. For, in order to make even internal change cognitable, we require to represent time, as the form of the internal sense, figuratively by a line, and the internal change by the drawing of that line (motion), and consequently are obliged to employ external intuition to be able to represent the successive existence of ourselves in different states. The proper ground of this fact is that all change to be perceived as change presupposes something permanent in intuition, while in the internal sense no permanent intuition is to be found. Lastly, the objective possibility of the category of *community* cannot be conceived by mere reason, and consequently its objective reality cannot be demonstrated without an intuition, and that external in space. For how can we conceive the possibility of community, that is, when several substances exist, that some effect on the existence of the one follows from the existence of the other, and reciprocally, and therefore that, because something exists in the latter, something else must exist in the former, which could not be understood from its own existence alone? For this is the very essence of community—which is inconceivable as a property of things which are perfectly isolated. Hence, Leibnitz, in attributing to the substances of the world—as cogitated by the understanding alone—a community, required the mediating aid of a divinity; for, from their existence, such a property seemed to him with justice inconceivable. But we can very easily conceive the possibility of community (of substances as phenomena) if we represent them to ourselves as in space, consequently in external intuition. For external intuition contains in itself *a priori* formal external relations, as the conditions of the possibility of the real relations of action and reaction, and therefore of the possibility of community. With the same ease can it be demonstrated, that the possibility of things as *quantities,* and consequently the objective reality of the category of *quantity,* can be grounded only in external intuition, and that by its means alone is the notion of quantity appropriated by the internal sense. But I must avoid prolixity, and leave the task of illustrating this by examples to the reader's own reflection.

The above remarks are of the greatest importance, not only for the confirmation of our previous confutation of idealism, but still more when the subject of *self-cognition* by mere internal consciousness and the determination of our own nature without the aid of external empirical intuitions is under discussion, for the indication of the grounds of the possibility of such a cognition.

The result of the whole of this part of the analytic of principles is, therefore: "All principles of the pure understanding are nothing more than *a priori* principles of the possibility of experience, and to experience alone do all *a priori* synthetical propositions apply and relate"; indeed, their possibility itself rests entirely on this relation.

Chapter III. *Of the Ground of the Division of all Objects into Phenomena and Noumena.*

We have now not only traversed the region of the pure understanding and carefully surveyed every part of it, but we have also measured it, and assigned to everything therein its proper place. But this land is an island, and enclosed by nature herself within unchangeable limits. It is the land of truth (an attractive word), surrounded by a wide and stormy ocean, the region of illusion, where many a fog-bank, many an iceberg, seems to the mariner, on his voyage of discovery, a new country, and, while constantly deluding him with vain hopes, engages him in dangerous adventures, from which he never can desist, and which yet he never can bring to a termination. But before venturing upon this sea, in order to explore it in its whole extent, and to arrive at a certainty whether anything is to be discovered there, it will not be without advantage if we cast our eyes upon the chart of the land that we are about to leave, and to ask ourselves, firstly, whether we cannot rest perfectly contented with what it contains, or whether we must not of necessity be contented with it, if we can find nowhere else a solid foundation to build upon; and, secondly, by what title we possess this land itself, and how we hold it secure against all hostile claims? Although, in the course of our analytic, we have already given sufficient answers to these questions, yet a summary recapitulation of these solutions may be useful in strengthening our conviction, by uniting in one point the momenta of the arguments.

We have seen that everything which the understanding draws from itself, without borrowing from experience, it nevertheless possesses only for the behoof and use of experience. The principles of the pure understanding, whether constitutive *a priori* (as the mathematical principles), or merely regulative (as the dynamical), contain nothing but the pure schema, as it were, of possible experience. For experience possesses its unity from the synthetical unity which the understanding, originally and from itself, imparts to the synthesis of the imagination in relation to apperception, and in *a priori* relation to and agreement with which phenomena, as data for a possible cognition, must stand. But although these rules of the understanding are not only *a priori* true, but the very source of all truth, that is, of the accordance of our cognition with objects, and on this ground, that they contain the basis of the possibility of experience, as the *ensemble* of all cognition, it seems to us not enough to propound what is true—we desire also to be told what we want to know. If, then, we learn nothing more by this critical examination than what we should have practised in the merely empirical use of the understanding, without any such subtle inquiry, the presumption is that the advantage we reap from it is not worth the labour bestowed upon it. It may certainly be answered that no rash curiosity is more prejudicial to the enlargement of our knowledge than that which must know beforehand the utility of this or that piece of information which we seek, before we have entered on the needful investigations, and before one could form the least conception of its utility, even though it were placed before our eyes. But there is one advantage in such transcendental inquiries which can be made comprehensible to the dullest and most reluctant learner—this, namely, that the understanding which is occupied merely with empirical exercise, and does not reflect on the sources of its own cognition, may exercise its functions very well and very successfully, but is quite unable to do one thing, and that of very great importance, to determine, namely, the bounds that limit its employment, and to know what lies within or without its own sphere. This purpose can be obtained only by such profound investigations as we have instituted. But if it cannot distinguish whether certain questions lie within its horizon or not, it can never be sure either as to its claims or possessions, but must lay its account with many humiliating corrections, when it transgresses, as it unavoidably will, the limits of its own territory, and loses itself in fanciful opinions and blinding illusions.

That the understanding, therefore, cannot make of its *a priori* principles, or even of its conceptions, other than an empirical use, is a proposition which leads to the most important results. A transcendental use is made of a conception in a fundamental proposition or principle, when it is referred to things *in general* and considered as things *in themselves;* an empirical use, when it is referred merely to *phenomena,* that is, to objects of a possible *experience.* That the latter use of a conception is the only admissible one is evident from the reasons following. For every conception are requisite, firstly, the logical form of a conception (of thought) in general; and, secondly, the possibility of presenting to this an object to which it may apply. Failing this latter, it has no sense, and is utterly void of content, although it may contain the logical function for constructing a conception from certain data. Now, object cannot be given to a conception otherwise than by intuition, and, even if a pure intuition antecedent to the object is *a priori* possible, this pure intuition can itself obtain objective validity only from empirical intuition, of which it is itself but the form. All conceptions, therefore, and with them all principles, however high the degree of their *a priori* possibility, relate to empirical intuitions, that is, to data towards a possible experience. Without this they possess no objective validity, but are mere play of imagination or of understanding with images or notions. Let us take, for example, the conceptions of mathematics, and first in its pure intuitions. "Space has three dimensions"—"Between two points there can be only one straight line," etc. Although all these principles, and the representation of the object with which this science occupies itself, are generated in the mind entirely *a priori,* they would nevertheless have no significance if we were not always able to exhibit their significance in and by means of phenomena (empirical objects). Hence it is requisite that an abstract conception be *made sensuous,* that is, that an object corresponding to it in intuition be forthcoming, otherwise the conception remains, as we say, without *sense,* that is, without meaning. Mathematics fulfils this requirement by the construction of the figure, which is a phenomenon evident to the senses. The same science finds support and significance in number; this in its turn finds it in the fingers, or in counters, or in lines and points. The conception itself is always produced *a priori,* together with the synthetical principles or formulas from such conceptions; but the proper employment of them, and their application to objects, can exist nowhere but in experience, the possibility of which, as regards its form, they contain *a priori*.

That this is also the case with all of the categories and the principles based upon them is evident from the fact that we cannot render intelligible the possibility of an object corresponding to them without having recourse to the conditions of sensibility, consequently, to the form of phenomena, to which, as their only proper objects, their use must therefore be confined, inasmuch as, if this condition is removed, all significance, that is, all relation to an object, disappears, and no example can be found to make it comprehensible what sort of things we ought to think under such conceptions.

The conception of quantity cannot be explained except by saying that it is the determination of a thing whereby it can be cogitated how many times one is placed in it. But this "how many times" is based upon successive repetition, consequently upon time and the synthesis of the homogeneous therein. Reality, in contradistinction to negation, can be explained only by cogitating a time which is either filled therewith or is void. If I leave out the notion of permanence (which is existence in all time), there remains in the conception of substance nothing but the logical notion of subject, a notion of which I endeavour to realize by representing to myself something that can exist only as a subject. But not only am I perfectly ignorant of any conditions under which this logical prerogative can belong to a thing, I can make nothing out of the notion, and draw no inference from it, because no object to which to apply the conception is determined, and we consequently do not know whether it has any meaning at all. In like manner, if I leave out the notion of time, in which something follows upon some other thing in conformity with a rule, I can find nothing in the pure category, except that there is a something of such a sort that from it a conclusion may be drawn as to the existence of some other thing. But in this case it would not only be impossible to distinguish between a cause and an effect, but, as this power to draw conclusions requires conditions of which I am quite ignorant, the conception is not determined as to the mode in which it ought to apply to an object. The so-called principle: "Everything that is contingent has a cause," comes with a gravity and self-assumed authority that seems to require no support from without. But, I ask, what is meant by contingent? The answer is that the non-existence of which is possible. But I should like very well to know by what means this possibility of non-existence is to be cognized, if we do not represent to ourselves a succession in the series of phenomena, and in this succession an existence which follows a non-existence, or conversely, consequently, change. For to say, that the non-existence of a thing is not self-contradictory is a lame appeal to a logical condition, which is no doubt a necessary condition of the existence of the conception, but is far from being sufficient for the real objective possibility of non-existence. I can annihilate in thought every existing substance without self-contradiction, but I cannot infer from this their objective contingency in existence, that is to say, the possibility of their non-existence in itself. As regards the category of community, it may easily be inferred that, as the pure categories of substance and causality are incapable of a definition and explanation sufficient to determine their object without the aid of intuition, the category of reciprocal causality in the relation of substances to each other (*commercium*) is just as little susceptible thereof. Possibility, existence, and necessity nobody has ever yet been able to explain without being guilty of manifest tautology, when the definition has been drawn entirely from the pure understanding. For the substitution of the logical possibility of the *conception*—the condition of which is that it be not self-contradictory, for the transcendental possibility of *things*—the condition of which is that there be an object corresponding to the conception, is a trick which can only deceive the inexperienced.[1]

It follows incontestably, that the pure conceptions of the understanding are incapable of *transcendental,* and must always be of *empirical* use alone, and that the principles of the pure understanding relate only to the general conditions of a possible experience, to objects of the senses, and never to things in general, apart from the mode in which we intuite them.

Transcendental analytic has accordingly this important result, to wit, that the understanding is competent to effect nothing *a priori,* except the anticipation of the form of a possible experience in general, and that, as that which is not phenomenon cannot be an object of ex-

[1] In one word, to none of these conceptions belongs a corresponding object, and consequently their real possibility cannot be demonstrated, if we take away sensuous intuition—the only intuition which we possess—and there then remains nothing but the *logical* possibility, that is, the fact that the conception or thought is possible—which, however, is not the question; what we want to know being, whether it relates to an object and thus possesses any meaning.

perience, it can never overstep the limits of sensibility, within which alone objects are presented to us. Its principles are merely principles of the exposition of phenomena, and the proud name of an *ontology,* which professes to present synthetical cognitions *a priori* of things in general in a systematic doctrine, must give place to the modest title of *analytic* of the pure understanding.

Thought is the act of referring a given intuition to an object. If the mode of this intuition is unknown to us, the object is merely transcendental, and the conception of the understanding is employed only transcendentally, that is, to produce unity in the thought of a manifold in general. Now a pure category, in which all conditions of sensuous intuition—as the only intuition we possess—are abstracted, does not determine an object, but merely expresses the thought of an object in general, according to different modes. Now, to employ a conception, the function of judgement is required, by which an object is subsumed under the conception, consequently the at least formal condition, under which something can be given in intuition. Failing this condition of judgement (schema), subsumption is impossible; for there is in such a case nothing given, which may be subsumed under the conception. The merely transcendental use of the categories is therefore, in fact, no use at all and has no determined, or even, as regards its form, determinable object. Hence it follows that the pure category is incompetent to establish a synthetical *a priori* principle, and that the principles of the pure understanding are only of empirical and never of transcendental use, and that beyond the sphere of possible experience no synthetical *a priori* principles are possible.

It may be advisable, therefore, to express ourselves thus. The pure categories, apart from the formal conditions of sensibility, have a merely transcendental *meaning,* but are nevertheless not of transcendental *use,* because this is in itself impossible, inasmuch as all the conditions of any employment or use of them (in judgements) are absent, to wit, the formal conditions of the subsumption of an object under these conceptions. As, therefore, in the character of pure categories, they must be employed empirically, and cannot be employed transcendentally, they are of no use at all, when separated from sensibility, that is, they cannot be applied to an object. They are merely the pure form of the employment of the understanding in respect of objects in general and of thought, without its being at the same time possible to think or to determine any object by their means.

But there lurks at the foundation of this subject an illusion which it is very difficult to avoid. The categories are not based, as regards their origin, upon sensibility, like the *forms of intuition,* space, and time; they seem, therefore, to be capable of an application beyond the sphere of sensuous objects. But this is not the case. They are nothing but mere *forms of thought,* which contain only the logical faculty of uniting *a priori* in consciousness the manifold given in intuition. Apart, then, from the only intuition possible for us, they have still less meaning than the pure sensuous forms, space and time, for through them an object is at least given, while a mode of connection of the manifold, when the intuition which alone gives the manifold is wanting, has no meaning at all. At the same time, when we designate certain objects as phenomena or sensuous existences, thus distinguishing our mode of intuiting them from their own nature as things in themselves, it is evident that by this very distinction we as it were place the latter, considered in this their own nature, although we do not so intuite them, in opposition to the former, or, on the other hand, we do so place other possible things, which are not objects of our senses, but are cogitated by the understanding alone, and call them intelligible existences (noumena). Now the question arises whether the pure conceptions of our understanding do possess significance in respect of these latter, and may possibly be a mode of cognizing them.

But we are met at the very commencement with an ambiguity, which may easily occasion great misapprehension. The understanding, when it terms an object in a certain relation phenomenon, at the same time forms out of this relation a representation or notion of an *object in itself,* and hence believes that it can form also *conceptions* of such objects. Now as the understanding possesses no other fundamental conceptions besides the categories, it takes for granted that an object considered as a thing in itself must be capable of being thought by means of these pure conceptions, and is thereby led to hold the perfectly undetermined conception of an intelligible existence, a something out of the sphere of our sensibility, for a *determinate* conception of an existence which we can cognize in some way or other by means of the understanding.

If, by the term *noumenon,* we understand a thing so far as it is *not an object of our sensu-*

ous intuition, thus making abstraction of our mode of intuiting it, this is a noumenon in the *negative* sense of the word. But if we understand by it an *object of a non-sensuous intuition,* we in this case assume a peculiar mode of intuition, an intellectual intuition, to wit, which does not, however, belong to us, of the very possibility of which we have no notion—and this is a noumenon in the *positive* sense.

The doctrine of sensibility is also the doctrine of noumena in the negative sense, that is, of things which the understanding is obliged to cogitate apart from any relation to our mode of intuition, consequently not as mere phenomena, but as things in themselves. But the understanding at the same time comprehends that it cannot employ its categories for the consideration of things in themselves, because these possess significance only in relation to the unity of intuitions in space and time, and that they are competent to determine this unity by means of general *a priori* connecting conceptions only on account of the pure ideality of space and time. Where this unity of time is not to be met with, as is the case with noumena, the whole use, indeed the whole meaning of the categories is entirely lost, for even the possibility of things to correspond to the categories is in this case incomprehensible. On this point, I need only refer the reader to what I have said at the commencement of the General Remark appended to the foregoing chapter. Now, the possibility of a thing can never be proved from the fact that the conception of it is not self-contradictory, but only by means of an intuition corresponding to the conception. If, therefore, we wish to apply the categories to objects which cannot be regarded as phenomena, we must have an intuition different from the sensuous, and in this case the objects would be a noumena *in the positive sense* of the word. Now, as such an intuition, that is, an intellectual intuition, is no part of our faculty of cognition, it is absolutely impossible for the categories to possess any application beyond the limits of experience. It may be true that there are intelligible existences to which our faculty of sensuous intuition has no relation, and cannot be applied, but our conceptions of the understanding, as mere forms of thought for our sensuous intuition, do not extend to these. What, therefore, we call *noumenon* must be understood by us as such in a *negative* sense.

If I take away from an empirial intuition all thought (by means of the categories), there remains no cognition of any object; for by means of mere intuition nothing is cogitated, and, from the existence of such or such an affection of sensibility in me, it does not follow that this affection or representation has any relation to an object without me. But if I take away all intuition, there still remains the form of thought, that is, the mode of determining an object for the manifold of a possible intuition. Thus the categories do in some measure really extend further than sensuous intuition, inasmuch as they think objects in general, without regard to the mode (of sensibility) in which these objects are given. But they do not for this reason apply to and determine a wider sphere of objects, because we cannot assume that such can be given, without presupposing the possibility of another than the sensuous mode of intuition, a supposition we are not justified in making.

I call a conception problematical which contains in itself no contradiction, and which is connected with other cognitions as a limitation of given conceptions, but whose objective reality cannot be cognized in any manner. The conception of a *noumenon,* that is, of a thing which must be cogitated not as an object of sense, but as a thing in itself (solely through the pure understanding), is not self-contradictory, for we are not entitled to maintain that sensibility is the only possible mode of intuition. Nay, further, this conception is necessary to restrain sensuous intuition within the bounds of phenomena, and thus to limit the objective validity of sensuous cognition; for things in themselves, which lie beyond its province, are called noumena for the very purpose of indicating that this cognition does not extend its application to all that the understanding thinks. But, after all, the possibility of such noumena is quite incomprehensible, and beyond the sphere of phenomena, all is for us a mere void; that is to say, we possess an understanding whose province does *problematically* extend beyond this sphere, but we do not possess an intuition, indeed, not even the conception of a possible intuition, by means of which objects beyond the region of sensibility could be given us, and in reference to which the understanding might be employed *assertorically.* The conception of a noumenon is therefore merely a *limitative conception* and therefore only of negative use. But it is not an arbitrary or fictitious notion, but is connected with the limitation of sensibility, without, however, being capable of presenting us with any positive datum beyond this sphere.

The division of objects into phenomena and

noumena, and of the world into a *mundus sensibilis* and *intelligibilis* is therefore quite inadmissible in a *positive sense,* although conceptions do certainly admit of such a division; for the class of noumena have no determinate object corresponding to them, and cannot therefore possess objective validity. If we abandon the senses, how can it be made conceivable that the categories (which are the only conceptions that could serve as conceptions for noumena) have any sense or meaning at all, inasmuch as something more than the mere unity of thought, namely, a possible intuition, is requisite for their application to an object? The conception of a noumenon, considered as merely problematical, is, however, not only admissible, but, as a limitative conception of sensibility, absolutely necessary. But, in this case, a noumenon is not a particular *intelligible object* for our understanding; on the contrary, the kind of understanding to which it could belong is itself a problem, for we cannot form the most distant conception of the possibility of an understanding which should cognize an object, not discursively by means of categories, but intuitively in a non-sensuous intuition. Our understanding attains in this way a sort of negative extension. That is to say, it is not limited by, but rather limits, sensibility, by giving the name of noumena to things, not considered as phenomena, but as things in themselves. But it at the same time prescribes limits to itself, for it confesses itself unable to cognize these by means of the categories, and hence is compelled to cogitate them merely as an unknown something.

I find, however, in the writings of modern authors, an entirely different use of the expressions, *mundus sensibilis* and *intelligibilis,* which quite departs from the meaning of the ancients —an acceptation in which, indeed, there is to be found no difficulty, but which at the same time depends on mere verbal quibbling. According to this meaning, some have chosen to call the complex of phenomena, in so far as it is intuited, *mundus sensibilis,* but in so far as the connection thereof is cogitated according to general laws of thought, *mundus intelligibilis.* Astronomy, in so far as we mean by the word the mere observation of the starry heaven, may represent the former; a system of astronomy, such as the Copernican or Newtonian, the latter. But such twisting of words is a mere sophistical subterfuge, to avoid a difficult question, by modifying its meaning to suit our own convenience. To be sure, understanding and reason are employed in the cognition of phenomena; but the question is, whether these can be applied when the object is not a phenomenon— and in this sense we regard it if it is cogitated as given to the understanding alone, and not to the senses. The question therefore is whether, over and above the empirical use of the understanding, a transcendental use is possible, which applies to the noumenon as an object. This question we have answered in the negative.

When therefore we say, the senses represent objects *as they appear,* the understanding *as they are,* the latter statement must not be understood in a transcendental, but only in an empirical signification, that is, as they must be represented in the complete connection of phenomena, and not according to what they may be, apart from their relation to possible experience, consequently not as objects of the pure understanding. For this must ever remain unknown to us. Nay, it is also quite unknown to us whether any such transcendental or extraordinary cognition is possible under any circumstances, at least, whether it is possible by means of our categories. *Understanding* and *sensibility,* with us, can determine objects only *in conjunction.* If we separate them, we have intuitions without conceptions, or conceptions without intuitions; in both cases, representations, which we cannot apply to any determinate object.

If, after all our inquiries and explanations, any one still hesitates to abandon the mere transcendental use of the categories, let him attempt to construct with them a synthetical proposition. It would, of course, be unnecessary for this purpose to construct an analytical proposition, for that does not extend the sphere of the understanding, but, being concerned only about what is cogitated in the conception itself, it leaves it quite undecided whether the conception has any relation to objects, or merely indicates the unity of thought—complete abstraction being made of the *modi* in which an object may be given: in such a proposition, it is sufficient for the understanding to know what lies in the conception—to what it applies is to it indifferent. The attempt must therefore be made with a synthetical and so-called transcendental principle, for example: "Everything that exists, exists as substance," or, "Everything that is contingent exists as an effect of some other thing, viz., of its cause." Now I ask, whence can the understanding draw these synthetical propositions, when the conceptions contained therein do not relate to possible experience but to things in themselves (noumena)? Where is to be found the *third term,* which is always requisite in a synthetical proposition, which may connect in the same proposition conceptions which have no logical (analytical) connection with each other? The proposition never will be demonstrated, nay, more, the possibility of any such pure assertion never can be shown, without making reference to the empirical use of the understanding, and thus, *ipso facto,* completely renouncing pure and non-sensuous judgement. Thus the conception of pure and merely intelligible objects is completely void of all principles of its application, because we cannot imagine any mode in which they might be given, and the problematical thought which leaves a place open for them serves only, like a void space, to limit the use of empirical principles, without containing at the same time any other object of cognition beyond their sphere.

APPENDIX

Of the Equivocal Nature or Amphiboly of the Conceptions of Reflection from the Confusion of the Transcendental with the Empirical use of the Understanding.

REFLECTION (*reflexio*) is not occupied about objects themselves, for the purpose of directly obtaining conceptions of them, but is that state of the mind in which we set ourselves to discover the subjective conditions under which we obtain conceptions. It is the consciousness of the relation of given representations to the different sources or faculties of cognition, by which alone their relation to each other can be rightly determined. The first question which occurs in considering our representations is to what faculty of cognition do they belong? To the understanding or to the senses? Many judgements are admitted to be true from mere habit or inclination; but, because reflection neither precedes nor follows, it is held to be a judgement that has its origin in the understanding. All judgements do not require *examination,* that is, investigation into the grounds of their truth. For, when they are immediately certain (for example: "Between two points there can be only one straight line"), no better or less mediate test of their truth can be found than that which they themselves contain and express. But all judgement, nay, all comparisons require *reflection,* that is, a distinction of the faculty of cognition to which the given conceptions belong. The act whereby I compare my representations with the faculty of cognition which originates them, and whereby I distinguish whether they are compared with each other as belonging to the pure understanding or to sensuous intuition, I term *transcendental reflection.* Now, the relations in which conceptions can stand to each other are those of *identity* and *difference, agreement* and *opposition,* of the *internal* and *external,* finally, of the *determinable* and the *determining* (matter and form). The proper determination of these relations rests on the question, to what faculty of cognition they *subjectively* belong, whether to sensibility or understanding? For, on the manner in which we solve this question depends the manner in which we must cogitate these relations.

Before constructing any objective judgement, we compare the conceptions that are to be placed in the judgement, and observe whether there exists *identity* (of many representations in one conception), if a *general* judgement is to be constructed, or *difference,* if a *particular;* whether there is *agreement* when *affirmative;* and *opposition* when *negative* judgements are to be constructed, and so on. For this reason we ought to call these conceptions, conceptions of comparison (*conceptus comparationis*). But as, when the question is not as to the logical form, but as to the content of conceptions, that is to say, whether the things themselves are identical or different, in agreement or opposition, and so on, the things can have a twofold relation to our faculty of cognition, to wit, a relation either to sensibility or to the understanding, and as on this relation depends their relation to each other, transcendental reflection, that is, the relation of given representations to one or the other faculty of cognition, can alone determine this latter relation. Thus we shall not be able to discover whether the things are identical or different, in agreement or opposition, etc., from the mere conception of the things by means of comparison (*comparatio*), but only by distinguishing the mode of cognition to which they belong, in other words, by means of transcendental reflection. We may, therefore, with justice say, that *logical reflection* is mere comparison, for in it no account is taken of the faculty of cognition to which the given conceptions belong, and they are consequently, as far as regards their origin, to be treated as homogeneous; while *transcendental reflection* (which applies to the objects themselves) contains the ground of the possibility of objective comparison of representations with each other, and is therefore very different from the former, because the faculties of cognition to which they belong are not even the same. Transcendental reflection is a duty which no one can neglect who wishes to establish an *a priori* judgement upon things. We shall now proceed to fulfil this duty, and thereby throw not a little light on the question as to the determination of the proper business of the understanding.

1. *Identity and Difference.* When an object is presented to us several times, but always with the same internal determinations (*qualitas et quantitas*), it, if an object of pure understanding, is always the same, not several things, but only one thing (*numerica identitas*); but if a phenomenon, we do not concern ourselves with comparing the conception of the thing with the conception of some other, but, although they may be in this respect perfectly the same, the difference of place at the same time is a sufficient ground for asserting the *numerical difference* of these objects (of sense). Thus, in the case of two drops of water, we may make complete abstraction of all internal difference (quality and quantity), and, the fact that they are intuited at the same time in different places, is sufficient to justify us in holding them to be numerically different. Leibnitz regarded phenomena as things in themselves, consequently as *intelligibilia,* that is, objects of pure understanding (although, on account of the confused nature of their representations, he gave them the name of phenomena), and in this case his principle of the indiscernible (*principium identatis indiscernibilium*) is not to be impugned. But, as phenomena are objects of sensibility, and, as the understanding, in respect of them, must be employed empirically and not purely or transcendentally, plurality and numerical difference are given by space itself as the condition of external phenomena. For one part of space, although it may be perfectly similar and equal to another part, is still without it, and for this reason alone is different from the latter, which is added to it in order to make up a greater space. It follows that this must hold good of all things that are in the different parts of space at the same time, however similar and equal one may be to another.

2. *Agreement and Opposition.* When reality is represented by the pure understanding (*realitas noumenon*), opposition between realities is incogitable—such a relation, that is, that when these realities are connected in one subject, they annihilate the effects of each other and may be represented in the formula $3 - 3 = 0$. On the other hand, the real in a phenomenon (*realitas phaenomenon*) may very well be in mutual opposition, and, when united in the same subject, the one may completely or in part annihilate the effect or *consequence of the other;* as in the case of two moving forces in the same straight line drawing or impelling a point in opposite directions, or in the case of a pleasure counterbalancing a certain amount of pain.

3. *The Internal and External.* In an object of the pure understanding, only that is internal which has no relation (as regards its existence) to anything different from itself. On the other hand, the internal determinations of a *substantia phaenomenon* in space are nothing but relations, and it is itself nothing more than a complex of mere relations. Substance in space we are cognizant of only through forces operative in it, either drawing others towards itself (attraction), or preventing others from forcing into itself (repulsion and impenetrability). We know no other properties that make up the conception of substance phenomenal in space, and which we term matter. On the other hand, as an object of the pure understanding, every substance must have internal determination and forces. But what other internal attributes of such an object can I think than those which my internal sense presents to me? That, to wit, which in either itself *thought,* or something analogous to it. Hence Leibnitz, who looked upon things as noumena, after denying them everything like external relation, and therefore also *composition* or combination, declared that all substances, even the component parts of matter, were simple substances with powers of representation, in one word, *monads.*

4. *Matter and Form.* These two conceptions lie at the foundation of all other reflection, so inseparably are they connected with every mode of exercising the understanding. The former denotes the determinable in general, the second its determination, both in a transcendental sense, abstraction being made of every difference in that which is given, and of the mode in which it is determined. Logicians formerly termed the universal, *matter,* the specific difference of this or that part of the universal, *form.* In a judgement one may call the given conceptions logical matter (for the judgement), the relation of these to each other (by means of the copula), the form of the judgement. In an object, the composite parts thereof (*essentialia*) are the matter; the mode in which they are connected in the object, the form. In respect to things in general, unlimited reality was regarded as the matter of all possibility, the limitation thereof (negation) as the form, by which one thing is distinguished from another according to transcendental con-

ceptions. The understanding demands that something be given (at least in the conception), in order to be able to determine it in a certain manner. Hence, in a conception of the pure understanding, the matter precedes the form, and for this reason Leibnitz first assumed the existence of things (monads) and of an internal power of representation in them, in order to found upon this their external relation and the community of their state (that is, of their representations). Hence, with him, space and time were possible—the former through the relation of substances, the latter through the connection of their determinations with each other, as causes and effects. And so would it really be, if the pure understanding were capable of an immediate application to objects, and if space and time were determinations of things in themselves. But being merely sensuous intuitions, in which we determine all objects solely as phenomena, the form of intuition (as a subjective property of sensibility) must antecede all matter (sensations), consequently space and time must antecede all phenomena and all data of experience, and rather make experience itself possible. But the intellectual philosopher could not endure that the form should precede the things themselves and determine their possibility; an objection perfectly correct, if we assume that we intuite things as they are, although with confused representation. But as sensuous intuition is a peculiar subjective condition, which is *a priori* at the foundation of all perception, and the form of which is primitive, the form must be given *per se,* and so far from matter (or the things themselves which appear) lying at the foundation of experience (as we must conclude, if we judge by mere conceptions), the very possibility of itself presupposes, on the contrary, a given formal intuition (space and time).

Remark on the Amphiboly of the Conceptions of Reflection

Let me be allowed to term the position which we assign to a conception either in the sensibility or in the pure understanding, the *transcendental place.* In this manner, the appointment of the position which must be taken by each conception according to the difference in its use, and the directions for determining this place to all conceptions according to rules, would be a *transcendental topic,* a doctrine which would thoroughly shield us from the surreptitious devices of the pure understanding and the delusions which thence arise, as it would always distinguish to what faculty of cognition each conception properly belonged. Every conception, every title, under which many cognitions rank together, may be called a *logical place.* Upon this is based the *logical topic* of Aristotle, of which teachers and rhetoricians could avail themselves, in order, under certain titles of thought, to observe what would best suit the matter they had to treat, and thus enable themselves to quibble and talk with fluency and an appearance of profundity.

Transcendental topic, on the contrary, contains nothing more than the above-mentioned four titles of all comparison and distinction, which differ from categories in this respect, that they do not represent the object according to that which constitutes its conception (quantity, reality), but set forth merely the comparison of representations, which precedes our conceptions of things. But this comparison requires a previous reflection, that is, a determination of the place to which the representations of the things which are compared belong, whether, to wit, they are cogitated by the pure understanding, or given by sensibility.

Conceptions may be logically compared without the trouble of inquiring to what faculty their objects belong, whether as noumena, to the understanding, or as phenomena, to sensibility. If, however, we wish to employ these conceptions in respect of objects, previous transcendental reflection is necessary. Without this reflection I should make a very unsafe use of these conceptions, and construct pretended synthetical propositions which critical reason cannot acknowledge and which are based solely upon a transcendental amphiboly, that is, upon a substitution of an object of pure understanding for a phenomenon.

For want of this doctrine of transcendental topic, and consequently deceived by the amphiboly of the conceptions of reflection, the celebrated Leibnitz constructed an *intellectual system of the world*, or rather, believed himself competent to cognize the internal nature of things, by comparing all objects merely with the understanding and the abstract formal conceptions of thought. Our table of the conceptions of reflection gives us the unexpected advantage of being able to exhibit the distinctive peculiarities of his system in all its parts, and at the same time of exposing the fundamental principle of this peculiar mode of thought, which rested upon naught but a misconception. He compared all things with each other merely by means of conceptions, and naturally found no other differences than those by which the understanding distinguishes its pure conceptions one from another. The conditions of sensuous intuition, which contain in themselves their own means of distinction, he did not look upon as primitive, because sensibility was to him but a confused mode of representation and not any particular source of representations. A phenomenon was for him the representation of the thing in itself, although distinguished from cognition by the understanding only in respect of the logical form—the former with its usual want of analysis containing, according to him, a certain mixture of collateral representations in its conception of a thing, which it is the duty of the understanding to separate and distinguish. In one word, Leibnitz *intellectualized* phenomena, just as Locke, in his system of *noogony* (if I may be allowed to make use of such expressions), *sensualized* the conceptions of the understanding, that is to say, declared them to be nothing more than empirical or abstract conceptions of reflection. Instead of seeking in the understanding and sensibility two different sources of representations, which, however, can present us with objective judgements of things only in *conjunction*, each of these great men recognized but one of these faculties, which, in their opinion, applied immediately to things in themselves, the other having no duty but that of confusing or arranging the representations of the former.

Accordingly, the objects of sense were compared by Leibnitz as things in general merely in the understanding.

1st. He compares them in regard to their identity or difference—as judged by the understanding. As, therefore, he considered merely the conceptions of objects, and not their position in intuition, in which alone objects can be given, and left quite out of sight the transcendental *locale* of these conceptions—whether, that is, their object ought to be classed among phenomena, or among things in themselves, it was to be expected that he should extend the application of the principle of indiscernibles, which is valid solely of conceptions of things in general, to objects of sense (*mundus phaenomenon*), and that he should believe that he had thereby contributed in no small degree to extend our knowledge of nature. In truth, if I cognize in all its inner determinations a drop of water as a thing in itself, I cannot look upon one drop as different from another, if the conception of the one is completely identical with that of the other. But if it is a phenomenon in space, it has a place not merely in the understanding (among conceptions), but also in sensuous external intuition (in space), and in this case, the physical *locale* is a matter of indifference in regard to the internal determinations of things, and one place, B, may contain a thing which is perfectly similar and equal to another in a place, A, just as well as if the two things were in every respect different from each other. Difference of place without any other conditions, makes the plurality and distinction of objects as phenomena, not only possible in itself, but even necessary. Consequently, the above so-called law is not a law of nature. It is merely an analytical rule for the comparison of things by means of mere conceptions.

2nd. The principle: "Realities (as simple affirmations) never logically contradict each other," is a proposition perfectly true respecting the relation of conceptions, but, whether as regards nature, or things in themselves (of which we have not the slightest conception), is without any the least meaning. For real opposition, in which $A - B$ is $= 0$, exists everywhere, an opposition, that is, in which one reality united with another in the same subject annihilates the effects of the other—a fact which is constantly brought before our eyes by the different antagonistic actions and operations in nature, which, nevertheless, as depending on real forces, must be called *realitates phaenomena*. General mechanics can even present us with the empirical condition of this opposition in an *a priori* rule, as it directs its attention to the opposition in the direction of forces—a condition of which the transcendental conception of reality can tell us nothing. Although M. Leibnitz did not announce this proposition with precisely the pomp of a new principle, he yet employed it for the establishment of new propositions, and his followers introduced it into their Leibnitzio-Wolfian system of philosophy. According to this principle, for example, all evils are but consequences of the limited nature of created beings, that is, negations, because these are the only opposite of reality. (In the mere conception of a thing in general this is really the case, but not in things as phenomena.) In like manner, the upholders of this system deem it not only possible, but natural also, to connect and unite all reality in one being, because they acknowledge no other sort of opposition than that of contradiction (by which the conception itself of a thing is annihilated), and find themselves unable to conceive an opposition of reciprocal destruction, so to speak, in which one real cause destroys the effect of another, and the conditions of whose representation we meet with only in sensibility.

3rd. The Leibnitzian monadology has really no better foundation than on this philosopher's mode of falsely representing the difference of the internal and external solely in relation to the understanding. Substances, in general, must have something *inward,* which is therefore free from external relations, consequently from that of composition also. The *simple*—that which can be represented by a unit—is therefore the foundation of that which is internal in things in themselves. The internal state of substances cannot therefore consist in place, shape, contact, or motion, determinations which are all external relations, and we can ascribe to them no other than that whereby we internally determine our faculty of sense itself, that is to say, the state of representation. Thus, then, were constructed the monads, which were to form the elements of the universe, the active force of which consists in representation, the effects of this force being thus entirely confined to themselves.

For the same reason, his view of the possible community of substances could not represent it but as a *predetermined harmony,* and by no means as a physical influence. For inasmuch as everything is occupied only internally, that is, with its own representations, the state of the representations of one substance could not stand in active and living connection with that of another, but some third cause operating on all without exception was necessary to make the different states correspond with one another. And this did not happen by means of assistance applied in each particular case (*systema assistentiae*), but through the unity of the idea of a cause occupied and connected with all substances, in which they necessarily receive, according to the Leibnitzian school, their existence and permanence, consequently also reciprocal correspondence, according to universal laws.

4th. This philosopher's celebrated *doctrine of space and time,* in which he intellectualized these forms of sensibility, originated in the same delusion of transcendental reflection. If I attempt to represent by the mere understanding, the external relations of things, I can do so only by employing the conception of their reciprocal action, and if I wish to connect one state of the same thing with another state, I must avail myself of the notion of the order of cause and effect. And thus Leibnitz regarded space as a certain order in the community of substances, and time as the dynamical sequence of their states. That which space and time possess proper to themselves and independent of things, he ascribed to a necessary *confusion* in our conceptions of them, whereby that which is a mere form of dynamical relations is held to be a self-existent intuition, antecedent even to things themselves. Thus space and time were the intelligible form of the connection of things (substances and their states) in themselves. But things were intelligible substances (*substantiae noumena*). At the same time, he made these conceptions valid of phenomena, because he did not allow to sensibility a peculiar mode of intuition, but sought all, even the empirical representation of objects, in the understanding, and left to sense naught but the despicable task of confusing and disarranging the representations of the former.

But even if we could frame any synthetical proposition concerning things in themselves by means of the pure understanding (which is impossible), it could not apply to phenomena, which do not represent things in themselves. In such a case I should be obliged in transcendental reflection to compare my conceptions only under the conditions of sensibility, and so space and time would not be determinations of things in themselves, but of phenomena. What things may be in themselves, I know not and need not know, because a thing is never presented to me otherwise than as a phenomenon.

I must adopt the same mode of procedure with the other conceptions of reflection. Matter is *substantia phaenomenon.* That in it which is internal I seek to discover in all parts of space which it occupies, and in all the functions and operations it performs, and which are indeed never anything but phenomena of the external sense. I cannot therefore find anything that is absolutely, but only what is comparatively internal, and which itself consists of external relations. The absolutely internal in matter, and as it should be according to the pure understanding, is a mere chimera, for matter is not an object for the pure understanding. But the transcendental object, which is the foundation of the phenomenon which we call matter, is a mere *nescio quid,* the nature of which we could not understand, even though someone were found able to tell us. For we can understand nothing that does not bring with it something in intuition corresponding to the expressions employed. If, by the complaint of being *unable to perceive the internal nature of things,* it is meant that we do not comprehend by the pure understanding what the things which appear to us may be in themselves, it is a silly and unreasonable complaint; for those who talk thus really desire that we should be able to cognize, consequently to intuite, things without senses, and therefore wish that we possessed a faculty of cognition perfectly different from the human faculty, not merely in degree, but even as regards intuition and the mode thereof, so that thus we should not be men, but belong to a class of beings, the possibility of whose existence, much less their nature and constitution, we have no means of cognizing. By observation and analysis of phenomena we penetrate into the interior of nature, and no one can say what progress this knowledge may make in time. But those transcendental questions which pass beyond the limits of nature, we could never answer, even although all nature were laid open to us, because we have not the power of observing our own mind with any other intuition than that of our internal sense. For herein lies the mystery of the origin and source of our faculty of sensibility. Its application to an object, and the transcendental ground of this unity of subjective and objective, lie too deeply concealed for us, who cognize ourselves only through the internal sense, consequently as phenomena, to be able to discover in our existence anything but phenomena, the non-sensuous cause of which we at the same time earnestly desire to penetrate to.

The great utility of this critique of conclusions arrived at by the processes of mere reflection consists in its clear demonstration of the nullity of all conclusions respecting objects which are compared with each other in the understanding alone, while it at the same time confirms what we particularly insisted on, namely, that, although phenomena are not included as things in themselves among the objects of the pure understanding, they are nevertheless the only things by which our cognition can possess objective reality, that is to say, which give us intuitions to correspond with our conceptions.

When we reflect in a purely logical manner, we do nothing more than compare conceptions in our understanding, to discover whether both have the same content, whether they are self-contradictory or not, whether anything is contained in either conception, which of the two is given, and which is merely a mode of thinking that given. But if I apply these conceptions to an object in general (in the transcendental sense), without first determining whether it is an object of sensuous or intellectual intuition, certain limitations present themselves, which forbid us to pass beyond the conceptions and render all empirical use of them impossible. And thus these limitations prove that the representation of an object as a thing in general is not only *insufficient,* but, without sensuous determination and independently of empirical conditions, *self-contradictory;* that we must therefore make abstraction of all objects, as in logic, or, admitting them, must think them under conditions of sensuous intuition; that, consequently, the intelligible requires an altogether peculiar intuition, which we do not possess, and in the absence of which it is for us nothing; while, on the other hand, phenomena cannot be objects in themselves. For, when I merely think things in general, the difference in their external relations cannot constitute a difference in the things themselves; on the contrary, the former presupposes the latter, and if the conception of one of two things is not internally different from that of the other, I am merely thinking the same thing in different relations. Further, by the addition of one affirmation (reality) to the other, the positive therein is really augmented, and nothing is abstracted or withdrawn from it; hence the real in things cannot be in contradiction with or opposition to itself—and so on.

The true use of the conceptions of reflection in the employment of the understanding has, as we have shown, been so misconceived by Leibnitz, one of the most acute philosophers of either ancient or modern times, that he has been misled into the construction of a baseless system of intellectual cognition, which professes to determine its objects without the intervention of the senses. For this reason, the exposition of the cause of the amphiboly of these conceptions, as the origin of these false principles, is of great utility in determining with certainty the proper limits of the understanding.

It is right to say whatever is affirmed or denied of the whole of a conception can be affirmed or denied of any part of it (*dictum de omni et nullo*); but it would be absurd so to alter this logical proposition as to say whatever is not contained in a general conception is likewise not contained in the particular conceptions which rank under it; for the latter are particular conceptions, for the very reason that their content is greater than that which is cogitated in the general conception. And yet the whole intellectual system of Leibnitz is based upon this false principle, and with it must necessarily fall to the ground, together with all the ambiguous principles in reference to the employment of the understanding which have thence originated.

Leibnitz's principle of the identity of indiscernibles or indistinguishables is really based on the presupposition that, if in the conception of a thing a certain distinction is not to be found, it is also not to be met with in things themselves; that, consequently, all things are completely identical (*numero eadem*) which are not distinguishable from each other (as to quality or quantity) in our conceptions of them. But, as in the mere conception of anything abstraction has been made of many necessary conditions of intuition, that of which abstraction has been made is rashly held to be non-existent, and nothing is attributed to the thing but what is contained in its conception.

The conception of a cubic foot of space, however I may think it, is in itself completely identical. But two cubic feet in space are nevertheless distinct from each other from the sole fact of their being in different places (they are *numero diversa*); and these places are conditions of intuition, wherein the object of this conception is given, and which do not belong to the conception, but to the faculty of sensibility. In like manner, there is in the conception of a thing no contradiction when a negative is not connected with an affirmative; and merely affirmative conceptions cannot, in conjunction, produce any negation. But in sensuous intuition, wherein reality (take for example, motion) is given, we find conditions (opposite directions)—of which abstraction has been made in the conception of motion in general—which render possible a contradiction or opposition (not indeed of a logical kind)—and which from pure positives produce zero=0. We are therefore not justified in saying that all reality is in perfect agreement and harmony, because no contradiction is discoverable among its conceptions.[1] According to mere conceptions, that which is internal is the substratum of all relations or external determinations. When, therefore, I abstract all conditions of intuition, and confine myself solely to the conception of a thing in general, I can make abstraction of all external relations, and there must nevertheless remain a conception of that which indicates no relation, but merely internal determinations. Now it seems to follow that in everything (substance) there is something which is absolutely internal and which antecedes all external determinations, inasmuch as it renders them possible; and that therefore this substratum is something which does not contain any external relations and is consequently simple (for corporeal things are never anything but relations, at least of their parts external to each other); and, inasmuch as we know of no other absolutely internal determinations than those of the internal sense, this substratum is not only simple, but also, analogously with our internal sense, determined through *representations*, that is to say, all things are properly *monads*, or simple beings endowed with the power of representation. Now all this would be perfectly correct, if the conception of a thing were the only necessary condition of the presentation of objects of external intuition. It is, on the contrary, manifest that a permanent phenomenon in space (impenetrable extension) can contain mere relations, and nothing that is absolutely internal, and yet be the primary substratum of all external perception. By mere conceptions I cannot think anything external, without, at the same time, thinking something internal, for the reason that conceptions of relations presuppose given things, and without these are impossible. But, as an intuition there is something (that is, space, which, with all it contains, consists of purely formal, or, indeed, real relations) which is not found in the mere conception of a thing in general, and this presents to us the substratum which could not be cognized through conceptions alone, I cannot say: because a thing cannot be represented *by mere conceptions* without something absolutely internal, there is also, in the things themselves which are contained under these conceptions, and in *their intuition* nothing external to which something absolutely internal does not serve as the foundation. For, when we have made abstraction of all the conditions of intuition, there certainly remains in the mere conception nothing but the internal in general, through which alone the external is possible. But this necessity, which is grounded upon abstraction alone, does not obtain in the case of things themselves, in so far as they are given in intuition with such determinations as express mere relations, without having anything internal as their foundation;

[1] If any one wishes here to have recourse to the usual subterfuge, and to say, that at least *realitates noumena* cannot be in opposition to each other, it will be requisite for him to adduce an example of this pure and non-sensuous reality, that it may be understood whether the notion represents something or nothing. But an example cannot be found except in experience, which never presents to us anything more than *phenomena;* and thus the proposition means nothing more than that the conception which contains only affirmatives does not contain anything negative—a proposition nobody ever doubted.

for they are not things in themselves, but only phenomena. What we cognize in matter is nothing but relations (what we call its internal determinations are but comparatively internal). But there are some self-subsistent and permanent, through which a determined object is given. That I, when abstraction is made of these relations, have nothing more to think, does not destroy the conception of a thing as phenomenon, nor the conception of an object *in abstracto,* but it does away with the possibility of an object that is determinable according to mere conceptions, that is, of a noumenon. It is certainly startling to hear that a thing consists solely of relations; but this thing is simply a phenomenon, and cannot be cogitated by means of the mere categories: it does itself consist in the mere relation of something in general to the senses. In the same way, we cannot cogitate relations of things *in abstracto,* if we commence with conceptions alone, in any other manner than that one is the cause of determinations in the other; for that is itself the conception of the understanding or category of relation. But, as in this case we make abstraction of all intuition, we lose altogether the mode in which the manifold determines to each of its parts its place, that is, the form of sensibility (space); and yet this mode antecedes all empirical causality.

If by *intelligible objects* we understand things which can be thought by means of the pure categories, without the need of the schemata of sensibility, such objects are impossible. For the condition of the objective use of all our conceptions of understanding is the mode of our sensuous intuition, whereby objects are given; and, if we make abstraction of the latter, the former can have no relation to an object. And even if we should suppose a different kind of intuition from our own, still our functions of thought would have no use or signification in respect thereof. But if we understand by the term, *objects of a non-sensuous intuition,* in respect of which our categories are not valid, and of which we can accordingly have no knowledge (neither intuition nor conception), in this merely negative sense noumena must be admitted. For this is no more than saying that our mode of intuition is not applicable to all things, but only to objects of our senses, that consequently its objective validity is limited, and that room is therefore left for another kind of intuition, and thus also for things that may be objects of it. But in this sense the conception of a noumenon is problematical, that is to say, it is the notion of a thing of which we can neither say that it is possible, nor that it is impossible, inasmuch as we do not know of any mode of intuition besides the sensuous, or of any other sort of conceptions than the categories—a mode of intuition and a kind of conception neither of which is applicable to a non-sensuous object. We are on this account incompetent to extend the sphere of our objects of thought beyond the conditions of our sensibility, and to assume the existence of objects of pure thought, that is, of noumena, inasmuch as these have no true positive signification. For it must be confessed of the categories that they are not of themselves sufficient for the cognition of things in themselves and, without the data of sensibility, are mere subjective forms of the unity of the understanding. Thought is certainly not a product of the senses, and in so far is not limited by them, but it does not therefore follow that it may be employed purely and without the intervention of sensibility, for it would then be without reference to an object. And we cannot call a noumenon an object of pure thought; for the representation thereof is but the problematical conception of an object for a perfectly different intuition and a perfectly different understanding from ours, both of which are consequently themselves problematical. The conception of a noumenon is therefore not the conception of an object, but merely a problematical conception inseparably connected with the limitation of our sensibility. That is to say, this conception contains the answer to the question: "Are there objects quite unconnected with, and independent of, our intuition?"—a question to which only an indeterminate answer can be given. That answer is: "Inasmuch as sensuous intuition does not apply to all things without distinction, there remains room for other and different objects." The existence of these problematical objects is therefore not absolutely denied, in the absence of a determinate conception of them, but, as no category is valid in respect of them, neither must they be admitted as objects for our understanding.

Understanding accordingly limits sensibility, without at the same time enlarging its own field. While, moreover, it forbids sensibility to apply its forms and modes to things in themselves and restricts it to the sphere of phenomena, it cogitates an object in itself, only, however, as a transcendental object, which is the cause of a phenomenon (consequently not itself a phenomenon), and which cannot be thought either as a quantity or as reality, or as substance (because these conceptions always require sensuous forms in which to determine an object)—an object, therefore, of which we are quite unable to say whether it can be met with in ourselves or out of us, whether it would be annihilated together with sensibility, or, if this were taken away, would continue to exist. If we wish to call this object a noumenon, because the representation of it is non-sensuous, we are at liberty to do so. But as we can apply to it none of the conceptions of our understanding, the representation is for us quite void, and is available only for the indication of the limits of our sensuous intuition, thereby leaving at the same time an empty space, which we are competent to fill by the aid neither of possible experience, nor of the pure understanding.

The critique of the pure understanding, accordingly, does not permit us to create for ourselves a new field of objects beyond those which are presented to us as phenomena, and to stray into intelligible worlds; nay, it does not even allow us to endeavour to form so much as a conception of them. The specious error which leads to this—and which is a perfectly excusable one—lies in the fact that the employment of the understanding, contrary to its proper purpose and destination, is made transcendental, and objects, that is, possible intuitions, are made to regulate themselves according to conceptions, instead of the conceptions arranging themselves according to the intuitions, on which alone their own objective validity rests. Now the reason of this again is that apperception, and with it thought, antecedes all possible determinate arrangement of representations. Accordingly we think something in general and determine it on the one hand sensuously, but, on the other, distinguish the general and *in abstracto* represented object from this particular mode of intuiting it. In this case there remains a mode of determining the object by mere thought, which is really but a logical form without content, which, however, seems to us to be a mode of the existence of the object in itself (noumenon), without regard to intuition which is limited to our senses.

Before ending this transcendental analytic, we must make an addition, which, although in itself of no particular importance, seems to be necessary to the completeness of the system. The highest conception, with which a transcendental philosophy commonly begins, is the division into possible and impossible. But as all division presupposes a divided conception, a still higher one must exist, and this is the conception of an object in general—problematically understood and without its being decided whether it is something or nothing. As the categories are the only conceptions which apply to objects in general, the distinguishing of an object, whether it is something or nothing, must proceed according to the order and direction of the categories.

1. To the categories of quantity, that is, the conceptions of all, many, and one, the conception which annihilates all, that is, the conception of *none,* is opposed. And thus the object of a conception, to which no intuition can be found to correspond, is=nothing. That is, it is a conception without an object (*ens rationis*), like noumena, which cannot be considered possible in the sphere of reality, though they must not therefore be held to be impossible—or like certain new fundamental forces in matter, the existence of which is cogitable without contradiction, though, as examples from experience are not forthcoming, they must not be regarded as possible.

2. Reality is *something*; negation is *nothing*, that is, a conception of the absence of an object, as cold, a shadow (*nihil privativum*).

3. The mere form of intuition, without substance, is in itself no object, but the merely formal condition of an object (as phenomenon), as pure space and pure time. These are certainly something, as forms of intuition, but are not themselves objects which are intuited (*ens imaginarium*).

4. The object of a conception which is self-contradictory, is nothing, because the conception is nothing—is impossible, as a figure composed of two straight lines (*nihil negativum*).

The table of this division of the conception of *nothing* (the corresponding division of the conception of *something* does not require special description) must therefore be arranged as follows:

NOTHING
As

1
Empty Conception
without object,
ens rationis

2	3
Empty object of a conception, *nihil privativum*	Empty intuition without object, *ens imaginarium*

4
Empty object
without conception,
nihil negativum

We see that the *ens rationis* is distinguished from the *nihil negativum* or pure nothing by the consideration that the former must not be reckoned among possibilities, because it is a mere fiction — though not self-contradictory, while the latter is completely opposed to all possibility, inasmuch as the conception annihilates itself. Both, however, are empty conceptions. On the other hand, the *nihil privativum* and *ens imaginarium* are empty *data* for conceptions. If light be not given to the senses, we cannot represent to ourselves darkness, and if extended objects are not perceived, we cannot represent space. Neither the negation, nor the mere form of intuition can, without something real, be an object.

Transcendental Logic. Second Division

Transcendental Dialectic

Introduction

I. *Of Transcendental Illusory Appearance*

We termed dialectic in general a *logic of appearance.* This does not signify a doctrine of *probability*; for probability is truth, only cognized upon insufficient grounds, and though the information it gives us is imperfect, it is not therefore deceitful. Hence it must not be separated from the analytical part of logic. Still less must *phenomenon* and *appearance* be held to be identical. For truth or illusory appearance does not reside in the object, in so far as it is intuited, but in the judgement upon the object, in so far as it is thought. It is, therefore, quite correct to say that the senses do not err, not because they always judge correctly, but because *they do not* judge at all. Hence truth and error, consequently also, illusory appearance as the cause of error, are only to be found in a judgement, that is, in the relation of an object to our understanding. In a cognition which completely harmonizes with the laws of the understanding, no error can exist. In a representation of the senses—as not containing any judgement—there is also no error. But no power of nature can of itself deviate from its own laws. Hence neither the understanding *per se* (without the influence of another cause), nor the senses *per se,* would fall into error; the former could not, because, if it acts only according to its own laws, the effect (the judgement) must necessarily accord with these laws. But in accordance with the laws of the understanding consists the formal element in all truth. In the senses there is no judgement—neither a true nor a false one. But, as we have no source of cognition besides these two, it follows that error is caused solely by the unobserved influence of the sensibility upon the understanding. And thus it happens that the subjective grounds of a judgement blend and are confounded with the objective, and cause them to deviate from their proper determination,[1] just as a body in motion would always of itself proceed in a straight line, but if another impetus gives to it a different direction, it will then start off into a curvilinear line of motion. To distinguish the peculiar action of the understanding from the power which mingles with it, it is necessary to consider an erroneous judgement as the diagonal between two forces, that determine the judgement in two different directions, which, as it were, form an angle, and to resolve this composite operation into the simple ones of the understanding and the sensibility. In pure *a priori* judgements this must be done by means of transcendental reflection, whereby, as has been already shown, each representation has its place appointed in the corresponding faculty of cognition, and consequently the influence of the one faculty upon the other is made apparent.

It is not at present our business to treat of empirical illusory appearance (for example, optical illusion), which occurs in the empirical application of otherwise correct rules of the understanding, and in which the judgement is misled by the influence of imagination. Our purpose is to speak of *transcendental illusory appearance,* which influences principles—that are not even applied to experience, for in this case we should possess a sure test of their correctness—but which leads us, in disregard of all the warnings of criticism, completely beyond the empirical employment of the categories and deludes us with the chimera of an extension of the sphere of the *pure understanding.* We shall term those principles the application of which is con-

[1] Sensibility, subjected to the understanding, as the object upon which the understanding employs its functions, is the source of real cognitions. But, in so far as it exercises an influence upon the action of the understanding and determines it to judgement, sensibility is itself the cause of error.

fined entirely within the limits of possible experience, *immanent;* those, on the other hand, which transgress these limits, we shall call *transcendent* principles. But by these latter I do not understand principles of the *transcendental* use or misuse of the categories, which is in reality a mere fault of the judgement when not under due restraint from criticism, and therefore not paying sufficient attention to the limits of the sphere in which the pure understanding is allowed to exercise its functions; but real principles which exhort us to break down all those barriers, and to lay claim to a perfectly new field of cognition, which recognizes no line of demarcation. Thus *transcendental* and *transcendent* are not identical terms. The principles of the pure understanding, which we have already propounded, ought to be of empirical and not of transcendental use, that is, they are not applicable to any object beyond the sphere of experience. A principle which removes these limits, nay, which authorizes us to overstep them, is called *transcendent.* If our criticism can succeed in exposing the illusion in these pretended principles, those which are limited in their employment to the sphere of experience may be called, in opposition to the others, *immanent* principles of the pure understanding.

Logical illusion, which consists merely in the imitation of the form of reason (the illusion in sophistical syllogisms), arises entirely from a want of due attention to logical rules. So soon as the attention is awakened to the case before us, this illusion totally disappears. Transcendental illusion, on the contrary, does not cease to exist, even after it has been exposed, and its nothingness clearly perceived by means of transcendental criticism. Take, for example, the illusion in the proposition: "The world must have a beginning in time." The cause of this is as follows. In our reason, subjectively considered as a faculty of human cognition, there exist fundamental rules and maxims of its exercise, which have completely the appearance of objective principles. Now from this cause it happens that the subjective necessity of a certain connection of our conceptions, is regarded as an objective necessity of the determination of things in themselves. This illusion it is impossible to avoid, just as we cannot avoid perceiving that the sea appears to be higher at a distance than it is near the shore, because we see the former by means of higher rays than the latter, or, which is a still stronger case, as even the astronomer cannot prevent himself from seeing the moon larger at its rising than some time afterwards, although he is not deceived by this illusion.

Transcendental dialectic will therefore content itself with exposing the illusory appearance in transcendental judgements, and guarding us against it; but to make it, as in the case of logical illusion, entirely disappear and cease to be illusion is utterly beyond its power. For we have here to do with a *natural* and unavoidable illusion, which rests upon subjective principles and imposes these upon us as objective, while logical dialectic, in the detection of sophisms, has to do merely with an error in the logical consequence of the propositions, or with an artificially constructed illusion, in imitation of the natural error. There is, therefore, a natural and unavoidable dialectic of pure reason—not that in which the bungler, from want of the requisite knowledge, involves himself, nor that which the sophist devises for the purpose of misleading, but that which is an inseparable adjunct of human reason, and which, even after its illusions have been exposed, does not cease to deceive, and continually to lead reason into momentary errors, which it becomes necessary continually to remove.

II. *Of Pure Reason as the Seat of the Transcendental Illusory Appearance*

A. OF REASON IN GENERAL

All our knowledge begins with sense, proceeds thence to understanding, and ends with reason, beyond which nothing higher can be discovered in the human mind for elaborating the matter of intuition and subjecting it to the highest unity of thought. At this stage of our inquiry it is my duty to give an explanation of this, the highest faculty of cognition, and I confess I find myself here in some difficulty. Of reason, as of the understanding, there is a merely formal, that is, logical use, in which it makes abstraction of all content of cognition; but there is also a real use, inasmuch as it contains in itself the source of certain conceptions and principles, which it does not borrow either from the senses or the understanding. The former faculty has been long defined by logicians as the faculty of mediate conclusion in contradistinction to immediate conclusions (*consequentiae immediatae*); but the nature of the latter, which itself generates conceptions, is not to be understood from this definition. Now as a division of reason into a logical and a transcendental faculty presents itself here, it becomes necessary to seek for a higher conception of this source of cognition which shall comprehend both conceptions. In this we may expect, according to the analogy of the conceptions of the understanding, that the logical conception will give us the key to the transcendental, and that the table of the functions of the former will present us with the clue to the conceptions of reason.

In the former part of our transcendental logic, we defined the understanding to be the faculty of rules; reason may be distinguished from understanding as the *faculty of principles.*

The term *principle* is ambiguous, and commonly signifies merely a cognition that may be employed as a principle, although it is not in itself, and as regards its proper origin, entitled to the distinction. Every general proposition, even if derived from experience by the process of induction, may serve as the major in a syllogism; but it is not for that reason a principle. Mathematical axioms (for example, there can be only one straight line between two points) are general *a priori* cognitions, and are therefore rightly denominated principles, relatively to the cases which can be subsumed under them. But I cannot for this reason say that I cognize this property of a straight line from principles —I cognize it only in pure intuition.

Cognition from principles, then, is that cognition in which I cognize the particular in the general by means of conceptions. Thus every syllogism is a form of the deduction of a cognition from a principle. For the major always gives a conception, through which everything that is subsumed under the condition thereof is cognized according to a principle. Now as every general cognition may serve as the major in a syllogism, and the understanding presents us with such general *a priori* propositions, they may be termed principles, in respect of their possible use.

But if we consider these principles of the pure understanding in relation to their origin, we shall find them to be anything rather than cognitions from conceptions. For they would not even be possible *a priori,* if we could not rely on the assistance of pure intuition (in mathematics), or on that of the conditions of a possible experience. That everything that happens has a cause, cannot be concluded from the general conception of that which happens; on the contrary the principle of causality instructs us as to the mode of obtaining from that which happens a determinate empirical conception.

Synthetical cognitions from conceptions the understanding cannot supply, and they alone are entitled to be called *principles*. At the same time, all general propositions may be termed *comparative* principles.

It has been a long-cherished wish—that (who knows how late) may one day be happily accomplished—that the principles of the endless variety of civil laws should be investigated and exposed; for in this way alone can we find the secret of simplifying legislation. But in this case, laws are nothing more than limitations of our freedom upon conditions under which it subsists in perfect harmony with itself; they consequently have for their object that which is completely our own work, and of which we ourselves may be the cause by means of these conceptions. But how objects as things in themselves—how the nature of things is subordinated to principles and is to be determined according to conceptions, is a question which it seems well nigh impossible to answer. Be this, however, as it may—for on this point our investigation is yet to be made—it is at least manifest from what we have said that cognition from principles is something very different from cognition by means of the understanding, which may indeed precede other cognitions in the form of a principle, but in itself—in so far as it is synthetical—is neither based upon mere thought, nor contains a general proposition drawn from conceptions alone.

The understanding may be a faculty for the production of unity of phenomena by virtue of rules; the reason is a faculty for the production of unity of rules (of the understanding) under principles. Reason, therefore, never applies directly to experience, or to any sensuous object; its object is, on the contrary, the understanding, to the manifold cognition of which it gives a unity *a priori* by means of conceptions—a unity which may be called rational unity, and which is of a nature very different from that of the unity produced by the understanding.

The above is the general conception of the faculty of reason, in so far as it has been possible to make it comprehensible in the absence of examples. These will be given in the sequel.

B. OF THE LOGICAL USE OF REASON

A distinction is commonly made between that which is immediately cognized and that which is inferred or concluded. That in a figure which is bounded by three straight lines there are three angles, is an immediate cognition; but that these angles are together equal to two right angles, is an inference or conclusion. Now, as we are constantly employing this mode of thought and have thus become quite accustomed to it, we no longer remark the above distinction, and, as in the case of the so-called deceptions of sense, consider as immediately perceived, what has really been inferred. In every reasoning or syllogism, there is a fundamental proposition, afterwards a second drawn from it, and finally the conclusion, which connects the truth in the first with the truth in the second—and that infallibly. If the judgement concluded is so contained in the first proposition that it can be deduced from it without the meditation of a third notion, the conclusion is called immediate (*consequentia immediata*); I prefer the term conclusion of the understanding. But if, in addition to the fundamental cognition, a second judgement is necessary for the production of the conclusion, it is called a conclusion of the reason. In the proposition: *All men are mortal,* are contained the propositions: *Some men are mortal, Nothing that is not mortal is a man,* and these are therefore immediate conclusions from the first. On the other hand, the proposition: *all the learned are mortal,* is not contained in the main proposition (for the conception of a learned man does not occur in it), and it can be deduced from the main proposition only by means of a mediating judgement.

In every syllogism I first cogitate a *rule* (*the major*) by means of the *understanding.* In the next place I *subsume* a cognition under the condition of the rule (and this is the *minor*) by means of the *judgement.* And finally I *determine* my cognition by means of the predicate of the rule (this is the *conclusio*), consequently, I determine it *a priori* by means of the *reason.* The relations, therefore, which the major proposition, as the rule, represents between a cognition and its condition, constitute the different kinds of syllogisms. These are just threefold—analogously with all judgements, in so far as they differ in the mode of expressing the relation of a cognition in the understanding—namely, *categorical, hypothetical, and disjunctive.*

When, as often happens, the conclusion is a judgement which may follow from other given judgements, through which a perfectly different object is cogitated, I endeavour to discover in the understanding whether the assertion in this conclusion does not stand under certain conditions according to a general rule. If I find such a condition, and if the object mentioned in the conclusion can be subsumed under the given condition, then this conclusion follows from a rule which is also valid for other objects of cognition. From this we see that reason endeavours to subject the great variety of the cognitions of the understanding to the smallest possible number of principles (general conditions), and thus to produce in it the highest unity.

C. OF THE PURE USE OF REASON

Can we isolate reason, and, if so, is it in this case a peculiar source of conceptions and judgements which spring from it alone, and through which it can be applied to objects; or is it merely a subordinate faculty, whose duty it is to give a certain form to given cognitions—a form which is called logical, and through which the cognitions of the understanding are subordinated to each other, and lower rules to higher (those, to wit, whose condition comprises in its sphere the condition of the others), in so far as this can be done by comparison? This is the question which we have at present to answer. Manifold variety of rules and unity of principles is a requirement of reason, for the purpose of bringing the understanding into complete accordance with itself, just as understanding subjects the manifold content of intuition to conceptions, and thereby introduces connection into it. But this principle prescribes no law to objects, and does not contain any ground of the possibility of cognizing or of determining them as such, but is merely a subjective law for the proper arrangement of the content of the understanding. The purpose of this law is, by a comparison of the conceptions of the understanding, to reduce them to the smallest possible number, although, at the same time, it does not justify us in demanding from objects themselves such a uniformity as might contribute to the convenience and the enlargement of the sphere of the understanding, or in expecting that it will itself thus receive from them objective validity. In one word, the question is: "does reason in itself, that is, does pure reason contain *a priori* synthetical principles and rules, and what are those principles?"

The formal and logical procedure of reason in syllogisms gives us sufficient information in regard to the ground on which the transcendental principle of reason in its pure synthetical cognition will rest.

1. Reason, as observed in the syllogistic process, is not applicable to intuitions, for the purpose of subjecting them to rules—for this is the province of the understanding with its categories—but to conceptions and judgements. If pure reason does apply to objects and the intuition of them, it does so not immediately, but mediately—through the understanding and its judgements, which have a direct relation to the

senses and their intuition, for the purpose of determining their objects. The unity of reason is therefore not the unity of a possible experience, but is essentially different from this unity, which is that of the understanding. That everything which happens has a cause, is not a principle cognized and prescribed by reason. This principle makes the unity of experience possible and borrows nothing from reason, which, without a reference to possible experience, could never have produced by means of mere conceptions any such synthetical unity.

2. Reason, in its logical use, endeavours to discover the general condition of its judgement (the conclusion), and a syllogism is itself nothing but a judgement by means of the subsumption of its condition under a general rule (the major). Now as this rule may itself be subjected to the same process of reason, and thus the condition of the condition be sought (by means of a prosyllogism) as long as the process can be continued, it is very manifest that the peculiar principle of reason in its logical use is to find for the conditioned cognition of the understanding the unconditioned whereby the unity of the former is completed.

But this logical maxim cannot be a principle of *pure reason,* unless we admit that, if the conditioned is given, the whole series of conditions subordinated to one another—a series which is consequently itself unconditioned—is also given, that is, contained in the object and its connection.

But this principle of pure reason is evidently *synthetical;* for, analytically, the conditioned certainly relates to some condition, but not to the unconditioned. From this principle also there must originate different synthetical propositions, of which the pure understanding is perfectly ignorant, for it has to do only with objects of a possible experience, the cognition and synthesis of which is always conditioned. The unconditioned, if it does really exist, must be especially considered in regard to the determinations which distinguish it from whatever is conditioned, and will thus afford us material for many *a priori* synthetical propositions.

The principles resulting from this highest principle of pure reason will, however, be *transcendent* in relation to phenomena, that is to say, it will be impossible to make any adequate empirical use of this principle. It is therefore completely different from all principles of the understanding, the use made of which is entirely *immanent,* their object and purpose being merely the possibility of experience. Now our duty in the transcendental dialectic is as follows. To discover whether the principle that the series of conditions (in the synthesis of phenomena, or of thought in general) extends to the unconditioned is objectively true, or not; what consequences result therefrom affecting the empirical use of the understanding, or rather whether there exists any such objectively valid proposition of reason, and whether it is not, on the contrary, a merely logical precept which directs us to ascend perpetually to still higher conditions, to approach completeness in the series of them, and thus to introduce into our cognition the highest possible unity of reason. We must ascertain, I say, whether this requirement of reason has not been regarded, by a misunderstanding, as a transcendental principle of pure reason, which postulates a thorough completeness in the series of conditions in objects themselves. We must show, moreover, the misconceptions and illusions that intrude into syllogisms, the major proposition of which pure reason has supplied—a proposition which has perhaps more of the character of a *petitio* than of a *postulatum* —and that proceed from experience upwards to its conditions. The solution of these problems is our task in transcendental dialectic, which we are about to expose even at its source, that lies deep in human reason. We shall divide it into two parts, the first of which will treat of the *transcendent conceptions* of pure reason, the second of transcendent and *dialectical syllogisms.*

BOOK I

Of the Conceptions of Pure Reason

The conceptions of pure reason—we do not here speak of the possibility of them—are not obtained by reflection, but by inference or conclusion. The conceptions of understanding are also cogitated *a priori* antecedently to experience, and render it possible; but they contain nothing but the unity of reflection upon phenomena, in so far as these must necessarily belong to a possible empirical consciousness. Through them alone are cognition and the determination of an object possible. It is from them, accordingly, that we receive material for reasoning, and antecedently to them we possess no *a priori* conceptions of objects from which they might be deduced. On the other hand, the sole basis of their objective reality consists in the necessity imposed on them, as containing the intellectual form of all experience, of restricting their application and influence to the sphere of experience.

But the term, *conception of reason,* or rational conception, itself indicates that it does not confine itself within the limits of experience, because its object-matter is a cognition, of which every empirical cognition is but a part—nay, the whole of possible experience may be itself but a part of it—a cognition to which no actual experience ever fully attains, although it does always pertain to it. The aim of rational conceptions is the *comprehension,* as that of the conceptions of understanding is the *understanding* of perceptions. If they contain the unconditioned, they relate to that to which all experience is subordinate, but which is never itself an object of experience—that towards which reason tends in all its conclusions from experience, and by the standard of which it estimates the degree of their empirical use, but which is never itself an element in an empirical synthesis. If, notwithstanding, such conceptions possess objective validity, they may be called *conceptus ratiocinati* (conceptions legitimately concluded); in cases where they do not, they have been admitted on account of having the appearance of being correctly concluded, and may be called *conceptus ratiocinantes* (sophistical conceptions). But as this can only be sufficiently demonstrated in that part of our treatise which relates to the dialectical conclusions of reason, we shall omit any consideration of it in this place. As we called the pure conceptions of the understanding *categories,* we shall also distinguish those of pure reason by a new name and call them *transcendental ideas.* These terms, however, we must in the first place explain and justify.

SECTION I—*Of Ideas in General*

DESPITE the great wealth of words which European languages possess, the thinker finds himself often at a loss for an expression exactly suited to his conception, for want of which he is unable to make himself intelligible either to others or to himself. To coin new words is a pretension to legislation in language which is seldom successful; and, before recourse is taken to so desperate an expedient, it is advisable to examine the dead and learned languages, with the hope and the probability that we may there meet with some adequate expression of the notion we have in our minds. In this case, even if the original meaning of the word has become somewhat uncertain, from carelessness or want of caution on the part of the authors of it, it is always better to adhere to and confirm its proper meaning—even although it may be doubtful whether it was formerly used in exactly this sense—than to make our labour vain by want of sufficient care to render ourselves intelligible.

For this reason, when it happens that there exists only a single word to express a certain conception, and this word, in its usual acceptation, is thoroughly adequate to the conception, the accurate distinction of which from related conceptions is of great importance, we ought not to employ the expression improvidently, or, for the sake of variety and elegance of style, use it as a synonym for other cognate words. It is our duty, on the contrary, carefully to preserve its peculiar signification, as otherwise it easily happens that when the attention of the reader is no longer particularly attracted to the expression, and it is lost amid the multitude of other words of very different import, the thought which it conveyed, and which it alone conveyed, is lost with it.

Plato employed the expression *idea* in a way that plainly showed he meant by it something which is never derived from the senses, but which far transcends even the conceptions of the understanding (with which Aristotle occupied himself), inasmuch as in experience nothing perfectly corresponding to them could be found. Ideas are, according to him, archetypes of things themselves, and not merely keys to possible experiences, like the categories. In his view they flow from the highest reason, by which they have been imparted to human reason, which, however, exists no longer in its original state, but is obliged with great labour to recall by reminiscence—which is called philosophy—the old but now sadly obscured ideas. I will not here enter upon any literary investigation of the sense which this sublime philosopher attached to this expression. I shall content myself with remarking that it is nothing unusual, in common conversation as well as in written works, by comparing the thoughts which an author has delivered upon a subject, to understand him better than he understood himself—inasmuch as he may not have sufficiently determined his conception, and thus have sometimes spoken, nay even thought, in opposition to his own opinions.

Plato perceived very clearly that our faculty of cognition has the feeling of a much higher vocation than that of merely spelling out phenomena according to synthetical unity, for the purpose of being able to read them as experience, and that our reason naturally raises itself to cognitions far too elevated to admit of the possibility of an object given by experience corresponding to them—cognitions which are nevertheless real, and are not mere phantoms of the brain.

This philosopher found his ideas especially in all that is practical,[1] that is, which rests upon freedom, which in its turn ranks under cognitions that are the peculiar product of reason. He who would derive from experience the conceptions of virtue, who would make (as many have really done) that, which at best can but serve as an imperfectly illustrative example, a model for the formation of a perfectly adequate idea on the subject, would in fact transform virtue into a nonentity changeable according to time and circumstance and utterly incapable of being employed as a rule. On the contrary, every one is conscious that, when any one is held up to him as a model of virtue, he compares this so-called model with the true original which he possesses in his own mind and values him according to this standard. But this standard is the idea of virtue, in relation to which all possible objects of experience are indeed serviceable as examples—proofs of the practicability in a certain degree of that which the conception of virtue demands—but certainly not as archetypes. That the actions of man will never be in perfect accordance with all the requirements of the pure ideas of reason, does not prove the thought to be chimerical. For only through this idea are all judgements as to moral merit or demerit possible; it consequently lies at the foundation of every approach to moral perfection, however far removed from it the obstacles in human nature—indeterminable as to degree—may keep us.

The Platonic Republic has become proverbial as an example—and a striking one—of imaginary perfection, such as can exist only in the brain of the idle thinker; and Brucker ridicules the philosopher for maintaining that a prince can never govern well, unless he is participant in *the ideas.* But we should do better to follow up this thought and, where this admirable thinker leaves us without assistance, employ new efforts to place it in clearer light, rather than carelessly fling it aside as useless, under the very miserable and pernicious pretext of impracticability. A constitution of *the greatest possible human freedom* according to laws, by which *the liberty of every individual can consist with the liberty of every other* (not of the greatest possible happiness, for this follows necessarily from the former), is, to say the least, a necessary idea, which must be placed at the foundation not only of the first plan of the constitution of a state, but of all its laws. And, in this, it is not necessary at the outset to take account of the obstacles which lie in our way—obstacles which perhaps do not necessarily arise from the character of human nature, but rather from the previous neglect of true ideas in legislation. For there is nothing more pernicious and more unworthy of a philosopher, than the vulgar appeal to a so-called adverse experience, which indeed would not have existed, if those institutions had been established at the proper time and in accordance with ideas; while, instead of this, conceptions, crude for the very reason that they have been drawn from experience, have marred and frustrated all our better views and intentions. The more legislation and government are in harmony with this idea, the more rare do punishments become and thus it is quite reasonable to maintain, as Plato did, that in a perfect state no punishments at all would be necessary. Now although a perfect state may never exist, the idea is not on that account the less just, which holds up this *maximum* as the archetype or standard of a constitution, in order to bring legislative government always nearer and nearer to the greatest possible perfection. For at what precise degree human nature must stop in its progress, and how wide must be the chasm which must necessarily exist between the idea and its realization, are problems which no one can or ought to determine—and for this reason, that it is the destination of freedom to overstep all assigned limits between itself and the idea.

But not only in that wherein human reason is a real causal agent and where ideas are operative causes (of actions and their objects), that is to say, in the region of ethics, but also in regard to nature herself, Plato saw clear proofs of an origin from ideas. A plant, and animal, the regular order of nature—probably also the disposition of the whole universe—give manifest evidence that they are possible only by means of and according to ideas; that, indeed, no one creature, under the individual conditions of its

[1] He certainly extended the application of his conception to speculative cognitions also, provided they were given pure and completely *a priori,* nay, even to mathematics, although this science cannot possess an object otherwhere than in *possible* experience. I cannot follow him in this, and as little can I follow him in his mystical deduction of these ideas, or in his hypostatization of them; although, in truth, the elevated and exaggerated language which he employed in describing them is quite capable of an interpretation more subdued and more in accordance with fact and the nature of things.

existence, perfectly harmonizes with the idea of the most perfect of its kind—just as little as man with the idea of humanity, which nevertheless he bears in his soul as the archetypal standard of his actions; that, notwithstanding, these ideas are in the highest sense individually, unchangeably, and completely determined, and are the original causes of things; and that the totality of connected objects in the universe is alone fully adequate to that idea. Setting aside the exaggerations of expression in the writings of this philosopher, the mental power exhibited in this ascent from the ectypal mode of regarding the physical world to the architectonic connection thereof according to ends, that is, ideas, is an effort which deserves imitation and claims respect. But as regards the principles of ethics, of legislation, and of religion, spheres in which ideas alone render experience possible, although they never attain to full expression therein, he has vindicated for himself a position of peculiar merit, which is not appreciated only because it is judged by the very empirical rules, the validity of which as principles is destroyed by ideas. For as regards nature, experience presents us with rules and is the source of truth, but in relation to ethical laws experience is the parent of illusion, and it is in the highest degree reprehensible to limit or to deduce the laws which dictate what I *ought to do,* from what *is done.*

We must, however, omit the consideration of these important subjects, the development of which is in reality the peculiar duty and dignity of philosophy, and confine ourselves for the present to the more humble but not less useful task of preparing a firm foundation for those majestic edifices of moral science. For this foundation has been hitherto insecure from the many subterranean passages which reason in its confident but vain search for treasures has made in all directions. Our present duty is to make ourselves perfectly acquainted with the transcendental use made of pure reason, its principles and ideas, that we may be able properly to determine and value its influence and real worth. But before bringing these introductory remarks to a close, I beg those who really have philosophy at heart—and their number is but small—if they shall find themselves convinced by the considerations following as well as by those above, to exert themselves to preserve to the expression *idea* its original signification, and to take care that it be not lost among those other expressions by which all sorts of representations are loosely designated—that the interests of science may not thereby suffer. We are in no want of words to denominate adequately every mode of representation, without the necessity of encroaching upon terms which are proper to others. The following is a graduated list of them. The genus is *representation* in general (*representatio*). Under it stands representation with consciousness (*perceptio*). A *perception* which relates solely to the subject as a modification of its state, is a *sensation* (*sensatio*), an objective perception is a *cognition* (*cognitio*). A cognition is either an *intuition* or a *conception* (*intuitus vel conceptus*). The former has an immediate relation to the object and is singular and individual; the latter has but a mediate relation, by means of a characteristic mark which may be common to several things. A conception is either *empirical* or *pure*. A pure conception, in so far as it has its origin in the understanding alone, and is not the conception of a pure sensuous image, is called *notio*. A conception formed from notions, which transcends the possibility of experience, is an *idea,* or a conception of reason. To one who has accustomed himself to these distinctions, it must be quite intolerable to hear the representation of the colour red called an idea. It ought not even to be called a notion or conception of understanding.

Section II. *Of Transcendental Ideas*

Transcendental analytic showed us how the mere logical form of our cognition can contain the origin of pure conceptions *a priori,* conceptions which represent objects antecedently to all experience, or rather, indicate the synthetical unity which alone renders possible an empirical cognition of objects. The form of judgements—converted into a conception of the synthesis of intuitions—produced the categories which direct the employment of the understanding in experience. This consideration warrants us to expect that the form of syllogisms, when applied to synthetical unity of intuitions, following the rule of the categories, will contain the origin of particular *a priori* conceptions, which we may call pure conceptions of reason or transcendental ideas, and which will determine the use of the understanding in the totality of experience according to principles.

The function of reason in arguments consists in the universality of a cognition according to conceptions, and the syllogism itself is a judgement which is determined *a priori* in the whole extent of its condition. The proposition: "Caius is mortal," is one which may be obtained from experience by the aid of the understanding alone; but my wish is to find a conception which contains the condition under which the predicate of this judgement is given—in this case, the conception of *man*—and after subsuming under this condition, taken in its whole extent (all men are mortal), I determine according to it the cognition of the object thought, and say: "Caius is mortal."

Hence, in the conclusion of a syllogism we restrict a predicate to a certain object, after having thought it in the major in its whole extent under a certain condition. This complete quantity of the extent in relation to such a condition is called *universality* (*universalitas*). To this corresponds *totality* (*universitas*) of conditions in the synthesis of intuitions. The transcendental conception of reason is therefore nothing else than the conception of the *totality of the conditions* of a given conditioned. Now as the *unconditioned* alone renders possible totality of conditions, and, conversely, the totality of conditions is itself always unconditioned; a pure rational conception in general can be defined and explained by means of the conception of the unconditioned, in so far as it contains a basis for the synthesis of the conditioned.

To the number of modes of relation which the understanding cogitates by means of the categories, the number of pure rational conceptions will correspond. We must therefore seek for, first, an *unconditioned* of the *categorical* synthesis in a *subject;* secondly, of the *hypothetical* synthesis of the members of a *series;* thirdly, of the *disjunctive* synthesis of parts in a *system.*

There are exactly the same number of modes of syllogisms, each of which proceeds through prosyllogisms to the unconditioned—one to the subject which cannot be employed as predicate, another to the presupposition which supposes nothing higher than itself, and the third to an aggregate of the members of the complete division of a conception. Hence the pure rational conceptions of totality in the synthesis of conditions have a necessary foundation in the nature of human reason—at least as modes of elevating the unity of the understanding to the unconditioned. They may have no valid application, corresponding to their transcendental employment, *in concreto,* and be thus of no greater utility than to direct the understanding how, while extending them as widely as possible, to maintain its exercise and application in perfect consistence and harmony.

But, while speaking here of the totality of conditions and of the unconditioned as the common title of all conceptions of reason, we again light upon an expression which we find it impossible to dispense with, and which nevertheless, owing to the ambiguity attaching to it from long abuse, we cannot employ with safety. The word *absolute* is one of the few words which, in its original signification, was perfectly adequate to the conception it was intended to convey—a conception which no other word in the same language exactly suits, and the loss—or, which is the same thing, the incautious and loose employment—of which must be followed by the loss of the conception itself. And, as it is a conception which occupies much of the attention of reason, its loss would be greatly to the detriment of all transcendental philosophy. The word *absolute* is at present frequently used to denote that something can be predicated of a thing considered *in itself* and intrinsically. In this sense *absolutely possible* would signify that which is possible in itself (*interne*)—which is, in fact, the *least* that one can predicate of an object. On the other hand, it is sometimes employed to indicate that a thing is valid in all respects—for example, absolute sovereignty. *Absolutely possible* would in this sense signify that which is *possible in all relations* and in every respect; and this is the most that can be predicated of the possibility of a thing. Now these significations do in truth frequently coincide. Thus, for example, that which is intrinsically impossible, is also impossible in all relations, that is, absolutely impossible. But in most cases they differ from each other *toto caelo,* and I can by no means conclude that, because a thing is in itself possible, it is also possible in all relations, and therefore absolutely. Nay, more, I shall in the sequel show that absolute necessity does not by any means depend on internal necessity, and that, therefore, it must not be considered as synonymous with it. Of an opposite which is intrinsically impossible, we may affirm that it is in all respects impossible, and that, consequently, the thing itself, of which this is the opposite, is absolutely necessary; but I cannot reason conversely and say, the opposite of that which is absolutely necessary is intrinsically impossible, that is, that the *absolute* necessity of things is an *internal* necessity. For this internal necessity is in certain cases a mere empty word with which the least conception cannot be connected, while the conception of the necessity of a thing in all relations possesses very peculiar determinations. Now as the loss of a conception of great utility in speculative science cannot be a matter of indifference to the philosopher, I trust that the proper determination and careful preservation of the expression on which the conception depends will likewise be not indifferent to him.

In this enlarged signification, then, shall I employ the word *absolute,* in opposition to that which is valid only in some particular respect; for the latter is restricted by conditions, the former is valid without any restriction whatever.

Now the transcendental conception of reason has for its object nothing else than absolute totality in the synthesis of conditions and does not rest satisfied till it has attained to the absolutely, that is, in all respects and relations, unconditioned. For pure reason leaves to the understanding everything that immediately relates to the object of intuition or rather to their synthesis in imagination. The former restricts itself to the absolute totality in the employment of the conceptions of the understanding and aims at carrying out the synthetical unity which is cogitated in the category, even to the unconditioned. This unity may hence be called the *rational unity* of phenomena, as the other, which the category expresses, may be termed the *unity of the understanding.* Reason, therefore, has an immediate relation to the use of the understanding, not indeed in so far as the latter contains the ground of possible experience (for the conception of the absolute totality of conditions is not a conception that can be employed in experience, because no experience is unconditioned), but solely for the purpose of directing it to a certain unity, of which the understanding has no conception, and the aim of which is to collect into an *absolute whole* all acts of the understanding. Hence the objective employment of the pure conceptions of reason is always *transcendent,* while that of the pure conceptions of the understanding must, according to their nature, be always *immanent,* inasmuch as they are limited to possible experience.

I understand by idea a necessary conception of reason, to which no corresponding object can be discovered in the world of sense. Accordingly, the pure conceptions of reason at present under consideration are *transcendental ideas.* They are conceptions of pure reason, for they regard all empirical cognition as determined by means of an absolute totality of conditions. They are not mere fictions, but natural and necessary products of reason, and have hence a necessary relation to the whole sphere of the exercise of the understanding. And, finally, they are transcendent, and overstep the limits of all experiences, in which, consequently, no object can ever be presented that would be perfectly adequate to a transcendental idea. When we use the word *idea,* we say, as regards its object (an object of the pure understanding), a great deal, but as regards its subject (that is, in respect of its reality under conditions of experience), exceedingly little, because the idea, as the conception of a maximum, can never be completely and adequately presented *in concreto.* Now, as in the merely speculative employment of reason the latter is properly the sole aim, and as in this case the approximation to a conception, which is never attained in practice, is the same thing as if the conception were nonexistent—it is commonly said of the conception of this kind, "it is only an idea." So we might very well say, "the absolute totality of all phenomena is only an idea," for, as we never can present an adequate representation of it, it remains for us a *problem* incapable of solution. On the other hand, as in the practical use of the understanding we have only to do with action and practice according to rules, an idea of pure reason can always be given really *in concreto,* although only partially, nay, it is the indispensable condition of all practical employment of reason. The practice or execution of the idea is always limited and defective, but nevertheless within indeterminable boundaries, consequently always under the influence of the conception of an absolute perfection. And thus the practical idea is always in the highest degree fruitful, and in relation to real actions indispensably necessary. In the idea, pure reason possesses even causality and the power of producing that which its conception contains. Hence we cannot say of wisdom, in a disparaging way, " it is only an idea." For, for the very reason that it is the idea of the necessary unity of all possible aims, it must be for all practical exertions and endeavours the primitive condition and rule—a rule which, if not constitutive, is at least limitative.

Now, although we must say of the transcendental conceptions of reason, *"they are only ideas,"* we must not, on this account, look upon them as superfluous and nugatory. For, although no object can be determined by them, they can be of great utility, unobserved and at the basis of the edifice of the understanding, as the canon for its extended and self-consistent exercise—a canon which, indeed, does not enable it to cognize more in an object than it would cognize by the help of its own conceptions, but which guides it more securely in its cognition. Not to mention that they perhaps render possible a transition from our conceptions of nature and the non-ego to the practical conceptions, and thus produce for even ethical ideas keeping, so to speak, and connection with the speculative cognitions of reason. The explication of all this must be looked for in the sequel.

But setting aside, in conformity with our original purpose, the consideration of the practical ideas, we proceed to contemplate reason in its speculative use alone, nay, in a still more restricted sphere, to wit, in the transcendental use; and here must strike into the same path which we followed in our deduction of the categories. That is to say, we shall consider the logical form of the cognition of reason, that we may see whether reason may not be thereby a source of conceptions which enables us to regard objects in themselves as determined synthetically *a priori*, in relation to one or other of the functions of reason.

Reason, considered as the faculty of a certain logical form of cognition, is the faculty of conclusion, that is, of mediate judgement—by means of the subsumption of the condition of a possible judgement under the condition of a given judgement. The given judgement is the general rule (major). The subsumption of the condition of another possible judgement under the condition of the rule is the minor. The actual judgement, which enounces the assertion of the rule in the subsumed case, is the conclusion (*conclusio*). The rule predicates something generally under a certain condition. The condition of the rule is satisfied in some particular case. It follows that what was valid in general under that condition must also be considered as valid in the particular case which satisfies this condition. It is very plain that reason attains to a cognition, by means of acts of the understanding which constitute a series of conditions. When I arrive at the proposition, "All bodies are changeable," by beginning with the more remote cognition (in which the conception of body does not appear, but which nevertheless contains the condition of that conception), "All compound is changeable," by proceeding from this to a less remote cognition, which stands under the condition of the former, "Bodies are compound," and hence to a third, which at length connects for me the remote cognition (changeable) with the one before me, "Consequently, bodies are changeable"—I have arrived at a cognition (conclusion) through a series of conditions (premisses). Now every series, whose exponent (of the categorical or hypothetical judgement) is given, can be continued; consequently the same procedure of reason conducts us to the *ratiocinatio polysyllogistica*, which is a series of syllogisms, that can be continued either on the side of the conditions (*per prosyllogismos*) or of the conditioned (*per episyllogismos*) to an indefinite extent.

But we very soon perceive that the chain or series of prosyllogisms, that is, of deduced cognitions on the side of the grounds or conditions of a given cognition, in other words, the *ascending series* of syllogisms must have a very different relation to the faculty of reason from that of the *descending series*, that is, the progressive procedure of reason on the side of the conditioned by means of episyllogisms. For, as in the former case the cognition (*conclusio*) is given only as conditioned, reason can attain to this cognition only under the presupposition that all the members of the series on the side of the conditions are given (totality in the series of premisses), because only under this supposition is the judgement we may be considering possible *a priori;* while on the side of the conditioned or the inferences, only an incomplete and *becoming*, and not a presupposed or given series, consequently only a potential progression, is cogitated. Hence, when a cognition is contemplated as conditioned, reason is compelled to consider the series of conditions in an ascending line as completed and given in their totality. But if the very same condition is considered at the same time as the condition of other cognitions, which together constitute a series of inferences or consequences in a descending line, reason may preserve a perfect indifference, as to how far this progression may extend *a parte posteriori*, and whether the totality of this series is possible, because it stands in no need of such a series for the purpose of arriving at the conclusion before it, inasmuch as this conclusion is sufficiently guaranteed and determined on grounds *a parte priori*. It may be the case, that upon the side of the conditions the series of premisses has a *first* or highest condition, or it may not possess this, and so be *a parte priori* unlimited; but it must, nevertheless, contain totality of conditions, even admitting that we never could succeed in completely apprehending it; and the whole series must be unconditionally true, if the conditioned, which is considered as an inference resulting from it, is to be held as true. This is a requirement of reason, which announces its cognition as determined *a priori* and as necessary, either in itself—and in this case it needs no grounds to rest upon—or, if it is deduced, as a member of a series of grounds, which is itself unconditionally true.

SECTION III. *System of Transcendental Ideas*

WE are not at present engaged with a logical dialectic, which makes complete abstraction of the content of cognition and aims only at unveiling the illusory appearance in the form of syllogisms. Our subject is transcendental dialectic, which must contain, completely *a priori,* the origin of certain cognitions drawn from pure reason, and the origin of certain deduced conceptions, the object of which cannot be given empirically and which therefore lie beyond the sphere of the faculty of understanding. We have observed, from the natural relation which the transcendental use of our cognition, in syllogisms as well as in judgements, must have to the logical, that there are three kinds of dialectical arguments, corresponding to the three modes of conclusion, by which reason attains to cognitions on principles; and that in all it is the business of reason to ascend from the conditioned synthesis, beyond which the understanding never proceeds, to the unconditioned which the understanding never can reach.

Now the most general relations which can exist in our representations are: 1st, the relation to the subject; 2nd, the relation to objects, either as phenomena, or as objects of thought in general. If we connect this subdivision with the main division, all the relations of our representations, of which we can form either a conception or an idea, are threefold: 1. The relation to the subject; 2. The relation to the manifold of the object as a phenomenon; 3. The relation to all things in general.

Now all pure conceptions have to do in general with the synthetical unity of representations; conceptions of pure reason (transcendental ideas), on the other hand, with the unconditional synthetical unity of all conditions. It follows that all transcendental ideas arrange themselves in three classes, the *first* of which contains the absolute (unconditioned) *unity of the thinking subject*, the *second* the absolute *unity of the series of the conditions* of a phenomenon, the *third* the absolute *unity of the condition of all objects of thought* in general.

The thinking subject is the object-matter of *Psychology;* the sum total of all phenomena (the world) is the object-matter of *Cosmology*; and the thing which contains the highest condition of the possibility of all that is cogitable (the being of all beings) is the object-matter of all *Theology.* Thus pure reason presents us with the idea of a transcendental doctrine of the soul (*psychologia rationalis*), of a transcendental science of the world (*cosmologia rationalis*), and finally of a transcendental doctrine of God (*theologia transcendentalis*). Understanding cannot originate even the outline of any of these sciences, even when connected with the highest logical use of reason, that is, all cogitable syllogisms—for the purpose of proceeding from one object (phenomenon) to all others, even to the utmost limits of the empirical synthesis. They are, on the contrary, pure and genuine products, or problems, of pure reason.

What modi of the pure conceptions of reason these transcendental ideas are will be fully exposed in the following chapter. They follow the guiding thread of the categories. For pure reason never relates immediately to objects, but to the conceptions of these contained in the understanding. In like manner, it will be made manifest in the detailed explanation of these ideas—how reason, merely through the synthetical use of the same function which it employs in a categorical syllogism, necessarily attains to the conception of the absolute unity of the *thinking subject*—how the logical procedure in hypothetical ideas necessarily produces the idea of the absolutely unconditioned *in a series* of given conditions, and finally—how the mere form of the disjunctive syllogism involves the highest conception of a *being of all beings*: a thought which at first sight seems in the highest degree paradoxical.

An *objective deduction,* such as we were able to present in the case of the categories, is impossible as regards these transcendental ideas. For they have, in truth, no relation to any object, in experience, for the very reason that they are only ideas. But a subjective deduction of them from the nature of our reason is possible, and has been given in the present chapter.

It is easy to perceive that the sole aim of pure reason is the absolute totality of the synthesis *on the side of the conditions,* and that it does not concern itself with the absolute completeness *on the part of the conditioned.* For of the former alone does she stand in need, in order to preposit the whole series of conditions, and thus present them to the understanding *a priori.* But if we once have a completely (and unconditionally) given condition, there is no further necessity, in proceeding with the series, for a conception of reason; for the understanding takes of itself every step downward, from the condition to the conditioned. Thus the transcendental ideas are available only for *ascending* in the series of conditions, till we reach the unconditioned, that is, principles. As regards *descending* to the conditioned, on the other hand, we find that there is a widely extensive logical use which reason makes of the laws of the understanding, but that a transcendental use thereof is impossible; and that when we form an idea of the absolute totality of such a synthesis, for example, of the whole series of all *future* changes in the world, this idea is a mere *ens rationis,* an arbitrary fiction of thought, and not a necessary presupposition of reason. For the possibility of the conditioned presupposes the totality of its conditions, but not of its consequences. Consequently, this conception is not a transcendental idea—and it is with these alone that we are at present occupied.

Finally, it is obvious that there exists among the transcendental ideas a certain connection and unity, and that pure reason, by means of them, collects all its cognitions into one system. From the cognition of self to the cognition of the world, and through these to the supreme being, the progression is so natural, that it seems to resemble the logical march of reason from the premisses to the conclusion.[1] Now whether there lies unobserved at the foundation of these ideas an analogy of the same kind as exists between the logical and transcendental procedure of reason, is another of those questions, the answer to which we must not expect till we arrive at a more advanced stage in our inquiries. In this cursory and preliminary view, we have, meanwhile, reached our aim. For we have dispelled the ambiguity which attached to the transcendental conceptions of reason, from their being commonly mixed up with other conceptions in the systems of philosophers, and not properly distinguished from the conceptions of the understanding; we have exposed their origin and, thereby, at the same time their determinate number, and presented them in a systematic connection, and have thus marked out and enclosed a definite sphere for pure reason.

Book II

Of the Dialectical Procedure of Pure Reason

It may be said that the object of a merely transcendental idea is something of which we have no conception, although the idea may be a necessary product of reason according to its original laws. For, in fact, a conception of an object that is adequate to the idea given by reason, is impossible. For such an object must be capable of being presented and intuited in a possible experience. But we should express our meaning better, and with less risk of being misunderstood, if we said that we can have no knowledge of an object, which perfectly corresponds to an idea, although we may possess a problematical conception thereof.

Now the transcendental (subjective) reality at least of the pure conceptions of reason rests upon the fact that we are led to such ideas by a necessary procedure of reason. There must therefore be syllogisms which contain no empirical premisses, and by means of which we conclude from something that we do know, to something of which we do not even possess a conception, to which we, nevertheless, by an unavoidable illusion, ascribe objective reality. Such arguments are, as regards their result, rather to be termed sophisms than syllogisms, although indeed, as regards their origin, they are very well entitled to the latter name, inasmuch as they are not fictions or accidental products of reason, but are necessitated by its very nature. They are sophisms, not of men, but of pure reason herself, from which the wisest cannot free himself. After long labour he may be able to guard against the error, but he can never be thoroughly rid of the illusion which continually mocks and misleads him.

Of these dialectical arguments there are three kinds, corresponding to the number of the ideas which their conclusions present. In the argument or syllogism of the *first class,* I conclude, from the transcendental conception of the subject which contains no manifold, the absolute unity of the subject itself, of which I cannot in this manner attain to a conception. This dialectical argument I shall call the transcendental *pa-*

[1] The science of Metaphysics has for the proper object of its inquiries only three grand ideas: God, Freedom, and Immortality, and it aims at showing, that the second conception, conjoined with the first, must lead to the third, as a necessary conclusion. All the other subjects with which it occupies itself, are merely means for the attainment and realization of these ideas. It does not require these ideas for the construction of a science of nature, but, on the contrary, for the purpose of passing beyond the sphere of nature. A complete insight into and comprehension of them would render *Theology, Ethics,* and, through the conjunction of both, *Religion,* solely dependent on the speculative faculty of reason. In a systematic representation of these ideas the above-mentioned arrangement—the *synthetical* one—would be the most suitable; but in the investigation which must necessarily precede it, the *analytical,* which reverses this arrangement, would be better adapted to our purpose, as in it we should proceed from that which experience immediately presents to us—psychology, to cosmology, and thence to theology.

ralogism. The *second class* of sophistical arguments is occupied with the transcendental conception of the absolute totality of the series of conditions for a given phenomenon, and I conclude, from the fact that I have always a self-contradictory conception of the unconditioned synthetical unity of the series upon one side, the truth of the opposite unity, of which I have nevertheless no conception. The condition of reason in these dialectical arguments, I shall term the *antinomy* of pure reason. Finally, according to the *third* kind of sophistical argument, I conclude, from the totality of the conditions of thinking objects in general, in so far as they can be given, the absolute synthetical unity of all conditions of the possibility of things in general; that is, from things which I do not know in their mere transcendental conception, I conclude a being of all beings which I know still less by means of a transcendental conception, and of whose unconditioned necessity I can form no conception whatever. This dialectical argument I shall call the *ideal* of pure reason.

Chapter I. *Of the Paralogisms of Pure Reason*

The logical paralogism consists in the falsity of an argument in respect of its form, be the content what it may. But a transcendental paralogism has a transcendental foundation, and concludes falsely, while the form is correct and unexceptionable. In this manner the paralogism has its foundation in the nature of human reason, and is the parent of an unavoidable, though not insoluble, mental illusion.

We now come to a conception which was not inserted in the general list of transcendental conceptions, and yet must be reckoned with them, but at the same time without in the least altering, or indicating a deficiency in that table. This is the conception, or, if the term is preferred, the judgement, "I think." But it is readily perceived that this thought is as it were the vehicle of all conceptions in general, and consequently of transcendental conceptions also, and that it is therefore regarded as a transcendental conception, although it can have no peculiar claim to be so ranked, inasmuch as its only use is to indicate that all thought is accompanied by consciousness. At the same time, pure as this conception is from empirical content (impressions of the senses), it enables us to distinguish two different kinds of objects. "I," as thinking, am an object of the internal sense, and am called *soul.* That which is an object of the external senses is called *body.* Thus the expression, "I," as a thinking being, designates the object-matter of psychology, which may be called "the rational doctrine of the soul," inasmuch as in this science I desire to know nothing of the soul but what, independently of all experience (which determines me *in concreto*), may be concluded from this conception "I," in so far as it appears in all thought.

Now, the *rational* doctrine of the soul is really an undertaking of this kind. For if the smallest empirical element of thought, if any particular perception of my internal state, were to be introduced among the grounds of cognition of this science, it would not be a rational, but an *empirical* doctrine of the soul. We have thus before us a pretended science, raised upon the single proposition, "I think," whose foundation or want of foundation we may very properly, and agreeably with the nature of a transcendental philosophy, here examine. It ought not to be objected that in this proposition, which expresses the perception of one's self, an internal experience is asserted, and that consequently the rational doctrine of the soul which is founded upon it, is not pure, but partly founded upon an empirical principle. For this internal perception is nothing more than the mere apperception, "I think," which in fact renders all transcendental conceptions possible, in which we say, "I think substance, cause, etc." For internal experience in general and its possibility, or perception in general, and its relation to other perceptions, unless some particular distinction or determination thereof is empirically given, cannot be regarded as empirical cognition, but as cognition of the empirical, and belongs to the investigation of the possibility of every experience, which is certainly transcendental. The smallest object of experience (for example, only pleasure or pain), that should be included in the general representation of self-consciousness, would immediately change the rational into an empirical psychology.

"I think" is therefore the only text of rational psychology, from which it must develop its whole system. It is manifest that this thought, when applied to an object (myself), can contain nothing but transcendental predicates thereof; because the least empirical predicate would destroy the purity of the science and its independence of all experience.

But we shall have to follow here the guidance of the categories—only, as in the present case a thing, "I," as thinking being, is at first given, we shall—not indeed change the order of the categories as it stands in the table—but begin at the category of substance, by which a thing in itself is represented, and proceed backwards through the series. The topic of the rational doctrine of the soul, from which everything else it may contain must be deduced, is accordingly as follows:

1

The Soul is SUBSTANCE

2

As regards its quality it is SIMPLE

3

As regards the different times in which it exists, it is numerically identical, that is UNITY, not Plurality

4

It is in relation to *possible* objects in space[1]

From these elements originate all the conceptions of pure psychology, by combination alone, without the aid of any other principle. This substance, merely as an object of the internal sense, gives the conception of *Immateriality;* as simple substance, that of *Incorruptibility;* its identity, as intellectual substance, gives the conception of *Personality;* all these three together, *Spirituality.* Its relation to objects in space gives us the conception of connection (*commercium*) with bodies. Thus it represents thinking substance as the principle of life in matter, that is, as a soul (*anima*), and as the ground of *Animality;* and this, limited and determined by the conception of spirituality, gives us that of *Immortality.*

Now to these conceptions relate four paralogisms of a transcendental psychology, which is falsely held to be a science of pure reason, touching the nature of our thinking being. We can, however, lay at the foundation of this science nothing but the simple and in itself perfectly contentless representation "I," which cannot even be called a conception, but merely a consciousness which accompanies all conceptions. By this "I," or "He," or "It," who or which thinks, nothing more is represented than a transcendental subject of thought=x, which is cognized only by means of the thoughts that are its predicates, and of which, apart from these, we cannot form the least conception. Hence we are obliged to go round this representation in a perpetual circle, inasmuch as we must always employ it, in order to frame any judgement respecting it. And this inconvenience we find it impossible to rid ourselves of, because consciousness in itself is not so much a representation distinguishing a particular object, as a form of representation in general, in so far as it may be termed cognition; for in and by cognition alone do I think anything.

It must, however, appear extraordinary at first sight that the condition under which I think, and which is consequently a property of my subject, should be held to be likewise valid for every existence which thinks, and that we can presume to base upon a seemingly empirical proposition a judgement which is apodeictic and universal, to wit, that everything which thinks is constituted as the voice of my consciousness declares it to be, that is, as a self-conscious being. The cause of this belief is to be found in the fact that we necessarily attribute to things *a priori* all the properties which constitute conditions under which alone we can cogitate them. Now I cannot obtain the least representation of a thinking being by means of external experience, but solely through self-consciousness. Such objects are consequently nothing more than the transference of this consciousness of mine to other things which can only thus be represented as thinking beings. The proposition, "I think," is, in the present case, understood in a problematical sense, not in so far as it contains a perception of an existence (like the Cartesian *"Cogito, ergo sum"*),[2] but in regard to its mere possibility—for the purpose of discovering what properties may be inferred from so simple a proposition and predicated of the subject of it.

If at the foundation of our pure rational cognition of thinking beings there lay more than the mere *Cogito*—if we could likewise call in aid observations on the play of our thoughts, and the thence derived natural laws of the thinking self, there would arise an empirical psychology which would be a kind of physiology of the internal sense and might possibly be capable of explaining the phenomena of that sense. But it could never be available for discovering those properties which do not belong to possible experience (such as the quality of simplicity), nor could it make any apodeictic enunciation on the nature of thinking beings:

[1] The reader, who may not so easily perceive the psychological sense of these expressions, taken here in their transcendental abstraction, and cannot guess why the latter attribute of the soul belongs to the category of *existence,* will find the expressions sufficiently explained and justified in the sequel. I have, moreover, to apologize for the Latin terms which have been employed, instead of their German synonyms, contrary to the rules of correct writing. But I judged it better to sacrifice elegance to perspicuity.

[2] ["I think, therefore I am."]

it would therefore not be a rational psychology.

Now, as the proposition "I think" (in the problematical sense) contains the form of every judgement in general and is the constant accompaniment of all the categories, it is manifest that conclusions are drawn from it only by a transcendental employment of the understanding. This use of the understanding excludes all empirical elements; and we cannot, as has been shown above, have any favourable conception beforehand of its procedure. We shall therefore follow with a critical eye this proposition through all the predicaments of pure psychology; but we shall, for brevity's sake, allow this examination to proceed in an uninterrupted connection.

Before entering on this task, however, the following general remark may help to quicken our attention to this mode of argument. It is not merely through my thinking that I cognize an object, but only through my determining a given intuition in relation to the unity of consciousness in which all thinking consists. It follows that I cognize myself, not through my being conscious of myself as thinking, but only when I am conscious of the intuition of myself as determined in relation to the function of thought. All the modi of self-consciousness in thought are hence not conceptions of objects (conceptions of the understanding—categories); they are mere logical functions, which do not present to thought an object to be cognized, and cannot therefore present my Self as an object. Not the consciousness of the *determining*, but only that of the *determinable* self, that is, of my internal intuition (in so far as the manifold contained in it can be connected conformably with the general condition of the unity of apperception in thought), is the object.

1. In all judgements I am the *determining* subject of that relation which constitutes a judgement. But that the I which thinks, must be considered as in thought always a *subject,* and as a thing which cannot be a predicate to thought, is an apodeictic and *identical* proposition. But this proposition does not signify that I, as an object, am, for myself, a *self-subsistent being* or *substance.* This latter statement—an ambitious one—requires to be supported by data which are not to be discovered in thought; and are perhaps (in so far as I consider the thinking self merely *as such*) not to be discovered in the thinking self at all.

2. That the *I* or *Ego* of apperception, and consequently in all thought, is *singular* or simple, and cannot be resolved into a plurality of subjects, and therefore indicates a logically simple subject—this is self-evident from the very conception of an Ego, and is consequently an analytical proposition. But this is not tantamount to declaring that the thinking Ego is a simple *substance*—for this would be a synthetical proposition. The conception of substance always relates to intuitions, which with me cannot be other than sensuous, and which consequently lie completely out of the sphere of the understanding and its thought: but to this sphere belongs the affirmation that the Ego is simple in thought. It would indeed be surprising, if the conception of "substance," which in other cases requires so much labour to distinguish from the other elements presented by intuition—so much trouble, too, to discover whether it can be simple (as in the case of the parts of matter)—should be presented immediately to me, as if by revelation, in the poorest mental representation of all.

3. The proposition of the identity of my Self amidst all the manifold representations of which I am conscious, is likewise a proposition lying in the conceptions themselves, and is consequently analytical. But this identity of the subject, of which I am conscious in all its representations, does not relate to or concern the intuition of the subject, by which it is given as an object. This proposition cannot therefore enounce the identity of the person, by which is understood the consciousness of the identity of its own substance as a thinking being in all change and variation of circumstances. To prove this, we should require not a mere analysis of the proposition, but synthetical judgements based upon a given intuition.

4. I distinguish my own existence, as that of a thinking being, from that of other things external to me—among which my body also is reckoned. This is also an analytical proposition, for *other* things are exactly those which I think as different or *distinguished* from myself. But whether this consciousness of myself is possible *without* things external to me; and whether therefore I can exist merely as a thinking being (without being man)—cannot be known or inferred from this proposition.

Thus we have gained nothing as regards the cognition of myself as object, by the analysis of the consciousness of my Self in thought. The logical exposition of thought in general is mistaken for a metaphysical determination of the object.

Our *Critique* would be an investigation utterly superfluous, if there existed a possibility of proving *a priori,* that all thinking beings are in themselves simple substances, as such, therefore, possess the inseparable attribute of personality, and are conscious of their existence apart from and unconnected with matter. For we should thus have taken a step beyond the world of sense, and have penetrated into the sphere of *noumena;* and in this case the right could not be denied us of extending our knowledge in this sphere, of establishing ourselves, and, under a favouring star, appropriating to ourselves possessions in it. For the proposition: "Every thinking being, as such, is simple substance," is an *a priori* synthetical proposition; because in the first place it goes beyond the conception which is the subject of it, and adds to the mere notion of a thinking being the *mode of its existence,* and in the second place annexes a predicate (that of simplicity) to the latter conception—a predicate which it could not have discovered in the sphere of experience. It would follow that *a priori* synthetical propositions are possible and legitimate, not only, as we have maintained, in relation to objects of possible experience, and as principles of the possibility of this experience itself, but are applicable to things in themselves—an inference which makes an end of the whole of this *Critique,* and obliges us to fall back on the old mode of metaphysical procedure. But indeed the danger is not so great, if we look a little closer into the question.

There lurks in the procedure of rational psychology a paralogism, which is represented in the following syllogism:

That which cannot be cogitated otherwise than as subject, does not exist otherwise than as subject, and is therefore substance.

A thinking being, considered merely as such, cannot be cogitated otherwise than as subject.

Therefore it exists also as such, that is, as substance.

In the major we speak of a being that can be cogitated generally and in every relation, consequently as it may be given in intuition. But in the minor we speak of the same being only in so far as it regards itself as subject, relatively to thought and the unity of consciousness, but not in relation to intuition, by which it is presented as an object to thought. Thus the conclusion is here arrived at by a *Sophisma figurae dictionis.*[1]

That this famous argument is a mere paralogism, will be plain to any one who will consider the general remark which precedes our exposition of the principles of the pure understanding, and the section on noumena. For it was there proved that the conception of a thing, which can exist *per se*—only as a subject and never as a predicate, possesses no objective reality; that is to say, we can never know whether there exists any object to correspond to the conception; consequently, the conception is nothing more than a conception, and from it we derive no proper knowledge. If this conception is to indicate by the term *substance,* an object that can be given, if it is to become a cognition, we must have at the foundation of the cognition a permanent intuition, as the indispensable condition of its objective reality. For through intuition alone can an object be given. But in internal intuition there is nothing permanent, for the Ego is but the consciousness of my thought. If then, we appeal merely to thought, we cannot discover the necessary condition of the application of the conception of substance—that is, of a subject existing *per se*—to the subject as a thinking being. And thus the conception of the simple nature of substance, which is connected with the objective reality of this conception, is shown to be also invalid, and to be, in fact, nothing more than the logical qualitative unity of self-consciousness in thought; whilst we remain perfectly ignorant whether the subject is composite or not.

Refutation of the Argument of Mendelssohn for the Substantiality or Permanence of the Soul

This acute philosopher easily perceived the insufficiency of the common argument which attempts to prove that the soul—it being granted that it is a simple being—cannot perish by *dissolution* or *decomposition;* he saw it is not impossible for it to cease to be by *extinction,* or *disappearance.* He endeavoured to prove in his *Phaedo,* that the soul cannot be annihilated, by showing that a simple being cannot

[1] *Thought* is taken in the two premisses in two totally different senses. In the major it is considered as relating and applying to objects in general, consequently to objects of intuition also. In the minor, we understand it as relating merely to self-consciousness. In this sense, we do not cogitate an object, but merely the relation to the self-consciousness of the subject, as the form of thought. In the former premiss we speak of things which cannot be cogitated otherwise than as subjects. In the second, we do not speak of *things,* but of *thought* (all objects being abstracted), in which the Ego is always the subject of consciousness. Hence the conclusion cannot be, "I cannot exist otherwise than as subject"; but only "I can, in cogitating my existence, employ my Ego only as the subject of the judgement." But this is an identical proposition, and throws no light on the mode of my existence.

cease to exist. Inasmuch as, he said, a simple existence cannot diminish, nor gradually lose portions of its being, and thus be by degrees reduced to nothing (for it possesses no parts, and therefore no multiplicity), between the moment in which it is, and the moment in which it is not, no time can be discovered—which is impossible. But this philosopher did not consider that, granting the soul to possess this simple nature, which contains no parts external to each other and consequently no extensive quantity, we cannot refuse to it any less than to any other being, intensive quantity, that is, a degree of reality in regard to all its faculties, nay, to all that constitutes its existence. But this degree of reality can become less and less through an infinite series of smaller degrees. It follows, therefore, that this supposed substance—this thing, the permanence of which is not assured in any other way, may, if not by decomposition, by gradual loss (*remissio*) of its powers (consequently by elanguescence, if I may employ this expression), be changed into nothing. For consciousness itself has always a degree, which may be lessened.[1] Consequently the faculty of being conscious may be diminished; and so with all other faculties. The permanence of the soul, therefore, as an object of the internal sense, remains undemonstrated, nay, even indemonstrable. Its permanence in life is evident, *per se*, inasmuch as the thinking being (as man) is to itself, at the same time, an object of the external senses. But this does not authorize the rational psychologist to affirm, from mere conceptions, its permanence beyond life.[2]

If, now, we take the above propositions—as they must be accepted as valid for all thinking beings in the system of rational psychology—in synthetical connection, and proceed, from the category of relation, with the proposition: "All thinking beings are, as such, substances," backwards through the series, till the circle is completed; we come at last to their existence, of which, in this system of rational psychology, substances are held to be conscious, independently of external things; nay, it is asserted that, in relation to the permanence which is a necessary characteristic of substance, they can of themselves determine external things. It follows that *idealism*—at least problematical idealism, is perfectly unavoidable in this rationalistic system. And, if the existence of outward things is not held to be requisite to the determination of the existence of a substance in time, the existence of these outward things at all, is a gratuitous assumption which remains without the possibility of a proof.

[1] Clearness is not, as logicians maintain, the consciousness of a representation. For a certain degree of consciousness, which may not, however, be sufficient for recollection, is to be met with in many dim representations. For without any consciousness at all, we should not be able to recognize any difference in the obscure representations we connect; as we really can do with many conceptions, such as those of right and justice, and those of the musician, who strikes at once several notes in improvising a piece of music. But a representation is clear, in which our consciousness is sufficient for the *consciousness of the difference* of this representation from others. If we are only conscious that there is a difference, but are not conscious of the difference—that is, what the difference is—the representation must be termed obscure. There is, consequently, an infinite series of degrees of consciousness down to its entire disappearance.

[2] There are some who think they have done enough to establish a new possibility in the mode of the existence of souls, when they have shown that there is no contradiction in their hypotheses on this subject. Such are those who affirm the possibility of thought—of which they have no other knowledge than what they derive from its use in connecting empirical intuitions presented in this our human life—after this life has ceased. But it is very easy to embarrass them by the introduction of counter-possibilities, which rest upon quite as good a foundation. Such, for example, is the possibility of the division of a *simple substance* into several substances; and conversely, of the coalition of several into one simple substance. For, although divisibility presupposes composition, it does not necessarily require a composition of substances, but only of the degrees (of the several faculties) of one and the same substance. Now we can cogitate all the powers and faculties of the soul—even that of consciousness—as diminished by one half, the substance still remaining. In the same way we can represent to ourselves without contradiction, this obliterated half as preserved, not in the soul, but without it; and we can believe that, as in this case everything that is real in the soul, and has a degree—consequently its entire existence—has been halved, a particular substance would arise out of the soul. For the multiplicity, which has been divided, formerly existed, but not as a multiplicity of substances, but of every reality as the quantum of existence in it; and the unity of substance was merely a mode of existence, which by this division alone has been transformed into a plurality of subsistence. In the same manner several simple substances might coalesce into one, without anything being lost except the plurality of subsistence, inasmuch as the one substance would contain the degree of reality of all the former substances. Perhaps, indeed, the simple substances, which appear under the form of matter, might (not indeed by a mechanical or chemical influence upon each other, but by an unknown influence, of which the former would be but the phenomenal appearance), by means of such a *dynamical* division of the parent-souls, as *intensive quantities*, produce other souls, while the former repaired the loss thus sustained with new matter of the same sort. I am far from allowing any value to such chimeras; and the principles of our analytic have clearly proved that no other than an empirical use of the categories—that of substance, for example—is possible. But if the rationalist is bold enough to construct, on the mere authority of the faculty of thought—without any intuition, whereby an object is given—a self-subsistent being, merely because the unity of apperception in thought cannot allow him to believe it a composite being, instead of declaring, as he ought to do, that he is unable to explain the possibility of a thinking nature; what ought to hinder the *materialist*, with as complete an independence of experience, to employ the principle of the rationalist in a directly opposite manner—still preserving the formal unity required by his opponent?

But if we proceed *analytically*—the "I think" as a proposition containing in itself an existence as given, consequently modality being the principle—and dissect this proposition, in order to ascertain its content, and discover whether and how this *Ego* determines its existence in time and space without the aid of anything external; the propositions of rationalistic psychology would not begin with the conception of a thinking being, but with a reality, and the properties of a thinking being in general would be deduced from the mode in which this reality is cogitated, after everything empirical had been abstracted; as is shown in the following table:

1

I think,

2 *as Subject,* 3 *as simple Subject,*

4

as identical Subject,
in every state of my thought.

Now, inasmuch as it is not determined in this second proposition, whether I can exist and be cogitated only as subject, and not also as a predicate of another being, the conception of a subject is here taken in a merely logical sense; and it remains undetermined, whether substance is to be cogitated under the conception or not. But in the third proposition, the absolute unity of apperception—the simple *Ego* in the representation to which all connection and separation, which constitute thought, relate, is of itself important; even although it presents us with no information about the constitution or subsistence of the subject. Apperception is something real, and the simplicity of its nature is given in the very fact of its possibility. Now in space there is nothing real that is at the same time simple; for points, which are the only simple things in space, are merely limits, but not constituent parts of space. From this follows the impossibility of a definition on the basis of materialism of the constitution of my *Ego* as a merely thinking subject. But, because my existence is considered in the first proposition as given, for it does not mean, "Every thinking being exists" (for this would be predicating of them absolute necessity), but only, "*I exist* thinking"; the proposition is quite empirical, and contains the determinability of my existence merely in relation to my representations in time. But as I require for this purpose something that is permanent, such as is not given in internal intuition; the mode of my existence, whether as substance or as accident, cannot be determined by means of this simple self-consciousness. Thus, if materialism is inadequate to explain the mode in which I exist, spiritualism is likewise as insufficient; and the conclusion is that we are utterly unable to attain to any knowledge of the constitution of the soul, in so far as relates to the possibility of its existence apart from external objects.

And, indeed, how should it be possible, merely by the aid of the unity of consciousness—which we cognize only for the reason that it is indispensable to the possibility of experience—to pass the bounds of experience (our existence in this life); and to extend our cognition to the nature of all thinking beings by means of the empirical—but in relation to every sort of intuition, perfectly undetermined—proposition, "I think"?

There does not then exist any rational psychology as a *doctrine* furnishing any addition to our knowledge of ourselves. It is nothing more than a *discipline,* which sets impassable limits to speculative reason in this region of thought, to prevent it, on the one hand, from throwing itself into the arms of a soulless materialism, and, on the other, from losing itself in the mazes of a baseless spiritualism. It teaches us to consider this refusal of our reason to give any satisfactory answer to questions which reach beyond the limits of this our human life, as a hint to abandon fruitless speculation; and to direct, to a practical use, our knowledge of ourselves—which, although applicable only to objects of experience, receives its principles from a higher source, and regulates its procedure as if our destiny reached far beyond the boundaries of experience and life.

From all this it is evident that rational psychology has its origin in a mere misunderstanding. The unity of consciousness, which lies at the basis of the categories, is considered to be an intuition of the subject as an object; and the category of substance is applied to the intuition. But this unity is nothing more than the unity in *thought,* by which no object is given; to which therefore the category of substance—which always presupposes a given intuition—cannot be applied. Consequently, the subject cannot be cognized. The subject of the categories cannot, therefore, for the very reason that it cogitates these, frame any conception of itself as an object of the categories; for, to cogitate these, it must lay at the foundation its own pure self-consciousness—the very thing that it wishes to explain and describe. In like manner, the subject, in which the representation of time has its basis, cannot determine, for this very reason, its own existence in time. Now, if the latter is impossible, the former, as an attempt to determine itself by means of the categories as a thinking being in general, is no less so.[1]

Thus, then, appears the vanity of the hope of establishing a cognition which is to extend its rule beyond the limits of experience—a cognition which is one of the highest interests of humanity; and thus is proved the futility of the attempt of speculative philosophy in this region of thought. But, in this interest of thought, the severity of criticism has rendered to reason a not unimportant service, by the demonstration of the impossibility of making any dogmatical affirmation concerning an object of experience beyond the boundaries of experience. She has thus fortified reason against all affirmations of the contrary. Now, this can be accomplished in only two ways. Either our proposition must be proved apodeictically; or, if this is unsuccessful, the sources of this inability must be sought for, and, if these are discovered to exist in the natural and necessary limitation of our reason, our opponents must submit to the same law of renunciation and refrain from advancing claims to dogmatic assertion.

But the right, say rather the necessity to admit a future life, upon principles of the practical conjoined with the speculative use of reason, has lost nothing by this renunciation; for the merely speculative proof has never had any influence upon the common reason of men. It stands upon the point of a hair, so that even the schools have been able to preserve it from falling only by incessantly discussing it and spinning it like a top; and even in their eyes it has never been able to present any safe foundation for the erection of a theory. The proofs which have been current among men, preserve their value undiminished; nay, rather gain in clearness and unsophisticated power, by the rejection of the dogmatical assumptions of speculative reason. For reason is thus confined within her own peculiar province—the arrangement of ends or aims, which is at the same time the arrangement of nature; and, as a practical faculty, without limiting itself to the latter, it is justified in extending the former, and with it our own existence, beyond the boundaries of experience and life. If we turn our attention to the *analogy of the nature* of living beings in this world, in the consideration of which reason is obliged to accept as a principle that no organ, no faculty, no appetite is useless, and that nothing is superfluous, nothing disproportionate to its use, nothing unsuited to its end; but that, on the contrary, everything is perfectly conformed to its destination in life—we shall find that man, who alone is the final end and aim of this order, is still the only animal that seems to be excepted from it. For his natural gifts — not merely as regards the talents and motives that may incite him to employ them, but especially the moral law in him—stretch so far beyond all mere earthly utility and advantage, that he feels himself bound to prize the mere consciousness of probity, apart from all advantageous consequences—even the shadowy gift of posthumous fame—above everything; and he is conscious of an inward call to constitute himself, by his conduct in this world—without regard to mere sublunary interests—the citizen of a better. This mighty, irresistible proof — accompanied by an ever-increasing knowledge of the conformability to a purpose in everything we see around us, by the conviction of the boundless immensity of creation, by the consciousness of a certain illimitableness in the possible ex-

[1] The "I think" is, as has been already stated, an empirical proposition, and contains the proposition, "I exist." But I cannot say, "Everything, which thinks, exists"; for in this case the property of thought would constitute all beings possessing it, necessary beings. Hence my existence cannot be considered as an inference from the proposition, "I think," as Descartes maintained—because in this case the major premiss, "Everything, which thinks, exists," must precede—but the two propositions are identical. The proposition, "I think," expresses an undetermined empirical intuition, that is, perception (proving consequently that sensation, which must belong to sensibility, lies at the foundation of this proposition); but it precedes experience, whose province it is to determine an object of perception by means of the categories in relation to time; and existence in this proposition is not a category, as it does not apply to an undetermined given object, but only to one of which we have a conception, and about which we wish to know whether it does or does not exist, out of, and apart from this conception. An undetermined perception signifies here merely something real that has been given, only, however, to thought in general—but not as a phenomenon, nor as a thing in itself (noumenon), but only as something that really exists, and is designated as such in the proposition, "I think." For it must be remarked that, when I call the proposition, "I think," an empirical proposition, I do not thereby mean that the *Ego* in the proposition is an empirical representation; on the contrary, it is purely intellectual, because it belongs to thought in general. But without some empirical representation, which presents to the mind material for thought, the mental act, "I think," would not take place; and the empirical is only the condition of the application or employment of the pure intellectual faculty.

tension of our knowledge, and by a desire commensurate therewith—remains to humanity, even after the theoretical cognition of ourselves has failed to establish the necessity of an existence after death.

Conclusion of the Solution of the Psychological Paralogism

The dialectical illusion in rational psychology arises from our confounding an idea of reason (of a pure intelligence) with the conception —in every respect undetermined—of a thinking being in general. I cogitate myself in behalf of a possible experience, at the same time making abstraction of all actual experience; and infer therefrom that I can be conscious of myself apart from experience and its empirical conditions. I consequently confound the possible *abstraction* of my empirically determined existence with the supposed consciousness of a possible *separate* existence of my thinking self; and I believe that I cognize what is substantial in myself as a transcendental subject, when I have nothing more in thought than the unity of consciousness, which lies at the basis of all determination of cognition.

The task of explaining the community of the soul with the body does not properly belong to the psychology of which we are here speaking; because it proposes to prove the personality of the soul apart from this communion (after death), and is therefore *transcendent* in the proper sense of the word, although occupying itself with an object of experience—only in so far, however, as it ceases to be an object of experience. But a sufficient answer may be found to the question in our system. The difficulty which lies in the execution of this task consists, as is well known, in the presupposed heterogeneity of the object of the internal sense (the soul) and the objects of the external senses; inasmuch as the formal condition of the intuition of the one is time, and of that of the other space also. But if we consider that both kinds of objects do not differ internally, but only in so far as the one *appears* externally to the other—consequently, that what lies at the basis of phenomena, as a thing in itself, may not be heterogeneous; this difficulty disappears. There then remains no other difficulty than is to be found in the question—how a community of substances is possible; a question which lies out of the region of psychology, and which the reader, after what in our *analytic* has been said of primitive forces and faculties, will easily judge to be also beyond the region of human cognition.

General Remark

On the Transition from Rational Psychology to Cosmology

The proposition, "I think," or, "I exist thinking," is an empirical proposition. But such a proposition must be based on empirical intuition, and the object cogitated as a phenomenon; and thus our theory appears to maintain that the soul, even in thought, is merely a phenomenon; and in this way our consciousness itself, in fact, abuts upon nothing.

Thought, *per se,* is merely the purely spontaneous logical function which operates to connect the manifold of a possible intuition; and it does not represent the subject of consciousness as a phenomenon—for this reason alone, that it pays no attention to the question whether the mode of intuiting it is sensuous or intellectual. I therefore do not represent myself in thought either as I am, or as I appear to myself; I merely cogitate myself as an object in general, of the mode of intuiting which I make abstraction. When I represent myself as the *subject* of thought, or as the *ground* of thought, these modes of representation are not related to the categories of substance or of cause; for these are functions of thought applicable only to our sensuous intuition. The application of these categories to the *Ego* would, however, be necessary, if I wished to make myself an object of knowledge. But I wish to be conscious of myself only as thinking; in what mode my Self is given in intuition, I do not consider, and it may be that I, who think, am a phenomenon —although not in so far as I am a thinking being; but in the consciousness of myself in mere thought I am a being, though this consciousness does not present to me any property of this being as material for thought.

But the proposition, "I think," in so far as it declares, "*I exist* thinking," is not the mere representation of a logical function. It determines the subject (which is in this case an object also) in relation to existence; and it cannot be given without the aid of the internal sense, whose intuition presents to us an object, not as a thing in itself, but always as a phenomenon. In this proposition there is therefore something more to be found than the mere spontaneity of thought; there is also the receptivity of intuition, that is, my thought of myself applied to the empirical intuition of myself. Now, in this intuition the thinking self must seek the conditions of the employment of its logical functions as categories of substance, cause, and so forth; not merely for the purpose of distinguishing itself as an object in itself by means of the representation "I," but also for the purpose of determining the mode of its existence, that is, of cognizing itself as noumenon. But this is impossible, for the internal empirical intuition is sensuous, and presents us with nothing but phenomenal data, which do not assist the object of pure consciousness in its attempt to cognize itself as a separate existence, but are useful only as contributions to experience.

But, let it be granted that we could discover, not in experience, but in certain firmly-established *a priori* laws of the use of pure reason—laws relating to our existence, authority to consider ourselves as legislating *a priori* in relation to our own existence and as determining this existence; we should, on this supposition, find ourselves possessed of a spontaneity, by which our actual existence would be determinable, without the aid of the conditions of empirical intuition. We should also become aware that in the consciousness of our existence there was an *a priori* content, which would serve to determine our own existence—an existence only sensuously determinable—relatively, however, to a certain internal faculty in relation to an intelligible world.

But this would not give the least help to the attempts of rational psychology. For this wonderful faculty, which the consciousness of the moral law in me reveals, would present me with a principle of the determination of my own existence which is purely intellectual—but by what predicates? By none other than those which are given in sensuous intuition. Thus I should find myself in the same position in rational psychology which I formerly occupied, that is to say, I should find myself still in need of sensuous intuitions, in order to give significance to my conceptions of substance and cause, by means of which alone I can possess a knowledge of myself: but these intuitions can never raise me above the sphere of experience. I should be justified, however, in applying these conceptions, in regard to their practical use, which is always directed to objects of experience—in conformity with their analogical significance when employed theoretically—to freedom and its subject. At the same time, I should understand by them merely the logical functions of subject and predicate, of principle and consequence, in conformity with which all actions are so determined, that they are capable of being explained along with the laws of nature, conformably to the categories of substance and cause, although they originate from a very different principle. We have made these observations for the purpose of guarding against misunderstanding, to which the doctrine of our intuition of self as a phenomenon is exposed. We shall have occasion to perceive their utility in the sequel.

Chapter II. *The Antinomy of Pure Reason*

We showed in the introduction to this part of our work, that all transcendental illusion of pure reason arose from dialectical arguments, the schema of which logic gives us in its three formal species of syllogisms—just as the categories find their logical schema in the four functions of all judgements. The first kind of these sophistical arguments related to the unconditioned unity of the *subjective* conditions of all representations in general (of the subject or soul), in correspondence with the *categorical* syllogisms, the major of which, as the principle, enounces the relation of a predicate to a subject. The second kind of dialectical argument will therefore be concerned, following the analogy with *hypothetical* syllogisms, with the unconditioned unity of the objective conditions in the phenomenon; and, in this way, the theme of the third kind to be treated of in the following chapter will be the unconditioned unity of the objective conditions of the possibility of objects in general.

But it is worthy of remark that the transcendental paralogism produced in the mind only a one-third illusion, in regard to the idea of the subject of our thought; and the conceptions of reason gave no ground to maintain the contrary proposition. The advantage is completely on the side of Pneumatism; although this theory itself passes into naught, in the crucible of pure reason.

Very different is the case when we apply reason to the *objective synthesis* of phenomena. Here, certainly, reason establishes, with much plausibility, its principle of unconditioned unity; but it very soon falls into such contradictions that it is compelled, in relation to cosmology, to renounce its pretensions.

For here a new phenomenon of human reason meets us—a perfectly natural antithetic, which does not require to be sought for by subtle sophistry, but into which reason of itself unavoidably falls. It is thereby preserved, to be sure, from the slumber of a fancied conviction —which a merely one-sided illusion produces; but it is at the same time compelled, either, on the one hand, to abandon itself to a despairing scepticism, or, on the other, to assume a dogmatical confidence and obstinate persistence in certain assertions, without granting a fair hearing to the other side of the question. Either is the death of a sound philosophy, although the former might perhaps deserve the title of the *euthanasia* of pure reason.

Before entering this region of discord and confusion, which the conflict of the laws of pure reason (antinomy) produces, we shall present the reader with some considerations, in explanation and justification of the method we intend to follow in our treatment of this subject. I term all transcendental ideas, in so far as they relate to the absolute totality in the synthesis of phenomena, *cosmical conceptions;* partly on account of this unconditioned totality, on which the conception of the world-whole is based—a conception, which is itself an idea—partly because they relate solely to the synthesis of phenomena—the empirical synthesis; while, on the other hand, the absolute totality in the synthesis of the conditions of all possible things gives rise to an ideal of pure reason, which is quite distinct from the cosmical conception, although it stands in relation with it. Hence, as the paralogisms of pure reason laid the foundation for a dialectical psychology, the antinomy of pure reason will present us with the transcendental principles of a pretended pure (rational) cosmology—not, however, to declare it valid and to appropriate it, but—as the very term of a conflict of reason sufficiently indicates, to present it as an idea which cannot be reconciled with phenomena and experience.

SECTION I. *System of Cosmological Ideas*

THAT we may be able to enumerate with systematic precision these ideas according to a principle, we must remark, *in the first place,* that it is from the understanding alone that pure and transcendental conceptions take their origin; that the reason does not properly give birth to any conception, but only frees the conception of the understanding from the unavoidable limitation of a possible experience, and thus endeavours to raise it above the empirical, though it must still be in connection with it. This happens from the fact that, for a given conditioned, reason demands absolute totality on the side of the conditions (to which the understanding submits all phenomena), and thus makes of the category a transcendental idea. This it does that it may be able to give absolute completeness to the empirical synthesis, by continuing it to the unconditioned (which is not to be found in experience, but only in the idea). Reason requires this according to the principle: *If the conditioned is given the whole of the conditions, and consequently the absolutely unconditioned, is also given,* whereby alone the former was possible. *First,* then, the transcendental ideas are properly nothing but categories elevated to the unconditioned; and they may be arranged in a table according to the titles of the latter. But, *secondly,* all the categories are not available for this purpose, but only those in which the synthesis constitutes a series—of conditions subordinated to, not co-ordinated with, each other. Absolute totality is required of reason only in so far as concerns the ascending series of the conditions of a conditioned; not, consequently, when the question relates to the descending series of consequences, or to the aggregate of the co-ordinated conditions of these consequences. For, in relation to a given conditioned, conditions are presupposed and considered to be given along with it. On the other hand, as the consequences do not render possible their conditions, but rather presuppose them—in the consideration of the procession of consequences (or in the descent from the given condition to the conditioned), we may be quite unconcerned whether the series ceases or not; and their totality is not a necessary demand of reason.

Thus we cogitate—and necessarily—a given time completely elapsed up to a given moment, although that time is not determinable by us. But as regards time future, which is not the condition of arriving at the present, in order to conceive it; it is quite indifferent whether we consider future time as ceasing at some point, or as prolonging itself to infinity. Take, for example, the series *m, n, o,* in which *n* is given as conditioned in relation to *m,* but at the same time as the condition of *o,* and let the series proceed upwards from the conditioned *n* to *m* (*l, k, i,* etc.), and also downwards from the condition *n* to the conditioned *o* (*p, q, r,* etc.)—I must presuppose the former series, to be able to consider *n* as given, and *n* is according to reason (the totality of conditions) possible only by means of that series. But its possibility does not rest on the following series *o, p, q, r,* which for this reason cannot be regarded as given, but only as capable of being given (*dabilis*).

I shall term the synthesis of the series on the side of the conditions—from that nearest to the given phenomenon up to the more remote—*regressive;* that which proceeds on the side of the conditioned, from the immediate consequence to the more remote, I shall call the *pro-*

gressive synthesis. The former proceeds *in antecedentia,* the latter *in consequentia.* The cosmological ideas are therefore occupied with the totality of the regressive synthesis, and proceed *in antecedentia,* not *in consequentia.* When the latter takes place, it is an arbitrary and not a necessary problem of pure reason; for we require, for the complete understanding of what is given in a phenomenon, not the consequences which succeed, but the grounds or principles which precede.

In order to construct the table of ideas in correspondence with the table of categories, we take first the two primitive *quanta* of all our intuitions, time and space. Time is in itself a series (and the formal condition of all series), and hence, in relation to a given present, we must distinguish *a priori* in it the *antecedentia* as conditions (time past) from the *consequentia* (time future). Consequently, the transcendental idea of the absolute totality of the series of the conditions of a given conditioned, relates merely to all past time. According to the idea of reason, the whole past time, as the condition of the given moment, is necessarily cogitated as given. But, as regards space, there exists in it no distinction between *progressus* and *regressus;* for it is an *aggregate* and not a series—its parts existing together at the same time. I can consider a given point of time in relation to past time only as conditioned, because this given moment comes into existence only through the past time—or rather through the passing of the preceding time. But as the parts of space are not subordinated, but co-ordinated to each other, one part cannot be the condition of the possibility of the other; and space is not in itself, like time, a series. But the synthesis of the manifold parts of space—(the syntheses whereby we apprehend space)—is nevertheless successive; it takes place, therefore, in time, and contains a series. And as in this series of aggregated spaces (for example, the feet in a rood), beginning with a given portion of space, those which continue to be annexed form the *condition of the limits* of the former—the measurement of a space must also be regarded as a synthesis of the series of the conditions of a given conditioned. It differs, however, in this respect from that of time, that the side of the conditioned is not in itself distinguishable from the side of the condition; and, consequently, *regressus* and *progressus* in space seem to be identical. But, inasmuch as one part of space is not given, but only limited, by and through another, we must also consider every limited space as conditioned, in so far as it presupposes some other space as the condition of its limitation, and so on. As regards limitation, therefore, our procedure in space is also a *regressus,* and the transcendental idea of the absolute totality of the synthesis in a series of conditions applies to space also; and I am entitled to demand the absolute totality of the phenomenal synthesis in space as well as in time. Whether my demand can be satisfied is a question to be answered in the sequel.

Secondly, the real in space—that is, matter—is conditioned. Its internal conditions are its parts, and the parts of parts its remote conditions; so that in this case we find a regressive synthesis, the absolute totality of which is a demand of reason. But this cannot be obtained otherwise than by a complete division of parts, whereby the real in matter becomes either nothing or that which is not matter, that is to say, the simple. Consequently we find here also a series of conditions and a progress to the unconditioned.

Thirdly, as regards the categories of a real relation between phenomena, the category *of substance* and its accidents is not suitable for the formation of a transcendental idea; that is to say, reason has no ground, in regard to it, to proceed regressively with conditions. For accidents (in so far as they inhere in a substance) are co-ordinated with each other, and do not constitute a series. And, in relation to substance, they are not properly subordinated to it, but are the mode of existence of the substance itself. The conception of the *substantial* might nevertheless seem to be an idea of the transcendental reason. But, as this signifies nothing more than the conception of an object in general, which subsists in so far as we cogitate in it merely a transcendental subject without any predicates; and as the question here is of an unconditioned in the series of phenomena—it is clear that the substantial can form no member thereof. The same holds good of substances in community, which are mere aggregates and do not form a series. For they are not subordinated to each other as conditions of the possibility of each other; which, however, may be affirmed of spaces, the limits of which are never determined in themselves, but always by some other space. It is, therefore, only in the category of *causality* that we can find a series of causes to a given effect, and in which we ascend from the latter, as the conditioned, to the former as the conditions, and thus answer the question of reason.

Fourthly, the conceptions of the *possible,*

the *actual*, and the *necessary* do not conduct us to any series—excepting only in so far as the contingent in existence must always be regarded as conditioned, and as indicating, according to a law of the understanding, a condition, under which it is necessary to rise to a higher, till in the totality of the series, reason arrives at unconditioned *necessity*.

There are, accordingly, only four cosmological ideas, corresponding with the four titles of the categories. For we can select only such as necessarily furnish us with a series in the synthesis of the manifold.

1

The absolute Completeness
of the
COMPOSITION
of the given totality of all phenomena

2

The absolute Completeness
of the
DIVISION
of a given totality
in a phenomenon

3

The absolute Completeness
of the
ORIGINATION
of a phenomenon

4

The absolute Completeness
of the DEPENDENCE *of the* EXISTENCE
of what is changeable in a phenomenon

We must here remark, in the first place, that the idea of absolute totality relates to nothing but the exposition of *phenomena*, and therefore not to the pure conception of a totality of things. Phenomena are here, therefore, regarded as given, and reason requires the absolute completeness of the conditions of their possibility, in so far as these conditions constitute a series—consequently an absolutely (that is, in every respect) complete synthesis, whereby a phenomenon can be explained according to the laws of the understanding.

Secondly, it is properly the unconditioned alone that reason seeks in this serially and regressively conducted synthesis of conditions. It wishes, to speak in another way, to attain to completeness in the series of premisses, so as to render it unnecessary to presuppose others. This *unconditioned* is always contained in the *absolute totality of the series*, when we endeavour to form a representation of it in thought. But this absolutely complete synthesis is itself but an idea; for it is impossible, at least beforehand, to know whether any such synthesis is possible in the case of phenomena. When we represent all existence in thought by means of pure conceptions of the understanding, without any conditions of sensuous intuition, we may say with justice that for a given conditioned the whole series of conditions subordinated to each other is also given; for the former is only given through the latter. But we find in the case of phenomena a particular limitation of the mode in which conditions are given, that is, through the successive synthesis of the manifold of intuition, which must be complete in the regress. Now whether this completeness is sensuously possible, is a problem. But the idea of it lies in the reason—be it possible or impossible to connect with the idea adequate empirical conceptions. Therefore, as in the absolute totality of the regressive synthesis of the manifold in a phenomenon (following the guidance of the categories, which represent it as a series of conditions to a given conditioned) the unconditioned is necessarily contained—it being still left unascertained whether and how this totality exists; reason sets out from the idea of totality, although its proper and final aim is the *unconditioned*—of the whole series, or of a part thereof.

This unconditioned may be cogitated—either as existing only in the entire series, all the members of which therefore would be without exception conditioned and only the totality absolutely unconditioned—and in this case the *regressus* is called infinite; or the absolutely unconditioned is only a part of the series, to which the other members are subordinated, but which is not itself submitted to any other condition.[1] In the former case the series is *a parte priori* unlimited (without beginning), that is, infinite, and nevertheless completely given. But the regress in it is never completed, and can only be called *potentially* infinite. In the second case there exists a first in the series. This first is called, in relation to past time, the *beginning of the world;* in relation to space, the *limit of the world;* in relation to the parts of a given

[1] The absolute totality of the series of conditions to a given conditioned is always unconditioned; because beyond it there exist no other conditions, on which it might depend. But the absolute totality of such a series is only an idea, or rather a problematical conception, the possibility of which must be investigated—particularly in relation to the mode in which the unconditioned, as the transcendental idea which is the real subject of inquiry, may be contained therein.

limited whole, the *simple;* in relation to causes, absolute *spontaneity* (liberty); and in relation to the existence of changeable things, absolute *physical necessity.*

We possess two expressions, *world* and *nature,* which are generally interchanged. The first denotes the mathematical total of all phenomena and the totality of their synthesis—in its progress by means of composition, as well as by division. And the world is termed nature,[1] when it is regarded as a dynamical whole—when our attention is not directed to the aggregation in space and time, for the purpose of cogitating it as a quantity, but to the unity in the *existence* of phenomena. In this case the condition of that which happens is called a cause; the unconditioned causality of the cause in a phenomenon is termed liberty; the conditioned cause is called in a more limited sense a natural cause. The conditioned in existence is termed contingent, and the unconditioned necessary. The unconditioned necessity of phenomena may be called *natural necessity.*

The ideas which we are at present engaged in discussing I have called cosmological ideas; partly because by the term *world* is understood the entire content of all phenomena, and our ideas are directed solely to the unconditioned among phenomena; partly also, because *world,* in the transcendental sense, signifies the absolute totality of the content of existing things, and we are directing our attention only to the completeness of the synthesis—although, properly, only in regression. In regard to the fact that these ideas are all transcendent, and, although they do not transcend phenomena as regards their mode, but are concerned solely with the world of sense (and not with noumena), nevertheless carry their synthesis to a degree far above all possible experience—it still seems to me that we can, with perfect propriety, designate them *cosmical conceptions.* As regards the distinction between the mathematically and the dynamically unconditioned which is the aim of the regression of the synthesis, I should call the two former, in a more limited signification, cosmical conceptions, the remaining two *transcendent physical conceptions.* This distinction does not at present seem to be of particular importance, but we shall afterwards find it to be of some value.

[1] Nature, understood *adjectivè (formaliter),* signifies the complex of the determinations of a thing, connected according to an internal principle of causality. On the other hand, we understand by nature, *substantive (materialiter),* the sum total of phenomena, in so far as they, by virtue of an internal principle of causality, are connected with each other throughout. In the former sense we speak of the nature of liquid matter, of fire, etc., and employ the word only *adjectivè;* while, if speaking of the objects of nature, we have in our minds the idea of a subsisting whole.

SECTION II. *Antithetic of Pure Reason*

THETIC is the term applied to every collection of dogmatical propositions. By antithetic I do not understand dogmatical assertions of the opposite, but the self-contradiction of seemingly dogmatical cognitions (*thesis cum antithesi*), in none of which we can discover any decided superiority. Antithetic is not, therefore, occupied with one-sided statements, but is engaged in considering the contradictory nature of the general cognitions of reason and its causes. Transcendental antithetic is an investigation into the antinomy of pure reason, its causes and result. If we employ our reason not merely in the application of the principles of the understanding to objects of experience, but venture with it beyond these boundaries, there arise certain sophistical propositions or theorems. These assertions have the following peculiarities: They can find neither confirmation nor confutation in experience; and each is in itself not only self-consistent, but possesses conditions of its necessity in the very nature of reason—only that, unluckily, there exist just as valid and necessary grounds for maintaining the contrary proposition.

The questions which naturally arise in the consideration of this dialectic of pure reason, are therefore: 1st. In what propositions is pure reason unavoidably subject to an antinomy? 2nd. What are the causes of this antinomy? 3rd. Whether and in what way can reason free itself from this self-contradiction?

A dialectical proposition or theorem of pure reason must, according to what has been said, be distinguishable from all sophistical propositions, by the fact that it is not an answer to an arbitrary question, which may be raised at the mere pleasure of any person, but to one which human reason must necessarily encounter in its progress. In the second place, a dialectical proposition, with its opposite, does not carry the appearance of a merely artificial illusion, which disappears as soon as it is investigated, but a natural and unavoidable illusion, which, even when we are no longer deceived by it, continues to mock us and, although rendered harmless, can never be completely removed.

This dialectical doctrine will not relate to the unity of understanding in empirical conceptions, but to the unity of reason in pure ideas. The conditions of this doctrine are—inasmuch as it must, as a synthesis according to rules, be conformable to the understanding, and at the same time as the absolute unity of the synthesis, to the reason—that, if it is adequate to the unity of reason, it is too great for the understanding, if according with the understanding, it is too small for the reason. Hence arises a mutual opposition, which cannot be avoided, do what we will.

These sophistical assertions of dialectic open, as it were, a battle-field, where that side obtains the victory which has been permitted to make the attack, and he is compelled to yield who has been unfortunately obliged to stand on the defensive. And hence, champions of ability, whether on the right or on the wrong side, are certain to carry away the crown of victory, if they only take care to have the right to make the last attack, and are not obliged to sustain another onset from their opponent. We can easily believe that this arena has been often trampled by the feet of combatants, that many victories have been obtained on both sides, but that the last victory, decisive of the affair between the contending parties, was won by him who fought for the right, only if his adversary was forbidden to continue the tourney. As impartial umpires, we must lay aside entirely the consideration whether the combatants are fighting for the right or for the wrong side, for the true or for the false, and allow the combat to be first decided. Perhaps, after they have wearied more than injured each other, they will discover the nothingness of their cause of quarrel and part good friends.

This method of watching, or rather of originating, a conflict of assertions, not for the purpose of finally deciding in favour of either side, but to discover whether the object of the struggle is not a mere illusion, which each strives in vain to reach, but which would be no gain even when reached—this procedure, I say, may be termed the *sceptical method*. It is thoroughly distinct from *scepticism*—the principle of a technical and scientific ignorance, which undermines the foundations of all knowledge, in order, if possible, to destroy our belief and confidence therein. For the sceptical method aims at certainty, by endeavouring to discover in a conflict of this kind, conducted honestly and intelligently on both sides, the point of misunderstanding; just as wise legislators derive, from the embarrassment of judges in lawsuits, information in regard to the defective and ill-defined parts of their statutes. The antinomy which reveals itself in the application of laws, is for our limited wisdom the best criterion of legislation. For the attention of reason, which in abstract speculation does not easily become conscious of its errors, is thus roused to the momenta in the determination of its principles.

But this sceptical method is essentially peculiar to transcendental philosophy, and can perhaps be dispensed with in every other field of investigation. In mathematics its use would be absurd; because in it no false assertions can long remain hidden, inasmuch as its demonstrations must always proceed under the guidance of pure intuition, and by means of an always evident synthesis. In experimental philosophy, doubt and delay may be very useful; but no misunderstanding is possible, which cannot be easily removed; and in experience means of solving the difficulty and putting an end to the dissension must at last be found, whether sooner or later. Moral philosophy can always exhibit its principles, with their practical consequences, *in concreto*—at least in possible experiences, and thus escape the mistakes and ambiguities of abstraction. But transcendental propositions, which lay claim to insight beyond the region of possible experience, cannot, on the one hand, exhibit their abstract synthesis in any *a priori* intuition, nor, on the other, expose a lurking error by the help of experience. Transcendental reason, therefore, presents us with no other criterion than that of an attempt to reconcile such assertions, and for this purpose to permit a free and unrestrained conflict between them. And this we now proceed to arrange.[1]

[1] The antinomies stand in the order of the four transcendental ideas above detailed.

First Conflict of The Transcendental Ideas

Thesis

The world has a beginning in time, and is also limited in regard to space.

PROOF

Granted that the world has no beginning in time; up to every given moment of time, an eternity must have elapsed, and therewith passed away an infinite series of successive conditions or states of things in the world. Now the infinity of a series consists in the fact that it never can be completed by means of a successive synthesis. It follows that an infinite series already elapsed is impossible and that, consequently, a beginning of the world is a necessary condition of its existence. And this was the first thing to be proved.

As regards the second, let us take the opposite for granted. In this case, the world must be an infinite given total of coexistent things. Now we cannot cogitate the dimensions of a quantity, which is not given within certain limits of an intuition,[1] in any other way than by means of the synthesis of its parts, and the total of such a quantity only by means of a completed synthesis, or the repeated addition of unity to itself. Accordingly, to cogitate the world, which fills all spaces, as a whole, the successive synthesis of the parts of an infinite world must be looked upon as completed, that is to say, an infinite time must be regarded as having elapsed in the enumeration of all co-existing things; which is impossible. For this reason an infinite aggregate of actual things cannot be considered as a given whole, consequently, not as a contemporaneously given whole. The world is consequently, as regards extension in space, *not infinite,* but enclosed in limits. And this was the second thing to be proved.

[1] We may consider an undetermined quantity as a whole, when it is enclosed within limits, although we cannot construct or ascertain its totality by measurement, that is, by the successive synthesis of its parts. For its limits of themselves determine its completeness as a whole.

Antithesis

The world has no beginning, and no limits in space, but is, in relation both to time and space, infinite.

PROOF

For let it be granted that it has a beginning. A beginning is an existence which is preceded by a time in which the thing does not exist. On the above supposition, it follows that there must have been a time in which the world did not exist, that is, a void time. But in a void time the origination of a thing is impossible; because no part of any such time contains a distinctive condition of being, in preference to that of non-being (whether the supposed thing originate of itself, or by means of some other cause). Consequently, many series of things may have a beginning in the world, but the world itself cannot have a beginning, and is, therefore, in relation to past time, infinite.

As regards the second statement, let us first take the opposite for granted—that the world is finite and limited in space; it follows that it must exist in a void space, which is not limited. We should therefore meet not only with a relation of things *in space,* but also a relation of things *to space.* Now, as the world is an absolute whole, out of and beyond which no object of intuition, and consequently no correlate to which can be discovered, this relation of the world to a void space is merely a relation to *no object.* But such a relation, and consequently the limitation of the world by void space, is nothing. Consequently, the world, as regards space, is not limited, that is, it is infinite in regard to extension.[2]

[2] Space is merely the form of external intuition (formal intuition), and not a real object which can be externally perceived. Space, prior to all things which determine it (fill or limit it), or, rather, which present an *empirical intuition* conformable to it, is, under the title of absolute space, nothing but the mere possibility of external phenomena, in so far as they either exist in themselves, or can annex themselves to given intuitions. Empirical intuition is therefore not a composition of phenomena and space (of perception and empty intuition). The one is not the correlate of the other in a synthesis, but they are vitally connected in the same empirical intuition, as matter and form. If we wish to set one of these two apart from the other—space from phenomena—there arise all sorts of empty determinations of external intuition, which are very far from being possible perceptions. For example, motion or rest of the world in an infinite empty space, or a determination of the mutual relation of both, cannot possibly be perceived, and is therefore merely the predicate of a notional entity.

Observations on the First Antinomy

On the Thesis

In bringing forward these conflicting arguments, I have not been on the search for sophisms, for the purpose of availing myself of special pleading, which takes advantage of the carelessness of the opposite party, appeals to a misunderstood statute, and erects its unrighteous claims upon an unfair interpretation. Both proofs originate fairly from the nature of the case, and the advantage presented by the mistakes of the dogmatists of both parties has been completely set aside.

The thesis might also have been unfairly demonstrated, by the introduction of an erroneous conception of the infinity of a given quantity. A quantity is infinite, if a greater than itself cannot possibly exist. The quantity is measured by the number of given units—which are taken as a standard—contained in it. Now no number can be the greatest, because one or more units can always be added. It follows that an infinite given quantity, consequently an infinite world (both as regards time and extension) is impossible. It is, therefore, limited in both respects. In this manner I might have conducted my proof; but the conception given in it does not agree with the true conception of an infinite whole. In this there is no representation of its quantity, it is not said how large it is; consequently its conception is not the conception of a *maximum*. We cogitate in it merely its relation to an arbitrarily assumed unit, in relation to which it is greater than any number. Now, just as the unit which is taken is greater or smaller, the infinite will be greater or smaller; but the infinity, which consists merely in the relation to this given unit, must remain always the same, although the absolute quantity of the whole is not thereby cognized.

The true (transcendental) conception of infinity is: that the successive synthesis of unity in the measurement of a given quantum can never be completed.[1] Hence it follows, without possibility of mistake, that an eternity of actual successive states up to a given (the present) moment cannot have elapsed, and that the world must therefore have a beginning.

In regard to the second part of the thesis, the difficulty as to an infinite and yet elapsed series

[1] The quantum in this sense contains a congeries of given units, which is greater than any number—and this is the mathematical conception of the infinite.

On the Antithesis

The proof in favour of the infinity of the cosmical succession and the cosmical content is based upon the consideration that, in the opposite case, a void time and a void space must constitute the limits of the world. Now I am not unaware, that there are some ways of escaping this conclusion. It may, for example, be alleged, that a limit to the world, as regards both space and time, is quite possible, without at the same time holding the existence of an absolute time before the beginning of the world, or an absolute space extending beyond the actual world—which is impossible. I am quite well satisfied with the latter part of this opinion of the philosophers of the Leibnitzian school. Space is merely the form of external intuition, but not a real object which can itself be externally intuited; it is not a correlate of phenomena, it is the form of phenomena itself. Space, therefore, cannot be regarded as absolutely and in itself something determinative of the existence of things, because it is not itself an object, but only the form of possible objects. Consequently, things, as phenomena, determine space; that is to say, they render it possible that, of all the possible predicates of space (size and relation), certain may belong to reality. But we cannot affirm the converse, that space, as something self-subsistent, can determine real things in regard to size or shape, for it is in itself not a real thing. Space (filled or void)[2] may therefore be limited by phenomena, but phenomena cannot be limited by an empty space without them. This is true of time also. All this being granted, it is nevertheless indisputable, that we must assume these two nonentities, void space without and void time before the world, if we assume the existence of cosmical limits, relatively to space or time.

For, as regards the subterfuge adopted by those who endeavour to evade the consequence—that, if the world is limited as to space and time, the infinite void must determine the existence of actual things in regard to their dimensions—it arises solely from the fact that, instead of a *sensuous world*, an *intelligible world*—of which nothing is known—is cogitated; instead

[2] It is evident that what is meant here is, that empty space, in so far as it is limited by phenomena—space, that is, *within* the world—does not at least contradict transcendental principles, and may therefore, as regards them, be admitted, although its possibility cannot on that account be affirmed.

THESIS

disappears; for the manifold of a world infinite in extension is contemporaneously given. But, in order to cogitate the total of this manifold, as we cannot have the aid of limits constituting by themselves this total in intuition, we are obliged to give some account of our conception, which in this case cannot proceed from the whole to the determined quantity of the parts, but must demonstrate the possibility of a whole by means of a successive synthesis of the parts. But as this synthesis must constitute a series that cannot be completed, it is impossible for us to cogitate prior to it, and consequently not by means of it, a totality. For the conception of totality itself is in the present case the representation of a completed synthesis of the parts; and this completion, and consequently its conception, is impossible.

ANTITHESIS

of a real beginning (an existence, which is preceded by a period in which nothing exists), an existence which presupposes *no other condition* than that of time; and, instead of limits of extension, boundaries of the universe. But the question relates to the *mundus phaenomenon,* and its quantity; and in this case we cannot make abstraction of the conditions of sensibility, without doing away with the essential reality of this world itself. The world of sense, if it is limited, must necessarily lie in the infinite void. If this, and with it space as the *a priori* condition of the possibility of phenomena, is left out of view, the whole world of sense disappears. In our problem is this alone considered as given. The *mundus intelligibilis* is nothing but the general conception of a world, in which abstraction has been made of all conditions of intuition, and in relation to which no synthetical proposition—either affirmative or negative—is possible.

SECOND CONFLICT OF THE TRANSCENDENTAL IDEAS

THESIS

Every composite substance in the world consists of simple parts; and there exists nothing that is not either itself simple, or composed of simple parts.

PROOF

For, grant that composite substances do not consist of simple parts; in this case, if all combination or composition were annihilated in thought, no composite part, and (as, by the supposition, there do not exist simple parts) no simple part would exist. Consequently, no substance; consequently, nothing would exist. Either, then, it is impossible to annihilate composition in thought; or, after such annihilation, there must remain something that subsists without composition, that is, something that is simple. But in the former case the composite could not itself consist of substances, because with substances composition is merely a contingent relation, apart from which they must still exist as self-subsistent beings. Now, as this case contradicts the supposition, the second must contain the truth—that the substantial composite in the world consists of simple parts.

It follows, as an immediate inference, that the things in the world are all, without exception, simple beings—that composition is merely an external condition pertaining to them—and that, although we never can separate and isolate the elementary substances from the state

ANTITHESIS

No composite thing in the world consists of simple parts; and there does not exist in the world any simple substance.

PROOF

Let it be supposed that a composite thing (as substance) consists of simple parts. Inasmuch as all external relation, consequently all composition of substances, is possible only in space; the space, occupied by that which is composite, must consist of the same number of parts as is contained in the composite. But space does not consist of simple parts, but of spaces. Therefore, every part of the composite must occupy a space. But the absolutely primary parts of what is composite are simple. It follows that what is simple occupies a space. Now, as everything real that occupies a space, contains a manifold the parts of which are external to each other, and is consequently composite—and a real composite, not of accidents (for these cannot exist external to each other apart from substance), but of substances—it follows that the simple must be a substantial composite, which is self-contradictory.

The second proposition of the antithesis—that there exists in the world nothing that is simple—is here equivalent to the following: The existence of the absolutely simple cannot be demonstrated from any experience or percep-

THESIS

of composition, reason must cogitate these as the primary subjects of all composition, and consequently, as prior thereto—and as simple substances.

ANTITHESIS

tion either external or internal; and the absolutely simple is a mere idea, the objective reality of which cannot be demonstrated in any possible experience; it is consequently, in the exposition of phenomena, without application and object. For, let us take for granted that an object may be found in experience for this transcendental idea; the empirical intuition of such an object must then be recognized to contain absolutely no manifold with its parts external to each other, and connected into unity. Now, as we cannot reason from the nonconsciousness of such a manifold to the impossibility of its existence in the intuition of an object, and as the proof of this impossibility is necessary for the establishment and proof of absolute simplicity; it follows that this simplicity cannot be inferred from any perception whatever. As, therefore, an absolutely simple object cannot be given in any experience, and the world of sense must be considered as the sum total of all possible experiences: nothing simple exists in the world.

This second proposition in the antithesis has a more extended aim than the first. The first merely banishes the simple from the intuition of the composite; while the second drives it entirely out of nature. Hence we were unable to demonstrate it from the conception of a given object of external intuition (of the composite), but we were obliged to prove it from the relation of a given object to a possible experience in general.

OBSERVATIONS ON THE SECOND ANTINOMY

THESIS

When I speak of a *whole,* which necessarily consists of simple parts, I understand thereby only a substantial whole, as the true composite; that is to say, I understand that contingent unity of the manifold which is given as perfectly isolated (at least in thought), placed in reciprocal connection, and thus constituted a unity. Space ought not to be called a *compositum* but a *totum,* for its parts are possible in the whole, and not the whole by means of the parts. It might perhaps be called a *compositum ideale,* but not a *compositum reale.* But this is of no importance. As space is not a composite of substances (and not even of real accidents), if I abstract all composition therein—nothing, not even a point, remains; for a point is possible only as the limit of a space—consequently of a composite. Space and time, therefore, do not consist of simple parts. That which belongs only to the condition or state of a substance, even although it possesses a quantity (motion

ANTITHESIS

Against the assertion of the infinite subdivisibility of matter, whose ground of proof is purely mathematical, objections have been alleged by the Monadists. These objections lay themselves open, at first sight, to suspicion, from the fact that they do not recognize the clearest mathematical proofs as propositions relating to the constitution of space, in so far as it is really the formal condition of the possibility of all matter, but regard them merely as inferences from abstract but arbitrary conceptions, which cannot have any application to real things. Just as if it were possible to imagine another mode of intuition than that given in the primitive intuition of space; and just as if its *a priori* determinations did not apply to everything, the existence of which is possible, from the fact alone of its filling space. If we listen to them, we shall find ourselves required to cogitate, in addition to the mathematical point, which is simple—not, however, a part, but a mere limit of space—

THESIS

or change, for example), likewise does not consist of simple parts. That is to say, a certain degree of change does not originate from the addition of many simple changes. Our inference of the simple from the composite is valid only of self-subsisting things. But the accidents of a state are not self-subsistent. The proof, then, for the necessity of the simple, as the component part of all that is substantial and composite, may prove a failure, and the whole case of this thesis be lost, if we carry the proposition too far, and wish to make it valid of everything that is composite without distinction—as indeed has really now and then happened. Besides, I am here speaking only of the simple, in so far as it is necessarily given in the composite—the latter being capable of solution into the former as its component parts. The proper signification of the word *monas* (as employed by Leibnitz) ought to relate to the simple, given *immediately* as simple substance (for example, in consciousness), and not as an element of the composite. As an element, the term *atomus* would be more appropriate. And as I wish to prove the existence of simple substances, only in relation to, and as the elements of, the composite, I might term the antithesis of the second Antinomy, transcendental *Atomistic*. But as this word has long been employed to designate a particular theory of corporeal phenomena (*moleculae*), and thus presupposes a basis of empirical conceptions, I prefer calling it the dialectical principle of *Monadology*.

ANTITHESIS

physical points, which are indeed likewise simple, but possess the peculiar property, as parts of space, of filling it merely by their aggregation. I shall not repeat here the common and clear refutations of this absurdity, which are to be found everywhere in numbers: every one knows that it is impossible to undermine the evidence of mathematics by mere discursive conceptions; I shall only remark that, if in this case philosophy endeavours to gain an advantage over mathematics by sophistical artifices, it is because it forgets that the discussion relates solely to *phenomena* and their conditions. It is not sufficient to find the conception of the simple for the pure *conception* of the composite, but we must discover for the *intuition* of the composite (matter), the intuition of the simple. Now this, according to the laws of sensibility, and consequently in the case of objects of sense, is utterly impossible. In the case of a whole composed of substances, which is cogitated solely by the pure understanding, it may be necessary to be in possession of the simple before composition is possible. But this does not hold good of the *Totum substantiale phaenomenon*, which, as an empirical intuition in space, possesses the necessary property of containing no simple part, for the very reason that no part of space is simple. Meanwhile, the Monadists have been subtle enough to escape from this difficulty, by presupposing intuition and the dynamical relation of substances as the condition of the possibility of space, instead of regarding space as the condition of the possibility of the objects of external intuition, that is, of bodies. Now we have a conception of bodies only as phenomena, and, as such, they necessarily presuppose space as the condition of all external phenomena. The evasion is therefore in vain; as, indeed, we have sufficiently shown in our *Aesthetic*. If bodies were *things in themselves*, the proof of the Monadists would be unexceptionable.

The second dialectical assertion possesses the peculiarity of having opposed to it a dogmatical proposition, which, among all such sophistical statements, is the only one that undertakes to prove in the case of an object of experience, that which is properly a transcendental idea—the absolute simplicity of substance. The proposition is that the object of the internal sense, the thinking Ego, is an absolute simple substance. Without at present entering upon this subject—as it has been considered at length in a former chapter—I shall merely remark that, if

THESIS

ANTITHESIS

something is cogitated merely as an object, without the addition of any synthetical determination of its intuition—as happens in the case of the bare representation, *I*—it is certain that no manifold and no composition can be perceived in such a representation. As, moreover, the predicates whereby I cogitate this object are merely intuitions of the internal sense, there cannot be discovered in them anything to prove the existence of a manifold whose parts are external to each other, and, consequently, nothing to prove the existence of real composition. Consciousness, therefore, is so constituted that, inasmuch as the thinking subject is at the same time its own object, it cannot divide itself—although it can divide its inhering determinations. For every object in relation to itself is absolute unity. Nevertheless, if the subject is regarded *externally*, as an object of intuition, it must, in its character of phenomenon, possess the property of composition. And it must always be regarded in this manner, if we wish to know whether there is or is not contained in it a manifold whose parts are external to each other.

THIRD CONFLICT OF THE TRANSCENDENTAL IDEAS

THESIS

Causality according to the laws of nature, is not the only causality operating to originate the phenomena of the world. A causality of freedom is also necessary to account fully for these phenomena.

PROOF

Let it be supposed, that there is no other kind of causality than that according to the laws of nature. Consequently, everything that happens presupposes a previous condition, which it follows with absolute certainty, in conformity with a rule. But this previous condition must itself be something that has happened (that has arisen in time, as it did not exist before), for, if it has always been in existence, its consequence or effect would not thus originate for the first time, but would likewise have always existed. The causality, therefore, of a cause, whereby something happens, is itself a thing that has *happened*. Now this again presupposes, in conformity with the law of nature, a previous condition and its causality, and this another anterior to the former, and so on. If, then, everything happens solely in accordance with the laws of nature, there cannot be any real first beginning of things, but only a subaltern or comparative beginning. There cannot, therefore, be a completeness of series on the side of

ANTITHESIS

There is no such thing as freedom, but everything in the world happens solely according to the laws of nature.

PROOF

Granted, that there does exist *freedom* in the transcendental sense, as a peculiar kind of causality, operating to produce events in the world—a faculty, that is to say, of originating a state, and consequently a series of consequences from that state. In this case, not only the series originated by this spontaneity, but the determination of this spontaneity itself to the production of the series, that is to say, the causality itself must have an absolute commencement, such that nothing can precede to determine this action according to unvarying laws. But every beginning of action presupposes in the acting cause a state of inaction; and a dynamically primal beginning of action presupposes a state, which has no connection—as regards causality—with the preceding state of the cause—which does not, that is, in any wise result from it. Transcendental freedom is therefore opposed to the natural law of cause and effect, and such a conjunction of successive states in effective causes is destructive of the

PROOF

the causes which originate the one from the other. But the law of nature is that nothing can happen without a sufficient *a priori* determined cause. The proposition therefore—if all causality is possible only in accordance with the laws of nature—is, when stated in this unlimited and general manner, self-contradictory. It follows that this cannot be the only kind of causality.

From what has been said, it follows that a causality must be admitted, by means of which something happens, without its cause being determined according to necessary laws by some other cause preceding. That is to say, there must exist an *absolute spontaneity* of cause, which of itself originates a series of phenomena which proceeds according to natural laws—consequently transcendental freedom, without which even in the course of nature the succession of phenomena on the side of causes is never complete.

PROOF

possibility of unity in experience and for that reason not to be found in experience—is consequently a mere fiction of thought.

We have, therefore, nothing but nature to which we must look for connection and order in cosmical events. Freedom—independence of the laws of nature—is certainly a deliverance from restraint, but it is also a relinquishing of the guidance of law and rule. For it cannot be alleged that, instead of the laws of nature, laws of freedom may be introduced into the causality of the course of nature. For, if freedom were determined according to laws, it would be no longer freedom, but merely nature. Nature, therefore, and transcendental freedom are distinguishable as conformity to law and lawlessness. The former imposes upon understanding the difficulty of seeking the origin of events ever higher and higher in the series of causes, inasmuch as causality is always conditioned thereby; while it compensates this labour by the guarantee of a unity complete and in conformity with law. The latter, on the contrary, holds out to the understanding the promise of a point of rest in the chain of causes, by conducting it to an unconditioned causality, which professes to have the power of spontaneous origination, but which, in its own utter blindness, deprives it of the guidance of rules, by which alone a completely connected experience is possible.

Observations on the Third Antinomy

On the Thesis

The transcendental idea of freedom is far from constituting the entire content of the psychological conception so termed, which is for the most part empirical. It merely presents us with the conception of spontaneity of action, as the proper ground for imputing freedom to the cause of a certain class of objects. It is, however, the true stumbling-stone to philosophy, which meets with unconquerable difficulties in the way of its admitting this kind of unconditioned causality. That element in the question of the freedom of the will, which has for so long a time placed speculative reason in such perplexity, is properly only transcendental, and concerns the question, whether there must be held to exist a faculty of *spontaneous* origination of a series of successive things or states. How such a faculty is possible is not a necessary inquiry; for in the case of natural causality itself, we are obliged to content ourselves with

On the Antithesis

The assertor of the all-sufficiency of nature in regard to causality (transcendental *Physiocracy*), in opposition to the doctrine of freedom, would defend his view of the question somewhat in the following manner. He would say, in answer to the sophistical arguments of the opposite party: *If you do not accept a mathematical first, in relation to time, you have no need to seek a dynamical first, in regard to causality.* Who compelled you to imagine an absolutely primal condition of the world, and therewith an absolute beginning of the gradually progressing successions of phenomena—and, as some foundation for this fancy of yours, to set bounds to unlimited nature? Inasmuch as the substances in the world have always existed—at least the unity of experience renders such a supposition quite necessary—there is no difficulty in believing also, that the changes in the conditions of these substances have always ex-

THESIS

the *a priori* knowledge that such a causality must be presupposed, although we are quite incapable of comprehending how the being of one thing is possible through the being of another, but must for this information look entirely to experience. Now we have demonstrated this necessity of a free first beginning of a series of phenomena, only in so far as it is required for the comprehension of an origin of the world, all following states being regarded as a succession according to laws of nature alone. But, as there has thus been proved the existence of a faculty which can of itself originate a series in time—although we are unable to explain how it can exist—we feel ourselves authorized to admit, even in the midst of the natural course of events, a beginning, as regards causality, of different successions of phenomena, and at the same time to attribute to all substances a faculty of free action. But we ought in this case not to allow ourselves to fall into a common misunderstanding, and to suppose that, because a successive series in the world can only have a comparatively first beginning—another state or condition of things always preceding—an absolutely first beginning of a series in the course of nature is impossible. For we are not speaking here of an absolutely first beginning in relation to time, but as regards causality alone. When, for example, I, completely of my own free will, and independently of the necessarily determinative influence of natural causes, rise from my chair, there commences with this event, including its material consequences *in infinitum*, an absolutely new series; although, in relation to time, this event is merely the continuation of a preceding series. For this resolution and act of mine do not form part of the succession of effects in nature, and are not mere continuations of it; on the contrary, the determining causes of nature cease to operate in reference to this event, which certainly *succeeds* the acts of nature, but does not *proceed* from them. For these reasons, the action of a free agent must be termed, in regard to causality, if not in relation to time, an absolutely primal beginning of a series of phenomena.

The justification of this need of reason to rest upon a free act as the first beginning of the series of natural causes is evident from the fact, that all philosophers of antiquity (with the exception of the Epicurean school) felt themselves obliged, when constructing a theory of the motions of the universe, to accept a *prime mover*,

ANTITHESIS

isted; and, consequently, that a first beginning, mathematical or dynamical, is by no means required. The possibility of such an infinite derivation, without any initial member from which all the others result, is certainly quite incomprehensible. But, if you are rash enough to deny the enigmatical secrets of nature for this reason, you will find yourselves obliged to deny also the existence of many fundamental properties of natural objects (such as fundamental forces), which you can just as little comprehend; and even the possibility of so simple a conception as that of change must present to you insuperable difficulties. For if experience did not teach you that it was real, you never could conceive *a priori* the possibility of this ceaseless sequence of being and non-being.

But if the existence of a transcendental faculty of freedom is granted—a faculty of originating changes in the world—this faculty must at least exist out of and apart from the world; although it is certainly a bold assumption, that, over and above the complete content of all possible intuitions, there still exists an object which cannot be presented in any possible perception. But, to attribute to substances in the world itself such a faculty, is quite inadmissible; for, in this case; the connection of phenomena reciprocally determining and determined according to general laws, which is termed nature, and along with it the criteria of empirical truth, which enable us to distinguish experience from mere visionary dreaming, would almost entirely disappear. In proximity with such a lawless faculty of freedom, a system of nature is hardly cogitable; for the laws of the latter would be continually subject to the intrusive influences of the former, and the course of phenomena, which would otherwise proceed regularly and uniformly, would become thereby confused and disconnected.

THESIS

that is, a freely acting cause, which spontaneously and prior to all other causes evolved this series of states. They always felt the need of going beyond mere nature, for the purpose of making a first beginning comprehensible.

ANTITHESIS

FOURTH CONFLICT OF THE TRANSCENDENTAL IDEAS

THESIS

There exists either in, or in connection with the world—either as a part of it, or as the cause of it—an absolutely necessary being.

PROOF

The world of sense, as the sum total of all phenomena, contains a series of changes. For, without such a series, the mental representation of the series of time itself, as the condition of the possibility of the sensuous world, could not be presented to us.[1] But every change stands under its condition, which precedes it in time and renders it necessary. Now the existence of a given condition presupposes a complete series of conditions up to the absolutely unconditioned, which alone is absolutely necessary. It follows that something that is absolutely necessary must exist, if change exists as its consequence. But this necessary thing itself belongs to the sensuous world. For suppose it to exist out of and apart from it, the series of cosmical changes would receive from it a beginning, and yet this necessary cause would not itself belong to the world of sense. But this is impossible. For, as the beginning of a series in time is determined only by that which precedes it in time, the supreme condition of the beginning of a series of changes must exist in the time in which this series itself did not exist; for a beginning supposes a time preceding, in which the thing that begins to be was not in existence. The causality of the necessary cause of changes, and consequently the cause itself, must for these reasons belong to time—and to phenomena, time being possible only as the form of phenomena. Consequently, it cannot be cogitated as separated from the world of sense—the sum total of all phenomena. There is, therefore, contained in the world, something that is absolutely necessary—whether it be the whole cosmical series itself, or only a part of it.

[1] *Objectively,* time, as the formal condition of the possibility of change, precedes all changes; but *subjectively,* and in consciousness, the representation of time, like every other, is given solely by *occasion* of perception.

ANTITHESIS

An absolutely necessary being does not exist, either in the world, or out of it—as its cause.

PROOF

Grant that either the world itself is necessary, or that there is contained in it a necessary existence. Two cases are possible. *First,* there must either be in the series of cosmical changes a beginning, which is unconditionally necessary, and therefore uncaused—which is at variance with the dynamical law of the determination of all phenomena in time; or, *secondly,* the series itself is without beginning, and, although contingent and conditioned in all its parts, is nevertheless absolutely necessary and unconditioned as a whole—which is self-contradictory. For the existence of an aggregate cannot be necessary, if no single part of it possesses necessary existence.

Grant, on the other hand, that an absolutely necessary cause exists out of and apart from the world. This cause, as the highest member in the series of the causes of cosmical changes, must originate or begin[2] the existence of the latter and their series. In this case it must also begin to act, and its causality would therefore belong to time, and consequently to the sum total of phenomena, that is, to the world. It follows that the cause cannot be out of the world; which is contradictory to the hypothesis. Therefore, neither in the world, nor out of it (but in causal connection with it), does there exist any absolutely necessary being.

[2] The word *begin* is taken in two senses. The first is active—the cause being regarded as beginning a series of conditions as its effect *(infit)*. The second is passive—the causality in the cause itself beginning to operate *(fit)*. I reason here from the first to the second.

Observations on the Fourth Antinomy

On the Thesis

To demonstrate the existence of a necessary being, I cannot be permitted in this place to employ any other than the *cosmological* argument, which ascends from the conditioned in phenomena to the unconditioned in conception—the unconditioned being considered the necessary condition of the absolute totality of the series. The proof, from the mere idea of a supreme being, belongs to another principle of reason and requires separate discussion.

The pure cosmological proof demonstrates the existence of a necessary being, but at the same time leaves it quite unsettled, whether this being is the world itself, or quite distinct from it. To establish the truth of the latter view, principles are requisite, which are not cosmological and do not proceed in the series of phenomena. We should require to introduce into our proof conceptions of contingent beings—regarded merely as objects of the understanding, and also a principle which enables us to connect these, by means of mere conceptions, with a necessary being. But the proper place for all such arguments is a *transcendent* philosophy, which has unhappily not yet been established.

But, if we begin our proof cosmologically, by laying at the foundation of it the series of phenomena, and the regress in it according to empirical laws of causality, we are not at liberty to break off from this mode of demonstration and to pass over to something which is not itself a member of the series. The condition must be taken in exactly the same signification as the relation of the conditioned to its condition in the series has been taken, for the series must conduct us in an unbroken regress to this supreme condition. But if this relation is sensuous, and belongs to the possible empirical employment of understanding, the supreme condition or cause must close the regressive series according to the laws of sensibility and consequently, must belong to the series of time. It follows that this necessary existence must be regarded as the highest member of the cosmical series.

Certain philosophers have, nevertheless, allowed themselves the liberty of making such a *saltus* (μετάβασις εἰς ἄλλο γένος). From the changes in the world they have concluded their empirical contingency, that is, their dependence on empirically-determined causes, and they thus admitted an ascending series of empirical con-

On the Antithesis

The difficulties which meet us, in our attempt to rise through the series of phenomena to the existence of an absolutely necessary supreme cause, must not originate from our inability to establish the truth of our mere conceptions of the necessary existence of a thing. That is to say, our objections must not be ontological, but must be directed against the causal connection with a series of phenomena of a condition which is itself unconditioned. In one word, they must be cosmological and relate to empirical laws. We must show that the regress in the series of causes (in the world of sense) cannot conclude with an empirically unconditioned condition, and that the cosmological argument from the contingency of the cosmical state—a contingency alleged to arise from change—does not justify us in accepting a first cause, that is, a prime originator of the cosmical series.

The reader will observe in this antinomy a very remarkable contrast. The very same grounds of proof which established in the thesis the existence of a supreme being, demonstrated in the antithesis—and with equal strictness—the non-existence of such a being. We found, first, that *a necessary being exists,* because the whole time past contains the series of all conditions, and with it, therefore, the unconditioned (the necessary); secondly, that *there does not exist any necessary being*, for the same reason, that the whole time past contains the series of all conditions—which are themselves, therefore, in the aggregate, conditioned. The cause of this seeming incongruity is as follows. We attend, in the first argument, solely to the *absolute totality* of the series of conditions, the one of which determines the other in time, and thus arrive at a necessary unconditioned. In the second, we consider, on the contrary, the *contingency* of everything that is determined in the *series of time*—for every event is preceded by a time, in which the condition itself must be determined as conditioned—and thus everything that is unconditioned or absolutely necessary disappears. In both, the mode of proof is quite in accordance with the common procedure of human reason, which often falls into discord with itself, from considering an object from two different points of view. Herr von Mairan regarded the controversy between two celebrated astronomers, which arose from a similar difficulty as to

THESIS

ditions: and in this they are quite right. But as they could not find in this series any primal beginning or any highest member, they passed suddenly from the empirical conception of contingency to the pure category, which presents us with a series—not sensuous, but intellectual—whose completeness does certainly rest upon the existence of an absolutely necessary cause. Nay, more, this intellectual series is not tied to any sensuous conditions; and is therefore free from the condition of time, which requires it spontaneously to begin its causality in time. But such a procedure is perfectly inadmissible, as will be made plain from what follows.

In the pure sense of the categories, that is contingent the contradictory opposite of which is possible. Now we cannot reason from empirical contingency to intellectual. The opposite of that which is changed—the opposite of its state—is actual at another time, and is therefore possible. Consequently, it is not the contradictory opposite of the former state. To be *that,* it is necessary that, in the same time in which the preceding state existed, its opposite could have existed in its place; but such a cognition is not given us in the mere phenomenon of change. A body that was in motion $= A$, comes into a state of rest $=$ *non-A*. Now it cannot be concluded from the fact that a state opposite to the state *A* follows it, that the contradictory opposite of *A* is possible; and that *A* is therefore contingent. To prove this, we should require to know that the state of rest could have existed in the very same time in which the motion took place. Now we know nothing more than that the state of rest was actual in the time that followed the state of motion; consequently, that it was also possible. But motion at one time, and rest at another time, are not contradictorily opposed to each other. It follows from what has been said that the succession of opposite determinations, that is, change, does not demonstrate the fact of contingency as represented in the conceptions of the pure understanding; and that it cannot, therefore, conduct us to the fact of the existence of a necessary being. Change proves merely empirical contingency, that is to say, that the new state could not have existed without a cause, which belongs to the preceding time. This cause—even although it is regarded as absolutely necessary—must be presented to us in time, and must belong to the series of phenomena.

ANTITHESIS

the choice of a proper standpoint, as a phenomenon of sufficient importance to warrant a separate treatise on the subject. The one concluded: *the moon revolves on its own axis,* because it constantly presents the same side to the earth; the other declared that *the moon does not revolve on its own axis,* for the same reason. Both conclusions were perfectly correct, according to the point of view from which the motions of the moon were considered.

SECTION III. *Of the Interest of Reason in these Self-contradictions*

We have thus completely before us the dialectical procedure of the cosmological ideas. No possible experience can present us with an object adequate to them in extent. Nay, more, reason itself cannot cogitate them as according with the general laws of experience. And yet they are not arbitrary fictions of thought. On the contrary, reason, in its uninterrupted progress in the empirical synthesis, is necessarily conducted to them, when it endeavours to free from all conditions and to comprehend in its unconditioned totality that which can only be determined conditionally in accordance with the laws of experience. These dialectical propositions are so many attempts to solve four natural and unavoidable problems of reason. There are neither more, nor can there be less, than this number, because there are no other series of synthetical hypotheses, limiting *a priori* the empirical synthesis.

The brilliant claims of reason striving to extend its dominion beyond the limits of experience, have been represented above only in dry formulae, which contain merely the grounds of its pretensions. They have, besides, in conformity with the character of a transcendental philosophy, been freed from every empirical element; although the full splendour of the promises they hold out, and the anticipations they excite, manifests itself only when in connection with empirical cognitions. In the application of them, however, and in the advancing enlargement of the employment of reason, while struggling to rise from the region of experience and to soar to those sublime ideas, philosophy discovers a value and a dignity, which, if it could but make good its assertions, would raise it far above all other departments of human knowledge—professing, as it does, to present a sure foundation for our highest hopes and the ultimate aims of all the exertions of reason. The questions: whether the world has a beginning and a limit to its extension in space; whether there exists anywhere, or perhaps, in my own thinking Self, an indivisible and indestructible unity—or whether nothing but what is divisible and transitory exists; whether I am a free agent, or, like other beings, am bound in the chains of nature and fate; whether, finally, there is a supreme cause of the world, or all our thought and speculation must end with nature and the order of external things—are questions for the solution of which the mathematician would willingly exchange his whole science; for in it there is no satisfaction for the highest aspirations and most ardent desires of humanity. Nay, it may even be said that the true value of mathematics—that pride of human reason—consists in this: that she guides reason to the knowledge of nature—in her greater as well as in her less manifestations—in her beautiful order and regularity—guides her, moreover, to an insight into the wonderful unity of the moving forces in the operations of nature, far beyond the expectations of a philosophy building only on experience; and that she thus encourages philosophy to extend the province of reason beyond all experience, and at the same time provides it with the most excellent materials for supporting its investigations, in so far as their nature admits, by adequate and accordant intuitions.

Unfortunately for speculation—but perhaps fortunately for the practical interests of humanity—reason, in the midst of her highest anticipations, finds herself hemmed in by a press of opposite and contradictory conclusions, from which neither her honour nor her safety will permit her to draw back. Nor can she regard these conflicting trains of reasoning with indifference as mere passages at arms, still less can she command peace; for in the subject of the conflict she has a deep interest. There is no other course left open to her than to reflect with herself upon the origin of this disunion in reason—whether it may not arise from a mere misunderstanding. After such an inquiry, arrogant claims would have to be given up on both sides; but the sovereignty of reason over understanding and sense would be based upon a sure foundation.

We shall at present defer this radical inquiry and, in the meantime, consider for a little what side in the controversy we should most willingly take, if we were obliged to become partisans at all. As, in this case, we leave out of sight altogether the logical criterion of truth, and merely consult our own interest in reference to the question, these considerations, although inadequate to settle the question of right in either party, will enable us to comprehend how those who have taken part in the struggle, adopt the one view rather than the other—no special insight into the subject, however, having influenced their choice. They will, at the same time, explain to us many other things by the way—for example, the fiery zeal on the one side and the cold maintenance of their cause on the other; why the one party has met with the warmest approbations, and the other has always been repulsed by irreconcilable prejudices.

There is one thing, however, that determines the proper point of view, from which alone this preliminary inquiry can be instituted and carried on with the proper completeness—and that is the comparison of the principles from which both sides, thesis and antithesis, proceed. My readers would remark in the propositions of the antithesis a complete uniformity in the mode of thought and a perfect unity of principle. Its principle was that of pure empiricism, not only in the explication of the phenomena in the world, but also in the solution of the transcendental ideas, even of that of the universe itself. The affirmations of the thesis, on the contrary, were based, in addition to the empirical mode of explanation employed in the series of phenomena, on intellectual propositions; and its principles were in so far not simple. I shall term the thesis, in view of its essential characteristic, the *dogmatism* of pure reason.

On the side of *Dogmatism,* or of the thesis, therefore, in the determination of the cosmological ideas, we find:

1. A *practical interest,* which must be very dear to every right-thinking man. That the word has a beginning—that the nature of my thinking self is simple, and therefore indestructible—that I am a free agent, and raised above the compulsion of nature and her laws—and, finally, that the entire order of things, which form the world, is dependent upon a Supreme Being, from whom the whole receives unity and connection—these are so many foundation-stones of morality and religion. The antithesis deprives us of all these supports—or, at least, seems so to deprive us.

2. A *speculative interest* of reason manifests itself on this side. For, if we take the transcendental ideas and employ them in the manner which the thesis directs, we can exhibit completely *a priori* the entire chain of conditions, and understand the derivation of the conditioned —beginning from the unconditioned. This the antithesis does not do; and for this reason does not meet with so welcome a reception. For it can give no answer to our question respecting the conditions of its synthesis—except such as must be supplemented by another question, and so on to infinity. According to it, we must rise from a given beginning to one still higher; every part conducts us to a still smaller one; every event is preceded by another event which is its cause; and the conditions of existence rest always upon other and still higher conditions, and find neither end nor basis in some self-subsistent thing as the primal being.

3. This side has also the advantage of *popularity;* and this constitutes no small part of its claim to favour. The common understanding does not find the least difficulty in the idea of the unconditioned beginning of all synthesis—accustomed, as it is, rather to follow our consequences than to seek for a proper basis for cognition. In the conception of an absolute first, moreover—the possibility of which it does not inquire into—it is highly gratified to find a firmly-established point of departure for its attempts at theory; while in the restless and continuous ascent from the conditioned to the condition, always with one foot in the air, it can find no satisfaction.

On the side of the antithesis, or *Empiricism,* in the determination of the cosmological ideas:

1. We cannot discover any such practical interest arising from pure principles of reason as morality and religion present. On the contrary, pure empiricism seems to empty them of all their power and influence. If there does not exist a Supreme Being distinct from the world—if the world is without beginning, consequently without a Creator—if our wills are not free, and the soul is divisible and subject to corruption just like matter—the ideas and principles of morality lose all validity and fall with the transcendental ideas which constituted their theoretical support.

2. But empiricism, in compensation, holds out to reason, in its speculative interests, certain important advantages, far exceeding any that the dogmatist can promise us. For, when employed by the empiricist, understanding is always upon its proper ground of investigation—the field of possible experience, the laws of which it can explore, and thus extend its cognition securely and with clear intelligence without being stopped by limits in any direction. Here can it and ought it to find and present to intuition its proper object—not only in itself, but in all its relations; or, if it employ conceptions, upon this ground it can always present the corresponding images in clear and unmistakable intuitions. It is quite unnecessary for it to renounce the guidance of nature, to attach itself to ideas, the objects of which it cannot know; because, as mere intellectual entities, they cannot be presented in any intuition. On the contrary, it is not even permitted to abandon its proper occupation, under the pretence that it has been brought to a conclusion (for it never can be), and to pass into the region of idealizing reason and transcendent

conceptions, which it is not required to observe and explore the laws of nature, but merely to *think* and to *imagine*—secure from being contradicted by facts, because they have not been called as witnesses, but passed by, or perhaps subordinated to the so-called higher interests and considerations of pure reason.

Hence the empiricist will never allow himself to accept any epoch of nature for the first—the absolutely primal state; he will not believe that there can be limits to his outlook into her wide domains, nor pass from the objects of nature, which he can satisfactorily explain by means of observation and mathematical thought—which he can determine synthetically in intuition, to those which neither sense nor imagination can ever present *in concreto;* he will not concede the existence of a faculty in nature, operating independently of the laws of nature—a concession which would introduce uncertainty into the procedure of the understanding, which is guided by necessary laws to the observation of phenomena; nor, finally, will he permit himself to seek a cause beyond nature, inasmuch as we know nothing but it, and from it alone receive an objective basis for all our conceptions and instruction in the unvarying laws of things.

In truth, if the empirical philosopher had no other purpose in the establishment of his antithesis than to check the presumption of a reason which mistakes its true destination, which boasts of its insight and its knowledge, just where all insight and knowledge cease to exist, and regards that which is valid only in relation to a practical interest, as an advancement of the speculative interests of the mind (in order, when it is convenient for itself, to break the thread of our physical investigations, and, under pretence of extending our cognition, connect them with transcendental ideas, by means of which we really know only that we know nothing)—if, I say, the empiricist rested satisfied with this benefit, the principle advanced by him would be a maxim recommending moderation in the pretensions of reason and modesty in its affirmations, and at the same time would direct us to the right mode of extending the province of the understanding, by the help of the only true teacher, experience. In obedience to this advice, intellectual *hypotheses* and *faith* would not be called in aid of our practical interests; nor should we introduce them under the pompous titles of science and insight. For speculative *cognition* cannot find an objective basis any other where than in experience; and, when we overstep its limits, our synthesis, which requires ever new cognitions independent of experience, has no substratum of intuition upon which to build.

But if—as often happens—empiricism, in relation to ideas, becomes itself dogmatic and boldly denies that which is above the sphere of its phenomenal cognition, it falls itself into the error of intemperance—an error which is here all the more reprehensible, as thereby the practical interest of reason receives an irreparable injury.

And this constitutes the opposition between Epicureanism[1] and Platonism.

Both Epicurus and Plato assert more in their systems than they know. The former encourages and advances science—although to the prejudice of the practical; the latter presents us with excellent principles for the investigation of the practical, but, in relation to everything regarding which we can attain to speculative cognition, permits reason to append idealistic explanations of natural phenomena, to the great injury of physical investigation.

3. In regard to the third motive for the preliminary choice of a party in this war of assertions, it seems very extraordinary that empiricism should be utterly unpopular. We should be inclined to believe that the common understanding would receive it with pleasure—promising as it does to satisfy it without passing the bounds of experience and its connected order; while transcendental dogmatism obliges it to rise to conceptions which far surpass the intelligence and ability of the most practised thinkers. But in this, in truth, is to be found its real motive. For the common understanding thus finds itself in a situation where not even the most learned can have the advantage of it. If it understands little or nothing about these transcendental conceptions, no one can boast of understanding any

[1] It is, however, still a matter of doubt whether Epicurus ever propounded these principles as directions for the objective employment of the understanding. If, indeed, they were nothing more than maxims for the speculative exercise of reason, he gives evidence therein of a more genuine philosophic spirit than any of the philosophers of antiquity. That, in the explanation of phenomena, we must proceed as if the field of inquiry had neither limits in space nor commencement in time; that we must be satisfied with the teaching of experience in reference to the material of which the world is composed; that we must not look for any other mode of the origination of events than that which is determined by the unalterable laws of nature; and finally, that we must not employ the hypothesis of a cause distinct from the world to account for a phenomenon or for the world itself—are principles for the extension of speculative philosophy, and the discovery of the true sources of the principles of morals, which, however little conformed to in the present day, are undoubtedly correct. At the same time, any one desirous of *ignoring,* in mere speculation, these dogmatical propositions, need not for that reason be accused of *denying* them.

more; and although it may not express itself in so scholastically correct a manner as others, it can busy itself with reasoning and arguments without end, wandering among mere ideas, about which one can always be very eloquent, because we know nothing about them; while, in the observation and investigation of nature, it would be forced to remain dumb and to confess its utter ignorance. Thus indolence and vanity form of themselves strong recommendations of these principles. Besides, although it is a hard thing for a philosopher to assume a principle, of which he can give to himself no reasonable account, and still more to employ conceptions, the objective reality of which cannot be established, nothing is more usual with the common understanding. It wants something which will allow it to go to work with confidence. The difficulty of even comprehending a supposition does not disquiet it, because—not knowing what comprehending means—it never even thinks of the supposition it may be adopting as a principle; and regards as known that with which it has become familiar from constant use. And, at last, all speculative interests disappear before the practical interests which it holds dear; and it fancies that it understands and knows what its necessities and hopes incite it to assume or to believe. Thus the empiricism of transcendentally idealizing reason is robbed of all popularity; and, however prejudicial it may be to the highest practical principles, there is no fear that it will ever pass the limits of the schools, or acquire any favour or influence in society or with the multitude.

Human reason is by nature architectonic. That is to say, it regards all cognitions as parts of a possible system, and hence accepts only such principles as at least do not incapacitate a cognition to which we may have attained from being placed along with others in a general system. But the propositions of the antithesis are of a character which renders the completion of an edifice of cognitions impossible. According to these, beyond one state or epoch of the world there is always to be found one more ancient; in every part always other parts themselves divisible; preceding every event another, the origin of which must itself be sought still higher; and everything in existence is conditioned, and still not dependent on an unconditioned and primal existence. As, therefore, the antithesis will not concede the existence of a first beginning which might be available as a foundation, a complete edifice of cognition, in the presence of such hypotheses, is utterly impossible. Thus the architectonic interest of reason, which requires a unity—not empirical, but *a priori* and rational—forms a natural recommendation for the assertions of the thesis in our antinomy.

But if any one could free himself entirely from all considerations of interest, and weigh without partiality the assertions of reason, attending only to their content, irrespective of the consequences which follow from them; such a person, on the supposition that he knew no other way out of the confusion than to settle the truth of one or other of the conflicting doctrines, would live in a state of continual hesitation. To-day, he would feel convinced that the human will is free; to-morrow, considering the indissoluble chain of nature, he would look on freedom as a mere illusion and declare *nature* to be all-in-all. But, if he were called to action, the play of the merely speculative reason would disappear like the shapes of a dream, and practical interest would dictate his choice of principles. But, as it well befits a reflective and inquiring being to devote certain periods of time to the examination of its own reason—to divest itself of all partiality, and frankly to communicate its observations for the judgement and opinion of others; so no one can be blamed for, much less prevented from, placing both parties on their trial, with permission to defend themselves, free from intimidation, before a sworn jury of equal condition with themselves—the condition of weak and fallible men.

SECTION IV. *Of the necessity imposed upon Pure Reason of presenting a Solution of its Transcendental Problems*

To avow an ability to solve all problems and to answer all questions would be a profession certain to convict any philosopher of extravagant boasting and self-conceit, and at once to destroy the confidence that might otherwise have been reposed in him. There are, however, sciences so constituted that every question arising within their sphere must necessarily be capable of receiving an answer from the knowledge already possessed, for the answer must be received from the same sources whence the question arose. In such sciences it is not allowable to excuse ourselves on the plea of necessary and unavoidable ignorance; a solution is absolutely requisite. The rule of *right* and *wrong* must help us to the knowledge of what is right or wrong in all possible cases; otherwise, the idea of obligation or duty would be utterly null, for we cannot have any obligation to that *which we cannot know.* On the other hand, in our investigations of the phenomena of nature, much must remain uncertain, and many questions continue insoluble; because what we know of nature is far from being sufficient to explain all the phenomena that are presented to our observation. Now the question is: "Whether there is in transcendental philosophy any question, relating to an object presented to pure reason, which is unanswerable by this reason; and whether we must regard the subject of the question as quite uncertain, so far as our knowledge extends, and must give it a place among those subjects, of which we have just so much conception as is sufficient to enable us to raise a question—faculty or materials failing us, however, when we attempt an answer."

Now I maintain that, among all speculative cognition, the peculiarity of transcendental philosophy is that there is no question, relating to an object presented to pure reason, which is insoluble by this reason; and that the profession of unavoidable ignorance—the problem being alleged to be beyond the reach of our faculties—cannot free us from the obligation to present a complete and satisfactory answer. For the very conception which enables us to raise the question must give us the power of answering it; inasmuch as the object, as in the case of right and wrong, is not to be discovered out of the conception.

But, in transcendental philosophy, it is only the cosmological questions to which we can demand a satisfactory answer in relation to the constitution of their object; and the philosopher is not permitted to avail himself of the pretext of necessary ignorance and impenetrable obscurity. These questions relate solely to the cosmological ideas. For the object must be given in experience, and the question relates to the adequateness of the object to an idea. If the object is transcendental and therefore itself unknown; if the question, for example, is whether the object—the something, the phenomenon of which (internal—in ourselves) is thought—that is to say, the soul, is in itself a simple being; or whether there is a cause of all things, which is absolutely necessary—in such cases we are seeking for our idea an object, of which we may confess that it is unknown to us, though we must not on that account assert that it is impossible.[1] The cosmological ideas alone possess the peculiarity that we can presuppose the object of them and the empirical synthesis requisite for the conception of that object to be given; and the question, which arises from these ideas, relates merely to the progress of this synthesis, in so far as it must contain absolute totality—which, however, is not empirical, as it cannot be given in any experience. Now, as the question here is solely in regard to a thing as the object of a possible experience and not as a thing in itself, the answer to the transcendental cosmological question need not be sought out of the idea, for the question does not regard an object in itself. The question in relation to a possible experience is not, "What can be given in an experience *in concreto*" but "what is contained in the idea, to which the empirical synthesis must approximate." The question must therefore be capable of solution from the idea alone. For the idea is a creation of reason itself, which therefore cannot disclaim the obligation to answer or refer us to the unknown object.

It is not so extraordinary, as it at first sight appears, that a science should demand and expect satisfactory answers to all the questions that may arise within its own sphere (*questiones domesticae*), although, up to a certain time, these answers may not have been discovered. There are, in addition to transcendental philosophy, only two pure sciences of reason; the one with a speculative, the other with a practical content—*pure mathematics* and *pure ethics.* Has any one ever heard it alleged that, from our complete and necessary ignorance of the conditions, it is *uncertain* what exact relation the diameter of a circle bears to the circle in rational or irrational numbers? By the former the sum cannot be given exactly, by the latter only approximately; and therefore we decide that the impossibility of a solution of the question is evident. Lambert presented us with a demonstration of this. In the general principles of morals there can be nothing uncertain, for the propositions are either utterly without meaning, or must originate solely in our rational conceptions. On the other hand, there must be in phys-

[1] The question, "What is the constitution of a transcendental object?" is unanswerable—we are unable to say *what it is;* but we can perceive that the *question* itself *is nothing;* because it does not relate to any object that can be presented to us. For this reason, we must consider all the questions raised in transcendental psychology as answerable and as really answered; for they relate to the transcendental subject of all internal phenomena, which is not itself phenomenon and consequently not given as an object, in which, moreover, none of the categories—and it is to them that the question is properly directed—find any conditions of its application. Here, therefore, is a case where no answer is the only proper answer. For a question regarding the constitution of a something which cannot be cogitated by any determined predicate, being completely beyond the sphere of objects and experience, is perfectly null and void.

ical science an infinite number of conjectures, which can never become certainties; because the phenomena of nature are not given as objects dependent on our conceptions. The key to the solution of such questions cannot, therefore, be found in our conceptions, or in pure thought, but must lie without us and for that reason is in many cases not to be discovered; and consequently a satisfactory explanation cannot be expected. The questions of transcendental analytic, which relate to the deduction of our pure cognition, are not to be regarded as of the same kind as those mentioned above; for we are not at present treating of the certainty of judgements in relation to the origin of our conceptions, but only of that certainty in relation to objects.

We cannot, therefore, escape the responsibility of at least a critical solution of the questions of reason, by complaints of the limited nature of our faculties, and the seemingly humble confession that it is beyond the power of our reason to decide, whether the world has existed from all eternity or had a beginning—whether it is infinitely extended, or enclosed within certain limits—whether anything in the world is simple, or whether everything must be capable of infinite divisibility—whether freedom can originate phenomena, or whether everything is absolutely dependent on the laws and order of nature—and, finally, whether there exists a being that is completely unconditioned and necessary, or whether the existence of everything is conditioned and consequently dependent on something external to itself, and therefore in its own nature contingent. For all these questions relate to an object, which can be given nowhere else than in thought. This object is the absolutely unconditioned totality of the synthesis of phenomena. If the conceptions in our minds do not assist us to some certain result in regard to these problems, we must not defend ourselves on the plea that the object itself remains hidden from and unknown to us. For no such thing or object can be given—it is not to be found out of the idea in our minds. We must seek the cause of our failure in our idea itself, which is an insoluble problem and in regard to which we obstinately assume that there exists a real object corresponding and adequate to it. A clear explanation of the dialectic which lies in our conception, will very soon enable us to come to a satisfactory decision in regard to such a question.

The pretext that we are unable to arrive at certainty in regard to these problems may be met with this question, which requires at least a plain answer: "From what source do the ideas originate, the solution of which involves you in such difficulties? Are you seeking for an explanation of certain phenomena; and do you expect these ideas to give you the principles or the rules of this explanation?" Let it be granted, that all nature was laid open before you; that nothing was hid from your senses and your consciousness. Still, you could not cognize *in concreto* the object of your ideas in any experience. For what is demanded is not only this full and complete intuition, but also a complete synthesis and the consciousness of its absolute totality; and this is not possible by means of any empirical cognition. It follows that your question—your idea—is by no means necessary for the explanation of any phenomenon; and the idea cannot have been in any sense given by the object itself. For such an object can never be presented to us, because it cannot be given by any possible experience. Whatever perceptions you may attain to, you are still surrounded by *conditions*—in space, or in time—and you cannot discover anything unconditioned; nor can you decide whether this unconditioned is to be placed in an absolute beginning of the synthesis, or in an absolute totality of the series without beginning. A whole, in the empirical signification of the term, is always merely comparative. The absolute whole of quantity (the universe), of division, of derivation, of the condition of existence, with the question—whether it is to be produced by finite or infinite synthesis, no possible experience can instruct us concerning. You will not, for example, be able to explain the phenomena of a body in the least degree better, whether you believe it to consist of simple, or of composite parts; for a simple phenomenon—and just as little an infinite series of composition—can never be presented to your perception. Phenomena require and admit of explanation, only in so far as the conditions of that explanation are given in perception; but the sum total of that which is given in phenomena, considered as an absolute whole, is itself a perception—and we cannot therefore seek for explanations of this whole beyond itself, in other perceptions. The explanation of this whole is the proper object of the transcendental problems of pure reason.

Although, therefore, the solution of these problems is unattainable through experience, we must not permit ourselves to say that it is uncertain how the object of our inquiries is constituted. For the object is in our own mind and cannot be discovered in experience; and we have only to take care that our thoughts are consistent with each other, and to avoid falling into the amphiboly of regarding our idea as a representation of an object empirically given, and therefore to be cognized according to the laws of experience. A dogmatical solution is therefore not only unsatisfactory but impossible. The critical solution, which may be a perfectly certain one, does not consider the question objectively, but proceeds by inquiring into the basis of the cognition upon which the question rests.

SECTION V. *Sceptical Exposition of the Cosmological Problems presented in the four Transcendental Ideas*

WE should be quite willing to desist from the demand of a dogmatical answer to our questions, if we understood beforehand that, be the answer what it may, it would only serve to increase our ignorance, to throw us from one incomprehensibility into another, from one obscurity into another still greater, and perhaps lead us into irreconcilable contradictions. If a dogmatical affirmative or negative answer is demanded, is it at all prudent to set aside the probable grounds of a solution which lie before us and to take into consideration what advantage we shall gain, if the answer is to favour the one side or the other? If it happens that in both cases the answer is mere nonsense, we have in this an irresistible summons to institute a critical investigation of the question, for the purpose of discovering whether it is based on a groundless presupposition and relates to an idea, the falsity of which would be more easily exposed in its application and consequences than in the mere representation of its content. This is the great utility of the sceptical mode of treating the questions addressed by pure reason to itself. By this method we easily rid ourselves of the confusions of dogmatism, and establish in its place a temperate criticism, which, as a genuine cathartic, will successfully remove the presumptuous notions of philosophy and their consequence—the vain pretension to universal science.

If, then, I could understand the nature of a cosmological idea and perceive, before I entered on the discussion of the subject at all, that, whatever side of the question regarding the unconditioned of the regressive synthesis of phenomena it favoured—it must either be *too great* or *too small* for every *conception of the understanding*—I would be able to comprehend how the idea, which relates to an object of experience—an experience which must be adequate to and in accordance with a possible conception of the understanding—must be completely void and without significance, inasmuch as its object is inadequate, consider it as we may. And this is actually the case with all cosmological conceptions, which, for the reason above mentioned, involve reason, so long as it remains attached to them, in an unavoidable antinomy. For suppose:

First, that *the world has no beginning*—in this case it is too large for our conception; for this conception, which consists in a successive regress, cannot overtake the whole eternity that has elapsed. Grant that *it has a beginning,* it is then too small for the conception of the understanding. For, as a beginning presupposes a time preceding, it cannot be unconditioned; and the law of the empirical employment of the understanding imposes the necessity of looking for a higher condition of time; and the world is, therefore, evidently too small for this law.

The same is the case with the double answer to the question regarding the extent, in space, of the world. For, if it is *infinite* and unlimited, it must be *too large* for every possible empirical conception. If it is *finite* and limited, we have a right to ask: "What determines these limits?" Void space is not a self-subsistent correlate of things, and cannot be a final condition—and still less an empirical condition, forming a part of a possible experience. For how can we have any experience or perception of an absolute void? But the absolute totality of the empirical synthesis requires that the unconditioned be an empirical conception. Consequently, a finite world is *too small* for our conception.

Secondly, if every phenomenon (matter) in space consists of an *infinite number of parts,* the regress of the division is always too great for our conception; and if the *division* of space must *cease* with some member of the division (the simple), it is too small for the idea of the unconditioned. For the member at which we have discontinued our division still admits a regress to many more parts contained in the object.

Thirdly, suppose that every event in the world happens in accordance with the laws of nature; the causality of a cause must itself be an event and necessitates a regress to a still higher cause, and consequently the unceasing prolongation of the series of conditions *a parte priori.* Operative nature is therefore too large for every conception we can form in the synthesis of cosmical events.

If we admit the existence of *spontaneously* produced events, that is, of *free* agency, we are driven, in our search for sufficient reasons, on an unavoidable law of nature and are compelled to appeal to the empirical law of causality, and we find that any such totality of connection in our synthesis is too small for our necessary empirical conception.

Fourthly, if we assume the existence of an *absolutely necessary being*—whether it be the world or something in the world, or the cause of the world—we must place it in a time at an infinite distance from any given moment; for, otherwise, it must be dependent on some other and higher existence. Such an existence is, in this case, too large for our empirical conception, and unattainable by the continued regress of any synthesis.

But if we believe that everything in the world—be it condition or conditioned—is *contingent;* every given existence is too small for our conception. For in this case we are compelled to seek for some other existence upon which the former depends.

We have said that in all these cases the cosmological idea is either too great or too small for the empirical regress in a synthesis, and consequently for every possible conception of the understanding. Why did we not express ourselves in a manner exactly the reverse of this and, instead of accusing the cosmological idea of overstepping or of falling short of its true aim, possible experience, say that, in the first case, the empirical conception is always too small for the idea, and in the second too great, and thus attach the blame of these contradictions to the empirical regress? The reason is this. Possible experience can alone give reality to our conceptions; without it a conception is merely an idea, without truth or relation to an object. Hence a possible empirical conception must be the standard by which we are to judge whether an idea is anything more than an idea and fiction of thought, or whether it relates to an object in the world. If we say of a thing that in relation to some other thing it is too large or too small, the former is considered as existing for the sake of the latter, and requiring to be adapted to it. Among the trivial subjects of discussion in the old schools of dialectics was this question: "If a ball cannot pass through a hole, shall we say that the ball is too large or the hole too small?" In this case it is indifferent what expression we employ; for we do not know which exists for the sake of the other. On the other hand, we cannot say: "The man is too long for his coat"; but: "The coat is too short for the man."

We are thus led to the well-founded suspicion that the cosmological ideas, and all the conflicting sophistical assertions connected with them, are based upon a false and fictitious conception of the mode in which the object of these ideas is presented to us; and this suspicion will probably direct us how to expose the illusion that has so long led us astray from the truth.

Section VI. *Transcendental Idealism as the Key to the Solution of Pure Cosmological Dialectic*

In the transcendental aesthetic we proved that everything intuited in space and time, all objects of a possible experience, are nothing but phenomena, that is, mere representations; and that these, as presented to us—as extended bodies, or as series of changes—have no self-subsistent existence apart from human thought. This doctrine I call *Transcendental Idealism.*[1] The realist in the transcendental sense regards these modifications of our sensibility, these mere representations, as things subsisting in themselves.

It would be unjust to accuse us of holding the long-decried theory of empirical idealism, which, while admitting the reality of space, denies, or at least doubts, the existence of bodies extended in it, and thus leaves us without a sufficient criterion of reality and illusion. The supporters of this theory find no difficulty in admitting the reality of the phenomena of the internal sense in time; nay, they go the length of maintaining that this internal experience is of itself a sufficient proof of the real existence of its object as a thing in itself.

Transcendental idealism allows that the objects of external intuition—as intuited in space, and all changes in time—as represented by the internal sense, are real. For, as space is the form of that intuition which we call external, and, without objects in space, no empirical representation could be given us, we can and ought to regard extended bodies in it as real. The case is the same with representations in time. But time and space, with all phenomena therein, are not in themselves *things.* They are nothing but representations and cannot exist out of and apart from the mind. Nay, the sensuous internal intuition of the mind (as the object of consciousness), the determination of which is represented by the succession of different states in time, is not the real, proper self, as it exists in itself—not the transcendental subject—but only a phe-

[1] I have elsewhere termed this theory *formal* idealism, to distinguish it from *material* idealism, which doubts or denies the existence of external things. To avoid ambiguity, it seems advisable in many cases to employ this term instead of that mentioned in the text.

nomenon, which is presented to the sensibility of this, to us, unknown being. This internal phenomenon cannot be admitted to be a self-subsisting thing; for its condition is time, and time cannot be the condition of a thing in itself. But the empirical truth of phenomena in space and time is guaranteed beyond the possibility of doubt, and sufficiently distinguished from the illusion of dreams or fancy—although both have a proper and thorough connection in an experience according to empirical laws. The objects of experience then are not things in themselves, but are given only in experience, and have no existence apart from and independently of experience. That there may be inhabitants in the moon, although no one has ever observed them, must certainly be admitted; but this assertion means only, that we may in the possible progress of experience discover them at some future time. For that which stands in connection with a perception according to the laws of the progress of experience is real. They are therefore really existent, if they stand in empirical connection with my actual or real consciousness, although they are not in themselves real, that is, apart from the progress of experience.

There is nothing actually given—we can be conscious of nothing as real, except a perception and the empirical progression from it to other possible perceptions. For phenomena, as mere representations, are real only in perception; and perception is, in fact, nothing but the reality of an empirical representation, that is, a phenomenon. To call a phenomenon a real thing prior to perception means either that we must meet with this phenomenon in the progress of experience, or it means nothing at all. For I can say only of a thing in itself that it exists without relation to the senses and experience. But we are speaking here merely of phenomena in space and time, both of which are determinations of sensibility, and not of things in themselves. It follows that phenomena are not things in themselves, but are mere representations, which if not given in us—in perception—are non-existent.

The faculty of sensuous intuition is properly a receptivity—a capacity of being affected in a certain manner by representations, the relation of which to each other is a pure intuition of space and time—the pure forms of sensibility. These representations, in so far as they are connected and determinable in this relation (in space and time) according to laws of the unity of experience, are called *objects*. The non-sensuous cause of these representations is completely unknown to us and hence cannot be intuited as an object. For such an object could not be represented either in space or in time; and without these conditions intuition or representation is impossible. We may, at the same time, term the non-sensuous cause of phenomena the transcendental object—but merely as a mental correlate to sensibility, considered as a receptivity. To this transcendental object we may attribute the whole connection and extent of our possible perceptions, and say that it is given and exists in itself prior to all experience. But the phenomena, corresponding to it, are not given as things in themselves, but in experience alone. For they are mere representations, receiving from perceptions alone significance and relation to a real object, under the condition that this or that perception—indicating an object—is in complete connection with all others in accordance with the rules of the unity of experience. Thus we can say: "The things that really existed in past time are given in the transcendental object of experience." But these are to me real objects, only in so far as I can represent to my own mind, that a regressive series of possible perceptions—following the indications of history, or the footsteps of cause and effect—in accordance with empirical laws—that, in one word, the course of the world conducts us to an elapsed series of time as the condition of the present time. This series in past time is represented as real, not in itself, but only in connection with a possible experience. Thus, when I say that certain events occurred in past time, I merely assert the possibility of prolonging the chain of experience, from the present perception, upwards to the conditions that determine it according to time.

If I represent to myself all objects existing in all space and time, I do not thereby place these in space and time prior to all experience; on the contrary, such a representation is nothing more than the notion of a possible experience, in its absolute completeness. In experience alone are those objects, which are nothing but representations, given. But, when I say they existed prior to my experience, this means only that I must begin with the perception present to me and follow the track indicated until I discover them in some part or region of experience. The cause of the empirical condition of this progression—and consequently at what member therein I must stop, and at what point in the regress I am to find this member—is transcendental, and hence necessarily incognizable. But with this we have not to do; our concern is only with the law of progression in experience, in which objects, that is, phenomena, are given. It is a matter of indifference, whether I say, "I may in the progress of experience discover stars, at a hundred times greater distance than the most distant of those now visible," or, "Stars at this distance may be met in space, although no one has, or ever will discover them." For, if they are given as things in themselves, without any relation to possible experience, they are for me non-existent, consequently, are not objects, for they are not contained in the regressive series of experience. But, if these phenomena must be employed in the construction or support of the cosmological idea of an absolute whole, and when we are discussing a question that oversteps the limits of possible experience, the proper distinction of the different theories of the reality of sensuous objects is of great importance, in order to avoid the illusion which must necessarily arise from the misinterpretation of our empirical conceptions.

Section VII. *Critical Solution of the Cosmological Problem*

The antinomy of pure reason is based upon the following dialectical argument: "If that which is conditioned is given, the whole series of its conditions is also given; but sensuous objects are given as conditioned; consequently . . ." This syllogism, the major of which seems so natural and evident, introduces as many cosmological ideas as there are different kinds of conditions in the synthesis of phenomena, in so far as these conditions constitute a series. These ideas require absolute totality in the series, and thus place reason in inextricable embarrassment. Before proceeding to expose the fallacy in this dialectical argument, it will be necessary to have a correct understanding of certain conceptions that appear in it.

In the first place, the following proposition is evident, and indubitably certain: "If the conditioned is given, a regress in the series of all its conditions is thereby imperatively *required*." For the very conception of a conditioned is a conception of something related to a condition, and, if this condition is itself conditioned, to another condition—and so on through all the members of the series. This proposition is, therefore, analytical and has nothing to fear from transcendental criticism. It is a logical postulate of reason: to pursue, as far as possible, the connection of a conception with its conditions.

If, in the second place, both the conditioned and the condition are things in themselves, and if the former is given, not only is the regress to the latter requisite, but the latter is really *given with* the former. Now, as this is true of all the members of the series, the entire series of conditions, and with them the unconditioned, is at the same time given in the very fact of the conditioned, the existence of which is possible only in and through that series, being given. In this case, the synthesis of the conditioned with its condition, is a synthesis of the understanding merely, which represents things *as they are,* without regarding whether and how we can cognize them. But if I have to do with phenomena, which, in their character of mere representations, are not given, if I do not attain to a cognition of them (in other words, to themselves, for they are nothing more than empirical cognitions), I am not entitled to say: "If the conditioned is given, all its conditions (as phenomena) are also given." I cannot, therefore, from the fact of a conditioned being given, infer the absolute totality of the series of its conditions. For phenomena are nothing but an empirical synthesis in apprehension or perception, and are therefore given only in it. Now, in speaking of phenomena, it does not follow that, if the conditioned is given, the synthesis which constitutes its empirical condition is also thereby given and presupposed; such a synthesis can be established only by an actual regress in the series of conditions. But we are entitled to say in this case that a *regress* to the conditions of a conditioned, in other words, that a continuous empirical synthesis is enjoined; that, if the conditions are not *given,* they are at least *required;* and that we are certain to discover the conditions in this regress.

We can now see that the major, in the above cosmological syllogism, takes the conditioned in the transcendental signification which it has in the pure category, while the minor speaks of it in the empirical signification which it has in the category as applied to phenomena. There is, therefore, a dialectical fallacy in the syllogism—a *sophisma figurae dictionis*. But this fallacy is not a consciously devised one, but a perfectly natural illusion of the common reason of man. For, when a thing is given as conditioned, we presuppose in the major its conditions and their series, unperceived, as it were, and unseen; because this is nothing more than the logical requirement of complete and satisfactory premisses for a given conclusion. In this case, time is altogether left out in the connection of the conditioned with the condition; they are supposed to be given in themselves, and *contemporaneously*. It is, moreover, just as natural to regard phenomena (in the minor) as things in themselves and as objects presented to the pure understanding, as in the major, in which complete abstraction was made of all conditions of intuition. But it is under these conditions alone that objects are given. Now we overlooked a remarkable distinction between the conceptions. The synthesis of the conditioned with its condition, and the complete series of the latter (in the major) are not limited by time, and do not contain the conception of succession. On the contrary, the empirical synthesis and the series of conditions in the phenomenal world—subsumed in the minor—are necessarily successive and given in time alone. It follows that I cannot presuppose in the minor, as I did in the major, the absolute *totality* of the synthesis and of the series therein represented; for in the major all the members of the series are given as things in themselves—without any limitations or conditions of time, while in the minor they are possible only in and through a successive regress, which cannot exist, except it be actually carried into execution in the world of phenomena.

After this proof of the viciousness of the argument commonly employed in maintaining cosmological assertions, both parties may now be justly dismissed, as advancing claims without grounds or title. But the process has not been ended by convincing them that one or both were in the wrong and had maintained an assertion which was without valid grounds of proof. Nothing seems to be clearer than that, if one maintains: "The world has a beginning," and another: "The world has no beginning," one of the two must be right. But it is likewise clear that, if the evidence on both sides is equal, it is impossible to discover on what side the truth lies; and the controversy continues, although the parties have been recommended to peace before the tribunal of reason. There remains, then, no other means of settling the question than to convince the parties, who refute each other with such conclusiveness and ability, that they are disputing about nothing, and that a transcendental illusion has been mocking them with visions of reality where there is none. The mode of adjusting a dispute which cannot be decided upon its own merits, we shall now proceed to lay before our readers.

Zeno of Elea, a subtle dialectician, was severely reprimanded by Plato as a sophist, who, merely from the base motive of exhibiting his skill in discussion, maintained and subverted the same proposition by arguments as powerful and convincing on the one side as on the other. He maintained, for example, that God (who was probably nothing more, in his view, than the world) is neither finite nor infinite, neither in motion nor in rest, neither similar nor dissimilar to any other thing. It seemed to those philosophers who criticized his mode of discussion that his purpose was to deny completely both of two self-contradictory propositions—which is absurd. But I cannot believe that there is any justice in this accusation. The first of these propositions I shall presently consider in a more detailed manner. With regard to the others, if by the word of *God* he understood merely the *Universe*, his meaning must have been—that it cannot be permanently present in one place—that is, at rest—nor be capable of changing its place—that is, of moving—because all places are in the universe, and the universe itself is, therefore, in no place. Again, if the universe contains in itself everything that exists, it cannot be similar or dissimilar to any *other* thing, because there is, in fact, no *other* thing with which it can be compared. If two opposite judgements presuppose a contingent impossible, or arbitrary condition, both—in spite of their opposition (which is, however, not properly or really a contradiction)—fall away; because the condition, which ensured the validity of both, has itself disappeared.

If we say: "Everybody has either a good or a bad smell," we have omitted a third possible judgement—it has no smell at all; and thus both conflicting statements may be false. If we say: "It is either good-smelling or not good-smelling (*vel suaveolens vel non-suaveolens*)," both judgements are contradictorily opposed; and the contradictory opposite of the former judgement—some bodies are not good-smelling—embraces also those bodies which have no smell at all. In the preceding pair of opposed judgements (*per disparata*), the contingent condition of the conception of body (smell) attached to both conflicting statements, instead of having been omitted in the latter, which is consequently not the contradictory opposite of the former.

If, accordingly, we say: "The world is either infinite in extension, or it is not infinite (*non est infinitus*)"; and if the former proposition is false, its contradictory opposite—the world is not infinite—must be true. And thus I should deny the existence of an infinite, without, however affirming the existence of a finite world. But if we construct our proposition thus: "The world is either infinite or finite (non-infinite)," both statements may be false. For, in this case, we consider the world as *per se* determined in regard to quantity, and while, in the one judgement, we deny its infinite and consequently, perhaps, its independent existence; in the other, we append to the world, regarded as a thing in itself, a certain determination—that of finitude; and the latter may be false as well as the former, if the world is not given as a *thing in itself,* and thus neither as finite nor as infinite in quantity. This kind of opposition I may be allowed to term *dialectical;* that of contradictories may be called *analytical opposition.* Thus then, of two dialectically opposed judgements both may be false, from the fact, that the one is not a mere contradictory of the other, but actually enounces more than is requisite for a full and complete contradiction.

When we regard the two propositions—"The world is infinite in quantity," and, "The world is finite in quantity," as contradictory opposites, we are assuming that the world—the complete series of phenomena—is a thing in itself. For it remains as a permanent quantity, whether I deny the infinite or the finite regress in the series of its phenomena. But if we dismiss this assumption—this transcendental illusion—and deny that it is a thing in itself, the contradictory opposition is metamorphosed into a merely dialectical one; and the world, as not existing in itself—independently of the regressive series of my representations—exists in like manner neither as a whole which is infinite nor as a whole which is finite in itself. The universe exists for me only in the empirical regress of the series of phenomena and not *per se.* If, then, it is always conditioned, it is never completely or as a whole; and it is, therefore, not an unconditioned whole and does not exist as such, either with an infinite, or with a finite quantity.

What we have here said of the first cosmological idea—that of the absolute totality of quantity in phenomena—applies also to the others. The series of conditions is discoverable only in the regressive synthesis itself, and not in the phenomenon considered as a thing in itself—given prior to all regress. Hence I am compelled to say: "The aggregate of parts in a given phenomenon is in itself neither finite nor infinite; and these parts are given only in the regressive synthesis of decomposition—a synthesis which is never given in absolute *completeness,* either as finite, or as infinite." The same is the case with the series of subordinated causes, or of the conditioned up to the unconditioned and necessary existence, which can never be regarded as in itself, and in its totality, either as finite or as infinite; because, as a series of subordinate representations, it subsists only in the dynamical regress and cannot be regarded as existing previously to this regress, or as a self-subsistent series of things.

Thus the antinomy of pure reason in its cosmological ideas disappears. For the above demonstration has established the fact that it is merely the product of a dialectical and illusory opposition, which arises from the application of the idea of absolute totality—admissible only as a condition of things in themselves—to phenomena, which exist only in our representations, and—when constituting a series—in a successive regress. This antinomy of reason may, however, be really profitable to our speculative interests, not in the way of contributing any dogmatical addition, but as presenting to us another material support in our critical investigations. For it furnishes us with an indirect proof of the transcendental ideality of phenomena, if our minds were not completely satisfied with the direct proof set forth in the *Trancendental Aesthetic.* The proof would proceed in the following dilemma. If the world is a whole existing in itself, it must be either finite or infinite. But it is neither finite nor infinite—as has been shown, on the one side, by the thesis, on the other, by the antithesis. Therefore the world—the content of all phenomena—is not a whole existing in itself. It follows that phenomena are nothing, apart from our representations. And this is what we mean by *transcendental ideality.*

This remark is of some importance. It enables us to see that the proofs of the fourfold antinomy are not mere sophistries — are not fallacious, but grounded on the nature of reason, and valid—under the supposition that phenomena are things in themselves. The opposition of the judgements which follow makes it evident that a fallacy lay in the initial supposition, and thus helps us to discover the true constitution of objects of sense. This transcendental dialectic does not favour scepticism, although it presents us with a triumphant demonstration of the advantages of the sceptical method, the great utility of which is apparent in the antinomy, where the arguments of reason were allowed to confront each other in undiminished force. And although the result of these conflicts of reason is not what we expected—although we have obtained no positive dogmatical addition to metaphysical science—we have still reaped a great advantage in the correction of our judgements on these subjects of thought.

SECTION VIII. *Regulative Principle of Pure Reason in relation to the Cosmological Ideas*

THE cosmological principle of totality could not give us any certain knowledge in regard to the *maximum* in the series of conditions in the world of sense, considered as a thing in itself. The actual regress in the series is the only means of approaching this maximum. This principle of pure reason, therefore, may still be considered as valid—not as an *axiom* enabling us to cogitate totality in the object as actual, but as a *problem* for the understanding, which requires it to institute and to continue, in conformity with the idea of totality in the mind, the regress in the series of the conditions of a given conditioned. For in the world of sense, that is, in space and time, every condition which we discover in our investigation of phenomena is itself conditioned; because sensuous objects are not things in themselves (in which case an absolutely unconditioned might be reached in the progress of cognition), but are merely empirical representations, the conditions of which must always be found in intuition. The principle of reason is therefore properly a mere rule—prescribing a regress in the series of conditions for given phenomena, and prohibiting any pause or rest on an absolutely unconditioned. It is, therefore, not a principle of the possibility of experience or of the empirical cognition of sensuous objects—consequently not a principle of the understanding; for every experience is confined within certain proper limits determined by the given intuition. Still less is it a *constitutive principle* of reason authorizing us to extend our conception of the sensuous world beyond all possible experience. It is merely a principle for the enlargement and extension of experience as far as is possible for human faculties. It forbids us to consider any empirical limits as absolute. It is, hence, a principle of reason, which, as a *rule*, dictates how we ought to proceed in our empirical regress, but is unable to *anticipate* or indicate prior to the empirical regress what is given in the object itself. I have termed it for this reason a *regulative* principle of reason; while the principle of the absolute totality of the series of conditions, as existing in itself and given in the object, is a constitutive cosmological principle. This distinction will at once demonstrate the falsehood of the constitutive principle, and prevent us from attributing (by a transcendental *subreptio*) objective reality to an idea, which is valid only as a rule.

In order to understand the proper meaning of this rule of pure reason, we must notice first that it cannot tell us *what the object is*, but only *how the empirical regress is to be proceeded with* in order to attain to the complete conception of the object. If it gave us any information in respect to the former statement, it would be a constitutive principle—a principle impossible from the nature of pure reason. It will not therefore enable us to establish any such conclusions as: "The series of conditions for a given conditioned is in itself finite." or, "It is infinite." For, in this case, we should be cogitating in the mere idea of absolute totality, an object which is not and cannot be given in experience; inasmuch as we should be attributing a reality objective and independent of the empirical synthesis, to a series of phenomena. This idea of reason cannot then be regarded as valid—except as a rule for the regressive synthesis in the series of conditions, according to which we must proceed from the conditioned, through all intermediate and subordinate conditions, up to the unconditioned; although this goal is unattained and unattainable. For the absolutely unconditioned cannot be discovered in the sphere of experience.

We now proceed to determine clearly our notion of a synthesis which can never be complete. There are two terms commonly employed for this purpose. These terms are regarded as expressions of different and distinguishable notions, although the ground of the distinction has never been clearly exposed. The term employed by the mathematicians is *progressus in infinitum.* The philosophers prefer the expression *progressus in indefinitum.* Without detaining the reader with an examination of the reasons for such a distinction, or with remarks on the right or wrong use of the terms, I shall endeavour clearly to determine these conceptions, so far as is necessary for the purpose in this *Critique.*

We may, with propriety, say of a straight line, that it may be produced to infinity. In this case the distinction between a *progressus in infinitum* and a *progressus in indefinitum* is a mere piece of subtlety. For, although when we say, "Produce a straight line," it is more correct to say *in indefinitum* than *in infinitum;* because the former means, "Produce it as far as you *please,*" the second, "You *must* not cease to produce it"; the expression *in infinitum* is, when we are speaking of the *power* to do it, perfectly correct, for we can always make it longer if we please—on to infinity. And this remark holds good in all cases, when we speak of a *progressus,* that is, an advancement from the condition to the conditioned; this possible advancement always proceeds to infinity. We may proceed from a given pair in the descending line of generation from father to son, and cogitate a never-ending line of descendants from it. For in such a case reason does not demand absolute totality in the series, because it does not presuppose it as a condition and as given (*datum*), but merely as conditioned, and as capable of being given (*dabile*).

Very different is the case with the problem: "How far the regress, which ascends from the given conditioned to the conditions, must extend"; whether I can say: "It is a *regress in infinitum*," or only *"in indefinitum"*; and whether, for example, setting out from the human beings at present alive in the world, I may ascend in the series of their ancestors, *in infinitum*—or whether all that can be said is, that so far as I have proceeded, I have discovered no empirical ground for considering the series limited, so that I am justified, and indeed, compelled to search for ancestors still further back, although I am not obliged by the idea of reason to presuppose them.

My answer to this question is: "If the series is given in empirical intuition as a whole, the regress in the series of its internal conditions proceeds *in infinitum;* but, if only one member of the series is given, from which the regress is to proceed to absolute totality, the regress is possible only *in indefinitum.*" For example, the division of a portion of matter given within certain limits—of a body, that is—proceeds *in infinitum.* For, as the condition of this whole is its part, and the condition of the part a part of the part, and so on, and as in this regress of decomposition an unconditioned indivisible member of the series of conditions is not to be found; there are no reasons or grounds in experience for stopping in the division, but, on the contrary, the more remote members of the division are actually and empirically given prior to this division. That is to say, the division proceeds to infinity. On the other hand, the series of ancestors of any given human being is not given, in its absolute totality, in any experience, and yet the regress proceeds from every genealogical member of this series to one still higher, and does not meet with any empirical limit presenting an absolutely unconditioned member of the series. But as the members of such a series are not contained in the empirical intuition of the whole, prior to the regress, this regress does not proceed to infinity, but only *in indefinitum,* that is, we are called upon to discover other and higher members, which are themselves always conditioned.

In neither case—the *regressus in infinitum,* nor the *regressus in indefinitum,* is the series of conditions to be considered as actually infinite in the object itself. This might be true of things in themselves, but it cannot be asserted of phenomena, which, as conditions of each other, are only given in the empirical regress itself. Hence, the question no longer is, "What is the quantity of this series of conditions in itself—is it finite or infinite?" for it is nothing in itself; but, "How is the empirical regress to be commenced, and how far ought we to proceed with it?" And here a signal distinction in the application of this rule becomes apparent. If the whole is given empirically, it is possible to recede in the series of its internal conditions *to infinity.* But if the whole is not given, and can only be given by and through the empirical regress, I can only say: "It is *possible to infinity,* to proceed to still higher conditions in the series." In the first case, I am justified in asserting that more members are empirically given in the object than I attain to in the regress (of decomposition). In the second case, I am justified only in saying, that I can always proceed further in the regress, because no member of the series is given as absolutely conditioned, and thus a higher member is possible, and an inquiry with regard to it is necessary. In the one case it is necessary to *find* other members of the series, in the other it is necessary to *inquire* for others, inasmuch as experience presents no absolute limitation of the regress. For, either you do not possess a perception which absolutely limits your empirical regress, and in this case the regress cannot be regarded as complete; or, you do possess such a limitative perception, in which case it is not a part of your series (for that which *limits* must be distinct from that which is *limited* by it), and it is incumbent on you to continue your regress up to this condition, and so on.

These remarks will be placed in their proper light by their application in the following section.

SECTION IX. *Of the Empirical Use of the Regulative Principle of Reason with regard to the Cosmological Ideas*

WE have shown that no transcendental use can be made either of the conceptions of reason or of understanding. We have shown, likewise, that the demand of absolute totality in the series of conditions in the world of sense arises from a transcendental employment of reason, resting on the opinion that phenomena are to be regarded as things in themselves. It follows that we are not required to answer the question respecting the absolute quantity of a series—whether it is *in itself* limited or unlimited. We are only called upon to determine how far we must proceed in the empirical regress from condition to condition, in order to discover, in conformity with the rule of reason, a full and correct answer to the questions proposed by reason itself.

This principle of reason is hence valid only as a rule for the *extension* of a possible experience—its invalidity as a principle constitutive of phenomena in themselves having been sufficiently demonstrated. And thus, too, the antinomial conflict of reason with itself is completely put an end to; inasmuch as we have not only presented a critical solution of the fallacy lurking in the opposite statements of reason, but have shown the true meaning of the ideas which gave rise to these statements. The *dialectical* principle of reason has, therefore, been changed into a *doctrinal* principle. But in fact, if this principle, in the subjective signification which we have shown to be its only true sense, may be guaranteed as a principle of the unceasing extension of the employment of our understanding, its influence and value are just as great as if it were an axiom for the *a priori* determination of objects. For such an axiom could not exert a stronger influence on the extension and rectification of our knowledge, otherwise than by procuring for the principles of the understanding the most widely expanded employment in the field of experience.

I. *Solution of the Cosmological Idea of the Totality of the Composition of Phenomena in the Universe*

Here, as well as in the case of the other cosmological problems, the ground of the regulative principle of reason is the proposition that in our empirical regress *no experience of an absolute limit,* and consequently no experience of a condition, which is itself *absolutely unconditioned,* is discoverable. And the truth of this proposition itself rests upon the consideration that such an experience must represent to us phenomena as limited by nothing or the mere void, on which our continued regress by means of perception must abut—which is impossible.

Now this proposition, which declares that every condition atttained in the empirical regress must itself be considered empirically conditioned, contains the rule *in terminis,* which requires me, to whatever extent I may have proceeded in the ascending series, always to look for some higher member in the series—whether this member is to become known to me through experience, or not.

Nothing further is necessary, then, for the solution of the first cosmological problem, than to decide, whether, in the regress to the unconditioned quantity of the universe (as regards space and time), this never limited ascent ought to be called a *regressus in infinitum* or *indefinitum.*

The general representation which we form in our minds of the series of all past states or conditions of the world, or of all the things which at present exist in it, is itself nothing more than a *possible* empirical regress, which is cogitated—although in an undetermined manner—in the mind, and which gives rise to the conception of a series of conditions for a given object.[1] Now I have a conception of the universe, but not an intuition—that is, not an intuition of it as a whole. Thus I cannot infer the magnitude of the regress from the quantity or magnitude of the world, and determine the former by means of the latter; on the contrary, I must first of all form a conception of the quantity or magnitude of the world from the magnitude of the empirical regress. But of this regress I know nothing more than that I ought to proceed from every given member of the series of conditions to one still higher. But the quantity of the universe is not thereby determined, and we cannot affirm that this regress proceeds *in infinitum.* Such an affirmation would *anticipate* the members of the series which have not yet been reached, and represent the number of them as beyond the grasp of any empirical synthesis; it would consequently *determine* the cosmical quantity prior to the regress (although only in a negative manner)—which is impossible. For the world is not given in its totality in any intuition: consequently, its quantity cannot be given prior to the regress. It follows that we are unable to make any declaration respecting the cosmical quantity in itself—not even that the regress in it is a regress *in infinitum;* we must only endeavour to attain to a conception of the quantity of the universe, in conformity with the rule which determines the empirical regress in it. But this rule merely requires us never to admit an absolute limit to our series—how far soever we may have proceeded in it, but always, on the contrary, to subordinate

[1] The cosmical series can neither be greater nor smaller than the possible empirical regress, upon which its conception is based. And as this regress cannot be a determinate infinite regress, still less a determinate finite (absolutely limited), it is evident that we cannot regard the world as either finite or infinite, because the regress, which gives us the representation of the world, is neither finite nor infinite.

every phenomenon to some other as its condition, and consequently to proceed to this higher phenomenon. Such a regress is, therefore, the *regressus in indefinitum,* which, as not determining a quantity in the object, is clearly distinguishable from the *regressus in infinitum.*

It follows from what we have said that we are not justified in declaring the world to be infinite in space, or as regards past time. For this conception of an infinite given quantity is empirical; but we cannot apply the conception of an infinite quantity to the world as an object of the senses. I cannot say, "The regress from a given perception to everything limited either in space or time, proceeds *in infinitum,*" for this presupposes an infinite cosmical quantity; neither can I say, "It is *finite,*" for an absolute limit is likewise impossible in experience. It follows that I am not entitled to make any assertion at all respecting the whole object of experience—the world of sense; I must limit my declarations to the rule according to which experience or empirical knowledge is to be attained.

To the question, therefore, respecting the cosmical quantity, the first and negative answer is: "The world has no beginning in time, and no absolute limit in space."

For, in the contrary case, it would be limited by a void time on the one hand, and by a void space on the other. Now, since the world, as a phenomenon, cannot be thus limited in itself—for a phenomenon is not a thing in itself; it must be possible for us to have a perception of this limitation by a void time and a void space. But such a perception—such an experience is impossible; because it has no content. Consequently, an absolute cosmical limit is empirically, and therefore absolutely, impossible.[1]

From this follows the *affirmative* answer: "The regress in the series of phenomena—as a determination of the cosmical quantity, proceeds *in indefinitum.*" This is equivalent to saying: "The world of sense has no absolute quantity, but the empirical regress (through which alone the world of sense is presented to us on the side of its conditions) rests upon a rule, which requires it to proceed from every member of the series, as conditioned, to one still more remote (whether through personal experience, or by means of history, or the chain of cause and effect), and not to cease at any point in this extension of the possible empirical employment of the understanding." And this is the proper and only use which reason can make of its principles.

The above rule does not prescribe an unceasing regress in one kind of phenomena. It does not, for example, forbid us, in our ascent from an individual human being through the line of his ancestors, to expect that we shall discover at some point of the regress a primeval pair, or to admit, in the series of heavenly bodies, a sun at the farthest possible distance from some centre. All that it demands is a perpetual progress from phenomena to phenomena, even although an actual perception is not presented by them (as in the case of our perceptions being so weak as that we are unable to become conscious of them), since they, nevertheless, belong to possible experience.

Every beginning is in time, and all limits to extension are in space. But space and time are in the world of sense. Consequently phenomena *in the world* are conditionally limited, but *the world* itself is not limited, either conditionally or unconditionally.

For this reason, and because neither the world nor the cosmical series of conditions to a given conditioned can be *completely given,* our conception of the cosmical quantity is given only in and through the regress and not prior to it—in a collective intuition. But the regress itself is really nothing more than the *determining* of the cosmical quantity, and cannot therefore give us any *determined* conception of it—still less a conception of a quantity which is, in relation to a certain standard, infinite. The regress does not, therefore, proceed to infinity (an infinity given), but only to an indefinite extent, for the purpose of presenting to us a quantity—realized only in and through the regress itself.

II. *Solution of the Cosmological Idea of the Totality of the Division of a Whole given in Intuition*

When I divide a whole which is given in intuition, I proceed from a conditioned to its conditions. The division of the parts of the whole (*subdivisio* or *decompositio*) is a regress in the series of these conditions. The absolute totality of this series would be actually attained and given to the mind, if the regress could arrive at

[1] The reader will remark that the proof presented above is very different from the dogmatical demonstration given in the antithesis of the first antinomy. In that demonstration, it was taken for granted that the world is a thing in itself—given in its totality prior to all regress, and a determined position in space and time was denied to it—if it was not considered as occupying all time and all space. Hence our conclusion differed from that given above; for we inferred in the antithesis the actual infinity of the world.

simple parts. But if all the parts in a continuous decomposition are themselves divisible, the division, that is to say, the regress, proceeds from the conditioned to its conditions *in infinitum;* because the conditions (the parts) are themselves contained in the conditioned, and, as the latter is given in a limited intuition, the former are all given along with it. This regress cannot, therefore, be called a *regressus in indefinitum,* as happened in the case of the preceding cosmological idea, the regress in which proceeded from the conditioned to the conditions not given contemporaneously and along with it, but discoverable only through the empirical regress. We are not, however, entitled to affirm of a whole of this kind, which is divisible *in infinitum,* that *it consists of an infinite number of parts.* For, although all the parts are contained in the intuition of the whole, the *whole division* is not contained therein. The division is contained only in the progressing decomposition—in the regress itself, which is the condition of the possibility and actuality of the series. Now, as this regress is infinite, all the members (parts) to which it attains must be contained in the given whole as an *aggregate.* But the complete *series of division* is not contained therein. For this series, being infinite in succession and always incomplete, cannot represent an infinite number of members, and still less a composition of these members into a whole.

To apply this remark to space. Every limited part of space presented to intuition is a whole, the parts of which are always spaces—to whatever extent subdivided. Every limited space is hence divisible to infinity.

Let us again apply the remark to an external phenomenon enclosed in limits, that is, a body. The divisibility of a body rests upon the divisibility of space, which is the condition of the possibility of the body as an extended whole. A body is consequently divisible to infinity, though it does not, for that reason, consist of an infinite number of parts.

It certainly seems that, as a body must be cogitated as substance in space, the law of divisibility would not be applicable to it as substance. For we may and ought to grant, in the case of space, that division or decomposition, to any extent, never can utterly annihilate composition (that is to say, the smallest part of space must still consist of spaces); otherwise space would entirely cease to exist—which is impossible. But, the assertion on the other hand, that when all composition in matter is annihilated in thought, nothing remains, does not seem to harmonize with the conception of substance, which must be properly the subject of all composition and must remain, even after the conjunction of its attributes in space—which constituted a body—is annihilated in thought. But this is not the case with substance in the phenomenal world, which is not a thing in itself cogitated by the pure category. Phenomenal substance is not an absolute subject; it is merely a permanent sensuous image, and nothing more than an intuition, in which the unconditioned is not to be found.

But, although this rule of progress to infinity is legitimate and applicable to the subdivision of a phenomenon, as a mere occupation or filling of space, it is not applicable to a whole consisting of a number of distinct parts and consituting a *quantum discretum*—that is to say, an organized body. It cannot be admitted that every part in an organized whole is itself organized, and that, in analysing it to infinity, we must always meet with organized parts; although we may allow that the parts of the matter which we decompose *in infinitum, may* be organized. For the infinity of the division of a phenomenon in space rests altogether on the fact that the divisibility of a phenomenon is given only in and through this infinity, that is, an undetermined number of parts is given, while the parts themselves are given and determined only in and through the subdivision; in a word, the infinity of the division necessarily presupposes that the whole is not already divided *in se.* Hence our division determines a number of parts in the whole—a number which extends just as far as the actual regress in the division; while, on the other hand, the very notion of a body organized to infinity represents the whole as already and in itself divided. We expect, therefore, to find in it a determinate, but at the same time, infinite, number of parts—which is self-contradictory. For we should thus have a whole containing a series of members which could not be completed in any regress—which is infinite, and at the same time complete in an organized composite. Infinite divisibility is applicable only to a *quantum continuum,* and is based entirely on the infinite divisibility of space. But in a *quantum discretum* the multitude of parts or units is always determined, and hence always equal to some number. To what extent a body may be organized, experience alone can inform us; and although, so far as our experience of this or that body has extended, we may not have discovered any inorganic part, such parts must exist in possible experience. But how far the transcendental division of a phenomenon must extend, we cannot know from experience—it is a question which experience cannot answer; it is answered only by the principle of reason which forbids us to consider the empirical regress, in the analysis of extended body, as ever absolutely complete.

Concluding Remark on the Solution of the Transcendental Mathematical Ideas—and Introductory to the Solution of the Dynamical Ideas

We presented the antinomy of pure reason in a tabular form, and we endeavoured to show the ground of this self-contradiction on the part of reason, and the only means of bringing it to a conclusion—namely, by declaring both contradictory statements to be false. We represented in these antinomies the conditions of phenomena as belonging to the conditioned according to relations of space and time—which is the usual supposition of the common understanding. In this respect, all dialectical representations of totality, in the series of conditions to a given conditioned, were perfectly *homogeneous*. The condition was always a member of the series along with the conditioned, and thus the homogeneity of the whole series was assured. In this case the regress could never be cogitated as complete; or, if this was the case, a member really conditioned was falsely regarded as a primal member, consequently as unconditioned. In such an antinomy, therefore, we did not consider the object, that is, the conditioned, but the series of conditions belonging to the object, and the magnitude of that series. And thus arose the difficulty—a difficulty not to be settled by any decision regarding the claims of the two parties, but simply by cutting the knot—by declaring the series proposed by reason to be either *too long* or *too short* for the understanding, which could in neither case make its conceptions adequate with the ideas.

But we have overlooked, up to this point, an essential difference existing between the conceptions of the understanding which reason endeavours to raise to the rank of ideas—two of these indicating a *mathematical,* and two a *dynamical* synthesis of phenomena. Hitherto, it was necessary to signalize this distinction; for, just as in our general representation of all transcendental ideas, we considered them under phenomenal conditions, so, in the two mathematical ideas, our discussion is concerned solely with an object in the world of phenomena. But as we are now about to proceed to the consideration of the *dynamical* conceptions of the understanding, and their adequateness with ideas, we must not lose sight of this distinction. We shall find that it opens up to us an entirely new view of the conflict in which reason is involved. For, while in the first two antinomies, both parties were *dismissed,* on the ground of having advanced statements based upon false hypothesis; in the present case the hope appears of discovering a hypothesis which may be consistent with the demands of reason, and, the judge completing the statement of the grounds of claim, which both parties had left in an unsatisfactory state, the question may be settled on its own merits, not by dismissing the claimants, but by a *comparison* of the arguments on both sides. If we consider merely their *extension,* and whether they are adequate with ideas, the series of conditions may be regarded as all homogeneous. But the conception of the understanding which lies at the basis of these ideas, contains either a *synthesis of the homogeneous* (presupposed in every quantity—in its composition as well as in its division) or of the *heterogeneous,* which is the case in the dynamical synthesis of cause and effect, as well as of the necessary and the contingent.

Thus it happens that in the mathematical series of phenomena no other than a *sensuous* condition is admissible—a condition which is itself a member of the series; while the dynamical series of sensuous conditions admits a heterogeneous condition, which is not a member of the series, but, as purely *intelligible,* lies out of and beyond it. And thus reason is satisfied, and an unconditioned placed at the head of the series of phenomena, without introducing confusion into or discontinuing it, contrary to the principles of the understanding.

Now, from the fact that the dynamical ideas admit a condition of phenomena which does not form a part of the series of phenomena, arises a result which we should not have expected from an antinomy. In former cases, the result was that both contradictory dialectical statements were declared to be false. In the present case, we find the conditioned in the dynamical series connected with an empirically unconditioned, but *non-sensuous* condition; and thus satisfaction is done to the *understanding* on the one hand and to the *reason* on the other.[1] While,

[1] For the understanding cannot admit *among phenomena* a condition which is itself empirically unconditioned. But if it is possible to cogitate an *intelligible* condition—one which is not a member of the series of phenomena—for a conditioned phenomenon, without breaking the series of empirical conditions, such a condition may be admissible as *empirically unconditioned,* and the empirical regress continue regular, unceasing, and intact.

moreover, the dialectical arguments for unconditioned totality in mere phenomena fall to the ground, *both* propositions of reason may be shown to be true in their proper signification. This could not happen in the case of the cosmological ideas which demanded a mathematically unconditioned unity; for no condition could be placed at the head of the series of phenomena, except one which was itself a phenomenon and consequently a member of the series.

III. *Solution of the Cosmological Idea of the Totality of the Deduction of Cosmical Events from their Causes*

There are only two modes of causality cogitable—the causality of *nature* or of *freedom.* The first is the conjunction of a particular state with another preceding it in the world of sense, the former following the latter by virtue of a law. Now, as the causality of phenomena is subject to conditions of time, and the preceding state, if it had always existed, could not have produced an effect which would make its first appearance at a particular time, the causality of a cause must itself be an effect—must itself have *begun to be,* and therefore, according to the principle of the understanding, itself requires a cause.

We must understand, on the contrary, by the term freedom, in the cosmological sense, a faculty of the *spontaneous* origination of a state; the causality of which, therefore, is not subordinated to another cause determining it in time. Freedom is in this sense a pure transcendental idea, which, in the first place, contains no empirical element; the object of which, in the second place, cannot be given or determined in any experience, because it is a universal law of the very possibility of experience, that everything which happens must have a cause, that consequently the causality of a cause, being itself something that has *happened,* must also have a cause. In this view of the case, the whole field of experience, how far soever it may extend, contains nothing that is not subject to the laws of nature. But, as we cannot by this means attain to an absolute totality of conditions in reference to the series of causes and effects, reason creates the idea of a spontaneity, which can begin to act of itself, and without any external cause determining it to action, according to the natural law of causality.

It is especially remarkable that the practical conception of freedom is based upon the *transcendental idea,* and that the question of the possibility of the former is difficult only as it involves the consideration of the truth of the latter. Freedom, in the *practical sense,* is the independence of the will of *coercion* by sensuous impulses. A will is *sensuous,* in so far as it is *pathologically affected* (by sensuous impulses); it is termed *animal* (*arbitrium brutum*), when it is *pathologically necessitated.* The human will is certainly an *arbitrium sensitivum,* not *brutum,* but *liberum;* because sensuousness does not necessitate its action, a faculty existing in man of self-determination, independently of all sensuous coercion.

It is plain that, if all causality in the world of sense were natural—and natural only—every event would be determined by another according to necessary laws, and that, consequently, phenomena, in so far as they determine the will, must necessitate every action as a natural effect from themselves; and thus all practical freedom would fall to the ground with the transcendental idea. For the latter presupposes that although a certain thing has not happened, it *ought* to have happened, and that, consequently, its phenomenal cause was not so powerful and determinative as to exclude the causality of our will—a causality capable of producing effects independently of and even in opposition to the power of natural causes, and capable, consequently, of *spontaneously* originating a series of events.

Here, too, we find it to be the case, as we generally found in the self-contradictions and perplexities of a reason which strives to pass the bounds of possible experience, that the problem is properly not *physiological,*[1] but *transcendental.* The question of the possibility of freedom does indeed concern psychology; but, as it rests upon dialectical arguments of pure reason, its solution must engage the attention of transcendental philosophy. Before attempting this solution, a task which transcendental philosophy cannot decline, it will be advisable to make a remark with regard to its procedure in the settlement of the question.

If phenomena were things in themselves, and time and space forms of the existence of things, condition and conditioned would always be members of the same series; and thus would arise in the present case the antinomy common to all transcendental ideas—that their series is either too great or too small for the understanding. The dynamical ideas, which we are about to discuss in this and the following section, possess the peculiarity of relating to an object, not con-

1 [Probably an error of the press, and that we should read *psychological.*]

sidered as a quantity, but as an *existence;* and thus, in the discussion of the present question, we may make abstraction of the quantity of the series of conditions, and consider merely the dynamical relation of the condition to the conditioned. The question, then, suggests itself, whether freedom is possible; and, if it is, whether it can consist with the universality of the natural law of causality; and, consequently, whether we enounce a proper disjunctive proposition when we say: "Every effect must have its origin either in nature or in freedom," or whether *both* cannot exist together in the same event in different relations. The principle of an unbroken connection between all events in the phenomenal world, in accordance with the unchangeable laws of nature, is a well-established principle of transcendental analytic which admits of no exception. The question, therefore, is: "Whether an effect, determined according to the laws of nature, can at the same time be produced by a free agent, or whether freedom and nature mutually exclude each other?" And here, the common but fallacious hypothesis of the *absolute reality* of phenomena manifests its injurious influence in embarrassing the procedure of reason. For if phenomena are things in themselves, freedom is impossible. In this case, nature is the complete and all-sufficient cause of every event; and condition and conditioned, cause and effect are contained in the same series, and necessitated by the same law. If, on the contrary, phenomena are held to be, as they are in fact, nothing more than mere representations, connected with each other in accordance with empirical laws, they must have a ground which is *not* phenomenal. But the causality of such an intelligible cause is not determined or determinable by phenomena; although its effects, as phenomena, must be determined by other phenomenal existences. This cause and its causality exist therefore out of and apart from the series of phenomena; while its effects do exist and are discoverable in the series of empirical conditions. Such an effect may therefore be considered to be free in relation to its intelligible cause, and necessary in relation to the phenomena from which it is a necessary consequence—a distinction which, stated in this perfectly general and abstract manner, must appear in the highest degree subtle and obscure. The sequel will explain. It is sufficient, at present, to remark that, as the complete and unbroken connection of phenomena is an unalterable law of nature, freedom is impossible—on the supposition that phenomena are absolutely real. Hence those philosophers who adhere to the common opinion on this subject can never succeed in reconciling the ideas of nature and freedom.

Possibility of Freedom in Harmony with the Universal Law of Natural Necessity

That element in a sensuous object which is not itself sensuous, I may be allowed to term *intelligible.* If, accordingly, an object which must be regarded as a sensuous phenomenon possesses a faculty which is not an object of sensuous intuition, but by means of which it is capable of being the cause of phenomena, the *causality* of an object or existence of this kind may be regarded from two different points of view. It may be considered to be *intelligible,* as regards its *action* —the action of a thing which is a thing in itself, and *sensuous,* as regards its *effects*—the effects of a phenomenon belonging to the sensuous world. We should accordingly, have to form both an empirical and an intellectual conception of the causality of such a faculty or power—both, however, having reference to the same effect. This twofold manner of cogitating a power residing in a sensuous object does not run counter to any of the conceptions which we ought to form of the world of phenomena or of a possible experience. Phenomena—not being things in themselves —must have a transcendental object as a foundation, which determines them as mere representations; and there seems to be no reason why we should not ascribe to this transcendental object, in addition to the property of self-phenomenization, a *causality* whose effects are to be met with in the world of phenomena, although it is not itself a phenomenon. But every effective cause must possess a *character,* that is to say, a law of its causality, without which it would cease to be a cause. In the above case, then, every sensuous object would possess an *empirical* character, which guaranteed that its actions, as phenomena, stand in complete and harmonious connection, conformably to unvarying natural laws, with all other phenomena, and can be deduced from these, as conditions, and that they do thus, in connection with these, constitute a series in the order of nature. This sensuous object must, in the second place, possess an *intelligible character,* which guarantees it to be the cause of those actions, as phenomena, although it is not itself a phenomenon nor subordinate to the conditions of the world of sense. The former may be termed the character of the thing as a phenomenon, the latter the character of the thing as a thing in itself.

Now this active subject would, in its character of intelligible subject, be subordinate to no conditions of time, for time is only a condition of phenomena, and not of things in themselves. No *action* would *begin* or *cease* to be in this subject; it would consequently be free from the law of all determination of time—the law of change, namely, that everything *which happens* must have a cause in the phenomena of a preceding state. In one word, the causality of the subject, in so far as it is intelligible, would not form part of the series of empirical conditions which determine and necessitate an event in the world of sense. Again, this intelligible character of a thing cannot be immediately cognized, because we can perceive nothing but phenomena, but it must be capable of being cogitated in harmony with the empirical character; for we always find ourselves compelled to place, in thought, a transcendental object at the basis of phenomena although we can never know what this object is in itself.

In virtue of its empirical character, this subject would at the same time be subordinate to all the empirical laws of causality, and, as a phenomenon and member of the sensuous world, its effects would have to be accounted for by a reference to preceding phenomena. Eternal phenomena must be capable of influencing it; and its actions, in accordance with natural laws, must explain to us how its empirical character, that is, the law of its causality, is to be cognized in and by means of experience. In a word, all requisites for a complete and necessary determination of these actions must be presented to us by experience.

In virtue of its intelligible character, on the other hand (although we possess only a general conception of this character), the subject must be regarded as free from all sensuous influences, and from all phenomenal determination. Moreover, as nothing *happens* in this subject—for it is a *noumenon,* and there does not consequently exist in it any change, demanding the dynamical determination of time, and for the same reason no connection with phenomena as causes—this active existence must in its actions be free from and independent of natural necessity, for this necessity exists only in the world of phenomena. It would be quite correct to say that it originates or begins its effects in the world of sense *from itself,* although the action productive of these effects does not begin *in itself*. We should not be in this case affirming that these sensuous effects began to exist of themselves, because they are always determined by prior empirical conditions —by virtue of the empirical character, which is the phenomenon of the intelligible character—and are possible only as constituting a continuation of the series of natural causes. And thus nature and freedom, each in the complete and absolute signification of these terms, can exist, without contradiction or disagreement, in the same action.

Exposition of the Cosmological Idea of Freedom in Harmony with the Universal Law of Natural Necessity

I have thought it advisable to lay before the reader at first merely a sketch of the solution of this transcendental problem, in order to enable him to form with greater ease a clear conception of the course which reason must adopt in the solution. I shall now proceed to exhibit the several momenta of this solution, and to consider them in their order.

The natural law that everything which happens must have a cause, that the causality of this cause, that is, the action of the cause (which cannot always have existed, but must be itself an *event,* for it precedes in time some effect which it has originated), must have itself a phenomenal cause, by which it is determined, and, consequently, that all events are empirically determined in an order of nature—this law, I say, which lies at the foundation of the possibility of experience, and of a connected system of phenomena or *nature,* is a law of the understanding, from which no departure, and to which no exception, can be admitted. For to except even a single phenomenon from its operation is to exclude it from the sphere of possible experience and thus to admit it to be a mere fiction of thought or phantom of the brain.

Thus we are obliged to acknowledge the existence of a chain of causes, in which, however, *absolute totality* cannot be found. But we need not detain ourselves with this question, for it has already been sufficiently answered in our discussion of the antinomies into which reason falls, when it attempts to reach the unconditioned in the series of phenomena. If we permit ourselves to be deceived by the illusion of transcendental idealism, we shall find that neither nature nor freedom exists. Now the question is: "Whether, admitting the existence of natural necessity in the world of phenomena, it is possible to consider an effect as at the same time an effect of nature and an effect of freedom—or, whether these two modes of causality are contradictory and incompatible?"

No phenomenal cause can absolutely and of itself begin a series. Every action, in so far as it is productive of an event, is itself an event or occurrence, and presupposes another preceding state, in which its cause existed. Thus everything that happens is but a continuation of a series, and an absolute beginning is impossible in the sensuous world. The actions of natural causes are, accordingly, themselves effects, and presuppose causes preceding them in time. A *primal* action which forms an absolute beginning, is beyond the causal power of phenomena.

Now, is it absolutely necessary that, granting that all effects are phenomena, the causality of the cause of these effects must also be a phenomenon and belong to the empirical world? Is it not rather possible that, although every effect in the phenomenal world must be connected with an empirical cause, according to the universal law of nature, this empirical causality may be itself the effect of a non-empirical and intelligible causality—its connection with natural causes remaining nevertheless intact? Such a causality would be considered, in reference to phenomena, as the primal action of a cause, which is in so far, therefore, not phenomenal, but, by reason of this faculty or power, intelligible; although it must, at the same time, as a link in the chain of nature, be regarded as belonging to the sensuous world.

A belief in the reciprocal causality of phenomena is necessary, if we are required to look for and to present the natural conditions of natural events, that is to say, their causes. This being admitted as unexceptionably valid, the requirements of the understanding, which recognizes nothing but nature in the region of phenomena, are satisfied, and our physical explanations of physical phenomena may proceed in their regular course, without hinderance and without opposition. But it is no stumbling-block in the way, even assuming the idea to be a pure fiction, to admit that there are some natural causes in the possession of a faculty which is not empirical, but intelligible, inasmuch as it is not determined to action by empirical conditions, but purely and solely upon grounds brought forward by the understanding—this action being still, when the cause is phenomenized, in perfect accordance with the laws of empirical causality. Thus the acting subject, as a *causal phenomenon,* would continue to preserve a complete connection with nature and natural conditions; and the *phenomenon* only of the subject (with all its phenomenal causality) would contain certain conditions, which, if we ascend from the empirical to the transcendental object, must necessarily be regarded as intelligible. For, if we attend, in our inquiries with regard to causes in the world of phenomena, to the directions of nature alone, we need not trouble ourselves about the relation in which the transcendental subject, which is completely unknown to us, stands to these phenomena and their connection in nature. The intelligible ground of phenomena in this subject does not concern empirical questions. It has to do only with pure thought; and, although the effects of this thought and action of the pure understanding are discoverable in phenomena, these phenomena must nevertheless be capable of a full and complete explanation, upon purely physical grounds and in accordance with natural laws. And in this case we attend solely to their empirical and omit all consideration of their intelligible character (which is the transcendental cause of the former) as completely unknown, except in so far as it is exhibited by the latter as its empirical symbol. Now let us apply this to experience. Man is a phenomenon of the sensuous world and, at the same time, therefore, a natural cause, the causality of which must be regulated by empirical laws. As such, he must possess an empirical character, like all other natural phenomena. We remark this empirical character in his actions, which reveal the presence of certain powers and faculties. If we consider inanimate or merely animal nature, we can discover no reason for ascribing to ourselves any other than a faculty which is determined in a purely sensuous manner. But man, to whom nature reveals herself only through sense, cognizes himself not only by his senses, but also through pure apperception; and this in actions and internal determinations, which he cannot regard as sensuous impressions. He is thus to himself, on the one hand, a phenomenon, but on the other hand, in respect of certain faculties, a purely intelligible object—intelligible, because its action cannot be ascribed to sensuous receptivity. These faculties are understanding and reason. The latter, especially, is in a peculiar manner distinct from all empirically-conditioned faculties, for it employs ideas alone in the consideration of its objects, and by means of these determines the understanding, which then proceeds to make an empirical use of its own conceptions, which, like the ideas of reason, are pure and non-empirical.

That reason possesses the faculty of causality, or that at least we are compelled so to represent it, is evident from the *imperatives,* which in the sphere of the practical we impose on many of our executive powers. The words *I ought* express a species of necessity, and imply a connection with grounds which nature does not and cannot present to the mind of man. Understanding knows nothing in nature but that *which is*, or has been, or will be. It would be absurd to say that anything in nature *ought* to be other than it is in the relations of time in which it stands; indeed, the *ought,* when we consider merely the course of nature, has neither application nor meaning. The question, "What ought to happen in the sphere of nature?" is just as absurd as the question, "What ought to be the properties of a circle?" All that we are entitled to ask is, "What takes place in nature?" or, in the latter case, "What *are* the properties of a circle?"

But the idea of an *ought* or of duty indicates a possible action, the ground of which is a pure conception; while the ground of a merely natural action is, on the contrary, always a phenomenon. This action must certainly be possible under physical conditions, if it is prescribed by the moral imperative *ought;* but these physical or natural conditions do not concern the determination of the will itself, they relate to its effects alone, and the consequences of the effect in the world of phenomena. Whatever number of motives nature may present to my will, whatever sensuous impulses—the moral *ought* it is beyond their power to produce. They may produce a volition, which, so far from being necessary, is always conditioned—a volition to which the *ought* enunciated by reason, sets an aim and a standard, gives permission or prohibition. Be the object what it may, purely sensuous—as pleasure, or presented by pure reason—as good, reason will not yield to grounds which have an empirical origin. Reason will not follow the order of things presented by experience, but, with perfect spontaneity, rearranges them according to ideas, with which it compels empirical conditions to agree. It declares, in the name of these ideas, certain actions to be necessary which nevertheless *have not taken place* and which perhaps never will take place; and yet presupposes that it possesses the faculty of causality in relation to these actions. For, in the absence of this supposition, it could not expect its ideas to produce certain effects in the world of experience.

Now, let us stop here and admit it to be at least possible that reason does stand in a really causal relation to phenomena. In this case it must—pure reason as it is—exhibit an empirical character. For every cause supposes a rule, according to which certain phenomena follow as effects from the cause, and every rule requires uniformity in these effects; and this is the proper ground of the conception of a cause—as a faculty or power. Now this conception (of a cause) may be termed the empirical character of reason; and this character is a permanent one, while the effects produced appear, in conformity with the various conditions which accompany and partly limit them, in various forms.

Thus the volition of every man has an empirical character, which is nothing more than the causality of his reason, in so far as its effects in the phenomenal world manifest the presence of a rule, according to which we are enabled to examine, in their several kinds and degrees, the actions of this causality and the rational grounds for these actions, and in this way to decide upon the subjective principles of the volition. Now we learn what this empirical character is only from phenomenal effects, and from the rule of these which is presented by experience; and for this reason all the actions of man in the world of phenomena are determined by his empirical character, and the co-operative causes of nature. If, then, we could investigate all the phenomena of human volition to their lowest foundation in the mind, there would be no action which we could not anticipate with certainty, and recognize to be absolutely necessary from its preceding conditions. So far as relates to this empirical character, therefore, there can be no freedom; and it is only in the light of this character that we can consider the human will, when we confine ourselves to simple *observation* and, as is the case in anthropology, institute a physiological investigation of the motive causes of human actions.

But when we consider the same actions in relation to reason—not for the purpose of *explaining* their origin, that is, in relation to speculative reason, but to practical reason, as the producing cause of these actions—we shall discover a rule and an order very different from those of nature and experience. For the declaration of this mental faculty may be that what *has* and could not but *take* place in the course of nature, *ought not* to have taken place. Sometimes, too, we discover, or believe that we discover, that the ideas of reason did actually stand in a causal relation to certain actions of man; and that these actions have taken place because they were determined, not by empirical causes, but by the act of the will upon grounds of reason.

Now, granting that reason stands in a causal relation to phenomena; can an action of reason be called free, when we know that, sensuously, in its empirical character, it is completely determined and absolutely necessary? But this empirical character is itself determined by the intelligible character. The latter we cannot cognize; we can only indicate it by means of phenomena, which enable us to have an immediate cognition only of the empirical character.[1] An action, then, in so far as it is to be ascribed to an intelligible cause, does not result from it in accordance with empirical laws. That is to say, not the conditions of pure reason, but only their effects in the internal sense, precede the act. Pure reason, as a purely intelligible faculty, is not subject to the conditions of time. The causality of reason in its intelligible character *does not begin to be;* it does not make its appearance at a certain time, for the purpose of producing an effect. If this were not the case, the causality of reason would be subservient to the natural law of phenomena, which determines them according to time, and as a series of causes and effects in time; it would consequently cease to be freedom and become a part of nature. We are therefore justified in saying: "If reason stands in a causal relation to phenomena, it is a faculty which originates the sensuous condition of an empirical series of effects." For the condition, which resides in the reason, is non-sensuous, and therefore cannot be originated, or begin to be. And thus we find—what we could not discover in any empirical series—a *condition* of a successive series of events itself empirically unconditioned. For, in the present case, the condition stands *out of* and beyond the series of phenomena—it is intelligible, and it consequently cannot be subjected to any sensuous condition, or to any time-determination by a preceding cause.

But, in another respect, the same cause belongs also to the series of phenomena. Man is himself a phenomenon. His will has an empirical character, which is the empirical cause of all his actions. There is no condition—determining man and his volition in conformity with this character—which does not itself form part of the series of effects in nature, and is subject to their law—the law according to which an empirically undetermined cause of an event in time cannot exist. For this reason no given action can have an absolute and spontaneous origination, all actions being phenomena, and belonging to the world of experience. But it cannot be said of reason, that the state in which it determines the will is always preceded by some other state determining it. For reason is not a phenomenon, and therefore not subject to sensuous conditions; and, consequently, even in relation to its causality, the sequence or conditions of time do not influence reason, nor can the dynamical law of nature, which determines the sequence of time according to certain rules, be applied to it.

Reason is consequently the permanent condition of all actions of the human will. Each of these is determined in the empirical character of the man, even before it has taken place. The intelligible character, of which the former is but the sensuous schema, knows no *before* or *after;* and every action, irrespective of the time-relation in which it stands with other phenomena, is the immediate effect of the intelligible character of pure reason, which, consequently, enjoys freedom of action, and is not dynamically determined either by internal or external preceding conditions. This freedom must not be described, in a merely negative manner, as independence of empirical conditions, for in this case the faculty of reason would cease to be a cause of phenomena; but it must be regarded, positively, as a faculty which can spontaneously originate a series of events. At the same time, it must not be supposed that any beginning can take place in reason; on the contrary, reason, as the unconditioned condition of all action of the will, admits of no time-conditions, although its effect does really begin in a series of phenomena—a beginning which is not, however, absolutely primal.

I shall illustrate this regulative principle of reason by an example, from its employment in the world of experience; proved it cannot be by any amount of experience, or by any number of facts, for such arguments cannot establish the truth of transcendental propositions. Let us take a voluntary action—for example, a falsehood—by means of which a man has introduced a certain degree of confusion into the social life of humanity, which is judged according to the motives from which it originated, and the blame of which and of the evil consequences arising from it, is imputed to the offender. We at first proceed to examine the empirical character of the offence, and for this purpose we endeavour to penetrate to the sources of that character, such as a defective education, bad company, a shameless and wicked disposition, frivolity, and want of reflection—not forgetting also the occasioning causes which prevailed at the moment of the transgression. In this the procedure is exactly the same as that pursued in the investigation of the series of causes which determine a given physical effect. Now, although we believe the action to have been determined by all these cir-

[1] The real morality of actions—their merit or demerit, and even that of our own conduct, is completely unknown to us. Our estimates can relate only to their empirical character. How much is the result of the action of free will, how much is to be ascribed to nature and to blameless error, or to a happy constitution of temperament (*merito fortunae*), no one can discover, nor, for this reason, determine with perfect justice.

cumstances, we do not the less blame the offender. We do not blame him for his unhappy disposition, nor for the circumstances which influenced him, nay, not even for his former course of life; for we presuppose that all these considerations may be set aside, that the series of preceding conditions may be regarded as having never existed, and that the action may be considered as completely unconditioned in relation to any state preceding, just as if the agent commenced with it an entirely new series of effects. Our blame of the offender is grounded upon a law of reason, which requires us to regard this faculty as a cause, which could have and ought to have otherwise determined the behaviour of the culprit, independently of all empirical conditions. This causality of reason we do not regard as a co-operating agency, but as complete in itself. It matters not whether the sensuous impulses favoured or opposed the action of this causality, the offence is estimated according to its intelligible character—the offender is decidedly worthy of blame, the moment he utters a falsehood. It follows that we regard reason, in spite of the empirical conditions of the act, as completely free, and therefore, as in the present case, culpable.

The above judgement is complete evidence that we are accustomed to think that reason is not affected by sensuous conditions, that in it no change takes place—although its phenomena, in other words, the mode in which it appears in its effects, are subject to change—that in it no preceding state determines the following, and, consequently, that it does not form a member of the series of sensuous conditions which necessitate phenomena according to natural laws. Reason is present and the same in all human actions and at all times; but it does not itself exist in time, and therefore does not enter upon any state in which it did not formerly exist. It is, relatively to new states or conditions, *determining*, but not *determinable*. Hence we cannot ask: "Why did not reason determine itself in a different manner?" The question ought to be thus stated: "Why did not reason employ its power of causality to determine certain *phenomena* in a different manner?" But this is a question which admits of no answer. For a different intelligible character would have exhibited a different empirical character; and, when we say that, in spite of the course which his whole former life has taken, the offender could have refrained from uttering the falsehood, this means merely that the act was subject to the power and authority —permissive or prohibitive—of reason. Now, reason is not subject in its causality to any conditions of phenomena or of time; and a difference in time may produce a difference in the relation of phenomena to each other—for these are not things and therefore not causes in themselves—but it cannot produce any difference in the relation in which the action stands to the faculty of reason.

Thus, then, in our investigation into free actions and the causal power which produced them, we arrive at an intelligible cause, beyond which, however, we cannot go; although we can recognize that it is free, that is, independent of all sensuous conditions, and that, in this way, it may be the sensuously unconditioned condition of phenomena. But for what reason the intelligible character generates such and such phenomena and exhibits such and such an empirical character under certain circumstances, it is beyond the power of our reason to decide. The question is as much above the power and the sphere of reason as the following would be: "Why does the transcendental object of our external sensuous intuition allow of no other form than that of intuition *in space?*" But the problem, which we were called upon to solve, does not require us to entertain any such questions. The problem was merely this—whether freedom and natural necessity can exist without opposition in the same action. To this question we have given a sufficient answer; for we have shown that, as the former stands in a relation to a different kind of condition from those of the latter, the law of the one does not affect the law of the other and that, consequently, both can exist together in independence of and without interference with each other.

The reader must be careful to remark that my intention in the above remarks has not been to prove the *actual existence* of freedom, as a faculty in which resides the cause of certain sensuous phenomena. For, not to mention that such an argument would not have a transcendental character, nor have been limited to the discussion of pure conceptions—all attempts at inferring from experience what cannot be cogitated in accordance with its laws, must ever be unsuccessful. Nay, more, I have not even aimed at demonstrating the *possibility* of freedom; for this too would have been a vain endeavour, inasmuch as it is beyond the power of the mind to cognize the possibility of a reality or of a causal power by the aid of mere *a priori* conceptions. Freedom has been considered in the foregoing remarks only as a transcendental idea, by means of which reason aims at originating a series of conditions in the world of phenomena with the help of that which is sensuously unconditioned, involving itself, however, in an antinomy with the laws which itself prescribes for the conduct of the understanding. That this antinomy is based upon a mere illusion, and that nature and freedom are at least *not opposed*—this was the only thing in our power to prove, and the question which it was our task to solve.

IV. *Solution of the Cosmological Idea of the Totality of the Dependence of Phenomenal Existences*

In the preceding remarks, we considered the changes in the world of sense as constituting a dynamical series, in which each member is subordinated to another—as its cause. Our present purpose is to avail ourselves of this series of states or conditions as a guide to an existence which may be the highest condition of all changeable phenomena, that is, to a *necessary being*. Our endeavour to reach, not the unconditioned causality, but the unconditioned existence, of substance. The series before us is therefore a series of conceptions, and not of intuitions (in which the one intuition is the condition of the other).

But it is evident that, as all phenomena are subject to change and conditioned in their existence, the series of dependent existences cannot embrace an unconditioned member, the existence of which would be absolutely necessary. It follows that, if phenomena were things in themselves, and—as an immediate consequence from this supposition—condition and conditioned belonged to the same series of phenomena, the existence of a necessary being, as the condition of the existence of sensuous phenomena, would be perfectly impossible.

An important distinction, however, exists between the dynamical and the mathematical regress. The latter is engaged solely with the combination of parts into a whole, or with the division of a whole into its parts; and therefore are the conditions of its series parts of the series, and to be consequently regarded as homogeneous, and for this reason, as consisting, without exception, of phenomena. If the former regress, on the contrary, the aim of which is not to establish the possibility of an unconditioned whole consisting of given parts, or of an unconditioned part of a given whole, but to demonstrate the possibility of the deduction of a certain state from its cause, or of the contingent existence of substance from that which exists necessarily, it is not requisite that the condition should form part of an empirical series along with the conditioned.

In the case of the apparent antinomy with which we are at present dealing, there exists a way of escape from the difficulty; for it is not impossible that both of the contradictory statements may be true in different relations. All sensuous phenomena may be contingent, and consequently possess only an empirically conditioned existence, and yet there may also exist a non-empirical condition of the whole series, or, in other words, a necessary being. For this necessary being, as an intelligible condition, would not form a member—not even the highest member—of the series; the whole world of sense would be left in its empirically determined existence uninterfered with and uninfluenced. This would also form a ground of distinction between the modes of solution employed for the third and fourth antinomies. For, while in the consideration of freedom in the former antinomy, the thing itself—the cause (*substantia phaenomenon*)—was regarded as belonging to the series of conditions, and only its *causality* to the intelligible world—we are obliged in the present case to cogitate this necessary being as purely intelligible and as existing entirely apart from the world of sense (as an *ens extramundanum*); for otherwise it would be subject to the phenomenal law of contingency and dependence.

In relation to the present problem, therefore, the *regulative principle* of reason is that everything in the sensuous world possesses an empirically conditioned existence—that no property of the sensuous world possesses unconditioned necessity—that we are bound to expect, and, so far as is possible, to seek for the empirical condition of every member in the series of conditions—and that there is no sufficient reason to justify us in deducing any existence from a condition which lies out of and beyond the empirical series, or in regarding any existence as independent and self-subsistent; although this should not prevent us from recognizing the possibility of the whole series being based upon a being which is intelligible, and for this reason free from all empirical conditions.

But it has been far from my intention, in these remarks, to prove the existence of this unconditioned and necessary being, or even to evidence the possibility of a purely intelligible condition of the existence of all sensuous phenomena. As bounds were set to reason, to prevent it from leaving the guiding thread of empirical conditions and losing itself in *transcendent* theories which are incapable of *concrete* presentation; so it was my purpose, on the other hand, to set bounds to the law of the purely empirical understanding, and to protest against any attempts on its part at deciding on the possibility of things, or declaring the existence of the intelligible to be *impossible,* merely on the ground that it is not available for the explanation and exposition of phenomena. It has been shown, at the same time, that the contingency of all the phenomena of nature and their empirical conditions is quite consistent with the arbitrary hypothesis of a necessary, although purely intelligible condition, that no real contradiction exists between them and that, consequently, *both may be true.* The existence of such an absolutely necessary being may be impossible; but this can never be demonstrated from the universal contingency and dependence of sensuous phenomena, nor from the principle which forbids us to discontinue the series at some member of it, or to seek for its cause in some sphere of existence beyond the world of nature. Reason goes its way in the empirical world, and follows, too, its peculiar path in the sphere of the transcendental.

The sensuous world contains nothing but phenomena, which are mere representations, and always sensuously conditioned; things in themselves are not, and cannot be, objects to us. It is not to be wondered at, therefore, that we are not justified in leaping from some member of an empirical series beyond the world of sense, as if empirical representations were things in themselves, existing apart from their transcendental ground in the human mind, and the cause of whose existence may be sought out of the empirical series. This would certainly be the case with contingent *things;* but it cannot be with mere *representations* of things, the contingency of which is itself merely a phenomenon and can relate to no other regress than that which determines phenomena, that is, the empirical. But to cogitate an intelligible ground of phenomena, as free, moreover, from the contingency of the latter, conflicts neither with the unlimited nature of the empirical regress, nor with the complete contingency of phenomena. And the demonstration of this was the only thing necessary for the solution of this apparent antinomy. For if the condition of every conditioned—as regards its existence—is sensuous, and for this reason a part of the same series, it must be itself conditioned, as was shown in the antithesis of the fourth antinomy. The embarrassments into which a reason, which postulates the unconditioned, necessarily falls, must, therefore, continue to exist; or the unconditioned must be placed in the sphere of the intelligible. In this way, its necessity does not require, nor does it even permit, the presence of an empirical condition: and it is, consequently, unconditionally necessary.

The empirical employment of reason is not affected by the assumption of a purely intelligible being; it continues its operations on the principle of the contingency of all phenomena, proceeding from empirical conditions to still higher and higher conditions, themselves empirical. Just as little does this regulative principle exclude the assumption of an intelligible cause, when the question regards merely the pure employment of reason—in relation to ends or aims. For, in this case, an intelligible cause signifies merely the transcendental and to us unknown ground of the possibility of sensuous phenomena, and its existence, necessary and independent of all sensuous conditions, is not inconsistent with the contingency of phenomena, or with the unlimited possibility of regress which exists in the series of empirical conditions.

Concluding Remarks on the Antinomy of Pure Reason

So long as the object of our rational conceptions is the totality of conditions in the world of phenomena, and the satisfaction, from this source, of the requirements of reason, so long are our ideas transcendental and *cosmological.* But when we set the unconditioned—which is the aim of all our inquiries—in a sphere which lies out of the world of sense and possible experience, our ideas become *transcendent.* They are then not merely serviceable towards the completion of the exercise of reason (which remains an idea, never executed, but always to be pursued); they detach themselves completely from experience and construct for themselves objects, the material of which has not been presented by experience, and the objective reality of which is not based upon the completion of the empirical series, but upon pure *a priori* conceptions. The intelligible object of these transcendent ideas may be conceded, as a transcendental object. But we cannot cogitate it as a thing determinable by certain distinct predicates relating to its internal nature, for it has no connection with empirical conceptions; nor are we justified in affirming the existence of any such object. It is, consequently, a mere product of the mind alone. Of all the cosmological ideas, however, it is that occasioning the fourth antinomy which compels us to venture upon this step. For the existence of phenomena, always conditioned and never self-subsistent, requires us to look for an object different from phenomena—an intelligible object, with which all contingency must cease. But, as we have allowed ourselves to assume the existence of a self-subsistent reality out of the field of experience, and are therefore obliged to regard phenomena as merely a contingent mode of representing intelligible objects employed by beings which are themselves intelligences—no other course remains for us than to follow analogy and employ the same mode in forming some conception of intelligible things, of which we have not the least knowledge, which nature taught us to use in the formation of empirical conceptions. Experience made us acquainted with the contingent. But we are at present engaged in the discussion of things which are not objects of experience; and must, therefore, deduce our knowledge of them from that which is necessary absolutely and in itself, that is, from pure conceptions. Hence the first step which we take out of the world of sense obliges us to begin our system of new cognition with the investigation of a necessary being, and to deduce from our conceptions of it all our conceptions of intelligible things. This we propose to attempt in the following chapter.

CHAPTER III. *The Ideal of Pure Reason*

SECTION I. *Of the Ideal in General*

WE have seen that pure conceptions do not present objects to the mind, except under sensuous conditions; because the conditions of objective reality do not exist in these conceptions, which contain, in fact, nothing but the mere form of thought. They may, however, when applied to phenomena, be presented *in concreto;* for it is phenomena that present to them the materials for the formation of empirical conceptions, which are nothing more than concrete forms of the conceptions of the understanding. But *ideas* are still further removed from objective reality than *categories;* for no phenomenon can ever present them to the human mind *in concreto*. They contain a certain perfection, attainable by no possible empirical cognition; and they give to reason a systematic unity, to which the unity of experience attempts to approximate, but can never completely attain.

But still further removed than the idea from objective reality is the *Ideal,* by which term I understand the idea, not *in concreto*, but *in individuo*—as an individual thing, determinable or determined by the idea alone. The idea of humanity in its complete perfection supposes not only the advancement of all the powers and faculties, which constitute our conception of human nature, to a complete attainment of their final aims, but also everything which is requisite for the complete determination of the idea; for of all contradictory predicates, only one can conform with the idea of the perfect man. What I have termed an ideal was in Plato's philosophy an *idea of the divine mind*—an individual object present to its pure intuition, the most perfect of every kind of possible beings, and the archetype of all phenomenal existences.

Without rising to these speculative heights, we are bound to confess that human reason contains not only ideas, but ideals, which possess, not, like those of Plato, creative, but certainly *practical* power—as regulative principles, and form the basis of the perfectibility of certain *actions*. Moral conceptions are not perfectly pure conceptions of reason, because an empirical element—of pleasure or pain—lies at the foundation of them. In relation, however, to the principle, whereby reason sets bounds to a freedom which is in itself without law, and consequently when we attend merely to their form, they may be considered as pure conceptions of reason. Virtue and wisdom in their perfect purity are ideas. But the wise man of the Stoics is an ideal, that is to say, a human being existing only in thought and in complete conformity with the idea of wisdom. As the idea provides a rule, so the ideal serves as an *archetype* for the perfect and complete determination of the copy. Thus the conduct of this wise and divine man serves us as a standard of action, with which we may compare and judge ourselves, which may help us to reform ourselves, although the perfection it demands can never be attained by us. Although we cannot concede objective reality to these ideals, they are not to be considered as chimeras; on the contrary, they provide reason with a standard, which enables it to estimate, by comparison, the degree of incompleteness in the objects presented to it. But to aim at realizing the ideal in an example in the world of experience—to describe, for instance, the character of the perfectly wise man in a romance—is impracticable. Nay more, there is something absurd in the attempt; and the result must be little edifying, as the natural limitations, which are continually breaking in upon the perfection and completeness of the idea, destroy the illusion in the story and throw an air of suspicion even on what is good in the idea, which hence appears fictitious and unreal.

Such is the constitution of the ideal of reason,

which is always based upon determinate conceptions, and serves as a rule and a model for limitation or of criticism. Very different is the nature of the ideals of the imagination. Of these it is impossible to present an intelligible conception; they are a kind of *monogram*, drawn according to no determinate rule, and forming rather a vague picture—the production of many diverse experiences—than a determinate image. Such are the ideals which painters and physiognomists profess to have in their minds, and which can serve neither as a model for production nor as a standard for appreciation. They may be termed, though improperly, sensuous ideals, as they are declared to be models of certain possible empirical intuitions. They cannot, however, furnish rules or standards for explanation or examination.

In its ideals, reason aims at complete and perfect determination according to *a priori* rules; and hence it cogitates an object, which must be completely determinable in conformity with principles, although all empirical conditions are absent, and the conception of the object is on this account transcendent.

SECTION II. *Of the Transcendental Ideal (Prototypon Trancendentale)*

EVERY conception is, in relation to that which is not contained in it, undetermined and subject to the principle of *determinability*. This principle is that, of *every two* contradictorily opposed predicates, only one can belong to a conception. It is a purely logical principle, itself based upon the principle of contradiction; inasmuch as it makes complete abstraction of the content and attends merely to the logical form of the cognition.

But again, everything, as regards its possibility, is also subject to the principle of complete determination, according to which one of *all the possible contradictory predicates* of things must belong to it. This principle is not based merely upon that of contradiction; for, in addition to the relation between two contradictory predicates, it regards everything as standing in a relation to the *sum of possibilities*, as the sum-total of all predicates of things, and, while presupposing this sum as an *a priori* condition, presents to the mind everything as receiving the possibility of its individual existence from the relation it bears to, and the share it possesses in, the aforesaid sum of possibilities.[1] The principle of complete determination relates therefore to the content and not to the logical form. It is the principle of the synthesis of all the predicates which are required to constitute the complete conception of a thing, and not a mere principle of analytical representation, which enounces that one of two contradictory predicates must belong to a conception. It contains, moreover, a transcendental presupposition—that, namely, of the material for *all possibility*, which must contain *a priori* the data for this or that *particular possibility*.

The proposition, *Everything which exists is completely determined*, means not only that one of every pair of *given* contradictory attributes, but that one of all *possible* attributes, is always predicable of the thing; in it the predicates are not merely compared logically with each other, but the thing itself is transcendentally compared with the sum-total of all possible predicates. The proposition is equivalent to saying: "To attain to a complete knowledge of a thing, it is necessary to possess a knowledge of everything that is possible, and to determine it thereby in a positive or negative manner." The conception of complete determination is consequently a conception which cannot be presented in its totality *in concreto*, and is therefore based upon an idea, which has its seat in the reason—the faculty which prescribes to the understanding the laws of its harmonious and perfect exercise.

Now, although this idea of the *sum-total of all possibility*, in so far as it forms the condition of the complete determination of everything, is itself undetermined in relation to the predicates which may constitute this sum-total, and we cogitate in it merely the sum-total of all possible predicates—we nevertheless find, upon closer examination, that this idea, as a primitive conception of the mind, excludes a large number of predicates—those deduced and those irreconcilable with others, and that it is evolved as a conception completely determined *a priori*. Thus it becomes the conception of an individual object, which is completely determined by and through the mere idea, and must consequently be termed an ideal of pure reason.

When we consider all possible predicates, not merely logically, but transcendentally, that is to

[1] Thus this principle declares everything to possess a relation to a common correlate—the sum-total of possibility, which, if discovered to exist in the idea of one individual thing, would establish the affinity of all possible things, from the identity of the ground of their complete determination. The *determinability* of every *conception* is subordinate to the *universality* (*Allgemeinheit, universalitas*) of the principle of excluded middle; the *determination* of a *thing* to the *totality* (*Allheit, universitas*) of all possible predicates.

say, with reference to the content which may be cogitated as existing in them *a priori,* we shall find that some indicate a being, others merely a non-being. The logical negation expressed in the word *not* does not properly belong to a conception, but only to the relation of one conception to another in a judgement, and is consequently quite insufficient to present to the mind the content of a conception. The expression *not mortal* does not indicate that a non-being is cogitated in the object; it does not concern the content at all. A transcendental negation, on the contrary, indicates non-being in itself, and is opposed to transcendental affirmation, the conception of which of itself expresses a being. Hence this affirmation indicates a reality, because in and through it objects are considered to be something—to be things; while the opposite negation, on the other hand, indicates a mere want, or privation, or absence, and, where such negations alone are attached to a representation, the non-existence of anything corresponding to the representation.

Now a negation cannot be cogitated as determined, without cogitating at the same time the opposite affirmation. The man born blind has not the least notion of darkness, because he has none of light; the vagabond knows nothing of poverty, because he has never known what it is to be in comfort;[1] the ignorant man has no conception of his ignorance, because he has no conception of knowledge. All conceptions of negatives are accordingly derived or deduced conceptions; and realities contain the *data,* and, so to speak, the material or transcendental content of the possibility and complete determination of all things.

If, therefore, a transcendental substratum lies at the foundation of the complete determination of things—a substratum which is to form the fund from which all possible predicates of things are to be supplied, this substratum cannot be anything else than the idea of a sum-total of reality (*omnitudo realitatis*). In this view, negations are nothing but *limitations*—a term which could not, with propriety, be applied to them, if the unlimited (the all) did not form the true basis of our conception.

This conception of a sum-total of reality is the conception of a *thing in itself,* regarded as completely determined; and the conception of an *ens realissimum* is the conception of an individual being, inasmuch as it is determined by that predicate of all possible contradictory predicates, which indicates and belongs to *being.* It is, therefore, a transcendental *ideal* which forms the basis of the complete determination of everything that exists, and is the highest material condition of its possibility—a condition on which must rest the cogitation of all objects with respect to their content. Nay, more, this ideal is the only proper ideal of which the human mind is capable; because in this case alone a general conception of a thing is completely determined by and through itself, and cognized as the representation of an individuum.

The logical determination of a conception is based upon a disjunctive syllogism, the major of which contains the logical division of the extent of a general conception, the minor limits this extent to a certain part, while the conclusion determines the conception by this part. The general conception of a reality cannot be divided *a priori,* because, without the aid of experience, we cannot know any determinate kinds of reality, standing under the former as the genus. The transcendental principle of the complete determination of all things is therefore merely the representation of the sum-total of all reality; it is not a conception which is the genus of all predicates *under itself,* but one which comprehends them all *within itself.* The complete determination of a thing is consequently based upon the limitation of this *total* of reality, so much being predicated of the thing, while all that remains over is excluded—a procedure which is in exact agreement with that of the disjunctive syllogism and the determination of the objects in the conclusion by one of the members of the division. It follows that reason, in laying the transcendental ideal at the foundation of its determination of all possible things, takes a course in exact analogy with that which it pursues in disjunctive syllogisms—a proposition which formed the basis of the systematic division of all transcendental ideas, according to which they are produced in complete parallelism with the three modes of syllogistic reasoning employed by the human mind.[2]

It is self-evident that reason, in cogitating the necessary complete determination of things, does not presuppose the existence of a being corresponding to its ideal, but merely the idea of the ideal—for the purpose of deducing from

[1] The investigations and calculations of astronomers have taught us much that is wonderful; but the most important lesson we have received from them is the discovery of the abyss of our *ignorance* in relation to the universe—an ignorance the magnitude of which reason, without the information thus derived, could never have conceived. This discovery of our deficiencies must produce a great change in the determination of the aims of human reason.

[2] See pages 115 and 120.

the unconditioned totality of complete determination, the conditioned, that is, the totality of limited things. The ideal is therefore the prototype of all things, which, as defective copies (*ectypa*), receive from it the material of their possibility, and approximate to it more or less, though it is impossible that they can ever attain to its perfection.

The possibility of things must therefore be regarded as derived—except that of the thing which contains in itself all reality, which must be considered to be primitive and original. For all negations—and they are the only predicates by means of which all other things can be distinguished from the *ens realissimum*—are mere limitations of a greater and a higher—nay, the highest reality; and they consequently presuppose this reality, and are, as regards their content, derived from it. The manifold nature of things is only an infinitely various mode of limiting the conception of the highest reality, which is their common substratum; just as all figures are possible only as different modes of limiting infinite space. The object of the ideal of reason—an object existing only in reason itself—is also termed the *primal being* (*ens originarium*); as having no existence superior to him, the *supreme being* (*ens summum*); and as being the condition of all other beings, which rank under it, the *being of all beings* (*ens entium*). But none of these terms indicate the objective relation of an actually existing object to other things, but merely that of an *idea to conceptions;* and all our investigations into this subject still leave us in perfect uncertainty with regard to the existence of this being.

A primal being cannot be said to consist of many other beings with an existence which is derivative, for the latter presuppose the former, and therefore cannot be constitutive parts of it. It follows that the ideal of the primal being must be cogitated as simple.

The deduction of the possibility of all other things from this primal being cannot, strictly speaking, be considered as a *limitation,* or as a kind of *division* of its reality; for this would be regarding the primal being as a mere aggregate—which has been shown to be impossible, although it was so represented in our first rough sketch. The highest reality must be regarded rather as the *ground* than as the *sum-total* of the possibility of all things, and the manifold nature of things be based, not upon the limitation of the primal being itself, but upon the complete series of effects which flow from it. And thus all our powers of sense, as well as all phenomenal reality, may be with propriety regarded as belonging to this series of effects, while they could not have formed parts of the idea, considered as an aggregate. Pursuing this track, and hypostatizing this idea, we shall find ourselves authorized to determine our notion of the Supreme Being by means of the mere conception of a highest reality, as one, simple, all-sufficient, eternal, and so on—in one word, to determine it in its unconditioned completeness by the aid of every possible predicate. The conception of such a being is the conception of *God* in its transcendental sense, and thus the ideal of pure reason is the object-matter of a transcendental *theology.*

But, by such an employment of the transcendental idea, we should be overstepping the limits of its validity and purpose. For reason placed it, as the *conception* of all reality, at the basis of the complete determination of things, without requiring that this conception be regarded as the conception of an objective existence. Such an existence would be purely fictitious, and the hypostatizing of the content of the idea into an ideal, as an individual being, is a step perfectly unauthorized. Nay, more, we are not even called upon to assume the possibility of such an hypothesis, as none of the deductions drawn from such an ideal would affect the complete determination of things in general—for the sake of which alone is the idea necessary.

It is not sufficient to circumscribe the procedure and the dialectic of reason; we must also endeavour to discover the sources of this dialectic, that we may have it in our power to give a rational explanation of this illusion, as a phenomenon of the human mind. For the ideal, of which we are at present speaking, is based, not upon an arbitrary, but upon a natural, idea. The question hence arises: How happens it that reason regards the possibility of all things as deduced from a single possibility, that, to wit, of the highest reality, and presupposes this as existing in an individual and primal being?

The answer is ready; it is at once presented by the procedure of transcendental analytic. The possibility of sensuous objects is a relation of these objects to thought, in which something (the empirical form) may be cogitated *a priori;* while that which constitutes the matter—the reality of the phenomenon (that element which corresponds to sensation)—must be given from without, as otherwise it could not even be cogitated by, nor could its possibility be presentable to the mind. Now, a sensuous object is completely determined, when it has been compared with all phenomenal predicates, and represented by means of these either positively or negatively. But, as that which constitutes the thing itself—the real in a phenomenon, must be given, and that, in which the real of *all phenomena* is given, is experience, one, sole, and all-embracing—the material of the possibility of all sensuous objects must be presupposed as given in a whole, and it is upon the limitation of this whole that the possibility of all empirical objects, their distinction from each other and their complete determination, are based. Now, no other objects are presented to us besides sensuous objects, and these can be given only in connection with a possible experience; it follows that a thing is not an object *to us,* unless it presupposes the whole or sum-total of empirical reality as the condition of its possibility. Now, a natural illusion leads us to consider this principle, which is valid only of sensuous objects, as valid with regard to things in general. And thus we are induced to hold the empirical principle of our conceptions of the possibility of things, as phenomena, by leaving out this limitative condition, to be a transcendental principle of the possibility of things in general.

We proceed afterwards to hypostatize this idea of the sum-total of all reality, by changing the *distributive* unity of the empirical exercise of the understanding into the *collective* unity of an empirical whole—a dialectical illusion, and by cogitating this whole or sum of experience as an individual thing, containing in itself all empirical reality. This individual thing or being is then, by means of the above-mentioned transcendental subreption, substituted for our notion of a thing which stands at the head of the possibility of all things, the real conditions of whose complete determination it presents.[1]

SECTION III. *Of the Arguments employed by Speculative Reason in Proof of the Existence of a Supreme Being*

NOTWITHSTANDING the pressing necessity which reason feels, to form some presupposition that shall serve the understanding as a proper basis for the complete determination of its conceptions, the idealistic and factitious nature of such a presupposition is too evident to allow reason for a moment to persuade itself into a belief of the objective existence of a mere creation of its own thought. But there are other considerations which compel reason to seek out some resting-place in the regress from the conditioned to the unconditioned, which is not given as an actual existence from the mere conception of it, although it alone can give completeness to the series of conditions. And this is the natural course of every human reason, even of the most uneducated, although the path at first entered it does not always continue to follow. It does not begin from conceptions, but from common experience, and requires a basis in actual existence. But this basis is insecure, unless it rests upon the immovable rock of the absolutely necessary. And this foundation is itself unworthy of trust, if it leave under and above it empty space, if it do not fill all, and leave no room for a *why* or a *wherefore,* if it be not, in one word, infinite in its reality.

If we admit the existence of some one thing, whatever it may be, we must also admit that there is something which exists *necessarily.* For what is contingent exists only under the condition of some other thing, which is its cause; and from this we must go on to conclude the existence of a cause which is not contingent, and which consequently exists necessarily and unconditionally. Such is the argument by which reason justifies its advances towards a primal being.

Now reason looks round for the conception of a being that may be admitted, without inconsistency, to be worthy of the attribute of absolute necessity, not for the purpose of inferring *a priori,* from the conception of such a being, its objective existence (for if reason allowed itself to take this course, it would not require a basis in given and actual existence, but merely the support of pure conceptions), but for the purpose of discovering, among all our conceptions of possible things, that conception which possesses no element inconsistent with the idea of absolute necessity. For that there must be some absolutely necessary existence, it regards as a truth already established. Now, if it can remove every existence incapable of supporting the attribute of absolute necessity, excepting one—this must be the absolutely necessary being, whether its necessity is comprehensible by us, that is, deducible from the conception of it alone, or not.

Now that, the conception of which contains a

[1] This ideal of the *ens realissimum*—although merely a mental representation—is first *objectivized,* that is, has an objective existence attributed to it, then *hypostatized,* and finally, by the natural progress of reason to the completion of unity, *personified,* as we shall show presently. For the regulative unity of experience is not based upon phenomena themselves, but upon the connection of the variety of phenomena by the *understanding* in a *consciousness,* and thus the unity of the supreme reality and the complete determinability of all things, seem to reside in a supreme understanding, and, consequently, in a conscious intelligence.

therefore to every *wherefore*, which is not defective in any respect whatever, which is all-sufficient as a condition, seems to be the being of which we can justly predicate absolute necessity—for this reason, that, possessing the conditions of all that is possible, it does not and cannot itself require any condition. And thus it satisfies, in one respect at least, the requirements of the conception of absolute necessity. In this view, it is superior to all other conceptions, which, as deficient and incomplete, do not possess the characteristic of independence of all higher conditions. It is true that we cannot infer from this that what does not contain in itself the supreme and complete condition—the condition of all other things—must possess only a conditioned existence; but as little can we assert the contrary, for this supposed being does not possess the only characteristic which can enable reason to cognize by means of an *a priori* conception the unconditioned and necessary nature of its existence.

The conception of an *ens realissimum* is that which best agrees with the conception of an unconditioned and necessary being. The former conception does not satisfy all the requirements of the latter; but we have no choice, we are obliged to adhere to it, for we find that we cannot do without the existence of a necessary being; and even although we admit it, we find it out of our power to discover in the whole sphere of possibility any being that can advance well-grounded claims to such a distinction.

The following is, therefore, the natural course of human reason. It begins by persuading itself of the existence of some necessary being. In this being it recognizes the characteristics of unconditioned existence. It then seeks the conception of that which is independent of all conditions, and finds it in that which is itself the sufficient condition of all other things—in other words, in that which contains all reality. But the unlimited all is an absolute unity, and is conceived by the mind as a being one and supreme; and thus reason concludes that the Supreme Being, as the primal basis of all things, possesses an existence which is absolutely necessary.

This conception must be regarded as in some degree satisfactory, if we admit the existence of a necessary being, and consider that there exists a necessity for a definite and final answer to these questions. In such a case, we cannot make a better choice, or rather we have no choice at all, but feel ourselves obliged to declare in favour of the absolute unity of complete reality, as the highest source of the possibility of things. But if there exists no motive for coming to a definite conclusion, and we may leave the question unanswered till we have fully weighed both sides—in other words, when we are merely called upon to decide how much we happen to know about the question, and how much we merely flatter ourselves that we know—the above conclusion does not appear to be so great advantage, but, on the contrary, seems defective in the grounds upon which it is supported.

For, admitting the truth of all that has been said, that, namely, the inference from a given existence (my own, for example) to the existence of an unconditioned and necessary being is valid and unassailable; that, in the second place, we must consider a being which contains all reality, and consequently all the conditions of other things, to be absolutely unconditioned; and admitting too, that we have thus discovered the conception of a thing to which may be attributed, without inconsistency, absolute necessity—it does not follow from all this that the conception of a limited being, in which the supreme reality does not reside, is therefore incompatible with the idea of absolute necessity. For, although I do not discover the element of the unconditioned in the conception of such a being—an element which is manifestly existent in the sum-total of all conditions—I am not entitled to conclude that its existence is therefore conditioned; just as I am not entitled to affirm, in a hypothetical syllogism, that where a certain condition does not exist (in the present, completeness, as far as pure conceptions are concerned), the conditioned does not exist either. On the contrary, we are free to consider all limited beings as likewise unconditionally necessary, although we are unable to infer this from the general conception which we have of them. Thus conducted, this argument is incapable of giving us the least notion of the properties of a necessary being, and must be in every respect without result.

This argument continues, however, to possess a weight and an authority, which, in spite of its objective insufficiency, it has never been divested of. For, granting that certain responsibilities lie upon us, which, as based on the ideas of reason, deserve to be respected and submitted to, although they are incapable of a real or practical application to our nature, or, in other words, would be responsibilities without motives, except upon the supposition of a Supreme Being to give effect and influence to the practical laws: in such a case we should be bound to obey our conceptions, which, although objectively insufficient, do, according to the standard of reason, preponderate over and are superior to any claims that may be advanced from any other quarter. The equilibrium of doubt would in this case be destroyed by a practical addition; indeed, Reason would be compelled to condemn herself, if she refused to comply with the demands of the judgement, no superior to which we know—however defective her understanding of the grounds of these demands might be.

This argument, although in fact transcendental, inasmuch as it rests upon the intrinsic insufficiency of the contingent, is so simple and natural, that the commonest understanding can appreciate its value. We see things around us change, arise, and pass away; they, or their condition, must therefore have a cause. The same demand must again be made of the cause itself—as a datum of experience. Now it is natural that we should place the *highest* causality just where we place *supreme* causality, in that being, which contains the conditions of all possible effects, and the conception of which is so simple as that of an all-embracing reality. This highest cause, then, we regard as absolutely necessary, because we find it absolutely necessary to rise to it, and do not discover any reason for proceeding beyond it. Thus, among all nations, through the darkest polytheism glimmer some faint sparks of monotheism, to which these idolaters have been led, not from reflection and profound thought, but by the study and natural progress of the common understanding.

There are only three modes of proving the existence of a Deity, on the grounds of speculative reason.

All the paths conducting to this end begin either from determinate experience and the peculiar constitution of the world of sense, and rise, according to the laws of causality, from it to the highest cause existing apart from the world—or from a purely indeterminate experience, that is, some empirical existence—or abstraction is made of all experience, and the existence of a supreme cause is concluded from *a priori* conceptions alone. The first is the *physico-theological* argument, the second the *cosmological,* the third the *ontological.* More there are not, and more there cannot be.

I shall show it is as unsuccessful on the one path—the empirical—as on the other—the transcendental—and that it stretches its wings in vain, to soar beyond the world of sense by the mere might of speculative thought. As regards the order in which we must discuss those arguments, it will be exactly the reverse of that in which reason, in the progress of its development, attains to them—the order in which they are placed above. For it will be made manifest to the reader that, although experience presents the occasion and the starting-point, it is the *transcendental idea* of reason which guides it in its pilgrimage and is the goal of all its struggles. I shall therefore begin with an examination of the transcendental argument, and afterwards inquire what additional strength has accrued to this mode of proof from the addition of the empirical element.

Section IV. *Of the Impossibility of an Ontological Proof of the Existence of God*

It is evident from what has been said that the conception of an absolutely necessary being is a mere idea, the objective reality of which is far from being established by the mere fact that it is a need of reason. On the contrary, this idea serves merely to indicate a certain unattainable perfection, and rather limits the operations than, by the presentation of new objects, extends the sphere of the understanding. But a strange anomaly meets us at the very threshold; for the inference from a given existence in general to an absolutely necessary existence seems to be correct and unavoidable, while the conditions of the *understanding* refuse to aid us in forming any conception of such a being.

Philosophers have always talked of an *absolutely necessary* being, and have nevertheless declined to take the trouble of conceiving whether—and how—a being of this nature is even cogitable, not to mention that its existence is actually demonstrable. A verbal definition of the conception is certainly easy enough: it is something the non-existence of which is impossible. But does this definition throw any light upon the conditions which render it impossible to cogitate the non-existence of a thing—conditions which we wish to ascertain, that we may discover whether we think anything in the conception of such a being or not? For the mere fact that I throw away, by means of the word *unconditioned,* all the conditions which the understanding habitually requires in order to regard anything as necessary, is very far from making clear whether by means of the conception of the unconditionally necessary I think of something, or really of nothing at all.

Nay, more, this chance-conception, now become so current, many have endeavoured to explain by examples which seemed to render any inquiries regarding its intelligibility quite needless. Every geometrical proposition—a triangle has three angles—it was said, is absolutely necessary; and thus people talked of an object which lay out of the sphere of our understanding as if it were perfectly plain what the conception of such a being meant.

All the examples adduced have been drawn, without exception, from *judgements,* and not from *things.* But the unconditioned necessity of a judgement does not form the absolute necessity of a thing. On the contrary, the absolute necessity of a judgement is only a conditioned necessity of a thing, or of the predicate in a judgement. The proposition above-mentioned does not enounce that three angles necessarily exist, but, upon condition that a triangle exists, three angles must necessarily exist—in it. And thus this logical necessity has been the source of the greatest delusions. Having formed an *a priori* conception of a thing, the content of which was made to embrace existence, we believed ourselves safe in concluding that, because existence belongs necessarily to the object of the conception (that is, under the condition of my positing this thing as given), the existence of the thing is also posited necessarily, and that it is therefore absolutely necessary—merely because its existence has been cogitated in the conception.

If, in an identical judgement, I annihilate the predicate in thought, and retain the subject, a contradiction is the result; and hence I say, the former belongs necessarily to the latter. But if I suppress both subject and predicate in thought, no contradiction arises; for there *is nothing* at all, and therefore no means of forming a contradiction. To suppose the existence of a triangle and not that of its three angles, is self-contradictory; but to suppose the non-existence of both triangle and angles is perfectly admissible. And so is it with the conception of an absolutely necessary being. Annihilate its existence in thought, and you annihilate the thing itself with all its predicates; how then can there be any room for contradiction? Externally, there is nothing to give rise to a contradiction, for a thing cannot be necessary externally; nor internally, for, by the annihilation or suppression of the thing itself, its internal properties are also annihilated. God is omnipotent—that is a necessary judgement. His omnipotence cannot be denied, if the existence of a Deity is posited —the existence, that is, of an infinite being, the two conceptions being identical. But when you say, *God does not exist,* neither omnipotence nor any other predicate is affirmed; they must all disappear with the subject, and in this judgement there cannot exist the least self-contradiction.

You have thus seen that when the predicate of a judgement is annihilated in thought along with the subject, no internal contradiction can arise, be the predicate what it may. There is no possibility of evading the conclusion—you find yourselves compelled to declare: There are certain subjects which cannot be annihilated in thought. But this is nothing more than saying: There exist subjects which are absolutely necessary—the very hypothesis which you are called upon to establish. For I find myself unable to form the slightest conception of a thing which when annihilated in thought with all its predicates, leaves behind a contradiction; and contradiction is the only criterion of impossibility in the sphere of pure *a priori* conceptions.

Against these general considerations, the justice of which no one can dispute, one argument is adduced, which is regarded as furnishing a satisfactory demonstration from the fact. It is affirmed that there is one and only one conception, in which the non-being or annihilation of the object is self-contradictory, and this is the conception of an *ens realissimum.* It possesses, you say, all reality, and you feel yourselves justified in admitting the possibility of such a being. (This I am willing to grant for the present, although the existence of a conception which is not self-contradictory is far from being sufficient to prove the possibility of an object.)[1] Now the notion of all reality embraces in it that of existence; the notion of existence lies, therefore, in the conception of this possible thing. If this thing is annihilated in thought, the internal possibility of the thing is also annihilated, which is self-contradictory.

I answer: It is absurd to introduce—under whatever term disguised—into the conception of a thing, which is to be cogitated solely in reference to its possibility, the conception of its existence. If this is admitted, you will have apparently gained the day, but in reality have enounced nothing but a mere tautology. I ask, is the proposition, *this or that thing* (which I am

[1] A conception is always possible, if it is not self-contradictory. This is the logical criterion of possibility, distinguishing the object of such a conception from the *nihil negativum.* But it may be, notwithstanding, an empty conception, unless the objective reality of this synthesis, but which it is generated, is demonstrated; and a proof of this kind must be based upon principles of possible experience, and not upon the principle of analysis or contradiction. This remark may be serviceable as a warning against concluding, from the possibility of a conception—which is logical—the possibility of a thing—which is real.

admitting to be possible) *exists,* an analytical or a synthetical proposition? If the former, there is no addition made to the subject of your thought by the affirmation of its existence; but then the conception in your minds is identical with the thing itself, or you have supposed the existence of a thing to be possible, and then inferred its existence from its internal possibility —which is but a miserable tautology. The word *reality* in the conception of the thing, and the word *existence* in the conception of the predicate, will not help you out of the difficulty. For, supposing you were to term all positing of a thing *reality,* you have thereby posited the thing with all its predicates in the conception of the subject and assumed its actual existence, and this you merely repeat in the predicate. But if you confess, as every reasonable person must, that every existential proposition is synthetical, how can it be maintained that the predicate of existence cannot be denied without contradiction?—a property which is the characteristic of analytical propositions, alone.

I should have a reasonable hope of putting an end for ever to this sophistical mode of argumentation, by a strict definition of the conception of existence, did not my own experience teach me that the illusion arising from our confounding a logical with a real predicate (a predicate which aids in the determination of a thing) resists almost all the endeavours of explanation and illustration. A *logical predicate* may be what you please, even the subject may be predicated of itself; for logic pays no regard to the content of a judgement. But the determination of a conception is a predicate, which adds to and enlarges the conception. It must not, therefore, be contained in the conception.

Being is evidently not a real predicate, that is, a conception of something which is added to the conception of some other thing. It is merely the positing of a thing, or of certain determinations in it. Logically, it is merely the copula of a judgement. The proposition, *God is omnipotent,* contains two conceptions, which have a certain object or content; the word *is,* is no additional predicate—it merely indicates the relation of the predicate to the subject. Now, if I take the subject (God) with all its predicates (omnipotence being one), and say: *God is,* or, *There is a God,* I add no new predicate to the conception of God, I merely posit or affirm the existence of the subject with all its predicates —I posit the *object* in relation to my *conception.* The content of both is the same; and there is no addition made to the conception, which expresses merely the possibility of the object, by my cogitating the object—in the expression, it *is*—as absolutely given or existing. Thus the real contains no more than the possible. A hundred real dollars contain no more than a hundred possible dollars. For, as the latter indicate the conception, and the former the object, on the supposition that the content of the former was greater than that of the latter, my conception would not be an expression of the whole object, and would consequently be an inadequate conception of it. But in reckoning my wealth there may be said to be more in a hundred real dollars than in a hundred possible dollars—that is, in the mere conception of them. For the real object—the dollars—is not analytically contained in my conception, but forms a synthetical addition to my conception (which is merely a determination of my mental state), although this objective reality—this existence —apart from my conceptions, does not in the least degree increase the aforesaid hundred dollars.

By whatever and by whatever number of predicates—even to the complete determination of it—I may cogitate a thing, I do not in the least augment the object of my conception by the addition of the statement: *This thing exists.* Otherwise, not exactly the same, but something more than what was cogitated in my conception, would exist, and I could not affirm that the exact object of my conception had real existence. If I cogitate a thing as containing all modes of reality except one, the mode of reality which is absent is not added to the conception of the thing by the affirmation that the thing exists; on the contrary, the thing exists—if it exist at all—with the same defect as that cogitated in its conception; otherwise not that which was cogitated, but something different, exists. Now, if I cogitate a being as the highest reality, without defect or imperfection, the question still remains—whether this being exists or not? For, although no element is wanting in the possible real content of my conception, there is a defect in its relation to my mental state, that is, I am ignorant whether the cognition of the object indicated by the conception is possible *a posteriori.* And here the cause of the present difficulty becomes apparent. If the question regarded an object of sense merely, it would be impossible for me to confound the conception with the existence of a thing. For the conception merely enables me to cogitate an object as according with the general conditions of experience; while the existence of the object permits me to cogitate it as contained in the sphere of actual experience. At the same time, this connection with the world of experience does not in the least augment the conception, although a possible perception has been added to the experience of the mind. But if we cogitate existence by the pure category alone, it is not to be wondered at, that we should find ourselves unable to present any criterion sufficient to distinguish it from mere possibility.

Whatever be the content of our conception of an object, it is necessary to go beyond it, if we wish to predicate existence of the object. In the case of sensuous objects, this is attained by their connection according to empirical laws with some one of my perceptions; but there is no means of cognizing the existence of objects of pure thought, because it must be cognized completely *a priori*. But all our knowledge of existence (be it immediately by perception, or by inferences connecting some object with a perception) belongs entirely to the sphere of experience—which is in perfect unity with itself; and although an existence out of this sphere cannot be absolutely declared to be impossible, it is a hypothesis the truth of which we have no means of ascertaining.

The notion of a Supreme Being is in many respects a highly useful idea; but for the very reason that it is an idea, it is incapable of enlarging our cognition with regard to the existence of things. It is not even sufficient to instruct us as to the possibility of a being which we do not know to exist. The analytical criterion of possibility, which consists in the absence of contradiction in propositions, cannot be denied it. But the connection of real properties in a thing is a synthesis of the possibility of which an *a priori* judgement cannot be formed, because these realities are not presented to us specifically; and even if this were to happen, a judgement would still be impossible, because the criterion of the possibility of synthetical cognitions must be sought for in the world of experience, to which the object of an idea cannot belong. And thus the celebrated Leibnitz has utterly failed in his attempt to establish upon *a priori* grounds the possibility of this sublime ideal being.

The celebrated ontological or Cartesian argument for the existence of a Supreme Being is therefore insufficient; and we may as well hope to increase our stock of knowledge by the aid of mere ideas, as the merchant to augment his wealth by the addition of noughts to his cash-account.

SECTION V. *Of the Impossibility of a Cosmological Proof of the Existence of God*

IT was by no means a natural course of proceeding, but, on the contrary, an invention entirely due to the subtlety of the schools, to attempt to draw from a mere idea a proof of the existence of an object corresponding to it. Such a course would never have been pursued, were it not for that need of reason which requires it to suppose the existence of a necessary being as a basis for the empirical regress, and that, as this necessity must be unconditioned and *a priori,* reason is bound to discover a conception which shall satisfy, if possible, this requirement, and enable us to attain to the *a priori* cognition of such a being. This conception was thought to be found in the idea of an *ens realissimum,* and thus this idea was employed for the attainment of a better defined knowledge of a necessary being, of the existence of which we were convinced, or persuaded, on other grounds. Thus reason was seduced from her natural course; and, instead of concluding with the conception of an *ens realissimum,* an attempt was made to begin with it, for the purpose of inferring from it that idea of a necessary existence which it was in fact called in to complete. Thus arose that unfortunate ontological argument, which neither satisfies the healthy common sense of humanity, nor sustains the scientific examination of the philosopher.

The *cosmological proof,* which we are about to examine, retains the connection between absolute necessity and the highest reality; but, instead of reasoning from this highest reality to a necessary existence, like the preceding argument, it concludes from the given unconditioned necessity of some being its unlimited reality. The track it pursues, whether rational or sophistical, is at least natural, and not only goes far to persuade the common understanding, but shows itself deserving of respect from the speculative intellect; while it contains, at the same time, the outlines of all the arguments employed in natural theology—arguments which always have been, and still will be, in use and authority. These, however adorned, and hid under whatever embellishments of rhetoric and sentiment, are at bottom identical with the arguments we are at present to discuss. This proof, termed by Leibnitz the *argumentum a contingentia mundi,* I shall now lay before the reader, and subject to a strict examination.

It is framed in the following manner: If something exists, an absolutely necessary being must likewise exist. Now I, at least, exist. Consequently, there exists an absolutely necessary being. The minor contains an experience, the major reasons from a general experience to the existence of a necessary being.[1] Thus this argument really begins at experience, and is not completely *a priori*, or ontological. The object of all possible experience being the world, it is called the *cosmological* proof. It contains no reference to any peculiar property of sensuous objects, by which this world of sense might be distinguished from other possible worlds; and in this respect it differs from the physico-theological proof, which is based upon the consideration of the peculiar constitution of our sensuous world.

The proof proceeds thus: A necessary being can be determined only in one way, that is, it can be determined by only one of all possible opposed predicates; consequently, it must be *completely* determined in and by its conception. But there is only a single conception of a thing possible, which completely determines the thing *a priori*: that is, the conception of the *ens realissimum*. It follows that the conception of the *ens realissimum* is the only conception by and in which we can cogitate a necessary being. Consequently, a Supreme Being necessarily exists.

In this cosmological argument are assembled so many sophistical propositions that speculative reason seems to have exerted in it all her dialectical skill to produce a transcendental illusion of the most extreme character. We shall postpone an investigation of this argument for the present, and confine ourselves to exposing the stratagem by which it imposes upon us an old argument in a new dress, and appeals to the agreement of two witnesses, the one with the credentials of pure reason, and the other with those of empiricism; while, in fact, it is only the former who has changed his dress and voice, for the purpose of passing himself off for an additional witness. That it may possess a secure foundation, it bases its conclusions upon experience, and thus appears to be completely distinct from the ontological argument, which places its confidence entirely in pure *a priori* conceptions. But this experience merely aids reason in making one step—to the existence of a necessary being. What the properties of this being are cannot be learned from experience; and therefore reason abandons it altogether, and pursues its inquiries in the sphere of pure conception, for the purpose of discovering what the properties of an absolutely necessary being ought to be, that is, what among all possible things contain the conditions (*requisita*) of absolute necessity. Reason believes that it has discovered these requisites in the conception of an *ens realissimum*—and in it alone, and hence concludes: The *ens realissimum* is an absolutely necessary being. But it is evident that reason has here presupposed that the conception of an *ens realissimum* is perfectly adequate to the conception of a being of absolute necessity, that is, that we may infer the existence of the latter from that of the former—a proposition which formed the basis of the ontological argument, and which is now employed in the support of the cosmological argument, contrary to the wish and professions of its inventors. For the existence of an absolutely necessary being is given in conceptions alone. But if I say: "The conception of the *ens realissimum* is a conception of this kind, and in fact the only conception which is adequate to our idea of a necessary being," I am obliged to admit, that the latter may be inferred from the former. Thus it is properly the ontological argument which figures in the cosmological, and constitutes the whole strength of the latter; while the spurious basis of experience has been of no further use than to conduct us to the conception of absolute necessity, being utterly insufficient to demonstrate the presence of this attribute in any determinate existence or thing. For when we propose to ourselves an aim of this character, we must abandon the sphere of experience, and rise to that of pure conceptions, which we examine with the purpose of discovering whether any one contains the conditions of the possibility of an absolutely necessary being. But if the possibility of such a being is thus demonstrated, its existence is also proved; for we may then assert that, of all possible beings there is one which possesses the attribute of necessity—in other words, this being possesses an absolutely necessary existence.

All illusions in an argument are more easily detected when they are presented in the formal manner employed by the schools, which we now proceed to do.

If the proposition: "Every absolutely necessary being is likewise an *ens realissimum*," is correct (and it is this which constitutes the *nervus probandi* of the cosmological argument), it must, like all affirmative judgements, be capable of conversion—the *conversio per accidens*, at least. It follows, then, that some *entia realissima*

[1] This inference is too well known to require more detailed discussion. It is based upon the spurious transcendental law of causality, that everything which is *contingent* has a cause, which, if itself contingent, must also have a cause; and so on, till the series of subordinated causes must end with an absolutely necessary cause, without which it would not possess completeness.

are absolutely necessary beings. But no *ens realissimum* is in any respect different from another, and what is valid of some is valid of all. In this present case, therefore, I may employ simple conversion, and say: "Every *ens realissimum* is a necessary being." But as this proposition is determined *a priori* by the conceptions contained in it, the mere conception of an *ens realissimum* must possess the additional attribute of absolute necessity. But this is exactly what was maintained in the ontological argument, and not recognized by the cosmological, although it formed the real ground of its disguised and illusory reasoning.

Thus the second mode employed by speculative reason of demonstrating the existence of a Supreme Being, is not only, like the first, illusory and inadequate, but possesses the additional blemish of an *ignoratio elenchi*—professing to conduct us by a new road to the desired goal, but bringing us back, after a short circuit, to the old path which we had deserted at its call.

I mentioned above that this cosmological argument contains a perfect nest of dialectical assumptions, which transcendental criticism does not find it difficult to expose and to dissipate. I shall merely enumerate these, leaving it to the reader, who must by this time be well practised in such matters, to investigate the fallacies residing therein.

The following fallacies, for example, are discoverable in this mode of proof: 1. The transcendental principle: "Everything that is contingent must have a cause"—a principle without significance, except in the sensuous world. For the purely intellectual conception of the contingent cannot produce any synthetical proposition, like that of causality, which is itself without significance or distinguishing characteristic except in the phenomenal world. But in the present case it is employed to help us beyond the limits of its sphere. 2. "From the impossibility of an infinite ascending series of causes in the world of sense a first cause is inferred"; a conclusion which the principles of the employment of reason do not justify even in the sphere of experience, and still less when an attempt is made to pass the limits of this sphere. 3. Reason allows itself to be satisfied upon insufficient grounds, with regard to the completion of this series. It removes all conditions (without which, however, no conception of Necessity can take place); and, as after this it is beyond our power to form any other conceptions, it accepts this as a completion of the conception it wishes to form of the series. 4. The logical possibility of a conception of the total of reality (the criterion of this possibility being the absence of contradiction) is confounded with the transcendental, which requires a principle of the practicability of such a synthesis—a principle which again refers us to the world of experience. And so on.

The aim of the cosmological argument is to avoid the necessity of proving the existence of a necessary being *a priori* from mere conceptions —a proof which must be ontological, and of which we feel ourselves quite incapable. With this purpose, we reason from an actual existence —an experience in general, to an absolutely necessary condition of that existence. It is in this case unnecessary to demonstrate its possibility. For after having proved that it exists, the question regarding its possibility is superfluous. Now, when we wish to define more strictly the nature of this necessary being, we do not look out for some being the conception of which would enable us to comprehend the necessity of its being—for if we could do this, an empirical presupposition would be unnecessary; no, we try to discover merely the negative condition (*conditio sine qua non*), without which a being would not be absolutely necessary. Now this would be perfectly admissible in every sort of reasoning, from a consequence to its principle; but in the present case it unfortunately happens that the condition of absolute necessity can be discovered in but a single being, the conception of which must consequently contain all that is requisite for demonstrating the presence of absolute necessity, and thus entitle me to infer this absolute necessity *a priori*. That is, it must be possible to reason conversely, and say: The thing, to which the conception of the highest reality belongs, is absolutely necessary. But if I cannot reason thus —and I cannot, unless I believe in the sufficiency of the ontological argument—I find insurmountable obstacles in my new path, and am really no farther than the point from which I set out. The conception of a Supreme Being satisfies all questions *a priori* regarding the internal determinations of a thing, and is for this reason an ideal without equal or parallel, the general conception of it indicating it as at the same time an *ens individuum* among all possible things. But the conception does not satisfy the question regarding its existence—which was the purpose of all our inquiries; and, although the existence of a necessary being were admitted, we should find it impossible to answer the question: What of all things in the world must be regarded as such?

It is certainly allowable to *admit* the existence

of an all-sufficient being—a cause of all possible effects—for the purpose of enabling reason to introduce unity into its mode and grounds of explanation with regard to phenomena. But to assert that such a being *necessarily exists,* is no longer the modest enunciation of an admissible hypothesis, but the boldest declaration of an apodeictic certainty; for the cognition of that which is absolutely necessary must itself possess that character.

The aim of the transcendental ideal formed by the mind is either to discover a conception which shall harmonize with the idea of absolute necessity, or a conception which shall contain that idea. If the one is possible, so is the other; for reason recognizes that alone as absolutely necessary which is necessary from its conception. But both attempts are equally beyond our power—we find it impossible to *satisfy* the understanding upon this point, and as impossible to induce it to remain at rest in relation to this incapacity.

Unconditioned necessity, which, as the ultimate support and stay of all existing things, is an indispensable requirement of the mind, is an abyss on the verge of which human reason trembles in dismay. Even the idea of eternity, terrible and sublime as it is, as depicted by Haller, does not produce upon the mental vision such a feeling of awe and terror; for, although it *measures* the duration of things, it does not *support* them. We cannot bear, nor can we rid ourselves of the thought that a being, which we regard as the greatest of all possible existences, should *say to himself*: I am from eternity to eternity; beside me there is nothing, except that which exists by my will; *but whence then am I*? Here all sinks away from under us; and the greatest, as the smallest, perfection, hovers without stay or footing in presence of the speculative reason, which finds it as easy to part with the one as with the other.

Many physical powers, which evidence their existence by their effects, are perfectly inscrutable in their nature; they elude all our powers of observation. The transcendental object which forms the basis of phenomena, and, in connection with it, the reason why our sensibility possesses this rather than that particular kind of conditions, are and must ever remain hidden from our mental vision; the fact is there, the reason of the fact we cannot see. But an ideal of pure reason cannot be termed mysterious or *inscrutable,* because the only credential of its reality is the need of it felt by reason, for the purpose of giving completeness to the world of synthetical unity. An ideal is not even given as a cogitable *object,* and therefore cannot be inscrutable; on the contrary, it must, as a mere idea, be based on the constitution of reason itself, and on this account must be capable of explanation and solution. For the very essence of reason consists in its ability to give an account, of all our conceptions, opinions, and assertions—upon objective, or, when they happen to be illusory and fallacious, upon subjective grounds.

Detection and Explanation of the Dialectical Illusion in all Transcendental Arguments for the Existence of a Necessary Being

Both of the above arguments are transcendental; in other words, they do not proceed upon empirical principles. For, although the cosmological argument professed to lay a basis of experience for its edifice of reasoning, it did not ground its procedure upon the peculiar constitution of experience, but upon pure principles of reason—in relation to an existence given by empirical consciousness; utterly abandoning its guidance, however, for the purpose of supporting its assertions entirely upon pure conceptions. Now what is the cause, in these transcendental arguments, of the dialectical, but natural, illusion, which connects the conceptions of necessity and supreme reality, and hypostatizes that which cannot be anything but an idea? What is the cause of this unavoidable step on the part of reason, of admitting that some one among all existing things must be necessary, while it falls back from the assertion of the existence of such a being as from an abyss? And how does reason proceed to explain this anomaly to itself, and from the wavering condition of a timid and reluctant approbation—always again withdrawn—arrive at a calm and settled insight into its cause?

It is something very remarkable that, on the supposition that something exists, I cannot avoid the inference that something exists necessarily. Upon this perfectly natural—but not on that account reliable—inference does the cosmological argument rest. But, let me form any conception whatever of a thing, I find that I cannot cogitate the existence of the thing as absolutely necessary, and that nothing prevents me—be the thing or being what it may—from cogitating its non-existence. I may thus be obliged to admit that all existing things have a necessary basis, while I cannot cogitate any single or individual thing as necessary. In other words, I can never *complete* the regress through the conditions of existence, without admitting the existence of a necessary being; but, on the other hand, I cannot make a *commencement* from this being.

If I must cogitate something as existing necessarily as the basis of existing things, and yet am not permitted to cogitate any individual thing as in itself necessary, the inevitable inference is that necessity and contingency are not properties of things themselves—otherwise an internal contradiction would result; that consequently neither of these principles are objective, but merely subjective principles of reason—the one requiring us to seek for a necessary ground for everything that exists, that is, to be satisfied with no other explanation than that which is complete *a priori*, the other forbidding us ever to hope for the attainment of this completeness, that is, to regard no member of the empirical world as unconditioned. In this mode of viewing them, both principles, in their purely heuristic and regulative character, and as concerning merely the formal interest of reason, are quite consistent with each other. The one says: "You must philosophize upon nature," as if there existed a necessary primal basis of all existing things, solely for the purpose of introducing systematic unity into your knowledge, by pursuing an idea of this character—a foundation which is arbitrarily admitted to be ultimate; while the other warns you to consider no individual determination, concerning the existence of things, as such an ultimate foundation, that is, as absolutely necessary, but to keep the way always open for further progress in the deduction, and to treat every determination as determined by some other. But if all that we perceive must be regarded as conditionally necessary, it is impossible that anything which is empirically given should be absolutely necessary.

It follows from this that you must accept the absolutely necessary as *out of* and beyond the world, inasmuch as it is useful only as a principle of the highest possible unity in experience, and you cannot discover any such necessary existence in the *world*, the second rule requiring you to regard all empirical causes of unity as themselves deduced.

The philosophers of antiquity regarded all the forms of nature as contingent; while matter was considered by them, in accordance with the judgement of the common reason of mankind, as primal and necessary. But if they had regarded matter, not relatively—as the substratum of phenomena, but absolutely and *in itself*—as an independent existence, this idea of absolute necessity would have immediately disappeared. For there is nothing absolutely connecting reason with such an existence; on the contrary, it can annihilate it in thought, always and without self-contradiction. But in thought alone lay the idea of absolute necessity. A regulative principle must, therefore, have been at the foundation of this opinion. In fact, extension and impenetrability—which together constitute our conception of matter—form the supreme empirical principle of the unity of phenomena, and this principle, in so far as it is empirically unconditioned, possesses the property of a regulative principle. But, as every determination of matter which constitutes what is real in it—and consequently impenetrability—is an effect, which must have a cause, and is for this reason always derived, the notion of matter cannot harmonize with the idea of a necessary being, in its character of the principle of all derived unity. For every one of its real properties, being derived, must be only conditionally necessary, and can therefore be annihilated in thought; and thus the whole existence of matter can be so annihilated or suppressed. If this were not the case, we should have found in the world of phenomena the highest ground or condition of unity—which is impossible, according to the second regulative principle. It follows that matter, and, in general, all that forms part of the world of sense, cannot be a necessary primal being, nor even a principle of empirical unity, but that this being or principle must have its place assigned without the world. And, in this way, we can proceed in perfect confidence to deduce the phenomena of the world and their existence from other phenomena, just as if there existed no necessary being; and we can at the same time, strive without ceasing towards the attainment of completeness for our deduction, just as if such a being—the supreme condition of all existences—were presupposed by the mind.

These remarks will have made it evident to the reader that the ideal of the Supreme Being, far from being an enouncement of the existence of a being in itself necessary, is nothing more than a *regulative principle* of reason, requiring us to regard all connection existing between phenomena as if it had its origin from an all-sufficient necessary cause, and basing upon this the rule of a systematic and necessary unity in the explanation of phenomena. We cannot, at the same time, avoid regarding, by a transcendental *subreptio*, this formal principle as constitutive, and hypostatizing this unity. Precisely similar is the case with our notion of space. Space is the primal condition of all forms, which are properly just so many different limitations of it; and thus, although it is merely a principle of sensibility, we cannot help regarding it as an absolutely necessary and self-subsistent thing—as an object given *a priori* in itself. In the same way, it is quite natural that, as the systematic unity of nature cannot be established as a principle for the empirical employment of reason, unless it is based upon the idea of an *ens realissimum,* as the supreme cause, we should regard this idea as a real object, and this object, in its character of supreme condition, as absolutely necessary, and that in this way a *regulative* should be transformed into a *constitutive* principle. This interchange becomes evident when I regard this supreme being, which, relatively to the world, was absolutely (unconditionally) necessary, as a thing *per se.* In this case, I find it impossible to represent this necessity in or by any conception, and it exists merely in my own mind, as the formal condition of thought, but not as a material and hypostatic condition of existence.

Section VI. *Of the Impossibility of a Physico-Theological Proof*

If, then, neither a pure conception nor the general experience of an existing being can provide a sufficient basis for the proof of the existence of the Deity, we can make the attempt by the only other mode—that of grounding our argument upon a *determinate experience* of the phenomena of the present world, their constitution and disposition, and discover whether we can thus attain to a sound conviction of the existence of a Supreme Being. This argument we shall term the *physico-theological* argument. If it is shown to be insufficient, speculative reason cannot present us with any satisfactory proof of the existence of a being corresponding to our transcendental idea.

It is evident from the remarks that have been made in the preceding sections, that an answer to this question will be far from being difficult or unconvincing. For how can any experience be adequate with an idea? The very essence of an idea consists in the fact that no experience can ever be discovered congruent or adequate with it. The transcendental idea of a necessary and all-sufficient being is so immeasurably great, so high above all that is empirical, which is always conditioned, that we hope in vain to find materials in the sphere of experience sufficiently ample for our conception, and in vain seek the unconditioned among things that are conditioned, while examples, nay, even guidance is denied us by the laws of empirical synthesis.

If the Supreme Being forms a link in the chain of empirical conditions, it must be a member of the empirical series, and, like the lower members which it precedes, have its origin in some higher member of the series. If, on the other hand, we disengage it from the chain, and cogitate it as an intelligible being, apart from the series of natural causes—how shall reason bridge the abyss that separates the latter from the former? All laws respecting the regress from effects to causes, all synthetical additions to our knowledge relate solely to possible experience and the objects of the sensuous world, and, apart from them, are without significance.

The world around us opens before our view so magnificent a spectacle of order, variety, beauty, and conformity to ends, that whether we pursue our observations into the infinity of space in the one direction, or into its illimitable divisions in the other, whether we regard the world in its greatest or its least manifestations—even after we have attained to the highest summit of knowledge which our weak minds can reach, we find that language in the presence of wonders so inconceivable has lost its force, and number its power to reckon, nay, even thought fails to conceive adequately, and our conception of the whole dissolves into an astonishment without power of expression—all the more eloquent that it is dumb. Everywhere around us we observe a chain of causes and effects, of means and ends, of death and birth; and, as nothing has entered of itself into the condition in which we find it, we are constantly referred to some other thing, which itself suggests the same inquiry regarding its cause, and thus the universe must sink into the abyss of nothingness, unless we admit that, besides this infinite chain of contingencies, there exists something that is primal and self-subsistent—something which, as the cause of this phenomenal world, secures its continuance and preservation.

This highest cause—what magnitude shall we attribute to it? Of the content of the world we are ignorant; still less can we estimate its magnitude by comparison with the sphere of the possible. But this supreme cause being a necessity of the human mind, what is there to prevent us from attributing to it such a degree of perfection as to place it above the sphere of *all that* is possible? This we can easily do, although only by the aid of the faint outline of an abstract conception, by representing this being to ourselves as containing in itself, as an individual substance, all possible perfection—a conception which satisfies that requirement of reason which demands parsimony in principles, which is free from self-contradiction, which even contributes to the extension of the employment of reason in experience, by means of the guidance afforded by this idea to order and system, and which in no respect conflicts with any law of experience.

This argument always deserves to be mentioned with respect. It is the oldest, the clearest, and that most in conformity with the common reason of humanity. It animates the study of nature, as it itself derives its existence and draws ever new strength from that source. It introduces aims and ends into a sphere in which our observation could not of itself have discovered them, and extends our knowledge of nature, by directing our attention to a unity, the principle of which lies beyond nature. This knowledge of nature again reacts upon this idea—its cause; and thus our belief in a divine author of the universe rises to the power of an irresistible conviction.

For these reasons it would be utterly hopeless to attempt to rob this argument of the authority it has always enjoyed. The mind, unceasingly elevated by these considerations, which, although empirical, are so remarkably powerful, and continually adding to their force, will not suffer itself to be depressed by the doubts suggested by subtle speculation; it tears itself out of this state of uncertainty, the moment it casts a look upon the wondrous forms of nature and the majesty of the universe, and rises from height to height, from condition to condition, till it has elevated itself to the supreme and unconditioned author of all.

But although we have nothing to object to the reasonableness and utility of this procedure, but have rather to commend and encourage it, we cannot approve of the claims which this argument advances to demonstrative certainty and to a reception upon its own merits, apart from favour or support by other arguments. Nor can it injure the cause of morality to endeavour to lower the tone of the arrogant sophist, and to teach him that modesty and moderation which are the properties of a belief that brings calm and content into the mind, without prescribing to it an unworthy subjection. I maintain, then, that the physico-theological argument is insufficient of itself to prove the existence of a Supreme Being, that it must entrust this to the ontological argument—to which it serves merely as an introduction, and that, consequently, this argument contains the *only possible ground of proof* (possessed by speculative reason) for the existence of this being.

The chief momenta in the physico-theological argument are as follow: 1. We observe in the world manifest signs of an arrangement full of purpose, executed with great wisdom, and existing in a whole of a content indescribably various, and of an extent without limits. 2. This arrangement of means and ends is entirely foreign to the things existing in the world—it belongs to them merely as a contingent attribute; in other words, the nature of different things could not of itself, whatever means were employed, harmoniously tend towards certain purposes, were they not chosen and directed for these purposes by a rational and disposing principle, in accordance with certain fundamental ideas. 3. There exists, therefore, a sublime and wise cause (or several), which is not merely a blind, all-powerful nature, producing the beings and events which fill the world in unconscious *fecundity*, but a *free* and intelligent cause of the world. 4. The unity of this cause may be inferred from the unity of the reciprocal relation existing between the parts of the world, as portions of an artistic edifice—an inference which all our observation favours, and all principles of analogy support.

In the above argument, it is inferred from the analogy of certain products of nature with those of human art, when it compels Nature to bend herself to its purposes, as in the case of a house, a ship, or a watch, that the same kind of causality—namely, understanding and will—resides in nature. It is also declared that the internal possibility of this freely-acting nature (which is the source of all art, and perhaps also of human reason) is derivable from another and superhuman art—a conclusion which would perhaps be found incapable of standing the test of subtle transcendental criticism. But to neither of these opinions shall we at present object. We shall only remark that it must be confessed that, if we are to discuss the subject of cause at all, we cannot proceed more securely than with the guidance of the analogy subsisting between nature and such products of design—these being the only products whose causes and modes of organization are completely known to us. Reason would be unable to satisfy her own requirements, if she passed from a causality which she does know, to obscure and indemonstrable principles of explanation which she does not know.

According to the physico-theological argument, the connection and harmony existing in the world evidence the contingency of the form merely, but not of the matter, that is, of the substance of the world. To establish the truth of the latter opinion, it would be necessary to prove that all things would be in themselves incapable of this harmony and order, unless they were, even as regards their *substance,* the product of a supreme wisdom. But this would require very different grounds of proof from those presented by the analogy with human art. This proof can at most, therefore, demonstrate the existence of an *architect of the world,* whose efforts are limited by the capabilities of the material with which he works, but not of a *creator of the world,* to whom all things are subject. Thus this argument is utterly insufficient for the task before us—a demonstration of the existence of an all-sufficient being. If we wish to prove the contingency of matter, we must have recourse to a transcendental argument, which the physico-theological was constructed expressly to avoid.

We infer, from the order and design visible in the universe, as a disposition of a thoroughly contingent character, the existence of a cause *proportionate thereto.* The conception of this cause must contain certain *determinate* qualities, and it must therefore be regarded as the conception of a being which possesses all power, wisdom, and so on, in one word, all perfection—the conception, that is, of an all-sufficient being. For the predicates of *very great,* astonishing, or immeasurable power and excellence, give us no determinate conception of the thing, nor do they inform us what the thing may be in itself. They merely indicate the relation existing between the magnitude of the object and the observer, who compares it with himself and with his own power of comprehension, and are mere expressions of praise and reverence, by which the object is either magnified, or the observing subject depreciated in relation to the object. Where we have to do with the magnitude (of the perfection) of a thing, we can discover no determinate conception, except that which comprehends all possible perfection or completeness, and it is only the total (*omnitudo*) of reality which is completely determined in and through its conception alone.

Now it cannot be expected that any one will be bold enough to declare that he has a perfect insight into the relation which the magnitude of the world he contemplates bears (in its extent as well as in its content) to omnipotence, into that of the order and design in the world to the highest wisdom, and that of the unity of the world to the absolute unity of a Supreme Being. Physico-theology is therefore incapable of presenting a determinate conception of a supreme cause of the world, and is therefore insufficient as a principle of theology—a theology which is itself to be the basis of religion.

The attainment of absolute totality is completely impossible on the path of empiricism. And yet this is the path pursued in the physico-theological argument. What means shall we employ to bridge the abyss?

After elevating ourselves to admiration of the magnitude of the power, wisdom, and other attributes of the author of the world, and finding we can advance no further, we leave the argument on empirical grounds, and proceed to infer the contingency of the world from the order and conformity to aims that are observable in it. From this contingency we infer, by the help of transcendental conceptions alone, the existence of something absolutely necessary; and, still advancing, proceed from the conception of the absolute necessity of the first cause to the completely determined or determining conception thereof—the conception of an all-embracing reality. Thus the physico-theological, failing in its undertaking, recurs in its embarrassment to the cosmological argument; and, as this is merely the ontological argument in disguise, it executes its design solely by the aid of pure reason, although it at first professed to have no connection with this faculty and to base its entire procedure upon experience alone.

The physico-theologians have therefore no reason to regard with such contempt the transcendental mode of argument, and to look down upon it, with the conceit of clear-sighted observers of nature, as the brain-cobweb of obscure speculatists. For, if they reflect upon and examine their own arguments, they will find that, after following for some time the path of nature and experience, and discovering themselves no nearer their object, they suddenly leave this path and pass into the region of pure possibility, where they hope to reach upon the wings of ideas what had eluded all their empirical investigations. Gaining, as they think, a firm footing after this immense leap, they extend their determinate conception—into the possession of which they have come, they know not how—over the whole sphere of creation, and explain their ideal, which is entirely a product of pure reason, by illustrations drawn from experience—though in a degree miserably unworthy of the grandeur of the object, while they refuse to acknowledge that they have arrived at this cognition or hypothesis by a very different road from that of experience.

Thus the physico-theological is based upon the cosmological, and this upon the ontological proof of the existence of a Supreme Being; and as besides these three there is no other path open to speculative reason, the ontological proof, on the ground of pure conceptions of reason, is the only possible one, if any proof of a proposition so far transcending the empirical exercise of the understanding is possible at all.

Section VII. *Critique of all Theology based upon Speculative Principles of Reason*

If by the term *theology* I understand the cognition of a primal being, that cognition is based either upon reason alone (*theologia rationalis*) or upon revelation (*theologia revelata*). The former cogitates its object either by means of pure transcendental conceptions, as an *ens originarium, realissimum, ens entium,* and is termed *transcendental theology*; or, by means of a conception derived from the nature of our own mind, as a supreme intelligence, and must then be entitled *natural* theology. The person who believes in a transcendental theology alone, is termed a *deist*; he who acknowledges the possibility of a *natural* theology also, a *theist.* The former admits that we can cognize by pure reason alone the existence of a Supreme Being, but at the same time maintains that our conception of this being is purely transcendental, and that all we can say of it is that it possesses all reality, without being able to define it more closely. The second asserts that reason is capable of presenting us, from the analogy with nature, with a more definite conception of this being, and that its operations, as the cause of all things, are the results of intelligence and free will. The former regards the Supreme Being as the *cause of the world*—whether by the necessity of his nature, or as a free agent, is left undetermined; the latter considers this being as the *author of the world.*

Transcendental theology aims either at inferring the existence of a Supreme Being from a general experience, without any closer reference to the world to which this experience belongs, and in this case it is called *cosmotheology*; or it endeavours to cognize the existence of such a being, through mere conceptions, without the aid of experience, and is then termed *ontotheology.*

Natural theology infers the attributes and the existence of an author of the world, from the constitution of, the order and unity observable in, the world, in which two modes of causality must be admitted to exist—those of nature and freedom. Thus it rises from this world to a supreme intelligence, either as the principle of all natural, or of all moral order and perfection. In the former case it is termed *physico-theology,* in the latter, *ethical* or *moral-theology.*[1]

As we are wont to understand by the term *God* not merely an eternal nature, the operations of which are insensate and blind, but a Supreme Being, who is the free and intelligent author of all things, and as it is this latter view alone that can be of interest to humanity, we might, in strict rigour, deny to the *deist* any belief in God at all, and regard him merely as a maintainer of the existence of a primal being or thing—the supreme cause of all other things. But, as no one ought to be blamed, merely because he does not feel himself justified in maintaining a certain opinion, as if he altogether denied its truth and asserted the opposite, it is more correct—as it is less harsh—to say, the deist believes in a God, the theist in a *living God* (*summa intelligentia*). We shall now proceed to investigate the sources of all these attempts of reason to establish the existence of a Supreme Being.

It may be sufficient in this place to define theoretical knowledge or cognition as knowledge of that which *is,* and practical knowledge as knowledge of that which *ought to be.* In this view, the theoretical employment of reason is that by which I cognize *a priori* (as necessary) that something is, while the practical is that by which I cognize *a priori* what ought to happen. Now, if it is an indubitably certain, though at the same time an entirely conditioned truth, that something is, or ought to happen, either a certain determinate condition of this truth is absolutely necessary, or such a condition may be arbitrarily presupposed. In the former case the condition is postulated (*per thesin*), in the latter supposed (*per hypothesin*). There are certain practical laws—those of morality—which are absolutely necessary. Now, if these laws necessarily presuppose the existence of some being, as the condition of the possibility of their *obligatory* power, this being must be *postulated,* because the conditioned, from which we reason to this determinate condition, is itself cognized *a priori* as absolutely necessary. We shall at some future time show that the moral laws not merely presuppose the existence of a Supreme Being, but also, as themselves absolutely necessary in a different relation, demand or postulate it—although only from a practical point of view. The discussion of this argument we postpone for the present.

[1] Not theological ethics; for this science contains ethical laws, which *presuppose* the existence of a Supreme Governor of the world; while moral-theology, on the contrary, is the expression of a conviction of the existence of a Supreme Being, founded upon ethical laws.

When the question relates merely to that which is, not to that which ought to be, the conditioned which is presented in experience is always cogitated as contingent. For this reason its condition cannot be regarded as absolutely necessary, but merely as relatively necessary, or rather as *needful;* the condition is in itself and *a priori* a mere arbitrary presupposition in aid of the cognition, by reason, of the conditioned. If, then, we are to possess a theoretical cognition of the absolute necessity of a thing, we cannot attain to this cognition otherwise than *a priori* by means of *conceptions;* while it is impossible in this way to cognize the existence of a cause which bears any relation to an existence given in experience.

Theoretical cognition is *speculative* when it relates to an object or certain conceptions of an object which is not given and cannot be discovered by means of experience. It is opposed to the *cognition of nature,* which concerns only those objects or predicates which can be presented in a possible experience.

The principle that everything which happens (the *empirically* contingent) must have a cause, is a principle of the cognition of nature, but not of speculative cognition. For, if we change it into an abstract principle, and deprive it of its reference to experience and the empirical, we shall find that it cannot with justice be regarded any longer as a synthetical proposition, and that it is impossible to discover any mode of transition from that which exists to something entirely different — termed *cause.* Nay, more, the conception of a cause—as likewise that of the contingent—loses, in this speculative mode of employing it, all significance, for its objective reality and meaning are comprehensible from experience alone.

When from the existence of the universe and the things in it the existence of a cause of the universe is inferred, reason is proceeding not in the *natural,* but in the *speculative* method. For the principle of the former enounces, not that things themselves or substances, but only that which *happens* or their *states*—as empirically contingent, have a cause: the assertion that the existence of substance itself is contingent is not justified by experience, it is the assertion of a reason employing its principles in a speculative manner. If, again, I infer from the form of the universe, from the way in which all things are connected and act and react upon each other, the existence of a cause entirely distinct from the universe—this would again be a judgement of purely speculative reason; because the object in this case—the cause—can never be an object of possible experience. In both these cases the principle of causality, which is valid only in the field of experience—useless and even meaningless beyond this region, would be diverted from its proper destination.

Now I maintain that all attempts of reason to establish a theology by the aid of speculation alone are fruitless, that the principles of reason as applied to nature do not conduct us to any theological truths, and, consequently, that a rational theology can have no existence, unless it is founded upon the laws of morality. For all synthetical principles of the understanding are valid only as *immanent* in experience; while the cognition of a Supreme Being necessitates their being employed transcendentally, and of this the understanding is quite incapable. If the empirical law of causality is to conduct us to a Supreme Being, this being must belong to the chain of empirical objects—in which case it would be, like all phenomena, itself conditioned. If the possibility of passing the limits of experience be admitted, by means of the dynamical law of the relation of an effect to its cause, what kind of conception shall we obtain by this procedure? Certainly not the conception of a Supreme Being, because experience never presents us with the greatest of all possible effects, and it is only an effect of this character that could witness to the existence of a corresponding cause. If, for the purpose of fully satisfying the requirements of Reason, we recognize her right to assert the existence of a perfect and absolutely necessary being, this can be admitted only from favour, and cannot be regarded as the result or irresistible demonstration. The physico-theological proof may add weight to others—if other proofs there are—by connecting speculation with experience; but in itself it rather prepares the mind for theological cognition, and gives it a right and natural direction, than establishes a sure foundation for theology.

It is now perfectly evident that transcendental questions admit only of transcendental answers—those presented *a priori* by pure conceptions without the least empirical admixture. But the question in the present case is evidently synthetical—it aims at the extension of our cognition beyond the bounds of experience—it requires an assurance respecting the existence of a being corresponding with the idea in our minds, to which no experience can ever be adequate. Now it has been abundantly proved that all *a priori* synthetical cognition is possible only as the expression of the formal conditions of a possible experience; and that the validity of all principles depends upon their immanence in the field of experience, that is, their relation to objects of empirical cognition or phenomena. Thus all transcendental procedure in reference to speculative theology is without result.

If any one prefers doubting the conclusiveness of the proofs of our analytic to losing the persuasion of the validity of these old and time-honoured arguments, he at least cannot decline answering the question—how he can pass the limits of all possible experience by the help of mere ideas. If he talks of new arguments, or of improvements upon old arguments, I request him to spare me. There is certainly no great choice in this sphere of discussion, as all speculative arguments must at last look for support to the ontological, and I have, therefore, very little to fear from the argumentative fecundity of the dogmatical defenders of a non-sensuous reason. Without looking upon myself as a remarkably combative person, I shall not decline the challenge to detect the fallacy and destroy the pretensions of every attempt of speculative theology. And yet the hope of better fortune never deserts those who are accustomed to the dogmatical mode of procedure. I shall, therefore, restrict myself to the simple and equitable demand that such reasoners will demonstrate, from the nature of the human mind as well as from that of the other sources of knowledge, how we are to proceed to extend our cognition completely *a priori,* and to carry it to that point where experience abandons us, and no means exist of guaranteeing the objective reality of our conceptions. In whatever way the understanding may have attained to a conception, the existence of the object of the conception cannot be discovered in it by analysis, because the cognition of the *existence* of the object depends upon the object's being posited and given in itself *apart from the conception.* But it is utterly impossible to go beyond our conception, without the aid of experience—which presents to the mind nothing but phenomena, or to attain by the help of mere conceptions to a conviction of the existence of new kinds of objects or supernatural beings.

But although pure speculative reason is far from sufficient to demonstrate the existence of a Supreme Being, it is of the highest utility in *correcting* our conception of this being—on the supposition that we can attain to the cognition of it by some other means—in making it consistent with itself and with all other conceptions of intelligible objects, clearing it from all that is incompatible with the conception of an *ens summum,* and eliminating from it all limitations or admixtures of empirical elements.

Transcendental theology is still therefore, notwithstanding its objective insufficiency, of importance in a negative respect; it is useful as a test of the procedure of reason when engaged with pure ideas, no other than a transcendental standard being in this case admissible. For if, from a practical point of view, the hypothesis of a Supreme and All-sufficient Being is to maintain its validity without opposition, it must be of the highest importance to define this conception in a correct and rigorous manner—as the transcendental conception of a necessary being, to eliminate all phenomenal elements (anthropomorphism in its most extended signification), and at the same time to overflow all contradictory assertions—be they *atheistic, deistic,* or *anthropomorphic.* This is of course very easy; as the same arguments which demonstrated the inability of human reason to *affirm* the existence of a Supreme Being must be alike sufficient to prove the invalidity of its denial. For it is impossible to gain from the pure speculation of reason demonstration that there exists no Supreme Being, as the ground of all that exists, or that this being possesses none of those properties which we regard as analogical with the dynamical qualities of a thinking being, or that, as the anthropomorphists would have us believe, it is subject to all the limitations which sensibility imposes upon those intelligences which exist in the world of experience.

A Supreme Being is, therefore, for the speculative reason, a mere ideal, though a *faultless* one—a conception which perfects and crowns the system of human cognition, but the objective reality of which can neither be proved nor disproved by pure reason. If this defect is ever supplied by a moral theology, the problematic transcendental theology which has preceded, will have been at least serviceable as demonstrating the mental necessity existing for the conception, by the complete determination of it which it has furnished, and the ceaseless testing of the conclusions of a reason often deceived by sense, and not always in harmony with its own ideas. The attributes of necessity, infinitude, unity, existence apart from the world (and not as a world-soul), eternity (free from conditions of time), omnipresence (free from conditions of space), omnipotence, and others, are pure transcendental predicates; and thus the accurate conception of a Supreme Being, which every theology requires, is furnished by transcendental theology alone.

APPENDIX

Of the Regulative Employment of the Ideas of Pure Reason

THE result of all the dialectical attempts of pure reason not only confirms the truth of what we have already proved in our Transcendental Analytic, namely, that all inferences which would lead us beyond the limits of experience are fallacious and groundless, but it at the same time teaches us this important lesson, that human reason has a natural inclination to overstep these limits, and that transcendental ideas are as much the natural property of the reason as categories are of the understanding. There exists this difference, however, that while the categories never mislead us, outward objects being always in perfect harmony therewith, ideas are the parents of irresistible illusions, the severest and most subtle criticism being required to save us from the fallacies which they induce.

Whatever is grounded in the nature of our powers will be found to be in harmony with the final purpose and proper employment of these powers, when once we have discovered their true direction and aim. We are entitled to suppose, therefore, that there exists a mode of employing transcendental ideas which is proper and *immanent;* although, when we mistake their meaning, and regard them as conceptions of actual things, their mode of application is *transcendent* and delusive. For it is not the idea itself, but only the employment of the idea in relation to possible experience, that is transcendent or immanent. An idea is employed transcendently, when it is applied to an object falsely believed to be adequate with and to correspond to it; immanently, when it is applied solely to the employment of the *understanding* in the sphere of experience. Thus all errors of *subreptio*—of misapplication, are to be ascribed to defects of judgement, and not to understanding or reason.

Reason never has an immediate relation to an object; it relates immediately to the understanding alone. It is only through the understanding that it can be employed in the field of experience. It does not *form* conceptions of objects, it merely *arranges* them and gives to them that unity which they are capable of possessing when the sphere of their application has been extended as widely as possible. Reason avails itself of the conception of the understanding for the sole purpose of producing totality in the different series. This totality the understanding does not concern itself with; its only occupation is the connection of experiences, by which *series* of conditions in accordance with conceptions are established. The object of reason is, therefore, the understanding and its proper destination. As the latter brings unity into the diversity of objects by means of its conceptions, so the former brings unity into the diversity of conceptions by means of ideas; as it sets the final aim of a collective unity to the operations of the understanding, which without this occupies itself with a distributive unity alone.

I accordingly maintain that transcendental ideas can never be employed as constitutive ideas, that they cannot be conceptions of objects, and that, when thus considered, they assume a fallacious and dialectical character. But, on the other hand, they are capable of an admirable and indispensably necessary application to objects—as regulative ideas, directing the understanding to a certain aim, the guiding lines towards which all its laws follow, and in which they all meet in one point. This point—though a mere idea (*focus imaginarius*), that is, not a point from which the conceptions of the understanding do really proceed, for it lies beyond the sphere of possible experience—serves, notwithstanding, to give to these conceptions the greatest possible unity combined with the greatest possible extension. Hence arises the natural illusion which induces us to believe that these lines proceed from an object which lies out of the sphere of empirical cognition, just as objects reflected in a mirror appear to be behind it. But this illusion—which we may hinder from imposing upon us—is necessary and unavoidable, if we desire to see, not only those objects which lie before us, but those which are at a great distance behind us; that is to say, when, in the present case, we direct the aims of the understanding, beyond every given experience, towards an extension as great as can possibly be attained.

If we review our cognitions in their entire extent, we shall find that the peculiar business of reason is to arrange them into a *system,* that is to say, to give them connection according to a principle. This unity presupposes an idea—the idea of the form of a whole (of cognition), preceding the determinate cognition of the parts, and containing the conditions which determine *a priori* to every part its place and relation to the other parts of the whole system. This idea, accordingly, demands complete unity in the cognition of the understanding—not the unity of a contingent aggregate, but that of a system connected according to necessary laws. It cannot be affirmed with propriety that this idea is a conception of an object; it is merely a conception of the complete unity of the conceptions of objects, in so far as this unity is available to the understanding as a rule. Such conceptions of reason are not derived from nature; on the contrary, we employ them for the interrogation and investigation of nature, and regard our cognition as defective so long as it is not adequate to them. We admit that such a thing as *pure earth, pure water,* or *pure air,* is not to be discovered. And yet we require these conceptions (which have their origin in the reason, so far as regards their absolute purity and completeness) for the purpose of determining the share which each of these natural causes has in every phenomenon. Thus the different kinds of matter are all referred to earths, as mere weight; to salts and inflammable bodies, as pure force; and finally, to water and air, as the *vehicula* of the former, or the machines employed by them in their operations —for the purpose of explaining the chemical action and reaction of bodies in accordance with the idea of a mechanism. For, although not actually so expressed, the influence of such ideas of reason is very observable in the procedure of natural philosophers.

If reason is the faculty of deducing the particular from the general, and if the general be certain *in se* and given, it is only necessary that the *judgement* should subsume the particular under the general, the particular being thus necessarily determined. I shall term this the *demonstrative* or *apodeictic* employment of reason. If, however, the general is admitted as *problematical* only, and is a mere idea, the particular case is certain, but the universality of the rule which applies to this particular case remains a problem. Several particular cases, the certainty of which is beyond doubt, are then taken and examined, for the purpose of discovering whether the rule is applicable to them; and if it appears that all the particular cases which can be collected follow from the rule, its universality is inferred, and at the same time, all the causes which have not, or cannot be presented to our observation, are concluded to be of the same character with those which we have observed. This I shall term the *hypothetical* employment of the reason.

The hypothetical exercise of reason by the aid of ideas employed as problematical conceptions is properly not *constitutive.* That is to say, if we consider the subject strictly, the truth of the rule, which has been employed as an hypothesis, does not follow from the use that is made of it by reason. For how can we know all the possible cases that may arise? some of which may, however, prove exceptions to the universality of the rule. This employment of reason is merely regulative, and its sole aim is the introduction of unity into the aggregate of our particular cognitions, and thereby the *approximating* of the rule to universality.

The object of the hypothetical employment of reason is therefore the systematic unity of cognitions; and this unity is the *criterion* of the *truth* of a rule. On the other hand, this systematic unity—as a mere idea—is in fact merely a unity *projected,* not to be regarded as given, but only in the light of a problem—a problem which serves, however, as a principle for the various and particular exercise of the understanding in experience, directs it with regard to those cases which are not presented to our observation, and introduces harmony and consistency into all its operations.

All that we can be certain of from the above considerations is that this systematic unity is a logical principle, whose aim is to assist the understanding, where it cannot of itself attain to rules, by means of ideas, to bring all these various rules under one principle, and thus to ensure the most complete consistency and connection that can be attained. But the assertion that objects and the understanding by which they are cognized are so constituted as to be determined to systematic unity, that this may be postulated *a priori,* without any reference to the interest of reason, and that we are justified in declaring all possible cognitions—empirical and others—to possess systematic unity, and to be subject to general principles from which, notwithstanding their various character, they are all derivable—such an assertion can be founded only upon a *transcendental* principle of reason, which would render this systematic unity not subjectively and logically—in its character of a method, but objectively necessary.

We shall illustrate this by an example. The conceptions of the understanding make us acquainted, among many other kinds of unity, with that of the causality of a substance, which is termed *power.* The different phenomenal manifestations of the same substance appear at first view to be so very dissimilar that we are inclined to assume the existence of just as many different powers as there are different effects—as, in the case of the human mind, we have feeling, consciousness, imagnination, memory, wit, analysis, pleasure, desire and so on. Now we are required by a logical maxim to reduce these differences to as small a number as possible, by comparing them and discovering the hidden identity which exists. We must inquire, for example, whether or not imagination (connected with consciousness), memory, wit, and analysis are not merely different forms of understanding and reason. The idea of a *fundamental power,* the existence of which no effort of logic can assure us of, is the problem to be solved, for the systematic representation of the existing variety of powers. The logical principle of reason requires us to produce as great a unity as is possible in the system of our cognitions; and the more the phenomena of this and the other power are found to be identical, the more probable does it become, that they are nothing but different manifestations of one and the same power, which may be called, relatively speaking, a *fundamental power*. And so with other cases.

These relatively fundamental powers must again be compared with each other, to discover, if possible, the one radical and *absolutely* fundamental power of which they are but the manifestations. But this unity is purely hypothetical. It is not maintained, that this unity does really exist, but that we must, in the interest of reason, that is, for the establishment of principles for the various rules presented by experience, try to discover and introduce it, so far as is practicable, into the sphere of our cognitions.

But the transcendental employment of the understanding would lead us to believe that this idea of a fundamental power is not problematical, but that it possesses objective reality, and thus the systematic unity of the various powers or forces in a substance is demanded by the understanding and erected into an apodeictic or necessary principle. For, without having attempted to discover the unity of the various powers existing in nature, nay, even after all our attempts have failed, we notwithstanding presuppose that it does exist, and may be, sooner or later, discovered. And this reason does, not only, as in the case above adduced, with regard to the unity of substance, but where many substances, although all to a certain extent homogeneous, are discoverable, as in the case of matter in general. Here also does reason presuppose the existence of the systematic unity of various powers—inasmuch as particular laws of nature are subordinate to general laws; and parsimony in principles is not merely an economical principle of reason, but an essential law of nature.

We cannot understand, in fact, how a logical principle of unity can of right exist, unless we presuppose a transcendental principle, by which such a systematic unity—as a property of objects themselves—is regarded as necessary *a priori.* For with what right can reason, in its logical exercise, require us to regard the variety of forces which nature displays, as in effect a disguised unity, and to deduce them from one fundamental force or power, when she is free to admit that it is just as possible that all forces should be different in kind, and that a systematic unity is not conformable to the design of nature? In this view of the case, reason would be proceeding in direct opposition to her own destination, by setting as an aim an idea which entirely conflicts with the procedure and arrangement of nature. Neither can we assert that reason has previously inferred this unity from the contingent nature of phenomena. For the law of reason which requires us to seek for this unity is a necessary law, inasmuch as without it we should not possess a faculty of reason, nor without reason a consistent and self-accordant mode of employing the understanding, nor, in the absence of this, any proper and sufficient criterion of empirical truth. In relation to this criterion, therefore, we must suppose the idea of the systematic unity of nature to possess objective validity and necessity.

We find this transcendental presupposition lurking in different forms in the principles of philosophers, although they have neither recognized it nor confessed to themselves its presence. That the diversities of individual things do not exclude identity of species, that the various species must be considered as merely different determinations of a few *genera,* and these again as divisions of still higher *races,* and so on—that, accordingly, a certain systematic unity of all possible empirical conceptions, in so far as they can be deduced from higher and more general conceptions, must be sought for, is a scholastic maxim or logical principle, without which reason could not be employed by us. For we can infer the particular from the general, only in so far as general properties of things constitute the foundation upon which the particular rest.

That the same unity exists in nature is presupposed by philosophers in the well-known scholastic maxim, which forbids us unnecessarily to augment the number of entities or principles (*entia praeter necessitatem non esse multiplicanda*). This maxim asserts that nature herself assists in the establishment of this unity of reason, and that the seemingly infinite diversity of phenomena should not deter us from the expectation of discovering beneath this diversity a unity of fundamental properties, of which the aforesaid variety is but a more or less determined form. This unity, although a mere idea, has been always pursued with so much zeal, that thinkers have found it necessary rather to moderate the desire than to encourage it. It was considered a great step when chemists were able to reduce all salts to two main genera—acids and alkalis; and they regard this difference as itself a mere variety, or different manifestation of one and the same fundamental material. The different kinds of earths (stones and even metals) chemists have endeavoured to reduce to three, and afterwards to two; but still, not content with this advance, they cannot but think that behind these diversities there lurks but one genus—nay, that even salts and earths have a common principle. It might be conjectured that this is merely an economical plan of reason, for the purpose of sparing itself trouble, and an attempt of a purely hypothetical character, which, when successful, gives an appearance of probability to the principle of explanation employed by the reason. But a selfish purpose of this kind is easily to be distinguished from the idea, according to which every one presupposes that this unity is in accordance with the laws of nature, and that reason does not in this case *request,* but *requires,* although we are quite unable to determine the proper limits of this unity.

If the diversity existing in phenomena—a diversity not of form (for in this they may be similar) but of content—were so great that the subtlest human reason could never by comparison discover in them the least similarity (which is not impossible), in this case the logical law of genera would be without foundation, the conception of a genus, nay, all general conceptions would be impossible, and the faculty of the understanding, the exercise of which is restricted to the world of conceptions, could not exist. The logical principle of genera, accordingly, if it is to be applied to nature (by which I mean objects presented to our senses), presupposes a transcendental principle. In accordance with this principle, homogeneity is necessarily presupposed in the variety of phenomena (although we are unable to determine *a priori* the degree of this homogeneity), because without it no empirical conceptions, and consequently no experience, would be possible.

The logical principle of genera, which demands identity in phenomena, is balanced by another principle—that of *species,* which requires variety and diversity in things, notwithstanding their accordance in the same genus, and directs the understanding to attend to the one no less than to the other. This principle (of the faculty of distinction) acts as a check upon the levity of the former (the faculty of wit); and reason exhibits in this respect a double and conflicting interest—on the one hand, the interest in the *extent* (the interest of generality) in relation to genera; on the other, that of the *content* (the interest of individuality) in relation to the variety of species. In the former case, the understanding cogitates more *under* its conceptions, in the latter it cogitates more *in* them. This distinction manifests itself likewise in the habits of thought peculiar to natural philosophers, some of whom—the remarkably speculative heads—may be said to be hostile to heterogeneity in phenomena, and have their eyes always fixed on the unity of genera, while others—with a strong empirical tendency—aim unceasingly at the analysis of phenomena, and almost destroy in us the hope of ever being able to estimate the character of these according to general principles.

The latter mode of thought is evidently based upon a logical principle, the aim of which is the systematic completeness of all cognitions. This principle authorizes me, beginning at the genus, to descend to the various and diverse contained under it; and in this way extension, as in the former case unity, is assured to the system. For if we merely examine the sphere of the conception which indicates a genus, we cannot discover how far it is possible to proceed in the division of that sphere; just as it is impossible, from the consideration of the space occupied by matter, to determine how far we can proceed in the division of it. Hence every *genus* must contain different *species,* and these again different *subspecies;* and as each of the latter must itself contain a sphere (must be of a certain extent, as a *conceptus communis*), reason demands that no species or sub-species is to be considered as the lowest possible. For a species or sub-species, being always a conception, which contains only what is common to a number of different things, does not completely determine any individual thing, or relate immediately to it, and must consequently contain other conceptions, that is, other sub-species under it. This law of specification may be thus expressed: *Entium varietates non temere sunt minuendae.*

But it is easy to see that this logical law would likewise be without sense or application, were it not based upon a transcendental *law of specification,* which certainly does not require that the differences existing in phenomena should be *infinite* in number, for the logical principle, which merely maintains the *indeterminate-*

ness of the logical sphere of a conception, in relation to its possible division, does not authorize this statement; while it does impose upon the understanding the duty of searching for sub-species to every species, and minor differences in every difference. For, were there no lower conceptions, neither could there be any higher. Now the understanding cognizes only by means of conceptions; consequently, how far soever it may proceed in division, never by mere intuition, but always by lower and lower conceptions. The cognition of phenomena in their complete determination (which is possible only by means of the understanding) requires an unceasingly continued specification of conceptions, and a progression to ever smaller differences, of which abstraction had been made in the conception of the species, and still more in that of the genus.

This law of specification cannot be deduced from experience; it can never present us with a principle of so universal an application. Empirical specification very soon stops in its distinction of diversities, and requires the guidance of the transcendental law, as a principle of the reason—a law which imposes on us the necessity of never ceasing in our search for differences, even although these may not present themselves to the senses. That absorbent earths are of different kinds could only be discovered by obeying the anticipatory law of reason, which imposes upon the understanding the task of discovering the differences existing between these earths, and supposes that nature is richer in substances than our senses would indicate. The faculty of the understanding belongs to us just as much under the presupposition of differences in the objects of nature, as under the condition that these objects are homogeneous, because we could not possess conceptions, nor make any use of our understanding, were not the phenomena included under these conceptions in some respects dissimilar, as well as similar, in their character.

Reason thus prepares the sphere of the understanding for the operations of this faculty: 1. By the principle of the *homogeneity* of the diverse in higher genera; 2. By the principle of the *variety* of the homogeneous in lower species; and, to complete the systematic unity, it adds, 3. A law of the *affinity* of all conceptions which prescribes a continuous transition from one species to every other by the gradual increase of diversity. We may term these the principles of the *homogeneity*, the *specification*, and the *continuity* of forms. The latter results from the union of the two former, inasmuch as we regard the systematic connection as complete in thought, in the ascent to higher genera, as well as in the descent to lower species. For all diversities must be related to each other, as they all spring from one highest genus, descending through the different gradations of a more and more extended determination.

We may illustrate the systematic unity produced by the three logical principles in the following manner. Every conception may be regarded as a point, which, as the standpoint of a spectator, has a certain horizon, which may be said to enclose a number of things that may be viewed, so to speak, from that centre. Within this horizon there must be an infinite number of other points, each of which has its own horizon, smaller and more circumscribed; in other words, every species contains sub-species, according to the principle of specification, and the logical horizon consists of smaller horizons (sub-species), but not of points (individuals), which possess no extent. But different horizons or genera, which include under them so many conceptions, may have one common horizon, from which, as from a mid-point, they may be surveyed; and we may proceed thus, till we arrive at the highest genus, or universal and true horizon, which is determined by the highest conception, and which contains under itself all differences and varieties, as genera, species, and sub-species.

To this highest standpoint I am conducted by the law of homogeneity, as to all lower and more variously-determined conceptions by the law of specification. Now as in this way there exists no void in the whole extent of all possible conceptions, and as out of the sphere of these the mind can discover nothing, there arises from the presupposition of the universal horizon above mentioned, and its complete division, the principle: *Non datur vacuum formarum.* This principle asserts that there are not different primitive and highest genera, which stand isolated, so to speak, from each other, but all the various genera are mere divisions and limitations of one highest and universal genus; and hence follows immediately the principle: *Datur continuum formarum.* This principle indicates that all differences of species limit each other, and do not admit of transition from one to another by a *saltus,* but only through smaller degrees of the difference between the one species and the other. In one word, there are no species or sub-species which (in the view of reason) are the nearest possible to each other; intermediate species or sub-species being always possible, the difference of which from each of the former is always smaller than the difference existing between these.

The first law, therefore, directs us to avoid the notion that there exist different primal genera, and enounces the fact of perfect homogeneity; the second imposes a check upon this tendency to unity and prescribes the distinction of sub-species, before proceeding to apply our general conceptions to individuals. The third unites both the former, by enouncing the fact of homogeneity as existing even in the most various diversity, by means of the gradual transition from one species to another. Thus it indicates a relationship between the different branches or species, in so far as they all spring from the same stem.

But this logical law of the *continuum specierum* (*formarum logicarum*) presupposes a transcendental principle (*lex continui in natura*), without which the understanding might be led into error, by following the guidance of the former, and thus perhaps pursuing a path contrary to that prescribed by nature. This law must, consequently, be based upon pure transcendental, and not upon empirical, considerations. For, in the latter case, it would come later than the system; whereas it is really itself the parent of all that is systematic in our cognition of nature. These principles are not mere hypotheses employed for the purpose of experimenting upon nature; although when any such connection is discovered, it forms a solid ground for regarding the hypothetical unity as valid in the sphere of nature—and thus they are in this respect not without their use. But we go farther, and maintain that it is manifest that these principles of parsimony in fundamental causes, variety in effects, and affinity in phenomena, are in accordance both with reason and nature, and that they are not mere methods or plans devised for the purpose of assisting us in our observation of the external world.

But it is plain that this continuity of forms is a mere idea, to which no adequate object can be discovered in experience. And this for two reasons. First, because the species in nature are really divided, and hence form *quanta discreta;* and, if the gradual progression through their affinity were continuous, the intermediate members lying between two given species must be infinite in number, which is impossible. Secondly, because we cannot make any determinate empirical use of this law, inasmuch as it does not present us with any criterion of affinity which could aid us in determining how far we ought to pursue the graduation of differences: it merely contains a general indication that it is our duty to seek for and, if possible, to discover them.

When we arrange these principles of systematic unity in the order conformable to their employment in experience, they will stand thus: *Variety, Affinity, Unity,* each of them, as ideas, being taken in the highest degree of their completeness. Reason presupposes the existence of cognitions of the understanding, which have a direct relation to experience, and aims at the ideal unity of these cognitions—a unity which far transcends all experience or empirical notions. The affinity of the diverse, notwithstanding the differences existing between its parts, has a relation to things, but a still closer one to the mere properties and powers of things. For example, imperfect experience may represent the orbits of the planets as circular. But we discover variations from this course, and we proceed to suppose that the planets revolve in a path which, if not a circle, is of a character very similar to it. That is to say, the movements of those planets which do not form a circle will approximate more or less to the properties of a circle, and probably form an ellipse. The paths of comets exhibit still greater variations, for, so far as our observation extends, they do not return upon their own course in a circle or ellipse. But we proceed to the conjecture that comets describe a parabola, a figure which is closely allied to the ellipse. In fact, a parabola is merely an ellipse, with its longer axis produced to an indefinite extent. Thus these principles conduct us to a unity in the genera of the forms of these orbits, and, proceeding farther, to a unity as regards the cause of the motions of the heavenly bodies—that is, gravitation. But we go on extending our conquests over nature, and endeavour to explain all seeming deviations from these rules, and even make additions to our system which no experience can ever substantiate—for example, the theory, in affinity with that of ellipses, of hyperbolic paths of comets, pursuing which, these bodies leave our solar system and, passing from sun to sun, unite the most distant parts of the infinite universe, which is held together by the same moving power.

The most remarkable circumstance connected with these principles is that they seem to be transcendental, and, although only containing ideas for the guidance of the empirical exercise of reason, and although this empirical employment stands to these ideas in an asymptotic relation alone (to use a mathematical term), that is, continually approximate, without ever being able to attain to them, they possess, notwithstanding, as *a priori* synthetical propositions, objective though undetermined validity, and are available as rules for possible experience. In the elaboration of our experience, they may also be employed with great advantage, as heuristic[1] principles. A transcendental deduction of them cannot be made; such a deduction being always impossible in the case of ideas, as has been already shown.

We distinguished, in the Transcendental Analytic, the *dynamical* principles of the understanding, which are regulative principles of *intuition*, from the mathematical, which are constitutive principles of intuition. These dynamical laws are, however, constitutive in relation to *experience*, inasmuch as they render the conceptions without which experience could not exist possible *a priori*. But the principles of pure reason cannot be constitutive even in regard to empirical *conceptions*, because no sensuous schema corresponding to them can be discovered, and they cannot therefore have an object *in concreto*. Now, if I grant that they cannot be employed in the sphere of experience, as constitutive principles, how shall I secure for them employment and objective validity as regulative principles, and in what way can they be so employed?

The understanding is the object of reason, as sensibility is the object of the understanding. The production of systematic unity in all the empirical operations of the understanding is the proper occupation of reason; just as it is the business of the understanding to connect the various content of phenomena by means of conceptions, and subject them to empirical laws. But the operations of the understanding are, without the schemata of sensibility, *undetermined;* and, in the same manner, the unity of reason is perfectly *undetermined* as regards the conditions under which, and the extent to which, the understanding ought to carry the systematic connection of its conceptions. But, although it is impossible to discover in *intuition* a schema for the complete systematic unity of all the conceptions of the understanding, there must be some *analogon* of this schema. This analogon is the idea of the *maximum* of the division and the connection of our cognition in one principle. For we may have a determinate notion of a *maximum* and an absolutely perfect, all the restrictive conditions which are connected with an indeterminate and various content having been abstracted. Thus the idea of reason is analogous with a sensuous schema, with this difference, that the application of the categories to the schema of reason does not present a cognition of any object (as is the case with the application of the categories to sensuous schemata), but merely provides us with a rule or principle for the systematic unity of the exercise of the understanding. Now, as every principle which imposes upon the exercise of the understanding *a priori* compliance with the rule of systematic unity also relates, although only in an indirect manner, to an object of experience, the principles of pure reason will also possess objective reality and validity in relation to experience. But they will not aim at *determining* our knowledge in regard to any empirical object; they will merely indicate the procedure, following which the empirical and determinate exercise of the understanding may be in complete harmony and connection with itself—a result which is produced by its being brought into harmony with the principle of systematic unity, so far as that is possible, and deduced from it.

I term all subjective principles, which are not derived from observation of the constitution of an object, but from the interest which Reason has in producing a certain completeness in her cognition of that object, *maxims* of reason. Thus there are maxims of speculative reason, which are based solely upon its speculative interest, although they appear to be objective principles.

When principles which are really regulative are regarded as constitutive, and employed as objective principles, contradictions must arise; but if they are considered as mere maxims, there is no room for contradictions of any kind, as they then merely indicate the different interests of reason, which occasion differences in the mode of thought. In effect, Reason has only one single interest, and the seeming contradiction existing between her maxims merely indicates a difference in, and a reciprocal limitation of, the methods by which this interest is satisfied.

This reasoner has at heart the interest of *diversity* — in accordance with the principle of specification; another, the interest of *unity*—in accordance with the principle of aggregation. Each believes that his judgement rests upon a thorough insight into the subject he is examining, and yet it has been influenced solely by a greater or less degree of adherence to some one of the two principles, neither of which are objective, but originate solely from the interest of reason, and on this account to be termed *max-*

[1] From the Greek *εὑρίσκω*.

ims rather than *principles*. When I observe intelligent men disputing about the distinctive characteristics of men, animals, or plants, and even of minerals, those on the one side assuming the existence of certain national characteristics, certain well-defined and hereditary distinctions of family, race, and so on, while the other side maintain that nature has endowed all races of men with the same faculties and dispositions, and that all differences are but the result of external and accidental circumstances—I have only to consider for a moment the real nature of the subject of discussion, to arrive at the conclusion that it is a subject far too deep for us to judge of, and that there is little probability of either party being able to speak from a perfect insight into and understanding of the nature of the subject itself. Both have, in reality, been struggling for the twofold interest of reason; the one maintaining the one interest, the other the other. But this difference between the maxims of diversity and unity may easily be reconciled and adjusted; although, so long as they are regarded as objective principles, they must occasion not only contradictions and polemic, but place hinderances in the way of the advancement of truth, until some means is discovered of reconciling these conflicting interests, and bringing reason into union and harmony with itself.

The same is the case with the so-called law discovered by Leibnitz,[1] and supported with remarkable ability by Bonnet[2]—the law of the *continuous gradation* of created beings, which is nothing more than an inference from the principle of affinity; for observation and study of the order of nature could never present it to the mind as an objective truth. The steps of this ladder, as they appear in experience, are too far apart from each other, and the so-called petty differences between different kinds of animals are in nature commonly so wide separations that no confidence can be placed in such views (particularly when we reflect on the great variety of things, and the ease with which we can discover resemblances), and no faith in the laws which are said to express the aims and purposes of nature. On the other hand, the method of investigating the order of nature in the light of this principle, and the maxim which requires us to regard this order—it being still undetermined how far it extends—as really existing in nature, is beyond doubt a legitimate and excellent principle of reason—a principle which extends farther than any experience or observation of ours and which, without giving us any positive knowledge of anything in the region of experience, guides us to the goal of systematic unity.

Of the Ultimate End of the Natural Dialectic of Human Reason

The ideas of pure reason cannot be, of themselves and in their own nature, dialectical; it is from their misemployment alone that fallacies and illusions arise. For they originate in the nature of reason itself, and it is impossible that this supreme tribunal for all the rights and claims of speculation should be itself undeserving of confidence and promotive of error. It is to be expected, therefore, that these ideas have a genuine and legitimate aim. It is true, the mob of sophists raise against reason the cry of inconsistency and contradiction, and affect to despise the government of that faculty, because they cannot understand its constitution, while it is to its beneficial influences alone that they owe the position and the intelligence which enable them to criticize and to blame its procedure.

We cannot employ an *a priori* conception with certainty, until we have made a transcendental deduction therefore. The ideas of pure reason do not admit of the same kind of deduction as the categories. But if they are to possess the least objective validity, and to represent anything but mere creations of thought (*entia rationis ratiocinantis*), a deduction of them must be possible. This deduction will complete the critical task imposed upon pure reason; and it is to this part of our labours that we now proceed.

There is a great difference between a thing's being presented to the mind as an *object in an absolute sense*, or merely as an *ideal object*. In the former case I employ my conceptions to determine the object; in the latter case nothing is present to the mind but a mere schema, which does not relate directly to an object, not even in a hypothetical sense, but which is useful only for the purpose of representing other objects to the mind, in a mediate and indirect manner, by means of their relation to the idea in the intellect. Thus I say the conception of a supreme intelligence is a mere idea; that is to say, its objective reality does not consist in the fact that it has an immediate relation to an object (for in this sense we have no means of establishing its objective validity), it is merely a schema constructed according to the necessary conditions of the unity of reason—the schema of a thing in general, which is useful towards the production of the highest degree of systematic unity

[1] Leibnitz, *Nouveaux Essais*, iii. 6.

[2] Bonnet, *Betrachtungen über die Natur*, pages 29-85.

in the empirical exercise of reason, in which we deduce this or that object of experience from the imaginary object of this idea, as the ground or cause of the said object of experience. In this way, the idea is properly a heuristic, and not an ostensive, conception; it does not give us any information respecting the constitution of an object, it merely indicates how, under the guidance of the idea, we ought to *investigate* the constitution and the relations of objects in the world of experience. Now, if it can be shown that the three kinds of transcendental ideas (psychological, cosmological, and theological), although not relating directly to any object nor determining it, do nevertheless, on the supposition of the existence of an *ideal object,* produce systematic unity in the laws of the empirical employment of the reason, and extend our empirical cognition, without ever being inconsistent or in opposition with it—it must be a necessary *maxim* of reason to regulate its procedure according to these ideas. And this forms the transcendental deduction of all speculative ideas, not as *constitutive* principles of the extension of our cognition beyond the limits of our experience, but as *regulative* principles of the systematic unity of empirical cognition, which is by the aid of these ideas arranged and emended within its own proper limits, to an extent unattainable by the operation of the principles of the understanding alone.

I shall make this plainer. Guided by the principles involved in these ideas, we must, in the *first* place, so connect all the phenomena, actions, and feelings of the mind, as if it were a simple substance, which, endowed with personal identity, possesses a permanent existence (in this life at least), while its states, among which those of the body are to be included as external conditions, are in continual change. *Secondly,* in cosmology, we must investigate the conditions of all natural phenomena, internal as well as external, as if they belonged to a chain infinite and without any prime or supreme member, while we do not, on this account, deny the existence of intelligible grounds of these phenomena, although we never employ them to explain phenomena, for the simple reason that they are not objects of our cognition. *Thirdly,* in the sphere of theology, we must regard the whole system of possible experience as forming an absolute, but dependent and sensuously-conditioned unity, and at the same time as based upon a sole, supreme, and all-sufficient ground existing apart from the world itself—a ground which is a self-subsistent, primeval and creative reason, in relation to which we so employ our reason in the field of experience, as if all objects drew their origin from that archetype of all reason. In other words, we ought not to deduce the internal phenomena of the mind from a simple thinking substance, but deduce them from each other under the guidance of the regulative idea of a simple being; we ought not to deduce the phenomena, order, and unity of the universe from a supreme intelligence, but merely draw from this idea of a supremely wise cause the rules which must guide reason in its connection of causes and effects.

Now there is nothing to hinder us from *admitting* these ideas to possess an objective and hyperbolic existence, except the cosmological ideas, which lead reason into an antinomy: the psychological and theological ideas are not antinomial. They contain no contradiction; and how, then, can any one dispute their objective reality, since he who denies it knows as little about their possibility as we who affirm? And yet, when we wish to admit the existence of a thing, it is not sufficient to convince ourselves that there is no positive obstacle in the way; for it cannot be allowable to regard mere creations of thought, which transcend, though they do not contradict, all our conceptions, as real and determinate objects, solely upon the authority of a speculative reason striving to compass its own aims. They cannot, therefore, be admitted to be real in themselves; they can only possess a comparative reality—that of a schema of the regulative principle of the systematic unity of all cognition. They are to be regarded not as actual things, but as in some measure analogous to them. We abstract from the object of the idea all the conditions which limit the exercise of our understanding, but which, on the other hand, are the sole conditions of our possessing a determinate conception of any given thing. And thus we cogitate a something, of the real nature of which we have not the least conception, but which we represent to ourselves as standing in a relation to the whole system of phenomena, analogous to that in which phenomena stand to each other.

By admitting these ideal beings, we do not really extend our cognitions beyond the objects of possible experience; we extend merely the empirical unity of our experience, by the aid of systematic unity, the schema of which is furnished by the idea, which is therefore valid—not as a constitutive, but as a regulative principle. For although we posit a thing corresponding to the idea—a something, an actual existence—we do not on that account aim at the extension of our cognition by means of transcendent conceptions. This existence is purely ideal, and not objective; it is the mere expression of the systematic unity which is to be the guide of reason in the field of experience. There are no attempts made at deciding what the ground of this unity may be, or what the real nature of this imaginary being.

Thus the transcendental and only determinate conception of God, which is presented to us by speculative reason, is in the strictest sense *deistic*. In other words, reason does not assure us of the objective validity of the conception; it merely gives us the idea of something, on which the supreme and necessary unity of all experience is based. This something we cannot, following the analogy of a real substance, cogitate otherwise than as the cause of all things operating in accordance with rational laws, if we regard it as an individual object; although we should rest contented with the idea alone as a regulative principle of reason, and make no attempt at completing the sum of the conditions imposed by thought. This attempt is, indeed, inconsistent with the grand aim of complete systematic unity in the sphere of cognition—a unity to which no bounds are set by reason.

Hence it happens that, admitting a divine being, I can have no conception of the internal possibility of its perfection, or of the necessity of its existence. The only advantage of this admission is that it enables me to answer all other questions relating to the contingent, and to give reason the most complete satisfaction as regards the unity which it aims at attaining in the world of experience. But I cannot satisfy reason with regard to this hypothesis itself; and this proves that it is not its intelligence and insight into the subject, but its speculative interest alone which induces it to proceed from a point lying far beyond the sphere of our cognition, for the purpose of being able to consider all objects as parts of a systematic whole.

Here a distinction presents itself, in regard to the way in which we may cogitate a presupposition—a distinction which is somewhat subtle, but of great importance in transcendental philosophy. I may have sufficient grounds to admit something, or the existence of something, in a relative point of view (*suppositio relativa*), without being justified in admitting it in an absolute sense (*suppositio absoluta*). This distinction is undoubtedly requisite, in the case of a regulative principle, the necessity of which we recognize, though we are ignorant of the source and cause of that necessity, and which we assume to be based upon some ultimate ground, for the purpose of being able to cogitate the universality of the principle in a more determinate way. For example, I cogitate the existence of a being corresponding to a pure transcendental idea. But I cannot admit that this being exists absolutely and in itself, because all of the conceptions by which I can cogitate an object in a determinate manner fall short of assuring me of its existence; nay, the conditions of the objective validity of my conceptions are excluded by the idea—by the very fact of its being an idea. The conceptions of reality, substance, causality, nay, even that of necessity in existence, have no significance out of the sphere of empirical cognition, and cannot, beyond that sphere, determine any object. They may, accordingly, be employed to explain the possibility of things in the world of sense, but they are utterly inadequate to explain the possibility of the *universe itself* considered as a whole; because in this case the ground of explanation must lie out of and beyond the world, and cannot, therefore, be an object of possible experience. Now, I may admit the existence of an incomprehensible being of this nature—the object of a mere idea, relatively to the world of sense; although I have no ground to admit its existence absolutely and in itself. For if an idea (that of a systematic and complete unity, of which I shall presently speak more particularly) lies at the foundation of the most extended empirical employment of reason, and if this idea cannot be adequately represented *in concreto*, although it is indispensably necessary for the approximation of empirical unity to the highest possible degree—I am not only authorized, but compelled, to realize this idea, that is, to posit a real object corresponding thereto. But I cannot profess to know this object; it is to me merely a something, to which, as the ground of systematic unity in cognition, I attribute such properties as are analogous to the conceptions employed by the understanding in the sphere of experience. Following the analogy of the notions of reality, substance, causality, and necessity, I cogitate a being, which possesses all these attributes in the highest degree; and, as this idea is the offspring of my reason alone, I cogitate this being as *self-subsistent reason*, and as the cause of the universe operating by means of ideas of the greatest possible harmony and unity. Thus I abstract all conditions that would limit my idea, solely for the purpose of rendering systematic unity possible in the world of empirical diversity, and thus securing the widest possible extension for the exercise of reason in that sphere. This I am enabled to do, by regarding all connections and relations in the world of sense, *as if* they were the dispositions of a supreme reason, of which our reason is but a faint image. I then proceed to cogitate this Supreme Being by conceptions which have, properly, no meaning or application, except in the world of sense. But as I am authorized to employ the transcendental hypothesis of such a being in a relative respect alone, that is, as the substratum of the greatest possible unity in experience—I may attribute to a being which I regard as distinct from the world, such properties as belong solely to the sphere of sense and experience. For I do not desire, and am not justified in desiring, to cognize this object of my idea, as it exists in itself; for I possess no conceptions sufficient for this task, those of reality, substance, causality, nay, even that of necessity in existence, losing all significance, and becoming merely the signs of conceptions, without content and without applicability, when I attempt to carry them beyond the limits of the world of sense. I cogitate merely the relation of a perfectly unknown being to the greatest possible systematic unity of experience, solely for the purpose of employing it as the schema of the regulative principle which directs reason in its empirical exercise.

It is evident, at the first view, that we cannot presuppose the reality of this transcendental object, by means of the conceptions of reality, substance, causality, and so on, because these conceptions cannot be applied to anything that is distinct from the world of sense. Thus the supposition of a Supreme Being or cause is purely relative; it is cogitated only in behalf of the systematic unity of experience; such a being is but a something, of whose existence in itself we have not the least conception. Thus, too, it becomes sufficiently manifest why we required the idea of a necessary being in relation to objects given by sense, although we can never have the least conception of this being, or of its absolute necessity.

And now we can clearly perceive the result of our transcendental dialectic, and the proper aim of the ideas of pure reason—which become dialectical solely from misunderstanding and inconsiderateness. Pure reason is, in fact, occupied with itself, and not with any object. Objects are not presented to it to be embraced in the unity of an empirical conception; it is only the cognitions of the understanding that are presented to it, for the purpose of receiving the unity of a rational conception, that is, of being connected according to a principle. The unity of reason is the unity of system; and this systematic unity is not an objective principle, extending its dominion over objects, but a subjective maxim, extending its authority over the empirical cognition of objects. The systematic connection which reason gives to the empirical employment of the understanding not only advances the extension of that employment, but ensures its correctness, and thus the principle of a systematic unity of this nature is also objective, although only in an indefinite respect (*principium vagum*). It is not, however, a constitutive principle, determining an object to which it directly relates; it is merely a regulative principle or maxim, advancing and strengthening the empirical exercise of reason, by the opening up of new paths of which the understanding is ignorant, while it never conflicts with the laws of its exercise in the sphere of experience.

But reason cannot cogitate this systematic unity, without at the same time cogitating an object of the idea—an object that cannot be presented in any experience, which contains no concrete example of a complete systematic unity. This being (*ens rationis ratiocinatae*) is therefore a mere idea and is not assumed to be a thing which is real absolutely and in itself. On the contrary, it forms merely the problematical foundation of the connection which the mind introduces among the phenomena of the sensuous world. We look upon this connection, in the light of the above-mentioned idea, as if it drew its origin from the supposed being which corresponds to the idea. And yet all we aim at is the possession of this idea as a secure foundation for the systematic unity of experience—a unity indispensable to reason, advantageous to the understanding, and promotive of the interests of empirical cognition.

We mistake the true meaning of this idea when we regard it as an enouncement, or even as a hypothetical declaration of the existence of a real thing, which we are to regard as the origin or ground of a systematic constitution of the universe. On the contrary, it is left completely undetermined what the nature or properties of this so-called ground may be. The idea is merely to be adopted as a point of view, from which this unity, so essential to reason and so beneficial to the understanding, may be regarded as radiating. In one word, this transcendental thing is merely the schema of a regulative principle, by means of which Reason, so far as in her lies, extends the dominion of systematic unity over the whole sphere of experience.

The first object of an idea of this kind is the

ego, considered merely as a thinking nature or soul. If I wish to investigate the properties of a thinking being, I must interrogate experience. But I find that I can apply none of the categories to this object, the schema of these categories, which is the condition of their application, being given only in sensuous intuition. But I cannot thus attain to the cognition of a systematic unity of all the phenomena of the internal sense. Instead, therefore, of an empirical conception of what the soul really is, reason takes the conception of the empirical unity of all thought, and, by cogitating this unity as unconditioned and primitive, constructs the rational conception or idea of a simple substance which is in itself unchangeable, possessing personal identity, and in connection with other real things external to it; in one word, it constructs the idea of a simple self-subsistent intelligence. But the real aim of reason in this procedure is the attainment of principles of systematic unity for the explanation of the phenomena of the soul. That is, reason desires to be able to represent all the determinations of the internal sense as existing in one subject, all powers as deduced from one fundamental power, all changes as mere varieties in the condition of a being which is permanent and always the same, and all *phenomena* in space as entirely different in their nature from the procedure of thought. Essential simplicity (with the other attributes predicated of the ego) is regarded as the mere schema of this regulative principle; it is not assumed that it is the actual ground of the properties of the soul. For these properties may rest upon quite different grounds, of which we are completely ignorant; just as the above predicates could not give us any knowledge of the soul as it is in itself, even if we regarded them as valid in respect of it, inasmuch as they constitute a mere idea, which cannot be represented *in concreto*. Nothing but good can result from a psychological idea of this kind, if we only take proper care not to consider it as more than an idea; that is, if we regard it as valid merely in relation to the employment of reason, in the sphere of the phenomena of the soul. Under the guidance of this idea, or principle, no empirical laws of corporeal phenomena are called in to explain that which is a phenomenon of the *internal sense* alone; no windy hypotheses of the generation, annihilation, and palingenesis of souls are admitted. Thus the consideration of this object of the internal sense is kept pure, and unmixed with heterogeneous elements; while the investigation of reason aims at reducing all the grounds of explanation employed in this sphere of knowledge to a single principle. All this is best effected, nay, cannot be effected otherwise than by means of such a schema, which requires us to regard this ideal thing as an actual existence. The psychological idea is, therefore, meaningless and inapplicable, except as the schema of a regulative conception. For, if I ask whether the soul is not really of a spiritual nature—it is a question which has no meaning. From such a conception has been abstracted, not merely all corporeal nature, but all nature, that is, all the predicates of a possible experience; and consequently, all the conditions which enable us to cogitate an object to this conception have disappeared. But, if these conditions are absent, it is evident that the conception is meaningless.

The second regulative idea of speculative reason is the conception of the universe. For nature is properly the only object presented to us, in regard to which reason requires regulative principles. Nature is twofold—thinking and corporeal nature. To cogitate the latter in regard to its internal possibility, that is, to determine the application of the categories to it, no idea is required—no representation which transcends experience. In this sphere, therefore, an idea is impossible, sensuous intuition being our only guide; while, in the sphere of psychology, we require the fundamental idea (I), which contains *a priori* a certain form of thought, namely, the unity of the ego. Pure reason has, therefore, nothing left but nature in general, and the completeness of conditions in nature in accordance with some principle. The absolute totality of the series of these conditions is an idea, which can never be fully realized in the empirical exercise of reason, while it is serviceable as a rule for the procedure of reason in relation to that totality. It requires us, in the explanation of given phenomena (in the regress or ascent in the series), to proceed as if the series were infinite in itself, that is, were prolonged *in indefinitum;* while on the other hand, where reason is regarded as itself the determining cause (in the region of freedom), we are required to proceed as if we had not before us an object of sense, but of the pure understanding. In this latter case, the conditions do not exist in the series of phenomena, but may be placed quite out of and beyond it, and the series of conditions may be regarded as if it had an absolute beginning from an intelligible cause. All this proves that the cosmological ideas are nothing but regulative principles, and not constitutive; and that their aim is not to realize an actual totality in such series. The full discussion of this subject will be found in its proper place in the chapter on the antinomy of pure reason.

The third idea of pure reason, containing the hypothesis of a being which is valid merely as a relative hypothesis, is that of the one and all-sufficient cause of all cosmological series, in other words, the idea of God. We have not the slightest ground absolutely to admit the existence of an object corresponding to this idea; for what can empower or authorize us to affirm the existence of a being of the highest perfection—a being whose existence is absolutely necessary—merely because we possess the conception of such a being? The answer is: It is the existence of the world which renders this hypothesis necessary. But this answer makes it perfectly evident that the idea of this being, like all other speculative ideas, is essentially nothing more than a demand upon reason that it shall regulate the connection which it and its subordinate faculties introduce into the phenomena of the world by principles of systematic unity and, consequently, that it shall regard all phenomena as originating from one all-embracing being, as the supreme and all-sufficient cause. From this it is plain that the only aim of reason in this procedure is the establishment of its own formal rule for the extension of its dominion in the world of experience; that it does not aim at an extension of its cognition *beyond the limits of experience;* and that, consequently, this idea does not contain any constitutive principle.

The highest formal unity, which is based upon ideas alone, is the unity of all things—a unity in accordance with an aim or purpose; and the speculative interest of reason renders it necessary to regard all order in the world as if it originated from the intention and design of a supreme reason. This principle unfolds to the view of reason in the sphere of experience new and enlarged prospects, and invites it to connect the phenomena of the world according to teleological laws, and in this way to attain to the highest possible degree of systematic unity. The hypothesis of a supreme intelligence, as the sole cause of the universe—an intelligence which has for us no more than an ideal existence—is accordingly always of the greatest service to reason. Thus, if we presuppose, in relation to the figure of the earth (which is round, but somewhat flattened at the poles),[1] or that of mountains or seas, wise designs on the part of an author of the universe, we cannot fail to make, by the light of this supposition, a great number of interesting discoveries. If we keep to this hypothesis, as a principle which is purely regulative, even error cannot be very detrimental. For, in this case, error can have no more serious consequences than that, where we expected to discover a teleological connection (*nexus finalis*), only a mechanical or physical connection appears. In such a case, we merely fail to find the additional form of unity we expected, but we do not lose the rational unity which the mind requires in its procedure in experience. But even a miscarriage of this sort cannot affect the law in its general and teleological relations. For although we may convict an anatomist of an error, when he connects the limb of some animal with a certain purpose, it is quite impossible to *prove* in a single case that any arrangement of nature, be it what it may, is entirely without aim or design. And thus medical physiology, by the aid of a principle presented to it by pure reason, extends its very limited empirical knowledge of the purposes of the different parts of an organized body so far that it may be asserted with the utmost confidence, and with the approbation of all reflecting men, that every organ or bodily part of an animal has its use and answers a certain design. Now, this is a supposition which, if regarded as of a constitutive character, goes much farther than any experience or observation of ours can justify. Hence it is evident that it is nothing more than a regulative principle of reason, which aims at the highest degree of systematic unity, by the aid of the idea of a causality according to design in a supreme cause—a cause which it regards as the highest intelligence.

If, however, we neglect this restriction of the idea to a purely regulative influence, reason is betrayed into numerous errors. For it has then left the ground of experience, in which alone are to be found the criteria of truth, and has ventured into the region of the incomprehensible and unsearchable, on the heights of which it loses its power and collectedness, because it has

[1] The advantages which a circular form, in the case of the earth, has over every other, are well known. But few are aware that the slight flattening at the poles, which gives it the figure of a spheroid, is the only cause which prevents the elevations of continents or even of mountains, perhaps thrown up by some internal convulsion, from continually altering the position of the axis of the earth—and that to some considerable degree in a short time. The great protuberance of the earth under the Equator serves to overbalance the impetus of all other masses of earth, and thus to preserve the axis of the earth, so far as we can observe, in its present position. And yet this wise arrangement has been unthinkingly explained from the equilibrium of the formerly fluid mass.

completely severed its connection with experience.

The first error which arises from our employing the idea of a Supreme Being as a constitutive (in repugnance to the very nature of an idea), and not as a regulative principle, is the error of inactive reason (*ignava ratio*).[1] We may so term every principle which requires us to regard our investigations of nature as absolutely complete, and allows reason to cease its inquiries, as if it had fully executed its task. Thus the psychological idea of the ego, when employed as a constitutive principle for the explanation of the phenomena of the soul, and for the extension of our knowledge regarding this subject beyond the limits of experience—even to the condition of the soul after death—is convenient enough for the purposes of pure reason, but detrimental and even ruinous to its interests in the sphere of nature and experience. The dogmatizing spiritualist explains the unchanging unity of our personality through all changes of condition from the unity of a thinking substance, the interest which we take in things and events that can happen only after our death, from a consciousness of the immaterial nature of our thinking subject, and so on. Thus he dispenses with all empirical investigations into the cause of these internal phenomena, and with all possible explanations of them upon purely natural grounds; while, at the dictation of a transcendent reason, he passes by the immanent sources of cognition in experience, greatly to his own ease and convenience, but to the sacrifice of all genuine insight and intelligence. These prejudicial consequences become still more evident, in the case of the dogmatical treatment of our idea of a Supreme Intelligence, and the theological system of nature (physico-theology) which is falsely based upon it. For, in this case, the aims which we observe in nature, and often those which we merely fancy to exist, make the investigation of causes a very easy task, by directing us to refer such and such phenomena immediately to the unsearchable will and counsel of the Supreme Wisdom, while we ought to investigate their causes in the general laws of the mechanism of matter. We are thus recommended to consider the labour of reason as ended, when we have merely dispensed with its employment, which is guided surely and safely only by the order of nature and the series of changes in the world—which are arranged according to immanent and general laws. This error may be avoided, if we do not merely consider from the view-point of final aims certain parts of nature, such as the division and structure of a continent, the constitution and direction of certain mountain-chains, or even the organization existing in the vegetable and animal kingdoms, but look upon this systematic unity of nature in a perfectly *general* way, in relation to the idea of a Supreme Intelligence. If we pursue this advice, we lay as a foundation for all investigation the conformity to aims of all phenomena of nature in accordance with universal laws, for which no particular arrangement of nature is exempt, but only cognized by us with more or less difficulty; and we possess a regulative principle of the systematic unity of a teleological connection, which we do not attempt to anticipate or predetermine. All that we do, and ought to do, is to follow out the physico-mechanical connection in nature according to general laws, with the hope of discovering, sooner or later, the teleological connection also. Thus, and thus only, can the principle of final unity aid in the extension of the employment of reason in the sphere of experience, without being in any case detrimental to its interests.

The second error which arises from the misconception of the principle of systematic unity is that of perverted reason (*perversa ratio, ὕστερον πρότερον rationis*). The idea of systematic unity is available as a regulative principle in the connection of phenomena according to general natural laws; and, how far soever we have to travel upon the path of experience to discover some fact or event, this idea requires us to believe that we have approached all the more nearly to the completion of its use in the sphere of nature, although that completion can never be attained. But this error reverses the procedure of reason. We begin by hypostatizing the principle of systematic unity, and by giving an anthropomorphic determination to the conception of a Supreme Intelligence, and then proceed forcibly to impose aims upon nature. Thus not only does teleology, which ought to aid in the completion of unity in accordance with general laws, operate to the destruction of its influence, but it hinders reason from attaining its proper aim, that is, the proof, upon natural grounds, of the existence of a supreme intelligent cause. For, if we cannot presuppose supreme finality in nature *a priori,* that is, as essentially belonging to

[1] This was the term applied by the old dialecticians to a sophistical argument, which ran thus: If it is your fate to die of this disease, you will die, whether you employ a physician or not. Cicero says that this mode of reasoning has received this appellation, because, if followed, it puts an end to the employment of reason in the affairs of life. For a similar reason, I have applied this designation to the sophistical argument of pure reason.

nature, how can we be directed to endeavour to discover this unity and, rising gradually through its different degrees, to approach the supreme perfection of an author of all—a perfection which is absolutely necessary, and therefore cognizable *a priori*? The regulative principle directs us to presuppose systematic unity absolutely and, consequently, as following from the essential nature of things—but only as a *unity of nature,* not merely cognized empirically, but presupposed *a priori,* although only in an indeterminate manner. But if I insist on basing nature upon the foundation of a supreme ordaining Being, the unity of nature is in effect lost. For, in this case, it is quite foreign and unessential to the nature of things, and cannot be cognized from the general laws of nature. And thus arises a vicious circular argument, what ought to have been proved having been presupposed.

To take the regulative principle of systematic unity in nature for a constitutive principle, and to hypostatize and make a cause out of that which is properly the ideal ground of the consistent and harmonious exercise of reason, involves reason in inextricable embarrassments. The investigation of nature pursues its own path under the guidance of the chain of natural causes, in accordance with the general laws of nature, and ever follows the light of the idea of an author of the universe—not for the purpose of deducing the finality, which it constantly pursues, from this Supreme Being, but to attain to the cognition of his existence from the finality which it seeks in the existence of the phenomena of nature, and, if possible, in that of all things—to cognize this being, consequently, as absolutely necessary. Whether this latter purpose succeed or not, the idea is and must always be a true one, and its employment, when merely regulative, must always be accompanied by truthful and beneficial results.

Complete unity, in conformity with aims, constitutes absolute perfection. But if we do not find this unity in the nature of the things which go to constitute the world of experience, that is, of objective cognition, consequently in the universal and necessary laws of nature, how can we infer from this unity the idea of the supreme and absolutely necessary perfection of a primal being, which is the origin of all causality? The greatest systematic unity, and consequently teleological unity, constitutes the very foundation of the possibility of the most extended employment of human reason. The idea of unity is therefore essentially and indissolubly connected with the nature of our reason. This idea is a legislative one; and hence it is very natural that we should assume the existence of a legislative reason corresponding to it, from which the systematic unity of nature—the object of the operations of reason—must be derived.

In the course of our discussion of the antinomies, we stated that it is always possible to answer all the questions which pure reason may raise; and that the plea of the limited nature of our cognition, which is unavoidable and proper in many questions regarding natural phenomena, cannot in this case be admitted, because the questions raised do not relate to the nature of things, but are necessarily originated by the nature of reason itself, and relate to its own internal constitution. We can now establish this assertion, which at first sight appeared so rash, in relation to the two questions in which reason takes the greatest interest, and thus complete our discussion of the dialectic of pure reason.

If, then, the question is asked, in relation to transcendental theology,[1] *first,* whether there is anything distinct from the world, which contains the ground of cosmical order and connection according to general laws? The answer is: *Certainly.* For the world is a sum of phenomena; there must, therefore, be some transcendental basis of these phenomena, that is, a basis cogitable by the pure understanding alone. If, *secondly,* the question is asked whether this being is substance, whether it is of the greatest reality, whether it is necessary, and so forth? I answer that *this question is utterly without meaning.* For all the categories which aid me in forming a conception of an object cannot be employed except in the world of sense, and are without meaning when not applied to objects of actual or possible experience. Out of this sphere, they are not properly conceptions, but the mere marks or indices of conceptions, which we may admit, although they cannot, without the help of experience, help us to understand any subject or thing. If, *thirdly,* the question is whether we may not cogitate this being, which is distinct from the world, in analogy with the objects of experience? The answer is: *Undoubtedly,* but only as an ideal, and not as a real object. That is, we must cogitate it only as an unknown substratum of the systematic unity, order, and finality of the world—a

[1] After what has been said of the psychological idea of the ego and its proper employment as a regulative principle of the operations of reason, I need not enter into details regarding the transcendental illusion by which the systematic unity of all the various phenomena of the internal sense is hypostatized. The procedure is in this case very similar to that which has been discussed in our remarks on the theological ideal.

unity which reason must employ as the regulative principle of its investigation of nature. Nay, more, we may admit into the idea certain anthropomorphic elements, which are promotive of the interests of this regulative principle. For it is no more than an idea, which does not relate directly to a being distinct from the world, but to the regulative principle of the systematic unity of the world, by means, however, of a schema of this unity—the schema of a Supreme Intelligence, who is the wisely-designing author of the universe. What this basis of cosmical unity may be in itself, we know not—we cannot discover from the idea; we merely know how we ought to employ the idea of this unity, in relation to the systematic operation of reason in the sphere of experience.

But, it will be asked again, *can* we on these grounds, admit the existence of a wise and omnipotent author of the world? *Without doubt;* and not only so, but we *must* assume the existence of such a being. But do we thus extend the limits of our knowledge beyond the field of possible experience? By *no means.* For we have merely presupposed a something, of which we have no conception, which we do not know as it is in itself; but, in relation to the systematic disposition of the universe, which we must presuppose in all our observation of nature, we have cogitated this unknown being *in analogy* with an intelligent existence (an empirical conception), that is to say, we have endowed it with those attributes, which, judging from the nature of our own reason, may contain the ground of such a systematic unity. This idea is therefore valid only relatively to the employment in experience of our reason. But if we attribute to it absolute and objective validity, we overlook the fact that it is merely an ideal being that we cogitate; and, by setting out from a basis which is not determinable by considerations drawn from experience, we place ourselves in a position which incapacitates us from applying this principle to the empirical employment of reason.

But, it will be asked further, can I make any use of this conception and hypothesis in my investigations into the world and nature? *Yes,* for this very purpose was the idea established by reason as a fundamental basis. But may I regard certain arrangements, which seemed to have been made in conformity with some fixed aim, as the arrangements of design, and look upon them as proceeding from the divine will, with the intervention, however, of certain other particular arrangements disposed to that end? Yes, you may do so; but at the same time you must regard it as indifferent, whether it is asserted that divine wisdom has disposed all things in conformity with his highest aims, or that the idea of supreme wisdom is a regulative principle in the investigation of nature, and at the same time a principle of the systematic unity of nature according to general laws, even in those cases where we are unable to discover that unity. In other words, it must be perfectly indifferent to you whether you say, when you have discovered this unity: God has wisely willed it so; or: Nature has wisely arranged this. For it was nothing but the systematic unity, which reason requires as a basis for the investigation of nature, that justified you in accepting the idea of a supreme intelligence as a schema for a regulative principle; and, the farther you advance in the discovery of design and finality, the more certain the validity of your idea. But, as the whole aim of this regulative principle was the discovery of a necessary and systematic unity in nature, we have, in so far as we attain this, to attribute our success to the idea of a Supreme Being; while, at the same time, we cannot, without involving ourselves in contradictions, overlook the general laws of nature, as it was in reference to them alone that this idea was employed. We cannot, I say, overlook the general laws of nature, and regard this conformity to aims observable in nature as contingent or hyperphysical in its origin; inasmuch as there is no ground which can justify us in the admission of a being with such properties distinct from and above nature. All that we are authorized to assert is that this idea may be employed as a principle, and that the properties of the being which is assumed to correspond to it may be regarded as systematically connected in analogy with the causal determination of phenomena.

For the same reasons we are justified in introducing into the idea of the supreme cause other anthropomorphic elements (for without these we could not predicate anything of it); we may regard it as allowable to cogitate this cause as a being with understanding, the feelings of pleasure and displeasure, and faculties of desire and will corresponding to these. At the same time, we may attribute to this being infinite perfection—a perfection which necessarily transcends that which our knowledge of the order and design in the world authorize us to predicate of it. For the regulative law of systematic unity requires us to study nature on the supposition that systematic and final unity *in infinitum* is everywhere discoverable, even in the highest diversity. For, although we may discover little of this cosmical perfection, it belongs to the legislative prerogative of reason to require us always to seek for and to expect it; while it must always be beneficial to institute all inquiries into nature in accordance with this principle. But it is evident that, by this idea of a supreme author of all, which I place as the foundation of all inquiries into nature, I do not mean to assert the existence of such a being, or that I have any knowledge of its existence; and, consequently, I do not really deduce anything from the existence of this being, but merely from its idea, that is to say, from the nature of things in this world, in accordance with this idea. A certain dim consciousness of the true use of this idea seems to have dictated to the philosophers of all times the moderate language used by them regarding the cause of the world. We find them employing the expressions *wisdom* and *care of nature,* and *divine wisdom,* as synonymous—nay, in purely speculative discussions, preferring the former, because it does not carry the appearance of greater pretensions than such as we are entitled to make, and at the same time directs reason to its proper field of action—nature and her phenomena.

Thus, pure reason, which at first seemed to promise us nothing less than the extension of our cognition beyond the limits of experience, is found, when thoroughly examined, to contain nothing but regulative principles, the virtue and function of which is to introduce into our cognition a higher degree of unity than the understanding could of itself. These principles, by placing the goal of all our struggles at so great a distance, realize for us the most thorough connection between the different parts of our cognition, and the highest degree of systematic unity. But, on the other hand, if misunderstood and employed as constitutive principles of transcendent cognition, they become the parents of illusions and contradictions, while pretending to introduce us to new regions of knowledge.

Thus all human cognition begins with intuitions, proceeds from thence to conceptions, and ends with ideas. Although it possesses, in relation to all three elements, *a priori* sources of cognition, which seemed to transcend the limits of all experience, a thoroughgoing criticism demonstrates that speculative reason can never, by the aid of these elements, pass the bounds of possible experience, and that the proper destination of this highest faculty of cognition is to employ all methods, and all the principles of these methods, for the purpose of penetrating into the innermost secrets of nature, by the aid of the principles of unity (among all kinds of which teleological unity is the highest), while it ought not to attempt to soar above the sphere of experience, beyond which there lies nought for us but the void inane. The critical examination, in our Transcendental Analytic, of all the propositions which professed to extend cognition beyond the sphere of experience, completely demonstrated that they can only conduct us to a possible experience. If we were not distrustful even of the clearest abstract theorems, if we were not allured by specious and inviting prospects to escape from the constraining power of their evidence, we might spare ourselves the laborious examination of all the dialectical arguments which a transcendent reason adduces in support of its pretensions; for we should know with the most complete certainty that, however honest such professions might be, they are null and valueless, because they relate to a kind of knowledge to which no man can by any possibility attain. But, as there is no end to discussion, if we cannot discover the true cause of the illusions by which even the wisest are deceived, and as the analysis of all our transcendent cognition into its elements is of itself of no slight value as a psychological study, while it is a duty incumbent on every philosopher—it was found necessary to investigate the dialectical procedure of reason in its primary sources. And as the inferences of which this dialectic is the parent are not only deceitful, but naturally possess a profound interest for humanity, it was advisable at the same time, to give a full account of the momenta of this dialectical procedure, and to deposit it in the archives of human reason, as a warning to all future metaphysicians to avoid these causes of speculative error.

II
TRANSCENDENTAL DOCTRINE OF METHOD

If we regard the sum of the cognition of pure speculative reason as an edifice, the idea of which, at least, exists in the human mind, it may be said that we have in the Transcendental Doctrine of Elements examined the materials and determined to what edifice these belong, and what its height and stability. We have found, indeed, that, although we had purposed to build for ourselves a tower which should reach to Heaven, the supply of materials sufficed merely for a habitation, which was spacious enough for all terrestrial purposes, and high enough to enable us to survey the level plain of experience, but that the bold undertaking designed necessarily failed for want of materials—not to mention the confusion of tongues, which gave rise to endless disputes among the labourers on the plan of the edifice, and at last scattered them over all the world, each to erect a separate building for himself, according to his own plans and his own inclinations. Our present task relates not to the materials, but to the plan of an edifice; and, as we have had sufficient warning not to venture blindly upon a design which may be found to transcend our natural powers, while, at the same time, we cannot give up the intention of erecting a secure abode for the mind, we must proportion our design to the material which is presented to us, and which is, at the same time, sufficient for all our wants.

I understand, then, by the transcendental doctrine of method, the determination of the formal conditions of a complete system of pure reason. We shall accordingly have to treat of the *discipline*, the *canon*, the *architectonic*, and, finally, the *history* of pure reason. This part of our *Critique* will accomplish, from the transcendental point of view, what has been usually attempted, but miserably executed, under the name of *practical logic*. It has been badly executed, I say, because general logic, not being limited to any particular kind of cognition (not even to the pure cognition of the understanding) nor to any particular objects, it cannot, without borrowing from other sciences, do more than present merely the titles or signs of *possible methods* and the technical expressions, which are employed in the systematic parts of all sciences; and thus the pupil is made acquainted with names, the meaning and application of which he is to learn only at some future time.

Chapter I. *The Discipline of Pure Reason*

Negative judgements—those which are so not merely as regards their logical form, but in respect of their content—are not commonly held in especial respect. They are, on the contrary, regarded as jealous enemies of our insatiable desire for knowledge; and it almost requires an apology to induce us to tolerate, much less to prize and to respect them.

All propositions, indeed, may be *logically* expressed in a negative form; but, in relation to the content of our cognition, the peculiar province of negative judgements is solely to *prevent error*. For this reason, too, negative propositions, which are framed for the purpose of correcting false cognitions where error is absolutely impossible, are undoubtedly true, but inane and senseless; that is, they are in reality purposeless and, for this reason, often very ridiculous. Such is the proposition of the schoolman that Alexander could not have subdued any countries without an army.

But where the limits of our possible cognition are very much contracted, the attraction to new fields of knowledge great, the illusions to which the mind is subject of the most deceptive character, and the evil consequences of error of no inconsiderable magnitude—the *negative* element in knowledge, which is useful only to guard us against error, is of far more importance than much of that positive instruction which makes additions to the sum of our knowledge. The *restraint* which is employed to repress, and finally to extirpate the constant inclination to depart from certain rules, is termed *discipline*. It is distinguished from *culture*, which aims at the formation of a certain degree of skill, without attempting to repress or to destroy any other mental power, already existing. In the cultivation of a talent, which has given evidence of an impulse towards self-development, discipline takes a negative,[1] culture and doctrine a positive, part.

That natural dispositions and talents (such as imagination and wit), which ask a free and unlimited development, require in many respects the corrective influence of discipline, every one will readily grant. But it may well appear strange that reason, whose proper duty it is to prescribe rules of discipline to all the other powers of the mind, should itself require this corrective. It has, in fact, hitherto escaped this humiliation, only because, in presence of its magnificent pretensions and high position, no one could readily suspect it to be capable of substituting fancies for conceptions, and words for things.

Reason, when employed in the field of experience, does not stand in need of criticism, because its principles are subjected to the continual test of empirical observations. Nor is criticism requisite in the sphere of mathematics, where the conceptions of reason must always be presented *in concreto* in pure intuition, and baseless or arbitrary assertions are discovered without difficulty. But where reason is not held in a plain track by the influence of empirical or of pure intuition, that is, when it is employed in the transcendental sphere of pure conceptions, it stands in great need of discipline, to restrain its propensity to overstep the limits of possible experience and to keep it from wandering into error. In fact, the utility of the philosophy of pure reason is entirely of this negative character. Particular errors may be corrected by particular animadversions, and the causes of these errors may be eradicated by criticism. But where we find, as in the case of pure reason, a complete system of illusions and fallacies, closely connected with each other and depending upon grand general principles, there seems to be required a peculiar and negative code of mental legislation, which, under the denomination of a *discipline*, and founded upon the nature of reason and the objects of its exercise, shall constitute a system of thorough examination and testing, which no fallacy will be able to withstand or escape from, under whatever disguise or concealment it may lurk.

But the reader must remark that, in this the second division of our transcendental *Critique* the discipline of pure reason is not directed to the content, but to the method of the cognition of pure reason. The former task has been completed in the doctrine of elements. But there is so much similarity in the mode of employing the faculty of reason, whatever be the object to which it is applied, while, at the same time, its employment in the transcendental sphere is so essentially different in kind from every other, that, without the warning negative influence of a discipline specially directed to that end, the errors are unavoidable which spring from the unskilful employment of the methods which are originated by reason but which are out of place in this sphere.

Section I. *The Discipline of Pure Reason in the Sphere of Dogmatism*

The science of mathematics presents the most brilliant example of the extension of the sphere of pure reason without the aid of experience. Examples are always contagious; and they exert an especial influence on the same faculty, which naturally flatters itself that it will have the same good fortune in other case as fell to its lot in one fortunate instance. Hence pure reason hopes to be able to extend its empire in the transcendental sphere with equal success and security, especially when it applies the same method which was attended with such brilliant results in the science of mathematics. It is, therefore, of the highest importance for us to know whether the method of arriving at demonstrative certainty, which is termed *mathematical*, be identical with that by which we endeavour to attain the same degree of certainty in philosophy, and which is termed in that science *dogmatical*.

Philosophical cognition is the *cognition* of *reason* by means of *conceptions;* mathematical cognition is cognition by means of the *construction* of conceptions. The *construction* of a conception is the presentation *a priori* of the intuition which corresponds to the conception. For this purpose a *non-empirical* intuition is requisite, which, as an intuition, is an *individual* object; while, as the construction of a conception (a general representation), it must be seen to be universally valid for all the possible intuitions which rank under that conception. Thus I construct a triangle, by the presentation of the object which corresponds to this conception,

[1] I am well aware that, in the language of the schools, the term *discipline* is usually employed as synonymous with *instruction*. But there are so many cases in which it is necessary to distinguish the notion of the former, as a course of corrective training, from that of the latter, as the communication of knowledge, and the nature of things itself demands the appropriation of the most suitable expressions for this distinction, that it is my desire that the former terms should never be employed in any other than a negative signification.

either by mere imagination, in pure intuition, or upon paper, in empirical intuition, in both cases completely *a priori,* without borrowing the type of that figure from any experience. The individual figure drawn upon paper is empirical; but it serves, notwithstanding, to indicate the conception, even in its universality, because in this empirical intuition we keep our eye merely on the act of the construction of the conception, and pay no attention to the various modes of determining it, for example, its size, the length of its sides, the size of its angles, these not in the least affecting the essential character of the conception.

Philosophical cognition, accordingly, regards the particular only in the general; mathematical the general in the particular, nay, in the individual. This is done, however, entirely *a priori* and by means of pure reason, so that, as this individual figure is determined under certain universal conditions of construction, the object of the conception, to which this individual figure corresponds as its schema, must be cogitated as universally determined.

The essential difference of these two modes of cognition consists, therefore, in this formal quality; it does not regard the difference of the matter or objects of both. Those thinkers who aim at distinguishing philosophy from mathematics by asserting that the former has to do with *quality* merely, and the latter with *quantity,* have mistaken the effect for the cause. The reason why mathematical cognition can relate only to quantity is to be found in its form alone. For it is the conception of quantities only that is capable of being constructed, that is, presented *a priori* in intuition; while qualities cannot be given in any other than an empirical intuition. Hence the cognition of qualities by reason is possible only through conceptions. No one can find an intuition which shall correspond to the conception of reality, except in experience; it cannot be presented to the mind *a priori* and antecedently to the empirical consciousness of a reality. We can form an intuition, by means of the mere conception of it, of a cone, without the aid of experience; but the colour of the cone we cannot know except from experience. I cannot present an intuition of a cause, except in an example which experience offers to me. Besides, philosophy, as well as mathematics, treats of quantities; as, for example, of totality, infinity, and so on. Mathematics, too, treats of the difference of lines and surfaces—as spaces of different quality, of the continuity of extension—as a quality thereof. But, although in such cases they have a common object, the mode in which reason considers that object is very different in philosophy from what it is in mathematics. The former confines itself to the general conceptions; the latter can do nothing with a mere conception, it hastens to intuition. In this intuition it regards the conception *in concreto,* not empirically, but in an *a priori* intuition, which it has constructed; and in which, all the results which follow from the general conditions of the construction of the conception are in all cases valid for the object of the constructed conception.

Suppose that the conception of a triangle is given to a philosopher and that he is required to discover, by the philosophical method, what relation the sum of its angles bears to a right angle. He has nothing before him but the conception of a figure enclosed within three right lines, and, consequently, with the same number of angles. He may analyse the conception of a right line, of an angle, or of the number three as long as he pleases, but he will not discover any properties not contained in these conceptions. But, if this question is proposed to a geometrician, he at once begins by constructing a triangle. He knows that two right angles are equal to the sum of all the contiguous angles which proceed from one point in a straight line; and he goes on to produce one side of his triangle, thus forming two adjacent angles which are together equal to two right angles. He then divides the exterior of these angles, by drawing a line parallel with the opposite side of the triangle, and immediately perceives that he has thus got an exterior adjacent angle which is equal to the interior. Proceeding in this way, through a chain of inferences, and always on the ground of intuition, he arrives at a clear and universally valid solution of the question.

But mathematics does not confine itself to the construction of quantities (*quanta*), as in the case of geometry; it occupies itself with pure quantity also (*quantitas*), as in the case of algebra, where complete abstraction is made of the properties of the object indicated by the conception of quantity. In algebra, a certain method of notation by signs is adopted, and these indicate the different possible constructions of quantities, the extraction of roots, and so on. After having thus denoted the general conception of quantities, according to their different relations, the different operations by which quantity or number is increased or diminished are presented in intuition in accordance with general rules. Thus, when one quantity is to be divided by another, the signs which denote both are placed in the form peculiar to the operation of division; and thus algebra, by means of a symbolical construction of quantity, just as geometry, with its ostensive or geometrical construction (a construction of the objects themselves), arrives at results which discursive cognition cannot hope to reach by the aid of mere conceptions.

Now, what is the cause of this difference in the fortune of the philosopher and the mathematician, the former of whom follows the path of conceptions, while the latter pursues that of intuitions, which he represents, *a priori*, in correspondence with his conceptions? The cause is evident from what has been already demonstrated in the introduction to this *Critique*. We do not, in the present case, want to discover analytical propositions, which may be produced merely by analysing our conceptions—for in this the philosopher would have the advantage over his rival; we aim at the discovery of synthetical propositions—such synthetical propositions, moreover, as can be cognized *a priori*. I must not confine myself to that which I actually cogitate in my conception of a triangle, for this is nothing more than the mere definition; I must try to go beyond that, and to arrive at properties which are not contained in, although they belong to, the conception. Now, this is impossible, unless I determine the object present to my mind according to the conditions, either of empirical, or of pure, intuition. In the former case, I should have an empirical proposition (arrived at by actual measurement of the angles of the triangle), which would possess neither universality nor necessity; but that would be of no value. In the latter, I proceed by geometrical construction, by means of which I collect, in a pure intuition, just as I would in an empirical intuition, all the various properties which belong to the schema of a triangle in general, and consequently to its conception, and thus construct synthetical propositions which possess the attribute of universality.

It would be vain to philosophize upon the triangle, that is, to reflect on it discursively; I should get no further than the definition with which I had been obliged to set out. There are certainly transcendental synthetical propositions which are framed by means of pure conceptions, and which form the peculiar distinction of philosophy; but these do not relate to any particular thing, but to a thing in general, and enounce the conditions under which the perception of it may become a part of possible experience. But the science of mathematics has nothing to do with such questions, nor with the question of existence in any fashion; it is concerned merely with the properties of objects in themselves, only in so far as these are connected with the conception of the objects.

In the above example, we have merely attempted to show the great difference which exists between the discursive employment of reason in the sphere of conceptions, and its intuitive exercise by means of the construction of conceptions. The question naturally arises: What is the cause which necessitates this twofold exercise of reason, and how are we to discover whether it is the philosophical or the mathematical method which reason is pursuing in an argument?

All our knowledge relates, finally, to possible intuitions, for it is these alone that present objects to the mind. An *a priori* or non-empirical conception contains either a pure intuition—and in this case it can be constructed; or it contains nothing but the synthesis of possible intuitions, which are not given *a priori*. In this latter case, it may help us to form synthetical *a priori* judgements, but only in the discursive method, by conceptions, not in the intuitive, by means of the construction of conceptions.

The only *a priori* intuition is that of the pure form of phenomena—space and time. A conception of space and time as *quanta* may be presented *a priori* in intuition, that is, constructed, either alone with their quality (figure), or as pure quantity (the mere synthesis of the homogeneous), by means of number. But the matter of phenomena, by which *things* are given in space and time, can be presented only in perception, *a posteriori*. The only conception which represents *a priori* this empirical content of phenomena is the conception of a *thing* in general; and the *a priori* synthetical cognition of this conception can give us nothing more than the rule for the synthesis of that which may be contained in the corresponding *a posteriori* perception; it is utterly inadequate to present an *a priori* intuition of the real object, which must necessarily be empirical.

Synthetical propositions, which relate to *things* in general, an *a priori* intuition of which is impossible, are transcendental. For this reason transcendental propositions cannot be framed by means of the construction of conceptions; they are *a priori*, and based entirely on conceptions themselves. They contain merely the rule, by which we are to seek in the world of perception or experience the synthetical unity of that which cannot be intuited *a priori*. But they are incompetent to present any of the conceptions which appear in them in an *a priori* intuition; these can be given only *a posteriori*, in experience, which, however, is itself possible only through these synthetical principles.

If we are to form a synthetical judgement regarding a conception, we must go beyond it, to the intuition in which it is given. If we keep to what is contained in the conception, the judgement is merely analytical—it is merely an explanation of what we have cogitated in the conception. But I can pass from the conception to the pure or empirical intuition which corresponds to it. I can proceed to examine my conception *in concreto*, and to cognize, either *a priori* or *a posteriori*, what I find in the object of the conception. The former—*a priori* cognition—is rational-mathematical cognition by means of the construction of the conception; the latter—*a posteriori* cognition—is purely empirical cognition, which does not possess the attributes of necessity and universality. Thus I may analyse the conception I have of gold; but I gain no new information from this analysis, I merely enumerate the different properties which I had connected with the notion indicated by the word. My knowledge has gained in logical clearness and arrangement, but no addition has been made to it. But if I take the matter which is indicated by this name, and submit it to the examination of my senses, I am enabled to form several synthetical—although still empirical—propositions. The mathematical conception of a triangle I should construct, that is, present *a priori* in intuition, and in this way attain to rational-synthetical cognition. But when the transcendental conception of reality, or substance, or power is presented to my mind, I find that it does not relate to or indicate either an empirical or pure intuition, but that it indicates merely the synthesis of empirical intuitions, which cannot of course be given *a priori*. The synthesis in such a conception cannot proceed *a priori*—without the aid of experience—to the intuition which corresponds to the conception; and, for this reason, none of these conceptions can produce a determinative synthetical proposition, they can never present more than a principle of the synthesis[1] of possible empirical intuitions. A transcendental proposition is, therefore, a synthetical cognition of reason by means of pure conceptions and the discursive method, and it renders possible all synthetical unity in empirical cognition, though it cannot present us with any intuition *a priori*.

There is thus a twofold exercise of reason. Both modes have the properties of universality and an *a priori* origin in common, but are, in their procedure, of widely different character. The reason of this is that in the world of phenomena, in which alone objects are presented to our minds, there are two main elements—the form of intuition (space and time), which can be cognized and determined completely *a priori*, and the matter or content—that which is presented in space and time, and which, consequently, contains a something—an existence corresponding to our powers of sensation. As regards the latter, which can never be given in a determinate mode except by experience, there are no *a priori* notions which relate to it, except the undetermined conceptions of the synthesis of possible sensations, in so far as these belong (in a possible experience) to the unity of consciousness. As regards the former, we can determine our conceptions *a priori* in intuition, inasmuch as we are ourselves the creators of the objects of the conceptions in space and time—these objects being regarded simply as *quanta*. In the one case, reason proceeds according to conceptions and can do nothing more than subject phenomena to these—which can only be determined empirically, that is, *a posteriori*—in conformity, however, with those conceptions as the rules of all empirical synthesis. In the other case, reason proceeds by the construction of conceptions; and, as these conceptions relate to an *a priori* intuition, they may be given and determined in pure intuition *a priori*, and without the aid of empirical data. The examination and consideration of everything that exists in space or time—whether it is a quantum or not, in how far the particular something (which fills space or time) is a primary substratum, or a mere determination of some other existence, whether it relates to anything else—either as cause or effect, whether its existence is isolated or in reciprocal connection with and dependence upon others, the possibility of this existence, its reality and necessity or their opposites—all these form part of the *cognition* of reason on the ground of concep-

[1] In the case of the conception of cause, I do really go beyond the empirical conception of an event—but not to the intuition which presents this conception *in concreto*, but only to the time-conditions, which may be found in experience to correspond to the conception. My procedure is, therefore, strictly according to conceptions; I cannot in a case of this kind employ the construction of conceptions, because the conception is merely a rule for the synthesis of perceptions, which are not pure intuitions, and which, therefore, cannot be given *a priori*.

tions, and this cognition is termed *philosophical.* But to determine *a priori* an intuition in space (its figure), to divide time into periods, or merely to cognize the quantity of an intuition in space and time, and to determine it by number—all this is an *operation of reason* by means of the construction of conceptions, and is called *mathematical.*

The success which attends the efforts of reason in the sphere of mathematics naturally fosters the expectation that the same good fortune will be its lot, if it applies the mathematical method in other regions of mental endeavour besides that of quantities. Its success is thus great, because it can support all its conceptions by *a priori* intuitions and, in this way, make itself a master, as it were, over nature; while pure philosophy, with its *a priori* discursive conceptions, bungles about in the world of nature, and cannot accredit or show any *a priori* evidence of the reality of these conceptions. Masters in the science of mathematics are confident of the success of this method; indeed, it is a common persuasion that it is capable of being applied to any subject of human thought. They have hardly ever reflected or philosophized on their favourite science—a task of great difficulty; and the specific difference between the two modes of employing the faculty of reason has never entered their thoughts. Rules current in the field of common experience, and which common sense stamps everywhere with its approval, are regarded by them as axiomatic. From what source the conceptions of space and time, with which (as the only primitive quanta) they have to deal, enter their minds, is a question which they do not trouble themselves to answer; and they think it just as unnecessary to examine into the origin of the pure conceptions of the understanding and the extent of their validity. All they have to do with them is to employ them. In all this they are perfectly right, if they do not overstep the limits of the sphere of *nature.* But they pass, unconsciously, from the world of sense to the insecure ground of pure transcendental conceptions (*instabilis tellus, innabilis unda*), where they can neither stand nor swim, and where the tracks of their footsteps are obliterated by time; while the march of mathematics is pursued on a broad and magnificent highway, which the latest posterity shall frequent without fear of danger or impediment.

As we have taken upon us the task of determining, clearly and certainly, the limits of pure reason in the sphere of transcendentalism, and as the efforts of reason in this direction are persisted in, even after the plainest and most expressive warnings, hope still beckoning us past the limits of experience into the splendours of the intellectual world—it becomes necessary to cut away the last anchor of this fallacious and fantastic hope. We shall, accordingly, show that the mathematical method is unattended in the sphere of philosophy by the least advantage—except, perhaps, that it more plainly exhibits its own inadequacy—that geometry and philosophy are two quite different things, although they go hand in hand in the field of natural science, and, consequently, that the procedure of the one can never be imitated by the other.

The evidence of mathematics rests upon definitions, axioms, and demonstrations. I shall be satisfied with showing that none of these forms can be employed or imitated in philosophy in the sense in which they are understood by mathematicians; and that the geometrician, if he employs his method in philosophy, will succeed only in building card-castles, while the employment of the philosophical method in mathematics can result in nothing but mere verbiage. The essential business of philosophy, indeed, is to mark out the limits of the science; and even the mathematician, unless his talent is naturally circumscribed and limited to this particular department of knowledge, cannot turn a deaf ear to the warnings of philosophy, or set himself above its direction.

1. *Of Definitions. A definition* is, as the term itself indicates, the representation, upon primary grounds, of the complete conception of a thing within its own limits.[1] Accordingly, an *empirical* conception cannot be defined, it can only be *explained.* For, as there are in such a conception only a certain number of marks or signs, which denote a certain class of sensuous objects, we can never be sure that we do not cogitate under the word which indicates the same object, at one time a greater, at another a smaller number of signs. Thus, one person may cogitate in his conception of gold, in addition to its properties of weight, colour, malleability, that of resisting rust, while another person may be ignorant of this quality. We employ certain signs only so long as we require them

[1] The definition must describe the conception *completely,* that is, omit none of the marks or signs of which it is composed; *within its own limits,* that is, it must be precise, and enumerate no more signs than belong to the conception; and *on primary grounds,* that is to say, the limitations of the bounds of the conception must not be deduced from other conceptions, as in this case a proof would be necessary, and the so-called definition would be incapable of taking its place at the head of all the judgements we have to form regarding an object.

for the sake of distinction; new observations abstract some and add new ones, so that an empirical conception never remains within permanent limits. It is, in fact, useless to define a conception of this kind. If, for example, we are speaking of water and its properties, we do not stop at what we actually think by the word *water,* but proceed to observation and experiment; and the word, with the few signs attached to it, is more properly a *designation* than a conception of the thing. A definition in this case would evidently be nothing more than a determination of the word. In the second place, no *a priori* conception, such as those of substance, cause, right, fitness, and so on, can be defined. For I can never be sure, that the clear representation of a given conception (which is given in a confused state) has been fully developed, until I know that the representation is adequate with its object. But, inasmuch as the conception, as it is presented to the mind, may contain a number of obscure representations, which we do not observe in our analysis, although we employ them in our application of the conception, I can never be sure that my analysis is complete, while examples may make this probable, although they can never demonstrate the fact. Instead of the word *definition,* I should rather employ the term *exposition*—a more modest expression, which the critic may accept without surrendering his doubts as to the completeness of the analysis of any such conception. As, therefore, neither empirical nor *a priori* conceptions are capable of definition, we have to see whether the only other kind of conceptions—arbitrary conceptions—can be subjected to this mental operation. Such a conception can always be defined; for I must know thoroughly what I wished to cogitate in it, as it was I who created it, and it was not given to my mind either by the nature of my understanding or by experience. At the same time, I cannot say that, by such a definition, I have defined a real object. If the conception is based upon empirical conditions, if, for example, I have a conception of a clock for a ship, this arbitrary conception does not assure me of the existence or even of the possibility of the object. My definition of such a conception would with more propriety be termed a declaration of a project than a definition of an object. There are no other conceptions which can bear definition, except those which contain an arbitrary synthesis, which can be constructed *a priori.* Consequently, the science of mathematics alone possesses definitions. For the object here thought is presented *a priori* in intuition; and thus it can never contain more or less than the conception, because the conception of the object has been given by the definition — and primarily, that is, without deriving the definition from any other source. Philosophical definitions are, therefore, merely expositions of given conceptions, while mathematical definitions are constructions of conceptions originally formed by the mind itself; the former are produced by analysis, the completeness of which is never demonstratively certain, the latter by a synthesis. In a mathematical definition the conception is *formed,* in a philosophical definition it is only *explained.* From this it follows:

(*a*) That we must not imitate, in philosophy, the mathematical usage of commencing with definitions—except by way of hypothesis or experiment. For, as all so-called philosophical definitions are merely analyses of given conceptions, these conceptions, although only in a confused form, must precede the analysis; and the incomplete exposition must precede the complete, so that we may be able to draw certain inferences from the characteristics which an incomplete analysis has enabled us to discover, before we attain to the complete exposition or definition of the conception. In one word, a full and clear definition ought, in philosophy, rather to form the conclusion than the commencement of our labours.[1] In mathematics, on the contrary, we cannot have a conception prior to the definition; it is the definition which gives us the conception, and it must for this reason form the commencement of every chain of mathematical reasoning.

(*b*) Mathematical definitions cannot be erroneous. For the conception is given only in and through the definition, and thus it contains only what has been cogitated in the definition. But although a definition cannot be incorrect, as regards its content, an error may sometimes, although seldom, creep into the form. This error consists in a want of precision. Thus the common definition of a circle—that it is a curved line, every point in which is equally distant from another point called the centre—is faulty,

[1] Philosophy abounds in faulty definitions, especially such as contain some of the elements requisite to form a complete definition. If a conception could not be employed in reasoning before it had been defined, it would fare ill with all philosophical thought. But, as incompletely defined conceptions may always be employed without detriment to truth, so far as our analysis of the elements contained in them proceeds, imperfect definitions, that is, propositions which are properly not definitions, but merely approximations thereto, may be used with great advantage. In mathematics, definition belongs *ad esse,* in philosophy *ad melius esse.* It is a difficult task to construct a proper definition. Jurists are still without a complete definition of the idea of right.

from the fact that the determination indicated by the word *curved* is superfluous. For there ought to be a particular theorem, which may be easily proved from the definition, to the effect that every line, which has all its points at equal distances from another point, must be a curved line—that is, that not even the smallest part of it can be straight. Analytical definitions, on the other hand, may be erroneous in many respects, either by the introduction of signs which do not actually exist in the conception, or by wanting in that completeness which forms the essential of a definition. In the latter case, the definition is necessarily defective, because we can never be fully certain of the completeness of our analysis. For these reasons, the method of definition employed in mathematics cannot be imitated in philosophy.

2. *Of Axioms.* These, in so far as they are immediately certain, are *a priori* synthetical principles. Now, one conception cannot be connected synthetically and yet immediately with another; because, if we wish to proceed out of and beyond a conception, a third mediating cognition is necessary. And, as philosophy is a cognition of reason by the aid of conceptions alone, there is to be found in it no principle which deserves to be called an axiom. Mathematics, on the other hand, may possess axioms, because it can always connect the predicates of an object *a priori,* and without any mediating term, by means of the construction of conceptions in intuition. Such is the case with the proposition: Three points can always lie in a plane. On the other hand, no synthetical principle which is based upon conceptions, can ever be immediately certain (for example, the proposition: Everything that happens has a cause), because I require a mediating term to connect the two conceptions of event and cause—namely, the condition of time-determination in an experience, and I cannot cognize any such principle immediately and from conceptions alone. Discursive principles are, accordingly, very different from intuitive principles or axioms. The former always require deduction, which in the case of the latter may be altogether dispensed with. Axioms are, for this reason, always self-evident, while philosophical principles, whatever may be the degree of certainty they possess, cannot lay any claim to such a distinction. No synthetical proposition of pure transcendental reason can be so evident, as is often rashly enough declared, as the statement, *twice two are four*. It is true that in the Analytic I introduced into the list of principles of the pure understanding, certain axioms of intuition; but the principle there discussed was not itself an axiom, but served merely to present the principle of the possibility of axioms in general, while it was really nothing more than a principle based upon conceptions. For it is one part of the duty of transcendental philosophy to establish the possibility of mathematics itself. Philosophy possesses, then, no axioms, and has no right to impose its *a priori* principles upon thought, until it has established their authority and validity by a thoroughgoing deduction.

3. *Of Demonstrations.* Only an apodeictic proof, based upon intuition, can be termed a *demonstration.* Experience teaches us what is, but it cannot convince us that it might not have been otherwise. Hence a proof upon empirical grounds cannot be apodeictic. *A priori* conceptions, in discursive cognition, can never produce intuitive certainty or evidence, however certain the judgement they present may be. Mathematics alone, therefore, contains demonstrations, because it does not deduce its cognition from conceptions, but from the construction of conceptions, that is, from intuition, which can be given *a priori* in accordance with conceptions. The method of algebra, in equations, from which the correct answer is deduced by reduction, is a kind of construction—not geometrical, but by symbols—in which all conceptions, especially those of the relations of quantities, are represented in intuition by signs; and thus the conclusions in that science are secured from errors by the fact that every proof is submitted to ocular evidence. Philosophical cognition does not possess this advantage, it being required to consider the general always *in abstracto* (by means of conceptions), while mathematics can always consider it *in concreto* (in an individual intuition), and at the same time by means of *a priori* representation, whereby all errors are rendered manifest to the senses. The former—discursive proofs—ought to be termed *acroamatic proofs,* rather than *demonstrations,* as only words are employed in them, while demonstrations proper, as the term itself indicates, always require a reference to the intuition of the object.

It follows from all these considerations that it is not consonant with the nature of philosophy, especially in the sphere of pure reason, to employ the dogmatical method, and to adorn itself with the titles and insignia of mathematical science. It does not belong to that order, and can only hope for a fraternal union with that science. Its attempts at mathematical evidence are vain pretensions, which can only keep it back from its true aim, which is to detect the illusory procedure of reason when transgressing its proper limits, and by fully explaining and analysing our conceptions, to conduct us from the dim regions of speculation to the clear region of modest self-knowledge. Reason must not, therefore, in its transcendental endeavours, look forward with such confidence, as if the path it is pursuing led straight to its aim, nor reckon with such security upon its premisses, as to consider it unnecessary to take a step back, or to keep a strict watch for errors, which, overlooked in the principles, may be detected in the arguments themselves—in which case it may be requisite either to determine these principles with greater strictness, or to change them entirely.

I divide all apodeictic propositions, whether demonstrable or immediately certain, into *dogmata* and *mathemata.* A direct synthetical proposition, based on conceptions, is a *dogma;* a proposition of the same kind, based on the construction of conceptions, is a *mathema.* Analytical judgements do not teach us any more about an object than what was contained in the conception we had of it; because they do not extend our cognition beyond our conception of an object, they merely elucidate the conception. They cannot therefore be with propriety termed *dogmas.* Of the two kinds of *a priori* synthetical propositions above mentioned, only those which are employed in philosophy can, according to the general mode of speech, bear this name; those of arithmetic or geometry would not be rightly so denominated. Thus the customary mode of speaking confirms the explanation given above, and the conclusion arrived at, that only those judgements which are based upon conceptions, not on the construction of conceptions, can be termed *dogmatical.*

Thus, pure reason, in the sphere of speculation, does not contain a single direct synthetical judgement based upon conceptions. By means of ideas, it is, as we have shown, incapable of producing synthetical judgements, which are objectively valid; by means of the conceptions of the understanding, it establishes certain indubitable principles, not, however, directly on the basis of conceptions, but only indirectly by means of the relation of these conceptions to something of a purely contingent nature, namely, possible experience. When experience is presupposed, these principles are apodeictically certain, but in themselves, and directly, they cannot even be cognized *a priori.* Thus the given conceptions of *cause* and *event* will not be sufficient for the demonstration of the proposition: Every event has a cause. For this reason, it is not a dogma; although from another point of view, that of experience, it is capable of being proved to demonstration. The proper term for such a proposition is *principle,* and not *theorem* (although it does require to be proved), because it possesses the remarkable peculiarity of being the condition of the possibility of its own ground of proof, that is, experience, and of forming a necessary presupposition in all empirical observation.

If then, in the speculative sphere of pure reason, no dogmata are to be found; all *dogmatical* methods, whether borrowed from mathematics, or invented by philosophical thinkers, are alike inappropriate and inefficient. They only serve to conceal errors and fallacies, and to deceive philosophy, whose duty it is to see that reason pursues a safe and straight path. A philosophical method may, however, be *systematical.* For our reason is, subjectively considered, itself a system, and, in the sphere of mere conceptions, a system of investigation according to principles of unity, the material being supplied by experience alone. But this is not the proper place for discussing the peculiar method of transcendental philosophy, as our present task is simply to examine whether our faculties are capable of erecting an edifice on the basis of pure reason, and how far they may proceed with the materials at their command.

SECTION II. *The Discipline of Pure Reason in Polemics*

REASON must be subject, in all its operations, to criticism, which must always be permitted to exercise its functions without restraint; otherwise its interests are imperilled and its influence obnoxious to suspicion. There is nothing, however useful, however sacred it may be, that can claim exemption from the searching examination of this supreme tribunal, which has no respect of persons. The very existence of reason depends upon this freedom; for the voice of reason is not that of a dictatorial and despotic power, it is rather like the vote of the citizens of a free state, every member of which must have the privilege of giving free expression to his doubts, and possess even the right of *veto.*

But while reason can never decline to submit itself to the tribunal of criticism, it has not always cause to *dread* the judgement of this court. Pure reason, however, when engaged in the sphere of dogmatism, is not so thoroughly conscious of a strict observance of its highest laws, as to appear before a higher judicial reason with perfect confidence. On the contrary, it must renounce its magnificent dogmatical pretensions in philosophy.

Very different is the case when it has to defend itself, not before a judge, but against an equal. If dogmatical assertions are advanced on the negative side, in opposition to those made by reason on the positive side, its justification κατ' ἄνθρωπον is complete, although the proof of its propositions is κατ' ἀλήθειαν unsatisfactory.

By the polemic of pure reason I mean the defence of its propositions made by reason, in opposition to the dogmatical counter-propositions advanced by other parties. The question here is not whether its own statements may not also be false; it merely regards the fact that reason proves that the opposite cannot be established with demonstrative certainty, nor even asserted with a higher degree of probability. Reason does not hold her possessions upon sufferance; for, although she cannot show a perfectly satisfactory title to them, no one can prove that she is *not* the rightful possessor.

It is a melancholy reflection that reason, in its highest exercise, falls into an antithetic; and that the supreme tribunal for the settlement of differences should not be at union with itself. It is true that we had to discuss the question of an apparent antithetic, but we found that it was based upon a misconception. In conformity with the common prejudice, phenomena were regarded as things in themselves, and thus an absolute completeness in their synthesis was required in the one mode or in the other (it was shown to be impossible in both); a demand entirely out of place in regard to phenomena. There was, then, no real self-contradiction of reason in the propositions: The series of phenomena *given in themselves* has an absolutely first beginning; and: This series is absolutely and *in itself* without beginning. The two propositions are perfectly consistent with each other, because phenomena as phenomena are *in themselves* nothing, and consequently the hypothesis that they are things in themselves must lead to self-contradictory inferences.

But there are cases in which a similar misunderstanding cannot be provided against, and the dispute must remain unsettled. Take, for example, the theistic proposition: There is a Supreme Being; and on the other hand, the atheistic counter-statement: There exists no Supreme Being; or, in psychology: Everything that thinks possesses the attribute of absolute and permanent unity, which is utterly different from the transitory unity of material phenomena; and the counter-proposition: The soul is not an immaterial unity, and its nature is transitory, like that of phenomena. The objects of these questions contain no heterogeneous or contradictory elements, for they relate to *things in themselves,* and not to phenomena. There would arise, indeed, a real contradiction, if reason came forward with a statement on the negative side of these questions alone. As regards the criticism to which the grounds of proof on the affirmative side must be subjected, it may be freely admitted, without necessitating the surrender of the affirmative propositions, which have, at least, the interest of reason in their favour—an advantage which the opposite party cannot lay claim to.

I cannot agree with the opinion of several admirable thinkers—Sulzer among the rest—that, in spite of the weakness of the arguments hitherto in use, we may hope, one day, to see sufficient demonstrations of the two cardinal propositions of pure reason—the existence of a Supreme Being, and the immortality of the soul. I am certain, on the contrary, that this will never be the case. For on what ground can reason base such synthetical propositions, which do not relate to the objects of experience and their internal possibility? But it is also demonstratively certain that no one will ever be able to maintain the contrary with the least show of probability. For, as he can attempt such a proof solely upon the basis of pure reason, he is bound to prove that a Supreme Being, and a thinking subject in the character of a pure intelligence, are *impossible.* But where will he find the knowledge which can enable him to enounce synthetical judgements in regard to things which transcend the region of experience? We may, therefore, rest assured that the opposite never will be demonstrated. We need not, then, have recourse to scholastic arguments; we may always admit the truth of those propositions which are consistent with the speculative interests of reason in the sphere of experience, and form, moreover, the only means of uniting the speculative with the practical interest. Our opponent, who must not be considered here as a critic solely, we can be ready to meet with a *non liquet* which cannot fail to disconcert him; while we cannot deny his right to a similar retort, as we have on our side the advantage of the support of the subjective maxim of reason, and can therefore look upon all his sophistical arguments with calm indifference.

From this point of view, there is properly no antithetic of pure reason. For the only arena for such a struggle would be upon the field of pure theology and psychology; but on this ground there can appear no combatant whom we need to fear. Ridicule and boasting can be his only weapons; and these may be laughed at, as mere child's play. This consideration restores to Reason her courage; for what source of confidence could be found, if she, whose vocation it is to destroy error, were at variance with herself and without any reasonable hope of ever reaching a state of permanent repose?

Everything in nature is good for some purpose. Even poisons are serviceable; they destroy the evil effects of other poisons generated in our system, and must always find a place in every complete pharmacopoeia. The objections raised against the fallacies and sophistries of speculative reason, are objections given by the nature of this reason itself, and must therefore have a destination and purpose which can only be for the good of humanity. For what purpose has Providence raised many objects, in which we have the deepest interest, so far above us, that we vainly try to cognize them with certainty, and our powers of mental vision are rather excited than satisfied by the glimpses we may chance to seize? It is very doubtful whether it is for our benefit to advance bold affirmations regarding subjects involved in such obscurity; perhaps it would even be detrimental to our best interests. But it is undoubtedly always beneficial to leave the investigating, as well as the critical reason, in perfect freedom, and permit it to take charge of its own interests, which are advanced as much by its limitation, as by its extension of its views, and which always suffer by the interference of foreign powers forcing it, against its natural tendencies, to bend to certain preconceived designs.

Allow your opponent to say what he thinks reasonable, and combat him only with the weapons of reason. Have no anxiety for the practical interests of humanity—these are never imperilled in a purely speculative dispute. Such a dispute serves merely to disclose the antinomy of reason, which, as it has its source in the nature of reason, ought to be thoroughly investigated. Reason is benefited by the examination of a subject on both sides, and its judgements are corrected by being limited. It is not the *matter* that may give occasion to dispute, but the *manner*. For it is perfectly permissible to employ, in the presence of reason, the language of a firmly-rooted *faith,* even after we have been obliged to renounce all pretensions to *knowledge.*

If we were to ask the dispassionate David Hume—a philosopher endowed, in a degree that few are, with a well-balanced judgement: What motive induced you to spend so much labour and thought in undermining the consoling and beneficial persuasion that reason is capable of assuring us of the existence, and presenting us with a determinate conception of a Supreme Being?—his answer would be: Nothing but the desire of teaching reason to know its own powers better, and, at the same time, a dislike of the procedure by which that faculty was compelled to support foregone conclusions, and prevented from confessing the internal weaknesses which it cannot but feel when it enters upon a rigid self-examination. If, on the other hand, we were to ask Priestley—a philosopher who had no taste for transcendental speculation, but was entirely devoted to the principles of *empiricism*—what his motives were for overturning those two main pillars of religion—the doctrines of the freedom of the will and the immortality of the soul (in his view the hope of a future life is but the expectation of the miracle of resurrection)—this philosopher, himself a zealous and pious teacher of religion, could give no other answer than this: I acted in the interest of reason, which always suffers, when certain objects are explained and judged by a reference to other supposed laws than those of material nature—the only laws which we know in a determinate manner. It would be unfair to decry the latter philosopher, who endeavoured to harmonize his paradoxical opinions with the interests of religion, and to undervalue an honest and reflecting man, because he finds himself at a loss the moment he has left the field of natural science. The same grace must be accorded to Hume, a man not less well-disposed, and quite as blameless in his moral character, and who pushed his abstract speculations to an extreme length, because, as he rightly believed, the object of them lies entirely beyond the bounds of natural science, and within the sphere of pure ideas.

What is to be done to provide against the danger which seems in the present case to menace the best interests of humanity? The course to be pursued in reference to this subject is a perfectly plain and natural one. Let each thinker pursue his own path; if he shows talent, if he gives evidence of profound thought, in one word, if he shows that he possesses the power of reasoning—reason is always the gainer. If you have recourse to other means, if you attempt to coerce reason, if you raise the cry of treason to humanity, if you excite the feelings of the crowd, which can neither understand nor sympathize with such subtle speculations—you will only make yourselves ridiculous. For the question does not concern the advantage or disadvantage which we are expected to reap from such inquiries; the question is merely how far reason can advance in the field of speculation, apart from all kinds of interest, and whether we may depend upon the exertions of speculative reason, or must renounce all reliance on it. Instead of joining the combatants, it is your part to be a tranquil spectator of the struggle—a laborious struggle for the parties engaged, but attended, in its progress as well as in its result, with the most advantageous consequences for the interests of thought and knowledge. It is absurd to expect to be enlightened by Reason, and at the same time to prescribe to her what side of the question she must adopt. Moreover, reason is sufficiently held in check by its own power, the limits imposed on it by its own nature are sufficient; it is unnecessary for you to place over it additional guards, as if its power were dangerous to the constitution of the intellectual state. In the dialectic of reason there is no victory gained which need in the least disturb your tranquillity.

The strife of dialectic is a necessity of reason, and we cannot but wish that it had been conducted long ere this with that perfect freedom which ought to be its essential condition. In this case, we should have had at an earlier period a matured and profound criticism, which must have put an end to all dialectical disputes, by exposing the illusions and prejudices in which they originated.

There is in human nature an unworthy propensity—a propensity which, like everything that springs from nature, must in its final purpose be conducive to the good of humanity—to conceal our real sentiments, and to give expression only to certain received opinions, which are regarded as at once safe and promotive of the common good. It is true, this tendency, not only to conceal our real sentiments, but to profess those which may gain us favour in the eyes of society, has not only *civilized*, but, in a certain measure, *moralized* us; as no one can break through the outward covering of respectability, honour, and morality, and thus the seemingly-good examples which we see around us form an excellent school for moral improvement, so long as our belief in their genuineness remains unshaken. But this disposition to represent ourselves as better than we are, and to utter opinions which are not our own, can be nothing more than a kind of *provisionary* arrangement of nature to lead us from the rudeness of an uncivilized state, and to teach us how to assume at least the appearance and *manner* of the good we see. But when true principles have been developed, and have obtained a sure foundation in our habit of thought, this conventionalism must be attacked with earnest vigour, otherwise it corrupts the heart, and checks the growth of good dispositions with the mischievous weed of fair appearances.

I am sorry to remark the same tendency to misrepresentation and hypocrisy in the sphere of speculative discussion, where there is less temptation to restrain the free expression of thought. For what can be more prejudicial to the interests of intelligence than to falsify our real sentiments, to conceal the doubts which we feel in regard to our statements, or to maintain the validity of grounds of proof which we well know to be insufficient? So long as mere personal vanity is the source of these unworthy artifices—and this is generally the case in speculative discussions, which are mostly destitute of practical interest, and are incapable of complete demonstration—the vanity of the opposite party exaggerates as much on the other side; and thus the result is the same, although it is not brought about so soon as if the dispute had been conducted in a sincere and upright spirit. But where the mass entertains the notion that the aim of certain subtle speculators is nothing less than to shake the very foundations of public welfare and morality—it seems not only prudent, but even praiseworthy, to maintain the good cause by illusory arguments, rather than to give to our supposed opponents the advantage of lowering our declarations to the moderate tone of a merely practical conviction, and of compelling us to confess our inability to attain to apodeictic certainty in speculative subjects. But we ought to reflect that there is nothing in the world more fatal to the maintenance of a good cause than deceit, misrepresentation, and falsehood. That the strictest laws of honesty should be observed in the discussion of a purely speculative subject is the least requirement that can be made. If we could reckon with security even upon so little, the conflict of speculative reason regarding the important questions of God, immortality, and freedom, would have been either decided long ago, or would very soon be brought to a conclusion. But, in general, the uprightness of the defence stands in an inverse ratio to the goodness of the cause; and perhaps more honesty and fairness are shown by those who deny than by those who uphold these doctrines.

I shall persuade myself, then, that I have readers who do not wish to see a righteous cause defended by unfair arguments. Such will now recognize the fact that, according to the principles of this *Critique,* if we consider not what is, but what ought to be the case, there can be really no polemic of pure reason. For how can two persons dispute about a thing, the reality of which neither can present in actual or even in possible experience? Each adopts the plan of meditating on his idea for the purpose of drawing from the idea, if he can, what is *more than the idea,* that is, the reality of the object which it indicates. How shall they settle the dispute, since neither is able to make his assertions directly comprehensible and certain, but must restrict himself to attacking and confuting those of his opponent? All statements enounced by pure reason transcend the conditions of possible experience, beyond the sphere of which we can discover no criterion of truth, while they are at the same time framed in accordance with the laws of the understanding, which are applicable only to experience; and thus it is the fate of all such speculative discussions that while the one party attacks the weaker side of his opponent, he infallibly lays open his own weaknesses.

The critique of pure reason may be regarded as the highest tribunal for all speculative disputes; for it is not involved in these disputes, which have an immediate relation to certain objects and not to the laws of the mind, but is instituted for the purpose of determining the rights and limits of reason.

Without the control of criticism, reason is, as it were, in a state of nature, and can only establish its claims and assertions by *war.* Criticism, on the contrary, deciding all questions according to the fundamental laws of its own institution, secures to us the peace of law and order, and enables us to discuss all differences in the more tranquil manner of a legal *process.* In the former case, disputes are ended by *victory,* which both sides may claim and which is followed by a hollow armistice; in the latter, by a *sentence,* which, as it strikes at the root of all speculative differences, ensures to all concerned a lasting peace. The endless disputes of a dogmatizing reason compel us to look for some mode of arriving at a settled decision by a critical investigation of reason itself; just as Hobbes maintains that the state of nature is a state of injustice and violence, and that we must leave it and submit ourselves to the constraint of law, which indeed limits individual freedom, but only that it may consist with the freedom of others and with the common good of all.

This freedom will, among other things, permit of our openly stating the difficulties and doubts which we are ourselves unable to solve, without being decried on that account as turbulent and dangerous citizens. This privilege forms part of the native rights of human reason, which recognizes no other judge than the universal reason of humanity; and as this reason is the source of all progress and improvement, such a privilege is to be held sacred and inviolable. It is unwise, moreover, to denounce as dangerous any bold assertions against, or rash attacks upon, an opinion which is held by the largest and most moral class of the community; for that would be giving them an importance which they do not deserve. When I hear that the freedom of the will, the hope of a future life, and the existence of God have been overthrown by the arguments of some able writer, I feel a strong desire to read his book; for I expect that he will add to my knowledge and impart greater clearness and distinctness to my views by the argumentative power shown in his writings. But I am perfectly certain, even before I have opened the book, that he has not succeeded in a single point, not because I believe I am in possession of irrefutable demonstrations of these important propositions, but because this transcendental critique, which has disclosed to me the power and the limits of pure reason, has fully convinced me that, as it is insufficient to establish the affirmative, it is as powerless, and even more so, to assure us of the truth of the negative answer to these questions. From what source does this free-thinker derive his knowledge that there is, for example, no Supreme Being? This proposition lies out of the field of possible experience, and, therefore, beyond the limits of human cognition. But I would not read at all the answer which the dogmatical maintainer of the good cause makes to his opponent, because I know well beforehand, that he will merely attack the fallacious grounds of his adversary, without being able to establish his own assertions. Besides, a new illusory argument, in the construction of which talent and acuteness are shown, is suggestive of new ideas and new trains of reasoning, and in this respect the old and everyday sophistries are quite useless. Again, the dogmatical opponent of religion gives employment to criticism, and enables us to test and correct its principles, while there is no occasion for anxiety in regard to the influence and results of his reasoning.

But, it will be said, must we not warn the youth entrusted to academical care against such writings, must we not preserve them from the knowledge of these dangerous assertions, until their judgement is ripened, or rather until the doctrines which we wish to inculcate are so firmly rooted in their minds as to withstand all attempts at instilling the contrary dogmas, from whatever quarter they may come?

If we are to confine ourselves to the dogmatical procedure in the sphere of pure reason, and find ourselves unable to settle such disputes otherwise than by becoming a party in them, and setting counter-assertions against the statements advanced by our opponents, there is certainly no plan more advisable *for the moment,* but, at the same time, none more absurd and inefficient *for the future,* than this retaining of the youthful mind under guardianship for a time, and thus preserving it—for so long at least—from seduction into error. But when, at a later period, either curiosity, or the prevalent fashion of thought places such writings in their hands, will the so-called convictions of their youth stand firm? The young thinker, who has in his armoury none but dogmatical weapons with which to resist the attacks of his opponent, and who cannot detect the latent dialectic which lies in his own opinions as well as in those of the opposite party, sees the advance of illusory arguments and grounds of proof which have the advantage of novelty, against as illusory grounds of proof destitute of this advantage, and which, perhaps, excite the suspicion that the natural credulity of his youth has been abused by his instructors. He thinks he can find no better means of showing that he has outgrown the discipline of his minority than by despising those well-meant warnings, and, knowing no system of thought but that of dogmatism, he drinks deep draughts of the poison that is to sap the principles in which his early years were trained.

Exactly the opposite of the system here recommended ought to be pursued in academical instruction. This can only be effected, however, by a thorough training in the critical investigation of pure reason. For, in order to bring the principles of this critique into exercise as soon as possible, and to demonstrate their perfect sufficiency, even in the presence of the highest degree of dialectical illusion, the student ought to examine the assertions made on both sides of speculative questions step by step, and to test them by these principles. It cannot be a difficult task for him to show the fallacies inherent in these propositions, and thus he begins early to feel his own power of securing himself against the influence of such sophistical arguments, which must finally lose, for him, all their illusory power. And, although the same blows which overturn the edifice of his opponent are as fatal to his own speculative structures, if such he has wished to rear; he need not feel any sorrow in regard to this seeming misfortune, as he has now before him a fair prospect into the practical region in which he may reasonably hope to find a more secure foundation for a rational system.

There is, accordingly, no proper polemic in the sphere of pure reason. Both parties beat the air and fight with their own shadows, as they pass beyond the limits of nature, and can find no tangible point of attack—no firm footing for their dogmatical conflict. Fight as vigorously as they may, the shadows which they hew down, immediately start up again, like the heroes in Walhalla, and renew the bloodless and unceasing contest.

But neither can we admit that there is any proper sceptical employment of pure reason, such as might be based upon the principle of *neutrality* in all speculative disputes. To excite reason against itself, to place weapons in the hands of the party on the one side as well as in those of the other, and to remain an undisturbed and sarcastic spectator of the fierce struggle that ensues, seems, from the dogmatical point of view, to be a part fitting only a malevolent disposition. But, when the sophist evidences an invincible obstinacy and blindness, and a pride which no criticism can moderate, there is no other practicable course than to oppose to this pride and obstinacy similar feelings and pretensions on the other side, equally well or ill founded, so that reason, staggered by the reflections thus forced upon it, finds it necessary to moderate its confidence in such pretensions and to listen to the advice of criticism. But we cannot stop at these doubts, much less regard the conviction of our ignorance, not only as a cure for the conceit natural to dogmatism, but as the settlement of the disputes in which reason is involved with itself. On the contrary, scepticism is merely a means of awakening reason from its dogmatic dreams and exciting it to a more careful investigation into its own powers and pretensions. But, as scepticism appears to be the shortest road to a permanent peace in the domain of philosophy, and as it is the track pursued by the many who aim at giving a philosophical colouring to their contemptuous dislike of all inquiries of this kind, I think it necessary to present to my readers this mode of thought in its true light.

Scepticism not a Permanent State for Human Reason

The consciousness of ignorance—unless this ignorance is recognized to be absolutely necessary—ought, instead of forming the conclusion of my inquiries, to be the strongest motive to the pursuit of them. All ignorance is either ignorance of things or of the limits of knowledge. If my ignorance is accidental and not necessary, it must incite me, in the first case, to a *dogmatical* inquiry regarding the objects of which I am ignorant; in the second, to a *critical* investigation into the bounds of all possible knowledge. But that my ignorance is absolutely necessary and unavoidable, and that it consequently absolves from the duty of all further investigation, is a fact which cannot be made out upon empirical grounds—from *observation*—but upon critical grounds alone, that is, by a thoroughgoing *investigation* into the primary sources of cognition. It follows that the determination of the bounds of reason can be made only on *a priori* grounds; while the empirical limitation of reason, which is merely an indeterminate cognition of an ignorance that can never be completely removed, can take place only *a posteriori*. In other words, our empirical knowledge is limited by that which yet remains for us to know. The former cognition of our ignorance, which is possible only on a rational basis, is a *science;* the latter is merely a *perception,* and we cannot say how far the inferences drawn from it may extend. If I regard the earth, as it really appears to my senses, as a flat surface, I am ignorant how far this surface extends. But experience teaches me that, how far soever I go, I always see before me a space in which I can proceed farther; and thus I know the limits—merely visual—of my actual knowledge of the earth, although I am ignorant of the limits of the earth itself. But if I have got so far as to know that the earth is a sphere, and that its surface is spherical, I can cognize *a priori* and determine upon principles, from my knowledge of a small part of this surface—say to the extent of a degree—the diameter and circumference of the earth; and although I am ignorant of the objects which this surface contains, I have a perfect knowledge of its limits and extent.

The sum of all the possible objects of our cognition seems to us to be a level surface, with an apparent horizon—that which forms the limit of its extent, and which has been termed by us the *idea of unconditioned totality*. To reach this limit by empirical means is impossible, and all attempts to determine it *a priori* according to a principle, are alike in vain. But all the questions raised by pure reason relate to that which lies beyond this horizon, or, at least, in its boundary line.

The celebrated David Hume was one of those geographers of human reason who believe that they have given a sufficient answer to all such questions by declaring them to lie beyond the horizon of our knowledge—a horizon which, however, Hume was unable to determine. His attention especially was directed to the principle of causality; and he remarked with perfect justice that the truth of this principle, and even the objective validity of the conception of a cause, was not commonly based upon clear insight, that is, upon *a priori* cognition. Hence he concluded that this law does not derive its authority from its universality and necessity, but merely from its general applicability in the course of experience, and a kind of subjective necessity thence arising, which he termed *habit*. From the inability of reason to establish this principle as a necessary law for the acquisition of all experience, he inferred the nullity of all the attempts of reason to pass the region of the empirical.

This procedure of subjecting the *facta* of reason to examination, and, if necessary, to disapproval, may be termed the *censura* of reason. This *censura* must inevitably lead us to *doubts* regarding *all* transcendent employment of principles. But this is only the second step in our inquiry. The first step in regard to the subjects of pure reason, and which marks the infancy of that faculty, is that of *dogmatism*. The second, which we have just mentioned, is that of *scepticism,* and it gives evidence that our judgement has been improved by experience. But a third step is necessary—indicative of the maturity and manhood of the judgement, which now lays a firm foundation upon universal and necessary principles. This is the period of *criticism,* in which we do not examine the *facta* of reason, but reason itself, in the whole extent of its powers, and in regard to its capability of *a priori* cognition; and thus we determine not merely the empirical and ever-shifting bounds of our knowledge, but its necessary and eternal limits. We demonstrate from indubitable principles, not merely our ignorance in respect to this or that subject, but in regard to all possible questions of a certain class. Thus scepticism is a resting-place for reason, in which it may reflect on its dogmatical wanderings and gain some knowledge of the region in which it happens to be, that it may pursue its way with greater certainty;

but it cannot be its permanent dwelling-place. It must take up its abode only in the region of complete certitude, whether this relates to the cognition of objects themselves, or to the limits which bound all our cognition.

Reason is not to be considered as an indefinitely extended plane, of the bounds of which we have only a general knowledge; it ought rather to be compared to a sphere, the radius of which may be found from the curvature of its surface —that is, the nature of *a priori* synthetical propositions—and, consequently, its circumference and extent. Beyond the sphere of experience there are no objects which it can cognize; nay, even questions regarding such supposititious objects relate only to the subjective principles of a complete determination of the relations which exist between the understanding-conceptions which lie within this sphere.

We are actually in possession of *a priori* synthetical cognitions, as is proved by the existence of the principles of the understanding, which anticipate experience. If any one cannot comprehend the possibility of these principles, he may have some reason to doubt whether they are really *a priori;* but he cannot on this account declare them to be impossible, and affirm the nullity of the steps which reason may have taken under their guidance. He can only say: If we perceived their origin and their authenticity, we should be able to determine the extent and limits of reason; but, till we can do this, all propositions regarding the latter are mere random assertions. In this view, the doubt respecting all dogmatical philosophy, which proceeds without the guidance of criticism, is well grounded; but we cannot therefore deny to reason the ability to construct a sound philosophy, when the way has been prepared by a thorough critical investigation. All the conceptions produced, and all the questions raised, by pure reason, do not lie in the sphere of experience, but in that of reason itself, and hence they must be solved, and shown to be either valid or inadmissible, by that faculty. We have no right to decline the solution of such problems, on the ground that the solution can be discovered only from the nature of things, and under pretence of the limitation of human faculties, for reason is the sole creator of all these ideas, and is therefore bound either to establish their validity or to expose their illusory nature.

The polemic of scepticism is properly directed against the dogmatist, who erects a system of philosophy without having examined the fundamental objective principles on which it is based, for the purpose of evidencing the futility of his designs, and thus bringing him to a knowledge of his own powers. But, in itself, scepticism does not give us any certain information in regard to the bounds of our knowledge. All unsuccessful dogmatical attempts of reason are *facta,* which it is always useful to submit to the censure of the sceptic. But this cannot help us to any decision regarding the expectations which reason cherishes of better success in future endeavours; the investigations of scepticism cannot, therefore, settle the dispute regarding the rights and powers of human reason.

Hume is perhaps the ablest and most ingenious of all sceptical philosophers, and his writings have, undoubtedly, exerted the most powerful influence in awakening reason to a thorough investigation into its own powers. It will, therefore, well repay our labours to consider for a little the course of reasoning which he followed and the errors into which he strayed, although setting out on the path of truth and certitude.

Hume was probably aware, although he never clearly developed the notion, that we proceed in judgements of a certain class beyond our conception of the object. I have termed this kind of judgement *synthetical.* As regard the manner in which I pass beyond my conception by the aid of experience, no doubts can be entertained. Experience is itself a synthesis of perceptions; and it employs perceptions to increment the conception, which I obtain by means of another perception. But we feel persuaded that we are able to proceed beyond a conception, and to extend our cognition *a priori.* We attempt this in two ways—either, through the pure understanding, in relation to that which may become an *object of experience,* or, through pure reason, in relation to such properties of things, or of the existence of things, as can never be presented in any experience. This sceptical philosopher did not distinguish these two kinds of judgements, as he ought to have done, but regarded this augmentation of conceptions, and, if we may so express ourselves, the spontaneous generation of understanding and reason, independently of the impregnation of experience, as altogether impossible. The so-called *a priori* principles of these faculties he consequently held to be invalid and imaginary, and regarded them as nothing but subjective habits of thought originating in experience, and therefore purely empirical and contingent rules, to which we attribute a spurious necessity and universality. In support of this strange assertion, he referred us to the generally acknowledged principle of the relation between cause and effect. No faculty of the mind can conduct us from the conception of a thing to the existence of something else; and hence he believed he could infer that, without experience, we possess no source from which we can augment a conception, and no ground sufficient to justify us in framing a judgement that is to extend our cognition *a priori*. That the light of the sun, which shines upon a piece of wax, at the same time melts it, while it hardens clay, no power of the understanding could infer from the conceptions which we previously possessed of these substances; much less is there any *a priori* law that could conduct us to such a conclusion, which experience alone can certify. On the other hand, we have seen in our discussion of transcendental logic, that, although we can never proceed *immediately* beyond the content of the conception which is given us, we can always cognize completely *a priori*—in relation, however, to a third term, namely, *possible* experience—the law of its connection with other things. For example, if I observe that a piece of wax melts, I can cognize *a priori* that there must have been something (the sun's heat) preceding, which this effect follows according to a fixed law; although, without the aid of experience, I could not cognize *a priori* and in a *determinate* manner either the cause from the effect, or the effect from the cause. Hume was, therefore, wrong in inferring, from the contingency of the determination *according to law*, the contingency of *the law* itself; and the passing beyond the conception of a thing to possible experience (which is an *a priori* proceeding, constituting the objective reality of the conception), he confounded with our synthesis of objects in actual experience, which is always, of course, empirical. Thus, too, he regarded the principle of affinity, which has its seat in the understanding and indicates a necessary connection, as a mere rule of association, lying in the imitative faculty of imagination, which can present only contingent, and not objective connections.

The sceptical errors of this remarkably acute thinker arose principally from a defect, which was common to him with the dogmatists, namely, that he had never made a systematic review of all the different kinds of *a priori* synthesis performed by the understanding. Had he done so, he would have found, to take one example among many, that the *principle of permanence* was of this character, and that it, as well as the principle of causality, anticipates experience. In this way he might have been able to describe the determinate limits of the *a priori* operations of understanding and reason. But he merely declared the understanding to be limited, instead of showing what its limits were; he created a general mistrust in the power of our faculties, without giving us any determinate knowledge of the bounds of our necessary and unavoidable ignorance; he examined and condemned some of the principles of the understanding, without investigating all its powers with the completeness necessary to criticism. He denies, with truth, certain powers to the understanding, but he goes further, and declares it to be utterly inadequate to the *a priori* extension of knowledge, although he has not fully examined all the powers which reside in the faculty; and thus the fate which always overtakes scepticism meets him too. That is to say, his own declarations are doubted, for his objections were based upon *facta*, which are contingent, and not upon principles, which can alone demonstrate the necessary invalidity of all dogmatical assertions.

As Hume makes no distinction between the well-grounded claims of the understanding and the dialectical pretensions of reason, against which, however, his attacks are mainly directed, reason does not feel itself shut out from all attempts at the extension of *a priori* cognition, and hence it refuses, in spite of a few checks in this or that quarter, to relinquish such efforts. For one naturally arms oneself to resist an attack, and becomes more obstinate in the resolve to establish the claims he has advanced. But a complete review of the powers of reason, and the conviction thence arising that we are in possession of a limited field of action, while we must admit the vanity of higher claims, puts an end to all doubt and dispute, and induces reason to rest satisfied with the undisturbed possession of its limited domain.

To the uncritical dogmatist, who has not surveyed the sphere of his understanding, nor determined, in accordance with principles, the limits of possible cognition, who, consequently, is ignorant of his own powers, and believes he will discover them by the attempts he makes in the field of cognition, these attacks of scepticism are not only dangerous, but destructive. For if there is one proposition in his chain of reasoning which he cannot prove, or the fallacy in which he cannot evolve in accordance with a principle, suspicion falls on all his statements, however plausible they may appear.

And thus scepticism, the bane of dogmatical philosophy, conducts us to a sound investigation into the understanding and the reason. When we are thus far advanced, we need fear no further attacks; for the limits of our domain are clearly marked out, and we can make no claims nor become involved in any disputes regarding the region that lies beyond these limits. Thus the sceptical procedure in philosophy does not present any *solution* of the problems of reason, but it forms an excellent *exercise* for its powers, awakening its circumspection, and indicating the means whereby it may most fully establish its claims to its legitimate possessions.

SECTION III. *The Discipline of Pure Reason in Hypothesis*

THIS critique of reason has now taught us that all its efforts to extend the bounds of knowledge, by means of pure speculation, are utterly fruitless. So much the wider field, it may appear, lies open to hypothesis; as, where we cannot know with certainty, we are at liberty to make guesses and to form suppositions.

Imagination may be allowed, under the strict surveillance of reason, to invent suppositions; but, these must be based on something that is perfectly certain—and that is the *possibility* of the object. If we are well assured upon this point, it is allowable to have recourse to supposition in regard to the reality of the object; but this supposition must, unless it is utterly groundless, be connected, as its ground of explanation, with that which is really given and absolutely certain. Such a supposition is termed a *hypothesis*.

It is beyond our power to form the least conception *a priori* of the possibility of dynamical connection in phenomena; and the category of the pure understanding will not enable us to excogitate any such connection, but merely helps us to understand it, when we meet with it in experience. For this reason we cannot, in accordance with the categories, imagine or invent any object or any property of an object not given, or that may not be given in experience, and employ it in a hypothesis; otherwise, we should be basing our chain of reasoning upon mere chimerical fancies, and not upon conceptions of things. Thus, we have no right to assume the existence of new powers, not existing in nature—for example, an understanding with a non-sensuous intuition, a force of attraction without contact, or some new kind of substances occupying space, and yet without the property of impenetrability—and, consequently, we cannot assume that there is any other kind of community among substances than that observable in experience, any kind of presence than that in space, or any kind of duration than that in time. In one word, the conditions of possible experience are for reason the only conditions of the possibility of things; reason cannot venture to form, independently of these conditions, any conceptions of things, because such conceptions, although not self-contradictory, are without object and without application.

The conceptions of reason are, as we have already shown, mere ideas, and do not relate to any object in any kind of experience. At the same time, they do not indicate imaginary or possible objects. They are purely problematical in their nature and, as aids to the heuristic exercise of the faculties, form the basis of the regulative principles for the systematic employment of the understanding in the field of experience. If we leave this ground of experience, they become mere fictions of thought, the possibility of which is quite indemonstrable; and they cannot, consequently, be employed as hypotheses in the explanation of real phenomena. It is quite admissible to *cogitate* the soul as simple, for the purpose of enabling ourselves to employ the idea of a perfect and necessary unity of all the faculties of the mind as the principle of all our inquiries into its internal phenomena, although we cannot cognize this unity *in concreto*. But to *assume* that the soul is a simple substance (a transcendental conception) would be enouncing a proposition which is not only indemonstrable—as many physical hypotheses are—but a proposition which is purely arbitrary, and in the highest degree rash. The simple is never presented in experience; and, if by substance is here meant the permanent object of sensuous intuition, the possibility of a *simple phenomenon* is perfectly inconceivable. Reason affords no good grounds for admitting the existence of intelligible beings, or of intelligible properties of sensuous things, although—as we have no conception either of their possibility or of their impossibility—it will always be out of our power to affirm dogmatically that they do not exist. In the explanation of given phenomena, no other things and no other grounds of explanation can be employed than those which stand in connection with the given phenomena according to the known laws of experience. A *transcendental hypothesis,* in which a mere idea of reason is employed to explain the phenomena of nature, would not give us any better insight into a phenomenon, as we should be trying to explain what we do not sufficiently understand from known empirical principles, by what we do not understand at all. The principles of such a hypothesis might conduce to the satisfaction of reason, but it would not assist the understanding in its application to objects. Order and conformity to aims in the sphere of nature must be themselves explained upon natural grounds and according to natural laws; and the wildest hypotheses, if they are only physical, are here more admissible than a hyperphysical hypothesis, such as that of a divine author. For such a hypothesis would introduce the principle of *ignava ratio,* which requires us to give up the search for causes that might be discovered in the course of experience and to rest satisfied with a mere idea. As regards the absolute totality of the grounds of explanation in the series of these causes, this can be no hindrance to the understanding in the case of phenomena; because, as they are to us nothing more than phenomena, we have no right to look for anything like completeness in the synthesis of the series of their conditions.

Transcendental hypotheses are therefore inadmissible; and we cannot use the liberty of employing, in the absence of physical, hyperphysical grounds of explanation. And this for two reasons; first, because such hypotheses do not advance reason, but rather stop it in its progress; secondly, because this licence would render fruitless all its exertions in its own proper sphere, which is that of experience. For, when the explanation of natural phenomena happens to be difficult, we have constantly at hand a transcendental ground of explanation, which lifts us above the necessity of investigating nature; and our inquiries are brought to a close, not because we have obtained all the requisite knowledge, but because we abut upon a principle which is incomprehensible and which, indeed, is so far back in the track of thought as to contain the conception of the absolutely primal being.

The next requisite for the admissibility of a hypothesis is its sufficiency. That is, it must determine *a priori* the consequences which are given in experience and which are supposed to follow from the hypothesis itself. If we require to employ auxiliary hypotheses, the suspicion naturally arises that they are mere fictions; because the necessity for each of them requires the same justification as in the case of the original hypothesis, and thus their testimony is invalid. If we suppose the existence of an infinitely perfect cause, we possess sufficient grounds for the explanation of the conformity to aims, the order and the greatness which we observe in the universe; but we find ourselves obliged, when we observe the evil in the world and the exceptions to these laws, to employ new hypotheses in support of the original one. We employ the idea of the simple nature of the human soul as the foundation of all the theories we may form of its phenomena; but when we meet with difficulties in our way, when we observe in the soul phenomena similar to the changes which take place in matter, we require to call in new auxiliary hypotheses. These may, indeed, not be false, but we do not know them to be true, because the only witness to their certitude is the hypothesis which they themselves have been called in to explain.

We are not discussing the above-mentioned assertions regarding the immaterial unity of the soul and the existence of a Supreme Being as dogmata, which certain philosophers profess to demonstrate *a priori,* but purely as hypotheses. In the former case, the dogmatist must take care that his arguments possess the apodeictic certainty of a demonstration. For the assertion that the reality of such ideas is *probable* is as absurd as a proof of the probability of a proposition in geometry. Pure abstract reason, apart from all experience, can either cognize nothing at all; and hence the judgements it enounces are never mere opinions, they are either apodeictic certainties, or declarations that nothing can be known on the subject. Opinions and probable judgements on the nature of things can only be employed to explain given phenomena, or they may relate to the effect, in accordance with empirical laws, of an actually existing cause. In other words, we must restrict the sphere of opinion to the world of experience and nature. Beyond this region *opinion* is mere invention; unless we are groping about for the truth on a path not yet fully known, and have some hopes of stumbling upon it by chance.

But, although hypotheses are inadmissible in answers to the questions of pure speculative reason, they may be employed in the defence of these answers. That is to say, hypotheses are admissible in polemic, but not in the sphere of dogmatism. By the defence of statements of this character, I do not mean an attempt at discovering new grounds for their support, but merely the refutation of the arguments of opponents. All *a priori* synthetical propositions possess the peculiarity that, although the philosopher who maintains the reality of the ideas contained in the proposition is not in possession of sufficient knowledge to establish the certainty of his statements, his opponent is as little able to prove the truth of the opposite. This equality of fortune does not allow the one party to be superior to the other in the sphere of speculative cognition; and it is this sphere, accordingly, that is the proper arena of these endless speculative conflicts. But we shall afterwards show that, in relation to its *practical exercise,* Reason has the right of admitting what, in the field of pure speculation, she would not be justified in supposing, except upon perfectly sufficient grounds; because all such suppositions destroy the necessary completeness of speculation—a condition which the practical reason, however, does not consider to be requisite. In this sphere, therefore, Reason is mistress of a possession, her title to which she does not require to prove —which, in fact, she could not do. The burden of proof accordingly rests upon the opponent. But as he has just as little knowledge regarding the subject discussed, and is as little able to prove the non-existence of the object of an idea, as the philosopher on the other side is to demonstrate its reality, it is evident that there is an advantage on the side of the philosopher who maintains his proposition as a practically necessary supposition (*melior est conditio possidentis*).[1] For he is at liberty to employ, in self-defence, the same weapons as his opponent makes use of in attacking him; that is, he has a right to use hypotheses not for the purpose of supporting the arguments in favour of his own propositions, but to show that his opponent knows no more than himself regarding the subject under discussion and cannot boast of any speculative advantage.

Hypotheses are, therefore, admissible in the sphere of pure reason only as weapons for self-defence, and not as supports to dogmatical assertions. But the opposing party we must always seek for in ourselves. For speculative reason is, in the sphere of transcendentalism, dialectical *in its own nature.* The difficulties and objections we have to fear lie in ourselves. They are like old but never superannuated claims; and we must seek them out, and settle them once and for ever, if we are to expect a permanent peace. External tranquillity is hollow and unreal. The root of these contradictions, which lies in the nature of human reason, must be destroyed; and this can only be done by giving it, in the first instance, freedom to grow, nay, by nourishing it, that it may send out shoots, and thus betray its own existence. It is our duty, therefore, to try to discover new objections, to put weapons in the hands of our opponent, and to grant him the most favourable position in the arena that he can wish. We have nothing to fear from these concessions; on the contrary, we may rather hope that we shall thus make ourselves master of a possession which no one will ever venture to dispute.

The thinker requires, to be fully equipped, the hypotheses of pure reason, which, although but leaden weapons (for they have not been steeled in the armoury of experience), are as useful as any that can be employed by his opponents. If, accordingly, we have assumed, from a non-speculative point of view, the immaterial nature of the soul, and are met by the objection that experience seems to prove that the growth and decay of our mental faculties are mere modifications of the sensuous organism—we can weaken the force of this objection by the assumption that the body is nothing but the fundamental phenomenon, to which, as a necessary condition, all sensibility, and consequently all thought, relates in the present state of our existence; and that the separation of soul and body forms the conclusion of the sensuous exercise of our power of cognition and the beginning of the intellectual. The body would, in this view of the question, be regarded, not as the cause of thought, but merely as its restrictive condition, as promotive of the sensuous and animal, but as a hindrance to the pure and spiritual life; and the dependence of the animal life on the constitution of the body, would not prove that the *whole* life of man was also dependent on the state of the organism. We might go still farther, and discover new objections, or carry out to their extreme consequences those which have already been adduced.

Generation, in the human race as well as among the irrational animals, depends on so many accidents—of occasion, of proper sustenance, of the laws enacted by the government of a country, of vice even, that it is difficult to believe in the eternal existence of a being whose life has begun under circumstances so mean and trivial, and so entirely dependent upon our own control. As regards the continuance of the existence of the whole race, we need have no difficulties, for accident in single cases is subject to general laws; but, in the case of each individual, it would seem as if we could hardly expect so wonderful an effect from causes so insignificant. But, in answer to these objections, we may adduce the transcendental hypothesis that all life is properly intelligible, and not subject to changes of time, and that it neither began in birth, nor will end in death. We may assume that this life is nothing more than a sensuous representation of pure spiritual life; that the

[1] ["The condition of the party in possession, or the defendant, is the better of the two."]

whole world of sense is but an image, hovering before the faculty of cognition which we exercise in this sphere, and with no more objective reality than a dream; and that if we could intuite ourselves and other things as they really are, we should see ourselves in a world of spiritual natures, our connection with which did not begin at our birth and will not cease with the destruction of the body. And so on.

We cannot be said to know what has been above asserted, nor do we seriously maintain the truth of these assertions; and the notions therein indicated are not even ideas of reason, they are purely *fictitious* conceptions. But this hypothetical procedure is in perfect conformity with the laws of reason. Our opponent mistakes the absence of empirical conditions for a proof of the complete impossibility of all that we have asserted; and we have to show him that he has not exhausted the whole sphere of possibility and that he can as little compass that sphere by the laws of experience and nature, as we can lay a secure foundation for the operations of reason beyond the region of experience. Such hypothetical defences against the pretensions of an opponent must not be regarded as declarations of opinion. The philosopher abandons them, so soon as the opposite party renounces its dogmatical conceit. To maintain a simply negative position in relation to propositions which rest on an insecure foundation, well befits the moderation of a true philosopher; but to uphold the objections urged against an opponent as proofs of the opposite statement is a proceeding just as unwarrantable and arrogant as it is to attack the position of a philosopher who advances affirmative propositions regarding such a subject.

It is evident, therefore, that hypotheses, in the speculative sphere, are valid, not as independent propositions, but only relatively to opposite transcendent assumptions. For, to make the principles of possible experience conditions of the possibility of things in general is just as transcendent a procedure as to maintain the objective reality of ideas which can be applied to no objects except such as lie without the limits of possible experience. The judgements enounced by pure reason must be necessary, or they must not be enounced at all. Reason cannot trouble herself with opinions. But the hypotheses we have been discussing are merely problematical judgements, which can neither be confuted nor proved; while, therefore, they are not personal opinions, they are indispensable as answers to objections which are liable to be raised. But we must take care to confine them to this function, and guard against any assumption on their part of absolute validity, a proceeding which would involve reason in inextricable difficulties and contradictions.

SECTION IV. *The Discipline of Pure Reason in Relation to Proofs*

IT is a peculiarity, which distinguishes the proofs of transcendental synthetical propositions from those of all other *a priori* synthetical cognitions, that reason, in the case of the former, does not apply its conceptions directly to an object, but is first obliged to prove, *a priori*, the objective validity of these conceptions and the possibility of their syntheses. This is not merely a prudential rule, it is essential to the very possibility of the proof of a transcendental proposition. If I am required to pass, *a priori*, beyond the conception of an object, I find that it is utterly impossible without the guidance of something which is not contained in the conception. In mathematics, it is *a priori* intuition that guides my synthesis; and, in this case, all our conclusions may be drawn immediately from pure intuition. In transcendental cognition, so long as we are dealing only with conceptions of the understanding, we are guided by possible experience. That is to say, a proof in the sphere of transcendental cognition does not show that the given conception (that of an event, for example) leads directly to another conception (that of a cause)—for this would be a *saltus* which nothing can justify; but it shows that experience itself, and consequently the object of experience, is impossible without the connection indicated by these conceptions. It follows that such a proof must demonstrate the possibility of arriving, synthetically and *a priori*, at a certain knowledge of things, which was not contained in our conceptions of these things. Unless we pay particular attention to this requirement, our proofs, instead of pursuing the straight path indicated by reason, follow the tortuous road of mere subjective association. The illusory conviction, which rests upon subjective causes of association, and which is considered as resulting from the perception of a real and objective natural affinity, is always open to doubt and suspicion. For this reason, all the attempts which have been made to prove the principle of sufficient reason, have, according to the universal admission of philosophers, been quite unsuccessful; and, before the appearance of transcendental criticism, it was considered better, as this principle could not be abandoned, to appeal boldly to the common sense of mankind (a proceeding which always proves that the problem, which reason ought to solve, is one in which philosophers find great difficulties), rather than attempt to discover new dogmatical proofs.

But, if the proposition to be proved is a proposition of pure reason, and if I aim at passing beyond my empirical conceptions by the aid of mere ideas, it is necessary that the proof should first show that such a step in synthesis is possible (which it is not), before it proceeds to prove the truth of the proposition itself. The so-called proof of the simple nature of the soul from the unity of apperception, is a very plausible one. But it contains no answer to the objection, that, as the notion of absolute simplicity is not a conception which is directly applicable to a perception, but is an idea which must be inferred—if at all—from observation, it is by no means evident how the mere fact of consciousness, which is contained *in all thought,* although in so far a simple representation, can conduct me to the consciousness and cognition of a thing which is purely a thinking substance. When I represent to my mind the power of my body as in motion, my body in this thought is so far absolute unity, and my representation of it is a simple one; and hence I can indicate this representation by the motion of a point, because I have made abstraction of the size or volume of the body. But I cannot hence infer that, given merely the moving power of a body, the body may be cogitated as simple substance, merely because the representation in my mind takes no account of its content in space, and is consequently simple. The simple, in abstraction, is very different from the objectively simple; and hence the Ego, which is simple in the first sense, may, in the second sense, as indicating the soul itself, be a very complex conception, with a very various content. Thus it is evident that in all such arguments there lurks a paralogism. We guess (for without some such surmise our suspicion would not be excited in reference to a proof of this character) at the presence of the paralogism, by keeping ever before us a criterion of the possibility of those synthetical propositions which aim at proving more than experience can teach us. This criterion is obtained from the observation that such proofs do not lead us directly from the subject of the proposition to be proved to the required predicate, but find it necessary to presuppose the possibility of extending our cognition *a priori* by means of ideas. We must, accordingly, always use the greatest caution; we require, before attempting any proof, to consider how it is possible to extend the sphere of cognition by the operations of pure reason, and from what source we are to derive knowledge, which is not obtained from the analysis of conceptions, nor relates, by anticipation, to possible experience. We shall thus spare ourselves much severe and fruitless labour, by not expecting from reason what is beyond its power, or rather by subjecting it to discipline, and teaching it to moderate its vehement desires for the extension of the sphere of cognition.

The first rule for our guidance is, therefore, not to attempt a transcendental proof, before we have considered from what source we are to derive the principles upon which the proof is to be based, and what right we have to expect that our conclusions from these principles will be veracious. If they are principles of the understanding, it is vain to expect that we should attain by their means to ideas of pure reason; for these principles are valid only in regard to objects of possible experience. If they are principles of pure reason, our labour is alike in vain. For the principles of reason, if employed as objective, are without exception dialectical and possess no validity or truth, except as regulative principles of the systematic employment of reason in experience. But when such delusive proofs are presented to us, it is our duty to meet them with the *non liquet* of a matured judgement; and, although we are unable to expose the particular sophism upon which the proof is based, we have a right to demand a deduction of the principles employed in it; and, if these principles have their origin in pure reason alone, such a deduction is absolutely impossible. And thus it is unnecessary that we should trouble ourselves with the exposure and confutation of every sophistical illusion; we may, at once, bring all dialectic, which is inexhaustible in the production of fallacies, before the bar of critical reason, which tests the principles upon which all dialectical procedure is based. The second peculiarity of transcendental proof is that a transcendental proposition cannot rest upon more than *a single* proof. If I am drawing conclusions, not from conceptions, but from intuition corresponding to a conception, be it pure intuition, as in mathematics, or empirical, as in natural science, the intuition which forms the basis of my inferences presents me with materials for many synthetical propositions, which I can connect in various modes, while, as it is allowable to proceed from different points in the intention, I can arrive by different paths at the same proposition.

But every transcendental proposition sets out from a conception, and posits the synthetical condition of the possibility of an object according to this conception. There must, therefore, be but one ground of proof, because it is the conception alone which determines the object; and thus the proof cannot contain anything more than the determination of the object according to the conception. In our Transcendental Analytic, for example, we inferred the principle: Every event has a cause, from the only condition of the objective possibility of our conception of an event. This is that an event cannot be determined in time, and consequently cannot form a part of experience, unless it stands under this dynamical law. This is the only possible ground of proof; for our conception of an event possesses objective validity, that is, is a true conception, only because the law of causality determines an object to which it can refer. Other arguments in support of this principle have been attempted—such as that from the contingent nature of a phenomenon; but when this argument is considered, we can discover no criterion of contingency, except the fact of an event—of something *happening,* that is to say, the existence which is preceded by the non-existence of an object, and thus we fall back on the very thing to be proved. If the proposition: "Every thinking being is simple," is to be proved, we keep to the conception of the ego, which is simple, and to which all thought has a relation. The same is the case with the transcendental proof of the existence of a Deity, which is based solely upon the harmony and reciprocal fitness of the conceptions of an *ens realissimum* and a necessary being, and cannot be attempted in any other manner.

This caution serves to simplify very much the criticism of all propositions of reason. When reason employs conceptions alone, only one proof of its thesis is possible, if any. When, therefore, the dogmatist advances with ten arguments in favour of a proposition, we may be sure that not one of them is conclusive. For if he possessed one which proved the proposition he brings forward to demonstration—as must always be the case with the propositions of pure reason—what need is there for any more? His intention can only be similar to that of the advocate who had different arguments for different judges; thus availing himself of the weakness of those who examine his arguments, who, without going into any profound investigation, adopt the view of the case which seems most probable at first sight and decide according to it.

The third rule for the guidance of pure reason in the conduct of a proof is that all transcendental proofs must never be *apagogic* or indirect, but always ostensive or direct. The direct or ostensive proof not only establishes the truth of the proposition to be proved, but exposes the grounds of its truth; the apagogic, on the other hand, may assure us of the truth of the proposition, but it cannot enable us to comprehend the grounds of its possibility. The latter is, accordingly, rather an auxiliary to an argument, than a strictly philosophical and rational mode of procedure. In one respect, however, they have an advantage over direct proofs, from the fact that the mode of arguing by contradiction, which they employ, renders our understanding of the question more clear, and approximates the proof to the certainty of an intuitional demonstration.

The true reason why indirect proofs are employed in different sciences is this. When the grounds upon which we seek to base a cognition are too various or too profound, we try whether or not we may not discover the truth of our cognition from its consequences. The *modus ponens* of reasoning from the truth of its inferences to the truth of a proposition would be admissible if all the inferences that can be drawn from it are known to be true; for in this case there can be only one possible ground for these inferences, and that is the true one. But this is a quite impracticable procedure, as it surpasses all our powers to discover all the possible inferences that can be drawn from a proposition. But this mode of reasoning is employed, under favour, when we wish to prove the truth of an hypothesis; in which case we admit the truth of the conclusion—which is supported by analogy—that, if all the inferences we have drawn and examined agree with the proposition assumed, all other possible inferences will also agree with it. But, in this way, an hypothesis can never be established as a demonstrated truth. The *modus tollens* of reasoning from known inferences to the unknown proposition, is not only a rigorous, but a very easy mode of proof. For, if it can be shown that but one inference from a proposition is false, then the proposition must itself be false. Instead, then, of examining, in an ostensive argument, the whole series of the grounds on which the truth of a proposition rests, we need only take the opposite of this proposition, and if one inference from it be false, then must the opposite be itself false; and, consequently, the proposition which we wished to prove must be true.

The apagogic method of proof is admissible only in those sciences where it is impossible to mistake a subjective representation for an objective cognition. Where this is possible, it is plain that the opposite of a given proposition may contradict merely the subjective conditions of thought, and not the objective cognition; or it may happen that both propositions contradict each other only under a subjective condition, which is incorrectly considered to be objective, and, as the condition is itself false, both propositions may be false, and it will, consequently, be impossible to conclude the truth of the one from the falseness of the other.

In mathematics such subreptions are impossible; and it is in this science, accordingly, that the indirect mode of proof has its true place. In the science of nature, where all assertion is based upon empirical intuition, such subreptions may be guarded against by the repeated comparison of observations; but this mode of proof is of little value in this sphere of knowledge. But the transcendental efforts of pure reason are all made in the sphere of the subjective, which is the real medium of all dialectical illusion; and thus reason endeavours, in its premisses, to impose upon us subjective representations for objective cognitions. In the transcendental sphere of pure reason, then, and in the case of synthetical propositions, it is inadmissible to support a statement by disproving the counter-statement. For only two cases are possible; either, the counter-statement is nothing but the enouncement of the inconsistency of the opposite opinion with the subjective conditions of reason, which does not affect the real case (for example, we cannot comprehend the unconditioned necessity of the existence of a being, and hence every speculative proof of the existence of such a being must be opposed on *subjective* grounds, while the possibility of this being *in itself* cannot with justice be denied); or, both propositions, being dialectical in their nature, are based upon an impossible conception. In this latter case the rule applies: *non entis nulla sunt predicata;* that is to say, what we affirm and what we deny, respecting such an object, are equally untrue, and the apagogic mode of arriving at the truth is in this case impossible. If, for example, we presuppose that the world of sense is given *in itself* in its totality, it is false, *either* that it is infinite, *or* that it is finite and limited in space. Both are false, because the hypothesis is false. For the notion of phenomena (as mere representations) which are given *in themselves* (as objects) is self-contradictory; and the infinitude of this imaginary whole would, indeed, be unconditioned, but would be inconsistent (as everything in the phenomenal world is conditioned) with the unconditioned determination and finitude of quantities which is presupposed in our conception.

The apagogic mode of proof is the true source of those illusions which have always had so strong an attraction for the admirers of dogmatical philosophy. It may be compared to a champion who maintains the honour and claims of the party he has adopted by offering battle to all who doubt the validity of these claims and the purity of that honour; while nothing can be proved in this way, except the respective strength of the combatants, and the advantage, in this respect, is always on the side of the attacking party. Spectators, observing that each party is alternately conqueror and conquered, are led to regard the subject of dispute as beyond the power of man to decide upon. But such an opinion cannot be justified; and it is sufficient to apply to these reasoners the remark:

Non defensoribus istis
Tempus eget.

Each must try to establish his assertions by a transcendental deduction of the grounds of proof employed in his argument, and thus enable us to see in what way the claims of reason may be supported. If an opponent bases his assertions upon subjective grounds, he may be refuted with ease; not, however to the advantage of the dogmatist, who likewise depends upon subjective sources of cognition and is in like manner driven into a corner by his opponent. But, if parties employ the direct method of procedure, they will soon discover the difficulty, nay, the impossibility of proving their assertions, and will be forced to appeal to prescription and precedence; or they will, by the help of criticism, discover with ease the dogmatical illusions by which they had been mocked, and compel reason to renounce its exaggerated pretensions to speculative insight and to confine itself within the limits of its proper sphere—that of practical principles.

CHAPTER II. *The Canon of Pure Reason*

IT is a humiliating consideration for human reason that it is incompetent to discover truth by means of pure speculation, but, on the contrary, stands in need of discipline to check its deviations from the straight path and to expose the illusions which it originates. But, on the other hand, this consideration ought to elevate and to give it confidence, for this discipline is exercised by itself alone, and it is subject to the censure of no other power. The bounds, moreover, which it is forced to set to its speculative exercise, form likewise a check upon the fallacious pretensions of opponents; and thus what remains of its possessions, after these exaggerated claims have been disallowed, is secure from attack or usurpation. The greatest, and perhaps the only, use of all philosophy of pure reason is, accordingly, of a purely negative character. It is not an organon for the extension, but a discipline for the determination, of the limits of its exercise; and without laying claim to the discovery of new truth, it has the modest merit of guarding against error.

At the same time, there must be some source of positive cognitions which belong to the domain of pure reason and which become the causes of error only from our mistaking their true character, while they form the goal towards which reason continually strives. How else can we account for the inextinguishable desire in the human mind to find a firm footing in some region beyond the limits of the world of experience? It hopes to attain to the possession of a knowledge in which it has the deepest interest. It enters upon the path of pure speculation; but in vain. We have some reason, however, to expect that, in the only other way that lies open to it—the path of *practical* reason—it may meet with better success.

I understand by a *canon* a list of the *a priori* principles of the proper employment of certain faculties of cognition. Thus general logic, in its analytical department, is a formal canon for the faculties of understanding and reason. In the same way, Transcendental Analytic was seen to be a canon of the pure *understanding;* for it alone is competent to enounce true *a priori* synthetical cognitions. But, when no proper employment of a faculty of cognition is possible, no canon can exist. But the synthetical cognition of pure speculative *reason* is, as has been shown, completely impossible. There cannot, therefore, exist any canon for the speculative exercise of this faculty—for its speculative exercise is entirely dialectical; and, consequently, transcendental logic, in this respect, is merely a discipline, and not a canon. If, then, there is any proper mode of employing the faculty of pure reason—in which case there must be a canon for this faculty—this canon will relate, not to the speculative, but to the *practical use of reason.* This canon we now proceed to investigate.

SECTION I. *Of the Ultimate End of the Pure Use of Reason*

THERE exists in the faculty of reason a natural desire to venture beyond the field of experience, to attempt to reach the utmost bounds of all cognition by the help of ideas alone, and not to rest satisfied until it has fulfilled its course and raised the sum of its cognitions into a self-subsistent systematic whole. Is the motive for this endeavour to be found in its speculative, or in its practical interests alone?

Setting aside, at present, the results of the labours of pure reason in its speculative exercise, I shall merely inquire regarding the problems the solution of which forms its ultimate aim, whether reached or not, and in relation to which all other aims are but partial and intermediate. These highest aims must, from the nature of reason, possess complete unity; otherwise the highest interest of humanity could not be successfully promoted.

The transcendental speculation of reason relates to three things: the freedom of the will, the immortality of the soul, and the existence of God. The speculative interest which reason has in those questions is very small; and, for its sake alone, we should not undertake the labour of transcendental investigation—a labour full of toil and ceaseless struggle. We should be loth to undertake this labour, because the discoveries we might make would not be of the smallest use in the sphere of concrete or physical investigation. We may find out that the will is free, but this knowledge only relates to the intelligible cause of our volition. As regards the phenomena or expressions of this will, that is, our actions, we are bound, in obedience to an inviolable maxim, without which reason cannot be employed in the sphere of experience, to explain these in the same way as we explain all the other phenomena of nature, that is to say, according to its unchangeable laws. We may have discovered the spirituality and immortality of the soul, but we cannot employ this knowledge to explain the phenomena of this life, nor the peculiar nature of the future, because our conception of an incorporeal nature is purely negative and does not add anything to our knowledge, and the only inferences to be drawn from it are purely fictitious. If, again, we prove the existence of a supreme intelligence, we should be able from it to make the conformity to aims existing in the arrangement of the world comprehensible; but we should not be justified in deducing from it any particular arrangement or disposition, or inferring any where it is not perceived. For it is a necessary rule of the speculative use of reason that we must not overlook natural causes, or refuse to listen to the teaching of experience, for the sake of deducing what we know and perceive from something that transcends all our knowledge. In one word, these three propositions are, for the speculative reason, always transcendent, and cannot be employed as immanent principles in relation to the objects of experience; they are, consequently, of no use to us in this sphere, being but the valueless results of the severe but unprofitable efforts of reason.

If, then, the actual *cognition* of these three cardinal propositions is perfectly useless, while Reason uses her utmost endeavours to induce us to admit them, it is plain that their real value and importance relate to our *practical,* and not to our speculative interest.

I term all that is possible through free will, practical. But if the conditions of the exercise of free volition are empirical, reason can have only a regulative, and not a constitutive, influence upon it, and is serviceable merely for the introduction of unity into its empirical laws. In the moral philosophy of prudence, for example, the sole business of reason is to bring about a union of all the ends, which are aimed at by our inclinations, into one ultimate end—that of *happiness*—and to show the agreement which should exist among the means of attaining that end. In this sphere, accordingly, reason cannot present to us any other than *pragmatical* laws of free action, for our guidance towards the aims set up by the senses, and is incompetent to give us laws which are pure and determined completely *a priori.* On the other hand, pure practical laws, the ends of which have been given by reason entirely *a priori,* and which are not empirically conditioned, but are, on the contrary, absolutely imperative in their nature, would be products of pure reason. Such are the *moral* laws; and these alone belong to the sphere of the practical exercise of reason, and admit of a canon.

All the powers of reason, in the sphere of what may be termed *pure* philosophy, are, in fact, directed to the three above-mentioned problems alone. These again have a still higher end —the answer to the question, *what we ought to do,* if the will is free, if there is a God and a future world. Now, as this problem relates to our conduct, in reference to the highest aim of humanity, it is evident that the ultimate intention of nature, in the constitution of our reason, has been directed to the *moral* alone.

We must take care, however, in turning our attention to an object which is foreign[1] to the sphere of transcendental philosophy, not to injure the unity of our system by digressions, nor, on the other hand, to fail in clearness, by saying too little on the new subject of discussion. I hope to avoid both extremes, by keeping as close as possible to the transcendental, and excluding all psychological, that is, empirical, elements.

I have to remark, in the first place, that at present I treat of the conception of freedom in the practical sense only, and set aside the corresponding transcendental conception, which cannot be employed as a ground of explanation in the phenomenal world, but is itself a problem for pure reason. A will is purely *animal* (*arbitrium brutum*) when it is determined by sensuous impulses or instincts only, that is, when it is determined in a *pathological* manner. A will, which can be determined independently of sensuous impulses, consequently by motives presented by reason alone, is called a *free will* (*arbitrium liberum*); and everything which is connected with this free will, either as principle or consequence, is termed *practical.* The existence of practical freedom can be proved from experience alone. For the human will is not determined by that alone which immediately affects the senses; on the contrary, we have the power, by calling up the notion of what is useful or hurtful in a more distant relation, of overcoming the immediate impressions on our sensuous faculty of desire. But these considerations of what is desirable in relation to our whole state, that is, is in the end good and useful, are based entirely upon reason. This faculty, accordingly, enounces laws, which are imperative or objective *laws of freedom* and which tell us what *ought to take place,* thus distinguishing themselves from the *laws of nature,* which relate to that which *does take place.* The laws of freedom or of free will are hence termed practical laws.

Whether reason is not itself, in the actual delivery of these laws, determined in its turn by other influences, and whether the action which, in relation to sensuous impulses, we call *free,* may not, in relation to higher and more remote operative causes, really form a part of *nature*—these are questions which do not here concern us. They are purely speculative questions; and

[1] All practical conceptions relate to objects of pleasure and pain, and consequently—in an indirect manner, at least—to objects of feeling. But as feeling is not a faculty of representation, but lies out of the sphere of our powers of cognition, the elements of our judgements, in so far as they relate to pleasure or pain, that is, the elements of our practical judgements, do not belong to transcendental philosophy, which has to do with pure *a priori* cognitions alone.

all we have to do, in the practical sphere, is to inquire into the *rule* of conduct which reason has to present. Experience demonstrates to us the existence of practical freedom as one of the causes which exist in nature, that is, it shows the causal power of reason in the determination of the will. The idea of transcendental freedom, on the contrary, requires that reason—in relation to its causal power of commencing a series of phenomena—should be independent of all sensuous determining causes; and thus it seems to be in opposition to the law of nature and to all possible experience. It therefore remains a problem for the human mind. But this problem does not concern reason in its practical use; and we have, therefore, in a canon of pure reason, to do with only two questions, which relate to the practical interest of pure reason: Is there a God? and, Is there a future life? The question of transcendental freedom is purely speculative, and we may therefore set it entirely aside when we come to treat of practical reason. Besides, we have already discussed this subject in the antinomy of pure reason.

Section II. *Of the Ideal of the Summum Bonum as a Determining Ground of the Ultimate End of Pure Reason*

Reason conducted us, in its speculative use, through the field of experience and, as it can never find complete satisfaction in that sphere, from thence to speculative ideas—which, however, in the end brought us back again to experience, and thus fulfilled the purpose of reason, in a manner which, though useful, was not at all in accordance with our expectations. It now remains for us to consider whether pure reason can be employed in a practical sphere, and whether it will here conduct us to those ideas which attain the highest ends of pure reason, as we have just stated them. We shall thus ascertain whether, from the point of view of its practical interest, reason may not be able to supply us with that which, on the speculative side, it wholly denies us.

The whole interest of reason, speculative as well as practical, is centred in the three following questions:

1. What can I know?
2. What ought I to do?
3. What may I hope?

The first question is purely speculative. We have, as I flatter myself, exhausted all the replies of which it is susceptible, and have at last found the reply with which reason must content itself, and with which it ought to be content, so long as it pays no regard to the practical. But from the two great ends to the attainment of which all these efforts of pure reason were in fact directed, we remain just as far removed as if we had consulted our ease and declined the task at the outset. So far, then, as *knowledge* is concerned, thus much, at least, is established, that, in regard to those two problems, it lies beyond our reach.

The second question is purely practical. As such it may indeed fall within the province of pure reason, but still it is not transcendental, but moral, and consequently cannot in itself form the subject of our criticism.

The third question: If I act as I ought to do, what may I then hope?—is at once practical and theoretical. The practical forms a clue to the answer of the theoretical, and—in its highest form—speculative question. For all *hoping* has happiness for its object and stands in precisely the same relation to the practical and the law of morality as *knowing* to the theoretical cognition of things and the law of nature. The former arrives finally at the conclusion that *something is* (which determines the ultimate end), because *something ought to take place;* the latter, that *something is* (which operates as the highest cause), because *something does take place.*

Happiness is the satisfaction of all our desires; *extensive,* in regard to their multiplicity; *intensive,* in regard to their degree; and *protensive,* in regard to their duration. The practical law based on the motive of *happiness* I term a pragmatical law (or prudential rule); but that law, assuming such to exist, which has no other motive than the *worthiness of being happy,* I term a moral or ethical law. The first tells us what we have to do, if we wish to become possessed of happiness; the second dictates how we ought to act, in order to deserve happiness. The first is based upon empirical principles; for it is only by experience that I can learn either what inclinations exist which desire satisfaction, or what are the natural means of satisfying them. The second takes no account of our desires or the means of satisfying them, and regards only the freedom of a rational being, and the necessary conditions under which alone this freedom can harmonize with the distribution of happiness according to principles. This second law may therefore rest upon mere ideas of pure reason, and may be cognized *a priori.*

I assume that there are pure moral laws which determine, entirely *a priori* (without regard to empirical motives, that is, to happiness), the conduct of a rational being, or in other words, to use which it makes of its freedom, and that these laws are *absolutely* imperative (not merely hypothetically, on the supposition of other empirical ends), and therefore in all respects necessary. I am warranted in assuming this, not only by the arguments of the most enlightened moralists, but by the moral judgement of every man who will make the attempt to form a distinct conception of such a law.

Pure reason, then, contains, not indeed in its speculative, but in its practical, or, more strictly, its moral use, principles of the *possibility of experience,* of such actions, namely, as, in accordance with ethical precepts, *might* be met with in the *history* of man. For since reason commands that such actions should take place, it must be possible for them to take place; and hence a particular kind of systematic unity—the moral—must be possible. We have found, it is true, that the systematic unity of nature could not be established according to speculative principles of reason, because, while reason possesses a causal power in relation to freedom, it has none in relation to the whole sphere of nature; and, while moral principles of reason can produce free actions, they cannot produce natural laws. It is, then, in its practical, but especially in its moral use, that the principles of pure reason possess objective reality.

I call the world *a moral world,* in so far as it may be in accordance with all the ethical laws—which, by virtue of the *freedom* of reasonable beings, it *can* be, and according to the necessary laws of *morality* it *ought to be.* But this world must be conceived only as an intelligible world, inasmuch as abstraction is therein made of all conditions (ends), and even of all impediments to morality (the weakness or pravity of human nature). So far, then, it is a mere idea—though still a practical idea—which may have, and ought to have, an influence on the world of sense, so as to bring it as far as possible into conformity with itself. The idea of a moral world has, therefore, objective reality, not as referring to an object of intelligible intuition—for of such an object we can form no conception whatever—but to the world of sense—conceived, however, as an object of pure reason in its practical use—and to a *corpus mysticum* of rational beings in it, in so far as the *liberum arbitrium* of the individual is placed, under and by virtue of moral laws, in complete systematic unity both with itself and with the freedom of all others.

That is the answer to the first of the two questions of pure reason which relate to its practical interest: *Do that which will render thee worthy of happiness.* The second question is this: If I conduct myself so as not to be unworthy of happiness, may I hope thereby to obtain happiness? In order to arrive at the solution of this question, we must inquire whether the principles of pure reason, which prescribe *a priori* the law, necessarily also connect this hope with it.

I say, then, that just as the moral principles are necessary according to reason in its *practical* use, so it is equally necessary according to reason in its *theoretical* use to assume that every one has ground to hope for happiness in the measure in which he has made himself worthy of it in his conduct, and that therefore the system of morality is inseparably (though only in the idea of pure reason) connected with that of happiness.

Now in an intelligible, that is, in the moral world, in the conception of which we make abstraction of all the impediments to morality (sensuous desires), such a system of happiness, connected with and proportioned to morality, may be conceived as necessary, because freedom of volition—partly incited, and partly restrained by moral laws—would be itself the cause of general happiness; and thus rational beings, under the guidance of such principles, would be themselves the authors both of their own enduring welfare and that of others. But such a system of self-rewarding morality is only an idea, the carrying out of which depends upon the condition that every one acts as he ought; in other words, that all actions of reasonable beings be such as they would be if they sprung from a Supreme Will, comprehending in, or under, itself all particular wills. But since the moral law is binding on each individual in the use of his freedom of volition, even if others should not act in conformity with this law, neither the nature of things, nor the causality of actions and their relation to morality, determine how the consequences of these actions will be related to happiness; and the necessary connection of the hope of happiness with the unceasing endeavour to become worthy of happiness, cannot be cognized by reason, if we take nature alone for our guide. This connection can be hoped for only on the assumption that the cause of nature is a supreme reason, which governs according to moral laws.

I term the idea of an intelligence in which the morally most perfect will, united with supreme blessedness, is the cause of all happiness in the world, so far as happiness stands in strict relation to morality (as the worthiness of being happy), *the Ideal of the Supreme Good.* It is only, then, in the ideal of the supreme *original* good, that pure reason can find the ground of the practically necessary connection of both elements of the highest *derivative* good, and accordingly of an intelligible, that is, *moral* world. Now since we are necessitated by reason to conceive ourselves as belonging to such a world, while the senses present to us nothing but a world of phenomena, we must assume the former as a consequence of our conduct in the world of sense (since the world of sense gives us no hint of it), and therefore as future in relation to us. Thus God and a future life are two hypotheses which, according to the principles of pure reason, are inseparable from the obligation which this reason imposes upon us.

Morality *per se* constitutes a system. But we can form no system of happiness, except in so far as it is dispensed in strict proportion to morality. But this is only possible in the intelligible world, under a wise author and ruler. Such a ruler, together with life in such a world, which we must look upon as future, reason finds itself compelled to assume; or it must regard the moral laws as idle dreams, since the necessary consequence which this same reason connects with them must, without this hypothesis, fall to the ground. Hence also the moral laws are universally regarded as *commands,* which they could not be did they not connect *a priori* adequate consequences with their dictates, and thus carry with them *promises* and *threats.* But this, again, they could not do, did they not reside in a necessary being, as the Supreme Good, which alone can render such a teleological unity possible.

Leibnitz termed the world, when viewed in relation to the rational beings which it contains, and the moral relations in which they stand to each other, under the government of the Supreme Good, *the kingdom of Grace,* and distinguished it from the *kingdom of Nature,* in which these rational beings live, under moral laws, indeed, but expect no other consequences from their actions than such as follow according to the course of nature in the world of sense. To view ourselves, therefore, as in the kingdom of grace, in which all happiness awaits us, except in so far as we ourselves limit our participation in it by actions which render us unworthy of happiness, is a practically necessary idea of reason.

Practical laws, in so far as they are subjective grounds of actions, that is, subjective principles, are termed *maxims.* The *judgements* of morality, in its purity and ultimate results, are framed according to *ideas*; the *observance* of its laws, according to *maxims.*

The whole course of our life must be subject to moral maxims; but this is impossible, unless with the moral law, which is a mere idea, reason connects an efficient cause which ordains to all conduct which is in conformity with the moral law an issue either in this or in another life, which is in exact conformity with our highest aims. Thus, without a God and without a world, invisible to us now, but hoped for, the glorious ideas of morality are, indeed, objects of approbation and of admiration, but cannot be the springs of purpose and action. For they do not satisfy all the aims which are natural to every rational being, and which are determined *a priori* by pure reason itself, and necessary.

Happiness alone is, in the view of reason, far from being the complete good. Reason does not approve of it (however much inclination may desire it), except as united with desert. On the other hand, morality alone, and with it, mere *desert,* is likewise far from being the complete good. To make it complete, he who conducts himself in a manner not unworthy of happiness, must be able to hope for the possession of happiness. Even reason, unbiased by private ends, or interested considerations, cannot judge otherwise, if it puts itself in the place of a being whose business it is to dispense all happiness to others. For in the practical idea both points are essentially combined, though in such a way that participation in happiness is rendered possible by the moral disposition, as its condition, and not conversely, the moral disposition by the prospect of happiness. For a disposition which should require the prospect of happiness as its necessary condition would not be moral, and hence also would not be worthy of complete happiness—a happiness which, in the view of reason, recognizes no limitation but such as arises from our own immoral conduct.

Happiness, therefore, in exact proportion with the morality of rational beings (whereby they are made worthy of happiness), constitutes alone the supreme good of a world into which we absolutely must transport ourselves according to the commands of pure but practical reason. This world is, it is true, only an intelligible world; for of such a systematic unity of ends as it requires, the world of sense gives us no hint. Its reality can be based on nothing else but the hypothesis of a supreme original good. In it independent reason, equipped with all the sufficiency of a supreme cause, founds, maintains, and fulfils the universal order of things, with the most perfect teleological harmony, however much this order may be hidden from us in the world of sense.

This moral theology has the peculiar advantage, in contrast with speculative theology, of leading inevitably to the conception of a *sole, perfect,* and *rational* First Cause, whereof speculative theology does not give us any *indication* on objective grounds, far less any convincing *evidence.* For we find neither in transcendental nor in natural theology, however far reason may lead us in these, any ground to warrant us in assuming the existence of *one only* Being, which stands at the head of all natural causes, and on which these are entirely dependent. On the other hand, if we take our stand on moral unity as a necessary law of the universe, and from this point of view consider what is necessary to give this law adequate efficiency and, for us, obligatory force, we must come to the conclusion that there is one only supreme will, which comprehends all these laws in itself. For how, under different wills, should we find complete unity of ends? This will must be omnipotent, that all nature and its relation to morality in the world may be subject to it; omniscient, that it may have knowledge of the most secret feelings and their moral worth; omnipresent, that it may be at hand to supply every necessity to which the highest weal of the world may give rise; eternal, that this harmony of nature and liberty may never fail; and so on.

But this systematic unity of ends in this world of intelligences—which, as mere nature, is only a world of sense, but, as a system of freedom of volition, may be termed an intelligible, that is, moral world (*regnum gratiae*)—leads inevitably also to the teleological unity of all things which constitute this great whole, according to universal natural laws—just as the unity of the former is according to universal and necessary moral laws—and unites the practical with the speculative reason. The world must be represented as having originated from an idea, if it is to harmonize with that use of reason without which we cannot even consider ourselves as worthy of reason—namely, the moral use, which rests entirely on the idea of the supreme good. Hence the investigation of nature receives a teleological direction, and becomes, in its widest extension, physico-theology. But this, taking its rise in moral order as a unity founded on the essence of freedom, and not accidentally instituted by external commands, establishes the teleological view of nature on grounds which must be inseparably connected with the internal possibility of things. This gives rise to a *transcendental theology,* which takes the ideal of the highest ontological perfection as a principle of systematic unity; and this principle connects all things according to universal and necessary natural laws, because all things have their origin in the absolute necessity of the one only Primal Being.

What *use* can we make of our understanding, even in respect of experience, if we do not propose ends to ourselves? But the highest ends are those of morality, and it is only pure reason that can give us the knowledge of these. Though supplied with these, and putting ourselves under their guidance, we can make no teleological use of the knowledge of nature, as regards *cognition,* unless nature itself has established teleological unity. For without this unity we should not even possess reason, because we should have no school for reason, and no cultivation through objects which afford the materials for its conceptions. But teleological unity is a necessary unity, and founded on the essence of the individual will itself. Hence this will, which is the condition of the application of this unity *in concreto,* must be so likewise. In this way the transcendental enlargement of our rational cognition would be, not the cause, but merely the effect of the practical teleology which pure reason imposes upon us.

Hence, also, we find in the history of human reason that, before the moral conceptions were sufficiently purified and determined, and before men had attained to a perception of the systematic unity of ends according to these conceptions and from necessary principles, the knowledge of nature, and even a considerable amount of intellectual culture in many other sciences, could produce only rude and vague conceptions of the Deity, sometimes even admitting of an astonishing indifference with regard to this question altogether. But the more enlarged treatment of moral ideas, which was rendered necessary by the extreme pure moral law of our religion, awakened the interest, and thereby quickened the perceptions of reason in relation to this object. In this way, and without the help either of an extended acquaintance with nature, or of a reliable transcendental insight (for these have been wanting in all ages), a conception of the Divine Being was arrived at, which we now hold to be the correct one, not because speculative reason convinces us of its correctness, but because it accords with the moral principles of reason. Thus it is to pure reason, but only in its practical use, that we must ascribe the merit of having connected with our highest interest a cognition, of which mere speculation was able only to form a conjecture, but the validity of which it was unable to establish—and of having thereby rendered it, not indeed a demonstrated dogma, but a hypothesis absolutely necessary to the essential ends of reason.

But if practical reason has reached this elevation, and has attained to the conception of a sole Primal Being as the supreme good, it must not, therefore, imagine that it has transcended the empirical conditions of its application, and risen to the immediate cognition of new objects; it must not presume to start from the conception which it has gained, and to deduce from it the moral laws themselves. For it was these very laws, the *internal* practical necessity of which led us to the hypothesis of an independent cause, or of a wise ruler of the universe, who should give them effect. Hence we are not entitled to regard them as accidental and derived from the mere will of the ruler, especially as we have no conception of such a will, except as formed in accordance with these laws. So far, then, as practical reason has the right to conduct us, we shall not look upon actions as binding on us, because they are the commands of God, but we shall regard them as divine commands, because we are internally bound by them. We shall study freedom under the teleological unity which accords with principles of reason; we shall look upon ourselves as acting in conformity with the divine will only in so far as we hold sacred the moral law which reason teaches us from the nature of actions themselves, and we shall believe that we can obey that will only by promoting the weal of the universe in ourselves and in others. Moral theology is, therefore, only of immanent use. It teaches us to fulfil our destiny here in the world, by placing ourselves in harmony with the general system of ends, and warns us against the fanaticism, nay, the crime of depriving reason of its legislative authority in the moral conduct of life, for the purpose of directly connecting this authority with the idea of the Supreme Being. For this would be, not an immanent, but a transcendent use of moral theology, and, like the transcendent use of mere speculation, would inevitably pervert and frustrate the ultimate ends of reason.

SECTION III. *Of Opinion, Knowledge, and Belief*

THE holding of a thing to be true is a phenomenon in our understanding which may rest on objective grounds, but requires, also, subjective causes in the mind of the person judging. If a judgement is valid for every rational being, then its ground is objectively sufficient, and it is termed a *conviction.* If, on the other hand, it has its ground in the particular character of the subject, it is termed a *persuasion.*

Persuasion is a mere illusion, the ground of the judgement, which lies solely in the subject, being regarded as objective. Hence a judgement of this kind has only private validity—is only valid for the individual who judges, and the holding of a thing to be true in this way cannot be communicated. But truth depends upon agreement with the object, and consequently the judgements of all understandings, if true, must be in agreement with each other (*consentientia uni tertio consentiunt inter se*). Conviction may, therefore, be distinguished, from an external point of view, from persuasion, by the possibility of communicating it and by showing its validity for the reason of every man; for in this case the presumption, at least, arises that the agreement of all judgements with each other, in spite of the different characters of individuals, rests upon the common ground of the agreement of each with the object, and thus the correctness of the judgement is established.

Persuasion, accordingly, cannot be *subjectively* distinguished from conviction, that is, so long as the subject views its judgement simply as a phenomenon of its own mind. But if we inquire whether the grounds of our judgement, which are valid for us, produce the same effect on the reason of others as on our own, we have then the means, though only subjective means, not, indeed, of producing conviction, but of detecting the merely private validity of the judgement; in other words, of discovering that there is in it the element of mere persuasion.

If we can, in addition to this, develop the *subjective causes* of the judgement, which we have taken for its *objective grounds,* and thus explain the deceptive judgement as a phenomenon in our mind, apart altogether from the objective character of the object, we can then expose the illusion and need be no longer deceived by it, although, if its subjective cause lies in our nature, we cannot hope altogether to escape its influence.

I can only *maintain,* that is, affirm as necessarily valid for every one, that which produces conviction. Persuasion I may keep for myself, if it is agreeable to me; but I cannot, and ought not, to attempt to impose it as binding upon others.

Holding for true, or the subjective validity of a judgement in relation to conviction (which is, at the same time, objectively valid), has the ıree following degrees: *opinion, belief,* and *ıowledge.* Opinion is a consciously insufficient ıdgement, subjectively as well as objectively. elief is subjectively sufficient, but is recognized being objectively insufficient. Knowledge is th subjectively and objectively sufficient. Subctive sufficiency is termed *conviction* (for mylf); objective sufficiency is termed *certainty* 'or all). I need not dwell longer on the explanaon of such simple conceptions.

I must never venture to *be of opinion,* withıt *knowing* something, at least, by which my ıdgement, in itself merely problematical, is ːought into connection with the truth—which nnection, although not perfect, is still someing more than an arbitrary fiction. Moreover, ıe law of such a connection must be certain. or if, in relation to this law, I have nothing ore than opinion, my judgement is but a play the imagination, without the least relation to uth. In the judgements of pure reason, opinn has no place. For, as they do not rest on npirical grounds and as the sphere of pure rean is that of necessary truth and *a priori* cognion, the principle of connection in it requires iiversality and necessity, and consequently erfect certainty—otherwise we should have no ıide to the truth at all. Hence it is absurd to ave an opinion in pure mathematics; we must now, or abstain from forming a judgement algether. The case is the same with the maxims morality. For we must not hazard an action n the mere opinion that it is allowed, but we ıust know it to be so.

In the transcendental sphere of reason, on the ther hand, the term opinion is too weak, while ıe word knowledge is too strong. From the mere- speculative point of view, therefore, we canot form a judgement at all. For the subjective rounds of a judgement, such as produce belief, ınnot be admitted in speculative inquiries, insmuch as they cannot stand without empirical ıpport and are incapable of being communiated to others in equal measure.

But it is only from the *practical* point of view ıat a *theoretically* insufficient judgement can e termed belief. Now the practical reference is ither to *skill* or to *morality;* to the former, hen the end proposed is arbitrary and accidenal, to the latter, when it is absolutely necessary.

If we propose to ourselves any end whatever, he conditions of its attainment are hypothetially necessary. The necessity is subjectively, but till only comparatively, sufficient, if I am acuainted with no other conditions under which he end can be attained. On the other hand, it is sufficient, absolutely and for every one, if I know for certain that no one can be acquainted with any other conditions under which the attainment of the proposed end would be possible. In the former case my supposition—my judgement with regard to certain conditions—is a merely accidental belief; in the latter it is a necessary belief. The physician must pursue some course in the case of a patient who is in danger, but is ignorant of the nature of the disease. He observes the symptoms, and concludes, according to the best of his judgement, that it is a case of phthisis. His belief is, even in his own judgement, only contingent: another man might, perhaps come nearer the truth. Such a belief, contingent indeed, but still forming the ground of the actual use of means for the attainment of certain ends, I term *pragmatical belief.*

The usual test, whether that which any one maintains is merely his persuasion, or his subjective conviction at least, that is, his firm belief, is a *bet.* It frequently happens that a man delivers his opinions with so much boldness and assurance, that he appears to be under no apprehension as to the possibility of his being in error. The offer of a bet startles him, and makes him pause. Sometimes it turns out that his persuasion may be valued at a ducat, but not at ten. For he does not hesitate, perhaps, to venture a ducat, but if it is proposed to stake ten, he immediately becomes aware of the possibility of his being mistaken—a possibility which has hitherto escaped his observation. If we imagine to ourselves that we have to stake the happiness of our whole life on the truth of any proposition, our judgement drops its air of triumph, we take the alarm, and discover the actual strength of our belief. Thus pragmatical belief has degrees, varying in proportion to the interests at stake.

Now, in cases where we cannot enter upon any course of action in reference to some object, and where, accordingly, our judgement is purely theoretical, we can still represent to ourselves, in thought, the possibility of a course of action, for which we suppose that we have sufficient grounds, if any means existed of ascertaining the truth of the matter. Thus we find in purely theoretical judgements an *analogon* of practical judgements, to which the word *belief* may properly be applied, and which we may term *doctrinal belief.* I should not hesitate to stake my all on the truth of the proposition — if there were any possibility of bringing it to the test of experience—that, at least, some one of the planets, which we see, is inhabited. Hence I say that I have not merely the opinion, but the strong belief, on the correctness of which I would stake even many of the advantages of life, that there are inhabitants in other worlds.

Now we must admit that the doctrine of the existence of God belongs to doctrinal belief. For, although in respect to the theoretical cognition of the universe I do not require to form any theory which necessarily involves this idea, as the condition of my explanation of the phenomena which the universe presents, but, on the contrary, am rather bound so to use my reason as if everything were mere nature, still teleological unity is so important a condition of the application of my reason to nature, that it is impossible for me to ignore it—especially since, in addition to these considerations, abundant examples of it are supplied by experience. But the sole condition, so far as my knowledge extends, under which this unity can be my guide in the investigation of nature, is the assumption that a supreme intelligence has ordered all things according to the wisest ends. Consequently, the hypothesis of a wise author of the universe is necessary for my guidance in the investigation of nature—is the condition under which alone I can fulfil an end which is contingent indeed, but by no means unimportant. Moreover, since the result of my attempts so frequently confirms the utility of this assumption, and since nothing decisive can be adduced against it, it follows that it would be saying far too little to term my judgement, in this case, a mere opinion, and that, even in this theoretical connection, I may assert that I firmly believe in God. Still, if we use words strictly, this must not be called a practical, but a doctrinal belief, which the theology of nature (physico-theology) must also produce in my mind. In the wisdom of a Supreme Being, and in the shortness of life, so inadequate to the development of the glorious powers of human nature, we may find equally sufficient grounds for a doctrinal belief in the future life of the human soul.

The expression of belief is, in such cases, an expression of modesty from the *objective* point of view, but, at the same time, of firm confidence, from the *subjective*. If I should venture to term this merely theoretical judgement even so much as a hypothesis which I am entitled to assume; a more complete conception, with regard to another world and to the cause of the world, might then be justly required of me than I am, in reality, able to give. For, if I assume anything, even as a mere hypothesis, I must, at least, know so much of the properties of *such* a being as will enable me, not to form the *conception*, but to imagine the *existence* of it. But the word *belief* refers only to the guidance which an idea gives me, and to its subjective influence on the conduct of my reason, which forces me to hold it fast, though I may not be in a position to give a speculative account of it.

But mere doctrinal belief is, to some extent, wanting in stability. We often quit our hold of it, in consequence of the difficulties which occur in speculation, though in the end we inevitably return to it again.

It is quite otherwise with *moral belief*. For in this sphere action is absolutely necessary, that is, I must act in obedience to the moral law in all points. The end is here incontrovertibly established, and there is only one condition possible, according to the best of my perception, under which this end can harmonize with all other ends, and so have practical validity—namely, the existence of a God and of a future world. I know also, to a certainty, that no one can be acquainted with any other conditions which conduct to the same unity of ends under the moral law. But since the moral precept is, at the same time, my maxim (as reason requires that it should be), I am irresistibly constrained to believe in the existence of God and in a future life; and I am sure that nothing can make me waver in this belief, since I should thereby overthrow my moral maxims, the renunciation of which would render me hateful in my own eyes.

Thus, while all the ambitious attempts of reason to penetrate beyond the limits of experience end in disappointment, there is still enough left to satisfy us in a practical point of view. No one, it is true, will be able to boast that he knows that there is a God and a future life; for, if he knows this, he is just the man whom I have long wished to find. All knowledge, regarding an object of mere reason, can be communicated; and I should thus be enabled to hope that my own knowledge would receive this wonderful extension, through the instrumentality of his instruction. No, my conviction is not *logical*, but *moral* certainty; and since it rests on subjective grounds (of the moral sentiment), I must not even say: *It is* morally certain that there is a God, etc. but: *I am* morally certain, that is, my belief in God and in another world is so interwoven with my moral nature that I am under as little apprehension of having the former torn from me as of losing the latter.

The only point in this argument that may appear open to suspicion is that this rational belief presupposes the existence of moral sentiments. If we give up this assumption, and take a man who is entirely indifferent with regard to moral laws, the question which reason proposes, becomes then merely a problem for speculation and may, indeed, be supported by strong grounds from analogy, but not by such as will compel the most obstinate scepticism to give way.[1] But in these questions no man is free from all interest. For though the want of good sentiments may place him beyond the influence of moral interests, still even in this case enough may be left to make him *fear* the existence of God and a future life. For he cannot pretend to any *certainty* of the non-existence of God and of a future life, unless—since it could only be proved by mere reason, and therefore apodeictically—he is prepared to establish the *impossibility* of both, which certainly no reasonable man would undertake to do. This would be a *negative* belief, which could not, indeed, produce morality and good sentiments, but still could produce an analogon of these, by operating as a powerful restraint on the outbreak of evil dispositions.

But, it will be said, is this all that pure reason can effect, in opening up prospects beyond the limits of experience? Nothing more than two articles of belief? Common sense could have done as much as this, without taking the philosophers to counsel in the matter!

I shall not here eulogize philosophy for the benefits which the laborious efforts of its criticism have conferred on human reason—even granting that its merit should turn out in the end to be only negative—for on this point something more will be said in the next section. But, I ask, do you require that that knowledge which concerns all men, should transcend the common understanding, and should only be revealed to you by philosophers? The very circumstance which has called forth your censure, is the best confirmation of the correctness of our previous assertions, since it discloses, what could not have been foreseen, that Nature is not chargeable with any partial distribution of her gifts in those matters which concern all men without distinction and that, in respect to the essential ends of human nature, we cannot advance further with the help of the highest philosophy, than under the guidance which nature has vouchsafed to the meanest understanding.

[1] The human mind (as, I believe, every rational being must of necessity do) takes a natural interest in morality, although this interest is not undivided, and may not be practically in preponderance. If you strengthen and increase it, you will find the reason become docile, more enlightened, and more capable of uniting the speculative interest with the practical. But if you do not take care at the outset, or at least midway, to make men good, you will never force them into an honest belief.

CHAPTER III. *The Architectonic of Pure Reason*

By the term *architectonic* I mean the art of constructing a system. Without systematic unity, our knowledge cannot become science; it will be an aggregate, and not a system. Thus architectonic is the doctrine of the scientific in cognition, and therefore necessarily forms part of our methodology.

Reason cannot permit our knowledge to remain in an unconnected and rhapsodistic state, but requires that the sum of our cognitions should constitute a system. It is thus alone that they can advance the ends of reason. By a *system* I mean the unity of various cognitions under one idea. This idea is the conception—given by reason—of the form of a whole, in so far as the conception determines *a priori* not only the limits of its content, but the place which each of its parts is to occupy. The scientific idea contains, therefore, the end and the form of the whole which is in accordance with that end. The unity of the end, to which all the parts of the system relate, and through which all have a relation to each other, communicates unity to the whole system, so that the absence of any part can be immediately detected from our knowledge of the rest; and it determines *a priori* the limits of the system, thus excluding all contingent or arbitrary additions. The whole is thus an organism (*articulatio*), and not an aggregate (*coacervatio*); it may grow from within (*per intussusceptionem*), but it cannot increase by external additions (*per appositionem*). It is, thus, like an animal body, the growth of which does not add any limb, but, without changing their proportions, makes each in its sphere stronger and more active.

We require, for the execution of the idea of a system, a *schema,* that is, a content and an arrangement of parts determined *a priori* by the principle which the aim of the system prescribes. A schema which is not projected in accordance with an idea, that is, from the standpoint of the highest aim of reason, but merely empirically, in accordance with accidental aims and purposes (the number of which cannot be predetermined), can give us nothing more than *technical* unity. But the schema which is originated from an idea (in which case reason presents us with aims *a priori,* and does not look for them to experience), forms the basis of *architectonical* unity. A science, in the proper acceptation of that term, cannot be formed *technically,* that is, from observation of the similarity existing between different objects, and the purely contingent use we make of our knowledge *in concreto* with reference to all kinds of arbitrary external aims; its constitution must be framed on architectonical principles, that is, its parts must be shown to possess an essential affinity, and be capable of being deduced from one supreme and internal aim or end, which forms the condition of the possibility of the scientific whole. The schema of a science must give *a priori* the plan of it (*monogramma*), and the division of the whole into parts, in conformity with the idea of the science; and it must also distinguish this whole from all others, according to certain understood principles.

No one will attempt to construct a science, unless he have some idea to rest on as a proper basis. But, in the elaboration of the science, he finds that the schema, nay, even the definition which he at first gave of the science, rarely corresponds with his idea; for this idea lies, like a germ, in our reason, its parts undeveloped and hid even from microscopical observation. For this reason, we ought to explain and define sciences, not according to the description which the originator gives of them, but according to the idea which we find based in reason itself, and which is suggested by the natural unity of the parts of the science already accumulated. For it will often be found that the originator of a science and even his latest successors remain attached to an erroneous idea, which they cannot render clear to themselves, and that they thus fail in determining the true content, the articulation or systematic unity, and the limits of their science.

It is unfortunate that, only after having occupied ourselves for a long time in the collection of materials, under the guidance of an idea which lies undeveloped in the mind, but not according to any definite plan of arrangement—nay, only after we have spent much time and labour in the technical disposition of our materials, does it become possible to view the idea of a science in a clear light, and to project, according to architectonical principles, a plan of the whole, in accordance with the aims of reason. Systems seem, like certain worms, to be formed by a kind of *generatio aequivoca*—by the mere confluence of conceptions, and to gain completeness only with the progress of time. But the schema or germ of all lies in reason; and thus is not only every system organized according to its own idea, but all are united into one grand system of human knowledge, of which they form members. For this reason, it is possible to frame an architectonic of all human cognition, the formation of which, at the present time, considering the immense materials collected or to be found in the ruins of old systems, would not indeed be very difficult. Our purpose at present is merely to sketch the plan of the *architectonic* of all cognition given by *pure reason;* and we begin from the point where the main root of human knowledge divides into two, one of which is *reason.* By *reason* I understand here the whole higher faculty of cognition, the *rational* being placed in contradistinction to the *empirical.*

If I make complete abstraction of the content of cognition, objectively considered, all cognition is, from a subjective point of view, either historical or rational. Historical cognition is *cognitio ex datis,* rational, *cognitio ex principiis.* Whatever may be the original source of a cognition, it is, in relation to the person who possesses it, merely historical, if he knows only what has been given him from another quarter, whether that knowledge was communicated by direct experience or by instruction. Thus the person who has *learned* a system of philosophy—say the Wolfian—although he has a perfect knowledge of all the principles, definitions, and arguments in that philosophy, as well as of the divisions that have been made of the system, possesses really no more than an *historical* knowledge of the Wolfian system; he knows only what has been told him, his judgements are only those which he has received from his teachers. Dispute the validity of a definition, and he is completely at a loss to find another. He has formed his mind on another's; but the imitative faculty is not the productive. His knowledge has not been drawn from reason; and although, objectively considered, it is rational knowledge, subjectively, it is merely historical. He has learned this or that philosophy and is merely a plaster-cast of a living man. Rational cognitions which are objective, that is, which have their source in reason, can be so termed from a subjective point of view, only when they have been drawn by the individual himself from the sources of reason, that is, from principles; and it is in this way alone that criticism, or even the rejection of what has been already learned, can spring up in the mind.

All rational cognition is, again, based either on conceptions, or on the construction of conceptions. The former is termed *philosophical,* the latter *mathematical.* I have already shown the essential difference of these two methods of cognition in the first chapter. A cognition may be objectively philosophical and subjectively historical—as is the case with the majority of scholars and those who cannot look beyond the limits of their system, and who remain in a state of pupilage all their lives. But it is remarkable that mathematical knowledge, when committed to memory, is valid, from the subjective point of view, as rational knowledge also, and that the same distinction cannot be drawn here as in the case of philosophical cognition. The reason is that the only way of arriving at this knowledge is through the essential principles of reason, and thus it is always certain and indisputable; because reason is employed *in concreto*—but at the same time *a priori*—that is, in pure and, therefore, infallible intuition; and thus all causes of illusion and error are excluded. Of all the *a priori* sciences of reason, therefore, mathematics alone can be learned. Philosophy—unless it be in an historical manner—cannot be learned; we can at most learn to *philosophize.*

Philosophy is the system of all philosophical cognition. We must use this term in an objective sense, if we understand by it the archetype of all attempts at philosophizing, and the standard by which all subjective philosophies are to be judged. In this sense, philosophy is merely the idea of a possible science, which does not exist *in concreto,* but to which we endeavour in various ways to approximate, until we have discovered the right path to pursue—a path overgrown by the errors and illusions of sense—and the image we have hitherto tried in vain to shape has become a perfect copy of the great prototype. Until that time, we cannot learn philosophy—it does not exist; if it does, where is it, who possesses it, and how shall we know it? We can only learn to philosophize; in other words, we can only exercise our powers of reasoning in accordance with general principles, retaining at the same time, the right of investigating the sources of these principles, of testing, and even of rejecting them.

Until then, our conception of philosophy is only a *scholastic conception*—a conception, that is, of a system of cognition which we are trying to elaborate into a science; all that we at present know being the systematic unity of this cognition, and consequently the *logical* completeness of the cognition for the desired end. But there is also a *cosmical conception* (*conceptus cosmicus*) of philosophy, which has always formed the true basis of this term, especially when philosophy was personified and presented to us in the ideal of a *philosopher*. In this view, philosophy is the science of the relation of all cognition to the ultimate and essential aims of human reason *(teleologia rationis humanae),* and the philosopher is not merely an artist—who occupies himself with conceptions—but a lawgiver, legislating for human reason. In this sense of the word, it would be in the highest degree arrogant to assume the title of philosopher, and to pretend that we had reached the perfection of the prototype which lies in the idea alone.

The mathematician, the natural philosopher, and the logician—how far soever the first may have advanced in rational, and the two latter in philosophical knowledge—are merely artists, engaged in the arrangement and formation of conceptions; they cannot be termed philosophers. Above them all, there is the ideal teacher, who employs them as instruments for the advancement of the essential aims of human reason. Him alone can we call philosopher; but he nowhere exists. But the idea of his legislative power resides in the mind of every man, and it alone teaches us what kind of systematic unity philosophy demands in view of the ultimate aims of reason. This idea is, therefore, a cosmical conception.[1]

In view of the complete systematic unity of reason, there can only be one ultimate end of all the operations of the mind. To this all other aims are subordinate, and nothing more than means for its attainment. This ultimate end is the destination of man, and the philosophy which relates to it is termed moral philosophy. The superior position occupied by moral philosophy, above all other spheres for the operations of reason, sufficiently indicates the reason why the ancients always included the idea—and in an especial manner—of moralist in that of philosopher. Even at the present day, we call a man who appears to have the power of self-government, even although his knowledge may be very limited, by the name of philosopher.

The legislation of human reason, or philosophy, has two objects—nature and freedom—and thus contains not only the laws of nature, but also those of ethics, at first in two separate systems, which, finally, merge into one grand philosophical system of cognition. The philosophy of nature relates to that *which is,* that of ethics to that which *ought to be.*

But all philosophy is either cognition on the basis of pure reason, or the cognition of reason

[1] By a *cosmical conception,* I mean one in which all men necessarily take an interest; the *aim* of a science must accordingly be determined according to *scholastic conceptions,* if it is regarded merely as a means to certain arbitrarily proposed ends.

on the basis of empirical principles. The former is termed *pure,* the latter *empirical* philosophy.

The philosophy of pure reason is either *propaedeutic,* that is, an inquiry into the powers of reason in regard to pure *a priori* cognition, and is termed *critical philosophy;* or it is, secondly, the system of pure reason—a science containing the systematic presentation of the whole body of philosophical knowledge, true as well as illusory, given by pure reason—and is called *metaphysic.* This name may, however, be also given to the whole system of pure philosophy, critical philosophy included, and may designate the investigation into the sources or possibility of *a priori* cognition, as well as the presentation of the *a priori* cognitions which form a system of pure philosophy—excluding, at the same time, all empirical and mathematical elements.

Metaphysic is divided into that of the *speculative* and that of the *practical* use of pure reason, and is, accordingly, either the *metaphysic of nature,* or the *metaphysic of ethics.* The former contains all the pure rational principles—based upon conceptions alone (and thus excluding mathematics)—of all *theoretical* cognition; the latter, the principles which determine and necessitate *a priori* all *action.* Now moral philosophy alone contains a code of laws—for the regulation of our actions—which are deduced from principles entirely *a priori.* Hence the metaphysic of ethics is the only pure moral philosophy, as it is not based upon anthropological or other empirical considerations. The metaphysic of speculative reason is what is commonly called *metaphysic* in the more limited sense. But as pure moral philosophy properly forms a part of this system of cognition, we must allow it to retain the name of *metaphysic,* although it is not requisite that we should insist on so terming it in our present discussion.

It is of the highest importance to separate those cognitions which differ from others both in kind and in origin, and to take great care that they are not confounded with those with which they are generally found connected. What the chemist does in the analysis of substances, what the mathematician in pure mathematics, is, in a still higher degree, the duty of the philosopher, that the value of each different kind of cognition, and the part it takes in the operations of the mind, may be clearly defined. Human reason has never wanted a metaphysic of some kind, since it attained the power of thought, or rather of reflection; but it has never been able to keep this sphere of thought and cognition pure from all admixture of foreign elements. The idea of a science of this kind is as old as speculation itself; and what mind does not speculate—either in the scholastic or in the popular fashion? At the same time, it must be admitted that even thinkers by profession have been unable clearly to explain the distinction between the two elements of our cognition—the one completely *a priori,* the other *a posteriori;* and hence the proper definition of a peculiar kind of cognition, and with it the just idea of a science which has so long and so deeply engaged the attention of the human mind, has never been established. When it was said: "Metaphysic is the science of the first principles of human cognition," this definition did not signalize a peculiarity in kind, but only a difference in degree; these first principles were thus declared to be more general than others, but no criterion of distinction from empirical principles was given. Of these some are more general, and therefore higher, than others; and—as we cannot distinguish what is completely *a priori* from that which is known to be *a posteriori*—where shall we draw the line which is to separate the higher and so-called first principles, from the lower and subordinate principles of cognition? What would be said if we were asked to be satisfied with a division of the epochs of the world into the earlier centuries and those following them? "Does the fifth, or the tenth century belong to the earlier centuries?" it would be asked. In the same way I ask: Does the conception of extension belong to metaphysics? You answer, "Yes." Well, that of body too? "Yes." And that of a fluid body? You stop, you are unprepared to admit this; for if you do, everything will belong to metaphysics. From this it is evident that the mere degree of subordination—of the particular to the general—cannot determine the limits of a science; and that, in the present case, we must expect to find a difference in the conceptions of metaphysics both in kind and in origin. The fundamental idea of metaphysics was obscured on another side by the fact that this kind of *a priori* cognition showed a certain similarity in character with the science of mathematics. Both have the property in common of possessing an *a priori* origin; but, in the one, our knowledge is based upon conceptions, in the other, on the construction of conceptions. Thus a decided dissimilarity between philosophical and mathematical cognition comes out—a dissimilarity which was always felt, but which could not be made distinct for want of an insight into the criteria of the difference. And thus it happened that, as philosophers themselves failed in the proper development of the idea of their science, the elaboration of the science could not proceed with a definite aim, or under trustworthy guidance. Thus, too, philosophers, ignorant of the path they ought to pursue and always disputing with each other regarding the discoveries which each asserted he had made, brought their science into disrepute with the rest of the world, and finally, even among themselves.

All pure *a priori* cognition forms, therefore, in view of the peculiar faculty which originates it, a peculiar and distinct unity; and metaphysic is the term applied to the philosophy which attempts to represent that cognition in this systematic unity. The speculative part of metaphysic, which has especially appropriated this appellation—that which we have called the *metaphysic* of *nature*—and which considers everything, as it is (not as it ought to be), by means of *a priori* conceptions, is divided in the following manner.

Metaphysic, in the more limited acceptation of the term, consists of two parts—*transcendental philosophy* and the *physiology* of pure reason. The former presents the system of all the conceptions and principles belonging to the understanding and the reason, and which relate to objects in general, but not to any particular given objects (*Ontologia*); the latter has *nature* for its subject-matter, that is, the sum of given objects—whether given to the senses, or, if we will, to some other kind of intuition—and is accordingly *physiology*, although only *rationalis*. But the use of the faculty of reason in this rational mode of regarding nature is either physical or hyperphysical, or, more properly speaking, *immanent* or *transcendent*. The former relates to nature, in so far as our knowledge regarding it may be applied in experience (*in concreto*); the latter to that connection of the objects of experience, which transcends all experience. *Transcendent physiology* has, again, an *internal* and an *external* connection with its object, both, however, transcending possible experience; the former is the physiology of nature as a whole, or *transcendental cognition of the world*, the latter of the connection of the whole of nature with a being above nature, or transcendental *cognition of God*.

Immanent physiology, on the contrary, considers nature as the sum of all sensuous objects, consequently, as it is presented to us—but still according to *a priori* conditions, for it is under these alone that nature can be presented to our minds at all. The objects of immanent physiology are of two kinds: 1. Those of the external senses, or *corporeal nature;* 2. The object of the internal sense, the soul, or, in accordance with our fundamental conceptions of it, *thinking nature.* The metaphysics of corporeal nature is called *physics;* but, as it must contain only the principles of an *a priori* cognition of nature, we must term it *rational physics.* The metaphysics of thinking nature is called *psychology,* and for the same reason is to be regarded as merely the *rational cognition* of the soul.

Thus the whole system of metaphysics consists of four principal parts: I. *Ontology;* 2. *Rational physiology;* 3. *Rational cosmology;* and 4. *Rational theology.* The second part—that of the rational doctrine of nature—may be subdivided into two, *physica rationalis*[1] and *psychologia rationalis.*

The fundamental idea of a philosophy of pure reason of necessity dictates this division; it is, therefore, *architectonical*—in accordance with the highest aims of reason, and not merely *technical,* or according to certain accidentally-observed similarities existing between the different parts of the whole science. For this reason, also, is the division immutable and of legislative authority. But the reader may observe in it a few points to which he ought to demur, and which may weaken his conviction of its truth and legitimacy.

In the first place, how can I desire an *a priori* cognition or metaphysic of objects, in so far as they are given *a posteriori?* and how is it possible to cognize the nature of things according to *a priori* principles, and to attain to a *rational* physiology? The answer is this. We take from experience nothing more than is requisite to present us with an object (in general) of the external or of the internal sense; in the former case, by the mere conception of matter (impenetrable and inanimate extension), in the latter, by the conception of a thinking being—given in the internal empirical representation, *I think.* As to the rest, we must not employ in our metaphysic of these objects any empirical principles (which add to the content of our conceptions by means of experience), for the purpose of forming by

[1] It must not be supposed that I mean by this appellation what is generally called *physica generalis,* and which is rather mathematics than a philosophy of nature. For the metaphysic of nature is completely different from mathematics, nor is it so rich in results, although it is of great importance as a critical test of the application of pure understanding-cognition to nature. For want of its guidance, even mathematicians, adopting certain common notions—which are, in fact, metaphysical—have unconsciously crowded their theories of nature with hypotheses, the fallacy of which becomes evident upon the application of the principles of this metaphysic, without detriment, however, to the employment of mathematics in this sphere of cognition.

their help any judgements respecting these objects.

Secondly, what place shall we assign to *empirical psychology,* which has always been considered a part of metaphysics, and from which in our time such important philosophical results have been expected, after the hope of constructing an *a priori* system of knowledge had been abandoned? I answer: It must be placed by the side of empirical physics or physics proper; that is, must be regarded as forming a part of *applied* philosophy, the *a priori* principles of which are contained in pure philosophy, which is therefore connected, although it must not be confounded, with psychology. Empirical psychology must therefore be banished from the sphere of metaphysics, and is indeed excluded by the very idea of that science. In conformity, however, with scholastic usage, we must permit it to occupy a place in metaphysics—but only as an appendix to it. We adopt this course from motives of economy; as psychology is not as yet full enough to occupy our attention as an independent study, while it is, at the same time, of too great importance to be entirely excluded or placed where it has still less affinity than it has with the subject of metaphysics. It is a stranger who has been long a guest; and we make it welcome to stay, until it can take up a more suitable abode in a complete system of anthropology—the pendant to empirical physics.

The above is the general idea of metaphysics, which, as more was expected from it than could be looked for with justice, and as these pleasant expectations were unfortunately never realized, fell into general disrepute. Our *Critique* must have fully convinced the reader that, although metaphysics cannot form the foundation of religion, it must always be one of its most important bulwarks, and that human reason, which naturally pursues a dialectical course, cannot do without this science, which checks its tendencies towards dialectic and, by elevating reason to a scientific and clear self-knowledge, prevents the ravages which a lawless speculative reason would infallibly commit in the sphere of morals as well as in that of religion. We may be sure, therefore, whatever contempt may be thrown upon metaphysics by those who judge a science not by its own nature, but according to the accidental effects it may have produced, that it can never be completely abandoned, that we must always return to it as to a beloved one who has been for a time estranged, because the questions with which it is engaged relate to the highest aims of humanity, and reason must always labour either to attain to settled views in regard to these, or to destroy those which others have already established.

Metaphysic, therefore—that of nature, as well as that of ethics, but in an especial manner the criticism which forms the propaedeutic to all the operations of reason—forms properly that department of knowledge which may be termed, in the truest sense of the word, *philosophy*. The path which it pursues is that of science, which, when it has once been discovered, is never lost, and never misleads. Mathematics, natural science, the common experience of men, have a high value as means, for the most part, to accidental ends—but at last also, to those which are necessary and essential to the existence of humanity. But to guide them to this high goal, they require the aid of rational cognition on the basis of pure conceptions, which, be it termed as it may, is properly nothing but metaphysics.

For the same reason, metaphysics forms likewise the completion of the *culture* of human reason. In this respect, it is indispensable, setting aside altogether the influence which it exerts as a science. For its subject-matter is the elements and highest maxims of reason, which form the basis of the *possibility* of some sciences and of the *use* of all. That, as a purely speculative science, it is more useful in preventing error than in the extension of knowledge, does not detract from its value; on the contrary, the supreme office of censor which it occupies assures to it the highest authority and importance. This office it administers for the purpose of securing order, harmony, and well-being to science, and of directing its noble and fruitful labours to the highest possible aim—the happiness of all mankind.

CHAPTER IV. *The History of Pure Reason*

THIS title is placed here merely for the purpose of designating a division of the system of pure reason of which I do not intend to treat at present. I shall content myself with casting a cursory glance, from a purely transcendental point of view—that of the nature of pure reason—on the labours of philosophers up to the present time. They have aimed at erecting an edifice of philosophy; but to my eye this edifice appears to be in a very ruinous condition.

It is very remarkable, although naturally it could not have been otherwise, that, in the infancy of philosophy, the study of the nature of God and the constitution of a future world formed the commencement, rather than the conclusion, as we should have it, of the speculative efforts of the human mind. However rude the religious conceptions generated by the remains of the old manners and customs of a less cultivated time, the intelligent classes were not thereby prevented from devoting themselves to free inquiry into the existence and nature of God; and they easily saw that there could be no surer way of pleasing the invisible ruler of the world, and of attaining to happiness in another world at least, than a good and honest course of life in this. Thus theology and morals formed the two chief motives, or rather the points of attraction in all abstract inquiries. But it was the former that especially occupied the attention of speculative reason, and which afterwards became so celebrated under the name of metaphysics.

I shall not at present indicate the periods of time at which the greatest changes in metaphysics took place, but shall merely give a hasty sketch of the different ideas which occasioned the most important revolutions in this sphere of thought. There are three different ends in relation to which these revolutions have taken place.

1. *In relation to the object* of the cognition of reason, philosophers may be divided into *sensualists* and *intellectualists*. Epicurus may be regarded as the head of the former, Plato of the latter. The distinction here signalized, subtle as it is, dates from the earliest times, and was long maintained. The former asserted that reality resides in sensuous objects alone, and that everything else is merely imaginary; the latter, that the senses are the parents of illusion and that truth is to be found in the understanding alone. The former did not deny to the conceptions of the understanding a certain kind of reality; but with them it was merely *logical*, with the others it was *mystical*. The former admitted *intellectual* conceptions, but declared that sensuous objects alone possessed real existence. The latter maintained that all real objects were *intelligible*, and believed that the pure understanding possessed a faculty of *intuition* apart from sense, which, in their opinion, served only to confuse the ideas of the understanding.

2. *In relation to the origin* of the pure cognitions of reason, we find one school maintaining that they are derived entirely from experience, and another that they have their origin in reason alone. Aristotle may be regarded as the head of the *empiricists*, and Plato of the *noologists*. Locke, the follower of Aristotle in modern times, and Leibnitz of Plato (although he cannot be said to have imitated him in his mysticism), have not been able to bring this question to a settled conclusion. The procedure of Epicurus in his sensual system, in which he always restricted his conclusions to the sphere of experience, was much more consequent than that of Aristotle and Locke. The latter especially, after having derived all the conceptions and principles of the mind from experience, goes so far, in the employment of these conceptions and principles, as to maintain that we can prove the existence of God and the immortality of the soul—both of them objects lying beyond the limits of possible experience—with the same force of demonstration as any mathematical proposition.

3. *In relation to method*. Method is procedure *according to principles*. We may divide the methods at present employed in the field of inquiry into the *naturalistic* and the *scientific*. The *naturalist* of pure reason lays it down as his principle that common reason, without the aid of science—which he calls sound reason, or common sense—can give a more satisfactory answer to the most important questions of metaphysics than speculation is able to do. He must maintain, therefore, that we can determine the content and circumference of the moon more certainly by the naked eye, than by the aid of mathematical reasoning. But this system is mere misology reduced to principles; and, what is the most absurd thing in this doctrine, the neglect of all scientific means is paraded as a *peculiar method* of extending our cognition. As regards those who are *naturalists* because they know no better, they are certainly not to be blamed. They follow common sense, without parading their ignorance as a method which is to teach us the wonderful secret, how we are to find the truth which lies at the bottom of the well of Democritus.

Quod sapio satis est mihi, non ego curo
Esse quod Arcesilas aerumnosique Solones. PERSIUS[1]

is their motto, under which they may lead a pleasant and praiseworthy life, without troubling themselves with science or troubling science with them.

As regards those who wish to pursue a *scientific* method, they have now the choice of following either the *dogmatical* or the *sceptical*, while they are bound never to desert the *systematic* mode of procedure. When I mention, in relation to the former, the celebrated Wolf, and as regards the latter, David Hume, I may leave,

[1] [*Satirae*, iii. 78-79. "What I know is enough for me; I don't care to be what Arcesilas was, and the wretched Solons."]

in accordance with my present intention, all others unnamed. The critical path alone is still open. If my reader has been kind and patient enough to accompany me on this hitherto untravelled route, he can now judge whether, if he and others will contribute their exertions towards making this narrow footpath a high road of thought, that which many centuries have failed to accomplish may not be executed before the close of the present—namely, to bring Reason to perfect contentment in regard to that which has always, but without permanent results, occupied her powers and engaged her ardent desire for knowledge.

CONTENTS

FUNDAMENTAL PRINCIPLES OF THE METAPHYSIC OF MORALS

PREFACE

ANCIENT Greek philosophy was divided into three sciences: physics, ethics, and logic. This division is perfectly suitable to the nature of the thing; and the only improvement that can be made in it is to add the principle on which it is based, so that we may both satisfy ourselves of its completeness, and also be able to determine correctly the necessary subdivisions.

All rational knowledge is either *material* or *formal:* the former considers some object, the latter is concerned only with the form of the understanding and of the reason itself, and with the universal laws of thought in general without distinction of its objects. Formal philosophy is called *logic.* Material philosophy, however, has to do with determinate objects and the laws to which they are subject, is again twofold; for these laws are either laws of *nature* or of *freedom.* The science of the former is *physics,* that of the latter, *ethics;* they are also called *natural philosophy* and *moral philosophy* respectively.

Logic cannot have any empirical part; that is, a part in which the universal and necessary laws of thought should rest on grounds taken from experience; otherwise it would not be logic, i.e., a canon for the understanding or the reason, valid for all thought, and capable of demonstration. Natural and moral philosophy, on the contrary, can each have their empirical part, since the former has to determine the laws of nature as an object of experience; the latter the laws of the human will, so far as it is affected by nature: the former, however, being laws according to which everything does happen; the latter, laws according to which everything ought to happen. Ethics, however, must also consider the conditions under which what ought to happen frequently does not.

We may call all philosophy *empirical,* so far as it is based on grounds of experience: on the other hand, that which delivers its doctrines from *a priori* principles alone we may call *pure* philosophy. When the latter is merely formal it is *logic;* if it is restricted to definite objects of the understanding it is *metaphysic.*

In this way there arises the idea of a twofold metaphysic—a *metaphysic of nature* and a *metaphysic of morals.* Physics will thus have an empirical and also a rational part. It is the same with Ethics; but here the empirical part might have the special name of *practical anthropology,* the name *morality* being appropriated to the rational part.

All trades, arts, and handiworks have gained by division of labour, namely, when, instead of one man doing everything, each confines himself to a certain kind of work distinct from others in the treatment it requires, so as to be able to perform it with greater facility and in the greatest perfection. Where the different kinds of work are not distinguished and divided, where everyone is a jack-of-all-trades, there manufactures remain still in the greatest barbarism. It might deserve to be considered whether pure philosophy in all its parts does not require a man specially devoted to it, and whether it would not be better for the whole business of science if those who, to please the tastes of the public, are wont to blend the rational and empirical elements together, mixed in all sorts of proportions unknown to themselves, and who call themselves independent thinkers, giving the name of *minute philosophers* to those who apply themselves to the rational part only—if these, I say, were warned not to carry on two employments together which differ widely in the treatment they demand, for each of which perhaps a special talent is required, and the combination of which in one person only produces bunglers. But I only ask here whether the nature of science does not require that we should always carefully separate the empirical from the rational part, and prefix to Physics proper (or empirical physics) a metaphysic of nature, and to practical anthropology a metaphysic of morals, which must be carefully cleared of everything empirical, so that we may know how much can be accomplished by pure reason in both cases, and from what sources it draws this its *a priori* teaching, and that whether the latter inquiry is conducted by all moralists (whose name is legion), or only by some who feel a calling thereto.

As my concern here is with moral philosophy, I limit the question suggested to this: Whether it is not of the utmost necessity to construct a pure moral philosophy, perfectly cleared of everything which is only empirical and which belongs to anthropology? for that such a philosophy must be possible is evident from the common idea of duty and of the moral laws. Everyone must admit that if a law is to have moral force, i.e., to be the basis of an obligation, it must carry with it absolute necessity; that, for example, the precept, "Thou shalt not lie," is not valid for men alone, as if other rational beings had no need to observe it; and so with all the other moral laws properly so called; that, therefore, the basis of obligation must not be sought in the nature of man, or in the circumstances in the world in which he is placed, but *a priori* simply in the conception of pure reason; and although any other precept which is founded on principles of mere experience may be in certain respects universal, yet in as far as it rests even in the least degree on an empirical basis, perhaps only as to a motive, such a precept, while it may be a practical rule, can never be called a moral law.

Thus not only are moral laws with their principles essentially distinguished from every other kind of practical knowledge in which there is anything empirical, but all moral philosophy rests wholly on its pure part. When applied to man, it does not borrow the least thing from the knowledge of man himself (anthropology), but gives laws *a priori* to him as a rational being. No doubt these laws require a judgement sharpened by experience, in order on the one hand to distinguish in what cases they are applicable, and on the other to procure for them access to the will of the man and effectual influence on conduct; since man is acted on by so many inclinations that, though capable of the idea of a practical pure reason, he is not so easily able to make it effective *in concreto* in his life.

A metaphysic of morals is therefore indispensably necessary, not merely for speculative reasons, in order to investigate the sources of the practical principles which are to be found *a priori* in our reason, but also because morals themselves are liable to all sorts of corruption, as long as we are without that clue and supreme canon by which to estimate them correctly. For in order that an action should be morally good, it is not enough that it *conform* to the moral law, but it must also be done for the sake of the law, otherwise that conformity is only very contingent and uncertain; since a principle which is not moral, although it may now and then produce actions conformable to the law, will also often produce actions which contradict it. Now it is only a pure philosophy that we can look for the moral law in its purity and genuineness (and, in a practical matter, this is of the utmost consequence): we must, therefore, begin with pure philosophy (metaphysic), and without it there cannot be any moral philosophy at all. That which mingles these pure principles with the empirical does not deserve the name of philosophy (for what distinguishes philosophy from common rational knowledge is that it treats in separate sciences what the latter only comprehends confusedly); much less does it deserve that of moral philosophy, since by this confusion it even spoils the purity of morals themselves, and counteracts its own end.

Let it not be thought, however, that what is here demanded is already extant in the propaedeutic prefixed by the celebrated Wolf to his moral philosophy, namely, his so-called *general practical philosophy,* and that, therefore, we have not to strike into an entirely new field. Just because it was to be a general practical philosophy, it has not taken into consideration a will of any particular kind—say one which should be determined solely from *a priori* principles without any empirical motives, and which we might call a pure will, but volition in general, with all the actions and conditions which belong to it in this general signification. By this it is distinguished from a metaphysic of morals, just as general logic, which treats of the acts and canons of thought *in general,* is distinguished from transcendental philosophy, which treats of the particular acts and canons of *pure* thought, i.e., that whose cognitions are altogether *a priori.* For the metaphysic of morals has to examine the idea and the principles of a possible *pure* will, and not the acts and conditions of human volition generally, which for the most part are drawn from psychology. It is true that moral laws and duty are spoken of in the general moral philosophy (contrary indeed to all fitness). But this is no objection, for in this respect also the authors of that science remain true to their idea of it; they do not distinguish the motives which are prescribed as such by reason alone altogether *a priori,* and which are properly moral, from the empirical motives which the understanding raises to general conceptions merely by comparison of experiences; but, without noticing the difference of their sources, and looking on them all as homogeneous, they consider only their greater or less amount. It is in this way they frame their notion of *obligation,* which, though anything but moral, is all that can be attained in a philosophy which passes no judgement at all on the *origin* of all possible practical concepts, whether they are *a priori,* or only *a posteriori.*

Intending to publish hereafter a metaphysic of morals, I issue in the first instance these fundamental principles. Indeed there is properly no other foundation for it than the *critical examination of a pure practical reason;* just as that of metaphysics is the critical examination of the pure speculative reason, already published. But in the first place the former is not so absolutely necessary as the latter, because in moral concerns human reason can easily be brought to a high degree of correctness and completeness, even in the commonest understanding, while on the contrary in its theoretic but pure use it is wholly dialectical; and in the second place if the critique of a pure practical reason is to be complete, it must be possible at the same time to show its identity with the speculative reason in a common principle, for it can ultimately be only one and the same reason which has to be distinguished merely in its application. I could not, however, bring it to such completeness here, without introducing considerations of a wholly different kind, which would be perplexing to the reader. On this account I have adopted the title of *Fundamental Principles of the Metaphysic of Morals* instead of that of a *Critical Examination of the pure practical reason.*

But in the third place, since a metaphysic of morals, in spite of the discouraging title, is yet capable of being presented in popular form, and one adapted to the common understanding, I find it useful to separate from it this preliminary treatise on its fundamental principles, in order that I may not hereafter have need to introduce these necessarily subtle discussions into a book of a more simple character.

The present treatise is, however, nothing more than the investigation and establishment of *the supreme principle of morality,* and this alone constitutes a study complete in itself and one which ought to be kept apart from every other moral investigation. No doubt my conclusions on this weighty question, which has hitherto been very unsatisfactorily examined, would receive much light from the application of the same principle to the whole system, and would be greatly confirmed by the adequacy which it exhibits throughout; but I must forego this advantage, which indeed would be after all more gratifying than useful, since the easy applicability of a principle and its apparent adequacy give no very certain proof of its soundness, but rather inspire a certain partiality, which prevents us from examining and estimating it strictly in itself and without regard to consequences.

I have adopted in this work the method which I think most suitable, proceeding analytically from common knowledge to the determination of its ultimate principle, and again descending synthetically from the examination of this principle and its sources to the common knowledge in which we find it employed. The division will, therefore, be as follows:

1 First section. Transition from the common rational knowledge of morality to the philosophical.

2 Second section. Transition from popular moral philosophy to the metaphysic of morals.

3 Third section. Final step from the metaphysic of morals to the critique of the pure practical reason.

FIRST SECTION

TRANSITION FROM THE COMMON RATIONAL KNOWLEDGE OF MORALITY TO THE PHILOSOPHICAL

NOTHING can possibly be conceived in the world, or even out of it, which can be called good, without qualification, except a good will. Intelligence, wit, judgement, and the other *talents* of the mind, however they may be named, or courage, resolution, perseverance, as qualities of temperament, are undoubtedly good and desirable in many respects; but these gifts of nature may also become extremely bad and mischievous if the will which is to make use of them, and which, therefore, constitutes what is called *character*, is not good. It is the same with the *gifts of fortune.* Power, riches, honour, even health, and the general well-being and contentment with one's condition which is called *happiness*, inspire pride, and often presumption, if there is not a good will to correct the influence of these on the mind, and with this also to rectify the whole principle of acting and adapt it to its end. The sight of a being who is not adorned with a single feature of a pure and good will, enjoying unbroken prosperity, can never give pleasure to an impartial rational spectator. Thus a good will appears to constitute the indispensable condition even of being worthy of happiness.

There are even some qualities which are of service to this good will itself and may facilitate its action, yet which have no intrinsic unconditional value, but always presuppose a good will, and this qualifies the esteem that we justly have for them and does not permit us to regard them as absolutely good. Moderation in the affections and passions, self-control, and calm deliberation are not only good in many respects, but even seem to constitute part of the intrinsic worth of the person; but they are far from deserving to be called good without qualification, although they have been so unconditionally praised by the ancients. For without the principles of a good will, they may become extremely bad, and the coolness of a villain not only makes him far more dangerous, but also directly makes him more abominable in our eyes than he would have been without it.

A good will is good not because of what it performs or effects, not by its aptness for the attainment of some proposed end, but simply by virtue of the volition; that is, it is good in itself, and considered by itself is to be esteemed much higher than all that can be brought about by it in favour of any inclination, nay even of the sum total of all inclinations. Even if it should happen that, owing to special disfavour of fortune, or the niggardly provision of a step-motherly nature, this will should wholly lack power to accomplish its purpose, if with its greatest efforts it should yet achieve nothing, and there should remain only the good will (not, to be sure, a mere wish, but the summoning of all means in our power), then, like a jewel, it would still shine by its own light, as a thing which has its whole value in itself. Its usefulness or fruitfulness can neither add nor take away anything from this value. It would be, as it were, only the setting to enable us to handle it the more conveniently in common commerce, or to attract to it the attention of those who are not yet connoisseurs, but not to recommend it to true connoisseurs, or to determine its value.

There is, however, something so strange in this idea of the absolute value of the mere will, in which no account is taken of its utility, that notwithstanding the thorough assent of even common reason to the idea, yet a suspicion must arise that it may perhaps really be the product of mere high-flown fancy, and that we may have misunderstood the purpose of nature in assigning reason as the governor of our will. Therefore we will examine this idea from this point of view.

In the physical constitution of an organized being, that is, a being adapted suitably to the purposes of life, we assume it as a fundamental principle that no organ for any purpose will be found but what is also the fittest and best adapted for that purpose. Now in a being which has reason and a will, if the proper object of nature were its *conservation*, its *welfare*, in a word, its *happiness*, then nature would have hit upon a very bad arrangement in selecting the reason of the creature to carry out this purpose. For all the actions which the creature has to perform with a view to this purpose, and the whole rule of its conduct, would be far more surely prescribed to it by instinct, and that end would have been attained thereby much more certainly than it ever can be by reason. Should reason have been communicated to this favoured creature over and above, it must only have served it to contemplate the happy constitution of its nature, to admire it, to congratulate itself thereon, and to feel thankful for it to the beneficent cause, but not that it should subject its desires to that weak and delusive guidance and meddle bunglingly with the purpose of nature. In a word, nature would have taken care that reason should not break forth into *practical exercise,* nor have the presumption, with its weak insight, to think out for itself the plan of happiness, and of the means of attaining it. Nature would not only have taken on herself the choice of the ends, but also of the means, and with wise foresight would have entrusted both to instinct.

And, in fact, we find that the more a cultivated reason applies itself with deliberate purpose to the enjoyment of life and happiness, so much the more does the man fail of true satisfaction. And from this circumstance there arises in many, if they are candid enough to confess it, a certain degree of *misology,* that is, hatred of reason, especially in the case of those who are most experienced in the use of it, because after calculating all the advantages they derive, I do not say from the invention of all the arts of common luxury, but even from the sciences (which seem to them to be after all only a luxury of the understanding), they find that they have, in fact, only brought more trouble on their shoulders, rather than gained in happiness; and they end by envying, rather than despising, the more common stamp of men who keep closer to the guidance of mere instinct and do not allow their reason much influence on their conduct. And this we must admit, that the judgement of those who would very much lower the lofty eulogies of the advantages which reason gives us in regard to the happiness and satisfaction of life, or who would even reduce them below zero, is by no means morose or ungrateful to the goodness with which the world is governed, but that there lies at the root of these judgements the idea that our existence has a different and far nobler end, for which, and not for happiness, reason is properly intended, and which must, therefore, be regarded as the supreme condition to which the private ends of man must, for the most part, be postponed.

For as reason is not competent to guide the will with certainty in regard to its objects and the satisfaction of all our wants (which it to some extent even multiplies), this being an end to which an implanted instinct would have led with much greater certainty; and since, nevertheless, reason is imparted to us as a practical faculty, i.e., as one which is to have influence on the *will,* therefore, admitting that nature generally in the distribution of her capacities has adapted the means to the end, its true destination must be to produce a *will,* not merely good as a *means* to something else, but *good in itself,* for which reason was absolutely necessary. This will then, though not indeed the sole and complete good, must be the supreme good and the condition of every other, even of the desire of happiness. Under these circumstances, there is nothing inconsistent with the wisdom of nature in the fact that the cultivation of the reason, which is requisite for the first and unconditional purpose, does in many ways interfere, at least in this life, with the attainment of the second, which is always conditional, namely, happiness. Nay, it may even reduce it to nothing, without nature thereby failing of her purpose. For reason recognizes the establishment of a good will as its highest practical destination, and in attaining this purpose is capable only of a satisfaction of its own proper kind, namely that from the attainment of an end, which end again is determined by reason only, notwithstanding that this may involve many a disappointment to the ends of inclination.

We have then to develop the notion of a will which deserves to be highly esteemed for itself and is good without a view to anything further, a notion which exists already in the sound natural understanding, requiring rather to be cleared up than to be taught, and which in estimating the value of our actions always takes the first place and constitutes the condition of all the rest. In order to do this, we will take the notion of duty, which includes that of a good will, although implying certain subjective restrictions and hindrances. These, however, far from concealing it, or rendering it unrecognizable, rather bring it out by contrast and make it shine forth so much the brighter.

I omit here all actions which are already recognized as inconsistent with duty, although they may be useful for this or that purpose, for with these the question whether they are done *from duty* cannot arise at all, since they even conflict with it. I also set aside those actions which really conform to duty, but to which men have *no* direct *inclination,* performing them because they are impelled thereto by some other inclination. For in this case we can readily distinguish whether the action which agrees with duty is done *from duty,* or from a selfish view. It is much harder to make this distinction when the action accords with duty and the subject has besides a *direct* inclination to it. For example, it is always a matter of duty that a dealer should not overcharge an inexperienced purchaser; and wherever there is much commerce the prudent tradesman does not overcharge, but keeps a fixed price for everyone, so that a child buys of him as well as any other. Men are thus *honestly* served; but this is not enough to make us believe that the tradesman has so acted from duty and from principles of honesty: his own advantage required it; it is out of the question in this case to suppose that he might besides have a direct inclination in favour of the buyers, so that, as it were, from love he should give no advantage to one over another. Accordingly the action was done neither from duty nor from direct inclination, but merely with a selfish view.

On the other hand, it is a duty to maintain one's life; and, in addition, everyone has also a direct inclination to do so. But on this account the often anxious care which most men take for it has no intrinsic worth, and their maxim has no moral import. They preserve their life *as duty requires,* no doubt, but not *because duty requires.* On the other hand, if adversity and hopeless sorrow have completely taken away the relish for life; if the unfortunate one, strong in mind, indignant at his fate rather than desponding or dejected, wishes for death, and yet preserves his life without loving it—not from inclination or fear, but from duty—then his maxim has a moral worth.

To be beneficent when we can is a duty; and besides this, there are many minds so sympathetically constituted that, without any other motive of vanity or self-interest, they find a pleasure in spreading joy around them and can take delight in the satisfaction of others so far as it is their own work. But I maintain that in such a case an action of this kind, however proper, however amiable it may be, has nevertheless no true moral worth, but is on a level with other inclinations, e.g., the inclination to honour, which, if it is happily directed to that which is in fact of public utility and accordant with duty and consequently honourable, deserves praise and encouragement, but not esteem. For the maxim lacks the moral import, namely, that such actions be done *from duty,* not from inclination. Put the case that the mind of that philanthropist were clouded by sorrow of his own, extinguishing all sympathy with the lot of others, and that, while he still has the power to benefit others in distress, he is not touched by their trouble because he is absorbed with his own; and now suppose that he tears himself out of this dead insensibility, and performs the action without any inclination to it, but simply from duty, then first has his action its genuine moral worth. Further still; if nature has put little sympathy in the heart of this or that man; if he, supposed to be an upright man, is by temperament cold and indifferent to the sufferings of others, perhaps because in respect of his own he is provided with the special gift of patience and fortitude and supposes, or even requires, that others should have the same—and such a man would certainly not be the meanest product of nature—but if nature had not specially framed him for a philanthropist, would he not still find in himself a source from whence to give himself a far higher worth than that of a good-natured temperament could be? Unquestionably. It is just in this that the moral worth of the character is brought out which is incomparably the highest of all, namely, that he is beneficent, not from inclination, but from duty.

To secure one's own happiness is a duty, at least indirectly; for discontent with one's condition, under a pressure of many anxieties and amidst unsatisfied wants, might easily become a great *temptation to transgression of duty.* But here again, without looking to duty, all men have already the strongest and most intimate inclination to happiness, because it is just in this idea that all inclinations are combined in one total. But the precept of happiness is often of such a sort that it greatly interferes with some inclinations, and yet a man cannot form any definite and certain conception of the sum of satisfaction of all of them which is called happiness. It is not then to be wondered at that a single inclination, definite both as to what it promises and as to the time within which it can be gratified, is often able to overcome such a fluctuating idea, and that a gouty patient, for instance, can choose to enjoy what he likes, and to suffer what he may, since, according to his calculation, on this occasion at least, he has not sacrificed the enjoyment of the present moment to a possibly mistaken expectation of a happiness which is supposed to be found in health. But even in this case, if the general desire for happiness did not influence his will, and supposing that in his particular case health was not a necessary element in this calculation, there yet remains in this, as in all other cases, this law, namely, that he should promote his happiness not from inclination but from duty, and by this would his conduct first acquire true moral worth.

It is in this manner, undoubtedly, that we are to understand those passages of Scripture also in which we are commanded to love our neighbour, even our enemy. For love, as an affection, cannot be commanded, but beneficence for duty's sake may; even though we are not impelled to it by any inclination—nay, are even repelled by a natural and unconquerable aversion. This is *practical* love and not *pathological*—a love which is seated in the will, and not in the propensions of sense—in principles of action and not of tender sympathy; and it is this love alone which can be commanded.

The second proposition is: That an action done from duty derives its moral worth, *not from the purpose* which is to be attained by it, but from the maxim by which it is determined, and therefore does not depend on the realization of the object of the action, but merely on the *principle of volition* by which the action has taken place, without regard to any object of desire. It is clear from what precedes that the purposes which we may have in view in our actions, or their effects regarded as ends and springs of the will, cannot give to actions any unconditional or moral worth. In what, then, can their worth lie, if it is not to consist in the will and in reference to its expected effect? It cannot lie anywhere but in the *principle of the will* without regard to the ends which can be attained by the action. For the will stands between its *a priori* principle, which is formal, and its *a posteriori* spring, which is material, as between two roads, and as it must be determined by something, it follows that it must be determined by the formal principle of volition when an action is done from duty, in which case every material principle has been withdrawn from it.

The third proposition, which is a consequence of the two preceding, I would express thus: *Duty is the necessity of acting from respect for the law.* I may have *inclination* for an object as the effect of my proposed action, but I cannot have *respect* for it, just for this reason, that it is an effect and not an energy of will. Similarly, I cannot have respect for inclination, whether my own or another's; I can at most, if my own, approve it; if another's, sometimes even love it; i.e., look on it as favourable to my own interest. It is only what is connected with my will as a principle, by no means as an effect—what does not subserve my inclination, but overpowers it, or at least in case of choice excludes it from its calculation—in other words, simply the law of itself, which can be an object of respect, and hence a command. Now an action done from duty must wholly exclude the influence of inclination and with it every object of the will, so that nothing remains which can determine the will except objectively the *law,* and subjectively *pure respect* for this practical law, and consequently the maxim[1] that I should follow this law even to the thwarting of all my inclinations.

Thus the moral worth of an action does not lie in the effect expected from it, nor in any principle of action which requires to borrow its motive from this expected effect. For all these effects—agreeableness of one's condition and even the promotion of the happiness of others—could have been also brought about by other causes, so that for this there would have been no need of the will of a rational being; whereas it is in this alone that the supreme and unconditional good can be found. The pre-eminent good which we call moral can therefore consist in nothing else than *the conception of law* in itself, *which certainly is only possible in a rational being,* in so far as this conception, and not the expected effect, determines the will. This is a good which is already present in the person who acts accordingly, and we have not to wait for it to appear first in the result.[2]

[1] A *maxim* is the subjective principle of volition. The objective principle (i.e., that which would also serve subjectively as a practical principle to all rational beings if reason had full power over the faculty of desire) is the practical *law*.

[2] It might be here objected to me that I take refuge behind the word *respect* in an obscure feeling, instead of giving a distinct solution of the question by a concept of the reason. But although respect is a feeling, it is not a feeling *received* through influence, but is *self-wrought* by a rational concept, and, therefore, is specifically distinct from all feelings of the former kind, which may be referred either to inclination or fear. What I recognise immediately as a law for me, I recognise with respect. This merely signifies the consciousness that my will is *subordinate* to a law, without the intervention of other influences on my sense. The immediate determination of the will by the law, and the consciousness of this, is called *respect,* so that this is regarded as an *effect* of the law on the subject, and not as the *cause* of it. Respect is properly the conception of a worth which thwarts my self-love. Accordingly it is something which is considered neither as an object of inclination nor of fear, although it has something analogous to both. The *object* of respect is the *law* only, and that the law which we impose on *ourselves* and yet recognise as necessary in itself. As a law, we are subjected to it without consulting self-love; as imposed by us on ourselves, it is a result of our will. In the former aspect it has an analogy to fear, in the latter to inclination. Respect for a person is properly only respect for the law

But what sort of law can that be, the conception of which must determine the will, even without paying any regard to the effect expected from it, in order that this will may be called good absolutely and without qualification? As I have deprived the will of every impulse which could arise to it from obedience to any law, there remains nothing but the universal conformity of its actions to law in general, which alone is to serve the will as a principle, i.e., I am never to act otherwise than so *that I could also will that my maxim should become a universal law.* Here, now, it is the simple conformity to law in general, without assuming any particular law applicable to certain actions, that serves the will as its principle and must so serve it, if duty is not to be a vain delusion and a chimerical notion. The common reason of men in its practical judgements perfectly coincides with this and always has in view the principle here suggested. Let the question be, for example: May I when in distress make a promise with the intention not to keep it? I readily distinguish here between the two significations which the question may have: Whether it is prudent, or whether it is right, to make a false promise? The former may undoubtedly often be the case. I see clearly indeed that it is not enough to extricate myself from a present difficulty by means of this subterfuge, but it must be well considered whether there may not hereafter spring from this lie much greater inconvenience than that from which I now free myself, and as, with all my supposed *cunning*, the consequences cannot be so easily foreseen but that credit once lost may be much more injurious to me than any mischief which I seek to avoid at present, it should be considered whether it would not be more *prudent* to act herein according to a universal maxim and to make it a habit to promise nothing except with the intention of keeping it. But it is soon clear to me that such a maxim will still only be based on the fear of consequences. Now it is a wholly different thing to be truthful from duty and to be so from apprehension of injurious consequences. In the first case, the very notion of the action already implies a law for me; in the second case, I must first look about elsewhere to see what results may be combined with it which would affect myself. For to deviate from the principle of duty is beyond all doubt wicked; but to be unfaithful to my maxim of prudence may often be very advantageous to me, although to abide by it is certainly safer. The shortest way, however, and an unerring one, to discover the answer to this question whether a lying promise is consistent with duty, is to ask myself, "Should I be content that my maxim (to extricate myself from difficulty by a false promise) should hold good as a universal law, for myself as well as for others? and should I be able to say to myself, "Every one may make a deceitful promise when he finds himself in a difficulty from which he cannot otherwise extricate himself?" Then I presently become aware that while I can will the lie, I can by no means will that lying should be a universal law. For with such a law there would be no promises at all, since it would be in vain to allege my intention in regard to my future actions to those who would not believe this allegation, or if they over hastily did so would pay me back in my own coin. Hence my maxim, as soon as it should be made a universal law, would necessarily destroy itself.

I do not, therefore, need any far-reaching penetration to discern what I have to do in order that my will may be morally good. Inexperienced in the course of the world, incapable of being prepared for all its contingencies, I only ask myself: Canst thou also will that thy maxim should be a universal law? If not, then it must be rejected, and that not because of a disadvantage accruing from it to myself or even to others, but because it cannot enter as a principle into a possible universal legislation, and reason extorts from me immediate respect for such legislation. I do not indeed as yet *discern* on what this respect is based (this the philosopher may inquire), but at least I understand this, that it is an estimation of the worth which far outweighs all worth of what is recommended by inclination, and that the necessity of acting from *pure* respect for the practical law is what constitutes duty, to which every other motive must give place, because it is the condition of a will being good *in itself*, and the worth of such a will is above everything.

Thus, then, without quitting the moral knowledge of common human reason, we have arrived at its principle. And although, no doubt, common men do not conceive it in such an abstract and universal form, yet they always have it really before their eyes and use it as the standard of their decision. Here it would be easy to show how, with this compass in hand,

---

(of honesty, etc.) of which he gives us an example. Since we also look on the improvement of our talents as a duty, we consider that we see in a person of talents, as it were, the *example of a law* (viz., to become like him in this by exercise), and this constitutes our respect. All so-called moral *interest* consists simply in *respect* for the law.

men are well able to distinguish, in every case that occurs, what is good, what bad, conformably to duty or inconsistent with it, if, without in the least teaching them anything new, we only, like Socrates, direct their attention to the principle they themselves employ; and that, therefore, we do not need science and philosophy to know what we should do to be honest and good, yea, even wise and virtuous. Indeed we might well have conjectured beforehand that the knowledge of what every man is bound to do, and therefore also to know, would be within the reach of every man, even the commonest. Here we cannot forbear admiration when we see how great an advantage the practical judgement has over the theoretical in the common understanding of men. In the latter, if common reason ventures to depart from the laws of experience and from the perceptions of the senses, it falls into mere inconceivabilities and self-contradictions, at least into a chaos of uncertainty, obscurity, and instability. But in the practical sphere it is just when the common understanding excludes all sensible springs from practical laws that its power of judgement begins to show itself to advantage. It then becomes even subtle, whether it be that it chicanes with its own conscience or with other claims respecting what is to be called right, or whether it desires for its own instruction to determine honestly the worth of actions; and, in the latter case, it may even have as good a hope of hitting the mark as any philosopher whatever can promise himself. Nay, it is almost more sure of doing so, because the philosopher cannot have any other principle, while he may easily perplex his judgement by a multitude of considerations foreign to the matter, and so turn aside from the right way. Would it not therefore be wiser in moral concerns to acquiesce in the judgement of common reason, or at most only to call in philosophy for the purpose of rendering the system of morals more complete and intelligible, and its rules more convenient for use (especially for disputation), but not so as to draw off the common understanding from its happy simplicity, or to bring it by means of philosophy into a new path of inquiry and instruction?

Innocence is indeed a glorious thing; only, on the other hand, it is very sad that it cannot well maintain itself and is easily seduced. On this account even wisdom—which otherwise consists more in conduct than in knowledge—yet has need of science, not in order to learn from it, but to secure for its precepts admission and permanence. Against all the commands of duty which reason represents to man as so deserving of respect, he feels in himself a powerful counterpoise in his wants and inclinations, the entire satisfaction of which he sums up under the name of happiness. Now reason issues its commands unyieldingly, without promising anything to the inclinations, and, as it were, with disregard and contempt for these claims, which are so impetuous, and at the same time so plausible, and which will not allow themselves to be suppressed by any command. Hence there arises a natural *dialectic,* i.e., a disposition, to argue against these strict laws of duty and to question their validity, or at least their purity and strictness; and, if possible, to make them more accordant with our wishes and inclinations, that is to say, to corrupt them at their very source, and entirely to destroy their worth—a thing which even common practical reason cannot ultimately call good.

Thus is the *common reason of man* compelled to go out of its sphere, and to take a step into the field of a *practical philosophy,* not to satisfy any speculative want (which never occurs to it as long as it is content to be mere sound reason), but even on practical grounds, in order to attain in it information and clear instruction respecting the source of its principle, and the correct determination of it in opposition to the maxims which are based on wants and inclinations, so that it may escape from the perplexity of opposite claims and not run the risk of losing all genuine moral principles through the equivocation into which it easily falls. Thus, when practical reason cultivates itself, there insensibly arises in it a dialetic which forces it to seek aid in philosophy, just as happens to it in its theoretic use; and in this case, therefore, as well as in the other, it will find rest nowhere but in a thorough critical examination of our reason.

SECOND SECTION

TRANSITION FROM POPULAR MORAL PHILOSOPHY TO THE METAPHYSIC OF MORALS

IF we have hitherto drawn our notion of duty from the common use of our practical reason, it is by no means to be inferred that we have treated it as an empirical notion. On the contrary, if we attend to the experience of men's conduct, we meet frequent and, as we ourselves allow, just complaints that one cannot find a single certain example of the disposition to act from pure duty. Although many things are done in *conformity* with what *duty* prescribes, it is nevertheless always doubtful whether they are done strictly *from duty,* so as to have a moral worth. Hence there have at all times been philosophers who have altogether denied that this disposition actually exists at all in human actions, and have ascribed everything to a more or less refined self-love. Not that they have on that account questioned the soundness of the conception of morality; on the contrary, they spoke with sincere regret of the frailty and corruption of human nature, which, though noble enough to take as its rule an idea so worthy of respect, is yet too weak to follow it and employs reason, which ought to give it the law only for the purpose of providing for the interest of the inclinations, whether singly or at the best in the greatest possible harmony with one another.

In fact, it is absolutely impossible to make out by experience with complete certainty a single case in which the maxim of an action, however right in itself, rested simply on moral grounds and on the conception of duty. Sometimes it happens that with the sharpest self-examination we can find nothing beside the moral principle of duty which could have been powerful enough to move us to this or that action and to so great a sacrifice; yet we cannot from this infer with certainty that it was not really some secret impulse of self-love, under the false appearance of duty, that was the actual determining cause of the will. We like them to flatter ourselves by falsely taking credit for a more noble motive; whereas in fact we can never, even by the strictest examination, get completely behind the secret springs of action; since, when the question is of moral worth, it is not with the actions which we see that we are concerned, but with those inward principles of them which we do not see.

Moreover, we cannot better serve the wishes of those who ridicule all morality as a mere chimera of human imagination overstepping itself from vanity, than by conceding to them that notions of duty must be drawn only from experience (as from indolence, people are ready to think is also the case with all other notions); for this is to prepare for them a certain triumph. I am willing to admit out of love of humanity that even most of our actions are correct, but if we look closer at them we everywhere come upon the dear self which is always prominent, and it is this they have in view and not the strict command of duty which would often require self-denial. Without being an enemy of virtue, a cool observer, one that does not mistake the wish for good, however lively, for its reality, may sometimes doubt whether true virtue is actually found anywhere in the world, and this especially as years increase and the judgement is partly made wiser by experience and partly, also, more acute in observation. This being so, nothing can secure us from falling away altogether from our ideas of duty, or maintain in the soul a well-grounded respect for its law, but the clear conviction that although there should never have been actions which really sprang from such pure sources, yet whether this or that takes place is not at all the question; but that reason of itself, independent on all experience, ordains what ought to take place, that accordingly actions of which perhaps the world has hitherto never given an example, the feasibility even of which might be very much doubted by one who founds everything on experience, are nevertheless inflexibly commanded by reason; that, e.g., even though there might never yet have been a sincere friend, yet not a whit the less is pure sincerity in friendship required of every man, because, prior to all experience, this duty is involved as duty in the idea of a reason determining the will by *a priori* principles.

When we add further that, unless we deny that the notion of morality has any truth or reference to any possible object, we must admit that its law must be valid, not merely for men but for all *rational creatures generally,* not merely under certain contingent conditions or with exceptions but *with absolute necessity,* then it is clear that no experience could enable us to infer even the possibility of such apodeictic laws. For with what right could we bring into unbounded respect as a universal precept for every rational nature that which perhaps holds only under the contingent conditions of humanity? Or how could laws of the determination of *our* will be regarded as laws of the determination of the will of rational beings generally, and for us only as such, if they were merely empirical and did not take their origin wholly *a priori* from pure but practical reason?

Nor could anything be more fatal to morality than that we should wish to derive it from examples. For every example of it that is set before me must be first itself tested by principles of morality, whether it is worthy to serve as an original example, i.e., as a pattern; but by no means can it authoritatively furnish the conception of morality. Even the Holy One of the Gospels must first be compared with our ideal of moral perfection before we can recognise Him as such; and so He says of Himself, "Why call ye Me (whom you see) good; none is good (the model of good) but God only (whom ye do not see)?" But whence have we the conception of God as the supreme good? Simply from the *idea* of moral perfection, which reason frames *a priori* and connects inseparably with the notion of a free will. Imitation finds no place at all in morality, and examples serve only for encouragement, i.e., they put beyond doubt the feasibility of what the law commands, they make visible that which the practical rule expresses more generally, but they can never authorize us to set aside the true original which lies in reason and to guide ourselves by examples.

If then there is no genuine supreme principle of morality but what must rest simply on pure reason, independent of all experience, I think it is not necessary even to put the question whether it is good to exhibit these concepts in their generality (*in abstracto*) as they are established *a priori* along with the principles belonging to them, if our knowledge is to be distinguished from the *vulgar* and to be called philosophical. In our times indeed this might perhaps be necessary; for if we collected votes whether pure rational knowledge separated from everything empirical, that is to say, metaphysic of morals, or whether popular practical philosophy is to be preferred, it is easy to guess which side would preponderate.

This descending to popular notions is certainly very commendable, if the ascent to the principles of pure reason has first taken place and been satisfactorily accomplished. This implies that we first *found* ethics on metaphysics, and then, when it is firmly established, procure a *hearing* for it by giving it a popular character. But it is quite absurd to try to be popular in the first inquiry, on which the soundness of the principles depends. It is not only that this proceeding can never lay claim to the very rare merit of a true *philosophical popularity,* since there is no art in being intelligible if one renounces all thoroughness of insight; but also it produces a disgusting medley of compiled observations and half-reasoned principles. Shallow pates enjoy this because it can be used for every-day chat, but the sagacious find in it only confusion, and being unsatisfied and unable to help themselves, they turn away their eyes, while philosophers, who see quite well through this delusion, are little listened to when they call men off for a time from this pretended popularity, in order that they might be rightfully popular after they have attained a definite insight.

We need only look at the attempts of moralists in that favourite fashion, and we shall find at one time the special constitution of human nature (including, however, the idea of a rational nature generally), at one time perfection, at another happiness, here moral sense, there fear of God, a little of this, and a little of that, in marvellous mixture, without its occurring to them to ask whether the principles of morality are to be sought in the knowledge of human nature at all (which we can have only from experience); or, if this is not so, if these principles are to be found altogether *a priori,* free from everything empirical, in pure rational concepts only and nowhere else, not even in the smallest degree; then rather to adopt the method of making this a separate inquiry, as pure practical philosophy, or (if one may use a name so decried) as metaphysic of morals,[1] to bring it by

[1] Just as pure mathematics are distinguished from applied, pure logic from applied, so if we choose we may also distinguish pure philosophy of morals (metaphysic) from applied (viz., applied to human nature). By this designation we are also at once reminded that moral principles are not based on properties of human

itself to completeness, and to require the public, which wishes for popular treatment, to await the issue of this undertaking.

Such a metaphysic of morals, completely isolated, not mixed with any anthropology, theology, physics, or hyperphysics, and still less with occult qualities (which we might call *hypophysical*), is not only an indispensable substratum of all sound theoretical knowledge of duties, but is at the same time a desideratum of the highest importance to the actual fulfilment of their precepts. For the pure conception of duty, unmixed with any foreign addition of empirical attractions, and, in a word, the conception of the moral law, exercises on the human heart, by way of reason alone (which first becomes aware with this that it can of itself be practical), an influence so much more powerful than all other springs[1] which may be derived from the field of experience, that, in the consciousness of its worth, it despises the latter, and can by degrees become their master; whereas a mixed ethics, compounded partly of motives drawn from feelings and inclinations, and partly also of conceptions of reason, must make the mind waver between motives which cannot be brought under any principle, which lead to good only by mere accident and very often also to evil.

From what has been said, it is clear that all moral conceptions have their seat and origin completely *a priori* in the reason, and that, moreover, in the commonest reason just as truly as in that which is in the highest degree speculative; that they cannot be obtained by abstraction from any empirical, and therefore merely contingent, knowledge; that it is just this purity of their origin that makes them worthy to serve as our supreme practical principle, and that just in proportion as we add anything empirical, we detract from their genuine influence and from the absolute value of actions; that it is not only of the greatest necessity, in a purely speculative point of view, but is also of the greatest practical importance, to derive these notions and laws from pure reason, to present them pure and unmixed, and even to determine the compass of this practical or pure rational knowledge, i.e., to determine the whole faculty of pure practical reason; and, in doing so, we must not make its principles dependent on the particular nature of human reason, though in speculative philosophy this may be permitted, or may even at times be necessary; but since moral laws ought to hold good for every rational creature, we must derive them from the general concept of a rational being. In this way, although for its *application* to man morality has need of anthropology, yet, in the first instance, we must treat it independently as pure philosophy, i.e., as metaphysic, complete in itself (a thing which in such distinct branches of science is easily done); knowing well that unless we are in possession of this, it would not only be vain to determine the moral element of duty in right actions for purposes of speculative criticism, but it would be impossible to base morals on their genuine principles, even for common practical purposes, especially of moral instruction, so as to produce pure moral dispositions, and to engraft them on men's minds to the promotion of the greatest possible good in the world.

But in order that in this study we may not merely advance by the natural steps from the common moral judgement (in this case very worthy of respect) to the philosophical, as has been already done, but also from a popular philosophy, which goes no further than it can reach by groping with the help of examples, to metaphysic (which does allow itself to be checked by anything empirical and, as it must measure the whole extent of this kind of rational knowledge, goes as far as ideal conceptions, where even examples fail us), we must follow and clearly describe the practical faculty of reason, from the general rules of its determination to the point where the notion of duty springs from it.

Everything in nature works according to laws. Rational beings alone have the faculty of acting according *to the conception* of laws, that is according to principles, i.e., have a *will*. Since the deduction of actions from principles requires *reason*, the will is nothing but practical

---

nature, but must subsist *a priori* of themselves, while from such principles practical rules must be capable of being deduced for every rational nature, and accordingly for that of man.

[1] I have a letter from the late excellent Sulzer, in which he asks me what can be the reason that moral instruction, although containing much that is convincing for the reason, yet accomplishes so little? My answer was postponed in order that I might make it complete. But it is simply this: that the teachers themselves have not got their own notions clear, and when they endeavour to make up for this by raking up motives of moral goodness from every quarter, trying to make their physic right strong, they spoil it. For the commonest understanding shows that if we imagine, on the one hand, an act of honesty done with steadfast mind, apart from every view to advantage of any kind in this world or another, and even under the greatest temptations of necessity or allurement, and, on the other hand, a similar act which was affected, in however low a degree, by a foreign motive, the former leaves far behind and eclipses the second; it elevates the soul and inspires the wish to be able to act in like manner oneself. Even moderately young children feel this impression, and one should never represent duties to them in any other light.

reason. If reason infallibly determines the will, then the actions of such a being which are recognised as objectively necessary are subjectively necessary also, i.e., the will is a faculty to choose *that only* which reason independent of inclination recognises as practically necessary, i.e., as good. But if reason of itself does not sufficiently determine the will, if the latter is subject also to subjective conditions (particular impulses) which do not always coincide with the objective conditions; in a word, if the will does not *in itself* completely accord with reason (which is actually the case with men), then the actions which objectively are recognised as necessary are subjectively contingent, and the determination of such a will according to objective laws is *obligation,* that is to say, the relation of the objective laws to a will that is not thoroughly good is conceived as the determination of the will of a rational being by principles of reason, but which the will from its nature does not of necessity follow.

The conception of an objective principle, in so far as it is obligatory for a will, is called a *command* (of reason), and the formula of the command is called an *imperative.*

All imperatives are expressed by the word *ought* [or *shall*], and thereby indicate the relation of an objective law of reason to a will, which from its subjective constitution is not necessarily determined by it (an obligation). They say that something would be good to do or to forbear, but they say it to a will which does not always do a thing because it is conceived to be good to do it. That is practically *good,* however, which determines the will by means of the conceptions of reason, and consequently not from subjective causes, but objectively, that is on principles which are valid for every rational being as such. It is distinguished from the *pleasant,* as that which influences the will only by means of sensation from merely subjective causes, valid only for the sense of this or that one, and not as a principle of reason, which holds for every one.[1]

A perfectly good will would therefore be equally subject to objective laws (viz., laws of good), but could not be conceived as *obliged* thereby to act lawfully, because of itself from its subjective constitution it can only be determined by the conception of good. Therefore no imperatives hold for the Divine will, or in general for a *holy* will; *ought* is here out of place, because the volition is already of itself necessarily in unison with the law. Therefore imperatives are only formulæ to express the relation of objective laws of all volition to the subjective imperfection of the will of this or that rational being, e.g., the human will.

Now all *imperatives* command either *hypothetically* or *categorically.* The former represent the practical necessity of a possible action as means to something else that is willed (or at least which one might possibly will). The categorical imperative would be that which represented an action as necessary of itself without reference to another end, i.e., as objectively necessary.

Since every practical law represents a possible action as good and, on this account, for a subject who is practically determinable by reason, necessary, all imperatives are formulae determining an action which is necessary according to the principle of a will good in some respects. If now the action is good only as a means *to something else,* then the imperative is *hypothetical;* if it is conceived as good *in itself* and consequently as being necessarily the principle of a will which of itself conforms to reason, then it is *categorical.*

Thus the imperative declares what action possible by me would be good and presents the practical rule in relation to a will which does not forthwith perform an action simply because it is good, whether because the subject does not always know that it is good, or because, even if it know this, yet its maxims might be opposed to the objective principles of practical reason.

Accordingly the hypothetical imperative only says that the action is good for some purpose, *possible* or *actual.* In the first case it is a *problematical,* in the second an *assertorial* practical principle. The categorical imperative which declares an action to be objectively necessary in itself without reference to any purpose, i.e.,

[1] The dependence of the desires on sensations is called inclination, and this accordingly always indicates a *want.* The dependence of a contingently determinable will on principles of reason is called an *interest.* This, therefore, is found only in the case of a dependent will which does not always of itself conform to reason; in the Divine will we cannot conceive any interest. But the human will can also *take an interest* in a thing without therefore acting *from interest.* The former signifies the *practical* interest in the action, the latter the *pathological* in the object of the action. The former indicates only dependence of the will on principles of reason in themselves; the second, dependence on principles of reason for the sake of inclination, reason supplying only the practical rules how the requirement of the inclination may be satisfied. In the first case the action interests me; in the second the object of the action (because it is pleasant to me). We have seen in the first section that in an action done from duty we must look not to the interest in the object, but only to that in the action itself, and in its rational principle (viz., the law).

without any other end, is valid as an *apodeictic* (practical) principle.

Whatever is possible only by the power of some rational being may also be conceived as a possible purpose of some will; and therefore the principles of action as regards the means necessary to attain some possible purpose are in fact infinitely numerous. All sciences have a practical part, consisting of problems expressing that some end is possible for us and of imperatives directing how it may be attained. These may, therefore, be called in general imperatives of *skill*. Here there is no question whether the end is rational and good, but only what one must do in order to attain it. The precepts for the physician to make his patient thoroughly healthy, and for a poisoner to ensure certain death, are of equal value in this respect, that each serves to effect its purpose perfectly. Since in early youth it cannot be known what ends are likely to occur to us in the course of life, parents seek to have their children taught a *great many things*, and provide for their *skill* in the use of means for all sorts of arbitrary ends, of none of which can they determine whether it may not perhaps hereafter be an object to their pupil, but which it is at all events *possible* that he might aim at; and this anxiety is so great that they commonly neglect to form and correct their judgement on the value of the things which may be chosen as ends.

There is *one* end, however, which may be assumed to be actually such to all rational beings (so far as imperatives apply to them, viz., as dependent beings), and, therefore, one purpose which they not merely *may* have, but which we may with certainty assume that they all actually *have* by a natural necessity, and this is *happiness*. The hypothetical imperative which expresses the practical necessity of an action as means to the advancement of happiness is *assertorial*. We are not to present it as necessary for an uncertain and merely possible purpose, but for a purpose which we may presuppose with certainty and *a priori* in every man, because it belongs to his being. Now skill in the choice of means to his own greatest well-being may be called *prudence*,[1] in the narrowest sense. And thus the imperative which refers to the choice of means to one's own happiness, i.e., the precept of prudence, is still always *hypothetical*; the action is not commanded absolutely, but only as means to another purpose.

Finally, there is an imperative which commands a certain conduct immediately, without having as its condition any other purpose to be attained by it. This imperative is *categorical*. It concerns not the matter of the action, or its intended result, but its form and the principle of which it is itself a result; and what is essentially good in it consists in the mental disposition, let the consequence be what it may. This imperative may be called that of *morality*.

There is a marked distinction also between the volitions on these three sorts of principles in the *dissimilarity* of the obligation of the will. In order to mark this difference more clearly, I think they would be most suitably named in their order if we said they are either *rules* of skill, or *counsels* of prudence, or *commands* (*laws*) of morality. For it is *law* only that involves the conception of an *unconditional* and objective necessity, which is consequently universally valid; and commands are laws which must be obeyed, that is, must be followed, even in opposition to inclination. *Counsels*, indeed, involve necessity, but one which can only hold under a contingent subjective condition, viz., they depend on whether this or that man reckons this or that as part of his happiness; the categorical imperative, on the contrary, is not limited by any condition, and as being absolutely, although practically, necessary, may be quite properly called a *command*. We might also call the first kind of imperatives *technical* (belonging to art), the second *pragmatic*[2] (to welfare), the third *moral* (belonging to free conduct generally, that is, to morals).

Now arises the question, how are all these imperatives possible? This question does not seek to know how we can conceive the accomplishment of the action which the imperative ordains, but merely how we can conceive the obligation of the will which the imperative expresses. No special explanation is needed to

[1] The word *prudence* is taken in two senses: in the one it may bear the name of *knowledge of the world*, in the other that of *private prudence*. The former is a man's ability to influence others so as to use them for his own purposes. The latter is the sagacity to combine all these purposes for his own lasting benefit. This latter is properly that to which the value even of the former is reduced, and when a man is prudent in the former sense, but not in the latter, we might better say of him that he is clever and cunning, but, on the whole, imprudent.

[2] It seems to me that the proper signification of the word *pragmatic* may be most accurately defined in this way. For *sanctions* are called pragmatic which flow properly not from the law of the states as necessary enactments, but from *precaution* for the general welfare. A history is composed pragmatically when it teaches *prudence*, i.e., instructs the world how it can provide for its interests better, or at least as well as, the men of former time.

show how an imperative of skill is possible. Whoever wills the end, wills also (so far as reason decides his conduct) the means in his power which are indispensably necessary thereto. This proposition is, as regards the volition, analytical; for, in willing an object as my effect, there is already thought the causality of myself as an acting cause, that is to say, the use of the means; and the imperative educes from the conception of volition of an end the conception of actions necessary to this end. Synthetical propositions must no doubt be employed in defining the means to a proposed end; but they do not concern the principle, the act of the will, but the object and its realization. E.g., that in order to bisect a line on an unerring principle I must draw from its extremities two intersecting arcs; this no doubt is taught by mathematics only in synthetical propositions; but if I know that it is only by this process that the intended operation can be performed, then to say that, if I fully will the operation, I also will the action required for it, is an analytical proposition; for it is one and the same thing to conceive something as an effect which I can produce in a certain way, and to conceive myself as acting in this way.

If it were only equally easy to give a definite conception of happiness, the imperatives of prudence would correspond exactly with those of skill, and would likewise be analytical. For in this case as in that, it could be said: "Whoever wills the end, wills also (according to the dictate of reason necessarily) the indispensable means thereto which are in his power." But, unfortunately, the notion of happiness is so indefinite that although every man wishes to attain it, yet he never can say definitely and consistently what it is that he really wishes and wills. The reason of this is that all the elements which belong to the notion of happiness are altogether empirical, i.e., they must be borrowed from experience, and nevertheless the idea of happiness requires an absolute whole, a maximum of welfare in my present and all future circumstances. Now it is impossible that the most clear-sighted and at the same time most powerful being (supposed finite) should frame to himself a definite conception of what he really wills in this. Does he will riches, how much anxiety, envy, and snares might he not thereby draw upon his shoulders? Does he will knowledge and discernment, perhaps it might prove to be only an eye so much the sharper to show him so much the more fearfully the evils that are now concealed from him, and that cannot be avoided, or to impose more wants on his desires, which already give him concern enough. Would he have long life? who guarantees to him that it would not be a long misery? would he at least have health? how often has uneasiness of the body restrained from excesses into which perfect health would have allowed one to fall? and so on. In short, he is unable, on any principle, to determine with certainty what would make him truly happy; because to do so he would need to be omniscient. We cannot therefore act on any definite principles to secure happiness, but only on empirical counsels, e.g. of regimen, frugality, courtesy, reserve, etc., which experience teaches do, on the average, most promote well-being. Hence it follows that the imperatives of prudence do not, strictly speaking, command at all, that is, they cannot present actions objectively as practically *necessary;* that they are rather to be regarded as counsels (*consilia*) than precepts (*praecepta*) of reason, that the problem to determine certainly and universally what action would promote the happiness of a rational being is completely insoluble, and consequently no imperative respecting it is possible which should, in the strict sense, command to do what makes happy; because happiness is not an ideal of reason but of imagination, resting solely on empirical grounds, and it is vain to expect that these should define an action by which one could attain the totality of a series of consequences which is really endless. This imperative of prudence would however be an analytical proposition if we assume that the means to happiness could be certainly assigned; for it is distinguished from the imperative of skill only by this, that in the latter the end is merely possible, in the former it is given; as however both only ordain the means to that which we suppose to be willed as an end, it follows that the imperative which ordains the willing of the means to him who wills the end is in both cases analytical. Thus there is no difficulty in regard to the possibility of an imperative of this kind either.

On the other hand, the question how the imperative of *morality* is possible, is undoubtedly one, the only one, demanding a solution, as this is not at all hypothetical, and the objective necessity which it presents cannot rest on any hypothesis, as is the case with the hypothetical imperatives. Only here we must never leave out of consideration that we *cannot* make out *by any example,* in other words empirically, whether there is such an imperative at all, but it is rather to be feared that all those which seem to be categorical may yet be at bottom hypothetical. For instance, when the precept is: "Thou shalt not promise deceitfully"; and it is assumed that the necessity of this is not a mere counsel to avoid some other evil, so that it should mean: "Thou shalt not make a lying promise, lest if it become known thou shouldst destroy thy credit," but that an action of this kind must be regarded as evil in itself, so that the imperative of the prohibition is categorical; then we cannot show with certainty in any example that the will was determined merely by the law, without any other spring of action, although it may appear to be so. For it is always possible that fear of disgrace, perhaps also obscure dread of other dangers, may have a secret influence on the will. Who can prove by experience the non-existence of a cause when all that experience tells us is that we do not perceive it? But in such a case the so-called moral imperative, which as such appears to be categorical and unconditional, would in reality be only a pragmatic precept, drawing our attention to our own interests and merely teaching us to take these into consideration.

We shall therefore have to investigate *a priori* the possibility of a categorical imperative, as we have not in this case the advantage of its reality being given in experience, so that [the elucidation of] its possibility should be requisite only for its explanation, not for its establishment. In the meantime it may be discerned beforehand that the categorical imperative alone has the purport of a practical *law;* all the rest may indeed be called *principles* of the will but not laws, since whatever is only necessary for the attainment of some arbitrary purpose may be considered as in itself contingent, and we can at any time be free from the precept if we give up the purpose; on the contrary, the unconditional command leaves the will no liberty to choose the opposite; consequently it alone carries with it that necessity which we require in a law.

Secondly, in the case of this categorical imperative or law of morality, the difficulty (of discerning its possibility) is a very profound one. It is an *a priori* synthetical practical proposition;[1] and as there is so much difficulty in discerning the possibility of speculative propositions of this kind, it may readily be supposed that the difficulty will be no less with the practical.

In this problem we will first inquire whether the mere conception of a categorical imperative may not perhaps supply us also with the formula of it, containing the proposition which alone can be a categorical imperative; for even if we know the tenor of such an absolute command, yet how it is possible will require further special and laborious study, which we postpone to the last section.

When I conceive a hypothetical imperative, in general I do not know beforehand what it will contain until I am given the condition. But when I conceive a categorical imperative, I know at once what it contains. For as the imperative contains besides the law only the necessity that the maxims[2] shall conform to this law, while the law contains no conditions restricting it, there remains nothing but the general statement that the maxim of the action should conform to a universal law, and it is this conformity alone that the imperative properly represents as necessary.

There is therefore but one categorical imperative, namely, this: *Act only on that maxim whereby thou canst at the same time will that it should become a universal law.*

Now if all imperatives of duty can be deduced from this one imperative as from their principle, then, although it should remain undecided what is called *duty* is not merely a vain notion, yet at least we shall be able to show what we understand by it and what this notion means.

Since the universality of the law according to which effects are produced constitutes what is properly called *nature* in the most general sense (as to form), that is the existence of things so far as it is determined by general laws, the imperative of duty may be expressed thus: *Act as if the maxim of thy action were to become by thy will a universal law of nature.*

We will now enumerate a few duties, adopting the usual division of them into duties to

[1] I connect the act with the will without presupposing any condition resulting from any inclination, but *a priori,* and therefore necessarily (though only objectively, i.e., assuming the idea of a reason possessing full power over all subjective motives). This is accordingly a practical proposition which does not deduce the willing of an action by mere analysis from another already presupposed (for we have not such a perfect will), but connects it immediately with the conception of the will of a rational being, as something not contained in it.

[2] A *maxim* is a subjective principle of action, and must be distinguished from the *objective principle,* namely, practical law. The former contains the practical rule set by reason according to the conditions of the subject (often its ignorance or its inclinations), so that it is the principle on which the subject *acts;* but the law is the objective principle valid for every rational being, and is the principle on which it *ought to act* that is an imperative.

ourselves and to others, and into perfect and imperfect duties.[1]

1. A man reduced to despair by a series of misfortunes feels wearied of life, but is still so far in possession of his reason that he can ask himself whether it would not be contrary to his duty to himself to take his own life. Now he inquires whether the maxim of his action could become a universal law of nature. His maxim is: "From self-love I adopt it as a principle to shorten my life when its longer duration is likely to bring more evil than satisfaction." It is asked then simply whether this principle founded on self-love can become a universal law of nature. Now we see at once that a system of nature of which it should be a law to destroy life by means of the very feeling whose special nature it is to impel to the improvement of life would contradict itself and, therefore, could not exist as a system of nature; hence that maxim cannot possibly exist as a universal law of nature and, consequently, would be wholly inconsistent with the supreme principle of all duty.

2. Another finds himself forced by necessity to borrow money. He knows that he will not be able to repay it, but sees also that nothing will be lent to him unless he promises stoutly to repay it in a definite time. He desires to make this promise, but he has still so much conscience as to ask himself: "Is it not unlawful and inconsistent with duty to get out of a difficulty in this way?" Suppose however that he resolves to do so: then the maxim of his action would be expressed thus: "When I think myself in want of money, I will borrow money and promise to repay it, although I know that I never can do so." Now this principle of self-love or of one's own advantage may perhaps be consistent with my whole future welfare; but the question now is, "Is it right?" I change then the suggestion of self-love into a universal law, and state the question thus: "How would it be if my maxim were a universal law?" Then I see at once that it could never hold as a universal law of nature, but would necessarily contradict itself. For supposing it to be a universal law that everyone when he thinks himself in a difficulty should be able to promise whatever he pleases, with the purpose of not keeping his promise, the promise itself would become impossible, as well as the end that one might have in view in it, since no one would consider that anything was promised to him, but would ridicule all such statements as vain pretences.

3. A third finds in himself a talent which with the help of some culture might make him a useful man in many respects. But he finds himself in comfortable circumstances and prefers to indulge in pleasure rather than to take pains in enlarging and improving his happy natural capacities. He asks, however, whether his maxim of neglect of his natural gifts, besides agreeing with his inclination to indulgence, agrees also with what is called duty. He sees then that a system of nature could indeed subsist with such a universal law although men (like the South Sea islanders) should let their talents rest and resolve to devote their lives merely to idleness, amusement, and propagation of their species—in a word, to enjoyment; but he cannot possibly *will* that this should be a universal law of nature, or be implanted in us as such by a natural instinct. For, as a rational being, he necessarily wills that his faculties be developed, since they serve him and have been given him, for all sorts of possible purposes.

4. A fourth, who is in prosperity, while he sees that others have to contend with great wretchedness and that he could help them, thinks: "What concern is it of mine? Let everyone be as happy as Heaven pleases, or as he can make himself; I will take nothing from him nor even envy him, only I do not wish to contribute anything to his welfare or to his assistance in distress!" Now no doubt if such a mode of thinking were a universal law, the human race might very well subsist, and doubtless even better than in a state in which everyone talks of sympathy and good-will, or even takes care occasionally to put it into practice, but, on the other side, also cheats when he can, betrays the rights of men, or otherwise violates them. But although it is possible that a universal law of nature might exist in accordance with that maxim, it is impossible to *will* that such a principle should have the universal validity of a law of nature. For a will which resolved this would contradict itself, inasmuch as many cases might occur in which one would have need of the love and sympathy of others, and in which, by such a law of nature, sprung from his own will, he would deprive himself of all hope of the aid he desires.

[1] It must be noted here that I reserve the division of duties for a future *metaphysic of morals;* so that I give it here only as an arbitrary one (in order to arrange my examples). For the rest, I understand by a *perfect duty* one that admits no exception in favour of inclination, and then I have not merely *external* but also *internal* perfect duties. This is contrary to the use of the word adopted in the schools; but I do not intend to justify it here, as it is all one for my purpose whether it is admitted or not.

These are a few of the many actual duties, or at least what we regard as such, which obviously fall into two classes on the one principle that we have laid down. We must be *able to will* that a maxim of our action should be a universal law. This is the canon of the moral appreciation of the action generally. Some actions are of such a character that their maxim cannot without contradiction be even *conceived* as a universal law of nature, far from it being possible that we should *will* that it should be so. In others this intrinsic impossibility is not found, but still it is impossible to *will* that their maxim should be raised to the universality of a law of nature, since such a will would contradict itself It is easily seen that the former violate strict or rigorous (inflexible) duty; the latter only laxer (meritorious) duty. Thus it has been completely shown how all duties depend as regards the nature of the obligation (not the object of the action) on the same principle.

If now we attend to ourselves on occasion of any transgression of duty, we shall find that we in fact do not will that our maxim should be a universal law, for that is impossible for us; on the contrary, we will that the opposite should remain a universal law, only we assume the liberty of making an *exception* in our own favour or (just for this time only) in favour of our inclination. Consequently if we considered all cases from one and the same point of view, namely, that of reason, we should find a contradiction in our own will, namely, that a certain principle should be objectively necessary as a universal law, and yet subjectively should not be universal, but admit of exceptions. As however we at one moment regard our action from the point of view of a will wholly conformed to reason, and then again look at the same action from the point of view of a will affected by inclination, there is not really any contradiction, but an antagonism of inclination to the precept of reason, whereby the universality of the principle is changed into a mere generality, so that the practical principle of reason shall meet the maxim half way. Now, although this cannot be justified in our own impartial judgement, yet it proves that we do really recognise the validity of the categorical imperative and (with all respect for it) only allow ourselves a few exceptions, which we think unimportant and forced from us.

We have thus established at least this much, that if duty is a conception which is to have any import and real legislative authority for our actions, it can only be expressed in categorical and not at all in hypothetical imperatives. We have also, which is of great importance, exhibited clearly and definitely for every practical application the content of the categorical imperative, which must contain the principle of all duty if there is such a thing at all. We have not yet, however, advanced so far as to prove *a priori* that there actually is such an imperative, that there is a practical law which commands absolutely of itself and without any other impulse, and that the following of this law is duty.

With the view of attaining to this, it is of extreme importance to remember that we must not allow ourselves to think of deducing the reality of this principle from the *particular attributes of human nature*. For duty is to be a practical, unconditional necessity of action; it must therefore hold for all rational beings (to whom an imperative can apply at all), and *for this reason only* be also a law for all human wills. On the contrary, whatever is deduced from the particular natural characteristics of humanity, from certain feelings and propensions, nay, even, if possible, from any particular tendency proper to human reason, and which need not necessarily hold for the will of every rational being; this may indeed supply us with a maxim, but not with a law; with a subjective principle on which we may have a propension and inclination to act, but not with an objective principle on which we should be *enjoined* to act, even though all our propensions, inclinations, and natural dispositions were opposed to it. In fact, the sublimity and intrinsic dignity of the command in duty are so much the more evident, the less the subjective impulses favour it and the more they oppose it, without being able in the slightest degree to weaken the obligation of the law or to diminish its validity.

Here then we see philosophy brought to a critical position, since it has to be firmly fixed, notwithstanding that it has nothing to support it in heaven or earth. Here it must show its purity as absolute director of its own laws, not the herald of those which are whispered to it by an implanted sense or who knows what tutelary nature. Although these may be better than nothing, yet they can never afford principles dictated by reason, which must have their source wholly *a priori* and thence their commanding authority, expecting everything from the supremacy of the law and the due respect for it, nothing from inclination, or else condemning the man to self-contempt and inward abhorrence.

Thus every empirical element is not only

quite incapable of being an aid to the principle of morality, but is even highly prejudicial to the purity of morals, for the proper and inestimable worth of an absolutely good will consists just in this, that the principle of action is free from all influence of contingent grounds, which alone experience can furnish. We cannot too much or too often repeat our warning against this lax and even mean habit of thought which seeks for its principle amongst empirical motives and laws; for human reason in its weariness is glad to rest on this pillow, and in a dream of sweet illusions (in which, instead of Juno, it embraces a cloud) it substitutes for morality a bastard patched up from limbs of various derivation, which looks like anything one chooses to see in it, only not like virtue to one who has once beheld her in her true form.[1]

The question then is this: "Is it a necessary law *for all rational beings* that they should always judge of their actions by maxims of which they can themselves will that they should serve as universal laws?" If it is so, then it must be connected (altogether *a priori*) with the very conception of the will of a rational being generally. But in order to discover this connexion we must, however reluctantly, take a step into metaphysic, although into a domain of it which is distinct from speculative philosophy, namely, the metaphysic of morals. In a practical philosophy, where it is not the reasons of what *happens* that we have to ascertain, but the laws of what *ought to happen*, even although it never does, i.e., objective practical laws, there it is not necessary to inquire into the reasons why anything pleases or displeases, how the pleasure of mere sensation differs from taste, and whether the latter is distinct from a general satisfaction of reason; on what the feeling of pleasure or pain rests, and how from it desires and inclinations arise, and from these again maxims by the co-operation of reason: for all this belongs to an empirical psychology, which would constitute the second part of physics, if we regard physics as the *philosophy* of nature, so far as it is based on *empirical laws*. But here we are concerned with objective practical laws and, consequently, with the relation of the will to itself so far as it is determined by reason alone, in which case whatever has reference to anything empirical is necessarily excluded; since if *reason of itself alone* determines the conduct (and it is the possibility of this that we are now investigating), it must necessarily do so *a priori.*

The will is conceived as a faculty of determining oneself to action *in accordance with the conception of certain laws.* And such a faculty can be found only in rational beings. Now that which serves the will as the objective ground of its self-determination is the *end,* and, if this is assigned by reason alone, it must hold for all rational beings. On the other hand, that which merely contains the ground of possibility of the action of which the effect is the end, this is called the *means.* The subjective ground of the desire is the *spring,* the objective ground of the volition is the *motive*; hence the distinction between subjective ends which rest on springs, and objective ends which depend on motives valid for every rational being. Practical principles are *formal* when they abstract from all subjective ends; they are *material* when they assume these, and therefore particular springs of action. The ends which a rational being proposes to himself at pleasure as *effects* of his actions (material ends) are all only relative, for it is only their relation to the particular desires of the subject that gives them their worth, which therefore cannot furnish principles universal and necessary for all rational beings and for every volition, that is to say practical laws. Hence all these relative ends can give rise only to hypothetical imperatives.

Supposing, however, that there were something *whose existence* has *in itself* an absolute worth, something which, being *an end in itself,* could be a source of definite laws; then in this and this alone would lie the source of a possible categorical imperative, i.e., a practical law.

Now I say: man and generally any rational being *exists* as an end in himself, *not merely as a means* to be arbitrarily used by this or that will, but in all his actions, whether they concern himself or other rational beings, must be always regarded at the same time as an end. All objects of the inclinations have only a conditional worth, for if the inclinations and the wants founded on them did not exist, then their object would be without value. But the inclinations, themselves being sources of want, are so far from having an absolute worth for which they should be desired that on the contrary it must be the universal wish of every rational being to be wholly free from them. Thus the worth of any object which is *to be acquired* by

[1] To behold virtue in her proper form is nothing else but to contemplate morality stripped of all admixture of sensible things and of every spurious ornament of reward or self-love. How much she then eclipses everything else that appears charming to the affections, every one may readily perceive with the least exertion of his reason, if it be not wholly spoiled for abstraction.

our action is always conditional. Beings whose existence depends not on our will but on nature's, have nevertheless, if they are irrational beings, only a relative value as means, and are therefore called *things;* rational beings, on the contrary, are called *persons,* because their very nature points them out as ends in themselves, that is as something which must not be used merely as means, and so far therefore restricts freedom of action (and is an object of respect). These, therefore, are not merely subjective ends whose existence has a worth *for us* as an effect of our action, but *objective ends,* that is, things whose existence is an end in itself; an end moreover for which no other can be substituted, which they should subserve *merely* as means, for otherwise nothing whatever would possess *absolute worth;* but if all worth were conditioned and therefore contingent, then there would be no supreme practical principle of reason whatever.

If then there is a supreme practical principle or, in respect of the human will, a categorical imperative, it must be one which, being drawn from the conception of that which is necessarily an end for everyone because it is *an end in itself,* constitutes an *objective* principle of will, and can therefore serve as a universal practical law. The foundation of this principle is: *rational nature exists as an end in itself.* Man necessarily conceives his own existence as being so; so far then this is a *subjective* principle of human actions. But every other rational being regards its existence similarly, just on the same rational principle that holds for me:[1] so that it is at the same time an objective principle, from which as a supreme practical law all laws of the will must be capable of being deduced. Acordingly the practical imperative will be as follows: *So act as to treat humanity, whether in thine own person or in that of any other, in every case as an end withal, never as means only.* We will now inquire whether this can be practically carried out.

To abide by the previous examples:

Firstly, under the head of necessary duty to oneself: He who contemplates suicide should ask himself whether his action can be consistent with the idea of humanity *as an end in itself.* If he destroys himself in order to escape from painful circumstances, he uses a person merely as *a mean* to maintain a tolerable condition up to the end of life. But a man is not a thing, that is to say, something which can be used merely as means, but must in all his actions be always considered as an end in himself. I cannot, therefore, dispose in any way of a man in my own person so as to mutilate him, to damage or kill him. (It belongs to ethics proper to define this principle more precisely, so as to avoid all misunderstanding, e. g., as to the amputation of the limbs in order to preserve myself, as to exposing my life to danger with a view to preserve it, etc. This question is therefore omitted here.)

Secondly, as regards necessary duties, or those of strict obligation, towards others: He who is thinking of making a lying promise to others will see at once that he would be using another man *merely as a mean,* without the latter containing at the same time the end in himself. For he whom I propose by such a promise to use for my own purposes cannot possibly assent to my mode of acting towards him and, therefore, cannot himself contain the end of this action. This violation of the principle of humanity in other men is more obvious if we take in examples of attacks on the freedom and property of others. For then it is clear that he who transgresses the rights of men intends to use the person of others merely as a means, without considering that as rational beings they ought always to be esteemed also as ends, that is, as beings who must be capable of containing in themselves the end of the very same action.[2]

Thirdly, as regards contingent (meritorious) duties to oneself: It is not enough that the action does not violate humanity in our own person as an end in itself, it must also *harmonize with* it. Now there are in humanity capacities of greater perfection, which belong to the end that nature has in view in regard to humanity in ourselves as the subject: to neglect these might perhaps be consistent with the *maintenance* of humanity as an end in itself, but not with the *advancement* of this end.

Fourthly, as regards meritorious duties towards others: The natural end which all men have is their own happiness. Now humanity

[1] This proposition is here stated as a postulate. The ground of it will be found in the concluding section.

[2] Let it not be thought that the common *"quod tibi non vis fieri, etc."* could serve here as the rule or principle. For it is only a deduction from the former, though with several limitations; it cannot be a universal law, for it does not contain the principle of duties to oneself, nor of the duties of benevolence to others (for many a one would gladly consent that others should not benefit him, provided only that he might be excused from showing benevolence to them), nor finally that of duties of strict obligation to one another, for on this principle the criminal might argue against the judge who punishes him, and so on.

might indeed subsist, although no one should contribute anything to the happiness of others, provided he did not intentionally withdraw anything from it; but after all this would only harmonize negatively not positively with *humanity as an end in itself*, if every one does not also endeavour, as far as in him lies, to forward the ends of others. For the ends of any subject which is an end in himself ought as far as possible to be *my* ends also, if that conception is to have its *full* effect with me.

This principle, that humanity and generally every rational nature is *an end in itself* (which is the supreme limiting condition of every man's freedom of action), is not borrowed from experience, *firstly,* because it is universal, applying as it does to all rational beings whatever, and experience is not capable of determining anything about them; *secondly,* because it does not present humanity as an end to men (subjectively), that is as an object which men do of themselves actually adopt as an end; but as an objective end, which must as a law constitute the supreme limiting condition of all our subjective ends, let them be what we will; it must therefore spring from pure reason. In fact the objective principle of all practical legislation lies (according to the first principle) in *the rule* and its form of universality which makes it capable of being a law (say, e. g., a law of nature); but the *subjective* principle is in the *end;* now by the second principle the subject of all ends is each rational being, inasmuch as it is an end in itself. Hence follows the third practical principle of the will, which is the ultimate condition of its harmony with universal practical reason, viz.: the idea of *the will of every rational being as a universally legislative will.*

On this principle all maxims are rejected which are inconsistent with the will being itself universal legislator. Thus the will is not subject simply to the law, but so subject that it must be regarded *as itself giving the law* and, on this ground only, subject to the law (of which it can regard itself as the author).

In the previous imperatives, namely, that based on the conception of the conformity of actions to general laws, as in a *physical system of nature,* and that based on the universal *prerogative* of rational beings as ends in themselves—these imperatives, just because they were conceived as categorical, excluded from any share in their authority all admixture of any interest as a spring of action; they were, however, only *assumed* to be categorical, because such an assumption was necessary to explain the conception of duty. But we could not prove independently that there are practical propositions which command categorically, nor can it be proved in this section; one thing, however, could be done, namely, to indicate in the imperative itself, by some determinate expression, that in the case of volition from duty all interest is renounced, which is the specific criterion of categorical as distinguished from hypothetical imperatives. This is done in the present (third) formula of the principle, namely, in the idea of the will of every rational being as a *universally legislating will.*

For although a will *which is subject to laws* may be attached to this law by means of an interest, yet a will which is itself a supreme lawgiver so far as it is such cannot possibly depend on any interest, since a will so dependent would itself still need another law restricting the interest of its self-love by the condition that it should be valid as universal law.

Thus the *principle* that every human will is *a will which in all its maxims gives universal laws,*[1] provided it be otherwise justified, would be very *well adapted* to be the categorical imperative, in this respect, namely, that just because of the idea of universal legislation it is *not based on any interest,* and therefore it alone among all possible imperatives can be *unconditional.* Or still better, converting the proposition, if there is a categorical imperative (i. e., a law for the will of every rational being), it can only command that everything be done from maxims of one's will regarded as a will which could at the same time will that it should itself give universal laws, for in that case only the practical principle and the imperative which it obeys are unconditional, since they cannot be based on any interest.

Looking back now on all previous attempts to discover the principle of morality, we need not wonder why they all failed. It was seen that man was bound to laws by duty, but it was not observed that the laws to which he is subject are *only those of his own giving,* though at the same time they are *universal,* and that he is only bound to act in conformity with his own will; a will, however, which is designed by nature to give universal laws. For when one has conceived man only as subject to a law (no matter what), then this law required some interest, either by way of attraction or constraint,

[1] I may be excused from adducing examples to elucidate this principle, as those which have already been used to elucidate the categorical imperative and its formula would all serve for the like purpose here.

since it did not originate as a law from *his own* will, but this will was according to a law obliged by *something else* to act in a certain manner. Now by this necessary consequence all the labour spent in finding a supreme principle of *duty* was irrevocably lost. For men never elicited duty, but only a necessity of acting from a certain interest. Whether this interest was private or otherwise, in any case the imperative must be conditional and could not by any means be capable of being a moral command. I will therefore call this the principle of *autonomy* of the will, in contrast with every other which I accordingly reckon as *heteronomy*.[1]

The conception of the will of every rational being as one which must consider itself as giving in all the maxims of its will universal laws, so as to judge itself and its actions from this point of view—this conception leads to another which depends on it and is very fruitful, namely that of *a kingdom of ends*.

By a *kingdom* I understand the union of different rational beings in a system by common laws. Now since it is by laws that ends are determined as regards their universal validity, hence, if we abstract from the personal differences of rational beings and likewise from all the content of their private ends, we shall be able to conceive all ends combined in a systematic whole (including both rational beings as ends in themselves, and also the special ends which each may propose to himself), that is to say, we can conceive a kingdom of ends, which on the preceding principles is possible.

For all rational beings come under the *law* that each of them must treat itself and all others *never merely as means*, but in every case *at the same time as ends in themselves*. Hence results a systematic union of rational being by common objective laws, i. e., a kingdom which may be called a kingdom of ends, since what these laws have in view is just the relation of these beings to one another as ends and means. It is certainly only an ideal.

A rational being belongs as a *member* to the kingdom of ends when, although giving universal laws in it, he is also himself subject to these laws. He belongs to it *as sovereign* when, while giving laws, he is not subject to the will of any other.

A rational being must always regard himself as giving laws either as member or as sovereign in a kingdom of ends which is rendered possible by the freedom of will. He cannot, however, maintain the latter position merely by the maxims of his will, but only in case he is a completely independent being without wants and with unrestricted power adequate to his will.

Morality consists then in the reference of all action to the legislation which alone can render a kingdom of ends possible. This legislation must be capable of existing in every rational being and of emanating from his will, so that the principle of this will is never to act on any maxim which could not without contradiction be also a universal law and, accordingly, always so to act *that the will could at the same time regard itself as giving in its maxims universal laws*. If now the maxims of rational beings are not by their own nature coincident with this objective principle, then the necessity of acting on it is called *practical necessitation*, i.e., *duty*. Duty does not apply to the sovereign in the kingdom of ends, but it does to every member of it and to all in the same degree.

The practical necessity of acting on this principle, i.e., duty, does not rest at all on feelings, impulses, or inclinations, but solely on the relation of rational beings to one another, a relation in which the will of a rational being must always be regarded as *legislative*, since otherwise it could not be conceived as *an end in itself*. Reason then refers every maxim of the will, regarding it as legislating universally, to every other will and also to every action towards oneself; and this not on account of any other practical motive or any future advantage, but from the idea of the *dignity* of a rational being, obeying no law but that which he himself also gives.

In the kingdom of ends everything has either value or dignity. Whatever has a value can be replaced by something else which is *equivalent*; whatever, on the other hand, is above all value, and therefore admits of no equivalent, has a dignity.

Whatever has reference to the general inclinations and wants of mankind has a *market value*; whatever, without presupposing a want, corresponds to a certain taste, that is to a satisfaction in the mere purposeless play of our faculties, has a *fancy value*; but that which constitutes the condition under which alone anything can be an end in itself, this has not merely a relative worth, i.e., value, but an intrinsic worth, that is, *dignity*.

Now morality is the condition under which alone a rational being can be an end in himself, since by this alone is it possible that he should be a legislating member in the kingdom of ends. Thus morality, and humanity as capable of it, is that which alone has dignity. Skill and diligence

[1] [Cf. *Critique of Practical Reason*, p. 328.]

in labour have a market value; wit, lively imagination, and humour, have fancy value; on the other hand, fidelity to promises, benevolence from principle (not from instinct), have an intrinsic worth. Neither nature nor art contains anything which in default of these it could put in their place, for their worth consists not in the effects which spring from them, not in the use and advantage which they secure, but in the disposition of mind, that is, the maxims of the will which are ready to manifest themselves in such actions, even though they should not have the desired effect. These actions also need no recommendation from any subjective taste or sentiment, that they may be looked on with immediate favour and satisfaction: they need no immediate propension or feeling for them; they exhibit the will that performs them as an object of an immediate respect, and nothing but reason is required to *impose* them on the will; not to *flatter* it into them, which, in the case of duties, would be a contradiction. This estimation therefore shows that the worth of such a disposition is dignity, and places it infinitely above all value, with which it cannot for a moment be brought into comparison or competition without as it were violating its sanctity.

What then is it which justifies virtue or the morally good disposition, in making such lofty claims? It is nothing less than the privilege it secures to the rational being of participating in the giving of universal laws, by which it qualifies him to be a member of a possible kingdom of ends, a privilege to which he was already destined by his own nature as being an end in himself and, on that account, legislating in the kingdom of ends; free as regards all laws of physical nature, and obeying those only which he himself gives, and by which his maxims can belong to a system of universal law, to which at the same time he submits himself. For nothing has any worth except what the law assigns it. Now the legislation itself which assigns the worth of everything must for that very reason possess dignity, that is an unconditional incomparable worth; and the word *respect* alone supplies a becoming expression for the esteem which a rational being must have for it. *Autonomy* then is the basis of the dignity of human and of every rational nature.

The three modes of presenting the principle of morality that have been adduced are at bottom only so many formulae of the very same law, and each of itself involves the other two. There is, however, a difference in them, but it is rather subjectively than objectively practical, intended namely to bring an idea of the reason nearer to intuition (by means of a certain analogy) and thereby nearer to feeling. All maxims, in fact, have:

1. A *form,* consisting in universality; and in this view the formula of the moral imperative is expressed thus, that the maxims must be so chosen as if they were to serve as universal laws of nature.

2. A *matter,* namely, an end, and here the formula says that the rational being, as it is an end by its own nature and therefore an end in itself, must in every maxim serve as the condition limiting all merely relative and arbitrary ends.

3. A *complete characterization* of all maxims by means of that formula, namely, that all maxims ought by their own legislation to harmonize with a possible kingdom of ends as with a kingdom of nature[1]. There is a progress here in the order of the categories of *unity* of the form of the will (its universality), *plurality* of the matter (the objects, i.e., the ends), and *totality* of the system of these. In forming our moral *judgement* of actions, it is better to proceed always on the strict method and start from the general formula of the categorical imperative: *Act according to a maxim which can at the same time make itself a universal law.* If, however, we wish to gain an *entrance* for the moral law, it is very useful to bring one and the same action under the three specified conceptions, and thereby as far as possible to bring it nearer to intuition.

We can now end where we started at the beginning, namely, with the conception of a will unconditionally good. *That will* is *absolutely good* which cannot be evil—in other words, whose maxim, if made a universal law, could never contradict itself. This principle, then, is its supreme law: "Act always on such a maxim as thou canst at the same time will to be a universal law"; this is the sole condition under which a will can never contradict itself; and such an imperative is categorical. Since the validity of the will as a universal law for possible actions is analogous to the universal connexion of the existence of things by general laws, which is the formal notion of nature in general, the categorical imperative can also be expressed

[1] Teleology considers nature as a kingdom of ends; ethics regards a possible kingdom of ends as a kingdom of nature. In the first case, the kingdom of ends is a theoretical idea, adopted to explain what actually is. In the latter it is a practical idea, adopted to bring about that which is not yet, but which can be realized by our conduct, namely, if it conforms to this idea.

thus: *Act on maxims which can at the same time have for their object themselves as universal laws of nature.* Such then is the formula of an absolutely good will.

Rational nature is distinguished from the rest of nature by this, that it sets before itself an end. This end would be the matter of every good will. But since in the idea of a will that is absolutely good without being limited by any condition (of attaining this or that end) we must abstract wholly from every end *to be effected* (since this would make every will only relatively good), it follows that in this case the end must be conceived, not as an end to be effected, but as an *independently* existing end. Consequently it is conceived only negatively, i.e., as that which we must never act against and which, therefore, must never be regarded merely as means, but must in every volition be esteemed as an end likewise. Now this end can be nothing but the subject of all possible ends, since this is also the subject of a possible absolutely good will; for such a will cannot without contradiction be postponed to any other object. The principle: "So act in regard to every rational being (thyself and others), that he may always have place in thy maxim as an end in himself," is accordingly essentially identical with this other: "Act upon a maxim which, at the same time, involves its own universal validity for every rational being." For that in using means for every end I should limit my maxim by the condition of its holding good as a law for every subject, this comes to the same thing as that the fundamental principle of all maxims of action must be that the subject of all ends, i.e., the rational being himself, be never employed merely as means, but as the supreme condition restricting the use of all means, that is in every case as an end likewise.

It follows incontestably that, to whatever laws any rational being may be subject, he being an end in himself must be able to regard himself as also legislating universally in respect of these same laws, since it is just this fitness of his maxims for universal legislation that distinguishes him as an end in himself; also it follows that this implies his dignity (prerogative) above all mere physical beings, that he must always take his maxims from the point of view which regards himself and, likewise, every other rational being as law-giving beings (on which account they are called *persons*). In this way a world of rational beings (*mundus intelligibilis*) is possible as a kingdom of ends, and this by virtue of the legislation proper to all persons as members. Therefore every rational being must so act as if he were by his maxims in every case a legislating member in the universal kingdom of ends. The formal principle of these maxims is: "So act as if thy maxim were to serve likewise as the universal law (of all rational beings)." A kingdom of ends is thus only possible on the analogy of a kingdom of nature, the former however only by maxims, that is self-imposed rules, the latter only by the laws of efficient causes acting under necessitation from without. Nevertheless, although the system of nature is looked upon as a machine, yet so far as it has reference to rational beings as its ends, it is given on this account the name of a kingdom of nature. Now such a kingdom of ends would be actually realized by means of maxims conforming to the canon which the categorical imperative prescribes to all rational beings, *if they were universally followed.* But although a rational being, even if he punctually follows this maxim himself, cannot reckon upon all others being therefore true to the same, nor expect that the kingdom of nature and its orderly arrangements shall be in harmony with him as a fitting member, so as to form a kingdom of ends to which he himself contributes, that is to say, that it shall favour his expectation of happiness, still that law: "Act according to the maxims of a member of a merely possible kingdom of ends legislating in it universally," remains in its full force, inasmuch as it commands categorically. And it is just in this that the paradox lies; that the mere dignity of man as a rational creature, without any other end or advantage to be attained thereby, in other words, respect for a mere idea, should yet serve as an inflexible precept of the will, and that it is precisely in this independence of the maxim on all such springs of action that its sublimity consists; and it is this that makes every rational subject worthy to be a legislative member in the kingdom of ends: for otherwise he would have to be conceived only as subject to the physical law of his wants. And although we should suppose the kingdom of nature and the kingdom of ends to be united under one sovereign, so that the latter kingdom thereby ceased to be a mere idea and acquired true reality, then it would no doubt gain the accession of a strong spring, but by no means any increase of its intrinsic worth. For this sole absolute lawgiver must, notwithstanding this, be always conceived as estimating the worth of rational beings only by their disinterested behaviour, as prescribed to themselves from that idea [the dignity of man] alone.

The essence of things is not altered by their external relations, and that which, abstracting from these, alone constitutes the absolute worth of man, is also that by which he must be judged, whoever the judge may be, and even by the Supreme Being. *Morality,* then, is the relation of actions to the autonomy of the will, that is, to the potential universal legislation by its maxims. An action that is consistent with the autonomy of the will is *permitted;* one that does not agree therewith is *forbidden.* A will whose maxims necessarily coincide with the laws of autonomy is a *holy* will, good absolutely. The dependence of a will not absolutely good on the principle of autonomy (moral necessitation) is obligation. This, then, cannot be applied to a holy being. The objective necessity of actions from obligation is called *duty.*

From what has just been said, it is easy to see how it happens that, although the conception of duty implies subjection to the law, we yet ascribe a certain *dignity* and sublimity to the person who fulfils all his duties. There is not, indeed, any sublimity in him, so far as he is *subject* to the moral law; but inasmuch as in regard to that very law he is likewise a *legislator,* and on that account alone subject to it, he has sublimity. We have also shown above that neither fear nor inclination, but simply respect for the law, is the spring which can give actions a moral worth. Our own will, so far as we suppose it to act only under the condition that its maxims are potentially universal laws, this ideal will which is possible to us is the proper object of respect; and the dignity of humanity consists just in this capacity of being universally legislative, though with the condition that it is itself subject to this same legislation.

The Autonomy of the Will as the Supreme Principle of Morality

Autonomy of the will is that property of it by which it is a law to itself (independently of any property of the objects of volition). The principle of autonomy then is: "Always so to choose that the same volition shall comprehend the maxims of our choice as a universal law." We cannot prove that this practical rule is an imperative, i.e., that the will of every rational being is necessarily bound to it as a condition, by a mere analysis of the conceptions which occur in it, since it is a synthetical proposition; we must advance beyond the cognition of the objects to a critical examination of the subject, that is, of the pure practical reason, for this synthetic proposition which commands apodeictically must be capable of being cognized wholly *a priori.* This matter, however, does not belong to the present section. But that the principle of autonomy in question is the sole principle of morals can be readily shown by mere analysis of the conceptions of morality. For by this analysis we find that its principle must be a categorical imperative and that what this commands is neither more nor less than this very autonomy.

Heteronomy of the Will as the Source of all spurious Principles of Morality

If the will seeks the law which is to determine it *anywhere else* than in the fitness of its maxims to be universal laws of its own dictation, consequently if it goes out of itself and seeks this law in the character of any of its objects, there always results *heteronomy.* The will in that case does not give itself the law, but it is given by the object through its relation to the will. This relation, whether it rests on inclination or on conceptions of reason, only admits of hypothetical imperatives: "I ought to do something *because I wish for something else.*" On the contrary, the moral, and therefore categorical, imperative says: "I ought to do so and so, even though I should not wish for anything else." E.g., the former says: "I ought not to lie, if I would retain my reputation"; the latter says: "I ought not to lie, although it should not bring me the least discredit." The latter therefore must so far abstract from all objects that they shall have no *influence* on the will, in order that practical reason (will) may not be restricted to administering an interest not belonging to it, but may simply show its own commanding authority as the supreme legislation. Thus, e.g., I ought to endeavour to promote the happiness of others, not as if its realization involved any concern of mine (whether by immediate inclination or by any satisfaction indirectly gained through reason), but simply because a maxim which excludes it cannot be comprehended as a universal law in one and the same volition.

Classification of all Principles of Morality which can be founded on the Conception of Heteronomy

Here as elsewhere human reason in its pure use, so long as it was not critically examined, has first tried all possible wrong ways before it succeeded in finding the one true way.

All principles which can be taken from this point of view are either *empirical* or *rational.*

The *former*, drawn from the principle of *happiness*, are built on physical or moral feelings; the *latter*, drawn from the principle of *perfection*, are built either on the rational conception of perfection as a possible effect, or on that of an independent perfection (the will of God) as the determining cause of our will.

Empirical principles are wholly incapable of serving as a foundation for moral laws. For the universality with which these should hold for all rational beings without distinction, the unconditional practical necessity which is thereby imposed on them, is lost when their foundation is taken from the *particular constitution of human nature*, or the accidental circumstances in which it is placed. The principle of *private happiness*, however, is the most objectionable, not merely because it is false, and experience contradicts the supposition that prosperity is always proportioned to good conduct, nor yet merely because it contributes nothing to the establishment of morality—since it is quite a different thing to make a prosperous man and a good man, or to make one prudent and sharp-sighted for his own interests and to make him virtuous—but because the springs it provides for morality are such as rather undermine it and destroy its sublimity, since they put the motives to virtue and to vice in the same class and only teach us to make a better calculation, the specific difference between virtue and vice being entirely extinguished. On the other hand, as to moral feeling, this supposed special sense,[1] the appeal to it is indeed superficial when those who cannot *think* believe that *feeling* will help them out, even in what concerns general laws: and besides, feelings, which naturally differ infinitely in degree, cannot furnish a uniform standard of good and evil, nor has anyone a right to form judgements for others by his own feelings: nevertheless this moral feeling is nearer to morality and its dignity in this respect, that it pays virtue the honour of ascribing to her *immediately* the satisfaction and esteem we have for her and does not, as it were, tell her to her face that we are not attached to her by her beauty but by profit.

Amongst the *rational* principles of morality, the ontological conception of *perfection*, notwithstanding its defects, is better than the theological conception which derives morality from a Divine absolutely perfect will. The former is, no doubt, empty and indefinite and consequently useless for finding in the boundless field of possible reality the greatest amount suitable for us; moreover, in attempting to distinguish specifically the reality of which we are now speaking from every other, it inevitably tends to turn in a circle and cannot avoid tacitly presupposing the morality which it is to explain; it is nevertheless preferable to the theological view, first, because we have no intuition of the divine perfection and can only deduce it from our own conceptions, the most important of which is that of morality, and our explanation would thus be involved in a gross circle; and, in the next place, if we avoid this, the only notion of the Divine will remaining to us is a conception made up of the attributes of desire of glory and dominion, combined with the awful conceptions of might and vengeance, and any system of morals erected on this foundation would be directly opposed to morality.

However, if I had to choose between the notion of the moral sense and that of perfection in general (two systems which at least do not weaken morality, although they are totally incapable of serving as its foundation), then I should decide for the latter, because it at least withdraws the decision of the question from the sensibility and brings it to the court of pure reason; and although even here it decides nothing, it at all events preserves the indefinite idea (of a will good in itself) free from corruption, until it shall be more precisely defined.

For the rest I think I may be excused here from a detailed refutation of all these doctrines; that would only be superfluous labour, since it is so easy, and is probably so well seen even by those whose office requires them to decide for one of these theories (because their hearers would not tolerate suspension of judgement). But what interests us more here is to know that the prime foundation of morality laid down by all these principles is nothing but heteronomy of the will, and for this reason they must necessarily miss their aim.

In every case where an object of the will has to be supposed, in order that the rule may be prescribed which is to determine the will, there the rule is simply heteronomy; the imperative is conditional, namely, *if* or *because* one wishes for this object, one should act so and so: hence it can never command morally, that is, categorically. Whether the object determines the will by means of inclination, as in the principle

[1] I class the principle of moral feeling under that of happiness, because every empirical interest promises to contribute to our well-being by the agreeableness that a thing affords, whether it be immediately and without a view to profit, or whether profit be regarded. We must likewise, with Hutcheson, class the principle of sympathy with the happiness of others under his assumed moral sense.

of private happiness, or by means of reason directed to objects of our possible volition generally, as in the principle of perfection, in either case the will never determines itself *immediately* by the conception of the action, but only by the influence which the foreseen effect of the action has on the will; *I ought to do something, on this account, because I wish for something else;* and here there must be yet another law assumed in me as its subject, by which I necessarily will this other thing, and this law again requires an imperative to restrict this maxim. For the influence which the conception of an object within the reach of our faculties can exercise on the will of the subject, in consequence of its natural properties, depends on the nature of the subject, either the sensibility (inclination and taste), or the understanding and reason, the employment of which is by the peculiar constitution of their nature attended with satisfaction. It follows that the law would be, properly speaking, given by nature, and, as such, it must be known and proved by experience and would consequently be contingent and therefore incapable of being an apodeictic practical rule, such as the moral rule must be. Not only so, but it is *inevitably only heteronomy;* the will does not give itself the law, but is given by a foreign impulse by means of a particular natural constitution of the subject adapted to receive it. An absolutely good will, then, the principle of which must be a categorical imperative, will be indeterminate as regards all objects and will contain merely the *form of volition* generally, and that as autonomy, that is to say, the capability of the maxims of every good will to make themselves a universal law, is itself the only law which the will of every rational being imposes on itself, without needing to assume any spring or interest as a foundation.

How such a synthetical practical a priori *proposition is possible,* and why it is necessary, is a problem whose solution does not lie within the bounds of the metaphysic of morals; and we have not here affirmed its truth, much less professed to have a proof of it in our power. We simply showed by the development of the universally received notion of morality that an autonomy of the will is inevitably connected with it, or rather is its foundation. Whoever then holds morality to be anything real, and not a chimerical idea without any truth, must likewise admit the principle of it that is here assigned. This section then, like the first, was merely analytical. Now to prove that morality is no creation of the brain, which it cannot be if the categorical imperative and with it the autonomy of the will is true, and as an *a priori* principle absolutely necessary, this supposes the *possibility of a synthetic use of pure practical reason,* which however we cannot venture on without first giving a critical examination of this faculty of reason. In the concluding section we shall give the principal outlines of this critical examination as far as is sufficient for our purpose.

THIRD SECTION

TRANSITION FROM THE METAPHYSIC OF MORALS TO THE CRITIQUE OF PURE PRACTICAL REASON

The Concept of Freedom is the Key that explains the Autonomy of the Will

THE *will* is a kind of causality belonging to living beings in so far as they are rational, and *freedom* would be this property of such causality that it can be efficient, independently of foreign causes *determining* it; just as *physical necessity* is the property that the causality of all irrational beings has of being determined to activity by the influence of foreign causes.

The preceding definition of freedom is *negative* and therefore unfruitful for the discovery of its essence, but it leads to a *positive* conception which is so much the more full and fruitful. Since the conception of causality involves that of laws, according to which, by something that we call *cause,* something else, namely the effect, must be produced; hence, although freedom is not a property of the will depending on physical laws, yet it is not for that reason lawless; on the contrary it must be a causality acting according to immutable laws, but of a peculiar kind; otherwise a free will would be an absurdity. Physical necessity is a heteronomy of the efficient causes, for every effect is possible only according to this law, that something else determines the efficient cause to exert its causality. What else then can freedom of the will be but autonomy, that is, the property of the will to be a law to itself? But the proposition: "The will is in every action a law to itself," only expresses the principle: "To act on no other maxim than that which can also have as an object itself as a universal law." Now this is precisely the formula of the categorical imperative and is the principle of morality, so that a free will and a will subject to moral laws are one and the same.

On the hypothesis, then, of freedom of the will, morality together with its principle follows from it by mere analysis of the conception. However, the latter is a synthetic proposition; viz., an absolutely good will is that whose maxim can always include itself regarded as a universal law; for this property of its maxim can never be discovered by analysing the conception of an absolutely good will. Now such synthetic propositions are only possible in this way: that the two cognitions are connected together by their union with a third in which they are both to be found. The *positive* concept of freedom furnishes this third cognition, which cannot, as with physical causes, be the nature of the sensible world (in the concept of which we find conjoined the concept of something in relation as cause to *something else* as effect). We cannot now at once show what this third is to which freedom points us and of which we have an idea *a priori,* nor can we make intelligible how the concept of freedom is shown to be legitimate from principles of pure practical reason and with it the possibility of a categorical imperative; but some further preparation is required.

Freedom must be presupposed as a Property of the Will of all Rational Beings

It is not enough to predicate freedom of our own will, from whatever reason, if we have not sufficient grounds for predicating the same of all rational beings. For as morality serves as a law for us only because we are *rational beings,* it must also hold for all rational beings; and as it must be deduced simply from the property of freedom, it must be shown that freedom also is a property of all rational beings. It is not enough, then, to prove it from certain supposed experiences of human nature (which indeed is quite impossible, and it can only be shown *a priori*), but we must show that it belongs to the activity of all rational beings endowed with a will. Now I say every being that cannot act except *under the idea of freedom* is just for that reason in a practical point of view really free, that is to say, all laws which are inseparably connected with freedom have the same force for him as if his will had been shown to be free in itself by a proof theoretically conclusive.[1] Now I affirm that we must attribute to every rational being which has a will that it has also the idea of freedom and acts entirely under this idea. For in such a being we conceive a reason that is practical, that is, has causality in reference to its objects. Now we cannot possibly conceive a reason consciously receiving a bias from any other quarter with respect to its judgements, for then the subject would ascribe the determination of its judgement not to its own reason, but to an impulse. It must regard itself as the author of its principles independent of foreign influences. Consequently as practical reason or as the will of a rational being it must regard itself as free, that is to say, the will of such a being cannot be a will of its own except under the idea of freedom. This idea must therefore in a practical point of view be ascribed to every rational being.

Of the Interest attaching to the Ideas of Morality

We have finally reduced the definite conception of morality to the idea of freedom. This latter, however, we could not prove to be actually a property of ourselves or of human nature; only we saw that it must be presupposed if we would conceive a being as rational and conscious of its causality in respect of its actions, i.e., as endowed with a will; and so we find that on just the same grounds we must ascribe to every being endowed with reason and will this attribute of determining itself to action under the idea of its freedom.

Now it resulted also from the presupposition of these ideas that we became aware of a law that the subjective principles of action, i.e., maxims, must always be so assumed that they can also hold as objective, that is, universal principles, and so serve as universal laws of our own dictation. But why then should I subject myself to this principle and that simply as a rational being, thus also subjecting to it all oth-

[1] I adopt this method of assuming freedom merely *as an idea* which rational beings suppose in their actions, in order to avoid the necessity of proving it in its theoretical aspect also. The former is sufficient for my purpose; for even though the speculative proof should not be made out, yet a being that cannot act except with the idea of freedom is bound by the same laws that would oblige a being who was actually free. Thus we can escape here from the onus which presses on the theory.

er being endowed with reason? I will allow that no interest *urges* me to this, for that would not give a categorical imperative, but I must *take* an interest in it and discern how this comes to pass; for this "I ought" is properly an "I would," valid for every rational being, provided only that reason determined his actions without any hindrance. But for beings that are in addition affected as we are by springs of a different kind, namely, sensibility, and in whose case that is not always done which reason alone would do, for these that necessity is expressed only as an "ought," and the subjective necessity is different from the objective.

It seems then as if the moral law, that is, the principle of autonomy of the will, were properly speaking only presupposed in the idea of freedom, and as if we could not prove its reality and objective necessity independently. In that case we should still have gained something considerable by at least determining the true principle more exactly than had previously been done; but as regards its validity and the practical necessity of subjecting oneself to it, we should not have advanced a step. For if we were asked why the universal validity of our maxim as a law must be the condition restricting our actions, and on what we ground the worth which we assign to this manner of acting—a worth so great that there cannot be any higher interest; and if we were asked further how it happens that it is by this alone a man believes he feels his own personal worth, in comparison with which that of an agreeable or disagreeable condition is to be regarded as nothing, to these questions we could give no satisfactory answer.

We find indeed sometimes that we can take an interest in a personal quality which does not involve any interest of external condition, provided this quality makes us capable of participating in the condition in case reason were to effect the allotment; that is to say, the mere being worthy of happiness can interest of itself even without the motive of participating in this happiness. This judgement, however, is in fact only the effect of the importance of the moral law which we before presupposed (when by the idea of freedom we detach ourselves from every empirical interest); but that we ought to detach ourselves from these interests, i.e., to consider ourselves as free in action and yet as subject to certain laws, so as to find a worth simply in our own person which can compensate us for the loss of everything that gives worth to our condition; this we are not yet able to discern in this way, nor do we see how it is possible so to act—in other words, *whence the moral law derives its obligation.*

It must be freely admitted that there is a sort of circle here from which it seems impossible to escape. In the order of efficient causes we assume ourselves free, in order that in the order of ends we may conceive ourselves as subject to moral laws: and we afterwards conceive ourselves as subject to these laws, because we have attributed to ourselves freedom of will: for freedom and self-legislation of will are both autonomy and, therefore, are reciprocal conceptions, and for this very reason one must not be used to explain the other or give the reason of it, but at most only logical purposes to reduce apparently different notions of the same object to one single concept (as we reduce different fractions of the same value to the lowest terms).

One resource remains to us, namely, to inquire whether we do not occupy different points of view when by means of freedom we think ourselves as causes efficient *a priori,* and when we form our conception of ourselves from our actions as effects which we see before our eyes.

It is a remark which needs no subtle reflection to make, but which we may assume that even the commonest understanding can make, although it be after its fashion by an obscure discernment of judgement which it calls *feeling,* that all the "ideas" that come to us involuntarily (as those of the senses) do not enable us to know objects otherwise than as they affect us; so that what they may be in themselves remains unknown to us, and consequently that as regards "ideas" of this kind even with the closest attention and clearness that the understanding can apply to them, we can by them only attain to the knowledge of *appearances,* never to that of *things in themselves.* As soon as this distinction has once been made (perhaps merely in consequence of the difference observed between the ideas given us from without, and in which we are passive, and those that we produce simply from ourselves, and in which we show our own activity), then it follows of itself that we must admit and assume behind the appearance something else that is not an appearance, namely, the things in themselves; although we must admit that as they can never be known to us except as they affect us, we can come no nearer to them, nor can we ever know what they are in themselves. This must furnish a distinction, however crude, between a *world of sense* and the *world of understanding,* of which the former may be different according to the difference of the sensuous impressions in various observers, while the second which is its basis always remains the same. Even as to himself, a man cannot pretend to know what he is in himself from the knowledge he has by internal sensation. For as he does not as it were create himself, and does not come by the conception of himself *a priori* but empirically, it naturally follows that he can obtain his knowledge even of himself only by the inner sense and, consequently, only through the appearances of his nature and the way in which his consciousness is affected. At the same time beyond these characteristics of his own subject, made up of mere appearances, he must necessarily suppose something else as their basis, namely, his *ego*, whatever its characteristics in itself may be. Thus in respect to mere perception and receptivity of sensations he must reckon himself as belonging to the *world of sense;* but in respect of whatever there may be of pure activity in him (that which reaches consciousness immediately and not through affecting the senses), he must reckon himself as belonging to the *intellectual world*, of which, however, he has no further knowledge. To such a conclusion the reflecting man must come with respect to all the things which can be presented to him: it is probably to be met with even in persons of the commonest understanding, who, as is well known, are very much inclined to suppose behind the objects of the senses something else invisible and acting of itself. They spoil it, however, by presently sensualizing this invisible again; that is to say, wanting to make it an object of intuition, so that they do not become a whit the wiser.

Now man really finds in himself a faculty by which he distinguishes himself from everything else, even from himself as affected by objects, and that is *reason.* This being pure spontaneity is even elevated above the *understanding.* For although the latter is a spontaneity and does not, like sense, merely contain intuitions that arise when we are affected by things (and are therefore passive), yet it cannot produce from its activity any other conceptions than those which merely serve *to bring the intuitions of sense under rules* and, thereby, to unite them in one consciousness, and without this use of the sensibility it could not think at all; whereas, on the contrary, reason shows so pure a spontaneity in the case of what I call *ideas* [ideal conceptions] that it thereby far transcends everything that the sensibility can give it, and exhibits its most important function in distinguishing the world of sense from that of understanding, and thereby prescribing the limits of the understanding itself.

For this reason a rational being must regard himself *qua* intelligence (not from the side of his lower faculties) as belonging not to the world of sense, but to that of understanding; hence he has two points of view from which he can regard himself, and recognise laws of the exercise of his faculties, and consequently of all his actions: *first,* so far as he belongs to the world of sense, he finds himself subject to laws of nature (heteronomy); *secondly,* as belonging to the intelligible world, under laws which being independent of nature have their foundation not in experience but in reason alone.

As a rational being, and consequently belonging to the intelligible world, man can never conceive the causality of his own will otherwise than on condition of the idea of freedom, for independence of the determinate causes of the sensible world (an independence which reason must always ascribe to itself) is freedom. Now the idea of freedom is inseparably connected with the conception of *autonomy,* and this again with the universal principle of morality which is ideally the foundation of all actions of *rational* beings, just as the law of nature is of all phenomena.

Now the suspicion is removed which we raised above, that there was a latent circle involved in our reasoning from freedom to autonomy, and from this to the moral law, viz.: that we laid down the idea of freedom because of the moral law only that we might afterwards in turn infer the latter from freedom, and that consequently we could assign no reason at all for this law, but could only [present] it as a *petitio principii* which well disposed minds would gladly concede to us, but which we could never put forward as a provable proposition. For now we see that, when we conceive ourselves as free, we transfer ourselves into the world of understanding as members of it and recognise the autonomy of the will with its consequence, morality; whereas, if we conceive ourselves as under obligation, we consider ourselves as belonging to the world of sense and at the same time to the world of understanding.

How is a Categorical Imperative Possible?

Every rational being reckons himself *qua* intelligence as belonging to the world of understanding, and it is simply as an efficient cause belonging to that world that he calls his causality a *will.* On the other side he is also conscious of himself as a part of the world of sense in which his actions, which are mere appearances [phenomena] of that causality, are displayed; we cannot, however, discern how they are possible from this causality which we do not know; but instead of that, these actions as belonging to the sensible world must be viewed as determined by other phenomena, namely, desires and inclinations. If therefore I were only a member of the world of understanding, then all my actions would perfectly conform to the principle of autonomy of the pure will; if I were only a part of the world of sense, they would necessarily be assumed to conform wholly to the natural law of desires and inclinations, in other words, to the heteronomy of nature. (The former would rest on morality as the supreme principle, the latter on happiness.) Since, however, *the world of understanding contains the foundation of the world of sense, and consequently of its laws also,* and accordingly gives the law to my will (which belongs wholly to the world of understanding) directly, and must be conceived as doing so, it follows that, although on the one side I must regard myself as a being belonging to the world of sense, yet on the other side I must recognize myself as subject as an intelligence to the law of the world of understanding, i.e., to reason, which contains this law in the idea of freedom, and therefore as subject to the autonomy of the will: consequently I must regard the laws of the world of understanding as imperatives for me and the actions which conform to them as duties.

And thus what makes categorical imperatives possible is this, that the idea of freedom makes me a member of an intelligible world, in consequence of which, if I were nothing else, all my actions *would* always conform to the autonomy of the will; but as I at the same time intuite myself as a member of the world of sense, they *ought* so to conform, and this *categorical* "ought" implies a synthetic *a priori* proposition, inasmuch as besides my will as affected by sensible desires there is added further the idea of the same will but as belonging to the world of the understanding, pure and practical of itself, which contains the supreme condition according to reason of the former will; precisely as to the intuitions of sense there are added concepts of the understanding which of themselves signify nothing but regular form in general and in this way synthetic *a priori* propositions become possible, on which all knowledge of physical nature rests.

The practical use of common human reason confirms this reasoning. There is no one, not even the most consummate villain, provided only that he is otherwise accustomed to the use of reason, who, when we set before him examples of honesty of purpose, of steadfastness in following good maxims, of sympathy and general benevolence (even combined with great sacrifices of advantages and comfort), does not wish that he might also possess these qualities. Only on account of his inclinations and impulses he cannot attain this in himself, but at the same time he wishes to be free from such inclinations which are burdensome to himself. He proves by this that he transfers himself in thought with a will free from the impulses of the sensibility into an order of things wholly different from that of his desires in the field of the sensibility; since he cannot expect to obtain by that wish any gratification of his desires, nor any position which would satisfy any of his actual or supposable inclinations (for this would destroy the pre-eminence of the very idea which wrests that wish from him): he can only expect a greater intrinsic worth of his own person. This better person, however, he imagines himself to be when he transfers himself to the point of view of a member of the world of the understanding, to which he is involuntarily forced by the idea of freedom, i.e., of independence on *determining* causes of the world of sense; and from this point of view he is conscious of a good will, which by his own confession constitutes the law for the bad will that he possesses as a member of the world of sense—a law whose authority he recognizes while transgressing it. What he morally "ought" is then what he necessarily "would," as a member of the world of the understanding, and is conceived by him as an "ought" only inasmuch as he likewise considers himself as a member of the world of sense.

Of the Extreme Limits of all Practical Philosophy.

All men attribute to themselves freedom of will. Hence come all judgements upon actions as being such as *ought to have been done,* although they *have not been* done. However, this freedom is not a conception of experience, nor can it be so, since it still remains, even though experience shows the contrary of what on supposition of freedom are conceived as its necessary consequences. On the other side it is equally necessary that everything that takes place should be fixedly determined according to laws of nature. This necessity of nature is likewise not an empirical conception, just for this reason, that it involves the motion of necessity and consequently of *a priori* cognition. But this conception of a system of nature is confirmed by experience; and it must even be inevitably presupposed if experience itself is to be possible, that is, a connected knowledge of the objects of sense resting on general laws. Therefore freedom is only an *idea* of reason, and its objective reality in itself is doubtful; while nature is a *concept* of the *understanding* which proves, and must necessarily prove, its reality in examples of experience.

There arises from this a dialectic of reason, since the freedom attributed to the will appears to contradict the necessity of nature, and placed between these two ways reason for *speculative purposes* finds the road of physical necessity much more beaten and more appropriate than that of freedom; yet for *practical purposes* the narrow footpath of freedom is the only one on which it is possible to make use of reason in our conduct; hence it is just as impossible for the subtlest philosophy as for the commonest reason of men to argue away freedom. Philosophy must then assume that no real contradiction will be found between freedom and physical necessity of the same human actions, for it cannot give up the conception of nature any more than that of freedom.

Nevertheless, even though we should never be able to comprehend how freedom is possible, we must at least remove this apparent contradiction in a convincing manner. For if the thought of freedom contradicts either itself or nature, which is equally necessary, it must in competition with physical necessity be entirely given up.

It would, however, be impossible to escape this contradiction if the thinking subject, which seems to itself free, conceived itself *in the same sense* or in *the very same relation* when it calls itself free as when in respect of the same action it assumes itself to be subject to the law of nature. Hence it is an indispensable problem of speculative philosophy to show that its illusion respecting the contradiction rests on this, that we think of man in a different sense and relation when we call him free and when we regard him as subject to the laws of nature as being part and parcel of nature. It must therefore show that not only *can* both these very well co-exist, but that both must be thought *as necessarily united* in the same subject, since otherwise no reason could be given why we should burden reason with an idea which, though it may possibly *without contradiction* be reconciled with another that is sufficiently established, yet entangles us in a perplexity which sorely embarrasses reason in its theoretic employment. This duty, however, belongs only to speculative philosophy. The philosopher then has no option whether he will remove the apparent contradiction or leave it untouched; for in the latter case the theory respecting this would be *bonum vacans,* into the possession of which the fatalist would have a right to enter and chase all morality out of its supposed domain as occupying it without title.

We cannot however as yet say that we are touching the bounds of practical philosophy. For the settlement of that controversy does not belong to it; it only demands from speculative reason that it should put an end to the discord in which it entangles itself in theoretical questions, so that practical reason may have rest and security from external attacks which might make the ground debatable on which it desires to build.

The claims to freedom of will made even by common reason are founded on the consciousness and the admitted supposition that reason is independent of merely subjectively determined causes which together constitute what belongs to sensation only and which consequently come under the general designation of sensibility. Man considering himself in this way as an intelligence places himself thereby in a different order of things and in a relation to determining grounds of a wholly different kind when on the one hand he thinks of himself as an intelligence endowed with a will, and consequently with causality, and when on the other he perceives himself as a phenomenon in the world of sense (as he really is also), and affirms that his causality is subject to external determination according to laws of nature. Now he soon becomes aware that both can hold good, nay, must hold good at the same time. For there is not the smallest contradiction in saying that a *thing in appearance* (belonging to the world of sense) is subject to certain laws, of which the very same *as a thing* or being *in itself* is independent, and that he must conceive and think of himself in this twofold way, rests as to the first on the consciousness of himself as an object affected through the senses, and as to the second on the consciousness of himself as an intelligence, i.e., as independent on sensible impressions in the employment of his reason (in other words as belonging to the world of understanding).

Hence it comes to pass that man claims the possession of a will which takes no account of anything that comes under the head of desires and inclinations and, on the contrary, conceives actions as possible to him, nay, even as necessary which can only be done by disregarding all desires and sensible inclinations. The causality of such actions lies in him as an intelligence and in the laws of effects and actions [which depend] on the principles of an intelligible world, of which indeed he knows nothing more than that in it pure reason alone independent of sensibility gives the law; moreover since it is only in that world, as an intelligence, that he is his proper self (being as man only the appearance of himself), those laws apply to him directly and categorically, so that the incitements of inclinations and appetites (in other words the whole nature of the world of sense) cannot impair the laws of his volition as an intelligence. Nay, he does not even hold himself responsible for the former or ascribe them to his proper self, i.e., his will: he only ascribes to his will any indulgence which he might yield them if he allowed them to influence his maxims to the prejudice of the rational laws of the will.

When practical reason *thinks* itself into a world of understanding, it does not thereby transcend its own limits, as it would if it tried to enter it by *intuition* or *sensation*. The former is only a negative thought in respect of the world of sense, which does not give any laws to reason in determining the will and is positive only in this single point that this freedom as a negative characteristic is at the same time conjoined with a (positive) faculty and even with a causality of reason, which we designate a *will*, namely a faculty of so acting that the principle of the actions shall conform to the essential character of a rational motive, i.e., the condition that the maxim have universal validity as a law. But were it to borrow an *object of will*, that is, a motive, from the world of understanding, then it would overstep its bounds and pretend to be acquainted with something of which it knows nothing. The conception of a world of the understanding is then only a *point of view* which reason finds itself compelled to take outside the appearances in order to *conceive itself as practical*, which would not be possible if the influences of the sensibility had a determining power on man, but which is necessary unless he is to be denied the consciousness of himself as an intelligence and, consequently, as a rational cause, energizing by reason, that is, operating freely. This thought certainly involves the idea of an order and a system of laws different from that of the mechanism of nature which belongs to the sensible world; and it makes the conception of an intelligible world necessary (that is to say, the whole system of rational beings as things in themselves). But it does not in the least authorize us to think of it further than as to its *formal* condition only, that is, the universality of the maxims of the will as laws, and consequently the autonomy of the latter, which alone is consistent with its freedom; whereas, on the contrary, all laws that refer to a definite object give heteronomy, which only belongs to laws of nature and can only apply to the sensible world.

But reason would overstep all its bounds if it undertook to *explain how* pure reason can be practical, which would be exactly the same problem as to explain *how freedom is possible*.

For we can explain nothing but that which we can reduce to laws, the object of which can be given in some possible experience. But freedom is a mere *idea*, the objective reality of which can in no wise be shown according to laws of nature, and consequently not in any possible experience; and for this reason it can never be comprehended or understood, because we cannot support it by any sort of example or analogy. It holds good only as a necessary hypothesis of reason in a being that believes itself conscious of a will, that is, of a faculty distinct from mere desire (namely, a faculty of determining itself to action as an intelligence, in other words, by laws of reason independently on natural instincts). Now where determination according to laws of nature ceases, there all *explanation* ceases also, and nothing remains but *defence*, i.e., the removal of the objections of those who pretend to have seen deeper into the nature of things, and thereupon boldly declare freedom impossible. We can only point out to them that the supposed contradiction that they have discovered in it arises only from this, that in order to be able to apply the law of nature to human actions, they must necessarily consider man as an appearance: then when we demand of them that they should also think of him *qua* intelligence as a thing in itself, they still persist in considering him in this respect also as an appearance. In this view it would no doubt be a contradiction to suppose the causality of the same subject (that is, his will) to be withdrawn from all the natural laws of the sensible world. But this contradiction disappears, if they would only bethink themselves and admit, as is reasonable, that behind the appearances there must also lie at their root (although hidden) the things in themselves, and that we cannot expect the laws of these to be the same as those that govern their appearances.

The subjective impossibility of explaining the freedom of the will is identical with the impossibility of discovering and explaining an interest[1] which man can take in the moral law. Nevertheless he does actually take an interest in it, the basis of which in us we call the *moral feeling,* which some have falsely assigned as the standard of our moral judgement, whereas it must rather be viewed as the *subjective* effect that the law exercises on the will, the objective principle of which is furnished by reason alone.

In order indeed that a rational being who is also affected through the senses should will what reason alone directs such beings that they ought to will, it is no doubt requisite that reason should have a power *to infuse a feeling of pleasure* or satisfaction in the fulfilment of duty, that is to say, that it should have a causality by which it determines the sensibility according to its own principles. But it is quite impossible to discern, i.e., to make it intelligible *a priori,* how a mere thought, which itself contains nothing sensible, can itself produce a sensation of pleasure or pain; for this is a particular kind of causality of which as of every other causality we can determine nothing whatever *a priori;* we must only consult experience about it. But as this cannot supply us with any relation of cause and effect except between two objects of experience, whereas in this case, although indeed the effect produced lies within experience, yet the cause is supposed to be pure reason acting through mere ideas which offer no object to experience, it follows that for us men it is quite impossible to explain how and why the *universality of the maxim as a law,* that is, morality, interests. This only is certain, that it is not *because it interests* us that it has validity for us (for that would be heteronomy and dependence of practical reason on sensibility, namely, on a feeling as its principle, in which case it could never give moral laws), but that it interests us because it is valid for us as men, inasmuch as it had its source in our will as intelligences, in other words, in our proper self, *and what belongs to mere appearance is necessarily subordinated by reason to the nature of the thing in itself.*

[1] Interest is that by which reason becomes practical, i.e., a cause determining the will. Hence we say of rational beings only that they take an interest in a thing; irrational beings only feel sensual appetites. Reason takes a direct interest in action then only when the universal validity of its maxims is alone sufficient to determine the will. Such an interest alone is pure. But if it can determine the will only by means of another object of desire or on the suggestion of a particular feeling of the subject, then reason takes only an indirect interest in the action, and, as reason by itself without experience cannot discover either objects of the will or a special feeling actuating it, this latter interest would only be empirical and not a pure rational interest. The logical interest of reason (namely, to extend its insight) is never direct, but presupposes purposes for which reason is employed.

The question then, "How a categorical imperative is possible," can be answered to this extent, that we can assign the only hypothesis on which it is possible, namely, the idea of freedom; and we can also discern the necessity of this hypothesis, and this is sufficient for the *practical exercise* of reason, that is, for the conviction of the *validity of this imperative,* and hence of the moral law; but how this hypothesis itself is possible can never be discerned by any human reason. On the hypothesis, however, that the will of an intelligence is free, its *autonomy,* as the essential formal condition of its determination, is a necessary consequence. Moreover, this freedom of will is not merely quite *possible* as a hypothesis (not involving any contradiction to the principle of physical necessity in the connexion of the phenomena of the sensible world) as speculative philosophy can show: but further, a rational being who is conscious of causality through reason, that is to say, of a will (distinct from desires), must *of necessity* make it practically, that is, in idea, the condition of all his voluntary actions. But to explain how pure reason can be of itself practical without the aid of any spring of action that could be derived from any other source, i.e., how the mere principle of the *universal validity of all its maxims as laws* (which would certainly be the form of a pure practical reason) can of itself supply a spring, without any matter (object) of the will in which one could antecedently take any interest; and how it can produce an interest which would be called purely *moral;* or in other words, *how pure reason can be practical*—to explain this is beyond the power of human reason, and all the labour and pains of seeking an explanation of it are lost.

It is just the same as if I sought to find out how freedom itself is possible as the causality of a will. For then I quit the ground of philosophical explanation, and I have no other to go upon. I might indeed revel in the world of intelligences which still remains to me, but although I have an *idea* of it which is well founded, yet I have not the least *knowledge* of it, nor can I ever attain to such knowledge with all the efforts of my natural faculty of reason. It signifies only a something that remains over when I have eliminated everything belonging to the world of sense from the actuating principles of my will, serving merely to keep in bounds the principle of motives taken from the field of sensibility; fixing its limits and showing that it does not contain all in all within itself, but that there is more beyond it; but this something more I know no further. Of pure reason which frames this ideal, there remains after the abstraction of all matter, i.e., knowledge of objects, nothing but the form, namely, the practical law of the universality of the maxims, and in conformity with this conception of reason in reference to a pure world of understanding as a possible efficient cause, that is a cause determining the will. There must here be a total absence of springs; unless this idea of an intelligible world is itself the spring, or that in which reason primarily takes an interest; but to make this intelligible is precisely the problem that we cannot solve.

Here now is the extreme limit of all moral inquiry, and it is of great importance to determine it even on this account, in order that reason may not on the one hand, to the prejudice of morals, seek about in the world of sense for the supreme motive and an interest comprehensible but empirical; and on the other hand, that it may not impotently flap its wings without being able to move in the (for it) empty space of transcendent concepts which we call the intelligible world, and so lose itself amidst chimeras. For the rest, the idea of a pure world of understanding as a system of all intelligences, and to which we ourselves as rational beings belong (although we are likewise on the other side members of the sensible world), this remains always a useful and legitimate idea for the purposes of rational belief, although all knowledge stops at its threshold, useful, namely, to produce in us a lively interest in the moral law by means of the noble ideal of a universal kingdom of *ends in themselves* (rational beings), to which we can belong as members then only when we carefully conduct ourselves according to the maxims of freedom as if they were laws of nature.

Concluding Remark

The speculative employment of reason *with respect to nature* leads to the absolute necessity of some supreme cause of *the world:* the practical employment of reason *with a view to freedom* leads also to absolute necessity, but only *of the laws of the actions* of a rational being as such. Now it is an essential *principle* of reason, however employed, to push its knowledge to a consciousness of its *necessity* (without which it would not be rational knowledge). It is, however, an equally essential *restriction* of the same reason that it can neither discern the *necessity* of what is or what happens, nor of what ought to happen, unless a condition is supposed on which it is or happens or ought to happen. In this way, however, by the constant inquiry for the condition, the satisfaction of reason is only further and further postponed. Hence it unceasingly seeks the unconditionally necessary and finds itself forced to assume it, although without any means of making it comprehensible to itself, happy enough if only it can discover a conception which agrees with this assumption. It is therefore no fault in our deduction of the supreme principle of morality, but an objection that should be made to human reason in general, that it cannot enable us to conceive the absolute necessity of an unconditional practical law (such as the categorical imperative must be). It cannot be blamed for refusing to explain this necessity by a condition, that is to say, by means of some interest assumed as a basis, since the law would then cease to be a supreme law of reason. And thus while we do not comprehend the practical unconditional necessity of the moral imperative, we yet comprehend its *incomprehensibility,* and this is all that can be fairly demanded of a philosophy which strives to carry its principles up to the very limit of human reason.

CONTENTS

CRITIQUE OF PRACTICAL REASON

PREFACE

THIS work is called the *Critique of Practical Reason,* not of the *pure* practical reason, although its parallelism with the speculative critique would seem to require the latter term. The reason of this appears sufficiently from the treatise itself. Its business is to show that *there is pure practical reason,* and for this purpose it criticizes the entire practical *faculty* of reason. If it succeeds in this, it has no need to criticize the *pure faculty itself* in order to see whether reason in making such a claim does not presumptuously *overstep* itself (as is the case with the speculative reason). For if, as pure reason, it is actually practical, it proves its own reality and that of its concepts by fact, and all disputation against the possibility of its being real is futile.

With this faculty, transcendental *freedom* is also established; freedom, namely, in that absolute sense in which speculative reason required it in its use of the concept of causality in order to escape the antinomy into which it inevitably falls, when in the chain of cause and effect it tries to think the *unconditioned.* Speculative reason could only exhibit this concept (of freedom) problematically as not impossible to thought, without assuring it any objective reality, and merely lest the supposed impossibility of what it must at least allow to be thinkable should endanger its very being and plunge it into an abyss of scepticism.

Inasmuch as the reality of the concept of freedom is proved by an apodeictic law of practical reason, it is the *keystone* of the whole system of pure reason, even the speculative, and all other concepts (those of God and immortality) which, as being mere ideas, remain in it unsupported, now attach themselves to this concept, and by it obtain consistence and objective reality; that is to say, their *possibility* is *proved* by the fact that freedom actually exists, for this idea is revealed by the moral law.

Freedom, however, is the only one of all the ideas of the speculative reason of which we *know* the possibility *a priori* (without, however, understanding it), because it is the condition of the moral law which we know.[1] The ideas of *God* and *immortality,* however, are not conditions of the moral law, but only conditions of the necessary object of a will determined by this law; that is to say, conditions of the practical use of our pure reason. Hence, with respect to these ideas, we cannot affirm that we *know* and *understand,* I will not say the actuality, but even the possibility of them. However they are the conditions of the application of the morally determined will to its object, which is given to it *a priori,* viz., the *summum bonum.* Consequently in this practical point of view their possibility must be *assumed,* although we cannot theoretically know and understand it. To justify this assumption it is sufficient, in a practical point of view, that they contain no intrinsic impossibility (contradiction). Here we have what, as far as speculative reason is concerned, is a merely *subjective* principle of assent, which, however, is *objectively* valid for a reason equally pure but practical, and this principle, by means of the concept of freedom, assures objective reality and authority to the ideas of God and immortality. Nay, there is a subjective necessity (a need of pure reason) to assume them. Nevertheless the theoretical knowledge of reason is not hereby enlarged, but only the possibility is given, which heretofore was merely a *problem* and now becomes *assertion,* and thus the practical use of reason is connected with the elements of theoretical reason. And this need is not a merely hypothetical one for the *arbitrary* purposes of speculation, that we must assume something if we *wish* in speculation to carry reason to its utmost limits, but it is a need which has the force of *law* to assume something without which that cannot be which we must inevitably set before us as the aim of our action.

[1] Lest any one should imagine that he finds an *inconsistency* here when I call freedom the condition of the moral law, and hereafter maintain in the treatise itself that the moral law is the condition under which we can first *become conscious* of freedom, I will merely remark that freedom is the *ratio essendi* of the moral law, while the moral law is the *ratio cognoscendi* of freedom. For had not the moral law been previously distinctly thought in our reason, we should never consider ourselves justified in *assuming* such a thing as freedom, although it be not contradictory. But were there no freedom it would be *impossible to trace* the moral law in ourselves at all.

It would certainly be more satisfactory to our speculative reason if it could solve these problems for itself without this circuit and preserve the solution for practical use as a thing to be referred to, but in fact our faculty of speculation is not so well provided. Those who boast of such high knowledge ought not to keep it back, but to exhibit it publicly that it may be tested and appreciated. They want to prove: very good, let them prove; and the critical philosophy lays its arms at their feet as the victors. *Quid statis? Nolint. Atqui licet esse beatis.* As they then do not in fact choose to do so, probably because they cannot, we must take up these arms again in order to seek in the mortal use of reason, and to base on this, the notions of *God, freedom,* and *immortality,* the *possibility* of which speculation cannot adequately prove.

Here first is explained the enigma of the critical philosophy, viz.: how we *deny* objective *reality* to the supersensible use of the *categories* in speculation and yet *admit* this *reality* with respect to the objects of pure practical reason. This must at first seem *inconsistent* as long as this practical use is only nominally known. But when, by a thorough analysis of it, one becomes aware that the reality spoken of does not imply any theoretical *determination of the categories* and extension of our knowledge to the supersensible; but that what is meant is that in this respect *an object* belongs to them, because either they are contained in the necessary determination of the will *a priori,* or are inseparably connected with its object; then this inconsistency disappears, because the use we make of these concepts is different from what speculative reason requires. On the other hand, there now appears an unexpected and very satisfactory proof of the *consistency* of the speculative critical philosophy. For whereas it insisted that the objects of experience as such, including our own subject, have only the value of *phenomena,* while at the same time things in themselves must be supposed as their basis, so that not everything supersensible was to be regarded as a fiction and its concept as empty; so now practical reason itself, without any concert with the speculative, assures reality to a supersensible object of the category of causality, viz., *freedom,* although (as becomes a practical concept) only for practical use; and this establishes on the evidence of a fact that which in the former case could only be conceived. By this the strange but certain doctrine of the speculative critical philosophy, that *the thinking subject is to itself in internal intuition only a phenomenon,* obtains in the critical examination of the practical reason its full confirmation, and that so thoroughly that we should be compelled to adopt this doctrine, even if the former had never proved it at all.[1]

By this also I can understand why the most considerable objections which I have as yet met with against the Critique turn about these two points, namely, on the one side, the objective reality of the categories as applied to noumena, which is in the theoretical department of knowledge denied, in the practical affirmed; and on the other side, the paradoxical demand to regard oneself *quâ* subject of freedom as a noumenon, and at the same time from the point of view of physical nature as a phenomenon in one's own empirical consciousness; for as long as one has formed no definite notions of morality and freedom, one could not conjecture on the one side what was intended to be the noumenon, the basis of the alleged phenomenon, and on the other side it seemed doubtful whether it was at all possible to form any notion of it, seeing that we had previously assigned all the notions of the pure understanding in its theoretical use exclusively to phenomena. Nothing but a detailed criticism of the practical reason can remove all this misapprehension and set in a clear light the consistency which constitutes its greatest merit.

So much by way of justification of the proceeding by which, in this work, the notions and principles of pure speculative reason which have already undergone their special critical examination are, now and then, again subjected to examination. This would not in other cases be in accordance with the systematic process by which a science is established, since matters which have been decided ought only to be cited and not again discussed. In this case, however, it was not only allowable but necessary, because reason is here considered in transition to a different use of these concepts from what it had made of them before. Such a transition necessitates a comparison of the old and the new usage, in order to distinguish well the new path from the old one and, at the same time, to allow their connection to be observed. Accordingly considerations of this kind, including those which are once more directed to the concept of

[1] The union of causality as freedom with causality as rational mechanism, the former established by the moral law, the latter by the law of nature in the same subject, namely, man, is impossible, unless we conceive him with reference to the former as a being in himself, and with reference to the latter as a phenomenon—the former in pure consciousness, the latter in empirical consciousness. Otherwise reason inevitably contradicts itself.

freedom in the practical use of the pure reason, must not be regarded as an interpolation serving only to fill up the gaps in the critical system of speculative reason (for this is for its own purpose complete), or like the props and buttresses which in a hastily constructed building are often added afterwards; but as true members which make the connexion of the system plain, and show us concepts, here presented as real, which there could only be presented problematically. This remark applies especially to the concept of freedom, respecting which one cannot but observe with surprise that so many boast of being able to understand it quite well and to explain its possibility, while they regard it only psychologically, whereas if they had studied it in a transcendental point of view, they must have recognized that it is not only *indispensable* as a problematical concept, in the complete use of speculative reason, but also quite *incomprehensible;* and if they afterwards came to consider its practical use, they must needs have come to the very mode of determining the principles of this, to which they are now so loth to assent. The concept of freedom is the stone of stumbling for all *empiricists,* but at the same time the key to the loftiest practical principles for *critical* moralists, who perceive by its means that they must necessarily proceed by a *rational* method. For this reason I beg the reader not to pass lightly over what is said of this concept at the end of the Analytic.

I must leave it to those who are acquainted with works of this kind to judge whether such a system as that of the practical reason, which is here developed from the critical examination of it, has cost much or little trouble, especially in seeking not to miss the true point of view from which the whole can be rightly sketched. It presupposes, indeed, the *Fundamental Principles of the Metaphysic of Morals,* but only in so far as this gives a preliminary acquaintance with the principle of duty, and assigns and justifies a definite formula thereof; in other respects it is independent.[1] It results from the nature of this practical faculty itself that the *complete classification* of all practical sciences cannot be added, as in the critique of the speculative reason. For it is not possible to define duties specially, as human duties, with a view to their classification, until the subject of this definition (viz., man) is known according to his actual nature, at least so far as is necessary with respect to duty; this, however, does not belong to a critical examination of the practical reason, the business of which is only to assign in a complete manner the principles of its possibility, extent, and limits, without special reference to human nature. The classification then belongs to the system of science, not to the system of criticism.

In the second part of the Analytic I have given, as I trust, a sufficient answer to the objection of a truth-loving and acute critic[2] of the *Fundamental Principles of the Metaphysic of Morals*—a critic always worthy of respect—the objection, namely, that *the notion of good was not established before the moral principle,* as he thinks it ought to have been.[3] I have

[1] A reviewer who wanted to find some fault with this work has hit the truth better, perhaps, than he thought, when he says that no new principle of morality is set forth in it, but only a *new formula.* But who would think of introducing a new principle of all morality and making himself as it were the first discoverer of it, just as if all the world before him were ignorant what duty was or had been in thorough-going error? But whoever knows of what importance to a mathematician a *formula* is, which defines accurately what is to be done to work a problem, will not think that a formula is insignificant and useless which does the same for all duty in general.

[2] [See Kant's *"Das mag in der Theorie richtig seyn,"* etc. *Werke,* vol. vii, p. 182.]

[3] It might also have been objected to me that I have not first defined the notion of the *faculty of desire,* or of the *feeling of pleasure,* although this reproach would be unfair, because this definition might reasonably be presupposed as given in psychology. However, the definition there given might be such as to found the determination of the faculty of desire on the feeling of pleasure (as is commonly done), and thus the supreme principle of practical philosophy would be necessarily made *empirical,* which, however, remains to be proved and in this critique is altogether refuted. It will, therefore, give this definition here in such a manner as it ought to be given, in order to leave this contested point open at the beginning, as it should be. LIFE is the faculty a being has of acting according to laws of the faculty of desire. The *faculty of* DESIRE is the being's *faculty of becoming by means of its ideas the cause of the actual existence of the objects of these ideas.* PLEASURE *is the idea of the agreement of the object, or the action with the subjective conditions of life,* i.e., with the faculty of *causality of an idea in respect of the actuality of its object* (or with the determination of the forces of the subject to action which produces it). I have no further need for the purposes of this critique of notions borrowed from psychology; the critique itself supplies the rest. It is easily seen that the question whether the faculty of desire is always based on pleasure, or whether under certain conditions pleasure only follows the determination of desire, is by this definition left undecided, for it is composed only of terms belonging to the pure understanding, i.e., of categories which contain nothing empirical. Such precaution is very desirable in all philosophy and yet is often neglected; namely, not to prejudge questions by adventuring definitions before the notion has been completely analysed, which is often very late. It may be observed through the whole course of the critical philosophy (of the theoretical as well as the practical reason) that frequent opportunity offers of supplying defects in the old dogmatic method of philosophy, and of correcting errors which are not observed until we make such rational use of these notions *viewing them as a whole.*

also had regard to many of the objections which have reached me from men who show that they have at heart the discovery of the truth, and I shall continue to do so (for those who have only their old system before their eyes, and who have already settled what is to be approved or disapproved, do not desire any explanation which might stand in the way of their own private opinion.)

When we have to study a particular faculty of the human mind in its sources, its content, and its limits; then from the nature of human knowledge we must begin with its *parts*, with an accurate and complete exposition of them; complete, namely, so far as is possible in the present state of our knowledge of its elements. But there is another thing to be attended to which is of a more philosophical and *architectonic* character, namely, to grasp correctly the *idea of the whole*, and from thence to get a view of all those parts as mutually related by the aid of pure reason, and by means of their derivation from the concept of the whole. This is only possible through the most intimate acquaintance with the system; and those who find the first inquiry too troublesome, and do not think it worth their while to attain such an acquaintance, cannot reach the second stage, namely, the general view, which is a synthetical return to that which had previously been given analytically. It is no wonder then if they find inconsistencies everywhere, although the gaps which these indicate are not in the system itself, but in their own incoherent train of thought.

I have no fear, as regards this treatise, of the reproach that I wish to introduce a *new language*, since the sort of knowledge here in question has itself somewhat of an everyday character. Nor even in the case of the former critique could this reproach occur to anyone who had thought it through and not merely turned over the leaves. To invent new words where the language has no lack of expressions for given notions is a childish effort to distinguish oneself from the crowd, if not by new and true thoughts, yet by new patches on the old garment. If, therefore, the readers of that work know any more familiar expressions which are as suitable to the thought as those seem to me to be, or if they think they can show the *futility* of these thoughts themselves and hence that of the expression, they would, in the first case, very much oblige me, for I only desire to be understood: and, in the second case, they would deserve well of philosophy. But, as long as these thoughts stand, I very much doubt that suitable and yet more common expressions for them can be found.[1]

In this manner, then, the *a priori* principles of two faculties of the mind, the faculty of cognition and that of desire, would be found and determined as to the conditions, extent, and limits of their use, and thus a sure foundation be paid for a scientific system of philosophy, both theoretic and practical.

Nothing worse could happen to these labours than that anyone should make the unexpected discovery that there neither is, nor can be, any *a priori* knowledge at all. But there is no danger of this. This would be the same thing as if one sought to prove by reason that there is no reason. For we only say that we know something by reason, when we are conscious that we could have known it, even if it had not been given to us in experience; hence rational knowledge and

[1] I am more afraid in the present treatise of occasional misconception in respect of some expressions which I have chosen with the greatest care in order that the notion to which they point may not be missed. Thus, in the table of categories of the *practical* reason under the title of *Modality*, the *permitted*, and *forbidden* (in a practical objective point of view, possible and impossible) have almost the same meaning in common language as the next category, *duty* and *contrary to duty*. Here, however, the *former* means what coincides with, or contradicts, a merely *possible* practical precept (for example, the solution of all problems of geometry and mechanics); the *latter*, what is similarly related to a law *actually* present in the reason; and this distinction is not quite foreign even to common language, although somewhat unusual. For example, it is *forbidden* to an orator, as such, to forge new words or constructions; in a certain degree this is *permitted* to a poet; in neither case is there any question of duty. For if anyone chooses to forfeit his reputation as an orator, no one can prevent him. We have here only to do with the distinction of *imperatives* into *problematical*, *assertorial*, and *apodeictic*. Similarly in the note in which I have compared the moral ideas of practical perfection in different philosophical schools, I have distinguished the idea of *wisdom* from that of *holiness*, although I have stated that essentially and objectively they are the same. But in that place I understand by the former only that wisdom to which man (the Stoic) lays claim; therefore I take it *subjectively* as an attribute alleged to belong to man. (Perhaps the expression *virtue*, with which also the Stoic made great show, would better mark the characteristic of his school.) The expression of a *postulate* of pure practical reason might give most occasion to misapprehension in case the reader confounded it with the signification of the postulates in pure mathematics, which carry apodeictic certainty with them. These, however, postulate the *possibility of an action*, the object of which has been previously recognized *a priori* in theory as *possible*, and that with perfect certainty. But the former postulates the possibility of an object itself (God and the immortality of the soul) from apodeictic *practical* laws, and therefore only for the purposes of a practical reason. This certainty of the postulated possibility then is not at all theoretic, and consequently not apodeictic; that is to say, it is not a known necessity as regards the object, but a necessary supposition as regards the subject, necessary for the obedience to its objective but practical laws. It is, therefore, merely a necessary hypothesis. I could find no better expression for this rational necessity, which is subjective, but yet true and unconditional.

knowledge *a priori* are one and the same. It is a clear contradiction to try to extract necessity from a principle of experience (*ex pumice aquam*), and to try by this to give a judgement true universality (without which there is no rational inference, not even inference from analogy, which is at least a presumed universality and objective necessity). To substitute subjective necessity, that is, custom, for objective, which exists only in *a priori* judgements, is to deny to reason the power of judging about the object, i.e., of knowing it, and what belongs to it. It implies, for example, that we must not say of something which often or always follows a certain antecedent state that we can *conclude* from this to that (for this would imply objective necessity and the notion of an *a priori* connexion), but only that we may expect similar cases (just as animals do), that is,that we reject the notion of cause altogether as *false* and a mere delusion. As to attempting to remedy this want of objective and consequently universal validity by saying that we can see no ground for attributing any other sort of knowledge to other rational beings, if this reasoning were valid, our ignorance would do more for the enlargement of our knowledge than all our meditation. For, then, on this very ground that we have no knowledge of any other rational beings besides man, we should have a right to suppose them to be of the same nature as we know ourselves to be: that is, we should really know them. I omit to mention that universal assent does not prove the objective validity of a judgement (i.e., its validity as a cognition), and although this universal assent should accidentally happen, it could furnish no proof of agreement with the object; on the contrary, it is the objective validity which alone constitutes the basis of a necessary universal consent.

Hume would be quite satisfied with this system of universal empiricism, for, as is well known, he desired nothing more than that, instead of ascribing any objective meaning to the necessity in the concept of cause, a merely subjective one should be assumed, viz., custom, in order to deny that reason could judge about God, freedom, and immortality; and if once his principles were granted, he was certainly well able to deduce his conclusions therefrom, with all logical coherence. But even Hume did not make his empiricism so universal as to include mathematics. He holds the principles of mathematics to be analytical; and if his were correct, they would certainly be apodeictic also: but we could not infer from this that reason has the faculty of forming apodeictic judgements in philosophy also—that is to say, those which are synthetical judgements, like the judgement of causality. But if we adopt a *universal* empiricism, then mathematics will be included.

Now if this science is in contradiction with a reason that admits only empirical principles, as it inevitably is in the antinomy in which mathematics prove the infinite divisibility of space, which empiricism cannot admit; then the greatest possible evidence of demonstration is in manifest contradiction with the alleged conclusions from experience, and we are driven to ask, like Cheselden's blind patient, "Which deceives me, sight or touch?" (for empiricism is based on a necessity *felt*, rationalism on a necessity *seen*). And thus universal empiricism reveals itself as absolute scepticism. It is erroneous to attribute this in such an unqualified sense to Hume,[1] since he left at least one certain touchstone (which can only be found in *a priori* principles), although experience consists not only of feelings, but also of judgements.

However, as in this philosophical and critical age such empiricism can scarcely be serious, and it is probably put forward only as an intellectual exercise and for the purpose of putting in a clearer light, by contrast, the necessity of rational *a priori* principles, we can only be grateful to those who employ themselves in this otherwise uninstructive labour.

[1] Names that designate the followers of a sect have always been accompanied with much injustice; just as if one said, "N is an Idealist." For although he not only admits, but even insists, that our ideas of external things have actual objects of external things corresponding to them, yet he holds that the form of the intuition does not depend on them but on the human mind.

INTRODUCTION

Of the Idea of a Critique of Practical Reason

THE theoretical use of reason was concerned with objects of the cognitive faculty only, and a critical examination of it with reference to this use applied properly only to the *pure* faculty of cognition; because this raised the suspicion, which was afterwards confirmed, that it might easily pass beyond its limits, and be lost among unattainable objects, or even contradictory notions. It is quite different with the practical use of reason. In this, reason is concerned with the grounds of determination of the will, which is a faculty either to produce objects corresponding to ideas, or to determine ourselves to the effecting of such objects (whether the physical power is sufficient or not); that is, to determine our causality. For here, reason can at least attain so far as to determine the will, and has always objective reality in so far as it is the volition only that is in question. The first question here then is whether pure reason of itself alone suffices to determine the will, or whether it can be a ground of determination only as dependent on empirical conditions. Now, here there comes in a notion of causality justified by the critique of the pure reason, although not capable of being presented empirically, viz., that of *freedom;* and if we can now discover means of proving that this property does in fact belong to the human will (and so to the will of all rational beings), then it will not only be shown that pure reason can be practical, but that it alone, and not reason empirically limited, is indubitably practical; consequently, we shall have to make a critical examination, not of *pure practical* reason, but only of *practical* reason generally. For when once pure reason is shown to exist, it needs no critical examination. For reason itself contains the standard for the critical examination of every use of it. The critique, then, of practical reason generally is bound to prevent the empirically conditioned reason from claiming exclusively to furnish the ground of determination of the will. If it is proved that there is a [practical] reason, its employment is alone immanent; the empirically conditioned use, which claims supremacy, is on the contrary transcendent and expresses itself in demands and precepts which go quite beyond its sphere. This is just the opposite of what might be said of pure reason in its speculative employment.

However, as it is still pure reason, the knowledge of which is here the foundation of its practical employment, the general outline of the classification of a critique of practical reason must be arranged in accordance with that of the speculative. We must, then, have the *Elements* and the *Methodology* of it; and in the former an *Analytic* as the rule of truth, and a *Dialectic* as the exposition and dissolution of the illusion in the judgements of practical reason. But the order in the subdivision of the Analytic will be the reverse of that in the critique of the pure speculative reason. For, in the present case, we shall commence with the *principles* and proceed to the *concepts,* and only then, if possible, to the senses; whereas in the case of the speculative reason we began with the senses and had to end with the principles. The reason of this lies again in this: that now we have to do with a will, and have to consider reason, not in its relation to objects, but to this will and its causality. We must, then, begin with the principles of a causality not empirically conditioned, after which the attempt can be made to establish our notions of the determining grounds of such a will, of their application to objects, and finally to the subject and its sense faculty. We necessarily begin with the law of causality from freedom, that is, with a pure practical principle, and this determines the objects to which alone it can be applied.

FIRST PART

ELEMENTS OF PURE PRACTICAL REASON

BOOK I. *The Analytic of Pure Practical Reason*

CHAPTER I. *Of the Principles of Pure Practical Reason*

§ I. DEFINITION

PRACTICAL principles are propositions which contain a general determination of the will, having under it several practical rules. They are subjective, or *maxims,* when the condition is regarded by the subject as valid only for his own will, but are objective, or practical *laws,* when the condition is recognized as objective, that is, valid for the will of every rational being.

REMARK

Supposing that *pure* reason contains in itself a practical motive, that is, one adequate to determine the will, then there are practical laws; otherwise all practical principles will be mere maxims. In case the will of a rational being is pathologically affected, there may occur a conflict of the maxims with the practical laws recognized by itself. For example, one may make it his maxim to let no injury pass unrevenged, and yet he may see that this is not a practical law, but only his own maxim; that, on the contrary, regarded as being in one and the same maxim a rule for the will of every rational being, it must contradict itself. In natural philosophy the principles of what happens, e.g., the principle of equality of action and reaction in the communication of motion) are at the same time laws of nature; for the use of reason there is theoretical and determined by the nature of the object. In practical philosophy, i.e., that which has to do only with the grounds of determination of the will, the principles which a man makes for himself are not laws by which one is inevitably bound; because reason in practical matters has to do with the subject, namely, with the faculty of desire, the special character of which may occasion variety in the rule. The practical rule is always a product of reason, because it prescribes action as a means to the effect. But in the case of a being with whom reason does not of itself determine the will, this rule is an *imperative,* i.e., a rule characterized by "shall," which expresses the objective necessitation of the action and signifies that, if reason completely determined the will, the action would inevitably take place according to this rule. Imperatives, therefore, are objectively valid, and are quite distinct from maxims, which are subjective principles. The former either determine the conditions of the causality of the rational being as an efficient cause, i.e., merely in reference to the effect and the means of attaining it; or they determine the will only, whether it is adequate to the effect or not. The former would be hypothetical imperatives, and contain mere precepts of skill; the latter, on the contrary, would be categorical, and would alone be practical laws. Thus maxims are *principles,* but not *imperatives.* Imperatives themselves, however, when they are conditional (i.e., do not determine the will simply as will, but only in respect to a desired effect, that is, when they are hypothetical imperatives), are practical *precepts* but not *laws.* Laws must be sufficient to determine the will as will, even before I ask whether I have power sufficient for a desired effect, or the means necessary to produce it; hence they are categorical: otherwise they are not laws at all, because the necessity is wanting, which, if it is to be practical, must be independent of conditions which are pathological and are therefore only contingently connected with the will. Tell a man, for example, that he must be industrious and thrifty in youth, in order that he may not want in old age; this is a correct and important practical precept of the will. But it is easy to see that in this case the will is directed to something *else* which it is presupposed that it desires; and as to this desire, we must leave it to the actor himself whether he looks forward to other resources than those of his own acquisition, or does not expect to be old, or thinks that in case of future necessity he will be able to make shift with little. Reason, from which alone can spring a rule involving necessity, does, indeed, give necessity to this precept (else it would not be an imperative), but this is a necessity dependent on subjective conditions, and cannot be supposed in the same degree in all subjects. But that reason may give laws it is necessary that it should only need to presuppose *itself*, because rules are objectively and universally valid only when they hold without any contingent subjective conditions, which distinguish one rational being from another. Now tell a man that he should never make a deceitful promise, this is a rule which only concerns his will, whether the purposes he may have can be attained thereby or not; it is the volition only which is to be determined *a priori* by that rule. If now it is found that this rule is practically right, then it is a law, because it is a categorical imperative. Thus, practical laws refer to the will only, without considering what is attained by its causality, and we may disregard this latter (as belonging to the world of sense) in order to have them quite pure.

§ II. Theorem I

All practical principles which presuppose an object (matter) of the faculty of desire as the ground of determination of the will are empirical and can furnish no practical laws.

By the matter of the faculty of desire I mean an object the realization of which is desired. Now, if the desire for this object *precedes* the practical rule and is the condition of our making it a principle, then I say (*in the first place*) this principle is in that case wholly empirical, for then what determines the choice is the idea of an object and that relation of this idea to the subject by which its faculty of desire is determined to its realization. Such a relation to the subject is called the *pleasure* in the realization of an object. This, then, must be presupposed as a condition of the possibility of determination of the will. But it is impossible to know *a priori* of any idea of an object whether it will be connected with *pleasure* or *pain*, or be indifferent. In such cases, therefore, the determining principle of the choice must be empirical and, therefore, also the practical material principle which presupposes it as a condition.

In the second place, since susceptibility to a pleasure or pain can be known only empirically and cannot hold in the same degree for all rational beings, a principle which is based on this subjective condition may serve indeed as a *maxim* for the subject which possesses this susceptibility, but not as a *law* even to him (because it is wanting in objective necessity, which must be recognized *a priori*); it follows, therefore, that such a principle can never furnish a practical law.

§ III. Theorem II

All material practical principles as such are of one and the same kind and come under the general principle of self-love or private happiness.

Pleasure arising from the idea of the existence of a thing, in so far as it is to determine the desire of this thing, is founded on the *susceptibility* of the subject, since it *depends* on the presence of an object; hence it belongs to sense (feeling), and not to understanding, which expresses a relation of the idea *to an object* according to concepts, not to the subject according to feelings. It is, then, practical only in so far as the faculty of desire is determined by the sensation of agreeableness which the subject expects from the actual existence of the object. Now, a rational being's consciousness of the pleasantness of life uninterruptedly accompanying his whole existence is happiness; and the principle which makes this the supreme ground of determination of the will is the principle of self-love. All material principles, then, which place the determining ground of the will in the pleasure or pain to be received from the existence of any object are all of the same kind, inasmuch as they all belong to the principle of self-love or private happiness.

COROLLARY

All *material* practical rules place the determining principle of the will in the *lower desires;* and if there were no *purely formal* laws of the will adequate to determine it, then we could not admit *any higher desire* at all.

REMARK I

It is surprising that men, otherwise acute, can think it possible to distinguish between *higher* and *lower desires,* according as the ideas which are connected with the feeling of pleasure have their origin in the *senses* or in the *understanding;* for when we inquire what are the determining grounds of desire, and place them in some expected pleasantness, it is of no consequence whence the *idea* of this pleasing object is derived, but only how much it *pleases.* Whether an idea has its seat and source in the understanding or not, if it can only determine the choice by presupposing a feeling of pleasure in the subject, it follows that its capability of determining the choice depends altogether on the nature of the inner sense, namely, that this can be agreeably affected by it. However dissimilar ideas of objects may be, though they be ideas of the understanding, or even of the reason in contrast to ideas of sense, yet the feeling of pleasure, by means of which they constitute the determining principle of the will (the expected satisfaction which impels the activity to the production of the object), is of one and the same kind, not only inasmuch as it can only be known empirically, but also inasmuch as it affects one and the same vital force which manifests itself in the faculty of desire, and in this respect can only differ in degree from every other ground of determination. Otherwise, how could we compare in respect of *magnitude* two principles of determination, the ideas of which depend upon different faculties, so as to prefer that which affects the faculty of desire in the highest degree. The same man may return unread an instructive book which he cannot again obtain, in order not to miss a hunt; he may depart in the midst of a fine speech, in order not to be late for dinner; he may leave a rational conversation, such as he otherwise values highly, to take his place at the gaming-table; he may even repulse a poor man whom he at other times takes pleasure in benefiting, because he has only just enough money in his pocket to pay for his admission to the theatre. If the determination of his will rests on the feeling of the agreeableness or disagreeableness that he expects from any cause, it is all the same to him by what sort of ideas he will be affected. The only thing that concerns him, in order to decide his choice, is, how great, how long continued, how easily obtained, and how often repeated, this agreeableness is. Just as to the man who wants money to spend, it is all the same whether the gold was dug out of the mountain or washed out of the sand, provided it is everywhere accepted at the same value; so the man who cares only for the enjoyment of life does not ask whether the ideas are of the understanding or the senses, but only *how much* and *how great pleasure* they will give for the longest time. It is only those that would gladly deny to pure reason the power of determining the will, without the presupposition of any feeling, who could deviate so far from their own exposition as to describe as quite heterogeneous what they have themselves previously brought under one and the same principle. Thus, for example, it is observed that we can find pleasure in the mere *exercise of power*, in the consciousness of our strength of mind in overcoming obstacles which are opposed to our designs, in the culture of our mental talents, etc.; and we justly call these more *refined* pleasures and enjoyments, because they are more in our power than others; they do not wear out, but rather increase the capacity for further enjoyment of them, and while they delight they at the same time cultivate. But to say on this account that they determine the will in a different way and not through sense, whereas the possibility of the pleasure presupposes a feeling for it implanted in us, which is the first condition of this satisfaction; this is just as when ignorant persons that like to dabble in metaphysics imagine matter so subtle, so supersubtle that they almost make themselves giddy with it, and then think that in this way they have conceived it as a *spiritual* and yet extended being. If with Epicurus we make virtue determine the will only by means of the pleasure it promises, we cannot afterwards blame him for holding that this pleasure is of the same kind as those of the coarsest senses. For we have no reason whatever to charge him with holding that the ideas by which this feeling is excited in us belong merely to the bodily senses. As far as can be conjectured, he sought the source of many of them in the use of the higher cognitive faculty, but this did not prevent him, and could not prevent him, from holding on the principle above stated, that the pleasure itself which those intellectual ideas give us, and by which alone they can determine the will, is just of the same kind. *Consistency* is the highest obligation of a philosopher, and yet the most rarely found. The ancient Greek schools give us more examples of it than we find in our *syncretistic* age, in which a certain shallow and dishonest *system of compromise* of contradictory principles is devised, because it commends itself better to a public which is content to know something of everything and nothing thoroughly, so as to please every party.

The principle of private happiness, however much understanding and reason may be used in it, cannot contain any other determining principles for the will than those which belong to the *lower* desires; and either there are no [higher] desires at all, or *pure* reason must of itself alone be practical; that is, it must be able to determine the will by the mere form of the practical rule without supposing any feeling, and consequently without any idea of the pleasant or unpleasant, which is the matter of the desire, and which is always an empirical condition of the principles. Then only, when reason of itself determines the will (not as the servant of the inclination), it is really a *higher* desire to which that which is pathologically determined is subordinate, and is really, and even specifically, distinct from the latter, so that even the slightest admixture of the motives of the latter impairs its strength and superiority; just as in a mathematical demonstration the least empirical condition would degrade and destroy its force and value. Reason, with its practical law, determines the will immediately, not by means of an intervening feeling of pleasure or pain, not even of pleasure in the law itself, and it is only because it can, as pure reason, be practical, that it is possible for it to be *legislative.*

REMARK II

To be happy is necessarily the wish of every finite rational being, and this, therefore, is inevitably a determining principle of its faculty of desire. For we are not in possession originally of satisfaction with our whole existence—a bliss which would imply a consciousness of our own independent self-sufficiency—this is a problem imposed upon us by our own finite nature, because we have wants and these wants regard the matter of our desires, that is, something that is relative to a subjective feeling of pleasure or pain, which determines what we need in order to be satisfied with our condition. But just because this material principle of determination can only be empirically known by the subject, it is impossible to regard this problem as a law; for a law being objective must contain the *very same principle of determination* of the will in all cases and for all rational beings. For, although the notion of happiness is *in every case* the foundation of practical relation of the *objects* to the desires, yet it is only a general name for the subjective determining principles, and determines nothing specifically; whereas this is what alone we are concerned with in this practical problem, which cannot be solved at all without such specific determination. For it is every man's own special feeling of pleasure and pain that decides in what he is to place his happiness, and even in the same subject this will vary with the difference of his wants according as this feeling changes, and thus a law which is *subjectively necessary* (as a law of nature) is *objectively* a very contingent practical principle, which can and must be very different in different subjects and therefore can never furnish a law; since, in the desire for happiness it is not the form (of conformity to law) that is decisive, but simply the matter, namely, whether I am to expect pleasure in following the law, and how much. Principles of self-love may, indeed, contain universal precepts of skill (how to find means to accomplish one's purpose), but in that case they are merely theoretical principles;[1] as, for example, how he who would like to eat bread should contrive a mill; but practical precepts founded on them can never be universal, for the determining principle of the desire is based on the feeling of pleasure and pain, which can never be supposed to be universally directed to the same objects.

Even supposing, however, that all finite rational beings were thoroughly agreed as to what were the objects of their feelings of pleasure and pain, and also as to the means which they must employ to attain the one and avoid the other; still, they could *by no means* set up the *principle of self-love* as a *practical law,* for this unanimity itself would be only contingent. The principle of determination would still be only subjectively valid and merely empirical, and would not possess the necessity which is conceived in every law, namely, an objective necessity arising from *a priori* grounds; unless, indeed, we hold this necessity to be not at all practical, but merely physical, viz., that our action is as inevitably determined by our inclination, as yawning when we see others yawn. It would be better to maintain that there are no practical laws at all, but only *counsels* for the service of our desires, than to raise merely subjective principles to the rank of practical laws, which have objective necessity, and not merely subjective, and which must be known by reason *a priori,* not by experience (however empirically universal this may be). Even the rules of corresponding phenomena are only called laws of nature (e.g., the mechanical laws), when we either know them really *a priori,* or (as in the case of chemical laws) suppose that they would be known *a priori* from objective grounds if our insight reached further. But in the case of merely subjective practical principles, it is expressly made a condition that they rest, not on objective, but on subjective conditions of choice, and hence that they must always be represented as mere maxims, never as practical laws. This second remark seems at first sight to be mere verbal refinement, but it defines the terms of the most important distinction which can come into consideration in practical investigations.

[1] Propositions which in mathematics or physics are called *practical* ought properly to be called *technical.* For they have nothing to do with the determination of the will; they only point out how a certain effect is to be produced and are, therefore, just as theoretical as any propositions which express the connection of a cause with an effect. Now whoever chooses the effect must also choose the cause.

§ IV. Theorem III

A rational being cannot regard his maxims as practical universal laws, unless he conceives them as principles which determine the will, not by their matter, but by their form only.

By the matter of a practical principle I mean the object of the will. This object is either the determining ground of the will or it is not. In the former case the rule of the will is subjected to an empirical condition (viz., the relation of the determining idea to the feeling of pleasure and pain), consequently it can not be a practical law. Now, when we abstract from a law all matter, i.e., every object of the will (as a determining principle), nothing is left but the mere *form* of a universal legislation. Therefore, either a rational being cannot conceive his subjective practical principles, that is, his maxims, as being at the same time universal laws, or he must suppose that their mere form, by which they are fitted for universal legislation, is alone what makes them practical laws.

REMARK

The commonest understanding can distinguish without instruction what form of maxim is adapted for universal legislation, and what is not. Suppose, for example, that I have made it my maxim to increase my fortune by every safe means. Now, I have a deposit in my hands, the owner of which is dead and has left no writing about it. This is just the case for my maxim. I desire then to know whether that maxim can also hold good as a universal practical law. I apply it, therefore, to the present case, and ask whether it could take the form of a law, and consequently whether I can by my maxim at the same time give such a law as this, that everyone may deny a deposit of which no one can produce a proof. I at once become aware that such a principle, viewed as a law, would annihilate itself, because the result would be that there would be no deposits. A practical law which I recognise as such must be qualified for universal legislation; this is an identical proposition and, therefore, self-evident. Now, if I say that my will is subject to a practical law, I cannot adduce my inclination (e. g., in the present case my avarice) as a principle of determination fitted to be a universal practical law; for this is so far from being fitted for a universal legislation that, if put in the form of a universal law, it would destroy itself.

It is, therefore, surprising that intelligent men could have thought of calling the desire of happiness a universal *practical law* on the ground that the desire is universal, and, therefore, also the *maxim* by which everyone makes this desire determine his will. For whereas in other cases a universal law of nature makes everything harmonious; here, on the contrary, if we attribute to the maxim the universality of a law, the extreme opposite of harmony will follow, the greatest opposition and the complete destruction of the maxim itself and its purpose. For, in that case, the will of all has not one and the same object, but everyone has his own (his private welfare), which may accidentally accord with the purposes of others which are equally selfish, but it is far from sufficing for a law; because the occasional exceptions which one is permitted to make are endless, and cannot be definitely embraced in one universal rule. In this manner, then, results a harmony like that which a certain satirical poem depicts as existing between a married couple bent on going to ruin, "O, marvellous harmony, what he wishes, she wishes also"; or like what is said of the pledge of Francis I to the Emperor Charles V, "What my brother Charles wishes that I wish also" (viz., Milan). Empirical principles of determination are not fit for any universal external legislation, but just as little for internal; for each man makes his own subject the foundation of his inclination, and in the same subject sometimes one inclination, sometimes another, has the preponderance. To discover a law which would govern them all under this condition, namely, bringing them all into harmony, is quite impossible.

§ V. Problem I

Supposing that the mere legislative form of maxims is alone the sufficient determining principle of a will, to find the nature of the will which can be determined by it alone.

Since the bare form of the law can only be conceived by reason, and is, therefore, not an object of the senses, and consequently does not belong to the class of phenomena, it follows that the idea of it, which determines the will, is distinct from all the principles that determine events in nature according to the law of causality, because in their case the determining principles must themselves be phenomena. Now, if no other determining principle can serve as a law for the will except that universal legislative form, such a will must be conceived as quite independent of the natural law of phenomena in their mutual relation, namely, the law of causality; such independence is called *freedom* in the strictest, that is, in the transcendental, sense;

consequently, a will which can have its law in nothing but the mere legislative form of the maxim is a free will.

§ VI. Problem II

Supposing that a will is free, to find the law which alone is competent to determine it necessarily.

Since the matter of the practical law, i.e., an object of the maxim, can never be given otherwise than empirically, and the free will is independent on empirical conditions (that is, conditions belonging to the world of sense) and yet is determinable, consequently a free will must find its principle of determination in the law, and yet independently of the matter of the law. But, besides the matter of the law, nothing is contained in it except the legislative form. It is the legislative form, then, contained in the maxim, which can alone constitute a principle of determination of the [free] will.

REMARK

Thus freedom and an unconditional practical law reciprocally imply each other. Now I do not ask here whether they are in fact distinct, or whether an unconditioned law is not rather merely the consciousness of a pure practical reason and the latter identical with the positive concept of freedom; I only ask, whence *begins* our *knowledge* of the unconditionally practical, whether it is from freedom or from the practical law? Now it cannot begin from freedom, for of this we cannot be immediately conscious, since the first concept of it is negative; nor can we infer it from experience, for experience gives us the knowledge only of the law of phenomena, and hence of the mechanism of nature, the direct opposite of freedom. It is therefore the moral law, of which we become directly conscious (as soon as we trace for ourselves maxims of the will), that *first* presents itself to us, and leads directly to the concept of freedom, inasmuch as reason presents it as a principle of determination not to be outweighed by any sensible conditions, nay, wholly independent of them. But how is the consciousness of that moral law possible? We can become conscious of pure practical laws just as we are conscious of pure theoretical principles, by attending to the necessity with which reason prescribes them and to the elimination of all empirical conditions, which it directs. The concept of a pure will arises out of the former, as that of a pure understanding arises out of the latter. That this is the true subordination of our concepts, and that it is morality that first discovers to us the notion of freedom, hence that it is *practical reason* which, with this concept, first proposes to speculative reason the most insoluble problem, thereby placing it in the greatest perplexity, is evident from the following consideration: Since nothing in phenomena can be explained by the concept of freedom, but the mechanism of nature must constitute the only clue; moreover, when pure reason tries to ascend in the series of causes to the unconditioned, it falls into an antinomy which is entangled in incomprehensibilities on the one side as much as the other; whilst the latter (namely, mechanism) is at least useful in the explanation of phenomena, therefore no one would ever have been so rash as to introduce freedom into science, had not the moral law, and with it practical reason, come in and forced this notion upon us. Experience, however, confirms this order of notions. Suppose some one asserts of his lustful appetite that, when the desired object and the opportunity are present, it is quite irresistible. [Ask him] — if a gallows were erected before the house where he finds this opportunity, in order that he should be hanged thereon immediately after the gratification of his lust, whether he could not then control his passion; we need not be long in doubt what he would reply. Ask him, however—if his sovereign ordered him, on pain of the same immediate execution, to bear false witness against an honourable man, whom the prince might wish to destroy under a plausible pretext, would he consider it possible in that case to overcome his love of life, however great it may be. He would perhaps not venture to affirm whether he would do so or not, but he must unhesitatingly admit that it is possible to do so. He judges, therefore, that he can do a certain thing because he is conscious that he ought, and he recognizes that he is free—a fact which but for the moral law he would never have known.

§ VII. Fundamental Law of the Pure Practical Reason

Act so that the maxim of thy will can always at the same time hold good as a principle of universal legislation.

REMARK

Pure geometry has postulates which are practical propositions, but contain nothing further than the assumption that we *can* do something if it is required that we *should* do it, and these are the only geometrical propositions that concern actual existence. They are, then, practical rules under a problematical condition of the will; but here the rule says: We absolutely must proceed in a certain manner. The practical rule is, therefore, unconditional, and hence it is conceived *a priori* as a categorically practical proposition by which the will is objectively determined absolutely and immediately (by the practical rule itself, which thus is in this case a law); for *pure reason practical of itself* is here directly legislative. The will is thought as independent on empirical conditions, and, therefore, as pure will determined by *the mere form of the law,* and this principle of determination is regarded as the supreme condition of all maxims. The thing is strange enough, and has no parallel in all the rest of our practical knowledge. For the *a priori* thought of a possible universal legislation which is therefore merely problematical, is unconditionally commanded as a law without borrowing anything from experience or from any external will. This, however, is not a precept to do something by which some desired effect can be attained (for then the will would depend on physical conditions), but a rule that determines the will *a priori* only so far as regards the forms of its maxims; and thus it is at least not impossible to conceive that a law, which only applies to the *subjective* form of principles, yet serves as a principle of determination by means of the *objective* form of law in general. We may call the consciousness of this fundamental law a fact of reason, because we cannot reason it out from antecedent data of reason, e. g., the consciousness of freedom (for this is not antecedently given), but it forces itself on us as a synthetic *a priori* proposition, which is not based on any intuition, either pure or empirical. It would, indeed, be analytical if the freedom of the will were presupposed, but to presuppose freedom as a positive *concept* would require an intellectual intuition, which cannot here be assumed; however, when we regard this law as *given,* it must be observed, in order not to fall into any misconception, that it is not an empirical fact, but the sole fact of the pure reason, which thereby announces itself as originally legislative (*sic volo, sic jubeo*).

COROLLARY

Pure reason is practical of itself alone and gives (to man) a universal law which we call the *moral law.*

REMARK

The fact just mentioned is undeniable. It is only necessary to analyse the judgement that men pass on the lawfulness of their actions, in order to find that, whatever inclination may say to the contrary, reason, incorruptible and self-constrained, always confronts the maxim of the will in any action with the pure will, that is, with itself, considering itself as *a priori* practical. Now this principle of morality, just on account of the universality of the legislation which makes it the formal supreme determining principle of the will, without regard to any subjective differences, is declared by the reason to be a law for all rational beings, in so far as they have a will, that is, a power to determine their causality by the conception of rules; and, therefore, so far as they are capable of acting according to principles, and consequently also according to practical *a priori* principles (for these alone have the necessity that reason requires in a principle). It is, therefore, not limited to men only, but applies to all finite beings that possess reason and will; nay, it even includes the Infinite Being as the supreme intelligence. In the former case, however, the law has the form of an imperative, because in them, as rational beings, we can suppose a *pure* will, but being creatures affected with wants and physical motives, not a *holy* will, that is, one which would be incapable of any maxim conflicting with the moral law. In their case, therefore, the moral law is an *imperative,* which commands categorically, because the law is unconditioned; the relation of such a will to this law is *dependence* under the name of *obligation,* which implies a *constraint* to an action, though only by reason and its objective law; and this action is called *duty,* because an elective will, subject to pathological affections (though not determined by them, and, therefore, still free), implies a wish that arises from *subjective* causes and, therefore, may often be opposed to the pure objective determining principle; whence it requires the moral constraint of a resistance of the practical reason, which may be called an internal, but intellectual, compulsion. In the supreme intelligence the elective will is rightly conceived as incapable of any maxim which could not at the same time be objectively a law; and the notion of *holiness,* which on that account belongs to it, places it, not indeed above all practical laws, but above all practically restrictive laws, and consequently above obligation and duty. This holiness of will is, however, a practical idea, which must necessarily serve as a type to which finite rational beings can only approximate indefinitely, and which the pure moral law, which is itself on this account called holy, constantly and rightly holds before their eyes. The utmost that finite practical reason can effect is to be certain of this indefinite progress of one's maxims and of their steady disposition to advance. This is virtue, and virtue, at least as a naturally acquired faculty, can never be perfect, because assurance in such a case never becomes apodeictic certainty and, when it only amounts to persuasion, is very dangerous.

§ VIII. Theorem IV

The *autonomy* of the will is the sole principle of all moral laws and of all duties which conform to them; on the other hand, *heteronomy* of the elective will not only cannot be the basis of any obligation, but is, on the contrary, opposed to the principle thereof and to the morality of the will.

In fact the sole principle of morality consists in the independence on all matter of the law (namely, a desired object), and in the determination of the elective will by the mere universal legislative form of which its maxim must be capable. Now this *independence* is *freedom* in the *negative* sense, and this *self-legislation* of the pure, and therefore practical, reason is freedom in the *positive* sense. Thus the moral law expresses nothing else than the *autonomy* of the pure practical reason; that is, freedom; and this is itself the formal condition of all maxims, and on this condition only can they agree with the supreme practical law. If therefore the matter of the volition, which can be nothing else than the object of a desire that is connected with the law, enters into the practical law, *as the condition of its possibility*, there results heteronomy of the elective will, namely, dependence on the physical law that we should follow some impulse or inclination. In that case the will does not give itself the law, but only the precept how rationally to follow pathological law; and the maxim which, in such a case, never contains the universally legislative form, not only produces no obligation, but is itself opposed to the principle of a pure practical reason and, therefore, also to the moral disposition, even though the resulting action may be conformable to the law.

REMARK

Hence a practical precept, which contains a material (and therefore empirical) condition, must never be reckoned a practical law. For the law of the pure will, which is free, brings the will into a sphere quite different from the empirical; and as the necessity involved in the law is not a physical necessity, it can only consist in the formal conditions of the possibility of a law in general. All the matter of practical rules rests on subjective conditions, which give them only a conditional universality (in case I *desire* this or that, what I must do in order to obtain it), and they all turn on the principle of *private happiness*. Now, it is indeed undeniable that every volition must have an object, and therefore a matter; but it does not follow that this is the determining principle and the condition of the maxim; for, if it is so, then this cannot be exhibited in a universally legislative form, since in that case the expectation of the existence of the object would be the determining cause of the choice, and the volition must presuppose the dependence of the faculty of desire on the existence of something; but this dependence can only be sought in empirical conditions and, therefore, can never furnish a foundation for a necessary and universal rule. Thus, the happiness of others may be the object of the will of a rational being. But if it were the determining principle of the maxim, we must assume that we find not only a rational satisfaction in the welfare of others, but also a want such as the sympathetic disposition in some men occasions. But I cannot assume the existence of this want in every rational being (not at all in God). The matter, then, of the maxim may remain, but it must not be the condition of it, else the maxim could not be fit for a law. Hence, the mere form of law, which limits the matter, must also be a reason for adding this matter to the will, not for presupposing it. For example, let the matter be my own happiness. This (rule), if I attribute it to everyone (as, in fact, I may, in the case of every finite being), can become an *objective* practical law only if I include the happiness of others. Therefore, the law that we should promote the happiness of others does not arise from the assumption that this is an object of everyone's choice, but merely from this, that the form of universality which reason requires as the condition of giving to a maxim of self-love the objective validity of a law is the principle that determines the will. Therefore it was not the object (the happiness of others) that determined the pure will, but it was the form of law only, by which I restricted my maxim, founded on inclination, so as to give it the universality of a law, and thus to adapt it to the practical reason; and it is this restriction alone, and not the addition of an external spring, that can give rise to the notion of the *obligation* to extend the maxim of my self-love to the happiness of others.

REMARK II

The direct opposite of the principle of morality is, when the principle of *private* happiness is made the determining principle of the will, and with this is to be reckoned, as I have shown above, everything that places the determining principle which is to serve as a law, anywhere but in the legislative form of the maxim. This contradiction, however, is not merely logical, like that which would arise between rules empirically conditioned, if they were raised to the rank of necessary principles of cognition, but is practical, and would ruin morality altogether were not the voice of reason in reference to the will so clear, so irrepressible, so distinctly audible, even to the commonest men. It can only, indeed, be maintained in the perplexing speculations of the schools, which are bold enough to shut their ears against that heavenly voice, in order to support a theory that costs no trouble.

Suppose that an acquaintance whom you otherwise liked were to attempt to justify himself to you for having borne false witness, first by alleging the, in his view, sacred duty of consulting his own happiness; then by enumerating the advantages which he had gained thereby, pointing out the prudence he had shown in securing himself against detection, even by yourself, to whom he now reveals the secret, only in order that he may be able to deny it at any time; and suppose he were then to affirm, in all seriousness, that he has fulfilled a true human duty; you would either laugh in his face, or shrink back from him with disgust; and yet, if a man has regulated his principles of action solely with a view to his own advantage, you would have nothing whatever to object against this mode of proceeding. Or suppose some one recommends you a man as steward, as a man to whom you can blindly trust all your affairs; and, in order to inspire you with confidence, extols him as a prudent man who thoroughly understands his own interest, and is so indefatigably active that he lets slip no opportunity of advancing it; lastly, lest you should be afraid of finding a vulgar selfishness in him, praises the good taste with which he lives; not seeking his pleasure in money-making, or in coarse wantonness, but in the enlargement of his knowledge, in instructive intercourse with a select circle, and even in relieving the needy; while as to the means (which, of course, derive all their value from the end), he is not particular, and is ready to use other people's money for the purpose as if it were his own, provided only he knows that he can do so safely, and without discovery; you would either believe that the recommender was mocking you, or that he had lost his senses. So sharply and clearly marked are the boundaries of morality and self-love that even the commonest eye cannot fail to distinguish whether a thing belongs to the one or the other. The few remarks that follow may appear superfluous where the truth is so plain, but at least they may serve to give a little more distinctness to the judgement of common sense.

The principle of happiness may, indeed, furnish maxims, but never such as would be competent to be laws of the will, even if *universal* happiness were made the object. For since the knowledge of this rests on mere empirical data, since every man's judgement on it depends very much on his particular point of view, which is itself moreover very variable, it can supply only *general* rules, not *universal;* that is, it can give rules which on the average will most frequently fit, but not rules which must hold good always and necessarily; hence, no practical *laws* can be founded on it. Just because in this case an object of choice is the foundation of the rule and must therefore precede it, the rule can refer to nothing but what is [felt], and therefore it refers to experience and is founded on it, and then the variety of judgement must be endless. This principle, therefore, does not prescribe the same practical rules to all rational beings, although the rules are all included under a common title, namely, that of happiness. The moral law, however, is conceived as objectively necessary, only because it holds for everyone that has reason and will.

The maxim of self-love (prudence) only *advises;* the law of morality *commands.* Now there is a great difference between that which we are *advised* to do and that to which we are *obliged.*

The commonest intelligence can easily and without hesitation see what, on the principle of autonomy of the will, requires to be done; but on supposition of heteronomy of the will, it is hard and requires knowledge of the world to see what is to be done. That is to say, what *duty* is, is plain of itself to everyone; but what is to bring true durable advantage, such as will extend to the whole of one's existence, is always veiled in impenetrable obscurity; and much prudence is required to adapt the practical rule founded on it to the ends of life, even tolerably, by making proper exceptions. But the moral law commands the most punctual obedience from everyone; it must, therefore, not be so difficult to judge what it requires to be done, that the commonest unpractised understanding, even without worldly prudence, should fail to apply it rightly.

It is always in everyone's power to satisfy the categorical command of morality; whereas it is seldom possible, and by no means so to everyone, to satisfy the empirically conditioned precept of happiness, even with regard to a single purpose. The reason is that in the former case there is question only of the maxim, which must be genuine and pure; but in the latter case there is question also of one's capacity and physical power to realize a desired object. A command that everyone should try to make himself happy would be foolish, for one never commands anyone to do what he of himself infallibly wishes to do. We must only command the means, or rather supply them, since he cannot do everything that he wishes. But to command morality under the name of duty is quite rational; for, in the first place, not everyone is willing to obey its precepts if they oppose his inclinations; and as to the means of obeying this law, these need not in this case be taught, for in this respect whatever he wishes to do he can do.

He who has *lost* at play may be *vexed* at himself and his folly, but if he is conscious of having *cheated* at play (although he has gained thereby), he must *despise* himself as soon as he compares himself with the moral law. This must, therefore, be something different from the principle of private happiness. For a man must have a different criterion when he is compelled to say to himself: "I am a *worthless* fellow, though I have filled my purse"; and when he approves himself, and says: "I am a *prudent* man, for I have enriched my treasure."

Finally, there is something further in the idea of our practical reason, which accompanies the transgression of a moral law—namely, its *ill desert.* Now the notion of punishment, as such, cannot be united with that of becoming a partaker of happiness; for although he who inflicts the punishment may at the same time have the benevolent purpose of directing this punishment to this end, yet it must first be justified in itself as punishment, i.e., as mere harm, so that if it stopped there, and the person punished could get no glimpse of kindness hidden behind this harshness, he must yet admit that justice was done him, and that his reward was perfectly suitable to his conduct. In every punishment, as such, there must first be justice, and this constitutes the essence of the notion. Benevolence may, indeed, be united with it, but the man who has deserved punishment has not the least reason to reckon upon this. Punishment, then, is a physical evil, which, though it be not connected with moral evil as a *natural* consequence, ought to be connected with it as a consequence by the principles of a moral legislation. Now, if every crime, even without regarding the physical consequence with respect to the actor, is in itself punishable, that is, forfeits happiness (at least partially), it is obviously absurd to say that the crime consisted just in this, that he has drawn punishment on himself, thereby injuring his private happiness (which, on the principle of self-love, must be the proper notion of all crime). According to this view, the punishment would be the reason for calling anything a crime, and justice would, on the contrary, consist in omitting all punishment, and even preventing that which naturally follows; for, if this were done, there would no longer be any evil in the action, since the harm which otherwise followed it, and on account of which alone the action was called evil, would now be prevented. To look, however, on all rewards and punishments as merely the machinery in the hand of a higher power, which is to serve only to set rational creatures striving after their final end (happiness), this is to reduce the will to a mechanism destructive of freedom; this is so evident that it need not detain us.

More refined, though equally false, is the theory of those who suppose a certain special moral sense, which sense and not reason determines the moral law, and in consequence of which the consciousness of virtue is supposed to be directly connected with contentment and pleasure; that of vice, with mental dissatisfaction and pain; thus reducing the whole to the desire of private happiness. Without repeating what has been said above, I will here only remark the fallacy they fall into. In order to imagine the vicious man as tormented with mental dissatisfaction by the consciousness of his transgressions, they must first represent him as in the main basis of his character, at least in some degree, morally good; just as he who is pleased with the consciousness of right conduct must be conceived as already virtuous. The notion of morality and duty must, therefore, have preceded any regard to this satisfaction, and cannot be derived from it. A man must first appreciate the importance of what we call *duty,* the authority of the moral law, and the immediate dignity which the following of it gives to the person in his own eyes, in order to feel that satisfaction in the consciousness of his conformity to it and the bitter remorse that accompanies the consciousness of its transgression. It is, therefore, impossible to feel this satisfaction or dissatisfaction prior to the knowledge of obligation, or to make it the basis of the latter. A man must be at least half honest in order even to be able to form a conception of these feelings. I do not deny that as the human will is, by virtue of liberty, capable of being immediately determined by the moral law, so frequent practice in accordance with this principle of determination can, at least, produce subjectively a feeling of satisfaction; on the contrary, it is a duty to establish and to cultivate this, which alone deserves to be called properly the moral feeling; but the notion of duty cannot be derived from it, else we should have to suppose a feeling for the law as such, and thus make that an object of sensation which can only be thought by the reason; and this, if it is not to be a flat contradiction, would destroy all notion of duty and put in its place a mere mechanical play of refined inclinations sometimes contending with the coarser.

If now we compare our *formal* supreme principle of pure practical reason (that of autonomy of the will) with all previous *material* principles of morality, we can exhibit them all in a table in which all possible cases are exhausted, except the one formal principle; and thus we can show visibly that it is vain to look for any other principle than that now proposed. In fact all possible principles of determination of the will are either merely *subjective*, and therefore empirical, or are also *objective* and rational; and both are either *external* or *internal*.

Practical Material Principles of Determination taken as the Foundation of Morality, are:

SUBJECTIVE

EXTERNAL	INTERNAL
Education (*Montaigne*)	Physical feeling (*Epicurus*)
The civil Constitution (*Mandeville*)	Moral feeling (*Hutcheson*)

OBJECTIVE

INTERNAL	EXTERNAL
Perfection (*Wolf* and the *Stoics*)	Will of God (*Crusius* and other *theological Moralists*)

Those of the upper table are all empirical and evidently incapable of furnishing the universal principle of morality; but those in the lower table are based on reason (for perfection as a quality of things, and the highest perfection conceived as *substance*, that is, God, can only be thought by means of rational concepts). But the former notion, namely, that of *perfection*, may either be taken in a *theoretic* signification, and then it means nothing but the completeness of each thing in its own kind (transcendental), or that of a thing merely as a thing (metaphysical); and with that we are not concerned here. But the notion of perfection in a *practical* sense is the fitness or sufficiency of a thing for all sorts of purposes. This perfection, as a *quality* of man and consequently internal, is nothing but *talent* and, what strengthens or completes this, *skill.* Supreme perfection conceived as *substance,* that is God, and consequently external (considered practically), is the sufficiency of this being for all ends. Ends then must first be given, relatively to which only can the notion of *perfection* (whether internal in ourselves or external in God) be the determining principle of the will. But an end—being an *object* which must precede the determination of the will by a practical rule and contain the ground of the possibility of this determination, and therefore contain also the matter of the will, taken as its determining principle—such an end is always empirical and, therefore, may serve for the *Epicurean* principle of the happiness theory, but not for the pure rational principle of morality and duty. Thus, talents and the improvement of them, because they contribute to the advantages of life; or the will of God, if agreement with it be taken as the object of the will, without any antecedent independent practical principle, can be motives only by reason of the *happiness* expected therefrom. Hence it follows, *first,* that all the principles here stated are *material; secondly,* that they include all possible material principles; and, finally, the conclusion, that since material principles are quite incapable of furnishing the supreme moral law (as has been shown), the *formal practical principle* of the pure reason (according to which the mere form of a universal legislation must constitute the supreme and immediate determining principle of the will) is the *only* one *possible* which is adequate to furnish categorical imperatives, that is, practical laws (which make actions a duty), and in general to serve as the principle of morality, both in criticizing conduct and also in its application to the human will to determine it.

I. *Of the Deduction of the Fundamental Principles of Pure Practical Reason*

This Analytic shows that pure reason can be practical, that is, can of itself determine the will independently of anything empirical; and this it proves by a fact in which pure reason in us proves itself actually practical, namely, the autonomy shown in the fundamental principle of morality, by which reason determines the will to action.

It shows at the same time that this fact is inseparably connected with the consciousness of freedom of the will, nay, is identical with it; and by this the will of a rational being, although as belonging to the world of sense it recognizes itself as necessarily subject to the laws of causality like other efficient causes; yet, at the same time, on another side, namely, as a being in itself, is conscious of existing in and being determined by an intelligible order of things; conscious not by virtue of a special intuition of itself, but by virtue of certain dynamical laws which determine its causality in the sensible world; for it has been elsewhere proved that if freedom is predicated of us, it transports us into an intelligible order of things.

Now, if we compare with this the analytical part of the critique of pure speculative reason, we shall see a remarkable contrast. There it was not fundamental principles, but pure, sensible *intuition* (space and time), that was the first *datum* that made *a priori* knowledge possible, though only of objects of the senses. Synthetical principles could not be derived from mere concepts without intuition; on the contrary, they could only exist with reference to this intuition, and therefore to objects of possible experience, since it is the concepts of the understanding, united with this intuition, which alone make that knowledge possible which we call experience. Beyond objects of experience, and therefore with regard to things as noumena, all positive knowledge was rightly disclaimed for speculative reason. This reason, however, went so far as to establish with certainty the concept of noumena; that is, the possibility, nay, the necessity, of thinking them; for example, it showed against all objections that the supposition of freedom, negatively considered, was quite consistent with those principles and limitations of pure theoretic reason. But it could not give us any definite enlargement of our knowledge with respect to such objects, but, on the contrary, cut off all view of them altogether.

On the other hand, the moral law, although it gives no *view*, yet gives us a fact absolutely inexplicable from any data of the sensible world, and the whole compass of our theoretical use of reason, a fact which points to a pure world of the understanding, nay, even defines it *positively* and enables us to know something of it, namely, a law.

This law (as far as rational beings are concerned) gives to the world of sense, which is a sensible system of nature, the form of a world of the understanding, that is, of a *supersensible system of nature,* without interfering with its mechanism. Now, a system of nature, in the most general sense, is the existence of things under laws. The sensible nature of rational beings in general is their existence under laws empirically conditioned, which, from the point of view of reason, is *heteronomy.* The supersensible nature of the same beings, on the other hand, is their existence according to laws which are independent of every empirical condition and, therefore, belong to the *autonomy* of pure reason. And, since the laws by which the existence of things depends on cognition are practical, supersensible nature, so far as we can form any notion of it, is nothing else than a *system of nature under the autonomy of pure practical reason.* Now, the law of this autonomy is the moral law, which, therefore, is the fundamental law of a supersensible nature, and of a pure world of understanding, whose counterpart must exist in the world of sense, but without interfering with its laws. We might call the former the *archetypal* world (*natura archetypa*), which we only know in the reason; and the latter the *ectypal* world (*natura ectypa*), because it contains the possible effect of the idea of the former which is the determining principle of the will. For the moral law, in fact, transfers us ideally into a system in which pure reason, if it were accompanied with adequate physical power, would produce the *summum bonum,* and it determines our will to give the sensible world the form of a system of rational beings.

The least attention to oneself proves that this idea really serves as the model for the determinations of our will.

When the maxim which I am disposed to follow in giving testimony is tested by the practical reason, I always consider what it would be if it were to hold as a universal law of nature. It is manifest that in this view it would oblige everyone to speak the truth. For it cannot hold as a universal law of nature that statements should be allowed to have the force of proof and yet to be purposely untrue. Similarly, the maxim which I adopt with respect to disposing freely of my life is at once determined, when I ask myself what it should be, in order that a system, of which it is the law, should maintain itself. It is obvious that in such a system no one could *arbitrarily* put an end to his own life, for such an arrangement would not be a permanent order of things. And so in all similar cases. Now, in nature, as it actually is an object of experience, the free will is not of itself determined to maxims which could of themselves be the foundation of a natural system of universal laws, or which could even be adapted to a system so constituted; on the contrary, its maxims are private inclinations which constitute, indeed, a natural whole in conformity with pathological (physical) laws, but could not form part of a system of nature, which would only be possible through our will acting in accordance with pure practical laws. Yet we are, through reason, conscious of a law to which all our maxims are subject, as though a natural order must be originated from our will. This law, therefore, must be the idea of a natural system not given in experience, and yet possible through freedom; a system, therefore, which is supersensible, and to which we give objective reality, at least in a practical point of view, since we look on it as an object of our will as pure rational beings.

Hence the distinction between the laws of a natural system to which the *will is subject,* and of a natural system which is *subject to a will* (as far as its relation to its free actions is concerned), rests on this, that in the former the objects must be causes of the ideas which determine the will; whereas in the latter the will is the cause of the objects; so that its causality has its determining principle solely in the pure faculty of reason, which may therefore be called a pure practical reason.

There are therefore two very distinct problems: how, on *the one side,* pure reason can *cognise* objects *a priori,* and how *on the other side* it can be an immediate determining principle of the will, that is, of the causality of the rational being with respect to the reality of objects (through the mere thought of the universal validity of its own maxims as laws).

The former, which belongs to the critique of the pure speculative reason, requires a previous explanation, how intuitions without which no object can be given, and, therefore, none known synthetically, are possible *a priori;* and its solution turns out to be that these are all only sensible and, therefore, do not render possible any speculative knowledge which goes further than possible experience reaches; and that therefore all the principles of that pure speculative reason avail only to make experience possible; either experience of given objects or of those that may be given *ad infinitum,* but never are completely given.

The latter, which belongs to the critique of practical reason, requires no explanation how the objects of the faculty of desire are possible, for that being a problem of the theoretical knowledge of nature is left to the critique of the speculative reason, but only how reason can determine the maxims of the will; whether this takes place only by means of empirical ideas as principles of determination, or whether pure reason can be practical and be the law of a possible order of nature, which is not empirically knowable. The possibility of such a supersensible system of nature, the conception of which can also be the ground of its reality through our own free will, does not require any *a priori* intuition (of an intelligible world) which, being in this case supersensible, would be impossible for us. For the question is only as to the determining principle of volition in its maxims, namely, whether it is empirical, or is a conception of the pure reason (having the legal character belonging to it in general), and how it can be the latter. It is left to the theoretic principles of reason to decide whether the causality of the will suffices for the realization of the objects or not, this being an inquiry into the possibility of the objects of the volition. Intuition of these objects is therefore of no importance to the practical problem. We are here concerned only with the determination of the will and the determining principles of its maxims as a free will, not at all with the result. For, provided only that the *will* conforms to the law of pure reason, then let its *power* in execution be what it may, whether according to these maxims of legislation of a possible system of nature any such system really results or not, this is no concern of the critique, which only inquires whether, and in what way, pure reason can be practical, that is directly determine the will.

In this inquiry criticism may and must begin with pure practical laws and their reality. But instead of intuition it takes as their foundation the conception of their existence in the intelligible world, namely, the concept of freedom. For this concept has no other meaning, and these laws are only possible in relation to freedom of the will; but freedom being supposed, they are necessary; or conversely freedom is necessary because those laws are necessary, being practical postulates. It cannot be further explained how this consciousness of the moral law, or, what is the same thing, of freedom, is possible; but that it is admissible is well established in the theoretical critique.

The *exposition* of the supreme principle of practical reason is now finished; that is to say, it has been shown first, what it contains, that it subsists for itself quite *a priori* and independent of empirical principles; and next in what it is distinguished from all other practical principles. With the *deduction*, that is, the justification of its objective and universal validity, and the discernment of the possibility of such a synthetical proposition *a priori*, we cannot expect to succeed so well as in the case of the principles of pure theoretical reason. For these referred to objects of possible experience, namely, to phenomena, and we could prove that these phenomena could be *known* as objects of experience only by being brought under the categories in accordance with these laws; and consequently that all possible experience must conform to these laws. But I could not proceed in this way with the deduction of the moral law. For this does not concern the knowledge of the properties of objects, which may be given to the reason from some other source; but a knowledge which can itself be the ground of the existence of the objects, and by which reason in a rational being has causality, i.e., pure reason, which can be regarded as a faculty immediately determining the will.

Now all our human insight is at an end as soon as we have arrived at fundamental powers or faculties, for the possibility of these cannot be understood by any means, and just as little should it be arbitrarily invented and assumed. Therefore, in the theoretic use of reason, it is experience alone that can justify us in assuming them. But this expedient of adducing empirical proofs, instead of a deduction from *a priori* sources of knowledge, is denied us here in respect to the pure practical faculty of reason. For whatever requires to draw the proof of its reality from experience must depend for the grounds of its possibility on principles of experience; and pure, yet practical, reason by its very notion cannot be regarded as such. Further, the moral law is given as a fact of pure reason of which we are *a priori* conscious, and which is apodeictically certain, though it be granted that in experience no example of its exact fulfilment can be found. Hence, the objective reality of the moral law cannot be proved by any deduction by any efforts of theoretical reason, whether speculative or empirically supported, and therefore, even if we renounced its apodeictic certainty, it could not be proved *a posteriori* by experience, and yet it is firmly established of itself.

But instead of this vainly sought deduction of the moral principle, something else is found which was quite unexpected, namely, that this moral principle serves conversely as the principle of the deduction of an inscrutable faculty which no experience could prove, but of which speculative reason was compelled at least to assume the possibility (in order to find amongst its cosmological ideas the unconditioned in the chain of causality, so as not to contradict itself) —I mean the faculty of freedom. The moral law, which itself does not require a justification, proves not merely the possibility of freedom, but that it really belongs to beings who recognize this law as binding on themselves. The moral law is in fact a law of the causality of free agents and, therefore, of the possibility of a supersensible system of nature, just as the metaphysical law of events in the world of sense was a law of causality of the sensible system of nature; and it therefore determines what speculative philosophy was compelled to leave undetermined, namely, the law for a causality, the concept of which in the latter was only negative; and therefore for the first time gives this concept objective reality.

This sort of credential of the moral law, viz., that it is set forth as a principle of the deduction of freedom, which is a causality of pure reason, is a sufficient substitute for all *a priori* justification, since theoretic reason was compelled to assume *at least* the possibility of freedom, in order to satisfy a want of its own. For the moral law proves its reality, so as even to satisfy the critique of the speculative reason, by the fact that it adds a positive definition to a causality previously conceived only negatively, the possibility of which was incomprehensible to speculative reason, which yet was compelled to suppose it. For it adds the notion of a reason that directly determines the will (by imposing on its maxims the condition of a universal legislative form); and thus it is able for the first time to give objective, though only practical, reality to reason, which always became transcendent when it sought to proceed speculatively with its ideas. It thus changes the *transcendent* use of reason into an *immanent*[1] use (so that reason is itself, by means of ideas, an efficient cause in the field of experience).

The determination of the causality of beings in the world of sense, as such, can never be unconditioned; and yet for every series of conditions there must be something unconditioned, and therefore there must be a causality which is determined wholly by itself. Hence, the idea of freedom as a faculty of absolute spontaneity

[1] [Cf. *Critique of Pure Reason*, p. 112.]

was not found to be a want, but, *as far as its possibility is concerned,* an analytic principle of pure speculative reason. But as it is absolutely impossible to find in experience any example in accordance with this idea, because amongst the causes of things as phenomena it would be impossible to meet with any absolutely unconditioned determination of causality, we were only able to *defend our supposition* that a freely acting cause might be a being in the world of sense, in so far as it is considered in the other point of view as a *noumenon,* showing that there is no contradiction in regarding all its actions as subject to physical conditions so far as they are phenomena, and yet regarding its causality as physically unconditioned, in so far as the acting being belongs to the world of understanding, and in thus making the concept of freedom the regulative principle of reason. By this principle I do not indeed learn what the object is to which that sort of causality is attributed; but I remove the difficulty, for, on the one side, in the explanation of events in the world, and consequently also of the actions of rational beings, I leave to the mechanism of physical necessity the right of ascending from conditioned to condition *ad infinitum,* while on the other side I keep open for speculative reason the place which for it is vacant, namely, the intelligible, in order to transfer the unconditioned thither. But I was not able to *verify* this *supposition;* that is, to change it into the *knowledge* of a being so acting, not even into the knowledge of the possibility of such a being. This vacant place is now filled by pure practical reason with a definite law of causality in an intelligible world (causality with freedom), namely, the moral law. Speculative reason does not hereby gain anything as regards its insight, but only as regards the *certainty* of its problematical notion of freedom, which here obtains *objective reality,* which, though only practical, is nevertheless undoubted. Even the notion of causality—the application, and consequently the signification, of which holds properly only in relation to phenomena, so as to connect them into experiences (as is shown by the *Critique of Pure Reason*) —is not so enlarged as to extend its use beyond these limits. For if reason sought to do this, it would have to show how the logical relation of principle and consequence can be used synthetically in a different sort of intuition from the sensible; that is how a *causa noumenon* is possible. This it can never do; and, as practical reason, it does not even concern itself with it, since it only places the *determining principle* of causality of man as a sensible creature (which is given) in *pure reason* (which is therefore called *practical*); and therefore it employs the notion of cause, not in order to know objects, but to determine causality in relation to objects in general. It can abstract altogether from the application of this notion to objects with a view to theoretical knowledge (since this concept is always found *a priori* in the understanding, even independently of any intuition). Reason, then, employs it only for a practical purpose, and hence we can transfer the determining principle of the will into the intelligible order of things, admitting, at the same time, that we cannot understand how the notion of cause can determine the knowledge of these things. But reason must cognise causality with respect to the actions of the will in the sensible world in a definite manner; otherwise, practical reason could not really produce any action. But as to the notion which it forms of its own causality as noumenon, it need not determine it theoretically with a view to the cognition of its supersensible existence, so as to give it significance in this way. For it acquires significance apart from this, though only for practical use, namely, through the moral law. Theoretically viewed, it remains always a pure *a priori* concept of the understanding, which can be applied to objects whether they have been given sensibly or not, although in the latter case it has no definite theoretical significance or application, but is only a formal, though essential, conception of the understanding relating to an object in general. The significance which reason gives it through the moral law is merely practical, inasmuch as the idea of the law of causality (of the will) has self causality, or is its determining principle.

II. *Of the Right that Pure Reason in its Practical use has to an Extension which is not possible to it in its Speculative Use.*

We have in the moral principle set forth a law of causality, the determining principle of which is set above all the conditions of the sensible world; we have it conceived how the will, as belonging to the intelligible world, is determinable, and therefore we have its subject (man) not merely *conceived* as belonging to a world of pure understanding, and in this respect unknown (which the critique of speculative reason enabled us to do), but also *defined* as regards his causality by means of a law which cannot be reduced to any physical law of the sensible world; and therefore our knowledge is *extended* beyond the limits of that world, a pretension which the *Critique of Pure Reason* declared to be futile in all speculation. Now, how is the practical use of pure reason here to be reconciled with the theoretical, as to the determination of the limits of its faculty?

David Hume, of whom we may say that he commenced the assault on the claims of pure reason, which made a thorough investigation of it necessary, argued thus: The notion of *cause* is a notion that involves the *necessity* of the connexion of the existence of different things (and that, in so far as they are different), so that, given A, I know that something quite distinct therefrom, namely B, must necessarily also exist. Now necessity can be attributed to a connection, only in so far as it is known *a priori,* for experience would only enable us to know of such a connection that it exists, not that it necessarily exists. Now, it is impossible, says he, to know *a priori* and as necessary the connection between one thing and another (or between one attribute and another quite distinct) when they have not been given in experience. Therefore the notion of a cause is fictitious and delusive and, to speak in the mildest way, is an illusion, only excusable inasmuch as the *custom* (a *subjective* necessity) of perceiving certain things, or their attributes as often associated in existence along with or in succession to one another, is insensibly taken for an objective necessity of supposing such a connection in the objects themselves; and thus the notion of a cause has been acquired surreptitiously and not legitimately; nay, it can never be so acquired or authenticated, since it demands a connection in itself vain, chimerical, and untenable in presence of reason, and to which no object can ever correspond. In this way was *empiricism* first introduced as the sole source of principles, as far as all knowledge of the existence of things is concerned (mathematics therefore remaining excepted); and with empiricism the most thorough scepticism, even with regard to the whole science of nature(as philosophy). For on such principles we can never conclude from given attributes of things as existing to a consequence (for this would require the notion of cause, which involves the necessity of such a connection); we can only, guided by imagination, expect similar cases—an expectation which is never certain, however often it has been fulfilled. Of no event could we say: a certain thing *must* have preceded it, on which it *necessarily* followed; that is, it must have a cause; and therefore, however frequent the cases we have known in which there was such an antecedent, so that a rule could be derived from them, yet we never could suppose it as always and necessarily so happening; we should, therefore, be obliged to leave its share to blind chance, with which all use of reason comes to an end; and this firmly establishes scepticism in reference to arguments ascending from effects to causes and makes it impregnable.

Mathematics escaped well, so far, because Hume thought that its propositions were analytical; that is, proceeded from one property to another, by virtue of identity and, consequently, according to the principle of contradiction. This, however, is not the case, since, on the contrary, they are synthetical; and although geometry, for example, has not to do with the existence of things, but only with their *a priori* properties in a possible intuition, yet it proceeds just as in the case of the causal notion, from one property (A) to another wholly distinct (B), as necessarily connected with the former. Nevertheless, mathematical science, so highly vaunted for its apodeictic certainty, must at last fall under this *empiricism* for the same reason for which Hume put custom in the place of objective necessity in the notion of cause and, in spite of all its pride, must consent to lower its bold pretension of claiming assent *a priori* and depend for assent to the universality of its propositions on the kindness of observers, who, when called as witnesses, would surely not hesitate to admit that what the geometer propounds as a theorem they have always perceived to be the fact, and, consequently, although it be not necessarily true, yet they would permit us to expect it to be true in the future. In this manner Hume's empiricism leads inevitably to scepticism, even with regard to mathematics, and consequently in every scientific theoretical use of reason (for this belongs either to philosophy or mathematics). Whether with such a terrible overthrow of the chief branches of knowledge, common reason will escape better, and will not rather become irrecoverably involved in this destruction of all knowledge, so that from the same principles a *universal* scepticism should follow (affecting, indeed, only the learned), this I will leave everyone to judge for himself.

As regards my own labours in the critical examination of pure reason, which were occasioned by Hume's sceptical teaching, but went much further and embraced the whole field of pure theoretical reason in its synthetic use and, consequently, the field of what is called metaphysics in general; I proceeded in the following manner with respect to the doubts raised by the Scottish philosopher touching the notion of causality. If Hume took the objects of experience for *things in themselves* (as is almost always done), he was quite right in declaring the notion of cause to be a deception and false illusion; for as to things in themselves, and their attributes as such, it is impossible to see why because A is given, B, which is different, must necessarily be also given, and therefore he could by no means admit such an *a priori* knowledge of things in themselves. Still less could this acute writer allow an empirical origin of this concept, since this is directly contradictory to the necessity of connection which constitutes the essence of the notion of causality; hence the notion was proscribed, and in its place was put custom in the observation of the course of perceptions.

It resulted, however, from my inquiries, that the objects with which we have to do in experience are by no means things in themselves, but merely phenomena; and that although in the case of things in themselves it is impossible to see how, if A is supposed, it should be contradictory that B, which is quite different from A, should not also be supposed (i.e., to see the necessity of the connection between A as cause and B as effect); yet it can very well be conceived that, as phenomena, they may be necessarily connected *in one experience* in a certain way (e.g., with regard to time-relations); so that they could not be separated without contradicting that connection, by means of which this experience is possible in which they are objects and in which alone they are cognisable by us. And so it was found to be in fact; so that I was able not only to prove the objective reality of the concept of cause in regard to objects of experience, but also to *deduce* it as an *a priori* concept by reason of the necessity of the connection it implied; that is, to show the possibility of its origin from pure understanding without any empirical sources; and thus, after removing the source of empiricism, I was able also to overthrow the inevitable consequence of this, namely, scepticism, first with regard to physical science, and then with regard to mathematics (in which empiricism has just the same grounds), both being sciences which have reference to objects of possible experience; herewith overthrowing the thorough doubt of whatever theoretic reason professes to discern.

But how is it with the application of this category of causality (and all the others; for without them there can be no knowledge of anything existing) to things which are not objects of possible experience, but lie beyond its bounds? For I was able to deduce the objective reality of these concepts only with regard to *objects of possible experience*. But even this very fact, that I have saved them, only in case I have proved that objects may by means of them be thought, though not determined *a priori;* this it is that gives them a place in the pure understanding, by which they are referred to objects in general (sensible or not sensible). If anything is still wanting, it is that which is the condition of the *application* of these categories, and especially that of causality, to objects, namely, intuition; for where this is not given, the application *with a view to theoretic knowledge of the object*, as a noumenon, is impossible and, therefore, if anyone ventures on it, is (as in the *Critique of Pure Reason*) absolutely forbidden. Still, the objective reality of the concept (of causality) remains, and it can be used even of noumena, but without our being able in the least to define the concept theoretically so as to produce knowledge. For that this concept, even in reference to an object, contains nothing impossible, was shown by this, that, even while applied to objects of sense, its seat was certainly fixed in the pure understanding; and although, when referred to things in themselves (which cannot be objects of experience), it is not capable of being determined so as to represent a *definite object* for the purpose of theoretic knowledge; yet for any other purpose (for instance, a practical) it might be capable of being determined so as to have such application. This could not be the case if, as Hume maintained, this concept of causality contained something absolutely impossible to be thought.

In order now to discover this condition of the application of the said concept to noumena, we need only recall why we are not content with its application to objects of experience, but desire also to apply it to things in themselves. It will appear, then, that it is not a theoretic but a practical purpose that makes this a necessity. In speculation, even if we were successful in it, we should not really gain anything in the knowledge of nature, or generally with regard to such objects as are given, but we should make a wide step from the sensibly conditioned (in which we have already enough to do to maintain ourselves, and to follow carefully the chain of causes) to the supersensible, in order to complete our knowledge of principles and to fix its limits; whereas there always remains an infinite chasm unfilled between those limits and what we know;

and we should have hearkened to a vain curiosity rather than a solid desire of knowledge.

But, besides the relation in which the *understanding* stands to objects (in theoretical knowledge), it has also a relation to the faculty of desire, which is therefore called the *will,* and the pure will, inasmuch as pure understanding (in this case called reason) is practical through the mere conception of a law. The objective reality of a pure will, or, what is the same thing, of a pure practical reason, is given in the moral law *a priori,* as it were, by a fact, for so we may name a determination of the will which is inevitable, although it does not rest on empirical principles. Now, in the notion of a will the notion of causality is already contained, and hence the notion of a pure will contains that of a causality accompanied with freedom, that is, one which is not determinable by physical laws, and consequently is not capable of any empirical intuition in proof of its reality, but, nevertheless, completely justifies its objective reality *a priori* in the pure practical law; not, indeed (as is easily seen) for the purposes of the theoretical, but of the practical use of reason. Now the notion of a being that has free will is the notion of a *causa noumenon,* and that this notion involves no contradiction, we are already assured by the fact—that inasmuch as the concept of cause has arisen wholly from pure understanding, and has its objective reality assured by the deduction, as it is moreover in its origin independent of any sensible conditions, it is, therefore, not restricted to phenomena (unless we wanted to make a definite theoretic use of it), but can be applied equally to things that are objects of the pure understanding. But, since this application cannot rest on any intuition (for intuition can only be sensible), therefore, *causa noumenon,* as regards the theoretic use of reason, although a possible and thinkable, is yet an empty notion. Now, I do not desire by means of this to *understand theoretically* the nature of a being, *in so far* as it has a *pure* will; it is enough for me to have thereby designated it as such, and hence to combine the notion of causality with that of freedom (and what is inseparable from it, the moral law, as its determining principle). Now, this right I certainly have by virtue of the pure, not-empirical origin of the notion of cause, since I do not consider myself entitled to make any use of it except in reference to the moral law which determines its reality, that is, only a practical use.

If, with Hume, I had denied to the notion of causality all objective reality in its [theoretic] use, not merely with regard to things in themselves (the supersensible), but also with regard to the objects of the senses, it would have lost all significance, and being a theoretically impossible notion would have been declared to be quite useless; and since what is nothing cannot be made any use of, the practical use of a concept *theoretically null* would have been absurd. But, as it is, the concept of a causality free from empirical conditions, although empty, i. e., without any appropriate intuition), is yet theoretically possible, and refers to an indeterminate object; but in compensation significance is given to it in the moral law and consequently in a practical sense. I have, indeed, no intuition which should determine its objective theoretic reality, but not the less it has a real application, which is exhibited *in concreto* in intentions or maxims; that is, it has a practical reality which can be specified, and this is sufficient to justify it even with a view to noumena.

Now, this objective reality of a pure concept of the understanding in the sphere of the supersensible, once brought in, gives an objective reality also to all the other categories, although only so far as they stand in *necessary* connexion with the determining principle of the will (the moral law); a reality only of practical application, which has not the least effect in enlarging our theoretical knowledge of these objects, or the discernment of their nature by pure reason. So we shall find also in the sequel that these categories refer only to beings as *intelligences,* and in them only to the relation of *reason* to the *will;* consequently, always only to the *practical,* and beyond this cannot pretend to any knowledge of these beings; and whatever other properties belonging to the theoretical representation of supersensible things may be brought into connexion with these categories, this is not to be reckoned as knowledge, but only as a right (in a practical point of view, however, it is a necessity) to admit and assume such beings, even in the case where we [conceive] supersensible beings (e.g., God) according to analogy, that is, a purely rational relation, of which we make a practical use with reference to what is sensible; and thus the application to the supersensible solely in a practical point of view does not give pure theoretic reason the least encouragement to run riot into the transcendent.

Chapter II. *Of the Concept of an Object of Pure Practical Reason*

By a concept of the practical reason I understand the idea of an object as an effect possible to be produced through freedom. To be an object of practical knowledge, as such, signifies, therefore, only the relation of the will to the action by which the object or its opposite would be realized; and to decide whether something is an object of *pure* practical reason or not is only to discern the possibility or impossibility of *willing* the action by which, if we had the required power (about which experience must decide), a certain object would be realized. If the object be taken as the determining principle of our desire, it must first be known whether it is *physically* possible by the free use of our powers, before we decide whether it is an object of practical reason or not. On the other hand, if the law can be considered *a priori* as the determining principle of the action, and the latter therefore as determined by pure practical reason, the judgement whether a thing is an object of pure practical reason or not does not depend at all on the comparison with our physical power; and the question is only whether we should *will* an action that is directed to the existence of an object, if the object were in our power; hence the previous question is only as the *moral possibility* of the action, for in this case it is not the object, but the law of the will, that is the determining principle of the action. The only objects of practical reason are therefore those of *good* and *evil*. For by the former is meant an object necessarily desired according to a principle of reason; by the latter one necessarily shunned, also according to a principle of reason.

If the notion of good is not to be derived from an antecedent practical law, but, on the contrary, is to serve as its foundation, it can only be the notion of something whose existence promises pleasure, and thus determines the causality of the subject to produce it, that is to say, determines the faculty of desire. Now, since it is impossible to discern *a priori* what idea will be accompanied with *pleasure* and what with *pain*, it will depend on experience alone to find out what is primarily good or evil. The property of the subject, with reference to which alone this experiment can be made, is the *feeling* of pleasure and pain, a receptivity belonging to the internal sense; thus that only would be primarily good with which the sensation of *pleasure* is immediately connected, and that simply evil which immediately excites *pain*. Since, however, this is opposed even to the usage of language, which distinguishes the *pleasant* from the *good*, the *unpleasant* from the *evil*, and requires that good and evil shall always be judged by reason, and, therefore, by concepts which can be communicated to everyone, and not by mere sensation, which is limited to individual [subjects] and their susceptibility; and, since nevertheless, pleasure or pain cannot be connected with any idea of an object *a priori*, the philosopher who thought himself obliged to make a feeling of pleasure the foundation of his practical judgements would call that *good* which is a *means* to the pleasant, and *evil*, what is a cause of unpleasantness and pain; for the judgement on the relation of means to ends certainly belongs to reason. But, although reason is alone capable of discerning the connexion of means with their ends (so that the will might even be defined as the faculty of ends, since these are always determining principles of the desires), yet the practical maxims which would follow from the aforesaid principle of the good being merely a means, would never contain as the object of the will anything good in itself, but only something good *for something;* the good would always be merely the useful, and that for which it is useful must always lie outside the will, in sensation. Now if this as a pleasant sensation were to be distinguished from the notion of good, then there would be nothing primarily good at all, but the good would have to be sought only in the means to something else, namely, some pleasantness.

It is an old formula of the schools: *Nihil appetimus nisi sub ratione boni; Nihil aversamur nisi sub ratione mali,* and it is used often correctly, but often also in a manner injurious to philosophy, because the expressions *boni* and *mali* are ambiguous, owing to the poverty of language, in consequence of which they admit a double sense, and, therefore, inevitably bring the practical laws into ambiguity; and philosophy, which in employing them becomes aware of the different meanings in the same word, but can find no special expressions for them, is driven to subtile distinctions about which there is subsequently no unanimity, because the distinction could not be directly marked by any suitable expression.[1]

The German language has the good fortune to possess expressions which do not allow this

[1] Besides this, the expression *sub ratione boni* is also ambiguous. For it may mean: "We represent something to ourselves as good, when and because we *desire* (will) it"; or "We desire something because we *represent* it to ourselves as *good,*" so that either the desire determines the notion of the object as a good, or the notion of good determines the desire (the will); so that in the first case *sub ratione boni* would mean, "We will something *under the idea* of the good"; in the second, *"In consequence of this idea,"* which, as determining the volition, must precede it.

difference to be overlooked. It possesses two very distinct concepts and especially distinct expressions for that which the Latins express by a single word, *bonum*. For *bonum* it has *das Gute* [good], and *das Wohl* [well, weal], for *malum das Böse* [evil], and *das Übel* [ill, bad], or *das Weh* [woe]. So that we express two quite distinct judgements when we consider in an action the *good* and *evil* of it, or our *weal* and *woe* (ill). Hence it already follows that the above quoted psychological proposition is at least very doubtful if it is translated: "We desire nothing except with a view to our *weal* or *woe*"; on the other hand, if we render it thus: "Under the direction of reason we desire nothing except so far as we esteem it good or evil," it is indubitably certain and at the same time quite clearly expressed.

Well or *ill* always implies only a reference to our condition, as *pleasant* or *unpleasant*, as one of pleasure or pain, and if we desire or avoid an object on this account, it is only so far as it is referred to our sensibility and to the feeling of pleasure or pain that it produces. But *good* or *evil* always implies a reference to the *will*, as determined by the *law of reason*, to make something its object; for it is never determined directly by the object and the idea of it, but is a faculty of taking a rule of reason for the motive of an action (by which an object may be realized). Good and evil therefore are properly referred to actions, not to the sensations of the person, and if anything is to be good or evil absolutely (i. e., in every respect and without any further condition), or is to be so esteemed, it can only be the manner of acting, the maxim of the will, and consequently the acting person himself as a good or evil man that can be so called, and not a thing.

However, then, men may laugh at the Stoic, who in the severest paroxysms of gout cried out: "Pain, however thou tormentest me, I will never admit that thou art an evil (*kakóv, malum*)": he was right. A bad thing it certainly was, and his cry betrayed that; but that any evil attached to him thereby, this he had no reason whatever to admit, for pain did not in the least diminish the worth of his person, but only that of his condition. If he had been conscious of a single lie, it would have lowered his pride, but pain served only to raise it, when he was conscious that he had not deserved it by any unrighteous action by which he had rendered himself worthy of punishment.

What we call *good* must be an object of desire in the judgement of every rational man, and *evil* an object of aversion in the eyes of everyone; therefore, in addition to sense, this judgement requires reason. So it is with truthfulness, as opposed to lying; so with justice, as opposed to violence, &c. But we may call a thing a bad [or ill] thing, which yet everyone must at the same time acknowledge to be good, sometimes directly, sometimes indirectly. The man who submits to a surgical operation feels it no doubt as a bad thing, but by their reason he and everyone acknowledge it to be good. If a man who delights in annoying and vexing peaceable people at last receives a right good beating, this is no doubt a bad thing; but everyone approves it and regards it as a good thing, even though nothing else resulted from it; nay, even the man who receives it must in his reason acknowledge that he has met justice, because he sees the proportion between good conduct and good fortune, which reason inevitably places before him, here put into practice.

No doubt our weal and woe are of *very great* importance in the estimation of our practical reason, and as far as our nature as sensible beings is concerned, our *happiness* is the only thing of *consequence*, provided it is estimated as reason especially requires, not by the transitory sensation, but by the influence that this has on our whole existence, and on our satisfaction therewith; but it is not *absolutely the only thing* of consequence. Man is a being who, as belonging to the world of sense, has wants, and so far his reason has an office which it cannot refuse, namely, to attend to the interest of his sensible nature, and to form practical maxims, even with a view to the happiness of this life, and if possible even to that of a future. But he is not so completely an animal as to be indifferent to what reason says on its own account, and to use it merely as an instrument for the satisfaction of his wants as a sensible being. For the possession of reason would not raise his worth above that of the brutes, if it is to serve him only for the same purpose that instinct serves in them; it would in that case be only a particular method which nature had employed to equip man for the same ends for which it has qualified brutes, without qualifying him for any higher purpose. No doubt once this arrangement of nature has been made for him he requires reason in order to take into consideration his weal and woe, but besides this he possesses it for a higher purpose also, namely, not only to take into consideration what is good or evil in itself, about which only pure reason, uninfluenced by any sensible interest, can judge, but also to distinguish this estimate thoroughly from the former and to make it the supreme condition thereof.

In estimating what is good or evil in itself, as distinguished from what can be so called only relatively, the following points are to be considered. Either a rational principle is already conceived, as of itself the determining principle of the will, without regard to possible objects of desire (and therefore by the more legislative form of the maxim), and in that case that principle is a practical *a priori* law, and pure reason is supposed to be practical of itself. The law in that case determines the will directly; the action conformed to it is *good in itself;* a will whose maxim always conforms to this law is *good absolutely in every respect* and is the *supreme condition of all good.* Or the maxim of the will is consequent on a determining principle of desire which presupposes an object of pleasure or pain, something therefore that *pleases* or *displeases,* and the maxim of reason that we should pursue the former and avoid the latter determines our actions as good relatively to our inclination, that is, good indirectly, i.e., relatively to a different end to which they are means), and in that case these maxims can never be called laws, but may be called rational practical precepts. The end itself, the pleasure that we seek, is in the latter case not a *good* but a *welfare;* not a concept of reason, but an empirical concept of an object of sensation; but the use of the means thereto, that is, the action, is nevertheless called good (because rational deliberation is required for it), not however, good absolutely, but only relatively to our sensuous nature, with regard to its feelings of pleasure and displeasure; but the will whose maxim is affected thereby is not a pure will; this is directed only to that in which pure reason by itself can be practical.

This is the proper place to explain the paradox of method in a critique of practical reason, namely, *that the concept of good and evil must not be determined before the moral law* (*of which it seems as if it must be the foundation*), *but only after it and by means of it.* In fact, even if we did not know that the principle of morality is a pure *a priori* law determining the will, yet, that we may not assume principles quite gratuitously, we must, at least at first, leave it *undecided,* whether the will has merely empirical principles of determination, or whether it has not also pure *a priori* principles; for it is contrary to all rules of philosophical method to assume as decided that which is the very point in question. Supposing that we wished to begin with the concept of good, in order to deduce from it the laws of the will, then this concept of an object (as a good) would at the same time assign to us this object as the sole determining principle of the will. Now, since this concept had not any practical *a priori* law for its standard, the criterion of good or evil could not be placed in anything but the agreement of the object with our feeling of pleasure or pain; and the use of reason could only consist in determining in the first place this pleasure or pain in connexion with all the sensations of my existence, and in the second place the means of securing to myself the object of the pleasure. Now, as experience alone can decide what conforms to the feeling of pleasure, and by hypothesis the practical law is to be based on this as a condition, it follows that the possibility of *a priori* practical laws would be at once excluded, because it was imagined to be necessary first of all to find an object the concept of which, as a good, should constitute the universal though empirical principle of determination of the will. But what it was necessary to inquire first of all was whether there is not an *a priori* determining principle of the will (and this could never be found anywhere but in a pure practical law, in so far as this law prescribes to maxims merely their form without regard to an object). Since, however, we laid the foundation of all practical law in an object determined by our conceptions of good and evil, whereas without a previous law that object could not be conceived by empirical concepts, we have deprived ourselves beforehand of the possibility of even conceiving a pure practical law. On the other hand, if we had first investigated the latter analytically, we should have found that it is not the concept of good as an object that determines the moral law and makes it possible, but that, on the contrary, it is the moral law that first determines the concept of good and makes it possible, so far as it deserves the name of *good* absolutely.

This remark, which only concerns the method of ultimate ethical inquiries, is of importance. It explains at once the occasion of all the mistakes of philosophers with respect to the supreme principle of morals. For they sought for an object of the will which they could make the matter and principle of a law (which consequently could not determine the will directly, but by means of that object referred to the feeling of pleasure or pain; whereas they ought first to have searched for a law that would determine the will *a priori* and directly, and afterwards determine the object in accordance with the will). Now, whether they placed this object of pleasure, which was to supply the supreme conception of goodness, in happiness, in perfection, in moral [feeling], or in the will of God, their principle in every case implied heteronomy, and they must inevitably come upon empirical conditions of a moral law, since their object, which was to be the immediate principle of the will, could not be called good or bad except in its immediate relation to feeling, which is always empirical. It is only a formal law—that is, one which prescribes to reason nothing more than the form of its universal legislation as the supreme condition of its maxims—that can be *a priori* a determining principle of practical reason. The ancients avowed this error without concealment by directing all their moral inquiries to the determination of the notion of the *summum bonum,* which they intended afterwards to make the determining principle of the will in the moral law; whereas it is only far later, when the moral law has been first established for itself, and shown to be the direct determining principle of the will, that this object can be presented to the will, whose form is now determined *a priori;* and this we shall undertake in the Dialectic of the pure practical reason. The moderns, with whom the question of the *summum bonum* has gone out of fashion, or at least seems to have become a secondary matter, hide the same error under vague (expressions as in many other cases). It shows itself, nevertheless, in their systems, as it always produces heteronomy of practical reason; and from this can never be derived a moral law giving universal commands.

Now, since the notions of good and evil, as consequences of the *a priori* determination of the will, imply also a pure practical principle, and therefore a causality of pure reason; hence they do not originally refer to objects (so as to be, for instance, special modes of the synthetic unity of the manifold of given intuitions in one consciousness)[1] like the pure concepts of the understanding or categories of reason in its theoretic employment; on the contrary, they presuppose that objects are given; but they are all modes (*modi*) of a single category, namely, that of causality, the determining principle of which consists in the rational conception of a law, which as a law of freedom reason gives to itself, thereby *a priori* proving itself practical. However, as the actions *on the one side* come under a law which is not a physical law, but a law of freedom, and consequently belong to the conduct of beings in the world of intelligence, yet on the *other side* as events in the world of sense they belong to phenomena; hence the determinations of a practical reason are only possible in reference to the latter and, therefore, in accordance with the categories of the understanding; not indeed with a view to any theoretic employment of it, i.e., so as to bring the manifold of (sensible) *intuition* under one consciousness *a priori;* but only to subject the manifold of *desires* to the unity of consciousness of a practical reason, giving it commands in the moral law, i.e., to a pure will *a priori.*

These *categories of freedom*—for so we choose to call them in contrast to those theoretic categories which are categories of physical nature—have an obvious advantage over the latter, inasmuch as the latter are only forms of thought which designate objects in an indefinite manner by means of universal concept of every possible intuition; the former, on the contrary, refer to the determination of a *free elective will* (to which indeed no exactly corresponding intuition can be assigned, but which has as its foundation a pure practical *a priori* law, which is not the case with any concepts belonging to the theoretic use of our cognitive faculties); hence, instead of the form of intuition (space and time), which does not lie in reason itself, but has to be drawn from another source, namely, the sensibility, these being elementary practical concepts have as their foundation the *form of a pure will,* which is given in reason and, therefore, in the thinking faculty itself. From this it happens that as all precepts of pure practical reason have to do only with the *determination of the will,* not with the physical conditions (of practical ability) of the *execution of one's purpose,* the practical *a priori* principles in relation to the supreme principle of freedom are at once cognitions, and have not to wait for intuitions in order to acquire significance, and that for this remarkable reason, because they themselves produce the reality of that to which they refer (the intention of the will), which is not the case with theoretical concepts. Only we must be careful to observe that these categories only apply to the practical reason; and thus they proceed in order from those which are as yet subject to sensible conditions and morally indeterminate to those which are free from sensible conditions and determined merely by the moral law.

[1] [See the *Critique of Pure Reason,* p. 52.]

Table of the Categories of Freedom relatively to the Notions of Good and Evil

I. Quantity

Subjective, according to maxims (*practical opinions of the individual*)
Objective, according to principles (*precepts*)
A priori both objective and subjective principles of freedom (*laws*)

II. Quality

Practical rules of *action (præceptivæ)*
Practical rules of *ommission (prohibitivæ)*
Practical rules of *exceptions (exceptivæ)*

III. Relation

To *personality*
To the *condition* of the person
Reciprocal, of one person to the condition of the others

IV. Modality

The *Permitted* and the *Forbidden*
Duty and the *contrary to duty*
Perfect and *imperfect duty*

It will at once be observed that in this table freedom is considered as a sort of causality not subject to empirical principles of determination, in regard to actions possible by it, which are phenomena in the world of sense, and that consequently it is referred to the categories which concern its physical possibility, whilst yet each category is taken so universally that the determining principle of that causality can be placed outside the world of sense in freedom as a property of a being in the world of intelligence; and finally the categories of modality introduce the transition from practical principles generally to those of morality, but only *problematically.* These can be established *dogmatically* only by the moral law.

I add nothing further here in explanation of the present table, since it is intelligible enough of itself. A division of this kind based on principles is very useful in any science, both for the sake of thoroughness and intelligibility. Thus, for instance, we know from the preceding table and its first number what we must begin from in practical inquiries; namely, from the maxims which every one founds on his own inclinations; the precepts which hold for a species of rational beings so far as they agree in certain inclinations; and finally the law which holds for all without regard to their inclinations, etc. In this way we survey the whole plan of what has to be done, every question of practical philosophy that has to be answered, and also the order that is to be followed.

Of the Typic of the Pure Practical Judgement

It is the notions of good and evil that first determine an object of the will. They themselves, however, are subject to a practical rule of reason which, if it is pure reason, determines the will *a priori* relatively to its object. Now, whether an action which is possible to us in the world of sense, comes under the rule or not, is a question to be decided by the practical judgement, by which what is said in the rule universally (*in abstracto*) is applied to an action *in concreto.* But since a practical rule of pure reason *in the first place* as *practical* concerns the existence of an object, and in *the second place* as a *practical rule* of pure reason implies necessity as regards the existence of the action and, therefore, is a practical law, not a physical law depending on empirical principles of determination, but a law of freedom by which the will is to be determined independently on anything empirical (merely by the conception of a law and its form), whereas all instances that can occur of possible actions can only be empirical, that is, belong to the experience of physical nature; hence, it seems absurd to expect to find in the world of sense a case which, while as such it depends only on the law of nature, yet admits of the application to it of a law of freedom, and to which we can apply the supersensible idea of the morally good which is to be exhibited in it *in concreto.* Thus, the judgement of the pure practical reason is subject to the same difficulties as that of the pure theoretical reason. The latter, however, had means at hand of escaping from these difficulties, because, in regard to the theoretical employment, intuitions were required to which pure concepts of the understanding could be applied, and such intuitions (though only of objects of the senses) can be given *a priori* and, therefore, as far as regards the union of the manifold in them, conforming to the pure *a priori* concepts of the understanding as *schemata.* On the other hand, the morally good is something whose object is supersensible; for which, therefore, nothing corresponding can be found in any sensible intuition. Judgement depending on laws of pure practical reason seems, therefore, to be subject to special difficulties arising from this, that a law of freedom is to be applied to actions, which are events taking place in the world of sense, and which, so far, belong to physical nature.

But here again is opened a favourable prospect for the pure practical judgement. When I subsume under a *pure practical* law an action possible to me in the world of sense, I am not concerned with the possibility of the *action* as an event in the world of sense. This is a matter that belongs to the decision of reason in its theoretic use according to the law of causality, which is a pure concept of the understanding, for which reason has a *schema* in the sensible intuition. Physical causality, or the condition under which it takes place, belongs to the physical concepts, the schema of which is sketched by transcendental imagination. Here, however, we have to do, not with the schema of a case that occurs according to laws, but with the schema of a law itself (if the word is allowable here), since the fact that the will (not the action relatively to its effect) is determined by the law alone without any other principle, connects the notion of causality with quite different conditions from those which constitute physical connection.

The physical law being a law to which the objects of sensible intuition, as such, are subject, must have a schema corresponding to it—that is, a general procedure of the imagination (by which it exhibits *a priori* to the senses the pure concept of the understanding which the law determines). But the law of freedom (that is, of a causality not subject to sensible conditions), and consequently the concept of the unconditionally good, cannot have any intuition, nor consequently any schema supplied to it for the purpose of its application *in concreto*. Consequently the moral law has no faculty but the understanding to aid its application to physical objects (not the imagination); and the understanding for the purposes of the judgement can provide for an idea of the reason, not a *schema* of the sensibility, but a law, though only as to its form as law; such a law, however, as can be exhibited *in concreto* in objects of the senses, and therefore a law of nature. We can therefore call this law the *type* of the moral law.

The rule of the judgement according to laws of pure practical reason is this: ask yourself whether, if the action you propose were to take place by a law of the system of nature of which you were yourself a part, you could regard it as possible by your own will. Everyone does, in fact, decide by this rule whether actions are morally good or evil. Thus, people say: "If *everyone* permitted himself to deceive, when he thought it to his advantage; or thought himself justified in shortening his life as soon as he was thoroughly weary of it; or looked with perfect indifference on the necessity of others; and if you belonged to such an order of things, would you do so with the assent of your own will?" Now everyone knows well that if he secretly allows himself to deceive, it does not follow that everyone else does so; or if, unobserved, he is destitute of compassion, others would not necessarily be so to him; hence, this comparison of the maxim of his actions with a universal law of nature is not the determining principle of his will. Such a law is, nevertheless, a *type* of the estimation of the maxim on moral principles. If the maxim of the action is not such as to stand the test of the form of a universal law of nature, then it is morally impossible. This is the judgement even of common sense; for its ordinary judgements, even those of experience, are always based on the law of nature. It has it therefore always at hand, only that in cases where *causality from freedom* is to be criticised, it makes that *law of nature* only the type of a *law of freedom*, because, without something which it could use as an example in a case of experience, it could not give the law of a pure practical reason its proper use in practice.

It is therefore allowable to use the *system of the world of sense* as the *type* of a *supersensible system of things*, provided I do not transfer to the latter the intuitions, and what depends on them, but merely apply to it the *form* of *law* in general (the notion of which occurs even in the commonest use of reason, but cannot be definitely known *a priori* for any other purpose than the pure practical use of reason); for laws, as such, are so far identical, no matter from what they derive their determining principles.

Further, since of all the supersensible absolutely nothing [is known] except freedom (through the moral law), and this only so far as it is inseparably implied in that law, and moreover all supersensible objects to which reason might lead us, following the guidance of that law, have still no reality for us, except for the purpose of that law, and for the use of mere practical reason; and as reason is authorized and even compelled to use physical nature (in its pure form as an object of the understanding) as the type of the judgement; hence, the present remark will serve to guard against reckoning amongst concepts themselves that which belongs only to the *typic* of concepts. This, namely, as a typic of the judgement, guards against the *empiricism* of practical reason, which founds the practical notions of good and evil merely on experienced consequences (so-called happiness). No doubt happiness and the infinite advantages which would result from a will determined by self-love, if this will at the same time erected itself into a universal law of nature, may certainly serve as a perfectly suitable type of the morally good, but it is not identical with it. The same typic guards also against the *mysticism* of practical reason, which turns what served only as a *symbol* into a *schema*, that is, proposes to provide for the moral concepts actual intuitions, which, however, are not sensible (intuitions of an invisible Kingdom of God), and thus plunges into the transcendent. What is befitting the use of the moral concepts is only the *rationalism* of the judgement, which takes from the sensible system of nature only what pure reason can also conceive of itself, that is, conformity to law, and transfers into the supersensible nothing but what can conversely be actually exhibited by actions in the world of sense according to the formal rule of a law of nature. However, the caution against *empiricism* of practical reason is much more important; for *mysticism* is quite reconcilable with the purity and sublimity of the moral law, and, besides, it is not very natural or agreeable to common habits of thought to strain one's imagination to supersensible intuitions; and hence the danger on this side is not so general. Empiricism, on the contrary, cuts up at the roots the morality of intentions (in which, and not in actions only, consists the high worth that men can and ought to give to themselves), and substitutes for duty something quite different, namely, an empirical interest, with which the inclinations generally are secretly leagued; and empiricism, moreover, being on this account allied with all the inclinations which (no matter what fashion they put on) degrade humanity when they are raised to the dignity of a supreme practical principle; and as these, nevertheless, are so favourable to everyone's feelings, it is for that reason much more dangerous than mysticism, which can never constitute a lasting condition of any great number of persons.

CHAPTER III. *Of the Motives of Pure Practical Reason*

WHAT is essential in the moral worth of actions is *that the moral law should directly determine the will.* If the determination of the will takes place in conformity indeed to the moral law, but only by means of a feeling, no matter of what kind, which has to be presupposed in order that the law may be sufficient to determine the will, and therefore not *for the sake of the law,* then the action will possess *legality,* but not *morality.* Now, if we understand by *motive* (*elater animi*) the subjective ground of determination of the will of a being whose reason does not necessarily conform to the objective law, by virtue of its own nature, then it will follow, first, that not motives can be attributed to the Divine will, and that the motives of the human will (as well as that of every created rational being) can never be anything else than the moral law, and consequently that the objective principle of determination must always and alone be also the subjectively sufficient determining principle of the action, if this is not merely to fulfil the *letter* of the law, without containing its *spirit.*[1]

Since, then, for the purpose of giving the moral law influence over the will, we must not seek for any other motives that might enable us to dispense with the motive of the law itself, because that would produce mere hypocrisy, without consistency; and it is even *dangerous* to allow other motives (for instance, that of interest) even to co-operate *along with* the moral law; hence nothing is left us but to determine carefully in what way the moral law becomes a motive, and what effect this has upon the faculty of desire. For as to the question how a law can be directly and of itself a determining principle of the will (which is the essence of morality), this is, for human reason, an insoluble problem and identical with the question: how a free will is possible. Therefore what we have to show *a priori* is not why the moral law in itself supplies a motive, but what effect it, as such, produces (or, more correctly speaking, must produce) on the mind.

The essential point in every determination of the will by the moral law is that being a free will it is determined simply by the moral law, not only without the co-operation of sensible impulses, but even to the rejection of all such, and to the checking of all inclinations so far as they might be opposed to that law. So far, then, the effect of the moral law as a motive is only negative, and this motive can be known *a priori* to be such. For all inclination and every sensible impulse is founded on feeling, and the negative effect produced on feeling (by the check on the inclinations) is itself feeling; consequently, we can see *a priori* that the moral law, as a determining principle of the will, must by thwarting all our inclinations produce a feeling which may be called *pain;* and in this we have the first, perhaps the only, instance in which we are able from *a priori* considerations to determine the

[1] We may say of every action that conforms to the law, but is not done for the sake of the law, that it is morally good in the *letter,* not in the *spirit* (the intention).

relation of a cognition (in this case of pure practical reason) to the feeling of pleasure or displeasure. All the inclinations together (which can be reduced to a tolerable system, in which case their satisfaction is called *happiness*) constitute *self-regard* (*solipsismus*). This is either the *self-love* that consists in an excessive *fondness* for oneself (*philautia*), or satisfaction with oneself (*arrogantia*). The former is called particularly *selfishness;* the latter *self-conceit.* Pure practical reason only *checks* selfishness, looking on it as natural and active in us even prior to the moral law, so far as to limit it to the condition of agreement with this law, and then it is called *rational self-love.* But self-conceit reason *strikes down* altogether, since all claims to self-esteem which precede agreement with the moral law are vain and unjustifiable, for the certainty of a state of mind that coincides with this law is the first condition of personal worth (as we shall presently show more clearly), and prior to this conformity any pretension to worth is false and unlawful. Now the propensity to self-esteem is one of the inclinations which the moral law checks, inasmuch as that esteem rests only on morality. Therefore the moral law breaks down self-conceit. But as this law is something positive in itself, namely, the form of an intellectual causality, that is, of freedom, it must be an object of respect; for, by opposing the subjective antagonism of the inclinations, it *weakens* self-conceit; and since it even *breaks down,* that is, humiliates, this conceit, it is an object of the highest respect and, consequently, is the foundation of a positive feeling which is not of empirical origin, but is known *a priori.* Therefore respect for the moral law is a feeling which is produced by an intellectual cause, and this feeling is the only one that we know quite *a priori* and the necessity of which we can perceive.

In the preceding chapter we have seen that everything that presents itself as an object of the will prior to the moral law is by that law itself, which is the supreme condition of practical reason, excluded from the determining principles of the will which we have called the unconditionally good; and that the mere practical form which consists in the adaptation of the maxims to universal legislation first determines what is good in itself and absolutely, and is the basis of the maxims of a pure will, which alone is good in every respect. However, we find that our nature as sensible beings is such that the matter of desire (objects of inclination, whether of hope or fear) first presents itself to us; and our pathologically affected self, although it is in its maxims quite unfit for universal legislation; yet, just as if it constituted our entire self, strives to put its pretensions forward first, and to have them acknowledged as the first and original. This propensity to make ourselves in the subjective determining principles of our choice serve as the objective determining principle of the will generally may be called *self-love;* and if this pretends to be legislative as an unconditional practical principle it may be called *self-conceit.* Now the moral law, which alone is truly objective (namely, in every respect), entirely excludes the influence of self-love on the supreme practical principle, and indefinitely checks the self-conceit that prescribes the subjective conditions of the former as laws. Now whatever checks our self-conceit in our own judgement humiliates; therefore the moral law inevitably humbles every man when he compares with it the physical propensities of his nature. That, the idea of which as a *determining principle of our will* humbles us in our self-consciousness, awakes *respect* for itself, so far as it is itself positive and a determining principle. Therefore the moral law is even subjectively a cause of respect. Now since everything that enters into self-love belongs to inclination, and all inclination rests on feelings, and consequently whatever checks all the feelings together in self-love has necessarily, by this very circumstance, an influence on feeling; hence we comprehend how it is possible to perceive *a priori* that the moral law can produce an effect on feeling, in that it excludes the inclinations and the propensity to make them the supreme practical condition, i. e., self-love, from all participation in the supreme legislation. This effect is on one side merely *negative,* but on the other side, relatively to the restricting principle of pure practical reason, it is *positive.* No special kind of feeling need be assumed for this under the name of a practical or moral feeling as antecedent to the moral law and serving as its foundation.

The negative effect on feeling (unpleasantness) is *pathological*, like every influence on feeling and like every feeling generally. But as an effect of the consciousness of the moral law, and consequently in relation to a supersensible cause, namely, the subject of pure practical reason which is the supreme lawgiver, this feeling of a rational being affected by inclinations is called *humiliation* (intellectual self-depreciation); but with reference to the positive source of this humiliation, the law, it is respect for it.

There is indeed no feeling for this law; but inasmuch as it removes the resistance out of the way, this removal of an obstacle is, in the judgement of reason, esteemed equivalent to a positive help to its causality. Therefore this feeling may also be called a *feeling of respect* for the moral law, and for both reasons together *a moral feeling*.

While the moral law, therefore, is a formal determining principle of action by practical pure reason, and is moreover a material though only objective determining principle of the objects of action as called *good* and *evil*, it is also a subjective determining principle, that is, a motive to this action, inasmuch as it has influence on the morality of the subject and produces a feeling conducive to the influence of the law on the will. There is here in the subject no *antecedent* feeling tending to morality. For this is impossible, since every feeling is sensible, and the motive of moral intention must be free from all sensible conditions. On the contrary, while the sensible feeling which is at the bottom of all our inclinations is the condition of that impression which we call *respect*, the cause that determines it lies in the pure practical reason; and this impression therefore, on account of its origin, must be called, not a pathological but a *practical effect*. For by the fact that the conception of the moral law deprives self-love of its influence, and self-conceit of its illusion, it lessens the obstacle to pure practical reason and produces the conception of the superiority of its objective law to the impulses of the sensibility; and thus, by removing the counterpoise, it gives relatively greater weight to the law in the judgement of reason (in the case of a will affected by the aforesaid impulses). Thus the respect for the law is not a motive to morality, but is morality itself subjectively considered as a motive, inasmuch as pure practical reason, by rejecting all the rival pretensions of self-love, gives authority to the law, which now alone has influence. Now it is to be observed that as respect is an effect on feeling, and therefore on the sensibility, of a rational being, it presupposes this sensibility, and therefore also the finiteness of such beings on whom the moral law imposes respect; and that respect for the *law* cannot be attributed to a supreme being, or to any being free from all sensibility, in whom, therefore, this sensibility cannot be an obstacle to practical reason.

This feeling (which we call the *moral feeling*) is therefore produced simply by reason. It does not serve for the estimation of actions nor for the foundation of the objective moral law itself, but merely as a motive to make this of itself a maxim. But what name could we more suitably apply to this singular feeling which cannot be compared to any pathological feeling? It is of such a peculiar kind that it seems to be at the disposal of reason only, and that pure practical reason.

Respect applies always to persons only—not to things. The latter may arouse inclination, and if they are animals (e. g., horses, dogs, etc.), even *love* or *fear,* like the sea, a volcano, a beast of prey; but never *respect.* Something that comes nearer to this feeling is *admiration,* and this, as an affection, astonishment, can apply to things also, e.g., lofty mountains, the magnitude, number, and distance of the heavenly bodies, the strength and swiftness of many animals, etc. But all this is not respect. A man also may be an object to me of love, fear, or admiration, even to astonishment, and yet not be an object of respect. His jocose humour, his courage and strength, his power from the rank he has amongst others, may inspire me with sentiments of this kind, but still inner respect for him is wanting. Fontenelle says, "I bow before a great man, but my mind does not bow." I would add, before an humble plain man, in whom I perceive uprightness of character in a higher degree than I am conscious of in myself, *my mind bows* whether I choose it or not, and though I bear my head never so high that he may not forget my superior rank. Why is this? Because his example exhibits to me a law that humbles my self-conceit when I compare it with my conduct: a law, the *practicability* of obedience to which I see proved by fact before my eyes. Now, I may even be conscious of a like degree of uprightness, and yet the respect remains. For since in man all good is defective, the law made visible by an example still humbles my pride, my standard being furnished by a man whose imperfections, whatever they may be, are not known to me as my own are, and who therefore appears to me in a more favourable light. *Respect* is a *tribute* which we cannot refuse to merit, whether we will or not; we may indeed outwardly withhold it, but we cannot help feeling it inwardly.

Respect is so *far from being* a feeling of pleasure that we only reluctantly give way to it as regards a man. We try to find out something that may lighten the burden of it, some fault to compensate us for the humiliation which such an example causes. Even the dead are not always secure from this criticism, especially if their example appears inimitable. Even the moral law itself in its *solemn majesty* is exposed to this endeavour to save oneself from yielding it respect. Can it be thought that it is for any other reason that we are so ready to reduce it to the level of our familiar inclination, or that it is for any other reason that we all take such trouble to make it out to be the chosen precept of our own interest well understood, but that we want to be free from the deterrent respect which shows us our own unworthiness with such severity? Nevertheless, on the other hand, so *little* is there *pain* in it that if once one has laid aside self-conceit and allowed practical influence to that respect, he can never be satisfied with contemplating the majesty of this law, and the soul believes itself elevated in proportion as it sees the holy law elevated above it and its frail nature. No doubt great talents and activity proportioned to them may also occasion respect or an analogous feeling. It is very proper to yield it to them, and then it appears as if this sentiment were the same thing as admiration. But if we look closer we shall observe that it is always uncertain how much of the ability is due to native talent, and how much to diligence in cultivating it. Reason represents it to us as probably the fruit of cultivation, and therefore as meritorious, and this notably reduces our self-conceit, and either casts a reproach on us or urges us to follow such an example in the way that is suitable to us. This respect, then, which we show to such a person (properly speaking, to the law that his example exhibits) is not mere admiration; and this is confirmed also by the fact that when the common run of admirers think they have learned from any source the badness of such a man's character (for instance Voltaire's) they give up all respect for him; whereas the true scholar still feels it at least with regard to his talents, because he is himself engaged in a business and a vocation which make imitation of such a man in some degree a law.

Respect for the moral law is, therefore, the only and the undoubted moral motive, and this feeling is directed to no object, except on the ground of this law. The moral law first determines the will objectively and directly in the judgement of reason; and freedom, whose causality can be determined only by the law, consists just in this, that it restricts all inclinations, and consequently self-esteem, by the condition of obedience to its pure law. This restriction now has an effect on feeling, and produces the impression of displeasure which can be known *a priori* from the moral law. Since it is so far only a *negative* effect which, arising from the influence of pure practical reason, checks the activity of the subject, so far as it is determined by inclinations, and hence checks the opinion of his personal worth (which, in the absence of agreement with the moral law, is reduced to nothing); hence, the effect of this law on feeling is merely humiliation. We can, therefore, perceive this *a priori,* but cannot know by it the force of the pure practical law as a motive, but only the resistance to motives of the sensibility. But since the same law is objectively, that is, in the conception of pure reason, an immediate principle of determination of the will, and consequently this humiliation takes place only relatively to the purity of the law; hence, the lowering of the pretensions of moral self-esteem, that is, humiliation on the sensible side, is an elevation of the moral, i.e., practical, esteem for the law itself on the intellectual side; in a word, it is respect for the law, and therefore, as its cause is intellectual, a positive feeling which can be known *a priori.* For whatever diminishes the obstacles to an activity furthers this activity itself. Now the recognition of the moral law is the consciousness of an activity of practical reason from objective principles, which only fails to reveal its effect in actions because subjective (pathological) causes hinder it. Respect for the moral law then must be regarded as a positive, though indirect, effect of it on feeling, inasmuch as this respect weakens the impeding influence of inclinations by humiliating self-esteem; and hence also as a subjective principle of activity, that is, as a *motive* to obedience to the law, and as a principle of the maxims of a life conformable to it. From the notion of a motive arises that of an *interest,* which can never be attributed to any being unless it possesses reason, and which signifies a *motive* of the will in so far as it is conceived by the reason. Since in a morally good will the law itself must be the motive, the *moral interest* is a pure interest of practical reason alone, independent of sense. On the notion of an interest is based that of a *maxim.* This, therefore, is morally good only in case it rests simply on the interest taken in obedience to the law. All three notions, however, that of a *motive,* of an *interest,* and of a *maxim,* can be applied only to finite beings. For they all suppose a limitation of the nature of the being, in that the subjective character of his choice does not of itself agree with the objective law of a practical reason; they suppose that the being requires to be impelled to action by something, because an internal obstacle opposes itself. Therefore they cannot be applied to the Divine will.

There is something so singular in the unbounded esteem for the pure moral law, apart from all advantage, as it is presented for our obedience by practical reason, the voice of which makes even the boldest sinner tremble and compels him to hide himself from it, that we cannot wonder if we find this influence of a mere intellectual idea on the feelings quite incomprehensible to speculative reason and have to be satisfied with seeing so much of this *a priori* that such a feeling is inseparably connected with the conception of the moral law in every finite rational being. If this feeling of respect were pathological, and therefore were a feeling of pleasure based on the inner *sense,* it would be in vain to try to discover a connection of it with any idea *a priori.* But [it] is a feeling that applies merely to what is practical, and depends on the conception of a law, simply as to its form, not on account of any object, and therefore cannot be reckoned either as pleasure or pain, and yet produces an *interest* in obedience to the law, which we call the *moral interest,* just as the capacity of taking such an interest in the law (or respect for the moral law itself) is properly the *moral feeling.*

The consciousness of a *free* submission of the will to the law, yet combined with an inevitable constraint put upon all inclinations, though only by our own reason, is respect for the law. The law that demands this respect and inspires it is clearly no other than the moral (for no other precludes all inclinations from exercising any direct influence on the will). An action which is objectively practical according to this law, to the exclusion of every determining principle of inclination, is *duty,* and this by reason of that exclusion includes in its concept practical *obligation,* that is, a determination to actions, however *reluctantly* they may be done. The feeling that arises from the consciousness of this obligation is not pathological, as would be a feeling produced by an object of the senses, but practical only, that is, it is made possible by a preceding (objective) determination of the will and a causality of the reason. As *submission* to the law, therefore, that is, as a command (announcing constraint for the sensibly affected subject), it contains in it no pleasure, but on the contrary, so far, pain in the action. On the other hand, however, as this constraint is exercised merely by the legislation of our *own* reason, it also contains something *elevating,* and this subjective effect on feeling, inasmuch as pure practical reason is the sole cause of it, may be called in this respect *self-approbation,* since we recognize ourselves as determined thereto solely by the law without any interest, and are now conscious of a quite different interest subjectively produced thereby, and which is purely practical and *free;* and our taking this interest in an action of duty is not suggested by any inclination, but is commanded and actually brought about by reason through the practical law; whence this feeling obtains a special name, that of *respect.*

The notion of duty, therefore, requires in the action, *objectively,* agreement with the law, and, subjectively in its maxim, that respect for the law shall be the sole mode in which the will is determined thereby. And on this rests the distinction between the consciousness of having acted *according to duty* and *from duty,* that is, from respect for the law. The former (*legality*) is possible even if inclinations have been the determining principles of the will; but the latter (*morality*), moral worth, can be placed only in this, that the action is done from duty, that is, simply for the sake of the law.[1]

It is of the greatest importance to attend with the utmost exactness in all moral judgements to the subjective principle of all maxims, that all the morality of actions may be placed in the necessity of acting *from duty* and from respect for the law, not from love and inclination for that which the actions are to produce. For men and all created rational beings moral necessity is constraint, that is obligation, and every action based on it is to be conceived as a duty, not as a proceeding previously pleasing, or likely to be pleasing to us of our own accord. As if indeed we could ever bring it about that without respect for the law, which implies fear, or at least apprehension of transgression, we of ourselves, like the independent Deity, could ever come into possession of *holiness* of will by the coincidence of our will with the pure moral law becoming as it were part of our nature, never to be shaken (in which case the law would cease to be a command for us, as we could never be tempted to be untrue to it).

[1] If we examine accurately the notion of respect for persons as it has been already laid down, we shall perceive that it always rests on the consciousness of a duty which an example shows us, and that respect, therefore, can never have any but a moral ground, and that it is very good and even, in a psychological point of view, very useful for the knowledge of mankind, that whenever we use this expression we should attend to this secret and marvellous, yet often recurring, regard which men in their judgement pay to the moral law.

The moral law is in fact for the will of a perfect being a law of *holiness,* but for the will of every finite rational being a law of *duty,* of moral constraint, and of the determination of its actions by *respect* for this law and reverence for its duty. No other subjective principle must be assumed as a motive, else while the action might chance to be such as the law prescribes, yet, as does not proceed from duty, the intention, which is the thing properly in question in this legislation, is not moral.

It is a very beautiful thing to do good to men from love to them and from sympathetic good will, or to be just from love of order; but this is not yet the true moral maxim of our conduct which is suitable to our position amongst rational beings as *men,* when we pretend with fanciful pride to set ourselves above the thought of duty, like volunteers, and, as if we were independent on the command, to want to do of our own good pleasure what we think we need no command to do. We stand under a *discipline* of reason and in all our maxims must not forget our subjection to it, nor withdraw anything therefrom, or by an egotistic presumption diminish aught of the authority of the law (although our own reason gives it) so as to set the determining principle of our will, even though the law be conformed to, anywhere else but in the law itself and in respect for this law. *Duty* and *obligation* are the only names that we must give to our relation to the moral law. We are indeed legislative members of a moral kingdom rendered possible by freedom, and presented to us by reason as an object of respect; but yet we are subjects in it, not the sovereign, and to mistake our inferior position as creatures, and presumptuously to reject the authority of the moral law, is already to revolt from it in spirit, even though the letter of it is fulfilled.

With this agrees very well the possibility of such a command as: *Love God above everything, and thy neighbour as thyself.*[1] For as a command it requires respect for a law which *commands love* and does not leave it to our own arbitrary choice to make this our principle. Love to God, however, considered as an inclination (pathological love), is impossible, for He is not an object of the senses. The same affection towards men is possible no doubt, but cannot be commanded, for it is not in the power of any man to love anyone at command; therefore it is only *practical love* that is meant in that pith of all laws. To love God means, in this sense, to like to do His commandments; to love one's neighbour means to like to practise all duties towards him. But the command that makes this a rule cannot command us to *have* this disposition in actions conformed to duty, but only to *endeavour* after it. For a command to like to do a thing is in itself contradictory, because if we already know of ourselves what we are bound to do, and if further we are conscious of liking to do it, a command would be quite needless; and if we do it not willingly, but only out of respect for the law, a command that makes this respect the motive of our maxim would directly counteract the disposition commanded. That law of all laws, therefore, like all the moral precepts of the Gospel, exhibits the moral disposition in all its perfection, in which, viewed as an ideal of holiness, it is not attainable by any creature, but yet is the pattern which we should strive to approach, and in an uninterrupted but infinite progress become like to. In fact, if a rational creature could ever reach this point, that he thoroughly *likes* to do all moral laws, this would mean that there does not exist in him even the possibility of a desire that would tempt him to deviate from them; for to overcome such a desire always costs the subject some sacrifice and therefore requires self-compulsion, that is, inward constraint to something that one does not quite like to do; and no creature can ever reach this stage of moral disposition. For, being a creature, and therefore always dependent with respect to what he requires for complete satisfaction, he can never be quite free from desires and inclinations, and as these rest on physical causes, they can never of themselves coincide with the moral law, the sources of which are quite different; and therefore they make it necessary to found the mental disposition of one's maxims on moral obligation, not on ready inclination, but on respect, which *demands* obedience to the law, even though one may not like it; not on love, which apprehends no inward reluctance of the will towards the law. Nevertheless, this latter, namely, love to the law (which would then cease to be a *command,* and then morality, which would have passed subjectively into holiness, would cease to be *virtue*) must be the constant though unattainable goal of his endeavours. For in the case of what we highly esteem, but yet (on account of the consciousness of our weakness) dread, the increased facility of satisfying it changes the most reverential awe into

[1] This law is in striking contrast with the principle of private happiness which some make the supreme principle of morality. This would be expressed thus: *Love thyself above everything, and God and thy neighbour for thine own sake.*

inclination, and respect into love; at least this would be the perfection of a disposition devoted to the law, if it were possible for a creature to attain it.

This reflection is intended not so much to clear up the evangelical command just cited, in order to prevent *religious fanaticism* in regard to love of God, but to define accurately the moral disposition with regard directly to our duties towards men, and to check, or if possible prevent, *a merely moral fanaticism* which infects many persons. The stage of morality on which man (and, as far as we can see, every rational creature) stands is respect for the moral law. The disposition that he ought to have in obeying this is to obey it from duty, not from spontaneous inclination, or from an endeavour taken up from liking and unbidden; and this proper moral condition in which he can always be is *virtue*, that is, moral disposition *militant*, and not *holiness* in the fancied *possession* of a perfect *purity* of the disposition of the will. It is nothing but moral fanaticism and exaggerated self-conceit that is infused into the mind by exhortation to actions as noble, sublime, and magnanimous, by which men are led into the delusion that it is not duty, that is, respect for the law, whose yoke (an easy yoke indeed, because reason itself imposes it on us) they *must* bear, whether they like it or not, that constitutes the determining principle of their actions, and which always humbles them while they *obey* it; fancying that those actions are expected from them, not from duty, but as pure merit. For not only would they, in imitating such deeds from such a principle, not have fulfilled the spirit of the law in the least, which consists not in the legality of the action (without regard to principle), but in the subjection of the mind to the law; not only do they make the motives *pathological* (seated in sympathy or self-love), not moral (in the law), but they produce in this way a vain, high-flying, fantastic way of thinking, flattering themselves with a spontaneous goodness of heart that needs neither spur nor bridle, for which no command is needed, and thereby forgetting their obligation, which they ought to think of rather than merit. Indeed actions of others which are done with great sacrifice, and merely for the sake of duty, may be praised as *noble* and *sublime,* but only so far as there are traces which suggest that they were done wholly out of respect for duty and not from excited feelings. If these, however, are set before anyone as examples to be imitated, respect for duty (which is the only true moral feeling) must be employed as the motive—this severe holy precept which never allows our vain self-love to dally with pathological impulses (however analogous they may be to morality), and to take a pride in *meritorious* worth. Now if we search we shall find for all actions that are worthy of praise a law of duty which *commands,* and does not leave us to choose what may be agreeable to our inclinations. This is the only way of representing things that can give a moral training to the soul, because it alone is capable of solid and accurately defined principles.

If *fanaticism* in its most general sense is a deliberate overstepping of the limits of human reason, then *moral fanaticism* is such an overstepping of the bounds that practical pure reason sets to mankind, in that it forbids us to place the subjective determining principle of correct actions, that is, their moral *motive,* in anything but the law itself, or to place the disposition which is thereby brought into the maxims in anything but respect for this law, and hence commands us to take as the supreme *vital principle* of all morality in men the thought of duty, which strikes down all *arrogance* as well as vain *self-love.*

If this is so, it is not only writers of romance or sentimental educators (although they may be zealous opponents of sentimentalism), but sometimes even philosophers, nay, even the severest of all, the Stoics, that have brought in *moral fanaticism* instead of a sober but wise moral discipline, although the fanaticism of the latter was more heroic, that of the former of an insipid, effeminate character; and we may, without hypocrisy, say of the moral teaching of the Gospel, that it first, by the purity of its moral principle, and at the same time by its suitability to the limitations of finite beings, brought all the good conduct of men under the discipline of a duty plainly set before their eyes, which does not permit them to indulge in dreams of imaginary moral perfections; and that it also set the bounds of humility (that is, self-knowledge) to self-conceit as well as to self-love, both which are ready to mistake their limits.

Duty! Thou sublime and mighty name that dost embrace nothing charming or insinuating, but requirest submission, and yet seekest not to move the will by threatening aught that would arouse natural aversion or terror, but merely holdest forth a law which of itself finds entrance into the mind, and yet gains reluctant reverence (though not always obedience), a law before which all inclinations are dumb, even though they secretly counter-work it; what origin is there worthy of thee, and where is to be found the root of thy noble descent which proudly rejects all kindred with the inclinations; a root to be derived from which is the indispensable condition of the only worth which men can give themselves?

It can be nothing less than a power which elevates man above himself (as a part of the world of sense), a power which connects him with an order of things that only the understanding can conceive, with a world which at the same time commands the whole sensible world, and with it the empirically determinable existence of man in time, as well as the sum total of all ends (which totality alone suits such unconditional practical laws as the moral). This power is nothing but *personality,* that is, freedom and independence on the mechanism of nature, yet, regarded also as a faculty of a being which is subject to special laws, namely, pure practical laws given by its own reason; so that the person as belonging to the sensible world is subject to his own personality as belonging to the intelligible [supersensible] world. It is then not to be wondered at that man, as belonging to both worlds, must regard his own nature in reference to its second and highest characteristic only with reverence, and its laws with the highest respect.

On this origin are founded many expressions which designate the worth of objects according to moral ideas. The moral law is *holy* (inviolable). Man is indeed unholy enough, but he must regard *humanity* in his own person as holy. In all creation every thing one chooses and over which one has any power, may be used *merely as means;* man alone, and with him every rational creature, is an *end in himself.* By virtue of the autonomy of his freedom he is the subject of the moral law, which is holy. Just for this reason every will, even every person's own individual will, in relation to itself, is restricted to the condition of agreement with the *autonomy* of the rational being, that is to say, that it is not to be subject to any purpose which cannot accord with a law which might arise from the will of the passive subject himself; the latter is, therefore, never to be employed merely as means, but as itself also, concurrently, an end. We justly attribute this condition even to the Divine will, with regard to the rational beings in the world, which are His creatures, since it rests on their *personality,* by which alone they are ends in themselves.

This respect-inspiring idea of personality which sets before our eyes the sublimity of our nature (in its higher aspect), while at the same time it shows us the want of accord of our conduct with it and thereby strikes down self-conceit, is even natural to the commonest reason and easily observed. Has not every even moderately honourable man sometimes found that, where by an otherwise inoffensive lie he might either have withdrawn himself from an unpleasant business, or even have procured some advantages for a loved and well-deserving friend, he has avoided it solely lest he should despise himself secretly in his own eyes? When an upright man is in the greatest distress, which he might have avoided if he could only have disregarded duty, is he not sustained by the consciousness that he has maintained humanity in its proper dignity in his own person and honoured it, that he has no reason to be ashamed of himself in his own sight, or to dread the inward glance of self-examination? This consolation is not happiness, it is not even the smallest part of it, for no one would wish to have occasion for it, or would, perhaps, even desire a life in such circumstances. But he lives, and he cannot endure that he should be in his own eyes unworthy of life. This inward peace is therefore merely negative as regards what can make life pleasant; it is, in fact, only the escaping the danger of sinking in personal worth, after everything else that is valuable has been lost. It is the effect of a respect for something quite different from life, something in comparison and contrast with which life with all its enjoyment has no value. He still lives only because it is his duty, not because he finds anything pleasant in life.

Such is the nature of the true motive of pure practical reason; it is no other than the pure moral law itself, inasmuch as it makes us conscious of the sublimity of our own supersensible existence and subjectively produces respect for their higher nature in men who are also conscious of their sensible existence and of the consequent dependence of their pathologically very susceptible nature. Now with this motive may be combined so many charms and satisfactions of life that even on this account alone the most prudent choice of a rational Epicurean reflecting on the greatest advantage of life would declare itself on the side of moral conduct, and it may even be advisable to join this prospect of a cheerful enjoyment of life with that supreme motive which is already sufficient of itself; but only as a counterpoise to the attractions which vice does not fail to exhibit on the opposite side, and not so as, even in the smallest degree, to place in this the proper moving power when duty is in question. For that would be just the same as to wish to taint the purity of the moral disposition in its source. The majesty of duty has nothing to do with enjoyment of life; it has its special law and its special tribunal, and though the two should be never so well shaken together to be given well mixed, like medicine, to the sick soul, yet they will soon separate of themselves; and if they do not, the former will not act; and although physical life might gain somewhat in force, the moral life would fade away irrecoverably.

Critical Examination of the Analytic of Pure Practical Reason

By the critical examination of a science, or of a portion of it, which constitutes a system by itself, I understand the inquiry and proof why it must have this and no other systematic form, when we compare it with another system which is based on a similar faculty of knowledge. Now practical and speculative reason are based on the same faculty, so far as both are *pure reason.* Therefore the difference in their systematic form must be determined by the comparison of both, and the ground of this must be assigned.

The Analytic of pure theoretic reason had to do with the knowledge of such objects as may have been given to the understanding, and was obliged therefore to begin from *intuition* and consequently (as this is always sensible) from sensibility; and only after that could advance to concepts (of the objects of this intuition), and could only end with *principles* after both these had preceded. On the contrary, since practical reason has not to do with objects so as to *know* them, but with its own faculty of *realizing* them (in accordance with the knowledge of them), that is, with a will which is a causality, inasmuch as reason contains its determining principle; since, consequently, it has not to furnish an object of intuition, but as practical reason has to furnish only a law (because the notion of causality always implies the reference to a law which determines the existence of the many in relation to one another); hence a critical examination of the Analytic of reason, if this is to be practical reason (and this is properly the problem), must begin with the *possibility of practical principles a priori.* Only after that can it proceed to *concepts* of the objects of a practical reason, namely, those of absolute good and evil, in order to assign them in accordance with those principles (for prior to those principles they cannot possibly be given as good and evil by any faculty of knowledge), and only then could the section be concluded with the last chapter, that, namely, which treats of the relation of the pure practical reason to the sensibility and of its necessary influence thereon, which is *a priori* cognisable, that is, of the *moral sentiment.* Thus the Analytic of the practical pure reason has the whole extent of the conditions of its use in common with the theoretical, but in reverse order. The Analytic of pure theoretic reason was divided into transcendental Aesthetic and transcendental Logic, that of the practical reversely into Logic and Aesthetic of pure practical reason (if I may, for the sake of analogy merely, use these designations, which are not quite suitable). This logic again was there divided into the Analytic of concepts and that of principles: here into that of principles and concepts. The Aesthetic also had in the former case two parts, on account of the two kinds of sensible intuition; here the sensibility is not considered as a capacity of intuition at all, but merely as feeling (which can be a subjective ground of desire), and in regard to it pure practical reason admits no further division.

It is also easy to see the reason why this division into two parts with its subdivision was not actually adopted here (as one might have been induced to attempt by the example of the former critique). For since it is *pure reason* that is here considered in its practical use, and consequently as proceeding from *a priori* principles, and not from empirical principles of determination, hence the division of the analytic of pure practical reason must resemble that of a syllogism; namely, proceeding from the universal in the *major premiss* (the moral principle), through a *minor premiss* containing a subsumption of possible actions (as good or evil) under the former, to the *conclusion,* namely, the subjective determination of the will (an interest in the possible practical good, and in the maxim founded on it). He who has been able to convince himself of the truth of the positions occurring in the Analytic will take pleasure in such comparisons; for they justly suggest the expectation that we may perhaps some day be able to discern the unity of the whole faculty of reason (theoretical as well as practical) and be able to derive all from one principle, which is what human reason inevitably demands, as it finds complete satisfaction only in a perfectly systematic unity of its knowledge.

If now we consider also the contents of the knowledge that we can have of a pure practical reason, and by means of it, as shown by the

Analytic, we find, along with a remarkable analogy between it and the theoretical, no less remarkable differences. As regards the theoretical, the *faculty of a pure rational cognition a priori* could be easily and evidently proved by examples from sciences (in which, as they put their principles to the test in so many ways by methodical use, there is not so much reason as in common knowledge to fear a secret mixture of empirical principles of cognition). But, that pure reason without the admixture of any empirical principle is practical of itself, this could only be shown from the *commonest practical use of reason,* by verifying the fact, that every man's natural reason acknowledges the supreme practical principle as the supreme law of his will—a law completely *a priori* and not depending on any sensible data. It was necessary first to establish and verify the purity of its origin, even in the *judgement of this common reason,* before science could take it in hand to make use of it, as a fact, that is, prior to all disputation about its possibility, and all the consequences that may be drawn from it. But this circumstance may be readily explained from what has just been said; because practical pure reason must necessarily begin with principles, which therefore must be the first data, the foundation of all science, and cannot be derived from it. It was possible to effect this verification of moral principles as principles of a pure reason quite well, and with sufficient certainty, by a single appeal to the judgement of common sense, for this reason, that anything empirical which might slip into our maxims as a determining principle of the will can be detected at once by the feeling of pleasure or pain which necessarily attaches to it as exciting desire; whereas pure practical reason positively *refuses* to admit this feeling into its principle as a condition. The heterogeneity of the determining principles (the empirical and rational) is clearly detected by this resistance of a practically legislating reason against every admixture of inclination, and by a peculiar kind of *sentiment,* which, however, does not precede the legislation of the practical reason, but, on the contrary, is produced by this as a constraint, namely, by the feeling of a respect such as no man has for inclinations of whatever kind but for the law only; and it is detected in so marked and prominent a manner that even the most uninstructed cannot fail to see at once in an example presented to him, that empirical principles of volition may indeed urge him to follow their attractions, but that he can never be expected to *obey* anything but the pure practical law of reason alone.

The distinction between the *doctrine of happiness* and the *doctrine of morality,* in the former of which empirical principles constitute the entire foundation, while in the second they do not form the smallest part of it, is the first and most important office of the Analytic of pure practical reason; and it must proceed in it with as much *exactness* and, so to speak, *scrupulousness,* as any geometer in his work. The philosopher, however, has greater difficulties to contend with here (as always in rational cognition by means of concepts merely without construction), because he cannot take any intuition as a foundation (for a pure noumenon). He has, however, this advantage that, like the chemist, he can at any time make an experiment with every man's practical reason for the purpose of distinguishing the moral (pure) principle of determination from the empirical; namely, by adding the moral law (as a determining principle) to the empirically affected will (e. g., that of the man who would be ready to lie because he can gain something thereby). It is as if the analyst added alkali to a solution of lime in hydrochloric acid, the acid at once forsakes the lime, combines with the alkali, and the lime is precipitated. Just in the same way, if to a man who is otherwise honest (or who for this occasion places himself only in thought in the position of an honest man), we present the moral law by which he recognises the worthlessness of the liar, his practical reason (in forming a judgement of what ought to be done) at once forsakes the advantage, combines with that which maintains in him respect for his own person (truthfulness), and the advantage after it has been separated and washed from every particle of reason (which is altogether on the side of duty) is easily weighed by everyone, so that it can enter into combination with reason in other cases, only not where it could be opposed to the moral law, which reason never forsakes, but most closely unites itself with.

But it does not follow that this distinction between the principle of happiness and that of morality is an *opposition* between them, and pure practical reason does not require that we should *renounce* all claim to happiness, but only that the moment duty is in question we should take *no account* of happiness. It may even in certain respects be a duty to provide for happiness; partly, because (including skill, wealth, riches) it contains means for the fulfilment of our duty; partly, because the absence of it (e.g., poverty) implies temptations to transgress our duty. But it can never be an immediate duty to promote our happiness, still less can it be the principle of all duty. Now, as all determining principles of the will, except the law of pure practical reason alone (the moral law), are all empirical and, therefore, as such, belong to the principle of happiness, they must all be kept apart from the supreme principle of morality and never be incorporated with it as a condition; since this would be to destroy all moral worth just as much as any empirical admixture with geometrical principles would destroy the certainty of mathematical evidence, which in Plato's opinion is the most excellent thing in mathematics, even surpassing their utility.

Instead, however, of the deduction of the supreme principle of pure practical reason, that is, the explanation of the possibility of such a knowledge *a priori,* the utmost we were able to do was to show that if we saw the possibility of the freedom of an efficient cause, we should also see not merely the possibility, but even the necessity, of the moral law as the supreme practical law of rational beings, to whom we attribute freedom of causality of their will; because both concepts are so inseparably united that we might define practical freedom as independence of the will on anything but the moral law. But we cannot perceive the possibility of the freedom of an efficient cause, especially in the world of sense; we are fortunate if only we can be sufficiently assured that there is no proof of its impossibility, and are now, by the moral law which postulates it, compelled and therefore authorized to assume it. However, there are still many who think that they can explain this freedom on empirical principles, like any other physical faculty, and treat it as a *psychological* property, the explanation of which only requires a more exact study of the *nature of the soul* and of the motives of the will, and not as a *transcendental* predicate of the causality of a being that belongs to the world of sense (which is really the point). They thus deprive us of the grand revelation which we obtain through practical reason by means of the moral law, the revelation, namely, of a supersensible world by the realization of the otherwise transcendent concept of freedom, and by this deprive us also of the moral law itself, which admits no empirical principle of determination. Therefore it will be necessary to add something here as a protection against this delusion and to exhibit *empiricism* in its naked superficiality.

The notion of causality as *physical necessity,* in opposition to the same notion as *freedom,* concerns only the existence of things so far as it is *determinable in time,* and, consequently, as phenomena, in opposition to their causality as things in themselves. Now if we take the attributes of existence of things in time for attributes of things in themselves (which is the common view), then it is impossible to reconcile the necessity of the causal relation with freedom; they are contradictory. For from the former it follows that every event, and consequently every action that takes place at a certain point of time, is a necessary result of what existed in time preceding. Now as time past is no longer in my power, hence every action that I perform must be the necessary result of certain determining grounds *which are not in my power,* that is, at the moment in which I am acting I am never free. Nay, even if I assume that my whole existence is independent on any foreign cause (for instance, God), so that the determining principles of my causality, and even of my whole existence, were not outside myself, yet this would not in the least transform that physical necessity into freedom. For at every moment of time I am still under the necessity of being determined to action by that which is *not in my power,* and the series of events infinite *a parte priori,* which I only continue according to a pre-determined order and could never begin of myself, would be a continuous physical chain, and therefore my causality would never be freedom.

If, then, we would attribute freedom to a being whose existence is determined in time, we cannot except him from the law of necessity as to all events in his existence and, consequently, as to his actions also; for that would be to hand him over to blind chance. Now as this law inevitably applies to all the causality of things, so far as their *existence* is determinable *in time,* it follows that if this were the mode in which we had also to conceive the *existence of these things in themselves,* freedom must be rejected as a vain and impossible conception. Consequently, if we would still save it, no other way remains but to consider that the existence of a thing, so far as it is determinable in time, and therefore its causality, according to the law of physical necessity, belong to *appearance,* and to attribute *freedom to the same being as a thing in itself.* This is certainly inevitable, if we would retain both these contradictory concepts together; but in application, when we try to explain their combination in one and the same action, great difficulties present themselves which seem to render such a combination impracticable.

When I say of a man who commits a theft that, by the law of causality, this deed is a necessary result of the determining causes in preceding time, then it was impossible that it could not have happened; how then can the judgement, according to the moral law, make any change, and suppose that it could have been omitted, because the law says that it ought to have been omitted; that is, how can a man be called quite free at the same moment, and with respect to the same action in which he is subject to an inevitable physical necessity? Some try to evade this by saying that the causes that determine his causality are of such a *kind* as to agree with a *comparative* notion of freedom. According to this, that is sometimes called a free effect, the determining physical cause of which lies *within* the acting thing itself, e. g., that which a projectile performs when it is in free motion, in which case we use the word *freedom*, because while it is in flight it is not urged by anything external; or as we call the motion of a clock a *free motion*, because it moves its hands itself, which therefore do not require to be pushed by external force; so although the actions of man are necessarily determined by causes which precede in time, we yet call them *free*, because these causes are ideas produced by our own faculties, whereby desires are evoked on occasion of circumstances, and hence actions are wrought according to our own pleasure. This is a wretched subterfuge with which some persons still let themselves be put off, and so think they have solved, with a petty word-jugglery, that difficult problem, at the solution of which centuries have laboured in vain, and which can therefore scarcely be found so completely on the surface. In fact, in the question about the freedom which must be the foundation of all moral laws and the consequent responsibility, it does not matter whether the principles which necessarily determine causality by a physical law reside *within* the subject or *without* him, or in the former case whether these principles are instinctive or are conceived by reason, if, as is admitted by these men themselves, these determining ideas have the ground of their existence in time and in the *antecedent state*, and this again in an antecedent, etc. Then it matters not that these are internal; it matters not that they have a psychological and not a mechanical causality, that is, produce actions by means of ideas and not by bodily movements; they are still *determining principles* of the causality of a being whose existence is determinable in time, and therefore under the necessitation of conditions of past time, which therefore, when the subject has to act, are *no longer in his power*. This may imply psychological freedom (if we choose to apply this term to a merely internal chain of ideas in the mind), but it involves physical necessity and, therefore, leaves no room for *transcendental freedom*, which must be conceived as independence on everything empirical, and, consequently, on nature generally, whether it is an object of the internal sense considered in time only, or of the external in time and space. Without this freedom (in the latter and true sense) which alone is practical *a priori*, no moral law and no moral imputation are possible. Just for this reason the necessity of events in time, according to the physical law of causality, may be called the *mechanism* of nature, although we do not mean by this that things which are subject to it must be really material *machines*. We look here only to the necessity of the connection of events in a time-series as it is developed according to the physical law, whether the subject in which this development takes place is called *automaton materiale* when the mechanical being is moved by matter, or with Leibnitz *spirituale* when it is impelled by ideas; and if the freedom of our will were no other than the latter (say the psychological and comparative, not also transcendental, that is, absolute), then it would at bottom be nothing better than the freedom of a turnspit, which, when once it is wound up, accomplishes its motions of itself.

Now, in order to remove in the supposed case the apparent contradiction between freedom and the mechanism of nature in one and the same action, we must remember what was said in the Critique of Pure Reason, or what follows therefrom; viz., that the necessity of nature, which cannot co-exist with the freedom of the subject, appertains only to the attributes of the thing that is subject to time-conditions, consequently only to those of the acting subject as a phenomenon; that therefore in this respect the determining principles of every action of the same reside in what belongs to past time and *is no longer in his power* (in which must be included his own past actions and the character that these may determine for him in his own eyes as a phenomenon). But the very same subject, being on the other side conscious of himself as a thing in himself, considers his existence also *in so far as it is not subject to time-conditions,* and regards himself as only determinable by laws which he gives himself through reason; and in this his existence nothing is antecedent to the determination of his will, but every action, and in general every modification of his existence, varying according to his internal sense, even the whole series of his existence as a sensible being is in the consciousness of his supersensible existence nothing but the result, and never to be regarded as the determining principle, of his causality as a *noumenon.* In this view now the rational being can justly say of every unlawful action that he performs, that he could very well have left it undone; although as appearance it is sufficiently determined in the past, and in this respect is absolutely necessary; for it, with all the past which determines it, belongs to the one single phenomenon of his character which he makes for himself, in consequence of which he imputes the causality of those appearances to himself as a cause independent of sensibility.

With this agree perfectly the judicial sentences of that wonderful faculty in us which we call *conscience.*[1] A man may use as much art as he likes in order to paint to himself an unlawful act, that he remembers, as an unintentional error, a mere oversight, such as one can never altogether avoid, and therefore as something in which he was carried away by the stream of physical necessity, and thus to make himself out innocent, yet he finds that the advocate who speaks in his favour can by no means silence the accuser within, if only he is conscious that at the time when he did this wrong he was in his senses, that is, in possession of his freedom; and, nevertheless, he accounts for his error from some bad habits, which by gradual neglect of attention he has allowed to grow upon him to such a degree that he can regard his error as its natural consequence, although this cannot protect him from the blame and reproach which he casts upon himself. This is also the ground of repentance for a long past action at every recollection of it; a painful feeling produced by the moral sentiment, and which is practically void in so far as it cannot serve to undo what has been done. (Hence Priestley, as a true and consistent *fatalist,* declares it absurd, and he deserves to be commended for this candour more than those who, while they maintain the mechanism of the will in fact, and its freedom in words only, yet wish it to be thought that they include it in their system of compromise, although they do not explain the possibility of such moral imputation.) But the pain is quite legitimate, because when the law of our intelligible [supersensible] existence (the moral law) is in question, reason recognizes no distinction of time, and only asks whether the event belongs to me, as my act, and then always morally connects the same feeling with it, whether it has happened just now or long ago. For in reference to the *supersensible* consciousness of its existence (i. e., freedom) the *life of sense* is but a single phenomenon, which, inasmuch as it contains merely manifestations of the mental disposition with regard to the moral law (i. e., of the character), must be judged not according to the physical necessity that belongs to it as phenomenon, but according to the absolute spontaneity of freedom. It may therefore be admitted that, if it were possible to have so profound an insight into a man's mental character as shown by internal as well as external actions as to know all its motives, even the smallest, and likewise all the external occasions that can influence them, we could calculate a man's conduct for the future with as great certainty as a lunar or solar eclipse; and nevertheless we may maintain that the man is free. In fact, if we were capable of a further glance, namely, an intellectual intuition of the same subject (which indeed is not granted to us, and instead of it we have only the rational concept), then we should perceive that this whole chain of appearances in regard to all that concerns the moral laws depends on the spontaneity of the subject as a thing in itself, of the determination of which no physical explanation can be given. In default of this intuition, the moral law assures us of this distinction between the relation of our actions as appearance to our sensible nature, and the relation of this sensible nature to the supersensible substratum in us. In this view, which is natural to our reason, though inexplicable, we can also justify some judgements which we passed with all conscientiousness, and which yet at first sight seem quite opposed to all equity. There are cases in which men, even with the same education which has been profitable to others, yet show such early depravity, and so continue to progress in it to years of manhood, that they are thought to be born villains, and their character altogether incapable of improvement; and nevertheless they are judged for what they do or leave undone, they are reproached for their faults as guilty; nay, they themselves (the children) regard these reproaches as well founded, exactly as if in spite

[1] [See Note on Conscience, p. 379.]

of the hopeless natural quality of mind ascribed to them, they remained just as responsible as any other man. This could not happen if we did not suppose that whatever springs from a man's choice (as every action intentionally performed undoubtedly does) has as its foundation a free causality, which from early youth expresses its character in its manifestations (i. e., actions). These, on account of the uniformity of conduct, exhibit a natural connection, which however does not make the vicious quality of the will necessary, but on the contrary, is the consequence of the evil principles voluntarily adopted and unchangeable, which only make it so much the more culpable and deserving of punishment. There still remains a difficulty in the combination of freedom with the mechanism of nature in a being belonging to the world of sense; a difficulty which, even after all the foregoing is admitted, threatens freedom with complete destruction. But with this danger there is also a circumstance that offers hope of an issue still favourable to freedom; namely, that the same difficulty presses much more strongly (in fact as we shall presently see, presses only) on the system that holds the existence determinable in time and space to be the existence of things in themselves; it does not therefore oblige us to give up our capital supposition of the ideality of time as a mere form of sensible intuition, and consequently as a mere manner of representation which is proper to the subject as belonging to the world of sense; and therefore it only requires that this view be reconciled with this idea.

The difficulty is as follows: Even if it is admitted that the supersensible subject can be free with respect to a given action, although, as a subject also belonging to the world of sense, he is under mechanical conditions with respect to the same action, still, as soon as we allow that *God* as universal first cause is also *the cause of the existence of substance* (a proposition which can never be given up without at the same time giving up the notion of God as the Being of all beings, and therewith giving up his all sufficiency, on which everything in theology depends), it seems as if we must admit that a man's actions have their determining principle in something *which is wholly out of his power*—namely, in the causality of a Supreme Being distinct from himself and on whom his own existence and the whole determination of his causality are absolutely dependent. In point of fact, if a man's actions as belonging to his modifications in time were not merely modifications of him as appearance, but as a thing in itself, freedom could not be saved. Man would be a marionette or an automaton, like Vaucanson's, prepared and wound up by the Supreme Artist. Self-consciousness would indeed make him a thinking automaton; but the consciousness of his own spontaneity would be mere delusion if this were mistaken for freedom, and it would deserve this name only in a comparative sense, since, although the proximate determining causes of its motion and a long series of their determining causes are internal, yet the last and highest is found in a foreign hand. Therefore I do not see how those who still insist on regarding time and space as attributes belonging to the existence of things in themselves, can avoid admitting the fatality of actions; or if (like the otherwise acute Mendelssohn) they allow them to be conditions necessarily belonging to the existence of finite and derived beings, but not to that of the infinite Supreme Being, I do not see on what ground they can justify such a distinction, or, indeed, how they can avoid the contradiction that meets them, when they hold that existence in time is an attribute necessarily belonging to finite things in themselves, whereas God is the cause of this existence, but cannot be the cause of time (or space) itself (since this must be presupposed as a necessary *a priori* condition of the existence of things); and consequently as regards the existence of these things. His causality must be subject to conditions and even to the condition of time; and this would inevitably bring in everything contradictory to the notions of His infinity and independence. On the other hand, it is quite easy for us to draw the distinction between the attribute of the divine existence of being independent on all time-conditions, and that of a being of the world of sense, the distinction being that between the *existence of a being in itself* and that of a *thing in appearance.* Hence, if this ideality of time and space is not adopted, nothing remains but Spinozism, in which space and time are essential attributes of the Supreme Being Himself, and the things dependent on Him (ourselves, therefore, included) are not substances, but merely accidents inhering in Him; since, if these things as His effects exist *in time* only, this being the condition of their existence in themselves, then the actions of these beings must be simply His actions which He performs in some place and time. Thus, Spinozism, in spite of the absurdity of its fundamental idea, argues more consistently than the creation theory can, when beings assumed to be substances, and beings in themselves *existing in time*, are regarded as effects of a Supreme Cause, and yet as not [belonging] to Him and His action, but as separate substances.

The above-mentioned difficulty is resolved briefly and clearly as follows: If existence *in time* is a mere sensible mode of representation belonging to thinking beings in the world and consequently does not apply to them as things in themselves, then the creation of these beings is a creation of things in themselves, since the notion of creation does not belong to the sensible form of representation of existence or to causality, but can only be referred to noumena. Consequently, when I say of beings in the world of sense that they are created, I so far regard them as noumena. As it would be a contradiction, therefore, to say that God is a creator of appearances, so also it is a contradiction to say that as creator He is the cause of actions in the world of sense, and therefore as appearances, although He is the cause of the existence of the acting beings (which are noumena). If now it is possible to affirm freedom in spite of the natural mechanism of actions as appearances (by regarding existence in time as something that belongs only to appearances, not to things in themselves), then the circumstance that the acting beings are creatures cannot make the slightest difference, since creation concerns their supersensible and not their sensible existence, and, therefore, cannot be regarded as the determining principle of the appearances. It would be quite different if the beings in the world as things in themselves existed *in time*, since in that case the creator of substance would be at the same time the author of the whole mechanism of this substance.

Of so great importance is the separation of time (as well as space) from the existence of things in themselves which was effected in the Critique of the Pure Speculative Reason.

It may be said that the solution here proposed involves great difficulty in itself and is scarcely susceptible of a lucid exposition. But is any other solution that has been attempted, or that may be attempted, easier and more intelligible? Rather might we say that the dogmatic teachers of metaphysics have shown more shrewdness than candour in keeping this difficult point out of sight as much as possible, in the hope that if they said nothing about it, probably no one would think of it. If science is to be advanced, all difficulties must be *laid open*, and we must even search for those that are hidden, for every difficulty calls forth a remedy, which cannot be discovered without science gaining either in extent or in exactness; and thus even obstacles become means of increasing the thoroughness of science. On the other hand, if the difficulties are intentionally concealed, or merely removed by palliatives, then sooner or later they burst out into incurable mischiefs, which bring science to ruin in an absolute scepticism.

Since it is, properly speaking, the notion of freedom alone amongst all the ideas of pure speculative reason that so greatly enlarges our knowledge in the sphere of the supersensible, though only of our practical knowledge, I ask myself *why it exclusively possesses so great fertility,* whereas the others only designate the vacant space for possible beings of the pure understanding, but are unable by any means to define the concept of them. I presently find that as I cannot think anything without a category, I must first look for a category for the rational idea of freedom with which I am now concerned; and this is the category of *causality;* and although freedom, a *concept of the reason,* being a transcendent concept, cannot have any intuition corresponding to it, yet the *concept of the understanding*—for the synthesis of which *the former*[1] demands the unconditioned —(namely, the concept of causality) must have a sensible intuition given, by which first its objective reality is assured. Now, the categories are all divided into two classes—the *mathematical,* which concern the unity of synthesis in the conception of objects, and the *dynamical,* which refer to the unity of synthesis in the conception of the existence of objects. The former (those of magnitude and quality) always contain a synthesis of the *homogeneous,* and it is not possible to find in this the unconditioned antecedent to what is given in sensible intuition as conditioned in space and time, as this would itself have to belong to space and time, and therefore be again still conditioned. Whence it resulted in the Dialectic of Pure Theoretic Reason that the opposite methods of attaining the unconditioned and the totality of the conditions were both wrong. The categories of the second class (those of causality and of the necessity of a thing) did not require this homogeneity (of the conditioned and the condition in synthesis), since here what we have to explain is not how the intuition is compounded from a manifold in it, but only how the existence of the condi-

[1] [Cf. *Critique of Pure Reason*, p. 177.]

tioned object corresponding to it is added to the existence of the condition (added, namely, in the understanding as connected therewith); and in that case it was allowable to suppose in the supersensible world the unconditioned antecedent to the altogether conditioned in the world of sense (both as regards the causal connection and the contingent existence of things themselves), although this unconditioned remained indeterminate, and to make the synthesis transcendent. Hence, it was found in the Dialectic of the Pure Speculative Reason that the two apparently opposite methods of obtaining for the conditioned the unconditioned were not really contradictory, e. g., in the synthesis of causality to conceive for the conditioned in the series of causes and effects of the sensible world, a causality which has no sensible condition, and that the same action which, as belonging to the world of sense, is always sensibly conditioned, that is, mechanically necessary, yet at the same time may be derived from a causality not sensibly conditioned—being the causality of the acting being as belonging to the supersensible world—and may consequently be conceived as free. Now, the only point in question was to change this *may be* into *is;* that is, that we should be able to show in an actual case, as it were by a fact, that certain actions imply such a causality (namely, the intellectual, sensibly unconditioned), whether they are actual or only commanded, that is, objectively necessary in a practical sense. We could not hope to find this connections in actions actually given in experience as events of the sensible world, since causality with freedom must always be sought outside the world of sense in the world of intelligence. But things of sense are the only things offered to our perception and observation. Hence, nothing remained but to find an incontestable objective principle of causality which excludes all sensible conditions: that is, a principle in which reason does not appeal further to something *else* as a determining ground of its causality, but contains this determining ground itself by means of that principle, and in which therefore it is itself as *pure reason* practical. Now, this principle had not to be searched for or discovered; it had long been in the reason of all men, and incorporated in their nature, and is the principle of *morality.* Therefore, that unconditioned causality, with the faculty of it, namely, freedom, is no longer merely indefinitely and problematically *thought* (this speculative reason could prove to be feasible), but is even *as regards the law of its causality* definitely and assertorially *known;* and with it the fact that a being (I myself), belonging to the world of sense, belongs also to the supersensible world, this is also positively *known,* and thus the reality of the supersensible world is established and in practical respects *definitely* given, and this definiteness, which for theoretical purposes would be *transcendent,* is for practical purposes *immanent.* We could not, however, make a similar step as regards the second dynamical idea, namely, that of a *necessary being.* We could not rise to it from the sensible world without the aid of the first dynamical idea. For if we attempted to do so, we should have ventured to leave at a bound all that is given to us, and to leap to that of which nothing is given us that can help us to effect the connection of such a supersensible being with the world of sense (since the necessary being would have to be known as given *outside ourselves*). On the other hand, it is now obvious that this connection is quite possible in relation to *our own* subject, inasmuch as I know myself to be *on the one side* as an intelligible [supersensible] being determined by the moral law (by means of freedom), and *on the other side* as acting in the world of sense. It is the concept of freedom alone that enables us to find the unconditioned and intelligible for the conditioned and sensible without going out of ourselves. For it is our own reason that by means of the supreme and unconditional practical law knows that itself and the being that is conscious of this law (our own person) belong to the pure world of understanding, and moreover defines the manner in which, as such, it can be active. In this way it can be understood why in the whole faculty of reason it is *the practical reason only* that can help us to pass beyond the world of sense and give us knowledge of a supersensible order and connection, which, however, for this very reason cannot be extended further than is necessary for pure practical purposes.

Let me be permitted on this occasion to make one more remark, namely, that every step that we make with pure reason, even in the practical sphere where no attention is paid to subtle speculation, nevertheless accords with all the material points of the Critique of the Theoretical Reason as closely and directly as if each step had been thought out with deliberate purpose to establish this confirmation. Such a thorough agreement, wholly unsought for and quite obvious (as anyone can convince himself, if he will only carry moral inquiries up to their principles), between the most important proposiion of practical reason and the often seemingly oo subtle and needless remarks of the Critique of the Speculative Reason, occasions surprise and astonishment, and confirms the maxim already recognized and praised by others, namely, that in every scientific inquiry we should pursue our way steadily with all possible exactness and frankness, without caring for any objections that may be raised from outside its sphere, but, as far as we can, to carry out our inquiry truthfully and completely by itself. Frequent observation has convinced me that, when such researches are concluded, that which in one part of them appeared to me very questionable, considered in relation to other extraneous doctrines, when I left this doubtfulness out of sight for a time and only attended to the business in hand until it was completed, at last was unexpectedly found to agree perfectly with what had been discovered separately without the least regard to those doctrines, and without any partiality or prejudice for them. Authors would save themselves many errors and much labour lost (because spent on a delusion) if they could only resolve to go to work with more frankness.

Book II. *Dialectic of Pure Practical Reason*

Chapter I. *Of a Dialectic of Pure Practical Reason Generally*

Pure reason always has its dialetic, whether it is considered in its speculative or its practical employment; for it requires the absolute totality of the conditions of what is given conditioned, and this can only be found in things in themselves. But as all conceptions of things in themselves must be referred to intuitions, and with us men these can never be other than sensible and hence can never enable us to know objects as things in themselves but only as appearances, and since the unconditioned can never be found in this chain of appearances which consists only of conditioned and conditions; thus from applying this rational idea of the totality of the conditions (in other words of the unconditioned) to appearances, there arises an inevitable illusion, as if these latter were things in themselves (for in the absence of a warning critique they are always regarded as such). This illusion would never be noticed as delusive if it did not betray itself by a *conflict* of reason with itself, when it applies to appearances its fundamental principle of presupposing the unconditioned to everything conditioned. By this, however, reason is compelled to trace this illusion to its source, and search how it can be removed, and this can only be done by a complete critical examination of the whole pure faculty of reason; so that the antinomy of the pure reason which is manifest in its dialectic is in fact the most beneficial error into which human reason could ever have fallen, since it at last drives us to search for the key to escape from this labyrinth; and when this key is found, it further discovers that which we did not seek but yet had need of, namely, a view into a higher and an immutable order of things, in which we even now are, and in which we are thereby enabled by definite precepts to continue to live according to the highest dictates of reason.

It may be seen in detail in the *Critique of Pure Reason* how in its speculative employment this natural dialectic is to be solved, and how the error which arises from a very natural illusion may be guarded against. But reason in its practical use is not a whit better off. As pure practical reason, it likewise seeks to find the unconditioned for the practically conditioned (which rests on inclinations and natural wants), and this is not as the determining principle of the will, but even when this is given (in the moral law) it seeks the unconditioned totality of the *object* of pure practical reason under the name of the *summum bonum.*

To define this idea practically, i.e., sufficiently for the maxims of our rational conduct, is the business of *practical wisdom,* and this again as a science is *philosophy,* in the sense in which the word was understood by the ancients, with whom it meant instruction in the conception in which the *summum bonum* was to be placed, and the conduct by which it was to be obtained. It would be well to leave this word in its ancient signification as a *doctrine of the summum bonum,* so far as reason endeavours to make this into a *science.* For on the one hand the restriction annexed would suit the Greek expression (which signifies the love of *wisdom*), and yet at the same time would be sufficient to embrace under the name of philosophy the love of *science:* that is to say, of all speculative rational knowledge, so far as it is serviceable to reason, both for that conception and also for the practical principle determining our conduct, without letting out of sight the main end, on account of which alone it can be called a doctrine of practical wisdom. On the other hand, it would be no harm to deter the self-conceit of one who ventures to claim the title of philosopher by holding before him in the very definition a standard of self-estimation which would very much lower his pretensions. For a *teacher of wisdom* would mean something more than a scholar who has not come so far as to guide himself, much less to guide others, with certain expectation of attaining so high an end: it would mean a *master in the knowledge of wisdom,* which implies more than a modest man would claim for himself. Thus philosophy as well as wisdom would always remain an ideal, which objectively is presented complete in reason alone, while subjectively for the person it is only the goal of his unceasing endeavours; and no one would be justified in professing to be in possession of it so as to assume the name of philosopher who could not also show its infallible effects in his own person as an example (in his self-mastery and the unquestioned interest that he takes pre-eminently in the general good), and this the ancients also required as a condition of deserving that honourable title.

We have another preliminary remark to make respecting the dialectic of the pure practical reason, on the point of the definition *of the summum bonum* (a successful solution of which dialectic would lead us to expect, as in case of that of the theoretical reason, the most beneficial effects, inasmuch as the self-contradictions of pure practical reason honestly stated, and not concealed, force us to undertake a complete critique of this faculty).

The moral law is the sole determining principle of a pure will. But since this is merely formal (viz., as prescribing only the form of the maxim as universally legislative), it abstracts as a determining principle from all matter—that is to say, from every object of volition. Hence, though the *summum bonum* may be the whole *object* of a pure practical reason, i.e., a pure will, yet it is not on that account to be regarded as its *determining principle;* and the moral law alone must be regarded as the principle on which that and its realization or promotion are aimed at. This remark is important in so delicate a case as the determination of moral principles, where the slightest misinterpretation perverts men's minds. For it will have been seen from the Analytic that, if we assume any object under the name of a good as a determining principle of the will prior to the moral law and then deduce from it the supreme practical principle, this would always introduce heteronomy and crush out the moral principle.

It is, however, evident that if the notion of the *summum bonum* includes that of the moral law as its supreme condition, then the *summum bonum* would not merely be an *object,* but the notion of it and the conception of its existence as possible by our own practical reason would likewise be the *determining principle* of the will, since in that case the will is in fact determined by the moral law which is already included in this conception, and by no other object as the principle of autonomy requires. This order of the conceptions of determination of the will must not be lost sight of, as otherwise we should misunderstand ourselves and think we had fallen into a contradiction, while everything remains in perfect harmony.

CHAPTER II. *Of the Dialectic of Pure Reason in defining the Conception of the "Summum Bonum"*

THE conception of the *summum* itself contains an ambiguity which might occasion needless disputes if we did not attend to it. The *summum* may mean either the supreme (*supremum*) or the perfect (*consummatum*). The former is that condition which is itself unconditioned, i.e., is not subordinate to any other (*originarium*); the second is that whole which is not a part of a greater whole of the same kind (*perfectissimum*). It has been shown in the Analytic that *virtue* (as worthiness to be happy) is the *supreme condition* of all that can appear to us desirable, and consequently of all our pursuit of happiness, and is therefore the *supreme* good. But it does not follow that it is the whole and perfect good as the object of the desires of rational finite beings; for this requires happiness also, and that not merely in the partial eyes of the person who makes himself an end, but even in the judgement of an impartial reason, which regards persons in general as ends in themselves. For to need happiness, to deserve it, and yet at the same time not to participate in it, cannot be consistent with the perfect volition of a rational being possessed at the same time of all power, if, for the sake of experiment, we conceive such a being. Now inasmuch as virtue and happiness together constitute the possession of the *summum bonum* in a person, and the distribution of happiness in exact proportion to morality (which is the worth of the person, and his worthiness to be happy) constitutes the *summum bonum* of a possible world; hence this *summum bonum* expresses the whole, the perfect good, in which, however, virtue as the condition is always the supreme good, since it has no condition above it; whereas happiness, while it is pleasant to the possessor of it, is not of itself absolutely and in all respects good, but always presupposes morally right behaviour as its condition.

When two elements are *necessarily* united in one concept, they must be connected as reason and consequence, and this either so that their unity is considered as *analytical* (logical connection), or as *synthetical* (real connection)—the former following the law of identity, the latter that of causality. The connection of virtue and happiness may therefore be understood in two ways: either the endeavour to be virtuous and the rational pursuit of happiness are not two distinct actions, but absolutely identical, in which case no maxim need be made the principle of the former, other than what serves for the latter; or the connection consists in this, that virtue produces happiness as something distinct from the consciousness of virtue, as a cause produces an effect.

The ancient Greek schools were, properly speaking, only two, and in determining the conception of the *summum bonum* these followed in fact one and the same method, inasmuch as they did not allow virtue and happiness to be regarded as two distinct elements of the *summum bonum*, and consequently sought the unity of the principle by the rule of identity; but they differed as to which of the two was to be taken as the fundamental notion. The Epicurean said: "To be conscious that one's maxims lead to happiness is virtue"; the Stoic said: "To be conscious of one's virtue is happiness." With the former, *Prudence* was equivalent to morality; with the latter, who chose a higher designation for virtue, morality alone was true wisdom.

While we must admire the men who in such early times tried all imaginable ways of extending the domain of philosophy, we must at the same time lament that their acuteness was unfortunately misapplied in trying to trace out identity between two extremely heterogeneous notions, those of happiness and virtue. But it agrees with the dialectical spirit of their times (and subtle minds are even now sometimes misled in the same way) to get rid of irreconcilable differences in principle by seeking to change them into a mere contest about words, and thus apparently working out the identity of the notion under different names, and this usually occurs in cases where the combination of heterogeneous principles lies so deep or so high, or would require so complete a transformation of the doctrines assumed in the rest of the philosophical system, that men are afraid to penetrate deeply into the real difference and prefer treating it as a difference in questions of form.

While both schools sought to trace out the identity of the practical principles of virtue and happiness, they were not agreed as to the way in which they tried to force this identity, but were separated infinitely from one another, the one placing its principle on the side of sense, the other on that of reason; the one in the consciousness of sensible wants, the other in the independence of practical reason on all sensible grounds of determination. According to the Epicurean, the notion of virtue was already involved in the maxim: "To promote one's own happiness"; according to the Stoics, on the other hand, the feeling of happiness was already contained in the consciousness of virtue. Now whatever is contained in another notion is identical with part of the containing notion, but not with the whole, and moreover two wholes may be specifically distinct, although they consist of the same parts; namely if the parts are united into a whole in totally different ways. The Stoic maintained that the virtue was the *whole summum bonum*, and happiness only the consciousness of possessing it, as making part of the state of the subject. The Epicurean maintained that happiness was the *whole summum bonum*, and virtue only the form of the maxim for its pursuit; viz., the rational use of the means for attaining it.

Now it is clear from the Analytic that the maxims of virtue and those of private happiness are quite heterogeneous as to their supreme practical principle, and, although they belong to one *summum bonum* which together they make possible, yet they are so far from coinciding that they restrict and check one another very much in the same subject. Thus the question: "*How is the summum bonum* practically possible?" still remains an unsolved problem, notwithstanding all the *attempts at coalition* that have hitherto been made. The Analytic has, however, shown what it is that makes the problem difficult to solve; namely, that happiness and morality are two specifically *distinct elements* of the *summum bonum* and, therefore, their combination *cannot* be *analytically* cognised (as if the man that seeks his own happiness should find by mere analysis of his conception that in so acting he is virtuous, or as if the man that follows virtue should in the consciousness of such conduct find that he is already happy *ipso facto*), but must be a *synthesis* of concepts. Now since this combination is recognised as *a priori,* and therefore as practically necessary, and consequently not as derived from experience, so that the possibility of the *summum bonum* does not rest on any empirical principle, it follows that the *deduction* [legitimation] of this concept must be *transcendental.* It is *a priori* (morally) necessary to *produce the summum bonum by freedom of will:* therefore the condition of its possibility must rest solely on *a priori* principles of cognition.

I. *The Antinomy of Practical Reason*

In the *summum bonum* which is practical for us, i.e., to be realized by our will, virtue and happiness are thought as necessarily combined, so that the one cannot be assumed by pure practical reason without the other also being attached to it. Now this combination (like every other) is either *analytical* or *synthetical.* It has been shown that it cannot be analytical; it must then be synthetical and, more particularly, must be conceived as the connection of cause and effect, since it concerns a practical good, i.e., one that is possible by means of action; consequently either the desire of happiness must be the motive to maxims of virtue, or the maxim of virtue must be the efficient cause of happiness. The first is *absolutely* impossible, because (as was proved in the Analytic) maxims which place the determining principle of the will in the desire of personal happiness are not moral at all, and no virtue can be founded on them. But the second is *also impossible,* because the practical connection of causes and effects in the world, as the result of the determination of the will, does not depend upon the moral dispositions of the will, but on the knowledge of the laws of nature and the physical power to use them for one's purposes; consequently we cannot expect in the world by the most punctilious observance of the moral laws any necessary connection of happiness with virtue adequate to the *summum bonum.* Now, as the promotion of this *summum bonum,* the conception of which contains this connection, is *a priori* a necessary object of our will and inseparably attached to the moral law, the impossibility of the former must prove the falsity of the latter. If then the supreme good is not possible by practical rules, then the moral law also which commands us to promote it is directed to vain imaginary ends and must consequently be false.

II. *Critical Solution of the Antinomy of Practical Reason*

The antinomy of pure speculative reason exhibits a similar conflict between freedom and physical necessity in the causality of events in the world. It was solved by showing that there is no real contradiction when the events and even the world in which they occur are regarded (as they ought to be) merely as appearances; since one and the same acting being, *as an appearance* (even to his own inner sense), has a causality in the world of sense that always conforms to the mechanism of nature, but with respect to the same events, so far as the acting person regards himself at the same time as a noumenon (as pure intelligence in an existence not dependent on the condition of time), he can contain a principle by which that causality acting according to laws of nature is determined, but which is itself free from all laws of nature.

It is just the same with the foregoing antinomy of pure practical reason. The first of the two propositions, "That the endeavour after happiness produces a virtuous mind," is *absolutely false;* but the second, "That a virtuous mind necessarily produces happiness," is *not absolutely* false, but only in so far as virtue is considered as a form of causality in the sensible world, and consequently only if I suppose existence in it to be the only sort of existence of a rational being; it is then only *conditionally* false. But as I am not only justified in thinking that I exist also as a noumenon in a world of the understanding, but even have in the moral law a purely intellectual determining principle of my causality (in the sensible world), it is not impossible that morality of mind should have a connection as cause with happiness (as an effect in the sensible world) if not immediate yet mediate (viz., through an intelligent author of nature), and moreover necessary; while in a system of nature which is merely an object of the senses, this combination could never occur except contingently and, therefore, could not suffice for the *summum bonum.*

Thus, notwithstanding this seeming conflict of practical reason with itself, the *summum bonum,* which is the necessary supreme end of a will morally determined, is a true object thereof; for it is practically possible, and the maxims of the will which as regards their matter refer to it have objective reality, which at first was threatened by the antinomy that appeared in the connection of morality with happiness by a general law; but this was merely from a misconception, because the relation between appearances was taken for a relation of the things in themselves to these appearances.

When we find ourselves obliged to go so far, namely, to the connection with an intelligible world, to find the possibility of the *summum bonum,* which reason points out to all rational beings as the goal of all their moral wishes, it must seem strange that, nevertheless, the philosophers both of ancient and modern times have been able to find happiness in accurate proportion to virtue even in *this life* (in the sensible world), or have persuaded themselves that they were conscious thereof. For Epicurus as well as the Stoics extolled above everything the happiness that springs from the consciousness of living virtuously; and the former was not so base in his practical precepts as one might infer from the principles of his theory, which he used for explanation and not for action, or as they were interpreted by many who were misled by his using the term *pleasure* for *contentment;* on the contrary, he reckoned the most disinterested practice of good amongst the ways of enjoying the most intimate delight, and his scheme of pleasure (by which he meant constant cheerfulness of mind) included the moderation and control of the inclinations, such as the strictest moral philosopher might require. He differed from the Stoics chiefly in making this pleasure the motive, which they very rightly refused to do. For, on the one hand, the virtuous Epicurus, like many well-intentioned men of this day who do not reflect deeply enough on their principles, fell into the error of presupposing the virtuous *disposition* in the persons for whom he wished to provide the springs to virtue (and indeed the upright man cannot be happy if he is not first conscious of his uprightness; since with such a character the reproach that his habit of thought would oblige him to make against himself in case of transgression and his moral self-condemnation would rob him of all enjoyment of the pleasantness which his condition might otherwise contain). But the question is: How is such a disposition possible in the first instance, and such a habit of thought in estimating the worth of one's existence, since prior to it there can be in the subject no feeling at all for moral worth? If a man is virtuous without being conscious of his integrity in every action, he will certainly not enjoy life, however favourable fortune may be to him in its physical circumstances; but can we make him virtuous in the first instance, in other words, before he esteems the moral worth of his existence so highly, by praising to him the peace of mind that would result from the consciousness of an integrity for which he has no sense?

On the other hand, however, there is here an occasion of a *vitium subreptionis,* and as it were of an optical illusion, in the self-consciousness of what one *does* as distinguished from what one *feels*—an illusion which even the most experienced cannot altogether avoid. The moral disposition of mind is necessarily combined with a consciousness that the will is determined *directly by the law.* Now the consciousness of a determination of the faculty of desire is always the source of a satisfaction in the resulting action; but this pleasure, this satisfaction in oneself, is not the determining principle of the action; on the contrary, the determination of the will directly by reason is the source of the feeling of pleasure, and this remains a pure practical not sensible determination of the faculty of desire. Now as this determination has exactly the same effect within in impelling to activity, that a feeling of the pleasure to be expected from the desired action would have had, we easily look on what we ourselves do as something which we merely passively feel, and take the moral spring for a sensible impulse, just as it happens in the so-called illusion of the senses (in this case the inner sense). It is a sublime thing in human nature to be determined to actions immediately by a purely rational law; sublime even is the illusion that regards the subjective side of this capacity of intellectual determination as something sensible and the effect of a special sensible feeling (for an intellectual feeling would be a contradiction). It is also of great importance to attend to this property of our personality and as much as possible to cultivate the effect of reason on this feeling. But we must beware lest by falsely extolling this moral determining principle as a spring, making its source lie in particular feelings of pleasure (which are in fact only results), we degrade and disfigure the true genuine spring, the law itself, by putting as it were a false foil upon it. Respect, not pleasure or enjoyment of happiness, is something for which it is not possible that reason should have any *antecedent* feeling as its foundation (for this would always be sensible and pathological); and consciousness of immediate obligation of the will by the law is by no means analogous to the feeling of pleasure, although in relation to the faculty of desire it produces the same effect, but from different sources: it is only by this mode of conception, however, that we can attain what we are seeking, namely, that actions be done not merely in accordance with duty (as a result of pleasant feelings), but from duty, which must be the true end of all moral cultivation.

Have we not, however, a word which does not express enjoyment, as happiness does, but indicates a satisfaction in one's existence, an analogue of the happiness which must necessarily accompany the consciousness of virtue? Yes! this word is *self-contentment* which in its proper signification always designates only a negative satisfaction in one's existence, in which one is conscious of needing nothing. Freedom and the consciousness of it as a faculty of following the moral law with unyielding resolution is *independence of inclinations,* at least as motives determining (though not as *affecting*) our desire, and so far as I am conscious of this freedom in following my moral maxims, it is the only source of an unaltered contentment which is necessarily connected with it and rests on no special feeling. This may be called *intellectual contentment.* The sensible contentment (improperly so-called) which rests on the satisfaction of the inclinations, however delicate they may be imagined to be, can never be adequate to the conception of it. For the inclinations change, they grow with the indulgence shown them, and always leave behind a still greater void than we had thought to fill. Hence they are always *burdensome* to a rational being, and, although he cannot lay them aside, they wrest from him the wish to be rid of them. Even an inclination to what is right (e.g., to beneficence), though it may much facilitate the efficacy of the *moral* maxims, cannot produce any. For in these all must be directed to the conception of the law as a determining principle, if the action is to contain *morality* and not merely *legality.* Inclination is blind and slavish, whether it be of a good sort or not, and, when morality is in question, reason must not play the part merely of guardian to inclination, but disregarding it altogether must attend simply to its own interest as pure practical reason. This very feeling of compassion and tender sympathy, if it precedes the deliberation on the question of duty and becomes a determining principle, is even annoying to right thinking persons, brings their deliberate maxims into confusion, and makes them wish to be delivered from it and to be subject to law-giving reason alone.

From this we can understand how the consciousness of this faculty of a pure practical reason produces by action (virtue) a consciousness of mastery over one's inclinations, and therefore of independence of them, and consequently also of the discontent that always accompanies them, and thus a negative satisfaction with one's state, i.e., *contentment,* which is primarily contentment with one's own person. Freedom itself becomes in this way (namely, indirectly) capable of an enjoyment which cannot be called happiness, because it does not depend on the positive concurrence of a feeling, nor is it, strictly speaking, *bliss,* since it does not include complete independence of inclinations and wants, but it resembles bliss in so far as the determination of one's will at least can hold itself free from their influence; and thus, at least in its origin, this enjoyment is analogous to the self-sufficiency which we can ascribe only to the Supreme Being.

From this solution of the antinomy of practical pure reason, it follows that in practical principles we may at least conceive as possible a natural and necessary connection between the consciousness of morality and the expectation of a proportionate happiness as its result, though it does not follow that we can know or perceive this connection; that, on the other hand, principles of the pursuit of happiness cannot possibly produce morality; that, therefore, morality is the *supreme* good (as the first condition of the *summum bonum*), while happiness constitutes its second element, but only in such a way that it is the morally conditioned, but necessary consequence of the former. Only with this subordination is the *summum bonum* the whole object of pure practical reason, which must necessarily conceive it as possible, since it commands us to contribute to the utmost of our power to its realization. But since the possibility of such connection of the conditioned with its condition belongs wholly to the supersensual relation of things and cannot be given according to the laws of the world of sense, although the practical consequences of the idea belong to the world of sense, namely, the actions that aim at realizing the *summum bonum;* we will therefore endeavour to set forth the grounds of that possibility, first, in respect of what is immediately in our power, and then, secondly, in that which is not in our power, but which reason presents to us as the supplement of our impotence, for the realization of the *summum bonum* (which by practical principles is necessary).

• • •

III. *Of the Primacy of Pure Practical Reason in its Union with the Speculative Reason*

By primacy between two or more things connected by reason, I understand the prerogative, belonging to one, of being the first determining principle in the connection with all the rest. In a narrower practical sense it means the prerogative of the interest of one in so far as the interest of the other is subordinated to it, while it is not postponed to any other. To every faculty of the mind we can attribute an interest, that is, a principle, that contains the condition on which alone the former is called into exercise. Reason, as the faculty of principles, determines the interest of all the powers of the mind and is determined by its own. The interest of its speculative employment consists in the *cognition* of the object pushed to the highest *a priori* principles: that of its practical employment, in the determination of the *will* in respect of the final and complete end. As to what is necessary for the possibility of any employment of reason at all, namely, that its principles and affirmations should not contradict one another, this constitutes no part of its interest, but is the condition of having reason at all; it is only its development, not mere consistency with itself, that is reckoned as its interest.

If practical reason could not assume or think as given anything further than what speculative reason of itself could offer it from its own insight, the latter would have the primacy. But supposing that it had of itself original *a priori* principles with which certain theoretical positions were inseparably connected, while these were withdrawn from any possible insight of speculative reason (which, however, they must not contradict); then the question is: Which interest is the superior (not which must give way, for they are not necessarily conflicting), whether speculative reason, which knows nothing of all that the practical offers for its acceptance, should take up these propositions and (although they transcend it) try to unite them with its own concepts as a foreign possession handed over to it, or whether it is justified in obstinately following its own separate interest and, according to the canonic of Epicurus, rejecting as vain subtlety everything that cannot accredit its objective reality by manifest examples to be shown in experience, even though it should be never so much interwoven with the interest of the practical (pure) use of reason, and in itself not contradictory to the theoretical, merely because it infringes on the interest of the speculative reason to this extent, that it removes the bounds which this latter had set to itself, and gives it up to every nonsense or delusion of imagination?

In fact, so far as practical reason is taken as dependent on pathological conditions, that is, as merely regulating the inclinations under the sensible principle of happiness, we could not require speculative reason to take its principles from such a source. Mohammed's paradise, or the absorption into the Deity of the theosophists and mystics would press their monstrosities on the reason according to the taste of each, and one might as well have no reason as surrender it in such fashion to all sorts of dreams. But if pure reason of itself can be practical and is actually so, as the consciousness of the moral law proves, then it is still only one and the same reason which, whether in a theoretical or a practical point of view, judges according to *a priori* principles; and then it is clear that although it is in the first point of view incompetent to establish certain propositions positively, which, however, do not contradict it, then, as soon as these propositions are *inseparably* attached *to the practical interest* of pure reason, it must accept them, though it be as something offered to it from a foreign source, something that has not grown on its own ground, but yet is sufficiently authenticated; and it must try to compare and connect them with everything that it has in its power as speculative reason. It must remember, however, that these are not additions to its insight, but yet are extensions of its employment in another, namely, a practical aspect; and this is not in the least opposed to its interest, which consists in the restriction of wild speculation.

Thus, when pure speculative and pure practical reason are combined in one cognition, the latter has the *primacy,* provided, namely, that this combination is not *contingent* and arbitrary, but founded *a priori* on reason itself and therefore *necessary.* For without this subordination there would arise a conflict of reason with itself; since, if they were merely co-ordinate, the former would close its boundaries strictly and admit nothing from the latter into its domain, while the latter would extend its bounds over everything and when its needs required would seek to embrace the former within them. Nor could we reverse the order and require pure practical reason to be subordinate to the speculative, since all interest is ultimately practical, and even that of speculative reason is conditional, and it is only in the practical employment of reason that it is complete.

IV. *The Immortality of the Soul as a Postulate of Pure Practical Reason*

The realization of the *summum bonum* in the world is the necessary object of a will determinable by the moral law. But in this will the *perfect accordance* of the mind with the moral law is the supreme condition of the *summum bonum.* This then must be possible, as well as its object, since it is contained in the command to promote the latter. Now, the perfect accordance of the will with the moral law is *holiness,* a perfection of which no rational being of the sensible world is capable at any moment of his existence. Since, nevertheless, it is required as practically necessary, it can only be found in a *progress in infinitum* towards that perfect accordance, and on the principles of pure practical reason it is necessary to assume such a practical progress as the real object of our will.

Now, this endless progress is only possible on the supposition of an *endless* duration of the *existence* and personality of the same rational being (which is called the *immortality of the soul*). The *summum bonum,* then, practically is only possible on the supposition of the immortality of the soul; consequently this immortality, being inseparably connected with the moral law, is a postulate of pure practical reason (by which I mean a *theoretical* proposition, not demonstrable as such, but which is an inseparable result of an unconditional *a priori practical* law.[1]

This principle of the moral destination of our nature, namely, that it is only in an endless progress that we can attain perfect accordance with the moral law, is of the greatest use, not merely for the present purpose of supplementing the impotence of speculative reason, but also with respect to religion. In default of it, either the moral law is quite degraded from its *holiness,* being made out to be *indulgent* and conformable to our convenience, or else men strain their notions of their vocation and their expectation to an unattainable goal, hoping to acquire complete holiness of will, and so they lose themselves in fanatical *theosophic* dreams, which wholly contradict self-knowledge. In both cases the unceasing *effort* to obey punctually and thoroughly a strict and inflexible command of reason, which yet is not ideal but real, is only hindered. For a rational but finite being, the only thing possible is an endless progress from the lower to higher degrees of moral perfection. The *Infinite* Being, to whom the condition of time is nothing, sees in this to us endless succession a whole of accordance with the moral law; and the holiness which his command inexorably requires, in order to be true to his justice in the share which He assigns to each in the *summum bonum,* is to be found in a single intellectual intuition of the whole existence of rational beings. All that can be expected of the creature in respect of the hope of this participation would be the consciousness of his tried character, by which from the progress he has hitherto made from the worse to the morally better, and the immutability of purpose which has thus become known to him, he may hope for a further unbroken continuance of the same, however long his existence may last, even beyond this life,[2] and thus he may hope, not indeed here, nor in any imaginable point of his future existence, but only in the endlessness of his duration (which God alone can survey) to be perfectly adequate to his will (without indulgence or excuse, which do not harmonize with justice).

[1] [See Preface, p. 294, *note.*]

V. *The Existence of God as a Postulate of Pure Practical Reason*

In the foregoing analysis the moral law led to a practical problem which is prescribed by pure reason alone, without the aid of any sensible motives, namely, that of the necessary completeness of the first and principle element of the *summum bonum,* viz., morality; and, as this can be perfectly solved only in eternity, to the postulate of *immortality.* The same law must also lead us to affirm the possibility of the second element of the *summum bonum,* viz., happiness proportioned to that morality, and this on grounds as disinterested as before, and solely

[2] It seems, nevertheless, impossible for a creature to have the *conviction* of his unwavering firmness of mind in the progress towards goodness. On this account the Christian religion makes it come only from the same Spirit that works sanctification, that is, this firm purpose, and with it the consciousness of steadfastness in the moral progress. But naturally one who is conscious that he has persevered through a long portion of his life up to the end in the progress to the better, and this from genuine moral motives, may well have the comforting hope, though not the certainty, that even in an existence prolonged beyond this life he will continue steadfast in these principles; and although he is never justified here in his own eyes, nor can ever hope to be so in the increased perfection of his nature, to which he looks forward, together with an increase of duties, nevertheless in this progress which, though it is directed to a goal infinitely remote, yet is in God's sight regarded as equivalent to possession, he may have a prospect of a *blessed* future; for this is the word that reason employs to designate perfect *well-being* independent of all contingent causes of the world, and which, like *holiness,* is an idea that can be contained only in an endless progress and its totality, and consequently is never fully attained by a creature.

from impartial reason; that is, it must lead to the supposition of the existence of a cause adequate to this effect; in other words, it must postulate the *existence of God,* as the necessary condition of the possibility of the *summum bonum* (an object of the will which is necessarily connected with the moral legislation of pure reason). We proceed to exhibit this connection in a convincing manner.

Happiness is the condition of a rational being in the world with whom *everything goes according to his wish and will;* it rests, therefore, on the harmony of physical nature with his whole end and likewise with the essential determining principle of his will. Now the moral law as a law of freedom commands by determining principles, which ought to be quite independent of nature and of its harmony with our faculty of desire (as springs). But the acting rational being in the world is not the cause of the world and of nature itself. There is not the least ground, therefore, in the moral law for a necessary connection between morality and proportionate happiness in a being that belongs to the world as part of it, and therefore dependent on it, and which for that reason cannot by his will be a cause of this nature, nor by his own power make it thoroughly harmonize, as far as his happiness is concerned, with his practical principles. Nevertheless, in the practical problem of pure reason, i.e., the necessary pursuit of the *summum bonum,* such a connection is postulated as necessary: we ought to endeavour to promote the *summum bonum,* which, therefore, must be possible. Accordingly, the existence of a cause of all nature, distinct from nature itself and containing the principle of this connection, namely, of the exact harmony of happiness with morality, is also *postulated.* Now this supreme cause must contain the principle of the harmony of nature, not merely with a law of the will of rational beings, but with the conception of this *law,* in so far as they make it the *supreme determining principle of the will,* and consequently not merely with the form of morals, but with their morality as their motive, that is, with their moral character. Therefore, the *summum bonum* is possible in the world only on the supposition of a Supreme Being having a causality corresponding to moral character. Now a being that is capable of acting on the conception of laws is an *intelligence* (a rational being), and the causality of such a being according to this conception of laws is his *will;* therefore the supreme cause of nature, which must be presupposed as a condition of the *summum bonum* is a being which is the cause of nature by *intelligence* and *will,* consequently its author, that is God. It follows that the postulate of the possibility of the *highest derived good* (the best world) is likewise the postulate of the reality of a *highest original good,* that is to say, of the existence of God. Now it was seen to be a duty for us to promote the *summum bonum;* consequently it is not merely allowable, but it is a necessity connected with duty as a requisite, that we should presuppose the possibility of this *summum bonum;* and as this is possible only on condition of the existence of God, it inseparably connects the supposition of this with duty; that is, it is morally necessary to assume the existence of God.

It must be remarked here that this moral necessity is *subjective,* that is, it is a want, and not *objective,* that is, itself a duty, for there cannot be a duty to suppose the existence of anything (since this concerns only the theoretical employment of reason). Moreover, it is not meant by this that it is necessary to suppose the existence of God *as a basis of all obligation in general* (for this rests, as has been sufficiently proved, simply on the autonomy of reason itself). What belongs to duty here is only the endeavour to realize and promote the *summum bonum* in the world, the possibility of which can therefore be postulated; and as our reason finds it not conceivable except on the supposition of a supreme intelligence, the admission of this existence is therefore connected with the consciousness of our duty, although the admission itself belongs to the domain of speculative reason. Considered in respect of this alone, as a principle of explanation, it may be called a *hypothesis,* but in reference to the intelligibility of an object given us by the moral law (the *summum bonum*), and consequently of a requirement for practical purposes, it may be called *faith,* that is to say a pure *rational faith,* since pure reason (both in its theoretical and practical use) is the sole source from which it springs.

From this *deduction* it is now intelligible why the Greek schools could never attain the solution of their problem of the practical possibility of the *summum bonum,* because they made the rule of the use which the will of man makes of his freedom the sole and sufficient ground of this possibility, thinking that they had no need for that purpose of the existence of God. No doubt they were so far right that they established the principle of morals of itself independently of this postulate, from the relation of reason only to the will, and consequently made it the *supreme* practical condition of the *summum bonum;* but it was not therefore the *whole* condition of its possibility. The Epicureans had indeed assumed as the supreme principle of morality a wholly false one, namely that of happiness, and had substituted for a law a maxim of arbitrary choice according to every man's inclination; they proceeded, however, *consistently* enough in this, that they degraded their *summum bonum* likewise, just in proportion to the meanness of their fundamental principle, and looked for no greater happiness than can be attained by human prudence (including temperance and moderation of the inclinations), and this as we know would be scanty enough and would be very different according to circumstances; not to mention the exceptions that their maxims must perpetually admit and which make them incapable of being laws. The Stoics, on the contrary, had chosen their supreme practical principle quite rightly, making virtue the condition of the *summum bonum;* but when they represented the degree of virtue required by its pure law as fully attainable in this life, they not only strained the moral powers of the *man* whom they called *the wise* beyond all the limits of his nature, and assumed a thing that contradicts all our knowledge of men, but also and principally they would not allow the second *element* of the *summum bonum,* namely, happiness, to be properly a special object of human desire, but made their *wise man,* like a divinity in his consciousness of the excellence of his person, wholly independent of nature (as regards his own contentment); they exposed him indeed to the evils of life, but made him not subject to them (at the same time representing him also as free from moral evil). They thus, in fact, left out the second element of the *summum bonum,* namely, personal happiness, placing it solely in action and satisfaction with one's own personal worth, thus including it in the consciousness of being morally minded, in which they might have been sufficiently refuted by the voice of their own nature.

The doctrine of Christianity,[1] even if we do not yet consider it as a religious doctrine, gives, touching this point, a conception of the *summum bonum* (the kingdom of God), which alone satisfies the strictest demand of practical reason. The moral law is holy (unyielding) and demands holiness of morals, although all the moral perfection to which man can attain is still only virtue, that is, a rightful disposition arising from *respect* for the law, implying consciousness of a constant propensity to transgression, or at least a want of purity, that is, a mixture of many spurious (not moral) motives of obedience to the law, consequently a self-esteem combined with humility. In respect, then, of the holiness which the Christian law requires, this leaves the creature nothing but a progress *in infinitum,* but for that very reason it justifies him in hoping for an endless duration of his existence. The *worth* of a character *perfectly* accordant with the moral law is infinite, since the only restriction on all possible happiness in the judgement of a wise and all powerful distributor of it is the absence of conformity of rational beings to their duty. But the moral law of itself does not *promise* any happiness, for according to our conceptions of an order of nature in general, this is not necessarily connected with obedience to the law. Now Christian morality supplies this defect (of the second indispensable element of the *summum bonum*) by represent-

[1] It is commonly held that the Christian precept of morality has no advantage in respect of purity over the moral conceptions of the Stoics; the distinction between them is, however, very obvious. The Stoic system made the consciousness of strength of mind the pivot on which all moral dispositions should turn; and although its disciples spoke of duties and even defined them very well, yet they placed the spring and proper determining principle of the will in an elevation of the mind above the lower springs of the senses, which owe their power only to weakness of mind. With them, therefore, virtue was a sort of heroism in the *wise man* who, raising himself above the animal nature of man, is sufficient for himself, and, while he prescribes duties to others, is himself raised above them, and is not subject to any temptation to transgress the moral law. All this, however, they could not have done if they had conceived this law in all its purity and strictness, as the precept of the Gospel does. When I give the name *idea* to a perfection to which nothing adequate can be given in experience, it does not follow that the moral ideas are something transcendent, that is something of which we could not even determine the concept adequately, or of which it is uncertain whether there is any object corresponding to it at all, as is the case with the ideas of speculative reason; on the contrary, being types of practical perfection, they serve as the indispensable rule of conduct and likewise as the *standard of comparison.* Now if I consider Christian morals on their philosophical side, then compared with the ideas of the Greek schools, they would appear as follows: the ideas of the Cynics, the Epicureans, the Stoics, and the Christians are: *simplicity of nature, prudence, wisdom,* and *holiness.* In respect of the way of attaining them, the Greek schools were distinguished from one another thus, that the Cynics only required *common sense,* the others the path of *science,* but both found the mere *use of natural powers* sufficient for the purpose. Christian morality, because its precept is framed (as a moral precept must be) so pure and unyielding, takes from man all confidence that he can be fully adequate to it, at least in this life, but again sets it up by enabling us to hope that if we act as well as it is in our *power* to do, then what is not in our power will come in to our aid from another source, whether we know how this may be or not. Aristotle and Plato differed only as to the *origin* of our moral conceptions.

ing the world in which rational beings devote themselves with all their soul to the moral law, as a *kingdom of God,* in which nature and morality are brought into a harmony foreign to each of itself, by a holy Author who makes the derived *summum bonum* possible. *Holiness* of life is prescribed to them as a rule even in this life, while the welfare proportioned to it, namely, *bliss,* is represented as attainable only in an eternity; because the *former* must always be the pattern of their conduct in every state, and progress towards it is already possible and necessary in this life; while the *latter,* under the name of *happiness,* cannot be attained at all in this world (so far as our own power is concerned), and therefore is made simply an object of hope. Nevertheless, the Christian principle of *morality* itself is not theological (so as to be heteronomy), but is autonomy of pure practical reason, since it does not make the knowledge of God and His will the foundation of these laws, but only of the attainment of the *summum bonum,* on condition of following these laws, and it does not even place the proper *spring* of this obedience in the desired results, but solely in the conception of duty, as that of which the faithful observance alone constitutes the worthiness to obtain those happy consequences.

In this manner, the moral laws lead through the conception of the *summum bonum* as the object and final end of pure practical reason to *religion,* that is, to the *recognition of all duties as divine commands, not as sanctions, that is to say, arbitrary ordinances of a foreign will and contingent in themselves,* but as essential *laws* of every free will in itself, which, nevertheless, must be regarded as commands of the Supreme Being, because it is only from a morally perfect (holy and good) and at the same time all-powerful will, and consequently only through harmony with this will, that we can hope to attain the *summum bonum* which the moral law makes it our duty to take as the object of our endeavours. Here again, then, all remains disinterested and founded merely on duty; neither fear nor hope being made the fundamental springs, which if taken as principles would destroy the whole moral worth of actions. The moral law commands me to make the highest possible good in a world the ultimate object of all my conduct. But I cannot hope to effect this otherwise than by the harmony of my will with that of a holy and good Author of the world; and although the conception of the *summum bonum* as a whole, in which the greatest happiness is conceived as combined in the most exact proportion with the highest degree of moral perfection (possible in creatures), includes *my own happiness,* yet it is not this that is the determining principle of the will which is enjoined to promote the *summum bonum,* but the moral law, which, on the contrary, limits by strict conditions my unbounded desire of happiness.

Hence also morality is not properly the doctrine how we should *make* ourselves happy, but how we should become *worthy* of happiness. It is only when religion is added that there also comes in the hope of participating some day in happiness in proportion as we have endeavoured to be not unworthy of it.

A man is *worthy* to possess a thing or a state when his possession of it is in harmony with the *summum bonum.* We can now easily see that all worthiness depends on moral conduct, since in the conception of the *summum bonum* this constitutes the condition of the rest (which belongs to one's state), namely, the participation of happiness. Now it follows from this that *morality* should never be treated as a *doctrine of happiness,* that is, an instruction how to become happy; for it has to do simply with the rational condition (*conditio sine qua non*) of happiness, not with the means of attaining it. But when morality has been completely expounded (which merely imposes duties instead of providing rules for selfish desires), then first, after the moral desire to promote the *summum bonum* (to bring the kingdom of God to us) has been awakened, a desire founded on a law, and which could not previously arise in any selfish mind, and when for the behoof of this desire the step to religion has been taken, then this ethical doctrine may be also called a doctrine of happiness because the *hope* of happiness first begins with religion only.

We can also see from this that, when we ask what is *God's ultimate end* in creating the world, we must not name the *happiness* of the rational beings in it, but the *summum bonum,* which adds a further condition to that wish of such beings, namely, the condition of being worthy of happiness, that is, the *morality* of these same rational beings, a condition which alone contains the rule by which only they can hope to share in the former at the hand of a *wise* Author. For as *wisdom,* theoretically considered, signifies *the knowledge of the summum bonum* and, practically, *the accordance of the will with the summum bonum,* we cannot attribute to a supreme independent wisdom an end based merely on *goodness*. For we cannot conceive the action of this goodness (in respect of the happiness of rational beings) as suitable to the highest original good, except under the restrictive conditions of harmony with the holiness[1] of his will. Therefore, those who placed the end of creation in the glory of God (provided that this is not conceived anthropomorphically as a desire to be praised) have perhaps hit upon the best expression. For nothing glorifies God more than that which is the most estimable thing in the world, respect for his command, the observance of the holy duty that his law imposes on us, when there is added thereto his glorious plan of crowning such a beautiful order of things with corresponding happiness. If the latter (to speak humanly) makes Him worthy of love, by the *former* He is an object of adoration. Even men can never acquire respect by benevolence alone, though they may gain love, so that the greatest beneficence only procures them honour when it is regulated by worthiness.

That in the order of ends, man (and with him every rational being) is *an end in himself*, that is, that he can never be used merely as a means by any (not even by God) without being at the same time an end also himself, that therefore *humanity* in our person must be *holy* to ourselves, this follows now of itself because he is the *subject of the moral law*, in other words, of that which is holy in itself, and on account of which and in agreement with which alone can anything be termed holy. For this moral law is founded on the autonomy of his will, as a free will which by its universal laws must necessarily be able to agree with that to which it is to submit itself.

VI. *Of the Postulates of Pure Practical Reason Generally*

They all proceed from the principle of morality, which is not a postulate but a law, by which reason determines the will directly, which will, because it is so determined as a pure will, requires these necessary conditions of obedience to its precept. These postulates are not theoretical dogmas but, suppositions practically necessary; while then they do [not] extend our speculative knowledge, they give objective reality to the ideas of speculative reason in general (by means of their reference to what is practical), and give it a right to concepts, the possibility even of which it could not otherwise venture to affirm.

These postulates are those *of immortality, freedom* positively considered (as the causality of a being so far as he belongs to the intelligible world), and the *existence of God*. The *first* results from the practically necessary condition of a duration adequate to the complete fulfilment of the moral law; the *second* from the necessary supposition of independence of the sensible world, and of the faculty of determining one's will according to the law of an intelligible world, that is, of freedom; the *third* from the necessary condition of the existence of the *summum bonum* in such an intelligible world, by the supposition of the supreme independent good, that is, the existence of God.

Thus the fact that respect for the moral law necessarily makes the *summum bonum* an object of our endeavours, and the supposition thence resulting of its objective reality, lead through the postulates of practical reason to conceptions which speculative reason might indeed present as problems, but could never solve. Thus it leads: 1. To that one in the solution of which the latter could do nothing but commit *paralogisms* (namely, that of immortality), because it could not lay hold of the character of permanence, by which to complete the psychological conception of an ultimate subject necessarily ascribed to the soul in self-consciousness, so as to make it the real conception of a substance, a character which practical reason furnishes by the postulate of a duration required for accordance with the moral law in the *summum bonum*, which is the whole end of practical reason. 2. It leads to that of which speculative reason contained nothing but *antinomy*, the solution of which it could only found on a notion problematically conceivable indeed, but whose objective reality it could not prove or determine, namely, the *cosmological* idea of an intelligible world and the consciousness of our existence in it, by means of the postulate of freedom (the reality of which it lays down by virtue of the moral law), and with it likewise

[1] In order to make these characteristics of these conceptions clear, I add the remark that whilst we ascribe to God various attributes, the quality of which we also find applicable to creatures, only that in Him they are raised to the highest degree, e. g., power, knowledge, presence, goodness, etc., under the designations of omnipotence, omniscience, omnipresence, etc., there are three that are ascribed to God exclusively, and yet without the addition of greatness, and which are all moral. He is the *only holy*, the *only blessed*, the *only wise*, because these conceptions already imply the absence of limitation. In the order of these attributes He is also the *holy lawgiver* (and creator), the *good governor* (and preserver) and the *just judge*, three attributes which include everything by which God is the object of religion, and in conformity with which the metaphysical perfections are added of themselves in the reason.

the law of an intelligible world, to which speculative reason could only point, but could not define its conception. 3. What speculative reason was able to think, but was obliged to leave undetermined as a mere transcendental *ideal*, viz., the *theological* conception of the first Being, to this it gives significance (in a practical view, that is, as a condition of the possibility of the object of a will determined by that law), namely, as the supreme principle of the *summum bonum* in an intelligible world, by means of moral legislation in it invested with sovereign power.

Is our knowledge, however, actually extended in this way by pure practical reason, and is that *immanent* in practical reason which for the speculative was only *transcendent?* Certainly, but *only in a practical point of view*. For we do not thereby take knowledge of the nature of our souls, nor of the intelligible world, nor of the Supreme Being, with respect to what they are in themselves, but we have merely combined the conceptions of them in the *practical* concept of the *summum bonum* as the object of our will, and this altogether *a priori*, but only by means of the moral law, and merely in reference to it, in respect of the object which it commands. But how freedom is possible, and how we are to conceive this kind of causality theoretically and positively, is not thereby discovered; but only that there is such a causality is postulated by the moral law and in its behoof. It is the same with the remaining ideas, the possibility of which no human intelligence will ever fathom, but the truth of which, on the other hand, no sophistry will ever wrest from the conviction even of the commonest man.

VII. *How is it possible to conceive an Extension of Pure Reason in a Practical point of view, without its Knowledge as Speculative being enlarged at the same time?*

In order not to be too abstract, we will answer this question at once in its application to the present case. In order to extend a pure cognition *practically*, there must be an *a priori purpose* given, that is, an end as object (of the will), which independently of all theological principle is presented as practically necessary by an imperative which determines the will directly (a categorical imperative), and in this case that is the *summum bonum*. This, however, is not possible without presupposing three theoretical conceptions (for which, because they are mere conceptions of pure reason, no corresponding intuition can be found, nor consequently by the path of theory any objective reality); namely, freedom, immortality, and God. Thus by the practical law which commands the existence of the highest good possible in a world, the possibility of those objects of pure speculative reason is postulated, and the objective reality which the latter could not assure them. By this the theoretical knowledge of pure reason does indeed obtain an accession; but it consists only in this, that those concepts which otherwise it had to look upon as problematical (merely thinkable) concepts, are now shown assertorially to be such as actually have objects; because practical reason indispensably requires their existence for the possibility of its object, the *summum bonum*, which practically is absolutely necessary, and this justifies theoretical reason in assuming them. But this extension of theoretical reason is no extension of speculative, that is, we cannot make any positive use of it in a *theoretical point of view*. For as nothing is accomplished in this by practical reason, further than that these concepts are real and actually have their (possible) objects, and nothing in the way of intuition of them is given thereby (which indeed could not be demanded), hence the admission of this reality does not render any synthetical proposition possible. Consequently, this discovery does not in the least help us to extend this knowledge of ours in a speculative point of view, although it does in respect of the practical employment of pure reason. The above three ideas of speculative reason are still in themselves not cognitions; they are however (transcendent) *thoughts*, in which there is nothing impossible. Now, by help of an apodeictic practical law, being necessary conditions of that which it commands *to be made an object*, they acquire objective reality; that is, we learn from it *that they have objects*, without being able to point out how the conception of them is related to an object, and this, too, is still not a cognition of *these objects;* for we cannot thereby form any synthetical judgement about them, nor determine their application theoretically; consequently, we can make no theoretical rational use of them at all, in which use all speculative knowledge of reason consists. Nevertheless, the theoretical knowledge, *not indeed of these objects*, but of reason generally, is so far enlarged by this, that by the practical postulates *objects were given* to those ideas, a merely problematical thought having by this means first acquired objective reality. There is therefore no extension of the knowledge *of given supersensible objects*, but an extension of theoretical reason and of its knowledge in respect of the supersensible generally; inasmuch as it is compelled to admit *that there are such objects,* although it is not able to define them more closely, so as itself to extend this knowledge of the objects (which have now been given it on practical grounds, and only for practical use). For this accession, then, pure theoretical reason, for which all those ideas are transcendent and without object, has simply to thank its practical faculty. In this they become *immanent and constitutive,* being the source of the possibility of *realizing the necessary object* of pure practical reason (the *summum bonum*); whereas apart from this they are transcendent, and merely *regulative* principles of speculative reason, which do not require it to assume a new object beyond experience, but only to bring its use in experience nearer to completeness. But when once reason is in possession of this accession, it will go to work with these ideas as speculative reason (properly only to assure the certainty of its practical use) in a negative manner: that is, not extending but clearing up its knowledge so as on one side to keep off *anthropomorphism,* as the source of *superstition,* or seeming extension of these conceptions by supposed experience; and on the other side *fanaticism,* which promises the same by means of supersensible intuition or feelings of the like kind. All these are hindrances to the practical use of pure reason, so that the removal of them may certainly be considered an extension of our knowledge in a practical point of view, without contradicting the admission that for speculative purposes reason has not in the least gained by this.

Every employment of reason in respect of an object requires pure concepts of the understanding (*categories*), without which no object can be conceived. These can be applied to the theoretical employment of reason, i. e., to that kind of knowledge, only in case an intuition (which is always sensible) is taken as a basis, and therefore merely in order to conceive by means of them an object of possible experience. Now here what have to be thought by means of the categories in order to be known are *ideas* of reason, which cannot be given in any experience. Only we are not here concerned with the theoretical knowledge of the objects of these ideas, but only with this, whether they have objects at all. This reality is supplied by pure practical reason, and theoretical reason has nothing further to do in this but to *think* those objects by means of categories. This, as we have elsewhere clearly shown, can be done well enough without needing any intuition (either sensible or supersensible) because the categories have their seat and origin in the pure understanding, simply as the faculty of thought, before and independently of any intuition, and they always only signify an object in general, *no matter in what way it may be given to us.* Now when the categories are to be applied to these ideas, it is not possible to give them any object in intuition; but *that such an object actually exists,* and consequently that the category as a mere form of thought is here not empty but has significance, this is sufficiently assured them by an object which practical reason presents beyond doubt in the concept of the *summum bonum,* the *reality of the conceptions* which are required for the possibility of the *summum bonum;* without, however, effecting by this accession the least extension of our knowledge on theoretical principles.

When these ideas of God, of an intelligible world (the kingdom of God), and of immortality are further determined by predicates taken from our own nature, we must not regard this determination as a *sensualizing* of those pure rational ideas (anthropomorphism), nor as a transcendent knowledge of *supersensible* objects; for these predicates are no others than understanding and will, considered too in the relation to each other in which they must be conceived in the moral law, and therefore, only so far as a pure practical use is made of them. As to all the rest that belongs to these conceptions psychologically, that is, so far as we observe these faculties of ours empirically *in their exercise* (e. g., that the understanding of man is discursive, and its notions therefore not intuitions but thoughts, that these follow one another in time, that his will has its satisfaction always dependent on the existence of its object, etc., which cannot be the case in the Supreme Being), from all this we abstract in that case, and then there remains of the notions by which we conceive a pure intelligence nothing more than just what is required for the possibility of conceiving a moral law. There is then a knowledge of God indeed, but only for practical purposes, and, if we attempt to extend it to a theoretical knowledge, we find an understanding that has *intuitions,* not thoughts, a will that is directed to objects on the existence of which its satisfaction does not in the least depend (not to mention the transcendental predicates, as, for example, a magnitude of existence, that is duration, which, however, is not in time, the only possible means we have of conceiving existence as magnitude). Now these are all attributes of which we can form no conception that would help to the *knowledge* of the object, and we learn from this that they can never be used for a *theory* of supersensible beings, so that on this side they are quite incapable of being the foundation of a speculative knowledge, and their use is limited simply to the practice of the moral law.

This last is so obvious, and can be proved so clearly by fact, that we may confidently challenge all pretended *natural theologians* (a singular name)[1] to specify (over and above the merely ontological predicates) one single attribute, whether of the understanding or of the will, determining this object of theirs, of which we could not show incontrovertibly that, if we abstract from it everything anthropomorphic, nothing would remain to us but the mere word, without our being able to connect with it the smallest notion by which we could hope for an extension of theoretical knowledge. But as to the practical, there still remains to us of the attributes of understanding and will the conception of a relation to which objective reality is given by the practical law (which determines *a priori* precisely this relation of the understanding to the will). When once this is done, then reality is given to the conception of the object of a will morally determined (the conception of the *summum bonum*), and with it to the conditions of its possibility, the ideas of God, freedom, and immortality, but always only relatively to the practice of the moral law (and not for any speculative purpose).

According to these remarks it is now easy to find the answer to the weighty question *whether the notion of God is one belonging to physics* (and therefore also to metaphysics, which contains the pure *a priori* principles of the former in their universal import) *or to morals*. If we have recourse to God as the Author of all things, in order to *explain* the arrangements of nature or its changes, this is at least not a physical explanation, and is a complete confession that our philosophy has come to an end, since we are obliged to assume something of which in itself we have otherwise no conception, in order to be able to frame a conception of the possibility of what we see before our eyes. Metaphysics, however, cannot enable us to attain *by certain inference* from the knowledge of *this* world to the conception of God and to the proof of His existence, for this reason, that in order to say that this world could be produced only by a God (according to the conception implied by this word) we should know this world as the most perfect whole possible; and for this purpose should also know all possible worlds (in order to be able to compare them with this); in other words, we should be omniscient. It is absolutely impossible, however, to know the existence of this Being from mere concepts, because every existential proposition, that is, every proposition that affirms the existence of a being of which I frame a concept, is a synthetic proposition, that is, one by which I go beyond that conception and affirm of it more than was thought in the conception itself; namely, that this concept *in the understanding* has an object corresponding to it *outside the understanding*, and this it is obviously impossible to elicit by any reasoning. There remains, therefore, only one single process possible for reason to attain this knowledge, namely, to start from the supreme principle of its pure practical use (which in every case is directed simply to the *existence* of something as a consequence of reason) and thus determine its object. Then its inevitable problem, namely, the necessary direction of the will to the *summum bonum*, discovers to us not only the necessity of assuming such a First Being in reference to the possibility of this good in the world, but, what is most remarkable, something which reason in its progress on the path of physical nature altogether failed to find, namely, an accurately defined conception of this First Being. As we can know only a small part of this world, and can still less compare it with all possible worlds, we may indeed from its order, design, and greatness, infer a wise, good, powerful, etc., Author of it, but not that He is all-wise, all-good, all-powerful, etc. It may indeed very well be granted that we should be justified in supplying this inevitable defect by a legitimate and reasonable hypothesis; namely, that when wisdom, goodness, etc., are displayed in all the parts that offer themselves to our nearer knowledge, it is just the same in all the rest, and that it would therefore be reasonable to ascribe all possible per-

[1] Learning is properly only the whole content of the *historical* sciences. Consequently it is only the teacher of revealed theology that can be called a learned theologian. If, however, we choose to call a man learned who is in possession of the rational sciences (mathematics and philosophy), although even this would be contrary to the signification of the word (which always counts as learning only that which one must be *"learned"* and which, therefore, he cannot discover of himself by reason), even in that case the philosopher would make too poor a figure with his knowledge of God as a positive science to let himself be called on that account a *learned* man.

fections to the Author of the world, but these are not strict *logical inferences* in which we can pride ourselves on our insight, but only permitted conclusions in which we may be indulged and which require further recommendation before we can make use of them. On the path of empirical inquiry then (physics), the conception of God remains always a conception of the perfection of the First Being not accurately enough determined to be held adequate to the conception of Deity. (With metaphysic in its transcendental part nothing whatever can be accomplished.)

When I now try to test this conception by reference to the object of practical reason, I find that the moral principle admits as possible only the conception of an Author of the world possessed *of the highest perfection.* He must be *omniscient,* in order to know my conduct up to the inmost root of my mental state in all possible cases and into all future time; *omnipotent,* in order to allot to it its fitting consequences; similarly He must be *omnipresent, eternal,* etc. Thus the moral law, by means of the conception of the *summum bonum* as the object of a pure practical reason, determines the concept of the First Being *as the Supreme Being;* a thing which the physical (and in its higher development the metaphysical), in other words, the whole speculative course of reason, was unable to effect. The conception of God, then, is one that belongs originally not to physics, i. e., to speculative reason, but to morals. The same may be said of the other conceptions of reason of which we have treated above as postulates of it in its practical use.

In the history of Grecian philosophy we find no distinct traces of a pure rational theology earlier than Anaxagoras; but this is not because the older philosophers had not intelligence or penetration enough to raise themselves to it by the path of speculation, at least with the aid of a thoroughly reasonable hypothesis. What could have been easier, what more natural, than the thought which of itself occurs to everyone, to assume instead of several causes of the world, instead of an indeterminate degree of perfection, a single rational cause having *all perfection?* But the evils in the world seemed to them to be much too serious objections to allow them to feel themselves justified in such a hypothesis. They showed intelligence and penetration then in this very point, that they did not allow themselves to adopt it, but on the contrary looked about amongst natural causes to see if they could not find in them the qualities and power required for a First Being. But when this acute people had advanced so far in their investigations of nature as to treat even moral questions philosophically, on which other nations had never done anything but talk, then first they found a new and practical want, which did not fail to give definiteness to their conception of the First Being: and in this the speculative reason played the part of spectator, or at best had the merit of embellishing a conception that had not grown on its own ground, and of applying a series of confirmations from the study of nature now brought forward for the first time, not indeed to strengthen the authority of this conception (which was already established), but rather to make a show with a supposed discovery of theoretical reason.

From these remarks, the reader of the Critique of Pure Speculative Reason will be thoroughly convinced how highly necessary that laborious *deduction* of the categories was, and how fruitful for theology and morals. For if, on the one hand, we place them in pure understanding, it is by this deduction alone that we can be prevented from regarding them, with Plato, as innate, and founding on them extravagant pretensions to theories of the supersensible, to which we can see no end, and by which we should make theology a magic lantern of chimeras; on the other hand, if we regard them as acquired, this deduction saves us from restricting, with Epicurus, all and every use of them, even for practical purposes, to the objects and motives of the senses. But now that the Critique has shown by that deduction, *first,* that they are not of empirical origin, but have their seat and source *a priori* in the pure understanding; *secondly,* that as they refer *to objects in general* independently of the intuition of them, hence, although they cannot effect *theoretical knowledge,* except in application to *empirical* objects, yet when applied to an object given by pure practical reason they enable us to *conceive the supersensible* definitely, only so far, however, as it is defined by such predicates as are necessarily connected with the pure *practical purpose* given *a priori* and with its possibility. The speculative restriction of pure reason and its practical extension bring it into that *relation of equality* in which reason in general can be employed suitably to its end, and this example proves better than any other that the path to *wisdom,* if it is to be made sure and not to be impassable or misleading, must with us men inevitably pass through science; but it is not till this is complete that we can be convinced that it leads to this goal.

VIII. *Of Belief from a Requirement of Pure Reason*

A want or requirement of pure reason in its speculative use leads only to a *hypothesis;* that of pure practical reason to a *postulate;* for in the former case I ascend from the result as high as I please in the series of causes, not in order to give objective reality to the result (e. g., the causal connection of things and changes in the world), but in order thoroughly to satisfy my inquiring reason in respect of it. Thus I see before me order and design in nature, and need not resort to speculation to assure myself of their *reality,* but to *explain* them I have *to presuppose* a Deity as their cause; and then since the inference from an effect to a definite cause is always uncertain and doubtful, especially to a cause so precise and so perfectly defined as we have to conceive in God, hence the highest degree of certainty to which this pre-supposition can be brought is that it is the most rational opinion for us men.[1] On the other hand, a requirement of pure *practical* reason is based on a *duty,* that of making something (the *summum bonum*) the object of my will so as to promote it with all my powers; in which case I must suppose its possibility and, consequently, also the conditions necessary thereto, namely, God, freedom, and immortality; since I cannot prove these by my speculative reason, although neither can I refute them. This duty is founded on something that is indeed quite independent of these suppositions and is of itself apodeictically certain, namely, the moral law; and so far it needs no further support by theoretical views as to the inner constitution of things, the secret final aim of the order of the world, or a presiding ruler thereof, in order to bind me in the most perfect manner to act in unconditional conformity to the law. But the subjective effect of this law, namely, the mental *disposition* conformed to it and made necessary by it, to promote the practically possible *summum bonum,* this pre-supposes at least that the latter is *possible,* for it would be practically impossible to strive after the object of a conception which at bottom was empty and had no object. Now the above-mentioned postulates concern only the physical or metaphysical conditions of the *possibility* of the *summum bonum;* in a word, those which lie in the nature of things; not, however, for the sake of an arbitrary speculative purpose, but of a practically necessary end of a pure rational will, which in this case does not *choose,* but *obeys* an inexorable command of reason, the foundation of which is *objective,* in the constitution of things as they must be universally judged by pure reason, and is not based on *inclination;* for we are in nowise justified in assuming, on account of what we *wish* on merely *subjective* grounds, that the means thereto are possible or that its object is real. This, then, is an absolutely necessary requirement, and what it pre-supposes is not merely justified as an allowable hypothesis, but as a postulate in a practical point of view; and admitting that the pure moral law inexorably binds every man as a command (not as a rule of prudence), the righteous man may say: "I *will* that there be a God, that my existence in this world be also an existence outside the chain of physical causes and in a pure world of the understanding, and lastly, that my duration be endless; I firmly abide by this, and will not let this faith be taken from me; for in this instance alone my interest, because I *must* not relax anything of it, inevitably determines my judgement, without regarding sophistries, however unable I may be to answer them or to oppose them with others more plausible."[2]

[1] But even here we should not be able to allege a requirement *of reason,* if we had not before our eyes a problematical, but yet inevitable, conception of reason, namely, that of an absolutely necessary being. This conception now seeks to be defined, and this, in addition to the tendency to extend itself, is the objective ground of a requirement of speculative reason, namely, to have a more precise definition of the conception of a necessary being which is to serve as the first cause of other beings, so as to make these latter knowable by some means. Without such antecedent necessary problems there are no *requirements*—at least not of *pure reason*—the rest are requirements of *inclination.*

[2] In the *Deutsches Museum,* February, 1787, there is a dissertation by a very subtle and clear-headed man, the late Wizenmann, whose early death is to be lamented, in which he disputes the right to argue from a want to the objective reality of its object, and illustrates the point by the example of *a man in love,* who having fooled himself into an idea of beauty, which is merely a chimera of his own brain, would fain conclude that such an object really exists somewhere. I quite agree with him in this, in all cases where the want is founded on *inclination,* which cannot necessarily postulate the existence of its object even for the man that is affected by it, much less can it contain a demand valid for everyone, and therefore it is merely a *subjective* ground of the wish. But in the present case we have a want of reason springing from an objective determining principle of the will, namely, the moral law, which necessarily binds every rational being, and therefore justifies him in assuming *a priori* in nature the conditions proper for it, and makes the latter inseparable from the complete practical use of reason. It is a duty to realize the *summum bonum* to the utmost of our power, therefore it must be possible, consequently it is unavoidable for every rational being in the world to assume what is necessary for its objective possibility. The assumption is as necessary as the moral law, in connection with which alone it is valid.

In order to prevent misconception in the use of a notion as yet so unusual as that of a faith of pure practical reason, let me be permitted to add one more remark. It might almost seem as if this rational faith were here announced as itself a *command,* namely, that we should assume the *summum bonum* as possible. But a faith that is commanded is nonsense. Let the preceding analysis, however, be remembered of what is required to be supposed in the conception of the *summum bonum,* and it will be seen that it cannot be commanded to assume this possibility, and no practical disposition of mind is required to *admit* it; but that speculative reason must concede it without being asked, for no one can affirm that it is *impossible* in itself that rational beings in the world should at the same time be worthy of happiness in conformity with the moral law and also possess this happiness proportionately. Now in respect of the first element of the *summum bonum,* namely, that which concerns morality, the moral law gives merely a command, and to doubt the possibility of that element would be the same as to call in question the moral law itself. But as regards the second element of that object, namely, happiness perfectly proportioned to that worthiness, it is true that there is no need of a command to admit its possibility in general, for theoretical reason has nothing to say against it; but *the manner* in which we have to conceive this harmony of the laws of nature with those of freedom has in it something in respect of which we have a *choice,* because theoretical reason decides nothing with apodeictic certainty about it, and in respect of this there may be a moral interest which turns the scale.

I had said above that in a mere course of nature in the world an accurate correspondence between happiness and moral worth is not to be expected and must be regarded as impossible, and that therefore the possibility of the *summum bonum* cannot be admitted from this side except on the supposition of a moral Author of the world. I purposely reserved the restriction of this judgement to the *subjective* conditions of our reason, in order not to make use of it until the manner of this belief should be defined more precisely. The fact is that the impossibility referred to is *merely subjective,* that is, our reason finds it *impossible for it* to render conceivable in the way of a mere course of nature a connection so exactly proportioned and so thoroughly adapted to an end, between two sets of events happening according to such distinct laws; although, as with everything else in nature that is adapted to an end, it cannot prove, that is, show by sufficient objective reason, that it is not possible by universal laws of nature.

Now, however, a deciding principle of a different kind comes into play to turn the scale in this uncertainty of speculative reason. The command to promote the *summum bonum* is established on an objective basis (in practical reason); the possibility of the same in general is likewise established on an objective basis (in theoretical reason, which has nothing to say against it). But reason cannot decide objectively in what way we are to conceive this possibility; whether by universal laws of nature without a wise Author presiding over nature, or only on supposition of such an Author. Now here there comes in a *subjective* condition of reason, the only way theoretically possible for it, of conceiving the exact harmony of the kingdom of nature with the kingdom of morals, which is the condition of the possibility of the *summum bonum;* and at the same time the only one conducive to morality (which depends on an objective law of reason). Now since the promotion of this *summum bonum,* and therefore the supposition of its possibility, are *objectively* necessary (though only as a result of practical reason), while at the same time the manner in which we would conceive it rests with our own choice, and in this choice a free interest of pure practical reason decides for the assumption of a wise Author of the world; it is clear that the principle that herein determines our judgement, though as a want it is *subjective,* yet at the same time being the means of promoting what is *objectively* (practically) necessary, is the foundation of a *maxim* of belief in a moral point of view, that is, a *faith of pure practical reason.* This, then, is not commanded, but being a voluntary determination of our judgement, conducive to the moral (commanded) purpose, and moreover harmonizing with the theoretical requirement of reason, to assume that existence and to make it the foundation of our further employment of reason, it has itself sprung from the moral disposition of mind; it may therefore at times waver even in the well-disposed, but can never be reduced to unbelief.

IX. *Of the Wise Adaptation of Man's Cognitive Faculties to his Practical Destination*

If human nature is destined to endeavour after the *summum bonum,* we must suppose also that the measure of its cognitive faculties, and particularly their relation to one another, is suitable to this end. Now the Critique of Pure

Speculative Reason proves that this is incapable of solving satisfactorily the most weighty problems that are proposed to it, although it does not ignore the natural and important hints received from the same reason, nor the great steps that it can make to approach to this great goal that is set before it, which, however, it can never reach of itself, even with the help of the greatest knowledge of nature. Nature then seems here to have provided us only in a *stepmotherly* fashion with the faculty required for our end.

Suppose, now, that in this matter nature had conformed to our wish and had given us that capacity of discernment or that enlightenment which we would gladly possess, or which some *imagine* they actually possess, what would in all probability be the consequence? Unless our whole nature were at the same time changed, our inclinations, which always have the first word, would first of all demand their own satisfaction, and, joined with rational reflection, the greatest possible and most lasting satisfaction, under the name of happiness; the moral law would afterwards speak, in order to keep them within their proper bounds, and even to subject them all to a higher end, which has no regard to inclination. But instead of the conflict that the moral disposition has now to carry on with the inclinations, in which, though after some defeats, moral strength of mind may be gradually acquired, *God* and *eternity* with their *awful majesty* would stand unceasingly *before our eyes* (for what we can prove perfectly is to us as certain as that of which we are assured by the sight of our eyes). Transgression of the law, would, no doubt, be avoided; what is commanded would be done; but the mental *disposition,* from which actions ought to proceed, cannot be infused by any command, and in this case the spur of action is ever active and *external,* so that reason has no need to exert itself in order to gather strength to resist the inclinations by a lively representation of the dignity of the law: hence most of the actions that conformed to the law would be done from fear, a few only from hope, and none at all from duty, and the moral worth of actions, on which alone in the eyes of supreme wisdom the worth of the person and even that of the world depends, would cease to exist. As long as the nature of man remains what it is, his conduct would thus be changed into mere mechanism, in which, as in a puppet-show, everything would *gesticulate* well, but there would be *no life* in the figures. Now, when it is quite otherwise with us, when with all the effort of our reason we have only a very obscure and doubtful view into the future, when the Governor of the world allows us only to conjecture his existence and his majesty, not to behold them or prove them clearly; and on the other hand, the moral law within us, without promising or threatening anything with certainty, demands of us disinterested respect; and only when this respect has become active and dominant, does it allow us by means of it a prospect into the world of the supersensible, and then only with weak glances: all this being so, there is room for true moral disposition, immediately devoted to the law, and a rational creature can become worthy of sharing in the *summum bonum* that corresponds to the worth of his person and not merely to his actions. Thus what the study of nature and of man teaches us sufficiently elsewhere may well be true here also; that the unsearchable wisdom by which we exist is not less worthy of admiration in what it has denied than in what it has granted.

SECOND PART

Methodology of Pure Practical Reason

BY the *methodology* of pure *practical* reason we are not to understand the mode of proceeding with pure practical principles (whether in study or in exposition), with a view to a scientific knowledge of them, which alone is what is properly called method elsewhere in *theoretical* philosophy (for popular knowledge requires a *manner*, science a *method*, i. e., a process *according to principles of reason* by which alone the manifold of any branch of knowledge can become a *system*). On the contrary, by this methodology is understood the mode in which we can give the laws of pure practical reason *access* to the human mind and *influence* on its maxims, that is, by which we can make the objectively practical reason *subjectively* practical also.

Now it is clear enough that those determining principles of the will which alone make maxims properly moral and give them a moral worth, namely, the direct conception of the law and the objective necessity of obeying it as our duty, must be regarded as the proper springs of actions, since otherwise *legality* of actions might be produced, but not *morality* of character. But it is not so clear; on the contrary, it must at first sight seem to every one very improbable that even subjectively that exhibition of pure virtue can have *more power* over the human mind, and supply a far stronger spring even for effecting that legality of actions, and can produce more powerful resolutions to prefer the law, from pure respect for it, to every other consideration, than all the deceptive allurements of pleasure or of all that may be reckoned as happiness, or even than all threatenings of pain and misfortune. Nevertheless, this is actually the case, and if human nature were not so constituted, no mode of presenting the law by roundabout ways and indirect recommendations would ever produce morality of character. All would be simple hypocrisy; the law would be hated, or at least despised, while it was followed for the sake of one's own advantage. The letter of the law (legality) would be found in our actions, but not the spirit of it in our minds (morality); and as with all our efforts we could not quite free ourselves from reason in our judgement, we must inevitably appear in our own eyes worthless, depraved men, even though we should seek to compensate ourselves for this mortification before the inner tribunal, by enjoying the pleasure that a supposed natural or divine law might be imagined to have connected with it a sort of police machinery, regulating its operations by what was done without troubling itself about the motives for doing it.

It cannot indeed be denied that in order to bring an uncultivated or degraded mind into the track of moral goodness some preparatory guidance is necessary, to attract it by a view of its own advantage, or to alarm it by fear of loss; but as soon as this mechanical work, these leading-strings have produced some effect, then we must bring before the mind the pure moral motive, which, not only because it is the only one that can be the foundation of a character (a practically consistent habit of mind with unchangeable maxims), but also because it teaches a man to feel his own dignity, gives the mind a power unexpected even by himself, to tear himself from all sensible attachments so far as they would fain have the rule, and to find a rich compensation for the sacrifice he offers, in the independence of his rational nature and the greatness of soul to which he sees that he is destined. We will therefore show, by such observations as every one can make, that this property of our minds, this receptivity for a pure moral interest, and consequently the moving force of the pure conception of virtue, when it is properly applied to the human heart, is the most powerful spring and, when a continued and punctual observance of moral maxims is in question, the only spring of good conduct. It must, however, be remembered that if these observations only prove the reality of such a feeling, but do not show any moral improvement brought about by it, this is no argument against the only method that exists of making the objectively practical laws of pure reason subjectively practical, through the mere force of the conception of duty; nor does it prove that this method is a vain delusion. For as it has never yet come into vogue, experience can say nothing of its results; one can only ask for proofs of the receptivity for such springs, and these I will now briefly present, and then sketch the method of founding and cultivating genuine moral dispositions.

When we attend to the course of conversation in mixed companies, consisting not merely of learned persons and subtle reasoners, but also of men of business or of women, we observe that, besides story-telling and jesting, another kind of entertainment finds a place in them, namely, argument; for stories, if they are to have novelty and interest, are soon exhausted, and jesting is likely to become insipid. Now of all argument there is none in which persons are more ready to join who find any other subtle discussion tedious, none that brings more liveliness into the company, than that which concerns the *moral worth* of this or that action by which the character of some person is to be made out. Persons, to whom in other cases anything subtle and speculative in theoretical questions is dry and irksome, presently join in when the question is to make out the moral import of a good or bad action that has been related, and they display an exactness, a refinement, a subtlety, in excogitating everything that can lessen the purity of purpose, and consequently the degree of virtue in it, which we do not expect from them in any other kind of speculation. In these criticisms, persons who are passing judgement on others often reveal their own character: some, in exercising their judicial office, especially upon the dead, seem inclined chiefly to defend the goodness that is related of this or that deed against all injurious charges of insincerity, and ultimately to defend the whole moral worth of the person against the reproach of dissimulation and secret wickedness; others, on the contrary, turn their thoughts more upon attacking this worth by accusation and fault finding. We cannot always, however, attribute to these latter the intention of arguing away virtue altogether out of all human examples in order to make it an empty name; often, on the contrary, it is only well-meant strictness in determining the true moral import of actions according to an uncompromising law. Comparison with such a law, instead of with examples, lowers self-conceit in moral matters very much, and not merely teaches humility, but makes every one feel it when he examines himself closely. Nevertheless, we can for the most part observe, in those who defend the purity of purpose in giving examples, that where there is the presumption of uprightness they are anxious to remove even the least spot, lest, if all examples had their truthfulness disputed, and if the purity of all human virtue were denied, it might in the end be regarded as a mere phantom, and so all effort to attain it be made light of as vain affectation and delusive conceit.

I do not know why the educators of youth have not long since made use of this propensity of reason to enter with pleasure upon the most subtle examination of the practical questions that are thrown up; and why they have not, after first laying the foundation of a purely moral catechism, searched through the biographies of ancient and modern times with the view of having at hand instances of the duties laid down, in which, especially by comparison of similar actions under different circumstances, they might exercise the critical judgement of their scholars in remarking their greater or less moral significance. This is a thing in which they would find that even early youth, which is still unripe for speculation of other kinds, would soon become very acute and not a little interested, because it feels the progress of its faculty of judgement; and, what is most important, they could hope with confidence that the frequent practice of knowing and approving good conduct in all its purity, and on the other hand of remarking with regret or contempt the least deviation from it, although it may be pursued only as a sport in which children may compete with one another, yet will leave a lasting impression of esteem on the one hand and disgust on the other; and so, by the mere habit of looking on such actions as deserving approval or blame, a good foundation would be laid for uprightness in the future course of life. Only I wish they would spare them the example of so-called *noble* (super-meritorious) actions, in which our sentimental books so much abound, and would refer all to duty merely, and to the worth that a man can and must give himself in his own eyes by the consciousness of not having transgressed it, since whatever runs up into empty wishes and longings after inaccessible perfection produces mere heroes of romance, who, while they pique themselves on their feeling for transcendent greatness, release themselves in return from the observance of common and every-day obligations, which then seem to them petty and insignificant.[1]

[1] It is quite proper to extol actions that display a great, unselfish, sympathizing mind or humanity. But, in this case, we must fix attention not so much on the *elevation of soul*, which is very fleeting and transitory, as on the *subjection of the heart to duty*, from which a more enduring impression may be expected, because this implies principle (whereas the former only implies ebullitions). One need only reflect a little and he will al-

But if it is asked: "What, then, is really *pure* morality, by which as a touchstone we must test the moral significance of every action," then I must admit that it is only philosophers that can make the decision of this question doubtful, for to common sense it has been decided long ago, not indeed by abstract general formulae, but by habitual use, like the distinction between the right and left hand. We will then point out the criterion of pure virtue in an example first, and, imagining that it is set before a boy, of say ten years old, for his judgement, we will see whether he would necessarily judge so of himself without being guided by his teacher. Tell him the history of an honest man whom men want to persuade to join the calumniators of an innocent and powerless person (say Anne Boleyn, accused by Henry VIII of England). He is offered advantages, great gifts, or high rank; he rejects them. This will excite mere approbation and applause in the mind of the hearer. Now begins the threatening of loss. Amongst these traducers are his best friends, who now renounce his friendship; near kinsfolk, who threaten to disinherit him (he being without fortune); powerful persons, who can persecute and harass him in all places and circumstances; a prince, who threatens him with loss of freedom, yea, loss of life. Then to fill the measure of suffering, and that he may feel the pain that only the morally good heart can feel very deeply, let us conceive his family threatened with extreme distress and want, *entreating him to yield;* conceive himself, though upright, yet with feelings not hard or insensible either to compassion or to his own distress; conceive him, I say, at the moment when he wishes that he had never lived to see the day that exposed him to such unutterable anguish, yet remaining true to his uprightness of purpose, without wavering or even doubting; then will my youthful hearer be raised gradually from mere approval to admiration, from that to amazement, and finally to the greatest veneration, and a lively wish that he himself could be such a man (though certainly not in such circumstances). Yet virtue is here worth so much only because it costs so much, not because it brings any profit. All the admiration, and even the endeavour to resemble this character, rest wholly on the purity of the moral principle, which can only be strikingly shown by removing from the springs of action everything that men may regard as part of happiness. Morality, then, must have the more power over the human heart the more purely it is exhibited. Whence it follows that if the law of morality and the image of holiness and virtue are to exercise any influence at all on our souls, they can do so only so far as they are laid to heart in their purity as motives, unmixed with any view to prosperity, for it is in suffering that they display themselves most nobly. Now that whose removal strengthens the effect of a moving force must have been a hindrance, consequently every admixture of motives taken from our own happiness is a hindrance to the influence of the moral law on the heart. I affirm further that even in that admired action, if the motive from which it was done was a high regard for duty, then it is just this respect for the law that has the greatest influence on the mind of the spectator, not any pretension to a supposed inward greatness of mind or noble meritorious sentiments; consequently duty, not merit, must have not only the most definite, but, when it is represented in the true light of its inviolability, the most penetrating, influence on the mind.

It is more necessary than ever to direct attention to this method in our times, when men hope to produce more effect on the mind with soft, tender feelings, or high-flown, puffing-up pretensions, which rather wither the heart than strengthen it, than by a plain and earnest representation of duty, which is more suited to human imperfection and to progress in goodness. To set before children, as a pattern, actions that are called noble, magnanimous, meritorious, with the notion of captivating them by infusing enthusiasm for such actions, is to defeat our end. For as they are still so backward in the observance of the commonest duty, and even in the correct estimation of it, this means simply to make them fantastical romancers betimes. But, even with the instructed and experienced part of mankind, this supposed spring has, if not an injurious, at least no genuine, moral effect on the heart, which, however, is what it was desired to produce.

All *feelings,* especially those that are to produce unwonted exertions, must accomplish their effect at the moment they are at their height and before the calm down; otherwise they effect nothing; for as there was nothing to strengthen the heart, but only to excite it, it naturally returns to its normal moderate tone and, thus,

---

ways find a debt that he has by some means incurred towards the human race (even if it were only this, that, by the inequality of men in the civil constitution, he enjoys advantages on account of which others must be the more in want), which will prevent the thought of *duty* from being repressed by the self-complacent imagination of *merit.*

falls back into its previous languor. *Principles* must be built on conceptions; on any other basis there can only be paroxysms, which can give the person no moral worth, nay, not even confidence in himself, without which the highest good in man, consciousness of the morality of his mind and character, cannot exist. Now if these conceptions are to become subjectively practical, we must not rest satisfied with admiring the objective law of morality, and esteeming it highly in reference to humanity, but we must consider the conception of it in relation to man as an individual, and then this law appears in a form indeed that is highly deserving of respect, but not so pleasant as if it belonged to the element to which he is naturally accustomed; but on the contrary as often compelling him to quit this element, not without self-denial, and to betake himself to a higher, in which he can only maintain himself with trouble and with unceasing apprehension of a relapse. In a word, the moral law demands obedience, from duty not from predilection, which cannot and ought not to be presupposed at all.

Let us now see, in an example, whether the conception of an action, as a noble and magnanimous one, has more subjective moving power than if the action is conceived merely as duty in relation to the solemn law of morality. The action by which a man endeavours at the greatest peril of life to rescue people from shipwreck, at last losing his life in the attempt, is reckoned on one side as duty, but on the other and for the most part as a meritorious action, but our esteem for it is much weakened by the notion of *duty to himself* which seems in this case to be somewhat infringed. More decisive is the magnanimous sacrifice of life for the safety of one's country; and yet there still remains some scruple whether it is a perfect duty to devote one's self to this purpose spontaneously and unbidden, and the action has not in itself the full force of a pattern and impulse to imitation. But if an indispensable duty be in question, the transgression of which violates the moral law itself, and without regard to the welfare of mankind, and as it were tramples on its holiness (such as are usually called duties to God, because in Him we conceive the ideal of holiness in substance), then we give our most perfect esteem to the pursuit of it at the sacrifice of all that can have any value for the dearest inclinations, and we find our soul strengthened and elevated by such an example, when we convince ourselves by contemplation of it that human nature is capable of so great an elevation above every motive that nature can oppose to it. Juvenal describes such an example in a climax which makes the reader feel vividly the force of the spring that is contained in the pure law of duty, as duty:

Esto bonus miles, tutor bonus, arbiter idem
Integer; ambiguæ si quando citabere testis
Incertæque rei, Phalaris licet imperet ut sis
Falsus, et admoto dictet periuria tauro,
Summum crede nefas animam præferre pudori,
Et propter vitam vivendi perdere causas.[1]

When we can bring any flattering thought of merit into our action, then the motive is already somewhat alloyed with self-love and has therefore some assistance from the side of the sensibility. But to postpone everything to the holiness of duty alone, and to be conscious that we *can* because our own reason recognises this as its command and says that we *ought* to do it, this is, as it were, to raise ourselves altogether above the world of sense, and there is inseparably involved in the same a consciousness of the law, as a spring of a faculty *that controls the sensibility;* and although this is not always attended with effect, yet frequent engagement with this spring, and the at first minor attempts at using it, give hope that this effect may be wrought, and that by degrees the greatest, and that a purely moral interest in it may be produced in us.

The method then takes the following course. At first we are only concerned to make the judging of actions by moral laws a natural employment accompanying all our own free actions, as well as the observation of those of others, and to make it as it were a habit, and to sharpen this judgement, asking first whether the action *conforms* objectively *to the moral law,* and to what law; and we distinguish the law that merely furnishes a *principle* of obligation from that which is really *obligatory* (*leges obligandi a legibus obligantibus*); as, for instance, the law of what men's *wants* require from me, as contrasted with that which their *rights* demand, the latter of which prescribes essential, the former only non-essential duties; and thus we teach how to distinguish different kinds of duties which meet in the same action. The other point to which attention must be directed

1 [Juvenal, *Satirae*, viii. 79–84. "Be you a good soldier, a faithful tutor, an uncorrupted umpire also; if you are summoned as a witness in a doubtful and uncertain thing, though Phalaris should command that you should be false, and should dictate perjuries with the bull brought to you, believe it the highest impiety to prefer life to reputation, and for the sake of life, to lose the causes of living."]

is the question whether the action was also (subjectively) done *for the sake of the moral law,* so that it not only is morally correct as a deed, but also, by the maxim from which it is done, has moral worth as a disposition. Now there is no doubt that this practice, and the resulting culture of our reason in judging merely of the practical, must gradually produce a certain interest even in the law of reason, and consequently in morally good actions. For we ultimately take a liking for a thing, the contemplation of which makes us feel that the use of our cognitive faculties is extended; and this extension is especially furthered by that in which we find moral correctness, since it is only in such an order of things that reason, with its faculty of determining *a priori* on principle what ought to be done, can find satisfaction. An observer of nature takes liking at last to objects that at first offended his senses, when he discovers in them the great adaptation of their organization to design, so that his reason finds food in its contemplation. So Leibnitz spared an insect that he had carefully examined with the microscope, and replaced it on its leaf, because he had found himself instructed by the view of it and had, as it were, received a benefit from it.

But this employment of the faculty of judgement, which makes us feel our own cognitive powers, is not yet the interest in actions and in their morality itself. It merely causes us to take pleasure in engaging in such criticism, and it gives to virtue or the disposition that conforms to moral laws a form of beauty, which is admired, but not on that account sought after (*laudatur et alget*); as everything the contemplation of which produces a consciousness of the harmony of our powers of conception, and in which we feel the whole of our faculty of knowledge (understanding and imagination) strengthened, produces a satisfaction, which may also be communicated to others, while nevertheless the existence of the object remains indifferent to us, being only regarded as the occasion of our becoming aware of the capacities in us which are elevated above mere animal nature. Now, however, the *second* exercise comes in, the living exhibition of morality of character by examples, in which attention is directed to purity of will, first only as a negative perfection, in so far as in an action done from duty no motives of inclination have any influence in determining it. By this the pupil's attention is fixed upon the consciousness of his *freedom,* and although this renunciation at first excites a feeling of pain, nevertheless, by its withdrawing the pupil from the constraint of even real wants, there is proclaimed to him at the same time a deliverance from the manifold dissatisfaction in which all these wants entangle him, and the mind is made capable of receiving the sensation of satisfaction from other sources. The heart is freed and lightened of a burden that always secretly presses on it, when instances of pure moral resolutions reveal to the man an inner faculty of which otherwise he has no right knowledge, *the inward freedom* to release himself from the boisterous importunity of inclinations, to such a degree that none of them, not even the dearest, shall have any influence on a resolution, for which we are now to employ our reason. Suppose a case where *I alone* know that the wrong is on my side, and although a free confession of it and the offer of satisfaction are so strongly opposed by vanity, selfishness, and even an otherwise not illegitimate antipathy to the man whose rights are impaired by me, I am nevertheless able to discard all these considerations; in this there is implied a consciousness of independence on inclinations and circumstances, and of the possibility of being sufficient for myself, which is salutary to me in general for other purposes also. And now the law of duty, in consequence of the positive worth which obedience to it makes us feel, finds easier access through the *respect for ourselves* in the consciousness of our freedom. When this is well established, when a man dreads nothing more than to find himself, on self-examination, worthless and contemptible in his own eyes, then every good moral disposition can be grafted on it, because this is the best, nay, the only guard that can keep off from the mind the pressure of ignoble and corrupting motives.

I have only intended to point out the most general maxims of the methodology of moral cultivation and exercise. As the manifold variety of duties requires special rules for each kind, and this would be a prolix affair, I shall be readily excused if in a work like this, which is only preliminary, I content myself with these outlines.

Conclusion

Two things fill the mind with ever new and increasing admiration and awe, the oftener and the more steadily we reflect on them: *the starry heavens above and the moral law within.* I have not to search for them and conjecture them as though they were veiled in darkness or were in the transcendent region beyond my horizon; I see them before me and connect them directly with the consciousness of my existence. The former begins from the place I occupy in the external world of sense, and enlarges my connection therein to an unbounded extent with worlds upon worlds and systems of systems, and moreover into limitless times of their periodic motion, its beginning and continuance. The second begins from my invisible self, my personality, and exhibits me in a world which has true infinity, but which is traceable only by the understanding, and with which I discern that I am not in a merely contingent but in a universal and necessary connection, as I am also thereby with all those visible worlds. The former view of a countless multitude of worlds annihilates as it were my importance as an *animal creature,* which after it has been for a short time provided with vital power, one knows not how, must again give back the matter of which it was formed to the planet it inhabits (a mere speck in the universe). The second, on the contrary, infinitely elevates my worth as an *intelligence* by my personality, in which the moral law reveals to me a life independent of animality and even of the whole sensible world, at least so far as may be inferred from the destination assigned to my existence by this law, a destination not restricted to conditions and limits of this life, but reaching into the infinite.

But though admiration and respect may excite to inquiry, they cannot supply the want of it. What, then, is to be done in order to enter on this in a useful manner and one adapted to the loftiness of the subject? Examples may serve in this as a warning and also for imitation. The contemplation of the world began from the noblest spectacle that the human senses present to us, and that our understanding can bear to follow in their vast reach; and it ended—in astrology. Morality began with the noblest attribute of human nature, the development and cultivation of which give a prospect of infinite utility; and ended—in fanaticism or superstition. So it is with all crude attempts where the principal part of the business depends on the use of reason, a use which does not come of itself, like the use of the feet, by frequent exercise, especially when attributes are in question which cannot be directly exhibited in common experience. But after the maxim had come into vogue, though late, to examine carefully beforehand all the steps that reason purposes to take, and not to let it proceed otherwise than in the track of a previously well considered method, then the study of the structure of the universe took quite a different direction, and thereby attained an incomparably happier result. The fall of a stone, the motion of a sling, resolved into their elements and the forces that are manifested in them, and treated mathematically, produced at last that clear and henceforward unchangeable insight into the system of the world which, as observation is continued, may hope always to extend itself, but need never fear to be compelled to retreat.

This example may suggest to us to enter on the same path in treating of the moral capacities of our nature, and may give us hope of a like good result. We have at hand the instances of the moral judgement of reason. By analysing these into their elementary conceptions, and in default of *mathematics* adopting a process similar to that of *chemistry,* the *separation* of the empirical from the rational elements that may be found in them, by repeated experiments on common sense, we may exhibit both *pure,* and learn with certainty what each part can accomplish of itself, so as to prevent on the one hand the errors of a still *crude* untrained judgement, and on the other hand (what is far more necessary) the *extravagances of genius,* by which, as by the adepts of the philosopher's stone, without any methodical study or knowledge of nature, visionary treasures are promised and the true are thrown away. In one word, science (critically undertaken and methodically directed) is the narrow gate that leads to the true *doctrine of practical wisdom,* if we understand by this not merely what one ought to *do,* but what ought to serve *teachers* as a guide to construct well and clearly the road to wisdom which everyone should travel, and to secure others from going astray. Philosophy must always continue to be the guardian of this science; and although the public does not take any interest in its subtle investigations, it must take an interest in the resulting *doctrines,* which such an examination first puts in a clear light.

CONTENTS
PREFACE AND INTRODUCTION TO THE METAPHYSICAL ELEMENTS OF ETHICS

PREFACE

TO THE METAPHYSICAL ELEMENTS OF ETHICS

IF there exists on any subject a *philosophy* (that is, a system of rational knowledge based on concepts), then there must also be for this philosophy a system of pure rational concepts, independent of any condition of intuition, in other words, a *metaphysic.* It may be asked whether *metaphysical elements* are required also for every *practical* philosophy, which is the doctrine of duties, and therefore also for Ethics, in order to be able to present it as a true science (systematically), not merely as an aggregate of separate doctrines (fragmentarily). As regards pure jurisprudence, no one will question this requirement; for it concerns only what is *formal* in the elective will, which has to be limited in its external relations according to laws of freedom; without regarding any *end* which is the matter of this will. Here, therefore, deontology is a mere *scientific doctrine* (*doctrina scientiae*).[1]

Now in this philosophy (of ethics) it seems contrary to the idea of it that we should go back to *metaphysical elements* in order to make the notion of duty purified from everything empirical (from every feeling) a motive of action. For what sort of notion can we form of the mighty power and herculean strength which would be sufficient to overcome the vice-breeding inclinations, if Virtue is to borrow her "arms from the armoury of metaphysics," which is a matter of speculation that only few men can handle? Hence all ethical teaching in lecture-rooms, pulpits, and popular books, when it is decked out with fragments of metaphysics, becomes ridiculous. But it is not, therefore, useless, much less ridiculous, to trace in metaphysics the first principles of ethics; for it is only as a philosopher that anyone can reach the first principles of this conception of duty, otherwise we could not look for either certainty or purity in the ethical teaching. To rely for this reason on a certain feeling which, on account of the effect expected from it, is called *moral,* may, perhaps, even satisfy the popular teacher, provided he desires as the criterion of a moral duty to consider the problem: "If everyone in every case made your maxim the universal law, how could this law be consistent with itself?" But if it were merely feeling that made it our duty to take this principle as a criterion, then this would not be dictated by reason, but only adopted instinctively and therefore blindly.

But in fact, whatever men imagine, no moral principle is based on any *feeling,* but such a principle is really nothing else than an obscurely conceived *metaphysic* which inheres in every man's reasoning faculty; as the teacher will easily find who tries to catechize his pupils in the Socratic method about the imperative of duty and its application to the moral judgement of his actions. The mode of stating it need not be always metaphysical, and the language need not necessarily be scholastic, unless the pupil is to be trained to be a philosopher. But the *thought* must go back to the elements of metaphysics, without which we cannot expect any certainty or purity, or even motive power in ethics.

If we deviate from this principle and begin from pathological, or purely sensitive, or even moral *feeling* (from what is subjectively practical instead of what is objective), that is, from the matter of the will, the *end,* not from its form that is the *law,* in order from thence to determine duties; then, certainly, there are no *metaphysical elements* of ethics, for feeling by whatever it may be excited is always physical.

[1] One who is *acquainted with practical philosophy* is not, therefore, a *practical philosopher.* The latter is he who makes the *rational end* the principle *of his actions,* while at the same time he joins with this the necessary knowledge which, as it aims at action, must not be spun out into the most subtile threads of metaphysic, unless a legal duty is in question; in which case *meum* and *tuum* must be accurately determined in the balance of justice, on the principle of equality of action and reaction, which requires something like mathematical proportion, but not in the case of a mere ethical duty. For in this case the question is not only to know what it is a duty to do (a thing which on account of the ends that all men naturally have can be easily decided), but the chief point is the inner principle of the will, namely, that the consciousness of this duty be also the *spring* of action, in order that we may be able to say of the man who joins to his knowledge this principle of wisdom that he is a *practical philosopher.*

But then ethical teaching, whether in schools, or lecture-rooms, etc., is corrupted in its source. For it is not a matter of indifference by what motives or means one is led to a good purpose (the obedience to duty). However disgusting, then, *metaphysics* may appear to those pretended philosophers who dogmatize *oracularly,* or even brilliantly, about the doctrine of duty, it is, nevertheless, an indispensable duty for those who oppose it to go back to its principles even in ethics, and to begin by going to school on its benches.

We may fairly wonder how, after all previous explanations of the principles of duty, so far as it is derived from pure reason, it was still possible to reduce it again to a *doctrine of happiness;* in such a way, however, that a certain *moral* happiness not resting on empirical causes was ultimately arrived at, a self-contradictory nonentity. In fact, when the thinking man has conquered the temptations to vice, and is conscious of having done his (often hard) duty, he finds himself in a state of peace and satisfaction which may well be called *happiness,* in which virtue is her own reward. Now, says the eudaemonist, this delight, this happiness, is the real motive of his acting virtuously. The notion of duty, says he, does not *immediately* determine his will; it is only by *means of* the happiness in prospect that he is moved to his duty. Now, on the other hand, since he can promise himself this reward of virtue only from the consciousness of having done his duty, it is clear that the latter must have preceded: that is, he must feel himself bound to do his duty before he thinks, and without thinking, that happiness will be the consequence of obedience to duty. He is thus involved in a *circle* in his *assignment of cause and effect.* He can only hope to be *happy* if he is conscious of his obedience to duty: and he can only be moved to obedience to duty if he foresees that he will thereby become happy. But in this reasoning there is also a *contradiction.* For, on the one side, he must obey his duty, without asking what effect this will have on his happiness, consequently, from a *moral* principle; on the other side, he can only recognize something as his duty when he can reckon on happiness which will accrue to him thereby, and consequently on a *pathological* principle, which is the direct opposite of the former.

I have in another place (the Berlin *Monatsschrift*[1]), reduced, as I believe, to the simplest expressions the distinction between *pathological* and *moral* pleasure. The pleasure, namely, *which must precede* the obedience to the law in order that one may act according to the law is *pathological,* and the process follows the *physical order of nature;* that which must *be preceded by* the law in order that it may be felt is in the *moral order.* If this distinction is not observed; if *eudaemonism* (the principle of happiness) is adopted as the principle instead of *eleutheronomy* (the principle of freedom of the inner legislation), the consequence is the *euthanasia* (quiet death) of all morality.

The cause of these mistakes is no other than the following: Those who are accustomed only to physiological explanations will not admit into their heads the categorical imperative from which these laws dictatorially proceed, notwithstanding that they feel themselves irresistibly forced by it. Dissatisfied at not being able to *explain* what lies wholly beyond that sphere, namely, *freedom* of the elective will, elevating as is this privilege, that man has of being capable of such an *idea.* They are stirred up by the proud claims of speculative reason, which feels its power so strongly in the fields, just as if they were allies leagued in defence of the omnipotence of theoretical reason and roused by a general call to arms to resist that idea; and thus they are at present, and perhaps for a long time to come, though ultimately in vain, to attack the moral concept of freedom and if possible render it doubtful.

1 [The essay referred to is that "On the Radical Evil in Human Nature."]

INTRODUCTION *to the Metaphysical Elements of Ethics*

ETHICS in ancient times signified *moral philosophy* (*philosophia moralis*) generally, which was also called the *doctrine of duties.* Subsequently it was found advisable to confine this name to a part of moral philosophy, namely, to the doctrine of duties which are not subject to external laws (for which in German the name *Tugendlehre* was found suitable). Thus the system of general deontology is divided into that of *jurisprudence* (*jurisprudentia*), which is capable of external laws, and of ethics, which is not thus capable, and we may let this division stand.

I. *Exposition of the Conception of Ethics*

The *notion of duty* is in itself already the notion of a *constraint* of the free elective will by the law; whether this constraint be an *external* one or be *self-constraint.* The moral *imperative,* by its categorical (the unconditional *ought*) anounces this constraint, which therefore does ot apply to all rational beings (for there may lso be *holy* beings), but applies to men as *ra-ional physical beings* who are unholy enough to e seduced by pleasure to the transgression of he moral law, although they themselves recog-ize its authority; and when they do obey it, to bey it *unwillingly* (with resistance of their in-lination); and it is in this that the constraint roperly consists.[1] Now, as man is a *free* moral) being, the notion of duty can contain nly *self-constraint* (by the idea of the law it-elf), when we look to the internal determina-ion of the will (the spring), for thus only is it ossible to combine that *constraint* (even if it vere external) with the freedom of the elective vill. The notion of duty then must be an ethical ne.

The impulses of nature, then, contain *hin-rances* to the fulfilment of duty in the mind of nan, and resisting forces, some of them power-ul; and he must judge himself able to combat hese and to conquer them by means of reason, ot in the future, but in the present, simulta-eously with the thought; he must judge that he *an* do what the law unconditionally commands hat he *ought*.

Now the power and resolved purpose to resist strong but unjust opponent is called *fortitude fortitudo*), and when concerned with the oppo-ent of the moral character *within us*, it is *vir-ue* (*virtus, fortitudo moralis*). Accordingly, eneral deontology, in that part which brings ot external, but internal, freedom under laws s the *doctrine of virtue*.

Jurisprudence had to do only with the *formal* ondition of external freedom (the condition f consistency with itself, if its maxim became universal law), that is, with *law*. Ethics, on he contrary, supplies us with a *matter* (an ob-ect of the free elective will), an *end* of pure eason which is at the same time conceived as n objectively necessary end, i.e., as duty for all men. For, as the sensible inclinations mislead us to ends (which are the matter of the elec-tive will) that may contradict duty, the legis-lating reason cannot otherwise guard against their influence than by an opposite moral end, which therefore must be given *a priori* inde-pendently on inclination.

An *end* is an object of the elective will (of a rational being) by the idea of which this will is determined to an action for the production of this object. Now I may be forced by others to actions which are directed to an end as means, but I cannot be forced *to have an end;* I can only *make* something an end to myself. If, how-ever, I am also bound to make something which lies in the notions of practical reason an end to myself, and therefore besides the formal deter-mining principle of the elective will (as con-tained in law) to have also a material principle, an end which can be opposed to the end derived from sensible impulses; then this gives the no-tion of an *end which is in itself a duty*. The doc-trine of this cannot belong to jurisprudence, but to ethics, since this alone includes in its conception *self-constraint* according to moral laws.

For this reason, ethics may also be defined as the system of the *ends* of the pure practical reason. The two parts of moral philosophy are distinguished as treating resepectively of ends and of duties of constraint. That ethics contains duties to the observance of which one cannot be (physically) forced by others, is merely the consequence of this, that it is a doctrine of *ends*, since to be *forced* to have ends or to set them before one's self is a contradiction.

Now that ethics is a *doctrine of virtue* (*doc-trina officiorum virtutis*) follows from the defi-nition of virtue given above compared with the obligation, the peculiarity of which has just been shown. There is in fact no other determi-nation of the elective will, except that to an *end*, which in the very notion of it implies that I cannot even *physically* be forced to it by the *elective will* of others. Another may indeed *force* me to do something which is not my end (but only means to the end of another), but he cannot force me to *make it my own end*, and yet I can have no end except of my own mak-ing. The latter supposition would be a con-tradiction—an act of freedom which yet at the same time would not be free. But there is no contradiction in setting before one's self an end which is also a duty: for in this case I constrain myself, and this is quite consistent with free-

[1] Man, however, *as at the same time a moral being*, hen he considers himself objectively, which he is quali-ed to do by his pure practical reason, (i.e., according) *humanity* in his own person), finds himself holy nough to transgress the law only *unwillingly;* for there no man so depraved who in this transgression would ot feel a resistance and an abhorrence of himself, so nat he must put a force on himself. It is impossible to xplain the phenomenon that at this parting of the ways where the beautiful fable places Hercules between vir-ie and sensuality) man shows more propensity to obey nclination than the law. For, we can only explain what appens by tracing it to a cause according to physical ws; but then we should not be able to conceive the lective will as free. Now this mutually opposed self-onstraint and the inevitability of it makes us recognize ie incomprehensible property of *freedom*.

dom.[1] But how is such an end possible? That is now the question. For the possibility of the notion of the thing (viz., that it is not self-contradictory) is not enough to prove the possibility of the thing itself (the objective reality of the notion).

II. *Exposition of the Notion of an End which is also a Duty*

We can conceive the relation of end to duty in two ways; either starting from the end to find the maxim of the dutiful actions; or conversely, setting out from this to find the end which is also duty. Jurisprudence proceeds in the former way. It is left to everyone's free elective will what end he will choose for his action. But its maxim is determined *a priori;* namely, that the freedom of the agent must be consistent with the freedom of every other according to a universal law.

Ethics, however, proceeds in the opposite way. It cannot start from the ends which the man may propose to himself, and hence give directions as to the maxims he should adopt, that is, as to his duty; for that would be to take empirical principles of maxims, and these could not give any notion of duty; since this, the categorical *ought,* has its root in pure reason alone. Indeed, if the maxims were to be adopted in accordance with those ends (which are all selfish), we could not properly speak of the notion of duty at all. Hence in ethics the *notion of duty* must lead to ends, and must on moral principles give the foundation of *maxims* with respect to the ends which we *ought* to propose to ourselves.

Setting aside the question what sort of end that is which is in itself a duty, and how such an end is possible, it is here only necessary to show that a duty of this kind is called a *duty of virtue,* and why it is so called.

To every duty corresponds a right of action (*facultas moralis generatim*), but all duties do not imply a corresponding *right* (*facultas juridica*) of another to compel any one, but only the duties called *legal duties.* Similarly to all ethical *obligation* corresponds the notion of virtue, but it does not follow that all ethical duties are duties of virtue. Those, in fact, are not s which do not concern so much a certain en (matter, object of the elective will), but merel that which is *formal* in the moral determinatio of the will (e.g., that the dutiful action mus also be done *from duty*). It is only an *end whic is also duty* that can be called a *duty of virtu* Hence there are several of the latter kind (an thus there are distinct virtues); on the contrary, there is only one duty of the forme kind, but it is one which is valid for all action (only one virtuous disposition).

The duty of virtue is essentially distinguished from the duty of justice in this respect that it is morally possible to be externally compelled to the latter, whereas the former rests o free self-constraint only. For finite *holy* being (which cannot even be tempted to the violatio of duty) there is no doctrine of virtue, but onl moral philosophy, the latter being an autonom of practical reason, whereas the former is als an *autocracy* of it. That is, it includes a consciousness—not indeed immediately perceived but rightly concluded, from the moral categorical imperative—of the *power* to become maste of one's inclinations which resist the law; s that human morality in its highest stage can ye be nothing more than virtue; even if it wer quite pure (perfectly free from the influence o a spring foreign to duty), a state which is poetically personified under the name of the *wis man* (as an ideal to which one should continually approximate).

Virtue, however, is not to be defined and esteemed merely as *habit,* and (as it is expresse in the prize essay of Cochius) as a long *custon* acquired by practice of morally good action For, if this is not an effect of well-resolved an firm principles ever more and more purified then, like any other mechanical arrangemen brought about by technical practical reason, i is neither armed for all circumstances nor adequately secured against the change that ma be wrought by new allurements.

REMARK

To virtue = + *a* is opposed as its *logical contradictory* (*contradictorie oppositum*) the *negative lack of virtue* (moral weakness) = 0; bu vice = − *a* is its *contrary* (*contrarie s. realite oppositum*); and it is not merely a needles question but an offensive one to ask whethe great *crimes* do not perhaps demand mor strength of mind than great virtues. For b strength of mind we understand the strength o purpose of a man, as a being endowed with free

[1] The less a man can be physically forced, and the more he can be morally forced (by the mere idea of duty), so much the freer he is. The man, for example, who is of sufficiently firm resolution and strong mind not to give up an enjoyment which he has resolved on, however much loss is shown as resulting therefrom, and who yet desists from his purpose unhesitatingly, though very reluctantly, when he finds that it would cause him to neglect an official duty or a sick father; this man proves his freedom in the highest degree by this very thing, that he cannot resist the voice of duty.

om, and consequently so far as he is master of imself (in his senses) and therefore in a *ealthy* condition of mind. But great crimes are aroxysms, the very sight of which makes the ıan of healthy mind shudder. The question vould therefore be something like this: whether man in a fit of madness can have more physi-al strength than if he is in his senses; and we ıay admit this, without on that account ascrib-ıg to him more strength of mind, if by mind ve understand the vital principle of man in the ree use of his powers. For since those crimes ave their ground merely in the power of the ıclinations that *weaken* reason, which does not rove strength of mind, this question would be early the same as the question whether a man ı a fit of illness can show more strength than ı a healthy condition; and this may be directly enied, since the want of health, which consists ı the proper balance of all the bodily forces of he man, is a weakness in the system of these orces, by which system alone we can estimate bsolute health.

III. *Of the Reason for conceiving an End which is also a Duty*

An *end* is an *object* of the free elective will, he idea of which determines this will to an ac-ion by which the object is produced. Accord-ıgly every action has its end, and as no one an have an end without *himself* making the ob-ect of his elective will his end, hence to have ome end of actions is an act of the *freedom* f the agent, not an affect of *physical nature.* Jow, since this act which determines an end is practical principle which commands not the ıeans (therefore not conditionally) but the nd itself (therefore unconditionally), hence it s a categorical imperative of pure practical rea-on and one, therefore, which combines *a con-ept of duty* with that of an end in general.

Now there must be such an end and a categor-cal imperative corresponding to it. For since here are free actions, there must also be ends o which as an object those actions are directed. mongst these ends there must also be some vhich are at the same time (that is, by their ery notion) duties. For if there were none uch, then since no actions can be without an nd, all ends which practical reason might have vould be valid only as means to other ends, and *categorical* imperative would be impossible; a upposition which destroys all moral philosophy.

Here, therefore, we treat not of ends which ıan actually *makes* to himself in accordance with the sensible impulses of his nature, but of objects of the free elective will under its own laws—objects which he *ought to make* his end. We may call the former technical (subjective), properly pragmatical, including the rules of prudence in the choice of its ends; but the latter we must call the moral (objective) doctrine of ends. This distinction is, however, superfluous here, since moral philosophy already by its very notion is clearly separated from the doctrine of physical nature (in the present instance, anthropology). The latter resting on empirical principles, whereas the moral doctrine of ends which treats of duties rests on principles given *a priori* in pure practical reason.

IV. *What are the Ends which are also Duties?*

They are: A. Our own Perfection, B. Happiness of Others.

We cannot invert these and make on one side our own happiness, and on the other the perfection of others, ends which should be in themselves duties for the same person.

For *one's own happiness* is, no doubt, an end that all men have (by virtue of the impulse of their nature), but this end cannot without contradiction be regarded as a duty. What a man of himself inevitably wills does not come under the notion of *duty,* for this is a *constraint* to an end reluctantly adopted. It is, therefore, a contradiction to say that a man *is in duty bound* to advance his own happiness with all his power.

It is likewise a contradiction to make the *perfection* of another my end, and to regard myself as in duty bound to promote it. For it is just in this that the *perfection* of another man as a person consists, namely, that he is able *of himself* to set before him his own end according to his own notions of duty; and it is a contradiction to require (to make it a duty for me) that I should do something which no other but himself can do.

V. *Explanation of these two Notions*

A. Our own Perfection

The word *perfection* is liable to many misconceptions. It is sometimes understood as a notion belonging to transcendental philosophy; viz., the notion of the *totality* of the manifold which taken together constitutes a thing; sometimes, again, it is understood as belonging to *teleology,* so that it signifies the correspondence of the properties of a thing to an *end.* Perfection in the former sense might be called *quantitative* (material), in the latter *qualitative* (formal) perfection. The former can be one only, for the whole of what belongs to the one thing is one. But of the latter there may be several in one thing; and it is of the latter property that we here treat.

When it is said of the perfection that belongs to man generally (properly speaking, to humanity), that it is in itself a duty to make this our end, it must be placed in that which may be the effect of one's *deed,* not in that which is merely an endowment for which we have to thank nature; for otherwise it would not be duty. Consequently, it can be nothing else than the *cultivation* of one's *power* (or natural capacity) and also of one's *will* (moral disposition) to satisfy the requirement of duty in general. The supreme element in the former (the power) is the understanding, it being the faculty of concepts, and, therefore, also of those concepts which refer to duty. First it is his duty to labour to raise himself out of the rudeness of his nature, out of his animal nature more and more to humanity, by which alone he is capable of setting before him ends to supply the defects of his ignorance by instruction, and to correct his errors; he is not merely *counselled* to do this by reason as technically practical, with a view to his purposes of other kinds (as art), but reason, as morally practical, absolutely *commands* him to do it, and makes this end his duty, in order that he may be worthy of the humanity that dwells in him. Secondly, to carry the cultivation of his *will* up to the purest virtuous disposition, that, namely, in which the *law* is also the spring of his dutiful actions, and to obey it from duty, for this is internal morally practical perfection. This is called the *moral sense* (as it were a special *sense, sensus moralis*), because it is a feeling of the effect which the legislative will within himself exercises on the faculty of acting accordingly. This is, indeed, often misused fanatically, as though (like the genius of Socrates) it preceded reason, or even could dispense with judgement of reason; but still it is a moral perfection, making every special end, which is also a duty, one's own end.

B. Happiness of Others

It is inevitable for human nature that a man should wish and seek for happiness, that is, satisfaction with his condition, with certainty of the continuance of this satisfaction. But for this very reason it is not an end that is also a duty. Some writers still make a distinction between moral and physical happiness (the former consisting in satisfaction with one's person and moral behaviour, that is, with what one *does* the other in satisfaction with that which natur confers, consequently with what one *enjoys* a a foreign gift). Without at present censurin the misuse of the word (which even involves contradiction), it must be observed that th feeling of the former belongs solely to the pre ceding head, namely, perfection. For he who i to feel himself happy in the mere consciousnes of his uprightness already possesses that per fection which in the previous section was de fined as that end which is also duty.

If happiness, then, is in question, which it i to be my duty to promote as my end, it must b the happiness of *other* men *whose* (permitted *end I hereby make also mine.* It still remain left to themselves to decide what they sha reckon as belonging to their happiness; onl that it is in my power to decline many thing which *they* so reckon, but which I do not so re gard, supposing that they have no right to de mand it from me as their own. A plausible ob jection often advanced against the division o duties above adopted consists in setting ove against that end a supposed obligation to stud my *own* (physical) happiness, and thus makin this, which is my natural and merely subjectiv end, my duty (and objective end). This re quires to be cleared up.

Adversity, pain, and want are great tempta tions to transgression of one's duty; according ly it would seem that strength, health, a com petence, and welfare generally, which are op posed to that influence, may also be regarde as ends that are also duties; that is, that it is duty to promote *our own* happiness not merel to make that of others our end. But in that cas the end is not happiness but the morality of th agent; and happiness is only the means of re moving the hindrances to morality; *permitte* means, since no one has a right to demand fron me the sacrifice of my not immoral ends. It i not directly a duty to seek a competence for one' self; but indirectly it may be so; namely, in or der to guard against poverty which is a grea temptation to vice. But then it is not my happi ness but my morality, to maintain which in it integrity is at once my end and my duty.

VI. *Ethics does not supply Laws for Action (which is done by Jurisprudence), but only for the Maxims of Action*

The notion of duty stands in immediate rela tion to a *law* (even though I abstract from ev ery end which is the matter of the law); as i shown by the formal principle of duty in th categorical imperative: "Act so that the maxims of thy action might become a universal *law*." But in ethics this is conceived as the law of *thy own will*, not of will in general, which might be that of others; for in the latter case it would give rise to a judicial duty which does not belong to the domain of ethics. In ethics, maxims are regarded as those subjective laws which merely have the specific character of universal legislation, which is only a negative principle (not to contradict a law in general). How, then, can there be further a law for the maxims of actions?

It is the notion of an *end* which is also a duty, a notion peculiar to ethics, that alone is the foundation of a law for the maxims of actions; by making the subjective end (that which every one has) subordinate to the objective end (that which every one ought to make his own). The imperative: "Thou shalt make this or that thy end (e. g., the happiness of others)" applies to the matter of the elective will (an object). Now since no free action is possible, without the agent having in view in it some end (as matter of his elective will), it follows that, if there is an end which is also a duty, the maxims of actions which are means to ends must contain only the condition of fitness for a possible universal legislation: on the other hand, the end which is also a duty can make it a law that we should have such a maxim, whilst for the maxim itself the possibility of agreeing with a universal legislation is sufficient.

For maxims of actions may be *arbitrary*, and are only limited by the condition of fitness for a universal legislation, which is the formal principle of actions. But a *law* abolishes the arbitrary character of actions, and is by this distinguished from *recommendation* (in which one only desires to know the best means to an end).

VII. *Ethical Duties are of indeterminate, Juridical Duties of strict, Obligation*

This proposition is a consequence of the foregoing; for if the law can only command the maxim of the actions, not the actions themselves, this is a sign that it leaves in the observance of it a latitude (*latitudo*) for the elective will; that is, it cannot definitely assign how and how much we should do by the action towards the end which is also duty. But by an indeterminate duty is not meant a permission to make exceptions from the maxim of the actions, but only the permission to limit one maxim of duty by another (e. g., the general love of our neighbour by the love of parents); and this in fact enlarges the field for the practice of virtue. The more indeterminate the duty, and the more imperfect accordingly the obligation of the man to the action, and the closer he nevertheless brings this maxim of obedience thereto (in his own mind) to the *strict* duty (of justice), so much the more perfect is his virtuous action.

Hence it is only imperfect duties that are *duties of virtue*. The fulfilment of them is *merit* (*meritum*) $= + a$; but their transgression is not necessarily *demerit* (*demeritum*) $= - a$, but only moral *unworth* $= 0$, unless the agent made it a principle not to conform to those duties. The strength of purpose in the former case is alone properly called *virtue* [*Tugend*] (*virtus*); the weakness in the latter case is not *vice* (*vitium*), but rather only *lack of virtue* [*Untugend*], a want of moral strength (*defectus moralis*). (As the word *Tugend* is derived from *taugen* [to be good for something], *Untugend* by its etymology signifies good for nothing.) Every action contrary to duty is called *transgression* (*peccatum*). Deliberate transgression which has become a principle is what properly constitutes what is called *vice* (*vitium*).

Although the conformity of actions to justice (i.e., to be an upright man) is nothing meritorious, yet the conformity of the maxim of such actions regarded as duties, that is, *reverence* for justice is *meritorious*. For by this the man makes the right of humanity or of men *his own end*, and thereby enlarges his notion of duty beyond that of *indebtedness* (*officium debiti*), since although another man by virtue of his rights can demand that my actions shall conform to the law, he cannot demand that the law shall also contain the spring of these actions. The same thing is true of the general ethical command, "Act dutifully from a sense of duty." To fix this disposition firmly in one's mind and to quicken it is, as in the former case, *meritorious*, because it goes beyond the law of duty in actions and makes the law in itself the spring.

But just for this reason, those duties also must be reckoned as of indeterminate obligation, in respect of which there exists a subjective principle which ethically *rewards* them; or to bring them as near as possible to the notion of a strict obligation, a principle of susceptibility of this reward according to the law of virtue; namely, a moral pleasure which goes beyond mere satisfaction with oneself (which may be merely negative), and of which it is proudly said that in this consciousness virtue is its own reward.

When this merit is a merit of the man in respect of other men of promoting their natural ends, which are recognized as such by all men (making their happiness his own), we might call it the *sweet merit,* the consciousness of which creates a moral enjoyment in which men are by sympathy inclined to *revel;* whereas the *bitter merit* of promoting the true welfare of other men, even though they should not recognize it as such (in the case of the unthankful and ungrateful), has commonly no such reaction, but only produces a *satisfaction* with one's self, although in the latter case this would be even greater.

VIII. *Exposition of the Duties of Virtue as Intermediate Duties*

(1) OUR OWN PERFECTION as an end which is also a duty

(*a*) Physical perfection; that is, *cultivation* of all our faculties generally for the promotion of the ends set before us by reason. That this is a duty, and therefore an end in itself, and that the effort to effect this even without regard to the advantage that it secures us, is based, not on a conditional (pragmatic), but an unconditional (moral) imperative, may be seen from the following consideration. The power of proposing to ourselves an end is the characteristic of humanity (as distinguished from the brutes). With the end of humanity in our own person is therefore combined the rational will, and consequently the duty of deserving well of humanity by culture generally, by acquiring or advancing the *power* to carry out all sorts of possible ends, so far as this power is to be found in man; that is, it is a duty to cultivate the crude capacities of our nature, since it is by that cultivation that the animal is raised to man, therefore it is a duty in itself.

This duty, however, is merely ethical, that is, of indeterminate obligation. No principle of reason prescribes how far one must go in this effort (in enlarging or correcting his faculty of understanding, that is, in acquisition of knowledge or technical capacity); and besides the difference in the circumstances into which men may come makes the choice of the kind of employment for which he should cultivate his talent very arbitrary. Here, therefore, there is no law of reason for actions, but only for the maxim of actions, viz.: "Cultivate thy faculties of mind and body so as to be effective for all ends that may come in thy way, uncertain which of them may become thy own."

(*b*) *Cultivation of Morality* in ourselves. The greatest moral perfection of man is to do his duty, and that *from duty* (that the law be not only the rule but also the spring of his actions). Now at first sight this seems to be a *strict* obligation, and as if the principle of duty commanded not merely the *legality* of every action, but also the *morality,* i.e., the mental disposition with the exactness and strictness of a law; but in fact the law commands even here only the *maxim of the action,* namely, that we should seek the ground of obligation, not in the sensible impulses (advantage or disadvantage), but wholly in the law; so that the action itself is not commanded. For it is not possible to man to see so far into the depth of his own heart that he could ever be thoroughly certain of the purity of his moral purpose and the sincerity of his mind even in *one single action,* although he has no doubt about the legality of it. Nay, often the weakness which deters a man from the risk of a crime is regarded by him as virtue (which gives the notion of strength). And how many there are who may have led a long blameless life, who are only *fortunate* in having escaped so many temptations. How much of the element of pure morality in their mental disposition may have belonged to each deed remains hidden even from themselves.

Accordingly, this duty to estimate the worth of one's actions not merely by their legality, but also by their morality (mental disposition), is only of *indeterminate* obligation; the law does not command this internal action in the human mind itself, but only the maxim of the action, namely, that we should strive with all our power that for all dutiful actions the thought of duty should be of itself an adequate spring.

(2) HAPPINESS OF OTHERS as an end which is also a duty

(*a*) *Physical Welfare. Benevolent wishes* may be unlimited, for they do not imply doing anything. But the case is more difficult with *benevolent action,* especially when this is to be done, not from friendly inclination (love) to others, but from duty, at the expense of the sacrifice and mortification of many of our appetites. That this beneficence is a duty results from this: that since our self-love cannot be separated from the need to be loved by others (to obtain help from them in case of necessity), we therefore make ourselves an end for others; and this maxim can never be obligatory except by having the specific character of a universal law, and consequently by means of a will that we should also make others our ends. Hence the happiness of others is an end that is also a duty.

I am only bound then to sacrifice to others a

part of my welfare without hope of recompense; because it is my duty, and it is impossible to assign definite limits how far that may go. Much depends on what would be the true want of each according to his own feelings, and it must be left to each to determine this for himself. For that one should sacrifice his own happiness, his true wants, in order to promote that of others, would be a self-contradictory maxim if made a universal law. This duty, therefore, is only *indeterminate;* it has a certain latitude within which one may do more or less without our being able to assign its limits definitely. The law holds only for the *maxims,* not for definite actions.

(b) Moral well-being of others (*salus moralis*) also belongs to the happiness of others, which it is our duty to promote, but only a negative duty. The pain that a man feels from remorse of conscience, although its origin is moral, is yet in its operation physical, like grief, fear, and every other diseased condition. To take care that he should not be deservedly smitten by this inward reproach is not indeed *my* duty but *his* business; nevertheless, it is my duty to do nothing which by the nature of man might seduce him to that for which his conscience may hereafter torment him, that is, it is my duty not to give him *occasion of stumbling.* But there are no definite limits within which this care for the moral satisfaction of others must be kept; therefore it involves only an indeterminate obligation.

IX. *What is a Duty of Virtue?*

Virtue is the strength of the man's maxim in his obedience to duty. All strength is known only by the obstacles that it can overcome; and in the case of virtue the obstacles are the natural inclinations which may come into conflict with the moral purpose; and as it is the man who himself puts these obstacles in the way of his maxims, hence virtue is not merely a self-constraint (for that might be an effort of one inclination to constrain another), but is also a constraint according to a principle of inward freedom, and therefore by the mere idea of duty, according to its formal law.

All duties involve a notion of *necessitation* by the law, and *ethical* duties involve a necessitation for which only an internal legislation is possible; juridical duties, on the other hand, one for which external legislation also is possible. Both, therefore, include the notion of constraint, either self-constraint or constraint by others. The moral power of the former is virtue, and the action springing from such a disposition (from reverence for the law) may be called a *virtuous* action (ethical), although the law expresses a juridical duty. For it is the doctrine of virtue that commands us to regard the rights of men as holy.

But it does not follow that everything the doing of which is virtue, is, properly speaking, a *duty of virtue.* The former may concern merely the *form* of the maxims; the latter applies to the *matter* of them, namely, to an *end* which is also conceived as duty. Now, as the ethical obligation to ends, of which there may be many, is only *indeterminate,* because it contains only a law for the maxim of actions, and the end is the matter (object) of elective will; hence there are many duties, differing according to the difference of lawful ends, which may be called *duties of virtue* (*officia honestatis*), just because they are subject only to free self-constraint, not to the constraint of other men, and determine the end which is also a duty.

Virtue, being a coincidence of the rational will, with every duty firmly settled in the character, is, like everything *formal,* only one and the same. But, as regards the *end* of actions, which is also duty, that is, as regards the matter which one *ought* to make an *end,* there may be several virtues; and as the obligation to its maxim is called a *duty of virtue,* it follows that there are also several duties of virtue.

The supreme principle of ethics (the doctrine of virtue) is: "Act on a maxim, the *ends* of which are such as it might be a universal law for everyone to have." On this principle a man is an end to himself as well as others, and it is not enough that he is not permitted to use either himself or others merely as means (which would imply that he might be indifferent to them), but it is in itself a duty of every man to make mankind in general his end.

The principle of ethics being a categorical imperative does not admit of proof, but it admits of a justification from principles of pure practical reason. Whatever in relation to mankind, to oneself, and others, *can* be an end, that *is* an end for pure practical reason: for this is a faculty of assigning ends in general; and to be indifferent to them, that is, to take no interest in them, is a contradiction; since in that case it would not determine the maxims of actions (which always involve an end), and consequently would cease to be practical reasons. Pure reason, however, cannot command any ends *a priori,* except so far as it declares the same to be also a duty, which duty is then called a *duty of virtue.*

X. *The Supreme Principle of Jurisprudence was Analytical; that of Ethics is Synthetical*

That external constraint, so far as it withstands that which hinders the external freedom that agrees with general laws (as an obstacle of the obstacle thereto), can be consistent with ends generally, is clear on the principle of contradiction, and I need not go beyond the notion of freedom in order to see it, let the end which each may be what he will. Accordingly, the supreme *principle of jurisprudence* is an analytical principle.[1] On the contrary the principle of ethics goes beyond the notion of external freedom and, by general laws, connects further with it an *end* which it makes a *duty*. This principle, therefore, is synthetic. The possibility of it is contained in the deduction (§ ix).

This enlargement of the notion of duty beyond that of external freedom and of its limitation by the merely formal condition of its constant harmony; this, I say, in which, instead of constraint from without, there is set up freedom *within*, the power of self-constraint, and that not by the help of other inclinations, but by pure practical reason (which scorns all such help), consists in this fact, which raises it above juridical duty; that by it *ends* are proposed from which jurisprudence altogether abstracts. In the case of the moral imperative, and the supposition of freedom which it necessarily involves, the *law*, the *power* (to fulfil it) and the *rational will* that determines the maxim, constitute all the elements that form the notion of juridical duty. But in the imperative, which commands the duty of virtue, there is added, besides the notion of self-constraint, that of an *end;* not one that we have, but that we ought to have, which, therefore, pure practical reason has in itself, whose highest, unconditional end (which, however, continues to be duty) consists in this: that virtue is its own end and, by deserving well of men, is also its own reward. Herein it shines so brightly as an ideal to human perceptions, it seems to cast in the shade even *holiness* itself, which is never tempted to transgression.[2] This, however, is an illusion arising from the fact that as we have no measure for the degree of strength, except the greatness of the obstacles which might have been overcome (which in our case are the inclinations), we are led to mistake the *subjective* conditions of estimation of a magnitude for the objective conditions of the magnitude itself. But when compared with *human ends,* all of which have their obstacles to be overcome, it is true that the worth of virtue itself, which is its own end, far outweighs the worth of all the utility and all the empirical ends and advantages which it may have as consequences.

We may, indeed, say that man is obliged to virtue (as a moral strength). For although the power (*facultas*) to overcome all imposing sensible impulses by virtue of his freedom can and must be *presupposed,* yet this power regarded as strength (*robur*) is something that must be acquired by the moral *spring* (the idea of the law) being elevated by contemplation of the dignity of the pure law of reason in us, and at the same time also by *exercise.*

XI. *According to the preceding Principles, the Scheme of Duties of Virtue may be thus exhibited*

The Material Element of the Duty of Virtue

Internal Duty of Virtue	1 *My Own End,* which is also my Duty (My own *Perfection*)	2 The *End of Others,* the promotion of which is also my Duty (The *Happiness* of Others)	External Duty of Virtue
	3 The *Law* which is also Spring On which the *Morality*	4 The *End* which is also Spring On which the *Legality*	

of every free determination of will rests

The Formal Element of the Duty of Virtue

XII. *Preliminary Notions of the Susceptibility of the Mind for Notions of Duty generally*

These are such moral qualities as, when a man does not possess them, he is not bound to acquire them. They are: the *moral feeling, conscience, love of one's neighbour,* and *respect for ourselves* (*self-esteem*). There is no obligation to have these, since they are *subjective* conditions of susceptibility for the notion of duty, not objective conditions of morality. They are all *sensitive* and antecedent, but natural capacities of mind (*prædispositio*) to be affected by notions of duty; capacities which it cannot be regarded as a duty to have, but which every man has, and by virtue of which he can be brought under obligation. The consciousness of them is not of empirical origin, but can only follow on that of a moral law, as an effect of the same on the mind.

[1] [Cf. *Science of Right,* p. 398.]

[2] So that one might vary two well-known lines of Haller thus:

> ***With all his failings, man is still***
> ***Better than angels void of will.***

A. The Moral Feeling

This is the susceptibility for pleasure or displeasure, merely from the consciousness of the agreement or disagreement of our action with the law of duty. Now, every determination of the elective will proceeds *from* the idea of the possible action *through* the feeling of pleasure or displeasure in taking an interest in it or its effect *to* the deed; and here the *sensitive* state (the affection of the internal sense) is either a *pathological* or a *moral* feeling. The former is the feeling that precedes the idea of the law, the latter that which may follow it.

Now it cannot be a duty to have a moral feeling, or to acquire it; for all consciousness of obligation supposes this feeling in order that one may become conscious of the necessitation that lies in the notion of duty; but every man (as a moral being) has it originally in himself; the obligation, then, can only extend to the *cultivation* of it and the strengthening of it even by admiration of its inscrutable origin; and this is effected by showing how it is just, by the mere conception of reason, that it is excited most strongly, in its own purity and apart from every pathological stimulus; and it is improper to call this feeling a moral *sense;* for the word *sense* generally means a theoretical power of perception directed to an object; whereas the moral feeling (like pleasure and displeasure in general) is something merely subjective, which supplies no knowledge. No man is wholly destitute of moral feeling, for if he were totally unsusceptible of this sensation he would be morally dead; and, to speak in the language of physicians, if the moral vital force could no longer produce any effect on this feeling, then his humanity would be dissolved (as it were by chemical laws) into mere animality and be irrevocably confounded with the mass of other physical beings. But we have no special *sense* for (moral) good and evil any more than for *truth,* although such expressions are often used; but we have a *susceptibility* of the free elective will for being moved by pure practical reason and its law; and it is this that we call the *moral feeling.*

B. Of Conscience

Similarly, conscience is not a thing to be acquired, and it is not a duty to acquire it; but every man, as a moral being, has it originally within him. To be bound to have a conscience would be as much as to say to be under a duty to recognize duties. For conscience is practical reason which, in every case of law, holds before a man his duty for acquittal or condemnation; consequently it does not refer to an object, but only to the subject (affecting the moral feeling by its own act); so that it is an inevitable fact, not an obligation and duty. When, therefore, it is said, "This man *has* no conscience," what is meant is that he pays no heed to its dictates. For if he really had none, he would not take credit to himself for anything done according to duty, nor reproach himself with violation of duty, and therefore he would be unable even to conceive the duty of having a conscience.

I pass by the manifold subdivisions of conscience, and only observe what follows from what has just been said, namely, that there is no such thing as an *erring* conscience. No doubt it is possible sometimes to err in the objective judgement whether something is a duty or not; but I cannot err in the subjective whether I have compared it with my practical (here judicially acting) reason for the purpose of that judgement: for if I erred I would not have exercised practical judgement at all, and in that case there is neither truth nor error. *Unconscientiousness* is not want of conscience, but the propensity not to heed its judgement. But when a man is conscious of having acted according to his conscience, then, as far as regards guilt or innocence, nothing more can be required of him, only he is bound to enlighten his *understanding* as to what is duty or not; but when it comes or has come to action, then conscience speaks involuntarily and inevitably. To act conscientiously can, therefore, not be a duty, since otherwise it would be necessary to have a second conscience, in order to be conscious of the act of the first.

The duty here is only to cultivate our conscience, to quicken our attention to the voice of the internal judge, and to use all means to secure obedience to it, and is thus our indirect duty.[1]

C. Of Love to Men

Love is a matter of *feeling,* not of will or volition, and I cannot love because I *will* to do so, still less because I *ought* (I cannot be necessitated to love); hence there is no such thing as a *duty to love. Benevolence,* however (*amor benevolentiæ*), as a mode of action, may be subject to a law of duty. Disinterested benevolence is often called (though very improperly) *love;* even where the happiness of the other is not concerned, but the complete and free surrender of all one's own ends to the ends of another (even a superhuman) being, love is spoken of as

[1] [Cf. Note on Conscience, p. 379.]

being also our duty. But all duty is *necessitation* or constraint, although it may be self-constraint according to a law. But what is done from constraint is not done from love.

It is a duty *to do good* to other men according to our power, whether we love them or not, and this duty loses nothing of its weight, although we must make the sad remark that our species, alas! is not such as to be found particularly worthy of love when we know it more closely. *Hatred of men,* however, is always hateful: even though without any active hostility it consists only in complete aversion from mankind (the solitary misanthropy). For benevolence still remains a duty even towards the manhater, whom one cannot love, but to whom we can show kindness.

To hate vice in men is neither duty nor against duty, but a mere feeling of horror of vice, the will having no influence on the feeling nor the feeling on the will. *Beneficence* is a duty. He who often practises this, and sees his beneficent purpose succeed, comes at last really to love him whom he has benefited. When, therefore, it is said: "Thou shalt *love* thy neighbour as thyself," this does not mean, "Thou shalt first of all love, and by means of this love (in the next place) do him good"; but: "*Do good* to thy neighbour, and this beneficence will produce in thee the love of men (as a settled habit of inclination to beneficence)."

The love of *complacency* (*amor complacentiæ*) would therefore alone be direct. This is a pleasure immediately connected with the idea of the existence of an object, and to have a duty to this, that is, to be necessitated to find pleasure in a thing, is a contradiction.

D. Of Respect

Respect (*reverentia*) is likewise something merely subjective; a feeling of a peculiar kind not a judgement about an object which it would be a duty to effect or to advance. For if considered as duty it could only be conceived as such by means of the *respect* which we have for it. To have a duty to this, therefore, would be as much as to say to be bound in duty to have a duty. When, therefore, it is said: "Man has a *duty* of *self-esteem*," this is improperly stated, and we ought rather to say: "The law within him inevitably forces from him *respect* for his own being, and this feeling (which is of a peculiar kind) is a basis of certain duties, that is, of certain actions which may be consistent with his duty to himself." But we cannot say that he has a duty of respect for himself; for he must have respect for the law within himself, in order to be able to conceive duty at all.

XIII. *General Principles of the Metaphysics of Morals in the treatment of* Pure *Ethics*

First. A duty can have only a *single* ground of obligation; and if two or more proofs of it are adduced, this is a certain mark that either no valid proof has yet been given, or that there are several distinct duties which have been regarded as one.

For all moral proofs, being philosophical, can only be drawn by means of rational knowledge *from concepts,* not like mathematics, through the construction of concepts. The latter science admits a variety of proofs of one and the same theorem; because in *intuition a priori* there may be several properties of an object, all of which lead back to the very same principle. If, for instance, to prove the duty of veracity, an argument is drawn first from the *harm* that a lie causes to other men; another from the *worthlessness* of a liar and the violation of his own self-respect, what is proved in the former argument is a duty of benevolence, not of veracity, that is to say, not the duty which required to be proved, but a different one. Now, if, in giving a variety of proofs for one and the same theorem, we flatter ourselves that the multitude of reasons will compensate the lack of weight in each taken separately, this is a very unphilosophical resource, since it betrays trickery and dishonesty; for several insufficient proofs placed *beside one another* do not produce certainty, nor even probability. They should *advance* as reason and consequence *in a series,* up to the sufficient reason, and it is only in this way that they can have the force of proof. Yet the former is the usual device of the rhetorician.

Secondly. The difference between virtue and vice cannot be sought in the *degree* in which certain maxims are followed, but only in the specific *quality* of the maxims (their relation to the law). In other words, the vaunted principle of Aristotle, that virtue is the *mean* between two vices, is false.[1] For instance, suppose that

[1] The common classical formulae of ethics—*medio tutissimus ibis; omne mimium vertitur in vitium; est modus in rebus,* etc., *medium tenuere beati; virtus est medium vitiorum et utrinque reductum*—["You will go most safely in the middle" (Virgil); "Every excess develops into a vice"; "There is a mean in all things, etc." (Horace); "Happy they who steadily pursue a middle course"; "Virtue is the mean between two vices and equally removed from either" (Horace).]—contain a poor sort of wisdom, which has no definite principles; for this mean between two extremes, who will assign it

good management is given as the *mean* between two vices, prodigality and avarice; then its origin as a virtue can neither be defined as the gradual diminution of the former vice (by saving), nor as the increase of the expenses of the miserly. These vices, in fact, cannot be viewed as if they, proceeding as it were in opposite directions, met together in good management; but each of them has its own maxim, which necessarily contradicts that of the other.

For the same reason, no vice can be defined as an *excess* in the practice of certain actions beyond what is proper (e.g., *Prodigalitas est excessus in consumendis opibus*); or, as a less exercise of them than is fitting (*Avaritia est defectus,* etc.). For since in this way the *degree* is left quite undefined, and the question whether conduct accords with duty or not, turns wholly on this, such an account is of no use as a definition.

Thirdly. Ethical virtue must not be estimated by the power we attribute to man of fulfilling the law; but, conversely, the moral power must be estimated by the law, which commands categorically; not, therefore, by the empirical knowledge that we have of men as they are, but by the rational knowledge how, according to the ideas of humanity, they ought to be. These three maxims of the scientific treatment of ethics are opposed to the older apophthegms:

1. There is only one virtue and only one vice.
2. Virtue is the observance of the mean path between two opposite vices.
3. Virtue (like prudence) must be learned from experience.

XIV. *Of Virtue in General*

Virtue signifies a moral strength of will. But this does not exhaust the notion; for such strength might also belong to a *holy* (superhuman) being, in whom no opposing impulse counteracts the law of his rational will; who therefore willingly does everything in accordance with the law. Virtue then is the moral strength of a *man's* will in his obedience to *duty;* and this is a moral *necessitation* by his own law giving reason, inasmuch as this constitutes itself a power *executing* the law. It is not itself a duty, nor is it a duty to possess it (otherwise we should be in duty bound to have a duty), but it commands, and accompanies its command with a moral constraint (one possible by laws of internal freedom). But since this should be irresistible, strength is requisite, and the degree of this strength can be estimated only by the magnitude of the hindrances which man creates for himself, by his inclinations. Vices, the brood of unlawful dispositions, are the monsters that he has to combat; wherefore this moral strength as *fortitude* (*fortitudo moralis*) constitutes the greatest and only true martial glory of man; it is also called the true *wisdom,* namely, the practical, because it makes the *ultimate end* of the existence of man on earth its own end. Its possession alone makes man free, healthy, rich, a king, etc., nor can either chance or fate deprive him of this, since he possesses himself, and the virtuous cannot lose his virtue.

All the encomiums bestowed on the ideal of humanity in its moral perfection can lose nothing of their practical reality by the examples of what men now are, have been, or will probably be hereafter; *anthropology* which proceeds from mere empirical knowledge cannot impair *anthroponomy* which is erected by the unconditionally legislating reason; and although virtue may now and then be called meritorious (in relation to men, not to the law), and be worthy of reward, yet in itself, as it is its own end, so also it must be regarded as its own reward.

Virtue considered in its complete perfection is, therefore, regarded not as if man possessed virtue, but as if virtue possessed the man, since in the former case it would appear as though he had still had the choice (for which he would then require another virtue, in order to select virtue from all other wares offered to him). To conceive a plurality of virtues (as we unavoidably must) is nothing else but to conceive various moral objects to which the (rational) will is led by the single principle of virtue; and it is the same with the opposite vices. The expression which personifies both is a contrivance for affecting the sensibility, pointing, however, to a moral sense. Hence it follows that an aesthetic of morals is not a part, but a subjective exposition of the Metaphysic of Morals; in which the emotions that accompany the necessitating force of the moral law make the efficiency of that force to be felt; for example: disgust, horror, etc., which gives a sensible form to the moral aversion in order to gain the precedence from the *merely* sensible incitement.

---

for me? Avarice (as a vice) is not distinguished from frugality (as a virtue) by merely being the latter pushed too far; but has a quite *different principle* (maxim), namely placing the end of economy not in the enjoyment of one's means, but in the mere *possession* of them, renouncing enjoyment; just as the vice of *prodigality* is not to be sought in the excessive enjoyment of one's means, but in the bad maxim which makes the use of them, without regard to their maintenance, the sole end.

XV. *Of the Principle on which Ethics is separated from Jurisprudence*

This separation on which the subdivision of *moral philosophy* in general rests, is founded on this: that the notion of *freedom*, which is common to both, makes it necessary to divide duties into those of external and those of internal freedom; the latter of which alone are ethical. Hence this internal freedom which is the condition of all *ethical duty* must be discussed as a preliminary *(discursus præliminaris)*, just as above the doctrine of conscience was discussed as the condition of all duty.

REMARKS

Of the Doctrine of Virtue on the Principle of Internal Freedom

Habit (*habitus*) is a facility of action and a subjective perfection of the *elective will*. But not every such *facility* is a *free habit* (*habitus libertatis*); for if it is *custom* (*assuetudo*), that is, a uniformity of action which, by frequent repetition, has become a *necessity*, then it is not a habit proceeding from freedom, and therefore not a moral habit. Virtue therefore cannot be *defined* as a habit of free law-abiding actions, unless indeed we add "determining itself in its action by the idea of the law"; and then this habit is not a property of the elective will, but of the *rational will*, which is a faculty that in adopting a rule also declares it to be a universal law, and it is only such a habit that can be reckoned as virtue. Two things are required for internal freedom: to be *master* of oneself in a given case *(animus sui compos)* and to have *command* over oneself (*imperium in semetipsum*), that is to *subdue* his emotions and to *govern* his passions. With these conditions, the *character* (*indoles*) is *noble* (*erecta*); in the opposite case, it is ignoble (*indoles abjecta serva*).

XVI. *Virtue requires, first of all, Command over Oneself*

Emotions and *passions* are essentially distinct; the former belong to *feeling* in so far as this coming before reflection makes it more difficult or even impossible. Hence emotion is called *hasty* (*animus præceps*). And reason declares through the notion of virtue that a man should *collect* himself; but this weakness in the life of one's understanding, joined with the strength of a mental excitement, is only a *lack of virtue* (*Untugend*), and as it were a weak and childish thing, which may very well consist with the best will, and has further this one good thing in it, that this storm soon subsides. A propensity to emotion (e. g., *resentment*) is therefore not so closely related to vice as passion is. *Passion*, on the other hand, is the sensible *appetite* grown into a permanent inclination (e. g., *hatred* in contrast to *resentment*). The calmness with which one indulges it leaves room for reflection and allows the mind to frame principles thereon for itself; and thus when the inclination falls upon what contradicts the law, to brood on it, to allow it to root itself deeply, and thereby to take up evil (as of set purpose) into one's maxim; and this is then specifically evil, that is, it is a true *vice*.

Virtue, therefore, in so far as it is based on internal freedom, contains a positive command for man, namely, that he should bring all his powers and inclinations under his rule (that of reason); and this is a positive precept of command over himself which is additional to the prohibition, namely, that he should not allow himself to be governed by his feelings and inclinations (the duty of *apathy*); since, unless reason takes the reins of government into its own hands, the feelings and inclinations play the master over the man.

XVII. *Virtue necessarily presupposes Apathy (considered as Strength)*

This word (apathy) has come into bad repute, just as if it meant *want of feeling*, and therefore subjective indifference with respect to the objects of the elective will; it is supposed to be a weakness. This misconception may be avoided by giving the name *moral apathy* to that want of emotion which is to be distinguished from indifference. In the former, the feelings arising from sensible impressions lose their influence on the moral feeling only because the respect for the law is more powerful than all of them together. It is only the apparent strength of a fever patient that makes even the lively sympathy with *good* rise to an emotion, or rather degenerate into it. Such an emotion is called *enthusiasm*, and it is with reference to this that we are to explain the *moderation* which is usually recommended in virtuous practices:

> *Insani sapiens nomen ferat, æquus uniqui*
> Ultra quam satis est *virtutem si petat ipsam.*[1]

For otherwise it is absurd to imagine that one could be *too wise* or *too virtuous*. The emotion

[1] Horace. ["Let the wise man bear the name of fool, and the just of unjust, if he pursue virtue herself beyond the proper bounds."]

always belongs to the sensibility, no matter by what sort of object it may be excited. The true strength of virtue is the *mind at rest,* with a firm, deliberate resolution to bring its law into practice. That is the state of *health* in the moral life; on the contrary, the emotion, even when it is excited by the idea of the *good,* is a momentary glitter which leaves exhaustion after it. We may apply the term *fantastically virtuous* to the man who will admit nothing to be *indifferent* in respect of morality (*adiaphora*), and who strews all his steps with duties, as with traps, and will not allow it to be indifferent whether a man eats fish or flesh, drink beer or wine, when both agree with him; a micrology which, if adopted into the doctrine of virtue, would make its rule a tyranny.

REMARK

Virtue is always in *progress,* and yet always begins *from the beginning.* The former follows from the fact that, *objectively* considered, it is an ideal and unattainable, and yet it is a duty constantly to approximate to it. The second is founded *subjectively* on the nature of man which is affected by inclinations, under the influence of which virtue, with its maxims adopted once for all, can never settle in a position of rest; but, if it is not rising, inevitably falls; because moral maxims cannot, like technical, be based on custom (for this belongs to the physical character of the determination of will); but even if the practice of them become a custom, the agent would thereby lose the *freedom* in the choice of his maxims, which freedom is the character of an action done from duty.

ON CONSCIENCE[1]

The consciousness of an internal *tribunal* in man (before which "his thoughts accuse or excuse one another") is CONSCIENCE.

Every man has a conscience, and finds himself observed by an inward judge which threatens and keeps him in awe (reverence combined with fear); and this power which watches over the laws within him is not something which he himself (arbitrarily) *makes,* but it is incorporated in his being. It follows him like his shadow, when he thinks to escape. He may indeed stupefy himself with pleasures and distractions, but cannot avoid now and then coming to himself or awaking, and then he at once perceives its awful voice. In his utmost depravity, he may, indeed, pay no attention to it, but he cannot avoid *hearing* it.

Now this original intellectual and (as a conception of duty) moral capacity, called *conscience,* has this peculiarity in it, that although its business is a business of man with himself, yet he finds himself compelled by his reason to transact it as if at the command *of another person.* For the transaction here is the conduct of a *trial* (*causa*) before a tribunal. But that he who is *accused* by his conscience should be conceived as *one* and *the same person* with the judge is an absurd conception of a judicial court; for then the complainant would always lose his case. Therefore, in all duties the conscience of the man must regard *another* than himself as the judge of his actions, if it is to avoid self-contradiction. Now this other may be an actual or a merely ideal person which reason frames to itself.[2] Such an idealized person (the authorized judge of conscience) must be one who knows the heart; for the tribunal is set up in the *inward part* of man; at the same time he must also be *all-obliging,* that is, must be or be conceived as a person in respect of whom all duties are to be regarded as his commands; since conscience is the inward judge of all free actions. Now, since such a moral being must at the same time possess all power (in heaven and earth), since otherwise he could not give his commands their proper effect (which the office of judge necessarily requires), and since such a moral being possessing power over all is called GOD, hence conscience must be conceived as the subjective principle of a responsibility for one's deeds before God; nay, this latter concept is contained (though it be only obscurely) in every moral self-consciousness.

[1] Not part of original text. From *Tugendlehre,* p. 293ff.

[2] [In a foot-note, Kant explains this double personality of a man as both the accuser and the judge, by reference to the *homo noumenon* and its specific difference from the rationally endowed *homo sensibilis.*]

CONTENTS

GENERAL INTRODUCTION TO THE METAPHYSIC OF MORALS

GENERAL DIVISIONS OF THE METAPHYSIC OF MORALS

I. DIVISION OF THE METAPHYSIC OF MORALS AS A SYSTEM OF DUTIES GENERALLY

1. All duties are either duties of right, that is, *juridical duties* (*officia juris*), or duties of virtue, that is, *ethical duties* (*officia virtutis s. ethica*). Juridical duties are such as may be promulgated by external legislation; ethical duties are those for which such legislation is not possible. The reason why the latter cannot be properly made the subject of external legislation is because they relate to an end or final purpose, which is itself, at the same time, embraced in these duties, and which it is a duty for the individual to have as such. But no external legislation can cause any one to adopt a particular intention, or to propose to himself a certain purpose; for this depends upon an internal condition or act of the mind itself. However, external actions conducive to such a mental condition may be commanded, without its being implied that the individual will of necessity make them an end to himself.

But why, then, it may be asked, is the science of morals, or moral philosophy, commonly entitled—especially by Cicero—the science of *duty* and not also the science of *right*, since duties and rights refer to each other? The reason is this. We know our own freedom—from which all moral laws and consequently all rights as well as all duties arise—only through the moral imperative, which is an immediate injunction of duty; whereas the conception of right as a ground of putting others under obligation has afterwards to be developed out of it.

2. In the doctrine of duty, man may and ought to be represented in accordance with the nature of his faculty of freedom, which is entirely supra-sensible. He is, therefore, to be represented purely according to his humanity as a personality independent of physical determinations (*homo noumenon*), in distinction from the same person as a man modified with these determinations (*homo phenomenon*). Hence the conceptions of right and end when referred to duty, in view of this twofold quality, give the following division:

DIVISION OF THE METAPHYSIC OF MORALS ACCORDING TO THE OBJECTIVE RELATION OF THE LAW OF DUTY

I. *Juridical Duties*	Oneself to or Others	I. *The Right of Humanity* in our own person (juridical duties towards oneself)	*Perfect Duty*
		II. *The Right of Mankind* in others (juridical duties towards others)	
II. *Ethical Duties*	Oneself to or Others	III. *The End of Humanity* in our person (ethical duties towards oneself)	*Imperfect Duty*
		IV. *The End of Mankind* in others (ethical duties towards others)	

II. DIVISION OF THE METAPHYSIC OF MORALS ACCORDING TO RELATIONS OF OBLIGATION

As the subjects between whom a relation of right and duty is apprehended—whether it actually exists or not—admit of being conceived in various juridical relations to each other, another division may be proposed from this point of view, as follows:

DIVISION POSSIBLE ACCORDING TO THE SUBJECTIVE RELATION OF THOSE WHO BIND UNDER OBLIGATIONS, AND THOSE WHO ARE BOUND UNDER OBLIGATIONS

1.

The juridical relation of man to beings *who have neither right nor duty:*

Vacat. There is no such relation, for such beings are irrational, and they neither put us under obligation, nor can we be put under obligation by them.

2.

The juridical relation of man to beings *who have both rights and duties:*

Adest. There is such a relation, for it is the relation of men to men.

3.

The juridical relation of man to beings *who have only duties and no rights:*

Vacat. There is no such relation, for such beings would be men without juridical personality, as slaves of bondsmen.

4.

The juridical relation of man to a being *who has only rights and no duties (God):*

Vacat. There is no such relation in mere philosophy, because such a being is not an object of possible experience.

A *real* relation between right and duty is therefore found, in this scheme, only in No. 2. The reason why such is not likewise found in No. 4 is because it would constitute a *transcendent* duty, that is, one to which no corresponding subject can be given that is external and capable of imposing obligation. Consequently the relation from the theoretical point of view is here merely *ideal;* that is, it is a relation to an object of thought which we form for ourselves. But the conception of this object is not entirely *empty*. On the contrary, it is a fruitful conception in relation to ourselves and the maxims of our inner morality, and therefore in relation to practice generally. And it is in this bearing that all the duty involved and practicable for us in such a merely ideal relation lies.

III. DIVISION OF THE METAPHYSIC OF MORALS AS A SYSTEM OF DUTIES GENERALLY

According to the constituent principles and the method of the system

I. *Principles*
- I. *Duties of Right*
  - I. *Private Right*
  - II. *Public Right*
- II. *Duties of Virtue, etc.* And so on, including all that refers not only to the materials, but also to the architectonic form of a scientific system of morals, when the metaphysical investigation of the elements has completely traced out the universal principles constituting the whole.

II. *Method*
- I. *Didactics*
- II. *Ascetics*

GENERAL INTRODUCTION TO THE METAPHYSIC OF MORALS

I. THE RELATION OF THE FACULTIES OF THE HUMAN MIND TO THE MORAL LAWS

THE *active faculty of the human mind,* as the faculty of desire in its widest sense, is the power which man has, through his mental representations, of becoming the cause of objects corresponding to these representations. The capacity of a being to act in conformity with his own representations is what constitutes the life of such a being.

It is to be observed, *first,* that with desire or aversion there is always connected *pleasure* or *pain,* the susceptibility for which is called *feeling.* But the converse does not always hold; for there may be a pleasure connected, not with the desire of an object, but with a mere mental representation, it being indifferent whether an object corresponding to the representation exist or not. And *second,* the pleasure or pain connected with the object of desire does not always precede the activity of desire; nor can it be regarded in every case as the cause, but it may as well be the effect of that activity. The capacity of experiencing pleasure or pain on the occasion of a mental representation is called "feeling," because pleasure and pain contain only what is *subjective* in the relations of our mental activity. They do not involve any relation to an object that could possibly furnish a knowledge of it as such; they cannot even give us a knowledge of our own mental state. For even sensations,[1] considered apart from the qualities which attach to them on account of the modifications of the subject—as, for instance, in reference to red, sweet, and such like—are referred as constituent elements of knowledge to objects, whereas pleasure or pain felt in connection with what is red or sweet express absolutely nothing that is in the object, but merely a relation to the subject. And for the reason just stated, pleasure and pain considered in themselves cannot be more precisely defined. All that can be further done with regard to them is merely to point out what consequences they may have in certain relations, in order to make the knowledge of them available practically.

The pleasure which is necessarily connected with the activity of desire, when the representation of the object desired affects the capacity of feeling, may be called *practical pleasure.* And this designation is applicable whether the pleasure is the cause or the effect of the desire. On the other hand, that pleasure which is not necessarily connected with the desire of an object, and which, therefore, is not a pleasure in the existence of the object, but is merely attached to a mental representation alone, may be called inactive complacency, or mere *contemplative pleasure.* The feeling of this latter kind of pleasure is what is called *taste.* Hence, in a system of practical philosophy, the contemplative pleasure of taste will not be discussed as an essential constituent conception, but need only be referred to incidentally or episodically. But as regards *practical* pleasure, it is otherwise. For the determination of the activity of the faculty of desire or appetency, which is necessarily preceded by this pleasure as its cause, is what properly constitutes *desire* in the strict sense of the term. Habitual desire, again, constitutes *inclination;* and the connection of pleasure with the

[1] The sensibility as the faculty of sense may be defined by reference to the subjective nature of our representations generally. It is the understanding that first refers the subjective representations to an object; it alone *thinks* anything by means of these representations. Now, the subjective nature of our representations might be of such a kind that they could be related to objects so as to furnish knowledge of them, either in regard to their form or matter—in the former relation by pure *perception,* in the latter by *sensation* proper. In this case, the sense-faculty, as the capacity for receiving objective representations, would be properly called *sense-perception.* But mere mental representation from its subjective nature cannot, in fact, become a constituent of objective knowledge, because it contains merely the relation of the representations to the subject, and includes nothing that can be used for attaining a knowledge of the object. In this case, then, this receptivity of the mind for subjective representations is called *feeling.* It includes the effect of the representations, whether sensible or intellectual, upon the subject; and it belongs to the sensibility, although the representation itself may belong to the understanding or the reason.

activity of desire, in so far as this connection is judged by the understanding to be valid according to a general rule holding good at least for the individual, is what is called *interest.* Hence, in such a case, the practical pleasure is an interest of the inclination of the individual. On the other hand, if the pleasure can only follow a preceding determination of the faculty of desire, it is an *intellectual pleasure,* and the interest in the object must be called a rational interest; for were the interest sensuous, and not based only upon pure principles of reason, sensation would necessarily be conjoined with the pleasure, and would thus determine the activity of the desire. Where an entirely pure interest of reason must be assumed, it is not legitimate to introduce into it an interest of inclination surreptitiously. However, in order to conform so far with the common phraseology, we may allow the application of the term "inclination" even to that which can only be the object of an "intellectual" pleasure in the sense of a habitual desire arising from a pure interest of reason. But such inclination would have to be viewed, not as the cause, but as the effect of the rational interest; and we might call it the *non-sensuous* or *rational inclination* (*propensio intellectualis*). Further, *concupiscence* is to be distinguished from the activity of desire itself, as a stimulus or incitement to its determination. It is always a sensuous state of the mind, which does not itself attain to the definiteness of an act of the power of desire.

The activity of the faculty of desire may proceed in accordance with conceptions; and in so far as the principle thus determining it to action is found in the mind, and not in its object, it constitutes *a power of acting or not acting according to liking.* In so far as the activity is accompanied with the consciousness of the power of the action to produce the object, it forms an act of *choice;* if this consciousness is not conjoined with it, the activity is called a *wish.* The faculty of desire, in so far as its inner principle of determination as the ground of its liking or predilection lies in the reason of the subject, constitutes the *will.* The will is therefore the faculty of active desire or appetency, viewed not so much in relation to the action—which is the relation of the act of choice—as rather in relation to the principle that determines the power of choice to the action. It has, in itself, properly no special principle of determination, but in so far as it may determine the voluntary act of choice, it is the *practical reason* itself.

Under the will, taken generally, may be included the volitional act of *choice,* and also the mere act of *wish,* in so far as reason may determine the faculty of desire in its activity. The act of choice that can be determined by *pure reason* constitutes the act of free-will. That act which is determinable only by inclination as a sensuous impulse or stimulus would be irrational brute choice (*arbitrium brutum*). The human act of choice, however, as human, is in fact *affected* by such impulses or stimuli, but is not *determined* by them; and it is, therefore, not pure in itself when taken apart from the acquired habit of determination by reason. But it may be determined to action by the pure will. The *freedom* of the act of volitional choice is its independence of being *determined* by sensuous impulses or stimuli. This forms the *negative* conception of the free-will. The *positive* conception of freedom is given by the fact that the will is the capability of pure reason to be practical of itself. But this is not possible otherwise than by the maxim of every action being subjected to the condition of being practicable as a universal law. Applied as pure reason to the act of choice, and considered apart from its objects, it may be regarded as the *faculty of principles;* and, in this connection, it is the source of *practical principles.* Hence it is to be viewed as a lawgiving faculty. But as the *material* upon which to construct a law is not furnished to it, it can only make the *form* of the maxim of the act of will, in so far as it is available as a universal law, the supreme law and determining principle of the will. And as the maxims, or rules of human action derived from subjective causes, do not of themselves necessarily agree with those that are objective and universal, reason can only prescribe this supreme law as an absolute imperative of prohibition or command.

The laws of freedom, as distinguished from the laws of nature, are *moral* laws. So far as they refer only to external actions and their lawfulness, they are called *juridical;* but if they also require that, as laws, they shall themselves be the determining principles of our actions, they are *ethical.* The agreement of an action with juridical laws is its *legality;* the agreement of an action with ethical laws is its *morality.* The freedom to which the former laws refer, can only be freedom in external practice; but the freedom to which the latter laws refer is freedom in the internal as well as the external exercise of the activity of the will in so far as it is determined by laws of reason. So, in theoretical philosophy, it is said that only the objects of the external senses are in space, but all the objects both of internal and external sense are in time; because the representations of both, as being representations, so far belong all to the internal sense. In like manner, whether freedom is viewed in reference to the external or the internal action of the will, its laws, as pure practical laws of reason for the free activity of the will generally, must at the same time be inner principles for its determination, although they may not always be considered in this relation.

II. THE IDEA AND NECESSITY OF A METAPHYSIC OF MORALS

It has been shown in *The Metaphysical Principles of the Science of Nature* that there must be principles *a priori* for the natural science that has to deal with the objects of the external senses. And it was further shown that it is possible, and even necessary, to formulate a system of these principles under the name of a "metaphysical science of nature," as a preliminary to experimental physics regarded as natural science applied to particular objects of experience. But this latter science, if care be taken to keep its generalizations free from error, may accept many propositions as universal on the evidence of experience, although if the term "universal" be taken in its strict sense, these would necessarily have to be deduced by the metaphysical science from principles *a priori*. Thus Newton accepted the principle of the equality of action and reaction as established by experience, and yet he extended it as a universal law over the whole of material nature. The chemists go even farther, grounding their most general laws regarding the combination and decomposition of the materials of bodies wholly upon experience; and yet they trust so completely to the universality and necessity of those laws that they have no anxiety as to any error being found in propositions founded upon experiments conducted in accordance with them.

But it is otherwise with *moral laws*. These, in contradistinction to natural laws, are only valid *as* laws, in so far as they can be rationally established *a priori* and comprehended as *necessary*. In fact, conceptions and judgements regarding ourselves and our conduct have no *moral* significance, if they contain only what may be learned from experience; and when any one is, so to speak, misled into making a moral principle out of anything derived from this latter source, he is already in danger of falling into the coarsest and most fatal errors.

If the philosophy of morals were nothing more than a theory of happiness (*eudaemonism*), it would be absurd to search after principles *a priori* as a foundation for it. For however plausible it may sound to say that reason, even prior to experience, can comprehend by what means we may attain to a lasting enjoyment of the real pleasures of life, yet all that is taught on this subject *a priori* is either tautological, or is assumed wholly without foundation. It is only experience that can show what will bring us enjoyment. The natural impulses directed towards nourishment, the sexual instinct, or the tendency to rest and motion, as well as the higher desires of honour, the acquisition of knowledge, and such like, as developed with our natural capacities, are alone capable of showing in what those enjoyments are to be *found*. And, further, the knowledge thus acquired is available for each individual merely in his own way; and it is only thus he can learn the means by which he has to *seek* those enjoyments. All specious rationalizing *a priori*, in this connection, is nothing at bottom but carrying facts of experience up to generalizations by induction (*secundum principia generalia non universalia*); and the generality thus attained is still so limited that numberless exceptions must be allowed to every individual in order that he may adapt the choice of his mode of life to his own particular inclinations and his capacity for pleasure. And, after all, the individual has really to acquire his prudence at the cost of his own suffering or that of his neighbors.

But it is quite otherwise with the principles of morality. They lay down commands for every one without regard to his particular inclinations, and merely because and so far as he is free, and has a practical reason. Instruction in the laws of morality is not drawn from observation of oneself or of our animal nature, nor from perception of the course of the world in regard to what happens, or how men act.[1] But reason commands how we *ought* to act, even al-

[1] This holds notwithstanding the fact that the term "morals," in Latin *mores*, and in German *sitten*, signifies originally only *manners* or *mode of life*.

though no example of such action were to be found; nor does reason give any regard to the advantage which may accrue to us by so acting, and which experience could alone actually show. For, although reason allows us to seek what is for our advantage in every possible way, and although, founding upon the evidence of experience, it may further promise that greater advantages will probably follow on the average from the observance of her commands than from their transgression, especially if prudence guides the conduct, yet the authority of her precepts as *commands* does not rest on such considerations. They are used by reason only as counsels, and by way of a counterpoise against seductions to an opposite course, when adjusting beforehand the equilibrium of a partial balance in the sphere of practical judgement, in order thereby to secure the decision of this judgement, according to the due weight of the *a priori* principles of a pure practical reason.

Metaphysics designates any system of knowledge *a priori* that consists of pure conceptions. Accordingly, a practical philosophy not having nature, but the freedom of the will for its object, will presuppose and require a *metaphysic of morals*. It is even a *duty* to have such a metaphysic; and every man does, indeed, possess it in himself, although commonly but in an obscure way. For how could any one believe that he has a source of universal law in himself, without principles *a priori?* And just as in a metaphysics of nature there must be principles regulating the application of the universal supreme principles of nature to objects of experience, so there cannot but be such principles in the metaphysic of morals; and we will often have to deal objectively with the particular *nature* of man as known only by experience, in order to show in it the consequences of these universal moral principles. But this mode of dealing with these principles in their particular applications will in no way detract from their rational purity, or throw doubt on their *a priori* origin. In other words, this amounts to saying that a metaphysic of morals cannot be founded on anthropology as the empirical science of man, but may be applied to it.

The counterpart of a metaphysic of morals, and the other member of the division of practical philosophy, would be a *moral anthropology*, as the empirical science of the moral nature of man. This science would contain only the subjective conditions that hinder or favor the *realization* in practice of the universal moral laws in human nature, with the means of propagating, spreading, and strengthening the moral principles—as by the education of the young and the instruction of the people—and all other such doctrines and precepts founded upon experience and indispensable in themselves, although they must neither precede the metaphysical investigation of the principles of reason, nor be mixed up with it. For, by doing so, there would be a great danger of laying down false, or at least very flexible moral laws, which would hold forth as unattainable what is not attached only because the law has not been comprehended and presented in its purity, in which also its strength consists. Or, otherwise, spurious and mixed motives might be adopted instead of what is dutiful and good in itself; and these would furnish no certain moral principles either for the guidance of the judgement or for the discipline of the heart in the practice of duty. It is only by pure reason, therefore, that duty can and must be prescribed.

The higher division of philosophy, under which the division just mentioned stands, is into *theoretical philosophy* and *practical philosophy*. Practical philosophy is just moral philosophy in its widest sense, as has been explained elsewhere.[1] All that is practicable and possible, according to natural laws, is the special subject of the activity of art, and its precepts and rules entirely depend on the theory of nature. It is only what is practicable according to laws of freedom that can have principles independent of theory, for there is no theory in relation to what passes beyond the determinations of nature. Philosophy therefore cannot embrace under its practical division a *technical* theory, but only a *morally practical* doctrine. But if the dexterity of the will in acting according to laws of freedom, in contradistinction to nature, were to be also called an *art*, it would necessarily indicate an art which would make a system of freedom possible like the system of nature. This would truly be a Divine art, if we were in a position by means of it to realize completely what reason prescribes to us, and to put the idea into practice.

[1] In the *Critique of Judgement* (1790).

III. THE DIVISION OF A METAPHYSIC OF MORALS

All *legislation,* whether relating to internal or external action, and whether prescribed *a priori* by mere reason or laid down by the will of another, involves *two elements: First,* a *law* which represents the action that ought to happen as necessary *objectively,* thus making the action a duty; *second,* a *motive* which connects the principle determining the will to this action with the mental representation of the law *subjectively,* so that the law makes duty the motive of the action. By the first element, the action is represented as a duty, in accordance with the mere theoretical knowledge of the possibility of determining the activity of the will by practical rules. By the second element, the obligation so to act is connected in the subject with a determining principle of the will as such. All legislation, therefore, may be differentiated by reference to its motive-principle.[1] The legislation which makes an action a duty, and this duty at the same time a motive, is *ethical.* That legislation which does not include the motive-principle in the law, and consequently admits another motive than the idea of duty itself, is *juridical.* In respect of the latter, it is evident that the motives distinct from the idea of duty, to which it may refer, must be drawn from the subjective (pathological) influences of inclination and of aversion, determining the voluntary activity, and especially from the latter; because it is a legislation which has to be compulsory, and not merely a mode of attracting or persuading. The agreement or non-agreement of an action with the law, without reference to its motive, is its *legality;* and that character of the action in which the idea of duty arising from the law at the same time forms the motive of the action, is its *morality.*

Duties specially in accord with a juridical legislation can only be external duties. For this mode of legislation does not require that the idea of the duty, which is internal, shall be of itself the determining principle of the act of will; and as it requires a motive suitable to the nature of its laws, it can only connect what is external with the law. Ethical legislation, on the other hand, makes internal actions also duties, but not to the exclusion of the external, for it embraces everything which is of the nature of duty. And just because ethical legislation includes within its law the internal motive of the action as contained in the idea of duty, it involves a characteristic which cannot at all enter into the legislation that is external. Hence, ethical legislation cannot as such be external, not even when proceeding from a Divine will, although it may receive duties which rest on an external legislation *as duties,* into the position of motives, within its own legislation.

From what has been said, it is evident that all duties, merely because they are duties, belong to *ethics;* and yet the legislation upon which they are founded is not on that account in all cases contained in ethics. On the contrary, the law of many of them lies outside of ethics. Thus ethics commands that I must fulfil a promise entered into by contract, although the other party might not be able to compel me to do so. It adopts the law (*pacta sunt servanda*) and the duty corresponding to it, from *jurisprudence* or the science of right, by which they are established. It is not in ethics, therefore, but in jurisprudence, that the principle of the legislation lies, that "promises made and accepted must be kept." Accordingly, ethics specially teaches that if the motive-principle of external compulsion which juridical legislation connects with a duty is even let go, the idea of duty alone is sufficient of itself as a motive. For were it not so, and were the legislation itself not juridical, and consequently the duty arising from it not specially a duty of right as distinguished from a duty of virtue, then fidelity in the performance of acts, to which the individual may be bound by the terms of a contract, would have to be classified with acts of benevolence and the obligation that underlies them, which cannot be correct. To keep one's promise is not properly a duty of virtue, but a duty of right, and the performance of it can be enforced by external compulsion. But to keep one's promise, even when no compulsion can be *applied* to enforce it, is, at the same time, a virtuous action, and a proof of virtue. Jurisprudence as the science of right, and ethics as the science of virtue, are therefore distinguished not so much by their different duties, as rather by the difference of the legislation which connects the one or the other kind of motive with their laws.

Ethical legislation is that which *cannot* be external, although the duties it prescribes *may* be external as well as internal. Juridical legislation is that which may also be external. Thus

[1] This ground of division will apply, although the action which it makes a duty may coincide with another action that may be otherwise looked at from another point of view. For instance, actions may in all cases be classified as external.

it is an external duty to keep a promise entered into by contract; but the injunction to do this merely because it is a duty, without regard to any other motive, belongs exclusively to the *internal* legislation. It does not belong thus to the ethical sphere as being a particular kind of duty or a particular mode of action to which we are bound—for it is an external duty in ethics as well as in jurisprudence—but it is because the legislation in the case referred to is internal, and cannot have an external lawgiver, that the obligation is reckoned as belonging to ethics. For the same reason, the duties of benevolence, although they are external duties as obligations to external actions, are, in like manner, reckoned as belonging to ethics, because they can only be enjoined by legislation that is internal. Ethics has no doubt its own peculiar duties—such as those towards oneself—but it has also duties in common with jurisprudence, only not under the same mode of *obligation.* In short, the peculiarity of ethical legislation is to enjoin the performance of certain actions merely because they are duties, and to make the principle of duty itself—whatever be its source or occasion—the sole sufficing motive of the activity of the will. Thus, then, there are many *ethical* duties that are *directly* such; and the inner legislation also makes the others—all and each of them—*indirectly* ethical.

The *deduction* of the division of a system is the proof of its completeness as well as of its continuity, so that there may be a logical transition from the general conception divided to the members of the division, and through the whole series of the subdivisions without any break or leap in the arrangement (*divisio per saltum*). Such a division is one of the most difficult conditions for the architect of a system to fulfil. There is even some doubt as to what is the *highest conception* that is primarily divided into *right* and *wrong* (*aut fas aut nefas*). It is assuredly the conception of the activity of the free-will in general. In like manner, the expounders of ontology start from *something* and *nothing,* without perceiving that these are already members of a division for which the highest divided conception is awanting, and which can be no other than that of *thing* in general.

IV. GENERAL PRELIMINARY CONCEPTIONS DEFINED AND EXPLAINED

(Philosophia practica universalis)

The conception of *freedom* is a conception of pure reason. It is therefore *transcendent* in so far as regards *theoretical* philosophy; for it is a conception for which no corresponding instance or example can be found or supplied in any possible experience. Accordingly freedom is not presented as an object of any theoretical knowledge that is possible for us. It is in no respect a constitutive, but only a regulative conception; and it can be accepted by the speculative reason as at most a merely negative principle. In the practical sphere of reason, however, the reality of freedom may be demonstrated by certain practical principles which, as laws, prove a causality of the pure reason in the process of determining the activity of the will that is independent of all empirical and sensible conditions. And thus there is established the fact of a pure will existing in us as the source of all moral conceptions and laws.

On this positive conception of freedom in the practical relation certain unconditional practical laws are founded, and they specially constitute *moral laws.* In relation to us as human beings, with an activity of will modified by sensible influences so as not to be conformable to the pure will, but as often contrary to it, these laws appear as *imperatives* commanding or prohibiting certain actions; and as such they are *categorical* or *unconditional imperatives.* Their categorical and unconditional character distinguishes them from the *technical imperatives* which express the prescriptions of art, and which always command only conditionally. According to these categorical imperatives, certain actions are *allowed* or *disallowed* as being morally possible or impossible; and certain of them or their opposites are morally necessary and obligatory. Hence, in reference to such actions, there arises the conception of a duty whose observance or transgression is accompanied with a pleasure or pain of a peculiar kind, known as moral feeling. We do not, however, take the moral feelings or sentiments into account in considering the practical laws of reason. For they do not form the foundation or principle of practical laws of reason, but only the subjective *effects* that arise in the mind on the occasion of our voluntary activity being determined by these laws. And while they neither add to nor take from the objective validity or influence of the moral laws in the judgement of reason, such sentiments may vary according to the differences of the individuals who experience them.

The following conceptions are common to jurisprudence and ethics as the two main divisions of the metaphysic of morals.

Obligation is the necessity of a free action when viewed in relation to a categorical imperative of reason. An *imperative* is a practical rule by which an action, otherwise contingent in itself, is *made* necessary. It is distinguished from a practical law in that such a law, while likewise representing the action as necessary, does not consider whether it is *internally* necessary as involved in the nature of the agent—say as a holy being—or is contingent to him, as in the case of man as we find him; for where the first condition holds good, there is in fact no imperative. Hence an imperative is a rule which not only represents but *makes* a subjectively contingent action necessary; and it, accordingly, represents the subject as being (morally) *necessitated* to act in accordance with this rule. A categorical or unconditional imperative is one which does not represent the action in any way *mediately* through the conception of an *end* that is to be attained by it; but it presents the action to the mind as objectively necessary by the mere representation of its form as an action, and thus makes it necessary. Such imperatives cannot be put forward by any other practical science than that which prescribes obligations, and it is only the science of morals that does this. All other imperatives are *technical*, and they are altogether conditional. The ground of the possibility of categorical imperatives lies in the fact that they refer to no determination of the activity of the will by which a purpose might be assigned to it, but solely to its *freedom*.

Every action is *allowed* (*licitum*) which is not contrary to obligation; and this freedom not being limited by an opposing imperative, constitutes a moral right as a warrant or title of action (*facultas moralis*). From this it is at once evident what actions are *disallowed* or illicit (*illicita*).

Duty is the designation of any action to which anyone is bound by an obligation. It is therefore the subject-matter of all obligation. Duty as regards the action concerned may be one and the same, and yet we may be bound to it in various ways.

The categorical imperative, as expressing an obligation in respect to certain actions, is a morally practical law. But because obligation involves not merely practical necessity expressed in a law as such, but also actual *necessitation*, the categorical imperative is a law either of command or prohibition, according as the doing or not doing of an action is represented as a duty. An action which is neither commanded nor forbidden is merely *allowed*, because there is no law restricting freedom, nor any duty in respect of it. Such an action is said to be *morally indifferent* (*indifferens, adiaphoron, res merae facultatis*). It may be asked whether there *are* such morally indifferent actions; and if there are, whether in addition to the preceptive and prohibitive law (*lex praeceptiva et prohibitiva, lex mandati et vetiti*), there is also required a permissive law (*lex permissiva*), in order that one may be free in such relations to act, or to forbear from acting, at his pleasure? If it were so, the moral right in question would not, in all cases, refer to actions that are indifferent in themselves (*adiaphora*); for no special law would be required to establish such a right, considered according to moral laws.

An action is called an *act*—or moral deed—in so far as it is subject to laws of obligation, and consequently in so far as the subject of it is regarded with reference to the freedom of his choice in the exercise of his will. The *agent*—as the actor or doer of the deed—is regarded as, through the act, the *author* of its effect; and this effect, along with the action itself, may be *imputed* to him, if he previously knew the law in virtue of which an obligation rested upon him.

A *person* is a subject who is capable of having his actions *imputed* to him. Moral personality is, therefore, nothing but the freedom of a rational being under moral laws; and it is to be distinguished from psychological freedom as the mere faculty by which we become conscious of ourselves in different states of the identity of our existence. Hence it follows that a person is properly subject to no other laws than those he lays down for himself, either alone or in conjunction with others.

A *thing* is what is incapable of being the subject of imputation. Every object of the free activity of the will, which is itself void of freedom, is therefore called a *thing* (*res corporealis*).

Right or *wrong* applies, as a general quality, to an act (*rectum aut minus rectum*), in so far as it is in accordance with duty or contrary to duty (*factum licitum aut illicitum*), no matter what may be the subject or origin of the duty itself. An act that is contrary to duty is called a *transgression* (*reatus*).

An *unintentional* transgression of a duty, which is, nevertheless, imputable to a person, is called a mere *fault* (*culpa*). An *intentional* transgression—that is, an act accompanied with the consciousness that it is a transgression—constitutes a *crime* (*dolus*).

Whatever is juridically in accordance with external laws is said to be *just* (*jus, instum*); and whatever is not juridically in accordance with external laws is *unjust* (*unjustum*).

A *collision of duties or obligations* (*collisio officiorum s. obligationum*) would be the result of such a relation between them that the one would annul the other, in whole or in part. Duty and obligation, however, are conceptions which express the objective practical *necessity* of certain actions, and two opposite rules cannot be objective and necessary at the same time; for if it is a duty to act according to one of them, it is not only no duty to act according to an opposite rule, but to do so would even be contrary to duty. Hence a *collision* of duties and obligations is entirely inconceivable (*obligationes non colliduntur*). There may, however, be two grounds of obligation (*rationes obligandi*), connected with an individual under a rule prescribed for himself, and yet neither the one nor the other may be sufficient to constitute an actual obligation (*rationes obligandi non obligantes*); and in that case the one of them is not a duty. If two such grounds of obligation are actually in collision with each other, practical philosophy does not say that the stronger *obligation* is to keep the upper hand (*fortior obligatio vincit*), but that the stronger *ground* of obligation is to maintain its place (*fortior obligandi ratio vincit*).

Obligatory Laws for which an external legislation is possible are called generally *external laws*. Those external laws, the obligatoriness of which can be recognised by reason *a priori* even without an external legislation, are called *natural laws*. Those laws, again, which are not obligatory without actual external legislation, are called *positive laws*. An external legislation, containing pure natural laws, is therefore conceivable; but in that case a previous natural law must be presupposed to establish the authority of the lawgiver by the right to subject others to obligation through his own act of will.

The principle which makes a certain action a duty is a practical law. The rule of the agent or actor, which he forms as a principle for himself on subjective grounds, is called his *maxim*. Hence, even when the law is one and invariable, the maxims of the agent may yet be very different.

The categorical imperative only expresses generally what constitutes obligation. It may b rendered by the following formula: "Act a cording to a maxim which can be adopted at th same time as a universal law." Actions mus therefore be considered, in the first place, ac cording to their subjective principle; but wheth er this principle is also valid objectively ca only be known by the criterion of the categor cal imperative. For reason brings the princip or maxim of any action to the test, by callin upon the agent to think of himself in connectio with it as at the same time laying down a uni versal law, and to consider whether his actio is so qualified as to be fit for entering into suc a universal legislation.

The simplicity of this law, in comparison wit the great and manifold consequences which ma be drawn from it, as well as its commandin authority and supremacy without the accom paniment of any visible motive or sanction, mus certainly at first appear very surprising. And w may well wonder at the power of our reason t determine the activity of the will by the mer idea of the qualification of a maxim for the *uni versality* of a practical law, especially when w are taught thereby that this practical moral lav first reveals a property of the will which th speculative reason would never have come up on either by principles *a priori*, or from any ex perience whatever; and even if it had ascertaine the fact, it could never have theoretically es tablished its possibility. This practical law, how ever, not only discovers the fact of that proper ty of the will, which is *freedom*, but irrefutabl establishes it. Hence it will be less surprising t find that the moral laws are *undemonstrable*, and yet *apodeictic*, like the mathematical postulates; and that they, at the same time, open up before us a whole field of practical knowledge, from which reason, on its theoretical side, must find itself entirely excluded with its speculative idea of freedom and all such ideas of the supersensible generally.

The conformity of an action to the law of duty constitutes its *legality*; the conformity of the maxim of the action with the law constitutes its morality. A *maxim* is thus a *subjective* principle of action, which the individual makes a rule for himself as to how in fact he *will* act.

On the other hand, the principle of duty is what reason absolutely, and therefore objectively and universally, lays down in the form of a command to the individual, as to how he *ought* to act.

The *supreme principle* of the science of morals accordingly is this: "Act according to a maxim which can likewise be valid as a universal law." Every maxim which is not qualified according to this condition is contrary to Morality.

Laws arise from the will, viewed generally as practical reason; maxims spring from the activity of the will in the process of choice. The latter in man is what constitutes free-will. The will which refers to nothing else than mere law can neither be called free nor not free, because it does not relate to actions immediately, but to the giving of a law for the maxim of actions; it is therefore the practical reason itself. Hence as a faculty, it is absolutely necessary in itself, and is not subject to any external necessitation. It is, therefore, only the act of *choice* in the voluntary process that can be called *free*.

The freedom of the act of will, however, is not to be defined as a liberty of indifference (*libertas indifferentae*), that, is, as a capacity of choosing to act for or against the law. The voluntary process, indeed, viewed as a *phenomenal* appearance, gives many examples of this choosing in experience; and some have accordingly so defined the free-will. For freedom, as it is first made knowable by the moral law, is known only as a *negative* property in us, as constituted by the fact of not being *necessitated* to act by sensible principles of determination. Regarded as a *noumenal* reality, however, in reference to man as a pure rational intelligence, the act of the will cannot be at all *theoretically* exhibited; nor can it therefore be explained how this power can act *necessitatingly* in relation to the sensible activity in the process of choice, or consequently in what the positive quality of freedom consists. Only thus much we can see into and comprehend, that although man, as a being *belonging to the world of sense*, exhibits—as experience shows—a capacity of choosing not only *conformably* to the law but also *contrary* to it, his freedom as a rational being *belonging to the world of intelligence* cannot be defined by reference merely to sensible appearances. For sensible phenomena cannot make a super-sensible object—such as free-will is—intelligible; nor can freedom ever be placed in the mere fact that the rational subject can make a choice in conflict with his own law-giving reason, although experience may prove that it happens often enough, notwithstanding our inability to conceive how it is possible. For it is one thing to admit a proposition as based on experience, and another thing to make it the *defining principle* and the universal differentiating mark of the act of free-will, in its distinction from the *arbitrium brutum s. servum;* because the empirical proposition does not assert that any particular characteristic *necessarily* belongs to the conception in question, but this is requisite in the process of definition. Freedom in relation to the internal legislation of reason can alone be properly called a power; the possibility of diverging from the law thus given is an incapacity or want of power. How then can the former be defined by the latter? It could only be by a definition which would add to the practical conception of the free-will, its *exercise* as shown by experience; but this would be a *hybrid definition* which would exhibit the conception in a false light.

A morally practical *law* is a proposition which contains a categorical imperative or command. He who commands by a law (*imperans*) is the lawgiver or *legislator*. He is the author of the obligation that accompanies the law, but he is not always the author of the law itself. In the latter case, the law would be positive, contingent, and arbitrary. The law which is imposed upon us *a priori* and unconditionally by our own reason may also be expressed as proceeding from the will of a supreme lawgiver or the Divine will. Such a will as supreme can consequently have only rights and not duties; and it only indicates the idea of a moral being whose will is law for all, without conceiving of him as the author of that will.

Imputation, in the moral sense, is the *judgement* by which anyone is declared to be the author or free cause of an action which is then regarded as his moral fact or deed, and is subjected to law. When the judgement likewise lays down the juridical consequences of the deed, it is judicial or valid (*imputatio judiciaria s. valida*); otherwise it would be only adjudicative or declaratory (*imputatio dijudicatoria*). That person—individual or collective—who is invested with the right to impute actions judicially, is called a *judge* or a court (*judex s. forum*).

When any one does, in conformity with duty, *more* than he can be compelled to do by the law, it is said to be *meritorious* (*meritum*). What is done only in exact conformity with the law, is *what is due* (*debitum*). And when *less* is done than can be demanded to be done by the law, the result is moral *demerit* (*demeritum*) or culpability.

The *juridical* effect or consequence of a culpable act of demerit is *punishment* (paena); that of a meritorious act is *reward* (*praemium*), assuming that this reward was promised in the law and that it formed the motive of the action. The coincidence or exact conformity of conduct to what is due has no juridical effect. Benevolent *remuneration* (*remuneratio s. repensio benefica*) has no place in *juridical* relations.

The good or bad consequences arising from the performance of an obligated action—as also the consequences arising from failing to perform a meritorious action—cannot be imputed to the agent (*modus imputationis tollens*). The good consequences of a meritorious action—as also the bad consequences of a wrongful action—may be imputed to the agent (*modus imputationis poneus*).

The degree of the imputability of actions is to be reckoned according to the magnitude of the hindrances or obstacles which it has been necessary for them to overcome. The greater the natural hindrances in the sphere of sense, and the less the moral hindrance of duty, so much the more is a good deed imputed as meritorious. This may be seen by considering such examples as rescuing a man who is an entire stranger from great distress, and at very considerable sacrifice. Conversely, the less the natural hindrance, and the greater the hindrance on the ground of duty, so much the more is a transgression imputable as culpable. Hence the state of mind of the agent or doer of a deed makes a difference in imputing its consequences, according as he did it in passion or performed it with coolness and deliberation.

CONTENTS
THE SCIENCE OF RIGHT

INTRODUCTION TO THE SCIENCE OF RIGHT

GENERAL DEFINITIONS AND DIVISIONS

A. *What the Science of Right is*

'HE Science of Right has for its object the rinciples of all the laws which it is possible to romulgate by external legislation. Where there s such a legislation, it becomes, in actual appliation to it, a system of *positive* right and law; nd he who is versed in the knowledge of this ystem is called a *jurist* or *jurisconsult* (*juris-onsultus*). A practical jurisconsult (*jurisperi-us*), or a professional lawyer, is one who is killed in the knowledge of positive external aws, and who can apply them to cases that nay occur in experience. Such practical knowldge of positive right, and law, may be regardd as belonging to *jurisprudence* (*jurispruden-ia*) in the original sense of the term. But the heoretical knowledge of right and law in prinple, as distinguished from positive laws and mpirical cases, belongs to the pure science of ight (*jurisscientia*). The science of right thus lesignates the philosophical and systematic nowledge of the principles of natural right. And it is from this science that the immutable rinciples of all positive legislation must be deived by practical jurists and lawgivers.

B. *What is Right?*

This question may be said to be about as emarrassing to the jurist as the well-known quesion, "What is truth?" is to the logician. It is ll the more so, if, on reflection, he strives to void tautology in his reply and recognise the act that a reference to what holds true merely f the laws of some one country at a particular ime is not a solution of the general problem hus proposed. It is quite easy to state what may e right in particular cases (*quid sit juris*), as eing what the laws of a certain place and of a ertain time say or may have said; but it is much nore difficult to determine whether what they have enacted is right in itself, and to lay down a niversal criterion by which right and wrong in general, and what is just and unjust, may be recognised. All this may remain entirely hidden even from the practical jurist until he abandon his empirical principles for a time and search in the pure reason for the sources of such judgements, in order to lay a real foundation for actual positive legislation. In this search, his empirical laws may, indeed, furnish him with excellent guidance; but a merely empirical system that is void of rational principles is, like the wooden head in the fable of Phaedrus, fine enough in appearance, but unfortunately it wants brain.

1. The conception of right—as referring to a corresponding obligation which is the moral aspect of it—in the *first* place, has regard only to the external and practical relation of one person to another, in so far as they can have influence upon each other, immediately or mediately, by their *actions* as facts. 2. In the *second* place, the conception of right does not indicate the relation of the action of an individual to the *wish* or the mere desire of another, as in acts of benevolence or of unkindness, but only the relation of his free action to the freedom of *action* of the other. 3. And, in the *third* place, in this reciprocal relation of voluntary actions, the conception of right does not take into consideration the *matter* of the act of will in so far as the end which any one may have in view in willing it is concerned. In other words, it is not asked in a question of right whether any one on buying goods for his own business realizes a profit by the transaction or not; but only the *form* of the transaction is taken into account, in considering the relation of the mutual acts of will. Acts of will or voluntary choice are thus regarded only in so far as they are *free*, and as to whether the action of one can harmonize with the freedom of another, according to a universal law.

Right, therefore, comprehends the whole of the conditions under which the voluntary actions of any one person can be harmonized in reality with the voluntary actions of every other person, according to a universal law of freedom.

C. *Universal Principle of Right*

"Every action is *right* which in itself, or in the maxim on which it proceeds, is such that it can coexist along with the freedom of the will of each and all in action, according to a universal law."

If, then, my action or my condition generally can coexist with the freedom of every other, according to a universal law, any one does me a wrong who hinders me in the performance of this action, or in the maintenance of this condition. For such a hindrance or obstruction cannot coexist with freedom according to universal laws.

It follows also that it cannot be demanded as a matter of right, that this universal principle of all maxims shall itself be adopted as my maxim, that is, that I shall make it the *maxim* of my actions. For any one may be free, although his freedom is entirely indifferent to me, or even if I wished in my heart to infringe it, so long as I do not actually violate that freedom by *my external action.* Ethics, however, as distinguished from jurisprudence, imposes upon me the obligation to make the fulfilment of right a *maxim* of my conduct.

The universal law of right may then be expressed thus: "Act externally in such a manner that the free exercise of thy will may be able to coexist with the freedom of all others, according to a universal law." This is undoubtedly a law which imposes obligation upon me; but it does not at all imply and still less command that I *ought,* merely on account of this obligation, to limit my freedom to these very conditions. Reason in this connection says only that it *is* restricted thus far by its idea, and may be likewise thus limited in fact by others; and it lays this down as a postulate which is not capable of further proof. As the object in view is not to teach virtue, but to explain what right *is,* thus far the law of right, as thus laid down, may not and should not be represented as a motive-principle of action.

D. *Right is Conjoined with the Title or Authority to Compel*

The resistance which is opposed to any hindrance of an effect is in reality a furtherance of this effect and is in accordance with its accomplishment. Now, everything that is wrong is a hindrance of freedom, according to universal laws; and compulsion or constraint of any kind is a hindrance or resistance made to freedom. Consequently, if a certain exercise of freedom is itself a hindrance of the freedom that is according to universal laws, it is wrong; and the compulsion of constraint which is opposed to it is right, as being a *hindering of a hindrance of freedom,* and as being in accord with the freedom which exists in accordance with universal laws. Hence, according to the logical principle of contradiction, all right is accompanied with an implied title or warrant to bring compulsion to bear on any one who may violate it in fact.

E. *Strict Right may be also Represented as the Possibility of a Universal Reciprocal Compulsion in harmony with the Freedom of All according to Universal Laws*

This proposition means the right is not to be regarded as composed of two different elements —obligation according to a law, and a title on the part of one who has bound another by his own free choice to compel him to perform. But it imports that the conception of right may be viewed as consisting immediately in the possibility of a universal reciprocal compulsion, in harmony with the freedom of all. As right in general has for its object only what is external in actions, strict right, as that with which nothing ethical is intermingled, requires no other motives of action than those that are merely external; for it is then pure right and is unmixed with any prescriptions of virtue. A *strict* right then, in the exact sense of the term, is that which alone can be called *wholly external.* Now such right is founded, no doubt, upon the consciousness of the obligation of every individual according to the law; but if it is to be pure as such, it neither may nor should refer to this consciousness as a motive by which to determine the free act of the will. For this purpose however, it founds upon the principle of the possibility of an external compulsion, such as may coexist with the freedom of every one according to universal laws. Accordingly, then where it is said that a creditor has a right to demand from a debtor the payment of his debt this does not mean merely that he can bring him to feel in his mind that reason obliges him to do this; but it means that he can apply an external compulsion to force any such one so to pay, and that this compulsion is quite consistent with the freedom of all, including the parties in question, according to a universal law

:ight and the title to compel, thus indicate the ame thing.

The law of right, as thus enunciated, is repreented as a reciprocal compulsion necessarily in ccordance with the freedom of every one, uner the principle of a universal freedom. It is ius, as it were, a representative *construction* f the conception of right, by exhibiting it in a ure intuitive perception *a priori*, after the analgy of the possibility of the free motions of odies under the physical law of *the equality f action and reaction*. Now, as in pure mathenatics, we cannot deduce the properties of its bjects immediately from a mere abstract coneption, but can only discover them by figuraive construction or representation of its coneptions; so it is in like manner with the prinziple of right. It is not so much the mere fornal *conception* of right, but rather that of a uniersal and equal reciprocal compulsion as harnonizing with it, and reduced under general aws, that makes representation of that concepion possible. But just as those conceptions preented in dynamics are founded upon a merely ormal representation of pure mathematics as resented in geometry, reason has taken care also to provide the understanding as far as posible with intuitive presentations *a priori* in beioof of a construction of the conception of ight. The right in geometrical lines (*rectum*) s opposed, as the straight, to that which is curved and to that which is oblique. In the first opposition, there is involved an *inner quality* of the lines of such a nature that there is only one *straight* or *right* line possible between two given points. In the second case, again, the *positions* of two intersecting or meeting *lines* are of such a nature that there can likewise be only *one* line called the perpendicular, which is not more inclined to the one side than the other, and it divides space on either side into two equal parts. After the manner of this analogy, the science of right aims at determining what every one shall have as his *own* with mathematical exactness; but this is not to be expected in the ethical science of virtue, as it cannot but allow a certain latitude for exceptions. But, without passing into the sphere of ethics, there are two cases—known as the equivocal right of equity and necessity—which claim a juridical decision, yet for which no one can be found to give such a decision, and which, as regards their relation to rights, belong, as it were, to the "*Intermundia*" of Epicurus. These we must at the outset take apart from the special exposition of the science of right, to which we are now about to advance; and we may consider them now by way of supplement to these introductory explanations, in order that their uncertain conditions may not exert a disturbing influence on the fixed principles of the proper doctrine of right.

F. *Supplementary Remarks on Equivocal Right* (Jus aequivocum)

With every right, in the strict acceptation (*jus strictum*), there is conjoined a right to compel. But it is possible to think of other rights of a *wider* kind (*jus latum*) in which the title to compel cannot be determined by any law. Now there are two real or supposed rights of this kind—equity and the right of necessity. The first alleges a right that is without compulsion; the second adopts a compulsion that is without right. This equivocalness, however, can be easily shown to rest on the peculiar fact that there are cases of doubtful right, for the decision of which no judge can be appointed.

I. *Equity*

Equity (aequitas), regarded objectively, does not properly constitute a claim upon the moral duty of benevolence or beneficence on the part of others; but whoever insists upon anything on the ground of equity, founds upon his *right* to the same. In this case, however, the conditions are awanting that are requisite for the function of a judge in order that he might determine what or what kind of satisfaction can be done to this claim. When one of the partners of a mercantile company, formed under the condition of equal profits, has, however, *done more* than the other members, and in consequence has also *lost more*, it is *in accordance with equity* that he should demand from the company more than merely an equal share of advantage with the rest. But, in relation to *strict right*—if we think of a judge considering his case—he can furnish no definite data to establish how much more belongs to him by the contract; and in case of an action at law, such a demand would be rejected. A domestic servant, again, who might be paid his wages due to the end of his year of service in a coinage that became depreciated within that period, so that it would not be of the same value to him as it was when he entered on his engagement, cannot claim by right to be kept from loss on account of the unequal value of the money if he receives the due amount of it. He can only make an appeal on the ground of equity,—a dumb goddess who cannot claim a hearing of right,—because there was nothing bearing on this point in the contract of service, and a judge cannot give a decree on the basis of vague or indefinite conditions.

Hence it follows, that a court of equity, for the decision of disputed questions of right, would involve a contradiction. It is only where his own proper rights are concerned, and in matters in which he can decide, that a judge may or ought to give a hearing to equity. Thus, if the Crown is supplicated to give an indemnity to certain persons for loss or injury sustained in its service, it may undertake the burden of doing so, although, according to strict right, the claim might be rejected on the ground of the pretext that the parties in question undertook the performance of the service occasioning the loss, at their own risk.

The *dictum* of equity may be put thus: "The strictest right is the greatest wrong" (*summum jus summa injuria*). But this evil cannot be obviated by the forms of right, although it relates to a matter of right; for the grievance that it gives rise to can only be put before a "court of conscience" (*forum poli*), whereas every question of right must be taken before a civil court (*forum soli*).

II. *The Right of Necessity*

The so-called right of necessity (*jus necessitatis*) is the supposed right or title, in case of the danger of losing my own life, to take away the life of another who has, in fact, done me no harm. It is evident that, viewed as a doctrine of right, this must involve a contradiction, For this is not the case of a *wrongful* aggressor making an unjust assault upon my life, and whom I anticipate by depriving him of his own (*jus inculpatae tutelae*); nor consequently is it a question merely of the recommendation of moderation which belongs to ethics as the doctrine of virtue, and not to jurisprudence as the doctrine of right. It is a question of the allowableness of using violence against one who has used none against me.

It is clear that the assertion of such a right is not to be understood objectively as being in accordance with what a law would prescribe, but merely subjectively, as proceeding on the assumption of how a sentence would be pronounced by a court in the case. There can, in fact, be no *criminal law* assigning the penalty of death to a man who, when shipwrecked and struggling in extreme danger for his life, and in order to save it, may thrust another from a plank on which he had saved himself. For the punishment threatened by the law could not possibly have greater power than the fear of the loss of life in the case in question. Such a penal law would thus fail altogether to exercise its intended effect; for the threat of an evil which is still *uncertain*—such as death by a judicial sentence—could not overcome the fear of an evil which is *certain*, as drowning is in such circumstances. An act of violent self-preservation, then, ought not to be considered as altogether beyond condemnation (*inculpabile*); it is only to be adjudged as exempt from punishment (*impunibile*). Yet this *subjective* condition of impunity, by a strange confusion of ideas, has been regarded by jurists as equivalent to *objective* lawfulness.

The *dictum* of the right of necessity is put in these terms: "Necessity has no law" (*Necessitas non habet legem*). And yet there cannot be a necessity that could make what is wrong lawful.

It is apparent, then, that in judgements relating both to "equity" and "the right of necessity," the *equivocations* involved arise from an interchange of the objective and subjective grounds that enter into the application of the principles of right, when viewed respectively by reason or by a judicial tribunal. What one may have good grounds for recognising as right in itself, may not find confirmation in a court of justice; and what he must consider to be wrong, in itself, may obtain recognition in such a court. And the reason of this is that the conception of right is not taken in the two cases in one and the same sense.

DIVISION OF THE SCIENCE OF RIGHT

A. *General Division of the Duties of Right* (Juridical Duties)

IN this division we may very conveniently follow Ulpian, if his three formulae are taken in a general sense, which may not have been quite clearly in his mind, but which they are capable of being developed into or of receiving. They are the following:

1. *Honeste vive.* "Live rightly." Juridical rectitude, or honour (*honestas juridica*), consists

in maintaining one's own worth as a man in relation to others. This duty may be rendered by the proposition: "Do not make thyself a mere means for the use of others, but be to them likewise an end." This duty will be explained in the next formula as an obligation arising out of the *right* of humanity in our own person (*lex justi*).

2. *Neminem laede.* "Do wrong to no one." This formula may be rendered so as to mean: "Do no wrong to any one, even if thou shouldst be under the necessity, in observing this duty, to cease from all connection with others and to avoid all society" (*lex juridica*).

3. *Suum cuique tribue.* "Assign to every one what is his own." This may be rendered, "Enter, if wrong cannot be avoided, into a society with others in which every one may have *secured* to him what is his own." If this formula were to be simply translated, "Give every one *his own*," it would express an absurdity, for we cannot *give* any one what he already has. If it is to have a definite meaning, it must therefore run thus: "Enter into a state in which every one can have what is his own secured against the action of every other" (*lex justitiae*).

These three classical formulae, at the same time, represent principles which suggest a division of the system of juridical duties into *internal duties, external duties,* and those *connecting duties* which contain the latter as deduced from the principle of the former by subsumption.

B. *Universal Division of Rights*

I. *Natural Right and Positive Right.* The system of rights, viewed as a scientific system of doctrines, is divided into natural right and positive right. Natural right rests upon pure rational principles *a priori;* positive or statutory right is what proceeds from the will of a legislator.

II. *Innate Right and Acquired Right.* The system of rights may again be regarded in reference to the implied powers of dealing morally with others as bound by obligations, that is, as furnishing a legal title of action in relation to them. Thus viewed, the system is divided into innate right and acquired right. Innate right is that right which belongs to every one by nature, independent of all juridical acts of experience. Acquired right is that right which is founded upon such juridical acts.

Innate right may also be called the "internal mine and thine" (*meum vel tuum internum*); for external right must always be acquired.

There is only one Innate Right, the Birthright of Freedom

Freedom is independence of the compulsory will of another; and in so far as it can coexist with the freedom of all according to a universal law, it is the one sole original, inborn right belonging to every man in virtue of his humanity. There is, indeed, an innate equality belonging to every man which consists in his right to be independent of being bound by others to anything more than that to which he may also reciprocally bind them. It is, consequently, the inborn quality of every man in virtue of which he ought to be *his own master by right* (*sui juris*). There is, also, the natural quality of justness attributable to a man as naturally of *unimpeachable right* (*justi*), because he has done no wrong to any one prior to his own juridical actions. And, further, there is also the innate right of common action on the part of every man, so that he may do towards others what does not infringe their rights or take away anything that is theirs unless they are willing to appropriate it; such as merely to communicate thought, to narrate anything, or to promise something whether truly and honestly, or untruly and dishonestly (*veriloquim aut falsiloquim*), for it rests entirely upon these others whether they will believe or trust in it or not.[1] But all these rights or titles are already included in the principle of innate freedom, and are not really distinguished from it, even as dividing members under a higher species of right.

The reason why such a division into separate rights has been introduced into the system of natural right, viewed as including all that is innate, was not without a purpose. Its object was to enable proof to be more readily put forward in case of any controversy arising about an acquired right, and questions emerging either with reference to a fact that might be in doubt, or, if

[1] It is customary to designate every untruth that is spoken *intentionally* as such, although it may be in a frivolous manner, a *lie,* or *falsehood (mendacium),* because it may do harm, at least in so far as any one who repeats it in good faith may be made a laughing-stock of to others on account of his easy credulity. But in the juridical sense, only that untruth is called a lie which immediately infringes the right of another, such as a false allegation of a contract having been concluded, when the allegation is put forward in order to deprive some one of what is his (*falsiloquim dolosum*). This distinction of conceptions so closely allied is not without foundation; because on the occasion of a simple statement of one's thoughts, it is always free for another to take them as he may; and yet the resulting repute, that such a one is a man whose word cannot be trusted, comes so close to the opprobrium of directly calling him a liar, that the boundary-line separating what, in such a case, belongs to jurisprudence, and what is special to ethics, can hardly be otherwise drawn.

that were established, in reference to a right under dispute. For the party repudiating an obligation, and on whom the burden of proof (*onus probandi*) might be incumbent, could thus methodically refer to his innate right of freedom as specified under various relations in detail, and could therefore found upon them equally as different titles of right.

In the relation of innate right, and consequently of the internal *mine* and *thine*, there is therefore not *rights*, but only one right. And, accordingly, this highest division of rights into *innate* and *acquired*, which evidently consists of two members extremely unequal in their contents is properly placed in the introduction; and the subdivisions of the science of right may be referred in detail to the *external mine* and *thine.*

C. *Methodical Division of the Science of Right*

The highest division of the system of natural right should not be—as it is frequently put—into "*natural* right" and "*social* right," but into natural right and civil right. The first constitutes private right; the second, public right. For it is not the "*social* state" but the "*civil* state" that is opposed to the "state of nature"; for in the "state of nature" there may well be society of some kind, but there is no "civil" society, as an institution securing the mine and thine by public laws. It is thus that right, viewed under reference to the state of nature, is specially called *private right.* The whole of the principles of right will therefore fall to be expounded under the two subdivisions of private right and public right.

THE SCIENCE OF RIGHT

FIRST PART. *PRIVATE RIGHT*

The System of Those Laws which Require no External Promulgation. The Principles of the External Mine and Thine Generally

Chapter I. Of the Mode of Having Anything External as One's Own

1. *The Meaning of "Mine" in Right* (Meum Juris)

Anything is *"mine" by right,* or is rightfully mine, when I am so connected with it, that if any other person should make use of it without my consent, he would do me a lesion or injury. The subjective condition of the use of anything is *possession* of it.

An *external* thing, however as such could only be mine, if I may assume it to be possible that I can be wronged by the use which another might make of it *when it is not actually in my possession.* Hence it would be a contradiction to have anything external as one's own, were not the conception of possession capable of two different meanings, as *sensible* possession that is perceivable by the senses, and *rational* possession that is perceivable only by the intellect. By the former is to be understood a *physical* possession, and by the latter, a purely *juridical* possession of the same object.

The description of an object as *"external* to me" may signify either that it is merely "different and distinct from me as a subject," or that it is also "a thing placed *outside* of me, and to be found elsewhere in space or time." Taken in the first sense, the term *possession* signifies *rational possession;* and, in the second sense, it must mean *empirical possession.* A rational or *intelligible* possession, if such be possible, is possession *viewed apart from physical holding or detention* (*detentio*).

2. *Juridical Postulate of the Practical Reason*

It is possible to have any external object of my will as mine. In other words, a maxim to this effect—were it to become law—that any object on which the will can be exerted must remain objectively in itself *without an owner,* as *res nullius,* is contrary to the principle of right.

For an object of any act of my will, is something that it would be *physically* within my power to use. Now, suppose there were things that *by right* should absolutely not be in our power, or, in other words, that it would be wrong or inconsistent with the freedom of all, according to universal law, to make use of them. On this supposition, freedom would so far be depriving itself of the use of its voluntary activity, in thus putting *useable* objects out of all possibility of *use.* In practical relations, this would be to annihilate them, by making them *res nullius,* notwithstanding the fact that acts of will in relation to such things would formally harmonize, in the actual use of them, with the external freedom of all according to universal laws. Now the pure practical reason lays down only formal laws as principles to regulate the exercise of the will; and therefore abstracts from the matter of the act of will, as regards the other qualities of the object, *which is considered only in so far as it is an object of the activity of the will.* Hence the practical reason cannot contain, in reference to such an object, an absolute prohibition of its use, because this would involve a contradiction of external freedom with itself. An object of my free will, however, is one which I have the physical capability of making some use of at will, since its *use* stands in my power (*in potentia*). This is to be distinguished from having the *object* brought under my disposal (*in potestatem meam reductum*), which supposes not a *capability* merely, but also a particular *act* of the free-will. But in order to consider something merely as an object of my will as such, it is sufficient to be conscious that I have it in my power. It is therefore an assumption *a priori* of the practical reason to regard and treat every object within the range of my free exercise of will as objectively a possible mine or thine.

This postulate may be called "a permissive law" of the practical reason, as giving us a special title which we could not evolve out of the mere conceptions of right generally. And this title constitutes the right to impose upon all others an obligation, not otherwise laid upon them, to abstain from the use of certain objects of our free choice, because we have already taken them into our possession. Reason wills that this shall be recognised as a valid principle, and it does so as *practical* reason; and it is enabled by means of this postulate *a priori* to enlarge its range of activity in practice.

3. *Possession and Ownership*

Any one who would assert the right to a thing as his must be in possession of it as an object. Were he not its actual possessor or owner, he could not be wronged or injured by the use which another might make of it without his consent. For, should anything external to him, and in no way connected with him by right, affect this object, it could not affect himself as a subject, nor do him any wrong, unless he stood in a relation of ownership to it.

4. *Exposition of the Conception of the External Mine and Thine*

There can only be *three* external objects of my will in the activity of choice:

(1) A corporeal *thing* external to me;

(2) The *free-will* of another in the performance of a particular act (*praestatio*);

(3) The *state* of another in relation to myself.

These correspond to the categories of *substance, causality, and reciprocity;* and they form the practical relations between me and external objects, according to the laws of freedom.

A. I can only call a corporeal thing or an object in *space* "mine," when, *even although not in physical possession of it,* I am able to assert that I am in possession of it in another real non-physical sense. Thus, I am not entitled to call an apple *mine* merely because I hold it in my hand or possess it physically; but only when I am entitled to say, "I possess it, although I have laid it out of my hand, and wherever it may lie." In like manner, I am not entitled to say of the ground, on which I may have laid myself down, that therefore it is *mine;* but only when I can rightly assert that it still remains in my possession, although I may have left the spot. For any one who, in the former appearances of empirical possession, might wrench the apple out of my hand, or drag me away from my resting-place, would, indeed, injure me in respect of the *inner* "mine" of freedom, but not in respect of the external "mine," unless I could assert that I was in the possession of the object, even when not actually holding it physically. And if I could not do this, neither could I call the apple or the spot mine.

B. I cannot call the *performance* of something by the action of the will of another "mine," if I can *only* say "it has come into my possession *at the same time* with a promise" (*pactum re initum*); but only if I am able to assert "I am in possession of the will of the other, so as to determine him to the performance of a particular act, although the time for the performance of it has not yet come." In the latter case, the promise belongs to the nature of things actually held as possessed, and as an *active obligation* I can reckon it mine; and this holds good not only if I have *the thing promised*—as in the first case—already in my possession, but even although I do not yet possess it in fact. Hence, I must be able to regard myself in thought as independent of that empirical form of possession that is limited by the condition of time and as being, nevertheless, in possession of the object.

C. I cannot call a wife, a child, a domestic, or, generally, any other person "mine" merely because I command them at present as belonging to my household, or because I have them under control, and in my power and possession. But I can call them mine, if, although they may have withdrawn themselves from my control and I do not therefore possess them empirically, I can still say "I possess them by my mere will, provided they exist anywhere in space or time; and, consequently, my possession of them is purely *juridical.*" They belong, in fact, to my possessions, only when and so far as I can assert this as a matter of right.

5. *Definition of the Conception of the External Mine and Thine*

Definitions are *nominal* or *real.* A nominal definition is sufficient merely to *distinguish* the object defined from all other objects, and it springs out of a complete and definite *exposition* of its conception. A real definition further suffices for a *deduction* of the conception defined, so as to furnish a knowledge of the reality of the object. The *nominal definition* of the external "mine" would thus be: "The external mine is anything outside of myself, such that any hindrance of my use of it at will would be doing me an injury or wrong as an infringement of that freedom of mine which may coexist with the freedom of all others according to a universal law." The *real definition* of this conception may be put thus: "The external mine is anything outside of myself, such that any prevention of my use of it would be a wrong, *although I may not be in possession of it* so as to be actually holding it as an object." I must be in some kind of possession of an external object, if the object is to be regarded as *mine;* for, otherwise, anyone interfering with this object would not, in doing so, affect me; nor, consequently, would he thereby do me any wrong. Hence, according to § 4, a *rational possession* (*possessio noumenon*) must be assumed as possible, if there is to be rightly an external *mine* and *thine*. Empirical possession is thus only phenomenal possession or holding (detention) of the object in the sphere of sensible *appearance* (*possessio phenomenon*), although the *object* which I possess is not regarded in this practical relation as itself a phenomenon—according to the exposition of the Transcendental Analytic in the *Critique of Pure Reason*—but as a thing in itself. For in the *Critique of Pure Reason* the interest of reason turns upon the *theoretical* knowledge of the nature of things and how far reason can go in such knowledge. But here reason has to deal with the practical determination of the action of the will according to laws of *freedom*, whether the object is perceivable through the senses or merely thinkable by the pure understanding. And right, as under consideration, is a pure practical conception of the reason in relation to the exercise of the will under laws of freedom.

And, hence, it is not quite correct to speak of "possessing" a right *to* this or that object, but it should rather be said that an object is possessed in a *purely juridical* way; for a right is itself the rational possession of an object, and to "possess a possession," would be an expression without meaning.

6. *Deduction of the Conception of a Purely Juridical Possession of an External Object* (Possessio Noumenon)

The question, "How is an *external mine and thine* possible?" resolves itself into this other question: "How is a *merely juridical* or *rational* possession possible?" And this second question resolves itself again into a third: "How is a *synthetic* proposition in right possible *a priori?*"

All propositions of right—as juridical propositions—are propositions *a priori*, for they are practical laws of reason (*dictamina rationis*). But the juridical proposition *a priori* respecting *empirical possession* is *analytical;* for it says nothing more than what follows by the principle of contradiction, from the conception of such possession; namely, that if I am the holder of a thing in the way of being physically connected with it, any one interfering with it without my consent—as, for instance, in wrenching an apple out of my hand—affects and detracts from my freedom as that which is internally mine; and consequently the maxim of his action is in direct contradiction to the axiom of right. The proposition expressing the principle of an empirical rightful possession does not therefore go beyond the right of a person in reference to himself.

On the other hand, the proposition expressing the possibility of the possession of a thing external to me, after abstraction of all the conditions of empirical possession in space and time—consequently presenting the assumption of the possibility of a *possessio noumenon*—goes beyond these limiting conditions; and because this proposition asserts a possession even without physical holding, as necessary to the conception of the external mine and thine, it is *synthetical*. And thus it becomes a problem for reason to show how such a proposition, extending its range beyond the conception of empirical possession, is possible *a priori*.

In this manner, for instance, the act of taking possession of a particular portion of the soil is a mode exercising the private free-will without being an act of *usurpation*. The possessor founds upon the innate right of *common possession* of the surface of the earth, and upon the universal will corresponding *a priori* to it, which allows a *private possession* of the soil; because what are mere things would be otherwise made in themselves and by a law into unappropriable objects. Thus a first appropriator acquires originally by primary possession a particular portion of the ground; and by right (*jure*) he resists every other person who would hinder him in the private use of it, although, while the "state of nature" continues, this cannot be done by juridical means (*de jure*), because a public law does not yet exist.

And although a piece of ground should be regarded as free, or declared to be such, so as to be for the public use of all without distinction, yet it cannot be said that it is thus free by nature and *originally* so, prior to any juridical act. For there would be a real relation already incorporated in such a piece of ground by the very fact that the possession of it was denied to any particular individual; and as this public freedom of the ground would be a prohibition of it to every particular individual, this presupposes a common possession of it which cannot take effect without a contract. A piece of ground, however, which can only become publicly free by contract, must actually be in the possession of all those associated together, who mutually interdict or suspend each other, from any particular or private use of it.

This *original* community of the soil and of the things upon it (*communio fundi originaria*), is an idea which has objective and practical juridical reality and is entirely different from the idea of a *primitive* community of things, which is a fiction. For the latter would have had to be *founded* as a form of society, and must have taken its rise from a contract by which all renounced the right of private possession, so that by uniting the property owned by each into a whole, it was thus transformed into a common possession. But had such an event taken place, history must have presented some evidence of it. To regard such a procedure as the original mode of taking possession, and to hold that the particular possessions of every individual may and ought to be grounded upon it, is evidently a contradiction.

Possession (*possessio*) is to be distinguished from habitation as mere *residence* (*sedes*); and the act of taking possession of the soil in the intention of acquiring it once for all, is also to be distinguished from *settlement* or *domicile* (*incolatus*), which is a continuous private possession of a place that is dependent on the presence of the individual upon it. We have not here to deal with the question of domiciliary settlement, as that is a secondary juridical act which may follow upon possession, or may not occur at all; for as such it could not involve an original possession, but only a secondary possession derived from the consent of others.

Simple physical possession, or holding of the soil, involves already certain relations of right to the thing, although it is certainly not sufficient to enable me to regard it as mine. Relative to others, so far as they know, it appears as a first possession in harmony with the law of external freedom; and, at the same time, it is embraced in the universal original possession which contains *a priori* the fundamental principle of the possibility of a private possession. Hence to disturb the first occupier or holder of a portion of the soil in his use of it is a lesion or wrong done to him. The first taking of possession has therefore a title of right (*titulus possessionis*) in its favour, which is simply the principle of the original common possession; and the saying that "It is well for those who are in possession" (*beati possidentes*), when one is not bound to authenticate his possession, is a principle of natural right that establishes the juridical act of taking possession, as a ground of acquisition upon which every first possessor may found.

It has been shown in the *Critique of Pure Reason* that in theoretical principles *a priori*, an intuitional perception *a priori* must be supplied in connection with any given conception; and, consequently, were it a question of a purely theoretical principle, something would have to be *added* to the conception of the possession of an object to make it real. But in respect of the *practical* principle under consideration, the procedure is just the converse of the theoretical process; so that all the conditions of perception which form the foundation of empirical possession must be abstracted or taken away in order to *extend* the range of the juridical conception beyond the empirical sphere, and in order to be able to apply the postulate, that every external object of the free activity of my will, so far as I have it in my power, although not in the possession of it, may be reckoned as juridically mine.

The possibility of such a possession, with consequent deduction of the conception of a non-empirical possession, is founded upon the juridical postulate of the practical reason, that "It is a juridical duty so to act towards others that what is external and useable may come into the possession or become the property of some one." And this postulate is conjoined with the exposition of the conception that what is externally one's own is founded upon a possession, that is *not physical*. The possibility of such a possession, thus conceived, cannot, however, be proved or comprehended in itself, because it is a *rational* conception for which no empirical perception can be furnished; but it follows as an immediate consequence from the postulate that has been enunciated. For, if it is necessary to act according to that juridical principle, the rational or intelligible condition of a purely juridical possession must also be possible. It need astonish no one, then, that the *theoretical* aspect of the principles of the external mine and thine is lost from view in the rational sphere of pure intelligence and presents no extension of knowledge; for the conception of freedom upon which they rest does not admit of any *theoretical* deduction of its possibility, and it can only be inferred from the practical law of reason, called the *categorical imperative*, viewed as a fact.

7. *Application of the Principle of the Possibility of an External Mine and Thine to Objects of Experience*

The conception of a purely juridical possession is not an empirical conception dependent on conditions of space and time, and yet it has practical reality. As such it must be applicable to objects of experience, the knowledge of which is independent of the conditions of space and time. The rational process by which the conception of right is brought into relation to such objects so as to constitute a possible external mine and thine, is as follows. The conception of right, being contained merely in reason, cannot be *immediately* applied to objects of experience, so as to give the conception of an empirical *possession*, but must be applied directly to the mediating conception, in the understanding, of *possession* in general; so that, instead of physical holding (*detentio*) as an empirical representation of possession, the formal conception or thought of *having*, abstracted from all conditions of space and time, is conceived by the mind, and only as implying that an object is in my power and at my disposal (*in potestate mea positum esse*). In this relation, the term *external* does not signify existence in *another place* than where I am, nor my resolution and acceptance at another time than the moment in which I have the offer of a thing: it signifies only an object *different* from or other than myself. Now the practical reason by its law of right wills, that I shall think the mine and thine in application to objects, not according to sensible conditions, but apart from these and from the possession they indicate; because they refer to determinations of the activity of the will that are in accordance with the laws of freedom. For it is only a *conception of the understanding* that can be brought under the rational conception of right. I may therefore say that I possess a field, although it is in quite a different place from that on which I actually find myself. For the question here is not concerning an intellectual relation to the object, but I have the thing practically *in my power* and at my disposal, which is a conception of possession realized by the understanding and independent of relations of space; and it is *mine*, because my will, in determining itself to any particular use of it, is not in conflict with the law of external freedom. Now it is just in abstraction from physical possession of the object of my free-will in the sphere of sense, that the practical reason wills that a rational possession of it shall be thought, according to intellectual conceptions which are not empirical, but contain *a priori* the conditions of rational possession. Hence it is in this fact, that we found the ground of the validity of such a rational conception of possession (*possessio noumenon*) as a principle of a universally valid *legislation*. For such a legislation is implied and contained in the expression, "This external object is *mine*," because an obligation is thereby imposed upon all others in respect of it, who would otherwise not have been obliged to abstain from the use of this object.

The mode, then, of having something external to myself as mine, consists in a specially juridical connection of the will of the subject with that object, independently of the empirical relations to it in space and in time, and in accordance with the conception of a rational possession. A particular spot on the earth is not externally mine because I occupy it with my body; for the question here discussed refers only to my external freedom, and consequently it affects only the possession of myself, which is not a thing external to me, and therefore only involves an internal right. But if I continue to be in possession of the spot, although I have taken myself away from it and gone to another place, only under that condition is my external right concerned in connection with it. And to make the continuous possession of this spot by my person a condition of having it as mine, must either be to assert that it is not possible at all to have anything external as one's own, which is contrary to the postulate in § 2, or to require, in order that this external possession may be possible, that I shall be in two places at the same time. But this amounts to saying that I must be in a place and also not in it, which is contradictory and absurb.

This position may be applied to the case in which I have accepted a promise; for my having and possession in respect of what has been promised become established on the ground of external right. This right is not to be annulled by the fact that the promiser having said at one time, "This thing shall be yours," again at a subsequent time says, "My will now is that the thing shall not be yours." In such relations of rational right, the conditions hold just the same as if the promiser had, without any interval of time between them, made the two declarations of his will, "This shall be yours," and also "This shall not be yours"; which manifestly contradicts itself.

The same thing holds, in like manner, of the conception of the juridical possession of a person as belonging to the *Having* of a subject, whether it be a wife, a child, or a servant. The relations of right involved in a household, and the reciprocal possession of all its members, are not annulled by the capability of separating from each other *in space;* because it is by *juridical* relations that they are connected, and the external *mine* and *thine,* as in the former cases, rests entirely upon the assumption of the possibility of a purely rational possession, without the accompaniment of physical detention or holding of the object.

Reason is forced to a critique of its juridically practical function in special reference to the conception of the external mine and thine, by the antinomy of the propositions enunciated regarding the possibility of such a form of possession. For these give rise to an inevitable dialectic, in which a thesis and an antithesis set up equal claims to the validity of two conflicting conditions. Reason is thus compelled, in its practical function in relation to right—as it was in its theoretical function—to make a distinction between possession as a phenomenal appearance presented to the senses, and that possession which is rational and thinkable only by the understanding.

Thesis.—The thesis, in this case, is: *"It is possible* to have something external as mine, although I am not in possession of it."

Antithesis.—The antithesis is: "*It is not possible* to have anything external as mine, if I am not in possession of it."

Solution.—The solution is: "Both Propositions are true"; the former when I mean empirical possession (*possessio phaenomenon,* the latter when I understand by the same term, a purely rational possession (*possessio noumenon*).

But the possibility of a rational possession, and consequently of an external mine and thine, cannot be comprehended by direct insight, but must be deduced from the practical reason. And in this relation it is specially noteworthy that the practical reason without intuitional perceptions, and even without requiring such an element *a priori,* can *extend* its range by the mere *elimination* of empirical conditions, as justified by the law of freedom, and can thus establish *synthetical* propositions *a priori.* The proof of this in the practical connection, as will be shown afterwards, can be adduced in an analytical manner.

8. *To Have Anything External as One's Own is only Possible in a Juridical or Civil State of Society under the Regulation of a Public Legislative Power*

If, by word or deed, I declare my will that some external thing shall be mine, I make a declaration that every other person is obliged to abstain from the use of this object of my exercise of will; and this imposes an obligation which no one would be under, without such a juridical act on my part. But the assumption of this act at the same time involves the admission that I am obliged reciprocally to observe a similar abstention towards every other in respect of what is externally theirs; for the obligation in question arises from a universal rule regulating the external juridical relations. Hence I am not obliged to let alone what another person declares to be externally his, unless every other person likewise secures me by a guarantee that he will act in relation to what is mine, upon the same principle. This guarantee of reciprocal and mutual abstention from what belongs to others does not require a special juridical act for its establishment, but is already involved in the conception of an external obligation of right, on account of the universality and consequently the reciprocity of the obligatoriness arising from a universal Rule. Now a single will, in relation to an external and consequently contingent possession, cannot serve as a compulsory law for all, because that would be to do violence to the freedom which is in accordance with universal laws. Therefore it is only a will that binds every one, and as such a common, collective, and authoritative will, that can furnish a guarantee of security to all. But the state of men under a universal, external, and public legislation, conjoined with authority and power, is called the civil state. There can therefore be an external mine and thine only in the civil state of society.

Consequence.—It follows, as a corollary, that, if it is juridically possible to have an external object as one's own, the individual subject of possession must be allowed *to compel* or constrain every person with whom a dispute as to the mine or thine of such a possession may arise, to enter along with himself into the relations of a civil constitution.

9. *There May, However, Be an External Mine and Thine Found as a Fact in the State of Nature, but it is only Provisory*

Natural right in the state of a civil constitution means the forms of right which may be deduced from principles *a priori* as the conditions of such a constitution. It is therefore not to be infringed by the statutory laws of such a constitution; and accordingly the juridical principle remains in force, that, "Whoever proceeds upon a maxim by which it becomes *impossible* for me to have an object of the exercise of my will as mine, does me a lesion or injury." For a civil constitution is only the juridical condition under which every one has what is his own merely secured to him, as distinguished from its being specially assigned and determined to him. All guarantee, therefore, assumes that everyone to whom a thing is secured is already in possession of it as his own. Hence, prior to the civil constitution—or *apart* from it—an external mine and thine must be assumed as possible, and along with it a right to compel everyone with whom we could come into any kind of intercourse to enter with us into a constitution in which what is mine or thine can be secured. There may thus be a possession in expectation or in preparation for such a state of security, as can only be established on the law of the common will; and as it is therefore in accordance with the *possibility* of such a state, it constitutes a *provisory* or temporary juridical possession; whereas that possession which is found in reality in the civil state of society will be a *peremptory* or guaranteed possession. Prior to entering into this state, for which he is naturally prepared, the individual rightfully resists those who will not adapt themselves to it, and who would disturb him in his provisory possession; because, if the will of all except himself were imposing upon him an obligation to withdraw from a certain possession, it would still be only a one-sided or *unilateral* will, and consequently it would have just as little *legal* title—which can be properly based only on the universalized will—to contest a claim of right as he would have to *assert* it. Yet he has the advantage on his side, of being in accord with the conditions requisite to the introduction and institution of a civil form of society. In a word, the mode in which anything external may be held as one's own in the *state of nature*, is just *physical* possession with a *presumption* of right thus far in its favour, that by union of the wills of all in a public legislation it will be made *juridical;* and in this expectation it holds *comparatively*, as a kind of potential juridical possession.

This prerogative of right, as arising from the fact of empirical possession, is in accordance with the formula: "It is well for those who are in possession" (*Beati possidentes*). It does not consist in the fact that, because the possessor has the presumption of being a *rightful man,* it is unnecessary for him to bring forward proof that he possesses a certain thing rightfully, for this position applies only to a case of disputed right. But it is because it accords with the postulate of the practical reason, that everyone is invested with the faculty of having as his own any external object upon which he has exerted his will; and, consequently, all actual possession is a state whose rightfulness is established upon that postulate by an anterior act of will. And such an act, if there be no prior possession of the same object by another opposed to it, does, therefore, provisionally justify and entitle me, according to the law of external freedom, to restrain anyone who refuses to enter with me into a state of public legal freedom from all pretension to the use of such an object. For such a procedure is requisite, in conformity with the postulate of reason, in order to subject to my proper use a thing which would otherwise be practically annihilated, as regards all proper use of it.

CHAPTER II. The Mode of Acquiring Anything External

10. *The General Principle of External Acquisition*

I acquire a thing when I act (*efficio*) so that it becomes *mine.* An external thing is *originally* mine when it is mine even without the intervention of a juridical act. An acquisition is *original* and *primary* when it is not derived from what another had already made his own.

There is nothing external that is as such originally mine; but anything external may be originally *acquired* when it is an object that no other person has yet made his. A state in which the mine and thine are in common cannot be conceived as having been at any time original. Such a state of things would have to be acquired by an external juridical act, although there may be an original and common possession of an external object. Even if we think hypothetically of a state in which the mine and thine would be *originally* in common as a *communio mei et tui originaria,* it would still have to be distinguished from a *primeval* communion (*communio primaeva*) with things in common, sometimes supposed to be founded in the first period of the relations of right among men, and which could not be regarded as based upon principles like the former, but only upon history. Even under that condition the historic *communio,* as a supposed primeval community, would always have to be viewed as acquired and derivative *(communio derivativa).*

The principle of external acquisition, then, may be expressed thus: "Whatever I bring under my power according to the law of external freedom, of which as an object of my free activity of will I have the capability of making use according to the postulate of the practical reason, and which I will to become mine in conformity with the idea of a possible united common will, *is* mine."

The practical elements *(momenta attendenda)* constitutive of the process of *original* acquisition are:

1. Prehension or seizure of an object which belongs to no one; for, if it belonged already to some one, the act would conflict with the freedom of others, that is, according to universal laws. This is the *taking possession* of an object of my free activity of will in space and time; the possession, therefore, into which I thus put myself is sensible or physical possession *(possessio phenomenon)*;

2. Declaration of the possession of this object by formal designation and the act of my free-will in interdicting every other person from using it as his;

3. Appropriation, as the act, in idea, of an externally legislative common will, by which all and each are obliged to respect and act in conformity with my act of will.

The validity of the last element in the process of acquisition, as that on which the conclusion that "the external object is mine" rests, is what makes the possession valid as a purely rational and *juridical* possession *(possessio noumenon).* It is founded upon the fact that, as all these acts are *juridical,* they consequently proceed from the practical reason, and therefore, in the question as to what is right, abstraction may be made of the empirical conditions involved, and the conclusion, "the external object is mine," thus becomes a correct inference from the external fact of sensible possession to the internal right of rational possession.

The original *primary* acquisition of an external object of the action of the will, is called *occupancy.* It can only take place in reference to substances or corporeal things. Now when this occupation of an external object does take place, the act presupposes, as a condition of such empirical possession, its priority in time before the act of any other who may also be willing to enter upon occupation of it. Hence the legal maxim: *"qui prior tempore, potior jure."* Such occupation as original or primary is, further, the effect only of a single or *unilateral* will; for were a bilateral or twofold will requisite for it, it would be derived from a contract of two or more persons with each other, and consequently it would be based upon what another or others had already made their own. It is not easy to see how such an act of free-will as this would be could really form a foundation for every one having his own. However, the *first* acquisition of a thing is on that account not quite exactly the same as the *original* acquisition of it. For the acquisition of a public juridical state by union of the wills of all in a universal legislation would be such an original acquisition, seeing that no other of the kind could precede it, and yet it would be *derived* from the particular wills of all the individuals, and consequently become all-sided or *omnilateral;* for a properly *primary acquisition* can only proceed from an individual or unilateral will.

Division of the Subject of the Acquisition of the External Mine and Thine

I. In respect of the matter of object of acquisition, I acquire either a corporeal thing (substance), or the performance of something by another (causality), or this other as a person in respect of his state, so far as I have a right to dispose of the same (in a relation of reciprocity with him).

II. In respect of the form or mode of acquisition, it is either a real right (*jus reale*), or a personal right (*jus personale*), or a real-personal right (*jus realiter personale*), to the possession although not to the use, of another person as if he were a thing.

III. In respect of the ground of right or the title (*titulus*) of acquisition—which, properly, is not a particular member of the division of rights, but rather a constituent element of the mode of exercising them—anything external is acquired by a certain free exercise of will that is either *unilateral,* as the act of a single will (*facto*), or *bilateral,* as the act of two wills (*pacto*), or *omnilateral,* as the act of all the wills of a community together (*lege*).

Section I. *Principles of Real Right*

11. *What is a Real Right?*

The usual definition of real right, or "right in a thing" (*jus reale, jus in re*), is that "it is a right as *against every possessor of it.*" This is a correct nominal definition. But what is it that entitles me to claim an external object from any one who may appear as its possessor, and to compel him, *per vindicationem,* to put me again, in place of himself, into possession of it? Is this external juridical relation of my will a kind of *immediate* relation to an external thing? If so, whoever might think of his right as referring not immediately to persons but to things would have to represent it, although only in an obscure way, somewhat thus. A right on one side has always a duty corresponding to it on the other, so that an external thing, although away from the hands of its first possessor, continues to be still connected with him by a continuing obligation; and thus it refuses to fall under the claim of any other possessor, because it is already bound to another. In this way my right, viewed as a kind of good genius accompanying a thing and preserving it from all external attack, would refer an alien possessor always to me! It is, however, absurb to think of an obligation of persons towards things, and conversely; although it may be allowed in any particular case to represent the juridical relation by a sensible image of this kind, and to express it in this way.

The real definition would run thus: "Right in a thing is a right to the private use of a thing, of which I am in possession—original or derivative—in common with all others." For this is the one condition under which it is alone possible that I can exclude every other possessor from the private use of the thing *(jus contra quemlibet hujus rei possessorem).* For, except by presupposing such a common collective possession, it cannot be conceived how, when I am not in actual possession of a thing, I could be injured or wronged by others who are in possession of it and use it. By an individual act of my own will I cannot oblige any other person to abstain from the use of a thing in respect of which he would otherwise be under no obligation; and, accordingly, such an obligation can only arise from the collective will of all united in a relation of common possession. Otherwise, I would have to think of a right in a thing, as if the *thing* has an obligation towards me, and as if the right as against every possessor of it had to be derived from this obligation in the thing, which is an absurb way of representing the subject.

Further, by the term *real right* (*jus reale*) is meant not only the *right in a thing (jus in re),* but also the *constitutive principle* of all the laws which relate to the real mine and thine. It is, however, evident that a man entirely alone upon the earth could properly neither have nor acquire any external thing as his own; because, between him as a person and all external things as material objects, there could be no relations of obligation. There is therefore, literally, no *direct* right in a thing, but only that right is to be properly called "real" which belongs to any one as constituted against a person, who is in common possession of things with all others in the civil state of society.

12. *The First Acquisition of a Thing can only be that of the Soil*

By the soil is understood all habitable Land. In relation to everything that is moveable upon it, it is to be regarded as a *substance,* and the mode of the existence of the moveables is viewed as an *inherence* in it. And just as, in the theoretical acceptance, accidents cannot exist apart from their substances, so, in the practical relation, moveables upon the soil cannot be regarded as belonging to any one unless he is supposed to have been previously in juridical possession of the soil, so that it is thus considered to be his.

For, let it be supposed that the soil belongs to no one. Then I would be entitled to remove every moveable thing found upon it from its place, even to total loss of it, in order to occupy that place, without infringing thereby on the freedom of any other; there being, by the hypothesis, no possessor of it at all. But everything that can be destroyed, such as a tree, a house, and such like—as regards its matter at least—is moveable; and if we call a thing which cannot be moved without destruction of its form an *immoveable,* the mine and thine in it is not understood as applying to its substance, but to that which is adherent to it and which does not essentially constitute the thing itself.

13. *Every Part of the Soil may be Originally Acquired; and the Principle of the Possibility of such Acquisition is the Original Community of the Soil Generally*

The first clause of this proposition is founded upon the postulate of the practical reason (§ 2); the second is established by the following proof.

All men are originally and before any juridical act of will in rightful possession of the soil; that is, they have a right to be wherever nature or chance has placed them without their will. Possession (*possessio*), which is to be distinguished from residential settlement (*sedes*) as a voluntary, acquired, and *permanent* possession, becomes *common* possession, on account of the connection with each other of all the places on the surface of the earth as a globe. For, had the surface of the earth been an infinite plain, men could have been so dispersed upon it that they might not have come into any necessary communion with each other, and a state of social community would not have been a necessary consequence of their existence upon the earth. Now that possession proper to all men upon the earth, which is prior to all their particular juridical acts, constitutes an *original possession in common* (*communio possessionis originaria*). The conception of such an original, common possession of things is not derived from experience, nor is it dependent on conditions of time, as is the case with the imaginary and indemonstrable fiction of *a primaeval community of possession* in actual history. Hence it is a practical conception of reason, involving in itself the only principle according to which men may use the place they happen to occupy on the surface of the earth, in accordance with laws of right.

14. *The Juridical Act of this Original Acquisition is Occupancy*

The act of taking possession (*apprehensio*), as being at its beginning the physical appropriation of a corporeal thing in space (*possessionis physicae*), can accord with the law of the external freedom of all, under no other condition than that of its *priority* in respect of time. In this relation it must have the characteristic of a first act in the way of taking possession, as a free exercise of will. The activity of will, however, as determining that the thing—in this case a definite separate place on the surface of the earth—shall be mine, being an act of appropriation, cannot be otherwise in the case of original acquisition than individual or *unilateral* (*voluntas unilateralis s. propria*). Now, occupancy is the acquisition of an external object by an individual act of will. The original acquisition of such an object as a limited portion of the soil can therefore only be accomplished by an act of occupation.

The possibility of this mode of acquisition cannot be intuitively apprehended by pure reason in any way, nor established by its principles, but is an immediate consequence from the postulate of the practical reason. The will as practical reason, however, cannot justify external acquisition otherwise than only in so far as it is itself included in an absolutely authoritative will, with which it is united by implication; or, in other words, only in so far as it is contained within a union of the wills of all who come into practical relation with each other. For an individual, unilateral will—and the same applies to a dual or other particular will—cannot impose on all an obligation which is contingent in itself. This requires an *omnilateral* or universal will, which is not contingent, but *a priori*, and which is therefore necessarily united and legislative. Only in accordance with such a principle can there be agreement of the active free-will of each individual with the freedom of all, and consequently rights in general, or even the possibility of an external mine and thine.

15. *It is Only within a Civil Constitution that Anything can be Acquired Peremptorily, whereas in the State of Nature Acquisition can only be Provisory*

A civil constitution is objectively necessary as a duty, although subjectively its reality is contingent. Hence, there is connected with it a real natural law of right, to which all external acquisition is subjected.

The *empirical title of acquisition* has been shown to be constituted by the taking physical possession (*apprehensio physica*) as founded upon an original community of right in all to the soil. And because a possession in the phenomenal sphere of sense can only be subordinated to that possession which is in accordance with rational conceptions of right, there must correspond to this physical act of possession a rational mode of taking possession by elimination of all the empirical conditions in space and time. This rational form of possession establishes the proposition that "whatever I bring under my power in accordance with laws of external freedom, and will that it shall be mine, becomes mine."

The *rational title of acquisition* can therefore only lie originally in the idea of the will of all united implicitly, or necessarily to be united, which is here tacitly assumed as an indispensable condition (*conditio sine qua non*). For by a single will there cannot be imposed upon others an obligation by which they would not have been otherwise bound. But the fact formed by wills actually and universally united in a legislation constitutes the civil state of society. Hence, it is only in conformity with the idea of a civil state of society, or in reference to it and its realization, that anything external can be acquired. Before such a state is realized, and in anticipation of it, acquisition, which would otherwise be derived, is consequently only *provisory*. The acquisition which is *peremptory* finds place only in the civil state.

Nevertheless, such provisory acquisition is

real acquisition. For, according to the postulate of the juridically practical reason, the possibility of acquisition in whatever state men may happen to be living beside one another, and therefore in the state of nature as well, is a principle of private right. And in accordance with this principle, every one is justified or entitled to exercise that compulsion by which it alone becomes possible to pass out of the state of nature and to enter into that state of civil society which alone can make all acquisition peremptory.

It is a question as to how far the right of taking possession of the soil extends. The answer is, So far as the capability of having it under one's power extends; that is, just as far as he who wills to appropriate it can defend it, as if the soil were to say: "If you cannot protect me, neither can you command me." In this way the controversy about what constitutes a *free* or *closed* sea must be decided. Thus, within the range of a cannon-shot no one has a right to intrude on the coast of a country that already belongs to a certain state, in order to fish or gather amber on the shore, or such like. Further, the question is put, "Is cultivation of the soil, by building, agriculture, drainage, etc., necessary in order to its acquisition?" *No*. For, as these processes as forms of specification are only accidents, they do not constitute objects of immediate possession and can only belong to the subject in so far as the substance of them has been already recognized as his. When it is a question of the first acquisition of a thing, the cultivation or modification of it by labour forms nothing more than an external sign of the fact that it has been taken into possession, and this can be indicated by many other signs that cost less trouble. Again: "May any one be hindered in the *act* of taking possession, so that neither one nor other of two competitors shall acquire the right of priority, and the soil in consequence may remain for all time free as belonging to no one?" *Not at all.* Such a hindrance cannot be allowed to take place, because the second of the two, in order to be enabled to do this, would himself have to be upon some neighbouring soil, where he also, in this manner, could be hindered from being, and such *absolute hindering* would involve a contradiction. It would, however, be quite consistent with the right of occupation, in the case of a certain intervening piece of the soil, to let it lie unused as a *neutral* ground for the separation of two neighbouring states; but under such a condition, that ground would actually belong to them both in common, and would not be without an owner (*res nullius*), just because it would be *used* by both in order to form a separation between them. Again: "May one have a thing as his, on a soil of which no one has appropriated any part as his own?" *Yes.* In Mongolia, for example, any one may let lie whatever baggage he has, or bring back the horse that has run away from him into his possession as his own, because the whole soil belongs to the people generally, and the use of it accordingly belongs to every individual. But that any one can have a moveable thing on the soil of another as his own is only possible by *contract.* Finally, there is the question: "May one of two neighbouring nations or tribes resist another when attempting to impose upon them a certain mode of using a particular soil; as, for instance, a tribe of hunters making such an attempt in relation to a pastoral people, or the latter to agriculturists and such like?" *Certainly.* For the mode in which such peoples or tribes may *settle* themselves upon the surface of the earth, provided they keep within their own boundaries, is a matter of mere pleasure and choice on their own part (*res merae facultatis*).

As a further question, it may be asked whether, when neither nature nor chance, but merely our own will, brings us into the neighbourhood of a people that gives no promise of a prospect of entering into civil union with us, we are to be considered entitled in any case to proceed with force in the intention of founding such a union, and bringing into a juridical state such men as the savage American Indians, the Hottentots, and the New Hollanders; or—and the case is not much better—whether we may establish colonies by deceptive purchase, and so become owners of their soil, and, in general, without regard to their first possession, make use at will of our superiority in relation to them? Further, may it not be held that Nature herself, as abhorring a vacuum, seems to demand such a procedure, and that large regions in other continents, that are now magnificently peopled, would otherwise have remained unpossessed by civilized inhabitants and might have for ever remained thus, so that the end of creation would have so far been frustrated? It is almost unnecessary to answer; for it is easy to see through all this flimsy veil of injustice, which just amounts to the Jesuitism of making a good end justify any means. This mode of acquiring the soil is, therefore, to be repudiated.

The indefiniteness of external acquirable objects in respect of their quantity, as well as their quality, makes the problem of the sole primary external acquisition of them one of the most difficult to solve. There must, however, be some one first acquisition of an external object; for every Acquisition cannot be derivative. Hence, the problem is not to be given up as insoluble or in itself as impossible. If it is solved by reference to the original contract, unless this contract is extended so as to include the whole human race, acquisition under it would still remain but provisional.

16. *Exposition of the Conception of a Primary Acquisition of the Soil*

All men are originally in a *common collective possession* of the soil of the whole earth (*communio fundi originaria*), and they have naturally each a will to use it (*lex justi*). But on account of the opposition of the free will of one to that of the other in the sphere of action, which is inevitable by nature, all use of the soil would be prevented did not every will contain at the same time a law for the regulation of the relation of all wills in action, according to which a *particular possession* can be determined to every one upon the common soil. This is the juridical law (*lex juridica*). But the distributive law of the mine and thine, as applicable to each individual on the soil, according to the axiom of external freedom, cannot proceed otherwise than from a *primarily* united will *a priori*—which does not presuppose any juridical act as requisite for this union. This Law can only take form in the civil state (*lex justitiae distributivae*); as it is in this state alone that the united common will determines what is *right,* what is *rightful,* and what is the constitution of *Right.* In reference to this state, however—and prior to its establishment and in view of it—it is *provisorily* a *duty* for every one to proceed according to the law of external acquisition; and accordingly it is a juridical procedure on the part of the will to lay every one under obligation to recognise the act of possessing and appropriating, although it be only unilaterally. Hence a provisory acquisition of the soil, with all its juridical consequences, is possible in the state of nature.

Such an acquisition, however, requires and also obtains the *favour* of a permissive law (*lex permissiva*), in respect of the determination of the limits of juridically possible possession. For it precedes the juridical state, and as merely introductory to it is not yet peremptory; and this favour does not extend farther than the date of the consent of the *other* co-operators in the establishment of the civil state. But if they are opposed to entering into the civil state, as long as this opposition lasts it carries all the effect of a guaranteed juridical acquisition with it, because the advance from the state of nature to the civil state is founded upon a duty.

17. *Deduction of the Conception of the Original Primary Acquisition*

We have found the *title* of acquisition in a universal original community of the soil, under the conditions of an external acquisition in space; and the *mode* of acquisition is contained in the empirical fact of taking possession (*apprehensio*), conjoined with the will to have an external object as one's own. It is further necessary to unfold, from the principles of the pure juridically practical reason involved in the conception, the juridical acquisition proper of an object—that is, the external mine and thine that follows from the two previous conditions, as rational possession (*possessio noumenon*).

The *juridical conception* of the *external* mine and thine, so far as it involves the category of *substance,* cannot by "that which is *external* to me" mean merely "*in a place* other than that in which I am"; for it is a *rational* conception. As under the conceptions of the reason only intellectual conceptions can be embraced, the expression in question can only signify "something that is different and distinct from me" according to the idea of a non-empirical possession through, as it were, a continuous activity in taking possession of an external object; and it involves only the notion of *having something in my power,* which indicates the connection of an object with myself, as a subjective condition of the possibility of making use of it. This forms a purely intellectual conception of the understanding. Now we can leave out or abstract from the sensible conditions of possession, as relations of a person to *objects* which have no obligation. This process of elimination just gives the rational relation of a person to *persons;* and it is such that he can bind them all by an obligation in reference to the use of things through his act of will, so far as it is conformable to the *axiom* of freedom, the *postulate* of right, and the universal *legislation* of the common will, conceived as united *a priori.* This is therefore the rational intelligible *possession* of things as by pure right, although they are objects of sense.

It is evident that the first modification, limitation, or *transformation* generally, of a portion of the soil cannot of itself furnish a title to its acquisition, since possession of an accident does not form a ground for legal possession of the substance. Rather, conversely, the inference as to the mine and thine must be drawn from ownership of the substance according to the rule: *Accessarium sequitur suum principale.* Hence one who has spent labour on a piece of ground that was not already his own, has lost his effort and work to the former owner. This position is so evident of itself that the old opinion to the opposite effect, that is still spread far and wide, can hardly be ascribed to any other than the prevailing illusion which unconsciously leads to the personification of things; and, then, as if they could be bound under an obligation by the labour bestowed upon them to be at the service of the person who does the labour, to regard them as his by *immediate* right. Otherwise it is probable that the natural question—already discussed—would not have been passed over with so light a tread, namely: "How is a right in a *thing* possible?" For, right as against every possible possessor of a thing means only the claim of a particular will to the use of an object so far as it may be included in the all-comprehending universal will, and can be thought as in harmony with its law.

As regards bodies situated upon a piece of ground which is already mine, if they otherwise belong to no other person, they belong to me without my requiring any particular juridical act for the purpose of this acquisition; they are mine not *facto,* but *lege.* For they may be regarded as accidents inhering in the substance of the soil, and they are thus mine *jure rei meae.* To this category also belongs everything which is so connected with anything of mine that it cannot be separated from what is mine without altering it substantially. Examples of this are gilding on an object, mixture of a material belonging to me with other things, alluvial deposit, or even alteration of the adjoining bed of a stream or river in my favour so as to produce an increase of my land, etc. By the same principles, the question must also be decided as to whether the acquirable soil may extend farther than the existing land, so as even to include part of the bed of the sea, with the right to fish on my own shores, to gather amber and such like. So far as I have the mechanical *capability* from my own *site,* as the place I occupy, to secure my soil from the attack of others—and, therefore, as far as cannon can carry from the shore—all is included in my *possession,* and the sea is thus far closed (*mare clausum*). But as there is no *site* for occupation upon the wide sea itself, possible possession cannot be extended so far, and the open sea is free (*mare liberum*). But in the case of men, or things that belong to them, becoming *stranded* on the shore, since the fact is not voluntary, it cannot be regarded by the owner of the shore as giving him a right of acquisition. For shipwreck is not an act of will, nor is its result a lesion to him; and things which may have come thus upon his soil, as still belonging to some one, are not to be treated as being without an owner or *res nullius.* On the other hand, a river, so far as possession of the bank reaches, may be originally acquired, like any other piece of ground, under the above restrictions, by one who is in possession of both its banks.

Property

An external object, which, in respect of its substance can be claimed by some one as his own, is called the *property* (*dominium*) of that person to whom all the rights in it as a thing belong—like the accidents inhering in a substance—and which, therefore, he as the proprietor (*dominus*) can dispose of at *will* (*jus disponendi de re sua*). But from this it follows at once that such an object can only be a corporeal thing towards which there is no direct personal obligation. Hence a man may be his own master (*sui juris*) but not the proprietor *of himself* (*sui dominus*), so as to be able to dispose of himself at will, to say nothing of the possibility of such a relation to other men; because he is responsible to humanity in his own person. This point, however, as belonging to the right of humanity as such, rather than to that of individual men, would not be discussed at its proper place here, but is only mentioned incidentally for the better elucidation of what has just been said. It may be further observed that there may be two full proprietors of one and the same thing, without there being a mine and thine in common, but only in so far as they are common possessors of what belongs only to *one* of them as *his own.* In such a case the whole possession, without the use of the thing, belongs to one only of the coproprietors (*condomini*); while to the others belongs all the use of the thing along with its possession. The former as the direct proprietor (*dominus directus*), therefore, restricts the latter as the proprietor in use (*dominus utilis*) to the condition of a certain continuous performance, with reference to the thing itself, without limiting him in the use of it.

SECTION II. *Principles of Personal Right*

18. *Nature and Acquisition of Personal Right*

The possession of the active free-will of another person, as the power to determine it by my will to a certain action, according to laws of freedom, is a form of right relating to the external mine and thine, as affected by the causality of another. It is possible to have several such rights in reference to the same person or to different persons. The principle of the system of laws, according to which I can be in such possession, is that of personal right, and there is only one such principle.

The acquisition of a personal right can never be primary or arbitrary; for such a mode of acquiring it would not be in accordance with the principle of the harmony of the freedom of my will with the freedom of every other, and it would therefore be wrong. Nor can such a right be acquired by means of any *unjust* act of another (*facto injusti alterius*), as being itself contrary to right; for if such a wrong as it implies were perpetrated on me, and I could demand satisfaction from the other, in accordance with right, yet in such a case I would only be entitled to maintain undiminished what was mine, and not to acquire anything more than what I formerly had.

Acquisition by means of the action of another, to which I determine his will according to laws of right, is therefore always derived from what that other has as his own. This derivation, as a juridical act, cannot be effected by a mere *negative relinquishment or renunciation* of what is his (*per derelictionem aut renunciationem*); because such a negative act would only amount to a cessation of *his* right, and not to the acquirement of a right on the part of another. It is therefore only by positive transference (*translatio*), or conveyance, that a personal right can be acquired; and this is only possible by means of a common will, through which objects come into the power of one or other, so that as one renounces a particular thing which he holds under the common right, the same object when accepted by another, in consequence of a positive act of will, becomes his. Such transference of the *property* of one to another is termed its *alienation*. The act of the united wills of two persons, by which what belonged to one passes to the other, constitutes *contract*.

19. *Acquisition by Contract*

In every contract there are *four juridical acts* of will involved; *two* of them being *preparatory acts*, and *two* of them *constitutive acts*. The two preparatory acts, as forms of treating in the transaction, are offer (*oblatio*) and approval (*approbatio*); the two constitutive acts, as the forms of *concluding* the transaction, are promise (*promissum*) and acceptance (*acceptatio*). For an offer cannot constitute a promise before it can be judged that the thing offered (*oblatum*) is something that is *agreeable* to the party to whom it is offered, and this much is shown by the first two declarations; but by them alone there is nothing as yet acquired.

Further, it is neither by the *particular* will of the promiser nor that of the acceptor that the property of the former passes over to the latter. This is effected only by the *combined* or united wills of both, and consequently so far only as the will of both is declared at the same time or simultaneously. Now, such simultaneousness is impossible by empirical acts of declaration, which can only *follow* each other in time and are never actually simultaneous. For if I have promised, and another person is now merely willing to accept, during the interval before actual acceptance, however short it may be, I may retract my offer, because I am thus far still free; and, on the other side, the acceptor, for the same reason, may likewise hold himself not to be bound, up till the moment of acceptance, by his counter-declaration following upon the promise. The external formalities or solemnities (*solemnia*) on the conclusion of a contract—such as shaking hands or breaking a straw (*stipula*) laid hold of by two persons—and all the various modes of confirming the declarations on either side, prove in fact the embarrassment of the contracting parties as to how and in what way they may represent declarations, which are always *successive*, as existing *simultaneously* at the same moment; and these forms fail to do this. They are, by their very nature, acts necessarily following each other in time, so that when the one act is, the other either is *not yet* or is *no longer*.

It is only the philosophical transcendental deduction of the conception of acquisition by contract that can remove all these difficulties. In a *juridical* external relation, my taking possession of the free-will of another, as the cause that determined it to a certain act, is conceived at first empirically by means of the declaration and counter-declaration of the free-will of each of us in time, as the sensible conditions of taking possession; and the two juridical acts must necessarily be regarded as following one another in time. But because this relation, viewed as juridical, is purely rational in itself, the will as a law-giving faculty of reason represents this possession as intelligible or rational (*possessio noumenon*), in accordance with conceptions of freedom and under abstraction of those empirical conditions. And now, the two acts of promise and acceptance are not regarded as *following* one another in time, but, in the manner of a *pactum re initum*, as proceeding from a *common* will, which is expressed by the term "at the same time," or "simultaneous," and the object promised (*promissum*) is represented, under elimination of empirical conditions, as acquired according to the law of the pure practical reason.

That this is the true and only possible deduction of the idea of acquisition by contract is sufficiently attested by the laborious yet always futile striving of writers on jurisprudence—such as Moses Mendelssohn in his *Jerusalem*—to adduce a proof of its rational possibility. The question is put thus: "Why *ought* I to keep my Promise?" For it is assumed as understood by all that I *ought* to do so. It is, however, absolutely impossible to give any further proof of the categorical imperative implied; just as it is impossible for the geometrician to prove by rational syllogisms that in order to construct a triangle I must take three lines—so far an analytical proposition—of which three lines any two together must be greater than the third—a synthetical proposition, and like the former *a priori*. It is a postulate of the pure reason that we ought to abstract from all the sensible conditions of space and time in reference to the conception of right; and the theory of the possibility of such abstraction from these conditions, without taking away the reality of the possession, just constitutes the transcendental deduction of the conception of acquisition by contract. It is quite akin to what was presented under the last title, as the theory of acquisition by occupation of the external object.

20. *What is Acquired by Contract?*

But what is that, designated as *external*, which I acquire by contract? As it is only the causality of the active will of another, in respect of the performance of something promised to me, I do not immediately acquire thereby an external thing, but an act of the will in question, whereby a thing is brought under my power so that I make it mine. By the contract, therefore, I acquire the promise of another, as distinguished from the thing promised; and yet something is thereby added to my having and possession. I have become the richer in possession (*locupletior*) by the acquisition of an active obligation that I can bring to bear upon the freedom and capability of another. This my *right*, however, is only a *personal* right, valid only to the effect of acting upon a *particular* physical person and specially upon the causality of his will, so that he shall *perform* something for me. It is not a *real* right upon that *moral person*, which is identified with the idea of the united *will of all* viewed *a priori*, and through which alone I can acquire a *right valid against every possessor of the thing*. For, it is in this that all right *in a thing* consists.

The transfer or transmission of what is mine to another by contract, takes place according to the law of continuity (*lex continui*). Possession of the object is not interrupted for a moment during this act; for, otherwise, I would acquire an object in this state as a thing that had no possessor, and it would thus be acquired originally, which is contrary to the idea of a contract. This continuity, however, implies that it is not the particular will of either the promiser or the acceptor, but their united will in common, that transfers what is mine to another. And hence it is not accomplished in such a manner that the promiser first relinquishes (*derelinquit*) his possession for the benefit of another, or renounces his right (*renunciat*), and thereupon the other at the same time enters upon it; or conversely. The transfer (*translatio*) is therefore an act in which the object belongs for a moment *at the same time* to both, just as in the parabolic path of a projectile the object on reaching its highest point may be regarded for a moment as *at the same time* both rising and falling, and as thus passing in fact from the ascending to the falling motion.

21. *Acceptance and Delivery*

A thing is not acquired in a case of contract by the acceptance (*acceptatio*) of the promise, but only by the delivery (*traditio*) of the object promised. For all promise is relative to *performance;* and if what was promised is a thing, the performance cannot be executed otherwise than by an act whereby the acceptor is put by the promiser into possession of the thing; and this is delivery. Before the delivery and the reception of the thing, the performance of the act required has not yet taken place; the thing has not yet passed from the one person to the other and, consequently, has not been acquired by that other. Hence the right arising from a contract is only a personal right; and it only becomes a real right by delivery.

A contract upon which delivery immediately follows (*pactum re initum*) excludes any interval of time between its conclusion and its execution; and as such it requires no further particular act in the future by which one person may transfer to another what is his. But if there is a time—definite or indefinite—agreed upon between them for the delivery, the question then arises whether the thing has already before that time become the acceptor's by the contract, so that his right is a right in the thing; *or* whether a further special contract regarding the delivery alone must be entered upon, so that the right that is acquired by mere acceptance is only a personal right, and thus it does not become a right in the thing until delivery? That the relation must be determined according to the latter alternative will be clear from what follows.

Suppose I conclude a contract about a thing that I wish to acquire—such as a horse—and that I take it immediately into my stable, or otherwise into my possession; then it is mine (*vi pacti re initi*), and my right is a right in the thing. But if I leave it in the hands of the seller without arranging with him specially in whose physical possession or holding (*detentio*) this thing shall be before my taking possession of it (*apprehensio*), and consequently, before the actual change of possession, the horse is not yet mine; and the right which I acquire is only a right against a particular person—namely, the seller of the horse—*to be put into possession* of the object (*poscendi traditionem*) as the subjective condition of any use of it at my will. My right is thus only a personal right to demand from the seller the *performance* of his promise (*praestatio*) to put me into possession of the thing. Now, if the contract does not contain the condition of delivery *at the same time*—as a *pactum re initum*—and consequently an interval of time intervenes between the conclusion of the contract and the taking possession of the object of acquisition, I cannot obtain possession of it during this interval otherwise than by exercising the particular juridical activity called *a possessory act* (*actum possessorium*), which constitutes a special contract. This act consists in my saying, "I will send to fetch the horse," to which the seller has to agree. For it is not self-evident or universally reasonable that any one will take a thing destined for the use of another into his charge at his own risk. On the contrary, a special contract is necessary for this arrangement, according to which the alienator of a thing continues to be its owner during a certain *definite* time, and must bear the risk of whatever may happen to it; while the acquirer can only be regarded by the seller as the owner when he has delayed to enter into possession beyond the date at which he agreed to take delivery. Prior to the possessory act, therefore, all that is acquired by the contract is only a personal right; and the acceptor can acquire an external thing only by delivery.

SECTION III. *Principles of Personal Right that is Real in Kind.* (Jus Realiter Personale)

22. *Nature of Personal Right of a Real Kind*

Personal right of a real kind is the right to the *possession* of an external object as a thing, and to the *use* of it as a person. The mine and thine embraced under this right relate specially to the family and household; and the relations involved are those of free beings in reciprocal real interaction with each other. Through their relations and influence as persons upon one another, in accordance with the principle of external freedom as the *cause* of it, they form a society composed as a whole of members standing in community with each other as persons; and this constitutes the household. The mode in which this social status is acquired by individuals, and the functions which prevail within it, proceed neither by arbitrary individual action (*facto*), nor by mere contract (*pacto*), but by law (*lege*). And this law as being not only a right, but also as constituting possession in reference to a person, is a right rising above all *mere* real and personal right. It must, in fact, form the right of humanity in our own person; and, as such, it has as its consequence a natural permissive law, by the favour of which such acquisition becomes possible to us.

23. *What is Acquired in the Household?*

The acquisition that is founded upon this law is, as regards its objects, threefold. The man acquires a wife; the husband and wife acquire children, constituting a family; and the family acquire domestics. All these objects, while acquirable, are inalienable; and the right of possession in these objects is *the most strictly personal of all rights.*

The Rights of the Family as a Domestic Society

Title I. *Conjugal Right. (Husband and Wife)*

24. *The Natural Basis of Marriage*

The domestic relations are founded on marriage, and marriage is founded upon the natural reciprocity or intercommunity (*commercium*) of the sexes.[1] This natural union of the sexes proceeds according to the mere animal nature (*vaga libido, venus vulgivaga, fornicatio*), or according to the law. The latter is marriage (*matrimonium*), which is the union of two persons of different sex for life-long reciprocal possession of their sexual faculties. The end of producing and educating children may be regarded as always the end of nature in implanting mutual desire and inclination in the sexes; but it is not necessary for the rightfulness of marriage that those who marry should set this before themselves as the end of their union, otherwise the marriage would be dissolved of itself when the production of children ceased.

And even assuming that enjoyment in the reciprocal use of the sexual endowments is an end of marriage, yet the contract of marriage is not on that account a matter of arbitrary will, but is a contract necessary in its nature by the law of humanity. In other words, if a man and a woman have the will to enter on reciprocal enjoyment in accordance with their sexual nature, they *must* necessarily marry each other; and this necessity is in accordance with the juridical laws of pure reason.

25. *The Rational Right of Marriage*

For, this natural *commercium*—as a *usus membrorum sexualium alterius*—is an enjoyment for which the one person is given up to the other. In this relation the human individual makes himself a *res*, which is contrary to the right of humanity in his own person. This, however, is only possible under the one condition, that as the one person is acquired by the other as a *res*, that same person also equally acquires the other reciprocally, and thus regains and reestablishes the rational personality. The acquisition of a part of the human organism being, on account of its unity, at the same time the acquisition of the whole person, it follows that the surrender and acceptation of, or by, one sex in relation to the other, is not only *permissible* under the condition of marriage, but is further *only* really possible under that condition. But the personal right thus acquired is, at the same time, *real in kind;* and this characteristic of it is established by the fact that if one of the married persons run away or enter into the possession of another, the other is entitled, at any time, and incontestably, to bring such a one back to the former relation, as if that person were a thing.

26. *Monogamy and Equality in Marriage*

For the same reasons, the relation of the married persons to each other is a relation of equality as regards the mutual possession of their persons, as well as of their goods. Consequently marriage is only truly realized in monogamy; for in the relation of polygamy the person who is given away on the one side, gains only a part of the one to whom that person is given up, and therefore becomes a mere *res*. But in respect of their goods, they have severally the right to renounce the use of any part of them, although only by a special contract.

From the principle thus stated, it also follows that concubinage is as little capable of being brought under a contract of right as the hiring of a person on any one occasion, in the way of a *pactum fornicationis*. For, as regards such a contract as this latter relation would imply, it must be admitted by all that any one who might enter into it could not be legally held to the fulfilment of their promise if they wished to resile from it. And as regards the former, a contract of concubinage would also fall as a *pactum turpe;* because as a contract of the *hire* (*locatio, conductio*), of a part for the use of another, on account of the inseparable unity of the members of a person, any one entering into such a contract would be actually surrendering as a *res* to the arbitrary will of another. Hence any party may annul a contract like this if entered into with any other, at any time and at pleasure; and that other would have no ground, in the circumstances, to complain of a lesion of his right. The same holds likewise of a morganatic or "left-hand" marriage, contracted in

[1] *Commercium sexuale est usus membrorum et facultatum sexualium alterius.* This "usus" is either natural, by which human beings may reproduce their own kind, or unnatural, which, again, refers either to a person of the same sex or to an animal of another species than man. These transgressions of all law, as *crimina carnis contra naturam*, are even "not to be named"; and, as wrongs against all humanity in the person, they cannot be saved, by any limitation or exception whatever, from entire reprobation.

order to turn the inequality in the social status of the two parties to advantage in the way of establishing the social supremacy of the one over the other; for, in fact, such a relation is not really different from concubinage, according to the principles of natural right, and therefore does not constitute a real marriage. Hence the question may be raised as to whether it is not contrary to the equality of married persons when the law says in any way of the husband in relation to the wife, "he shall be thy master," so that he is represented as the one who commands, and she is the one who obeys. This, however, cannot be regarded as contrary to the natural equality of a human pair, if such legal supremacy is based only upon the natural superiority of the faculties of the husband compared with the wife, in the effectuation of the common interest of the household, and if the right to command is based merely upon this fact. For this right may thus be deduced from the very duty of unity and equality in relation to the *end* involved.

27. *Fulfilment of the Contract of Marriage*

The contract of marriage is completed only by conjugal cohabitation. A contract of two persons of different sex, with the secret understanding either to abstain from conjugal cohabitation or with the consciousness on either side of incapacity for it, is a *simulated contract;* it does not constitute a marriage, and it may be dissolved by either of the parties at will. But if the incapacity only arises after marriage, the right of the contract is not annulled or diminished by a contingency that cannot be legally blamed.

The acquisition of a spouse, either as a husband or as a wife, is therefore not constituted *facto*—that is, by cohabitation—without a preceding contract; nor even *pacto*—by a mere contract of marriage, without subsequent cohabitation; but only *lege,* that is, as a juridical consequence of the obligation that is formed by two persons entering into a sexual union solely on the basis of a reciprocal *possession* of each other, which possession at the same time is only effected in reality by the reciprocal *usus facultatum sexualium alterius.*

Title II. *Parental Right.* (*Parent and Child*)

28. *The Relation of Parent and Child*

From the duty of man towards himself—that is, towards the humanity in his own person—there thus arises a personal right on the part of the members of the opposite sexes, as persons, to acquire one another really and reciprocally by marriage. In like manner, from the fact of *procreation* in the union thus constituted, there follows the duty of preserving and rearing *children* as the products of this union. Accordingly, children, as persons, have, at the same time, an original congenital right—distinguished from mere hereditary right—to be reared by the care of their parents till they are capable of maintaining themselves; and this provision becomes immediately theirs by law, without any particular juridical act being required to determine it.

For what is thus produced is a *person,* and it is impossible to think of a being endowed with personal freedom as produced merely by a physical process. And hence, *in the practical relation,* it is quite a correct and even a necessary idea to regard the act of generation as a process by which a person is brought without his consent into the world and placed in it by the responsible free will of others. This act, therefore, attaches an obligation to the parents to make their children—as far as their power goes—contented with the condition thus acquired. Hence parents cannot regard their child as, in a manner, a thing *of their own making;* for a being endowed with freedom cannot be so regarded. Nor, consequently, have they a right to destroy it as if it were their own property, or even to leave it to chance; because they have brought a being into the world who becomes in fact a citizen of the world, and they have placed that being in a state which they cannot be left to treat with indifference, even according to the natural conceptions of right.

We cannot even conceive how it is possible that God *can create* free beings; for it appears as if all their future actions, being predetermined by that first act, would be contained in the chain of natural necessity, and that, therefore, they could not be free. But as men we *are* free in fact, as is proved by the categorical imperative in the moral and practical relation as an authoritative decision of reason; yet reason cannot make the possibility of such a relation of cause to effect conceivable from the theoretical point of view, because they are both suprasensible. All that can be demanded of reason under these conditions would merely be to prove that there is *no contradiction* involved in the conception of a creation of free beings; and this may be done by showing that contradiction only arises when, along with the category of causality, the *condition of time* is transferred to the relation of suprasensible things. This condition, as implying that the cause of an effect must precede the effect as its reason, is inevitable in thinking the relation of objects of sense to one another; and if this conception of causality were to have objective reality given to it in the theoretical bearing, it would also have to be referred to the suprasensible sphere. But the contradiction vanishes when the pure category, apart from any sensible conditions, is applied from the moral and practical point of view, and consequently as in a non-sensible relation to the conception of creation.

The philosophical jurist will not regard this investigation, when thus carried back even to the ultimate principles of the transcendental philosophy, as an unnecessary subtlety in a metaphysic of morals, or as losing itself in aimless obscurity, when he takes into consideration the difficulty of doing justice in this inquiry to the ultimate relations of the principles of right.

29. *The Rights of the Parent*

From the duty thus indicated, there further necessarily arises the right of the parents to the management and training of the child, so long as it is itself incapable of making proper use of its body as an organism, and of its mind as an understanding. This involves its nourishment and the care of its education. This includes, in general, the function of forming and developing it *practically*, that it may be able in the future to maintain and advance itself, and also its moral culture and development, the guilt of neglecting it falling upon the parents. All this training is to be continued till the child reaches the period of emancipation (*emancipatio*), as the age of practicable self-support. The parents then virtually renounce the parental right to command, as well as all claim to repayment for their previous care and trouble; for which care and trouble, after the process of education is complete, they can only appeal to the children, by way of any claim, on the ground of the obligation of gratitude as a duty of virtue.

From the fact of personality in the children, it further follows that they can never be regarded as the property of the parents, but only as belonging to them by way of being in their *possession*, like other things that are held apart from the possession of all others and that can be brought back even against the will of the subjects. Hence the right of the parents is not a purely real right, and it is not alienable (*jus personalissimum*). But neither is it a *merely* personal right; it is a personal right of a *real* kind, that is, a personal right that is constituted and exercised after the *manner* of a real right.

It is therefore evident that the title of a *personal right of a real kind* must necessarily be added, in the science of right, to the titles of real right and personal right, the division of rights into these two being not complete. For, if the right of the parents to the children were treated as if it were merely a real right to a part of what belongs to their house, they could not found only upon the duty of the children to return to them in claiming them when they run away, but they would be then entitled to seize them and impound them like things or runaway cattle.

TITLE III. *Household Right. (Master and Servant)*

30. *Relation and Right of the Master of a Household*

The children of the house, who, along with the parents, constitute a family, attain *majority*, and become masters of themselves (*majorennes, sui juris*), even without a contract of release from their previous state of dependence, by their actually attaining to the capability of self-maintenance. This attainment arises, on the one hand, as a state of natural majority, with the advance of years in the general course of nature; and, on the other hand, it takes form, as a state in accordance with their own natural condition. They thus acquire the right of being their own masters, without the interposition of any special juridical act, and therefore merely by law (*lege*); and they owe their parents nothing by way of legal debt for their education, just as the parents, on their side, are now released from their obligations to the children in the same way. Parents and children thus gain or regain their natural freedom; and the domestic society, which was necessary according to the law of right, is thus naturally dissolved.

Both parties, however, may resolve to continue the household, but under another mode of obligation. It may assume the form of a relation between the head of the house, as its master, and the other members as domestic servants, male or female; and the connection between them in this new *regulated* domestic economy (*societas herilis*) may be determined by contract. The master of the house, actually or virtually, enters into contract with the children, now become major and masters of themselves; or, if there be no children in the family, with other free persons constituting the membership of the household; and thus there is established a domestic relationship not founded on social equality, but such that one *commands* as master, and another *obeys* as servant (*imperantis et subjecti domestici*).

The domestics or servants may then be regarded by the master of the household as thus far his. As regards the *form* or mode of his possession of them, they belong to him as if by a real right; for if any of them run away, he is entitled to bring them again under his power by a unilateral act of his will. But as regards the *matter* of his right, or the *use* he is entitled to make of such persons as his domestics, he is not entitled to conduct himself towards them as if he was their proprietor or owner (*dominus servi*); because they are only subjected to his power by contract, and by a contract under certain definite restrictions. For a contract by which the one party renounced his *whole* freedom for the advantage of the other, ceasing thereby to be a person and consequently having no duty even to observe a contract, is self-contradictory, and is therefore of itself null and void. The question as to the right of property in relation to one who has lost his legal personality by a crime does not concern us here.

This contract, then, of the master of a household with his domestics, cannot be of such a nature that the *use* of them could ever rightly become an *abuse* of them; and the judgement as to what constitutes *use* or *abuse* in such circumstances is not left merely to the master, but is also competent to the servants, who ought never to be held in bondage or bodily servitude as slaves or serfs. Such a contract cannot, therefore, be concluded for life, but in all cases only for a definite period, within which one party may intimate to the other a termination of their connection. Children, however, including even the children of one who has become enslaved owing to a crime, are always free. For every man is born free, because he has at birth as yet broken no law; and even the cost of his education till his maturity cannot be reckoned as a debt which he is bound to pay. Even a slave, if it were in his power, would be bound to educate his children without being entitled to count and reckon with them for the cost; and in view of his own incapacity for discharging this function, the possessor of a slave, therefore, enters upon the obligation which he has rendered the slave himself unable to fulfil.

Here, again, as under the first two titles, it is clear that there is a personal right of a *real* kind, in the relation of the master of a house to his domestics. For he can legally demand them as belonging to what is externally his, from any other possessor of them; and he is entitled to fetch them back to his house, even before the reasons that may have led them to run away, and their particular right in the circumstances, have been juridically investigated.

Systematic Division of all the Rights Capable of Being Acquired by Contract

31. *Division of Contracts. Juridical Conceptions of Money and a Book*

It is reasonable to demand that a metaphysical science of right shall completely and definitely determine the members of a logical division of its conceptions *a priori*, and thus establish them in a genuine system. All *empirical* division, on the other hand, is merely *fragmentary partition*, and it leaves us in uncertainty as to whether there may not be more members still required to complete the whole sphere of the divided conception. A division that is made according to a principle *a priori* may be called, in contrast to all empirical partitions, a *dogmatic* division.

Every contract, regarded in itself *objectively*, consists of two juridical acts: the promise and its acceptance. Acquisition by the latter, unless it be a *pactum re initum* which requires delivery, is not a *part*, but the juridically necessary *consequence* of the contract. Considered again *subjectively*, or as to whether the *acquisition*, which *ought* to happen as a necessary consequence according to reason, will also follow, in fact, as a *physical* consequence, it is evident that I have no *security* or guarantee that this will happen by the mere acceptance of a promise. There is, therefore, something externally required connected with the mode of the contract, in reference to the *certainty* of acquisition by it; and this can only be some element completing and determining the means necessary to the attainment of acquisition as realizing the purpose of the contract. And in his connection and behoof, three persons are required to intervene—the promiser, the acceptor, and the cautioner or surety. The importance of the cautioner is evident; but by his intervention and his special contract with the promiser, the acceptor gains nothing in respect of the object but the means of compulsion that enable him to obtain what is his own.

According to these rational principles of logical division, there are properly only *three* pure and simple *modes of contract.* There are, however, innumerable mixed and empirical modes, adding statutory and conventional forms to the principles of mine and thine that are in accordance with rational laws. But they lie outside of the circle of the metaphysical science of right, whose rational modes of contract can alone be indicated here.

All contracts are founded upon a purpose of acquisition, and are either:

A. Gratuitous contracts, *with unilateral acquisition; or*

B. Onerous contracts, *with reciprocal acquisition; or*

C. Cautionary contracts, *with no acquisition, but only guarantee of what has been already acquired.* These contracts may be *gratuitous* on the one side, and yet, at the same time, *onerous* on the other.

A. The gratuitous contracts (*pacta gratuita*) are:

1. Depositation (*depositum*), involving the preservation of some valuable deposited in trust;

2. Commodate (*commodatum*) a loan of the *use* of a thing;

3. Donation (*donatio*), a free gift.

B. The onerous contracts are contracts either of permutation or of hiring.

I. Contracts of permutation or reciprocal exchange (*permutatio late sic dicta*):

1. Barter, or strictly real exchange (*permutatio stricte sic dicta*). Goods exchanged for goods.

2. Purchase and sale (*emptio venditio*). Goods exchanged for money.

3. Loan (*mutuum*). Loan of a fungible under condition of its being returned in kind: corn for corn, or money for money.

II. Contracts of letting and hiring (*locatio conductio*):

1. Letting of a thing on hire to another person who is to make use of it (*locatio rei*). If the thing can only be restored *in specie*, it may be the subject of an onerous contract combining the consideration of *interest* with it (*pactum usurarium*).

2. Letting of work on hire (*locatio operae*). Consent to the use of my powers by another for a certain price (*merces*). The worker under this contract is a hired servant (*mercenarius*).

3. Mandate (*mandatum*). The contract of mandate is an engagement to perform or execute a certain business in place and in *name* of another person. If the action is merely done in the place of another, but not, at the same time, in his *name*, it is *performance without commission* (*gestio negotii*); but if it is rightfully performed in name of the other, it constitutes *mandate*, which as a contract of procuration is an *onerous* contract (*mandatum onerosum*).

C. The cautionary contracts (*cautiones*) are:

1. Pledge (*pignus*). Caution by a moveable deposited as security.

2. Suretyship (*fidejussio*). Caution for the fulfilment of the promise of another.

3. Personal security (*praestatio obsidis*). Guarantee of personal performance.

This list of all modes in which the property of one person may be transferred or conveyed to another includes conceptions of certain objects or instruments required for such transference (*translatio*). These appear to be entirely empirical, and it may therefore seem questionable whether they are entitled to a place in a *metaphysical* science of right. For, in such a science, the divisions must be made according to principles *a priori;* and hence the *matter* of the juridical relation, which may be *conventional,* ought to be left out of account, and only its form should be taken into consideration.

Such conceptions may be illustrated by taking the instance of *money,* in contradistinction from all other exchangeable things as wares and merchandise; or by the case of a *book.* And considering these as illustrative examples in this connection, it will be shown that the conception of money as the *greatest* and most *useable* of all the means of human intercommunication through things, in the way of purchase and sale in commerce, as well as that of books as the greatest means of carrying on the interchange of thought, resolve themselves into relations that are purely intellectual and rational. And hence it will be made evident that such conceptions do not really detract from the purity of the given scheme of pure rational contracts, by empirical admixture.

Illustration of Relations of Contract by the Conceptions of Money and a Book

I. *What is Money?*

Money is a thing which can only be made *use* of, by being *alienated* or exchanged. This is a good *nominal* definition, as given by Achenwall; and it is sufficient to distinguish objects of the will of this kind from all other objects. But it gives us no information regarding the rational possibility of such a thing as money is. Yet we see thus much by the definition: (1) that the alienation in this mode of human intercommunication and exchange is not viewed as a gift, but is intended as a mode of *reciprocal* acquisition by an onerous contract; and (2) that it is regarded as a mere means of carrying on *commerce,* universally adopted by the people, but having no value as such of itself, in contrast to other things as mercantile goods or wares which have a particular value in relation to special wants existing among the people. It therefore *represents* all exchangeable things.

A bushel of corn has the greatest direct value as a means of satisfying human wants. Cattle may be fed by it; and these again are subservient to our nourishment and locomotion, and they even labour in our stead. Thus, by means of corn, men are multiplied and supported, who not only act again in reproducing such natural products, but also by other artificial products they can come to the relief of all our proper wants. Thus are men enabled to build dwellings, to prepare clothing, and to supply all the ingenious comforts and enjoyments which make up the products of industry. On the other hand, the value of money is only indirect. It cannot be itself enjoyed, nor be used directly for enjoyment; it is, however, a means towards this, and of all outward things it is of the highest utility.

We may found a *real* definition of money provisionally upon these considerations. It may thus be defined as *the universal means of carrying on the* industry *of men in exchanging intercommunications with each other.* Hence national wealth, in so far as it can be acquired by means of money, is properly only the sum of the industry or applied labour with which men pay each other, and which is represented by the money in circulation among the people.

The thing which is to be called *money* must, therefore, have cost as much industry to produce it, or even to put it into the hands of others, as may be equivalent to the industry or labour required for the acquisition of the goods or wares or merchandise, as natural or artificial products, for which it is exchanged. For if it were easier to procure the material which is called money than the goods that are required, there would be more money in the market than goods to be sold; and because the seller would then have to expend more labour upon his goods than the buyer on the equivalent, the money coming in to him more rapidly, the labour applied to the preparation of goods and industry generally, with the industrial productivity which is the source of the public wealth, would at the same time dwindle and be cut down. Hence bank notes and assignations are not to be regarded as money, although they may take its place by way of representing it for a time; because it costs almost no labour to prepare them, and their value is based merely upon the opinion prevailing as to the further continuance of the previous possibility of changing them into ready money. But on its being in any way found out that there is not ready money in sufficient quantity for easy and safe conversion of such notes or assignations, the opinion gives way, and a fall in their value becomes inevitable. Thus the industrial labour of those who work the gold and silver mines in Peru and Mexico —especially on account of the frequent failures in the application of fruitless efforts to discover new veins of these precious metals—is probably even greater than what is expended in the manufacture of goods in Europe. Hence such mining labour, as unrewarded in the circumstances, would be abandoned of itself, and the countries mentioned would in consequence soon sink into poverty, did not the industry of Europe, stimulated in turn by these very metals, proportionally expand at the same time so as constantly to keep up the zeal of the miners in their work by the articles of luxury thereby offered to them. It is thus that the concurrence of industry with industry, and of labour with labour, is always maintained.

But how is it possible that what at the beginning constituted only goods or wares, at length became money? This has happened wherever a sovereign as great and powerful consumer of a particular substance, which he at first used merely for the adornment and decoration of his servants and court, has enforced the tribute of his subjects in this kind of material. Thus it may have been gold, or silver, or copper, or a species of beautiful shells called *cowries,* or even a sort of mat called *makutes,* as in Congo; or ingots of iron, as in Senegal; or Negro slaves, as on the Guinea Coast. When the ruler of the country demanded such things as imposts, those whose labour had to be put in motion to procure them were also paid by means of them, according to certain regulations of commerce then established, as in a market or exchange. As it appears to me, it is only thus that a particular species of goods came to be made a legal means of carrying on the industrial labour of the subjects in their commerce with each other, and thereby forming the medium of the national wealth. And thus it practically became money.

The rational conception of money, under which the empirical conception is embraced, is therefore that of a thing which, in the course of the public permutation or exchange of possessions (*permutatio publica*), determines the *price* of all the other things that form products or goods—under which term even the sciences are included, in so far as they are not taught *gratis* to others. The quantity of it among a people constitutes their wealth (*opulentia*). For price (*pretium*) is the public judgement about the *value* of a thing, in relation to the proportionate abundance of what forms the universal representative means in circulation for carrying on the reciprocal interchange of the products of industry or labour.[1] The precious metals, when they are not merely weighed but also stamped or provided with a sign indicating how much they are worth, form legal money, and are called *coin*.

According to Adam Smith: "Money has become, in all civilized nations, the universal instrument of commerce, by the intervention of which goods of all kinds are bought and sold or exchanged for one another." This definition expands the empirical conception of money to the rational idea of it, by taking regard only to the implied *form* of the reciprocal performances in the onerous contracts, and thus abstracting from their matter. It is thus conformable to the conception of right in the permutation and exchange of the mine and thine generally (*commutatio late sic dicta*). The definition, therefore, accords with the representation in the above synopsis of a dogmatic division of contracts *a priori*, and consequently with the metaphysical principle of right in general.

[1] Hence where commerce is extensive neither gold nor copper is specially used as money, but only as constituting wares; because there is too little of the first and too much of the second for them to be easily brought into circulation, so as at once to have the former in such small pieces as are necessary in payment for particular goods and not to have the latter in great quantity in case of the smallest acquisitions. Hence silver—more or less alloyed with copper—is taken as the proper material of money and the measure of the calculation of all prices in the great commercial intercommunications of the world; and the other metals—and still more nonmetallic substances—can only take its place in the case of a people of limited commerce.

II. *What is a Book?*

A book is a writing which contains a discourse addressed by some one to the public, through visible signs of speech. It is a matter of indifference to the present considerations whether it is written by a pen or imprinted by types, and on few or many pages. He who speaks to the public in his own name is the author. He who addresses the writing to the public in the name of the author is the publisher. When a publisher does this with the permission or authority of the author, the act is in accordance with right, and he is the rightful publisher; but if this is done without such permission or authority, the act is contrary to right, and the publisher is a counterfeiter or unlawful publisher. The whole of a set of copies of the original document is called an *edition*.

The Unauthorized Publishing of Books is Contrary to the Principles of Right, and is Rightly Prohibited

A *writing* is not an immediate direct presentation of a conception, as is the case, for instance, with an engraving that exhibits a portrait, or a bust or cast by a sculptor. It is a *discourse* addressed in a particular form to the public; and the author may be said to *speak* publicly by means of his publisher. The publisher, again, speaks by the aid of the printer as his workman (*operarius*), yet not in his own name, for otherwise he would be the author, but in the name of the author; and he is only entitled to do so in virtue of a mandate given him to that effect by the author. Now the unauthorized printer and publisher speaks by an assumed authority in his publication; in the name indeed of the author, but without a mandate to that effect (*gerit se mandatarium absque mandato*). Consequently such an unauthorized publication is a wrong committed upon the authorized and only lawful publisher, as it amounts to a pilfering of the profits which the latter was entitled and able to draw from the use of his proper right (*furtum usus*). Unauthorized printing and publication of books is, therefore, forbidden—as an act of counterfeit and piracy—on the ground of right.

There seems, however, to be an impression that there is a sort of common right to print and publish books; but the slightest reflection must convince any one that this would be a great injustice. The reason of it is found simply in the fact that a book, regarded from *one* point of view, is an external product of mechanical art (*opus mechanicum*), that can be imitated by any one who may be in rightful possession of a copy; and it is therefore his by a *real right*.

But, from *another* point of view, a book is not merely an external thing, but is a *discourse* of the publisher to the public, and he is only entitled to do this publicly under the mandate of the author (*praestatio operae*); and this constitutes a *personal right*. The error underlying the impression referred to, therefore, arises from an interchange and confusion of these two kinds of right in relation to books.

Confusion of Personal Right and Real Right

The confusion of personal right with real right may be likewise shown by reference to a difference of view in connection with another contract, falling under the head of contracts of hiring (B II. 1), namely, the contract of lease (*jus incolatus*). The question is raised as to whether a proprietor when he has sold a house or a piece of ground held on lease, before the expiry of the period of lease, was bound to add the condition of the continuance of the lease to the contract of purchase; *or* whether it should be held that "purchase breaks hire," of course under reservation of a period of warning determined by the nature of the subject in use. In the former view, a house or farm would be regarded as having a *burden* lying upon it, constituting a real right acquired in it by the lessee; and this might well enough be carried out by a clause merely indorsing or ingrossing the contract of lease in the deed of sale. But as it would no longer then be a simple lease; another contract would properly be required to be conjoined, a matter which few lessors would be disposed to grant. The proposition, then, that "Purchase breaks hire" holds in principle; for the full right in a thing as a property overbears all personal right, which is inconsistent with it. But there remains a right of action to the lessee, on the ground of a personal right for indemnification on account of any loss arising from breaking of the contract.

EPISODICAL SECTION. *The Ideal Acquisition of External Objects of the Will*

32. *The Nature and Modes of Ideal Acquisition*

I call that mode of acquisition *ideal* which involves no causality in time, and which is founded upon a mere idea of pure reason. It is nevertheless *actual*, and not merely imaginary acquisition; and it is not called *real* only because the act of acquisition is not empirical. This character of the act arises from the peculiarity that the person acquiring acquires from another who either is *not yet*, and who can only be regarded as a *possible* being, or who *is just ceasing to be*, or who *no longer is*. Hence such a mode of attaining to possession is to be regarded as a mere practical idea of reason.

There are three modes of ideal acquisition:

I. Acquisition by usucapion;

II. Acquisition by inheritance or succession;

III. Acquisition by undying merit (*meritum immortale*), or the claim by right to a good name at death.

These three modes of acquisition can, as a matter of fact, only have effect in a public juridical state of existence, but they are *not founded* merely upon the civil constitution or upon arbitrary statutes; they are already contained *a priori* in the conception of the state of nature, and are thus necessarily conceivable prior to their empirical manifestation. The laws regarding them in the civil constitution ought to be regulated by that rational conception.

33.—I. *Acquisition by Usucapion.* (Acquisitio per Usucapionem)

I may acquire the property of another merely by *long possession* and use of it (*usucapio*). Such property is not acquired, because I may legitimately *presume* that his consent is given to this effect (*per consensum praesumptum*); nor because I can assume that, as he does not oppose my acquisition of it, he has *relinquished* or abandoned it as his (*rem derelictam*). But I acquire it thus because, even if there were any one actually raising a claim to this property as its true owner, I may *exclude* him on the ground of my long possession of it, ignore his previous existence, and proceed as if he existed during the time of my possession as a mere abstraction, although I may have been subsequently apprized of his reality as well as of his claim. This mode of acquisition is not quite correctly designated *acquisition by prescription* (*per praescriptionem*); for the exclusion of all other claimants is to be regarded as only the consequence of the usucapion; and the process of acquisition must have gone before the right of exclusion. The rational possibility of such a mode of acquisition has now to be proved.

Any one who does not exercise a continuous *possessory activity* (*actus possessorius*) in relation to a thing as his is regarded with good right as one who does not at all exist as its possessor. For he cannot complain of lesion so long as he does not qualify himself with a title as its possessor. And even if he should afterwards lay claim to the thing when another has already taken possession of it, he only says he was once on a time owner of it, but not that he is so still, or that his possession has continued without interruption as a juridical fact. It can, therefore, only be a juridical process of possession, that has been maintained without interruption and is proveable by documentary fact, that any one can secure for himself what is his own after ceasing for a long time to make use of it.

For, suppose that the neglect to exercise this possessory activity had not the effect of enabling another to found upon his hitherto lawful, undisputed and *bona fide* possession, and irrefragable right to continue in its possession so that he may regard the thing that is thus in his possession as acquired by him. Then no acquisition would ever become peremptory and secured, but all acquisition would only be provisory and temporary. This is evident on the ground that there are no historical records available to carry the investigation of a title back to the first possessor and his act of acquisition. The presumption upon which acquisition by usucapion is founded is, therefore, not merely its conformity to *right* as allowed and just, but also the presumption of its *being* right (*praesumtio juris et de jure*), and its being assumed to be in accordance with compulsory laws (*suppositio legalis*). Anyone who has neglected to embody his possessory act in a documentary title has lost his claim to the right of being possessor for the time; and the length of the period of his neglecting to do so—which need not necessarily be particularly defined—can be referred to only as establishing the certainty of this neglect. And it would contradict the postulate of the juridically practical reason to maintain that one hitherto unknown as a possessor, and whose possessory activity has at least been interrupted, whether by or without fault of his own, could always at any time re-acquire a property; for this would be to make all ownership uncertain (*dominia rerum incerta facere*).

But if he is a member of the commonwealth or civil union, the state may maintain his possession for him vicariously, although it may be interrupted as private possession; and in that case the actual possessor will not be able to prove a title of acquisition even from a first occupation, nor to found upon a title of usucapion. But, in the state of nature, usucapion is universally a rightful ground of holding, not properly as a juridical mode of requiring a thing, but as a ground for maintaining oneself in possession of it where there are no juridical acts. A release from juridical claims is commonly also called acquisition. The prescriptive title of the older possessor, therefore, belongs to the sphere of natural right (*est juris naturae*).

34.—II. *Acquisition by Inheritance.* (Acquisitio haereditatis)

Inheritance is constituted by the transfer (*translatio*) of the property or goods of one who is dying to a survivor, through the consent of the will of both. The acquisition of the heir who takes the estate (*haeredis instituti*) and the relinquishment of the testator who leaves it, being the acts that constitute the exchange of the mine and thine, take place in the same moment of time—*in articulo mortis*—and just when the testator ceases to be. There is therefore no special act of transfer (*translatio*) in the empirical sense; for that would involve two successive acts, by which the one would first divest himself of his possession, and the other would thereupon enter into it. Inheritance as constituted by a simultaneous double act is, therefore, an ideal mode of acquisition. Inheritance is inconceivable in the state of nature without a testamentary disposition (*dispositio ultimae voluntatis*); and the question arises as to whether this mode of acquisition is to be regarded as a *contract of succession*, or a *unilateral act instituting an heir by a will* (*testamentum*). The determination of this question depends on the further question, whether and how, in the very same moment in which one individual ceases to be, there can be a transition of his property to another person. Hence the problem, as to how a mode of acquisition by inheritance is *possible*, must be investigated independently of the various possible forms in which it is practically carried out, and which can have place only in a commonwealth.

"It is *possible* to acquire by being instituted or appointed heir in a testamentary disposition." For the testator *Caius* promises and declares in his last will to *Titius*, who knows nothing of this promise, to transfer to him his estate in case of death, but thus continuing as long as he lives sole owner of it. Now by a mere unilateral act of will, nothing can in fact be transmitted to another person, as in addition to the promise of the one party there is required acceptance (*acceptatio*) on the part of the other, and a simultaneous bilateral act of will (*voluntas simultanea*) which, however, is here awanting. So long as Caius lives, Titius cannot expressly accept in order to enter on acquisition, because Caius has only promised in case of death; otherwise the property would be for a moment at least in common possession, which is not the will of the testator. However, Titius acquires *tacitly* a special right to the inheritance as a real right. This is constituted by the sole and exclusive right to *accept* the estate (*jus in re jacente*), which is therefore called at that point of time a *haereditas jacens*. Now as every man—because he must always gain and never lose by it—necessarily, although tacitly, accepts such a right, and as Titius after the death of Caius is in this position, he may acquire the succession as heir by acceptance of the promise. And the estate is not in the meantime entirely without an owner (*res nullius*), but is only *in abeyance* or vacant (*vacua*); because he has exclusively the right of choice as to whether he will actually make the estate bequeathed to him his own or not.

Hence testaments are valid according to mere natural right (*sunt juris naturae*). This assertion however, is to be understood in the sense that they are capable and worthy of being introduced and sanctioned in the civil state, whenever it is instituted. For it is only the common will in the civil state that maintains the possession of the inheritance or succession, while it hangs between acceptance or rejection and specially belongs to no particular individual.

35.—III. *The Continuing Right of a Good Name after Death.* (Bona fama Defuncti)

It would be absurd to think that a dead person could possess anything after his death, when he no longer exists in the eye of the law, if the matter in question were a mere thing. But a good name is a congenital and external, although merely ideal, possession, which attaches inseparably to the individual as a person. Now we can and must abstract here from all consideration as to whether the persons cease to be after death or still continue as such to exist; because, in considering their juridical relation to others, we regard persons merely according to their humanity and as rational beings (*homo noumenon*). Hence any attempt to bring the reputation or good name of a person into evil and false repute after death, is always questionable, even although a well-founded charge may be allowed —for to that extent the brocard *"De mortuis nil nisi bene"*[1] is wrong. Yet to spread charges against one who is absent and cannot defend himself, shows at least a want of magnanimity.

By a blameless life and a death that worthily ends it, it is admitted that a man may acquire a (negatively) good reputation constituting something that is his own, even when he no longer exists in the world of sense as a visible person (*homo phaenomenon*). It is further held that his survivors and successors—whether relatives or strangers—are entitled to defend his good name as a matter of right, on the ground that unproved accusations subject them all to the danger of similar treatment after death. Now that a man when dead can yet acquire such a right is a peculiar and, nevertheless, an undeniable manifestation in fact, of the *a priori* lawgiving reason thus extending its law of command or prohibition beyond the limits of the present life. If some one then spreads a charge regarding a dead person that would have dishonoured him when living, or even made him despicable, any one who can adduce a proof that this accusation is intentionally false and untrue may publicly declare him who thus brings the dead person into ill repute to be a calumniator, and affix dishonour to him in turn. This would not be allowable unless it were legitimate to assume that the dead person was injured by the accusation, although he is dead, and that a certain just satisfaction was done to him by an apology, although he no longer sensibly exists. A title to act the part of the vindicator of the dead person does not require to be established; for every one necessarily claims this of himself, not merely as a duty of virtue regarded ethically, but as a right belonging to him in virtue of his humanity. Nor does the vindicator require to show any special personal damage, accruing to him as a friend or relative, from a stain on the character of the deceased, to justify him in proceeding to censure it. That such a form of ideal acquisition, and even a right in an individual after death against survivors, is thus actually founded, cannot, therefore, be disputed, although the possibility of such a right is not capable of logical deduction.

There is no ground for drawing visionary inferences from what has just been stated, to the presentiment of a future life and invisible relations to departed souls. For the considerations connected with this right turn on nothing more than the purely moral and juridical relation which subsists among men, even in the present life, as rational beings. Abstraction is, however, made from all that belongs physically to their existence in space and time; that is, men are considered logically apart from these physical concomitants of their nature, not as to their

1 ["Let nothing be said of the dead but what is favourable."]

state when actually deprived of them, but only in so far as being spirits they are in a condition that might realize the injury done them by calumniators. Any one who may falsely say something against me a hundred years hence injures me even now. For in the pure juridical relation, which is entirely rational and surprasensible, abstraction is made from the physical conditions of time, and the calumniator is as culpable as if he had committed the offence in my lifetime; only this will not be tried by a criminal process, but he will only be punished with that loss of honour he would have caused to another, and this is inflicted upon him by public opinion according to the *lex talionis*. Even a *plagiarism* from a dead author, although it does not tarnish the honour of the deceased, but only deprives him of a part of his property, is yet properly regarded as a lesion of his human right.

Chapter III. Acquisition Conditioned by the Sentence of a Public Judicatory

36. *How and What Acquisition is Subjectively Conditioned by the Principle of a Public Court.*

Natural right, understood simply as that right which is not statutory, and which is knowable purely *a priori*, by every man's reason, will include distributive justice as well as commutative justice. It is manifest that the latter, as constituting the justice that is valid between persons in their reciprocal relations of intercourse with one another, must belong to natural right. But this holds also of distributive justice, in so far as it can be known *a priori;* and decisions or sentences regarding it must be regulated by the law of natural right.

The moral person who presides in the sphere of justice and administers it is called the Court of Justice, and, as engaged in the process of official duty, the *judicatory;* the sentence delivered in a case, is the judgement (*judicium*). All this is to be here viewed *a priori,* according to the rational conditions of right, without taking into consideration how such a constitution is to be actually established or organized, for which particular statutes, and consequently empirical principles, are requisite.

The question, then, in this connection, is not merely "What is *right in itself?*" in the sense in which every man must determine it by the judgement of reason; but "What is right as applied to this case?" that is, "What is right and just as viewed by a court?" The rational and the judicial points of view are therefore to be distinguished; and there are *four cases* in which the two forms of judgement have a different and opposite issue. And yet they may co-exist with each other, because they are delivered from two different, yet respectively true, points of view: the one from regard to private right, the other from the idea of public right. They are: I. The contract of donation (*pactum donationis*); II. The contract of loan (*commodatum*); III. The action of real revindication (*vindicatio*); and IV. Guarantee by oath (*juramentum*).

It is a common error on the part of the jurist to fall here into the fallacy of begging the question by a tacit assumption (*vitium subreptionis*). This is done by assuming as objective and absolute the juridical principle which a public court of justice is entitled and even bound to adopt in its own behoof, and only from the *subjective* purpose of qualifying itself to decide and judge upon all the rights pertaining to individuals. It is therefore of no small importance to make this specific difference intelligible, and to draw attention to it.

37.—I. *The Contract of Donation.* (Pactum Donationis)

The contract of donation signifies the *gratuitous* alienation (*gratis*) of a thing or right that is mine. It involves a relation between me as the donor (*donans*), and another person as the donatory (*donatarius*), in accordance with the principle of private right, by which what is mine is transferred to the latter, on his acceptance of it, as a gift (*donum*). However, it is not to be presumed that I have voluntarily bound myself thereby so as to be *compelled* to keep my promise, and that I have thus given away my *freedom* gratuitously, and, as it were, to that extent thrown myself away. *Nemo suum jactare praesumitur*. But this is what would happen, under such circumstances, according to the principle of right in the civil state; for in this sphere the donatory can *compel* me, under certain conditions, to perform my promise. If, then, the case comes before a court, according to the conditions of public right, it must either be presumed that the donor has consented to such compulsion, or the court would give no regard, in the sentence, to the consideration as to whether he intended to reserve the right to resile from his promise or not; but would only refer to what is certain, namely, the condition of the promise and the acceptance of the donatory. Although the promiser, therefore, thought—as may easily be supposed—that he could not be bound by his promise in any case, if he "rued" it before it was actually carried out, yet the court assumes that he ought *expressly* to have reserved this condition if such was his mind; and if he did not make such an express reservation, it will be held that he can be compelled to implement his promise. And this principle is assumed by the court, because the administration of justice would otherwise be endlessly impeded, or even made entirely impossible.

38.—II. *The Contract of Loan.* (Commodatum)

In the contract of commodate-loan (*commodatum*) I give some one the gratuitous *use* of something that is mine. If it is a thing that is given on loan, the contracting parties agree that the borrower will restore *the very same thing* to the power of the lender. But the receiver of the loan (*commodatarius*) cannot, at the same time, assume that the owner of the thing lent (*commodans*) will take upon himself all risk (*casus*) of any possible loss of it, or of its useful quality, that may arise from having given it into the possession of the receiver. For it is not to be understood of itself that the owner, besides the *use* of the thing, which he has granted to the receiver, and the detriment that is inseparable from such use, also gives a *guarantee* or warrandice against all damage that may arise from such use. On the contrary, a special accessory contract would have to be entered into for this purpose. The only question, then, that can be raised is this: "Is it incumbent on the lender or the borrower to add expressly the condition of undertaking the risk that may accrue to the thing lent; *or*, if this is not done, which of the parties is to be presumed to have *consented and agreed* to guarantee the property of the lender, up to restoration of the very same thing or its equivalent?" Certainly not the lender; because it cannot be presumed that he has gratuitously agreed to give more than the mere use of the thing, so that he cannot be supposed to have also undertaken the risk of loss of his property. But this may be assumed on the side of the borrower; because he thereby undertakes and performs nothing more than what is implied in the contract.

For example, I enter a house, when overtaken by a shower of rain, and ask the loan of a cloak. But through accidental contact with colouring matter, it becomes entirely spoiled while in my possession; or on entering another house, I lay it aside and it is stolen. Under such circumstances, everybody would think it absurd for me to assert that I had no further concern with the cloak but to return it as it was, or, in the latter case, only to mention the fact of the theft; and that, in any case, anything more required would be but an act of courtesy in expressing sympathy with the owner on account of his loss, seeing he can claim nothing on the ground of right. It would be otherwise, however, if, on asking the use of an article, I discharged myself beforehand from all responsibility, in case of its coming to grief while in my hands, on the ground of my being poor and unable to compensate any incidental loss. No one could find such a condition superfluous or ludicrous, unless the borrower were, in fact, known to be a well-to-do and well-disposed man; because in such a case it would almost be an insult not to act on the presumption of generous compensation for any loss sustained.

Now by the very nature of this contract, the possible damage (*casus*) which the thing lent may undergo cannot be exactly determined in any agreement. Commodate is therefore an uncertain contract (*pactum incertum*), because the consent can only be so far presumed. The judgement, in any case, deciding upon whom the incidence of any loss must fall, cannot therefore be determined from the conditions of the contract in itself, but only *by the principle of the court* before which it comes, and which can only consider what is certain in the contract; and the only thing certain is always the fact as to the possession of the thing as property. Hence the judgement passed in the state of nature will be different from that given by a court of justice in the civil state. The judgement from the standpoint of natural right will be determined by regard to the inner rational quality of the thing, and will run thus: "Loss arising from damage accruing to a thing lent falls upon the *borrower*" (*casum sentit commodatarius*); whereas the sentence of a court of justice in the civil state will run thus: "The loss falls upon the *lender*" (*casum sentit dominus*). The latter judgement turns out differently from the former as the sentence of the mere sound reason, because a public judge cannot found upon presumptions as to what either party may have thought; and thus the one who has not obtained release from all loss in the thing, by a special accessory contract, must bear the loss. Hence the difference between the judgement as the court must deliver it and the form in which each individual is entitled to hold it for himself, by his private reason, is a matter of importance, and is not to be overlooked in the consideration of juridical judgements.

39.—III. *The Revindication of what has been Lost.* (Vindicatio)

It is clear from what has been already said that a thing of mine which continues to exist remains mine, although I may not be in continuous occupation of it; and that it does not cease to be mine without a juridical act of dereliction or alienation. Further, it is evident that a right in this thing (*jus reale*) belongs in consequence to me (*jus personale*), against *every* holder of it, and not merely against some particular person. But the question now arises as to whether this right must be regarded by *every* other person as a continuous right of property *per se,* if I have not in any way *renounced* it, although the thing is in the possession of another.

A thing may be lost (*res amissa*) and thus come into other hands in an honourable *bona fide* way as a supposed "find"; or it may come to me by formal transfer on the part of one who is in possession of it, and who professes to be its owner, although he is not so. Taking the latter case, the question arises whether, since I cannot acquire a thing from one who is not its owner (*a non domino*), I am excluded by the fact from all right in the thing itself, and have merely a personal right against a wrongful possessor? This is manifestly so, if the acquisition is judged purely according to its inner justifying grounds and viewed according to the state of nature, and not according to the convenience of a court of justice.

For everything alienable must be capable of being acquired by anyone. The rightfulness of acquisition, however, rests entirely upon the form in accordance with which what is in possession of another, is transferred to me and accepted by me. In other words, rightful acquisition depends upon the formality of the juridical act of commutation or interchange between the possessor of the thing and the acquirer of it, without its being required to ask how the former came by it; because this would itself be an injury, on the ground that: *Quilibet praesumitur bonus.* Now suppose it turned out that the said possessor was not the real owner, I cannot admit that the real owner is entitled to hold me directly responsible, or so entitled with regard to any one who might be holding the thing. For I have myself taken nothing away from him, when, for example, I bought his horse according to the law (*titulo empti venditi*) when it was offered for sale in the public market. The title of acquisition is therefore unimpeachable on my side; and as buyer I am not bound, nor even have I the right, to investigate the title of the seller; for this process of investigation would have to go on in an ascending series *ad infinitum.* Hence on such grounds I ought to be regarded, in virtue of a regular and formal purchase, as not merely the *putative,* but the *real* owner of the horse.

But against this position, there immediately start up the following juridical principles. Any acquisition derived from one who is not the owner of the thing in question is null and void. I cannot derive from another anything more than what he himself rightfully has; and although as regards the form of the acquisition—the *modus acquirendi*—I may proceed in accordance with all the conditions of right when I deal in a stolen horse exposed for sale in the market, yet a real title warranting the acquisition was awanting; for the horse was not really the property of the seller in question. However I may be a *bona fide* possessor of a thing under such conditions, I am still only a *putative* owner, and the real owner has the right *of vindication* against me (*rem suam vindicandi*).

Now, it may be again asked, what is right and just *in itself* regarding the acquisition of external things among men in their intercourse with one another—viewed in the state of nature—according to the principles of commutative justice? And it must be admitted in this connection that whoever has a purpose of acquiring anything must regard it as absolutely necessary to investigate whether the thing which he wishes to acquire does not already belong to another person. For although he may carefully observe the formal conditions required for appropriating what may belong to the property of another, as in buying a horse according to the usual terms in a market, yet he can, at the most, acquire only a *personal right in relation* to a thing (*jus ad rem*) so long as it is still unknown to him whether another than the seller may not be the real owner. Hence, if some other person were to come forward and prove by documentary evidence a prior right of property in the thing, nothing would remain for the putative new owner but the advantage which he has drawn as a *bona fide* possessor of it up to that moment. Now it is frequently impossible to discover the absolutely first original owner of a thing in the series of putative owners, who derive their right from one another. Hence no mere exchange of external things, however well it may agree with the formal conditions of commutative justice, can ever guarantee an absolutely certain acquisition.

Here, however, the juridically law-giving reason comes in again with the principle of *distributive justice;* and it adopts as a criterion of the rightfulness of possession, not what is *in itself* in reference to the private will of each individual in the state of nature, but only the consideration of how it would be adjudged by a *court of justice* in a civil state, constituted by the united will of all. In this connection, fulfilment of the formal conditions of acquisition, that in themselves only establish a personal right, is postulated as sufficient; and they stand as an equivalent for the material conditions which properly establish the derivation of property from a prior putative owner, to the extent of making what is *in itself* only a personal right, valid *before a court,* as a real right. Thus the horse which I bought when exposed for sale in the public market, under conditions regulated by the municipal law, becomes my property if all the conditions of purchase and sale have been exactly observed in the transaction; but always under the reservation that the real owner continues to have the right of a claim against the seller, on the ground of his prior unalienated possession. My otherwise personal right is thus transmuted into a real right, according to which I may take and vindicate the object as mine wherever I may find it, without being responsible for the way in which the Seller had come into possession of it.

It is therefore only in behoof of the requirements of juridical decision in a court (*in favorem justitae distributivae*) that the right in respect of a thing is regarded, not as personal, which it is *in itself,* but as real, because it can thus be *most easily and certainly adjudged;* and it is thus accepted and dealt with according to a pure principle *a priori.* Upon this principle, various statutory laws come to be founded which specially aim at laying down the conditions under which alone a mode of acquisition shall be legitimate, so that the judge may be able to assign every one his own as *easily* and *certainly* as possible. Thus, in the brocard, "Purchase breaks hire," what by the nature of the subject is a real right—namely the hire—is taken to hold as a merely personal right; and, conversely, as in the case referred to above, what is in itself merely a personal right is held to be valid as a real right. And this is done only when the question arises as to the principles by which a court of justice in the civil state is to be guided, in order to proceed with all possible safety in delivering judgement on the rights of individuals.

40—IV. *Acquisition of Security by the Taking of an Oath.* (Cautio Juratoria)

Only one ground can be assigned on which it could be held that men are bound in the juridical relation to *believe* and to confess that there are gods, or that there is a God. It is that they may be able to swear an oath; and that thus by the fear of an all-seeing Supreme Power, whose revenge they must solemnly invoke upon themselves in case their utterance should be false, they may be constrained to be truthful in statement and faithful in promising. It is not morality but merely blind superstition that is reckoned upon in this process; for it is evident it implies that no certainty is to be expected from a mere *solemn* declaration in matters of right before a court, although the duty of truthfulness must have always appeared self-evident to all, in a matter which concerns the holiest that can be among men—namely, the right of man. Hence recourse has been had to a motive founded on mere myths and fables as imaginary guarantees. Thus among the *Rejangs,* a heathen people in Sumatra, it is the custom—according to the testimony of Marsden—to swear by the bones of their dead relatives, although they have no belief in a life after death. In like manner the negroes of *Guinea* swear by their *fetish,* a bird's feather, which they imprecate under the belief that it will break their neck. And so in other cases. The belief underlying these oaths is that an invisible power—whether it has understanding or not—by its very nature possesses magical power that can be put into action by such invocations. Such a belief—which is commonly called *religion,* but which ought to be called *superstition*—is, however, indispensable for the administration of justice; because, without referring to it, a court of justice would not have adequate means to ascertain facts otherwise kept secret, and to determine rights. A law making an oath obligatory is therefore only given in behoof of the judicial authority.

But then the question arises as to what the obligation could be founded upon that would bind any one in a court of justice to accept the oath of another person as a right and valid proof of the truth of his statements which are to put an end to all dispute. In other words, what obliges me juridically to believe that another person when taking an oath has any religion at all, so that I should subordinate or entrust my right to his oath? And, on like grounds, conversely, can I be bound at all to take an oath? It is evident that both these questions point to what is in itself morally wrong.

But in relation to a court of justice—and generally in the civil state—if it be assumed there are no other means of getting to the truth in certain cases than by an oath, it must be adopted. In regard to religion, under the supposition that every one has it, it may be utilized as a necessary means *(in causu necessitatis),* in behoof of the legitimate procedure of a court of justice. The court uses this form of spiritual compulsion (*tortura spiritualis*) as an available means, in conformity with the superstitious propensity of mankind, for the ascertainment of what is concealed; and therefore holds itself justified in so doing. The legislative power, however, is fundamentally wrong in assigning this authority to the judicial power, because even in the civil state any compulsion with regard to the taking of oaths is contrary to the inalienable freedom of man.

Official oaths, which are usually *promissory,* being taken on entering upon an office, to the effect that the individual has sincere *intention* to administer his functions dutifully, might well be changed into *assertory* oaths, to be taken at the end of a year or more of actual administration, the official swearing to the faithfulness of his discharge of duty during that time. This would bring the conscience more into action than the promissory oath, which always gives room for the internal pretext that, with the best intention, the difficulties that arose during the administration of the official function were not foreseen. And, further, violations of duty, under the prospect of their being summed up by future censors, would give rise to more anxiety as to censure than when they are merely represented, one after the other, and forgotten.

As regards an oath taken concerning a matter of belief (*de credulitate*), it is evident that no such oath can be demanded by a court. 1. For, *first,* it contains in itself a contradiction. Such belief, as intermediate between opinion and knowledge, is a thing on which one might venture to lay a *wager* but not to swear an *oath.* 2. And, *second,* the judge who imposes an oath of belief, in order to ascertain anything pertinent to his own purpose or even to the common good, commits a great offence against the conscientiousness of the party taking such an oath. This he does in regard both to the levity of mind, which he thereby helps to engender, and to the stings of conscience which a man must feel who to-day regards a subject from a certain point of view, but who will very probably to-morrow find it quite improbable from another point of view. Any one, therefore, who is compelled to take such an oath, is subjected to an injury.

Transition from the Mine and Thine in the State of Nature to the Mine and Thine in the Juridical State Generally

41. *Public Justice as Related to the Natural and the Civil State*

The juridical state is that relation of men to one another which contains the conditions under which it is alone possible for every one to obtain the right that is his due. The formal principle of the possibility of actually *participating* in such right, viewed in accordance with the idea of a universally legislative will, is public justice. Public justice may be considered in relation either to the possibility, or actuality, or necessity of the possession of objects—regarded as the matter of the activity of the will—according to laws. It may thus be divided into *protective justice* (*justitia testatrix*), *commutative justice (justitia commutativa),* and *distributive justice* (*justitia distributiva*), in the *first* mode of justice, the law declares merely what relation is internally *right* in respect of form (*lex justi*); in the *second,* it declares what is likewise externally in accord with a law in respect of the object, and what possession is rightful (*lex juridica*); and in the *third,* it declares what is right, and what is *just,* and to what extent, by the judgement of a court in any particular case coming under the given law. In this latter relation, the public court is called the *justice* of the country; and the question whether there actually is or is not such an administration of public justice may be regarded as the most important of all juridical interests.

The non-juridical state is that condition of society in which there is no distributive justice. It is commonly called the *natural* state (*status naturalis*), or the state of nature. It is not the *social state,* as Achenwall puts it, for this may be in itself an *artificial* state (*status artificialis*), that is to be contradistinguished from the "natural" state. The opposite of the state of nature is the *civil* state (*status civilis*) as the condition of a society standing under a distributive justice. In the state of nature, there may even be juridical forms of society—such as marriage, parental authority, the household, and such like. For none of these, however, does any law *a priori* lay it down as an incumbent obligation:

"Thou *shalt* enter into this state." But it may be said of the *juridical* state that: "All men who *may* even involuntarily come into relations of right with one another *ought* to enter into this state."

The natural or non-juridical social state may be viewed as the sphere of private right, and the civil state may be specially regarded as the sphere of public right. The latter state contains no more and no other duties of men towards each other than what may be conceived in connection with the former state; the matter of private right is, in short, the very same in both. The laws of the civil state, therefore, only turn upon the juridical form of the coexistence of men under a common constitution; and, in this respect, these laws must necessarily be regarded and conceived as public laws.

The civil union (*unio civilis*) cannot, in the strict sense, be properly called a *society;* for there is no sociality in common between the ruler (*imperans*) and the subject (*subditus*) under a civil constitution. They are not co-ordinated as associates in a society with each other, but the one is *subordinated* to the other. Those who may be co-ordinated with one another must consider themselves as mutually equal, in so far as they stand under common laws. The civil union may therefore be regarded not so much as *being,* but rather as *making* a society.

42. *The Postulate of Public Right*

From the conditions of private right in the natural state, there arises the postulate of public right. It may be thus expressed: "In the relation of unavoidable coexistence with others, thou shalt pass from the state of nature into a juridical union constituted under the condition of a distributive justice." The principle of this postulate may be unfolded analytically from the conception of *right* in the external relation, contradistinguished from mere *might* as violence.

No one is under obligation to abstain from interfering with the possession of others, unless they give him a reciprocal guarantee for the observance of a similar abstention from interference with his possession. Nor does he require to wait for proof by experience of the need of this guarantee, in view of the antagonistic disposition of others. He is therefore under no obligation to wait till he acquires practical prudence at his own cost; for he can perceive in himself evidence of the natural inclination of men to play the master over others, and to disregard the claims of the right of others, when they feel themselves their superiors by might or fraud. And thus it is not necessary to wait for the melancholy experience of actual hostility; the individual is from the first entitled to exercise a rightful compulsion towards those who already threaten him by their very nature. *Quilibet praesumitur malus, donec securitatem dederit oppositi.*

So long as the intention to live and continue in this state of externally lawless freedom prevails, men may be said to do no wrong or injustice at all *to one another,* even when they wage war against each other. For what seems competent as good for the one is equally valid for the other, as if it were so by mutual agreement. *Uti partes de jure suo disponunt, ita jus est.* But generally they must be considered as being in the highest state of wrong, as being and willing to be in a condition which is not juridical, and in which, therefore, no one can be secured against violence, in the possession of his own.

The distinction between what is only *formally* and what is also *materially* wrong, and unjust, finds frequent application in the science of right. An enemy who, on occupying a besieged fortress, instead of honourably fulfilling the conditions of a capitulation, maltreats the garrison on marching out, or otherwise violates the agreement, cannot complain of injury or wrong if on another occasion the same treatment is inflicted upon themselves. But, in fact, all such actions fundamentally involve the commission of wrong and injustice, in the highest degree; because they take all validity away from the conception of right, and give up everything, as it were by law itself, to savage violence, and thus overthrow the rights of men generally.

SECOND PART. *PUBLIC RIGHT*

THE SYSTEM OF THOSE LAWS WHICH REQUIRE PUBLIC PROMULGATION. THE PRINCIPLES OF RIGHT IN CIVIL SOCIETY

43. *Definition and Division of Public Right*

PUBLIC right embraces the whole of the laws that require to be universally promulgated in order to produce a juridical state of society. It is therefore a system of those laws that are requisite for a people as a multitude of men forming a nation, or for a number of nations, in their relations to each other. Men and nations, on account of their mutual influence on one another, require a juridical *constitution* uniting them under one will, in order that they may participate in what is right. This relation of the individuals of a nation to each other constitutes the civil union in the social state; and, viewed as a whole in relation to its constituent members, it forms the political state (*civitas*).

1. The state, as constituted by the common interest of all to live in a juridical union, is called, in view of its form, the commonwealth or the republic in the wider sense of the term (*res publica latius sic dicta*). The principles of right in this sphere thus constitute the first department of public right as the right of the state (*jus civitatis*) or national right. 2. The state, again, viewed in relation to other peoples, is called a power (*potentia*), whence arises the idea of potentates. Viewed in relation to the supposed hereditary unity of the people composing it, the state constitutes a nation (*gens*). Under the general conception of public right, in addition to the right of the individual state, there thus arises another department of right, constituting the right of nations (*jus gentium*) or international right. 3. Further, as the surface of the earth is not unlimited in extent, but is circumscribed into a unity, national right and international right necessarily culminate in the idea of a universal right of mankind, which may be called *Cosmopolitical Right* (*jus cosmopoliticum*). And national, international, and cosmopolitical right are so interconnected, that, if any one of these three possible forms of the juridical relation fails to embody the essential principles that ought to regulate external freedom by law, the structure of legislation reared by the others will also be undermined, and the whole system would at last fall to pieces.

I. Right of the State and Constitutional Law. (Jus Civitatis)

44. *Origin of the Civil Union and Public Right*

It is not from any experience prior to the appearance of an external authoritative legislation that we learn of the maxim of natural violence among men and their evil tendency to engage in war with each other. Nor is it assumed here that it is merely some particular historical condition or fact, that makes public legislative constraint necessary; for however well-disposed or favourable to right men may be considered to be of themselves, the rational idea of a state of society not yet regulated by right, must be taken as our starting-point. This idea implies that before a legal state of society can be publicly established, individual men, nations, and states, can never be safe against violence from each other; and this is evident from the consideration that every one of his own will naturally does *what seems good and right in his own eyes*, entirely independent of the opinion of others. Hence, unless the institution of right is to be renounced, the first thing incumbent on men is to accept the principle that it is necessary to leave the state of nature, in which every one follows his own inclinations, and to form a union of all those who cannot avoid coming into reciprocal communication, and thus subject themselves in common to the external restraint of public compulsory laws. Men thus enter into a civil union, in which every one has it determined by law what shall be recognized as his; and this is secured to him by a competent external power distinct from his own individuality. Such is the primary obligation, on the part of all men, to enter into the relations of a civil state of society.

The natural condition of mankind need not, on this ground, be represented as a state of absolute *injustice*, as if there could have been no other relation originally among men but what was merely determined by force. But this natural condition must be regarded, if it ever existed, as a state of society that was void of regulation by right (*status justitiae vacuus*), so that if a matter of right came to be *in dispute* (*jus controversum*), no competent judge was found to give an authorized legal decision upon it. It is therefore reasonable that any one should constrain another by force, to pass from such a non-juridical state of life and enter within the jurisdiction of a civil state of society. For, although on the basis of the *ideas of right* held by individuals as such, external things may be acquired by occupancy or contract, yet such acquisition is only *provisory* so long as it has not yet obtained the sanction of a public law. Till this sanction is reached, the condition of possession is not determined by any public distributive justice, nor is it secured by any power exercising public right.

If men were not disposed to recognize any acquisition at all as rightful—even in a provisional way—prior to entering into the civil state, this state of society would itself be impossible. For the laws regarding the mine and thine in the state of nature, contain formally the very same thing as they prescribe in the civil state, when it is viewed merely according to rational conceptions: only that in the forms of the civil state the conditions are laid down under which the formal prescriptions of the state of nature attain realization conformable to distributive justice. Were there, then, not even *provisionally,* an external *meum* and *tuum* in the state of nature, neither would there be any juridical duties in relation to them; and, consequently, there would be no obligation to pass out of that state into another.

45. *The Form of the State and its Three Powers*

A state *(civitas)* is the union of a number of men under juridical laws. These laws, as such, are to be regarded as necessary *a priori*—that is, as following of themselves from the conceptions of external right generally—and not as merely established by statute. The form of the state is thus involved in the *idea* of the state, viewed as it ought to be according to pure principles of right; and this ideal form furnishes the normal criterion of every real union that constitutes a commonwealth.

Every state contains in itself three powers, the universal united will of the people being thus personified in a political triad. These are *the legislative power, the executive power,* and *the judiciary power.*—1. The *legislative* power of the sovereignty in the state is embodied in the person of the lawgiver; 2. the *executive* power is embodied in the person of the ruler who administers the Law; and 3. the *judiciary* power, embodied in the person of the judge, is the function of assigning every one what is his own, according to the law *(potestas legislatoria, rectoria, et judiciaria).* These three powers may be compared to the three propositions in a practical syllogism: the major as the sumption laying down the universal *law* of a will, the minor presenting the *command* applicable to an action according to the law as the principle of the subsumption, and the conclusion containing the sentence, or judgement of right, in the particular case under consideration.

46. *The Legislative Power and the Members of the State*

The legislative power, viewed in its rational principle, can only belong to the united will of the people. For, as all right ought to proceed from this power, it is necessary that its laws should be unable to do wrong to any one whatever. Now, if any *one* individual determines anything in the state in contradistinction to *another,* it is always possible that he may perpetrate a wrong on that other; but this is never possible when *all* determine and decree what is to be Law to themselves. *Volenti non fit injuria.* Hence it is only the united and consenting will of all the people—in so far as each of them determines the same thing about all, and all determine the same thing about each—that ought to have the power of enacting law in the state.

The members of a civil society thus united for the purpose of legislation, and thereby constituting a state, are called its *citizens;* and there are three juridical attributes that inseparably belong to them by right. These are:—1. constitutional freedom, as the right of every citizen to have to obey no other law than that to which he has given his consent or approval; 2. civil equality, as the right of the citizen to recognise no one as a superior among the people in relation to himself, except in so far as such a one is as subject to *his* moral power to impose obligations, as that other has power to impose obligations upon him; and 3. political independence, as the right to owe his existence and continuance in society not to the arbitrary will of another, but to his own rights and powers as a member of the commonwealth, and, consequently, the possession of a civil personality, which cannot be represented by any other than himself.

The capability of voting by possession of the suffrage properly constitutes the political qualification of a citizen as a member of the state. But this, again, presupposes the independence or self-sufficiency of the individual citizen among the people, as one who is not a mere incidental part of the commonwealth, but a member of it acting of his own will in community with others. The last of the three qualities involved necessarily constitutes the distinction between *active* and *passive* citizenship; although the latter conception appears to stand in contradiction to the definition of a citizen as such. The following examples may serve to remove this difficulty. The apprentice of a merchant or tradesman, a servant who is not in the employ of the state, a minor (*naturaliter vel civiliter*), all women, and, generally, every one who is compelled to maintain himself not according to his own industry, but as it is arranged by others (the state excepted), are without civil personality, and their existence is only, as it were, incidentally included in the state. The woodcutter whom I employ on my estate; the smith in India who carries his hammer, anvil, and bellows into the houses where he is engaged to work in iron, as distinguished from the European carpenter or smith, who can offer the independent products of his labour as wares for public sale; the resident tutor as distinguished from the schoolmaster; the ploughman as distinguished from the farmer and such like, illustrate the distinction in question. In all these cases, the former members of the contrast are distinguished from the latter by being mere subsidiaries of the commonwealth and not active independent members of it, because they are of necessity commanded and protected by others, and consequently possess no political self-sufficiency in themselves. Such dependence on the will of others and the consequent inequality are, however, not inconsistent with the freedom and equality of the individuals *as men* helping to constitute the people. Much rather is it the case that it is only under such conditions that a people can become a state and enter into a civil constitution. But all are not equally qualified to exercise the right of suffrage under the constitution, and to be full citizens of the state, and not mere passive subjects under its protection. For, although they are entitled to demand to be treated by all the other citizens according to laws of natural freedom and equality, as *passive* parts of the state, it does not follow that they ought themselves to have the right to deal with the state as active members of it, to reorganize it, or to take action by way of introducing certain laws. All they have a right in their circumstances to claim may be no more than that whatever be the mode in which the positive laws are enacted, these laws must not be contrary to the natural laws that demand the freedom of all the people and the equality that is conformable thereto; and it must therefore be made possible for them to raise themselves from this passive condition in the state to the condition of active citizenship.

47. *Dignities in the State and the Original Contract*

All these three powers in the state are dignities; and, as necessarily arising out of the idea of the state and essential generally to the foundation of its constitution, they are to be regarded as political dignities. They imply the relation between a universal sovereign as head of the state—which according to the laws of freedom can be none other than the people itself united into a nation—and the mass of the individuals of the nation as subjects. The former member of the relation is the *ruling* power, whose function is to govern (*imperans*); the latter is the *ruled* constituents of the state, whose function is to obey (*subditi*).

The act by which a people is represented as constituting itself into a state, is termed the *original contract.* This is properly only an outward mode of representing the idea by which the rightfulness of the process of organizing the constitution may be made conceivable. According to this representation, all and each of the people give up their external freedom in order to receive it immediately again as members of a commonwealth. The commonwealth is the people viewed as united altogether into a state. And thus it is not to be said that the individual in the state has sacrificed *a part* of his inborn external freedom for a particular purpose; but he has abandoned his wild lawless freedom wholly, in order to find all his proper freedom again entire and undiminished, but in the form of a regulated order of dependence, that is, in a civil state regulated by laws of right. This relation of dependence thus arises out of his own regulative law giving will.

48. *Mutual Relations and Characteristics of the Three Powers*

The three powers in the state, as regards their relations to each other, are, therefore: (1) *coordinate* with one another as so many moral persons, and the one is thus the complement of the other in the way of completing the constitution of the state; (2) they are likewise *subordinate* to one another, so that the one cannot at the same time usurp the function of the other by whose side it moves, each having its own principle and maintaining its authority in a particular person, but under the condition of the will of a superior; and further, (3) by the *union* of both these relations, they assign distributively to every subject in the state his own rights.

Considered as to their respective dignity, the three powers may be thus described. The will of the *sovereign legislator,* in respect of what constitutes the external mine and thine, is to be regarded as *irreprehensible;* the executive function of the *supreme ruler* is to be regarded as *irresistible;* and the judicial sentence of the *supreme judge* is to be regarded as *irreversible,* being beyond appeal.

49. *Distinct Functions of the Three Powers. Autonomy of the State*

1. The executive power belongs to the *governor* or *regent* of the state, whether it assumes the form of a moral or individual person, as the king or prince (*rex, princeps*). This executive authority, as the supreme *agent* of the state, appoints the magistrates, and prescribes the rules to the people, in accordance with which individuals may acquire anything or maintain what is their own conformably to the law, each case being brought under its application. Regarded as a moral person, this executive authority constitutes the government. The orders issued by the government to the people and the magistrates, as well as to the higher ministerial *administrators* of the state (*gubernatio*), are rescripts or *decrees,* and not laws; for they terminate in the decision of particular cases, and are given forth as unchangeable. A government acting as an executive, and at the same time laying down the law as the legislative power, would be a *despotic* government, and would have to be contradistinguished from a *patriotic* government. A *patriotic* government, again, is to be distinguished from a *paternal* government (*regimen paternale*) which is the most despotic government of all, the citizens being dealt with by it as mere children. A patriotic government, however, is one in which the state, while dealing with the subjects as if they were members of a family, still treats them likewise as citizens, and according to laws that recognize their independence, each individual possessing himself and not being dependent on the absolute will of another beside him or above him.

2. The legislative authority ought not at the same time to be the executive or governor; for the governor, as administrator, should stand under the authority of the law, and is bound by it under the supreme control of the legislator. The legislative authority may therefore deprive the governor of his power, depose him, or reform his administration, but not *punish* him. This is the proper and only meaning of the common saying in England, "The King—as the supreme executive power—can do no wrong." For any such application of punishment would necessarily be an act of that very executive power to which the supreme right to *compel* according to law pertains, and which would itself be thus subjected to coercion; which is self-contradictory.

3. Further, neither the legislative power nor the executive power ought to exercise the *judicial* function, but only appoint judges as magistrates. It is the people who ought to judge themselves, through those of the citizens who are elected by free choice as their representatives for this purpose, and even specially for every process or cause. For the judicial sentence is a special act of public distributive justice performed by a judge or court as a constitutional administrator of the law, to a subject as one of the people. Such an act is not invested inherently with the power to determine and assign to any one what is his. Every individual among the people being merely passive in this relation to the supreme power, either the executive or the legislative authority might do him wrong in their determinations in cases of dispute regarding the property of individuals. It would not be the people themselves who thus determined, or who pronounced the judgements of "guilty" or "not guilty" regarding their fellow-citizens. For it is to the determination of this issue in a cause that the court has to apply the law; and it is by means of the executive authority, that the judge holds power to assign to every one his own. Hence it is only the *people* that properly can judge in a cause—although indirectly—by representatives elected and deputed by themselves, as in a jury. It would even be beneath the dignity of the sovereign head of the state to play the judge; for this would be to put himself into a position in which it would be possible to do wrong, and thus to subject himself to the demand for an appeal to a still higher power (*a rege male informato ad regem melius informandum*).

It is by the co-operation of these three powers—the legislative, the executive, and the judicial—that the state realizes its *autonomy.* This autonomy consists in its organizing, forming, and maintaining itself in accordance with the laws of freedom. In their union the *welfare* of the state is realized. *Salus reipublicae suprema lex.*[1] By this is not to be understood merely the

1 ["The health of the state is the highest law."]

individual *well-being* and *happiness* of the citizens of the state; for—as Rousseau asserts—this end may perhaps be more agreeably and more desirably attained in the state of nature, or even under a despotic government. But the welfare of the state, as its own highest good, signifies that condition in which the greatest harmony is attained between its constitution and the principles of right—a condition of the state which reason by a categorical imperative makes it obligatory upon us to strive after.

Constitutional and Juridical Consequences arising from the Nature of the Civil Union

A. *Right of the Supreme Power; Treason; Dethronement; Revolution; Reform*

The origin of the supreme power is *practically inscrutable* by the people who are placed under its authority. In other words, the subject need not *reason too curiously* in regard to its origin in the practical relation, as if the right of the obedience due to it were to be doubted *(jus controversum)*. For as the people, in order to be able to abjudicate with a title of right regarding the supreme power in the state, must be regarded as already united under one common legislative will, it cannot judge otherwise than as the present supreme head of the state *(summus imperans)* wills. The question has been raised as to whether an actual contract of subjection (*pactum subjectionis civilis*) originally preceded the civil government as a fact; or whether the power arose first, and the law only followed afterwards, or may have followed in this order. But such questions, as regards the people already actually living under the civil law, are either entirely aimless, or even fraught with subtle danger to the state. For, should the subject, after having dug down to the ultimate origin of the state, rise in opposition to the present ruling authority, he would expose himself as a citizen, according to the law and with full right, to be punished, destroyed, or outlawed. A law which is so holy and inviolable that it is *practically* a crime even to cast doubt upon it, or to suspend its operation for a moment, is represented of itself as necessarily derived from some supreme, unblameable lawgiver. And this is the meaning of the maxim, "All authority is from God", which proposition does not express the *historical foundation* of the civil constitution, but an ideal principle of the practical reason. It may be otherwise rendered thus: "It is a duty to obey the law of the existing legislative power, be its origin what it may."

Hence it follows, that the supreme power in the state has only rights, and no (compulsory) duties towards the subject. Further, if the ruler or regent, as the organ of the supreme power, proceeds in violation of the laws, as in imposing taxes, recruiting soldiers, and so on, contrary to the law of equality in the distribution of the political burdens, the subject may oppose *complaints* and *objections* (*gravamina*) to this injustice, but not active resistance.

There cannot even be an Article contained in the political constitution that would make it possible for a power in the state, in case of the transgression of the constitutional laws by the supreme authority, to resist or even to restrict it in so doing. For, whoever would restrict the supreme power of the state must have more, or at least equal, power as compared with the power that is so restricted; and if competent to command the subjects to resist, such a one would also have to be able to *protect* them, and if he is to be considered capable of judging what is right in every case, he may also publicly order resistance. But such a one, and not the actual authority, would then be the supreme power; which is contradictory. The supreme sovereign power, then, in proceeding by a minister who is at the same time the ruler of the state, consequently becomes despotic; and the expedient of giving the people to imagine—when they have properly only legislative influence—that they act by their deputies by way of limiting the sovereign authority, cannot so mask and disguise the actual despotism of such a government that it will not appear in the measures and means adopted by the minister to carry out his function. The people, while represented by their deputies in parliament, under such conditions, may have in these warrantors of their freedom and rights, persons who are keenly interested on their own account and their families, and who look to such a minister for the benefit of his influence in the army, navy, and public offices. And hence, instead of offering resistance to the undue pretensions of the government—whose public declarations ought to carry a prior accord on the part of the people, which, however, cannot be allowed in peace, they are rather always ready to play into the hands of the government. Hence the so-called *limited* political constitution, as a constitution of the internal rights of the state, is an unreality; and instead of being consistent with right, it is only a principle of expediency. And its aim is not so much to throw all possible obstacles in the way of a powerful violator of popular rights by his arbitrary influence upon the government, as rather to cloak it over under the illusion of a right of opposition conceded to the people.

Resistance on the part of the people to the supreme legislative power of the state is in no case legitimate; for it is only by submission to the universal legislative will, that a condition of law and order is possible. Hence there is no right of sedition, and still less of rebellion, belonging to the people. And least of all, when the supreme power is embodied in an individual monarch, is there any justification, under the pretext of his abuse of power, for seizing his person or taking away his life (*monarchomachismus sub specie tyrannicidii*). The slightest attempt of this kind is *high treason* (*proditio eminens*); and a traitor of this sort who aims at the *overthrow* of his country may be punished, as a political parricide, even with death. It is the duty of the people to bear any abuse of the supreme power, even then though it should be considered to be unbearable. And the reason is that any resistance of the highest legislative authority can never but be contrary to the law, and must even be regarded as tending to destroy the whole legal constitution. In order to be entitled to offer such resistance, a public law would be required to permit it. But the supreme legislation would by such a law cease to be supreme, and the people as subjects would be made sovereign over that to which they are subject; which is a contradiction. And the contradiction becomes more apparent when the question is put: "Who is to be the judge in a controversy between the people and the sovereign?" For the people and the sovereign are to be constitutionally or juridically regarded as two different moral persons; but the question shows that the people would then have to be the judge in their own cause.

The *dethronement* of a monarch may be also conceived as a *voluntary* abdication of the crown, and a resignation of his power into the hands of the people; or it might be a deliberate surrender of these without any assault on the royal person, in order that the monarch may be relegated into private life. But, however it happen, forcible compulsion of it, on the part of the people, cannot be justified under the pretext of a *right of necessity* (*casus necessitatis*); and least of all can the slightest right be shown for punishing the sovereign on the ground of previous maladministration. For all that has been already done in the quality of a sovereign must be regarded as done outwardly by right; and, considered as the source of the laws, the sovereign himself can do no wrong. Of all the abominations in the overthrow of a state by revolution, even the murder or *assassination* of the monarch is not the worst. For that may be done by the people out of fear, lest, if he is allowed to live, he may again acquire power and inflict punishment upon them; and so it may be done, not as an act of punitive justice, but merely from regard to self-preservation. It is the formal *execution* of a monarch that horrifies a soul filled with ideas of human right; and this feeling occurs again and again as often as the mind realizes the scenes that terminated the fate of Charles I or Louis XVI. Now how is this feeling to be explained? It is not a mere aesthetic feeling, arising from the working of the imagination, nor from sympathy, produced by fancying ourselves in the place of the sufferer. On the contrary, it is a *moral* feeling arising from the entire subversion of all our notions of right. Regicide, in short, is regarded as a crime which always remains such and can never be expiated (*crimen immortale, inexpiabile*); and it appears to resemble that sin which the theologians declare can neither be forgiven in this world nor in the next. The explanation of this phenomenon in the human mind appears to be furnished by the following reflections upon it; and they even shed some light upon the principles of political right.

Every transgression of a law only can and must be explained as arising from a maxim of the transgressor making such wrong-doing his rule of action; for were it not committed by him as a free being, it could not be imputed to him. But it is absolutely impossible to explain how any rational individual forms such a maxim against the clear prohibition of the law-giving reason; for it is only events which happen according to the mechanical laws of nature that are capable of explanation. Now a transgressor or criminal may commit his wrong-doing either according to the maxim of a rule supposed to be valid objectively and universally, or only as an exception from the rule by dispensing with its obligation for the occasion. In the *latter* case, he only *diverges* from the law, although intentionally. He may, at the same time, abhor his own transgression, and without formally renouncing his obedience to the law only wish to avoid it. In the *former* case, however, he rejects the authority of the law itself, the validity of which, however, he cannot repudiate before his own reason, even while he makes it his rule to act against it. His maxim is, therefore, not merely defective as being *negatively* contrary to the aw, but it is even positively illegal, as being *diametrically* contrary and in hostile opposition to it. So far as we can see into and understand the relation, it would appear as if it were impossible for men to commit wrongs and crimes of a wholly useless form of wickedness, and yet the idea of such extreme perversity cannot be overlooked in a system of moral philosophy.

There is thus a feeling of horror at the thought of the formal execution of a monarch *by his people*. And the reason it is that, whereas an act of assassination must be considered as only an *exception* from the rule which has been constituted a maxim, such an *execution* must be regarded as a complete *perversion* of the principles that should regulate the relation between a sovereign and his people. For it makes the people, who owe their constitutional existence to the legislation that issued from the sovereign, to be the ruler over him. Hence mere violence is thus elevated with bold brow, and as it were by principle, above the holiest right; and, appearing like an abyss to swallow up everything without recall, it seems like suicide committed by the state upon itself and a crime that is capable of no atonement. There is therefore reason to assume that the consent that is accorded to such executions is not really based upon a supposed principle of right, but only springs from fear of the vengeance that would be taken upon the people were the same power to revive again in the state. And hence it may be held that the formalities accompanying them have only been put forward in order to give these deeds a look of punishment from the accompaniment of a *judicial process,* such as could not go along with a mere murder or assassination. But such a cloaking of the deed entirely fails of its purpose, because this pretension on the part of the people is even worse than murder itself, as it implies a principle which would necessarily make the restoration of a state, when once overthrown, an impossibility.

An alteration of the still defective constitution of the state may sometimes be quite necessary. But all such changes ought only to proceed from the sovereign power in the way of *reform,* and are not to be brought about by the people in the way of *revolution;* and when they take place, they should only effect the *executive,* and not the *legislative,* power. A political constitution which is so modified that the people by their representatives in parliament can legally *resist* the executive power, and its representative minister, is called a *limited constitution.* Yet even under such a constitution there is no right of *active* resistance, as by an arbitrary combination of the people to coerce the government into a certain active procedure; for this would be to assume to perform an act of the executive itself. All that can rightly be allowed, is only a *negative* resistance, amounting to an act of *refusal* on the part of the people to concede all the demands which the executive may deem it necessary to make in behoof of the political administration. And if this right were never exercised, it would be a sure sign that the people were corrupted, their representatives venal, the supreme head of the government despotic, and his ministers practically betrayers of the people.

Further, when on the success of a revolution a new constitution has been founded, the unlawfulness of its beginning and of its institution cannot release the subjects from the obligation of adapting themselves, as good citizens, to the new order of things; and they are not entitled to refuse honourably to obey the authority that has thus attained the power in the state. A dethroned monarch, who has survived such a revolution, is not to be called to account on the ground of his former administration; and still less may he be punished for it, when withdrawing into the private life of a citizen he prefers his own quiet and the peace of the state to the uncertainty of exile, with the intention of maintaining his claims for restoration at all hazards, and pushing these either by secret counter-revolution or by the assistance of other powers. However, if he prefers to follow the latter course, his rights remain, because the rebellion that drove him from his position was inherently unjust. But the question then emerges as to whether other powers have the right to form themselves into an alliance in behalf of such a dethroned monarch merely in order not to leave the crime committed by the people unavenged, or to do away with it as a scandal to all the states; and whether they are therefore justified and called upon to restore by force to another state a formerly existing constitution that has been removed by a *revolution.* The discussion of this question, however, does not belong to this department of public right, but to the following section, concerning the right of nations.

B. *Land Rights. Secular and Church Lands, Rights of Taxation; Finance; Police; Inspection*

Is the sovereign, viewed as embodying the legislative power, to be regarded as the supreme proprietor of the soil, or only as the highest ruler of the people by the laws? As the soil is the supreme condition under which it is alone possible to have external things as one's own, its possible possession and use constitute the first acquirable basis of external right. Hence it is that all such rights must be derived from the sovereign as overlord and paramount superior of the soil, or, as it may be better put, as the supreme proprietor of the land (*dominus territorii*). The people, as forming the mass of the subjects, belong to the sovereign as a people; not in the sense of his being their proprietor in the way of real right, but as their supreme commander or chief in the way of personal right. This supreme proprietorship, however, is only an idea of the civil constitution, objectified to represent, in accordance with juridical conceptions, the necessary union of the private property of all the people under a public universal possessor. The relation is so represented in order that it may form a basis for the determination of particular rights in property. It does not proceed, therefore, upon the principle of mere *aggregation,* which advances empirically from the parts to the whole, but from the necessary formal principle of a division of the soil according to conceptions of right. In accordance with this principle, the supreme universal proprietor cannot have any private property in any part of the soil; for otherwise he would make himself a private person. Private property in the soil belongs only to the people, taken distributively and not collectively; from which condition, however, a nomadic people must be excepted as having no private property at all in the soil. The supreme proprietor accordingly ought not to hold private *estates,* either for private use or for the support of the court. For, as it would depend upon his own pleasure how far these should extend, the state would be in danger of seeing all property in the land taken into the hands of the government, and all the subjects treated as *bondsmen of the soil* (*glebae adscripti*). As possessors only of what was the private property of another, they might thus be deprived of all freedom and regarded as serfs or slaves. Of the supreme proprietor of the land, it may be said that *he possesses nothing* as his own, except himself; for if he possessed things in the state alongside of others, dispute and litigation would be possible with these others regarding those things, and there would be no independent judge to settle the cause. But it may also be said that *he possesses everything;* for he has the supreme right of sovereignty over the whole people, to whom all external things severally (*divisim*) belong; and as such he assigns distributively to every one what is to be his.

Hence there cannot be any corporation in the state, nor any class or order, that as proprietors can transmit the land for a sole exclusive use to the following generations for all time (*ad infinitum*), according to certain fixed statutes. The state may annul and abrogate all such statutes at any time, only under the condition of indemnifying survivors for their interests. The order of *knights,* constituting the nobility regarded as a mere rank or class of specially titled individuals, as well as the order of the *clergy,* called *the church,* are both subject to this relation. They can never be entitled by any hereditary privileges with which they may be favoured, to acquire an absolute property in the soil transmissible to their successors. They can only acquire the use of such property for the time being. If public opinion has ceased, on account of other arrangements, to impel the state to protect itself from negligence in the national defence by appeal to the *military honour* of the knightly order, the estates granted on that condition may be recalled. And, in like manner, the church lands or spiritualities may be reclaimed by the state without scruple, if public opinion has ceased to impel the members of the state to maintain masses for the souls of the dead, prayers for the living, and a multitude of clergy, as means to protect themselves from eternal fire. But in both cases, the condition of indemnifying existing interests must be observed. Those who in this connection fall under the movement of reform are not entitled to complain that their property is taken from them; for the foundation of their previous possession lay only in the *opinion of the people,* and it can be valid only so long as this opinion lasts. As soon as this public opinion in favour of such institutions dies out, or is even extinguished in the judgement of those who have the greatest claim by their acknowledged merit to lead and represent it, the putative proprietorship in question must cease, as if by a public appeal made regarding it to the state (*a rege male informato ad regem melius informandum*).

On this primarily acquired supreme proprietorship in the land rests the right of the sovereign, as universal proprietor of the country, to *assess* the private proprietors of the soil, and to demand taxes, excise, and dues, or the performance of service to the state such as may be required in war. But this is to be done so that it is actually the people that assess themselves, this being the only mode of proceeding according to laws of right. This may be effected through the medium of the body of deputies who represent the people. It is also permissible, in circumstances in which the state is in imminent danger, to proceed by a forced loan, as a right vested in the sovereign, although this may be a divergence from the existing law.

Upon this principle is also founded the right of administering the national economy, including the finance and the police. The police has specially to care for the public *safety, convenience,* and *decency.* As regards the last of these —the feeling or negative taste for public propriety—it is important that it be not deadened by such influences as begging, disorderly noises, offensive smells, public prostitution (*Venus vulgivaga*), or other offences against the moral sense, as it greatly facilitates the government in the task of regulating the life of the people by law.

For the preservation of the state there further belongs to it a right of *inspection* (*jus inspectionis*), which entitles the public authority to see that no secret society, political or religious, exists among the people that can exert a prejudicial influence upon the *public* weal. Accordingly, when it is required by the police, no such secret society may refuse to lay open its constitution. But the visitation and search of private houses by the police can only be justified in a case of necessity; and in every particular instance, it must be authorized by a higher authority.

C. *Relief of the Poor. Foundling Hospitals. The Church*

The sovereign, as undertaker of the duty of the people, has the right to tax them for purposes essentially connected with their own preservation. Such are, in particular, the relief of the poor, foundling asylums, and ecclesiastical establishments, otherwise designated *charitable* or *pious* foundations.

1. The people have in fact united themselves by their common will into a society, which has to be perpetually maintained; and for this purpose they have subjected themselves to the internal power of the state, in order to preserve the members of this society even when they are not able to support themselves. By the fundamental principle of the state, the government is justified and entitled to compel those who are able, to furnish the means necessary to preserve those who are not themselves capable of providing for the most necessary wants of nature. For the existence of persons with property in the state implies their submission under it for protection and the provision by the state of what is necessary for their existence; and accordingly the state founds a right upon an obligation on their part to contribute of their means for the preservation of their fellow-citizens. This may be carried out by taxing the property or the commercial industry of the citizens, or by establishing funds and drawing interest from them, not for the wants of the state as such, which is rich, but for those of the people. And this is not to be done merely by *voluntary* contributions, but by *compulsory* exactions as state-burdens, for we are here considering only the *right* of the state in relation to the people. Among the *voluntary* modes of raising such contributions, *lotteries* ought not to be allowed, because they increase the number of those who are poor, and involve danger to the public property. It may be asked whether the relief of the poor ought to be administered out of *current contributions,* so that every age should maintain its own poor; or whether this were better done by means of *permanent funds* and charitable institutions, such as widows' homes, hospitals, etc.? And if the former method is the better, it may also be considered whether the means necessary are to be raised by a legal assessment rather than by begging, which is generally nigh akin to robbing. The former method must in reality be regarded as the only one that is conformable to the right of the state, which cannot withdraw its connection from any one who has to live. For a legal current provision does not make the profession of poverty a means of gain for the indolent, as is to be feared is the case with pious foundations when they grow with the number of the poor; nor can it be charged with being an unjust or unrighteous burden imposed by the government on the people.

2. The state has also a right to impose upon the people the duty of preserving children exposed from want or shame, and who would otherwise perish; for it cannot knowingly allow this increase of its power to be destroyed, however unwelcome in some respects it may be. But it is a difficult question to determine how this may most justly be carried out. It might be considered whether it would not be right to exact contributions for this purpose from the unmarried persons of both sexes who are possessed of means, as being in part responsible for the evil; and further, whether the end in view would be best carried out by foundling hospitals, or in

what other way consistent with right. But this is a problem of which no solution has yet been offered that does not in some measure offend against right or morality.

3. The church is here regarded as an ecclesiastical establishment merely, and as such it must be carefully distinguished from religion, which as an internal mode of feeling lies wholly beyond the sphere of the action of the civil power. Viewed as an institution for public *worship* founded for the people—to whose opinion or conviction it owes its origin—the church establishment responds to a real want in the state. This is the need felt by the people to regard themselves as also subjects of a Supreme *Invisible* Power to which they must pay homage, and which may often be brought into a very undesirable collision with the civil power. The state has therefore a right in this relation; but it is not to be regarded as the right of constitutional legislation in the church, so as to organize it as may seem most advantageous for itself, or to prescribe and command its faith and ritual forms of worship (*ritus*); for all this must be left entirely to the teachers and rulers which the church has chosen for itself. The function of the state in this connection, only includes the *negative* right of regulating the influence of these public teachers upon the *visible* political commonwealth, that it may not be prejudicial to the public peace and tranquillity. Consequently the state has to take measures, on occasion of any internal conflict in the church, or on occasion of any collision of the several churches with each other, that civil concord is not endangered; and this right falls within the province of the police. It is *beneath the dignity* of the supreme power to interpose in determining what particular faith the church shall profess, or to decree that a certain faith shall be unalterably held, and that the church may not reform itself. For in doing so, the supreme power would be mixing itself up in a scholastic wrangle, on a footing of equality with its subjects; the monarch would be making himself a priest; and the churchmen might even reproach the supreme power with understanding nothing about matters of faith. Especially would this hold in respect of any prohibition of internal reform in the church; for what the people as a whole cannot determine upon for themselves cannot be determined for the people by the legislator. But no people can ever rationally determine that they will never advance farther in their insight into matters of faith, or resolve that they will never reform the institutions of the church; because this would be opposed to the humanity in their own persons and to their highest rights. And therefore the supreme power cannot of itself resolve and decree in these matters for the people. As regards the cost of maintaining the ecclesiastical establishment, for similar reasons this must be derived not from the public funds of the state, but from the section of the people who profess the particular faith of the church; and thus only ought it to fall as a burden on the community.

D. *The Right of Assigning Offices and Dignities in the State*

The right of the supreme authority in the state also includes:

1. The distribution of *offices,* as public and paid employments;

2. The conferring of *dignities,* as unpaid distinctions of rank, founded merely on honour, but establishing a gradation of higher and lower orders in the political scale; the latter, although free in themselves, being under obligation determined by the public law to obey the former so far as they are also entitled to command;

3. Besides these relatively beneficent rights, the supreme power in the state is also invested with the right of administering *punishment.*

As regards *civil offices,* the question arises as to whether the sovereign has the right, after bestowing an office on an individual, to take it again away at his mere pleasure, without any crime having been committed by the holder of the office. I say, *"No."* For what the united will of the people would never resolve, regarding their civil officers, cannot (constitutionally) be determined by the sovereign regarding them. The people have to bear the cost incurred by the appointment of an official, and undoubtedly it must be their will that any one in office should be completely competent for its duties. But such competency can only be acquired by a long preparation and training, and this process would necessarily occupy the time that would be required for acquiring the means of support by a different occupation. Arbitrary and frequent changes would therefore, as a rule, have the effect of filling offices with functionaries who have not acquired the skill required for their duties, and whose judgements had not attained maturity by practice. All this is contrary to the purpose of the state. And besides it is requisite in the interest of the people that it should be possible for every individual to rise from a lower office to the higher offices, as these latter would otherwise fall into incompetent hands, and that competent officials generally should have some guarantee of life-long provision.

Civil dignities include not only such as are connected with a public office, but also those which make the possessors of them, without any accompanying services to the state, members of a higher class or rank. The latter constitute the *nobility,* whose members are distinguished from the common citizens who form the mass of the people. The rank of the nobility is inherited by male descendants; and these again communicate it to wives who are not nobly born. Female descendants of noble families, however, do not communicate their rank to husbands who are not of noble birth, but they descend themselves into the common civil status of the people. This being so, the question then emerges as to whether the sovereign has the right to found a *hereditary* rank and class, intermediate between himself and the other citizens? The import of this question does not turn on whether it is conformable to the prudence of the sovereign, from regard to his own and the people's interests, to have such an institution; but whether it is in accordance with the right of the people that they should have a class of persons above them, who, while being subjects like themselves, are yet born as their commanders, or at least as privileged superiors? The answer to this question, as in previous instances, is to be derived from the principle that "what the people, as constituting the whole mass of the subjects, could not determine regarding themselves and their associated citizens, cannot be constitutionally determined by the sovereign regarding the people." Now a *hereditary* nobility is a rank which takes precedence of merit and is hoped for without any good reason—a thing of the imagination without genuine reality. For if an ancestor had merit, he could not transmit it to his posterity, but they must always acquire it for themselves. Nature has in fact not so arranged that the talent and will which give rise to merit in the state, are hereditary. And because it cannot be supposed of any individual that he will throw away his *freedom,* it is impossible that the common will of all the people should agree to such a groundless prerogative, and hence the sovereign cannot make it valid. It may happen, however, that such an anomaly as that of subjects who would be more than citizens, in the manner of born officials, or hereditary professors, has slipped into the mechanism of government in olden times, as in the case of the feudal system, which was almost entirely organized with reference to war. Under such circumstances, the state cannot deal otherwise with this error of a wrongly instituted rank in its midst, than by the remedy of a gradual extinction through hereditary positions being left unfilled as they fall vacant. The state has therefore the right provisorily to let a dignity in title continue, until the public opinion matures on the subject. And this will thus pass from the threefold division into sovereign, nobles, and people, to the twofold and only natural division into sovereign and people.

No individual in the state can indeed be entirely without dignity; for he has at least that of being a citizen, except when he has lost his civil status by a crime. As a criminal he is still maintained in life, but he is made the mere instrument of the will of another, whether it be the state or a particular citizen. In the latter position, in which he could only be placed by a juridical judgement, he would practically become a *slave,* and would belong as property (*dominium*) to another, who would be not merely his master (*herus*) but his owner (*dominus*). Such an owner would be entitled to exchange or alienate him as a thing, to use him at will except for shameful purposes, and to *dispose of his powers,* but not of his life and members. No one can bind himself to such a condition of dependence, as he would thereby cease to be a person, and it is only as a person that he can make a contract. It may, however, appear that one man may bind himself to another by a contract of hire, to discharge a certain service that is permissible in its kind, but is left entirely *undetermined* as regards its measure or amount; and that as receiving wages or board or protection in return, he thus becomes only a servant subject to the will of a master (*subditus*) and not a slave (*servus*). But this is an illusion. For if masters are entitled to use the powers of such subjects at will, they may exhaust these powers —as has been done in the case of Negroes in the Sugar Island—and they may thus reduce their servants to despair and death. But this would imply that they had actually given themselves away to their masters as property; which, in the case of persons, is impossible. A person can, therefore, only contract to perform work that is defined both in quality and quantity, either as a day-labourer or as a domiciled subject. In the latter case he may enter into a contract of lease for the use of the land of a superior, giving a definite rent or annual return for its utilization by himself, or he may contract for his service as a labourer upon the land. But he does not thereby make himself a slave, or a bondsman, or a serf attached to the soil (*glebae ad-*

scriptus), as he would thus divest himself of his personality; he can only enter into a temporary or at most a heritable lease. And even if by committing a crime he has *personally* become subjected to another, this subject-condition does not become *hereditary;* for he has only brought it upon himself by his own wrongdoing. Neither can one who has been begotten by a slave be claimed as property on the ground of the cost of his rearing, because such rearing is an absolute duty naturally incumbent upon parents; and in case the parents be slaves, it devolves upon their masters or owners, who, in undertaking the possession of such subjects, have also made themselves responsible for the performance of their duties.

E. *The Right of Punishing and of Pardoning*

1. *The Right of Punishing*

The right of administering punishment is the right of the sovereign as the supreme power to inflict pain upon a subject on account of a crime committed by him. The head of the state cannot therefore be punished; but his supremacy may be withdrawn from him. Any transgression of the public law which makes him who commits it incapable of being a citizen, constitutes a *crime,* either simply as a private crime (*crimen*), or also as a *public* crime (*crimen publicum*). Private crimes are dealt with by a civil court; public crimes by a criminal court. Embezzlement or speculation of money or goods entrusted in trade, fraud in purchase or sale, if done before the eyes of the party who suffers, are private crimes. On the other hand, coining false money or forging bills of exchange, theft, robbery, etc., are public crimes, because the commonwealth, and not merely some particular individual, is endangered thereby. Such crimes may be divided into those of a *base* character (*indolis abjectae*) and those of a *violent* character (*indolis violentiae*).

Judicial or juridical punishment (*poena forensis*) is to be distinguished from natural punishment (*poena naturalis*), in which crime as vice punishes itself, and does not as such come within the cognizance of the legislator. Juridical punishment can never be administered merely as a means for promoting another good either with regard to the criminal himself or to civil society, but must in all cases be imposed only because the individual on whom it is inflicted *has committed a crime.* For one man ought never to be dealt with merely as a means subservient to the purpose of another, nor be mixed up with the subjects of real right. Against such treatment his inborn personality has a right to protect him, even although he may be condemned to lose his civil personality. He must first be found guilty and *punishable,* before there can be any thought of drawing from his punishment any benefit for himself or his fellow-citizens. The penal law is a categorical imperative; and woe to him who creeps through the serpent-windings of utilitarianism to discover some advantage that may discharge him from the justice of punishment, or even from the due measure of it, according to the Pharisaic maxim: "It is better that *one* man should die than that the whole people should perish." For if justice and righteousness perish, human life would no longer have any value in the world. What, then, is to be said of such a proposal as to keep a criminal alive who has been condemned to death, on his being given to understand that, if he agreed to certain dangerous experiments being performed upon him, he would be allowed to survive if he came happily through them? It is argued that physicians might thus obtain new information that would be of value to the commonweal. But a court of justice would repudiate with scorn any proposal of this kind if made to it by the medical faculty; for justice would cease to be justice, if it were bartered away for any consideration whatever.

But what is the mode and measure of punishment which public justice takes as its principle and standard? It is just the principle of equality, by which the pointer of the scale of justice is made to incline no more to the one side than the other. It may be rendered by saying that the undeserved evil which any one commits on another is to be regarded as perpetrated on himself. Hence it may be said: "If you slander another, you slander yourself; if you steal from another, you steal from yourself; if you strike another, you strike yourself; if you kill another, you kill yourself." This is the right of retaliation (*jus talionis*); and, properly understood, it is the only principle which in regulating a public court, as distinguished from mere private judgement, can definitely assign both the quality and the quantity of a just penalty. All other standards are wavering and uncertain; and on account of other considerations involved in them, they contain no principle conformable to the sentence of pure and strict justice. It may appear, however, that difference of social status would not admit the application of the principle of retaliation, which is that of "like with like." But although the application may not in all cases be possible according to the letter, yet as regards the effect it may always be attained in practice, by due regard being given to the disposition and sentiment of the parties in the higher social sphere. Thus a pecuniary penalty on account of a verbal injury may have no direct proportion to the injustice of slander; for one who is wealthy may be able to indulge himself in this offence for his own gratification. Yet the attack committed on the honour of the party aggrieved may have its equivalent in the pain inflicted upon the pride of the aggressor, especially if he is condemned by the judgement of the court, not only to retract and apologize, but to submit to some meaner ordeal, as kissing the hand of the injured person. In like manner, if a man of the highest rank has violently assaulted an innocent citizen of the lower orders, he may be condemned not only to apologize but to undergo a solitary and painful imprisonment, whereby, in addition to the discomfort endured, the vanity of the offender would be painfully affected, and the very shame of his position would constitute an adequate retaliation after the principle of "like with like." But how then would we render the statement: "If you *steal* from another, you steal from yourself?" In this way, that whoever steals anything makes the property of all insecure; he therefore robs himself of all security in property, according to the right of retaliation. Such a one has nothing, and can acquire nothing, but he has the will to live; and this is only possible by others supporting him. But as the state should not do this gratuitously, he must for this purpose yield his powers to the state to be used in penal labour; and thus he falls for a time, or it may be for life, into a condition of slavery. But whoever has committed murder, must *die*. There is, in this case, no juridical substitute or surrogate, that can be given or taken for the satisfaction of justice. There is no *likeness* or proportion between life, however painful, and death; and therefore there is no equality between the crime of murder and the retaliation of it but what is judicially accomplished by the execution of the criminal. His death, however, must be kept free from all maltreatment that would make the humanity suffering in his person loathsome or abominable. Even if a civil society resolved to dissolve itself with the consent of all its members—as might be supposed in the case of a people inhabiting an island resolving to separate and scatter themselves throughout the whole world—the last murderer lying in the prison ought to be executed before the resolution was carried out. This ought to be done in order that every one may realize the desert of his deeds, and that bloodguiltiness may not remain upon the people; for otherwise they might all be regarded as participators in the murder as a public violation of justice.

The equalization of punishment with crime is therefore only possible by the cognition of the judge extending even to the penalty of death, according to the right of retaliation. This is manifest from the fact that it is only thus that a sentence can be pronounced over all criminals proportionate to their internal *wickedness;* as may be seen by considering the case when the punishment of death has to be inflicted, not on account of a murder, but on account of a political crime that can only be punished capitally. A hypothetical case, founded on history, will illustrate this. In the last Scottish rebellion there were various participators in it—such as Balmerino and others—who believed that in taking part in the rebellion they were only discharging their duty to the house of Stuart; but there were also others who were animated only by private motives and interests. Now, suppose that the judgement of the supreme court regarding them had been this: that every one should have liberty to choose between the punishment of death or penal servitude for life. In view of such an alternative, I say that the man of honour would choose death, and the knave would choose servitude. This would be the effect of their human nature as it is; for the honourable man values his honour more highly than even life itself, whereas a knave regards a life, although covered with shame, as better in his eyes than not to be.[1] The former is, without gainsaying, less guilty than the other; and they can only be proportionately punished by death being inflicted equally upon them both; yet to the one it is a mild punishment when his nobler temperament is taken into account, whereas it is a hard punishment to the other in view of his baser temperament. But, on the other hand, were they all equally condemned to penal servitude for life, the honourable man would be too severely punished, while the other, on account of his baseness of nature, would be too mildly punished. In the judgement to be pronounced over a number of criminals united in such a conspiracy, the best equalizer of punishment and crime in the form of public justice is death. And besides all this, it has never been heard of that a criminal condemned to death on account

[1] *Animam praeferre pudori,* Juvenal. [*Satirae,* viii. 83. "To prefer life to reputation."]

of a murder has complained that the sentence inflicted on him more than was right and just; and any one would treat him with scorn if he expressed himself to this effect against it. Otherwise it would be necessary to admit that, although wrong and injustice are not done to the criminal by the law, yet the legislative power is not entitled to administer this mode of punishment; and if it did so, it would be in contradiction with itself.

However many they may be who have committed a murder, or have even commanded it, or acted as art and part in it, they ought all to suffer death; for so justice wills it, in accordance with the idea of the juridical power, as founded on the universal laws of reason. But the number of the accomplices (*correi*) in such a deed might happen to be so great that the state, in resolving to be without such criminals, would be in danger of soon also being deprived of subjects. But it will not thus dissolve itself, neither must it return to the much worse condition of nature, in which there would be no external justice. Nor, above all, should it deaden the sensibilities of the people by the spectacle of justice being exhibited in the mere carnage of a slaughtering bench. In such circumstances the sovereign must always be allowed to have it in his power to take the part of the judge upon himself as a case of necessity—and to deliver a judgement which, instead of the penalty of death, shall assign some other punishment to the criminals and thereby preserve a multitude of the people. The penalty of deportation is relevant in this connection. Such a form of judgement cannot be carried out according to a public law, but only by an authoritative act of the royal prerogative, and it may only be applied as an act of grace in individual cases.

Against these doctrines, the Marquis Beccaria has given forth a different view. Moved by the compassionate sentimentality of a humane feeling, he has asserted that all capital punishment is wrong in itself and unjust. He has put forward this view on the ground that the penalty of death could not be contained in the original civil contract; for, in that case, every one of the people would have had to consent to lose his life if he murdered any of his fellow-citizens. But, it is argued, such a consent is impossible, because no one can thus dispose of his own life. All this is mere sophistry and perversion of right. No one undergoes punishment because he has willed to be punished, but because he has willed *a punishable action;* for it is in fact no punishment when any one experiences what he wills, and it is impossible for any one to *will* to be punished. To say, "I will to be punished, if I murder any one," can mean nothing more than, "I submit myself along with all the other citizens to the laws"; and if there are any criminals among the people, these laws will include penal laws. The individual who, as a co-legislator, enacts *penal law* cannot possibly be the same person who, as a subject, is punished according to the law; for, *qua* criminal, he cannot possibly be regarded as having a voice in the legislation, the legislator being rationally viewed as just and holy. If any one, then, enact a penal law against himself as a criminal, it must be the pure juridically law-giving reason (*homo noumenon*), which subjects him as one capable of crime, and consequently as another person (*homo phenomenon*), along with all the others in the civil union, to this penal law. In other words, it is not the people taken distributively, but the tribunal of public justice, as distinct from the criminal, that prescribes capital punishment; and it is not to be viewed as if the social contract contained the promise of all the individuals to allow themselves to be punished, thus disposing of themselves and their lives. For if the right to punish must be grounded upon a promise of the wrongdoer, whereby he is to be regarded as being willing to be punished, it ought also to be left to him to find himself deserving of the punishment; and the criminal would thus be his own judge. The chief error (πρῶτον ψεῦδος) of this sophistry consists in regarding the judgement of the criminal himself, necessarily determined by his reason, that he is under obligation to undergo the loss of his life, as a judgement that must be grounded on a resolution of his *will* to take it away himself; and thus the execution of the right in question is represented as united in one and the same person with the adjudication of the right.

There are, however, two crimes worthy of death, in respect of which it still remains doubtful whether the legislature have the right to deal with them capitally. It is the sentiment of honour that induces their perpetration. The one originates in a regard for *womanly* honour, the other in a regard for *military* honour; and in both cases there is a genuine feeling of honour incumbent on the individuals as a duty. The former is the crime of maternal infanticide (*infanticidium maternale*); the latter is the crime of killing a fellow-soldier in a duel (*commilitonicidium*). Now legislation cannot take away the shame of an illegitimate birth, nor wipe off the stain attaching from a suspicion of cowardice, to an officer who does not resist an act that would bring him into contempt, by an effort of his own that is superior to the fear of death. Hence it appears that, in such circumstances, the individuals concerned are remitted to the state of nature; and their acts in both cases must be called *homicide,* and not *murder,* which involves evil intent (*homicidium dolosum*). In all instances the acts are undoubtedly punishable; but they cannot be punished by the supreme power with death. An illegitimate child comes into the world outside of the law which properly regulates marriage, and it is thus born beyond the pale or constitutional protection of the law. Such a child is introduced, as it were, like prohibited goods, into the commonwealth, and as it has no legal right to existence in this way, its destruction might also be ignored; nor can the shame of the mother, when her unmarried confinement is known, be removed by any legal ordinance. A subordinate officer, again, on whom an insult is inflicted, sees himself compelled by the public opinion of his associates to obtain satisfaction; and, as in the state of nature, the punishment of the offender can only be effected by a duel, in which his own life is exposed to danger, and not by means of the law in a court of justice. The duel is therefore adopted as the means of demonstrating his courage as that characteristic upon which the honour of his profession essentially rests; and this is done even if it should issue in the killing of his adversary. But as such a result takes place publicly and under the consent of both parties, although it may be done unwillingly, it cannot properly be called murder (*homicidium dolosum*). What then is the right in both cases as relating to criminal justice? Penal justice is here in fact brought into great straits, having apparently either to declare the notion of honour, which is certainly no mere fancy here, to be nothing in the eye of the law, or to exempt the crime from its due punishment; and thus it would become either remiss or cruel. The knot thus tied is to be resolved in the following way. The categorical imperative of penal justice, that the killing of any person contrary to the law must be punished with death, remains in force; but the legislation itself and the civil constitution generally, so long as they are still barbarous and incomplete, are at fault. And this is the reason why the subjective motive-principles of honour among the people do not coincide with the standards which are objectively conformable to another purpose; so that the public justice issuing from the state becomes injustice relatively to that which is upheld among the people themselves.

II. The Right of Pardoning

The right of pardoning (*jus aggratiandi*), viewed in relation to the criminal, is the right of mitigating or entirely remitting his punishment. On the side of the sovereign this is the most delicate of all rights, as it may be exercised so as to set forth the splendour of his dignity, and yet so as to do a great wrong by it. It ought not to be exercised in application to the crimes of the subjects against each other; for exemption from punishment (*impunitas criminis*) would be the greatest wrong that could be done to them. It is only an occasion of some form of treason (*crimen laesae majestatis*), as a lesion against himself, that the sovereign should make use of this right. And it should not be exercised even in this connection, if the safety of the people would be endangered by remitting such punishment. This right is the only one which properly deserves the name of a "right of majesty."

50. *Juridical Relations of the Citizen to his Country and to Other Countries. Emigration; Immigration; Banishment; Exile*

The land or territory whose inhabitants—in virtue of its political constitution and without the necessary intervention of a special juridical act—are, by birth, fellow-citizens of one and the same commonwealth, is called their *country* or *fatherland. A foreign* country is one in which they would not possess this condition, but would be living *abroad.* If a country abroad form part of the territory under the same government as at home, it constitutes a *province,* according to the Roman usage of the term. It does not constitute an incorporated portion of the empire (*imperii*) so as to be the *abode* of equal fellow-citizens, but is only a *possession* of the government, like a *lower house*; and it must therefore honour the domain of the ruling state as the "mother country" (*regio domina*).

1. A subject, even regarded as a citizen, has the right of *emigration;* for the state cannot retain him as if he were its property. But he may only carry away with him his moveables as distinguished from his fixed possessions. However, he is entitled to sell his immovable property, and take the value of it in money with him.

2. The supreme power, as master of the country, has the right to favour *immigration* and the settlement of strangers and colonists. This will hold even although the natives of the country

may be unfavourably disposed to it, if their private property in the soil is not diminished or interfered with.

3. In the case of a subject who has committed a crime that renders all society of his fellow-citizens with him prejudicial to the state, the supreme power has also the right of inflicting *banishment* to a country abroad. By such deportation, he does not acquire any share in the rights of citizens of the territory to which he is banished.

4. The supreme power has also the right of imposing *exile* generally (*jus exilii*), by which a citizen is sent abroad into the wide world as the "out-land." And because the supreme authority thus withdraws all legal protection from the citizen, this amounts to making him an "outlaw" within the territory of his own country.

51. *The Three Forms of the State. Autocracy; Aristocracy; Democracy*

The three powers in the state, involved in the conception of a public government generally (*res publica latius dicta*), are only so many relations of the united will of the people which emanates from the *a priori* reason; and viewed as such it is the objective practical realization of the pure idea of a supreme head of the state. This supreme head is the sovereign; but conceived only as a representation of the whole people, the idea still requires physical embodiment in a person, who may exhibit the supreme power of the state and bring the idea actively to bear upon the popular will. The relation of the supreme power to the people is conceivable in three different forms: either *one* in the state rules over all; or *some*, united in relation of equality with each other, rule over all the others; or *all* together rule over each and all individually, including themselves. The form of the state is therefore either *autocratic*, or *aristocratic, or democratic*. The expression *monarchic* is not so suitable as *autocratic* for the conception here intended; for a monarch is one who has the *highest* power, an autocrat is one who has *all* power, so that this latter *is* the sovereign, whereas the former merely represents the sovereignty.

It is evident that an autocracy is the *simplest* form of government in the state, being constituted by the relation of one, as king, to the people, so that there is one only who is the lawgiver. An aristocracy, as a form of government, is, however, *compounded* of the union of two relations: that of the nobles in relation to one another as the lawgivers, thereby constituting the sovereignty, and that of this sovereign power to the people. A democracy, again, is the most *complex* of all the forms of the state, for it has to begin by uniting the will of all so as to form a people; and then it has to appoint a sovereign over this common union, which sovereign is no other than the united will itself. The consideration of the ways in which these forms are adulterated by the intrusion of violent and illegitimate usurpers of power, as in *oligarchy* and *ochlocracy*, as well as the discussion of the so-called *mixed* constitutions, may be passed over here as not essential, and as leading into too much detail.

As regards the *administration* of right in the state, it may be said that the simplest mode is also the best; but as regards its bearing on right itself, it is also the most dangerous for the people, in view of the despotism to which simplicity of administration so naturally gives rise. It is undoubtedly a rational maxim to aim at simplification in the machinery which is to unite the people under compulsory laws, and this would be secured were all the people to be passive and to obey only one person over them; but the method would not give subjects who were also citizens of the state. It is sometimes said that the people should be satisfied with the reflection that monarchy, regarded as an autocracy, is the best political constitution, *if the monarch is good*, that is, if he has the judgement as well as the will to do right. But this is a mere evasion and belongs to the common class of wise tautological phrases. It only amounts to saying that "the best constitution is that by which the supreme administrator of the state is made the best ruler"; that is, that the best constitution *is* the best!

52. *Historical Origin and Changes. A Pure Republic. Representative Government*

It is vain to inquire into the historical origin of the political mechanism; for it is no longer possible to discover historically the point of time at which civil society took its beginning. Savages do not draw up a documentary record of their having submitted themselves to law; and it may be inferred from the nature of uncivilized men that they must have set out from a state of violence. To prosecute such an inquiry in the intention of finding a pretext for altering the existing constitution by violence is no less than penal. For such a mode of alteration would amount to revolution, that could only be carried out by an insurrection of the people, and not by constitutional modes of legislation. But insurrection against an already existing constitution, is an overthrow of all civil and juridical relations, and of right generally; and hence it is not a mere alteration of the civil constitution, but a dissolution of it. It would thus form a mode of transition to a better constitution by palingenesis and not by mere metamorphosis; and it would require a new social contract, upon which the former original contract, as then annulled, would have no influence.

It must, however, be possible for the sovereign to change the existing constitution, if it is not actually consistent with the idea of the original contract. In doing so it is essential to give existence to that form of government which will properly constitute the people into a state. Such a change cannot be made by the state deliberately altering its constitution from one of the three forms to one of the other two. For example, political changes should not be carried out by the aristocrats combining to subject themselves to an autocracy, or resolving to fuse all into a democracy, or conversely; as if it depended on the arbitrary choice and liking of the sovereign what constitution he may impose on the people. For, even if as sovereign he resolved to alter the constitution into a democracy, he might be doing wrong to the people, because they might hold such a constitution in abhorrence, and regard either of the other two as more suitable to them in the circumstances.

The forms of the state are only the *letter* (*littera*) of the original constitution in the civil union; and they may therefore remain so long as they are considered, from ancient and long habit (and therefore only subjectively), to be necessary to the machinery of the political constitution. But the *spirit* of that original contract (*anima pacti originarii*) contains and imposes the obligation on the constituting power to make the mode of the *government* conformable to its idea; and, if this cannot be effected at once, to change it gradually and continuously till it harmonize *in its working* with the only rightful constitution, which is that of a *pure republic*. Thus the old empirical and statutory forms, which serve only to effect the political *subjection* of the people, will be resolved into the original and rational forms which alone take freedom as their principle, and even as the condition of all compulsion and constraint. Compulsion is in fact requisite for the realization of a juridical constitution, according to the proper idea of the state; and it will lead at last to the realization of that idea, even according to the letter. This is the only enduring political constitution, as in it the law is itself sovereign, and is no longer attached to a particular person. This is the ultimate end of all public right, and the state in which every citizen can have what is his own *peremptorily* assigned to him. But so long as the form of the state has to be represented, according to the letter, by many different moral persons invested with the supreme power, there can only be a *provisory* internal right, and not an absolutely juridical state of civil society.

Every true republic is and can only be constituted by a *representative system* of the people. Such a representative system is instituted in name of the people, and is constituted by all the citizens being united together, in order, by means of their deputies, to protect and secure their rights. But as soon as a supreme head of the state in person—be it as king, or nobility, or the whole body of the people in a democratic union—becomes also representative, the united people then does not merely *represent* the sovereignty, but they *are* themselves sovereign. It is in the people that the supreme power originally resides, and it is accordingly from this power that all the rights of individual citizens as mere subjects, and especially as officials of the state, must be derived. When the sovereignty of the people themselves is thus realized, the republic is established; and it is no longer necessary to give up the reins of government into the hands of those by whom they have been hitherto held, especially as they might again destroy all the new institutions by their arbitrary and absolute will.

It was therefore a great error in judgement on the part of a powerful ruler in our time, when he tried to extricate himself from the embarrassment arising from great public debts, by transferring this burden to the people, and leaving them to undertake and distribute them among themselves as they might best think fit. It thus became natural that the legislative power, not only in respect of the taxation of the subjects, but in respect of the government, should come into the hands of the people. It was requisite that they should be able to prevent the incurring of new debts by extravagance or war; and in consequence, the supreme power of the monarch entirely disappeared, not by being merely suspended, but by passing over in fact to the people, to whose legislative will the property of every subject thus became subjected. Nor can it be said that a tacit and yet obligatory promise must be assumed as having, under such circumstances, been given by the national assembly, not to constitute themselves into a sovereignty, but only to administer the affairs of the sovereign for the time, and after this was done to deliver the reins of the government again into the monarch's hands. Such a supposed contract would be null and void. The right of the supreme legislation in the commonwealth is not an alienable right, but is the most personal of all rights. Whoever possesses it can only dispose by the collective will of the people, in respect of the people; he cannot dispose in respect of the collective will itself, which is the ultimate foundation of all public contracts. A contract, by which the people would be bound to give back their authority again, would not be consistent with their position as a legislative power, and yet it would be made binding upon the people; which, on the principle that "No one can serve two masters," is a contradiction.

II. The Right of Nations and International Law. (Jus Gentium)

53. *Nature and Division of the Right of Nations*

The individuals, who make up a people, may be regarded as natives of the country sprung by natural descent from a common ancestry (*congeniti*), although this may not hold entirely true in detail. Again, they may be viewed according to the intellectual and juridical relation, as born of a common political mother, the republic, so that they constitute, as it were, a public family or nation (*gens, natio*) whose members are all related to each other as citizens of the state. As members of a state, they do not mix with those who live beside them in the state of nature, considering such to be ignoble. Yet these savages, on account of the lawless freedom they have chosen, regard themselves as superior to civilized peoples; and they constitute tribes and even races, but not states. The public right of *states* (*jus publicum civitatum*), in their relations to one another, is what we have to consider under the designation of the "right of nations." Wherever a state, viewed as a moral person, acts in relation to another existing in the condition of natural freedom, and consequently in a state of continual war, such right takes it rise.

The right of nations in relation to the state of war may be divided into: 1. the right of *going to* war; 2. right *during* war; and 3. right *after* war, the object of which is to constrain the nations mutually to pass from this state of war and to found a common constitution establishing perpetual peace. The difference between the right of individual men or families as related to each other in the state of nature, and the right of the nations among themselves, consists in this, that in the right of nations we have to consider not merely a relation of one state to another as a whole, but also the relation of the individual persons in one state to the individuals of another state, as well as to that state as a whole. This difference, however, between the right of nations and the right of individuals in the mere state of nature, requires to be determined by elements which can easily be deduced from the conception of the latter.

54. *Elements of the Right of Nations*

The elements of the right of nations are as follows:

1. States, viewed as nations, in their external relations to one another—like lawless savages—are naturally in a non-juridical condition;
2. This natural condition is a state of war in which the right of the stronger prevails; and although it may not in fact be always found as a state of actual war and incessant hostility, and although no real wrong is done to any one therein, yet the condition is wrong in itself in the highest degree, and the nations which form states contiguous to each other are bound mutually to pass out of it;
3. An alliance of nations, in accordance with the idea of an original social contract, is necessary to protect each other against external aggression and attack, but not involving interference with their several internal difficulties and disputes;
4. This mutual connection by alliance must dispense with a distinct sovereign power, such as is set up in the civil constitution; it can only take the form of a federation, which as such may be revoked on any occasion, and must consequently be renewed from time to time.

This is therefore a right which comes in as an accessory (*in subsidium*) of another original right, in order to prevent the nations from falling from right and lapsing into the state of actual war with each other. It thus issues in the idea of a *foedus amphictyonum.*

55. *Right of Going to War as related to the Subjects of the State*

We have then to consider, in the first place, the original right of free states *to go to war* with each other as being still in a state of nature, but as exercising this right in order to establish some condition of society approaching the juridical state. And, first of all, the question arises as to what right the state has in *relation to its own subjects,* to use them in order to make war against other states, to employ their property and even their lives for this purpose, or at least to expose them to hazard and danger; and all this in such a way that it does not depend upon their own personal judgement whether they will march into the field of war or not, but the supreme command of the sovereign claims to settle and dispose of them thus.

This right appears capable of being easily established. It may be grounded upon the right which every one has to do with what is his own as he will. Whatever one has *made* substantially for himself, he holds as his incontestable property. The following, then, is such a deduction as a mere jurist would put forward.

There are various *natural products* in a country which, as regards the *number* and *quantity* in which they exist, must be considered as specially *produced* (*artefacta*) by the work of the state; for the country would not yield them to such extent were it not under the constitution of the state and its regular administrative government, or if the inhabitants were still living in the state of nature. Sheep, cattle, domestic fowl—the most useful of their kind—swine, and such like, would either be used up as necessary food or destroyed by beasts of prey in the district in which I live, so that they would entirely disappear, or be found in very scant supplies, were it not for the government securing to the inhabitants their acquisitions and property. This holds likewise of the population itself, as we see in the case of the American deserts; and even were the greatest industry applied in those regions—which is not yet done—there might be but a scanty population. The inhabitants of any country would be but sparsely sown here and there were it not for the protection of government; because without it they could not spread themselves with their households upon a territory which was always in danger of being devastated by enemies or by wild beasts of prey; and further, so great a multitude of men as now live in any one country could not otherwise obtain sufficient means of support. Hence, as it can be said of vegetable growths, such as potatoes, as well as of domesticated animals, that because the abundance in which they are found is a *product* of human labour, they may be used, destroyed, and consumed by man; so it seems that it may be said of the sovereign, as the supreme power in the state, that he has the right to lead his subjects, as being for the most part productions of his own, to war, as if it were to the chase, and even to march them to the field of battle, as if it were on a pleasure excursion.

This principle of right may be supposed to float dimly before the mind of the monarch, and it certainly holds true at least of the lower animals which may become the property of man. But such a principle will not at all apply to men, especially when viewed as citizens who must be regarded as members of the state, with a share in the legislation, and not merely as means for others but as ends in themselves. As such they must give their free consent, through their representatives, not only to the carrying on of war generally, but to every separate declaration of war; and it is only under this limiting condition that the state has a right to demand their services in undertakings so full of danger.

We would therefore deduce this right rather from the duty of the sovereign to the people than conversely. Under this relation, the people must be regarded as having given their sanction; and, having the right of voting, they may be considered, although thus passive in reference to themselves individually, to be active in so far as they represent the sovereignty itself.

56. *Right of Going to War in relation to Hostile States*

Viewed as in the state of nature, the right of nations *to go to war* and to carry on hostilities is the legitimate way by which they prosecute their rights by their own power when they regard themselves as injured; and this is done because in that state the method of a juridical *process,* although the only one proper to settle such disputes, cannot be adopted.

The *threatening of war* is to be distinguished from the active injury of a first aggression, which again is distinguished from the general outbreak of hostilities. A threat or menace may be given by the active preparation of *armaments,* upon which a right of prevention (*jus praeventionis*) is founded on the other side, or merely by the *formidable increase* of the power of another state (*potestas tremenda*) by acquisition of territory. Lesion of a less powerful country may be involved merely in the condition of a more powerful neighbour *prior* to any action at all; and in the state of nature an attack under such circumstances would be warrantable. This international relation is the foundation of the right of equilibrium, or of the "balance of power," among all the states that are in active contiguity to each other.

The *right to go to war* is constituted by any

overt *act* of injury. This includes any arbitrary retaliation or act of *reprisal* (*retorsio*) as a satisfaction taken by one people for an offence committed by another, without any attempt being made to obtain reparation in a peaceful way. Such an act of retaliation would be similar in kind to an outbreak of hostilities without a previous declaration of war. For if there is to be any right at all during the state of war, something analogous to a contract must be assumed, involving *acceptance* on the side of the declaration on the other, and amounting to the fact that they both will to seek their right in this way.

57. *Right during War*

The determination of what constitutes right *in* war, is the most difficult problem of the right of nations and international law. It is very difficult even to form a conception of such a right, or to think of any law in this lawless state without falling into a contradiction. *Inter arma silent leges.*[1] It must then be just the right to carry on war according to such principles as render it always still possible to pass out of that natural condition of the states in their external relations to each other, and to enter into a condition of right.

No war of independent states against each other can rightly be a war of punishment (*bellum punitivum*). For punishment is only in place under the relation of a superior (*imperantis*) to a subject (*subditum*); and this is not the relation of the states to one another. Neither can an international war be "a war of extermination" (*bellum internicinum*), nor even "a war of subjugation" (*bellum subjugatorium*); for this would issue in the moral extinction of a state by its people being either fused into one mass with the conquering state, or being reduced to slavery. Not that this necessary means of attaining to a condition of peace is itself contradictory to the right of a state; but because the idea of the right of nations includes merely the conception of an antagonism that is in accordance with principles of external freedom, in order that the state may maintain what is properly its own, but not that it may acquire a condition which, from the aggrandizement of its power, might become threatening to other states.

Defensive measures and means of all kinds are allowable to a state that is forced to war, except such as by their use would make the subjects using them unfit to be citizens; for the state would thus make itself unfit to be regarded as a person capable of participating in equal rights in the international relations according to the right of nations. Among these forbidden means are to be reckoned the appointment of subjects to act as spies, or engaging subjects or even strangers to act as assassins, or poisoners (in which class might well be included the so-called sharpshooters who lurk in ambush for individuals), or even employing agents to spread false news. In a word, it is forbidden to use any such malignant and perfidious means as would destroy the confidence which would be requisite to establish a lasting peace thereafter.

It is permissible in war to impose exactions and contributions upon a conquered enemy; but it is not legitimate to plunder the people in the way of forcibly depriving individuals of their property. For this would be robbery, seeing it was not the conquered people but the state under whose government they were placed that carried on the war by means of them. All exactions should be raised by regular *requisition*, and receipts ought to be given for them, in order that when peace is restored the burden imposed on the country or the province may be proportionately borne.

58. *Right after War*

The right that follows *after* war, begins at the moment of the treaty of peace and refers to the consequences of the war. The conqueror lays down the conditions under which he will agree with the conquered power to form the conclusion of peace. Treaties are drawn up; not indeed according to any right that it pertains to him to protect, on account of an alleged lesion by his opponent, but as taking this question upon himself, he bases the right to decide it upon his own power. Hence the conqueror may not demand restitution of the cost of the war; because he would then have to declare the war of his opponent to be unjust. And even although he should adopt such an argument, he is not entitled to apply it; because he would have to declare the war to be punitive, and he would thus in turn inflict an injury. To this right belongs also the exchange of prisoners, which is to be carried out without ransom and without regard to equality of numbers.

Neither the conquered state nor its subjects lose their political liberty by conquest of the country, so as that the former should be degraded to a colony, or the latter to slaves; for otherwise it would have been a penal war, which is contradictory in itself. A *colony* or a prov-

[1] ["In the midst of arms the laws are silent." Cicero.]

ince is constituted by a people which has its own constitution, legislation, and territory, where persons belonging to another state are merely strangers, but which is nevertheless subject to the supreme *executive* power of another state. This other state is called the *mother-country*. It is ruled as a daughter, but has at the same time its own form of government, as in a separate parliament under the presidency of a viceroy (*civitas hybrida*). Such was Athens in relation to different islands; and such is at present (1796) the relation of Great Britain to Ireland.

Still less can *slavery* be deduced as a rightful institution, from the conquest of a people in war; for this would assume that the war was of a punitive nature. And least of all can a basis be found in war for a *hereditary* slavery, which is absurd in itself, since guilt cannot be inherited from the criminality of another.

Further, that an *amnesty* is involved in the conclusion of a treaty of peace is already implied in the very idea of a peace.

59. *The Rights of Peace*

The rights of peace are:

1. The right to be in peace when war is in the neighbourhood, or the right of *neutrality*.
2. The right to have peace secured so that it may continue when it has been concluded, that is, the right of *guarantee*.
3. The right of the several states to enter into a mutual *alliance*, so as to *defend* themselves in common against all external or even internal attacks. This right of federation, however, does not extend to the formation of any league for external aggression or internal aggrandizement.

60. *Right as against an Unjust Enemy*

The right of a state against an *unjust* enemy has no limits, at least in respect of quality as distinguished from quantity or degree. In other words, the injured state may use—not, indeed *any* means, but yet—all those means that are permissible and in reasonable measure in so far as they are in its power, in order to assert its right to what is its own. But what then is an *unjust* enemy according to the conceptions of the right of nations, when, as holds generally of the state of nature, every state is judge in its own cause? It is one whose publicly expressed will, whether in word or deed, betrays a maxim which, if it were taken as a universal rule, would make a state of peace among the nations impossible, and would necessarily perpetuate the state of nature. Such is the violation of public treaties, with regard to which it may be assumed that any such violation concerns all nations by threatening their freedom, and that they are thus summoned to unite against such a wrong and to take away the power of committing it. But this does not include the right *to partition and appropriate the country*, so as to make a state as it were disappear from the earth; for this would be an injustice to the people of that state, who cannot lose their original right to unite into a commonwealth, and to adopt such a new constitution as by its nature would be unfavourable to the inclination for war.

Further, it may be said that the expression "an unjust enemy in the state of nature" is *pleonastic;* for the state of nature is itself a state of injustice. A just enemy would be one to whom I would do wrong in offering resistance; but such a one would really not be my enemy.

61. *Perpetual Peace and a Permanent Congress of Nations*

The natural state of nations as well as of individual men is a state which it is a duty to pass out of, in order to enter into a legal state. Hence, before this transition occurs, all the right of nations and all the external property of states acquirable or maintainable by war are merely *provisory;* and they can only become *peremptory* in a universal union of states analogous to that by which a nation becomes a state. It is thus only that a real *state of peace* could be established. But with the too great extension of such a union of states over vast regions, any government of it, and consequently the protection of its individual members, must at last become impossible; and thus a multitude of such corporations would again bring round a state of war. Hence the *perpetual peace*, which is the ultimate end of all the right of nations, becomes in fact an impracticable idea. The political principles, however, which aim at such an end, and which enjoin the formation of such unions among the states as may promote a continuous *approximation* to a perpetual peace, are not impracticable; they are as practicable as this approximation itself, which is a practical problem involving a duty, and founded upon the right of individual men and states.

Such a *union of states*, in order to maintain peace, may be called a *permanent congress of nations;* and it is free to every neighbouring state to join in it. A union of this kind, so far at least as regards the formalities of the right of nations in respect of the preservation of peace, was presented in the first half of this century, in the Assembly of the States-General at the Hague. In this Assembly most of the European courts, and even the smallest republics, brought forward their complaints about the hostilities which were carried on by the one against the other. Thus the whole of Europe appeared like a single federated state, accepted as umpire by the several nations in their public differences. But in place of this agreement, the right of nations afterwards survived only in books; it disappeared from the cabinets, or, after force had been already used, it was relegated in the form of theoretical deductions to the obscurity of archives.

By such a *congress* is here meant only a voluntary combination of different states that would be *dissoluble* at any time, and not such a union as is embodied in the United States of America, founded upon a political constitution, and therefore indissoluble. It is only by a congress of this kind that the idea of a public right of nations can be established, and that the settlement of their differences by the mode of a civil process, and not by the barbarous means of war, can be realized.

III. The Universal Right of Mankind. (Jus Cosmopoliticum)

62. *Nature and Conditions of Cosmopolitical Right*

The rational idea of a universal, *peaceful,* if not yet friendly, union of all the nations upon the earth that may come into active relations with each other, is a *juridical* principle, as distinguished from philanthropic or ethical principles. Nature has enclosed them altogether within definite boundaries, in virtue of the spherical form of their abode as a *globus terraqueus*; and the possession of the soil upon which an inhabitant of the earth may live can only be regarded as possession of a part of a limited whole and, consequently, as a part to which every one has originally a right. Hence all nations *originally* hold a community of the soil, but not a *juridical* community of possession (*communio*), nor consequently of the use or proprietorship of the soil, but only of a possible physical *intercourse* (*commercium*) by means of it. In other words, they are placed in such thoroughgoing relations of each to all the rest that they may claim to enter into *intercourse* with one another, and they have a right to make an attempt in this direction, while a foreign nation would not be entitled to treat them on this account as enemies. This right, in so far as it relates to a possible union of all nations, in respect of certain laws universally regulating their intercourse with each other, may be called "cosmopolitical right" (*jus cosmopoliticum*).

It may appear that seas put nations out of all communion with each other. But this is not so; for by means of commerce, seas form the happiest natural provision for their intercourse. And the more there are of neighbouring coastlands, as in the case of the Mediterranean Sea, this intercourse becomes the more animated. And hence communications with such lands, especially where there are settlements upon them connected with the mother countries giving occasion for such communications, bring it about that evil and violence committed in one place of our globe are felt in all. Such possible abuse cannot, however, annul the right of man as a citizen of the world to *attempt* to enter into communion with all others, and for this purpose to *visit* all the regions of the earth, although this does not constitute a right of *settlement* upon the territory of another people (*jus incolatus*), for which a special contract is required.

But the question is raised as to whether, in the case of newly discovered countries, a people may claim the right to settle (*accolatus*), and to occupy possessions in the neighbourhood of another people that has already settled in that region; and to do this without their consent.

Such a right is indubitable, if the new settlement takes place at such a distance from the seat of the former that neither would restrict or injure the other in the use of their territory. But in the case of nomadic peoples, or tribes of shepherds and hunters (such as the Hottentots, the Tungusi, and most of the American Indians), whose support is derived from wide desert tracts, such occupation should never take place by force, but only by contract; and any such contract ought never to take advantage of the ignorance of the original dwellers in regard to the cession of their lands. Yet it is commonly alleged that such acts of violent appropriation may be justified as subserving the general good of the world. It appears as if sufficiently justifying grounds were furnished for them, partly by reference to the civilization of barbarous peoples (as by a pretext of this kind even Busching tries to excuse the bloody introduction of the Christian religion into Germany), and partly by founding upon the necessity of purging one's own country from depraved criminals, and the hope of their improvement or that of their posterity, in another continent like New Holland. But all these alleged good purposes cannot wash out the stain of injustice in the means employed to attain them. It may be objected that, had such scrupulousness about making a beginning in founding a legal state with force been always maintained, the whole earth would still have been in a state of lawlessness. But such an objection would as little annul the conditions of right in question as the pretext of the political revolutionaries that, when a constitution has become degenerate, it belongs to the people to transform it by force. This would amount generally to being unjust once and for all, in order thereafter to found justice the more surely, and to make it flourish.

Conclusion

If one cannot prove that a thing *is*, he may try to prove that it is *not*. And if he succeeds in doing neither (as often occurs), he may still ask whether it is in his *interest* to *accept* one or other of the alternatives hypothetically, from the theoretical or the practical point of view. In other words, a hypothesis may be accepted either in order to explain a certain phenomenon (as in astronomy to account for the retrogression and stationariness of the planets), or in order to attain a certain end, which again may be either *pragmatic,* as belonging merely to the sphere of art, or *moral,* as involving a purpose which it is a duty to adopt as a maxim of action. Now it is evident that the assumption (*suppositio*) of the practicability of such an end, though presented merely as a theoretical and problematical judgement, may be regarded as constituting a duty; and hence it is so regarded in this case. For although there may be no positive obligation to believe in such an end, yet even if there were not the least theoretical probability of action being carried out in accordance with it, so long as its impossibility cannot be demonstrated, there still remains a duty incumbent upon us with regard to it.

Now, as a matter of fact, the morally practical reason utters within us its irrevocable veto: *There shall be no war.* So there ought to be no war, neither between me and you in the condition of nature, nor between us as members of states which, although internally in a condition of law, are still externally in their relation to each other in a condition of lawlessness; for this is not the way by which any one should prosecute his right. Hence the question no longer is as to whether perpetual peace is a real thing or not a real thing, or as to whether we may not be deceiving ourselves when we adopt the former alternative, but we must *act* on the supposition of its being real. We must work for what may perhaps not be realized, and establish that constitution which yet seems best adapted to bring it about (mayhap republicanism in all states, together and separately). And thus we may put an end to the evil of wars, which have been the chief interest of the internal arrangements of all the states without exception. And although the realization of this purpose may always remain but a pious wish, yet we do certainly not deceive ourselves in adopting the maxim of action that will guide us in working incessantly for it; for it is a duty to do this. To suppose that the moral law within us is itself deceptive, would be sufficient to excite the horrible wish rather to be deprived of all reason than to live under such deception, and even to see oneself, according to such principles, degraded like the lower animals to the level of the mechanical play of nature.

It may be said that the universal and lasting establishment of peace constitutes not merely a part, but the whole final purpose and end of the science of right as viewed within the limits of reason. The state of peace is the only condition of the mine and thine that is secured and guaranteed by *laws* in the relationship of men living in numbers contiguous to each other, and who are thus combined in a constitution whose rule is derived not from the mere experience of those who have found it the best as a normal guide for others, but which must be taken by the reason *a priori* from the ideal of a juridical union of men under public laws generally. For all particular examples or instances, being able only to furnish illustration but not proof, are deceptive, and at all events require a metaphysic to establish them by its necessary principles. And this is conceded indirectly even by those who turn metaphysics into ridicule, when they say, as they often do: "The best constitution is that in which not men but laws exercise the power." For what can be more metaphysically sublime in its own way than this very idea of theirs, which according to their own assertion has, notwithstanding, the most objective reality? This may be easily shown by reference to actual instances. And it is this very idea which alone can be carried out practically, if it is not forced on in a revolutionary and sudden way by violent overthrow of the existing defective constitution; for this would produce for the time the momentary annihilation of the whole juridical state of society. But if the idea is carried forward by gradual reform and in accordance with fixed principles, it may lead by a continuous approximation to the highest political good, and to perpetual peace.

CONTENTS

THE CRITIQUE OF JUDGEMENT

PREFACE TO THE FIRST EDITION 1790

THE faculty of knowledge from *a priori* principles may be called *pure reason,* and the general investigation into its possibility and bounds the *Critique of Pure Reason.* This is permissible although "pure reason," as was the case with the same use of terms in our first work, is only intended to denote reason in its theoretical employment, and although there is no desire to bring under review its faculty as practical reason and its special principles as such. That *Critique* is, then, an investigation addressed simply to our faculty of knowing things *a priori.* Hence it makes our *cognitive faculties* its sole concern, to the exclusion of the feeling of pleasure or displeasure and the faculty of desire; and among the cognitive faculties it confines its attention to *understanding* and its *a priori* principles, to the exclusion of *judgement* and *reason,* (faculties that also belong to theoretical cognition,) because it turns out in the sequel that there is no cognitive faculty other than understanding capable of affording constitutive *a priori* principles of knowledge. Accordingly the critique which sifts these faculties one and all, so as to try the possible claims of each of the other faculties to a share in the clear possession of knowledge from roots of its own, retains nothing but what *understanding* prescribes *a priori* as a law for nature as the complex of phenomena—the form of these being similarly furnished *a priori.* All other pure concepts it relegates to the rank of ideas,[1] which for our faculty of theoretical cognition are transcendent; though they are not without their use nor redundant, but discharge certain functions as regulative principles.[2] For these concepts serve partly to restrain the officious pretentions of understanding, which, presuming on its ability to supply *a priori* the conditions of the possibility of all things which it is capable of knowing, behaves as if it had thus determined these bounds as those of the possibility of all things generally, and partly also to lead understanding, in its study of nature, according to a principle of completeness, unattainable as this remains for it, and so to promote the ultimate aim of all knowledge.

Properly, therefore, it was *understanding*—which, so far as it contains constitutive *a priori* cognitive principles, has its special realm, and one, moreover, in our *faculty of knowledge*—that the Critique, called in a general way that of pure reason was intended to establish in secure but particular possession against all other competitors. In the same way *reason,* which contains constitutive *a priori* principles solely in respect of the *faculty of desire,* gets its holding assigned to it by *The Critique of Practical Reason.*

But now comes *judgement,* which in the order of our cognitive faculties forms a middle term between understanding and reason. Has *it* also got independent *a priori* principles? If so, are they constitutive, or are they merely regulative, thus indicating no special realm? And do they give a rule *a priori* to the feeling of pleasure and displeasure, as the middle term between the faculties of cognition and desire, just as understanding prescribes laws *a priori* for the former and reason for the latter? This is the topic to which the present Critique is devoted.

A critique of pure reason, i.e., of our faculty of judging on *a priori* principles, would be incomplete if the critical examination of judgement, which is a faculty of knowledge, and as such lays claim to independent principles, were not dealt with separately. Still, however, its principles cannot, in a system of pure philosophy, form a separate constituent part intermediate between the theoretical and practical divisions, but may when needful be annexed to one or other as occasion requires. For if such a system is some day worked out under the general name of *metaphysic*—and its full and complete execution is both possible and of the utmost importance for the employment of reason in all departments of its activity—the critical examination of the ground for this edifice must have been previously carried down to the very

1 [The word is defined on pp. 489, 542. See *Critique of Pure Reason,* pp. 113–118: "I understand by *idea* a necessary conception of reason, to which no corresponding object can be discovered in the world of sense." (*Ibid.,* p. 117.) "They contain a certain perfection, attainable by no possible empirical cognition; and they give to reason a systematic unity, to which the unity of experience attempts to approximate, but can never completely attain." (*Ibid.,* p. 173.)]

2 [Cf. *Critique of Pure Reason,* pp. 193–200.]

depths of the foundations of the faculty of principles independent of experience, lest in some quarter it might give way, and sinking, inevitably bring with it the ruin of all.

We may readily gather, however, from the nature of the faculty of judgement (whose correct employment is so necessary and universally requisite that it is just this faculty that is intended when we speak of sound understanding) that the discovery of a peculiar principle belonging to it—and some such it must contain in itself *a priori,* for otherwise it would not be a cognitive faculty the distinctive character of which is obvious to the most commonplace criticism—must be a task involving considerable difficulties. For this principle is one which must not be derived from *a priori* concepts, seeing that these are the property of understanding, and judgement is only directed to their application. It has, therefore, itself to furnish a concept, and one from which, properly, we get no cognition of a thing, but which it can itself employ as a rule only—but not as an objective rule to which it can adapt its judgement, because, for that, another faculty of judgement would again be required to enable us to decide whether the case was one for the application of the rule or not.[1]

It is chiefly in those estimates that are called *aesthetic,* and which relate to the beautiful and sublime, whether of nature or of art, that one meets with the above difficulty about a principle (be it subjective or objective). And yet the critical search for a principle of judgement in their case is the most important item in a critique of this faculty. For, although they do not of themselves contribute a whit to the knowledge of things, they still belong wholly to the faculty of knowledge, and evidence an immediate bearing of this faculty upon the feeling of pleasure or displeasure according to some *a priori* principle, and do so without confusing this principle with what is capable of being a determining ground of the faculty of desire, for the latter has its principles *a priori* in concepts of reason. Logical estimates of nature, however, stand on a different footing. They deal with cases in which experience presents a conformity to law in things, which the understanding's general concept of the sensible is no longer adequate to render intelligible or explicable, and in which judgement may have recourse to itself for a principle of the reference of the natural thing to the unknowable supersensible and, indeed, must employ some such principle, though with a regard only to itself and the knowledge of nature. For in these cases the application of such an *a priori* principle for the *cognition* of what is in the world is both possible and necessary, and withal opens out prospects which are profitable for practical reason. But here there is no immediate reference to the feeling of pleasure or displeasure. But this is precisely the riddle in the principle of judgement that necessitates a separate division for this faculty in the critique—for there was nothing to prevent the formation of logical estimates according to concepts (from which no immediate conclusion can ever be drawn to the feeling of pleasure or displeasure) having been treated, with a critical statement of its limitations, in an appendage to the theoretical part of philosophy.

The present investigation of taste, as a faculty of aesthetic judgement, not being undertaken with a view to the formation or culture of taste (which will pursue its course in the future, as in the past, independently of such inquiries), but being merely directed to its transcendental aspects, I feel assured of its indulgent criticism in respect of any shortcomings on that score. But in all that is relevant to the transcendental aspect it must be prepared to stand the test of the most rigorous examination. Yet even here I venture to hope that the difficulty of unravelling a problem so involved in its nature may serve as an excuse for a certain amount of hardly avoidable obscurity in its solution, provided that the accuracy of our statement of the principle is proved with all requisite clearness. I admit that the mode of deriving the phenomena of judgement from that principle has not all the lucidity that is rightly demanded elsewhere, where the subject is cognition by concepts, and that I believe I have in fact attained in the second part of this work.

With this, then, I bring my entire critical undertaking to a close. I shall hasten to the doctrinal part, in order, as far as possible, to snatch from my advancing years what time may yet be favourable to the task. It is obvious that no separate division of doctrine is reserved for the faculty of judgement, seeing that, with judgement, critique takes the place of theory; but, following the division of philosophy into theoretical and practical, and of pure philosophy in the same way, the whole ground will be covered by the metaphysics of nature and of morals.

[1] [See Kant's general remarks on judgement in the *Critique of Pure Reason,* pp. 60–61.]

INTRODUCTION

I. *Division of Philosophy*

PHILOSOPHY may be said to contain the principles of the rational cognition that concepts afford us of things (not merely, as with logic, the principles of the form of thought in general irrespective of the objects), and, thus interpreted, the course, usually adopted, of dividing it into *theoretical* and *practical* is perfectly sound. But this makes imperative a specific distinction on the part of the concepts by which the principles of this rational cognition get their object assigned to them, for if the concepts are not distinct they fail to justify a division, which always presupposes that the principles belonging to the rational cognition of the several parts of the science in question are themselves mutually exclusive.

Now there are but two kinds of concepts, and these yield a corresponding number of distinct principles of the possibility of their objects. The concepts referred to are those *of nature* and that *of freedom*. By the first of these, a *theoretical* cognition from *a priori* principles becomes possible. In respect of such cognition, however, the second, by its very concept, imports no more than a negative principle (that of simple antithesis), while for the determination of the will, on the other hand, it establishes fundamental principles which enlarge the scope of its activity, and which on that account are called *practical*. Hence the division of philosophy falls properly into two parts, quite distinct in their principles—a theoretical, as *philosophy of nature*, and a practical, as *philosophy of morals* (for this is what the practical legislation of reason by the concept of freedom is called). Hitherto, however, in the application of these expressions to the division of the different principles, and with them to the division of philosophy, a gross misuse of the terms has prevailed; for what is practical according to concepts of nature has been taken as identical with what is practical according to the concept of freedom, with the result that a division has been made under these heads of theoretical and practical, by which, in effect, there has been no division at all (seeing that both parts might have similar principles).

The will—for this is what is said—is the faculty of desire and, as such, is just one of the many natural causes in the world, the one, namely, which acts by concepts; and whatever is represented as possible (or necessary) through the efficacy of will is called *practically possible* (or *necessary*): the intention being to distinguish its possibility (or necessity) from the physical possibility or necessity of an effect the causality of whose cause is not determined to its production by concepts (but rather, as with lifeless matter, by mechanism, and, as with the lower animals, by instinct). Now, the question in respect of the practical faculty: whether, that is to say, the concept, by which the causality of the will gets its rule, is a concept of nature or of freedom, is here left quite open.

The latter distinction, however, is essential. For, let the concept determining the causality be a concept of nature, and then the principles are *technically-practical;* but, let it be a concept of freedom, and they are *morally-practical.* Now, in the division of a rational science the difference between objects that require different principles for their cognition is the difference on which everything turns. Hence technically-practical principles belong to theoretical philosophy (natural science), whereas those morally-practical alone form the second part, that is, practical philosophy (ethical science).

All technically-practical rules (i.e., those of art and skill generally, or even of prudence, as a skill[1] in exercising an influence over men and their wills) must, so far as their principles rest upon concepts, be reckoned only as corollaries to theoretical philosophy. For they only touch the possibility of things according to concepts of nature, and this embraces, not alone the means discoverable in nature for the purpose, but even the will itself (as a faculty of desire, and consequently a natural faculty), so far as it is determinable on these rules by natural motives. Still these practical rules are not called laws (like physical laws), but only precepts. This is due to the fact that the will does not stand simply under the natural concept, but also under the concept of freedom. In the latter connection its principles are called laws, and these

[1] [Cf. *Fundamental Principles of the Metaphysic of Morals*. p. 266; also *Critique of Pure Reason*, 235.)

principles, with the addition of what follows from them, alone constitute the second or practical part of philosophy.

The solution of the problems of pure geometry is not allocated to a special part of that science, nor does the art of land-surveying merit the name of practical, in contradistinction to pure, as a second part of the general science of geometry, and with equally little, or perhaps less, right can the mechanical or chemical art of experiment or of observation be ranked as a practical part of the science of nature, or, in fine, domestic, agricultural, or political economy, the art of social intercourse, the principles of dietetics, or even general instruction as to the attainment of happiness, or as much as the control of the inclinations or the restraining of the affections with a view thereto, be denominated practical philosophy—not to mention forming these latter in a second part of philosophy in general. For, between them all, the above contain nothing more than rules of skill, which are thus only technically practical—the skill being directed to producing an effect which is possible according to natural concepts of causes and effects. As these concepts belong to theoretical philosophy, they are subject to those precepts as mere corollaries of theoretical philosophy (i.e., as corollaries of natural science), and so cannot claim any place in any special philosophy called practical. On the other hand, the morally practical precepts, which are founded entirely on the concept of freedom, to the complete exclusion of grounds taken from nature for the determination of the will, form quite a special kind of precepts. These, too, like the rules obeyed by nature, are, without qualification, called laws—though they do not, like the latter, rest on sensible conditions, but upon a supersensible principle—and they must needs have a separate part of philosophy allotted to them as their own, corresponding to the theoretical part, and termed *practical philosophy*.

Hence it is evident that a complex of practical precepts furnished by philosophy does not form a special part of philosophy, co-ordinate with the theoretical, by reason of its precepts being practical—for that they might be, notwithstanding that their principles were derived wholly from the theoretical knowledge of nature (as technically-practical rules). But an adequate reason only exists where their principle, being in no way borrowed from the concept of nature, which is always sensibly conditioned, rests consequently on the supersensible, which the concept of freedom alone makes cognizable by means of its formal laws, and where, therefore they are morally-practical, i. e., not merely precepts and rules in this or that interest, but laws independent of all antecedent reference to ends or aims.

II. *The Realm of Philosophy in General*

THE employment of our faculty of cognition from principles, and with it philosophy, is coextensive with the applicability of *a priori* concepts.

Now a division of the complex of all the objects to which those concepts are referred for the purpose, where possible, of compassing their knowledge, may be made according to the varied competence or incompetence of our faculty in that connection.

Concepts, so far as they are referred to objects apart from the question of whether knowledge of them is possible or not, have their field, which is determined simply by the relation in which their object stands to our faculty of cognition in general. The part of this field in which knowledge is possible for us is a territory (*territorium*) for these concepts and the requisite cognitive faculty. The part of the territory over which they exercise legislative authority is the realm (*ditio*) of these concepts, and their appropriate cognitive faculty. Empirical concepts have, therefore, their territory, doubtless, in nature as the complex of all sensible objects, but they have no realm (only a dwelling-place, *domicilium*), for, although they are formed according to law, they are not themselves legislative, but the rules founded on them are empirical and, consequently, contingent.

Our entire faculty of cognition has two realms, that of natural concepts and that of the concept of freedom, for through both it prescribes laws *a priori*. In accordance with this distinction, then, philosophy is divisible into theoretical and practical. But the territory upon which its realm is established, and over which it *exercises* its legislative authority, is still always confined to the complex of the objects of all possible experience, taken as no more than mere phenomena, for otherwise legislation by the understanding in respect of them is unthinkable.

The function of prescribing laws by means of concepts of nature is discharged by understanding and is theoretical. That of prescribing laws by means of the concept of freedom is discharged by reason and is merely practical. It is only in the practical sphere that reason can prescribe laws; in respect of theoretical knowledge (of nature) it can only (as by the understanding advised in the law) deduce from given laws their logical consequences, which still always remain restricted to nature. But we cannot reverse this and say that where rules are practical reason is then and there *legislative*, since the rules might be technically practical.

Understanding and reason, therefore, have two distinct jurisdictions over one and the same territory of experience. But neither can interfere with the other. For the concept of freedom just as little disturbs the legislation of nature, as the concept of nature influences legislation through the concept of freedom. That it is possible for us at least to think without contradiction of both these jurisdictions, and their appropriate faculties, as co-existing in the same subject, was shown by the *Critique of Pure Reason*, since it disposed of the objections on the other side by detecting their dialectical illusion.

Still, how does it happen that these two different realms do not form *one* realm, seeing that, while they do not limit each other in their legislation, they continually do so in their effects in the sensible world? The explanation lies in the fact that the concept of nature represents its objects in intuition doubtless, yet not as things-in-themselves, but as mere phenomena, whereas the concept of freedom represents in its object what is no doubt a thing-in-itself, but it does not make it intuitable, and further that neither the one nor the other is capable, therefore, of furnishing a theoretical cognition of its object (or even of the thinking subject) as a thing-in-itself, or, as this would be, of the supersensible—the idea of which has certainly to be introduced as the basis of the possibility of all those objects of experience, although it cannot itself ever be elevated or extended into a cognition.

Our entire cognitive faculty is, therefore, presented with an unbounded, but, also, inaccessible field—the field of the supersensible—in which we seek in vain for a territory, and on which, therefore, we can have no realm for theoretical cognition, be it for concepts of understanding or of reason. This field we must indeed occupy with ideas in the interest as well of the theoretical as the practical employment of reason, but, in connection with the laws arising from the concept of freedom, we cannot procure for these ideas any but practical reality, which, accordingly, fails to advance our theoretical cognition one step towards the supersensible.

Albeit, then, between the realm of the natural concept, as the sensible, and the realm of the concept of freedom, as the supersensible, there is a great gulf fixed, so that it is not possible to pass from the former to the latter (by means of the theoretical employment of reason), just as if they were so many separate worlds, the first of which is powerless to exercise influence on the second: still the latter is *meant* to influence the former—that is to say, the concept of freedom is meant to actualize in the sensible world the end proposed by its laws; and nature must consequently also be capable of being regarded in such a way that in the conformity to law of its form it at least harmonizes with the possibility of the ends to be effectuated in it according to the laws of freedom. There must, therefore, be a ground of the *unity* of the supersensible that lies at the basis of nature, with what the concept of freedom contains in a practical way, and although the concept of this ground neither theoretically nor practically attains to a knowledge of it, and so has no peculiar realm of its own, still it renders possible the transition from the mode of thought according to the principles of the one to that according to the principles of the other.[1]

III. *The Critique of Judgement as a means of connecting the two parts of Philosophy in a whole*

THE critique which deals with what our cognitive faculties are capable of yielding *a priori* has properly speaking no realm in respect of objects; for it is not a doctrine, its sole business being to investigate whether, having regard to the general bearings of our faculties, a doctrine is possible by their means, and if so, how. Its field extends to all their pretentions, with a view to confining them within their legitimate bounds. But what is shut out of the division of philosophy may still be admitted as a principal part into the general critique of our faculty of pure cognition, in the event, namely, of its containing principles which are not in themselves available either for theoretical or practical employment.

Concepts of nature contain the ground of all theoretical cognition *a priori* and rest, as we saw, upon the legislative authority of understanding. The concept of freedom contains the ground of all sensuously unconditioned practical precepts *a priori*, and rests upon that of reason. Both

[1] [Cf. p. 473, *et seq.*; also *Critique of Pure Reason*, pp. 236–37. This problem is discussed in the *Critique of Practical Reason* under the heading "Of the Typic of the Pure Practical Judgement," p. 319, *et seq.*; "It seems absurd to expect to find in the world of sense a case which, while as such it depends only on the law of nature, yet admits of the application to it of a law of freedom, and to which we can apply the supersensible idea of the morally good which is to be exhibited *in concreto*."]

faculties, therefore, besides their application in point of logical form to principles of whatever origin, have, in addition, their own peculiar jurisdiction in the matter of their content, and so, there being no further (*a priori*) jurisdiction above them, the division of philosophy into theoretical and practical is justified.

But there is still further in the family of our higher cognitive faculties a middle term between understanding and reason. This is *judgement,* of which we may reasonably presume by analogy that it may likewise contain, if not a special authority to prescribe laws, still a principle peculiar to itself upon which laws are sought, although one merely subjective *a priori.* This principle, even if it has no field of objects appropriate to it as its realm, may still have some territory or other with a certain character, for which just this very principle alone may be valid.

But in addition to the above considerations there is yet (to judge by analogy) a further ground, upon which judgement may be brought into line with another arrangement of our powers of representation, and one that appears to be of even greater importance than that of its kinship with the family of cognitive faculties. For all faculties of the soul, or capacities, are reducible to three, which do not admit of any further derivation from a common ground: the *faculty of knowledge,* the *feeling of pleasure or displeasure,* and the *faculty of desire.*[1] For the faculty of cognition understanding alone is legislative, if (as must be the case where it is considered on its own account free of confusion with the faculty of desire) this faculty, as that of *theoretical cognition,* is referred to nature, in respect of which alone (as phenomenon) it is possible for us to prescribe laws by means of *a priori* concepts of nature, which are properly pure concepts of understanding. For the faculty of desire, as a higher faculty operating under the concept of freedom, only reason (in which alone this concept has a place) prescribes laws *a priori.* Now between the faculties of knowledge and desire stands the feeling of pleasure, just as judgement is intermediate between understanding and reason. Hence we may, provisionally at least, assume that judgement likewise contains an *a priori* principle of its own, and that, since pleasure or displeasure is necessarily combined with the faculty of desire (be it antecedent to its principle, as with the lower desires, or, as with the higher, only supervening upon its determination by the moral law), it will effect a transition from the faculty of pure knowledge, i.e., from the realm of concepts of nature, to that of the concept of freedom, just as in its logical employment it makes possible the transition from understanding to reason.

Hence, despite the fact of philosophy being only divisible into two principal parts, the theoretical and the practical, and despite the fact of all that we may have to say of the special principles of judgement having to be assigned to its theoretical part, i.e., to rational cognition ac-

[1] Where one has reason to suppose that a relation subsists between concepts that are used as empirical principles and the faculty of pure cognition *a priori,* it is worth while attempting, in consideration of this connection, to give them a transcendental definition—a definition, that is, by pure categories, so far as these by themselves adequately indicate the distinction of the concept in question from others. This course follows that of the mathematician, who leaves the empirical data of his problem indeterminate, and only brings their relation in pure synthesis under the concepts of pure arithmetic, and thus generalizes his solution.—I have been taken to task for adopting a similar procedure (*Critique of Practical Reason,* Preface, p. 291) and fault had been found with my definition of the faculty of desire as *a faculty which by means of its representations is the cause of the actuality of the objects of those representations:* for mere *wishes* would still be desires, and yet in their case every one is ready to abandon all claim to being able by means of them alone to call their object into existence.—But this proves no more than the presence of desires in man by which he is in contradiction with himself. For in such a case he seeks the production of the object by means of his representation alone, without any hope of its being effectual, since he is conscious that his mechanical powers (if I may so call those which are not psychological), which would have to be determined by that representation, are either unequal to the task of realizing the object (by the intervention of means, therefore) or else are addressed to what is quite impossible, as, for example, to undo the past (*O mihi praeteritos, etc.*) or, to be able to annihilate the interval that, with intolerable delay, divides us from the wished-for moment.—Now, conscious as we are in such fantastic desires of the inefficiency of our representations (or even of their futility), as *causes* of their objects, there is still involved in every *wish* a reference of the same as cause, and therefore the representation of its *causality,* and this is especially discernible where the wish, as *longing,* is an affection. For such affections, since they dilate the heart and render it inert and thus exhaust its powers, show that a strain is kept on being exerted and re-exerted on these powers by the representations, but that the mind is allowed continually to relapse and get languid upon recognition of the impossibility before it. Even prayers for the aversion of great, and, so far as we can see, inevitable evils, and many superstitious means for attaining ends impossible of attainment by natural means, prove the causal reference of representations to their objects—a causality which not even the consciousness of inefficiency for producing the effect can deter from straining towards it. But why our nature should be furnished with a propensity to consciously vain desires is a teleological problem of anthropology. It would seem that were we not to be determined to the exertion of our power before we had assured ourselves of the efficiency of our faculty for producing an object, our power would remain to a large extent unused. For as a rule we only first learn to know our powers by making trial of them. This deceit of vain desires is therefore only the result of a beneficent disposition in our nature.

cording to concepts of nature: still the *Critique of Pure Reason,* which must settle this whole question before the above system is taken in hand, so as to substantiate its possibility, consists of three parts: the Critique of pure understanding, of pure judgement, and of pure reason, which faculties are called pure on the ground of their being legislative *a priori.*

IV. *Judgement as a Faculty by which Laws are prescribed* a priori

JUDGEMENT in general is the faculty of thinking the particular as contained under the universal. If the universal (the rule, principle, or law) is given, then the judgement which subsumes the particular under it *is determinant.* This is so even where such a judgement is transcendental and, as such, provides the conditions *a priori* in conformity with which alone subsumption under that universal can be effected. If, however, only the particular is given and the universal has to be found for it, then the judgement is simply *reflective.*

The determinant judgement determines under universal transcendental laws furnished by understanding and is subsumptive only; the law is marked out for it *a priori,* and it has no need to devise a law for its own guidance to enable it to subordinate the particular in nature to the universal. But there are such manifold forms of nature, so many modifications, as it were, of the universal transcendental concepts of nature, left undetermined by the laws furnished by pure understanding *a priori* as above mentioned, and for the reason that these laws only touch the general possibility of a nature (as an object of sense), that there must needs also be laws in this behalf. These laws, being empirical, may be contingent as far as the light of *our* understanding goes, but still, if they are to be called laws (as the concept of a nature requires), they must be regarded as necessary on a principle, unknown though it be to us, of the unity of the manifold. The reflective judgement which is compelled to ascend from the particular in nature to the universal stands, therefore, in need of a principle. This principle it cannot borrow from experience, because what it has to do is to establish just the unity of all empirical principles under higher, though likewise empirical, principles, and thence the possibility of the systematic subordination of higher and lower. Such a transcendental principle, therefore, the reflective judgement can only give as a law from and to itself. It cannot derive it from any other quarter (as it would then be a determinant judgement). Nor can it prescribe it to nature, for reflection on the laws of nature adjusts itself to nature, and not nature to the conditions according to which we strive to obtain a concept of it—a concept that is quite contingent in respect of these conditions.

Now the principle sought can only be this: as universal laws of nature have their ground in our understanding, which prescribes them to nature (though only according to the universal concept of it as nature), particular empirical laws must be regarded, in respect of that which is left undetermined in them by these universal laws, according to a unity such as they would have if an understanding (though it be not ours) had supplied them for the benefit of our cognitive faculties, so as to render possible a system of experience according to particular natural laws. This is not to be taken as implying that such an understanding must be actually assumed (for it is only the reflective judgement which avails itself of this idea as a principle for the purpose of reflection and not for determining anything); but this faculty rather gives by this means a law to itself alone and not to nature.

Now the concept of an object, so far as it contains at the same time the ground of the actuality of this object, is called its *end,* and the agreement of a thing with that constitution of things which is only possible according to ends, is called the *finality* of its form. Accordingly the principle of judgement, in respect of the form of the things of nature under empirical laws generally, is the *finality of nature* in its multiplicity. In other words, by this concept nature is represented as if an understanding contained the ground of the unity of the manifold of its empirical laws.

The finality of nature is, therefore, a particular *a priori* concept, which has its origin solely in the reflective judgement. For we cannot ascribe to the products of nature anything like a reference of nature in them to ends, but we can only make use of this concept to reflect upon them in respect of the nexus of phenomena in nature—a nexus given according to empirical laws. Furthermore, this concept is entirely different from practical finality (in human art or even morals), though it is doubtless thought after this analogy.

V. *The Principle of the formal finality of Nature is a transcendental Principle of Judgement*

A TRANSCENDENTAL principle is one through which we represent *a priori* the universal condition under which alone things can become objects of our cognition generally. A principle, on the other hand, is called *metaphysical* where it represents *a priori* the condition under which alone objects whose concept has to be given empirically may become further determined *a priori*. Thus the principle of the cognition of bodies as substances, and as changeable substances, is transcendental where the statement is that their change must have a cause: but it is metaphysical where it asserts that their change must have an *external* cause. For, in the first case, bodies need only be thought through ontological predicates (pure concepts of understanding) e.g., as substance, to enable the proposition to be cognized *a priori;* whereas, in the second case, the empirical concept of a body (as a movable thing in space) must be introduced to support the proposition, although, once this is done, it may be seen quite *a priori* that the latter predicate (movement only by means of an external cause) applies to body. In this way, as I shall show presently, the principle of the finality of nature (in the multiplicity of its empirical laws) is a transcendental principle. For the concept of objects, regarded as standing under this principle, is only the pure concept of objects of possible empirical cognition generally, and involves nothing empirical. On the other hand, the principle of practical finality, implied in the idea of the *determination* of a free *will,* would be a metaphysical principle, because the concept of a faculty of desire, as will, has to be given empirically, i.e., is not included among transcendental predicates. But both these principles are, none the less, not empirical, but *a priori* principles; because no further experience is required for the synthesis of the predicate with the empirical concept of the subject of their judgements, but it may be apprehended quite *a priori*.

That the concept of a finality of nature belongs to transcendental principles is abundantly evident from the maxims of judgement upon which we rely *a priori* in the investigation of nature, and which yet have to do with no more than the possibility of experience, and consequently of the knowledge of nature—but of nature not merely in a general way, but as determined by a manifold of particular laws. These maxims crop up frequently enough in the course of this science, though only in a scattered way. They are aphorisms of metaphysical wisdom, making their appearance in a number of rules the necessity of which cannot be demonstrated from concepts. "Nature takes the shortest way (*lex parsimoniae*); yet it makes no leap, either in the sequence of its changes, or in the juxtaposition of specifically different forms (*lex continui in natura*); its vast variety in empirical laws is for all that, unity under a few principles (*principia praeter necessitatem non sunt multiplicanda*)"; and so forth.

If we propose to assign the origin of these elementary rules, and attempt to do so on psychological lines, we go straight in the teeth of their sense. For they tell us, not what happens, i.e., according to what rule our powers of judgement actually discharge their functions, and how we judge, but how we ought to judge; and we cannot get this logical objective necessity where the principles are merely empirical. Hence the finality of nature for our cognitive faculties and their employment, which manifestly radiates from them, is a transcendental principle of judgements, and so needs also a transcendental deduction, by means of which the ground for this mode of judging must be traced to the *a priori* sources of knowledge.

Now, looking at the grounds of the possibility of an experience, the first thing, of course, that meets us is something necessary—namely, the universal laws apart from which nature in general (as an object of sense) cannot be thought. These rest on the categories, applied to the formal conditions of all intuition possible for us, so far as it is also given *a priori*. Under these laws, judgement is determinant; for it has nothing else to do than to subsume under given laws. For instance, understanding says: all change has its cause (universal law of nature); transcendental judgement has nothing further to do than to furnish *a priori* the condition of subsumption under the concept of understanding placed before it: this we get in the succession of the determinations of one and the same thing. Now for nature in general, as an object of possible experience, that law is cognized as absolutely necessary. But besides this formal time-condition, the objects of empirical cognition are determined, or, so far as we can judge *a priori,* are determinable, in divers ways, so that specifically differentiated natures, over and above what they have in common as things of nature in general, are further capable of being causes in an infinite variety of ways; and each of these modes must, on the concept of a cause in general, have its rule, which is a law, and, consequently, imports necessity: although owing to the constitution and limitations of our faculties of cognition we may entirely fail to see this necessity. Accordingly, in respect of nature's merely empirical laws, we must think in nature a possibility of an endless multiplicity of empirical laws, which yet are contingent so far as our insight goes, i.e., cannot be cognized *a priori*. In respect of these we estimate the unity of nature according to empirical laws, and the possibility of the unity of experience, as a system according to empirical laws, to be contingent. But, now, such a unity is one which must be necessarily presupposed and assumed, as otherwise we should not have a thoroughgoing connection of empirical cognition in a whole of experience. For the universal laws of nature, while providing, certainly, for such a connection among things generically, as things of nature in general, do not do so for them specifically as such particular things of nature. Hence judgement is compelled, for its own guidance, to adopt it as an *a priori* principle, that what is for human insight contingent in the particular (empirical) laws of nature contains nevertheless unity of law in the synthesis of its manifold in an intrinsically possible experience—unfathomable, though still thinkable, as such unity may, no doubt, be for us. Consequently, as the unity of law in a synthesis, which is cognized by us in obedience to a necessary aim (a need of understanding), though recognized at the same time as contingent, is represented as a finality of objects (here of nature), so judgement, which, in respect of things under possible (yet to be discovered) empirical laws, is merely reflective, must regard nature in respect of the latter according to a *principle of finality* for our cognitive faculty, which then finds expression in the above maxims of judgement. Now this transcendental concept of a finality of nature is neither a concept of nature nor of freedom, since it attributes nothing at all to the object, i.e., to nature, but only represents the unique mode in which we must proceed in our reflection upon the objects of nature with a view to getting a thoroughly interconnected whole of experience, and so is a subjective principle, i.e., maxim, of judgement. For this reason, too, just as if it were a lucky chance that favoured us, we are rejoiced (properly speaking, relieved of a want) where we meet with such systematic unity under merely empirical laws: although we must necessarily assume the presence of such a unity, apart from any ability on our part to apprehend or prove its existence.

In order to convince ourselves of the correctness of this deduction of the concept before us, and the necessity of assuming it as a transcendental principle of cognition, let us just bethink ourselves of the magnitude of the task. We have to form a connected experience from given perceptions of a nature containing a maybe endless multiplicity of empirical laws, and this problem has its seat *a priori* in our understanding. This understanding is no doubt *a priori* in possession of universal laws of nature, apart from which nature would be incapable of being an object of experience at all. But over and above this it needs a certain order of nature in its particular rules which are only capable of being brought to its knowledge empirically, and which, so far as it is concerned are contingent. These rules, without which we would have no means of advance from the universal analogy of a possible experience in general to a particular, must be regarded by understanding as laws, i.e., as necessary—for otherwise they would not form an order of nature—though it be unable to cognize or ever get an insight into their necessity. Albeit, then, it can determine nothing *a priori* in respect of these (objects), it must, in pursuit of such empirical so-called laws, lay at the basis of all reflection upon them an *a priori* principle, to the effect, namely, that a cognizable order of nature is possible according to them. A principle of this kind is expressed in the following propositions. There is in nature a subordination of genera and species comprehensible by us: Each of these genera again approximates to the others on a common principle, so that a transition may be possible from one to the other, and thereby to a higher genus: While it seems at the outset unavoidable for our understanding to assume for the specific variety of natural operations a like number of various kinds of causality, yet these may all be reduced to a small number of principles, the quest for which is our business; and so forth. This adaptation of nature to our cognitive faculties is presupposed *a priori* by judgement on behalf of its reflection upon it according to empirical laws. But understanding all the while recognizes it objectively as contingent, and it is merely judgement that attributes it to nature as transcendental finality, i.e., a finality in respect of the subject's faculty of cognition. For, were it not for this presupposition, we should have no order of nature in accordance with empirical laws, and, consequently, no guiding-thread for an experience that has to be brought to bear upon these in all their variety, or for an investigation of them.

For it is quite conceivable that, despite all the uniformity of the things of nature according to universal laws, without which we would not have the form of general empirical knowledge at all, the specific variety of the empirical laws of nature, with their effects, might still be so great as to make it impossible for our understanding to discover in nature an intelligible order, to divide its products into genera and species so as to avail ourselves of the principles of explanation and comprehension of one for explaining and interpreting another, and out of material coming to hand in such confusion (properly speaking only infinitely multiform and ill-adapted to our power of apprehension) to make a consistent context of experience.

Thus judgement, also, is equipped with an *a priori* principle for the possibility of nature, but only in a subjective respect. By means of this it prescribes a law, not to nature (as autonomy), but to itself (as heautonomy), to guide its reflection upon nature. This law may be called *the law of the specification of nature* in respect of its empirical laws. It is not one cognized *a priori* in nature, but judgement adopts it in the interests of a natural order, cognizable by our understanding, in the division which it makes of nature's universal laws when it seeks to subordinate to them a variety of particular laws. So when it is said that nature specifies its universal laws on a principle of finality for our cognitive faculties, i.e., of suitability for the human understanding and its necessary function of finding the universal for the particular presented to it by perception, and again for varieties (which are, of course, common for each species) connection in the unity of principle, we do not thereby either prescribe a law to nature, or learn one from it by observation—although the principle in question may be confirmed by this means. For it is not a principle of the determinant but merely of the reflective judgement. All that is intended is that, no matter what is the order and disposition of nature in respect of its universal laws, we must investigate its empirical laws throughout on that principle and the maxims founded thereon, because only so far as that principle applies can we make any headway in the employment of our understanding in experience, or gain knowledge.

VI. *The Association of the Feeling of Pleasure with the Concept of the Finality of Nature*

The conceived harmony of nature in the manifold of its particular laws with our need of finding universality of principles for it must, so far as our insight goes, be deemed contingent, but withal indispensable for the requirements of our understanding, and, consequently, a finality by which nature is in accord with our aim, but only so far as this is directed to knowledge. The universal laws of understanding, which are equally laws of nature, are, although arising from spontaneity, just as necessary for nature as the laws of motion applicable to matter. Their origin does not presuppose any regard to our cognitive faculties, seeing that it is only by their means that we first come by any conception of the meaning of a knowledge of things (of nature), and they of necessity apply to nature as object of our cognition in general. But it is contingent, so far as we can see, that the order of nature in its particular laws, with their wealth of at least possible variety and heterogeneity transcending all our powers of comprehension, should still in actual fact be commensurate with these powers. To find out this order is an undertaking on the part of our understanding, which pursues it with a regard to a necessary end of its own, that, namely, of introducing into nature unity of principle. This end must, then, be attributed to nature by judgement, since no law can be here prescribed to it by understanding.

The attainment of every aim is coupled with a feeling of pleasure. Now where such attainment has for its condition a representation *a priori*—as here a principle for the reflective judgement in general—the feeling of pleasure also is determined by a ground which is *a priori* and valid for all men: and that, too, merely by virtue of the reference of the object to our faculty of cognition. As the concept of finality here takes no cognizance whatever of the faculty of desire, it differs entirely from all practical finality of nature.

As a matter of fact, we do not, and cannot, find in ourselves the slightest effect on the feeling of pleasure from the coincidence of perceptions with the laws in accordance with the universal concepts of nature (the categories), since in their case understanding necessarily follows the bent of its own nature without ulterior aim. But, while this is so, the discovery, on the other hand, that two or more empirical heterogeneous laws of nature are allied under one principle that embraces them both, is the ground of a very appreciable pleasure, often even of admiration, and such, too, as does not wear off even though we are already familiar enough with its object. It is true that we no longer notice any decided pleasure in the comprehensibility of nature, or in the unity of its divisions into genera and species, without which the empirical concepts, that afford us our knowledge of nature in its particular laws, would not be possible. Still it is certain that the pleasure appeared in due course, and only by reason of the most ordinary experience being impossible without it, has it become gradually fused with simple cognition, and no longer arrests particular attention. Something, then, that makes us attentive in our estimate of nature to its finality for our understanding—an endeavour to bring, where possible, its heterogeneous laws under higher, though still always empirical, laws—is required, in order that, on meeting with success, pleasure may be felt in this their accord with our cognitive faculty, which accord is regarded by us as purely contingent. As against this, a representation of nature would be altogether displeasing to us, were we to be forewarned by it that, on the least investigation carried beyond the commonest experience, we should come in contact with such a heterogeneity of its laws as would make the union of its particular laws under universal empirical laws impossible for our understanding. For this would conflict with the principle of the subjectively final specification of nature in its genera, and with our own reflective judgement in respect thereof.

Yet this presupposition of judgement is so indeterminate on the question of the extent of the prevalence of that ideal finality of nature for our cognitive faculties, that if we are told that a more searching or enlarged knowledge of nature, derived from observation, must eventually bring us into contact with a multiplicity of laws that no human understanding could reduce to a principle, we can reconcile ourselves to the thought. But still we listen more gladly to others who hold out to us the hope that the more intimately we come to know the secrets of nature, or the better we are able to compare it with external members as yet unknown to us, the more simple shall we find it in its principles, and the further our experience advances the more harmonious shall we find it in the apparent heterogeneity of its empirical laws. For our judgement makes it imperative upon us to proceed on the principle of the conformity of nature to our faculty of cognition, so far as that principle extends, without deciding—for the rule is not given to us by a determinant judgement—whether bounds are anywhere set to it or not. For, while in respect of the rational employment of our cognitive faculty, bounds may be definitely determined, in the empirical field no such determination of bounds is possible.

VII. *The Aesthetic Representation of the Finality of Nature*

THAT which is purely subjective in the representation of an object, i.e., what constitutes its reference to the subject, not to the object, is its aesthetic quality. On the other hand, that which in such a representation serves, or is available, for the determination of the object (for the purpose of knowledge), is its logical validity. In the cognition of an object of sense, both sides are presented conjointly. In the sense-representation of external things, the quality of space in which we intuite them is the merely subjective side of my representation of them (by which what the things are in themselves as objects is left quite open), and it is on account of that reference that the object in being intuited in space is also thought merely as phenomenon. But despite its purely subjective quality, space is still a constituent of the knowledge of things as phenomena. *Sensation* (here external) also agrees in expressing a merely subjective side of our representations of external things, but one which is properly their matter (through which we are given something with real existence), just as space is the mere *a priori* form of the possibility of their intuition; and so sensation is, none the less, also employed in the cognition of external objects.

But that subjective side of a representation *which is incapable of becoming an element of cognition,* is the *pleasure* or *displeasure* connected with it;[1] for through it I cognize nothing in the object of the representation, although it may easily be the result of the operation of some cognition or other. Now the finality of a thing, so far as represented in our perception of it, is in no way a quality of the object itself (for a quality of this kind is not one that can be perceived), although it may be inferred from a cognition of things. In the finality, therefore, which is prior to the cognition of an object, and which, even apart from any desire to make use of the representation of it for the purpose of a cognition, is yet immediately connected with it, we have the subjective quality belonging to it that is incapable of becoming a constituent of knowledge. Hence we only apply the term *final* to the object on account of its representation being immediately coupled with the feeling of pleasure: and this representation itself is an aesthetic representation of the finality. The only question is whether such a representation of finality exists at all.

If pleasure is connected with the mere apprehension (*apprehensio*) of the form of an object of intuition, apart from any reference it may have to a concept for the purpose of a definite cognition, this does not make the representation

[1] [Cf. *Critique of Pure Reason,* p. 32: "All in our cognition that belongs to intuition contains nothing more than mere relations. The feelings of pain and pleasure, and the will are not cognitions, are excepted." Also see *ibid.*, p. 235.]

referable to the object, but solely to the subject. In such a case, the pleasure can express nothing but the conformity of the object to the cognitive faculties brought into play in the reflective judgement, and so far as they are in play, and hence merely a subjective formal finality of the object. For that apprehension of forms in the imagination can never take place without the reflective judgement, even when it has no intention of so doing, comparing them at least with its faculty of referring intuitions to concepts. If, now, in this comparison, imagination (as the faculty of intuitions *a priori*) is undesignedly brought into accord with understanding (as the faculty of concepts), by means of a given representation, and a feeling of pleasure is thereby aroused, then the object must be regarded as final for the reflective judgement. A judgement of this kind is an aesthetic judgement upon the finality of the object, which does not depend upon any present concept of the object, and does not provide one. When the form of an object (as opposed to the matter of its representation, as sensation) is, in the mere act of reflecting upon it, without regard to any concept to be obtained from it, estimated as the ground of a pleasure in the representation of such an object, then this pleasure is also judged to be combined necessarily with the representation of it, and so not merely for the subject apprehending this form, but for all in general who pass judgement. The object is then called beautiful; and the faculty of judging by means of such a pleasure (and so also with universal validity) is called *taste*. For since the ground of the pleasure is made to reside merely in the form of the object for reflection generally, consequently not in any sensation of the object, and without any reference, either, to any concept that might have something or other in view, it is with the conformity to law in the empirical employment of judgement generally (unity of imagination and understanding) in the subject, and with this alone, that the representation of the object in reflection, the conditions of which are universally valid *a priori*, accords. And, as this accordance of the object with the faculties of the subject is contingent, it gives rise to a representation of a finality on the part of the object in respect of the cognitive faculties of the subject.

Here, now, is a pleasure which—as is the case with all pleasure or displeasure that is not brought about through the agency of the concept of freedom (i.e., through the antecedent determination of the higher faculty of desire by means of pure reason)—no concepts could ever enable us to regard as necessarily connected with the representation of an object. It must always be only through reflective perception that it is cognized as conjoined with this representation. As with all empirical judgements, it is, consequently, unable to announce objective necessity or lay claim to *a priori* validity. But, then, the judgement of taste in fact only lays claim, like every other empirical judgement, to be valid for every one, and, despite its inner contingency this is always possible. The only point that is strange or out of the way about it is that it is not an empirical concept, but a feeling of pleasure (and so not a concept at all), that is yet exacted from every one by the judgement of taste, just as if it were a predicate united to the cognition of the object, and that is meant to be conjoined with its representation.

A singular empirical judgement, as for example, the judgement of one who perceives a movable drop of water in a rock-crystal, rightly looks to every one finding the fact as stated, since the judgement has been formed according to the universal conditions of the determinant judgement under the laws of a possible experience generally. In the same way, one who feels pleasure in simple reflection on the form of an object, without having any concept in mind, rightly lays claim to the agreement of every one, although this judgement is empirical and a singular judgement. For the ground of this pleasure is found in the universal, though subjective, condition of reflective judgements, namely the final harmony of an object (be it a product of nature or of art) with the mutual relation of the faculties of cognition (imagination and understanding), which are requisite for every empirical cognition. The pleasure in judgements of taste is, therefore, dependent doubtless on an empirical representation, and cannot be united *a priori* to any concept (one cannot determine *a priori* what object will be in accordance with taste or not—one must find out the object that is so); but then it is only made the determining ground of this judgement by virtue of our consciousness of its resting simply upon reflection and the universal, though only subjective, conditions of the harmony of that reflection with the knowledge of objects generally, for which the form of the object is final.

This is why judgements of taste are subjected to a critique in respect of their possibility. For their possibility presupposes an *a priori* principle, although that principle is neither a cognitive principle for understanding nor a practical principle for the will, and is thus in no way determinant *a priori.*

Susceptibility to pleasure arising from reflection on the forms of things (whether of nature or of art) betokens, however, not only a finality on the part of objects in their relation to the reflective judgement in the subject, in accordance with the concept of nature, but also, conversely, a finality on the part of the subject, answering to the concept of freedom, in respect of the form, or even formlessness of objects. The result is that the aesthetic judgement refers not merely, as a judgement of taste, to the beautiful, but also, as springing from a higher intellectual feeling, to the *sublime.* Hence the above-mentioned Critique of Aesthetic Judgement must be divided on these lines into two main parts.

VIII. *The Logical Representation of the Finality of Nature*

THERE are two ways in which finality may be represented in an object given in experience. It may be made to turn on what is purely subjective. In this case the object is considered in respect of its form as present in *apprehension* (*apprehensio*) prior to any concept;[1] and the harmony of this form with the cognitive faculties, promoting the combination of the intuition with concepts for cognition generally, is represented as a finality of the form of the object. Or, on the other hand, the representation of finality may be made to turn on what is objective, in which case it is represented as the harmony of the form of the object with the possibility of the thing itself according to an antecedent concept of it containing the ground of this form. We have seen that the representation of the former kind of finality rests on the pleasure immediately felt in mere reflection on the form of the object. But that of the latter kind of finality, as it refers the form of the object, not to the subject's cognitive faculties engaged in its apprehension, but to a definite cognition of the object under a given concept, has nothing to do with a feeling of pleasure in things, but only understanding and its estimate of them. Where the concept of an object is given, the function of judgement, in its employment of that concept for cognition, consists in *presentation* (*exhibitio*), i. e., in placing beside the concept an intuition corresponding to it. Here it may be that our own imagination is the agent employed, as in the case of art, where we realize a preconceived concept of an object which we set before ourselves as an end. Or the agent may be nature in its technic (as in the case of organic bodies), when we read into it our own concept of an end to assist our estimate of its product. In this case what is represented is not a mere *finality* of nature in the form of the thing, but this very product as a *natural end.* Although our concept that nature, in its empirical laws, is subjectively final in its forms is in no way a concept of the object, but only a principle of judgement for providing itself with concepts in the vast multiplicity of nature, so that it may be able to take its bearings, yet, on the analogy of an end, as it were a regard to our cognitive faculties is here attributed to nature. *Natural beauty* may, therefore, be looked on as the *presentation* of the concept of formal, i. e., merely subjective, finality and *natural ends* as the presentation of the concept of a real, i.e., objective, finality. The former of these we estimate by taste (aesthetically by means of the feeling of pleasure), the latter by understanding and reason (logically according to concepts).

On these considerations is based the division of the Critique of Judgement into that of the *aesthetic* and the *teleological* judgement. By the first is meant the faculty of estimating formal finality (otherwise called subjective) by the feeling of pleasure or displeasure, by the second, the faculty of estimating the real finality (objective) of nature by understanding and reason.

In a Critique of Judgement the part dealing with aesthetic judgement is essentially relevant, as it alone contains a principle introduced by judgement completely *a priori* as the basis of its reflection upon nature. This is the principle of nature's formal finality for our cognitive faculties in its particular (empirical) laws—a principle without which understanding could not feel itself at home in nature: whereas no reason is assignable *a priori,* nor is so much as the possibility of one apparent from the concept of nature as an object of experience, whether in its universal or in its particular aspects, why there should be objective ends of nature, i. e., things only possible as natural ends. But it is only judgement that, without being itself possessed *a priori* of a principle in that behalf, in actually occurring cases (of certain products) contains the rule for making use of the concept of ends in the interest of reason, after that the above transcendental principle has already prepared understanding to apply to nature the concept of an end (at least in respect of its form).

But the transcendental principle by which a

[1] [Cf. *Critique of Pure Reason,* pp. 41, 42, 86, 87.]

finality of nature in its subjective reference to our cognitive faculties, is represented in the form of a thing as a principle of its estimation, leaves quite undetermined the question of where and in what cases we have to make our estimate of the object as a product according to a principle of finality, instead of simply according to universal laws of nature. It resigns to the *aesthetic* judgement the task of deciding the conformity of this product (in its form) to our cognitive faculties as a question of taste (a matter which the aesthetic judgement decides, not by any harmony with concepts, but by feeling). On the other hand, judgement as teleologically employed assigns the determinate conditions under which something (e. g., an organized body) is to be estimated after the idea of an end of nature. But it can adduce no principle from the concept of nature, as an object of experience, to give it its authority to ascribe *a priori* to nature a reference to ends, or even only indeterminately to assume them from actual experience in the case of such products. The reason of this is that, in order to be able merely empirically to cognize objective finality in a certain object, many particular experiences must be collected and reviewed under the unity of their principle. Aesthetic judgement is, therefore, a special faculty of estimating according to a rule, but not according to concepts. The teleological is not a special faculty, but only general reflective judgement proceeding, as it always does in theoretical cognition, according to concepts, but in respect of certain objects of nature, following special principles—those, namely, of a judgement that is merely reflective and does not determine objects. Hence, as regards its application, it belongs to the theoretical part of philosophy, and on account of its special principles, which are not determinant, as principles belonging to doctrine have to be, it must also form a special part of the Critique. On the other hand, the aesthetic judgement contributes nothing to the cognition of its objects. Hence it must *only* be allocated to the Critique of the judging subject and of its faculties of knowledge so far as these are capable of possessing *a priori* principles, be their use (theoretical or practical) otherwise what it may—a Critique which is the propaedeutic of all philosophy.

IX. *Joinder of the Legislations of Understanding and Reason by means of Judgement*

UNDERSTANDING prescribes laws *a priori* for nature as an object of sense, so that we may have a theoretical knowledge of it in a possible experience. Reason prescribes laws *a priori* for freedom and its peculiar causality as the supersensible in the subject, so that we may have a purely practical knowledge. The realm of the concept of nature under the one legislation, and that of the concept of freedom under the other, are completely cut off from all reciprocal influence, that they might severally (each according to its own principles) exert upon the other, by the broad gulf that divides the supersensible from phenomena. The concept of freedom determines nothing in respect of the theoretical cognition of nature; and the concept of nature likewise nothing in respect of the practical laws of freedom. To that extent, then, it is not possible to throw a bridge from the one realm to the other. Yet although the determining grounds of causality according to the concept of freedom (and the practical rule that this contains) have no place in nature, and the sensible cannot determine the supersensible in the subject; still the converse is possible (not, it is true, in respect of the knowledge of nature, but of the consequences arising from the supersensible and bearing on the sensible). So much indeed is implied in the concept of a causality by freedom, the *operation* of which, in conformity with the formal laws of freedom, is to take effect in the word. The word *cause,* however, in its application to the supersensible only signifies the *ground* that determines the causality of things of nature to an effect in conformity with their appropriate natural laws, but at the same time also in unison with the formal principle of the laws of reason—a ground which, while its possibility is impenetrable, may still be completely cleared of the charge of contradiction that it is alleged to involve.[1] The effect in accordance with the concept of freedom is the final end which (or the manifestation of which in the sensible world) is to exist, and this presupposes

[1] One of the various supposed contradictions in this complete distinction of the causality of nature from that through freedom is expressed in the objection that when I speak of *hindrances* opposed by nature to causality according to laws of freedom (moral laws) or of *assistance* lent to it by nature, I am all the time admitting an *influence* of the former upon the latter. But the misinterpretation is easily avoided, if attention is only paid to the meaning of the statement. The resistance or furtherance is not between nature and freedom, but between the former as phenomenon and *the effects* of the latter as phenomena in the world of sense. Even the causality of freedom (of pure and practical reason) is the causality of a natural cause subordinated to freedom (a causality of the subject regarded as man, and consequently as a phenomenon), and one, the ground of whose determination is contained in the intelligible, that is thought under freedom, in a manner that is not further or otherwise explicable (just as in the case of that intelligible that forms the supersensible substrate of nature.)

the condition of the possibility of that end in nature (i. e., in the nature of the subject as a being of the sensible world, namely, as man). It is so presupposed *a priori,* and without regard to the practical, by judgement. This faculty, with its concept of a *finality* of nature, provides us with the mediating concept between concepts of nature and the concept of freedom—a concept that makes possible the transition from the pure theoretical [legislation of understanding] to the pure practical [legislation of reason] and from conformity to law in accordance with the former to final ends according to the latter. For through that concept we cognize the possibility of the final end that can only be actualized in nature and in harmony with its laws.

Understanding, by the possibility of its supplying *a priori* laws for nature, furnishes a proof of the fact that nature is cognized by us only as phenomenon, and in so doing points to its having a supersensible substrate; but this substrate it leaves quite *undetermined.* Judgement by the *a priori* principle of its estimation of nature according to its possible particular laws provides this supersensible substrate (within as well as without us) with *determinability through the intellectual faculty.* But reason gives *determination* to the same *a priori* by its practical law. Thus judgement makes possible the transition from the realm of the concept of nature to that of the concept of freedom.

In respect of the faculties of the soul generally, regarded as higher faculties, i. e., as faculties containing an autonomy, understanding is the one that contains the *constitutive a priori* principles for the *faculty of cognition* (the theoretical knowledge of nature). The *feeling of pleasure and displeasure* is provided for by the judgement in its independence from concepts and from sensations that refer to the determination of the faculty of desire and would thus be capable of being immediately practical. For the *faculty of desire* there is reason, which is practical without mediation of any pleasure of whatsoever origin, and which determines for it, as a higher faculty, the final end that is attended at the same time with pure intellectual delight in the object. Judgement's concept of a finality of nature falls, besides, under the head of natural concepts, but only as a regulative principle of the cognitive faculties—although the aesthetic judgement on certain objects (of nature or of art) which occasions that concept, is a constitutive principle in respect of the feeling of pleasure or displeasure. The spontaneity in the play of the cognitive faculties whose harmonious accord contains the ground of this pleasure, makes the concept in question, in its consequences, a suitable mediating link connecting the realm of the concept of nature with that of the concept of freedom, as this accord at the same time promotes the sensibility of the mind for moral feeling.[1] The following table may facilitate the review of all the above faculties in their systematic unity.[2]

List of Mental Faculties	*Cognitive Faculties*
Cognitive faculties	Understanding
Feeling of pleasure and displeasure	Judgement
Faculty of desire	Reason

A priori Principles	*Application*
Conformity to law	Nature
Finality	Art
Final End	Freedom

[1] [Cf. p. 548.]

[2] It has been thought somewhat suspicious that my divisions in pure philosophy should almost always come out threefold. But it is due to the nature of the case. If a division is to be *a priori* it must be either analytic, according to the law of contradiction—and then it is always twofold *(quodlibet ens est aut A aut non A)*—or else it is *synthetic.* If it is to be derived in the latter case from *a priori* concepts (not, as in mathematics, from the *a priori* intuition corresponding to the concept), then, to meet the requirements of synthetic unity in general, namely (1) a condition, (2) a conditioned, (3) the concept arising from the union of the conditioned with its condition, the division must of necessity be trichotomous.

FIRST PART
CRITIQUE OF AESTHETIC JUDGEMENT

SECTION I. *ANALYTIC OF AESTHETIC JUDGEMENT*

BOOK I. *Analytic of the Beautiful*

FIRST MOMENT. *Of the Judgement of Taste:*[1] *Moment of Quality*

§ I. *The judgement of taste is aesthetic*

IF we wish to discern whether anything is beautiful or not, we do not refer the representation of it to the object by means of understanding with a view to cognition, but by means of the imagination[2] (acting perhaps in conjunction with understanding) we refer the representation to the subject and its feeling of pleasure or displeasure. The judgement of taste, therefore, is not a cognitive judgement, and so not logical, but is aesthetic—which means that it is one whose determining ground *cannot be other than subjective*. Every reference of representations is capable of being objective, even that of sensations (in which case it signifies the real in an empirical representation). The one exception to this is the feeling of pleasure or displeasure. This denotes nothing in the object, but is a feeling which the subject has of itself and of the manner in which it is affected by the representation.

To apprehend a regular and appropriate building with one's cognitive faculties, be the mode of representation clear or confused, is quite a different thing from being conscious of this representation with an accompanying sensation of delight. Here the representation is referred wholly to the subject, and what is more to its feeling of life[3]—under the name of the feeling of pleasure or displeasure—and this forms the basis of a quite separate faculty of discriminating and estimating, that contributes nothing to knowledge. All it does is to compare the given representation in the subject with the entire faculty of representations of which the mind is conscious in the feeling of its state. Given representations in a judgement may be empirical, and so aesthetic; but the judgement which is pronounced by their means is logical, provided it refers them to the object. Conversely, be the given representations even rational, but referred in a judgement solely to the subject (to its feeling), they are always to that extent aesthetic.

§ 2. *The delight which determines the judgement of taste is independent of all interest*

THE delight which we connect with the representation of the real existence of an object is called *interest*. Such a delight, therefore, always involves a reference to the faculty of desire, either as its determining ground, or else as necessarily implicated with its determining ground. Now, where the question is whether something is beautiful, we do not want to know, whether we, or any one else, are, or even could be, concerned in the real existence of the thing, but rather what estimate we form of it on mere contemplation (intuition or reflection). If any one asks me whether I consider that the palace I see before me is beautiful, I may, perhaps, reply that I do not care for things of that sort that are merely made to be gaped at. Or I may reply in the same strain as that Iroquois *sachem* who said that nothing in Paris pleased him better than the eating-houses. I may even go a step further and inveigh with the vigour of a Rousseau against the vanity of the great who spend the sweat of the people on such superfluous things. Or, in fine, I may quite easily persuade myself that if I found myself on an uninhabited island, without hope of ever again coming among men, and could conjure such a palace

[1] The definition of taste here relied upon is that it is the faculty of estimating the beautiful. But the discovery of what is required for calling an object beautiful must be reserved for the analysis of judgements of taste. In my search for the moments to which attention is paid by this judgement in its reflection, I have followed the guidance of the logical functions of judging (for a judgement of taste always involves a reference to understanding). I have brought the moment of quality first under review, because this is what the aesthetic judgement on the beautiful looks to in the first instance.

[2] [Cf. p. 493.]

[3] [Cf. p. 495.]

into existence by a mere wish, I should still not trouble to do so, so long as I had a hut there that was comfortable enough for me. All this may be admitted and approved; only it is not the point now at issue. All one wants to know is whether the mere representation of the object is to my liking, no matter how indifferent I may be to the real existence of the object of this representation. It is quite plain that in order to say that the object *is beautiful*, and to show that I have taste, everything turns on the meaning which I can give to this representation, and not on any factor which makes me dependent on the real existence of the object. Every one must allow that a judgement on the beautiful which is tinged with the slightest interest, is very partial and not a pure judgement of taste.[1] One must not be in the least prepossessed in favour of the real existence of the thing, but must preserve complete indifference in this respect, in order to play the part of judge in matters of taste.

This proposition, which is of the utmost importance, cannot be better explained than by contrasting the pure disinterested[2] delight which appears in the judgement of taste with that allied to an interest—especially if we can also assure ourselves that there are no other kinds of interest beyond those presently to be mentioned.

§ 3. *Delight* IN THE AGREEABLE *is coupled with interest*

That is AGREEABLE *which the senses find pleasing in sensation.* This at once affords a convenient opportunity for condemning and directing particular attention to a prevalent confusion of the double meaning of which the word *sensation* is capable. All delight (as is said or thought) is itself sensation (of a pleasure). Consequently everything that pleases, and for the very reason that it pleases, is agreeable—and according to its different degrees, or its relations to other agreeable sensations, is attractive, charming, delicious, enjoyable, etc. But if this is conceded, then impressions of sense, which determine inclination, or principles of reason, which determine the will, or mere contemplated forms of intuition, which determine judgement, are all on a par in everything relevant to their effect upon the feeling of pleasure, for this would be agreeableness in the sensation of one's state; and since, in the last resort, all the elaborate work of our faculties must issue in and unite in the practical as its goal, we could credit our faculties with no other appreciation of things and the worth of things, than that consisting in the gratification which they promise. How this is attained is in the end immaterial; and, as the choice of the means is here the only thing that can make a difference, men might indeed blame one another for folly or imprudence, but never for baseness or wickedness; for they are all, each according to his own way of looking at things, pursuing one goal, which for each is the gratification in question.

When a modification of the feeling of pleasure or displeasure is termed *sensation,* this expression is given quite a different meaning to that which it bears when I call the representation of a thing (through sense as a receptivity pertaining to the faculty of knowledge) sensation. For in the latter case the representation is referred to the object, but in the former it is referred solely to the subject and is not available for any cognition, not even for that by which the subject *cognizes* itself.

Now in the above definition the word *sensation* is used to denote an objective representation of sense; and, to avoid continually running the risk of misinterpretation, we shall call that which must always remain purely subjective, and is absolutely incapable of forming a representation of an object, by the familiar name of *feeling.*[3] The green colour of the meadows belongs to *objective* sensation, as the perception of an object of sense; but its agreeableness to *subjective* sensation, by which no object is represented; i.e., to feeling, through which the object is regarded as an object of delight (which involves no cognition of the object).

Now, that a judgement on an object by which its agreeableness is affirmed, expresses an interest in it, is evident from the fact that through sensation it provokes a desire for similar objects, consequently the delight presupposes, not the simple judgement about it, but the bearing its real existence has upon my state so far as affected by such an object. Hence we do not merely say of the agreeable that it *pleases*, but that it *gratifies*. I do not accord it a simple approval, but inclination is aroused by it, and where agreeableness is of the liveliest type a

[1] [Cf. pp. 485, 520.]

[2] A judgement upon an object of our delight may be wholly *disinterested* but withal very *interesting*,* i.e., it relies on no interest, but it produces one. Of this kind are all pure moral judgements. But, of themselves judgements of taste do not even set up any interest whatsoever. Only in society is it *interesting* to have taste—a point which will be explained in the sequel.

* [Cf. pp. 520, *et seq.;* 522, *et seq.* Also Cf. *Fundamental Principles of the Metaphysic of Morals*, p. 265.]

[3] [Cf. footnote in the first section of the *Introduction to the Metaphysic of Morals,* p. 385.]

judgement on the character of the object is so entirely out of place that those who are always intent only on enjoyment (for that is the word used to denote intensity of gratification) would fain dispense with all judgement.

§4. *Delight* IN THE GOOD *is coupled with interest*

THAT is *good* which by means of reason commends itself by its mere concept. We call that *good for something* (useful) which only pleases as a means; but that which pleases on its own account we call *good in itself*. In both cases the concept of an end is implied, and consequently the relation of reason to (at least possible) willing, and thus a delight in the *existence* of an object or action, i.e., some interest or other.

To deem something good, I must always know what sort of a thing the object is intended to be, i. e., I must have a concept of it. That is not necessary to enable me to see beauty in a thing. Flowers, free patterns, lines aimlessly intertwining—technically termed foliage—have no signification, depend upon no definite concept, and yet please. Delight in the beautiful must depend upon the reflection on an object precursory to some (not definitely determined) concept. It is thus also differentiated from the agreeable, which rests entirely upon sensation.

In many cases, no doubt, the *agreeable* and the *good* seem convertible terms. Thus it is commonly said that all (especially lasting) gratification is of itself good; which is almost equivalent to saying that to be permanently agreeable and to be good are identical. But it is readily apparent that this is merely a vicious confusion of words, for the concepts appropriate to these expressions are far from interchangeable. The agreeable, which, as such, represents the object solely in relation to sense, must in the first instance be brought under principles of reason through the concept of an end, to be, as an object of will, called good. But that the reference to delight is wholly different where what gratifies is at the same time called *good*, is evident from the fact that with the good the question always is whether it is mediately or immediately good, i. e., useful or good in itself; whereas with the agreeable this point can never arise, since the word always means what pleases immediately—and it is just the same with what I call *beautiful*.

Even in everyday parlance, a distinction is drawn between the agreeable and the good. We do not scruple to say of a dish that stimulates the palate with spices and other condiments that it is agreeable—owning all the while that it is not good: because, while it immediately *satisfies* the senses, it is mediately displeasing, i. e., in the eye of reason that looks ahead to the consequences. Even in our estimate of health, this same distinction may be traced. To all that possess it, it is immediately agreeable—at least negatively, i. e., as remoteness of all bodily pains. But, if we are to say that it is good, we must further apply to reason to direct it to ends, that is, we must regard it as a state that puts us in a congenial mood for all we have to do. Finally, in respect of happiness every one believes that the greatest aggregate of the pleasures of life, taking duration as well as number into account, merits the name of a true, nay even of the highest, good. But reason sets its face against this too. Agreeableness is enjoyment. But if this is all that we are bent on, it would be foolish to be scrupulous about the means that procure it for us—whether it be obtained passively by the bounty of nature or actively and by the work of our own hands. But that there is any intrinsic worth in the real existence of a man who merely lives for *enjoyment*, however busy he may be in this respect, even when in so doing he serves others—all equally with himself intent only on enjoyment —as an excellent means to that one end, and does so, moreover, because through sympathy he shares all their gratifications—this is a view to which reason will never let itself be brought round. Only by what a man does heedless of enjoyment, in complete freedom, and independently of what he can procure passively from the hand of nature, does he give to his existence, as the real existence of a person, an absolute worth. Happiness, with all its plethora of pleasures, is far from being an unconditioned good.[1]

But, despite all this difference between the agreeable and the good, they both agree in being invariably coupled with an interest in their object. This is true, not alone of the agreeable, § 3, and of the mediately good, i. e., the useful, which pleases as a means to some pleasure, but also of that which is good absolutely and from every point of view, namely the moral good which carries with it the highest interest. For the good is the object of will, i. e., of a rationally determined faculty of desire). But to will

[1] An obligation to enjoyment is a patent absurdity. And the same, then, must also be said of a supposed obligation to actions that have merely enjoyment for their aim, no matter how spiritually this enjoyment may be refined in thought (or embellished), and even if it be a mystical, so-called heavenly, enjoyment.

something, and to take a delight in its existence, i.e., to take an interest in it, are identical.

§ 5. *Comparison of the three specifically different kinds of delight*

Both the agreeable and the good involve a reference to the faculty of desire, and are thus attended, the former with a delight pathologically conditioned (by stimuli), the latter with a pure practical delight. Such delight is determined not merely by the representation of the object, but also by the represented bond of connection between the subject and the real existence of the object. It is not merely the object, but also its real existence, that pleases. On the other hand, the judgement of taste is simply *contemplative*, i. e., it is a judgement which is indifferent as to the existence of an object, and only decides how its character stands with the feeling of pleasure and displeasure. But not even is this contemplation itself directed to concepts; for the judgement of taste is not a cognitive judgement (neither a theoretical one nor a practical), and hence, also, is not *grounded* on concepts, nor yet *intentionally directed* to them.

The agreeable, the beautiful, and the good thus denote three different relations of representations to the feeling of pleasure and displeasure, as a feeling in respect of which we distinguish different objects or modes of representation. Also, the corresponding expressions which indicate our satisfaction in them are different. The *agreeable* is what GRATIFIES a man; the *beautiful* what simply PLEASES him; the *good* what is ESTEEMED (*approved*), i.e., that on which he sets an objective worth. Agreeableness is a significant factor even with irrational animals; beauty has purport and significance only for human beings, i.e., for beings at once animal and rational (but not merely for them as rational—intelligent beings—but only for them as at once animal and rational); whereas the good is good for every rational being in general—a proposition which can only receive its complete justification and explanation in the sequel. Of all these three kinds of delight, that of taste in the beautiful may be said to be the one and only disinterested and *free* delight; for, with it, no interest, whether of sense or reason, extorts approval. And so we may say that delight, in the three cases mentioned, is related to *inclination*, to *favour*, or to *respect*. For FAVOUR is the only free liking. An object of inclination, and one which a law of reason imposes upon our desire, leaves us no freedom to turn anything into an object of pleasure. All interest presupposes a want, or calls one forth; and, being a ground determining approval, deprives the judgement on the object of its freedom.

So far as the interest of inclination in the case of the agreeable goes, every one says "Hunger is the best sauce; and people with a healthy appetite relish everything, so long as it is something they can eat." Such delight, consequently, gives no indication of taste having anything to say to the choice. Only when men have got all they want can we tell who among the crowd has taste or not. Similarly there may be correct habits (conduct) without virtue, politeness without good-will, propriety without honour, etc. For where the moral law dictates, there is, objectively, no room left for free choice as to what one has to do; and to show taste in the way one carries out these dictates, or in estimating the way others do so, is a totally different matter from displaying the moral frame of one's mind. For the latter involves a command and produces a need of something, whereas moral taste only plays with the objects of delight without devoting itself sincerely to any.

Definition of the Beautiful derived from the First Moment

Taste is the faculty of estimating an object or a mode of representation by means of a delight or aversion *apart from any interest*. The object of such a delight is called *beautiful*.

Second Moment. *Of the Judgement of Taste: Moment of Quantity*

§ 6. *The beautiful is that which, apart from concepts, is represented as the Object of a* UNIVERSAL *delight.*

This definition of the beautiful is deducible from the foregoing definition of it as an object of delight apart from any interest. For where any one is conscious that his delight in an object is with him independent of interest, it is inevitable that he should look on the object as one containing a ground of delight for all men. For, since the delight is not based on any inclination of the subject (or on any other deliberate interest), but the subject feels himself completely *free* in respect of the liking which he accords to the object, he can find as reason for his delight no personal conditions to which his own subjective self might alone be party. Hence he must regard it as resting on what he may also presuppose in every other person; and therefore he must believe that he has reason for demanding a similar delight from every one. Accordingly he will speak of the beautiful as if beauty were a quality of the object and the judgement logical (forming a cognition of the object by concepts of it); although it is only aesthetic, and contains merely a reference of the representation of the object to the subject; because it still bears this resemblance to the logical judgement, that it may be presupposed to be valid for all men. But this universality cannot spring from concepts. For from concepts there is no transition to the feeling of pleasure or displeasure (save in the case of pure practical laws, which, however, carry an interest with them; and such an interest does not attach to the pure judgement of taste). The result is that the judgement of taste, with its attendant consciousness of detachment from all interest, must involve a claim to validity for all men, and must do so apart from universality attached to objects, i. e., there must be coupled with it a claim to subjective universality.

§ 7. *Comparison of the beautiful with the agreeable and the good by means of the above characteristic*

As regards the *agreeable*, every one concedes that his judgement, which he bases on a private feeling, and in which he declares that an object pleases him, is restricted merely to himself personally. Thus he does not take it amiss if, when he says that Canary-wine is agreeable, another corrects the expression and reminds him that he ought to say: "It is agreeable *to me*." This applies not only to the taste of the tongue, the palate, and the throat, but to what may with any one be agreeable to eye or ear. A violet colour is to one soft and lovely: to another dull and faded. One man likes the tone of wind instruments, another prefers that of string instruments. To quarrel over such points with the idea of condemning another's judgement as incorrect when it differs from our own, as if the opposition between the two judgements were logical, would be folly. With the agreeable, therefore, the axiom holds good: *Every one has his own taste* (that of sense).

The beautiful stands on quite a different footing. It would, on the contrary, be ridiculous if any one who plumed himself on his taste were to think of justifying himself by saying: "This object (the building we see, the dress that person has on, the concert we hear, the poem submitted to our criticism) is beautiful *for me*." For if it merely pleases *him*, he must not call it *beautiful*. Many things may for him possess charm and agreeableness—no one cares about that; but when he puts a thing on a pedestal and calls it beautiful, he demands the same delight from others. He judges not merely for himself, but for all men, and then speaks of beauty as if it were a property of things. Thus he says the *thing* is beautiful; and it is not as if he counted on others agreeing in his judgement of liking owing to his having found them in such agreement on a number of occasions, but he *demands* this agreement of them. He blames them if they judge differently, and denies them taste, which he still requires of them as something they ought to have; and to this extent it is not open to men to say: "Every one has his own taste." This would be equivalent to saying that there is no such thing at all as taste, i. e., no aesthetic judgement capable of making a rightful claim upon the assent of all men.

Yet even in the case of the agreeable, we find that the estimates men form do betray a prevalent agreement among them, which leads to our crediting some with taste and denying it to others, and that, too, not as an organic sense but as a critical faculty in respect of the agreeable generally. So of one who knows how to entertain his guests with pleasures (of enjoyment through all the senses) in such a way that one and all are pleased, we say that he has taste. But the universality here is only understood in a comparative sense; and the rules that apply are, like all empirical rules, *general* only, not *universal*, the latter being what the judgement of taste upon the beautiful deals or claims to deal in. It is a judgement in respect of sociability so far as resting on empirical rules. In respect of the good, it is true that judgements also rightly assert a claim to validity for every one; but the good is only represented as an object of universal delight *by means of a concept*, which is the case neither with the agreeable nor the beautiful.

§ 8. *In a judgement of taste the universality of delight is only represented as subjective*

THIS particular form of the universality of an aesthetic judgement, which is to be met in a judgement of taste, is a significant feature, not for the logician certainly, but for the transcendental philosopher. It calls for no small effort on his part to discover its origin, but in return it brings to light a property of our cognitive faculty which, without this analysis, would have remained unknown.

First, one must get firmly into one's mind that by the judgement of taste (upon the beautiful) the delight in an object is imputed to *every one,* yet without being founded on a concept (for then it would be the good), and that this claim to universality is such an essential factor of a judgement by which we describe anything as *beautiful,* that were it not for its being present to the mind it would never enter into any one's head to use this expression, but everything that pleased without a concept would be ranked as agreeable. For in respect of the agreeable, every one is allowed to have his own opinion, and no one insists upon others agreeing with his judgement of taste, which is what is invariably done in the judgement of taste about beauty. The first of these I may call the *taste of sense,* the second, the *taste of reflection:* the first laying down judgements merely private, the second, on the other hand, judgements ostensibly of general validity (public), but both alike being aesthetic (not practical) judgements about an object merely in respect of the bearings of its representation on the feeling of pleasure or displeasure. Now it does seem strange that while with the taste of sense it is not alone experience that shows that its judgement (of pleasure or displeasure in something) is not universally valid, but every one willingly refrains from imputing this agreement to others (despite the frequent actual prevalence of a considerable consensus of general opinion even in these judgements), the taste of reflection, which, as experience teaches, has often enough to put up with a rude dismissal of its claims to universal validity of its judgement (upon the beautiful), can (as it actually does) find it possible for all that to formulate judgements capable of demanding this agreement in its universality. Such agreement it does in fact require from every one for each of its judgements of taste—the persons who pass these judgements not quarreling over the possibility of such a claim, but only failing in particular cases to come to terms as to the correct application of this faculty.

First of all we have here to note that a universality which does not rest upon concepts of the object (even though these are only empirical) is in no way logical, but aesthetic, i. e., does not involve any objective quantity of the judgement, but only one that is subjective. For this universality I use the expression *general validity,* which denotes the validity of the reference of a representation, not to the cognitive faculties, but to the feeling of pleasure or displeasure for every subject. (The same expression, however, may also be employed for the logical quantity of the judgement, provided we add *objective* universal validity, to distinguish it from the merely subjective validity which is always aesthetic.)

Now a judgement that has *objective universal validity* has always got the subjective also, i.e., if the judgement is valid for everything which is contained under a given concept, it is valid also for all who represent an object by means of this concept. But from a *subjective universal validity,* i. e., the aesthetic, that does not rest on any concept, no conclusion can be drawn to the logical; because judgements of that kind have no bearing upon the object. But for this very reason the aesthetic universality attributed to a judgement must also be of a special kind, seeing that it does not join the predicate of beauty to the concept of the *object* taken in its entire logical sphere, and yet does extend this predicate over the whole sphere of *judging subjects.*

In their logical quantity, all judgements of taste are *singular* judgements.[1] For, since I must present the object immediately to my feeling of pleasure or displeasure, and that, too, without the aid of concepts, such judgements cannot have the quantity of judgements with objective general validity. Yet by taking the singular representation of the object of the judgement of taste, and by comparison converting it into a concept according to the conditions determining that judgement, we can arrive at a logically universal judgement. For instance, by a judgement of the taste I describe the rose at which I am looking as beautiful. The judgement, on the other hand, resulting from the comparison of a number of singular representations: "Roses in general are beautiful,"[2] is no longer pronounced as a purely aesthetic judgement, but as a logical judgement founded on one that is aesthetic. Now the judgement, "The rose is agreeable" (to smell) is also, no doubt, an aesthetic and singular judgement, but then it is not one of taste but of sense. For it has this point of difference from a judgement of taste, that the latter imports an *aesthetic quantity* of universality, i. e., of validity for everyone which is not to be met with in a judgement upon the agreeable. It is only judgements upon the good which, while also determining the delight in an object, possess logical and not mere aesthetic universality; for it is as involving a cognition of the object that they are valid of it, and on that account valid for everyone.

In forming an estimate of objects merely

[1] [Cf. p. 515.]
[2] [Cf. p. 485, p. 486, and p. 515.]

from concepts, all representation of beauty goes by the board. There can, therefore, be no rule according to which any one is to be compelled to recognize anything as beautiful. Whether a dress, a house, or a flower is beautiful is a matter upon which one declines to allow one's judgement to be swayed by any reasons or principles. We want to get a look at the object with our own eyes, just as if our delight depended on sensation.[1] And yet, if upon so doing, we call the object beautiful, we believe ourselves to be speaking with a universal voice, and lay claim to the concurrence of everyone, whereas no private sensation would be decisive except for the observer alone and *his* liking.

Here, now, we may perceive that nothing is postulated in the judgement of taste but such a *universal voice* in respect of delight that it is not mediated by concepts; consequently, only the *possibility* of an aesthetic judgement capable of being at the same time deemed valid for everyone. The judgement of taste itself does not *postulate* the agreement of everyone (for it is only competent for a logically universal judgement to do this, in that it is able to bring forward reasons); it only *imputes* this agreement to everyone, as an instance of the rule in respect of which it looks for confirmation, not from concepts, but from the concurrence of others. The universal voice is, therefore, only an idea—resting upon grounds the investigation of which is here postponed. It may be a matter of uncertainty whether a person who thinks he is laying down a judgement of taste is, in fact, judging in conformity with that idea; but that this idea is what is contemplated in his judgement, and that, consequently, it is meant to be a judgement of taste, is proclaimed by his use of the expression "beauty." For himself he can be certain on the point from his mere consciousness of the separation of everything belonging to the agreeable and the good from the delight remaining to him; and this is all for which he promises himself the agreement of everyone—a claim which, under these conditions, he would also be warranted in making, were it not that he frequently sinned against them, and thus passed an erroneous judgement of taste.

§ 9. *Investigation of the question of the relative priority in a judgement of taste of the feeling of pleasure and the estimating of the object*

THE solution of this problem is the key to the Critique of taste, and so is worthy of all attention.

Were the pleasure in a given object to be the antecedent, and were the universal communicability of this pleasure to be all that the judgement of taste is meant to allow to the representation of the object, such a sequence would be self-contradictory. For a pleasure of that kind would be nothing but the feeling of mere agreeableness to the senses, and so, from its very nature, would possess no more than private validity, seeing that it would be immediately dependent on the representation through which the object *is given*.

Hence it is the universal capacity for being communicated incident to the mental state in the given representation which, as the subjective condition of the judgement of taste, must be, fundamental, with the pleasure in the object as its consequent.[2] Nothing, however, is capable of being universally communicated but cognition and representation so far as appurtenant to cognition. For it is only as thus appurtenant that the representation is objective, and it is this alone that gives it a universal point of reference with which the power of representation of every one is obliged to harmonize. If, then, the determining ground of the judgement as to this universal communicability of the representation is to be merely subjective, that is to say, to be conceived independently of any concept of the object, it can be nothing else than the mental state that presents itself in the mutual relation of the powers of representation so far as they refer a given representation *to cognition in general.*

The cognitive powers brought into play by this representation are here engaged in a free play, since no definite concept restricts them to a particular rule of cognition. Hence the mental state in this representation must be one of a feeling of the free play of the powers of representation in a given representation for a cognition in general. Now a representation, whereby an object is given, involves, in order that it may become a source of cognition at all, *imagination* for bringing together the manifold of intuition, and *understanding* for the unity of the concept uniting the representations. This state of *free play* of the cognitive faculties attending a representation by which an object is given must admit of universal communication: because cognition, as a definition of the object with which given representations (in any subject whatever) are to accord, is the one and only representation which is valid for everyone.

As the subjective universal communicability

[1] [Cf. p. 514.]

[2] [Cf. § 37.]

of the mode of representation in a judgement of taste is to subsist apart from the presupposition of any definite concept, it can be nothing else than the mental state present in the free play of imagination and understanding (so far as these are in mutual accord, as is requisite for *cognition in general*); for we are conscious that this subjective relation suitable for a cognition in general must be just as valid for every one, and consequently as universally communicable, as is any indeterminate cognition, which always rests upon that relation as its subjective condition.

Now this purely subjective (aesthetic) estimating of the object, or of the representation through which it is given, is antecedent to the pleasure in it, and is the basis of this pleasure in the harmony of the cognitive faculties. Again, the above-described universality of the subjective conditions of estimating objects forms the sole foundation of this universal subjective validity of the delight which we connect with the representation of the object that we call *beautiful.*

That an ability to communicate one's mental state, even though it be only in respect of our cognitive faculties, is attended with a pleasure, is a fact which might easily be demonstrated from the natural propensity of mankind to social life, i.e., empirically and psychologically. But what we have here in view calls for something more than this. In a judgement of taste, the pleasure felt by us is exacted from every one else as necessary, just as if, when we call something beautiful, beauty was to be regarded as a quality of the object forming part of its inherent determination according to concepts; although beauty is for itself, apart from any reference to the feeling of the subject, nothing. But the discussion of this question must be reserved until we have answered the further one of whether, and how, aesthetic judgements are possible *a priori*.

At present we are exercised with the lesser question of the way in which we become conscious, in a judgement of taste, of a reciprocal subjective common accord of the powers of cognition. Is it aesthetically by sensation and our mere internal sense? Or is it intellectually by consciousness of our intentional activity in bringing these powers into play?

Now if the given representation occasioning the judgement of taste were a concept which united understanding and imagination in the estimate of the object so as to give a cognition of the object, the consciousness of this relation would be intellectual (as in the objective schematism of judgement dealt with in the Critique). But, then, in that case the judgement would not be laid down with respect to pleasure and displeasure, and so would not be a judgement of taste. But, now, the judgement of taste determines the object, independently of concepts, in respect of delight and of the predicate of beauty. There is, therefore, no other way for the subjective unity of the relation in question to make itself known than by sensation. The quickening of both faculties (imagination and understanding) to an indefinite, but yet, thanks to the given representation, harmonious activity, such as belongs to cognition generally, is the sensation whose universal communicability is postulated by the judgement of taste. An objective relation can, of course, only be thought, yet in so far as, in respect of its conditions, it is subjective, it may be felt in its effect upon the mind, and, in the case of a relation (like that of the powers of representation to a faculty of cognition generally) which does not rest on any concept, no other consciousness of it is possible beyond that through sensation of its effect upon the mind—an effect consisting in the more facile play of both mental powers (imagination and understanding) as quickened by their mutual accord. A representation which is singular and independent of comparison with other representations, and, being such, yet accords with the conditions of the universality that is the general concern of understanding, is one that brings the cognitive faculties into that proportionate accord which we require for all cognition and which we therefore deem valid for every one who is so constituted as to judge by means of understanding and sense conjointly (i.e., for every man).

Definition of the Beautiful drawn from the Second Moment

The *beautiful* is that which, apart from a concept, pleases universally.

THIRD MOMENT. *Of Judgements of Taste: Moment of the* RELATION *of the Ends brought under Review in such Judgements*

§ 10. *Finality in general*

LET us define the meaning of "an end" in transcendental terms (i.e., without presupposing anything empirical, such as the feeling of pleasure). An end is the object of a concept so far as this concept is regarded as the cause of the object (the real ground of its possibility);

and the causality of a *concept* in respect of its *object* is finality (*forma finalis*). Where, then, not the cognition of an object merely, but the object itself (its form or real existence) as an effect, is thought to be possible only through a concept of it, there we imagine an end. The representation of the effect is here the determining ground of its cause and takes the lead of it. The consciousness of the causality of a representation in respect of the state of the subject as one tending *to preserve a continuance* of that state, may here be said to denote in a general way what is called pleasure; whereas displeasure is that representation which contains the ground for converting the state of the representations into their opposite (for hindering or removing them).[1]

The faculty of desire, so far as determinable only through concepts, i.e., so as to act in conformity with the representation of an end, would be the will.[2] But an object, or state of mind, or even an action may, although its possibility does not necessarily presuppose the representation of an end, be called final simply on account of its possibility being only explicable and intelligible for us by virtue of an assumption on our part of fundamental causality according to ends, i.e., a will that would have so ordained it according to a certain represented rule. Finality, therefore, may exist apart from an end, in so far as we do not locate the causes of this form in a will, but yet are able to render the explanation of its possibility intelligible to ourselves only by deriving it from a will. Now we are not always obliged to look with the eye of reason into what we observe (i.e., to consider it in its possibility). So we may at least observe a finality of form, and trace it in objects—though by reflection only—without resting it on an end (as the material of the *nexus finalis*).

§ 11. *The sole foundation of the judgement of taste is the* FORM OF FINALITY *of an object (or mode of representing it)*

WHENEVER an end is regarded as a source of delight, it always imports an interest as determining ground of the judgement on the object of pleasure. Hence the judgement of taste cannot rest on any subjective end as its ground. But neither can any representation of an objective end, i.e., of the possibility of the object itself on principles of final connection, determine the judgement of taste, and, consequently, neither can any concept of the good. For the judgement of taste is an aesthetic and not a cognitive judgement, and so does not deal with any *concept* of the nature or of the internal or external possibility, by this or that cause, of the object, but simply with the relative bearing of the representative powers so far as determined by a representation.

Now this relation, present when an object is characterized as beautiful, is coupled with the feeling of pleasure. This pleasure is by the judgement of taste pronounced valid for every one; hence an agreeableness attending the representation is just as incapable of containing the determining ground of the judgement as the representation of the perfection of the object or the concept of the good. We are thus left with the subjective finality in the representation of an object, exclusive of any end (objective or subjective)—consequently the bare form of finality in the representation whereby an object is *given* to us, so far as we are conscious of it—as that which is alone capable of constituting the delight which, apart from any concept, we estimate as universally communicable, and so of forming the determining ground of the judgement of taste.

§ 12. *The judgement of taste rests upon* a priori *grounds*

To determine *a priori* the connection of the feeling of pleasure or displeasure as an effect, with some representation or other (sensation or concept) as its cause, is utterly impossible; for that would be a causal relation which (with objects of experience) is always one that can only be cognized *a posteriori* and with the help of experience. True, in the *Critique of Practical Reason* we did actually derive *a priori* from universal moral concepts the feeling of respect (as a particular and peculiar modification of this feeling which does not strictly answer either to the pleasure or displeasure which we receive from empirical objects). But there we were further able to cross the border of experience and call in aid a causality resting on a supersensible attribute of the subject, namely that of freedom. But even there it was not this *feeling* exactly that we deduced from the idea of the moral as cause, but from this was derived simply the determination of the will. But the mental state present in the determination of the will by any means is at once in itself a feeling of pleasure and identical with it, and so does not issue from it as an effect. Such an effect must only be assumed where the concept of the moral as a good precedes the determination of the will by the

[1] [Cf. p. 485.]
[2] [Cf. *Introduction to the Metaphysic of Morals*, sect. i., pp. 385–387.]

aw; for in that case it would be futile to derive the pleasure combined with the concept from this concept as a mere cognition.

Now the pleasure in aesthetic judgements stands on a similar footing: only that here it is merely contemplative and does not bring about an interest in the object; whereas in the moral judgement it is practical. The consciousness of mere formal finality in the play of the cognitive faculties of the subject attending a representation whereby an object is given, is the pleasure itself, because it involves a determining ground of the subject's activity in respect of the quickening of its cognitive powers, and thus an internal causality (which is final) in respect of cognition generally, but without being limited to a definite cognition, and consequently a mere form of the subjective finality of a representation in an aesthetic judgement. This pleasure is also in no way practical, neither resembling that form the pathological ground of agreeableness nor that from the intellectual ground of the represented good. But still it involves an inherent causality, that, namely, of *preserving a continuance* of the state of the representation itself and the active engagement of the cognitive powers without ulterior aim. We *dwell* on the contemplation of the beautiful because this contemplation strengthens and reproduces itself. The case is analogous (but analogous only) to the way we linger on a charm in the representation of an object which keeps arresting the attention, the mind all the while remaining passive.

§ 13. *The pure judgement of taste is independent of charm and emotion*

Every interest vitiates the judgement of taste and robs it of its impartiality. This is especially so where, instead of, like the interest of reason, making finality take the lead of the feeling of pleasure, it grounds it upon this feeling—which is what always happens in aesthetic judgements upon anything so far as it gratifies or pains. Hence judgements so influenced can either lay no claim at all to a universally valid delight, or else must abate their claim in proportion as sensations of the kind in question enter into the determining grounds of taste. Taste that requires an added element of *charm* and *emotion* for its delight, not to speak of adopting this as the measure of its approval, has not yet emerged from barbarism.

And yet charms are frequently not alone ranked with beauty (which ought properly to be a question merely of the form) as supplementary to the aesthetic universal delight, but they have been accredited as intrinsic beauties, and consequently the matter of delight passed off for the form. This is a misconception which, like many others that have still an underlying element of truth, may be removed by a careful definition of these concepts.

A judgement of taste which is uninfluenced by charm or emotion (though these may be associated[1] with the delight in the beautiful), and whose determining ground, therefore, is simply finality of form, is *a pure judgement of taste.*

§ 14. *Exemplification*

Aesthetic, just like theoretical (logical) judgements, are divisible into empirical and pure. The first are those by which agreeableness or disagreeableness, the second those by which beauty is predicated of an object or its mode of representation. The former are judgements of sense (material aesthetic judgements), the latter (as formal) alone judgements of taste proper.

A judgement of taste, therefore, is only pure so far as its determining ground is tainted with no merely empirical delight. But such a taint is always present where charm or emotion have a share in the judgement by which something is to be described as beautiful.

Here now there is a recrudescence of a number of specious pleas that go the length of putting forward the case that charm is not merely a necessary ingredient of beauty, but is even of itself sufficient to merit the name of beautiful. A mere colour, such as the green of a plot of grass, or a mere tone (as distinguished from sound or noise), like that of a violin, is described by most people as in itself beautiful, notwithstanding the fact that both seem to depend merely on the matter of the representations—in other words, simply on sensation—which only entitles them to be called agreeable. But it will at the same time be observed that sensations of colour as well as of tone are only entitled to be immediately regarded as beautiful where, in either case, they are *pure*. This is a determination which at once goes to their form, and it is the only one which these representations possess that admits with certainty of being universally communicated. For it is not to be assumed that even the quality of the sensations agrees in all subjects, and we can hardly take it for granted that the agreeableness of a colour, or of the tone of a musical instrument, which we judge to be preferable to that of another, is given a like preference in the estimate of every one.

Assuming with Euler that colours are isoch-

[1] [Cf. pp. 486, 495.]

ronous vibrations (*pulsus*) of the aether, as tones are of the air set in vibration by sound, and, what is most important, that the mind not alone perceives by sense their effect in stimulating the organs, but also, by reflection, the regular play of the impressions (and consequently the form in which different representations are united)—which I, still, in no way doubt—then colour and tone would not be mere sensations. They would be nothing short of formal determinations of the unity of a manifold of sensations, and in that case could even be ranked as intrinsic beauties.

But the purity of a simple mode of sensation means that its uniformity is not disturbed or broken by any foreign sensation. It belongs merely to the form; for abstraction may there be made from the quality of the mode of such sensation (what colour or tone, if any, it represents). For this reason, all simple colours are regarded as beautiful so far as pure. Composite colours have not this advantage, because, not being simple, there is no standard for estimating whether they should be called pure or impure.

But as for the beauty ascribed to the object on account of its form, and the supposition that it is capable of being enhanced by charm, this is a common error and one very prejudicial to genuine, uncorrupted, sincere taste. Nevertheless charms may be added to beauty to lend to the mind, beyond a bare delight, an adventitious interest in the representation of the object, and thus to advocate taste and its cultivation. This applies especially where taste is as yet crude and untrained. But they are positively subversive of the judgement of taste, if allowed to obtrude themselves as grounds of estimating beauty. For so far are they from contributing to beauty that it is only where taste is still weak and untrained that, like aliens, they are admitted as a favour, and only on terms that they do not violate that beautiful form.

In painting, sculpture, and in fact in all the formative arts, in architecture and horticulture, so far as fine arts, the *design* is what is essential. Here it is not what gratifies in sensation but merely what pleases by its form, that is the fundamental prerequisite for taste. The colours which give brilliancy to the sketch are part of the charm. They may no doubt, in their own way, enliven the object for sensation, but make it really worth looking at and beautiful they cannot. Indeed, more often than not the requirements of the beautiful form restrict them to a very narrow compass, and, even where charm is admitted, it is only this form that gives them a place of honour.

All form of objects of sense (both of external and also, mediately, of internal sense) is either *figure* or *play*. In the latter case it is either play of figures (in space: mimic and dance), or mere play of sensations (in time). The *charm* of colours, or of the agreeable tones of instruments, may be added: but the *design* in the former and the *composition* in the latter constitute the proper object of the pure judgement of taste. To say that the purity alike of colours and of tones, or their variety and contrast, seem to contribute to beauty, is by no means to imply that, because in themselves agreeable, they therefore yield an addition to the delight in the form and one on a par with it. The real meaning rather is that they make this form more clearly, definitely, and completely intuitable, and besides stimulate the representation by their charm, as they excite and sustain the attention directed to the object itself.

Even what is called *ornamentation* (*parerga*), i.e., what is only an adjunct and not an intrinsic constituent in the complete representation of the object, in augmenting the delight of taste does so only by means of its form. Thus it is with the frames of pictures or the drapery on statues, or the colonnades of palaces. But if the ornamentation does not itself enter into the composition of the beautiful form—if it is introduced like a gold frame merely to win approval for the picture by means of its charm—it is then called *finery* and takes away from the genuine beauty.

Emotion—a sensation where an agreeable feeling is produced merely by means of a momentary check followed by a more powerful outpouring of the vital force—is quite foreign to beauty. Sublimity (with which the feeling of emotion is connected) requires, however, a different standard of estimation from that relied upon by taste. A pure judgement of taste has, then, for its determining ground neither charm nor emotion, in a word, no sensation as matter of the aesthetic judgement.

§ 15. *The judgement of taste is entirely independent of the concept of perfection*

Objective finality can only be cognized by means of a reference of the manifold to a definite end, and hence only through a concept. This alone makes it clear that the beautiful, which is estimated on the ground of a mere formal finality, i.e., a finality apart from an end, is wholly independent of the representation of the good. For the latter presupposes an objective finality, i.e., the reference of the object to a definite end.

Objective finality is either external, i.e., the *utility*, or internal, i. e., the *perfection*, of the object. That the delight in an object on account of which we call it beautiful is incapable of resting on the representation of its utility, is abundantly evident from the two preceding articles; for in that case, it would not be an immediate delight in the object, which latter is the essential condition of the judgement upon beauty. But in an objective, internal finality, i.e., perfection, we have what is more akin to the predicate of beauty, and so this has been held even by philosophers of reputation to be convertible with beauty, though subject to the qualification: *where it is thought in a confused way.*[1] In a critique of taste it is of the utmost importance to decide whether beauty is really reducible to the concept of perfection.

For estimating objective finality we always require the concept of an end, and, where such finality has to be, not an external one (utility), but an internal one, the concept of an internal end containing the ground of the internal possibility of the object. Now an end is in general that, the *concept* of which may be regarded as the ground of the possibility of the object itself. So in order to represent an objective finality in a thing we must first have a concept of *what sort of a thing it is to be.* The agreement of the manifold in a thing with this concept (which supplies the rule of its synthesis) is the *qualitative perfection* of the thing. *Quantitative* perfection is entirely distinct from this. It consists in the completeness of anything after its kind, and is a mere concept of quantity (of totality). In its case the question of *what the thing is to be* is regarded as definitely disposed of, and we only ask whether it is possessed of *all* the requisites that go to make it such. What is formal in the representation of a thing, i.e., the agreement of its manifold with a unity (i.e., irrespective of what it is to be), does not, of itself, afford us any cognition whatsoever of objective finality. For since abstraction is made from this unity as *end* (what the thing is to be), nothing is left but the subjective finality of the representations in the mind of the subject intuiting. This gives a certain finality of the representative state of the subject, in which the subject feels itself quite at home in its effort to grasp a given form in the imagination, but no perfection of any object, the latter not being here thought through any concept. For instance, if in a forest I light upon a plot of grass, round which trees stand in a circle, and if I do not then form any representation of an end, as that it is meant to be used, say, for country dances, then not the least hint of a concept of perfection is given by the mere form. To suppose a formal *objective* finality that is yet devoid of an end, i.e., the mere form of a *perfection* (apart from any matter or *concept* of that to which the agreement relates, even though there was the mere general idea of a conformity to law) is a veritable contradiction.

Now the judgement of taste is an aesthetic judgement, i.e., one resting on subjective grounds. No concept can be its determining ground, and hence not one of a definite end. Beauty, therefore, as a formal subjective finality, involves no thought whatsoever of a perfection of the object, as a would-be formal finality which yet, for all that, is objective: and the distinction between the concepts of the beautiful and the good, which represents both as differing only in their logical form, the first being merely a confused, the second a clearly defined, concept of perfection, while otherwise alike in content and origin, all goes for nothing: for then there would be no *specific* difference between them, but the judgement of taste would be just as much a cognitive judgement as one by which something is described as good—just as the man in the street, when he says that deceit is wrong, bases his judgement on confused, but the philosopher on clear grounds, while both appeal in reality to identical principles of reason. But I have already stated that an aesthetic judgement is quite unique, and affords absolutely no (not even a confused) knowledge of the object. It is only through a logical judgement that we get knowledge. The aesthetic judgement, on the other hand, refers the representation, by which an object is given, solely to the subject, and brings to our notice no quality of the object, but only the final form in the determination of the powers of representation engaged upon it. The judgement is called *aesthetic* for the very reason that its determining ground cannot be a concept, but is rather the feeling (of the internal sense) of the concert in the play of the mental powers as a thing only capable of being felt. If, on the other hand, confused concepts, and the objective judgement based on them, are going to be called *aesthetic*, we shall find ourselves with an understanding judging by sense, or a sense representing its objects by concepts—a mere choice of contradictions. The faculty of concepts, be they confused or be they clear, is understanding; and although understanding has (as in all judgements) its role in the judgement of taste, as an

[1] [Cf. *Critique of Pure Reason*, pp. 29–31.]

aesthetic judgement, its role there is not that of a faculty for cognizing an object, but of a faculty for determining that judgement and its representation (without a concept) according to its relation to the subject and its internal feeling, and for doing so in so far as that judgement is possible according to a universal rule.

§ 16. *A judgement of taste by which an object is described as beautiful, under the condition of a definite concept, is not pure*

THERE are two kinds of beauty: free beauty (*pulchritudo vaga*), or beauty which is merely dependent (*pulchritudo adhaerens*). The first presupposes no concept of what the object should be; the second does presuppose such a concept and, with it, an answering perfection of the object. Those of the first kind are said to be (self-subsisting) beauties of this thing or that thing; the other kind of beauty, being attached to a concept (conditioned beauty), is ascribed to objects which come under the concept of a particular end.

Flowers are free beauties of nature. Hardly anyone but a botanist knows the true nature of a flower, and even he, while recognizing in the flower the reproductive organ of the plant, pays no attention to this natural end when using his taste to judge of its beauty. Hence no perfection of any kind—no internal finality, as something to which the arrangement of the manifold is related—underlies this judgement. Many birds (the parrot, the humming-bird, the bird of paradise), and a number of crustacea, are self-subsisting beauties which are not appurtenant to any object defined with respect to its end, but please freely and on their own account. So designs *à la grecque*, foliage for framework or on wall-papers, etc., have no intrinsic meaning; they represent nothing—no object under a definite concept—and are free beauties.[1] We may also rank in the same class what in music are called *fantasias* (without a theme), and, indeed, all music that is not set to words.

In the estimate of a free beauty (according to mere form) we have the pure judgement of taste. No concept is here presupposed of any end for which the manifold should serve the given object, and which the latter, therefore, should represent—an incumbrance which would only restrict the freedom of the imagination that, as it were, is at play in the contemplation of the outward form.

But the beauty of man (including under this head that of a man, woman, or child), the beauty of a horse, or of a building (such as a church palace, arsenal, or summer-house), presuppose a concept of the end that defines what the thing has to be, and consequently a concept of it perfection; and is therefore merely appendant beauty. Now, just as it is a clog on the purity o the judgement of taste to have the agreeable (o sensation) joined with beauty to which properly only the form is relevant, so to combine the good with beauty (the good, namely, of the manifold to the thing itself according to its end) mars its purity.

Much might be added to a building that would immediately please the eye, were it not intended for a church. A figure might be beautified with all manner of flourishes and light but regular lines, as is done by the New Zealanders with their tattooing, were we dealing with anything but the figure of a human being. And here is one whose rugged features might be softened and given a more pleasing aspect, only he has got to be a man, or is, perhaps, a warrior that has to have a warlike appearance.

Now the delight in the manifold of a thing, in reference to the internal end that determines its possibility, is a delight based on a concept, whereas delight in the beautiful is such as does not presuppose any concept, but is immediately coupled with the representation through which the object is given (not through which it is thought). If, now, the judgement of taste in respect of the latter delight is made dependent upon the end involved in the former delight as a judgement of reason, and is thus placed under a restriction, then it is no longer a free and pure judgement of taste.

Taste, it is true, stands to gain by this combination of intellectual delight with the aesthetic. For it becomes fixed, and, while not universal, it enables rules to be prescribed for it in respect of certain definite final objects. But these rules are then not rules of taste, but merely rules for establishing a union of taste with reason, i.e., of the beautiful with the good—rules by which the former becomes available as an intentional instrument in respect of the latter, for the purpose of bringing that temper of the mind which is self-sustaining and of subjective universal validity to the support and maintenance of that mode of thought which, while possessing objective universal validity, can only be preserved by a resolute effort. But, strictly speaking, perfection neither gains by beauty, nor beauty by perfection. The truth is rather this, when we compare the representation through which an object is given to us with the object (in respect of what

[1] [Cf. p. 478, *et seq.*]

t is meant to be) by means of a concept, we cannot help reviewing it also in respect of the sensation in the subject. Hence there results a gain to the *entire faculty* of our representative power when harmony prevails between both states of mind.

In respect of an object with a definite internal end, a judgement of taste would only be pure where the person judging either has no concept of this end, or else makes abstraction from it in his judgement. But in cases like this, although such a person should lay down a correct judgement of taste, since he would be estimating the object as a free beauty, he would still be found fault with by another who saw nothing in its beauty but a dependent quality (i.e., who looked to the end of the object) and would be accused by him of false taste, though both would, in their own way, be judging correctly: the one according to what he had present to his senses, the other according to what was present in his thoughts. This distinction enables us to settle many disputes about beauty on the part of critics; for we may show them how one side is dealing with free beauty, and the other with that which is dependent: the former passing a pure judgement of taste, the latter one that is applied intentionally.

§ 17. *The Ideal of beauty*

THERE can be no objective rule of taste by which what is beautiful may be defined by means of concepts. For every judgement from that source is aesthetic, i.e., its determining ground is the feeling of the subject, and not any concept of an object. It is only throwing away labour to look for a principle of taste that affords a universal criterion of the beautiful by definite concepts; because what is sought is a thing impossible and inherently contradictory. But in the universal communicability of the sensation (of delight or aversion)—a communicability, too, that exists apart from any concept —in the accord, so far as possible, of all ages and nations as to this feeling in the representation of certain objects, we have the empirical criterion, weak indeed and scarce sufficient to raise a presumption, of the derivation of a taste, thus confirmed by examples, from grounds deep-seated and shared alike by all men, underlying their agreement in estimating the forms under which objects are given to them.

For this reason some products of taste are looked on as *exemplary*—not meaning thereby that by imitating others taste may be acquired. For taste must be an original faculty; whereas one who imitates a model, while showing skill commensurate with his success, only displays taste as himself a critic of this model.[1] Hence it follows that the highest model, the archetype of taste, is a mere idea, which each person must beget in his own consciousness, and according to which he must form his estimate of everything that is an object of taste, or that is an example of critical taste, and even of universal taste itself. Properly speaking, an *idea* signifies a concept of reason, and an *ideal* the representation of an individual existence as adequate to an idea. Hence this archetype of taste—which rests, indeed, upon reason's indeterminate idea of a maximum, but is not, however, capable of being represented by means of concepts, but only in an individual presentation—may more appropriately be called the *ideal of the beautiful.* While not having this ideal in our possession, we still strive to beget it within us. But it is bound to be merely an ideal of the imagination, seeing that it rests, not upon concepts, but upon the presentation—the faculty of presentation being the imagination. Now, how do we arrive at such an ideal of beauty? Is it *a priori* or empirically? Further, what species of the beautiful admits of an ideal?

First of all, we do well to observe that the beauty for which an ideal has to be sought cannot be a beauty that is *free and at large,* but must be one *fixed* by a concept of objective finality.[2] Hence it cannot belong to the object of an altogether pure judgement of taste, but must attach to one that is partly intellectual. In other words, where an ideal is to have place among the grounds upon which any estimate is formed, then beneath grounds of that kind there must lie some idea of reason according to determinate concepts, by which the end underlying the internal possibility of the object is determined *a priori.* An ideal of beautiful flowers, of a beautiful suite of furniture, or of a beautiful view, is unthinkable. But, it may also be impossible to represent an ideal of a beauty dependent on definite ends, e.g., a beautiful residence, a beautiful tree, a beautiful garden, etc., presumably because their ends are not sufficiently defined and fixed by their concept, with the result that their

1 Models of taste with respect to the arts of speech must be composed in a dead and learned language; the first, to prevent their having to suffer the changes that inevitably overtake living ones, making dignified expressions become degraded, common ones antiquated, and ones newly coined after a short currency obsolete: the second to ensure its having a grammar that is not subject to the caprices of fashion, but has fixed rules of its own.

2 [Cf. § 16.]

finality is nearly as free as with beauty that is quite *at large*. Only what has in itself the end of its real existence—only *man* that is able himself to determine his ends by reason, or, where he has to derive them from external perception, can still compare them with essential and universal ends, and then further pronounce aesthetically upon their accord with such ends, only he, among all objects in the world, admits, therefore, of an ideal of *beauty*, just as humanity in his person, as intelligence, alone admits of the ideal of *perfection*.

Two factors are here involved. *First*, there is the aesthetic *normal idea*, which is an individual intuition (of the imagination). This represents the norm by which we judge of a man as a member of a particular animal species. *Secondly*, there is the *rational idea*. This deals with the ends of humanity so far as capable of sensuous representation, and converts them into a principle for estimating his outward form, through which these ends are revealed in their phenomenal effect. The normal idea must draw from experience the constituents which it requires for the form of an animal of a particular kind. But the greatest finality in the construction of this form—that which would serve as a universal norm for forming an estimate of each individual of the species in question—the image that, as it were, forms an intentional basis underlying the technic of nature, to which no separate individual, but only the race as a whole, is adequate, has its seat merely in the idea of the judging subject. Yet it is, with all its proportions, an aesthetic idea, and, as such, capable of being fully presented *in concreto* in a model image. Now, how is this effected? In order to render the process to some extent intelligible (for who can wrest nature's whole secret from her?), let us attempt a psychological explanation.

It is of note that the imagination, in a manner quite incomprehensible to us, is able on occasion, even after a long lapse of time, not alone to recall the signs for concepts, but also to reproduce the image and shape of an object out of a countless number of others of a different, or even of the very same, kind. And, further, if the mind is engaged upon comparisons, we may well suppose that it can in actual fact, though the process is unconscious, superimpose as it were one image upon another, and from the coincidence of a number of the same kind arrive at a mean contour which serves as a common standard for all. Say, for instance, a person has seen a thousand full-grown men. Now if he wishes to judge normal size determined upon a comparative estimate, then imagination (to my mind) allows a great number of these images (perhaps the whole thousand) to fall one upon the other, and, if I may be allowed to extend to the case the analogy of optical presentation, in the space where they come most together, and within the contour where the place is illuminated by the greatest concentration of colour, one gets a perception of the *average size*, which alike in height and breadth is equally removed from the extreme limits of the greatest and smallest statures; and this is the stature of a beautiful man. (The same result could be obtained in a mechanical way, by taking the measures of all the thousand, and adding together their heights, and their breadths [and thicknesses], and dividing the sum in each case by a thousand.) But the power of imagination does all this by means of a dynamical effect upon the organ of internal sense, arising from the frequent apprehension of such forms. If, again, for our average man we seek on similar lines for the average head, and for this the average nose, and so on, then we get the figure that underlies the normal idea of a beautiful man in the country where the comparison is instituted. For this reason a Negro must necessarily (under these empirical conditions) have a different normal idea of the beauty of forms from what a white man has, and the Chinaman one different from the European. And the process would be just the same with the *model* of a beautiful horse or dog (of a particular breed). This *normal idea* is not derived from proportions taken from experience *as definite rules*:[1] rather is it according to this idea that rules for forming estimates first become possible. It is an intermediate between all singular intuitions of individuals, with their manifold variations—a floating image for the whole genus, which nature has set as an archetype underlying those of her products that belong to the same species, but which in no single case she

[1] [Cf. p. 489. A partial anticipation of this section is contained in the *Critique of Pure Reason*, p. 173–4. "Such is the constitution of the ideal of reason, which is always based upon determinate conceptions, and serves as a rule and a model for imitation or for criticism. Very different is the nature of the ideals of the imagination. Of these it is impossible to present an intelligible conception; they are a kind of monogram, drawn according to no determinate rule, and forming rather a vague picture—the production of many diverse experiences—than a determinate image. Such are the ideals which painters and physiognomists profess to have in their minds, and which can serve neither as a model for production nor as a standard for appreciation. They may be termed, though improperly, *sensuous ideals*, as they are declared to be models of certain possible empirical intuitions. They cannot, however, furnish rules or standards for explanation or examination."]

seems to have completely attained. But the normal idea is far from giving the complete *archetype* of *beauty* in the genus. It only gives the form that constitutes the indispensable condition of all beauty, and, consequently, only *correctness* in the presentation of the genus. It is, as the famous "Doryphorus" of Polycletus was called, the *rule* (and Myron's "Cow" might be similarly employed for its kind). It cannot, for that very reason, contain anything specifically characteristic; for otherwise it would not be the *normal idea* for the genus. Further, it is not by beauty that its presentation pleases, but merely because it does not contradict any of the conditions under which alone a thing belonging to this genus can be beautiful. The presentation is merely academically correct.[1]

But the *ideal* of the beautiful is still something different from its *normal idea*. For reasons already stated it is only to be sought in the *human figure*. Here the ideal consists in the expression of the *moral*, apart from which the object would not please at once universally and positively (not merely negatively in a presentation academically correct). The visible expression of moral ideas[2] that govern men inwardly can, of course, only be drawn from experience; but their combination with all that our reason connects with the morally good in the idea of the highest finality — benevolence, purity, strength, or equanimity, etc.—may be made, as it were, visible in bodily manifestation (as effect of what is internal), and this embodiment involves a union of pure ideas of reason and great imaginative power, in one who would even form an estimate of it, not to speak of being the author of its presentation. The correctness of such an ideal of beauty is evidenced by its not permitting any sensuous charm to mingle with the delight in its object, in which it still allows us to take a great interest. This fact in turn shows that an estimate formed according to such a standard can never be purely aesthetic, and that one formed according to an ideal of beauty cannot be a simple judgement of taste.

Definition of the Beautiful derived from this Third Moment

Beauty is the form of *finality* in an object, so far as perceived in it *apart from the representation of an end.*[3]

FOURTH MOMENT. *Of the Judgement of Taste: Moment of the Modality of the Delight in the Object*

§ 18. *Nature of the modality in a judgement of taste*

I MAY assert in the case of every representation that the synthesis of a pleasure with the representation (as a cognition) is at least *possible*. Of what I call *agreeable* I assert that it *actually* causes pleasure in me. But what we have in mind in the case of the *beautiful* is a *necessary* reference on its part to delight. However, this necessity is of a special kind. It is not a theoretical objective necessity—such as would let us cognize *a priori* that every one *will feel* this delight in the object that is called beautiful by me. Nor yet is it a practical necessity, in which case, thanks to concepts of a pure rational will in which free agents are supplied with a rule, this delight is the necessary consequence of an objective law, and simply means that one ought absolutely (without ulterior object) to act in a certain way. Rather, being such a necessity as is thought in an aesthetic judgement, it can only be termed *exemplary*. In other words it is a necessity of the assent of *all* to a judgement regarded as exemplifying a universal rule incapable of formulation. Since an aesthetic judgement is not an objective or cognitive judgement, this necessity is not derivable from definite concepts, and so is not apodeictic. Much less is it inferable from universality of experience

[1] It will be found that a perfectly regular face—one that a painter might fix his eye on for a model—ordinarily conveys nothing. This is because it is devoid of anything characteristic, and so the idea of the race is expressed in it rather than the specific qualities of a person. The exaggeration of what is characteristic in this way, i.e., exaggeration violating the normal idea (the finality of the race), is called *caricature*. Also experience shows that these quite regular faces indicate as a rule internally only a mediocre type of man; presumably—if one may assume that nature in its external form expresses the proportions of the internal—because, where none of the mental qualities exceed the proportion requisite to constitute a man free from faults, nothing can be expected in the way of what is called *genius*, in which nature seems to make a departure from its wonted relations of the mental powers in favour of some special one. [Cf. p. 527, *et seq.*]

[2] [Cf. p. 549.]

[3] As telling against this explanation, the instance may be adduced that there are things in which we see a form suggesting adaptation to an end,* without any end being cognized in them—as, for example, the stone implements frequently obtained from sepulchral tumuli and supplied with a hole, as if for [inserting] a handle; and although these by their shape manifestly indicate a finality, the end of which is unknown, they are not on that account described as beautiful. But the very fact of their being regarded as art-products involves an immediate recognition that their shape is attributed to some purpose or other and to a definite end. For this reason there is no immediate delight whatever in their contemplation. A flower, on the other hand, such as a tulip, is regarded as beautiful, because we meet with a certain finality in its perception, which, in our estimate of it, is not referred to any end whatever.

* [Cf. p. 523, *et seq.*]

(of a thoroughgoing agreement of judgements about the beauty of a certain object). For, apart from the fact that experience would hardly furnish evidences sufficiently numerous for this purpose, empirical judgements do not afford any foundation for a concept of the necessity of these judgements.

§ 19. *The subjective necessity attributed to a judgement of taste is conditioned*

The judgement of taste exacts agreement from every one; and a person who describes something as beautiful insists that every one *ought* to give the object in question his approval and follow suit in describing it as beautiful. The *ought* in aesthetic judgements, therefore, despite an accordance with all the requisite data for passing judgement, is still only pronounced conditionally. We are suitors for agreement from every one else, because we are fortified with a ground common to all. Further, we would be able to count on this agreement, provided we were always assured of the correct subsumption of the case under that ground as the rule of approval.

§ 20. *The condition of the necessity advanced by a judgement of taste is the idea of a common sense*

Were judgements of taste (like cognitive judgements) in possession of a definite objective principle, then one who in his judgement followed such a principle would claim unconditioned necessity for it. Again, were they devoid of any principle, as are those of the mere taste of sense, then no thought of any necessity on their part would enter one's head. Therefore they must have a subjective principle, and one which determines what pleases or displeases, by means of feeling only and not through concepts, but yet with universal validity. Such a principle, however, could only be regarded as a *common sense.* This differs essentially from common understanding, which is also sometimes called common sense (*sensus communis*): for the judgement of the latter is not one by feeling, but always one by concepts, though usually only in the shape of obscurely represented principles.

The judgement of taste, therefore, depends on our presupposing the existence of a common sense. (But this is not to be taken to mean some external sense, but the effect arising from the free play of our powers of cognition.) Only under the presupposition, I repeat, of such a common sense, are we able to lay down a judgement of taste.

§ 21. *Have we reason for presupposing a common sense?*

Cognitions and judgements must, together with their attendant conviction,[1] admit of being universally communicated; for otherwise a correspondence with the object would not be due to them. They would be a conglomerate constituting a mere subjective play of the powers of representation, just as scepticism would have it. But if cognitions are to admit of communication, then our mental state, i.e., the way the cognitive powers are attuned for cognition generally, and, in fact, the relative proportion suitable for a representation (by which an object is given to us) from which cognition is to result, must also admit of being universally communicated, as, without this, which is the subjective condition of the act of knowing, knowledge, as an effect, would not arise. And this is always what actually happens where a given object, through the intervention of sense, sets the imagination at work in arranging the manifold, and the imagination, in turn, the understanding in giving to this arrangement the unity of concepts. But this disposition of the cognitive powers has a relative proportion differing with the diversity of the objects that are given. However, there must be one in which this internal ratio suitable for quickening (one faculty by the other) is best adapted for both mental powers in respect of cognition (of given objects) generally; and this disposition can only be determined through feeling (and not by concepts). Since, now this disposition itself must admit of being universally communicated, and hence also the feeling of it (in the case of a given representation), while again, the universal communicability of a feeling presupposes a common sense: it follows that our assumption of it is well founded. And here, too, we do not have to take our stand on psychological observations, but we assume a common sense as the necessary condition of the universal communicability of our knowledge, which is presupposed in every logic and every principle of knowledge that is not one of scepticism.

§ 22. *The necessity of the universal assent that is thought in a judgement of taste, is a subjective necessity which, under the presupposition of a common sense, is represented as objective*

In all judgements by which we describe anything as beautiful, we tolerate no one else being of a different opinion, and in taking up this position we do not rest our judgement upon con-

[1] [Cf. *Critique of Pure Reason*, pp. 240–43.]

epts, but only on our feeling. Accordingly we introduce this fundamental feeling not as a private feeling, but as a public sense. Now, for this purpose, experience cannot be made the ground of his common sense, for the latter is invoked to justify judgements containing an "ought." The assertion is not that every one *will* fall in with our judgement, but rather that every one *ought* to agree with it. Here I put forward my judgement of taste as an example of the judgement of common sense, and attribute to it on that account *exemplary* validity. Hence common sense is a mere ideal norm. With this as presupposition, a judgement that accords with it, as well as the delight in an object expressed in that judgement, is rightly converted into a rule for everyone. For the principle, while it is only subjective, being yet assumed as subjectively universal (a necessary idea for everyone), could, in what concerns the consensus of different judging subjects, demand universal assent like an objective principle, provided we were assured of our subsumption under it being correct.

This indeterminate norm of a common sense is, as a matter of fact, presupposed by us; as is shown by our presuming to lay down judgements of taste. But does such a common sense[1] in fact exist as a constitutive principle of the possibility of experience, or is it formed for us as a regulative principle by a still higher principle of reason, that for higher ends first seeks to beget in us a common sense? Is taste, in other words, a natural and original faculty, or is it only the idea of one that is artificial and to be acquired by us, so that a judgement of taste, with its demand for universal assent, is but a requirement of reason for generating such a con*sensus*, and does the "ought," i. e., the objective necessity of the coincidence of the feeling of all with the particular feeling of each, only betoken the possibility of arriving at some sort of unanimity in these matters, and the judgement of taste only adduce an example of the application of this principle? These are questions which as yet we are neither willing nor in a position to investigate. For the present we have only to resolve the faculty of taste into its elements, and to unite these ultimately in the idea of a common sense.

Definition of the Beautiful drawn from the Fourth Moment

The beautiful is that which, apart from a concept, is cognized as object of a *necessary* delight.

1 [Cf. §40; also pp. 482, 505, *et seq.*; 543, *et seq.*; 549.]

General Remark on the First Section of the Analytic

The result to be extracted from the foregoing analysis is in effect this: That everything runs up into the concept of taste as a critical faculty by which an object is estimated in reference to the *free conformity to law* of the imagination. If, now, imagination must in the judgement of taste be regarded in its freedom, then, to begin with, it is not taken as reproductive, as in its subjection to the laws of association, but as productive and exerting an activity of its own (as originator of arbitrary forms of possible intuitions).[2] And although in the apprehension of a given object of sense it is tied down to a definite form of this object and, to that extent, does not enjoy free play (as it does in poetry),[3] still it is easy to conceive that the object may supply ready-made to the imagination just such a form of the arrangement of the manifold as the imagination, if it were left to itself, would freely protect in harmony with the general *conformity to law of the understanding*. But that the *imagination* should be both *free* and *of itself conformable to law*, i. e., carry autonomy with it, is a contradiction. The understanding alone gives the law. Where, however, the imagination is compelled to follow a course laid down by a definite law, then what the form of the product is to be is determined by concepts; but, in that case, as already shown, the delight is not delight in the beautiful, but in the good (in perfection, though it be no more than formal perfection), and the judgement is not one due to taste. Hence it is only a conformity to law without a law, and a subjective harmonizing of the imagination and the understanding without an objective one—which latter would mean that the representation was referred to a definite concept of the object—that can consist with the free conformity to law of the understanding (which has also been called finality apart from an end) and with the specific character of a judgement of taste.

Now geometrically regular figures, a circle, a square, a cube, and the like, are commonly brought forward by critics of taste as the most simple and unquestionable examples of beauty. And yet the very reason why they are called regular, is because the only way of representing them is by looking on them as mere presentations of a determinate concept by which the figure has its rule (according to which alone it

2 [Cf. p. 528, *et seq.*]
3 [Cf. pp. 528; 530, *et seq.*; 533, *et seq.*]

is possible) prescribed for it. One or other of these two views must, therefore, be wrong: either the verdict of the critics that attributes beauty to such figures, or else our own, which makes finality apart from any concept necessary for beauty.

One would scarce think it necessary for a man to have taste to take more delight in a circle than in a scrawled outline, in an equilateral and equiangular quadrilateral than in one that is all lop-sided, and, as it were, deformed. The requirements of common understanding ensure such a preference without the least demand upon taste. Where some purpose is perceived, as, for instance, that of forming an estimate of the area of a plot of land, or rendering intelligible the relation of divided parts to one another and to the whole, then regular figures, and those of the simplest kind, are needed; and the delight does not rest immediately upon the way the figure strikes the eye, but upon its serviceability for all manner of possible purposes. A room with the walls making oblique angles, a plot laid out in a garden in a similar way, even any violation of symmetry, as well in the figure of animals (e. g., being one-eyed) as in that of buildings, or of flower-beds, is displeasing because of its perversity of form, not alone in a practical way in respect of some definite use to which the thing may be put, but for an estimate that looks to all manner of possible purposes. With the judgement of taste the case is different. For, when it is pure, it combines delight or aversion immediately with the bare *contemplation* of the object irrespective of its use or of any end.

The regularity that conduces to the concept of an object is, in fact, the indispensable condition (*conditio sine qua non*) of grasping the object as a single representation and giving to the manifold its determinate form. This determination is an end in respect of knowledge; and in this connection it is invariably coupled with delight (such as attends the accomplishment of any, even problematical, purpose). Here, however, we have merely the value set upon the solution that satisfies the problem, and not a free and indeterminately final entertainment of the mental powers with what is called beautiful. In the latter case, understanding is at the service of imagination, in the former, this relation is reversed.

With a thing that owes its possibility to a purpose, a building, or even an animal, its regularity, which consists in symmetry, must express the unity of the intuition accompanying the concept of its end, and belongs with it to cognition. But where all that is intended is the maintenance of a free play of the powers of representation (subject, however, to the condition that there is to be nothing for understanding to take exception to), in ornamental gardens, in the decoration of rooms, in all kinds of furniture that shows good taste, etc., regularity in the shape of constraint is to be avoided as far as possible. Thus English taste in gardens, and fantastic taste in furniture, push the freedom of imagination to the verge of what is grotesque—the idea being that in this divorce from all constraint of rules the precise instance is being afforded where taste can exhibit its perfection in projects of the imagination to the fullest extent.

All stiff regularity (such as borders on mathematical regularity) is inherently repugnant to taste, in that the contemplation of it affords us no lasting entertainment. Indeed, where it has neither cognition nor some definite practical end expressly in view, we get heartily tired of it. On the other hand, anything that gives the imagination scope for unstudied and final play is always fresh to us. We do not grow to hate the very sight of it. *Marsden*, in his description of Sumatra, observes that the free beauties of nature so surround the beholder on all sides that they cease to have much attraction for him.[1] On the other hand he found a pepper garden full of charm, on coming across it in mid-forest with its rows of parallel stakes on which the plant twines itself. From all this he infers that wild, and in its appearance quite irregular beauty, is only pleasing as a change to one whose eyes have become surfeited with regular beauty. But he need only have made the experiment of passing one day in his pepper garden to realize that once the regularity has enabled the understanding to put itself in accord with the order that is the constant requirement, instead of the object diverting him any longer, it imposes an irksome constraint upon the imagination: whereas nature subject to no constraint of artificial rules, and lavish, as it there is, in its luxuriant variety can supply constant food for his taste. Even a bird's song, which we can reduce to no musical rule, seems to have more freedom in it, and thus to be richer for taste, than the human voice singing in accordance with all the rules that the art of music prescribes; for we grow tired much sooner of frequent and lengthy repetitions of the latter. Yet here most likely our sympathy with the mirth of a dear little creature is confused with

[1] [*The History of Sumatra*, by W. Marsden (London, 1783), p. 113.]

the beauty of its song, for if exactly imitated by man (as has been sometimes done with the notes of the nightingale)[1] it would strike our ear as wholly destitute of taste.

Further, beautiful objects have to be distinguished from beautiful views of objects (where the distance often prevents a clear perception).[2] In the latter case, taste appears to fasten, not so much on what the imagination *grasps* in this field, as on the incentive it receives to indulge in poetic fiction, i. e., in the peculiar fancies with which the mind entertains itself as it is being continually stirred by the variety that strikes the eye. It is just as when we watch the changing shapes of the fire or of a rippling brook: neither of which are things of beauty, but they convey a charm to the imagination, because they sustain its free play.

BOOK II. *Analytic of the Sublime*

§ 23. *Transition from the faculty of estimating the beautiful to that of estimating the sublime*

THE beautiful and the sublime agree on the point of pleasing on their own account. Further they agree in not presupposing either a judgement of sense or one logically determinant, but one of reflection. Hence it follows that the delight does not depend upon a sensation, as with the agreeable, nor upon a definite concept, as does the delight in the good, although it has, for all that, an indeterminate reference to concepts. Consequently the delight is connected with the mere presentation or faculty of presentation, and is thus taken to express the accord, in a given intuition, of the faculty of presentation, or the imagination, with the *faculty of concepts* that belongs to understanding or reason, in the sense of the former assisting the latter. Hence both kinds of judgements are *singular*, and yet such as profess to be universally valid in respect of every subject, despite the fact that their claims are directed merely to the feeling of pleasure and not to any knowledge of the object.

There are, however, also important and striking differences between the two. The beautiful in nature is a question of the form of the object, and this consists in limitation, whereas the sublime is to be found in an object even devoid of form, so far as it immediately involves, or else by its presence provokes a representation of *limitlessness*, yet with a superadded thought of its totality. Accordingly, the beautiful seems to be regarded as a presentation of an indeterminate concept of understanding, the sublime as a presentation of an indeterminate concept of reason. Hence the delight is in the former case coupled with the representation of *quality*, but in this case with that of *quantity*. Moreover, the former delight is very different from the latter in kind. For the beautiful is directly attended with a feeling of the furtherance of life, and is thus compatible with charms and a playful imagination. On the other hand, the feeling of the sublime is a pleasure that only arises indirectly, being brought about by the feeling of a momentary check to the vital forces followed at once by a discharge all the more powerful, and so it is an emotion that seems to be no sport, but dead earnest in the affairs of the imagination. Hence charms are repugnant to it; and, since the mind is not simply attracted by the object, but is also alternately repelled thereby, the delight in the sublime does not so much involve positive pleasure as admiration or respect, i. e., merits the name of a negative pleasure.

But the most important and vital distinction between the sublime and the beautiful is certainly this: that if, as is allowable, we here confine our attention in the first instance to the sublime in objects of nature (that of art being always restricted by the conditions of an agreement with nature), we observe that whereas natural beauty (such as is self-subsisting) conveys a finality in its form making the object appear, as it were, preadapted to our power of judgement, so that it thus forms of itself an object of our delight, that which, without our indulging in any refinements of thought, but, simply in our apprehension of it, excites the feeling of the sublime, may appear, indeed, in point of form to contravene the ends of our power of judgement, to be ill-adapted to our faculty of presentation, and to be, as it were, an outrage on the imagination, and yet it is judged all the more sublime on that account.

From this it may be seen at once that we express ourselves on the whole inaccurately if we term any *object of nature* sublime, although we may with perfect propriety call many such objects beautiful. For how can that which is apprehended as inherently contra-final be noted with an expression of approval? All that we can say is that the object lends itself to the presentation of a sublimity discoverable in the mind.

[1] [Cf. p. 523, *et seq.*]
[2] [Cf. p. 533.]

For the sublime, in the strict sense of the word, cannot be contained in any sensuous form, but rather concerns ideas of reason, which, although no adequate presentation of them is possible, may be excited and called into the mind by that very inadequacy itself which does admit of sensuous presentation. Thus the broad ocean agitated by storms cannot be called sublime. Its aspect is horrible, and one must have stored one's mind in advance with a rich stock of ideas, if such an intuition is to raise it to the pitch of a feeling which is itself sublime—sublime because the mind has been incited to abandon sensibility and employ itself upon ideas involving higher finality.

Self-subsisting natural beauty reveals to us a technic of nature which shows it in the light of a system ordered in accordance with laws the principle of which is not to be found within the range of our entire faculty of understanding.[1] This principle is that of a finality relative to the employment of judgement in respect of phenomena which have thus to be assigned, not merely to nature regarded as aimless mechanism, but also to nature regarded after the analogy of art. Hence it gives a veritable extension, not, of course, to our knowledge of objects of nature, but to our conception of nature itself—nature as mere mechanism being enlarged to the conception of nature as art—an extension inviting profound inquiries as to the possibility of such a form. But in what we are wont to call sublime in nature there is such an absence of anything leading to particular objective principles and corresponding forms of nature that it is rather in its chaos, or in its wildest and most irregular disorder and desolation, provided it gives signs of magnitude and power, that nature chiefly excites the ideas of the sublime. Hence we see that the concept of the sublime in nature is far less important and rich in consequences than that of its beauty. It gives on the whole no indication of anything final in nature itself, but only in the possible *employment* of our intuitions of it in inducing a feeling in our own selves of a finality quite independent of nature. For the beautiful in nature we must seek a ground external to ourselves, but for the sublime one merely in ourselves and the attitude of mind that introduces sublimity into the representation of nature. This is a very needful preliminary remark. It entirely separates the ideas of the sublime from that of a finality of *nature*, and makes the theory of the sublime a mere appendage to the aesthetic estimate of the finality of nature, because it does not give a representation of any particular form in nature, but involves no more than the development of a final employment by the imagination of its own representation.

§ 24. *Subdivision of an investigation of the feeling of the sublime*

In the division of the moments of an aesthetic estimate of objects in respect of the feeling of the sublime, the course of the Analytic will be able to follow the same principle as in the analysis of judgements of taste. For, the judgement being one of the aesthetic reflective judgement, the delight in the sublime, just like that in the beautiful, must in its *quantity* be shown to be universally valid, in its *quality* independent of interest, in its *relation* subjective finality, and the latter, in its *modality*, necessary. Hence the method here will not depart from the lines followed in the preceding section: unless something is made of the point that there, where the aesthetic judgement bore on the form of the object, we began with the investigation of its quality, whereas here, considering the formlessness that may belong to what we call sublime, we begin with that of its quantity, as first moment of the aesthetic judgement on the sublime—a divergence of method the reason for which is evident from § 23.

But the analysis of the sublime obliges a division not required by that of the beautiful, namely one into the *mathematically* and the *dynamically* sublime.

For the feeling of sublime involves as its characteristic feature a mental *movement* combined with the estimate of the object, whereas taste in respect of the beautiful presupposes that the mind is in *restful* contemplation, and preserves it in this state. But this movement has to be estimated as subjectively final (since the sublime pleases). Hence it is referred through the imagination either to the *faculty of cognition* or to that of *desire;* but to whichever faculty the reference is made, the finality of the given representation is estimated only in respect of these faculties (apart from end or interest). Accordingly the first is attributed to the object as a *mathematical,* the second as a *dynamical,* affection of the imagination. Hence we get the above double mode of representing an object as sublime.[2]

[1] [This may be compared with the first paragraph of the Introduction to the *Critique of Teleological Judgement;* p. 550, below. Cf. pp. 487, 512, *et seq.;* 516, *et seq.;* 518, *et seq.;* 531.]

[2] [Cf. p. 507. Also Cf. *Critique of Pure Reason,* pp. 43, 67.]

A. The Mathematically Sublime

§ 25. *Definition of the term "sublime"*

Sublime is the name given to what is *absolutely great.* But to be great and to be a magnitude are entirely different concepts (*magnitudo* and *quantitas*). In the same way, to *assert without qualification* (*simpliciter*) that something is great is quite a different thing from saying that it is *absolutely great* (*absolute, non comparative magnum*). The latter is *what is beyond all comparison great.* What, then, is the meaning of the assertion that anything is great, or small, or of medium size? What is indicated is not a pure concept of understanding, still less an intuition of sense; and just as little is it a concept of reason, for it does not import any principle of cognition. It must, therefore, be a concept of judgement, or have its source in one, and must introduce as basis of the judgement a subjective finality of the representation with reference to the power of judgement. Given a multiplicity of the homogeneous together constituting one thing, and we may at once cognize from the thing itself that it is a *magnitude* (*quantum*). No comparison with other things is required. But to determine *how great* it is always requires something else, which itself has magnitude, for its measure. Now, since in the estimate of magnitude we have to take into account not merely the multiplicity (number of units) but also the magnitude of the unit (the measure), and since the magnitude of this unit in turn always requires something else as its measure and as the standard of its comparison, and so on, we see that the computation of the magnitude of phenomena is, in all cases, utterly incapable of affording us any absolute concept of a magnitude, and can, instead, only afford one that is always based on comparison.

If, now, I assert without qualification that anything is great, it would seem that I have nothing in the way of a comparison present to my mind, or at least nothing involving an objective measure, for no attempt is thus made to determine how great the object is. But, despite the standard of comparison being merely subjective, the claim of the judgement is none the less one to universal agreement; the judgements: "That man is beautiful" and "He is tall" do not purport to speak only for the judging subject, but, like theoretical judgements, they demand the assent of everyone.

Now in a judgement that without qualification describes anything as great, it is not merely meant that the object has a magnitude, but greatness is ascribed to it pre-eminently among many other objects of a like kind, yet without the extent of this pre-eminence being determined. Hence a standard is certainly laid at the basis of the judgement, which standard is presupposed to be one that can be taken as the same for every one, but which is available only for an aesthetic estimate of the greatness, and not for one that is logical (mathematically determined), for the standard is a merely subjective one underlying the reflective judgement upon the greatness. Furthermore, this standard may be empirical, as, let us say, the average size of the men known to us, of animals of a certain kind, of trees, of houses, of mountains, and so forth. Or it may be a standard given *a priori,* which by reason of the imperfections of the judging subject is restricted to subjective conditions of presentation *in concreto;* as, in the practical sphere, the greatness of a particular virtue,[1] or of public liberty and justice in a country; or, in the theoretical sphere, the greatness of the accuracy or inaccuracy of an experiment or measurement, etc.

Here, now, it is of note that, although we have no interest whatever in the object, i. e., its real existence may be a matter of no concern to us, still its mere greatness, regarded even as devoid of form, is able to convey a universally communicable delight and so involve the consciousness of a subjective finality in the employment of our cognitive faculties, but not, be it remembered, a delight in the object, for the latter may be formless, but, in contradistinction to what is the case with the beautiful, where the reflective judgement finds itself set to a key that is final in respect of cognition generally, a delight in an extension affecting the imagination itself.

If (subject as above) we say of an object, without qualification, that it is great, this is not a mathematically determinant, but a mere reflective judgement upon its representation, which is subjectively final for a particular employment of our cognitive faculties in the estimation of magnitude, and we then always couple with the representation a kind of respect, just as we do a kind of contempt with what we call absolutely small. Moreover, the estimate of things as great or small extends to everything, even to all their qualities. Thus we call even their beauty great or small. The reason of this is to be found in the fact that we have only got to present a thing in intuition, as the precept of judgement directs (consequently to represent it

1 [Cf. p. 497, *et seq.*]

aesthetically), for it to be in its entirety a phenomenon, and hence a quantum.

If, however, we call anything not alone great, but, without qualification, absolutely, and in every respect (beyond all comparison) great, that is to say, *sublime,* we soon perceive that for this it is not permissible to seek an appropriate standard outside itself, but merely in itself. It is a greatness comparable to itself alone. Hence it comes that the sublime is not to be looked for in the things of nature, but only in our own ideas. But it must be left to the deduction to show in which of them it resides.

The above definition may also be expressed in this way: *that is sublime in comparison with which all else is small.* Here we readily see that nothing can be given in nature, no matter how great we may judge it to be, which, regarded in some other relation, may not be degraded to the level of the infinitely little, and nothing so small which in comparison with some still smaller standard may not for our imagination be enlarged to the greatness of a world. Telescopes have put within our reach an abundance of material to go upon in making the first observation, and microscopes the same in making the second. Nothing, therefore, which can be an object of the senses is to be termed *sublime* when treated on this footing. But precisely because there is a striving in our imagination towards progress *ad infinitum,* while reason demands absolute totality, as a real idea, that same inability on the part of our faculty for the estimation of the magnitude of things of the world of sense to attain to this idea, is the awakening of a feeling of a supersensible faculty within us; and it is the use to which judgement naturally puts particular objects on behalf of this latter feeling, and not the object of sense, that is absolutely great, and every other contrasted employment small. Consequently it is the disposition of soul evoked by a particular representation engaging the attention of the reflective judgement, and not the object, that is to be called sublime.

The foregoing formulae defining the sublime may, therefore, be supplemented by yet another: *The sublime is that, the mere capacity of thinking which evidences a faculty of mind transcending every standard of sense.*

§ 26. *The estimation of the magnitude of natural things requisite for the idea of the sublime*

THE estimation of magnitude by means of concepts of number (or their signs in algebra) is mathematical, but that in mere intuition (by the eye) is aesthetic. Now we can only get definite concepts of *how great* anything is by having recourse to numbers (or, at any rate, by getting approximate measurements by means of numerical series progressing *ad infinitum*), the unit being the measure; and to this extent all logical estimation of magnitude is mathematical. But, as the magnitude of the measure has to be assumed as a known quantity, if, to form an estimate of this, we must again have recourse to numbers involving another standard for their unit, and consequently must again proceed mathematically, we can never arrive at a first or fundamental measure, and so cannot get any definite concept of a given magnitude. The estimation of the magnitude of the fundamental measure must, therefore, consist merely in the immediate grasp which we can get of it in intuition, and the use to which our imagination can put this in presenting the numerical concepts: i. e., all estimation of the magnitude of objects of nature is in the last resort aesthetic (i.e., subjectively and not objectively determined).

Now for the mathematical estimation of magnitude there is, of course, no *greatest* possible (for the power of numbers extends to infinity), but for the aesthetic estimation there certainly is and of it I say that where it is considered an absolute measure beyond which no greater is possible subjectively (i.e., for the judging subject), it then conveys the idea of the sublime and calls forth that emotion which no mathematical estimation of magnitudes by numbers can evoke (unless in so far as the fundamental aesthetic measure is kept vividly present to the imagination): because the latter presents only the relative magnitude due to comparison with others of a like kind, whereas the former presents magnitude absolutely, so far as the mind can grasp it in an intuition.

To take in a quantum intuitively in the imagination so as to be able to use it as a measure, or unit for estimating magnitude by numbers, involves two operations of this faculty: *apprehension (apprehensio)* and *comprehension (comprehensio aesthetica*). Apprehension presents no difficulty: for this process can be carried on *ad infinitum;* but with the advance of apprehension comprehension becomes more difficult at every step and soon attains its maximum, and this is the aesthetically greatest fundamental measure for the estimation of magnitude. For if the apprehension has reached a point beyond which the representations of sensuous intuition in the case of the parts first apprehended begin to disappear from the imagination as this advances to the apprehension of yet others, as much, then, is lost at one end as is gained at the other, and for comprehension we get a maximum which the imagination cannot exceed.

This explains Savary's observations in his account of Egypt,[1] that in order to get the full emotional effect of the size of the Pyramids we must avoid coming too near just as much as remaining too far away. For in the latter case the representation of the apprehended parts (the tiers of stones) is but obscure, and produces no effect upon the aesthetic judgement of the Subject. In the former, however, it takes the eye some time to complete the apprehension from the base to the summit; but in this interval the first tiers always in part disappear before the imagination has taken in the last, and so the comprehension is never complete. The same explanation may also sufficiently account for the bewilderment, or sort of perplexity, which, as is said, seizes the visitor on first entering St. Peter's in Rome. For here a feeling comes home to him of the inadequacy of his imagination for presenting the idea of a whole within which that imagination attains its maximum, and, in its fruitless efforts to extend this limit, recoils upon itself, but in so doing succumbs to an emotional delight.

At present I am not disposed to deal with the ground of this delight, connected, as it is, with a representation in which we would least of all look for it—a representation, namely, that lets us see its own inadequacy, and consequently its subjective want of finality for our judgement in the estimation of magnitude—but confine myself to the remark that if the aesthetic judgement is to be *pure (unmixed with any teleological judgement* which, as such, belongs to reason), and if we are to give a suitable example of it for the Critique of *aesthetic* judgement, we must not point to the sublime in works of art, e.g., buildings, statues and the like, where a human end determines the form as well as the magnitude, nor yet in things of nature, *that in their very concept import a definite end,* e.g., animals of a recognized natural order, but in rude nature merely as involving magnitude (and only in this so far as it does not convey any charm or any emotion arising from actual danger). For, in a representation of this kind, nature contains nothing monstrous (nor what is either magnificent or horrible)—the magnitude apprehended may be increased to any extent provided imagination is able to grasp it all in one whole. An object is *monstrous* where by its size it defeats the end that forms its concept. The *colossal* is the mere presentation of a concept which is almost too great for presentation, i.e., borders on the relatively monstrous; for the end to be attained by the presentation of a concept is made harder to realize by the intuition of the object being almost too great for our faculty of apprehension. A pure judgement upon the sublime must, however, have no end belonging to the object as its determining ground, if it is to be aesthetic and not to be tainted with any judgement of understanding or reason.

[1] [*Lettres sur l'Egypte,* 1787.]

Since whatever is to be a source of pleasure, apart from interest, to the merely reflective judgement must involve in its representation subjective, and, as such, universally valid finality—though here, however, no finality of the *form* of the object underlies our estimate of it (as it does in the case of the beautiful)—the question arises: What is the subjective finality, and what enables it to be prescribed as a norm so as to yield a ground for universally valid delight in the mere estimation of magnitude, and that, too, in a case where it is pushed to the point at which our faculty of imagination breaks down in presenting the concept of a magnitude, and proves unequal to its task?

In the successive aggregation of units requisite for the representation of magnitudes, the imagination of itself advances *ad infinitum* without let or hindrance—understanding, however, conducting it by means of concepts of number for which the former must supply the schema. This procedure belongs to the logical estimation of magnitude, and, as such, is doubtless something objectively final according to the concept of an end (as all measurement is), but it is not anything which for the aesthetic judgement is final or pleasing. Further, in this intentional finality there is nothing compelling us to tax the utmost powers of the imagination, and drive it as far as ever it can reach in its presentations, so as to enlarge the size of the measure, and thus make the single intuition holding the many in one (the *comprehension)* as great as possible. For, in the estimation of magnitude by the understanding (arithmetic), we get just as far, whether the comprehension of the units is pushed to the number 10 (as in the decimal scale) or only to 4 (as in the quaternary); the further production of magnitude being carried out by the succesive aggregation of units, or, if the quantum is given in intuition, by apprehension, merely progressively (not comprehensively), according to an adopted principle of progression. In this mathematical estimation of magnitude, understanding is as well served and as satisfied whether imagination selects for the unit a magnitude which one can take in at a glance, e.g., a foot, or a perch, or else a German mile, or even the earth's diameter, the apprehension of which is indeed possible, but not its comprehension in an intuition of the imagination (i.e., it is not possible by means of a *comprehensio aesthetica,* thought quite so by means of a *comprehensio logica* in a numerical concept). In each case the logical estimation of magnitude advances *ad infinitum* with nothing to stop it.

The mind, however, hearkens now to the voice of reason, which for all given magnitudes —even for those which can never be completely apprehended, though (in sensuous representation) estimated as completely given—requires totality, and consequently comprehension in *one* intuition, and which calls for a *presentation* answering to all the above members of a progressively increasing numerical series, and does not exempt even the infinite (space and time past)[1] from this requirement, but rather renders it inevitable for us to regard this infinite (in the judgement of common reason) as *completely given* (i.e., given in its totality).

But the infinite is absolutely (not merely comparatively) great. In comparison with this all else (in the way of magnitudes of the same order) is small. But the point of capital importance is that the mere ability even to think it as *a whole* indicates a faculty of mind transcending every standard of sense. For the latter would entail a comprehension yielding as unit a standard bearing to the infinite ratio expressible in numbers, which is impossible. Still the *mere ability even to think* the given infinite without contradiction, is something that requires the presence in the human mind of a faculty that is itself supersensible. For it is only through this faculty and its idea of a noumenon, which latter, while not itself admitting of any intuition, is yet introduced as substrate underlying the intuition of the world as mere phenomenon, that the infinite of the world of sense, in the pure intellectual estimation of magnitude, is *completely* comprehended *under* a concept, although in the mathematical estimation *by means of numerical concepts* it can never be completely thought. Even a faculty enabling the infinite of supersensible intuition to be regarded as given (in its intelligible substrate), transcends every standard of sensibility and is great beyond all comparison even with the faculty of mathematical estimation: not, of course, from a theoretical point of view that looks to the interests of our faculty of knowledge, but as a broadening of the mind that from another (the practical) point of view feels itself empowered to pass beyond the narrow confines of sensibility.

[1] [Cf. *Critique of Pure Reason,* pp. 130–1.]

Nature, therefore, is sublime in such of its phenomena as in their intuition convey the idea of their infinity. But this can only occur through the inadequacy of even the greatest effort of our imagination in the estimation of the magnitude of an object. But, now, in the case of the mathematical estimation of magnitude, imagination is quite competent to supply a measure equal to the requirements of any object. For the numerical concepts of the understanding can by progressive synthesis make any measure adequate to any given magnitude. Hence it must be the *aesthetic* estimation of magnitude in which we get at once a feeling of the effort towards a comprehension that exceeds the faculty of imagination for mentally grasping the progressive apprehension in a whole of intuition, and, with it, a perception of the inadequacy of this faculty, which has no bounds to its progress, for taking in and using for the estimation of magnitude a fundamental measure that understanding could turn to account without the least trouble. Now the proper unchangeable fundamental measure of nature is its absolute whole, which, with it, regarded as a phenomenon, means infinity comprehended. But, since this fundamental measure is a self-contradictory concept (owing to the impossibility of the absolute totality of an endless progression), it follows that where the size of a natural object is such that the imagination spends its whole faculty of comprehension upon it in vain, it must carry our concept of nature to a supersensible substrate (underlying both nature and our faculty of thought) which is great beyond every standard of sense. Thus, instead of the object, it is rather the cast of the mind in appreciating it that we have to estimate as *sublime.*

Therefore, just as the aesthetic judgement in its estimate of the beautiful refers the imagination in its free play to the *understanding,* to bring out its agreement with the *concepts* of the latter in general (apart from their determination): so in its estimate of a thing as sublime it refers that faculty to *reason* to bring out its subjective accord with *ideas* of reason (indeterminately indicated), i.e., to induce a temper of mind conformable to that which the influence of definite (practical) ideas would produce upon feeling, and in common accord with it.

This makes it evident that true sublimity must be sought only in the mind of the judging subject, and not in the object of nature that occasions this attitude by the estimate formed of it. Who would apply the term "sublime" even to shapeless mountain masses towering one above the other in wild disorder, with their pyramids of ice, or to the dark tempestuous ocean, or such like things? But in the contemplation of them, without any regard to their form, the mind abandons itself to the imagination and to a reason placed, though quite apart from any definite end, in conjunction therewith, and merely broadening its view, and it feels itself elevated in its own estimate of itself on finding all the might of imagination still unequal to its ideas.

We get examples of the mathematically sublime of nature in mere intuition in all those instances where our imagination is afforded, not so much a greater numerical concept as a large unit as measure (for shortening the numerical series). A tree judged by the height of man gives, at all events, a standard for a mountain; and, supposing this is, say, a mile high, it can serve as unit for the number expressing the earth's diameter, so as to make it intuitable; similarly the earth's diameter for the known planetary system; this again for the system of the Milky Way; and the immeasurable host of such systems, which go by the name of *nebulae*, and most likely in turn themselves form such a system, holds out no prospect of a limit. Now in the aesthetic estimate of such an immeasurable whole, the sublime does not lie so much in the greatness of the number, as in the fact that in our onward advance we always arrive at proportionately greater units. The systematic division of the cosmos conduces to this result. For it represents all that is great in nature as in turn becoming little; or, to be more exact, it represents our imagination in all its boundlessness, and with it nature, as sinking into insignificance before the ideas of reason, once their adequate presentation is attempted.

§ 27. *Quality of the delight in our estimate of the sublime*

THE feeling of our incapacity to attain to an idea *that is a law for us,* IS RESPECT.[1] Now the idea of the comprehension of any phenomenon whatever, that may be given us, in a whole of intuition, is an idea imposed upon us by a law of reason, which recognizes no definite, universally valid and unchangeable measure except the absolute whole. But our imagination, even when taxing itself to the uttermost on the score of this required comprehension of a given object in a whole of intuition (and so with a view to the presentation of the idea of reason), betrays its limits and its inadequacy, but still, at the same time, its proper vocation of making itself adequate to the same as law. Therefore the feeling of the sublime in nature is respect for our own vocation, which we attribute to an object of nature by a certain subreption (substitution of a respect for the object in place of one for the idea of humanity in our own self—the subject); and this feeling renders, as it were, intuitable the supremacy of our cognitive faculties on the rational side over the greatest faculty of sensibility.

The feeling of the sublime is, therefore, at once a feeling of displeasure, arising from the inadequacy of imagination in the aesthetic estimation of magnitude to attain to its estimation by reason, and a simultaneously awakened pleasure, arising from this very judgement of the inadequacy of the greatest faculty of sense being in accord with ideas of reason, so far as the effort to attain to these is for us a law. It is, in other words, for us a law (of reason), which goes to make us what we are, that we should esteem as small in comparison with ideas of reason everything which for us is great in nature as an object of sense; and that which makes us alive to the feeling of this supersensible side of our being harmonizes with that law. Now the greatest effort of the imagination in the presentation of the unit for the estimation of magnitude involves in itself a reference to something *absolutely great*, consequently a reference also to the law of reason that this alone is to be adopted as the supreme measure of what is great. Therefore the inner perception of the inadequacy of every standard of sense to serve for the rational estimation of magnitude is a coming into accord with reason's laws, and a displeasure that makes us alive to the feeling of the supersensible side of our being, according to which it is final, and consequently a pleasure, to find every standard of sensibility falling short of the ideas of reason.

The mind feels itself *set in motion* in the representation of the sublime in nature; whereas in the aesthetic judgement upon what is beautiful therein it is in *restful* contemplation. This movement, especially in its inception, may be compared with vibration, i.e., with a rapidly alternating repulsion and attraction produced by

[1] [Cf. *Critique of Practical Reason,* p. 323, *et seq.*]

one and the same object.[1] The point of excess for the imagination (towards which it is driven in the apprehension of the intuition) is like an abyss in which it fears to lose itself, yet again for the rational idea of the supersensible it is not excessive, but conformable to law, and directed to drawing out such an effort on the part of the imagination: and so in turn as much a source of attraction as it was repellent to mere sensibility. But the judgement itself all the while steadfastly preserves its aesthetic character, because it represents, without being grounded on any definite concept of the object, merely the subjective play of the mental powers (imagination and reason) as harmonious by virtue of their very contrast. For just as in the estimate of the beautiful imagination and *understanding* by their concert generate subjective finality of the mental faculties, so imagination and *reason* do so here by their conflict—that is to say they induce a feeling of our possessing a pure and self-sufficient reason, or a faculty for the estimation of magnitude, whose preeminence can only be made intuitively evident by the inadequacy of that faculty which in the presentation of magnitudes (of objects of sense) is itself unbounded.

Measurement of a space (as apprehension) is at the same time a description of it, and so an objective movement in the imagination and a progression. On the other hand, the comprehension of the manifold in the unity, not of thought, but of intuition, and consequently the comprehension of the successively apprehended parts at one glance, is a retrogression that removes the time-condition in the progression of the imagination, and renders *coexistence* intuitable. Therefore, since the time-series is a condition of the internal sense and of an intuition, it is a subjective movement of the imagination by which it does violence to the internal sense —a violence which must be proportionately more striking the greater the quantum which the imagination comprehends in one intuition. The effort, therefore, to receive in a single intuition a measure for magnitudes which it takes an appreciable time to apprehend, is a mode of representation which, subjectively considered, is contra-final, but objectively, is requisite for the estimation of magnitude, and is consequently final. Here the very same violence that is wrought on the subject through the imagination is estimated as final *for the whole province* of the mind.

[1] [Cf. p. 537, *et seq.*; p. 509, *et seq.*]

The *quality* of the feeling of the sublime consists in its being, in respect of the faculty of forming aesthetic estimates, a feeling of displeasure at an object, which yet, at the same time, is represented as being final—a representation which derives its possibility from the fact that the subject's very incapacity betrays the consciousness of an unlimited faculty of the same subject, and that the mind can only form an aesthetic estimate of the latter faculty by means of that incapacity.

In the case of the logical estimation of magnitude, the impossibility of ever arriving at absolute totality by the progressive measurement of things of the sensible world in time and space was cognized as an objective impossibility, i. e., one of *thinking* the infinite as given, and not as simply subjective, i.e., an incapacity for *grasping* it; for nothing turns there on the amount of the comprehension in one intuition, as measure, but everything depends on a numerical concept. But in an aesthetic estimation of magnitude the numerical concept must drop out of count or undergo a change. The only thing that is final for such estimation is the comprehension on the part of imagination in respect of the unit of measure (the concept of a law of the successive production of the concept of magnitude being consequently avoided). If, now, a magnitude begins to tax the utmost stretch of our faculty of comprehension in an intuition, and still numerical magnitudes—in respect of which we are conscious of the boundlessness of our faculty—call upon the imagination for aesthetic comprehension in a greater unit, the mind then gets a feeling of being aesthetically confined within bounds. Nevertheless, with a view to the extension of imagination necessary for adequacy with what is unbounded in our faculty of reason, namely the idea of the absolute whole, the attendant displeasure, and, consequently, the want of finality in our faculty of imagination, is still represented as final for ideas of reason and their animation. But in this very way the aesthetic judgement itself is subjectively final for reason as source of ideas, i.e., of such an intellectual comprehension as makes all aesthetic comprehension small, and the object is received as sublime with a pleasure that is only possible through the mediation of a displeasure.

B. The Dynamically Sublime in Nature

§ 28. *Nature as Might*

Might is a power which is superior to great hindrances. It is termed *dominion* if it is also superior to the resistance of that which itself possesses might. Nature, considered in an aesthetic judgement as might that has no dominion over us, is *dynamically sublime.*

If we are to estimate nature as dynamically sublime, it must be represented as a source of fear (though the converse, that every object that is a source of fear, in our aesthetic judgement, sublime, does not hold). For in forming an aesthetic estimate (no concept being present) the superiority to hindrances can only be estimated according to the greatness of the resistance. Now that which we strive to resist is an evil, and, if we do not find our powers commensurate to the task, an object of fear. Hence the aesthetic judgement can only deem nature a might, and so dynamically sublime, in so far as it is looked upon as an object of fear.

But we may look upon an object as *fearful,* and yet not be afraid *of* it, if, that is, our estimate takes the form of our simply *picturing to ourselves* the case of our wishing to offer some resistance to it and recognizing that all such resistance would be quite futile. So the righteous man fears God without being afraid of Him, because he regards the case of his wishing to resist God and His commandments as one which need cause *him* no anxiety. But in every such case, regarded by him as not intrinsically impossible, he cognizes Him as One to be feared.

One who is in a state of fear can no more play the part of a judge of the sublime of nature than one captivated by inclination and appetite can of the beautiful. He flees from the sight of an object filling him with dread; and it is impossible to take delight in terror that is seriously entertained. Hence the agreeableness arising from the cessation of an uneasiness is *a state of joy.* But this, depending upon deliverance from a danger, is a rejoicing accompanied with a resolve never again to put oneself in the way of the danger: in fact we do not like bringing back to mind how we felt on that occasion—not to speak of going in search of an opportunity for experiencing it again.

Bold, overhanging, and, as it were, threatening rocks, thunderclouds piled up the vault of heaven, borne along with flashes and peals, volcanoes in all their violence of destruction, hurricanes leaving desolation in their track, the boundless ocean rising with rebellious force, the high waterfall of some mighty river, and the like, make our power of resistance of trifling moment in comparison with their might. But, provided our own position is secure, their aspect is all the more attractive for its fearfulness; and we readily call these objects sublime, because they raise the forces of the soul above the height of vulgar commonplace, and discover within us a power of resistance of quite another kind, which gives us courage to be able to measure ourselves against the seeming omnipotence of nature.

In the immeasurableness of nature and the incompetence of our faculty for adopting a standard proportionate to the aesthetic estimation of the magnitude of its *realm,* we found our own limitation. But with this we also found in our rational faculty another non-sensuous standard, one which has that infinity itself under it as a unit, and in comparison with which everything in nature is small, and so found in our minds a pre-eminence over nature even in it immeasurability. Now in just the same way the irresistibility of the might of nature forces upon us the recognition of our physical helplessness as beings of nature, but at the same time reveals a faculty of estimating ourselves as independent of nature, and discovers a pre-eminence above nature that is the foundation of a self-preservation of quite another kind from that which may be assailed and brought into danger by external nature. This saves humanity in our own person from humiliation, even though as mortal men we have to submit to external violence. In this way, external nature is not estimated in our aesthetic judgement as sublime so far as exciting fear, but rather because it challenges our power (one not of nature) to regard as small those things of which we are wont to be solicitous (worldly goods, health, and life), and hence to regard its might (to which in these matters we are no doubt subject) as exercising over us and our personality no such rude dominion that we should bow down before it, once the question becomes one of our highest principles and of our asserting or forsaking them. Therefore nature is here called *sublime* merely because it raises the imagination to a presentation of those cases in which the mind can make itself sensible of the appropriate sublimity of the sphere of its own being, even above nature.

This estimation of ourselves loses nothing by the fact that we must see ourselves safe in order to feel this soul-stirring delight—a fact from which it might be plausibly argued that, as there is no seriousness in the danger, so there is just as little seriousness in the sublimity of our faculty of soul. For here the delight only concerns the *province* of our faculty disclosed in such a case, so far as this faculty has its root in our nature; notwithstanding that its development and exercise is left to ourselves and remains an obligation. Here indeed there is truth—no matter how conscious a man, when he stretches his reflection so far abroad, may be of his actual present helplessness.

This principle has, doubtless, the appearance of being too far-fetched and subtle, and so of lying beyond the reach of an aesthetic judgement. But observation of men proves the reverse, and that it may be the foundation of the commonest judgements, although one is not always conscious of its presence. For what is it that, even to the savage, is the object of the greatest admiration? It is a man who is undaunted, who knows no fear, and who, therefore, does not give way to danger, but sets manfully to work with full deliberation. Even where civilization has reached a high pitch, there remains this special reverence for the soldier; only that there is then further required of him that he should also exhibit all the virtues of peace[1]—gentleness, sympathy, and even becoming thought for his own person; and for the reason that in this we recognize that his mind is above the threats of danger.[2] And so, comparing the statesman and the general, men may argue as they please as to the pre-eminent respect which is due to either above the other; but the verdict of the aesthetic judgement is for the latter. War itself, provided it is conducted with order and a sacred respect for the rights of civilians, has something sublime about it, and gives nations that carry it on in such a manner a stamp of mind only the more sublime the more numerous the dangers to which they are exposed, and which they are able to meet with fortitude. On the other hand, a prolonged peace favours the predominance of a mere commercial spirit, and with it a debasing self-interest, cowardice, and effeminacy, and tends to degrade the character of the nation.

So far as sublimity is predicated of might, this solution of the concept of it appears at variance with the fact that we are wont to represent God in the tempest, the storm, the earthquake, and the like, as presenting Himself in His wrath, but at the same time also in His sublimity, and yet here it would be alike folly and presumption to imagine a pre-eminence of our minds over the operations and, as it appears, even over the direction of such might. Here, instead of a feeling of the sublimity of our own nature, submission, prostration, and a feeling of utter helplessness seem more to constitute the attitude of mind befitting the manifestation of such an object, and to be that also more customarily associated with the idea of it on the occasion of a natural phenomenon of this kind. In religion, as a rule, prostration, adoration with bowed head, coupled with contrite, timorous posture and voice, seems to be the only becoming demeanour in presence of the Godhead, and accordingly most nations have assumed and still observe it. Yet this cast of mind is far from being intrinsically and necessarily involved in the idea of the *sublimity* of a religion and of its object. The man that is actually in a state of fear, finding in himself good reason to be so, because he is conscious of offending with his evil disposition against a might directed by a will at once irresistible and just, is far from being in the frame of mind for admiring divine greatness, for which a temper of calm reflection and a quite free judgement are required. Only when he becomes conscious of having a disposition that is upright and acceptable to God, do those operations of might serve to stir within him the idea of the sublimity of this Being, so far as he recognizes the existence in himself of a sublimity of disposition consonant with His will, and is thus raised above the dread of such operations of nature, in which he no longer sees God pouring forth the vials of the wrath. Even humility, taking the form of an uncompromising judgement upon his shortcomings, which, with consciousness of good intentions, might readily be glossed over on the ground of the frailty of human nature, is a sublime temper of the mind voluntarily to undergo the pain of remorse as a means of more and more effectually eradicating its cause. In this way religion is intrinsically distinguished from superstition, which latter rears in the mind, not reverence for the sublime, but dread and apprehension of the all-powerful Being to whose will terror-stricken man sees himself subjected, yet without according Him due honour. From this nothing can arise but grace-begging and vain adulation, instead of a religion consisting in a good life.

Sublimity, therefore, does not reside in any of the things of nature, but only in our own mind, in so far as we may become conscious of our superiority over nature within, and thus also over nature without us (as exerting influence upon us). Everything that provokes this feeling in us, including the *might* of nature which challenges our strength, is then, though improperly, called sublime, and it is only under presuppo-

[1] [Cf. King Henry's address before Harfleur; Shakespeare, *King Henry V*, Act III, Scene i.]

[2] [Cf. Aristotle's remarks on Courage, in the *Ethics*, III, 6, *et seq.*]

tion of this idea within us, and in relation to it, that we are capable of attaining to the idea of the sublimity of that Being which inspires deep respect in us, not by the mere display of its might in nature, but more by the faculty which is planted in us of estimating that might without fear, and of regarding our estate as exalted above it.

§ 29. *Modality of the judgement on the sublime in nature*

BEAUTIFUL nature contains countless things as to which we at once take every one as in their judgement concurring with our own, and as to which we may further expect this concurrence without facts finding us far astray. But in respect of our judgement upon the sublime in nature, we cannot so easily vouch for ready acceptance by others. For a far higher degree of culture,[1] not merely of the aesthetic judgement, but also of the faculties of cognition which lie at its basis, seems to be requisite to enable us to lay down a judgement upon this high distinction of natural objects.

The proper mental mood for a feeling of the sublime postulates the mind's susceptibility for ideas, since it is precisely in the failure of nature to attain to these—and consequently only under presupposition of this susceptibility and of the straining of the imagination to use nature as a schema for ideas—that there is something forbidding to sensibility, but which, for all that, has an attraction for us, arising from the fact of its being a dominion which reason exercises over sensibility with a view to extending it to the requirements of its own realm (the practical) and letting it look out beyond itself into the infinite, which for it is an abyss. In fact, without the development of moral ideas, that which, thanks to preparatory culture, we call sublime, merely strikes the untutored man as terrifying. He will see in the evidences which the ravages of nature give of her dominion, and in the vast scale of her might, compared with which his own is diminished to insignificance, only the misery, peril, and distress that would compass the man who was thrown to its mercy. So the simple-minded, and, for the most part, intelligent, Savoyard peasant, (as Herr von Sassure relates), unhesitatingly called all lovers of snow-mountains *fools*. And who can tell whether he would have been so wide of the mark, if that student of nature had taken the risk of the dangers to which he exposed himself merely, as most travellers do, for a fad, or so as some day to be able to give a thrilling account of his adventures? But the mind of Sassure was bent on the instruction of mankind, and soul-stirring sensations that excellent man indeed had, and the reader of his travels got them thrown into the bargain.

But the fact that culture is requisite for the judgement upon the sublime in nature (more than for that upon the beautiful) does not involve its being an original product of culture and something introduced in a more or less conventional way into society.[2] Rather is it in human nature that its foundations are laid, and, in fact, in that which, at once with common understanding, we may expect every one to possess and may require of him, namely, a native capacity for the feeling for (practical) ideas, i.e., for moral feeling.

This, now, is the foundation of the necessity of that agreement between other men's judgements upon the sublime and our own, which we make our own imply. For just as we taunt a man who is quite inappreciative when forming an estimate of an object of nature in which we see beauty, with want *of taste*, so we say of a man who remains unaffected in the presence of what we consider sublime, that he has no *feeling*.[3] But we demand both taste and feeling of every man, and, granted some degree of culture, we give him credit for both. Still, we do so with this difference: that, in the case of the former, since judgement there refers the imagination merely to the understanding, as the faculty of concepts, we make the requirement as a matter of course, whereas in the case of the latter, since here the judgement refers the imagination to reason, as a faculty of ideas, we do so only under a subjective presupposition (which, however, we believe we are warranted in making), namely, that of the moral feeling in man. And, on this assumption, we attribute necessity to the latter aesthetic judgement also.

In this modality of aesthetic judgements, namely, their assumed necessity, lies what is for the Critique of Judgement a moment of capital importance. For this is exactly what makes an *a priori* principle apparent in their case, and lifts them out of the sphere of empirical psychology, in which otherwise they would remain buried amid the feelings of gratification and pain (only with the senseless epithet of *finer* feeling), so as to place them, and, thanks to them, to place the faculty of judgement itself, in the class of judgements of which the basis of an *a priori*

1 [Cf. p. 518, *et seq.*]

2 [Cf. p. 493.]

3 [Cf. pp. 523; 549, *et seq.*]

principle is the distinguishing feature, and, thus distinguished, to introduce them into transcendental philosophy.

General Remark upon the Exposition of Aesthetic Reflective Judgements

In relation to the feeling of pleasure an object is to be counted either as *agreeable*, or *beautiful*, or *sublime*, or *good* (absolutely), *(incundum, pulchrum, sublime, honestum)*.

As the motive of desires the *agreeable* is invariably of one and the same kind, no matter what its source or how specifically different the representation (of sense and sensation objectively considered). Hence in estimating its influence upon the mind, the multitude of its charms (simultaneous or successive) is alone revelant, and so only, as it were, the mass of the agreeable sensation, and it is only by the *quantity*, therefore, that this can be made intelligible. Further it in no way conduces to our culture, but belongs only to mere enjoyment. The *beautiful*, on the other hand, requires the representation of a certain *quality* of the object, that permits also of being understood and reduced to concepts (although in the aesthetic judgement it is not so reduced), and it cultivates, as it instructs us to attend to finality in the feeling of pleasure. The *sublime* consists merely in the *relation* exhibited by the estimate of the serviceability of the sensible in the representation of nature for a possible supersensible employment. The *absolutely good*, estimated subjectively according to the feeling it inspires (the object of the moral feeling), as the determinability of the powers of the subject by means of the representation of an *absolutely necessitating* law, is principally distinguished by the *modality* of a necessity resting upon concepts *a priori*, and involving not a mere *claim*, but a *command* upon every one to assent, and belongs intrinsically not to the aesthetic, but to the pure intellectual judgement. Further, it is not ascribed to nature but to freedom, and that in a determinant and not a merely reflective judgement. But the *determinability of the subject* by means of this idea, and, what is more, that of a subject which can be sensible, in the way of a *modification of its state*, to *hindrances* on the part of sensibility, while, at the same time, it can by surmounting them feel superiority over them—a determinability, in other words, as moral feeling—is still so allied to aesthetic judgement and its *formal conditions* as to be capable of being pressed into the service of the aesthetic representation of the conformity to law of action from duty, i.e., of the representation of this as sublime, or even as beautiful, without forfeiting its purity—an impossible result were one to make it naturally bound up with the feeling of the agreeable.

The net result to be extracted from the exposition so far given of both kinds of aesthetic judgements may be summed up in the following brief definitions:

The *beautiful* is what pleases in the mere estimate formed of it (consequently not by intervention of any feeling of sense in accordance with a concept of the understanding). From this it follows at once that it must please apart from all interest.

The *sublime* is what pleases immediately by reason of its opposition to the interest of sense.

Both, as definitions of aesthetic universally valid estimates, have reference to subjective grounds. In the one case the reference is to grounds of sensibility, in so far as these are final on behalf of the contemplative understanding, in the other case in so far as, in their *opposition* to sensibility, they are, on the contrary, final in reference to the ends of practical reason. Both, however, as united in the same subject, are final in reference to the moral feeling. The beautiful prepares us to love something, even nature, apart from any interest: the sublime to esteem something highly even in opposition to our (sensible) interest.

The sublime may be described in this way: It is an object (of nature) the *representation of which determines the mind to regard the elevation of nature beyond our reach as equivalent to a presentation of ideas.*

In a literal sense and according to their logical import, ideas cannot be presented. But if we enlarge our empirical faculty of representation (mathematical or dynamical) with a view to the intuition of nature, reason inevitably steps forward, as the faculty concerned with the independence of the absolute totality, and calls forth the effort of the mind, unavailing though it be, to make representation of sense adequate to this totality. This effort, and the feeling of the unattainability of the idea by means of imagination, is itself a presentation of the subjective finality of our mind in the employment of the imagination in the interests of the mind's supersensible province, and compels us subjectively to *think* nature itself in its totality as a presentation of something supersensible, without our being able to effectuate this presentation *objectively*.

For we readily see that nature in space and

time falls entirely short of the unconditioned, consequently also of the absolutely great, which still the commonest reason demands. And by this we are also reminded that we have only to do with nature as phenomenon, and that this itself must be regarded as the mere presentation of a nature-in-itself (which exists in the idea of reason). But this idea of the supersensible, which no doubt we cannot further determine—so that we cannot *cognize* nature as its presentation, but only *think* it as such—is awakened in us by an object the aesthetic estimating of which strains the imagination to its utmost, whether in respect of its extension (mathematical), or of its might over the mind (dynamical). For it is founded upon the feeling of a sphere of the mind which altogether exceeds the realm of nature (i.e., upon the moral feeling), with regard to which the representation of the object is estimated as subjectively final.

As a matter of fact, a feeling for the sublime in nature is hardly thinkable unless in association with an attitude of mind resembling the moral. And though, like that feeling, the immediate pleasure in the beautiful in nature presupposes and cultivates a certain *liberality* of thought, i.e., makes our delight independent of any mere enjoyment of sense, still it represents freedom rather as in *play* than as exercising a law-ordained *function*, which is the genuine characteristic of human morality, where reason has to impose its dominion upon sensibility. There is, however, this qualification, that in the aesthetic judgement upon the sublime this dominion is represented as exercised through the imagination itself as an instrument of reason.

Thus, too, delight in the sublime in nature is only *negative* (whereas that in the beautiful is *positive*): that is to say, it is a feeling of imagination by its own act depriving itself of its freedom by receiving a final determination in accordance with a law other than that of its empirical employment. In this way it gains an extension and a might greater than that which it sacrifices. But the ground of this is concealed from it, and in its place it *feels* the sacrifice or deprivation, as well as its cause, to which it is subjected. The *astonishment* amounting almost to terror, the awe and thrill of devout feeling, that takes hold of one when gazing upon the prospect of mountains ascending to heaven, deep ravines and torrents raging there, deep-shadowed solitudes that invite to brooding melancholy, and the like—all this, when we are assured of our own safety, is not actual fear. Rather is it an attempt to gain access to it through imagination, for the purpose of feeling the might of this faculty in combining the movement of the mind thereby aroused with its serenity, and of thus being superior to internal and, therefore, to external, nature, so far as the latter can have any bearing upon our feeling of well-being. For the imagination, in accordance with laws of association, makes our state of contentment dependent upon physical conditions. But acting in accordance with principles of the schematism of judgement (consequently so far as it is subordinated to freedom), it is at the same time an instrument of reason and its ideas. But in this capacity it is a might enabling us to assert our independence as against the influences of nature, to degrade what is great in respect of the latter to the level of what is little, and thus to locate the absolutely great only in the proper estate of the subject. This reflection of aesthetic judgement by which it raises itself to the point of adequacy with reason, though without any determinate concept of reason, is still a representation of the object as subjectively final, by virtue even of the objective inadequacy of the imagination in its greatest extension for meeting the demands of reason (as the faculty of ideas).

Here we have to attend generally to what has been already adverted to, that in the transcendental aesthetic of judgement there must be no question of anything but pure aesthetic judgements. Consequently examples are not to be selected from such beautiful or sublime objects as presuppose the concept of an end. For then the finality would be either teleological, or based upon mere sensations of an object (gratification or pain) and so, in the first case, not aesthetic, and, in the second, not merely formal. So, if we call the sight of the starry heaven *sublime*, we must not found our estimate of it upon any concepts of worlds inhabited by rational beings, with the bright spots, which we see filling the space above us, as their suns moving in orbits prescribed for them with the wisest regard to ends. But we must take it, just as it strikes the eye, as a broad and all-embracing canopy: and it is merely under such a representation that we may posit the sublimity which the pure aesthetic judgement attributes to this object. Similarly, as to the prospect of the ocean, we are not to regard it as we, with our minds stored with knowledge on a variety of matters (which, however, is not contained in the immediate intuition), are wont to represent it in *thought*, as, let us say, a spacious realm of aquatic creatures, or as the mighty reservoirs from which are drawn the vapours that fill the air with clouds of moisture for the good of the land, or yet as an element which no doubt divides continent from continent, but at the same time affords the means of the greatest commercial intercourse between them—for in this way we get nothing beyond teleological judgements. Instead of this we must be able to see sublimity in the ocean, regarding it, as the poets do, according to what the impression upon the eye reveals, as, let us say, in its calm, a clear mirror of water bounded only by the heavens, or, be it disturbed, as threatening to overwhelm and engulf everything. The same is to be said of the sublime and beautiful in the human form. Here, for determining grounds of the judgement, we must not have recourse to concepts of ends *subserved* by all its limbs and members, or allow their accordance with these ends to *influence* our aesthetic judgement (in such case no longer pure), although it is certainly also a necessary condition of aesthetic delight that they should not conflict with these ends. Aesthetic finality is the conformity to law of judgement in its *freedom.* The delight in the object depends upon the reference which we seek to give to the imagination, subject to the proviso that it is to entertain the mind in a free activity. If, on the other hand, something else—be it sensation or concept of the understanding—determines the judgement, it is then conformable to law, no doubt, but not an act of *free* judgement.

Hence to speak of intellectual beauty or sublimity is to use expressions which, in the *first* place, are not quite correct. For these are aesthetic modes of representation which would be entirely foreign to us were we merely pure intelligences (or if we even put ourselves in thought in the position of such). *Secondly,* although both, as objects of an intellectual (moral) delight, are compatible with aesthetic delight to the extent of not *resting* upon any interest, still, on the other hand, there is a difficulty in the way of their alliance with such delight, since their function is to *produce* an interest, and, on the assumption that the presentation has to accord with delight in the aesthetic estimate, this interest could only be effected by means of an interest of sense combined with it in the presentation. But in this way the intellectual finality would be violated and rendered impure.

The object of a pure and unconditioned intellectual delight is the moral law in the might which it exerts in us over all *antecedent* motives of the mind. Now, since it is only through sacrifices that this might makes itself known to us aesthetically (and this involves a deprivation of something—though in the interest of inner freedom—whilst in turn it reveals in us an unfathomable depth of this supersensible faculty, the consequences of which extend beyond reach of the eye of sense), it follows that the delight, looked at from the aesthetic side (in reference to sensibility) is negative, i.e., opposed to this interest, but from the intellectual side, positive and bound up with an interest. Hence it follows that the intellectual and intrinsically final (moral) good, estimated aesthetically, instead of being represented as beautiful, must rather be represented as sublime, with the result that it arouses more a feeling of respect (which disdains charm) than of love or of the heart being drawn towards it—for human nature does not of its own proper motion accord with the good, but only by virtue of the dominion which reason exercises over sensibility. Conversely, that, too, which we call sublime in external nature, or even internal nature (e.g., certain affections) is only represented as a might of the mind enabling it to overcome this or that hindrance of sensibility by means of moral principles, and it is from this that it derives its interest.

I must dwell a while on the latter point. The idea of the good to which affection is superadded is *enthusiasm.* This state of mind appears to be sublime: so much so that there is a common saying that nothing great can be achieved without it. But now every affection[1] is blind either as to the choice of its end, or, supposing this has been furnished by reason, in the way it is effected—for it is that mental movement whereby the exercise of free deliberation upon fundamental principles, with a view to determining oneself accordingly, is rendered impossible. On this account it cannot merit any delight on the part of reason. Yet, from an aesthetic point of view, enthusiasm is sublime, because it is an effort of one's powers called forth by ideas which give to the mind an impetus of far stronger and more enduring efficacy than the stimulus afforded by sensible representations. But (as seems strange) even *freedom from affection* (*apatheia, phlegma in significatu bono)* in a mind that strenuously follows its unswerving principles is sublime, and

[1] There is a specific distinction between *affections* and *passions.* Affections are related merely to feeling; passions belong to the faculty of desire, and are inclinations that hinder or render impossible all determinability of the elective will by principles. Affections are impetuous and irresponsible; passions are abiding and deliberate. Thus resentment, in the form of anger, is an affection: but in the form of hatred (vindictiveness) it is a passion. Under no circumstances can the latter be called sublime; for, while the freedom of the mind is, no doubt, *impeded* in the case of affection, in passion it is abrogated.

that, too, in a manner vastly superior, because it has at the same time the delight of pure reason on its side. Such a stamp of mind is alone called *noble*. This expression, however, comes in time to be applied to things—such as buildings, a garment, literary style, the carriage of one's person, and the like—provided they do not so much excite *astonishment* (the affection attending the representation of novelty exceeding expectation) as *admiration* (an astonishment which does not cease when the novelty wears off)—and this obtains where ideas undesignedly and artlessly accord in their presentation with aesthetic delight.

Every affection of the STRENUOUS TYPE (such, that is, as excites the consciousness of our power of overcoming every resistance [*animus strenuus*]) is *aesthetically sublime*, e.g., anger, even desperation (the *rage of forlorn hope* but not *faint-hearted* despair). On the other hand, affection of the LANGUID TYPE (which converts the very effort of resistance into an object of displeasure [*animus languidus*] has nothing noble about it, though it may take its rank as possessing beauty of the sensuous order. Hence the *emotions* capable of attaining the strength of an affection are very diverse. We have *spirited*, and we have *tender* emotions. When the strength of the latter reaches that of an affection they can be turned to no account. The propensity to indulge in them is *sentimentality*. A sympathetic grief that refuses to be consoled, or one that has to do with imaginary misfortune to which we deliberately give way so far as to allow our fancy to delude us into thinking it actual fact, indicates and goes to make a tender, but at the same time weak, soul, which shows a beautiful side, and may no doubt be called *fanciful*, but never *enthusiastic*. Romances, maudlin dramas, shallow homilies, which trifle with so-called (though falsely so) noble sentiments, but in fact make the heart enervated, insensitive to the stern precepts of duty, and incapable of respect for the worth of humanity in our own person and the rights of men (which is something quite other than their happiness), and in general incapable of all firm principles; even a religious discourse which recommends a cringing and abject grace-begging and favour-seeking, abandoning all reliance on our own ability to resist the evil within us, in place of the vigorous resolution to try to get the better of our inclinations by means of those powers which, miserable sinners though we be, are still left to us; that false humility by which self-abasement, whining hypocritical repentance and a merely passive frame of mind are set down as the method by which alone we can become acceptable to the Supreme Being—these have neither lot nor fellowship with what may be reckoned to belong to beauty, not to speak of sublimity, of mental temperament.

But even impetuous movements of the mind —be they allied under the name of *edification* with ideas of religion, or, as pertaining merely to culture, with ideas involving a social interest— no matter what tension of the imagination they may produce, can in no way lay claim to the honour of a *sublime* presentation, if they do not leave behind them a temper of mind which, though it be only indirectly, has an influence upon the consciousness of the mind's strength and resoluteness in respect of that which carries with it pure intellectual finality (the supersensible). For, in the absence of this, all these emotions belong only to *motion*, which we welcome in the interests of good health. The agreeable lassitude that follows upon being stirred up in that way by the play of the affections, is a fruition of the state of well-being arising from the restoration of the equilibrium of the various vital forces within us. This, in the last resort, comes to no more than what the Eastern voluptuaries find so soothing when they get their bodies massaged, and all their muscles and joints softly pressed and bent; only that in the first case the principle that occasions the movement is chiefly internal, whereas here it is entirely external. Thus, many a man believes himself edified by a sermon in which there is no establishment of anything (no system of good maxims); or thinks himself improved by a tragedy, when he is merely glad at having got well rid of the feeling of being bored. Thus the sublime must in every case have reference to our *way of thinking*, i.e., to maxims directed to giving the intellectual side of our nature and the ideas of reason supremacy over sensibility.

We have no reason to fear that the feeling of the sublime will suffer from an abstract mode of presentation like this, which is altogether negative as to what is sensuous. For though the imagination, no doubt, finds nothing beyond the sensible world to which it can lay hold, still this thrusting aside of the sensible barriers gives it a feeling of being unbounded; and that removal is thus a presentation of the infinite. As such it can never be anything more than a negative presentation—but still it expands the soul. Perhaps there is no more sublime passage in the Jewish Law than the commandment: "Thou shalt not make unto thee any graven image, or any likeness of any thing that is in heaven or on earth, or under the earth, etc." This commandment can alone explain the enthusiasm which the Jewish people, in their moral period, felt for their religion when comparing themselves with others, or the pride inspired by Mohammedanism. The very same holds good of our representation of the moral law and of our native capacity for morality. The fear that, if we divest this representation of everything that can commend it to the senses, it will thereupon be attended only with a cold and lifeless approbation and not with any moving force or emotion, is wholly unwarranted. The very reverse is the truth. For when nothing any longer meets the eye of sense, and the unmistakable and ineffaceable idea of morality is left in possession of the field, there would be need rather of tempering the ardour of an unbounded imagination to prevent it rising to enthusiasm, than of seeking to lend these ideas the aid of images and childish devices for fear of their being wanting in potency. For this reason, governments have gladly let religion be fully equipped with these accessories, seeking in this way to relieve their subjects of the exertion, but to deprive them, at the same time, of the ability, required for expanding their spiritual powers beyond the limits arbitrarily laid down for them, and which facilitate their being treated as though they were merely passive.

This pure, elevating, merely negative presentation of morality involves, on the other hand, no fear of *fanaticism,* which is a *delusion* that would *will some* VISION *beyond all the bounds of sensibility;* i.e., would dream according to principles (rational raving). The safeguard is the purely negative character of the presentation. For *the inscrutability of the idea of freedom* precludes all positive presentation. The moral law, however, is a sufficient and original source of determination within us: so it does not for a moment permit us to cast about for a ground of determination external to itself. If enthusiasm is comparable to *delirium,* fanaticism may be compared to *mania.* Of these, the latter is least of all compatible with the sublime, for it is *profoundly* ridiculous. In enthusiasm, as an affection, the imagination is unbridled; in fanaticism, as a deep-seated, brooding passion, it is anomalous. The first is a transitory accident to which the healthiest understanding is liable to become at times the victim; the second is an undermining disease.

Simplicity (artless finality) is, as it were, the style adopted by nature in the sublime. It is also that of morality. The latter is a second (supersensible) nature, whose laws alone we know, without being able to attain to an intuition of the supersensible faculty within us—that which contains the ground of this legislation.

One further remark. The delight in the sublime, no less than in the beautiful, by reason of its universal *communicability* not alone is plainly distinguished from other aesthetic judgements, but also from this same property acquires an interest in society (in which it admits of such communication). Yet, despite this, we have to note the fact that *isolation from all society* is looked upon as something sublime, provided it rests upon ideas which disregard all sensible interest. To be self-sufficing, and so not to stand in need of society, yet without being unsociable, i.e., without shunning it, is something approaching the sublime—a remark applicable to all superiority to wants. On the other hand, to shun our fellow men from *misanthropy,* because of enmity towards them, or from *anthropophobia,* because we imagine the hand of every man is against us, is partly odious, partly contemptible. There is, however, a misanthropy (most improperly so called), the tendency towards which is to be found with advancing years in many right-minded men, that, as far as *good will* goes, is no doubt, philanthropic enough, but as the result of long and sad experience, is widely removed from *delight* in mankind. We see evidences of this in the propensity to recluseness, in the fanciful desire for a retired country seat, or else (with the young) in the dream of the happiness of being able to spend one's life with a little family on an island unknown to the rest of the world—material of which novelists or writers of Robinsonades know how to make such good use. Falsehood, ingratitude, injustice, the puerility of the ends which we ourselves look upon as great and momentous, and to compass which man inflicts upon his brother man all imaginable evils—these all so contradict the idea of what men might be if they only would, and are so at variance with our active wish to see them better, that, to avoid hating where we cannot love, it seems but a slight sacrifice to forego all the joys of fellowship with our kind. This sadness, which is not directed to the evils which fate brings down upon others (a sadness which springs from sympathy), but to those which they inflict upon themselves (one which is based on antipathy in questions of principle), is sublime because it is founded on ideas, whereas that springing from sympathy can only be accounted beautiful. Sassure, who was no less ingenious than profound, in the description of his Alpine travels remarks of Bonhomme, one of the Savoy mountains: "There reigns there a certain *insipid sadness.*" He recognized, therefore, that, besides this, there is an *interesting* sadness, such as is inspired by the sight of some desolate place into which men might fain withdraw themselves so as to hear no more of the world without, and be no longer versed in its affairs, a place, however, which must yet not be so altogether inhospitable as only to afford a most miserable retreat for a human being. I only make this observation as a reminder that even melancholy, (but not dispirited sadness), may take its place among the *vigorous* affections, provided it has its root in moral ideas. If, however, it is grounded upon sympathy, and, as such, is lovable, it belongs only to the *languid* affections. And this serves to call attention to the mental temperament which in the first case alone is *sublime.*

The transcendental exposition of aesthetic judgements now brought to a close may be compared with the physiological, as worked out by Burke and many acute men among us, so that we may see where a merely empirical exposition of the sublime and beautiful would bring us. Burke,[1] who deserves to be called the foremost author in this method of treatment, deduces, on these lines, "that the feeling of the sublime is grounded on the impulse towards self-preservation and on *fear,* i.e., on a pain, which, since it does not go the length of disordering the bodily parts, calls forth movements which, as they clear the vessels, whether fine or gross, of a dangerous and troublesome encumbrance, are capable of producing delight; not pleasure but a sort of delightful horror, a sort of tranquillity tinged with terror." The beautiful, which he grounds on love (from which, still, he would have desire kept separate), he reduces to "the relaxing, slackening, and enervating of the fibres of the body, and consequently a softening, a dissolving, a languor, and a fainting, dying, and melting away for pleasure." And this explanation he supports, not alone by instances in which the feeling of the beautiful as well as of the sublime is capable of being excited in us by the imagination in conjunction with the understanding, but even by instances when it is in conjunction with sensations. As psychological observations, these analyses of our mental phenomena are extremely fine, and supply a wealth of material for the favourite investigations of empirical anthropology. But, besides that, there is no denying the fact that all representations within us, no matter whether they are objectively merely sensible or wholly intellectual, are still subjectively associable with gratification or pain, however imperceptible either of these may be. (For these representations one and all have an influence on the feeling of life, and none of them, so far as it is a modification of the subject, can be indifferent.) We must even admit that, as Epicurus maintained, *gratification* and *pain* though proceeding from the imagination or even from representations of the understanding, are always in the last resort corporeal, since apart from any feeling of the bodily organ life would be merely a consciousness of one's existence, and could not include any feeling of well-being or the reverse, i.e., of the furtherance or hindrance of the vital forces. For, of itself alone, the mind is all life (the life-principle itself), and hindrance or furtherance has to be sought outside it, and yet in the man himself consequently in the connection with his body.

But if we attribute the delight in the object wholly and entirely to the gratification which it affords through charm or emotion, then we must not exact from *any one else* agreement with the aesthetic judgement passed by *us.* For, in such matters each person rightly consults his own personal feeling alone. But in that case there is an end of all censorship of taste—unless the example afforded by others as the result of a contingent coincidence of their judgements is to be held over us as *commanding* our assent. But this principle we would presumably resent, and appeal to our natural right of submitting a judgement to our own sense, where it rests upon the immediate feeling of personal well-being, instead of submitting it to that of others.

Hence if the import of the judgement of taste, where we appraise it as a judgement entitled to require the concurrence of every one, cannot be *egoistic,* but must necessarily, from its inner nature, be allowed a *pluralistic* validity, i.e., on account of what taste itself is, and not on account of the examples which others give of their taste, then it must found upon some *a priori* principle (be it subjective or objective), and no amount of prying into the empirical laws of the changes that go on within the mind can succeed in establishing such a principle. For these laws only yield a knowledge of how we do judge, but they do not give us a command as to how we ought to judge, and, what is more, such a command as is *unconditioned*—and commands of this kind are presupposed by judgements of taste, inasmuch

[1] See p. 223 of the German translation of his work: *Philosophical Investigations as to the Origin of our Conceptions of the Beautiful and Sublime.* Riga, published by Hartknock, 1773.

as they require delight to be taken as *immediately* connected with a representation. Accordingly, though the empirical exposition of aesthetic judgements may be a first step towards accumulating the material for a higher investigation, yet a transcendental examination of this faculty is possible, and forms an essential part of the Critique of Taste. For, were not taste in possession of *a priori* principles, it could not possibly sit in judgement upon the judgements of others and pass sentence of commendation or condemnation upon them, with even the least semblance of authority.

The remaining part of the Analytic of the aesthetic judgement contains first of all the:

Deduction of Pure Aesthetic Judgements

§ 30. *The deduction of aesthetic judgements upon objects of nature must not be directed to what we call sublime in nature, but only to the beautiful*

THE claim of an aesthetic judgement to universal validity for every subject, being a judgement which must rely on some *a priori* principle, stands in need of a deduction (i.e., a derivation of its title). Further, where the delight or aversion turns on the *form of the object* this has to be something over and above the exposition of the judgement. Such is the case with judgements of taste upon the beautiful in nature. For there the finality has its foundation in the object and its outward form—although it does not signify the reference of this to other objects according to concepts (for the purpose of cognitive judgements), but is merely concerned in general with the apprehension of this form so far as it proves accordant in the mind with the *faculty* of concepts as well as with that of their presentation (which is identical with that of apprehension). With regard to the beautiful in nature, therefore, we may start a number of questions touching the cause of this finality of their forms: e.g., how we are to explain why nature has scattered beauty abroad with so lavish a hand, even in the depth of the ocean where it can but seldom be reached by the eye of man—for which alone it is final?

But the sublime in nature—if we pass upon it a pure aesthetic judgement unmixed with concepts of perfection, as objective finality, which would make the judgement teleological—may be regarded as completely wanting in form or figure, and none the less be looked upon as an object of pure delight, and indicate a subjective finality of the given representation. So, now, the question suggests itself, whether in addition to the exposition of what is thought in an aesthetic judgement of this kind, we may be called upon to give a deduction of its claim to some (subjective) *a priori* principle.

This we may meet with the reply that the sublime in nature is improperly so called, and that sublimity should, in strictness, be attributed merely to the attitude of thought, or, rather, to that which serves as basis for this in human nature. The apprehension of an object otherwise formless and in conflict with ends supplies the mere occasion[1] for our coming to a consciousness of this basis; and the object is in this way put to a subjectively-final *use*, but it is not estimated as subjectively-final *on its own account* and because of its form. (It is, as it were, a *species finalis accepta, non data.*) Consequently the exposition we gave of judgements upon the sublime in nature was at the same time their deduction. For, in our analysis of the reflection on the part of judgement in this case, we found that in such judgements there is a final relation of the cognitive faculties, which has to be laid *a priori* at the basis of the faculty of ends (the will), and which is therefore itself *a priori* final. This, then, at once involves the deduction, i.e., the justification of the claim of such a judgement to universally-necessary validity.

Hence we may confine our search to one for the deduction of judgements of taste, i.e., of judgements upon the beauty of things of nature, and this will satisfactorily dispose of the problem for the entire aesthetic faculty of judgement.

§ 31. *Of the method of the deduction of judgements of taste*

THE obligation to furnish a deduction, i.e., a guarantee of the legitimacy of judgements of a particular kind, only arises where the judgement lays claim to necessity. This is the case even where it requires subjective universality, i.e., the concurrence of every one, albeit the judgement is not a cognitive judgement, but only one of pleasure or displeasure in a given object, i.e., an assumption of a subjective finality that has a thoroughgoing validity for every one, and which, since the judgement is one of taste, is not to be grounded upon any concept of the thing.

Now, in the latter case, we are not dealing with a judgement of cognition—neither with a theoretical one based on the concept of a *nature* in general, supplied by understanding, nor

[1] [Cf. p. 518.]

with a (pure) practical one based on the idea of *freedom*, as given *a priori* by reason—and so we are not called upon to justify *a priori* the validity of a judgement which represents either what a thing is, or that there is something which I ought to do in order to produce it. Consequently, if for judgement generally we demonstrate the *universal validity* of a *singular* judgement expressing the subjective finality of an empirical representation of the form of an object, we shall do all that is needed to explain how it is possible that something can please in the mere formation of an estimate of it (without sensation or concept), and how, just as the estimate of an object for the sake of a *cognition* generally has universal rules, the delight of any one person may be pronounced as a rule for every other.

Now if this universal validity is not to be based on a collection of votes and interrogation of others as to what sort of sensations they experience, but is to rest, as it were, upon an autonomy of the subject passing judgement on the feeling of pleasure (in the given representation), i.e., upon his own taste, and yet is also not to be derived from concepts; then it follows that such a judgement—and such the judgement of taste in fact is—has a double and also logical peculiarity. For, *first*, it has universal validity *a priori*, yet without having a logical universality according to concepts, but only the universality of a singular judgement. *Secondly*, it has a necessity (which must invariably rest upon *a priori* grounds), but one which depends upon no *a priori* proofs by the representation of which it would be competent to enforce the assent which the judgement of taste demands of every one.

The solution of these logical peculiarities, which distinguish a judgement of taste from all cognitive judgements, will of itself suffice for a deduction of this strange faculty, provided we abstract at the outset from all content of the judgement, viz., from the feeling of pleasure, and merely compare the aesthetic form with the form of objective judgements as prescribed by logic.[1] We shall first try, with the help of examples, to illustrate and bring out these characteristic properties of taste.

§ 32. *First peculiarity of the judgement of taste*

THE judgement of taste determines its object in respect of delight (as a thing of beauty) with a claim to the agreement of *every one*, just as if it were objective.

To say: "This flower is beautiful," is tantamount to repeating its own proper claim to the delight of everyone. The agreeableness of its smell gives it no claim at all. One man revels in it, but it gives another a headache. Now what else are we to suppose from this than that its beauty is to be taken for a property of the flower itself[2] which does not adapt itself to the diversity of heads and the individual senses of the multitude, but to which they must adapt themselves, if they are going to pass judgement upon it. And yet this is not the way the matter stands. For the judgement of taste consists precisely in a thing being called beautiful solely in respect of that quality in which it adapts itself to our mode of taking it in.

Besides, every judgement which is to show the taste of the individual, is required to be an independent judgement of the individual himself. There must be no need of groping about among other people's judgements and getting previous instruction from their delight in or aversion to the same object. Consequently his judgement should be given out *a priori*, and not as an imitation relying on the general pleasure a thing gives as a matter of fact. One would think, however, that a judgement *a priori* must involve a concept of the object for the cognition of which it contains the principle. But the judgement of taste is not founded on concepts, and is in no way a cognition, but only an aesthetic judgement.

Hence it is that a youthful poet refuses to allow himself to be dissuaded from the conviction that his poem is beautiful, either by the judgement of the public or of his friends. And even if he lends them an ear, he does so, not because he has now come to a different judgement, but because, though the whole public, at least so far as his work is concerned, should have false taste, he still, in his desire for recognition, finds good reason to accommodate himself to the popular error (even against his own judgement). It is only in aftertime, when his judgement has been sharpened by exercise, that of his own free will and accord he deserts his former judgements—behaving in just the same way as with those of his judgements which depend wholly upon reason. Taste lays claim simply to autonomy. To make the judgements of others the determining ground of one's own would be heteronomy.

The fact that we recommend the works of the ancients as models, and rightly too, and call their authors *classical*, as constituting a sort of nobility among writers that leads the way and thereby gives laws to the people, seems to indi-

[1] [Cf. p. 476.]

[2] [Cf. pp. 480, 544.]

cate *a posteriori* sources of taste and to contradict the autonomy of taste in each individual. But we might just as well say that the ancient mathematicians, who, to this day, are looked upon as the almost indispensable models of perfect thoroughness and elegance in synthetic methods, prove that reason also is on our part only imitative, and that it is incompetent with the deepest intuition to produce of itself rigorous proofs by means of the construction of concepts. There is no employment of our powers, no matter how free, not even of reason itself (which must create all its judgements from the common *a priori* source), which, if each individual had always to start afresh with the crude equipment of his natural state, would not get itself involved in blundering attempts, did not those of others lie before it as a warning. Not that predecessors make those who follow in their steps mere imitators, but by their methods they set others upon the track of seeking in themselves for the principles, and so of adopting their own, often better, course. Even in religion—where undoubtedly every one has to derive his rule of conduct from himself, seeing that he himself remains responsible for it and, when he goes wrong, cannot shift the blame upon others as teachers or leaders—general precepts learned at the feet either of priests or philosophers, or even drawn from ones' own resources, are never so efficacious as an example of virtue or holiness, which, historically portrayed, does not dispense with the autonomy of virtue drawn from the spontaneous and original idea of morality *(a priori),* or convert this into a mechanical process of imitation. *Following* which has reference to a precedent, and not imitation, is the proper expression for all influence which the products of an exemplary *author* may exert upon others—and this means no more than going to the same sources for a creative work as those to which he went for his creations, and learning from one's predecessor no more than the mode of availing oneself of such sources. Taste, just because its judgement cannot be determined by concepts or precepts, is among all faculties and talents the very one that stands most in need of examples of what has in the course of culture maintained itself longest in esteem. Thus it avoids an early lapse into crudity and a return to the rudeness of its earliest efforts.

§ 33. *Second peculiarity of the judgement of taste*

Proofs are of no avail whatever for determining the judgement of taste, and in this connection matters stand just as they would were that judgement simply *subjective.*

If any one does not think a building, view, or poem beautiful, then, *in the first place,* he refuses, so far as his inmost conviction goes, to allow approval to be wrung from him by a hundred voices all lauding it to the skies. Of course he may affect to be pleased with it, so as not to be considered as wanting in taste. He may even begin to harbour doubts as to whether he has formed his taste upon an acquaintance with a sufficient number of objects of a particular kind (just as one who in the distance recognizes, as he believes, something as a wood which every one else regards as a town, becomes doubtful of the judgement of his own eyesight). But, for all that, he clearly perceives that the approval of others affords no valid proof, available for the estimate of beauty. He recognizes that others, perchance, may see and observe for him, and that what many have seen in one and the same way may, for the purpose of a theoretical, and therefore logical, judgement, serve as an adequate ground of proof for him, albeit he believes he saw otherwise, but that what has pleased others can never serve him as the ground of an aesthetic judgement. The judgement of others, where unfavourable to ours, may, no doubt, rightly make us suspicious in respect of our own, but convince us that it is wrong it never can. Hence there is no empirical *ground of proof* that can coerce any one's judgement of taste.

In the second place, a proof *a priori* according to definite rules is still less capable of determining the judgement as to beauty. If any one reads me his poem, or brings me to a play, which, all said and done, fails to commend itself to my taste, then let him adduce Batteux or Lessing, or still older and more famous critics of taste, with all the host of rules laid down by them, as a proof of the beauty of his poem; let certain passages particularly displeasing to me accord completely with the rules of beauty (as set out by these critics and universally recognized): I stop my ears: I do not want to hear any reasons or any arguing about the matter. I would prefer to suppose that those rules of the critics were at fault, or at least have no application, than to allow my judgement to be determined by *a priori* proofs. I take my stand on the ground that my judgement is to be one of taste, and not one of understanding or reason.

This would appear to be one of the chief reasons why this faculty of aesthetic judgement has been given the name of *taste.* For a man may recount to me all the ingredients of a dish, and observe of each and every one of them that it is just what I like, and, in addition, rightly commend the wholesomeness of the food; yet I am deaf to all these arguments. I try the dish with *my own* tongue and palate, and I pass judgement according to their verdict (not according to universal principles).

As a matter of fact, the judgement of taste is invariably laid down as a singular judgement upon the object. The understanding can, from the comparison of the object, in point of delight, with the judgements of others, form a universal judgement, e.g.: "All tulips are beautiful." But that judgement is then not one of taste, but is a logical judgement which converts the reference of an object to our taste into a predicate belonging to things of a certain kind. But it is only the judgement whereby I regard an individual given tulip as beautiful, i.e., regard my delight in it as of universal validity, that is a judgement of taste. Its peculiarity, however, consists in the fact, that, although it has merely subjective validity, still it extends its claims to *all* subjects, as unreservedly as it would if it were an objective judgement, resting on grounds of cognition and capable of being proved to demonstration.

§ 34. *An objective principle of taste is not possible*

A PRINCIPLE of taste would mean a fundamental premiss under the condition of which one might subsume the concept of an object, and then, by a syllogism, draw the inference that it is beautiful. That, however, is absolutely impossible. For I must feel the pleasure immediately in the representation of the object, and I cannot be talked into it by any grounds of proof. Thus although critics, as Hume says, are able to reason more plausibly than cooks, they must still share the same fate. For the determining ground of their judgement they are not able to look to the force of demonstrations, but only to the reflection of the subject upon his own state (of pleasure or displeasure), to the exclusion of precepts and rules.

There is, however, a matter upon which it is competent for critics to exercise their subtlety, and upon which they ought to do so, so long as it tends to the rectification and extension of our judgements of taste. But that matter is not one of exhibiting the determining ground of aesthetic judgements of this kind in a universally applicable formula—which is impossible. Rather is it the investigation of the faculties of cognition and their function in these judgements, and the illustration, by the analysis of examples, of their mutual subjective finality, the form of which in a given representation has been shown above to constitute the beauty of their object. Hence with regard to the representation whereby an object is given, the critique of taste itself is only subjective; viz., it is the art or science of reducing the mutual relation of the understanding and the imagination in the given representation (without reference to antecedent sensation or concept), consequently their accordance or discordance, to rules, and of determining them with regard to their conditions. It is *art* if it only illustrates this by examples; it is *science* if it deduces the possibility of such an estimate from the nature of these faculties as faculties of knowledge in general. It is only with the latter, as trancendental critique, that we have here any concern. Its proper scope is the development and justification of the subjective principle of taste, as an *a priori* principle of judgement. As an art, critique merely looks to the physiological (here psychological) and, consequently, empirical rules, according to which in actual fact taste proceeds (passing by the question of their possibility) and seeks to apply them in estimating its objects. The latter critique criticizes the products of fine art, just as the former does the faculty of estimating them.

§ 35. *The principle of taste is the subjective principle of the general power of judgement*

THE judgement of taste is differentiated from logical judgement by the fact that, whereas the latter subsumes a representation under a concept of the object, the judgement of taste does not subsume under a concept at all—for, if it did, necessary and universal approval would be capable of being enforced by proofs. And yet it does bear this resemblance to the logical judgement, that it asserts a universality and necessity, not, however, according to concepts of the object, but a universality and necessity that are, consequently, merely subjective. Now the concepts in a judgement constitute its content (what belongs to the cognition of the object). But the judgement of taste is not determinable by means of concepts. Hence it can only have its ground in the subjective formal condition of a judgement in general. The subjective condition of all judgements is the judging faculty itself, or judgement. Employed in respect of a representation whereby an object is given, this requires the harmonious accordance of two powers of representation. These are: the imagination (for the intuition and the arrangement of the manifold of intuition), and the understanding (for the concept as a representation of the unity of this arrangement). Now, since no concept of the object underlies the judgement here, it can consist only in the subsumption of the imagination itself (in the case of a representation whereby an object is given) under the conditions enabling the understanding in general to advance from the intuition to concepts. That is to say, since the freedom of the imagination consists precisely in the fact that it schematizes without a concept, the judgement of taste must found upon a mere sensation of the mutually quickening activity of the imagination in its *freedom,* and of the understanding with its *conformity to law.* It must therefore rest upon a feeling that allows the object to be estimated by the finality of the representation (by which an object is given) for the furtherance of the cognitive faculties in their free play. Taste, then, as a subjective power of judgement, contains a principle of subsumption, not of intuitions under *concepts,* but of the *faculty* of intuitions or presentations, i.e., of the imagination, under the *faculty* of concepts, i.e., the understanding, so far as the former *in its freedom* accords with the latter *in its conformity to law.*[1]

For the discovery of this title by means of a deduction of judgements of taste, we can only avail ourselves of the guidance of the formal peculiarities of judgements of this kind, and consequently the mere consideration of their logical form.

§ 36. *The problem of a deduction of judgements of taste*

To form a cognitive judgement we may immediately connect with the perception of an object the concept of an object in general, the empirical predicates of which are contained in that perception. In this way, a judgement of experience is produced. Now this judgement rests on the foundation of *a priori* concepts of the synthetical unity of the manifold of intuition, enabling it to be thought as the determination of an object. These concepts (the categories) call for a deduction, and such was supplied in the *Critique of Pure Reason.* That deduction enabled us to solve the problem: How are synthetical *a priori* cognitive judgements possible? This problem had, accordingly, to do with the *a priori* principles of pure understanding and its theoretical judgements.

But we may also immediately connect with a perception a feeling of pleasure (or displeasure) and a delight attending the representation of the object and serving it instead of a predicate. In this way there arises a judgement which is aesthetic and not cognitive. Now, if such a judgement is not merely one of sensation, but a formal judgement of reflection that exacts this delight from everyone as necessary, something must lie at its basis as its *a priori* principle. This principle may, indeed, be a mere subjective one (supposing an objective one should be impossible for judgements of this kind), but, even as such, it requires a deduction to make it intelligible how an aesthetic judgement can lay claim to necessity. That, now, is what lies at the bottom of the problem upon which we are at present engaged, i.e.: How are judgements of taste possible? This problem, therefore, is concerned with the *a priori* principles of pure judgement in *aesthetic* judgements, i.e., not those in which (as in theoretical judgements) it has merely to subsume under objective concepts of understanding, and in which it comes under a law, but rather those in which it is itself, subjectively, object as well as law.

We may also put the problem in this way: How a judgement possible which, going merely upon the individual's *own* feeling of pleasure in an object independent of the concept of it, estimates this as a pleasure attached to the representation of the same object *in every other individual,* and does so *a priori,* i.e., without being allowed to wait and see if other people will be of the same mind?

It is easy to see that judgements of taste are synthetic, for they go beyond the concept and even the intuition of the object, and join as predicate to that intuition something which is not even a cognition at all, namely, the feeling of pleasure (or displeasure). But, although the predicate (the *personal* pleasure that is connected with the representation) is empirical, still we need not go further than what is involved in the expressions of their claim to see that, so far as concerns the agreement required of *everyone,* they are *a priori* judgements, or mean to pass for such. This problem of the Critique of Judgement, therefore, is part of the general problem of transcendental philosophy: How are synthetic *a priori* judgements possible?

§ 37. *What exactly it is that is asserted* a priori *of an object in a judgement of taste*

THE immediate synthesis of the representation of an object with pleasure can only be a matter of internal perception, and, were noth-

[1] [Cf. pp. 471, 476, 495, 512.]

ing more than this sought to be indicated, would only yield a mere empirical judgement. For with no representation can I *a priori* connect a determinate feeling (of pleasure or displeasure) except where I rely upon the basis of an *a priori* principle in reason determining the will. The truth is that the pleasure (in the moral feeling) is the consequence of the determination of the will by the principle. It cannot, therefore, be compared with the pleasure in taste. For it requires a determinate concept of a law: whereas the pleasure in taste has to be connected immediately with the sample estimate prior to any concept. For the same reason, also, all judgements of taste are singular judgements, for they unite their predicate of delight, not to a concept, but to a given singular empirical representation.

Hence, in a judgement of taste, what is represented *a priori* as a universal rule for the judgement and as valid for everyone, is not the pleasure but the *universal validity* of this pleasure perceived, as it is, to be combined in the mind with the mere estimate of an object.[1] A judgement to the effect that it is with pleasure that I perceive and estimate some object is an empirical judgement. But if it asserts that I think the object beautiful, i.e., that I may attribute that delight to everyone as necessary, it is then an *a priori* judgement.

§ 38. *Deduction of judgements of taste*

ADMITTING that in a pure judgement of taste the delight in the object is connected with the mere estimate of its form, then what we feel to be associated in the mind with the representation of the object is nothing else than its subjective finality for judgement. Since, now, in respect of the formal rules of estimating, apart from all matter (whether sensation or concept), judgement can only be directed to the subjective conditions of its employment in general (which is not restricted to the particular mode of sense nor to a particular concept of the understanding), and so can only be directed to that subjective factor which we may presuppose in all men (as requisite for a possible experience generally), it follows that the accordance of a representation with these conditions of the judgement must admit of being assumed valid *a priori* for every one. In other words, we are warranted in exacting from every one the pleasure or subjective finality of the representation in respect of the relation of the cognitive faculties engaged in the estimate of a sensible object in general.[2]

[1] [Cf. p. 482, *et seq.*]

Remark

What makes this deduction so easy is that it is spared the necessity of having to justify the objective reality of a concept. For beauty is not a concept of the object, and the judgement of taste is not a cognitive judgement. All that it holds out for is that we are justified in presupposing that the same subjective conditions of judgement which we find in ourselves are universally present in every man, and further that we have rightly subsumed the given object under these conditions. The latter, no doubt, has to face unavoidable difficulties which do not affect the logical judgement. (For there the subsumption is under concepts; whereas in the aesthetic judgement it is under a mere sensible relation of the imagination and understanding mutually harmonizing with one another in the represented form of the object, in which case the subsumption may easily prove fallacious.) But this in no way detracts from the legitimacy of the claim of the judgement to count upon universal agreement—a claim which amounts to no more than this: the correctness of the principle of judging validly for every one upon subjective grounds. For as to the difficulty and uncertainty concerning the correctness of the subsumption under that principle, it no more casts a doubt upon the legitimacy of the claim to this validity on the part of an aesthetic judgement generally, or, therefore, upon the principle itself, than the mistakes (though not so often or easily incurred), to which the subsumption of the logical judgement under its principle is similarly liable, can render the latter principle, which is objective, open to doubt. But if the question were: How is it possible to assume *a priori* that nature is a complex of objects of taste? the problem would then have reference to teleology, because it would have to be regarded as an end of na-

[2] In order to be justified in claiming universal agreement for an aesthetic judgement merely resting on subjective grounds, it is sufficient to assume: (1) that the subjective conditions of this faculty of aesthetic judgement are identical with all men in what concerns the relation of the cognitive faculties, there brought into action, with a view to a cognition in general. This must be true, as otherwise men would be incapable of communicating their representations or even their knowledge; (2) that the judgement has paid regard merely to this relation (consequently merely to the *formal condition* of the faculty of judgement), and is pure, i.e., is free from confusion either with concepts of the object or sensations as determining grounds. If any mistake is made in this latter point, this only touches the incorrect application to a particular case of the right which a law gives us, and does not do away with the right generally.

ture belonging essentially to its concept that it should exhibit forms that are final for our judgement. But the correctness of this assumption may still be seriously questioned, while the actual existence of beauties of nature is patent to experience.

§ 39. *The communicability of a sensation*

SENSATION, as the real in perception, where referred to knowledge, is called *organic sensation* and its specific quality may be represented as completely communicable to others in a like mode, provided we assume that every one has a like sense to our own. This, however, is an absolutely inadmissible presupposition in the case of an organic sensation. Thus a person who is without a sense of smell cannot have a sensation of this kind communicated to him, and, even if he does not suffer from this deficiency, we still cannot be certain that he gets precisely the same sensation from a flower that we get from it. But still more divergent must we consider men to be in respect of the *agreeableness* or *disagreeableness* derived from the sensation of one and the same object of sense, and it is absolutely out of the question to require that pleasure in such objects should be acknowledged by every one. Pleasure of this kind, since it enters into the mind through sense—our role, therefore, being a passive one—may be called the pleasure of *enjoyment*.

On the other hand, delight in an action on the score of its moral character is not a pleasure of enjoyment, but one of self-asserting activity and in this coming up to the idea of what it is meant to be. But this feeling, which is called the *moral feeling*, requires concepts and is the presentation of a finality, not free, but according to law. It, therefore, admits of communication only through the instrumentality of reason and, if the pleasure is to be of the same kind for everyone, by means of very determinate practical concepts of reason.

The pleasure in the sublime in nature, as one of rationalizing contemplation, lays claim also to universal participation, but still it presupposes another feeling, that, namely, of our supersensible sphere, which feeling, however obscure it may be, has a moral foundation. But there is absolutely no authority for my presupposing that others will pay attention to this and take a delight in beholding the uncouth dimensions of nature (one that in truth cannot be ascribed to its aspect, which is terrifying rather than otherwise). Nevertheless, having regard to the fact that attention ought to be paid upon every appropriate occasion to this moral birthright, we may still demand that delight from everyone; but we can do so only through the moral law, which, in its turn, rests upon concepts of reason.

The pleasure in the beautiful is, on the other hand, neither a pleasure of enjoyment nor of an activity according to law, nor yet one of a rationalizing contemplation according to ideas, but rather of mere reflection. Without any guiding-line of end or principle, this pleasure attends the ordinary apprehension of an object by means of the imagination, as the faculty of intuition, but with a reference to the understanding as faculty of concepts, and through the operation of a process of judgement which has also to be invoked in order to obtain the commonest experience. In the latter case, however, its functions are directed to perceiving an empirical objective concept, whereas in the former (in the aesthetic mode of estimating) merely to perceiving the adequacy of the representation for engaging both faculties of knowledge in their freedom in an harmonious (subjectively final) employment, i.e., to feeling with pleasure the subjective bearings of the representation. This pleasure must of necessity depend for every one upon the same conditions, seeing that they are the subjective conditions of the possibility of a cognition in general, and the proportion of these cognitive faculties which is requisite for taste is requisite also for ordinary sound understanding, the presence of which we are entitled to presuppose in every one. And, for this reason also, one who judges with taste (provided he does not make a mistake as to this consciousness, and does not take the matter for the form, or charm for beauty) can impute the subjective finality, i.e., his delight in the object, to everyone else and suppose his feeling universally communicable, and that, too, without the mediation of concepts.

§ 40. *Taste as a kind* of sensus communis

THE name of *sense* is often given to judgement where what attracts attention is not so much its reflective act as merely its result. So we speak of a sense of truth, of a sense of propriety, or of justice, etc. And yet, of course, we know, or at least ought well enough to know, that a sense cannot be the true abode of these concepts, not to speak of its being competent, even in the slightest degree, to pronounce universal rules. On the contrary, we recognize that a representation of this kind, be it of truth, propriety, beauty, or justice, could never enter our thoughts were we not able to raise ourselves above the level of the senses to that of higher faculties of cognition. *Common human understanding* which as mere sound (not yet cultivated) understanding, is looked upon as the least we can expect from any one claiming the name of man, has therefore the doubtful honour of having the name of common sense (*sensus communis*) bestowed upon it; and bestowed, too, in an acceptation of the word *common* (not merely in our own language, where it actually has a double meaning, but also in many others) which makes it amount to what is *vulgar*—what is everywhere to be met with—a quality which by no means confers credit or distinction upon its possessor.

However, by the name *sensus communis* is to be understood the idea of a *public* sense, i. e., a critical faculty which in its reflective act takes account (*a priori*) of the mode of representation of everyone else, in order, *as it were*, to weigh its judgement with the collective reason of mankind, and thereby avoid the illusion arising from subjective and personal conditions which could readily be taken for objective, an illusion that would exert a prejudicial influence upon its judgement. This is accomplished by weighing the judgement, not so much with actual, as rather with the merely possible, judgements of others, and by putting ourselves in the position of everyone else, as the result of a mere abstraction from the limitations which contingently affect our own estimate. This, in turn, is effected by so far as possible letting go the element of matter, i. e., sensation, in our general state of representative activity, and confining attention to the formal peculiarities of our representation or general state of representative activity. Now it may seem that this operation of reflection is too artificial to be attributed to the faculty which we call *common* sense. But this is an appearance due only to its expression in abstract formulae. In itself nothing is more natural than to abstract from charm and emotion where one is looking for a judgement intended to serve as a universal rule.

While the following maxims of common human understanding do not properly come in here as constituent parts of the critique of taste, they may still serve to elucidate its fundamental propositions. They are these: (1) to think for oneself; (2) to think from the standpoint of everyone else; (3) always to think consistently. The first is the maxim of *unprejudiced* thought, the second that of *enlarged* thought, the third that of *consistent* thought. The first is the maxim of a never-*passive* reason. To be given to such passivity, consequently to heteronomy of reason, is called *prejudice;* and the greatest of all prejudices is that of fancying nature not to be subject to rules which the understanding by virtue of its own essential laws lays at its basis, i. e., *superstition.* Emancipation from superstition is called *enlightenment;*[1] for although this term applies also to emancipation from prejudices generally, still superstition deserves pre-eminently (*in sensu eminenti*) to be called a prejudice. For the condition of blindness into which superstition puts one, which is as much as demands from one as an obligation, makes the need of being led by others, and consequently the passive state of the reason, pre-eminently conspicuous. As to the second maxim belonging to our habits of thought, we have quite got into the way of calling a man narrow (*narrow,* as opposed to being *of enlarged mind*) whose talents fall short of what is required for employment upon work of any magnitude (especially that involving intensity). But the question here is not one of the faculty of cognition, but of the *mental habit* of making a final use of it. This, however small the range and degree to which man's natural endowments extend, still indicates a man of *enlarged mind:* if he detaches himself from the subjective personal conditions of his judgement, which cramp the minds of so many others, and reflects upon his own judgement from a *universal standpoint* (which he can only determine by shifting his ground to the standpoint of others). The third maxim—that, namely, of *consistent* thought—is the hardest of attainment, and is only attainable by the union of both the former, and after constant attention to them has made one at home in their observance. We may say: The first of these is the maxim of understanding, the second that of judgement, the third of that reason.

I resume the thread of the discussion interrupted by the above digression, and I say that taste can with more justice be called a *sensus communis* than can sound understanding; and that the aesthetic, rather than the intellectual,

[1] We readily see that enlightenment, while easy, no doubt, *in thesi, in hypothesi* is difficult and slow of realization. For not to be passive with one's reason, but always to be self-legislative, is doubtless quite an easy matter for a man who only desires to be adapted to his essential end, and does not seek to know what is beyond his understanding. But as the tendency in the latter direction is hardly avoidable, and others are always coming and promising with full assurance that they are able to satisfy one's curiosity, it must be very difficult to preserve or restore in the mind (and particularly in the public mind) that merely negative attitude (which constitutes enlightenment proper).

judgement can bear the name of a public sense,[1] i. e., taking it that we are prepared to use the word *sense* of an effect that mere reflection has upon the mind; for then by sense we mean the feeling of pleasure. We might even define taste as the faculty of estimating what makes our feeling in a given representation *universally communicable* without the mediation of a concept.

The aptitude of men for communicating their thoughts requires, also, a relation between the imagination and the understanding, in order to connect intuitions with concepts, and concepts, in turn, with intuitions, which both unite in cognition. But there the agreement of both mental powers is *according to law,* and under the constraint of definite concepts. Only when the imagination in its freedom stirs the understanding, and the understanding apart from concepts puts the imagination into regular play, does the representation communicate itself not as thought, but as an internal feeling of a final state of the mind.

Taste is, therefore, the faculty of forming an *a priori* estimate of the communicability of the feeling that, without the mediation of a concept, are connected with a given representation.

Supposing, now, that we could assume that the mere universal communicability of our feeling must of itself carry with it an interest for us (an assumption, however, which we are not entitled to draw as a conclusion from the character of a merely reflective judgement), we should then be in a position to explain how the feeling in the judgement of taste comes to be exacted from everyone as a sort of duty.

§ 41. *The empirical interest in the beautiful*[2]

ABUNDANT proof has been given above to show that the judgement of taste by which something is declared beautiful must have no interest *as its determining ground.* But it does not follow from this that, after it has once been posited as a pure aesthetic judgement, an interest cannot then enter into combination with it. This combination, however, can never be anything but indirect. Taste must, that is to say, first of all be represented in conjunction with something else, if the delight attending the mere reflection upon an object is to admit of having further conjoined with it *a pleasure in the real existence* of the object (as that wherein all interest consists). For the saying, *a posse ad esse non valet consequentia,*[3] which is applied to cognitive judgements, holds good here in the case of aesthetic judgements. Now this "something else" may be something empirical, such as an inclination proper to the nature of human beings, or it may be something intellectual, as a property of the will whereby it admits of rational determination *a priori.* Both of these involve a delight in the existence of the object, and so can lay the foundation for an interest in what has already pleased of itself and without regard to any interest whatsoever.

The empirical interest in the beautiful exists only in *society.* And if we admit that the impulse to society is natural to mankind, and that the suitability for and the propensity towards it, i.e., *sociability,* is a property essential to the requirements of man as a creature intended for society, and one, therefore, that belongs to *humanity,* it is inevitable that we should also look upon taste in the light of a faculty for estimating whatever enables us to communicate even our *feeling* to every one else, and hence as a means of promoting that upon which the natural inclination of everyone is set.

With no one to take into account but himself, a man abandoned on a desert island would not adorn either himself or his hut, nor would he look for flowers, and still less plant them, with the object of providing himself with personal adornments. Only in society does it occur to him to be not merely a man, but a man refined after the manner of his kind (the beginning of civilization)—for that is the estimate formed of one who has the bent and turn for communicating his pleasure to others, and who is not quite satisfied with an object unless his feeling of delight in it can be shared in communion with others. Further, a regard to universal communicability is a thing which every one expects and requires from every one else, just as if it were part of an original compact dictated by humanity itself. And thus, no doubt, at first only charms, e. g., colours for painting oneself (roucou among the Caribs and cinnabar among the Iroquois), or flowers, sea-shells, beautifully coloured feathers, then, in the course of time, also beautiful forms (as in canoes, wearing-apparel, etc.) which convey no gratification, i. e., delight of enjoyment, become of moment in society and attract a considerable interest. Eventually, when civilization has reached its height it makes this work of communication almost the main business of refined inclination, and the entire value of sensations is placed in the degree to which

[1] Taste may be designated a *sensus communis aestheticus,* common human understanding a *sensus communis logicus.*

[2] [Cf. p. 510, *et seq.*]

[3] ["From possibility to actuality."]

they permit of universal communication. At this stage, then, even where the pleasure which each one has in an object is but insignificant and possesses of itself no conspicuous interest, still the idea of its universal communicability almost indefinitely augments its value.

This interest, indirectly attached to the beautiful by the inclination towards society, and, consequently, empirical, is, however, of no importance for us here. For that to which we have alone to look is what can have a bearing *a priori*, even though indirect, upon the judgement of taste. For, if even in this form an associated interest should betray itself, taste would then reveal a transition on the part of our critical faculty from the enjoyment of sense to the moral feeling.[1] This would not merely mean that we should be supplied with a more effectual guide for the final employment of taste, but taste would further be presented as a link in the chain of the human faculties *a priori* upon which all legislation must depend. This much may certainly be said of the empirical interest in objects of taste, and in taste itself, that as taste thus pays homage to inclination, however refined, such interest will nevertheless readily fuse also with all inclinations and passions, which in society attain to their greatest variety and highest degree, and the interest in the beautiful, if this is made its ground, can but afford a very ambiguous transition from the agreeable to the good. We have reason, however, to inquire whether this transition may not still in some way be furthered by means of taste when taken in its purity.

§ 42. *The intellectual interest in the beautiful*

It has been with the best intentions that those who love to see in the ultimate end of humanity, namely the morally good, the goal of all activities to which men are impelled by the inner bent of their nature, have regarded it as a mark of a good moral character to take an interest in the beautiful generally. But they have, not without reason, been contradicted, by others, who appeal to the fact of experience, that *virtuosi* in matters of taste, being not alone often, but one might say as a general rule, vain, capricious, and addicted to injurious passions, could perhaps more rarely than others lay claim to any pre-eminent attachment to moral principles. And so it would seem, not only that the feeling for the beautiful is specifically different from the moral feeling (which as a matter of fact is the case), but also that the interest which we may combine with it will hardly consort with the moral, and certainly not on grounds of inner affinity.

Now I willingly admit that the interest in the *beautiful of art* (including under this heading the artificial use of natural beauties for personal adornment, and so from vanity) gives no evidence at all of a habit of mind attached to the morally good, or even inclined that way. But, on the other hand, I do maintain that to take an *immediate interest* in the beauty of *nature* (not merely to have taste in estimating it) is always a mark of a good soul; and that, where this interest is habitual, it is at least indicative of a temper of mind favourable to the moral feeling that it should readily associate itself with the *contemplation of nature*. It must, however, be borne in mind that I mean to refer strictly to the beautiful *forms* of nature, and to put to one side the *charms* which she is wont so lavishly to combine with them; because, though the interest in these is no doubt immediate, it is nevertheless empirical.

One who alone (and without any intention of communicating his observations to others) regards the beautiful form of a wild flower, a bird, an insect, or the like, out of admiration and love of them, and being loath to let them escape him in nature, even at the risk of some misadventure to himself—so far from there being any prospect of advantage to him—such a one takes an immediate, and in fact intellectual, interest in the beauty of nature. This means that he is not alone pleased with nature's product in respect of its form, but is also pleased at its existence, and is so without any charm of sense having a share in the matter, or without his associating with it any end whatsoever.

In this connection, however, it is of note that were we to play a trick on our lover of the beautiful, and plant in the ground artificial flowers (which can be made so as to look just like natural ones), and perch artfully carved birds on the branches of trees, and he were to find out how he had been taken in, the immediate interest which these things previously had for him would at once vanish—though, perhaps, a different interest might intervene in its stead, that, namely, of vanity in decorating his room with them for the eyes of others. The fact is that our intuition and reflection must have as their concomitant the thought that the beauty in question is nature's handiwork; and this is the sole basis of the immediate interest that is taken in it. Failing this, we are either left with a bare judgement of taste void of all interest

[1] [Cf. p. 548.]

whatever, or else only with one that is combined with an interest that is mediate, involving, namely, a reference to society; which latter affords no reliable indication of morally good habits of thought.

The superiority which natural beauty has over that of art, even where it is excelled by the latter in point of form, in yet being alone able to awaken an immediate interest, accords with the refined and well-grounded habits of thought of all men who have cultivated their moral feeling. If a man with taste enough to judge of works of fine art with the greatest correctness and refinement readily quits the room in which he meets with those beauties that minister to vanity or, at least, social joys, and betakes himself to the beautiful in nature, so that he may there find as it were a feast for his soul in a train of thought which he can never completely evolve, we will then regard this his choice even with veneration, and give him credit for a beautiful soul, to which no connoisseur or art collector can lay claim on the score of the interest which his objects have for him. Here, now, are two kinds of objects which in the judgement of mere taste could scarcely contend with one another for a superiority. What then, is the distinction that makes us hold them in such different esteem?

We have a faculty of judgement which is merely aesthetic—a faculty of judging of forms without the aid of concepts, and of finding, in the mere estimate of them, a delight that we at the same time make into a rule for every one, without this judgement being founded on an interest, or yet producing one. On the other hand, we have also a faculty of intellectual judgement for the mere forms of practical maxims (so far as they are of themselves qualified for universal legislation)—a faculty of determining an *a priori* delight, which we make into a law for everyone, without our judgement being founded on any interest, *though here it produces one.* The pleasure or displeasure in the former judgement is called that of *taste;* the latter is called that of the *moral feeling.*

But, now, reason is further interested in ideas (for which in our moral feeling it brings about an immediate interest), having also objective reality.[1] That is to say, it is of interest to reason that nature should at least show a trace or give a hint that it contains in itself some ground or other[2] for assuming a uniform accordance of its products with our wholly disinterested delight (a delight which we cognize *a priori* as a law for every one without being able to ground it upon proofs). That being so, reason must take an interest in every manifestation on the part of nature of some such accordance. Hence the mind cannot reflect on the beauty of *nature* without at the same time finding its interest engaged. But this interest is akin to the moral. One, then, who takes such an interest in the beautiful in nature can only do so in so far as he has previously set his interest deep in the foundations of the morally good. On these grounds we have reason for presuming the presence of at least the germ of a good moral disposition in the case of a man to whom the beauty of nature is a matter of immediate interest.

It will be said that this interpretation of aesthetic judgements on the basis of kinship with our moral feeling has far too studied an appearance to be accepted as the true construction of the cypher in which nature speaks to us figuratively in its beautiful forms. But, first of all, this immediate interest in the beauty of nature is not in fact common. It is peculiar to those whose habits of thought are already trained to the good or else are eminently susceptible of such training; and under the circumstances the analogy[3] in which the pure judgement of taste that, without relying upon any interest, gives us a feeling of delight, and at the same time represents it *a priori* as proper to mankind in general, stands to the moral judgement that does just the same from concepts, is one which, without any clear, subtle, and deliberate reflection, conduces to a like immediate interest being taken in the objects of the former judgement as in those of the latter—with this one difference, that the interest in the first case is free, while in the latter it is one founded on objective laws. In addition to this, there is our admiration of Nature, which in her beautiful products displays herself as art, not as mere matter of chance, but, as it were, designedly, according to a law-directed arrangement, and as finality apart from any end. As we never meet with such an end outside ourselves, we naturally look for it in ourselves, and, in fact, in that which constitutes the ultimate end of our existence—the moral side of our being. (The inquiry into the ground of the possibility of such a natural finality will, however, first come under discussion in the Teleology.)

The fact that the delight in beautiful art does not, in the pure judgement of taste, involve an

[1] [Cf. pp. 517, 528, 546; also p. 496.]
[2] [Cf. p. 548.]
[3] [Cf. pp. 547, 548.]

immediate interest, as does that in beautiful nature, may be readily explained. For the former is either such an imitation of the latter as goes the length of deceiving us, in which case it acts upon us in the character of a natural beauty, which we take it to be; or else it is an intentional art obviously directed to our delight. In the latter case, however, the delight in the product would, it is true, be brought about immediately by taste, but there would be nothing but a mediate interest in the cause that lay beneath—an interest, namely, in an art only capable of interesting by its end, and never in itself. It will, perhaps, be said that this is also the case where an object of nature only interests by its beauty so far as a moral idea is brought into partnership therewith. But it is not the object that is of immediate interest, but rather the inherent character of the beauty qualifying it for such a partnership—a character, therefore, that belongs to the very essence of beauty.

The charms in natural beauty,[1] which are to be found blended, as it were, so frequently with beauty of form, belong either to the modifications of light (in colouring) or of sound (in tones). For these are the only sensations which permit not merely of a feeling of the senses, but also of reflection upon the form of these modifications of sense, and so embody as it were a language in which nature speaks to us and which has the semblance of a higher meaning. Thus the white colour of the lily seems to dispose the mind to ideas of innocence, and the other seven colours, following the series from the red to the violet, similarly to ideas of (1) sublimity, (2) courage, (3) candour, (4) amiability, (5) modesty, (6) constancy, (7) tenderness. The bird's song tells of joyousness and contentment with its existence. At least so we interpret nature—whether such be its purpose or not. But it is the indispensable requisite of the interest which we here take in beauty, that the beauty should be that of nature, and it vanishes completely as soon as we are conscious of having been deceived, and that it is only the work of art—so completely that even taste can then no longer find in it anything beautiful nor sight anything attractive. What do poets set more store on than the nightingale's bewitching and beautiful note, in a lonely thicket on a still summer evening by the soft light of the moon? And yet we have instances of how, where no such songster was to be found, a jovial host has played a trick on the guests with him on a visit to enjoy the country air, and has done so to their huge satisfaction, by hiding in a thicket a rogue of a youth who (with a reed or rush in his mouth) knew how to reproduce this note so as to hit off nature to perfection. But the instant one realizes that it is all a fraud no one will long endure listening to this song that before was regarded as so attractive. And it is just the same with the song of any other bird. It must be nature, or be mistaken by us for nature, to enable us to take an immediate *interest* in the beautiful as such; and this is all the more so if we can even call upon others to take a similar interest. And such a demand we do in fact make, since we regard as coarse and low the habits of thought of those who have no *feeling* for beautiful nature (for this is the word we use for susceptibility to an interest in the contemplation of beautiful nature), and who devote themselves to the mere enjoyments of sense found in eating and drinking.

1 [Cf. p. 521, *et seq.*]

§ 43. *Art in general*

(1.) *Art* is distinguished from *nature* as making (*facere*) is from acting or operating in general (*agere*), and the product or the result of the former is distinguished from that of the latter as *work* (*opus*) from *operation* (*effectus*).

By right it is only production through freedom, i.e., through an act of will that places reason at the basis of its action, that should be termed *art*. For, although we are pleased to call what bees produce (their regularly constituted cells) a work of art, we only do so on the strength of an analogy with art; that is to say, as soon as we call to mind that no rational deliberation forms the basis of their labour, we say at once that it is a product of their nature (of instinct), and it is only to their Creator that we ascribe it as art.

If, as sometimes happens, in a search through a bog, we light on a piece of hewn wood, we do not say it is a product of nature but of art. Its producing cause had an end in view to which the object owes its form. Apart from such cases, we recognize an art in everything formed in such a way that its actuality must have been preceded by a representation of the thing in its cause (as even in the case of the bees), although the effect could not have been *thought* by the cause. But where anything is called absolutely a work of art, to distinguish it from a natural product, then some work of man is always understood.

(2.) *Art,* as human skill, is distinguished also from *science* (as *ability* from *knowledge*), as a practical from a theoretical faculty, as technic from theory (as the art of surveying from geometry). For this reason, also, what one *can* do the moment one only *knows* what is to be done, hence without anything more than sufficient knowledge of the desired result, is not called art. To art that alone belongs for which the possession of the most complete knowledge does not involve one's having then and there the skill to do it. Camper[1] describes very exactly how the best shoe must be made, but he, doubtless, was not able to turn one out himself.[2]

(3.) *Art* is further distinguished from *handicraft*. The first is called *free*, the other may be called *industrial art*. We look on the former as something which could only prove final (be a success) as play, i.e., an occupation which is agreeable on its own account; but on the second as labour, i.e., a business, which on its own account is disagreeable (drudgery), and is only attractive by means of what it results in (e.g., the pay), and which is consequently capable of being a compulsory imposition. Whether in the list of arts and crafts we are to rank watchmakers as artists, and smiths on the contrary as craftsmen, requires a standpoint different from that here adopted—one, that is to say, taking account of the proposition of the talents which the business undertaken in either case must necessarily involve. Whether, also, among the so-called seven free arts some may not have been included which should be reckoned as sciences, and many, too, that resemble handicraft, is a matter I will not discuss here. It is not amiss, however, to remind the reader of this: that in all free arts something of a compulsory character is still required, or, as it is called, a *mechanism*, without which the *soul*, which in art must be *free*, and which alone gives life to the work, would be bodyless and evanescent (e.g., in the poetic art there must be correctness and wealth of language, likewise prosody and metre). For not a few leaders of a newer school[3] believe that the best way to promote a free art is to sweep away all restraint and convert it from labour into mere play.

1 [Peter Camper (1722–89), a Dutch physician and scientist, and author of anatomical and medical works.]

2 In my part of the country, if you set a common man a problem like that of Columbus and his egg, he says, "There is no art in that, it is only science": i.e., you *can* do it if you know *how;* and he says just the same of all the would-be arts of jugglers. To that of the tight-rope dancer, on the other hand, he has not the least compunction in giving the name of *art*.

3 [Cf. pp. 525; 526, *et seq.;* 531, *et seq.;* 538, *et seq.*]

§ 44. *Fine art*

THERE is no science of the beautiful, but only a critique. Nor, again, is there an elegant (*schöne*) science, but only a fine (*schöne*) art. For a science of the beautiful would have to determine scientifically, i.e., by means of proofs, whether a thing was to be considered beautiful or not; and the judgement upon beauty, consequently, would, if belonging to science, fail to be a judgement of taste. As for a beautiful science—a science which, as such, is to be beautiful, is a nonentity. For if, treating it as a science, we were to ask for reasons and proofs, we would be put off with elegant phrases (*bons mots*). What has given rise to the current expression *elegant sciences* is, doubtless, no more than this, that common observation has, quite accurately, noted the fact that for fine art, in the fulness of its perfection, a large store of science is required, as, for example, knowledge of ancient languages, acquaintance with classical authors, history, antiquarian learning, etc. Hence these historical sciences, owing to the fact that they form the necessary preparation and groundwork for fine art, and partly also owing to the fact that they are taken to comprise even the knowledge of the products of fine art (rhetoric and poetry), have by a confusion of words, actually got the name of elegant sciences.

Where art, merely seeking to actualize a possible object to the *cognition* of which it is adequate, does whatever acts are required for that purpose, then it is *mechanical*. But should the feeling of pleasure be what it has immediately in view, it is then termed *aesthetic* art. As such it may be either *agreeable* or *fine* art. The description "agreeable art" applies where the end of the art is that the pleasure should accompany the representations considered as mere *sensations*, the description "fine art" where it is to accompany them considered as *modes of cognition.*

Agreeable arts are those which have mere enjoyment for their object. Such are all the charms that can gratify a dinner party: entertaining narrative, the art of starting the whole table in unrestrained and sprightly conversation, or with jest and laughter inducing a certain air of gaiety. Here, as the saying goes, there may be much loose talk over the glasses, without a person wishing to be brought to book for all he utters, because it is only given out for the entertainment of the moment, and not as a lasting matter to be made the subject of reflection or repetition. (Of the same sort is also the art of arranging the table for enjoyment, or, at large banquets, the music of the orchestra—a quaint idea intended to act on the mind merely as an agreeable noise fostering a genial spirit, which, without any one paying the smallest attention to the composition, promotes the free flow of conversation between guest and guest.) In addition must be included play of every kind which is attended with no further interest than that of making the time pass by unheeded.

Fine art, on the other hand, is a mode of representation which is intrinsically final, and which, although devoid of an end, has the effect of advancing the culture of the mental powers in the interests of social communication.

The universal communicability of a pleasure involves in its very concept that the pleasure is not one of enjoyment arising out of mere sensation, but must be one of reflection. Hence aesthetic art, as art which is beautiful, is one having for its standard the reflective judgement and not organic sensation.

§ 45. *Fine art is an art, so far as it has at the same time the appearance of being nature*

A PRODUCT of fine art must be recognized to be art and not nature. Nevertheless the finality in its form must appear just as free from the constraint of arbitrary rules as if it were a product of mere nature. Upon this feeling of freedom in the play of our cognitive faculties—which play has at the same time to be final—rests that pleasure which alone is universally communicable without being based on concepts. Nature proved beautiful when it wore the appearance of art; and art can only be termed *beautiful*, where we are conscious of its being art, while yet it has the appearance of nature.

For, whether we are dealing with beauty of nature or beauty of art, we may make the universal statement: *That is beautiful which pleases in the mere estimate of it* (not in sensation or by means of a concept). Now art has always got a definite intention of producing something.[1] Were this "something," however, to be mere sensation (something merely subjective), intended to be accompanied with pleasure, then such product would, in our estimation of it, only please through the agency of the feeling of the senses. On the other hand, were the intention one directed to the production of a definite object, then, supposing this were attained by art, the object would only please by means of a concept. But in both cases the art would please, not in *the mere estimate of it,* i.e., not as fine art, but rather as mechanical art.

Hence the finality in the product of fine art, intentional though it be, must not have the appearance of being intentional; i.e., fine art must be clothed *with the aspect* of nature, although we recognize it to be art. But the way in which a product of art seems like nature is by the presence of perfect *exactness* in the agreement with rules prescribing how alone the product can be what it is intended to be, but with an absence of *laboured effect* (without academic form betraying itself), i.e., without a trace appearing of the artist having always had the rule present to him and of its having fettered his mental powers.

§ 46. *Fine art is the art of genius*

Genius is the talent (natural endowment) which gives the rule to art. Since talent, as an innate productive faculty of the artist, belongs itself to nature, we may put it this way: *Genius* is the innate mental aptitude (*ingenium*) *through which* nature gives the rule to art.

Whatever may be the merits of this definition, and whether it is merely arbitrary, or whether it is adequate or not to the concept usually associated with the word *genius* (a point which the following sections have to clear up), it may still be shown at the outset that, according to this acceptation of the word, fine arts must necessarily be regarded as arts of *genius.*

For every art presupposes rules which are laid down as the foundation which first enables a product, if it is to be called one of art, to be represented as possible. The concept of fine art, however, does not permit of the judgement upon the beauty of its product being derived from any rule that has a *concept* for its determining ground, and that depends, consequently, on a concept of the way in which the product is possible. Consequently fine art cannot of its own self excogitate the rule according to which it is to effectuate its product. But since, for all that, a product can never be called art unless there is a preceding rule, it follows that nature in the individual (and by virtue of the harmony of his faculties) must give the rule to art, i.e., fine art is only possible as a product of genius.

From this it may be seen that genius (1) is a *talent* for producing that for which no definite rule can be given,[2] and not an aptitude in the way of cleverness for what can be learned ac-

[1] [Cf. pp. 526, 527, 528, 530, 532, *et seq.;* 546, *et seq.;* 549, *et seq.*]

[2] [Cf. pp. 530, 543, *et seq.*]

cording to some rule; and that consequently *originality* must be its primary property. (2) Since there may also be original nonsense, its products must at the same time be models, i.e., be *exemplary;* and, consequently, though not themselves derived from imitation, they must serve that purpose for others, i.e., as a standard or rule of estimating. (3) It cannot indicate scientifically how it brings about its product, but rather gives the rule as *nature.* Hence, where an author owes a product to his genius, he does not himself know how the *ideas* for it have entered into his head, nor has he it in his power to invent the like at pleasure, or methodically, and communicate the same to others in such precepts as would put them in a position to produce similar products. (Hence, presumably, our word *Genie* is derived from *genius,* as the peculiar guardian and guiding spirit given to a man at his birth, by the inspiration of which those original ideas were obtained.) (4) Nature prescribes the rule through genius not to science but to art, and this also only in so far as it is to be fine art.[1]

§ 47. *Elucidation and confirmation of the above explanation of genius*

EVERY one is agreed on the point of the complete opposition between genius and the *spirit of imitation.* Now since learning is nothing but imitation, the greatest ability, or aptness as a pupil (capacity), is still, as such, not equivalent to genius. Even though a man weaves his own thoughts or fancies, instead of merely taking in what others have thought, and even though he go so far as to bring fresh gains to art and science, this does not afford a valid reason for calling such a man of *brains,* and often great brains, a *genius,* in contradistinction to one who goes by the name of *shallow-pate,* because he can never do more than merely learn and follow a lead. For what is accomplished in this way is something that *could* have been learned. Hence it all lies in the natural path of investigation and reflection according to rules, and so is not specifically distinguishable from what may be acquired as the result of industry backed up by imitation. So all that Newton has set forth in his immortal work on the *Principles of Natural Philosophy* may well be learned, however great a mind it took to find it all out, but we cannot learn to write in a true poetic vein, no matter how complete all the precepts of the poetic art may be, or however excellent its models. The reason is that all the steps that Newton had to take from the first elements of geometry to his greatest and most profound discoveries were such as he could make intuitively evident and plain to follow, not only for himself but for every one else. On the other hand, no Homer or Wieland can show how his ideas, so rich at once in fancy and in thought, enter and assemble themselves in his brain, for the good reason that he does not himself know, and so cannot teach others. In matters of science, therefore, the greatest inventor differs only in degree from the most laborious imitator and apprentice, whereas he differs specifically from one endowed by nature for fine art. No disparagement, however, of those great men, to whom the human race is so deeply indebted, is involved in this comparison of them with those who on the score of their talent for fine art are the elect of nature. The talent for science is formed for the continued advances of greater perfection in knowledge, with all its dependent practical advantages, as also for imparting the same to others. Hence scientists can boast a ground of considerable superiority over those who merit the honour of being called geniuses, since genius reaches a point at which art must make a halt, as there is a limit imposed upon it which it cannot transcend. This limit has in all probability been long since attained. In addition, such skill cannot be communicated, but requires to be bestowed directly from the hand of nature upon each individual, and so with him it dies, awaiting the day when nature once again endows another in the same way—one who needs no more than an example to set the talent of which he is conscious at work on similar lines.

Seeing, then, that the natural endowment of art (as fine art) must furnish the rule, what kind of rule must this be? It cannot be one set down in a formula and serving as a precept—for then the judgement upon the beautiful would be determinable according to concepts. Rather must the rule be gathered from the performance,[2] i.e., from the product, which others may use to put their own talent to the test, so as to let it serve as a model, not for *imitation,* but for *following.* The possibility of this is difficult to explain. The artist's ideas arouse like ideas on the part of his pupil, presuming nature to have visited him with a like proportion of the mental powers. For this reason, the models of fine art are the only means of handing down this art to posterity. This is something which cannot be done by mere descriptions (especially not in

[1] [Cf. pp. 490, 527.]

[2] [Cf. p. 548, *et seq.*]

the line of the arts of speech), and in these arts, furthermore, only those models can become classical of which the ancient, dead languages, preserved as learned, are the medium.

Despite the marked difference that distinguishes mechanical art, as an art merely depending upon industry and learning, from fine art, as that of genius, there is still no fine art in which something mechanical, capable of being at once comprehended and followed in obedience to rules, and consequently something *academic*, does not constitute the essential condition of the art. For the thought of something as end must be present, or else its product would not be ascribed to an art at all, but would be a mere product of chance. But the effectuation of an end necessitates determinate rules which we cannot venture to dispense with. Now, seeing that originality of talent is one (though not the sole) essential factor that goes to make up the character of genius, shallow minds fancy that the best evidence they can give of their being full-blown geniuses is by emancipating themselves from all academic constraint of rules, in the belief that one cuts a finer figure on the back of an ill-tempered than of a trained horse. Genius can do no more than furnish rich *material* for products of fine art; its elaboration and its *form* require a talent academically trained, so that it may be employed in such a way as to stand the test of judgement. But, for a person to hold forth and pass sentence like a genius in matters that fall to the province of the most patient rational investigation, is ridiculous in the extreme.[1] One is at a loss to know whether to laugh more at the impostor who envelops himself in such a cloud—in which we are given fuller scope to our imagination at the expense of all use of our critical faculty—or at the simple-minded public which imagines that its inability clearly to cognize and comprehend this masterpiece of penetration is due to its being invaded by new truths *en masse*, in comparison with which, detail, due to carefully weighed exposition and an academic examination of root-principles, seems to it only the work of a tyro.

§ 48. *The relation of genius to taste*

FOR *estimating* beautiful objects, as such, what is required is *taste;* but for fine art, i.e., the *production* of such objects, one needs *genius.*[2]

If we consider genius as the talent for fine art (which the proper signification of the word imports), and if we would analyse it from this point of view into the faculties which must concur to constitute such a talent, it is imperative at the outset accurately to determine the difference between beauty of nature, which it only requires taste to estimate, and beauty of art, which requires genius for its possibility (a possibility to which regard must also be paid in estimating such an object).

A beauty of nature is a *beautiful thing;* beauty of art is a *beautiful representation* of a thing.

To enable me to estimate a beauty of nature, as such, I do not need to be previously possessed of a concept of what sort of a thing the object is intended to be, i.e., I am not obliged to know its material finality (the end), but, rather, in forming an estimate of it apart from any knowledge of the end, the mere form pleases on its own account. If, however, the object is presented as a product of art, and is as such to be declared beautiful, then, seeing that art always presupposes an end in the cause (and its causality), a concept of what the thing is intended to be must first of all be laid at its basis. And, since the agreement of the manifold in a thing with an inner character belonging to it as its end constitutes the perfection of the thing, it follows that in estimating beauty of art the perfection of the thing must be also taken into account—a matter which in estimating a beauty of nature, as beautiful, is quite irrevelant. It is true that in forming an estimate, especially of animate objects of nature, e.g., of a man or a horse, objective finality is also commonly taken into account with a view to judgement upon their beauty; but then the judgement also ceases to be purely aesthetic, i.e., a mere judgement of taste. Nature is no longer estimated as it appears like art, but rather in so far as it actually *is* art, though superhuman art; and the teleological judgement serves as a basis and condition of the aesthetic, and one which the latter must regard. In such a case, where one says, for example, "That is a beautiful woman," what one in fact thinks is only this, that in her form nature excellently portrays the ends present in the female figure. For one has to extend one's view beyond the mere form to a concept, to enable the object to be thought in such manner by means of an aesthetic judgement logically conditioned.

Where fine art evidences its superiority is in the beautiful descriptions it gives of things that

[1] [In the *Critique of Practical Reason,* p. 361, Kant spoke of "the extravagances of genius, by which, as by the adepts of the philosopher's stone, without any methodical study or knowledge of nature, visionary treasures are promised and the true are thrown away."]

[2] [Cf. pp. 491, 548.]

in nature would be ugly or displeasing.[1] The Furies, diseases, devastations of war, and the like, can (as evils) be very beautifully described, nay even represented in pictures. One kind of ugliness alone is incapable of being represented conformably to nature without destroying all aesthetic delight, and consequently artistic beauty, namely, that which excites *disgust.* For, as in this strange sensation, which depends purely on the imagination, the object is represented as insisting, as it were, upon our enjoying it, while we still set our face against it, the artificial representation of the object is no longer distinguishable from the nature of the object itself in our sensation, and so it cannot possibly be regarded as beautiful. The art of sculpture, again, since in its products art is almost confused with nature, has excluded from its creations the direct representation of ugly objects, and, instead, only sanctions, for example, the representation of death (in a beautiful genius), or of the warlike spirit (in Mars), by means of an allegory, or attributes which wear a pleasant guise, and so only indirectly, through an interpretation on the part of reason, and not for the pure aesthetic judgement.

So much for the beautiful representation of an object, which is properly only the form of the presentation of a concept and the means by which the latter is universally communicated. To give this form, however, to the product of fine art, taste merely is required. By this the artist, having practised and corrected his taste by a variety of examples from nature or art, controls his work and, after many, and often laborious, attempts to satisfy taste, finds the form which commends itself to him. Hence this form is not, as it were, a matter of inspiration, or of a free swing of the mental powers, but rather of a slow and even painful process of improvement, directed to making the form adequate to his thought without prejudice to the freedom in the play of those powers.

Taste is, however, merely a critical, not a productive faculty; and what conforms to it is not, merely on that account, a work of fine art. It may belong to useful and mechanical art, or even to science, as a product following definite rules which are capable of being learned and which must be closely followed. But the pleasing form imparted to the work is only the vehicle of communication and a mode, as it were, of execution, in respect of which one remains to a certain extent free, notwithstanding being otherwise tied down to a definite end. So we demand that table appointments, or even a moral dissertation, and, indeed, a sermon, must bear this form of fine art, yet without its appearing *studied.* But one would not call them on this account works of fine art. A poem, a musical composition, a picture-gallery, and so forth, would, however, be placed under this head; and so in a would-be work of fine art we may frequently recognize genius without taste, and in another taste without genius.

§ 49. *The faculties of the mind which constitute genius*

Of certain products which are expected, partly at least, to stand on the footing of fine art, we say they are *soul*less; and this, although we find nothing to censure in them as far as taste goes. A poem may be very pretty and elegant, but is soulless. A narrative has precision and method, but is soulless. A speech on some festive occasion may be good in substance and ornate withal, but may be soulless. Conversation frequently is not devoid of entertainment, but yet soulless. Even of a woman we may well say, she is pretty, affable, and refined, but soulless. Now what do we here mean by "soul"?

Soul (*Geist*) in an aesthetical sense, signifies the animating principle in the mind. But that whereby this principle animates the psychic substance (*Seele*)— the material which it employs for that purpose—is that which sets the mental powers into a swing that is final, i.e., into a play which is self-maintaining and which strengthens those powers for such activity.[2]

Now my proposition is that this principle is nothing else than the faculty of presenting *aesthetic ideas.* But, by an aesthetic idea I mean that representation of the imagination which induces much thought, yet without the possibility of any definite thought whatever, i.e., *concept,* being adequate to it, and which language, consequently, can never get quite on level terms with or render completely intelligible. It is easily seen, that an aesthetic idea is the counterpart (pendant) of a *rational idea,* which, conversely, is a concept, to which no *intuition* (representation of the imagination) can be adequate.

The imagination (as a productive faculty of cognition) is a powerful agent for creating, as it were, a second nature out of the material supplied to it by actual nature. It affords us entertainment where experience proves too commonplace; and we even use it to remodel

[1] [Cf. Aristotle's *Poetics,* iv; and *Rhetoric,* I, xi.]

[2] [Cf. pp. 483, 484.]

experience, always following, no doubt, laws that are based on analogy, but still also following principles which have a higher seat in reason (and which are every whit as natural to us as those followed by the understanding in laying hold of empirical nature). By this means we get a sense of our freedom from the law of association[1] (which attaches to the empirical employment of the imagination), with the result that the material can be borrowed by us from nature in accordance with that law, but be worked up by us into something else—namely, what surpasses nature.

Such representations of the imagination may be termed *ideas*. This is partly because they at least strain after something lying out beyond the confines of experience, and so seek to approximate to a presentation of rational concepts (i.e., intellectual ideas), thus giving to these concepts the semblance of an objective reality. But, on the other hand, there is this most important reason, that no concept can be wholly adequate to them as internal intuitions. The poet essays the task of interpreting to sense the rational ideas of invisible beings, the kingdom of the blessed, hell, eternity, creation, etc. Or, again, as to things of which examples occur in experience, e.g., death, envy, and all vices, as also love, fame, and the like, transgressing the limits of experience he attempts with the aid of an imagination which emulates the display of reason in its attainment of a maximum, to body them forth to sense with a completeness of which nature affords no parallel; and it is in fact precisely in the poetic art that the faculty of aesthetic ideas can show itself to full advantage. This faculty, however, regarded solely on its own account, is properly no more than a talent (of the imagination).[2]

If, now, we attach to a concept a representation of the imagination belonging to its presentation, but inducing solely on its own account such a wealth of thought as would never admit of comprehension in a definite concept, and, as a consequence, giving aesthetically an unbounded expansion to the concept itself, then the imagination here displays a creative activity, and it puts the faculty of intellectual ideas (reason) into motion—a motion, at the instance of a representation, towards an extension of thought, that, while germane, no doubt, to the concept of the object, exceeds what can be laid hold of in that representation or clearly expressed.

[1] [Cf. p. 493.]
[2] [Cf. pp. 525, 530.]

Those forms which do not constitute the presentation of a given concept itself, but which, as secondary representations of the imagination, express the derivatives connected with it, and its kinship with other concepts, are called (aesthetic) *attributes* of an object, the concept of which, as an idea of reason, cannot be adequately presented. In this way Jupiter's eagle, with the lightning in its claws, is an attribute of the mighty king of heaven, and the peacock of its stately queen. They do not, like *logical* (aesthetic) *attributes* of an object, the concept of the sublimity and majesty of creation, but rather something else—something that gives the imagination an incentive to spread its flight over a whole host of kindred representations that provoke more thought than admits of expression in a concept determined by words. They furnish an *aesthetic idea*, which serves the above rational idea as a substitute for logical presentation,[3] but with the proper function, however, of animating the mind by opening out for it a prospect into a field of kindred representations stretching beyond its ken. But it is not alone in the arts of painting or sculpture, where the name of *attribute* is customarily employed, that fine art acts in this way; poetry and rhetoric also drive the soul that animates their work wholly from the aesthetic attributes of the objects—attributes which go hand in hand with the logical, and give the imagination an impetus to bring more thought into play in the matter, though in an undeveloped manner, than allows of being brought within the embrace of a concept, or, therefore, of being definitely formulated in language. For the sake of brevity I must confine myself to a few examples only. When the great king expresses himself in one of his poems by saying:

Oui, finissons sans trouble, et mourons sans regrets,
En laissant l'Univers comblé de nos bienfaits.
Ainsi l'Astre du jour, au bout de sa carrière,
Répand sur l'horizon une douce lumière,
Et les derniers rayons qu'il darde dans les airs
Sont les derniers soupirs qu'il donne à l'Univers;

he kindles in this way his rational idea of a cosmopolitan sentiment even at the close of life, with the help of an attribute which the imagination (in remembering all the pleasures of a

[3] [Cf. p. 506.]

fair summer's day that is over and gone—a memory of which pleasures is suggested by a serene evening) annexes to that representation, and which stirs up a crowd of sensations and secondary representations for which no expression can be found. On the other hand, even an intellectual concept may serve, conversely, as attribute for a representation of sense, and so animate the latter with the idea of the supersensible; but only by the aesthetic factor subjectively attaching to the consciousness of the supersensible being employed for the purpose. So, for example, a certain poet says in his description of a beautiful morning: "The sun arose, as out of virtue rises peace." The consciousness of virtue, even where we put ourselves only in thought in the position of a virtuous man, diffuses in the mind a multitude of sublime and tranquillizing feelings, and gives a boundless outlook into a happy future, such as no expression within the compass of a definite concept completely attains.[1]

In a word, the aesthetic idea is a representation of the imagination, annexed to a given concept, with which, in the free employment of imagination, such a multiplicity of partial representations are bound up, that no expression indicating a definite concept can be found for it—one which on that account allows a concept to be supplemented in thought by much that is indefinable in words, and the feeling of which quickens the cognitive faculties, and with language, as a mere thing of the letter, binds up the spirit (soul) also.

The mental powers whose union in a certain relation constitutes *genius* are imagination and understanding. Now, since the imagination, in its employment on behalf of cognition, is subjected to the constraint of the understanding and the restriction of having to be conformable to the concept belonging thereto, whereas aesthetically it is free to furnish of its own accord, over and above that agreement with the concept, a wealth of undeveloped material for the understanding, to which the latter paid no regard in its concept, but which it can make use of, not so much objectively for cognition, as subjectively for quickening the cognitive faculties, and hence also indirectly for cognitions, it may be seen that genius properly consists in the happy relation, which science cannot teach nor industry learn, enabling one to find out ideas for a given concept, and, besides, to hit upon the *expression* for them—the expression by means of which the subjective mental condition induced by the ideas as the concomitant of a concept may be communicated to others. This latter talent is properly that which is termed *soul.* For to get an expression for what is indefinable in the mental state accompanying a particular representation and to make it universally communicable—be the expression in language or painting or statuary—is a thing requiring a faculty for laying hold of the rapid and transient play of the imagination, and for unifying it in a concept (which for that very reason is original, and reveals a new rule which could not have been inferred from any preceding principles or examples) that admits of communication without any constraint of rules.

If, after this analysis, we cast a glance back upon the above definition of what is called *genius,* we find: *First,* that it is a talent for art—not one for science, in which clearly known rules must take the lead and determine the procedure. *Secondly,* being a talent in the line of art, it presupposes a definite concept of the product—as its end. Hence it presupposes understanding, but, in addition, a representation, indefinite though it be, of the material, i.e., of the intuition, required for the presentation of that concept, and so a relation of the imagination to the understanding. *Thirdly,* it displays itself, not so much in the working out of the projected end in the presentation of a definite *concept,* as rather in the portrayal, or expression of *aesthetic ideas* containing a wealth of material for effecting that intention. Consequently the imagination is represented by it in its freedom from all guidance of rules, but still as final for the presentation of the given concept. *Fourthly,* and lastly, the unsought and undesigned subjective finality in the free harmonizing of the imagination with the understanding's conformity to law presupposes a proportion and accord between these faculties such as cannot be brought about by any observance of rules, whether of science or mechanical imitation, but can only be produced by the nature of the individual.

Genius, according to these presuppositions,

[1] Perhaps there has never been a more sublime utterance, or a thought more sublimely expressed, than the well-known inscription upon the Temple of Isis (Mother *Nature*): "I am all that is, and that was, and that shall be, and no mortal hath raised the veil from before my face." Segner* made use of this idea in a suggestive vignette on the frontispiece of his *Natural Philosophy,* in order to inspire his pupil at the threshold of that temple into which he was about to lead him, with such a holy awe as would dispose his mind to serious attention.

* [Johann Andreas V. Segner, 1704-1777, Professor of Physics and Mathematics at the University of Gottingen.]

is the exemplary originality of the natural endowments of an individual in the *free* employment of his cognitive faculties. On this showing, the product of a genius (in respect of so much in this product as is attributable to genius, and not to possible learning or academic instruction) is an example, not for imitation (for that would mean the loss of the element of genius, and just the very soul of the work), but to be followed by another genius—one whom it arouses to a sense of his own originality in putting freedom from the constraint of rules so into force in his art that for art itself a new rule is won[1]—which is what shows a talent to be exemplary. Yet, since the genius is one of nature's elect—a type that must be regarded as but a rare phenomenon—for other clever minds his example gives rise to a school, that is to say a methodical instruction according to rules, collected, so far as the circumstances admit, from such products of genius and their peculiarities. And, to that extent, fine art is for such persons a matter of imitation, for which nature, through the medium of a genius, gave the rule.

But this imitation becomes *aping* when the pupil *copies* everything down to the deformities which the genius only of necessity suffered to remain, because they could hardly be removed without loss of force to the idea. This courage has merit only in the case of a genius. A certain *boldness* of expression and, in general, many a deviation from the common rule becomes him well, but in no sense is it a thing worthy of imitation. On the contrary it remains all through intrinsically a blemish, which one is bound to try to remove, but for which the genius is, as it were, allowed to plead a privilege, on the ground that a scrupulous carefulness would spoil what is inimitable in the impetuous ardour of his soul. *Mannerism* is another kind of aping—an aping of *peculiarity* (originality) in general, for the sake of removing oneself as far as possible from imitators, while the talent requisite to enable one to be at the same time *exemplary* is absent. There are, in fact, two modes (*modi*) in general of arranging one's thoughts for utterance. The one is called a *manner* (*modus aestheticus*), the other a *method* (*modus logicus*). The distinction between them is this: the former possesses no standard other than the *feeling* of unity in the presentation, whereas the latter here follows definite *principles*. As a consequence, the former is alone admissible for fine art. It is only, however, where the manner of carrying the idea into execution in a product of art is *aimed at* singularity, instead of being made appropriate to the idea, that *mannerism* is properly ascribed to such a product. The ostentatious (*précieux*), forced, and affected styles, intended to mark one out from the common herd (though soul is wanting), resemble the behaviour of a man who, as we say, hears himself talk, or who stands and moves about as if he were on a stage to be gaped at—action which invariably betrays a tyro.

[1] [Cf. p. 530.]

§ 50. *The combination of taste and genius in products of fine art*

To ask whether more stress should be laid in matters of fine art upon the presence of genius or upon that of taste, is equivalent to asking whether more turns upon imagination or upon judgement. Now, imagination rather entitles an art to be called an *inspired* (*geistreiche*) than a *fine* art. It is only in respect of judgement that the name of fine art is deserved. Hence it follows that judgement, being the indispensable condition (*conditio sine qua non*), is at least what one must look to as of capital importance in forming an estimate of art as fine art. So far as beauty is concerned, to be fertile and original in ideas is not such an imperative requirement as it is that the imagination in its freedom should be in accordance with the understanding's conformity to law. For, in lawless freedom, imagination, with all its wealth, produces nothing but nonsense; the power of judgement, on the other hand, is the faculty that makes it consonant with understanding.

Taste, like judgement in general, is the discipline (or corrective) of genius. It severely clips its wings, and makes it orderly or polished; but at the same time it gives it guidance directing and controlling its flight, so that it may preserve its character of finality. It introduces a clearness and order into the plenitude of thought, and in so doing gives stability to the ideas, and qualifies them at once for permanent and universal approval, for being followed by others, and for a continually progressive culture. And so, where the interests of both these qualities clash in a product, and there has to be a sacrifice of something, then it should rather be on the side of genius; and judgement, which in matters of fine art bases its decision on its own proper principles, will more readily endure an abatement of the freedom and wealth of the imagination than that the understanding should be compromised.

The requisites for fine art are, therefore, *imagination, understanding, soul,* and *taste.*[1]

§ 51. *The division of the fine arts*

BEAUTY (whether it be of nature or of art)[2] may in general be termed the *expression* of aesthetic ideas. But the provision must be added that with beauty of art this idea must be excited through the medium of a concept of the object, whereas with beauty of nature the bare reflection upon a given intuition, apart from any concept of what the object is intended to be, is sufficient for awakening and communicating the idea of which that object is regarded as the *expression.*

Accordingly, if we wish to make a division of the fine arts, we can choose for that purpose, tentatively at least, no more convenient principle than the analogy which art bears to the mode of expression of which men avail themselves in speech with a view to communicating themselves to one another as completely as possible, i.e., not merely in respect of their concepts but in respect of their sensations also.[3] Such expression consists in *word, gesture,* and *tone* (articulation, gesticulation, and modulation). It is the combination of these three modes of expression which alone constitutes a complete communication of the speaker. For thought, intuition, and sensation are in this way conveyed to others simultaneously and in conjunction.

Hence there are only three kinds of fine art: the art of *speech, formative* art, and the art of the *play of sensations* (as external sense impressions). This division might also be arranged as a dichotomy, so that fine art would be divided into that of the expression of thoughts or intuitions, the latter being subdivided according to the distinction between the form and the matter (sensation). It would, however, in that case appear too abstract, and less in line with popular conceptions.

(1) The arts of SPEECH are *rhetoric* and *poetry. Rhetoric* is the art of transacting a serious business of the understanding as if it were a free play of the imagination; *poetry* that of conducting a free play of the imagination as if it were a serious business of the understanding.

Thus the *orator* announces a serious business, and for the purpose of entertaining his audience conducts it as if it were a mere *play* with ideas. The *poet* promises merely an entertaining *play* with ideas, and yet for the understanding there enures as much as if the promotion of its business had been his one intention. The combination and harmony of the two faculties of cognition, sensibility and understanding, which, though doubtless indispensable to one another, do not readily permit of being united without compulsion and reciprocal abatement, must have the appearance of being undesigned and a spontaneous occurrence—otherwise it is not *fine* art. For this reason, what is studied and laboured must be here avoided.[4] For fine art must be free art in a double sense: i.e., not alone in a sense opposed to contract work, as not being a work the magnitude of which may be estimated, exacted, or paid for, according to a definite standard, but free also in the sense that, while the mind, no doubt, occupies itself, still it does so without ulterior regard to any other end, and yet with a feeling of satisfaction and stimulation (independent of reward).

The orator, therefore, gives something which he does not promise, viz., an entertaining play of the imagination. On the other hand, there is something in which he fails to come up to his promise, and a thing, too, which is his avowed business, namely, the engagement of the understanding to some end. The poet's promise, on the contrary, is a modest one, and a mere play with ideas is all he holds out to us, but he accomplishes something worthy of being made a serious business, namely, the using of play to provide food for the understanding, and the giving of life to its concepts by means of the imagination. Hence the orator in reality performs less than he promises, the poet more.

(2) The FORMATIVE arts, or those for the expression of ideas in *sensuous intuition* (not by means of representations of mere imagination that are excited by words) are arts either of *sensuous truth* or of *sensuous semblance.* The first is called *plastic* art, the second *painting.* Both use figures in space for the expression of ideas: the former makes figures discernible to two senses, sight and touch (though, so far as the latter sense is concerned, without regard to beauty), the latter makes them so to the former sense alone. The aesthetic idea (archetype, original) is the fundamental basis of both in the imagination; but the figure which constitutes its

[1] The first three faculties are first *brought into union* by means of the fourth. Hume, in his history, informs the English that although they are second in their works to no other people in the world in respect of the evidences they afford of the three first qualities *separately* considered, still in what unites them they must yield to their neighbours, the French.

[2] [Cf. p. 543, *et seq.*]

[3] The reader is not to consider this scheme for a possible division of the fine arts as a deliberate theory. It is only one of the various attempts that can and ought to be made.

[4] [Cf. p.. 525.]

expression (the ectype, the copy) is given either in its bodily extension (the way the object itself exists) or else in accordance with the picture which it forms of itself in the eye (according to its appearance when projected on a flat surface). Or, whatever the archetype is, either the reference to an actual end or only the semblance of one may be imposed upon reflection as its condition.

To *plastic* art, as the first kind of formative fine art, belong *sculpture* and *architecture*. The first is that which presents concepts of things corporeally, as they *might exist in nature* (though as fine art it directs its attention to aesthetic finality). The *second* is the art of presenting concepts of things which are possible *only through art*, and the determining ground of whose form is not nature but an orbitrary end—and of presenting them both with a view to this purpose and yet, at the same time, with aesthetic finality. In architecture the chief point is a certain *use* of the artistic object to which, as the condition, the aesthetic ideas are limited. In sculpture the mere *expression* of aesthetic ideas is the main intention. Thus statues of men, gods, animals, etc., belong to sculpture; but temples, splendid buildings for public concourse, or even dwelling-houses, triumphal arches, columns, mausoleums, etc., erected as monuments, belong to architecture, and in fact all household furniture (the work of cabinetmakers, and so forth—things meant to be used) may be added to the list, on the ground that adaptation of the product to a particular use is the essential element in a *work of architecture*. On the other hand, a mere *piece of sculpture*, made simply to be looked at and intended to please on its own account, is, as a corporeal presentation, a mere imitation of nature, though one in which regard is paid to aesthetic ideas, and in which, therefore, *sensuous truth* should not go the length of losing the appearance of being an art and a product of the elective will.

Painting, as the second kind of formative art, which presents the *sensuous semblance* in artful combination with ideas, I would divide into that of the beautiful *portrayal of nature*, and that of the beautiful *arrangement* of its *products*. The first is *painting proper*, the second *landscape gardening*. For the first gives only the semblance of bodily extension; whereas the second, giving this, no doubt, according to its truth, gives only the semblance of utility and employment for ends other than the play of the imagination in the contemplation of its forms.[1] The latter consists in no more than decking out the ground with the same manifold variety (grasses, flowers, shrubs, and trees, and even water, hills, and dales) as that with which nature presents it to our view, only arranged differently and in obedience to certain ideas. The beautiful arrangement of corporeal things, however, is also a thing for the eye only, just like painting—the sense of touch can form no intuitable representation of such a form. In addition I would place under the head of painting, in the wide sense, the decoration of rooms by means of hangings, ornamental accessories, and all beautiful furniture the sole function of which is *to be looked at;* and in the same way the art of tasteful dressing (with rings, snuffboxes, etc.). For a *parterre* of various flowers, a room with a variety of ornaments (including even the ladies' attire), go to make at a festal gathering a sort of picture which, like pictures in the true sense of the word (those which are not intended *to teach* history or natural science), has no business beyond appealing to the eye, in order to entertain the imagination in free play with ideas, and to engage actively the aesthetic judgement independently of any definite end. No matter how heterogeneous, on the mechanical side, may be the craft involved in all this decoration, and no matter what a variety of artists may be required, still the judgement of taste, so far as it is one upon what is beautiful in this art, is determined in one and the same way: namely, as a judgement only upon the forms (without regard to any end) as they present themselves to the eye, singly or in combination, according to their effect upon the imagination. The justification, however, of bringing formative art (by analogy) under a common head with gesture in a speech, lies in the fact that through these figures the soul of the artists furnishes a bodily expression for the substance and character of his thought, and makes the

[1] It seems strange that landscape gardening may be regarded as a kind of painting, notwithstanding that it presents its forms corporeally. But, as it takes its forms bodily from nature (the trees, shrubs, grasses, and flowers taken, originally at least, from wood and field) it is to that extent not an art such as, let us say, plastic art. Further, the arrangement which it makes is not conditioned by any concept of the object or of its end (as is the case in sculpture), but by the mere free play of the imagination in the act of contemplation. Hence it bears a degree of resemblance to simple aesthetic painting that has no definite theme (but by means of light and shade makes a pleasing composition of atmosphere, land, and water.)* Throughout, the reader is to weigh the above only as an effort to connect the fine arts under a principle, which, in the present instance, is intended to be that of the expression of aesthetic ideas (following the analogy of a language), and not as a positive and deliberate derivation of the connection.

* [Cf. p. 488.]

thing itself speak, as it were, in mimic language—a very common play of our fancy, that attributes to lifeless things a soul suitable to their form, and that uses them as its mouthpiece.

(3) The art of the BEAUTIFUL PLAY OF SENSATIONS (sensations that arise from external stimulation), which is a play of sensations that has nevertheless to permit of universal communication, can only be concerned with the proportion of the different degrees of tension in the sense to which the sensation belongs, i.e., with its tone. In this comprehensive sense of the word, it may be divided into the artificial play of sensations of hearing and of sight, consequently into *music* and the *art of colour*. It is of note that these two senses, over and above such susceptibility for impressions as is required to obtain concepts of external objects by means of these impressions, also admit of a peculiar associated sensation of which we cannot well determine whether it is based on sense or reflection; and that this sensibility may at times be wanting, although the sense, in other respects, and in what concerns its employment for the cognition of objects, is by no means deficient but particularly keen. In other words, we cannot confidently assert whether a colour or a tone (sound) is merely an agreeable sensation, or whether they are in themselves a beautiful play of sensations, and in being estimated aesthetically, convey, as such, a delight in their form. If we consider the velocity of the vibrations of light, or, in the second case, of the air, which in all probability far outstrips any capacity on our part for forming an immediate estimate in perception of the time interval between them, we should be led to believe that it is only the *effect* of those vibrating movements upon the elastic parts of our body, that can be evident to sense, but that the *time-interval* between them is not noticed nor involved in our estimate, and that, consequently, all that enters into combination with colours and tones is agreeableness, and not beauty, of their composition. But, let us consider, on the other hand, *first,* the mathematical character both of the proportion of those vibrations in music, and of our judgement upon it, and, as is reasonable, form an estimate of colour contrasts on the analogy of the latter. *Secondly,* let us consult the instances, albeit rare, of men who, with the best of sight, have failed to distinguish colours, and, with the sharpest hearing, to distinguish tones, while for men who have this ability the perception of an altered quality (not merely of the degree of the sensation) in the case of the different intensities in the scale of colours or tones is definite, as is also the number of those which may be *intelligibly* distinguished. Bearing all this in mind, we may feel compelled to look upon the sensations afforded by both, not as mere sense-impressions, but as the effect of an estimate of form in the play of a number of sensations. The difference which the one opinion or the other occasions in the estimate of the basis of music would, however, only give rise to this much change in its definition, that either it is to be interpreted, as we have done, as the *beautiful* play of sensations (through hearing), or else as one of *agreeable* sensations. According to the former interpretation, alone, would music be represented out and out as a *fine* art, whereas according to the latter it would be represented as (in part at least) an *agreeable* art.

§ 52. *The combination of the fine arts in one and the same product*

RHETORIC may in a *drama* be combined with a pictorial presentation as well of its subjects as of objects; as may poetry with music in a *song;* and this again with a pictorial (theatrical) presentation in an *opera;* and so may the play of sensations in a piece of music with the play of figures in a *dance,* and so on. Even the presentation of the sublime, so far as it belongs to fine art, may be brought into union with beauty in a *tragedy in verse,* a *didactic poem* or an *oratorio,* and in this combination fine art is even more artistic. Whether it is also more beautiful (having regard to the multiplicity of different kinds of delight which cross one another) may in some of these instances be doubted. Still in all fine art the essential element consists in the form which is final for observation and for estimating. Here the pleasure is at the same time culture, and disposes the soul to ideas, making it thus susceptible of such pleasure and entertainment in greater abundance. The matter of sensation (charm or emotion) is not essential. Here the aim is merely enjoyment, which leaves nothing behind it in the idea, and renders the soul dull, the object in the course of time distasteful, and the mind dissatisfied with itself and ill-humoured, owing to a consciousness that in the judgement of reason its disposition is perverse.

Where fine arts are not, either proximately or remotely, brought into combination with moral ideas, which alone are attended with a self-sufficing delight, the above is the fate that ultimately awaits them. They then only serve for a diversion, of which one continually feels an increasing need in proportion as one has availed oneself of it as a means of dispelling the discontent of one's mind, with the result that one makes oneself ever more and more unprofitable and dissatisfied with oneself. With a view to the purpose first named, the beauties of nature are in general the most beneficial, if one is early habituated to observe, estimate, and admire them.

§ 53. *Comparative estimate of the aesthetic worth of the fine arts*

Poetry (which owes its origin almost entirely to genius and is least willing to be led by precepts or example) holds the first rank among all the arts. It expands the mind by giving freedom to the imagination and by offering, from among the boundless multiplicity of possible forms accordant with a given concept, to whose bounds it is restricted, that one which couples with the presentation of the concept a wealth of thought to which no verbal expression is completely adequate, and by thus rising aesthetically to ideas. It invigorates the mind by letting it feel its faculty—free, spontaneous, and independent of determination by nature—of regarding and estimating nature as phenomenon in the light of aspects which nature of itself does not afford us in experience, either for sense or understanding, and of employing it accordingly in behalf of, and as a sort of schema for, the supersensible. It plays with semblance, which it produces at will, but not as an instrument of deception; for its avowed pursuit is merely one of play, which, however, understanding may turn to good account and employ for its own purpose. Rhetoric, so far as this is taken to mean the art of persuasion, i.e., the art of deluding by means of a fair semblance (as *ars oratoria*), and not merely excellence of speech (eloquence and style), is a dialectic, which borrows from poetry only so much as is necessary to win over men's minds to the side of the speaker before they have weighed the matter, and to rob their verdict of its freedom. Hence it can be recommended neither for the bar nor the pulpit. For where civil laws, the right of individual persons, or the permanent instruction and determination of men's minds to a correct knowledge and a conscientious observance of their duty is at stake, then it is below the dignity of an undertaking of such moment to exhibit even a trace of the exuberance of wit and imagination, and, still more, of the art of talking men round and prejudicing them in favour of any one. For although such art is capable of being at times directed to ends intrinsically legitimate and praiseworthy, still it becomes reprehensible on account of the subjective injury done in this way to maxims and sentiments, even where objectively the action may be lawful. For it is not enough to do what is right, but we should practise it solely on the ground of its being right. Further, the simple lucid concept of human concerns of this kind, backed up with lively illustrations of it, exerts of itself, in the absence of any offence against the rules of euphony of speech or of propriety in the expression of ideas of reason (all which together make up excellence of speech), a sufficient influence upon human minds to obviate the necessity of having recourse here to the machinery of persuasion, which, being equally available for the purpose of putting a fine gloss or a cloak upon vice and error, fails to rid one completely of the lurking suspicion that one is being artfully hoodwinked. In poetry everything is straight and above board. It shows its hand: it desires to carry on a mere entertaining play with the imagination, and one consonant, in respect of form, with the laws of understanding, and it does not seek to steal upon and ensnare the understanding with a sensuous presentation.[1]

After poetry, *if we take charm and mental stimulation into account,* I would give the next place to that art which comes nearer to it than to any other art of speech, and admits of very natural union with it, namely the art of *tone.* For though it speaks by means of mere sensations without concepts, and so does not, like poetry, leave behind it any food for reflection, still it moves the mind more diversely, and, although with transient, still with intenser effect. It is certainly, however, more a matter of enjoyment than of culture—the play of thought

[1] I must confess to the pure delight which I have ever been afforded by a beautiful poem; whereas the reading of the best speech of a Roman forensic orator, a modern parliamentary debater, or a preacher, has invariably been mingled with an unpleasant sense of disapproval of an insidious art that knows how, in matters of moment, to move men like machines to a judgement that must lose all its weight with them upon calm reflection. Force and elegance of speech (which together constitute rhetoric) belong to fine art; but oratory *(ars oratoria),* being the art of playing for one's own purpose upon the weaknesses of men (let this purpose be ever so good in intention or even in fact) merits no *respect* whatever. Besides, both at Athens and at Rome, it only attained its greatest height at a time when the state was hastening to its decay, and genuine patriotic sentiment was a thing of the past. One who sees the issue clearly, and who has a command of language in its wealth and its purity, and who is possessed of an imagination that is fertile and effective in presenting his ideas, and whose heart, withal, turns with lively sympathy to what is truly good—he is the *vir bonus dicendi peritus,* the orator without art, but of great impressiveness, as Cicero would have him, though he may not himself always have remained faithful to this ideal.

incidentally excited by it being merely the effect of a more or less mechanical association—and it possesses less worth in the eyes of reason than any other of the fine arts. Hence, like all enjoyment, it calls for constant change, and does not stand frequent repetition without inducing weariness. Its charm, which admits of such universal communication, appears to rest on the following facts. Every expression in language has an associated tone suited to its sense. This tone indicates, more or less, a mode in which the speaker is affected, and in turn evokes it in the hearer also, in whom conversely it then also excites the idea which in language is expressed with such a tone. Further, just as modulation is, as it were, a universal language of sensations intelligible to every man, so the art of tone wields the full force of this language wholly on its own account, namely, as a language of the affections, and in this way, according to the law of association, universally communicates the aesthetic ideas that are naturally combined therewith. But, further, inasmuch as those aesthetic ideas are not concepts or determinate thoughts, the form of the arrangement of these sensations (harmony and melody), taking the place of the form of a language, only serves the purpose of giving an expression to the aesthetic idea of an integral whole of an unutterable wealth of thought that fills the measure of a certain theme forming the dominant *affection* in the piece. This purpose is effectuated by means of a proposition in the accord of the sensations (an accord which may be brought mathematically under certain rules, since it rests, in the case of tones, upon the numerical relation of the vibrations of the air in the same time, so far as there is a combination of the tones simultaneously or in succession). Although this mathematical form is not represented by means of determinate concepts, to it alone belongs the delight which the mere reflection upon such a number of concomitant or consecutive sensations couples with this their play, as the universally valid condition of its beauty, and it is with reference to it alone that taste can lay claim to a right to anticipate the judgement of every man.

But mathematics, certainly, does not play the smallest part in the charm and movement of the mind produced by music. Rather is it only the indispensable condition (*conditio sine qua non*) of that proportion of the combining as well as changing impressions which makes it possible to grasp them all in one and prevent them from destroying one another, and to let them, rather, conspire towards the production of a continuous movement and quickening of the mind by affections that are in unison with it, and thus towards a serene self-enjoyment.

If, on the other hand, we estimate the worth of the fine arts by the culture they supply to the mind, and adopt for our standard the expansion of the faculties whose confluence, in judgement, is necessary for cognition, music, then, since it plays merely with sensations, has the lowest place among the fine arts—just as it has perhaps the highest among those valued at the same time for their agreeableness. Looked at in this light, it is far excelled by the formative arts. For, in putting the imagination into a play which is at once free and adapted to the understanding, they all the while carry on a serious business, since they execute a product which serves the concepts of understanding as a vehicle, permanent and appealing to us on its own account, for effectuating their union with sensibility, and thus for promoting, as it were, the urbanity of the higher powers of cognition. The two kinds of art pursue completely different courses. Music advances from sensations to indefinite ideas: formative art from definite ideas to sensations. The latter gives a *lasting* impression, the former one that is only *fleeting*. The former sensations imagination can recall and agreeably entertain itself with, while the latter either vanish entirely, or else, if involuntarily repeated by the imagination, are more annoying to us than agreeable. Over and above all this, music has a certain lack of urbanity about it. For owing chiefly to the character of its instruments, it scatters its influence abroad to an uncalled-for extent (through the neighbourhood), and thus, as it were, becomes obtrusive and deprives others, outside the musical circle, of their freedom. This is a thing that the arts that address themselves to the eye do not do, for if one is not disposed to give admittance to their impressions, one has only to look the other way. The case is almost on a par with the practice of regaling oneself with a perfume that exhales its odours far and wide. The man who pulls his perfumed handkerchief from his pocket gives a treat to all around whether they like it or not, and compels them, if they want to breathe at all, to be parties to the enjoyment, and so the habit has gone out of fashion.[1]

[1] Those who have recommended the singing of hymns at family prayers have forgotten the amount of annoyance which they give to the general public by such *noisy* (and, as a rule, for that very reason, pharisaical) worship, for they compel their neighbours either to join in the singing or else abandon their meditations.

Among the formative arts I would give the palm to *painting:* partly because it is the art of design and, as such, the groundwork of all the other formative arts; partly because it can penetrate much further into the region of ideas, and in conformity with them give a greater extension to the field of intuition than it is open to the others to do.

§ 54. *Remark*

As we have often shown, an essential distinction lies between what *pleases simply in the estimate formed of it* and what *gratifies* (pleases in sensation). The latter is something which, unlike the former, we cannot demand from every one. Gratification (no matter whether its cause has its seat even in ideas) appears always to consist in a feeling of the furtherance of the entire life of the man, and hence, also of his bodily well-being, i.e., his health. And so, perhaps, Epicurus was not wide of the mark when he said that at bottom all gratification is bodily sensation, and only misunderstood himself in ranking intellectual and even practical delight under the head of gratification. Bearing in mind the latter distinction, it is readily explicable how even the gratification a person feels is capable of displeasing him (as the joy of a necessitous but good-natured individual on being made the heir of an affectionate but penurious father), or how deep pain may still give pleasure to the sufferer (as the sorrow of a widow over the death of her deserving husband), or how there may be pleasure over and above gratification (as in scientific pursuits), or how a pain (as, for example, hatred, envy, and desire for revenge) may in addition be a source of displeasure. Here the delight or aversion depends upon reason, and is one with *approbation* or *disapprobation.* Gratification and pain, on the other hand, can only depend upon feeling, or upon the prospect of a possible *well-being* or the *reverse* (irrespective of source).

The changing free play of sensations (which do not follow any preconceived plan) is always a source of gratification, because it promotes the feeling of health; and it is immaterial whether or not we experience delight in the object of this play or even in the gratification itself when estimated in the light of reason. Also this gratification may amount to an affection, although we take no interest in the object itself, or none, at least, proportionate to the degree of the affection. We may divide the above play into that of *games of chance* (*Glückspiel*), *harmony* (*Tonspiel*), and *wit* (*Gedankenspiel*). The *first* stands in need of an *interest,* be it of vanity or self-seeking, but one which falls far short of that centered in the adopted mode of procurement. All that the *second* requires is the change of *sensations,* each of which has its bearing on affection, though without attaining to the degree of an affection, and excites aesthetic ideas. The *third* springs merely from the change of the representations in the judgement, which, while unproductive of any thought conveying an interest, yet enlivens the mind.

What a fund of gratification must be afforded by play, without our having to fall back upon any consideration of interest, is a matter to which all our evening parties bear witness—for without play they hardly ever escape falling flat. But the affections of hope, fear, joy, anger, and derision here engage in play, as every moment they change their parts and are so lively that, as by an internal motion, the whole vital function of the body seems to be furthered by the process—as is proved by a vivacity of the mind produced—although no one comes by anything in the way of profit or instruction. But as the play of chance is not one that is beautiful, we will here lay it aside. Music, on the contrary, and what provokes laughter are two kinds of play with aesthetic ideas, or even with representations of the understanding, by which, all said and done, nothing is thought. By mere force of change they yet are able to afford lively gratification. This furnishes pretty clear evidence that the quickening effect of both is physical, despite its being excited by ideas of the mind, and that the feeling of health, arising from a movement of the intestines answering to that play, makes up that entire gratification of an animated gathering upon the spirit and refinement of which we set such store. Not any estimate of harmony in tones or flashes of wit, which, with its beauty, serves only as a necessary vehicle, but rather the stimulated vital functions of the body, the affection stirring the intestines and the diaphragm, and, in a word, the feeling of health (of which we are only sensible upon some such provocation) are what constitute the gratification we experience at being able to reach the body through the soul and use the latter as the physician of the former.

In music, the course of this play is from bodily sensation to aesthetic ideas (which are the objects for the affections), and then from these back again, but with gathered strength, to the body. In jest (which just as much as the former deserves to be ranked rather as an agreeable than a fine art) the play sets out from thoughts which collectively, so far as seeking sensuous expression, engage the activity of the body. In this presentation the understanding, missing what it expected, suddenly lets go its hold, with the result that the effect of this slackening is felt in the body by the oscillation of the organs. This favours the restoration of the equilibrium of the latter, and exerts a beneficial influence upon the health.

Something absurd (something in which, therefore, the understanding can of itself find no delight) must be present in whatever is to raise a hearty convulsive laugh. *Laughter is an affection arising from a strained expectation being suddenly reduced to nothing.* This very reduction, at which certainly understanding cannot rejoice, is still indirectly a source of very lively enjoyment for a moment. Its cause must consequently lie in the influence of the representation upon the body and the reciprocal effect of this upon the mind. This, moreover, cannot depend upon the representation being objectively an object of gratification (for how can we derive gratification from a disappointment?) but must rest solely upon the fact that the reduction is a mere play of representations, and, as such, produces an equilibrium of the vital forces of the body.

Suppose that some one tells the following story: An Indian at an Englishman's table in Surat saw a bottle of ale opened, and all the beer turned into froth and flowing out. The repeated exclamations of the Indian showed his great astonishment. "Well, what is so wonderful in that?" asked the Englishman. "Oh, I'm not surprised myself," said the Indian, "at its getting out, but at how you ever managed to get it all in." At this we laugh, and it gives us hearty pleasure. This is not because we think ourselves, maybe, more quick-witted than this ignorant Indian, or because our understanding here brings to our notice any other ground of delight. It is rather that the bubble of our expectation was extended to the full and suddenly went off into nothing. Or, again, take the case of the heir of a wealthy relative being minded to make preparations for having the funeral obsequies on a most imposing scale, but complaining that things would not go right for him, because (as he said) "the more money I give my mourners to look sad, the more pleased they look." At this we laugh outright, and the reason lies in the fact that we had an expectation which is suddenly reduced to nothing. We must be careful to observe that the reduction is not one into the positive contrary of an expected object—for that is always something, and may frequently pain us—but must be a reduction to nothing. For where a person arouses great expectation by recounting some tale, and at the close its untruth becomes at once apparent to us, we are displeased at it. So it is, for instance, with the tale of people whose hair from excess of grief is said to have turned white in a single night. On the other hand, if a wag, wishing to cap the story, tells with the utmost circumstantiality of a merchant's grief, who, on his return journey from India to Europe with all his wealth in merchandise, was obliged by stress of storm to throw everything overboard, and grieved to such an extent that in the selfsame night his *wig* turned grey, we laugh and enjoy the tale. This is because we keep for a time playing on our own mistake about an object otherwise indifferent to us, or rather on the idea we ourselves were following out, and, beating it to and fro, just as if it were a ball eluding our grasp, when all we intend to do is just to get it into our hands and hold it tight. Here our gratification is not excited by a knave or a fool getting a rebuff: for, even on its own account, the latter tale told with an air of seriousness would of itself be enough to set a whole table into roars of laughter; and the other matter would ordinarily not be worth a moment's thought.

It is observable that in all such cases the joke must have something in it capable of momentarily deceiving us. Hence, when the semblance vanishes into nothing, the mind looks back in order to try it over again, and thus by a rapidly succeeding tension and relaxation it is jerked to and fro and put in oscillation. As the snapping of what was, as it were, tightening up the string takes place suddenly (not by a gradual loosening), the oscillation must bring about a mental movement and a sympathetic internal movement of the body. This continues involuntarily and produces fatigue, but in so doing it also affords recreation (the effects of a motion conducive to health).

For supposing we assume that some movement in the bodily organs is associated sympathetically with all our thoughts, it is readily intelligible how the sudden act above referred to, of shifting the mind now to one standpoint and now to the other, to enable it to contemplate its object, may involve a corresponding and reciprocal straining and slackening of the elastic parts of our intestines, which communicates itself to the diaphragm (and resembles that felt by ticklish people), in the course of which the lungs expel the air with rapidly succeeding interruptions, resulting in a movement conducive to health. This alone, and not what goes on in the mind, is the proper cause of the gratification in a thought that at bottom represents nothing. Voltaire[1] said that heaven has given us two things to compensate us for the many miseries of life, *hope* and *sleep*. He might have added *laughter* to the list—if only the means of exciting it in men of intelligence were as ready to hand, and the wit or originality of humour which it requires were not just as rare as the talent is common for inventing stuff *that splits the head,* as mystic speculators do, or *that breaks your neck,* as the genius does, or that *harrows the heart* as sentimental novelists do (aye, and moralists of the same type).

We may, therefore as I conceive, make Epicurus a present of the point that all gratification, even when occasioned by concepts that evoke aesthetic ideas, is *animal,* i.e., bodily sensation. For from this admission the *spiritual* feeling of respect for moral ideas, which is not one of gratification, but a self-esteem (an esteem for humanity within us) that raises us above the need of gratification, suffers not a whit—no nor even the less noble feeling of *taste.*

In *naïveté* we meet with a joint product of both the above. *Naïveté* is the breaking forth of the ingenuousness originally natural to humanity, in opposition to the art of disguising oneself that has become a second nature. We laugh at the simplicity that is as yet a stranger to dissimulation, but we rejoice the while over the simplicity of nature that thwarts that art. We await the commonplace manner of artificial utterance, thoughtfully addressed to a fair show, and lo! nature stands before us in unsullied innocence—nature that we were quite unprepared to meet, and that he who laid it bare had also no intention of revealing. That the outward appearance, fair but false, that usually assumes such importance in our judgement, is here, at a stroke, turned to a nullity, that, as it were, the rogue in us is nakedly exposed, calls forth the movement of the mind, in two successive and opposite directions, agitating the body at the same time with wholesome motion. But that something infinitely better than any accepted code of manners, namely purity of mind (or at least a vestige of such purity), has not become wholly extinct in human nature, infuses seriousness and reverence into this play of judgement. But since it is only a manifestation that obtrudes itself for a moment, and the veil of a dissembling art is soon drawn over it again, there enters into the above feelings a touch of pity. This is an emotion of tenderness, playful in its way, that thus readily admits of combination with this sort of genial laughter. And, in fact, this emotion is as a rule associated with it, and, at the same time, is wont to make amends to the person who provides such food for our merriment for his embarrassment at not being wise after the manner of men. For that reason an art of being *naïf* is a contradiction. But it is quite possible to give a representation of *naïveté* in a fictitious personage, and, rare as the art is, it is a fine art. With this *naïveté* we must not confuse homely simplicity, which only avoids spoiling nature by artificiality, because it has no notion of the conventions of good society.

The *humorous* manner may also be ranked as a thing which in its enlivening influence is clearly allied to the gratification provoked by laughter. It belongs to originality of mind (*des Geistes*), though not to the talent for fine art. *Humour,* in a good sense, means the talent for being able to put oneself at will into a certain frame of mind in which everything is estimated on lines that go quite off the beaten track (a topsy-turvy view of things), and yet on lines that follow certain principles, rational in the case of such a mental temperament. A person with whom such variations are not a matter of choice is said *to have humours;* but if a person can assume them voluntarily and of set purpose (on behalf of a lively presentation drawn from a ludicrous contrast), he and his way of speaking are termed *humorous.* This manner belongs, however, to agreeable rather than to fine art, because the object of the latter must always have an evident intrinsic worth about it, and thus demands a certain seriousness in its presentation, as taste does in estimating it.[2]

1 [*Henriade,* chant 7.]

2 [Cf. pp. 534, 536.]

SECTION II. *DIALECTIC OF AESTHETIC JUDGEMENT*

§ 55

For a power of judgement to be dialectical it must first of all be rationalizing; that is to say, its judgements must lay claim to universality,[1] and do so *a priori,* for it is in the antithesis of such judgements that dialectic consists. Hence there is nothing dialectical in the irreconcilability of aesthetic judgements of sense (upon the agreeable and disagreeable). And in so far as each person appeals merely to his own private taste, even the conflict of judgements of taste does not form a dialectic of taste—for no one is proposing to make his own judgement into a universal rule. Hence the only concept left to us of a dialectic affecting taste is one of a dialectic of the *critique* of taste (not of taste itself) in respect of its *principles:* for, on the question of the ground of the possibility of judgements of taste in general, mutually conflicting concepts naturally and unavoidably make their appearance. The transcendental critique of taste will, therefore, only include a part capable of bearing the name of a dialectic of the aesthetic judgement if we find an antinomy of the principles of this faculty which throws doubt upon its conformity to law, and hence also upon its inner possibility.

§ 56. *Representation of the antinomy of taste*

The first commonplace of taste is contained in the proposition under cover of which every one devoid of taste thinks to shelter himself from reproach: *every one has his own taste.* This is only another way of saying that the determining ground of this judgement is merely subjective (gratification or pain), and that the judgement has no right to the necessary agreement of others.

Its second commonplace, to which even those resort who concede the right of the judgement of taste to pronounce with validity for every one, is: *there is no disputing about taste.* This amounts to saying that, even though the determining ground of a judgement of taste be objective, it is not reducible to definite concepts, so that in respect of the judgement itself no *decision* can be reached by proofs, although it is quite open to us to *contend* upon the matter, and to contend with right. For though *contention* and *dispute* have this point in common, that they aim at bringing judgements into accordance out of and by means of their mutual opposition; yet they differ in the latter hoping to effect this from definite concepts, as grounds of proof, and, consequently, adopting *objective concepts* as grounds of the judgement. But where this is considered impracticable, dispute is regarded as alike out of the question.

Between these two commonplaces an intermediate proposition is readily seen to be missing. It is one which has certainly not become proverbial, but yet it is at the back of every one's mind. It is that *there may be contention about taste* (although not a dispute). This proposition, however, involves the contrary of the first one. For in a manner in which contention is to be allowed, there must be a hope of coming to terms. Hence one must be able to reckon on grounds of judgement that possess more than private validity and are thus not merely subjective. And yet the above principle (*Every one has his own taste*) is directly opposed to this.

The principle of taste, therefore, exhibits the following antinomy:

1. *Thesis.* The judgement of taste is not based upon concepts; for, if it were, it would be open to dispute (decision by means of proofs).

2. *Antithesis.* The judgement of taste is based on concepts; for otherwise, despite diversity of judgement, there could be no room even for contention in the matter (a claim to the necessary agreement of others with this judgement).

§ 57. *Solution of the antinomy of taste*

There is no possibility of removing the conflict of the above principles, which underlie every judgement of taste (and which are only the two peculiarities of the judgement of taste previously set out in the Analytic) except by showing that the concept to which the object is made to refer in a judgement of this kind is not taken in the same sense in both maxims of the

[1] Any judgement which sets up to be universal may be termed a *rationalizing* judgement *(indicium ratiocinans);* for so far as universal it may serve as the major premiss of a syllogism. On the other hand, only a judgement which is thought as the conclusion of a syllogism, and, therefore, as having an *a priori* foundation, can be called rational *(indicium ratiocinatum).*

aesthetic judgement; that this double sense, or point of view, in our estimate, is necessary for our power of transcendental judgement; and that nevertheless the false appearance arising from the confusion of one with the other is a natural illusion, and so unavoidable.

The judgement of taste must have reference to some concept or other, as otherwise it would be absolutely impossible for it to lay claim to necessary validity for every one. Yet it need not on that account be provable from a concept. For a concept may be either determinable, or else at once intrinsically undetermined and indeterminable. A concept of the understanding, which is determinable by means of predicates borrowed from sensible intuition and capable of corresponding to it, is of the first kind. But of the second kind is the transcendental rational concept of the supersensible, which lies at the basis of all that sensible intuition and is, therefore, incapable of being further determined theoretically.

Now the judgement of taste applies to objects of sense, but not so as to determine a *concept* of them for the understanding; for it is not a cognitive judgement. Hence it is a singular representation of intuition referable to the feeling of pleasure, and, as such, only a private judgement. And to that extent it would be limited in its validity to the individual judging: the object is *for me* an object of delight, for others it may be otherwise; every one to his taste.

For all that, the judgement of taste contains beyond doubt an enlarged reference on the part of the representation of the object (and at the same time on the part of the subject also), which lays the foundation of an extension of judgements of this kind to necessity for every one. This must of necessity be founded upon some concept or other, but such a concept as does not admit of being determined by intuition, and affords no knowledge of anything. Hence, too, it is a concept *which does not afford any proof* of the judgement of taste. But the mere pure rational concept of the supersensible lying at the basis of the object (and of the judging subject for that matter) as object of sense, and thus as phenomenon, is just such a concept. For unless such a point of view were adopted there would be no means of saving the claim of the judgement of taste to universal validity. And if the concept forming the required basis were a concept of understanding, though a mere confused one, as, let us say, of perfection, answering to which the sensible intuition of the beautiful might be adduced, then it would be at least intrinsically possible to found the judgement of taste upon proofs, which contradicts the thesis.

All contradiction disappears, however, if I say: The judgement of taste does depend upon a concept (of a general ground of the subjective finality of nature for the power of judgement), but one from which nothing can be cognized in respect of the object, and nothing proved, because it is in itself indeterminable and useless for knowledge. Yet, by means of this very concept, it acquires at the same time validity for every one (but with each individual, no doubt, as a singular judgement immediately accompanying his intuition): because its determining ground lies, perhaps, in the concept of what may be regarded as the supersensible substrate of humanity.

The solution of an antinomy turns solely on the possibility of two apparently conflicting propositions not being in fact contradictory, but rather being capable of consisting together, although the explanation of the possibility of their concept transcends our faculties of cognition. That this illusion is also natural and for human reason unavoidable, as well as why it is so, and remains so, although upon the solution of the apparent contradiction it no longer misleads us, may be made intelligible from the above considerations.

For the concept, which the universal validity of a judgement must have for its basis, is taken in the same sense in both the conflicting judgements, yet two opposite predicates are asserted of it. The thesis should therefore read: The judgement of taste is not based on *determinate* concepts; but the antithesis: The judgement of taste does rest upon a concept, although an *indeterminate* one (that, namely, of the supersensible substrate of phenomena); and then there would be no conflict between them.

Beyond removing this conflict between the claims and counter-claims of taste we can do nothing. To supply a determinate objective principle of taste in accordance with which its judgements might be derived, tested, and proved, is an absolute impossibility, for then it would not be a judgement of taste. The subjective principle—that is to say, the indeterminate idea of the supersensible within us—can only be indicated as the unique key to the riddle of this faculty, itself concealed from us in its sources; and there is no means of making it any more intelligible.

The antinomy here exhibited and resolved rests upon the proper concept of taste as a merely reflective aesthetic judgement, and the two seemingly conflicting principles are reconciled on the ground that *they may both be true*, and this is sufficient. If, on the other hand, owing to the fact that the representation lying at the basis of the judgement of taste is singular, the determining ground of taste is taken, as by some it is, to be *agreeableness*, or, as others, looking to its universal validity, would have it, the principle of *perfection*, and if the definition of taste is framed accordingly, the result is an antinomy which is absolutely irresolvable unless we show *the falsity of both propositions* as contraries (not as simple contradictories). This would force the conclusion that the concept upon which each is founded is self-contradictory. Thus it is evident that the removal of the antinomy of the aesthetic judgement pursues a course similar to that followed by the Critique in the solution of the antinomies of pure theoretical reason; and that the antinomies, both here and in the *Critique of Practical Reason*, compel us, whether we like it or not, to look beyond the horizon of the sensible, and to seek in the supersensible the point of union of all our faculties *a prori:* for we are left with no other expedient to bring reason into harmony with itself.

Remark I

We find such frequent occasion in transcendental philosophy for distinguishing ideas from concepts of the understanding that it may be of use to introduce technical terms answering to the distinction between them. I think that no objection will be raised to my proposing some. Ideas, in the most comprehensive sense of the word, are representations referred to an object according to a certain principle (subjective or objective), in so far as they can still never become a cognition of it. They are either referred to an intuition, in accordance with a merely subjective principle of the harmony of the cognitive faculties (imagination and understanding), and are then called *aesthetic;* or else they are referred to a concept according to an objective principle and yet are incapable of ever furnishing a cognition of the object, and are called *rational ideas*. In the latter case, the concept is a *transcendent* concept, and, as such, differs from a concept of understanding, for which an adequately answering experience may always be supplied, and which, on that account, is called *immanent*.

An *aesthetic idea* cannot become a cognition, because it is an *intuition* (of the imagination) for which an adequate concept can never be found. A *rational idea* can never become a cognition, because it involves a *concept* (of the supersensible), for which a commensurate intuition can never be given.

Now the aesthetic idea might, I think, be called an *inexponible* representation of the imagination, the rational idea, on the other hand, an *indemonstrable* concept of reason. The production of both is presupposed to be not altogether groundless, but rather (following the above explanation of an idea in general) to take place in obedience to certain principles of the cognitive faculties to which they belong (subjective principles in the case of the former and objective in that of the latter).

Concepts of the understanding must, as such, always be demonstrable (if, as in anatomy, demonstration is understood in the sense merely of *presentation*). In other words, the object answering to such concepts must always be capable of being given an intuition (pure or empirical); for only in this way can they become cognitions. The concept of *magnitude* may be given *a priori* in the intuition of space, e.g., of the right line, etc.; the concept of *cause* in impenetrability, in the impact of bodies, etc. Consequently both may be verified by means of an empirical intuition, i.e., the thought of them may be indicated (demonstrated, exhibited) in an example; and this it must be possible to do: for otherwise there would be no certainty of the thought not being empty, i.e., having no object.

In logic the expressions *demonstrable* or *indemonstrable* are ordinarily employed only in respect of *propositions*. A better designation would be to call the former propositions only *mediately*, and the latter, propositions *immediately, certain*. For pure philosophy, too, has propositions of both these kinds—meaning thereby true propositions which are in the one case capable, and in the other incapable, of proof. But, in its character of philosophy, while it can, no doubt, prove on *a priori* grounds, it cannot demonstrate—unless we wish to give the complete go-by to the meaning of the word which makes demonstrate (*ostendere, exhibere*) equivalent to giving an accompanying presentation of the concept in intuition (be it in a proof or in a definition). Where the intuition is *a priori* this is called its *construction*, but when even the intuition is empirical, we have still got the illustration of the object, by which means objective reality is assured to the concept. Thus an anatomist is said to demonstrate the human eye when he renders the concept, of which he has previously given a discursive exposition, intuitable by means of the dissection of that organ.

It follows from the above that the rational concept of the supersensible substrate of all phenomena generally, or even of that which must be laid at the basis of our elective will in respect of moral laws, i.e., the rational concept of transcendental freedom, is at once specifically an indemonstrable concept, and a rational idea, whereas virtue is so in a measure. For nothing can be given which in itself qualitatively answers in experience to the rational concept of the former, while in the case of virtue no empirical product of the above causality attains the degree that the rational idea prescribes as the rule.

Just as the *imagination,* in the case of a rational idea, fails with its intuitions to attain to the given concept, so *understanding,* in the case of an aesthetic idea, fails with its concepts ever to attain to the completeness of the internal intuition which imagination conjoins with a given representation. Now since the reduction of a representation of the imagination to concepts is equivalent to giving its *exponents,* the aesthetic idea may be called on *inexponible* representation of the imagination (in its free play). I shall have an opportunity hereafter of dealing more fully with ideas of this kind. At present I confine myself to the remark, that both kinds of ideas, aesthetic ideas as well as rational, are bound to have their principles, and that the seat of these principles must in both cases be reason—the latter depending upon the objective, the former upon the subjective, principles of its employment.

Consonantly with this, GENIUS may also be defined as the faculty of *aesthetic ideas.* This serves at the same time to point out the reason why it is nature (the nature of the individual) and not a set purpose, that in products of genius gives the rule to art (as the production of the beautiful). For the beautiful must not be estimated according to concepts, but by the final mode in which the imagination is attuned so as to accord with the faculty of concepts generally; and so rule and precept are incapable of serving as the requisite subjective standard for that aesthetic and unconditioned finality in fine art which has to make a warranted claim to being bound to please every one. Rather must such a standard be sought in the element of mere nature in the subject, which cannot be comprehended under rules or concepts, that is to say, the supersensible substrate of all the subject's faculties (unattainable by any concept of understanding), and consequently in that which forms the point of reference for the harmonious accord of all our faculties of cognition—the production of which accord is the ultimate end set by the intelligible basis of our nature. Thus alone is it possible for a subjective and yet universally valid principle *a priori* to lie at the basis of that finality for which no objective principle can be prescribed.

Remark 2

The following important observation here naturally presents itself: There are *three kinds of antinomies* of pure reason, which, however, all agree in forcing reason to abandon the otherwise very natural assumption which takes the objects of sense for things-in-themselves, and to regard them, instead, merely as phenomena, and to lay at their basis an intelligible substrate (something supersensible, the concept of which is only an idea and affords no proper knowledge). Apart from some such antinomy, reason could never bring itself to take such a step as to adopt a principle so severely restricting the field of its speculation, and to submit to sacrifices involving the complete dissipation of so many otherwise brilliant hopes. For even now that it is recompensed for this loss by the prospect of a proportionately wider scope of action from a practical point of view, it is not without a pang of regret that it appears to part company with those hopes, and to break away from the old ties.

The reason for there being three kinds of antinomies is to be found in the fact that there are three faculties of cognition, understanding, judgement, and reason, each of which, being a higher faculty of cognition, must have its *a priori* principles. For, so far as reason passes judgement upon these principles themselves and their employment, it inexorably requires the unconditioned for the given conditioned in respect of them all. This can never be found unless the sensible, instead of being regarded as inherently appurtenant to things-in-themselves, is treated as a mere phenomenon, and, as such, being made to rest upon something supersensible (the intelligible substrate of external and internal nature) as the thing-in-itself. There is then (1) *for the cognitive faculty* an antinomy of reason in respect of the theoretical employment of understanding carried to the point of the unconditioned; (2) *for the feeling of pleasure and displeasure* an antinomy of reason in respect of the aesthetic employment of judgement; (3) *for the faculty of desire* an antinomy in respect of the practical employment of self-legislative reason. For all these faculties have their fundamental *a priori* principles, and, following an imperative demand of reason, must be able to judge and to determine their object *unconditionally* in accordance with these principles.

As to two of the antinomies of these higher cognitive faculties, those, namely, of their theoretical and of their practical employment, we have already shown elsewhere both that they are *inevitable,* if no cognisance is taken in such judgements of a supersensible substrate of the given objects as phenomena, and, on the other hand, that they *can be solved* the moment this is done. Now, as to the antinomy incident to the employment of judgement in conformity with the demand of reason, and the solution of it here given, we may say that to avoid facing it there are but the following alternatives. It is open to us to deny that any *a priori* principle lies at the basis of the aesthetic judgement of taste, with the result that all claim to the necessity of a universal consensus of opinion is an idle and empty delusion, and that a judgement of taste only deserves to be considered to this extent correct, that *it so happens* that a number share the same opinion, and even this, not, in truth, because an *a priori* principle is *presumed* to lie at the back of this agreement, but rather (as with the taste of the palate) because of the contingently resembling organization of the individuals. *Or else,* in the alternative, we should have to suppose that the judgement of taste is in fact a disguised judgement of reason on the perfection discovered in a thing and the reference of the manifold in it to an end, and that it is consequently only called *aesthetic* on account of the confusion that here besets our reflection, although fundamentally it is teleological. In this latter case the solution of the antinomy with the assistance of transcendental ideas might be declared otiose and nugatory, and the above laws of taste thus reconciled with the objects of sense, not as mere phenomena, but even as things-in-themselves. How unsatisfactory both of those alternatives alike are as a means of escape has been shown in several places in our exposition of judgements of taste.

If, however, our deduction is at least credited with having been worked out on correct lines, even though it may not have been sufficiently clear in all its details, three ideas then stand out in evidence. *Firstly,* there is the supersensible in general, without further determination, as substrate of nature; *secondly,* this same supersensible as principle of the subjective finality of nature for our cognitive faculties; *thirdly,* the same supersensible again, as principle of the ends of freedom, and principle of the common accord of these ends with freedom in the moral sphere.

§ 58. *The idealism of the finality alike of nature and of art, as the unique principle of the aesthetic judgement*

THE principle of taste may, to begin with, be placed on either of two footings. For taste may be said invariably to judge on empirical grounds of determination and such, therefore, as are only given *a posteriori* through sense, or else it may be allowed to judge on an *a priori* ground. The former would be the *empiricism* of the critique of taste, the latter its *rationalism.* The first would obliterate the distinction that marks off the object of our delight from the *agreeable;* the *second,* supposing the judgement rested upon determinate concepts, would obliterate its distinction from the *good.* In this way *beauty* would have its *locus standi* in the world completely denied, and nothing but the dignity of a separate name, betokening, maybe, a certain blend of both the above-named kinds of delight, would be left in its stead. But we have shown the existence of grounds of delight which are *a priori,* and which therefore, can consist with the principle of rationalism, and which are yet incapable of being grasped by *definite concepts.*

As against the above, we may say that the rationalism of the principle of taste may take the form either of the *realism* of finality or of its *idealism.* Now, as a judgement of taste is not a cognitive judgement, and as beauty is not a property of the object considered in its own account, the rationalism of the principle of taste can never be placed in the fact that the finality in this judgement is regarded in thought as objective. In other words, the judgement is not directed theoretically, nor, therefore, logically, either (no matter if only in a confused estimate), to the perfection of the object, but only *aesthetically* to the harmonizing of its representation in the imagination with the essential principles of judgement generally in the subject. For this reason the judgement of taste, and the distinction between its realism and its idealism, can only, even on the principle of rationalism, depend upon its subjective finality interpreted in one or other of two ways. Either such subjective finality is, in the first case, a harmony with our judgement pursued as an actual (intentional) *end* of nature (or of art), or else, in the second case, it is only a supervening final harmony with the needs of our faculty of judgement in its relation to nature and the forms which nature produces in accordance with particular laws, and one that is independent of an end, spontaneous and contingent.

The beautiful forms displayed in the organic world all plead eloquently on the side of the realism of the aesthetic finality of nature in support of the plausible assumption that beneath the production of the beautiful there must lie a preconceived idea in the producing cause—that is to say an *end* acting in the interest of our imagination. Flowers, blossoms, even the shapes of plants as a whole, the elegance of animal formations of all kinds, unnecessary for the discharge of any function on their part, but chosen as it were with an eye to our taste; and, beyond all else, the variety and harmony in the array of colours (in the pheasant, in crustacea, in insects, down even to the meanest flowers), so pleasing and charming to the eyes, but which, inasmuch as they touch the bare surface, and do not even here in any way affect the structure, of these creatures—a matter which might have a necessary bearing on their internal ends—seem to be planned entirely with a view to outward appearance: all these lend great weight to the mode of explanation which assumes actual ends of nature in favour of our aesthetic judgement.

On the other hand, not alone does reason, with its maxims enjoining upon us in all cases to avoid, as far as possible, any unnecessary multiplication of principles, set itself against this assumption, but we have nature in its free formations displaying on all sides extensive mechanical proclivity to producing forms seemingly made, as it were, for the aesthetic employment of our judgement, without affording the least support to the supposition of a need for anything over and above its mechanism, as mere nature, to enable them to be final for our judgement apart from their being grounded upon any idea. The above expression, "*free formations*" of nature, is, however, here used to denote such as are originally set up in a *fluid at rest* where the volatilization or separation of some constituent (sometimes merely of caloric) leaves the residue on solidification to assume a definite shape or structure (figure or texture) which differs with specific differences of the matter, but for the same matter is invariable. Here, however, it is taken for granted that, as the true meaning of a fluid requires, the matter in the fluid is completely dissolved and not a mere admixture of solid particles simply held there in suspension.

The formation, then, takes place by a *concursion,* i.e., by a sudden solidification—not by a gradual transition from the fluid to the solid state, but, as it were, by a leap. This transition is termed *crystallization.* Freezing water offers the most familiar instance of a formation of this kind. There the process begins by straight threads of ice forming. These unite at angles of 60°, whilst others similarly attach themselves to them at every point until the whole has turned into ice. But while this is going on, the water between the threads of ice does not keep getting gradually more viscous, but remains as thoroughly fluid as it would be at a much higher temperature, although it is perfectly ice-cold. The matter that frees itself—that makes its sudden escape at the moment of solidification—is a considerable quantum of caloric. As this was merely required to preserve fluidity, its disappearance leaves the existing ice not a whit colder than the water which but a moment before was there as fluid.

There are many salts and also stones of a crystalline figure which owe their origin in like manner to some earthly substance being dissolved in water under the influence of agencies little understood. The drusy configurations of many minerals, of the cubical sulphide of lead, of the red silver ore, etc., are presumably also similarly formed in water, and by the concursion of their particles, on their being forced by some cause or other to relinquish this vehicle and to unite among themselves in definite external shapes.

But, further, all substances rendered fluid by heat, which have become solid as the result of cooling, give, when broken, internal evidences of a definite texture, thus suggesting the inference that only for the interference of their own weight or the disturbance of the air, the exterior would also have exhibited their proper specific shape. This has been observed in the case of some metals where the exterior of a molten mass has hardened, but the interior remained fluid, and then, owing to the withdrawal of the still fluid portion in the interior, there has been an undisturbed concursion of the remaining parts on the inside. A number of such mineral crystallizations, such as *spars, hematite, aragonite,* frequently present extremely beautiful shapes such as it might take art all its time to devise; and the halo in the grotto of

Antiparos is merely the work of water percolating through strata of gypsum.

The fluid state is, to all appearance, on the whole older than the solid, and plants as well as animal bodies are built up out of fluid nutritive substance, so far as this takes form undisturbed—in the case of the latter, admittedly, in obedience, primarily, to a certain original bent of nature directed to ends (which, as will be shown in Part II, must not be judged aesthetically, but teleologically by the principle of realism); but still all the while, perhaps, also following the universal law of the affinity of substances in the way they shoot together and form in freedom. In the same way, again, where an atmosphere, which is a composite of different kinds of gas, is charged with watery fluids, and these separate from it owing to a reduction of the temperature, they produce snow-figures of shapes differing with the actual composition of the atmosphere. These are frequently of very artistic appearance and of extreme beauty. So without at all derogating from the teleological principle by which an organization is judged, it is readily conceivable how with beauty of flowers, of the plumage of birds, of crustacea, both as to their shape and their colour, we have only what may be ascribed to nature and its capacity for originating in free activity aesthetically final forms, independently of any particular guiding ends, according to chemical laws, by means of the chemical integration of the substance requisite for the organization.

But what shows plainly that the principle of the *ideality* of the finality in the beauty of nature is the one upon which we ourselves invariably take our stand in our aesthetic judgements, forbidding us to have recourse to any realism of a natural end in favour of our faculty of representation as a principle of explanation, is that in our general estimate of beauty we seek its standard *a priori* in ourselves, and, that the aesthetic faculty is itself legislative in respect of the judgement whether anything is beautiful or not. This could not be so on the assumption of a realism of the finality of nature; because in that case we should have to go to nature for instruction as to what we should deem beautiful, and the judgement of taste would be subject to empirical principles. For in such an estimate the question does not turn on what nature is, or even on what it is for us in the way of an end, but on how we receive it. For nature to have fashioned its forms for our delight would inevitably imply an objective finality on the part of nature, instead of a subjective finality resting on the play of imagination in its freedom, where it is we who receive nature with favour, and not nature that does us a favour. That nature affords us an opportunity for perceiving the inner finality in the relation of our mental powers engaged in the estimate of certain of its products, and, indeed, such a finality as arising from a supersensible basis is to be pronounced necessary and of universal validity, is a property of nature which cannot belong to it as its end, or rather, cannot be estimated by us to be such an end. For otherwise the judgement that would be determined by reference to such an end would found upon heteronomy, instead of founding upon autonomy and being free, as befits a judgement of taste.

The principle of the idealism of finality is still more clearly apparent in fine art. For the point that sensations do not enable us to adopt an aesthetic realism of finality (which would make art merely agreeable instead of beautiful) is one which it enjoys in common with beautiful nature. But the further point that the delight arising from aesthetic ideas must not be made dependent upon the successful attainment of determinate ends (as an art mechanically directed to results), and that, consequently, even in the case of the rationalism of the principle, an ideality of the ends and not their reality is fundamental, is brought home to us by the fact that fine art, as such, must not be regarded as a product of understanding and science, but of genius, and must, therefore, derive its rule from *aesthetic* ideas, which are essentially different from rational ideas of determinate ends.

Just as the *ideality* of objects of sense as phenomena is the only way of explaining the possibility of their forms admitting of *a priori* determination, so, also, the *idealism* of the finality in estimating the beautiful in nature and in art is the only hypothesis upon which a critique can explain the possibility of a judgement of taste that demands *a priori* validity for every one (yet without basing the finality represented in the object upon concepts).

§ 59. *Beauty as the symbol of morality*

Intuitions are always required to verify the reality of our concepts. If the concepts are empirical, the intuitions are called *examples:* if they are pure concepts of the understanding, the intuitions go by the name of *schemata.* But to call for a verification of the objective reality of rational concepts, i.e., of ideas, and, what is more, on behalf of the theoretical cognition of such a reality, is to demand an impossibility, because absolutely no intuition adequate to them can be given.

All *hypotyposis* (presentation, *subjectio sub adspectum*) as a rendering in terms of sense, is twofold. Either it is *schematic*, as where the intuition corresponding to a concept comprehended by the understanding is given *a priori*, or else it is *symbolic*, as where the concept is one which only reason can think, and to which no sensible intuition can be adequate. In the latter case the concept is supplied with an intuition such that the procedure of judgement in dealing with it is merely analogous to that which it observes in schematism. In other words, what agrees with the concept is merely the rule of this procedure, and not the intuition itself. Hence the agreement is merely in the form of reflection, and not in the content.

Notwithstanding the adoption of the word *symbolic* by modern logicians in a sense opposed to an *intuitive* mode of representation, it is a wrong use of the word and subversive of its true meaning; for the symbolic is only a *mode* of any intrinsic connection with the intuition of sentation is, in fact, divisible into the *schematic* and the *symbolic*. Both are hypotyposes, i.e., presentations (*exhibitiones*), not mere *marks*. Marks are merely designations of concepts by the aid of accompanying sensible signs devoid of any intrinsic connection with the intuition of the object. Their sole function is to afford a means of reinvoking the concepts according to the imagination's law of association—a purely subjective role. Such marks are either words or visible (algebraic or even mimetic) signs, simply as *expressions* for concepts.[1]

All intuitions by which *a priori* concepts are given a foothold are, therefore, either *schemata* or *symbols*. Schemata contain direct, symbols indirect, presentations of the concept. Schemata effect this presentation demonstratively, symbols by the aid of an analogy (for which recourse is had even to empirical intuitions), in which analogy judgement performs a double function: first in applying the concept to the object of a sensible intuition, and then, secondly, in applying the mere rule of its reflection upon that intuition to quite another object, of which the former is but the symbol. In this way, a monarchical state is represented as a living body when it is governed by constitutional laws, but as a mere machine (like a hand-mill) when it is governed by an individual absolute will; but in both cases the representation is merely *symbolic*. For there is certainly no likeness between a despotic state and a hand-mill, whereas there surely is between the rules of reflection upon both and their causality. Hitherto this function has been but little analysed, worthy as it is of a deeper study. Still this is not the place to dwell upon it. In language we have many such indirect presentations modelled upon an analogy enabling the expression in question to contain, not the proper schema for the concept, but merely a symbol for reflection. Thus the words *ground* (support, basis), *to depend* (to be held up from above), to *flow* from (instead of to follow), *substance* (as Locke puts it: the support of accidents), and numberless others, are not schematic, but rather symbolic hypotyposes, and express concepts without employing a direct intuition for the purpose, but only drawing upon an analogy with one, i.e., transferring the reflection upon an object of intuition to quite a new concept, and one with which perhaps no intuition could ever directly correspond. Supposing the name of *knowledge* may be given to what only amounts to a mere mode of representation (which is quite permissible where this is not a principle of the theoretical determination of the object in respect of what it is in itself, but of the practical determination of what the idea of it ought to be for us and for its final employment), then all our knowledge of God is merely symbolic; and one who takes it, with the properties of understanding, will, and so forth, which only evidence their objective reality in beings of this world, to be schematic, falls into anthropomorphism, just as, if he abandons every intuitive element, he falls into Deism which furnishes no knowledge whatsoever—not even from a practical point of view.

Now, I say, the beautiful is the symbol of the morally good, and only in this light (a point of view natural to every one, and one which every one exacts from others as a duty) does it give us pleasure with an attendant claim to the agreement of every one else, whereupon the mind becomes conscious of a certain ennoblement and elevation above mere sensibility to pleasure from impressions of sense, and also appraises the worth of others on the score of a like maxim of their judgement. This is that *intelligible* to which taste, as noticed in the preceding paragraph, extends its view. It is, that

[1] The intuitive mode of knowledge must be contrasted with the discursive mode (not with the symbolic). The former is either *schematic*, by means of *demonstration*, or *symbolic*, as a representation following a mere *analogy*.

is to say, what brings even our higher cognitive faculties into common accord, and is that apart from which sheer contradiction would arise between their nature and the claims put forward by taste. In this faculty, judgement does not find itself subjected to a heteronomy of laws of experience as it does in the empirical estimate of things—in respect of the objects of such a pure delight it gives the law to itself, just as reason does in respect of the faculty of desire.[1] Here, too, both on account of this inner possibility in the subject, and on account of the external possibility of a nature harmonizing therewith, it finds a reference in itself to something in the subject itself and outside it, and which is not nature, nor yet freedom, but still is connected with the ground of the latter, i.e., the supersensible—a something in which the theoretical faculty gets bound up into unity with the practical in an intimate and obscure manner. We shall bring out a few points of this analogy, while taking care, at the same time, not to let the points of difference escape us.

(1) The beautiful pleases *immediately* (but only in reflective intuition, not, like morality, in its concept).[2] (2) It pleases *apart from all interest* (pleasure in the morally good is no doubt necessarily bound up with an interest, but not with one of the kind that are antecedent to the judgement upon the delight, but with one that judgement itself for the first time calls into existence). (3) *The freedom* of the imagination (consequently of our faculty in respect of its sensibility) is, in estimating the beautiful, represented as in accord with the understanding's conformity to law (in moral judgements the freedom of the will is thought as the harmony of the latter with itself according to universal laws of Reason). (4) The subjective principles of the estimate of the beautiful is represented as *universal*, i.e., valid for every man, but as incognizable by means of any universal concept (the objective principle of morality is set forth as also universal, i.e., for all individuals, and, at the same time, for all actions of the same individual, and, besides, as cognizable by means of a universal concept). For this reason the moral judgement not alone admits of definite constitutive principles, but is *only* possible by adopting these principles and their universality as the ground of its maxims.

Even common understanding is wont to pay regard to this analogy; and we frequently apply to beautiful objects of nature or of art names that seem to rely upon the basis of a moral estimate. We call buildings or trees *majestic* and *stately*, or plains *laughing* and *gay;* even colours are called *innocent, modest, soft,* because they excite sensations containing something analogous to the consciousness of the state of mind produced by moral judgements. Taste makes, as it were, the transition from the charm of sense to habitual moral interest possible without too violent a leap, for it represents the imagination, even in its freedom, as amenable to a final determination for understanding, and teaches us to find, even in sensuous objects, a free delight apart from any charm of sense.

§ 60. APPENDIX. *The methodology of taste*

THE division of a critique into elementology and methodology—a division which is introductory to science—is one inapplicable to the critique of taste. For there neither is, nor can be, a science of the beautiful, and the judgement of taste is not determinable by principles. For, as to the element of science in every art—a matter which turns upon *truth* in the presentation of the object of the art—while this is, no doubt, the indispensable condition (*conditio sine qua non*) of fine art, it is not itself fine art. Fine art, therefore, has only got a *manner* (*modus*), and not a *method* of teaching (*methodus*). The master must illustrate what the pupil is to achieve and how achievement is to be attained, and the proper function of the universal rules to which he ultimately reduces his treatment is rather that of supplying a convenient text for recalling its chief moments to the pupil's mind, than of prescribing them to him. Yet, in all this, due regard must be paid to a certain ideal which art must keep in view, even though complete success ever eludes its happiest efforts. Only by exciting the pupil's imagination to conformity with a given concept, by pointing out how the expression falls short of the idea to which, as aesthetic, the concept itself fails to attain, and by means of severe criticism, is it possible to prevent his promptly looking upon the examples set before him as the prototypes of excellence, and as models for him to imitate, without submission to any higher standard or to his own critical judgement. This would result in genius being stifled, and, with it, also the freedom of the imagination in its very conformity to law—a freedom without which a fine art is not possible, nor even as much as a correct taste of one's own for estimating it.

[1] [Cf. the reference to heteronomy and autonomy, p. 546.]

[2] [Cf. pp. 488, 512.]

The propaedeutic to all fine art, so far as the highest degree of its perfection is what is in view, appears to lie, not in precepts, but in the culture of the mental powers produced by a sound preparatory education in what are called the *humaniora*—so called, presumably, because *humanity* signifies, on the one hand, the universal *feeling of sympathy*, and, on the other, the faculty of being able to *communicate* universally one's inmost self—properties constituting in conjunction the befitting *social spirit* of mankind, in contradistinction to the narrow life of the lower animals. There was an age and there were nations in which the active impulse towards a social life *regulated by laws*—what converts a people into a permanent community—grappled with the huge difficulties presented by the trying problem of bringing freedom (and therefore equality also) into union with constraining force (more that of respect and dutiful submission than of fear). And such must have been the age, and such the nation, that first discovered the art of reciprocal communication of ideas between the more cultured and ruder sections of the community, and how to bridge the difference between the amplitude and refinement of the former and the natural simplicity and originality of the latter—in this way hitting upon that mean between higher culture and the modest worth of nature, that forms for taste also, as a sense common to all mankind, that true standard which no universal rules can supply.

Hardly will a later age dispense with those models. For nature will ever recede farther into the background, so that eventually, with no permanent example retained from the past, a future age would scarce be in a position to form a concept of the happy union, in one and the same people, of the law-directed constraint belonging to the highest culture, with the force and truth of a free nature sensible of its proper worth.

However, taste is, in the ultimate analysis, a critical faculty that judges of the rendering of moral ideas in terms of sense (through the intervention of a certain analogy in our reflection on both); and it is this rendering also, and the increased sensibility, founded upon it, for the feeling which these ideas evoke (termed *moral sense*), that are the origin of that pleasure which taste declares valid for mankind in general and not merely for the private feeling of each individual. This makes it clear that the true propaedeutic for laying the foundations of taste is the development of moral ideas and the culture of the moral feeling. For only when sensibility is brought into harmony with moral feeling can genuine taste assume a definite unchangeable form.

SECOND PART

CRITIQUE OF TELEOLOGICAL JUDGEMENT[1]

§ 61. *Objective finality in nature.* [*Introduction*][1]

We do not need to look beyond the critical explanation of the possibility of knowledge to find ample reason for assuming a subjective finality on the part of nature in its particular laws. This is a finality relative to comprehensibility—man's power of judgement being such as it is—and to the possibility of uniting particular experiences into a connected system of nature. In this system, then, we may further anticipate the possible existence of some among the many products of nature that, as if put there with quite a special regard to our judgement, are of a form particularly adapted to that faculty. Forms of this kind are those which by their combination of unity and heterogeneity serve as it were to strengthen and entertain the mental powers that enter into play in the exercise of the faculty of judgement, and to them the name of *beautiful forms* is accordingly given.

But the universal idea of nature, as the complex of objects of sense, gives us no reason whatever for assuming that things of nature serve one another as means to ends,[2] or that their very possibility[3] is only made fully intelligible by a causality of this sort. For since, in the case of the beautiful forms above mentioned, the representation of the things is something in ourselves, it can quite readily be thought even *a priori* as one well-adapted and convenient for disposing our cognitive faculties to an inward and final harmony. But where the ends are not ends of our own, and do not belong even to nature (which we do not take to be an intelligent being), there is no reason at all for presuming *a priori* that they may or ought nevertheless to constitute a special kind of causality or at least a quite peculiar order of nature. What is more, the actual existence of these ends cannot be proved by experience—save on the assumption of an antecedent process of mental jugglery that only reads the conception of an end into the nature of the things, and that, not deriving this conception from the objects and what it knows of them from experience makes use of it more for the purpose of rendering nature intelligible to us by an analogy to a subjective ground upon which our representations are brought into inner connection, than for that of cognizing nature from objective grounds.

Besides, objective finality, as a principle upon which physical objects are possible, is so far from attaching *necessarily* to the conception of nature that it is the stock example adduced to show the contingency of nature and its form. So where the structure of a bird, for instance, the hollow formation of its bones, the position of its wings for producing motion and of its tail for steering, are cited, we are told that all this is in the highest degree contingent if we simply look to the *nexus effectivus* in nature, and do not call in aid a special kind of causality, namely, that of ends (*nexus finalis*). This means that nature, regarded as mere mechanism, could have fashioned itself in a thousand other different ways without lighting precisely on the unity based on a principle like this, and that, accordingly, it is only outside the conception of nature, and not in it, that we may hope to find some shadow of ground *a priori* for that unity.

We are right, however, in applying the teleological estimate, at least problematically, to the investigation of nature; but only with a view to bringing it under principles of observation and research by *analogy* to the causality that looks to ends, while not pretending to *explain* it by this means. Thus it is an estimate of the reflective, not of the determinant, judgement. Yet the conception of combinations and forms in nature that are determined by ends is at least *one more principle* for reducing its phenomena to rules in cases where the laws of its purely mechanical causality do not carry us sufficiently far. For we are bringing forward a teleological ground where we endow a conception of an ob-

1 [For passages dealing with the teleological judgement in the Preface and Introduction, Cf. above, pp. 462, and 473–4. The table of faculties at p. 475 should also be considered. The first paragraph of § 70, below p. 562, repeats a portion of the introductory matter.]

2 [Cf. p. 554.]

3 [Cf. above, p. 473.]

ject—as if that conception were to be found in nature instead of in ourselves—with causality in respect of the object, or rather where we picture to ourselves the possibility of the object on the analogy of a causality of this kind—a causality such as we experience in ourselves—and so regard nature as possessed of a capacity of its own for acting *technically;* whereas if we did not ascribe such a mode of operation to nature its causality would have to be regarded as blind mechanism. But this is a different thing from crediting nature with causes acting *designedly,* to which it may be regarded as subjected in following its particular laws. The latter would mean that teleology is based, not merely on a *regulative* principle, directed to the simple *estimate* of phenomena, but is actually based on a *constitutive* principle available for *deriving* natural products from their causes: with the result that the conception of a physical end no longer exists for the reflective, but for the determinant, judgement. But in that case the conception would not really be specially connected with the power of judgement, as is the conception of beauty as a formal subjective finality. It would, on the contrary, be a conception of reason, and would introduce a new causality into science—one which we are borrowing all the time solely from ourselves and attributing to other beings, although we do not mean to assume that they and we are similarly constituted.

. . .

First Division. *Analytic of Teleological Judgement*

§ 62. *Purely formal, as distinguished from material, objective finality*

All geometrical figures drawn on a principle display an objective finality which takes many directions and has often been admired.[1] This finality is one of convenience on the part of the figure for solving a number of problems by a single principle, and even for solving each one of the problems in an infinite variety of ways. Here the finality is manifestly objective and intellectual, not simply subjective and aesthetic. For it expresses the way the figure lends itself to the production of many proposed figures, and it is cognized through reason. Yet this finality does not make the conception of the object itself possible, this is to say, we do not regard the object as possible simply because it may be turned to such use.

In such a simple figure as the circle lies the key to the solution of a host of problems every one of which would separately require elaborate materials, and this solution follows, we might say, directly as one of the infinite number of excellent properties of that figure. For instance, suppose we have to construct a triangle, being given the base and vertical angle. The problem is indeterminate, i.e., it admits of solution in an endless variety of ways. But the circle embraces them all in one, as the geometrical locus of all triangles satisfying this condition. Or two lines have to intersect one another so that the rectangle under the two parts of the one shall be equal to the rectangle under the two parts of the other. The solution of the problem is apparently full of difficulty. But all lines intersecting within a circle whose circumference passes through their extremities are divided directly in this ratio. The remaining curves similarly suggest to us other useful solutions, never contemplated in the rule upon which they are constructed. All conic sections, taken separately or compared with one another, are, however simple their definition, fruitful in principles for solving a host of possible problems. It is a real joy to see the ardour with which the older geometricians investigated these properties of such lines, without allowing themselves to be troubled by the question which shallow minds raise, as to the supposed use of such knowledge. Thus they investigated the properties of the parabola in ignorance of the law of terrestrial gravitation which would have shown them its application to the trajectory of heavy bodies (for the direction of their gravitation when in motion may be regarded as parallel to the curve of a parabola). So again they investigated the properties of the ellipse without a suspicion that a gravitation was also discoverable in the celestial bodies, and without knowing the law that governs it as the distance from the point of attraction varies, and that makes the bodies describe this curve in free motion. While in all these labours they were working unwittingly for those who were to come after them, they delighted themselves with a finality which, although belonging to the nature of the things, they were able to present completely *a priori* as necessary. Plato, himself a master of this

[1] [Cf. pp. 561, 594.]

science, was fired with the idea of an original constitution of things, for the discovery of which we could dispense with all experience, and of a power of the mind enabling it to derive the harmony of real things from their supersensible principle (and with these real things he classed the properties of numbers with which the mind plays in music). Thus inspired, he transcended the conceptions of experience and rose to ideas that seemed only explicable to him on the assumption of a community of intellect with the original source of all things real. No wonder that he banished from his school the man that was ignorant of geometry, since he thought that from the pure intuition residing in the depths of the human soul he could derive all that Anaxagoras inferred from the objects of experience and their purposive combination. For it is the necessity of that which, while appearing to be an original attribute belonging to the essential nature of things regardless of service to us, is yet final, and formed as if purposely designed for our use, that is the source of our great admiration of nature—a source not so much external to ourselves as seated in our reason. Surely we may pardon this admiration if, as the result of a misapprehension, it is inclined to rise by degrees to fanatical heights.

This intellectual finality is simply formal, not real. In other words, it is a finality which does not imply an underlying end, and which, therefore, does not stand in need of teleology. As such, and although it is objective, not subjective like aesthetic finality, its possibility is readily comprehensible, though only in the abstract. The figure of a circle is an intuition which understanding has determined according to a principle. This principle, which is arbitrarily assumed and made a fundamental conception, is applied to space, a form of intuition which similarly, is only found in ourselves, and found *a priori,* as a representation. It is the unity of this principle that explains the unity of the numerous rules resulting from the construction of that conception. These rules display finality from many possible points of view, but we must not rest this finality on an *end,* or resort to any explanation beyond the above. This is different from finding order and regularity in complexes of external *things* enclosed within definite bounds, as, for instance, order and regularity in the trees, flower-beds, and walks in a garden, which is one that I cannot hope to deduce *a priori* from any delimitation I may make of space according to some rule out of my own head. For these are things having real existence—things that to be cognized must be given empirically—and not a mere representation in myself defined *a priori* on a principle. Hence the latter (empirical) finality is *real,* and, being real, is dependent on the conception of an end.

But we can also quite easily see the reason for the admiration, and, in fact, regard it as justified, even where the finality admired is perceived in the essential nature of the things, they being things whose conceptions are such as we can construct. The various rules whose unity, derived from a principle, excites this admiration are one and all synthetic and do not follow from any *conception* of the object, as, for instance, from the conception of a circle, but require to have this object given in intuition. This gives the unity the appearance of having an external source of its rules distinct from our faculty of representation, just as if it were empirical. Hence the way the object answers to the understanding's own peculiar need for rules appears intrinsically contingent and, therefore, only possible by virtue of an end expressly directed to its production. Now since this harmony, despite all the finality mentioned, is not cognized empirically, but *a priori,* it is just what should bring home to us the fact that space, by the limitation of which (by means of the imagination acting in accordance with a conception) the object was alone possible, is not a quality of the things outside me, but a mere mode of representation existing in myself. Hence, where I draw a figure *in accordance with a conception,* or, in other words, when I form my own representation of what is given to me externally, be its own intrinsic nature what it may, what really happens is that I *introduce the finality* into that figure or representation. I derive no empirical instruction as to the finality from what is given to me externally, and consequently the figure is not one for which I require any special end external to myself and residing in the object. But this reflection presupposes a critical use of reason, and, therefore, it cannot be involved then and there in the estimate of the object and its properties. Hence all that this estimate immediately suggests to me is a unification of heterogeneous rules (united even in their intrinsic diversity) in a principle the truth of which I can cognize *a priori,* without requiring for that purpose some special explanation lying beyond my conception, or, to put it more generally, beyond my own *a priori* representation. Now *astonishment* is a shock that the mind receives from a representation and the rule given through it being incompatible with the mind's existing fund of root principles, and that accordingly makes one doubt one's own eyesight or question one's judgement; but *admiration* is an astonishment that keeps continually recurring despite the disappearance of this doubt. Admiration is consequently quite a natural effect of observing the above-mentioned finality in the essence of things (as phenomena), and so far there is really nothing to be said against it. For the agreement of the above form of sensuous intuition, which is called space, with the faculty of conceptions, namely understanding, not alone leaves it inexplicable why it is this particular form of agreement and not some other, but, in addition, produces an expansion of the mind in which it gets, so to speak, the secret feeling of the existence of something lying beyond the confines of such sensuous representations, in which, perhaps, although unknown to us, the ultimate source of that accordance could be found. It is true that we have also no need to know this source where we are merely concerned with the formal finality of our *a priori* representations; but even the mere fact that we are compelled to look out in that direction excites an accompanying admiration for the object which obliges us to do so.

The name of *beauty* is customarily given to the properties above referred to—both those of geometrical figures and also those of numbers—on account of a certain finality which they possess for employment in all kinds of ways in the field of knowledge, which finality the simplicity of their construction would not lead us to expect. Thus people speak of this or that *beautiful* property of the circle, brought to light in this or that manner. But it is not by means of any aesthetic appreciation that we consider such properties final. There is no estimate apart from a conception, making us take not of a purely *subjective* finality in the free play of our cognitive faculties. On the contrary it is an intellectual estimate according to conceptions, in which we clearly recognize an objective finality, that is to say, adaptability for all sorts of ends, i.e., an infinite manifold of ends. Such properties should rather be termed a *relative perfection,* than a beauty, of the mathematical figure. We cannot even properly allow the expression *intellectual beauty* at all: as, if we do, the word beauty must lose all definite meaning, and the delight of the intellect all superiority over that of the senses. The term beautiful could be better applied to a *demonstration* of the properties in question; since here understanding, as the faculty of conceptions, and imagination, as the faculty of presenting them *a priori,* get a feeling of invigoration (which, with the addition of the precision introduced by reason, is called the *elegance* of the demonstration): for in this case the delight, although founded on conceptions, is at least subjective, whereas perfection involves an objective delight.

§ 63. *Relative, as distinguished from intrinsic, finality of nature*

There is only one case in which experience leads our judgement to the conception of an objective and material finality, that is to say, to the conception of an end of nature. This is where the relation in which some cause stands to its effect is under review,[1] and where we are only able to see uniformity in this relation on introducing into the causal principle the idea of the effect and making it the source of the causality and the basal condition on which the effect is possible. Now this can be done in two ways. We may regard the effect as being, as it stands, an art-product, or we may only regard it as what other possible objects in nature may employ for the purposes of their art. We may, in other words, look upon the effect either as an end, or else as a means which other causes use in the pursuit of ends. The latter finality is termed *utility,* where it concerns human beings, and *adaptability* where it concerns any other creatures. It is a purely relative finality. The former, on the contrary, is an intrinsic finality belonging to the thing itself as a natural object.

For example, rivers in their course carry down earth of all kinds good for the growth of plants, and this they deposit sometimes inland, sometimes at their mouths. On some coasts the high-tide carries this alluvial mud inland, or deposits it along the sea-shore. Thus the fruitful soil is increased, especially where man helps to hinder the ebb tide carrying the detritus off again, and the vegetable kingdom gains a home in the former abode of fish and crustaceans. Nature has in this way itself effected most accretions to the land, and is still, though slowly, continuing the process. There now arises the question if this result is to be considered an end on the part of nature, since it is fraught with benefit to man. I say "to man," for the benefit to the vegetable kingdom cannot be taken into

[1] Pure mathematics can never deal with the real existence of things, but only with their possibility, that is to say, with the possibility of an intuition answering to the conceptions of the things. Hence it cannot touch the question of cause and effect, and consequently, all the finality there observed must always be regarded simply as formal, and never as a physical end.

account, inasmuch as against the gain to the land there is, as a set off, as much loss to sea-life.

Or we may give an example of the adaptability of particular things of nature as means for other forms of life—setting out with the assumption that these latter are ends. Thus there is no healthier soil for pine trees than a sandy soil. Now before the primeval sea withdrew from the land it left numerous sand tracts behind it in our northern regions. The result was that upon this soil, generally so unfavourable for cultivation of any kind, extensive pine forests were able to spring up—forests which we frequently blame our ancestors for having wantonly destroyed. Now it may be asked if this primordial deposit of sand tracts was not an end that nature had in view for the benefit of the possible pine forests that might grow on them. This much is clear: that if the pine forests are assumed to be a natural end, then the sand must be admitted to be an end also—though only a relative end—and one for which, in turn, the primeval sea's beach and its withdrawal were means; for in the series of the mutually subordinated members of a final nexus each intermediate member must be regarded as an end, though not a final end, to which its proximate cause stands as means. Similarly, if it is granted that cattle, sheep, horses, and the like, were to be in the world, then there had to be grass on the earth, while alkaline plants had to grow in the deserts if camels were to thrive. Again, these and other herbivora had to abound if wolves, tigers, and lions were to exist. Consequently objective finality based on adaptability is not an immanent objective finality of things, as though the sand, as simple sand, could not be conceived as the effect of its cause, the sea, unless we made this cause look to an end, and treated the effect, namely the sand, as an art-product. It is a purely relative finality, and merely contingent to the thing itself to which it is ascribed; and although among the examples cited, the various kinds of herbs or plants, considered in their own right, are to be estimated as organized products of nature, and, therefore, as things of art, yet, in relation to the animals that feed on them, they are to be regarded as mere raw material.

Moreover, the freedom of man's causality enables him to adapt physical things to the purposes he has in view. These purposes are frequently foolish—as when he uses the gay-coloured feathers of birds for adorning his clothes, and coloured earths or juices of plants for painting himself. Sometimes they are reasonable, as when he uses the horse for riding, and the ox or, as in Minorca, even the ass or pig for ploughing. But we cannot here assume even a relative end of nature—relative, that is, to such uses. For man's reason informs him how to adapt things to his own arbitrary whims—whims for which he was not himself at all predestined by nature. All we can say is that *if* we assume that it is intended that men should live on the earth, then at least, those means without which they could not exist as animals, and even, on however low a plane, as rational animals, must also not be absent. But in that case, those natural things that are indispensable for such existence must equally be regarded as ends of nature.

From what has been said we can easily see that the only condition on which extrinsic finality, that is, the adaptability of a thing for other things, can be looked on as an extrinsic physical end, is that the existence of the thing for which it is proximately or remotely adapted is itself, and in its own right, an end of nature. But this is a matter that can never be decided by any mere study of nature. Hence it follows that relative finality, although, on a certain supposition, it points to natural finality, does not warrant any absolute teleological judgement.[1]

In cold countries the snow protects the seeds from the frost. It facilitates human intercourse through the use of sleighs. The Laplander finds animals in these regions, namely reindeer, to bring about this intercourse. The latter find sufficient food to live on in a dry moss which they have to scrape out for themselves from under the snow, yet they submit to being tamed without difficulty, and readily allow themselves to be deprived of the freedom in which they could quite well have supported themselves. For other dwellers in these ice-bound lands, the sea is rich in its supply of animals that afford them fuel for heating their huts; in addition to which there are the food and clothing that these animals provide and the wood which the sea itself, as it were, washes in for them as material for their homes. Now here we have a truly marvellous assemblage of many relations of nature to an end—the end being the Greenlanders, Laplanders, Samoyedes, Jakutes, and the like. But we do not see why men should live in these places at all. To say, therefore, that the *facts* that vapour falls from the atmosphere in the form of snow, that the ocean has its currents that wash into these regions the wood grown in warmer lands, and that sea-monsters containing

[1] [Cf. p. 337.]

quantities of oil are to be found there, *are due* to the idea of some benefit to certain poor creatures underlying the cause that brings together all these natural products, would be a very hazardous and arbitrary assertion. For supposing that all this utility on the part of nature were absent, then the capacity of the natural causes to serve this order of existence would not be missed. On the contrary it would seem audacious and inconsiderate on our part even to ask for such a capacity, or demand such an end from nature—for nothing but the greatest want of social unity in mankind could have dispersed men into such inhospitable regions.

§ 64. *The distinctive character of things considered as physical ends*

A THING is possible only as an end where the causality to which it owes its origin must not be sought in the mechanism of nature, but in a cause whose capacity of acting is determined by conceptions. What is required in order that we may perceive that a thing is only possible in this way is that its form is not possible on purely natural laws[1]—that is to say, such laws as we may cognize by means of unaided understanding applied to objects of sense—but that, on the contrary, even to know it empirically in respect of its cause and effect presupposes conceptions of reason.[2] Here we have, as far as any empirical laws of nature go, a *contingency* of the form of the thing in relation to reason. Now reason in every case insists on cognizing the necessity of the form of a natural product, even where it only desires to perceive the conditions involved in its production. In the given form above mentioned, however, it cannot get this necessity. Hence the contingency is itself a ground for making us look upon the origin of the thing as if, just because of that contingency, it could only be possible through reason. But the causality, so construed, becomes the faculty of acting according to ends—that is to say, a will; and the object, which is represented as only deriving its possibility from such a will, will be represented as possible only as an end.

Suppose a person was in a country that seemed to him uninhabited and was to see a geometrical figure, say a regular hexagon, traced on the sand. As he reflected, and tried to get a conception of the figure, his reason would make him conscious, though perhaps obscurely, that in the production of this conception there was unity of principle. His reason would then forbid him to consider the sand, the neighbouring sea, the winds, or even animals with their footprints, as causes familiar to him, or any other irrational cause, as the ground of the possibility of such a form. For the contingency of coincidence with a conception like this, which is only possible in reason, would appear to him so infinitely great that there might just as well be no law of nature at all in the case. Hence it would seem that the cause of the production of such an effect could not be contained in the mere mechanical operation of nature, but that, on the contrary, a conception of such an object, as a conception that only reason can give and compare the object with, must likewise be what alone contains that causality. On these grounds, it would appear to him that this effect was one that might without reservation be regarded as an end, though not as a natural end. In other words he would regard it as a product of *art—vestigium hominis video.*

But where a thing is recognized to be a product of nature, then something more is required —unless, perhaps, our very estimate involves a contradiction—if, despite its being such a product, we are yet to estimate it as an end, and, consequently, as a *physical end*. As a provisional statement I would say that a thing exists as a physical end *if it is* (though in a double sense) *both cause and effect of itself*. For this involves a kind of causality that we cannot associate with the mere conception of a nature unless we make that nature rest on an underlying end, but which can then, though incomprehensible, be thought without contradiction. Before analysing the component factors of this idea of a physical end, let us first illustrate its meaning by an example.

A tree produces, in the first place, another tree, according to a familiar law of nature. But the tree which it produces is of the same genus. Hence, in its *genus*, it produces itself. In the genus, now as effect, now as cause, continually generated from itself and likewise generating itself, it preserves itself generically.

Secondly, a tree produces itself even as an *individual*. It is true that we only call this kind of effect growth; but growth is here to be understood in a sense that makes it entirely different from any increase according to mechanical laws, and renders it equivalent, though under another name, to generation. The plant first prepares the matter that it assimilates and bestows upon it a specifically distinctive quality which the mechanism of nature outside it cannot supply, and it develops itself by means of a material which, in its composite character, is its own product. For, although in respect of the

[1] [Cf. pp. 569, 572, 574, 579.]
[2] [Cf. pp. 556, 562, 568, 569, 578.]

constituents that it derives from nature outside, it must be regarded as only an educt, yet in the separation and recombination of this raw material we find an original capacity of selection and construction on the part of natural beings of this kind such as infinitely outdistances all the efforts of art, when the latter attempts to reconstitute those products of the vegetable kingdom out of the elements which it obtains through their analysis, or else out of the material which nature supplies for their nourishment.

Thirdly, a part of a tree also generates itself in such a way that the preservation of one part is reciprocally dependent on the preservation of the other parts. An eye taken from the sprig of one tree and set in the branch of another produces in the alien stock a growth of its own species, and similarly a scion grafted on the body of a different tree. Hence even in the case of the same tree each branch or leaf may be regarded as engrafted or inoculated into it, and, consequently, as a tree with a separate existence of its own, and only attaching itself to another and living parasitically on it. At the same time the leaves are certainly products of the tree, but they also maintain it in turn; for repeated defoliation would kill it, and its growth is dependent upon the action of the leaves on the trunk. The way nature comes, in these forms of life, to her own aid in the case of injury, where the want of one part necessary for the maintenance of the neighbouring parts is made good by the rest; the abortions or malformations in growth, where, on account of some chance defect or obstacle, certain parts adopt a completely new formation, so as to preserve the existing growth, and thus produce an anomalous form: are matters which I only desire to mention here in passing, although they are among the most wonderful properties of the forms of organic life.

§ 65. *Things considered as physical ends are organisms*

WHERE a thing is a product of nature and yet, so regarded, has to be cognized as possible only as a physical end, it must, from its character as set out in the preceding section, stand to itself reciprocally in the relation of cause and effect. This is, however, a somewhat inexact and indeterminate expression that needs derivation from a definite conception.

In so far as the causal connection is thought merely by means of understanding, it is a nexus constituting a series, namely of causes and effects, that is invariable progressive. The things that as effects presuppose others as their causes cannot themselves in turn be also causes of the latter. This causal connection is termed that of *efficient causes* (*nexus effectivus*). On the other hand, however, we are also able to think a causal connection according to a rational concept, that of ends, which, if regarded as a series, would involve regressive as well as progressive dependency. It would be one in which the thing that for the moment is designated *effect* deserves none the less, if we take the series regressively, to be called the *cause* of the thing of which it was said to be the effect. In the domain of practical matters, namely in art, we readily find examples of a nexus of this kind. Thus a house is certainly the cause of the money that is received as rent, but yet, conversely, the representation of this possible income was the cause of the building of the house. A causal nexus of this kind is termed that of *final causes* (*nexus finalis*). The former might, perhaps, more appropriately be called the nexus of *real,* and the latter the nexus of *ideal* causes, because with this use of terms it would be understood at once that there cannot be more than these two kinds of causality.

Now the *first* requisite of a thing, considered as a physical end, is that its parts, both as to their existence and form, are only possible by their relation to the whole. For the thing is itself an end, and is, therefore, comprehended under a conception or an idea that must determine *a priori* all that is to be contained in it. But so far as the possibility of a thing is only thought in this way, it is simply a work of art. It is the product, in other words, of an intelligent cause, distinct from the matter, or parts, of the thing, and of one whose causality, in bringing together and combining the parts, is determined by its idea of a whole made possible through that idea and, consequently, not by external nature.

But if a thing is a product of nature, and in this character is notwithstanding to contain intrinsically and in its inner possibility a relation to ends, in other words, is to be possible only as a physical end and independently of the causality of the conceptions of external rational agents, then this *second* requisite is involved, namely, that the parts of the thing combine of themselves into the unity of a whole by being reciprocally cause and effect of their form. For this is the only way in which it is possible that the idea of the whole may conversely, or reciprocally, determine in its turn the form and combination of all the parts, not as cause—for that would make it an art-product—but as the epistemological basis upon which the systematic unity of the form and combination of all the manifold contained in the given matter becomes cognizable for the person estimating it.

What we require, therefore, in the case of a body which in its intrinsic nature and inner possibility has to be estimated as a physical end, is as follows. Its parts must in their collective unity reciprocally produce one another alike as to form and combination, and thus by their own causality produce a whole, the conception of which, conversely—in a being possessing the causality according to conceptions that is adequate for such a product—could in turn be the cause of the whole according to a principle, so that, consequently, the nexus of *efficient causes* might be no less estimated as an *operation brought about by final* causes.

In such a natural product as this every part is thought as *owing* its presence to the *agency* of all the remaining parts, and also as existing *for the sake of the others* and of the whole, that is as an instrument, or organ. But this is not enough—for it might be an instrument of art, and thus have no more than its general possibility referred to an end. On the contrary the part must be an organ *producing* the other parts—each, consequently, reciprocally producing the others. No instrument of art can answer to this description, but only the instrument of that nature from whose resources the materials of every instrument are drawn—even the materials for instruments of art. Only under these conditions and upon these terms can such a product be an *organized* and *self-organized being,* and, as such, be called a *physical end.*

In a watch, one part is the instrument by which the movement of the others is effected, but one wheel is not the efficient cause of the production of the other. One part is certainly present for the sake of another, but it does not owe its presence to the agency of that other. For this reason, also, the producing cause of the watch and its form is not contained in the nature of this material, but lies outside the watch in a being that can act according to ideas of a whole which its causality makes possible. Hence one wheel in the watch does not produce the other, and, still less, does one watch produce other watches, by utilizing, or organizing, foreign material; hence it does not of itself replace parts of which it has been deprived, nor, if these are absent in the original construction, does it make good the deficiency by the subvention of the rest; nor does it, so to speak, repair its own casual disorders. But these are all things which we are justified in expecting from organized nature. An organized being is, therefore, not a mere machine. For a machine has solely *motive power,* whereas an organized being possesses inherent *formative* power, and such, moreover, as it can impart to material devoid of it—material which it organizes. This, therefore, is a self-propagating formative power,[1] which cannot be explained by the capacity of movement alone, that is to say, by mechanism.

We do not say half enough of nature and her capacity in organized products when we speak of this capacity as being the *analogue of art.* For what is here present to our minds is an artist—a rational being—working from without. But nature, on the contrary, organizes itself, and does so in each species of its organized products—following a single pattern, certainly, as to general features, but nevertheless admitting deviations calculated to secure self-preservation under particular circumstances. We might perhaps come nearer to the description of this impenetrable property if we were to call it an *analogue of life.* But then either we should have to endow matter as mere matter with a property (hylozoism) that contradicts its essential nature; or else we should have to associate with it a foreign principle *standing in community* with it (a soul). But, if such a product is to be a natural product, then we have to adopt one or other of two courses in order to bring in a soul. Either we must presuppose organized matter as the instrument of such a soul, which makes organized matter no whit more intelligible, or else we must make the soul the artificer of this structure, in which case we must withdraw the product from (corporal) nature. Strictly speaking, therefore, the organization of nature has nothing analogous to any causality known to us.[2] Natural beauty may justly be termed the *analogue* of art, for it is only ascribed to the objects in respect of reflection upon the *external* intuition of them and, therefore, only on account of their superficial form. But *intrinsic natural perfection,*[3] as possessed by things that are only pos-

1 [Cf. "formative impulse," p. 582.]

2 We may, on the other hand, make use of an analogy to the above mentioned immediate physical ends to throw light on a certain union, which, however, is to be found more often in idea than in fact. Thus in the case of a complete transformation, recently undertaken, of a great people into a state, the word *organization* has frequently, and with much propriety, been used for the constitution of the legal authorities and even of the entire body politic. For in a whole of this kind certainly no member should be a mere means, but should also be an end, and, seeing that he contributes to the possibility of the entire body, should have his position and function in turn defined by the idea of the whole.

3 [See § 15, p. 487; Cf. *Preface to the Metaphysical Elements of Ethics,* p. 370.]

sible as *physical ends,* and that are therefore called *organisms,* is unthinkable and inexplicable on any analogy to any known physical, or natural, agency, not even excepting—since we ourselves are part of nature in the widest sense—the suggestion of any strictly apt analogy to human art.

The concept of a thing as intrinsically a physical end is, therefore, not a constitutive conception either of understanding or of reason, but yet it may be used by reflective judgement as a regulative conception for guiding our investigation of objects of this kind by a remote analogy with our own causality according to ends generally, and as a basis of reflection upon their supreme source. But in the latter connection it cannot be used to promote our knowledge either of nature or of such original source of those objects, but must on the contrary be confined to the service of just the same practical faculty of reason in analogy with which we considered the cause of the finality in question.

Organisms are, therefore, the only beings in nature that, considered in their separate existence and apart from any relation to other things, cannot be thought possible except as ends of nature. It is they, then, that first afford objective reality to the conception of an *end* that is an end *of nature* and not a practical end. Thus they supply natural science with the basis for a teleology, or, in other words, a mode of estimating its objects on a special principle that it would otherwise be absolutely unjustifiable to introduce into that science—seeing that we are quite unable to perceive *a priori* the possibility of such a kind of causality.

§ 66. *The principle on which the intrinsic finality in organisms is estimated*

THIS principle, the statement of which serves to define what is meant by organisms, is as follows: *an organized natural product is one in which every part is reciprocally both end and means.* In such a product nothing is in vain, without an end, or to be ascribed to a blind mechanism of nature.[1]

It is true that the occasion for adopting this principle must be derived from experience—from such experience, namely, as is methodically arranged and is called *observation.* But owing to the universality and necessity which that principle predicates of such finality, it cannot rest merely on empirical grounds, but must have some underlying *a priori* principle. This principle, however, may be one that is merely regulative, and it may be that the ends in question only reside in the idea of the person forming the estimate and not in any efficient cause whatever. Hence the above named principle may be called a *maxim* for estimating the intrinsic finality of organisms.

It is common knowledge that scientists who dissect plants and animals, seeking to investigate their structure and to see into the reasons why and the end for which they are provided with such and such parts, why the parts have such and such a position and interconnection, and why the internal form is precisely what it is, adopt the above maxim as absolutely necessary. So they say that nothing in such forms of life is in *vain,* and they put the maxim on the same footing of validity as the fundamental principle of all natural science, that *nothing* happens *by chance.* They are, in fact, quite as unable to free themselves from this teleological principle as from that of general physical science. For just as the abandonment of the latter would leave them without any experience at all, so the abandonment of the former would leave them with no clue to assist their observation of a type of natural things that have once come to be thought under the conception of physical ends.

Indeed this conception leads reason into an order of things entirely different from that of a mere mechanism of nature, which *mere mechanism* no longer proves adequate in this domain. An idea has to underlie the possibility of the natural product. But this idea is an absolute unity of the representation, whereas the material is a plurality of things that of itself can afford no definite unity of composition. Hence, if that unity of the idea is actually to serve as the *a priori* determining ground of a natural law of the causality of such a form of the composite, the end of nature must be made to extend to *everything* contained in its product.[2] For if once we lift such an effect out of the sphere of the blind mechanism of nature and relate it *as a whole* to a supersensible ground of determination, we must then estimate it out and out on this principle. We have no reason for assuming the form of such a thing to be still partly dependent on blind mechanism, for with such confusion of heterogeneous principles every reliable rule for estimating things would disappear.

It is no doubt the case that in an animal body, for example, many parts might be explained as accretions on simple mechanical laws (as skin, bone, hair). Yet the cause that accumulates the appropriate material, modifies and fashions it,

1 [Cf. p. 580.]

2 [Cf. p. 558.]

and deposits it in its proper place, must always be estimated teleologically. Hence, everything in the body must be regarded as organized, and everything, also, in a certain relation to the thing is itself in turn an organ.

§ 67. *The principle on which nature in general is estimated teleologically as a system of ends*

We have said above that the *extrinsic* finality of natural things affords no adequate justification for taking them as ends of nature to explain the reason of their existence, or for treating their contingently final effects as ideally the grounds of their existence on the principle of final causes. Thus we are not entitled to consider *rivers* as physical ends then and there, because they facilitate international intercourse in inland countries, or *mountains*, because they contain the sources of the rivers and hold stores of snow for the maintenance of their flow in dry seasons, or, similarly, the *slope* of the land, that carries down these waters and leaves the country dry. For, although this configuration of the earth's surface is very necessary for the origination and sustenance of the vegetable and animal kingdoms, yet intrinsically it contains nothing the possibility of which should make us feel obliged to invoke a causality according to ends. The same applies to plants utilized or enjoyed by man; or to animals, as the camel, the ox, the horse, dog, etc., which are so variously employed, sometimes as servants of man, sometimes as food for him to live on, and mostly found quite indispensable. The external relationship of things that we have no reason to regard as ends in their own right can only be hypothetically estimated as final.

There is an essential distinction between estimating a thing as a physical end in virtue of its intrinsic form and regarding the real existence of this thing as an end of nature. To maintain the latter view we require, not merely the conception of a possible end, but a knowledge of the final end (*scopus*) of nature. This involves our referring nature to something supersensible, a reference that far transcends any teleological knowledge we have of nature; for, to find the end of the real existence of nature itself, we must look beyond nature. That the origin of a simple blade of grass is only possible on the rule of ends is, to our human critical faculty, sufficiently proved by its internal form. But let us lay aside this consideration and look only to the use to which the thing is put by other natural beings—which means that we abandon the study of the internal organization and look only to external adaptations to ends. We see, then, that the grass is required as a means of existence by cattle, and cattle, similarly, by man. But we do not see why after all it should be necessary that men should in fact exist (a question that might not be so easy to answer if the specimens of humanity that we had in mind were, say, the New Hollanders or Fuegians). We do not then arrive in this way at any categorical end. On the contrary, all this adaptation is made to rest on a condition that has to be removed to an ever-retreating horizon. This condition is the unconditional condition—the existence of a thing as a final end—which, as such, lies entirely outside the study of the world on physico-teleological lines. But, then, such a thing is not a physical end either, since it (or its entire genus) is not to be regarded as a product of nature.

Hence it is only in so far as matter is organized that it necessarily involves the conception of it as a physical end, because here it possesses a form that is at once specific and a product of nature. But, brought so far, this conception necessarily leads us to the idea of aggregate nature as a system following the rule of ends, to which idea, again, the whole mechanism of nature has to be subordinated on principles of reason—at least for the purpose of testing phenomenal nature by this idea. The principle of reason is one which it is competent for reason to use as a merely subjective principle, that is, as a maxim: everything in the world is good for something or other; nothing in it is in vain; we are entitled, nay incited, by the example that nature affords us in its organic products, to expect nothing from it and its laws but what is final when things are viewed as a whole.

It is evident that this is a principle to be applied not by the determinant, but only by the reflective, judgement, that it is regulative and not constitutive, and that all that we obtain from it is a clue to guide us in the study of natural things. These things it leads us to consider in relation to a ground of determination already given, and in the light of a new uniformity, and it helps us to extend physical science according to another principle, that, namely, of final causes, yet without interfering with the principle of the mechanism of physical causality. Furthermore, this principle is altogether silent on the point of whether anything estimated according to it is, or is not, an end of nature *by design:* whether, that is, the grass exists for the sake of the ox or the sheep, and whether these and the other things of nature exist for the sake of man. We do well to consider even things that are unpleasant to us, and that in particular connections are contra-final, from this point of view also. Thus, for example, one might say that the vermin which plague men in their clothes, hair, or beds, may, by a wise provision of nature, be an incitement towards cleanliness, which is of itself an important means for preserving health. Or the mosquitoes and other stinging insects that make the wilds of America so trying for the savages, may be so many goads to urge these primitive men to drain the marshes and bring light into the dense forests that shut out the air, and, by so doing, as well as by the tillage of the soil, to render their abodes more sanitary. Even what appears to man to be contrary to nature in his internal organization affords, when treated on these lines, an interesting, and sometimes even instructive, outlook into a teleological order of things, to which mere unaided study from a physical point of view apart from such a principle would not lead us. Some persons say that men or animals that have a tapeworm receive it as a sort of compensation to make good some deficiency in their vital organs. Now, just in the same way, I would ask if dreams (from which our sleep is never free, although we rarely remember what we have dreamed), may not be a regulation of nature adapted to ends. For, when all the muscular forces of the body are relaxed, dreams serve the purpose of internally stimulating the vital organs by means of the imagination and the great activity which it exerts—an activity that in this state generally rises to psycho-physical agitation. This seems to be why imagination is usually more actively at work in the sleep of those who have gone to bed at night with a loaded stomach, just when this stimulation is most needed. Hence, I would suggest that without this internal stimulating force and fatiguing unrest that makes us complain of our dreams, which in fact, however, are probably curative, sleep, even in a sound state of health, would amount to a complete extinction of life.

Once the teleological estimate of nature, supported by the physical ends actually presented to us in organic beings, has entitled us to form the idea of a vast system of natural ends, we may regard even natural beauty from this point of view, such beauty being an accordance of nature with the free play of our cognitive faculties as engaged in grasping and estimating its appearance. For then we may look upon it as an objective finality of nature in its entirety as a system of which man is a member. We may regard it as a favour[1] that nature has extended to us, that besides giving us what is useful it has dispensed beauty and charms in such abundance, and for this we may love it, just as we view it with respect because of its immensity, and feel ourselves ennobled by such contemplation—just as if nature had erected and decorated its splendid stage with this precise purpose in its mind.

The general purport of the present section is simply this: once we have discovered a capacity in nature for bringing forth products that can only be thought by us according to the conception of final causes, we advance a step farther. Even products which do not (either as to themselves or the relation, however final, in which they stand) make it necessarily incumbent upon us to go beyond the mechanism of blind efficient causes and seek out some other principle on which they are possible, may nevertheless be justly estimated as forming part of a system of ends. For the idea from which we started is one which, when we consider its foundation, already leads beyond the world of sense,[2] and then the unity of the supersensible principle must be treated, not as valid merely for certain species of natural beings, but as similarly valid for the whole of nature as a system.

§ 68. *The principle of teleology considered as an inherent principle of natural science*

THE principles of a science may be inherent in that science itself, and are then termed *domestic* (*principia domestica*). Or they may rest on conceptions that can only be vouched outside that science, and are *foreign* principles (*peregrina*). Sciences containing the latter principles rest their doctrines on auxiliary propositions (*lemmata*), that is, they obtain some conception or other, and with this conception some basis for a regular procedure, on credit from another science.

Every science is a system in its own right; and it is not sufficient that in it we construct according to principles, and so proceed technically, but we must also set to work architectonically with it as a separate and independent

[1] In the Part on Aesthetics, the statement was made: "*we regard nature with favour,*" because we take a delight in its form that is altogether free (disinterested). For in this judgement of mere taste, no account is taken of any end for which these natural beauties exist: whether to excite pleasure in us, or irrespective of us as ends. But in teleological judgement we pay attention to this relation; and so we can *regard it as a favour of nature,* that it has been disposed to promote our culture by exhibiting so many beautiful forms. [Cf. above, p. 546.]

[2] [Cf. p. 558.]

building. We must treat is as a self-subsisting whole, and not as a wing or section of another building—although we may subsequently make a passage to or fro from one part to another.

Hence if we supplement natural science by introducing the conception of God into its context for the purpose of rendering the finality of nature explicable, and if, having done so, we turn round and use this finality for the purpose of proving that there is a God, then both natural science and theology are deprived of all intrinsic substantiality. This deceptive crossing and recrossing from one side to the other involves both in uncertainty, because their boundaries are thus allowed to overlap.

The expression *an end of nature* is of itself sufficient to obviate this confusion and prevent our confounding natural science or the occasion it affords for a *teleological* estimate of its objects with the contemplation of God, and hence with a *theological derivation.* It is not to be regarded as a matter of no consequence that the above expression should be confused with that of a divine end in the appointment of nature, or that the latter should even be passed off as the more appropriate and the one more becoming to a pious soul, on the ground that, say what we will, it must eventually come back to our deriving these final forms in nature from a wise Author of the universe. On the contrary, we must scrupulously and modestly restrict ourselves to the term that expresses just as much as we know, and no more—namely, an end of nature. For before we arrive at the question of the cause of nature itself, we find in nature and in the course of its generative processes examples of these final products produced in nature according to known empirical laws. It is according to these laws that natural science must estimate its objects, and, consequently, it must seek within itself for this causality according to the rule of ends. Therefore this science must not overlap its bounds for the purpose of drawing into its own bosom, as a domestic principle, one to whose conception no experience can be adequate, and upon which we are not authorized to venture until after natural science has said its last word.

Natural qualities that are demonstrable *a priori,* and so reveal their possibility on universal principles without any aid from experience, may involve a technical finality. Yet, being absolutely necessary, they cannot be credited to natural teleologic at all. Natural teleology forms part of physics, and is a method applicable to the solution of the problems of physics. Arithmetical and geometrical analogies, also universal mechanical laws, however strange and worthy of our admiration the union in a single principle of a variety of rules apparently quite disconnected may seem, have no claim on that account to rank as teleological grounds of explanation in physics. They may deserve to be brought under review in the universal theory of the finality of the things of nature in general, but, if so, this is a theory that would have to be assigned to another science, namely metaphysics. It would not form an inherent principle of natural science: whereas in the case of the empirical laws of the physical ends which organisms present it is not alone permissible, but even unavoidable, to use teleological *criticism* as a principle of natural science in respect of a peculiar class of its objects.

For the purpose of keeping strictly within its own bounds physics entirely ignores the question whether physical ends are ends *designedly* or *undesignedly.* To deal with that question would be to meddle in the affairs of others—namely, in what is the business of metaphysics. Suffice it that there are objects whose one and only *explanation* is on natural laws that we are unable to conceive otherwise than by adopting the idea of ends as principle, objects which, in their intrinsic form, and with nothing more in view than their internal relations, are *cognizable* in this way alone. It is true that in teleology we speak of nature as if its finality were a thing of design. But to avoid all suspicion of presuming in the slightest to mix up with our sources of knowledge something that has no place in physics at all, namely a supernatural cause, we refer to design in such a way that, in the same breath, we attribute this design to nature, that is, to matter. Here no room is left for misinterpretation, since, obviously, no one would ascribe *design,* in the proper sense of the term, to a lifeless material. Hence our real intention is to indicate that the word *design,* as here used, only signifies a principle of the reflective, and not of the determinant, judgement, and consequently is not meant to introduce any special ground of causality, but only to assist the employment of reason by supplementing investigation on mechanical laws by the addition of another method of investigation, so as to make up for the inadequacy of the former even as a method of empirical research that has for its object all particular laws of nature. Therefore, when teleology is applied to physics, we speak with perfect justice of the wisdom, the economy, the forethought, the beneficence of nature.

But in so doing we do not convert nature into an intelligent being, for that would be absurd; but neither do we dare to think of placing another being, one that is intelligent, above nature as its architect, for that would be extravagant.[1] On the contrary, our only intention is to designate in this way a kind of natural causality on an analogy with our own causality in the technical employment of reason, for the purpose of keeping in view the rule upon which certain natural products are to be investigated.

But why, then, is it that teleology does not usually form a special part of theoretical natural science, but is relegated to theology by way of a propaedeutic or transition? This is done in order to keep the study of the mechanical aspect of nature in close adherence to what we are able so to subject to our observation or experiment that we could ourselves produce it like nature, or at least produce it according to similar laws. For we have complete insight only into what we can make and accomplish according to our conceptions. But to effect by means of art a presentation similar to organization, as an intrinsic end of nature, infinitely surpasses all our powers. And as for such extrinsic adjustments of nature as are considered final (e.g., winds, rains, etc.), physics certainly studies their mechanism, but it is quite unable to exhibit their relation to ends so far as this relation purports to be a condition necessarily attaching to a cause. For this necessity in the nexus does not touch the constitution of things, but turns wholly on the combination of our conceptions.

Second Division. *Dialectic of Teleological Judgement*

§ 69. *Nature of an antinomy of judgement*

The *determinant* judgement does not possess as its own separate property any principles upon which *conceptions of objects* are founded. It is not an autonomy; for it *subsumes* merely under given laws, or concepts, as principles. Just for this reason, it is not exposed to any danger from inherent antinomy and does not run the risk of a conflict of its principles. Thus transcendental judgement, which was shown to contain the conditions of subsumption under categories, was not independently *nomothetic*. It only specified the conditions of sensuous intuition upon which reality, that is, application, can be afforded to a given conception as a law of understanding. In the discharge of this office it could never fall into a state of internal disunion, at least in the matter of principles.

But the *reflective* judgement has to subsume under a law that is not yet given. It has, therefore, in fact only a principle of reflection upon objects for which we are objectively at a complete loss for a law, or conception of the object, sufficient to serve as a principle covering the particular cases as they come before us. Now as there is no permissible employment of the cognitive faculties apart from principles, the reflective judgement must in such cases be a principle to itself. As this principle is not objective and is unable to introduce any basis of cognition of the object sufficient for the required purpose of subsumption, it must serve as a mere subjective principle for the employment of our cognitive faculties in a final manner, namely, for reflecting upon objects of a particular kind. The reflective judgement has, therefore, its maxims applicable to such cases—maxims that are in fact necessary for obtaining a knowledge of the natural laws to be found in experience, and which are directed to assist us in attaining to conceptions, be these even conceptions of reason, wherever such conceptions are absolutely required for the mere purpose of getting to know nature in its empirical laws. Between these necessary maxims of the reflective judgement a conflict may arise, and consequently an antinomy.[2] This affords the basis of a dialectic; and if each of the mutually conflicting maxims has its foundation in the nature of our cognitive faculties, this dialectic may be called a *natural* dialectic, and it constitutes an unavoidable illusion which it is the duty of critical philosophy to expose and to resolve lest it should deceive us.

§ 70. *Exposition of this antinomy*

In dealing with nature as the complex of objects of external sense, reason is able to rely

[1] [The German word *vermessen* (presumptuous) is a good word and full of meaning. A judgement in which we forget to take stock of the extent of our powers of understanding may sometimes sound very modest, while yet it presumes a great deal, and is really very presumptuous. Of this type are the majority of those by which we purport to exalt divine wisdom by underlaying the works of creation and preservation with designs that are really intended to do honour to the individual wisdom of our own subtle intellects.]

[2] [Cf. *Critique of Practical Reason*, pp. 337.]

upon laws some of which are prescribed by understanding itself *a priori* to nature, while others are capable of indefinite extension by means of the empirical determinations occurring in experience. For the application of the laws prescribed *a priori* by understanding, that is, of the *universal* laws of material nature in general, judgement does not need any special principle of reflection; for there it is determinant, an objective principle being furnished to it by understanding. But in respect of the particular laws with which we can become acquainted through experience alone, there is such a wide scope for diversity and heterogeneity that judgement must be a principle to itself, even for the mere purpose of searching for a law and tracking one out in the phenomena of nature. For it needs such a principle as a guiding thread, if it is even to hope for a consistent body of empirical knowledge based on a thoroughgoing uniformity of nature—that is a unity of nature in its empirical laws. Now from the fact of this contingent unity of particular laws it may come to pass that judgement acts upon two maxims in its reflection, one of which it receives *a priori* from mere understanding, but the other of which is prompted by particular experiences that bring reason into play to institute an estimate of corporeal nature and its laws according to a particular principle. What happens then is that these two different maxims seem to all appearance unable to run in the same harness, and a dialectic arises that throws judgement into confusion as to the principle of its reflection.

The first maxim of such reflection is the *thesis:* All production of material things and their forms must be estimated as possible on mere mechanical laws.

The second maxim is the *antithesis:* Some products of material nature cannot be estimated as possible on mere mechanical laws (that is, for estimating them quite a different law of causality is required, namely, that of final causes).

If now these regulative principles of investigation were converted into constitutive principles of the possibility of the objects themselves, they would read thus:

Thesis: All production of material things is possible on mere mechanical laws.

Antithesis: Some production of such things is not possible on mere mechanical laws.

In this latter form, as objective principles for the determinant judgement, they would contradict one another, so that one of the pair would necessarily be false. But that would then be an antinomy certainly, though not one of judgement, but rather a conflict in the legislation of reason. But reason is unable to prove either one or the other of these principles: seeing that we can have no *a priori* determining principle of the possibility of things on mere empirical laws of nature.

On the other hand, looking to the maxims of a reflective judgement as first set out, we see that they do not in fact contain any contradiction at all. For if I say: "I must *estimate* the possibility of all events in material nature, and, consequently, also all forms considered as its products, on mere mechanical laws," I do not thereby assert that they *are solely possible in this way,* that is, to the exclusion of every other kind of causality. On the contrary this assertion is only intended to indicate that I *ought* at all times to *reflect* upon these things *according to the principle* of the simple mechanism of nature, and, consequently, push my investigation with it as far as I can, because unless I make it the basis of research there can be no knowledge of nature in the true sense of the term at all. Now this does not stand in the way of the second maxim when a proper occasion for its employment presents itself—that is to say, in the case of some natural forms (and, at their instance, in the case of entire nature), we may, in our reflection upon them, follow the trail of a principle which is radically different from explanation by the mechanism of nature, namely the principle of final causes. For reflection according to the first maxim is not in this way superseded. On the contrary, we are directed to pursue it as far as we can. Further, it is not asserted that those forms were not possible on the mechanism of nature. It is only maintained that *human reason,* adhering to this maxim and proceeding on these lines, could never discover a particle of foundation for what constitutes the specific character of a physical end, whatever additions it might make in this way to its knowledge of natural laws. This leaves it an open question whether, in the unknown inner basis of nature itself, the physico-mechanical and the final nexus present in the same things may not cohere in a single principle; it being only our reason that is not in a position to unite them in such a principle, so that our judgement, consequently, remains *reflective,* not determinant, that is, acts on a subjective ground, and not according to an objective principle of the possibility of things in their inherent nature, and, accordingly, is compelled to conceive a different principle from that of the mechanism of nature as a ground of the possibility of certain forms in nature.

§ 71. *Introduction to the solution of the above antinomy*

We are wholly unable to prove the impossibility of the production of organized natural products in accordance with the simple mechanism of nature. For we cannot see into the first and inner ground of the infinite multiplicity of the particular laws of nature, which, being only known empirically, are for us contingent, and so we are absolutely incapable of reaching the intrinsic and all-sufficient principle of the possibility of a nature—a principle which lies in the supersensible. But may not the productive capacity of nature be just as adequate for what we estimate to be formed or connected according to the idea of ends as it is for what we believe merely calls for mechanical functions on the part of nature? Or may it be that in fact things are genuine physical ends (as we must necessarily estimate them to be), and as such founded upon an original causality of a completely different kind, which cannot be an incident of material nature or of its intelligible substrate, namely, the causality of an architectonic understanding? What has been said shows that these are questions upon which our reason, very narrowly restricted in respect of the conception of causality if this conception has to be specified *a priori,* can give absolutely no information. But that, relatively to our cognitive faculties, the mere mechanism of nature is also unable to furnish any explanation of the production of organisms, is a matter just as indubitably certain. *For the reflective judgement,* therefore, this is a perfectly sound principle: that for the clearly manifest nexus of things according to final causes, we must think a causality distinct from mechanism, namely a world-cause acting according to ends, that is, an intelligent cause—however rash and undemonstrable a principle this might be *for the determinant judgement.* In the first case the principle is a simple maxim of judgement. The conception of causality which it involves is a mere idea to which we in no way undertake to concede reality, but only make use of it to guide a reflection that still leaves the door open for any available mechanical explanation, and that never strays from the world of sense. In the second case, the principle would be an objective principle. Reason would prescribe it and judgement would have to be subject to it and determine itself accordingly. But in that case, reflection wanders from the world of sense into transcendent regions and possibly gets led astray.

All semblance of an antinomy between the maxims of the strictly physical, or mechanical, mode of explanation and the teleological, or technical, rests, therefore, on our confusing a principle of the reflective with one of the determinant judgement. The *autonomy* of the former, which is valid merely subjectively for the use of our reason in respect of particular empirical laws, is mistaken for the *heteronomy* of the second, which has to conform to the laws, either universal or particular, given by understanding.

§ 72. *The various kinds of systems dealing with the finality of nature*

No one has ever yet questioned the correctness of the principle that when judging certain things in nature, namely organisms and their possibility, we must look to the conception of final causes. Such a principle is admittedly necessary even where we require no more than a *guiding-thread* for the purpose of becoming acquainted with the character of these things by means of observation, without trenching upon an investigation into their first origin. Hence the question can only be, whether this principle is merely subjectively valid, that is, a mere maxim of judgement, or is an objective principle of nature. On the latter alternative there would belong to nature another type of causality beyond its mechanism and its simple dynamical laws, namely, the causality of final causes, under which natural causes (dynamical forces) would stand only as intermediate causes.

Now this speculative question or problem might well be left without any answer or solution. For, if we content ourselves with speculation within the bounds of the mere knowledge of nature, the above maxims are ample for its study as far as human powers extend, and for probing its deepest secrets. So it must be that reason wakens some suspicion, or that nature, so to speak, gives us a hint. With the help of this conception of final causes, might we not be able to take a step, we are prompted to think, beyond and above nature, and connect it to the supreme point in the series of causes? Why not relinquish the investigation of nature (although we have not advanced so very far with it) or, at least, lay it temporarily aside, and try first to discover whither that stranger in natural science, the conception of physical ends, would lead us?

Now at this point, certainly, the undisputed

maxim above mentioned would have to merge in a problem that opens up a wide field for controversy. For it may be alleged that the nexus of natural finality *proves* the existence of a special kind of causality for nature. Or it may be contended that this nexus, considered in its true nature and on objective principles, is, on the contrary, identical with the mechanism of nature, or rests on one and the same ground, though in the case of many natural products this ground often lies too deeply buried for our investigation. Hence, as is contended, we have recourse to a subjective principle, namely art, or causality according to ideas, in order to introduce it, on an analogy, as the basis of nature —an expedient that in fact proves successful in many cases, in some certainly seems to fail, but in no case entitles us to introduce into natural science a mode of operation different from causality on mere mechanical laws of nature. Now, in giving to the procedure, or causal operation of nature, the name of *technic,* on account of the suggestion of an end which we find in its products, we propose to divide this technic into such as is *designed* (*technica intentionalis*) and such as is *undesigned* (*technica naturalis*). The former is intended to convey that nature's capacity for production by final causes must be considered a special kind of causality; the latter, that this capacity is at bottom identical with natural mechanism, and that the contingent coincidence with our artificial conceptions and their rules is a mere subjective condition of our estimating this capacity, and is thus erroneously interpreted as a special mode of natural production.

To speak now of the systems that offer an explanation of nature on the point of final causes, one cannot fail to perceive that they all, without exception, controvert one another dogmatically. In other words, they are at issue upon objective principles of the possibility of things, be this possibility one due to causes acting designedly or merely undesignedly. They do not attack the subjective maxim of mere judgement upon the cause of the final products in question. In the latter case, *disparate* principle might very well be reconciled, whereas, in *the former, contradictorily opposed* principles annul one another and are mutually inconsistent.

The systems in respect of the technic of nature, that is, of nature's power of production on the rule of ends, are of two kinds: that of the *idealism* and that of the *realism* of physical ends. The former maintains that all finality on the part of nature is *undesigned;* the latter, that some, namely finality in organized beings, is *designed.* From the latter the hypothetical consequence may be inferred, that the technic of nature is also designed in what concerns all its other products relatively to entire nature, that is, is an end.

1. The *idealism* of finality (I am here all along referring to objective finality) is either that of the *accidentality* or *fatality* of the determination of nature in the final form of its products. The former principle fixes on the relation of matter to the physical basis of its form, namely dynamical laws; the latter on its relation to the hyperphysical basis of matter and entire nature. The system of *accidentality,* which is attributed to Epicurus or Democritus, is, in its literal interpretation, so manifestly absurd that it need not detain us. On the other hand, the system of *fatality,* of which Spinoza is the accredited author, although it is to all appearances much older, rests upon something supersensible, into which our insight, accordingly, is unable to penetrate. It is not so easy to refute: the reason being that its conception of the original being is quite unintelligible. But this much is clear, that on this system the final nexus in the world must be regarded as undesigned. For, while it is derived from an original being, it is not derived from its intelligence, and consequently not from any design on its part, but from the necessity of the nature of this being and the world-unity flowing from that nature. Hence it is clear, too, that the fatalism of finality is also an idealism of finality.

2. The *realism* of the finality of nature is also either physical or hyperphysical. The *former* bases natural ends on the analogue of a faculty acting designedly, that is, on the *life of matter*—this life being either inherent in it or else bestowed upon it by an inner animating principle or world-soul. This is called *hylozoism.* The *latter* derives such ends from the original source of the universe. This source it regards as an intelligent Being producing with design—or essentially and fundamentally living. It is *theism.*[1]

[1] We see from this how, as in most speculative matters of pure reason, the schools of philosophy have, in the way of dogmatic assertions, usually attempted every possible solution of the problem before them. Thus in the case of the finality of nature, at one time a *lifeless matter,* or again a *lifeless God,* at another, a *living matter,* or else a *living God,* have been tried. Nothing is left to us except, if needs be, to break away from all these *objective assertions,* and weigh our judgement *critically* in its mere relation to our cognitive faculties. By so doing, we may procure for their principle a validity which, if not dogmatic, is yet that of a maxim, and ample for the reliable employment of our reason.

§ 73. *None of the above systems does what it professes to do*

WHAT is the aim and object of all the above systems? It is to explain our teleological judgements about nature. To do so, they adopt one or other of two courses. One side denies their truth, and consequently, describes them as an idealism of nature (represented as art). The other side recognizes their truth and promises to demonstrate the possibility of a nature according to the idea of final causes.

1. The systems that contend for the idealism of the final causes in nature fall into two classes. One class does certainly concede to the principle of these causes a causality according to dynamical laws (to which causality the natural things owe their final existence). But it denies to it *intentionality*—that is, it denies that this causality is determined designedly to this its final production, or, in other words, that an end is the cause. This is the explanation adopted by Epicurus. It completely denies and abolishes the distinction between a technic of nature and its mere mechanism. Blind chance is accepted as the explanation, not alone of the agreement of the generated products with our conception, and, consequently, of the technic of nature, but even of the determination of the causes of this development on dynamical laws, and, consequently, of its mechanism. Hence nothing is explained, not even the illusion in our teleological judgements, so that the alleged idealism in them is left altogether unsubstantiated.

Spinoza, as the representative of the other class, seeks to release us from any inquiry into the ground of possibility of ends of nature, and to deprive this idea of all reality, by refusing to allow that such ends are to be regarded as products at all. They are, rather, accidents inhering in an original being. This being, he says, is the substrate of the natural things, and, as such, he does not ascribe to it causality in respect of them, but simply subsistence. Thanks, then, to the unconditional necessity both of this being and of all the things of nature, as its inherent accidents, he assures to the natural forms, it is true, that unity of ground necessary for all finality, but he does so at the expense of their contingency, apart from which no *unity of end* is thinkable. In eliminating this unity, he eliminates all *trace of design* and leaves the original ground of the things of nature divested of all intelligence.

But Spinozism does not effect what it intends. It intends to furnish an explanation of the final nexus of natural things, which it does not deny, and it refers us simply to the unity of the subject in which they all inhere. But suppose we grant it this mode of existence for its beings of the world, such ontological unity is not then and there a *unity of end* and does not make it in any way intelligible. The latter is, in fact, quite a special kind of unity. It does not follow from the nexus of things in one subject, or of the beings of the world in an original being. On the contrary, it implies emphatically relation to a *cause* possessed of intelligence. Even if all the things were to be united in one *simple* subject, yet such unity would never exhibit a final relation unless these things were understood to be, first, inner *effects* of the substance as a *cause,* and, secondly, effects of it as cause by *virtue of its intelligence.* Apart from these formal conditions, all unity is mere necessity of nature, and, when it is ascribed nevertheless to things that we represent as outside one another, blind necessity. But if what the scholastics[1] call the *transcendental perfection* of things, in relation to their own proper essence—a perfection according to which all things have inherent in them all the requisites for being the thing they are and not any other thing—is to be termed a *natural finality,* we then get a childish playing with words in the place of conceptions. For if all things must be thought as ends, then to be a thing and to be an end are identical, so that, all said and done, there is nothing that specially deserves to be represented as an end.

This makes it evident that, by resolving our conception of natural finality into the consciousness of our own inherence in an all-embracing, though at the same time simple, being, and by seeking the form of finality in the unity of that being, Spinoza must have intended to maintain the idealism of the finality and not its realism. But even this he was unable to accomplish, for the mere representation of the unity of the substrate can never produce the idea of finality, be it even undesigned.

2. Those who not merely maintain the *realism* of physical ends, but purport even to explain it, think they can detect a special type of causality, namely that of causes operating intentionally. Or, at least, they think they are able to perceive the possibility of such causality—for unless they did they could not set

1 [Cf. *Critique of Pure Reason,* p. 44.]

about trying to explain it. For even the most daring hypothesis must rely at least on the *possibility* of its assumed foundation being *certain,* and the conception of this foundation must be capable of being assured its objective reality.

But the possibility of a living matter is quite inconceivable. The very conception of it involves self-contradiction, since lifelessness, *inertia,* constitutes the essential characteristic of matter. Then if the possibility of a matter endowed with life and of aggregate naturè conceived as an animal is invoked in support of the hypothesis of a finality of nature in the macrocosm, it can only be used with the utmost reserve in so far as it is manifested empirically in the organization of nature in the microcosm. Its possibility can in no way be perceived *a priori.* Hence there must be a vicious circle in the explanation, if the finality of nature in organized beings is sought to be derived from the life of matter and if this life in turn is only to be known in organized beings, so that no conception of its possibility can be formed apart from such experience. Hence hylozoism does not perform what it promises.

Finally *theism* is equally incapable of substantiating dogmatically the possibility of physical ends as a key to teleology. Yet the source of its explanation of them has this advantage over all others, that, by attributing an intelligence to the original Being, it adopts the best mode of rescuing the finality of nature from idealism and introduces an intentional causality for its production.

For theism would first have to succeed in proving to the satisfaction of the determinant judgement that the unity of end in matter is an impossible result of the mere mechanism of nature. Otherwise it is not entitled definitely to locate its ground beyond and above nature. But the farthest we can get is this. The first and inner ground of this very mechanism being beyond our ken, the constitution and limits of our cognitive faculties are such as to preclude us from in any way looking to matter with a view to finding in it a principle of determinate final relations. We are left, on the contrary, with no alternative mode of estimating nature's products as natural ends other than that which resorts to a supreme Intelligence as the cause of the world. But this is not a ground for the determinant judgement, but only for the reflective judgement, and it is absolutely incapable of authorizing us to make any objective assertion.

§ 74. *The impossibility of treating the concept of a technic of nature dogmatically springs from the inexplicability of a physical end*

Even though a conception is to be placed under an empirical condition, we deal dogmatically with it, if we regard it as contained under another conception of the object—this conception forming a principle of reason—and determine it in accordance with the latter. But we deal merely critically with the conception if we only regard it in relation to our cognitive faculties and, consequently, to the subjective conditions of thinking it, without undertaking to decide anything as to its object. Hence the dogmatic treatment of a conception is treatment which is authoritative for the determinant judgement; the critical treatment is such as is authoritative merely for the reflective judgement.

Now the conception of a thing as a physical end is one that subsumes nature under a causality that is only thinkable by the aid of reason, and so subsumes it for the purpose of letting us judge on the principle of what is given of the object in experience. But in order to make use of this conception dogmatically for the determinant judgement, we should have first to be assured of its objective reality, as otherwise we could not subsume any natural thing under it. The conception of a thing as a physical end is, however, certainly one that is empirically conditioned, that is, is one only possible under certain conditions given in experience. Yet it is not one to be abstracted from these conditions, but, on the contrary, it is only possible on a rational principle in the estimating of the object. Being such a principle we have no insight into its objective reality, that is to say, we cannot perceive that an object answering to it is possible. We cannot establish it dogmatically; and we do not know whether it is a mere logical fiction and an objectively empty conception (*conceptus ratiocinans*), or whether it is a rational conception, supplying a basis of knowledge and substantiated by reason (*conceptus ratiocinatus*). Hence it cannot be treated dogmatically on behalf of the determinant judgement. In other words, not alone is it impossible to decide whether or not things of nature, considered as physical ends, require for their production a causality of a quite peculiar kind, namely an intentional causality, but the very question is quite out of order. For the conception of a physical end is altogether unprovable by reason in respect of its objective reality, which means that it is not constitutive for the determinant judgement, but merely regulative for the reflective judgement.

That it is not provable is clear from the following considerations. Being a conception of a *natural product* it involves necessity. Yet it also involves in one and the same thing, considered as an end, an accompanying contingency in the form of the object in respect of mere laws of nature. Hence, if it is to escape self-contradiction, besides containing a basis of the possibility of the thing in nature it must further contain a basis of the possibility of this nature itself and of its reference to something that is not an empirically cognizable nature, namely to something supersensible, and, therefore, to what is not cognizable by us at all. Otherwise, in judging of its possibility, we should not have to estimate it in the light of a kind of causality different from that of natural mechanism. Accordingly the conception of a thing as a natural end is transcendent *for the determinant judgement,* if its object is viewed by reason—albeit for the reflective judgement it may be immanent in respect of objects of experience. Objective reality, therefore, cannot be procured for it on behalf of the determinant judgement. Hence we can understand how it is that all systems that are ever devised with a view to the dogmatic treatment of the conception of physical ends or of nature as a whole that owes its consistency and coherence to final causes, fail to decide anything whatever either by their objective affirmations or by their objective denials. For, if things are subsumed under a conception that is merely problematic, the synthetic predicates attached to this conception—as, for example, in the present case, whether the physical end which we suppose for the production of the thing is designed or undesigned—must yield judgements about the object of a like problematic character, be they affirmative or negative, since one does not know whether one is judging about what is something or nothing. The conception of a causality through ends, that is, ends of art, has certainly objective reality, just as that of a causality according to the mechanism of nature has. But the conception of a physical causality following the rule of ends, and still more of such a Being as is utterly incapable of being given to us in experience—a Being regarded as the original source of nature—while it may no doubt be thought without self-contradiction, is nevertheless useless for the purpose of dogmatic definitive assertions. For, since it is incapable of being extracted from experience, and besides is unnecessary for its possibility, there is nothing that can give any guarantee of its objective reality.[1] But even if this could be assured, how can I reckon among products of nature things that are definitely posited as products of divine art, when it was the very incapacity of nature to produce such things according to its own laws that necessitated the appeal to a cause distinct from nature?

§ 75. *The conception of an objective finality of nature is a critical principle of reason for the use of the reflective judgement*

BUT then it is one thing to say: The production of certain things of nature, or even of entire nature, is only possible through the agency of a cause that pursues designs in determining itself to action. It is a perfectly different thing to say: *By the peculiar constitution of my cognitive faculties,* the only way I can judge of the possibility of those things and of their production is by conceiving for that purpose a cause working designedly, and, consequently, a being whose productivity is analogous to the causality of an understanding. In the former case I desire to ascertain something about the object, and I am bound to prove the objective reality of a conception I have assumed. In the latter case it is only the employment of my cognitive faculties that is determined by reason in accordance with their peculiar character and the essential conditions imposed both by their range and their limitations. The first principle is, therefore, an *objective* principle intended for the determinant judgement. The second is a subjective principle for the use merely of the reflective judgement, of which it is, consequently, a maxim that reason prescribes.

In fact, if we desire to pursue the investigation of nature with diligent observation, be it only in its organized products, we cannot get rid of the necessity of adopting the conception of a design as basal. We have in this conception, therefore, a maxim absolutely necessary for the empirical employment of our reason. But once such a guide for the study of nature has been adopted, and its application verified, it is obvious that we must at least try this maxim of judgement also on nature as a whole, because many of its laws might be discoverable in the light of this maxim which otherwise, with the limitations of our insight into its mechanism, would remain hidden from us. But in respect

1 [Cf. p. 550.]

of the latter employment, useful as this maxim of judgement is, it is not indispensable. For nature as a whole is not given to us as organized—in the very strict sense above assigned to the word. On the other hand, in respect of those natural products that can only be estimated as designedly formed in the way they are, and not otherwise, the above maxim or reflective judgement is essentially necessary, if for no other purpose, to obtain an empirical knowledge of their intrinsic character. For the very notion that they are organized things is itself impossible unless we associate with it the notion of a production by design.

Now where the possibility of the real existence or form of a thing is represented to the mind as subject to the condition of an end, there is bound up indissolubly with the conception of the thing the conception of its contingency on natural laws. For this reason, those natural things which we consider to be only possible as ends constitute the foremost proof of the contingency of the universe. Alike for the popular understanding and for the philosopher they are, too, the only valid argument for its dependence upon and its origin from an extramundane Being, and from one, moreover, that the above final form shows to be intelligent. Thus they indicate that teleology must look to a theology for a complete answer to its inquiries.

But suppose teleology brought to the highest pitch of perfection, what would it all prove in the end? Does it prove, for example, that such an intelligent Being really exists? No; it proves no more than this, that by the constitution of our cognitive faculties, and, therefore, in bringing experience into touch with the highest principles of reason, we are absolutely incapable of forming any conception of the possibility of such a world unless we imagine a highest cause *operating designedly*. We are unable, therefore, objectively to substantiate the proposition: There is an intelligent original Being. On the contrary, we can only do so subjectively for the employment of our power of judgement in its reflection on the ends in nature, which are incapable of being thought on any other principle than that of the intentional causality of a highest cause.

Should we desire to establish the major premiss dogmatically from teleological grounds, we should become entangled in inextricable difficulties. For then these reasonings would have to be supported by the thesis: The organized beings in the world are not possible otherwise than by virtue of a cause operating designedly. But are we to say that, because we can only push forward our investigation into the causal nexus of these things and recognize the conformity to law which it displays by following the idea of ends, we are also entitled to presume that for every thinking and perceiving being the same holds true as a necessary condition, and as one, therefore, attaching to the object instead of merely to the subject, that is, to our own selves? For this is the inevitable position that we should have to be prepared to take up. But we could not succeed in carrying such a point. For, strictly speaking, we do not *observe* the ends in nature as designed. We only *read* this conception *into* the facts as a guide to judgement in its reflection upon the products of nature. Hence these ends are not given to us by the object. It is even impossible for us *a priori* to warrant the eligibility of such a conception if taken to possess objective reality. We can get absolutely nothing, therefore, out of the thesis beyond a proposition resting only on subjective conditions, that is to say the conditions of a reflective judgement adapted to our cognitive faculties. Were this proposition to be expressed in objective terms and as valid dogmatically, it would read: There is a God. But all that is permissible for us men is the narrow formula: We cannot conceive or render intelligible to ourselves the finality that must be introduced as the basis even of our knowledge of the intrinsic possibility of many natural things, except by representing it, and, in general, the world, as the product of an intelligent cause—in short, of a God.

Now supposing that this proposition, founded as it is upon an indispensably necessary maxim of our power of judgement, is perfectly satisfactory from every *human* point of view and for any use to which we can put our reason, whether speculative or practical, I should like to know what loss we suffer from our inability to prove its validity for higher beings also—that is to say, to substantiate it on pure objective grounds, which unfortunately are beyond our reach.[1] It is, I mean, quite certain that we can never get a sufficient knowledge of organized beings and their inner possibility, much less get an explanation of them, by looking merely to mechanical principles of nature. Indeed, so certain is it, that we may confidently assert that it is absurd for men even to entertain any thought of so doing or to hope that maybe another Newton may some day arise, to make intelligible to us even the genesis of

[1] [Cf. p. 571.]

but a blade of grass from natural laws that no design has ordered. Such insight we must absolutely deny to mankind. But, then, are we to think that a source of the possibility of organized beings amply sufficient to explain their origin without having recourse to a design, *could* never be found buried among the secrets even of nature, were we able to penetrate to the principle upon which it specifies its familiar universal laws? This, in its turn, would be a presumptuous judgement on our part. For how do we expect to get any knowledge on the point? Probabilities drop entirely out of count in a case like this, where the question turns on judgements of pure reason. On the question, therefore, whether or not any being acting designedly stands behind what we properly term *physical ends,* as a world cause, and consequently, as Author of the world, we can pass no objective judgement whatever, be it affirmative or negative. This much alone is certain, that if we ought, for all that, to form our judgement on what our own proper nature permits us to see, that is, subject to the conditions and restrictions of our reason, we are utterly unable to ascribe the possibility of such physical ends to any other source than an intelligent Being. This alone squares with the maxim of our reflective judgement, and, therefore, with a subjective ground that is nevertheless ineradicably fixed in the human race.

§ 76. *Remark*

THE following survey is one that justly merits detailed elaboration in transcendental philosophy, but it can only be introduced here as an explanatory digression, and not as a step in the main argument.

Reason is a faculty of principles, and the unconditioned is the ultimate goal at which it aims. Understanding, on the other hand, is at its disposal, but always only under a certain condition that must be given. But, without conceptions of understanding, to which objective reality must be given, reason can pass no objective (synthetical) judgements whatever. As theoretical reason, it is absolutely devoid of any constitutive principles of its own. Its principles, on the contrary, are merely regulative. It will readily be perceived that once reason advances beyond pursuit of understanding it becomes transcendent. It displays itself in ideas—that have certainly a foundation as regulative principles—but not in objectively valid conceptions. Understanding, however, unable to keep pace with it and yet requisite in order to give validity in respect of objects, restricts the validity of these ideas to the judging subject, though to the subject in a comprehensive sense, as inclusive of all who belong to the human race. In other words, it limits their validity to the terms of this condition: "From the nature of our human faculty of knowledge, or, to speak in the broadest terms, even according to any conception that we are able *to form for ourselves* of the capacity of a finite intelligent being in general, it must be conceived to be so and cannot be conceived otherwise"—terms which involve no assertion that the foundation of such a judgement lies in the object. We shall submit some examples which, while they certainly possess too great importance and are also too full of difficulty to be here forced at once on the reader as propositions that have been proved, may yet give him some food for reflection, and may elucidate the matters upon which our attention is here specially engaged.

Human understanding cannot avoid the necessity of drawing a distinction between the possibility and the actuality of things. The reason of this lies in our own selves and the nature of our cognitive faculties. For were it not that two entirely heterogeneous factors, understanding for conceptions and sensuous intuition for the corresponding objects, are required for the exercise of these faculties, there would be no such distinction between the possible and the actual. This means that if our understanding were intuitive it would have no objects but such as are actual. Conceptions, which are merely directed to the possibility of an object, and sensuous intuitions, which give us something and yet do not thereby let us cognize it as an object, would both cease to exist. Now the whole distinction which we draw between the merely possible and the actual rests upon the fact that possibility signifies the position of the representation of a thing relatively to our conception, and, in general, to our capacity of thinking, whereas actuality signifies the positing of the thing in its immediate self-existence apart from this conception. Accordingly, the distinction of possible from actual things is one that is merely valid subjectively for human understanding. It arises from the fact that even if something does not exist, we may yet always give it a place in our thoughts, or if there is something of which we have no conception we may nevertheless imagine it given. To say, therefore, that things may be possible without being actual, that from mere possibility, therefore, no conclusion whatever as to actuality can be drawn, is to state propositions that hold true for human reason, without such validity proving that this distinction lies in the things themselves. That this inference is not to be drawn from the propositions stated, and that, consequently, while these are certainly valid even of objects, so far as our cognitive faculties in their subjection to sensuous conditions are also occupied with objects of sense, they are not valid of things generally, is apparent when we look to the demands of reason. For reason never withdraws its challenge to us to adopt something or other existing with unconditioned necessity—a root origin—in which there is no longer to be any difference between possibility and actuality, and our understanding has absolutely no conception to answer to this idea—that is, it can discover no way of representing to itself any such thing or of forming any notion of its mode of existence. For if understanding *thinks* it—let it think it how it will—then the thing is represented merely as possible. If it is conscious of it as given in intuition, then it is actual, and no thought of any possibility enters into the case. Hence the conception of an absolutely necessary being, while doubtless an indispensable idea of reason, is for human understanding an unattainable problematic conception. Nevertheless it is valid for the employment of our cognitive faculties according to their peculiar structure; consequently not so for the object nor, as that would mean, for every knowing being. For I cannot take for granted that thought and intuition are two distinct conditions subject to which every being exercises its cognitive faculties, and, therefore, that things have a possibility and actuality. An understanding into whose mode of cognition this distinction did not enter would express itself by saying: "All objects that I know *are*, that is, exist"; and the possibility of some that did not exist, in other words, their contingency supposing them to exist, and therefore, the necessity that would be placed in contradistinction to this contingency, would never enter into the imagination of such a being. But what makes it so hard for our understanding with its conceptions to rival reason is simply this, that the very thing that reason regards as constitutive of the object and adopts as principle is for understanding, in its human form, transcendent, that is, impossible under the subjective conditions of its knowledge. In this state of affairs, then, this maxim always holds true, that once the knowledge of objects exceeds the capacity of understanding we must always conceive them according to the subjective conditions necessarily attaching to our human nature in the exercise of its faculties.[1] And if—as must needs be the case with transcendent conceptions—judgements passed in this manner cannot be constitutive principles determining the character of the object, we shall yet be left with regulative principles whose function is immanent and reliable, and which are adapted to the human point of view.

We have seen that, in the theoretical study of nature, reason must assume the idea of an unconditioned necessity of the original ground of nature. Similarly, in the practical sphere, it must presuppose its own causality as unconditioned in respect of nature, in other words, its freedom, since it is conscious of its own moral command. Now here the objective necessity of action as duty is, however, regarded as opposed to that which it would have as an event if its source lay in nature instead of in freedom or rational causality. So the action, with its absolute necessity of the moral order, is looked on as physically wholly contingent—that is, we recognize that what *ought* necessarily to happen frequently does not happen. Hence it is clear that it only springs from the subjective character of our practical faculty that the moral laws must be represented as commands, and the actions conformable to them as duties, and that reason expresses this necessity, not by an *is* or "happens" (being or fact), but by an "ought to be" (obligation). This would not occur if reason and its causality were considered as independent of sensibility, that is, as free from the subjective condition of its application to objects in nature, and as being, consequently, a cause in an intelligible world perfectly harmonizing with the moral law. For in such a world there would be no difference between obligation and act, or between a practical law as to what is possible through our agency and a theoretical law as to what we make actual. However, although an intelligible world in which everything is actual by reason of the simple fact that, being something good, it is possible, is for us a transcendent conception—as is also freedom itself, the formal condition of that world—yet it has its proper function. For while, as transcendent, it is useless for the purpose of any constitutive principle determining an object and its objective reality, it yet serves as a universal *regulative principle*. This is due to the constitution of our partly sensuous nature and capacity, which makes it valid for us and, so far as we can imagine from the constitution of our rea-

[1] [Cf. pp. 562, 563.]

son, for all intelligent beings that are in any way bound to this world of sense. But this principle does not objectively determine the nature of freedom as a form of causality: it converts, and converts with no less validity than if it did so determine the nature of that freedom, the rule of actions according to that idea into a command for every one.

Similarly, as to the case before us, we may admit that we should find no distinction between the mechanism and the technic of nature, that is, its final nexus, were it not for the type of our understanding. Our understanding must move from the universal to the particular. In respect of the particular, therefore, judgement can recognize no finality, or, consequently, pass any determinate judgements, unless it is possessed of a universal law under which it can subsume that particular. But the particular by its very nature contains something contingent in respect of the universal. Yet reason demands that there shall also be unity in the synthesis of the particular laws of nature, and, consequently, conformity to law—and a derivation *a priori* of the particular from the universal laws in point of their contingent content is not possible by any defining of the conception of the object. Now the above conformity to law on the part of the contingent is termed *finality*. Hence it follows that the conception of a finality of nature in its products, while it does not touch the determination of objects, is a necessary conception for the human power of judgement, in respect of nature. It is, therefore, a subjective principle of reason for the use of judgement, and one which, taken as regulative and not as constitutive, is as necessarily valid for our *human judgement* as if it were an objective principle.

§ 77. *The peculiarity of human understanding that makes the conception of a physical end possible for us*

In the foregoing Remark, we have noted peculiarities belonging to our faculty of cognition—even to our higher faculty of cognition—which we are easily misled into treating as objective predicates to be transferred to the things themselves. But these peculiarities relate to ideas to which no commensurate object can be given in experience, and which thus could only serve as regulative principles in the pursuit of experience. The conception of a physical end stands, no doubt, on the same footing as regards the source of the possibility of a predicate like this—a source which can only be ideal.[1] But the result attributable to this source, namely, the product itself, is nevertheless given in nature, and the conception of a causality of nature, regarded as a being acting according to ends, seems to convert the idea of a physical end into a constitutive teleological principle. Herein lies a point of difference between this and all other ideas.

But this difference lies in the fact that the idea in question is a principle of reason for the use, not of understanding, but of judgement, and is, consequently, a principle solely for the application of an understanding in the abstract to possible objects of experience. Moreover, this application only affects a field where the judgement passed cannot be determinant but simply reflective. Consequently, while the object may certainly be given in experience, it cannot even be *judged definitely*—to say nothing of being judged with complete adequacy—in accordance with the idea, but can only be made an object of reflection.

The difference turns, therefore, on a peculiarity of *our* (human) understanding relative to our power of judgement in reflecting on things in nature. But, if that is the case, then we must have here an underlying idea of a possible understanding different from the human. (And there was a similar implication in the *Critique of Pure Reason*. We were bound to have present to our minds the thought of another possible form of intuition, if ours was to be deemed one of a special kind, one, namely, for which objects were only to rank as phenomena.) Were this not so, it could not be said that certain natural products *must*, from the particular constitution of our understanding, be *considered by us*—if we are to conceive the possibility of their production—as having been produced designedly and as ends, yet without this statement involving any demand that there should, as a matter of fact, be a particular cause present in which the representation of an end acts as determining ground, or, therefore, without involving any assertion as to the powers of an understanding different from the human. This is to say, the statement does not deny that a superhuman understanding may be able to discover the source of the possibility of such natural products even in the mechanism of nature, that is, in the mechanism of a casual nexus for which an understanding is not positively assumed as cause.

Hence what we are here concerned with is the relation which *our* understanding bears to

[1] [Cf. p. 558.]

judgement. We have, in fact, to examine this relation with a view to finding a certain element of contingency in the constitution of our understanding, so as to note it as a peculiarity of our own in contradistinction to other possible understandings.

This contingency turns up quite naturally in the *particular* which judgement has to bring under the *universal* supplied by the conceptions of understanding. For the particular is not determined by the universal of *our* (human) understanding. Though different things may agree in a common characteristic, the variety of forms in which they may be presented to our perception is contingent. Our understanding is a faculty of conceptions. This means that it is a discursive understanding for which the character and variety to be found in the particular given to it in nature and capable of being brought under its conceptions must certainly be contingent. But now intuition is also a factor in knowledge, and a faculty of *complete spontaneity of intuition* would be a cognitive faculty distinct from sensibility and wholly independent of it. Hence it would be an understanding in the widest sense of the term. Thus we are also able to imagine an *intuitive* understanding—negatively, or simply as not discursive[1]—which does not move, as ours does with its conceptions, from the universal to the particular and so to the individual. Such an understanding would not experience the above contingency in the way nature and understanding accord in natural products subject to *particular laws*. But it is just this contingency that makes it so difficult for our understanding to reduce the multiplicity of nature to the unity of knowledge. Our understanding can only accomplish this task through the harmonizing of natural features with our faculty of conceptions—a most contingent accord. But an intuitive understanding has no such work to perform.

Accordingly our understanding is peculiarly circumstanced in respect of judgement. For in cognition by means of understanding, the particular is not determined by the universal. Therefore the particular cannot be derived from the universal alone. Yet in the multiplicity of nature, and through the medium of conception and laws, this particular has to accord with the universal in order to be capable of being subsumed under it. But, under the circumstances mentioned, this accord must be very contingent and must exist without any determinate principle to guide our judgement.

Nevertheless we are able at least to conceive the possibility of such an accord of the things in nature with the power of judgement—an accord which we represent as contingent, and, consequently, as only possible by means of an end directed to its production. But, to do so, we must at the same time imagine an understanding different from our own, relative to which—and, what is more, without starting to attribute an end to it—we may represent the above accord of natural laws with our power of judgement, which for our understanding is only thinkable when ends are introduced as a middle term effecting the connection, as *necessary*.

It is, in fact, a distinctive characteristic of our understanding, that in its cognition—as, for instance, of the cause of the product—it moves from the *analytic universal* to the particular, or, in other words, from conceptions to given empirical intuitions. In this process, therefore, it determines nothing in respect of the multiplicity of the particular. On the contrary, understanding must wait for the subsumption of the empirical intuition—supposing that the object is a natural product—under the conception, to furnish this determination for the faculty of judgement. But now we are able to form a notion of an understanding which, not being discursive like ours, but intuitive, moves from the *synthetic universal*, or intuition of a whole as a whole, to the particular—that is to say, from the whole to the parts. To render possible a definite form of the whole a *contingency* in the synthesis of the parts is not implied by such an understanding or its representation of the whole. But that is what our understanding requires. It must advance from the parts as the universally conceived principles to different possible forms to be subsumed thereunder as consequences. Its structure is

[1] "The logical negation expressed in the word *not* does not properly belong to a conception, but only to the relation of one conception to another in a judgement, and is consequently quite insufficient to present to the mind the content of a conception." *Critique of Pure Reason*, p. 175. "Our understanding attains in this way a sort of negative extension. That is to say, it is not limited by, but rather limits, sensibility, by giving the name of *noumena* to things, not considered as phenomena, but as things in themselves. But it at the same time prescribes limits to itself, for it confesses itself unable to cognize these by means of the categories, and hence is compelled to cogitate them merely as an unknown something." p. 98. "Even if we should suppose a different kind of intuition from our own, still our functions of thought would have no use or significance in respect thereof." p. 106. "We have no right to assume the existence of new powers, not existing in nature—for example, an understanding with a non-sensuous intuition." p. 227.

such that we can only regard a real whole in nature as the effect of the concurrent dynamical forces of the parts. How, then, may we avoid having to represent the possibility of the whole as dependent upon the parts in a manner conformable to our discursive understanding? May we follow what the standard of the intuitive or archetypal understanding prescribes, and represent the possibility of the parts as both in their form and synthesis dependent upon the whole? The very peculiarity of our understanding in question prevents this being done in such a way that the whole contains the source of the possibility of the nexus of the parts. This would be self-contradictory in knowledge of the discursive type. But the *representation* of a whole may contain the source of the possibility of the form of that whole and of the nexus of the parts which that form involves. This is our only road. But, now, the whole would in that case be an effect or product the *representation* of which is looked on as the *cause* of its possibility. But the product of a cause whose determining ground is merely the representation of its effect is termed an *end*. Hence it follows that it is simply a consequence flowing from the particular character of our understanding that we should figure to our minds products of nature as possible according to a different type of causality from that of the physical laws of matter, that is, as only possible according to ends and final causes. In the same way, we explain the fact that this principle does not touch the question of how such things themselves, even considered as phenomena, are possible on this mode of production, but only concerns the estimate of them possible to our understanding. On this view we see at the same time why it is that in natural science we are far from being satisfied with an explanation of natural products by means of a causality according to ends. For in such an explanation all we ask for is an estimate of physical generation adapted to our critical faculty, or reflective judgement, instead of one adapted to the things themselves on behalf of the determinant judgement. Here it is also quite unnecessary to prove that an *intellectus archetypus* like this is possible. It is sufficient to show that we are led to this idea of an *intellectus archetypus* by contrasting with it our discursive understanding that has need of images (*intellectus ectypus*) and noting the contingent character of a faculty of this form, and that this idea involves nothing self-contradictory.

Now where we consider a material whole and regard it as in point of form a product resulting from the parts and their powers and capacities of self-integration (including as parts any foreign material introduced by the co-operative action of the original parts), what we represent to ourselves in this way is a mechanical generation of the whole. But from this view of the generation of a whole we can elicit no conception of a whole as end—a whole whose intrinsic possibility emphatically presupposes the idea of a whole as that upon which the very nature and action of the parts depend. Yet this is the representation which we must form of an organized body. But, as has just been shown, we are not to conclude from this that the mechanical generation of an organized body is impossible. For that would amount to saying that it is impossible, or, in other words, self-contradictory, *for any understanding* to form a representation of such a unity in the conjunction of the manifold without also making the idea of this unity its producing cause, that is, without representing the production as designed. At the same time this is the conclusion that we should in fact have to draw were we entitled to look on material beings as things in themselves. For in that case the unity constituting the basis of the possibility of natural formations would only be the unity of space. But space is not a real ground of the generation of things. It is only their formal condition—although from the fact that no part in it can be determined except in relation to the whole (the representation of which, therefore, underlies the possibility of the parts) it has some resemblance to the real ground of which we are in search. But then it is at least possible to regard the material world as a mere phenomenon, and to think something which is not a phenomenon, namely a thing-in-itself, as its substrate. And this we may rest upon a corresponding intellectual intuition, albeit it is not the intuition we possess. In this way a supersensible real ground, although for us unknowable, would be procured for nature, and for the nature of which we ourselves form part. Everything, therefore, which is necessary in this nature as an object of sense we should estimate according to mechanical laws. But the accord and unity of the particular laws and of their resulting subordinate forms, which we must deem contingent in respect of mechanical laws—these things which exist in nature as an object of reason, and, indeed, nature in its entirety as a system, we should also consider in the light of teleological laws. Thus we should estimate nature on two kinds of principles. The mechanical mode of explanation would not be excluded by the teleological as if the two principles contradicted one another.

Further, this gives us an insight into what we might doubtless have easily conjectured independently, but which we should have found it difficult to assert or prove with certainty. It shows us that, while the principle of a mechanical derivation of natural products displaying finality is consistent with the teleological, it in no way enables us to dispense with it. We may apply to a thing which we have to estimate as a physical end, that is, to an organized being, all the laws of mechanical generation known or yet to be discovered, we may even hope to make good progress in such researches, but we can never get rid of the appeal to a completely different source of generation for the possibility of a product of this kind, namely that of a causality by ends. It is utterly impossible for human reason, or for any finite reason qualitatively resembling ours, however much it may surpass it in degree, to hope to understand the generation even of a blade of grass from mere mechanical causes. For if judgement finds the teleological nexus of causes and effects quite indispensable for the possibility of an object like this, be it only for the purpose of studying it under the guidance of experience, and if a ground involving relation to ends and adequate for external objects as phenomena altogether eludes us, so that we are compelled, although this ground lies in nature, to look for it in the supersensible substrate of nature, all possible insight into which is, however, cut off from us: it is absolutely impossible for us to obtain any explanation at the hand of nature itself to account for any synthesis displaying finality. So by the constitution of our human faculty of knowledge it becomes necessary to look for the supreme source of this finality in an original understanding as the cause of the world.

§ 78. *The union of the principle of the universal mechanism of matter with the teleological principle in the technic of nature*

It is of endless importance to reason to keep in view the mechanism which nature employs in its productions, and to take due account of it in explaining them, since no insight into the nature of things can be attained apart from that principle. Even the concession that a supreme Architect has directly created the forms of nature in the way they have existed from all time, or has predetermined those which in their course of evolution regularly conform to the same type, does not further our knowledge of nature one whit. The reason is that we are wholly ignorant of the manner in which the supreme Being acts and of His ideas, in which the principles of the possibility of the natural beings are supposed to be contained, and so cannot explain nature from Him by moving from above downwards, that is *a priori*. On the other hand, our explanation would be simply tautological if, relying on the finality found, as we believe, in the forms of objects of experience, we should set out from these forms and move from below upwards, that is *a posteriori*, and with a view to explaining such finality should appeal to a cause acting in accordance with ends. We should be cheating reason with mere words—not to mention the fact that where, by resorting to explanation of this kind, we get lost in the transcendent, and thus stray beyond the pursuit of natural science, reason is betrayed into poetic extravagance, the very thing which it is its pre-eminent vocation to prevent.

On the other hand, it is an equally necessary maxim of reason not to overlook the principle of ends in the products of nature. For although this principle does not make the mode in which such products originate any more comprehensible to us, yet it is a heuristic principle for the investigation of the particular laws of nature. And this remains true even though it be understood that, as we confine ourselves rigorously to the term physical ends, even where such products manifestly exhibit a designed final unity, we do not intend to make any use of the principle for the purpose of explaining nature itself—that is to say, in speaking of physical ends, pass beyond the bounds of nature in quest of the source of the possibility of those products. However, inasmuch as the question of this possibility must be met sooner or later, it is just as necessary to conceive a special type of causality for it—one not to be found in nature—as to allow that the mechanical activity of natural causes has its special type. For the receptivity for different forms over and above those which matter is capable of producing by virtue of such mechanism must be supplemented by a spontaneity of some cause—which cannot, therefore, be matter—as in its absence no reason can be assigned for those forms. Of course, before reason takes this step it must exercise due caution and not seek to explain as teleological every technic of nature—meaning by this a formative capacity of nature which displays (as in the case of regularly constructed bodies) finality of structure for our mere apprehension. On the contrary, it must continue to regard such technic as possible on purely mechanical principles. But to go so far as to exclude the teleological principle, and to want to keep always to mere mechanism, even where reason, in its investigation into the manner in which natural forms are rendered possible by their causes, finds a finality of a character whose relation to a different type of causality is apparent beyond all denial, is equally unscientific. It inevitably sends reason on a roving expedition among capacities of nature that are only cobwebs of the brain and quite unthinkable, in just the same way as a merely teleological mode of explanation that pays no heed to the mechanism of nature makes it visionary.

These two principles are not capable of being applied in conjunction to one and the same thing in nature as co-ordinate truths available for the explanation or deduction of one thing by or from another. In other words, they are not to be united in that way as dogmatic and constitutive principles affording insight into nature on behalf of the determinant judgement. If I suppose, for instance, that a maggot is to be regarded as a product of the mere mechanism of matter, that is of a new formative process which a substance brings about by its own unaided resources when its elements are liberated as the result of decomposition, I cannot then turn round and derive the same product from the same substance as a causality that acts from ends. Conversely, if I suppose that this product is a physical end, I am precluded from relying on its mechanical generation, or adopting such generation as a constitutive principle for estimating the product in respect of its possibility, and thus uniting the two principles. For each mode of explanation excludes the other—even supposing that objectively both grounds of the possibility of such a product rest on a single foundation, provided this foundation was not what we were thinking of. The principle which is to make possible the compatibility of the above pair of principles, as principles to be followed in estimating nature, must be placed in what lies beyond both (and consequently beyond the possible empirical representation of nature), but in what nevertheless contains the ground of the representation of nature. It must, in other words, be placed in the supersensible, and to this each of the two modes of explanation must be referred. Now the only conception we can have of the supersensible is the indeterminate conception of a ground that makes possible the estimate of nature according to empirical laws. Beyond this we cannot go: by no predicate can we determine this conception any further. Hence it follows that the union of the two principles cannot rest on one basis of *explanation* setting out in so many terms how a product is possible on given laws so as to satisfy the *determinant* judgement, but can only rest on a single basis of *exposition* elucidating this possibility for the *reflective* judgement. For explanation means derivation from a principle, which must, therefore, be capable of being clearly cognized and specified. Now the principle of the mechanism of nature and that of its causality according to ends, when applied to one and the same product of nature, must cohere in a single higher principle and flow from it as their common source, for if this were not so they could not both enter consistently into the same survey of nature. But if this principle, which is objectively common to both, and which, therefore, justifies the association of its dependent maxims of natural research, is of such a kind that, while it can be indicated, it can never be definitely cognized or clearly specified for employment in particular cases as they arise, then no explanation can be extracted from such a principle. There can be no clear and definite derivation, in other words, of the possibility of a natural product, as one possible on those two heterogeneous principles. Now the principle common to the mechanical derivation, on the one hand, and the teleological, on the other, is the *supersensible,* which we must introduce as the basis of nature as phenomenon. But of this we are unable from a theoretical point of view to form the slightest positive determinate conception. How, therefore, in the light of the supersensible as principle, nature in its particular laws constitutes a system for us, and one capable of being cognized as possible both on the principle of production from physical causes and on that of final causes, is a matter which does not admit of any explanation. All we can say is that if it happens that objects of nature present themselves, whose possibility is incapable of being conceived by us on the principle of mechanism —which has always a claim upon a natural being —unless we rely on teleological principles, it is then to be presumed that we may confidently study natural laws on lines following both principles—according as the possibility of the natural product is cognizable to our understandings from one or other principle—without being disturbed by the apparent conflict that arises between the principles upon which our estimate of the product is formed. For we are at least assured of the possibility of both being reconciled, even objectively, in a single principle, inasmuch as they deal with phenomena, and these presuppose a supersensible ground.

We have seen that the principles both of nature's mechanical operation and of its teleological or designed technique, as bearing upon one and the same product and its possibility, may alike be subordinated to a common higher principle of nature in its particular laws. Nevertheless, this principle being *transcendent,* the narrow capacity of our understanding is such that the above subordination does not enable us to unite the two principles *in the explanation* of the same natural generation, even where, as is the case with organized substances, the intrinsic possibility of the product is only *intelligible* by means of a causality according to ends. Hence we must keep to the statement of the principle of teleology above given. So we say that, by the constitution of our human understanding, no causes but those acting by design can be adopted as grounds of the possibility of organized beings in nature, and the mere mechanism of nature is quite insufficient to explain these its products; and we add that this implies no desire to decide anything by that principle in respect of the possibility of such things themselves.

This principle, we mean to say, is only a maxim of the reflective, not of the determinant judgement. Hence, it is only valid subjectively for us, not objectively to explain the possibility of things of this kind themselves—in which things themselves both modes of generation might easily spring consistently from one and the same ground. Furthermore, unless the teleologically-conceived mode of generation were supplemented by a conception of an concomitantly presented mechanism of nature, such genesis could not be estimated as a product of nature at all. Hence, we see that the above maxim immediately involves the necessity of a union of both principles in the estimate of things as physical ends. But this union is not to be directed to substituting one principle, either wholly or in part, in the place of the other. For in the room of what is regarded, by us at least, as only possible by design, mechanism cannot be assumed, and in the room of what is cognized as necessary in accordance with mechanism, such contingency as would require an end as its determining ground cannot be assumed. On the contrary, we can only subordinate one to the other, namely mechanism to designed technique. And on the trancendental principle of the finality of nature this may readily be done.

For where ends are thought as the sources of the possibility of certain things, means have also to be supposed. Now the law of the efficient causality of a means, considered *in its own right,* requires nothing that presupposes an end, and, consequently, may be both mechanical and yet a subordinate cause of designed effects. Hence, looking only to organic products of nature, but still more if, impressed by the endless multitude of such products, we go on and adopt, at least on an allowable hypothesis, the principle of design, in the connection of natural causes following particular laws, as a *universal principle* of the reflective judgement in respect of the whole of nature, namely the world, we may imagine a vast and even universal interconnection of mechanical and teleological laws in the generative processes of nature. Here we neither confuse nor transpose the principles upon which such processes are estimated. For in a teleological estimate, even if the form which the matter assumes is estimated as only possible by design, yet the matter itself, considered as to its nature, may also be subordinated, conformably to mechanical laws, as means to the represented end. At the same time, inasmuch as the basis of this compatibility lies in what is neither the one nor the other, neither mechanism nor final nexus, but is the supersensible substrate of nature which is shut out from our view, for our human reason the two modes of representing the possibility of such objects are not to be fused into one. On the contrary, we are unable to estimate their possibility otherwise than as one founded in accordance with the nexus of final causes on a supreme understanding. Thus the teleological mode of explanation is in no way prejudiced.

But now it is an open question, and for our reason must always remain an open question, how much the mechanism of nature contributes as means to each final design in nature. Further, having regard to the above-mentioned intelligible principle of the possibility of a nature in general, we may even assume that nature is possible in all respects on both kinds of law, the physical laws and those of final causes, as universally consonant laws, although we are quite unable to see how this is so. Hence, we are ignorant how far the mechanical mode of explanation possible for us may penetrate. This much only is certain, that no matter what progress we may succeed in making with it, it must still always remain inadequate for things that we have once recognized to be physical ends. Therefore, by the constitution of our understanding we must subordinate such mechanical grounds, one and all, to a teleological principle.

Now this is the source of a privilege and, owing to the importance of the study of nature on the lines of the principle of mechanism for the theoretical employment of our reason, the source also of a duty. We may and should explain all products and events of nature, even the most purposive, so far as in our power lies, on mechanical lines—and it is impossible for us to assign the limits of our powers when confined to the pursuit of inquiries of this kind. But in so doing we must never lose sight of the fact that among such products there are those which we cannot even subject to investigation except under the conception of an end of reason. These, if we respect the essential nature of our reason, we are obliged, despite those mechanical causes, to subordinate in the last resort to causality according to ends.[1]

APPENDIX. *Theory of the Method of Applying the Teleological Judgement*

§ 79. *Whether teleology must be treated as a branch of natural science*

EVERY science must have its definite position in the complete encyclopedia of the sciences. If it is a philosophical science, its position must be assigned to it either in the theoretical or the practical division. Further, if its place is in the theoretical division, then the position assigned to it must either be in natural science—which is its proper position when it considers things capable of being objects of experience—consequently in physics proper, psychology, or cosmology, or else in theology— as the science of the original source of the world as complex of all objects of experience.

Now the question arises: What position does teleology deserve? Is it a branch of natural science, properly so called, or of theology? A branch of one or the other it must be; for no science can belong to the transition from one to the other, because this only signifies the articulation or the organization of the system and not a position in it.

That it does not form a constituent part of theology, although the use that may there be made of it is most important, is evident from the nature of the case. For its objects are physical generations and their cause; and, although it points to this cause as a ground residing beyond and above nature, namely a Divine Author, yet it does not do so for the determinant judgement. It only points to this cause in the interests of the reflective judgement engaged in surveying nature, its purpose being to guide our estimate of the things in the world by means of the idea of such a ground, as a regulative principle, in a manner adapted to our human understanding.

But just as little does it appear to form a part of natural science. For this science requires determinant, and not merely reflective, principles for the purpose of assigning objective grounds of physical effects. As a matter of fact, also, the theory of nature, or the mechanical explanation of its phenomena by efficient causes, is in no way helped by considering them in the light of the correlation of ends. The exposition of the ends pursued by nature in its products, so far as such ends form a system according to teleological conceptions, is strictly speaking only incident to a description of nature that follows a particular guiding star. Here reason does fine work, and work that is full of practical finality from various points of view. But it gives no information whatever as to the origin and intrinsic possibility of these forms. Yet this is what specially concerns the theoretical science of nature.

Teleology, therefore, in the form of a science, is not a branch of doctrine at all, but only of critique, and of the critique of a particular cognitive faculty, namely judgement. But it does contain *a priori* principles, and to that extent it may, and in fact must, specify the method by which nature has to be judged according to the principle of final causes. In this way, the science of its methodical application exerts at least a negative influence upon the procedure to be adopted in the theoretical science of nature. It also in the same way affects the metaphysical bearing which this science may have on theology, when the former is treated as a propaedeutic to the latter.

§ 80. *The necessary subordination of the principle of mechanism to the teleological principle in the explanation of a thing regarded as a physical end*

OUR *right to aim at* an explanation of all natural products on simply mechanical lines is in itself quite unrestricted. But the constitution of our understanding, as engaged upon things in the shape of physical ends, is such that our *power* of *meeting all demands* from the unaided resources of mechanical explanation is not alone very limited, but is also circumscribed within clearly marked bounds. For by a principle of

[1] [Cf. *Critique of Pure Reason*, pp. 180–1.]

judgement that adopts the above procedure alone nothing whatever can be accomplished in the way of explaining physical ends. For this reason our estimate of such products must at all times be subordinated to a concurrent teleological principle.

Hence there is reason, and indeed merit, in pursuing the mechanism of nature for the purpose of explaining natural products so far as this can be done with probable success, and in fact never abandoning this attempt on the ground that it is *intrinsically* impossible to encounter the finality of nature along this road, but only on the ground that it is impossible *for us* as men. For in order to get home along this line of investigation we should require an intuition different from our sensuous intuition and a determinate knowledge of the intelligible substrate of nature—a substrate from which we could show the reason of the very mechanism of phenomena in their particular laws. But this wholly surpasses our capacity.

So where it is established beyond question that the conception of a physical end applies to things, as in the case of organized beings, if the naturalist is not to throw his labour away, he must always, in forming an estimate of them, accept some original organization or other as fundamental. He must consider that this organization avails itself of the very mechanism above mentioned for the purpose of producing other organic forms, or for evolving new structures from those given—such new structures, however, always issuing from and in accordance with the end in question.

It is praiseworthy to employ a comparative anatomy and go through the vast creation of organized beings in order to see if there is not discoverable in it some trace of a system, and indeed of a system following a genetic principle.[1] For otherwise we should be obliged to content ourselves with the mere critical principle—which tells us nothing that gives any insight into the production of such beings—and to abandon in despair all claim to *insight into nature* in this field. When we consider the agreement of so many genera of animals in a certain common schema, which apparently underlies not only the structure of their bones, but also the disposition of their remaining parts, and when we find here the wonderful simplicity of the original plan, which has been able to produce such an immense variety of species by the shortening of one member and the lengthening of another, by the involution of this part and the evolution of that, there gleams upon the mind a ray of hope, however faint, that the principle of the mechanism of nature, apart from which there can be no natural science at all, may yet enable us to arrive at some explanation in the case of organic life. This analogy of forms, which in all their differences seem to be produced in accordance with a common type, strengthens the suspicion that they have an actual kinship due to descent from a common parent. This we might trace in the gradual approximation of one animal species to another, from that in which the principle of ends seems best authenticated, namely from man, back to the polyp, and from this back even to mosses and lichens, and finally to the lowest perceivable stage of nature. Here we come to crude matter; and from this, and the forces which it exerts in accordance with mechanical laws (laws resembling those by which it acts in the formation of crystals)[2] seems to be developed the whole technic of nature, which, in the case of organized beings, is so incomprehensible to us that we feel obliged to imagine a different principle for its explanation.

Here the *archaeologist* of nature is at liberty to go back to the traces that remain of nature's earliest revolutions, and, appealing to all he knows of or can conjecture about its mechanism, to trace the genesis of that great family of living things (for it must be pictured as a family if there is to be any foundation for the consistently coherent affinity mentioned). He can suppose that the womb of mother earth as it first emerged, like a huge animal, from its chaotic state, gave birth to creatures whose form displayed less finality, and that these again bore others which adapted themselves more perfectly to their native surroundings and their relations to each other, until this womb, becoming rigid and ossified, restricted its birth to definite species incapable of further modification, and the multiplicity of forms was fixed as it stood when the operation of that fruitful formative power had ceased. Yet, for all that, he is obliged eventually to attribute to this universal mother an organization suitably constituted with a view to all these forms of life, for unless he does so, the possibility of the final form of the products of the animal and plant kingdoms is quite unthinkable.[3] But when he does attribute all this to

[1] [Cf. p. 555.]

[2] [Cf. p. 545, above.]

[3] An hypothesis of this kind may be called a daring venture on the part of reason; and there are probably few even among the most acute scientists to whose minds it has not sometimes occurred. For it cannot be said to be absurd, like the *generatio aequivoca*, which means the generation of an organized being from crude inor-

nature, he has only pushed the explanation a stage farther back. He cannot pretend to have made the genesis of those two kingdoms intelligible independently of the condition of final causes.

Even as regards the alteration which certain individuals of the organized genera contingently undergo, where we find that the character thus altered is transmitted and taken up into the generative power, we can form no other plausible estimate of it than that it is an occasional development of a purposive capacity originally present in the species with a view to the preservation of the race. For in the complete inner finality of an organized being, the generation of its like is intimately associated with the condition that nothing shall be taken up into the generative force which does not also belong, in such a system of ends, to one of its undeveloped native capacities. Once we depart from this principle we cannot know with certainty whether many constituents of the form at present found in a species may not be of equally contingent and purposeless origin, and the principle of teleology, that nothing in an organized being which is preserved in the propagation of the species should be estimated as devoid of finality, would be made very unreliable and could only hold good for the parent stock, to which our knowledge does not go back.

In reply to those who feel obliged to adopt a teleological principle of critical judgement, that is, an architectonic understanding in the case of all such physical ends, Hume raises the objection that one might ask with equal justice how such an understanding is itself possible. By this he means that one may also ask how it is possible that there should be such a teleological coincidence in one being of the manifold faculties and properties presupposed in the very conception of an understanding possessing at once intellectual and executive capacity. But there is nothing in this point. For the whole difficulty that besets the question as to the genesis of a thing that involves ends and that is solely comprehensible by their means rests upon the demand for unity in the source of the synthesis of the multiplicity of *externally existing* elements in this product. For, if this source is laid in the understanding of a productive cause regarded as a simple substance, the above question, as a teleological problem, is abundantly answered, whereas if the cause is merely sought in matter, as an aggregate of many externally existing substances, the unity of principle requisite for the intrinsically final form of its complex structures is wholly absent. The *autocracy* of matter in productions, that by our understanding are only conceivable as ends, is a word with no meaning.

This is the reason why those who look for a supreme ground of the possibility of the objectively final forms of matter, and yet do not concede an understanding to this ground, choose nevertheless to make the world-whole either an all-embracing substance (Pantheism), or else—what is only the preceding in more defined form—a complex of many determinations inhering in a single *simple substance* (Spinozism). Their object is to derive from this substance that *unity* of source which all finality presupposes. And in fact, thanks to their purely ontological conception of a simple substance, they really do something to satisfy *one* condition of the problem—namely, that of the unity implied in the reference to an end. But they have nothing to say on the subject of the *other* condition, namely the relation of the substance to its consequence regarded as an *end*, this relation being what gives to their ontological ground the more precise determination which the problem demands. The result is that they in no way answer the *entire* problem. Also for our understanding it remains absolutely unanswerable except on the following terms. First, the original source of things must be pictured by us as a simple substance. Then its attribute, as simple substance, in its relation to the specific character of the natural forms whose source it is—the character, namely, of final unity—must be pictured as the attribute of an intelligent substance. Lastly, the relation of this intelligent substance to the natural forms must, owing to the contingency which we find in everything which we imagine to be possible only as an end, be pictured as one of *causality*.

ganic matter. It never ceases to be *generatio univoca* in the widest acceptation of the word, as it only implies the generation of something organic from something else that is also organic, although, within the class of organic beings, differing specifically from it. It would be as if we supposed that certain water animals transformed themselves by degrees into marsh animals, and from these after some generations into land animals. In the judgement of plain reason there is nothing *a priori* self-contradictory in this. But experience offers no example of it. On the contrary, as far as experience goes, all generation known to us is *generatio homonyma*. It is not merely *univoca* in contradistinction to generation from an unorganized substance, but it brings forth a product which in its very organization is of like kind with that which produced it, and a *generatio heteronyma* is not met with anywhere within the range of our experience.

§ 81. *The association of mechanism with the teleological principle which we apply to the explanation of a physical end considered as a product of nature*

We have seen from the preceding section[1] that the mechanism of nature is not sufficient to enable us to conceive the possibility of an organized being, but that in its root origin it must be subordinated to a cause acting by design—or, at least, that the type of our cognitive faculty is such that we must conceive it to be so subordinated. But just as little can the mere teleological source of a being of this kind enable us to consider and to estimate it as at once an end and a product of nature. With that teleological source we must further associate the mechanism of nature as a sort of instrument of a cause acting by design and contemplating an end to which nature is subordinated even in its mechanical laws. The possibility of such a union of two completely different types of causality, namely, that of nature in its universal conformity to law and that of an idea which restricts nature to a particular form of which nature, as nature, is in no way the source, is something which our reason does not comprehend. For it resides in the supersensible substrate of nature, of which we are unable to make any definite affirmation, further than that it is the self-subsistent being of which we know merely the phenomenon. Yet, for all that, this principle remains in full and undiminished force, that everything which we assume to form part of phenomenal nature and to be its product must be thought as linked with nature on mechanical laws. For, apart from this type of causality, organized beings, although they are ends of nature, would not be natural products.

Now supposing we adopt the teleological principle of the production of organized beings, as indeed we cannot avoid doing, we may base their internally final form either on the *occasionalism* or on the *pre-establishment* of the cause. According to occasionalism, the Supreme Cause of the world would directly supply the organic formation, stamped with the impress of His idea, on the occasion of each impregnation, to the commingling substances united in the generative process. On the system of pre-establishment, the Supreme Cause would only endow the original products of His wisdom with the inherent capacity by means of which an organized being produces another after its own kind, and the species preserves its continuous existence, whilst the loss of individuals is ever being repaired through the agency of a nature that concurrently labours towards their destruction. If the occasionalism of the production of organized beings is assumed, all co-operation of nature in the process is entirely lost, and no room is left for the exercise of reason in judging of the possibility of products of this kind. So we may take it for granted that no one will embrace this system who cares anything for philosophy.

Again the system of pre-establishment may take either of two forms. Thus it treats every organized being produced from one of its own kind either as its *educt* or as its *product.* The system which regards the generations as educts is termed that of *individual preformation,* or, sometimes, the *theory of evolution;* that which regards them as products is called the system of *epigenesis.* The latter may also be called the system of *generic preformation,* inasmuch as it regards the productive capacity of the parents, in respect of the inner final tendency that would be part of their original stock, and, therefore, the specific form, as still having been *virtualiter* preformed. On this statement the opposite theory of individual preformation might also more appropriately be called the *theory of involution* (or *encasement*).

The advocates of the *theory of evolution* exclude all individuals from the formative force of nature, for the purpose of deriving them directly from the hand of the Creator. Yet they would not venture to describe the occurrence on the lines of the hypothesis of occasionalism, so as to make the impregnation an idle formality, which takes place whenever a supreme intelligent Cause of the world has made up His mind to form a foetus directly with His own hand and relegate to the mother the mere task of developing and nourishing it. They would avow adherence to the theory of preformation; as if it were not a matter of indifference whether a supernatural origin of such forms is allowed to take place at the start or in the course of the world-process. They fail to see that, in fact, a whole host of supernatural contrivances would be spared by acts of creation as occasion arose, which would be required if an embryo formed at the beginning of the world had to be preserved from the destructive forces of nature, and had to keep safe and sound all through the long ages till the day arrived for its development, and also that an incalculably greater number of such preformed entities would be created than would be destined ever to

[1] [Cf. pp. 579, 580.]

develop, and that all those would be so many creations thus rendered superfluous and in vain. Yet they would like to leave nature some role in these operations, so as not to lapse into unmitigated hyperphysic that can dispense with all explanation on naturalistic lines. Of course they would still remain unshaken in their hyperphysic; so much so that they would discover even in abortions—which yet cannot possibly be deemed ends of nature—a marvellous finality, be it even directed to no better purpose than that of being a meaningless finality intended to set some chance anatomist at his wit's end and make him fall on his knees with admiration. However, they would be absolutely unable to make the generation of hybrids fit in with the system of preformation, but would be compelled to allow to the seed of the male creature, to which in other cases they had denied all but the mechanical property of serving as the first means of nourishment for the embryo, a further and additional formative force directed to ends. And yet they would not concede this force to either of the two parents when dealing with the complete product of two creatures of the same genus.

As against this, even supposing we failed to see the enormous advantage on the side of the advocate of *epigenesis* in the matter of empirical evidences in support of his theory, still reason would antecedently be strongly prepossessed in favour of his line of explanation. For as regards things the possibility of whose origin can only be represented to the mind according to a causality of ends, epigenesis none the less regards nature as at least itself productive in respect of the continuation of the process, and not as merely unravelling something. Thus, with the least possible expenditure of the supernatural, it entrusts to nature the explanation of all steps subsequent to the original beginning. But it refrains from determining anything as to this original beginning, which is what baffles all the attempts of physics, no matter what chain of causes it adopts.

No one has rendered more valuable services in connection with this theory of epigenesis than Herr Hofr. Blumenbach. This is as true of what he has done towards establishing the correct principles of its application—partly by setting due bounds to an over liberal employment of it—as it is of his contributions to its proof. He makes organic substance the starting-point for physical explanation of these formations. For to suppose that crude matter, obeying mechanical laws, was originally its own architect, that life could have sprung up from the nature of what is void of life, and matter have spontaneously adopted the form of a self-maintaining finality, he justly declares to be contrary to reason. But, at the same time, he leaves to the mechanism of nature, in its subordination to this inscrutable *principle* of a primordial *organization*, an indeterminable yet also unmistakable function. The capacity of matter here required he terms—in contradistinction to the simply mechanical *formative force* universally residing in it—in the case of an organized body a *formative impulse*, standing, so to speak, under the higher guidance and direction of the above principle.

§ 82. *The teleological system in the extrinsic relations of organisms*

By *extrinsic finality* I mean the finality that exists where one things in nature subserves another as means to an end. Now even things which do not possess any intrinsic finality, and whose possibility does not imply any, such as earth, air, water, and the like, may nevertheless extrinsically, that is, in relation to other beings, be very well adapted to ends. But then those other beings must in all cases be organized, that is, be physical ends, for unless they are ends the former could not be considered means. Thus water, air, and earth cannot be regarded as means to the upgrowth of mountains. For intrinsically there is nothing in mountains that calls for a source of their possibility according to ends. Hence their cause can never be referred to such a source and represented under the predicate of a means subservient thereto.

Extrinsic finality is an entirely different conception from that of intrinsic finality, the latter being connected with the possibility of an object irrespective of whether its actuality is itself an end or not. In the case of an organism we may further inquire: For what end does it exist? But we can hardly do so in the case of things in which we recognize the simple effect of the mechanism of nature. The reason is that in the case of organisms we have already pictured to ourselves a causality according to ends—a creative understanding—to account for their intrinsic finality, and have referred this active faculty to its determining ground, the design. One extrinsic finality is the single exception—and it is one intimately bound up with the intrinsic finality of an organization. It does not leave open the question as to the ulterior end for which the nature so organized must have existed, and yet it lies in the extrinsic relation of a means to an end. This is the organization of the two sexes in their mutual relation with a view to the propagation of their species. For here we may always ask, just as in the case of an individual: Why was it necessary for such a pair to exist? The answer is: In this pair we have what first forms an *organizing* whole, though not an organized whole in a single body.

Now when it is asked to what end a thing exists, the answer may take one or other of two forms. It may be said that its existence and generation have no relation whatever to a cause acting designedly. Its origin is then always understood to be derived from the mechanism of nature. Or it may be said that its existence, being that of a contingent natural entity, has some ground or other involving design. And this is a thought which it is difficult for us to separate from the conception of a thing that is organized. For inasmuch as we are compelled to rest its intrinsic possibility on the causality of final causes and an idea underlying this causality, we cannot but think that the real existence of this product is also an end. For where the representation of an effect is at the same time the ground determining an intelligent efficient cause to its production, the effect so represented is termed an *end*. Here, therefore, we may either say that the end of the real existence of a natural being of this kind is inherent in itself, that is, that it is not merely an end, but also a *final end;* or we may say that the final end lies outside it in other natural beings, that is, that its real existence, which is adapted to ends, is not itself a final end, but is necessitated by its being at the same time a means.

But, if we go through the whole of nature, we do not find in it, as nature, any being capable of laying claim to the distinction of being the final end of creation. In fact it may even be proved *a priori* that what might do perhaps as an *ultimate end* for nature, endowing it with any conceivable qualities or properties we choose, could nevertheless in its character of a natural thing never be a final end.

Looking to the vegetable kingdom, we might at first be induced by the boundless fertility with which it spreads itself abroad upon almost every soil to think that it should be regarded as a mere product of the mechanism which nature displays in its formations in the mineral kingdom. But a more intimate knowledge of its indescribably wise organization precludes us from entertaining this view, and drives us to ask: For what purpose do these forms of life exist? Suppose we reply: For the animal kingdom, which is thus provided with the means of sustenance, so that it has been enabled to spread over the face of the earth in such a manifold variety of genera. The question again arises: For what purpose then do these herbivora exist? The answer would be something like this: For the carnivora, which are only able to live on what itself has animal life. At last we get down to the question: What is the end and purpose of these and all the preceding natural kingdoms? For man, we say, and the multifarious uses to which his intelligence teaches him to put all these forms of life. He is the ultimate end of creation here upon earth, because he is the one and only being upon it that is able to form a conception of ends and, from an aggregate of things purposively fashioned, to construct by the aid of his reason a system of ends.

We might also follow the chevalier Linné and take the seemingly opposite course. Thus we might say: The herbivorous animals exist for the purpose of checking the profuse growth of the vegetable kingdom by which many species of that kingdom would be choked; the carnivora for the purpose of setting bounds to the voracity of the herbivora; and finally man exists so that by pursuing the latter and reducing their numbers a certain equilibrium between the productive and destructive forces of nature may be established. So, on this view, however much man might in a certain relation be esteemed as end, in a different relation he would in turn only rank as a means.

If we adopt the principle of an objective finality in the manifold variety of the specific forms of terrestrial life and in their extrinsic relations to one another as beings with a structure adapted to ends, it is only rational to go on and imagine that in this extrinsic relation there is also a certain organization and a system of the whole kingdom of nature following final causes. But experience seems here to give the lie to the maxim of reason, more especially as regards an ultimate end of nature—an end which nevertheless is necessary to the possibility of such a system, and which we can only place in man. For, so far from making man, regarded as one of the many animal species, an ultimate end, nature has no more exempted him from its destructive than from its productive forces, nor has it made the smallest exception to its subjection of everything to a mechanism of forces devoid of an end.

The first thing that would have to be expressly appointed in a system ordered with a view to a final whole of natural beings upon the earth would be their habitat—the soil or the element upon or in which they are intended to thrive. But a more intimate knowledge of the nature of this basal condition of all organic production shows no trace of any causes but those acting altogether without design, and in fact tending towards destruction rather than calculated to promote genesis of forms, order, and ends. Land and seat not alone contain memorials of mighty primeval disasters that have overtaken both them and all their brood of living forms, but their entire structure—the strata of the land and the coast lines of the sea—has all the appearance of being the outcome of the wild and all-subduing forces of a nature working in a state of chaos. However wisely the configuration, elevation and slope of the land may now seem to be adapted for the reception of water from the air, for the subterranean channels of the springs that well up between the diverse layers of earth (suitable for various products), and for the course of the rivers, yet a closer investigation of them shows that they have resulted simply as the effect partly of volcanic eruptions, partly of floods, or even of invasions of the ocean. And this is not alone true as regards the genesis of this configuration, but more particularly of its subsequent transformation, attended with the disappearance of its primitive organic productions.[1] If now the abode for all these forms of life—the lap of the land and the bosom of the deep—points to none but a wholly undesigned mechanical generation, how can we, or what right have we to ask for or to maintain a different origin for these latter products? And even if man, as the most minute examination of the remains of those devastations of nature seems, in Camper's judgement, to prove, was not comprehended in such revolutions, yet his dependence upon the remaining forms of terrestrial life is such that, if a mechanism of nature whose power overrides these others is admitted, he must be regarded as included within its scope, although his intelligence, to a large extent at least, has been able to save him from its work of destruction.

[1] If the name of *natural history,* now that it has once been adopted, is to continue to be used for the description of nature, we may give the name of *archaeology* of *nature,* as contrasted with art, to that which the former literally indicates, namely an account of the bygone or *ancient* state of the earth—a matter on which, though we dare not hope for any certainty, we have good ground for conjecture. Fossil remains would be objects for the archaeology of nature, just as rudely cut stones, and things of that kind, would be for the archaeology of art. For, as work is actually being done in this department, under the name of a *theory of the earth,* steadily though, as we might expect, slowly, this name would not be given to a purely imaginary study of nature, but to one to which nature itself invites and summons us.

But this argument seems to go beyond what it was directed to prove. For it would seem to show not merely that man could not be an ultimate end of nature or, for the same reason, the aggregate of the organized things of terrestrial nature be a system of ends, but that even the products of nature previously deemed to be physical ends could have no other origin than the mechanism of nature.

But, then, we must bear in mind the results of the solution above given of the antinomy of the principles of the mechanical and teleological generation of organic natural beings. These principles, as we there saw, are merely principles of reflective judgement in respect of formative nature and its particular laws, the key to whose systematic correlation is not in our possession. They tell us nothing definite as to the origin of the things in their own intrinsic nature. They only assert that by the constitution of our understanding and our reason we are unable to conceive the origin in the case of beings of this kind otherwise than in the light of final causes. The utmost persistence possible, nay even a boldness, is allowed us in our endeavours to explain them on mechanical lines. More than that, we are even summoned by reason to do so, albeit we know we can never get home with such an explanation—not because there is an inherent inconsistency between the mechanical generation and an origin according to ends, but for subjective reasons involved in the particular type and limitations of our understanding. Lastly, we saw that the reconciliation of the two modes of picturing the possibility of nature might easily lie in the supersensible principle of nature, both external and internal. For the mode of representation based on final causes is only a subjective condition of the exercise of our reason in cases where it is not seeking to know the proper estimate to form of objects arranged merely as phenomena, but is bent rather on referring these phenomena, principles and all, to their supersensible substrate, for the purpose of recognizing the possibility of certain laws of their unity, which are incapable of being figured by the minds otherwise than by means of ends (of which reason also possesses examples of the supersensuous type).

§ 83. *The ultimate end of nature as a teleological system*

We have shown in the preceding section that, looking to principles of reason, there is ample ground—for the reflective, though not of course for the determinant, judgment—to make us estimate man as not merely a physical end, such as all organized beings are, but as the being upon this earth who is the *ultimate end* of nature, and the one in relation to whom all other natural things constitute a system of ends.[1] What now is the end in man, and the end which, as such, is intended to be promoted by means of his connection with nature? If this end is something which must be found in man himself, it must either be of such a kind that man himself may be satisfied by means of nature and its beneficence, or else it is the aptitude and skill for all manner of ends for which he may employ nature both external and internal. The former end of nature would be the *happiness* of man, the latter his *culture*.

The conception of happiness is not one which man abstracts more or less from his instincts and so derives from his animal nature. It is, on the contrary, a mere *idea* of a state, and one to which he seeks to make his actual state of being adequate under purely empirical conditions—an impossible task. He projects this idea himself, and, thanks to his understanding and its complicated relations with imagination and sense, projects it in such different ways, and even alters his conception so often, that were nature a complete slave to his elective will, it would nevertheless be utterly unable to adopt any definite, universal, and fixed law by which to accommodate itself to this fluctuating conception and so bring itself into accord with the end that each individual arbitrarily sets before himself. But even if we sought to reduce this conception to the level of the true wants of nature in which our species is in complete and fundamental accord, or trying the other alternative, sought to increase to the highest level man's skill in compassing his imagined ends, nevertheless what man means by happiness, and what in fact constitutes his peculiar ultimate physical end, as opposed to the end of freedom, would never be attained by him. For his own nature is not so constituted as to rest or be satisfied in any possession or enjoyment whatever. Then external nature is far from having made a particular favourite of man or from having preferred him to all other animals as the object of its beneficence. For we see that in its destructive operations—plague, famine, flood, cold, attacks from animals great and small, and all such things—it has as little spared him as any other animal.

[1] [Cf. p. 554.]

But, besides all this, the discord of inner *natural tendencies* betrays him into further misfortunes of his own invention, and reduces other members of his species, through the oppression of lordly power, the barbarism of wars, and the like, to such misery, while he himself does all he can to work ruin to his race, that, even with the utmost goodwill on the part of external nature, its end, supposing it were directed to the happiness of our species, would never be attained in a system of terrestrial nature, because our own nature is not capable of it. Man, therefore, is ever but a link in the chain of physical ends. True, he is a principle in respect of many ends to which nature seems to have predetermined him, seeing that he makes himself so; but, nevertheless, he is also a means towards the preservation of the finality in the mechanism of the remaining members. As the single being upon earth that possesses understanding, and, consequently, a capacity for setting before himself ends of his deliberate choice, he is certainly titular lord of nature, and, supposing we regard nature as a teleological system, he is born to be its ultimate end. But this is always on the terms that he has the intelligence and the will to give to it and to himself such a reference to ends as can be self-sufficing independently of nature, and, consequently, a final end. Such an end, however, must not be sought in nature.

But, where in man, at any rate, are we to place this *ultimate end* of nature? To discover this we must seek out what nature can supply for the purpose of preparing him for what he himself must do in order to be a final end, and we must segregate it from all ends whose possibility rests upon conditions that man can only await at the hand of nature. Earthly happiness is an end of the latter kind. It is understood to mean the complex of all possible human ends attainable through nature, whether in man or external to him. In other words, it is the material substance of all his earthly ends and what, if he converts it into his entire end, renders him incapable of positing a final end for his own real existence and of harmonizing therewith. Therefore, of all his ends in nature, we are left only with a formal, subjective condition, that, namely, of the aptitude for setting ends before himself at all, and, independent of nature in his power of determining ends, of employing nature as a means in accordance with the maxims of his free ends generally. This alone remains as what nature can effect relative to the final end that lies outside it, and as what may therefore be regarded as its ultimate end. The production in a rational being of an aptitude for any ends whatever of his own choosing, consequently of the aptitude of a being in his freedom, is *culture*. Hence it is only culture that can be the ultimate end which we have cause to attribute to nature in respect of the human race. His individual happiness on earth and, we may say, the mere fact that he is the chief instrument for instituting order and harmony in irrational external nature, are ruled out.

But not every form of culture can fill the office of this ultimate end of nature. *Skill* is a culture that is certainly the principal subjective condition of the aptitude for the furthering of ends of all kinds, yet it is incompetent for giving assistance to the *will* in its determination and choice of its ends. But this is an essential factor, if an aptitude for ends is to have its full meaning. This latter condition of aptitude, involving what might be called *culture* by way of discipline, is negative. It consists in the liberation of the will from the despotism of desires whereby, in our attachment to certain natural things, we are rendered incapable of exercising a choice of our own. This happens when we allow ourselves to be enchained by impulses with which nature only provided us that they might serve as leading strings to prevent our neglecting, or even impairing, the animal element in our nature, while yet we are left free enough to tighten or slacken them, to lengthen or shorten them, as the ends of our reason dictate.

Skill can hardly be developed in the human race otherwise than by means of inequality among men. For the majority, in a mechanical kind of way that calls for no special art, provide the necessaries of life for the ease and convenience of others who apply themselves to the less necessary branches of culture in science and art. These keep the masses in a state of oppression, with hard work and little enjoyment, though in the course of time much of the culture of the higher classes spreads to them also. But with the advance of this culture—the culminating point of which, where devotion to what is superfluous begins to be prejudicial to what is indispensable, is called *luxury*—misfortunes increase equally on both sides. With the lower classes they arise by force of domination from without, with the upper from seeds of discontent within. Yet this splendid misery is connected with the development of natural tendencies in the human race, and the end pursued by nature itself, though it be not our end, is thereby attained. The formal condition under which nature can alone attain this, its real end, is the existence of a constitution so regulating the mutual relations of men that the abuse of freedom by individuals striving one against another is opposed by a lawful authority centred in a whole, called a *civil community*. For it is only in such a constitution that the greatest development of natural tendencies can take place. In addition to this, we should also need a *cosmopolitan* whole—had men but the ingenuity to discover such a constitution and the wisdom voluntarily to submit themselves to its constraint. It would be a system of all states that are in danger of acting injuriously to one another. In its absence, and with the obstacles that ambition, love of power, and avarice, especially on the part of those who hold the reins of authority, put in the way even of the possibility of such a scheme, *war* is inevitable. Sometimes this results in states splitting up and resolving themselves into lesser states, sometimes one state absorbs other smaller states and endeavours to build up a larger unit. But if on the part of men war is a thoughtless undertaking, being stirred up by unbridled passions, it is nevertheless a deep-seated, maybe far-seeing, attempt on the part of supreme wisdom, if not to found, yet to prepare the way for a rule of law governing the freedom of states, and thus bring about their unity in a system established on a moral basis. And, in spite of the terrible calamities which it inflicts on the human race, and the hardships, perhaps even greater, imposed by the constant preparation for it in time of peace, yet—as the prospect of the dawn of an abiding reign of national happiness keeps ever retreating farther into the distance—it is one further spur for developing to the highest pitch all talents that minister to culture.

We turn now to the discipline of inclinations. In respect of these our natural equipment is very purposively adapted to the performance of our essential functions as an animal species, but they are a great impediment to the development of our humanity. Yet here again, in respect of this second requisite for culture, we see nature striving on purposive lines to give us that education that opens the door to higher ends than it can itself afford. The preponderance of evil which a taste refined to the extreme of idealization, and which even luxury in the sciences, considered as food for vanity, diffuses among us as the result of the crowd of insatiable inclinations which they beget, is indisputable. But, while that is so, we cannot fail to recognize the end of nature—ever more and more to prevail over the rudeness and violence of inclinations that belong more to the animal part of our nature and are most inimical to education that would fit us for our higher vocation (inclinations towards enjoyment), and to make way for the development of our humanity. Fine art and the sciences, if they do not make man morally better, yet, by conveying a pleasure that admits of universal communication and by introducing polish and refinement into society, make him civilized. Thus they do much to overcome the tyrannical propensities of sense, and so prepare man for a sovereignty in which reason alone shall have sway. Meanwhile the evils visited upon us, now by nature, now by the truculent egoism of man, evoke the energies of the soul, and give it strength and courage to submit to no such force, and at the same time quicken in us a sense that in the depths of our nature there is an aptitude for higher ends.[1]

§ 84. *The final end of the existence of a world, that is, of creation itself*

A *final end* is an end that does not require any other end as condition of its possibility.

If the simple mechanism of nature is accepted as the explanation of its finality, it is not open to us to ask: For what end do the things in the world exist? For, on such an idealistic system, we have only to reckon with the physical possibility of things—and things that it would be mere empty sophistry to imagine as ends.[2] Whether we refer this form of things to chance, or whether we refer it to blind necessity, such a question would in either case be meaningless. But if we suppose the final nexus in the world to be real, and assume a special type of causality for it, namely the activity of a cause *acting designedly*, we cannot then stop short at the question: What is the end for which things in the world, namely organized beings, possess this or that form, or are placed by nature in this or that relation to other things? On the contrary, once we have conceived an understanding that must be regarded as the cause of the possibility of such forms as they are actually found in things, we must go on and seek in this understanding for an objective ground capable of determining such productive understanding to the production of an effect of this kind. That ground is then the final end for which such things exist.

I have said before that the final end is not an end which nature would be competent to realize or produce in terms of its idea, because it is one that is unconditioned. For in nature, as a thing of sense, there is nothing whose determining ground, discoverable in nature itself, is not always in turn conditioned. This is not merely true of external or material nature, but also of internal or thinking nature—it being of course understood that I am only considering what in us is strictly nature. But a thing which by virtue of its objective characterization is to exist necessarily as the final end of an intelligent cause, must be of such a kind that in the order of ends it is dependent upon no further or other condition than simply its idea.

Now we have in the world beings of but one kind whose causality is teleological, or directed to ends, and which at the same time are beings of such a character that the law according to which they have to determine ends for themselves is represented by them themselves as unconditioned and not dependent on anything in nature, but as necessary in itself. The being of this kind is man, but man regarded as noumenon. He is the only natural creature whose peculiar objective characterization is nevertheless such as to enable us to recognize in him a supersensible faculty—his *freedom*—and to perceive both the law of the causality and the object of freedom which that faculty is able to set before itself as the highest end—the supreme good in the world.

Now it is not open to use in the case of man, considered as a moral agent, or similarly in the case of any rational being in the world, to ask the further question: For what end (*quem in finem*) does he exist? His existence inherently involves the highest end—the end to which, as far as in him lies, he may subject the whole of nature, or contrary to which at least he must not deem himself subjected to any influence on its part. Now assuming that things in the world

[1] The value of life for us, measured simply by *what we enjoy* (by the natural end of the sum of all our inclinations, that is by happiness), is easy to decide. It is less than nothing. For who would enter life afresh under the same conditions? Who would even do so according to a new, self-devised plan (which should, however, follow the course of nature), if it also were merely directed to enjoyment? We have shown above what value life receives from what it involves when lived according to the end with which nature is occupied in us, and which consists in *what we do,* not merely what we enjoy, we being, however, in that case always but a means to an undetermined final end. There remains then nothing but the worth which we ourselves assign to our life by what we not alone do, but do with a view to an end so independent of nature that the very existence of nature itself can only be an end subject to the condition so imposed.

[2] [Cf. p. 565.]

are beings that are dependent in point of their real existence, and, as such, stand in need of a supreme cause acting according to ends, then man is the final end of creation. For, without man, the chain of mutually subordinated ends would have no ultimate point of attachment.[1] Only in man, and only in him as the individual being to whom the moral law applies, do we find unconditional legislation in respect of ends. This legislation, therefore, is what alone qualifies him to be a final end to which entire nature is teleologically subordinated.[2]

§ 85. *Physico-Theology*

Physico-theology is the attempt on the part of reason to infer the supreme cause of nature and its attributes from the *ends* of nature—ends which can only be known empirically. A *moral theology,* or ethico-theology, would be the attempt to infer that cause and its attributes from the moral end of rational beings in nature—an end which can be known *a priori.*

The former naturally precedes the latter. For if we seek to infer a world-cause from the things in the world by *teleological* arguments, we must first of all be given ends of nature. Then, for these ends so given, we must afterwards look for a final end, and this final end obliges us to seek the principle of the causality of the supreme cause in question.

Much natural research can, and indeed must, be conducted in the light of the teleological principle without our having occasion to inquire into the source of the possibility of the final action which we meet with in various products of nature. But should we now desire to have also a conception of this source, we are then in the position of having absolutely no available insight that can penetrate beyond our mere maxim of reflective judgement. According to this maxim, given but a single organized product of nature, then the structure of our cognitive faculty is such that the only source which we can conceive it to have is one that is a cause of nature itself—be it of entire nature or even only of this particular portion of it—and that derives from an understanding the requisite causality for such a product. This is a critical principle which doubtless brings us no whit farther in the explanation of natural things or their origin. Yet it discloses to our view a prospect that extends beyond the horizon of nature and points to our being able perhaps to determine more closely the conception of an original being otherwise so unfruitful.

Now I say that, no matter how far physico-teleology may be pushed, it can never disclose to us anything about a *final end* of creation; for it never even begins to look for a final end. Thus it can justify, no doubt, the conception of an intelligent world-cause as a conception which subjectively—that is in relation to the nature of our cognitive faculty alone—is effective to explain the possibility of things that we can render intelligible to ourselves in the light of ends. But neither from a theoretical nor a practical point of view can it determine this conception any farther. Its attempt falls short of its proposed aim of affording a basis of theology. To the last, it remains nothing but a physical teleology: for the final nexus which it recognizes is only, and must only, be regarded as subject to natural conditions. Consequently it can never institute an inquiry into the end for which nature itself exists—this being an end whose source must be sought outside nature. Yet it is upon the definite idea of this end that the definite conception of such a supreme intelligent World-Cause, and, consequently, the possibility of a theology, depend.

Of what use are the things in the world to one another? What good is the manifold in a thing to this thing? How are we entitled to assume that nothing in the world is in vain, but that,

[1] [Cf. pp. 559, 590, 591.]

[2] It would be possible for the happiness of the rational beings in the world to be an end of nature, and, were it so, it would also be the *ultimate* end of nature. At least it is not obvious *a priori* why nature should not be so ordered, for, so far as we can see, happiness is an effect which it would be quite possible for nature to produce by means of its mechanism. But morality, or a causality according to ends that is subordinate to morality, is an absolutely impossible result of natural causes. For the principle that determines such causality to action is supersensible. In the order of ends, therefore, it is the sole principle possible which is absolutely unconditioned in respect of nature, and it is what alone qualifies the subject of such causality to be the *final end* of creation, and the one to which entire nature is subordinated. *Happiness,* on the other hand, as an appeal to the testimony of experience showed in the preceding section, so far from being a *final end of creation,* is not even an *end of nature* as regards man in preference to other creatures. It may ever be that individual men will make it their ultimate subjective end. But if, seeking for the final end of creation, I ask: "For what end was it necessary that men should exist?" my question then refers to an objective supreme end, such as the highest reason would demand for their creation. If, then, to this question we reply: "So that beings may exist upon whom that supreme Cause may exercise this beneficence," we then belie the condition to which the reason of man subjects, even his own inmost wish for happiness, namely, harmony with his own inner moral legislation. This proves that happiness can only be a conditional end, and, therefore, that it is only as a moral being that man can be the final end of creation; while, as regards his state of being, happiness is only incident thereto as a consequence proportionate to the measure of his harmony with that end, as the end of his existence.

provided we grant that certain things, regarded as ends, ought to exist, everything serves some purpose or other *in nature*? All these questions imply that, in respect of our judgement, reason has at its command no other principle of the possibility of the object which it is obliged to estimate teleologically than that of subordinating the mechanism of nature to the architectonic of an intelligent Author of the world; and directed to all these issues the teleological survey of the world plays its part nobly and fills us with intense admiration. But inasmuch as the data, and, consequently, the principles, for determining such a conception of an intelligent World-Cause, regarded as the supreme Artist, are merely empirical, they do not allow us to infer any other attributes belonging to it than those which experience reveals to us as manifested in its operations. But as experience is unable to embrace aggregate nature as a system, it must frequently find support for arguments which, to all appearances, conflict with that conception and with one another. Yet it can never lift us above nature to the end of its real existence or thus raise us to a definite conception of such a higher intelligence—not though it were in our power empirically to review the entire system in its purely physical aspect.

If the problem which physico-theology has to solve is set to a lower key, then its solution seems an easy matter. Thus we may think of an intelligent being possessing a number of superlative attributes, without the full complement of those necessary for establishing a nature harmonizing with the greatest possible end, and to all beings of this description—of whom there may be one or more—we might be extravagant enough to apply the conception of a *Deity*. Or, if we let it pass as of no importance to supplement by arbitrary additions the proofs of a theory where the grounds of proof are deficient; and if, therefore, where we have only reason to assume *much* perfection (and what, pray, is much for us?) we deem ourselves entitled to take *all possible* perfection for granted: then physical teleology has important claims to the distinction of affording the basis of a theology. But what is there to lead and, more than that, authorize us to supplement the facts of the case in this way? If we are called on to point out what it is, we shall seek in vain for any ground of justification in the principles of the theoretical employment of reason. For such employment emphatically demands that, for the purpose of explaining an object of experience, we are not to ascribe to it more attributes than we find in the empirical data for the possibility of the object. On closer investigation, we should see that underlying our procedure is an idea of a Supreme Being, which rests on an entirely different employment of reason, namely, its practical employment, and that it is this idea, which exists in us *a priori*, that impels us to supplement the defective representation of an original ground of the ends in nature afforded by physical teleology, and enlarge it to the conception of a Deity. When we saw this, we should not erroneously imagine that we had evolved this idea, and, with it, a theology by means of the theoretical employment of reason in the physical cognition of the world—much less that we had proved its reality.

One cannot blame the ancients so very much for imagining that, while there was great diversity among their gods, both in respect of their power and of their purposes and dispositions, they were all, not excepting the sovereign head of the gods himself, invariably limited in human fashion. For, on surveying the order and course of the things in nature, they certainly found ample reason for assuming something more than mere mechanism as its cause and for conjecturing the existence of purposes on the part of certain higher causes, which they could only conceive to be superhuman, behind the machinery of this world. But, since they encountered both the good and evil, the final and the contra-final, very much interspersed, at least to human eyes, and could not take the liberty of assuming, for the sake of the arbitrary idea of an all-perfect author, that there were nevertheless mysteriously wise and beneficent ends, of which they did not see the evidence, underlying all this apparent antagonism, their judgement on the supreme world-cause could hardly be other than it was, so long, that is, as they followed maxims of the mere theoretical employment of reason with strict consistency. Others who were physicists and in that character desired to be theologians also, thought that they would give full satisfaction to reason by providing for the absolute unity of the principle of natural things, which reason demands, by means of the idea of a being in which, as sole substance, the whole assemblage of those natural things would be contained only as inhering modes. While this substance would not be the cause of the world by virtue of its intelligence, it would nevertheless be a subject in which all the intelligence on the part of the beings in the world would reside. Hence, although it would not be a being that produced anything according to ends, it would be one in which all things—owing to the unity of the subject of which they are mere determinations—must necessarily be interconnected in a final manner, though apart from end or design. Thus they introduced the idealism of final Causes, by converting the unity, so difficult to deduce, of a number of substances standing in a final connection, from a causal dependence *on one* substance into the unity of inherence *in one*. Looked at from the side of the beings that inhere, this system became *pantheism*, and from the side of the sole subsisting subject, as original being, it became, by a later development, *Spinozism*. Thus in the end, instead of solving the problem of the primary source of the finality of nature, it represented the whole question as idle, for the conception of such finality, being shorn of all reality, was reduced to a simple misinterpretation of the universal ontological conception of a thing in the abstract.[1]

So we see that the conception of a Deity, such as would meet the demands of our teleological estimate of nature, can never be evolved according to mere theoretical principles of the employment of reason—and these are the only principles upon which physico-theology relies. For, suppose we assert that all teleology is a delusion on the part of judgement in its estimate of the causal nexus of things and take refuge in the sole principle of a mere mechanism of nature. Then nature only appears to us to involve a universal relation to ends, owing to the unity of the substance that contains it as no more than the multiplicity of its modes. Or, suppose that instead of adopting this idealism of final causes, we wish to adhere to the principle of the realism of this particular type of causality. Then—no matter whether we base natural ends on a number of intelligent original beings or on a single one—the moment we find ourselves with nothing upon which to found the conception of realism but empirical principles drawn from the actual nexus of ends in the world, on the one hand we cannot help accepting the fact of the discordance with final unity of which nature presents many examples, and, on the other hand, we can never obtain a sufficiently definite conception of a single intelligent Cause—so long as we keep to what mere experience entitles us to extract—to satisfy any sort of theology whatever which will be of use theoretically or practically.

It is true that physical teleology urges us to go in quest of a theology. But it cannot produce one—however far we carry our investigations of nature, or help out the nexus of ends discovered in it with ideas of reason (which for physical problems must be theoretical). We may pose the reasonable question: What is the use of our basing all these arrangements on a great, and for us unfathomable, intelligence, and supposing it to order this world according to purposes, if nature does not and cannot ever tell us anything as to the final purpose in view? For apart from a final purpose we are unable to relate all these natural ends to a common point, or form an adequate teleological principle, be it for combining all the ends in a known system, or be it for framing such a conception of the supreme Intelligence, as cause of a nature like this, as could act as a standard for our judgement in its teleological reflection upon nature. I should have, it is true, in that case an *art intelligence* for miscellaneous ends, but no *wisdom* for a final end, which nevertheless is what must, properly speaking, contain the ground by which such intelligence is determined. I require a final end, and it is only pure reason that *a priori* can supply this—for all ends in the world are empirically conditioned and can contain nothing that is absolutely good, but only what is good for this or that purpose regarded as contingent. Such a final end alone would instruct me how I am to conceive the supreme cause of nature—what attributes I am to assign to it, and in what degree, and how I am to conceive its relation to nature—if I am to estimate nature as a teleological system. In the absence, then, of a final end, what liberty or what authority have I to extend at will such a very limited conception of that original intelligence as I can base on my own poor knowledge of the world, or my conception of the power of this original being to realize its ideas, or of its will to do so, etc., and expand it to the idea of an allwise and infinite Being? Were I able to do this theoretically it would presuppose omniscience in myself to enable me to see into the ends of nature in their entire context, and in addition to conceive all other possible schemes, as compared with which the present would have to be estimated on reasonable grounds to be the best. For without this perfected knowledge of the effect, my reasoning can arrive at no definite conception of the supreme cause—which is only to be found in that of an intelligence in every respect infinite, that is, in the conception of a Deity—or establish a basis for theology.

Hence, allowing for all possible extension of physical teleology, we may keep to the principle set out above and say that the constitution and

[1] [Cf. p. 566.]

principles of our cognitive faculty are such that we can only conceive nature, in respect of those of its adjustments that are familiar to us and display finality, as the product of an intelligence to which it is subjected. But whether this intelligence may also have had a final purpose in view in the production of nature and in its constitution as a whole, which final purpose in that case would not reside in nature as the world of sense, is a matter that the theoretical study of nature can never disclose. On the contrary, however great our knowledge of nature, it remains an open question whether that supreme cause is the original source of nature as a cause acting throughout according to a final end, or whether it is not rather such a source by virtue of an intelligence that is determined by the simple necessity of its nature to the production of certain forms (by analogy to what we call the artistic instinct in the lower animals). The latter version does not involve our ascribing even wisdom to such intelligence, much less wisdom that is supreme and conjoined with all other properties requisite for ensuring the perfection of its product.

Hence physico-theology is a physical teleology misunderstood. It is of no use to theology except as a preparation or propaedeutic, and is only sufficient for this purpose when supplemented by a further principle on what it can rely. But it is not, as its name would suggest, sufficient, even as a propaedeutic, if taken by itself.

§ 86. *Ethico-Theology*

THERE is a judgement which even the commonest understanding finds irresistible when it reflects upon the existence of the things in the world and the real existence of the world itself. It is the verdict that all the manifold forms of life, co-ordinated though they may be with the greatest art and concatenated with the utmost variety of final adaptations, and even the entire complex that embraces their numerous systems, incorrectly called *worlds,* would all exist for nothing, if man, or rational beings of some sort, were not to be found in their midst. Without man, in other words, the whole of creation would be a mere wilderness, a thing in vain, and have no final end. Yet it is not man's cognitive faculty, that is, theoretical reason, that forms the point of reference which alone gives its worth to the existence of all else in the world—as if the meaning of his presence in the world was that there might be some one in it that could make it an object of *contemplation.*[1] For if this contemplation of the world brought to light nothing but things without a final end, the existence of the world could not acquire a worth from the fact of its being known. A final end of the world must be presupposed as that in relation to which the contemplation of the world may itself possess a worth. Neither is it in relation to the feeling of pleasure or the sum of such feelings that we can think that there is a given final end of creation, that is to say, it is not by well-being, not by enjoyment, whether bodily or mental, not, in a word, by happiness, that we value that absolute worth. For the fact that man, when he does exist, makes happiness his own final purpose, affords us no conception of any reason why he should exist at all, or of any worth he himself possesses, for which his real existence should be made agreeable to him. Hence man must already be presupposed to be the final end of creation, in order that we may have a rational ground to explain why nature, when regarded as an absolute whole according to principles of ends, must be in accord with the conditions of his happiness. Accordingly, it is only the faculty of desire that can give the required point of reference—yet not that faculty which makes man dependent upon nature (through impulses of sense), that is, not that in respect of which the worth of his existence is dependent upon what he receives and enjoys. On the contrary, it is the worth which he alone can give to himself, and which consists in what he does—in the manner in which and the principles upon which he acts in the *freedom* of his faculty of desire, and not as a link in the chain of nature. In other words, a good will is that whereby man's existence can alone possess an absolute worth, and in relation to which the existence of the world can have a *final end.*

Even the popular verdict of sound human reason, once its reflection is directed to this question and pressed to its consideration, is in complete accord with the judgement that it is only as a moral being that man can be a final end of creation. What, it will be said, does it all avail, that this man has so much talent, that he is even so active in its employment and thus exerts a useful influence upon social and public life, and that he possesses, therefore, considerable worth alike in relation to his own state of happiness and in relation to what is good for others, if he has not a good will? Looked at from the point of view of his inner self, he is a contemptible object; and, if creation is not to be altogether devoid of a final end, such a man, though as man he is part of creation, must nev-

[1] [Cf. p. 609.]

ertheless, as a bad man dwelling in a world subject to moral laws, forfeit, in accordance with those laws, his own subjective end, that is happiness, as the sole condition under which his real existence can consist with the final end.

Now if we find instances in the world of an order adapted to ends, and if, as reason inevitably requires, we subordinate the ends which are only conditionally ends to one that is unconditioned and supreme, that is to a final end, we readily see, to begin with, that we are not dealing with an end of nature, included in nature taken as existent, but with the end of the real existence of nature, with all its orderly adaptations included. Consequently we see that the question is one of the ultimate *end of creation,* and, more precisely, of the supreme condition under which alone there can be a final end, or, in other words, of the ground that determines a highest intelligence to the production of the beings in the world.

It is, then, only as a moral being that we acknowledge man to be the end of creation. Hence we have, first of all, a reason, or at least the primary condition, for regarding the world as a consistent whole of interconnected ends, and as a *system* of final causes. Now the structure of our reason is such that we necessarily refer natural ends to an intelligent world-cause. Above all, then, we have *one principle* applicable to this relation, enabling us to think the nature and attributes of this first cause considered as supreme ground in the kingdom of ends, and to form a definite conception of it. This is what could not be done by physical teleology, which was only able to suggest vague conceptions of such a ground—conceptions which this vagueness made as useless for practical as for theoretical employment.

With such a definite principle as this, of the causality of the original being, we shall not have to regard it merely as an intelligence and as legislating for nature, but as the Sovereign Head legislating in a moral Kingdom of Ends. In relation to the *summum bonum,* which is alone possible under His sovereignty, namely the real existence of rational beings under moral laws, we shall conceive this Original Being to be *omniscient,* so that even our inmost sentiments—wherein lies the distinctive moral worth in the actions of rational beings in the world—may not be hid from Him. We shall conceive Him as *omnipotent,* so that He may be able to adapt entire nature to this highest end; as both *all-good* and *just,* since these two attributes, which unite to form *wisdom,* constitute the conditions under which a supreme cause of the world can be the source of the greatest good under moral laws. Similarly the other remaining transcendental attributes, such as *eternity, omnipresence,* and so forth (for goodness and justice are moral attributes), all attributes that are presupposed in relation to such a final end, will have to be regarded as belonging to this Original Being. In this way, *moral* teleology supplements the deficiency of *physical* teleology, and for the first time establishes a *theology.* For physical teleology, if it is not to borrow secretly from moral teleology, but is to proceed with strict logical rigour, can from its own unaided resources establish nothing but a demonology, which does not admit of any definite conception.

But the principle which, because of the moral and teleological significance of certain beings in the world, refers the world to a Supreme Cause as Deity, does not establish this relation by being simply a completion of the physico-teleological argument, and therefore by adopting this necessarily as its foundation. On the contrary, it can rely on *its own* resources and urges attention to the ends of nature and inquiry after the incomprehensibly great art that lies hidden behind its forms, so as to give to the ideas produced by pure practical reason an incidental confirmation in physical ends. For the conception of beings of the world subject to moral laws is an *a priori* principle upon which man must necessarily estimate himself. Furthermore, if there is a world-cause acting designedly and directed to an end, the moral relation above mentioned must just as necessarily be the condition of the possibility of a creation as is the relation determined by physical laws—that is, supposing that such an intelligent cause has also a final end. This is a principle which reason regards even *a priori* as one that is necessary for its teleological estimate of the real existence of things. The whole question, then, is reduced to this: Have we any ground capable of satisfying reason, speculative or practical, to justify our attributing a *final end* to the supreme cause that acts according to ends? For that, judging by the subjective frame of our reason, or even by aught we can at all imagine of the reason of other beings, such final end could be nothing but *man as subject to moral laws,* may be taken *a priori* as a matter of certainty; whereas we are wholly unable to cognize *a priori* what are the ends of nature in the physical order, and above all it is impossible to see that a nature could not exist apart from such ends.

Remark

Imagine a man at the moment when his mind is disposed to moral feeling! If, amid beautiful natural surroundings, he is in calm and serene enjoyment of his existence, he feels within him a need—a need of being grateful for it to some one. Or, at another time, in the same frame of mind, he may find himself in the stress of duties which he can only perform and will perform by submitting to a voluntary sacrifice; then he feels within him a need—a need of having, in so doing, carried out some command and obeyed a Supreme Lord. Or he may in some thoughtless manner have diverged from the path of duty, though not so as to have made himself answerable to man; yet words of stern self-reproach will then fall upon an inward ear, and he will seem to hear the voice of a judge to whom he has to render account. In a word, he needs a moral intelligence; because he exists for an end, and this end demands a Being that has formed both him and the world with that end in view. It is waste of labour to go burrowing behind these feelings for motives; for they are immediately connected with the purest moral sentiment: *gratitude, obedience,* and *humiliation*—that is, submission before a deserved chastisement—being special modes of a mental disposition towards duty. It is merely that the mind inclined to give expansion to its moral sentiment here voluntarily imagines an object that is not in the world, in order, if possible, to prove its dutifulness in the eyes of such an object also. Hence it is at least possible—and, besides, there is in our moral habits of thought a foundation for so doing—to form a representation depicting a pure moral need for the real existence of a Being, whereby our morality gains in strength or even obtains—at least on the side of our representation—an extension of area, that is to say, is given a new object for its exercise. In other words, it is possible to admit a moral Legislator existing apart from the world, and to do so without regard to the theoretical proof, and still less to self-interest, but on a purely moral ground, which, while of course only subjective, is free from all foreign influence, on the mere recommendation of a pure practical reason that legislates for itself alone. It may be that such a disposition of the mind is but a rare occurrence, or, again, does not last long, but rather is fleeting and of no permanent effect, or, it may be, passes away without the mind bestowing a single thought upon the object so shadowed forth, and without troubling to reduce it to clear conceptions. Yet the source of this disposition is unmistakable. It is the original moral bent of our nature, as a subjective principle, that will not let us be satisfied, in our review of the world, with the finality which it derives through natural causes, but leads us to introduce into it an underlying supreme Cause governing nature according to moral laws. In addition to the above, there is the fact that we feel ourselves urged by the moral law to strive after a universal highest end, while yet we feel ourselves, and all nature too, incapable of its attainment. Further, it is only so far as we strive after this end that we can judge ourselves to be in harmony with the final end of an intelligent world-cause—if such there be. Thus we have a pure moral ground derived from practical reason for admitting this Cause (since we may do so without self-contradiction), if for no better reason, in order that we may not run the risk of regarding such striving as quite idle in its effects, and of allowing it to flag in consequence.

Let us restate what we intended to convey here by all these remarks. While *fear* doubtless in the first instance may have been able to produce *gods,* that is demons, it is only *reason* by its moral principles that has been able to produce the conception of *God*—and it has been able to do so despite the great ignorance that has prevailed in what concerns the teleology of nature, or the considerable doubt that arises from the difficulty of reconciling by a sufficiently established principle the mutually conflicting phenomena that nature presents. Further, the inner *moral* destination of man's existence supplements the shortcomings of natural knowledge, by directing us to join to the thought of the final end of the existence of all things—an end the principle of which only satisfies reason from an *ethical* point of view—the thought of the supreme cause as endowed with attributes whereby it is empowered to subject entire nature to that single purpose, and make it merely instrumental thereto. In other words it directs us to think the supreme cause as a *Deity.*

§ 87. *The moral proof of the existence of God*

We have a *physical teleology* that affords evidence sufficient for our theoretical reflective judgement to enable us to admit the existence of an intelligent world-cause. But in ourselves, and still more in the general conception of a rational being endowed with freedom of its causality, we find a *moral teleology.* But as our own relation to an end, together with the law governing it, may be determined *a priori,* and consequently cognized as necessary, moral teleology does not stand in need of any intelligent cause outside ourselves to explain this intrinsic conformity to law any more than what we consider final in the geometrical properties of figures (their adaptation for all possible kinds of employment by art) lets us look beyond to a supreme understanding that imparts this finality to them. But this moral teleology deals with us for all that as beings of the world and, therefore, as beings associated with other things in the world; and the same moral laws enjoin us to turn our consideration to these other things in the world, regarded either as ends, or as objects in respect of which we ourselves are the final end. This moral teleology, then, which deals with the relation of our own causality to ends, or even to a final end that must be proposed by us in the world, as well as with the reciprocal relation subsisting between the world and that moral end and the possibility of realizing it under external conditions—a matter upon which no physical teleology can give us any guidance—raises a necessary question. For we must ask: Does this moral teleology oblige our rational critical judgement to go beyond the world and seek for an intelligent supreme principle in respect of the relation of nature to the moral side of our being, so that we may form a representation of nature as displaying finality in relation also to our inner moral legislation and its possible realization? Hence there is certainly a moral teleology. It is as necessarily implicated with the *nomothetic* of freedom on the one hand, and that of nature on the other, as with civil legislation is implicated the question of where the executive authority is to be sought. In fact there is here the same implication as is to be found in everything in which reason has to assign a principle of the actuality of a certain uniform order of things that is only possible according to ideas. We shall begin by exhibiting how, from the above moral teleology and its relation to physical teleology, reason advances to *theology.* Having done so, we shall make some observations on the possibility and conclusiveness of this mode of reasoning.

If we assume the existence of certain things, or even only of certain forms of things, to be contingent, and consequently to be only possible by means of something else as their cause, we may then look for the supreme source of this causality, and, therefore, for the unconditioned ground of the conditioned, either in the physical or the teleological order—that is, we may look either to the *nexus effectivus* or to the *nexus finalis.* In other words, we may ask which is the supreme efficient cause, or we may ask what is the supreme or absolutely unconditioned end of such cause, that is, what in general is the final end for which it produces these or all its products. In the latter question, it is obviously taken for granted that this cause can form a representation of the end, and is consequently an intelligent being, or at least that it must be conceived by us as acting according to the laws of such a being.

Now, supposing we follow the teleological order, there is a *fundamental principle* to which even the most ordinary human intelligence is obliged to give immediate assent. It is the principle that if there is to be a *final end* at all, which reason must assign *a priori,* then it can only be *man*—or any rational being in the world—*subject to moral laws.*[1] For—and this is the verdict of everyone—if the world only consisted of lifeless beings, or even consisted partly of living, but yet irrational beings, the existence of such a world would have no worth whatever, because there would exist in it no being with the least conception of what worth is. On the other hand, if there were even rational beings,

[1] I say deliberately: *under* moral laws. It is not man *in accordance* with moral laws, that is to say, human beings living in conformity with such laws, that is the final end of creation. For to use the latter expression would be to assert more than we know, namely, that it is in the power of an author of the world to ensure that man should always conform to the moral laws. But this presupposes a conception of freedom and of nature—of which latter alone we can think an external author—that implies an insight into the supersensible substrate of nature and its identity with what is rendered possible in the world by causality through freedom. Such insight far exceeds that of our reason. It is only of *man under moral laws* that we are able to affirm, without transcending the limits of our insight, that his existence forms the final end of the world. This statement also accords perfectly with the verdict of human reason in its reflection upon the course of the world from a moral standpoint. We believe that even in the case of the wicked we perceive the traces of a wise design in things, if we see that the wanton criminal does not die before he has suffered the just punishment of his misdeeds. According to our conceptions of free causality, good or bad conduct depends upon ourselves. But where we think that the supreme wisdom in the government of the world lies, is in the fact that the occasion for the former, and the result following from both, is ordained according to moral laws. In the latter consists, properly speaking, the glory of God, which is therefore not inappropriately termed by theologians the *ultimate end* of creation. We should add that when we make use of the word *creation,* we only take it to mean what is spoken of here, namely, the cause of the *existence of a world,* or of the things in it, that is, substances. This is also what the strict meaning of the word conveys—*actuatio substantiae est creatio.* Consequently it implies no assumption of a cause that acts freely and that is therefore intelligent. The existence of such an intelligent cause is what we are set upon proving.

and if nevertheless their reason were only able to set the worth of the existence of things in the bearing which nature has upon them, that is, in their well-being, instead of being able to procure such a worth for themselves from original sources, that is, in their freedom, then there would be, it is true, relative ends in the world, but no absolute end, since the existence of rational beings of this kind would still always remain devoid of an end. It is, however, a distinctive feature of the moral laws that they prescribe something for reason in the form of an end apart from any condition and, consequently, in the very form that the conception of a final end requires. Therefore the real existence of a reason like this, that in the order of ends can be the supreme law to itself, in other words, the real existence of rational beings subject to moral laws, can alone be regarded as the final end of the existence of a world. But if this is not so, then either no end whatsoever in the cause underlies the existence of the world, or else only ends without a final end.

The moral law is the formal rational condition of the employment of our freedom, and, as such, of itself alone lays its obligation upon us, independently of any end as its material condition. But it also defines for us a final end, and does so *a priori*, and makes it obligatory upon us to strive towards its attainment. This end is the *summum bonum*, as the highest good *in the world* possible through freedom.

The subjective condition under which man, and, as far as we can at all conceive, every rational finite being also, is able under the above law to set before himself a final end, is happiness. Consequently the highest possible physical good in the world, and the one to be furthered so far as in us lies as the final end, is *happiness* —subject to the objective condition that the individual harmonizes with the law of *morality*, regarded as worthiness to be happy.

But by no faculty of our reason can we represent to ourselves these two requisites for the final end proposed to us by the moral law to be *conjoined* by means of mere natural causes and also conformed to the idea of the final end in contemplation. Accordingly, if we do not bring the causality of any other means besides nature into alliance with our freedom, the conception of the *practical necessity* of such an end through the application of our powers does not accord with the theoretical conception of *physical possibility* of its effectuation.

Consequently we must assume a moral world-cause, that is, an Author of the world, if we are to set before ourselves a final end in conformity with the requirements of the moral law. And as far as it is necessary to set such an end before us, so far, that is in the same degree and upon the same ground, it is necessary to assume an Author of the world, or, in other words, that there is a God.[1]

This proof, to which we may easily give the form of logical precision, does not imply that it is as necessary to assume the existence of God as it is to recognize the validity of the moral law, and that, consequently, one who is unable to convince himself of the former may deem himself absolved from the obligations imposed by the latter. No! all that must be abandoned in that case is the *premeditation* of the final end in the world to be effectuated by the pursuit of the moral law, that is, the premeditation of a happiness of rational beings harmoniously associated with such pursuit, as the highest good in the world. Every rational being would have to continue to recognize himself as firmly bound by the precept of morals, for their laws are formal and command unconditionally, paying no regard to ends (as the subject-matter of volition). But the one requirement of the final end, as prescribed by practical reason to the beings of the world, is an irresistible end planted in them by their nature as finite beings. Reason refuses to countenance this end except as subject to the moral law *as* inviolable *condition*, and would only have it made universal in accordance with this condition. Thus it makes the furtherance of happiness, in agreement with morality, the final end. To promote this end—so far, in respect of happiness, as lies in our power—is commanded us by the moral law, whatever the outcome of this endeavour may be. The fulfilment of duty consists in the form of the earnest will, not in the intervening causes that contribute to success.

Suppose, then, that a man, influenced partly by the weakness of all the speculative arguments that are thought so much of, and partly by the number of irregularities he finds in nature and the moral world, becomes persuaded of the prop-

[1] This moral argument is not intended to supply an *objectively* valid proof of the existence of God. It is not meant to demonstrate to the sceptic that there is a God, but that he *must adopt* the assumption of this proposition as a maxim of his practical reason, if he wishes to think in a manner consistent with morality. Further, the argument is not intended to affirm that it is necessary *for the purpose of morality* to assume that the happiness of all rational beings in the world is proportioned to their morality. On the contrary it is *by virtue of morality* that the assumption is necessitated. Consequently it is an argument that is sufficient *subjectively* and for moral persons.

osition: "There is no God"; nevertheless in his own eyes he would be a worthless creature if he chose on that account to regard the laws of duty as simply fanciful, invalid, and inobligatory, and resolved boldly to transgress them. Again, let us suppose that such a man were able subsequently to convince himself of the truth of what he had at first doubted; he would still remain worthless if he held to the above way of thinking. This is so, were he even to fulfil his duty as punctiliously as could be desired, so far as actual actions are concerned, but were to do so from fear or with a view to reward, and without an inward reverence for duty. Conversely, if, as a believer in God, he observes his duty according to his conscience, uprightly and disinterestedly, yet if whenever, to try himself, he puts before himself the case of his haply being able to convince himself that there is no God, he straightway believes himself free from all moral obligation, the state of his inner moral disposition could then only be bad.

Let us then, as we may, take the case of a righteous man, such, say, as Spinoza, who considers himself firmly persuaded that there is no God and—since in respect of the object of morality a similar result ensues—no future life either. How will he estimate his individual intrinsic finality that is derived from the moral law which he reveres in practice? He does not require that its pursuit should bring him any personal benefit either in this or any other world. On the contrary, his will is disinterestedly to establish only that good to which the holy law directs all his energies. But he is circumscribed in his endeavour. He may, it is true, expect to find a chance concurrence now and again, but he can never expect to find in nature a uniform agreement—a consistent agreement according to fixed rules, answering to what his maxims are and must be subjectively, with that end which yet he feels himself obliged and urged to realize. Deceit, violence, and envy will always be rife around him, although he himself is honest, peaceable, and benevolent; and the other righteous men that he meets in the world, no matter how deserving they may be of happiness, will be subjected by nature, which takes no heed of such deserts, to all the evils of want, disease, and untimely death, just as are the other animals on the earth. And so it will continue to be until one wide grave engulfs them all—just and unjust, there is no distinction in the grave—and hurls them back into the abyss of the aimless chaos of matter from which they were taken—they that were able to believe themselves the final end of creation. Thus the end which this right-minded man would have, and ought to have, in view in his pursuit of the moral law, would certainly have to be abandoned by him as impossible. But perhaps he resolves to remain faithful to the call of his inner moral vocation and would fain not let the respect with which he is immediately inspired to obedience by the moral law be weakened owing to the nullity of the one ideal final end that answers to its high demand—which could not happen without doing injury to moral sentiment. If so, he must assume the existence of a *moral* author of the world, that is, of a God. As this assumption at least involves nothing intrinsically self-contradictory he may quite readily make it from a practical point of view, that is to say, at least for the purpose of framing a conception of the possibility of the final end morally prescribed to him.

§ 88. *Limitation of the validity of the moral proof*

PURE reason, regarded as a practical faculty, a capacity, that is to say, for determining the pure employment of our causality by means of ideas, or pure rational conceptions, not alone possesses in its moral law a principle which is regulative of our actions, but by virtue of that law it furnishes at the same time an additional principle which, from a subjective point of view, is constitutive. This principle is contained in the conception of an object which reason alone is able to think, and which is meant to be realized in the world through our actions in conformity to that law. The idea of a final end in the employment of freedom in obedience to moral laws has, therefore, a reality that is subjectively *practical*. We are determined *a priori* by reason to further the *summum bonum* as far as in us lies. This *summum bonum* is formed by the union of the greatest welfare of the rational beings in the world with the supreme condition of their good, or, in other words, by the union of universal happiness with the strictest morality. Now the possibility of one of the factors of this final end, namely that of happiness, is empirically conditioned. It depends upon how nature is constituted—on whether nature harmonizes or not with this end. It is, therefore, from a theoretical point of view problematic; whereas the other factor, namely morality, in respect of which we are independent of the co-operation of nature, is *a priori* assured of its possibility and is dogmatically certain. Accordingly, the fact that we have a final end set before us *a priori* does not meet all the requirements of the objective and theoretical reality of the conception of the final end of rational beings in the world. It is further requisite that creation, that is, the world itself, should, in respect of its real existence, have a final end. Were we able to prove *a priori* that it has such an end, this would supplement the subjective reality of the final end by a reality that is objective. For, if creation has a final end at all, we cannot conceive it otherwise than as harmonizing necessarily with our moral faculty, which is what alone makes the conception of an end possible. But, now, we do find in the world what are certainly ends. In fact physical teleology exhibits ends in such abundance that if we let reason guide our judgement we have after all justification for assuming, as a principle upon which to investigate nature, that there is nothing whatever in nature that has not got its end. Yet in nature itself we search in vain for its own final end. Hence, just as the idea of this final end resides only in reason, so it is only in rational beings that such an end itself can and must be sought as an objective possibility. But the practical reason of these beings does not merely assign this final end: it also determines this conception in respect of the conditions under which a final end of creation can alone be thought by us.

Now the question arises: Is it not possible to substantiate the objective reality of the conception of a final end in a manner that will meet the theoretical requirements of pure reason? This cannot indeed be done apodeictically for the determinant judgement. Yet may it not be done sufficiently for the maxims of theoretical judgement so far as reflective? This is the least that could be demanded of speculative philosophy, which undertakes to connect the ethical end with physical ends by means of the idea of a single end. Yet even this little is still far more than it can ever accomplish.

Let us look at the matter from the standpoint of the principle of the theoretical reflective judgement. To account for the final products of nature, are we not justified in assuming a supreme cause of nature, whose causality in respect of the actuality of nature, or whose act of creation, must be regarded as specifically different from that which is required for the mechanism of nature, or, in other words, as the causality of an understanding? If we are, then, on the above principle, we should say that we were also sufficiently justified in attributing to this original being, not merely ends prevalent throughout nature, but also a final end. This does not serve the purpose of proving the existence of such a being, yet, at least, as was the case in the physical teleology, it is a justification sufficient to convince us that to make the possibility of such a world intelligible to ourselves we must not merely look to ends, but must also ascribe its real existence to an underlying final end.

But a final end is simply a conception of our practical reason and cannot be inferred from any data of experience for the purpose of forming a theoretical estimate of nature, nor can it be applied to the cognition of nature. The only possible use of this conception is for practical reason according to moral laws; and the final end of creation is such a constitution of the world as harmonizes with what we can only definitely specify according to laws, namely, with the final end of our pure practical reason and of this, moreover, so far as intended to be practical. Now, by virtue of the moral law which enjoins this final end upon us, we have reason for assuming from a practical point of view, that is, for the direction of our energies towards the realization of that end, that it is possible, or, in other words, practicable. Consequently we are also justified in assuming a nature of things harmonizing with such a possibility—for this possibility is subject to a condition which does not lie in our power, and unless nature played into our hands the realization of the final end would be impossible. Hence, we have a moral justification for supposing that where we have a world we have also a final end of creation.

This does not yet bring us to the inference from moral teleology to a theology, that is, to the existence of a moral Author of the world, but only to a final end of creation, which is defined in the above manner. Now must we, to account for this creation, that is, for the real existence of things conformable to a *final end,* in the first place admit an intelligent being, and, in the second place, not merely an intelligent being—as had to be admitted to account for the possibility of such things in nature as we are compelled to estimate as *ends*—but one that is also *moral,* as Author of the world, and consequently a *God?* This admission involves a further inference, and one of such a nature that we see that it is intended for the power of judging by conceptions of practical reason, and, being so, is drawn for the reflective, not for the determinant judgement. It is true that with us morally practical reason is essentially different in its principles from technically practical reason. But, while this is so, we cannot pretend to see that the same distinction must also hold in the case of the supreme world-cause, if it is assumed to be an intelligence, and that a particular type of causality is required on its part for the final end, different from that which is requisite simply for natural ends, or that we have, consequently, in our final end, not merely a *moral ground* for admitting a final end of creation, as an effect, but also a *moral being,* as the original source of creation. But it is quite competent for us to assert that *the nature of our faculty of reason is such* that without an Author and Governor of the world, who is also a moral Lawgiver, we are wholly unable to render intelligible to ourselves the possibility of a finality, related *to the moral law* and its object, such as exists in this final end.

The actuality of a supreme morally legislative Author is, therefore, sufficiently proved simply *for the practical employment* of our reason, without determining anything theoretically in respect of its existence. For reason has an end which is prescribed independently by its own peculiar legislation. To make this end possible it requires an idea which removes, sufficiently for the reflective judgement, the obstacle which arises from our inability to carry such legislation into effect when we have a mere physical conception of the world. In that way this idea acquires practical reality, although for speculative knowledge it fails of every means that would procure it reality from a theoretical point of view for explaining nature or determining its supreme cause. For theoretical reflective judgement an intelligent world-cause was sufficiently proved by physical teleology from the ends of nature. For the practical reflective judgement, moral teleology effects the same by means of the conception of a final end, which it is obliged to ascribe to creation from a practical point of view. The objective reality of the idea of God, regarded as a moral Author of the world, cannot, it is true, be substantiated by means of physical ends *alone*. Nevertheless, when the knowledge of those ends is associated with that of the moral end, the maxim of pure reason, which directs us to pursue unity of principles so far as we are able to do so, lends considerable importance to these ends for the purpose of reinforcing the practical reality of that idea by the reality which it already possesses from a theoretical point of view for judgement.

In this connection there are two points which it is most necessary to note for the purpose of preventing a misunderstanding which might easily arise. In the first place, these attributes of the Supreme Being can only be *conceived* by us on an analogy. For how are we to investigate its nature when experience can show us nothing similar? In the second place, such attributes also only enable us to conceive a Supreme Being, not to *cognize* it or to predicate them of it in more or less theoretical manner. For this could only be done on behalf of the determinant judgement, as a faculty of our reason in its speculative aspect, and for the purpose of discerning the *intrinsic nature* of the supreme world-cause. But the only question that concerns us here is as to what conception we have, by the structure of our cognitive faculties, to form of this Being, and whether we have to admit its existence on account of an end, which pure practical reason, apart from any such assumption, enjoins upon us to realize as far as in us lies, and for which we seek likewise to procure simply practical reality, that is to say, merely to be able to regard a contemplated effect as possible. It may well be that the above conception is transcendent for speculative reason. The attributes also which by means of it we ascribe to the Being in question may, objectively used, involve a latent anthropomorphism. Yet the object which we have in view in employing them is not that we wish to determine the nature of that Being by reference to them —a nature which is inaccessible to us—but rather that we seek to use them for determining our own selves and our will. We may name a cause after the conception which we have of its effect—though only in respect of the relation in which it stands to this effect. And we may do this without on that account seeking to define intrinsically the inherent nature of that cause by the only properties known to us of causes of that kind, which properties must be given to us by experience. We may, for instance, ascribe to the soul, among other properties, a *vis locomotiva,* because physical movements are actually started the cause of which lies in the mental representation of them. But this we do without on that account meaning to attribute to the soul the only kind of dynamical force of which we have any knowledge—that is, force exerted by attraction, pressure, impact, and, consequently, by means of a movement, which forces always presuppose a being extended in space. Now in just the same way we have to assume *something* that contains the ground of the possibility and practical reality, or practicability, of a necessary moral final end.

But, looking to the character of the effect expected therefrom, we may conceive this "something" as a wise Being ruling the world according to moral laws. And, conformably to the frame of our cognitive faculties, we are obliged to conceive it as a cause of things that is distinct from nature, for the sole purpose of expressing the *relation* in which this being that transcends all our cognitive faculties stands to the object of *our* practical reason. Yet in so doing we do not mean on that account to ascribe to this being theoretically the only causality of this kind familiar to us, namely an understanding and a will. Nay more, even as to the causality which we think exists in this Being in respect of what is *for us* a final end, we do not mean to differentiate it objectively, as it exists in this being itself, from the causality in respect of nature and all its final modes. On the contrary, we only presume to be able to admit this distinction as one subjectively necessary for our cognitive faculty, constituted as it is, and as valid for the reflective, and not for the objectively determinant, judgement. But, once the question touches practical matters, a *regulative* principle of this kind—one for prudence or wisdom to follow—which directs us to act in conformity with something, as an end, the possibility of which, by the frame of our cognitive faculties, can only be conceived by us in a certain manner, then becomes also *constitutive*. In other words, it is practically determinant, whereas the very same principle regarded as one upon which to estimate the objective possibility of things is in no way theoretically determinant, or, in other words, does not imply that the only type of possibility which our thinking faculty recognizes may also be predicated of the object of our thought. On the contrary, it is a mere *regulative* principle for the use of reflective judgement.

Remark

This moral proof is not in any sense a newly discovered argument, but at the most only an old one in a new form. For its germ was lying in the mind of man when his reason first quickened into life, and it only grew and ever developed with the progressive culture of that faculty. The moment mankind began to reflect upon right and wrong—at a time when men's eyes as yet cast but a heedless regard at the finality of nature, and when they took advantage of it without imagining the presence of anything but nature's accustomed course—one inevitable judgement must have forced itself upon them. It could never be that the issue is all alike, whether a man has acted fairly or falsely, with equity or with violence, albeit to his life's end, as far at least as human eye can see, his virtues have brought him no reward, his transgressions no punishment. It seems as though they perceived a voice within them say that it must make a difference. So there must also have been a lurking notion, however obscure, of something after which they felt themselves bound to strive, and with which such a result would be wholly discordant, or with which, once they regarded the course of the natural world as the sole order of things, they would then be unable to reconcile that significant bent of their minds. Now crude as are the various notions they might form of the way in which such an irregularity could be put straight—and it is one that must be far more revolting to the human mind than the blind chance which some have sought to make the underlying principle of their estimate of nature—there is only one principle upon which they could even conceive it possible for nature to harmonize with the moral law dwelling within them. It is that of a Supreme Cause ruling the world according to moral laws. For a final end within, that is set before them as a duty, and a nature without, that has no final end, though in it the former end is to be actualized, are in open contradiction. I admit they might hatch many absurdities anent the inner nature of that world-cause. But that relation to the moral order in the government of the world always remained the same as is universally comprehensible to the most untutored reason, so far as it treats itself as practical, though speculative reason is far from being able to keep pace with it. Further, in all probability, it was this moral interest that first aroused attentiveness to beauty and the ends of nature. This would be admirably calculated to strengthen the above idea, though it could not supply its foundation. Still less could it dispense with the moral interest;[1] for it is only in relation to the final end that the very study of the ends of nature acquires that immediate interest displayed to so great an extent in the admiration bestowed upon nature without regard to any accruing advantage.

§ 89. *The use of the moral argument*

THE fact that, in respect of all our ideas of the supersensible, reason is restricted to the conditions of its practical employment, is of obvious use in connection with the idea of God.

[1] [Cf. above, p. 522.]

It prevents *theology* from losing itself in the clouds of THEOSOPHY, i.e., in transcendent conceptions that confuse reason, or from sinking into the depths of DEMONOLOGY, i.e., an anthropomorphic mode of representing the Supreme Being. Also it keeps *religion* from falling into *theurgy,* which is a fanatical delusion that a feeling can be communicated to us from other supersensible beings and that we in turn can exert an influence on them, or into *idolatry,* which is a superstitious delusion that one can make oneself acceptable to the Supreme Being by other means than that of having the moral law at heart.[1]

For if the vanity or presumption of those who would argue about what lies beyond the world of sense is allowed to determine even the smallest point theoretically, and so as to extend our knowledge; if any boast is permitted of light upon the existence and constitution of the divine nature, its intelligence and will, and the laws of both these and the attributes which issue therefrom and influence the world: I should like to know at what precise point the line is going to be drawn for these pretensions of reason. From whatever source such light is derived, still more may be expected—if, as the idea is, we only rack our brains. Yet it is only on some principle that bounds can be set to such claims—it is not enough simply to appeal to our experience of the fact that all attempts of the sort have so far miscarried; for that is no disproof of the possibility of a better result. But the only principle possible in this case is either that of admitting that in respect of the supersensible absolutely nothing can be determined theoretically (unless solely by way of bare negation), or that of supposing the existence in our reason of an as yet unopened mine of who knows how vast and enlightening information reserved for us and our posterity. But the result, so far as concerns religion—that is, morality in relation to God as Lawgiver—would be that morality, supposing that the theoretical knowledge of God has to take the lead, must then conform to theology. Thus not alone will an extrinsic and arbitrary legislation on the part of a Supreme Being have to be introduced in place of an immanent and necessary legislation of reason, but, even in such legislation, all the defects of our insight into the divine nature must spread to the ethical code, and religion in this way be divorced from morality and perverted.

What now of the hope of a future life? It is open to us to look to the final end which, in obedience to the injunction of the moral law, we have ourselves to fulfil, and to adopt it as a guide to the verdict of reason on our destination—a verdict which is therefore only regarded as necessary or worthy of acceptance from a practical point of view. But if, instead of so doing, we consult our faculty of theoretical knowledge, then the same lot befalls psychology in this connection as befell theology in the case above. It supplies no more than a negative conception of our thinking being. It tells us that not one of the operations of the mind or manifestations of the internal sense can be explained on materialistic lines; that, accordingly, no enlightening or determinant judgement as to the separate nature of what thinks, or of the continuance or discontinuance of its personality after death, can possibly be passed on speculative grounds by any exercise of our faculty of theoretical knowledge. Thus everything is here left to the teleological estimate of our existence from a point of view that is necessary in the practical sphere, and to the assumption of the continuance of our existence, as a condition required by the final end that is absolutely imposed upon us by reason. Hence in our negative result we see at once a gain—a gain that at first sight no doubt appears a loss. For just as theology can never become theosophy, so rational *psychology* can never become *pneumatology,* as a science that extends our knowledge, nor yet, on the other hand, be in danger of lapsing into any sort of *materialism.* On the contrary, we see that it is really a mere anthropology of the internal sense, a knowledge, that is to say, of our thinking self *as alive,* and that, in the form of a theoretical cognition, it also remains merely empirical. But, as concerned with the problem of our eternal existence, rational psychology is not a theoretical science at all. It rests upon a single inference of moral teleology, just as the entire necessity of its employment arises out of moral teleology and our practical vocation.

§ 90. *The type of assurance in a teleological proof of the existence of God*

WHETHER a proof is derived from immediate empirical presentation of what is to be proved,

[1] A religion is never free from the imputation of idolatry, in a practical sense, so long as the attributes with which it endows the Supreme Being are such that anything that man may do can be taken as in accordance with God's will on any other all-sufficing condition than that of morality. For, however pure and free from sensuous images the form of that conception may be from a theoretical point of view, yet, with such attributes, it is from a practical point of view depicted as an idol—the nature of God's will, that is to say, is represented anthropomorphically.

as in the case of proof by observation of the object or by experiment, or whether it is derived *a priori* by reason from principles, what is primarily required of it is that it should not *persuade,* but *convince,* or at least tend to convince. The argument or inference, in other words, should not be simply a subjective, or aesthetic, ground of assent—a mere semblance—but should be objectively valid and a logical source of knowledge. If it is not this, intelligence is taken in, not won over. An illusory proof of the type in question is brought forward in natural theology—maybe with the best of intentions, but nevertheless with a deliberate concealment of its weakness. The whole host of evidences of an origin of the things of nature according to the principle of ends is marshalled before us, and capital is made out of the purely subjective foundation of human reason. The latter is inclined of its own proper motion, wherever it can do so without contradiction, to think one single principle in place of several. Also, where this principle only provides one, or, it may be, a large proportion, of the terms necessary for defining a conception, it supplements this or these by adding the others, so as to complete the conception of the thing by an arbitrary integration. For naturally, when we find such a number of products of nature pointing us to an intelligent cause, should we not suppose one single such cause in preference to supposing a plurality of them? And why, then, stop at great intelligence, might, and so forth, in this cause, and not rather endow it with omniscience and omnipotence, and, in a word, regard it as one that contains an ample source of such attributes for all possible things? And why not go on and ascribe to this single all-powerful primordial being, not merely the intelligence necessary for the laws and products of nature, but also the supreme ethical and practical reason that belongs to a moral world-cause? For by this completion of the concept we are supplied with a principle that meets the joint requirements alike of insight into nature and moral wisdom—and no objection of the least substance can be brought against the possibility of such an idea. If now, in the course of this argument, the moral springs that stir the mind are touched, and a lively interest imparted to them with all the force of rhetoric—of which they are quite worthy—a persuasion arises of the objective sufficiency of the proof, and, in most cases where it is used, an even beneficent illusion that disdains any examination of its logical accuracy, and in fact abhors and sets its face against logical criticism, as if it sprang from some impious misgiving. Now there is really nothing to say against all this, so long as we only take popular expediency into consideration. But we cannot and should not be deterred from the analysis of the proof into the two heterogeneous elements which this argument involves, namely into so much as pertains to physical, and so much as pertains to moral, teleology. For the fusing of both elements prevents our recognizing where the real nerve of the proof lies, or in what part or in what way it must be reshaped, so that its validity may be able to be upheld under the most searching examination—even though on some points we should be compelled to confess that reason sees but a short way. Hence, the philosopher finds it his duty—supposing that he were even to pay no regard to what he owes to sincerity—to expose the illusion, however wholesome, which such a confusion can produce. He must segregate what is mere matter of persuasion from what leads to conviction—two modes of assent that differ not merely in degree but in kind—so as to be able to present openly in all its clearness the attitude which the mind adopts in this proof, and to subject it frankly to the most rigorous test.

Now a proof which is directed towards conviction may be of one or other of two kinds. It may be intended to decide what the object is *in itself,* or else what it is *for us,* that is, for man in the abstract, according to the rational principles on which it is necessarily estimated by us. It may, in other words, be a proof κατ' ἀλήθειαν or one κατ' ἄνθρωπον—taking the latter word in the broad sense of man in the abstract. In the first case, is is founded on principles adequate for the determinant judgement, in the second, on such as are adequate merely for the reflective judgement. Where, in the latter case, a proof rests simply on theoretical principles, it can never tend towards conviction. But if it is founded on a practical principle of reason, one which, consequently, is universal and necessary, it may well lay claim to a conviction that is sufficient from a practical point of view, that is, to a moral conviction. But a proof *tends towards conviction,* though without producing conviction, if it merely puts us on the road to conviction. This it does where it only involves objective sources of conviction which, while as yet insufficient to produce certitude, are nevertheless of such a kind that they are not subjective grounds of judgement, which, as such, serve merely for persuasion.

Now all arguments that establish a theoretical proof are sufficient either: (1) for proof by logically rigorous *syllogistic inferences;* or, where this is not the case, (2) for inference by *analogy;* or, should even such inference be absent, still (3) for *probable opinion;* or, finally, for what is least of all, (4) the assumption of a merely possible source of explanation as an *hypothesis.* Now I assert that all arguments, without exception, that tend towards theoretical conviction, are powerless to produce any assurance of the above type, from its highest degree to its lowest, *where* the proposition that is to be proved is the real existence of an original being, regarded as a God in the sense appropriate to the complete content of this conception, that is to say, regarded as a *moral* Author of the world, and, consequently, in such a way that the final end of creation is at once derived from Him.

1. The Critique has abundantly shown how the matter stands as regards proof in *strict logical form*—advancing, that is, from universal to particular. No intuition corresponding to the conception of a being which has to be sought beyond nature is possible for us. So far, therefore, as that conception has to be determined theoretically by synthetic predicates, it always remains for us a problematical conception. Hence, there exists absolutely no cognition of such a being that would in the smallest degree enlarge the compass of our theoretical knowledge. The particular conception of a supersensible being cannot possibly be subsumed in any way under the universal principles of the nature of things, so as to allow of its being determined by inference from those principles, for they are solely valid for nature as an object of sense.

2. In the case of two dissimilar things, we may admittedly form some *conception* of one of them by an *analogy*[1] which one bears to the other, and do so even on the point on which they are dissimilar; but from that in which they are dissimilar we cannot draw any *inference* from one to the other on the strength of the analogy—that is, we cannot transfer the mark of the specific difference to the second. Thus, on the analogy of the law of the equality of action and reaction in the mutual attraction and repulsion of bodies, I am able to picture to my mind the social relations of the members of a commonwealth regulated by civil laws; but I cannot transfer to these relations the former specific modes, that is, physical attraction and repulsion, and ascribe them to the citizens, so as to constitute a system called a *state.* In the same way, the causality of the original being may, in its relation to the things of the world, regarded as physical ends, quite properly be conceived on the analogy of an intelligence, regarded as the source of the forms of certain products that we call works of art. For this is only done in the interests of the theoretical or practical use which our cognitive faculty has to make of this conception when dealing with the things in the world. But from the fact that, with the beings of the world, intelligence must be ascribed to the cause of an effect that is considered artificial, we are wholly unable to infer by analogy that, in relation to nature, the very same causality that we perceive in man belongs also to the being which is entirely distinct from nature. The reason is that this touches the precise point of dissimilarity between a cause that is sensuously conditioned in respect of its effects and a supersensible origi-

[1] *Analogy,* in a qualitative sense, is the identity of the relation subsisting between grounds and consequences—causes and effects—so far as such identity subsists despite the specific difference of the things, or of those properties, considered in themselves (i.e., apart from this relation), which are the source of similar consequences. Thus when we compare the formative operations of the lower animals with those of man, we regard the unknown source of such effects in the former case, as compared with the known source of similar effects produced by man, that is by reason, as the analogon of reason. By this we mean to imply that, while the source of the formative capacity of the lower animals, to which we give the name of *instinct,* is in fact specifically different from reason, yet, comparing, say, the constructive work of beavers and men, it stands in a like relation to its effect. But this does not justify me in inferring that, because man employs *reason* for that he constructs, beavers must possess reason also, and in calling this an *inference* from analogy. But from the similar mode of operation on the part of the lower animals, the source of which we are unable directly to perceive, compared with that of man, of which we are immediately conscious, we may quite correctly infer, *on the strength of the analogy,* that the lower animals, like man, act according to *representations,* and are not machines, as Descartes contends, and that, despite their specific difference, they are living beings and as such generally kindred to man. The principle that authorizes us to draw this inference lies in the fact that we have exactly the same reason for putting the lower animals in this respect in the same genus with men as in man for putting men, so far as we look at them from the outside and compare their acts, in the same genus with one another. There is *par ratio.* In the same way the causality of the supreme world-cause may be conceived on the analogy of an understanding, if we compare its final products in the world with the formative works of man, but we cannot, on the strength of the analogy, infer such human attributes in the world-cause. For the principle that would make such a mode of reasoning possible is absent in this case, namely the *paritas rationis* for including the supreme being and man, in relation to their respective causalities, in one and the same genus. The causality of the beings in the world which, like causality by means of understanding, is always sensuously conditioned, cannot be transferred to a being which has no generic conception in common with man beyond that of a thing in the abstract.

nal being. This dissimilarity is implied in the very conception of such a supersensible being, and the distinguishing feature cannot therefore be transferred to it. In this very fact, that I am required to conceive the causality of the Deity only on the analogy of an understanding —a faculty which is not known to us in any other being besides man, subject, as he is, to the conditions of sense—lies the prohibition that forbids me to ascribe to God an understanding in the proper sense of the word.[1]

3. There is no room for *opinion* in *a priori* judgements. Such judgements, on the contrary, enable us to cognize something as quite certain, or else give us no cognition at all. But even where the given premisses from which we start are empirical, as are the natural ends in the present case, yet they cannot help us to form any opinion that extends beyond the world of sense, and to such rash judgements we cannot accord the least claim to probability. For probability is a fraction of a possible certainty distributed over a particular series of grounds—the grounds of the possibility within the series being compared with the sufficient ground of certainty, as a part is compared with a whole. Here the insufficient ground must be capable of being increased to the point of sufficiency. But these grounds, being the determining grounds of the certainty of one and the same judgement, must be of the same order. For unless they are, they would not, when taken together, form a quantum—such as certainty is. Thus one component part cannot lie within the bounds of possible experience and another lie beyond all possible experience. Consequently, since premisses that are simply empirical do not lead to anything supersensible, nothing can supplement the imperfection of such an empirical series. Not the smallest approximation, therefore, occurs in the attempt to reach the supersensible, or a knowledge of it, from such premisses; and consequently no probability enters into a judgement about the supersensible, when it rests on arguments drawn from experience.

4. If anything is intended to serve as an *hypothesis* for explaining the possibility of a given phenomenon, then at least the possibility of that thing must be perfectly certain. We give away enough when, in the case of an hypothesis, we waive the knowledge of actual existence—which is affirmed in an opinion put forward as probable—and more than this we cannot surrender. At least the possibility of what we make the basis of an explanation must be open to no doubt, otherwise there would be no end to empty fictions of the brain. But it would be taking things for granted without anything whatever to go upon, if we were to assume the possibility of a supersensible Being defined according to positive conceptions, for no one of the conditions requisite for cognition, so far as concerns the element dependent on intuition, is given. Hence, all that is left as the criterion of this possibility is the principle of contradiction—which can only prove the possibility of the thought and not of the thought object itself.

The net result is that for the existence of the original being regarded as a Deity, or of the psychic substance, regarded as an immortal soul, it is absolutely impossible for human reason to obtain any proof from a theoretical point of view, so as to produce the smallest degree of assurance. And there is a perfectly intelligible reason for this, since we have no available material for defining the idea of the supersensible, seeing that we should have to draw that material from things in the world of sense, and then its character would make it utterly inappropriate to the supersensible. In the absence, therefore, of all definition, we are left merely with the conception of a not-sensible something containing the ultimate ground of the world of sense. This constitutes no cognition of its intrinsic nature, such as would amplify the conception.

§ 91. *The type of assurance produced by a practical faith*[2]

If we look merely to the manner in which something can be an object of knowledge (*res cognoscibilis*) *for us*, that is, having regard to the subjective nature of our powers of representation, we do not in that case compare our conceptions with the objects, but merely with our faculties of cognition and the use that they are able to make of the given representation from a theoretical or practical point of view. So the question whether something is a cognizable entity or not, is a question which touches, not the possibility of the things themselves, but the possibility of our knowledge of them.

Things *cognizable* are of three kinds: *matters of opinion* (*opiniabile*), *matters of fact* (*scibile*), *and matters of faith* (*mere credibile*).

[1] This does not involve the smallest loss to our representation of the relation in which this Being stands to the world, so far as concerns the consequences, theoretical or practical, of this conception. To seek to inquire into the intrinsic nature of this Being is a curiosity as senseless as idle.

[2] [See the section on "Opinion, Knowledge, and Belief," *Critique of Pure Reason*, p. 240–3.]

1. The objects of mere ideas of reason, being wholly incapable of presentation, on behalf of theoretical knowledge, in any possible experience whatever, are to that extent also things altogether *unknowable*, and, consequently, we cannot even *form an opinion* about them. For to form an opinion *a priori* is absurd on the face of it and the straight road to pure figments of the brain. Either our *a priori* proposition is certain, therefore, or it involves no element of assurance at all. Hence, *matters of opinion* are always objects of an empirical knowledge that is at least intrinsically possible. They are, in other words, objects belonging to the world of sense, but objects of which an empirical knowledge is impossible *for us*, because the degree of empirical knowledge we possess is as it is. Thus the ether of our modern physicists—an elastic fluid interpenetrating all other substances and completely permeating them—is a mere matter of opinion, yet it is in all respects of such a kind that it could be perceived if our external senses were sharpened to the highest degree, but its presentation can never be the subject of any observation or experiment. To assume rational inhabitants of other planets is a matter of opinion; for if we could get nearer the planets, which is intrinsically possible, experience would decide whether such inhabitants are there or not; but as we never shall get so near to them, the matter remains one of opinion. But to entertain an opinion that there exist in the material universe pure embodied thinking spirits is mere romancing—supposing, I mean, that we dismiss from our notice, as well we may, certain phenomena that have been passed off for such. Such a notion is not a matter of opinion at all, but an idea pure and simple. It is what remains over when we take away from a thinking being all that is material and yet let it keep its thought. But whether, when we have taken away everything else, the thought—which we only know in man, that is, in connection with a body—would still remain, is a matter we are unable to decide. A thing like this is a *fictitious logical entity* (*ens rationis ratiocinantis*),[1] not a *rational entity* (*ens rationis ratiocinatae*). With the latter it is anyway possible to substantiate the objective reality of its conception, at least in a manner sufficient for the practical employment of reason, for this employment, which has its peculiar and apodeictically certain *a priori* principles, in fact demands and postulates that conception.

2. The objects that answer to conceptions whose objective reality can be proved are *matters of fact*[2] (*res facti*). Such proof may be afforded by pure reason or by experience, and in the former case may be from theoretical or practical data of reason, but in all cases it must be effected by means of an intuition corresponding to the conceptions. Examples of matters of fact are the mathematical properties of geometrical magnitudes, for they admit of *a priori presentation* for the theoretical employment of reason. Further, things or qualities of things that are capable of being verified by experience, be it one's own personal experience or that of others (supported by evidence), are in the same way matters of fact. But there is this notable point, that one idea of reason, strange to say, is to be found among the matters of fact—an idea which does not of itself admit of any presentation in intuition, or, consequently, of any theoretical proof of its possibility. The idea in question is that of *freedom*. Its reality is the reality of a particular kind of causality (the conception of which would be transcendent if considered theoretically), and as a causality of that kind it admits of verification by means of practical laws of pure reason and in the actual actions that take place in obedience to them, and, consequently, in experience. It is the only one of all the ideas of pure reason whose object is a matter of fact and must be included among the *scibilia*.

3. Objects that must be thought *a priori*, either as consequences or as grounds, if pure practical reason is to be used as duty commands, but which are transcendent for the theoretical use of reason, are mere *matters of faith*. Such is the *summum bonum* which has to be realized in the world through freedom—a conception whose objective reality cannot be proved in any experience possible for us, or, consequently, so as to satisfy the requirements of the theoretical employment of reason, while at the same time we are enjoined to use it for the purpose of realizing that end through pure practical reason in the best way possible, and, accordingly, its possibility must be assumed. This effect which is commanded, *together with the only conditions on which its possibility is conceivable by us*, namely the existence of God and the immortality of the soul, are *matters of faith* (*res fidei*)

[1] [Cf. p. 567.]

[2] I here extend the conception of a matter of fact beyond the usual meaning of the term, and, I think, rightly. For it is not necessary, and indeed not practicable, to restrict this expression to actual experience where we are speaking of the relation of things to our cognitive faculties, as we do not need more than a merely possible experience to enable us to speak of things as objects of a definite kind of knowledge.

and, moreover, are of all objects the only ones that can be so called.[1] For although we have to believe what we can only learn by *testimony* from the experience of others, yet that does not make what is so believed in itself a matter of faith, for with *one* of those witnesses it was personal experience and matter of fact, or is assumed to have been so. In addition it must be possible to arrive at knowledge by this path—the path of historical faith; and the objects of history and geography, as, in general, everything that the nature of our cognitive faculties makes at least a possible subject of knowledge, are to be classed among matters of fact, not matters of faith. It is only objects of pure reason that can be matters of faith at all, and even they must then not be regarded as objects simply of pure speculative reason; for this does not enable them to be reckoned with any certainty whatever among matters, or objects, of that knowledge which is possible for us. They are ideas, that is conceptions, whose objective reality cannot be guaranteed theoretically. On the other hand, the supreme final end to be realized by us, which is all that can make us worthy of being ourselves the final end of a creation, is an idea that has objective reality for us in practical matters, and is a matter. But since we cannot procure objective reality for this conception from a theoretical point of view, it is a mere matter of faith on the part of pure reason, as are also God and immortality, they being the sole conditions under which, owing to the frame of our human reason, we are able to conceive the possibility of that effect of the use of our freedom according to law. But assurance in matters of faith is an assurance from a purely practical point of view. It is a moral faith that proves nothing for pure rational knowledge as theoretical, but only for it as practical and directed to the fulfilment of its obligations. It in no way extends either speculation or the practical rules of prudence actuated by the principle of self-love. If the supreme principle of all moral laws is a postulate, this involves the possibility of its supreme object, and, consequently, the condition under which we are able to conceive such possibility, being also postulated. This does not make the cognition of the latter any knowledge or any opinion of the existence or nature of these conditions, as a mode of theoretical knowledge, but a mere assumption, confined to matters practical and commanded in practical interests, on behalf of the moral use of our reason.

Were we able with any plausibility to make the ends of nature which physical teleology sets before us in such abundance the basis of a *determinate* conception of an intelligent world-cause, the existence of this being would not even then be a matter of faith. For as it would not be assumed on behalf of the performance of our duty, but only for the purpose of explaining nature, it would simply be the opinion and hypothesis best suited to our reason. Now the teleology in question does not lead in any way to a determinate conception of God. On the contrary, such a conception can only be found in that of a moral author of the world, because this alone assigns the final end to which we can attach ourselves only so far as we live in accordance with what the moral law prescribes to us as the final end and, consequently, imposes upon us as a duty. Hence, it is only by relation to the object of our duty, as the condition which makes its final end possible, that the conception of God acquires the privilege of figuring in our assurance as a matter of faith. On the other hand, this very same conception cannot make its object valid as a matter of fact, for, although the necessity of duty is quite plain for practical reason, yet the attainment of its final end, so far as it does not lie entirely in our own hands, is merely assumed in the interests of the practical employment of reason, and, therefore, is not practically necessary in the way duty itself is.[2]

[1] Being a matter of faith does not make a thing an *article of faith,* if by articles of faith we mean such matters of faith as one can be bound to *acknowledge,* inwardly or outwardly—a kind therefore that does not enter into natural theology. For, being matters of faith, they cannot, like matters of fact, depend on theoretical proofs, and, therefore, the assurance is a free assurance, and it is only as such that it is compatible with the morality of the subject.

[2] The final end which we are enjoined by the moral law to pursue is not the foundation of duty. For duty lies in the moral law which, being a formal practical principle, directs categorically, irrespective of the objects of the faculty of desire—the subject-matter of volition—and, consequently, of any end whatever. This formal character of our action—their subordination to the principle of universal validity—which alone constitutes their intrinsic moral worth, lies entirely in our own power; and we can quite easily make abstraction from the possibility or the impracticability of the ends that we are obliged to promote in accordance with that law—for they only form the extrinsic worth of our actions. Thus we put them out of consideration, as what does not lie altogether in our own power, in order to concentrate our attention on what rests in our own hands. But the object in view—the furthering of the final end of all rational beings, namely, happiness so far as consistent with duty—is nevertheless imposed upon us by the law of duty. But speculative reason does not in any way perceive the practicability of that object—whether we look at it from the standpoint of our own physical power or from that of the co-operation of nature. On the contrary, so far as we are able to form a rational judge-

Faith as *habitus,* not as *actus,* is the moral attitude of reason in its assurance of the truth of what is beyond the reach of theoretical knowledge. It is the steadfast principle of the mind, therefore, according to which the truth of what must necessarily be presupposed as the condition of the supreme final end being possible is assumed as true in consideration of the fact that we are under an obligation to pursue that end[1]—and assumed notwithstanding that we have no insight into its possibility, though likewise none into its impossibility. *Faith,* in the plain acceptation of the term, is a confidence of attaining a purpose the furthering of which is a duty, but whose achievement is a thing of which we are unable to *perceive* the possibility—or, consequently, the possibility of what we can alone conceive to be its conditions. Thus the faith that has reference to particular objects is entirely a matter of morality, provided such objects are not objects of possible knowledge or opinion, in which latter case, and above all in matters of history, it must be called *credulity* and not faith. It is a free assurance, not of any matter for which dogmatic proofs can be found for the theoretical determinant judgement, nor of what we consider a matter of obligation, but of that which we assume in the interests of a purpose which we set before ourselves in accordance with laws of freedom. But this does not mean that it is adopted like an opinion formed on inadequate grounds. On the contrary, it is something that has a foundation in reason (though only in relation to its practical employment), and *a foundation that satisfies the purpose of reason.* For without it, when the moral attitude comes into collision with theoretical reason and fails to satisfy its demand for a proof of the possibility of the object of morality, it loses all its stability and wavers between practical commands and theoretical doubts. To be *incredulous* is to adhere to the maxim of placing no reliance on testimony; but a person is *unbelieving* who denies all validity to the above ideas of reason because their reality has no theoretical foundation. Hence, such a person judges dogmatically. But a dogmatic *unbelief* cannot stand side by side with a moral maxim governing the attitude of the mind—for reason cannot command one to pursue an end that is recognized to be nothing but a fiction of the brain. But the case is different with a *doubtful faith.* For, with such a faith, the want of conviction from grounds of speculative reason is only an obstacle—one which a critical insight into the limits of this faculty can deprive of any influence upon conduct and for which it can make amends by a paramount practical assurance.

If we desire to replace certain mistaken efforts in philosophy, and to introduce a different principle, and gain influence for it, it gives great satisfaction to see just how and why such attempts were bound to miscarry.

God, freedom, and the *immortality of the soul* are the problems to whose solution, as their ultimate and unique goal, all the laborious preparations of metaphysics are directed. Now it was believed that the doctrine of freedom was only necessary as a negative condition for practical philosophy, whereas that of God and the nature of the soul, being part of theoretical philosophy, had to be proved independently and separately. Then each of those two conceptions was subsequently to be united with what is commanded by the moral law (which is only possible on terms of freedom) and a religion was to be arrived at in this way. But we perceive at once that such attempts were bound to miscarry. For from simple ontological conceptions of things in the abstract, or of the existence of a

ment on the point, speculative reason must, apart from the assumption of the existence of God and immortality, regard it as a baseless and idle, though well-intentioned, expectation, to hope that mere nature, internal or external, will from such causes bring about such a result of our good conduct, and could it have perfect certainty as to the truth of this judgement, it would have to look on the moral law itself as a mere delusion of our reason in respect of practical matters. But speculative reason is fully convinced that the latter can never happen, whereas those ideas whose object lies beyond nature may be thought without contradiction. Hence for the sake of its own practical law and the task which it imposes, and, therefore, in respect of moral concerns, it must recognize those ideas to be real, in order not to fall into self-contradiction.

[1] It is a confidence in the promise of the moral law. But this promise is not regarded as one involved in the moral law itself, but rather as one which we import into it, and so import on morally adequate grounds. For a final end cannot be commanded by any law of reason, unless reason, though it be with uncertain voice, also promises its attainability, and at the same time authorizes assurance as to the sole conditions under which our reason can imagine such attainability. The very word *fides* expresses this; and it must seem suspicious how this expression and this particular idea get a place in moral philosophy, since it was first introduced with Christianity, and its acceptance might perhaps seem only a flattering imitation of the language of the latter. But this is not the only case in which this wonderful religion has in the great simplicity of its statement enriched philosophy with far more definite and purer conceptions of morality than morality itself could have previously supplied. But once these conceptions are found, they are *freely* approved by reason, which adopts them as conceptions at which it could quite well have arrived itself and which it might and ought to have introduced.

necessary being, we can form absolutely no conception of an original being determined by predicates which admit of being given in experience and which are therefore available for cognition. But should the conception be founded on experience of the physical finality of nature, it could then in turn supply no proof adequate for morality or, consequently, the cognition of a God. Just as little could knowledge of the soul drawn from experience—which we can only obtain in this life—furnish a conception of its spiritual and immortal nature, or, consequently, one that would satisfy morality. *Theology* and *pneumatology,* regarded as problems framed in the interests of sciences pursued by a speculative reason, are in their very implication transcendent for all our faculties of knowledge and cannot, therefore, be established by means of any empirical data or predicates. These two conceptions, both that of God and that of the soul (in respect of its immortality), can only be defined by means of predicates which, although they themselves derive their possibility entirely from a supersensible source, must, for all that, prove their reality in experience, for this is the only way in which they can make possible a cognition of a wholly supersensible being. Now the only conception of this kind to be found in human reason is that of the freedom of man subject to moral laws and, in conjunction therewith, to the final end which freedom prescribes by means of these laws. These laws and this final end enable us to ascribe, the former to the author of nature, the latter to man, the properties which contain the necessary conditions of the possibility of both. Thus it is from this idea that an inference can be drawn to the real existence and the nature of both God and the soul —beings that otherwise would be entirely hidden from us.

Hence, the source of the failure of the attempt to attain to a proof of God and immortality by the merely theoretical route lies in the fact that no knowledge of the supersensible is possible if the path of natural conceptions is followed. The reason why the proof succeeds, on the other hand, when the path of morals, that is, of the conception of freedom, is followed, is because from the supersensible, which in morals is fundamental (i.e., as freedom), there issues a definite law of causality. By means of this law, the supersensible here not alone provides material for the knowledge of the other supersensible, that is of the moral final end and the conditions of its practicability, but it also substantiates its own reality, as a matter of fact, in actions.[1] For that very reason, however, it is unable to afford any valid argument other than from a practical point of view—which is also the only one needful for religion.

There is something very remarkable in the way this whole matter stands. Of the three ideas of pure reason—God, freedom, and immortality—that of freedom is the one and one conception of the supersensible which (owing to the causality implied in it) proves its objective reality in nature by its possible effect there. By this means it makes possible the connection of the two other ideas with nature, and the connection of all three to form a religion. We are thus ourselves possessed of a principle which is capable of determining the idea of the supersensible within us, and, in that way, also of the supersensible without us, so as to constitute knowledge—a knowledge, however, which is only possible from a practical point of view. This is something of which mere speculative philosophy—which can only give a simply negative conception even of freedom—must despair. Consequently the conception of freedom, as the root-conception of all unconditionally-practical laws, can extend reason beyond the bounds to which every natural, or theoretical, conception must remain hopelessly restricted.

General Remark on Teleology

If we ask how the moral argument, which only proves the existence of God as a matter of faith for practical pure reason, ranks with the other arguments in philosophy, the value of the entire stock of the latter may be readily estimated. It turns out that we are left with no choice here, but that philosophy in its theoretical capacity must of its own accord resign all its claims in the face of an impartial critique.

Philosophy must lay the first foundations of all assurance on what is matter of fact, unless such assurance is to be entirely baseless. Hence, the only difference that can arise in the proof is on the point of whether an assurance in the consequence inferred from this matter of fact may be based upon it in the form of *knowledge* for theoretical cognition or in the form of *faith* for practical cognition. All matters of fact come under the head either of the *conception of nature,* which proves its reality in objects of sense that are given, or might be given, antecedently to all conceptions of nature; or else of the *conception*

[1] [Cf. pp. 604, 608; Also: *Fundamental Principles of the Metaphysic of Morals,* pp. 253, 254, 264, 270, 272, 273, 275; Also: *The Critique of Practical Reason,* pp. 291, 297, 302, 308, 310, 314, 336.]

of freedom, which sufficiently substantiates its reality by the causality of reason in respect of certain effects in the world of sense that are possible by means of that causality—a causality which reason indisputably postulates in the moral law. Now the conception of nature—which pertains merely to theoretical cognition—is either metaphysical and wholly *a priori;* or physical, that is *a posteriori* and of necessity only conceivable by means of determinate experience. Hence, the metaphysical conception of nature—which does not presuppose any determinate experience—is ontological.

Now *the ontological proof* of the existence of God, drawn from the conception of an original being, may take one or other of two lines. It may start from the ontological predicates which alone enable that being to be completely defined in thought, and thence infer its absolutely necessary existence. Or it may start from the absolute necessity of the existence of something or other, whatever it may be, and thence infer the predicates of the original being. For an original being implies by its very conception—so that it may not be derived—the unconditional necessity of its existence and—so that this necessity may be formulated to the mind—its determination through and through by its conception. Now these two requirements were both supposed to be found in the conception of the ontological idea of an *ens realissimum* or *superlatively real being.* Thus there arose two metaphysical arguments.

The proof which is based on the purely metaphysical conception of nature—the strictly ontological proof, as it is called—started from the conception of the superlatively real being and thence inferred its absolutely necessary real existence, the argument being that unless it existed it would lack one reality, namely, real existence. The other, which is also called the metaphysico-*cosmological* proof, started from the necessity of the real existence of something or other—and as much as that I must certainly concede, since an existence is given to me in my own self-consciousness—and thence inferred its complete determination as the superlatively real being. For, as was argued, while all that has real existence is determined in all respects, what is absolutely necessary—that is, what we have to cognize as such, and, consequently, cognize *a priori*—must be completely determined *by its conception;* but such thorough determination can only be found in the conception of a superlatively real thing. The sophistries in both these inferences need not be exposed here, as that has already been done in another place. All I need now say is that, let such proofs be defended with all the forms of dialectical subtlety you please, yet they will never descend from the schools and enter into every-day life or be able to exert the smallest influence on ordinary healthy intelligence.

The proof which is founded on a conception of nature, which, while it can only be empirical, is yet intended to lead beyond the bounds of nature as the complex of objects of sense, can only be the proof derived from the *ends* of nature. Though the conception of these ends, no doubt, cannot be given *a priori,* but only through experience, this proof promises such a conception of the original ground of nature as alone, of all those that we can conceive, is appropriate to the supersensible—the conception, namely, of a supreme intelligence as cause of the world. And in point of fact, so far as principles of the reflective judgement go, that is to say, in respect of our human faculty of cognition, it is as good as its word. But, now, is this proof in a position to give us that conception of a *supreme* or independent, intelligent being, when further understood as that of a God, that is an Author of a world subject to moral laws, and so as, therefore, to be sufficiently definite for the idea of a final end of the existence of the world? That is the question on which everything turns, whether we are looking for a theoretically adequate conception of the Original Being on behalf of our knowledge of nature as a whole, or for a practical conception for religion.

This argument, drawn from physical teleology, is deserving of all respect. It appeals to the intelligence of the man in the street with the same convincing force as it does to the most subtle thinker; and a Reimarus won undying honour for himself by elaborating this line of thought, which he did with his characteristic profundity and clearness in that work of his which has not yet been excelled. But what is the source of the powerful influence which this proof exerts upon the mind, and exerts especially on a calm and perfectly voluntary assent arising from the cool judgement of reason—for emotion and exaltation of the mind produced by the wonders of nature may be put down to persuasion? Is it physical ends, which all point to an inscrutable intelligence in the world-cause? No, they would be an inadequate source, as they do not satisfy the needs of reason or an inquiring mind. For reason asks: For what end do all those things of nature exist which exhibit art-forms? And for what end does man himself exist—man with whose consideration we are inevitably brought to a halt, he being the ultimate end of nature, so far as we can conceive? Why does this universal nature exist, and what is the final end of all its wealth and variety of art? To suggest that it was made for enjoyment, or to be gazed at, surveyed and admired—which, if the matter ends there, amounts to no more than enjoyment of a particular kind—as though enjoyment was the ultimate and final end of the presence here of the world and of man himself, cannot satisfy reason. For a personal worth, which man can only give to himself, is pre-supposed by reason, as the sole condition upon which he and his existence can be a final end. In the absence of this personal worth—which alone admits of a definite conception—the ends of nature do not dispose of the question. In particular they cannot offer any *definite conception* of the supreme being as an all-sufficient (and for that reason one and, in the strict sense of the term, *Supreme*) Being, or of the laws according to which its intelligence is cause of the world.

That the physico-teleological proof[1] produces conviction just as if it were also a theological proof is, therefore, not due to the use of ends of nature as so many empirical evidences of a *supreme* intelligence. On the contrary it is the moral evidence, which dwells in every man and affects him so deeply, that insinuates itself into the reasoning. One does not stop at the being that manifests itself with such incomprehensible art in the ends of nature, but one goes on to ascribe to it a final end and, consequently, wisdom—although the perception of such physical ends does not entitle one to do this. Thus the above argument is arbitrarily supplemented in respect of its inherent defect. It is, therefore, really the moral proof that alone produces the conviction, and even this only does so from the point of view of moral considerations to which every one in the depth of his heart assents. The sole merit of the physico-teleological proof is that it leads the mind in its survey of the world to take the path of ends, and guides it in this way to an *intelligent* author of the world. At this point, then, the moral relation to ends and the idea of a like lawgiver and author of the world, in the form of a theological conception, though in truth purely an extraneous addition, seems to grow quite naturally out of the physico-teleological evidence.

Here the matter may be let rest at the popular *statement of the case*. For where ordinary sound understanding confuses two distinct principles, and draws its correct conclusion in point of fact only from one of them, it generally finds it difficult, if their separation calls for much reflection, to dissociate one from the other as heterogeneous principles. But, besides, the moral argument for the existence of God does not, strictly speaking, merely as it were *supplement* the physico-teleological so as to make it a complete proof. Rather is it a distinct proof which *compensates* for the failure of the latter to produce conviction. For the physico-teleological argument cannot in fact do anything more than direct reason in its estimate of the source of nature and its contingent but admirable order, which is only known to us through experience, and draw its attention to a cause that acts according to ends and is as such the source of nature—a cause which by the structure of our cognitive faculty we must conceive as intelligent—and in this way make it more susceptible to the influence of the moral proof. For what the latter conception needs is so essentially different from anything that is to be found in or taught by physical conceptions that it requires a special premiss and proof entirely independent of the foregoing if the conception of the original being is to be specified sufficiently for theology and its existence inferred. The moral proof (which of course only proves the existence of God when we take the practical, though also indispensable, side of reason into account) would, therefore, continue to retain its full force were we to meet with no material at all in the world, or only ambiguous material, for physical teleology. We can imagine rational beings finding themselves in the midst of a nature such as to show no clear trace of organization, but only the effects of a mere mechanism of crude matter, so that, looking to them and to the variability of some merely contingently final forms and relations, there would appear to be no reason for inferring an intelligent author. In this nature there would then be nothing to suggest a physical teleology. And yet reason, while receiving no instruction here from physical conceptions, would find in the conception of freedom, and the ethical ideas founded thereon, a ground, sufficient for practice, for postulating the conception of the original being appropriate to those ideas, that is, as a Deity, and nature, including even our own existence, as a final end answering to freedom and its laws, and for doing so in consideration of the indispensable command of practical reason. However the fact that in the actual world abundant material for

[1] [Cf. *Critique of Pure Reason*, p. 187.]

physical teleology exists to satisfy the rational beings in it—a fact not antecedently necessary—serves as a desirable confirmation of the moral argument, so far as nature can adduce anything analogous to the ideas of reason (moral ideas in this case). For the conception of a supreme cause that possesses intelligence—a conception that is far from sufficient for a theology—acquires by that means such reality as is sufficient for the reflective judgement. But this conception is not required as a foundation of the moral proof; nor can the latter proof be used for completing the former, which of itself does not point to morality at all, and making it *one* entire proof by continuing the train of reasoning on the same fundamental lines. Two such heterogeneous principles as nature and freedom cannot but yield two different lines of proof—while the attempt to derive the proof in question from nature will be found inadequate for what is meant to be proved.

If the premisses of the physico-teleological argument went the length of the proof sought, the result would be very gratifying to speculative reason. For they would afford hope of producing a theology—that being the name one would have to give to a theoretical knowledge of the divine nature and its existence sufficient for explaining both the constitution of the world and the distinctive scope of the moral laws. Similarly, if psychology was sufficient to enable us to attain to a knowledge of the immortality of the soul, it would open the door to a pneumatology which would be equally acceptable to reason. But, however much it might flatter the vanity of an idle curiosity,[1] neither of the two fulfil the desire of reason in respect of theory, which would have to be based on a knowledge of the nature of things. But whether they do not better fulfil their final objective purpose, the first in the form of theology, the second in the form of anthropology, when both founded on the moral principle, namely that of freedom, and adapted, therefore, to the practical employment of reason, is a different question, and one which we have here no need to pursue farther.

But the reason why the physico-teleological argument does not go the length that theology requires is that it does not, and cannot, give any conception of the original being that is sufficiently definite for that purpose. Such a conception has to be derived entirely from a different quarter, or (at least) you must look elsewhere to supplement the defects of the conception by what is an arbitrary addition. You infer an intelligent world-cause from the great finality of natural forms and their relations. But what is the degree of this intelligence? Beyond doubt, you cannot assume that it is the highest possible intelligence; for to do so you would have to see that a greater intelligence than that of which you perceive evidences in the world is inconceivable, which means attributing omniscience to yourself. In the same way you infer from the greatness of the world a very great might on the part of its author. But you will acknowledge that this has only comparative significance for your power of comprehension and that, since you do not know all that is possible, so as to compare it with the magnitude of the world, so far as known to you, you cannot infer the omnipotence of its author from so small a standard, and so forth. Now this does not bring you to any definite conception of an original being suitable for a theology. For that conception can only be found in the thought of the totality of the perfections associated with an intelligence, and for this merely *empirical* data can give you no assistance whatever. But, apart from a determinate conception of this kind, you can draw no inference to a *single* intelligent original being; whatever your purpose, you can only suppose one. Now, certainly, one may quite readily give you the liberty of making an arbitrary addition—since reason raises no valid objection—and saying that where one meets with so much perfection one may well suppose all perfection to be united in a unique world-cause; because reason can turn such a definite principle to better account both theoretically and practically. But then you cannot cry up this conception of the original being as one which you have proved, since you have only assumed it in the interests of a better employment of reason. Hence all lament or impotent rage on account of the supposed enormity of casting a doubt on the conclusiveness of your chain of reasoning is idle bluster. It would much like us to believe that the doubt that is freely expressed as to the validity of your argument is a questioning of sacred truth, so that under this cover its weakness may pass unnoticed.

On the other hand, moral teleology, whose foundations are no less firm than those of physical teleology, and which in fact should be regarded as in a better position, seeing that it rests *a priori* on principles that are inseparable from our reason, leads to what the possibility of a theology requires, namely to a definite

[1] [Cf. p. 603 note.]

conception of the supreme cause as one that is the cause of the world in its accordance with moral laws, and, consequently, of such a cause as satisfies our moral final end. Now that is a cause that requires nothing less than omniscience, omnipotence, omnipresence, and so forth, as the natural attributes characterizing its operation. These attributes must be thought as annexed to the moral final end which is infinite, and, accordingly, as adequate to that end. Thus moral teleology can alone furnish the conception of a *unique* Author of the world suitable for a theology.

In this way, theology also leads directly to *religion,* that is *the recognition of our duties as divine commands.* For it is only the recognition of our duty and of its content—the final end enjoined upon us by reason—that was able to produce a definite conception of God. This conception is, therefore, from its origin indissolubly connected with obligation to that Being. On the other hand, even supposing that by pursuing the theoretical path one could arrive at a definite conception of the original being, namely, as simple cause of nature, one would afterwards encounter considerable difficulty in finding valid proofs for ascribing to this being a causality in accordance with moral laws, and might, perhaps, not be able to do so at all without resorting to arbitrary interpolation. Yet, if the conception of such causality is left out, that would-be theological conception can form no basis for the support of religion. Even if a religion could be established on these theoretical lines, yet in what touches disposition, which is the essential element in religion, it would really be a different religion from one in which the conception of God and the practical conviction of His existence springs from root-ideas of morality. For if omnipotence, omniscience, and so forth, on the part of an Author of the world, were conceptions given to us from another quarter, and if, regarded in that light, we had to take them for granted for the purpose only of applying our conceptions of duties to our relation to such Author, then these latter conceptions would inevitably betray strong traces of compulsion and forced submission. But what of the alternative? What if the final end of our true being is delineated to our minds quite freely, and in virtue of the precept of our own reason, by a reverence for the moral law? Why, then, we accept into our moral perspective a cause harmonizing with that end and with its accomplishment, and accept it with deepest veneration—wholly different from any pathological fear—and we willingly bow down before it.[1]

But why should it be of any consequence to us to have a theology at all? Well, as to this, it is quite obvious that it is not necessary for the extension or rectification of our knowledge of nature or, in fact, for any theory whatever. We need theology solely on behalf of religion, that is to say, the practical or, in other words, moral employment of our reason, and need it as a subjective requirement. Now if it turns out that the one and only argument which leads to a definite conception of the object of theology is itself a moral argument, the result will not seem strange. But, more than that, we shall not feel that the assurance produced by this line of proof falls in any way short of the final purpose it has in view, provided we are clear on the point that an argument of this kind only proves the existence of God in a way that satisfies the moral side of our nature, that is, from a practical point of view. Speculation does not here display its force in any way, nor does it enlarge the borders of its realm. Also the surprise at the fact that we here assert the possibility of a theology, and the alleged contradiction in that assertion with what the Critique of speculative reason said of the categories, will disappear on close inspection. What that Critique said was that the categories can only produce knowledge when applied to objects of sense, and that they can in no way do so when applied to the supersensible. But, be it observed that while the categories are here used on behalf of the knowledge of God, they are so used solely for practical, not for theoretical purposes, that is they are not directed to the intrinsic, and for us inscrutable, nature of God. Let me take this opportunity of putting an end to the misinterpretation of the above doctrine in the Critique—a doctrine which is very necessary, but which, to the chagrin of blind dogmatists, relegates reason to its proper bounds. With this object I here append the following elucidation.

If I ascribe *motive* force to a body, and conceive it, therefore, by means of the category of *causality,* then at the same time and by the

[1] Both the admiration for beauty and the emotion excited by the profuse variety of ends of nature, which a reflective mind is able to feel prior to any clear representation of an intelligent author of the world, have something about them akin to a *religious* feeling. Hence they seem primarily to act upon the moral feeling (of gratitude and veneration towards the unknown cause) by means of a mode of critical judgement analogous to the moral mode, and therefore to affect the mind by exciting moral ideas. It is then that they inspire that admiration which is fraught with far more interest than mere theoretical observation can produce.

same means I *cognize* it; that is to say, I determine the conception which I have of it as an object in general by means of what applies to it in the concrete as an object of sense (this being the condition of the possibility of the relation in question). Thus, suppose the dynamical force that I ascribe to it is that of repulsion, then—even though I do not as yet place beside it another body against which it exerts this force—I may predicate of it a place in space, further an extension or space possessed by the body itself, and, besides, a filling of this space by the repelling forces of its parts, and, finally, the law regulating this filling of space—I mean the law that the force of repulsion in the parts must decrease in the same ratio as the extension of the body increases, and as the space which it fills with the same parts and by means of this force is enlarged. On the other hand, if I form a notion of a supersensible being as *prime mover,* and thus employ the category of causality in consideration of the same mode of action in the world, namely, the movement of matter, I must not then conceive it to be at any place in space, or to be extended, nay I am not even to conceive it as existing in time at all or as coexistent with other beings. Accordingly, I have no forms of thought whatever that could interpret to me the condition under which movement derived from this being as its source is possible. Consequently, from the predicate of cause, as prime mover, I do not get the least concrete cognition of it: I have only the representation of a something containing the source of the movements in the world. And as the relation in which this something, as cause stands to these movements, does not give me anything further that belongs to the constitution of the thing which is cause, it leaves the conception of this cause quite empty. The reason is that with predicates that only get their object in the world of sense I may no doubt advance to the existence of something that must contain the source of these predicates, but I cannot advance to the determination of the conception of this something as a supersensible being, a conception that excludes all those predicates. If, therefore, I make the category of causality determinate by means of the conception of a *prime mover,* it does not help me in the slightest to cognize what God is. But maybe I shall fare better if I take a line from the order of the world and proceed, not merely to *conceive* the causality of the supersensible being as that of a supreme *intelligence,* but also to *cognize* it by means of this determination of the conception in question; for then the troublesome terms of space and extension drop out. Beyond all doubt, the great finality present in the world compels us to *conceive* that there is a supreme cause of this finality and one whose causality has an intelligence behind it. But this in no way entitles us to *ascribe* such intelligence to that cause. (Thus, for instance, we are obliged to conceive the eternity of God as an existence in all time, because we can form no other conception of mere existence than that of a magnitude, or, in other words, than as duration. Similarly we have to conceive the divine omnipotence as an existence in all places, in order to interpret to ourselves God's immediate presence in respect of things external to one another. All this we do without, however, being at liberty to ascribe any of these thought-forms to God as something cognized in Him.) If I determine the causality of man in respect of certain products that are only explicable by reference to intentional finality, by conceiving it as an intelligence on his part, I need not stop there, but I can ascribe this predicate to him as a familiar attribute of man and thereby cognize him. For I know that intuitions are given to the senses of man, and by means of understanding are brought under a conception and thus under a rule; that this conception contains only the common mark, letting the particular drop out, and is therefore discursive; that the rules for bringing representations under the general form of a consciousness are given by understanding antecedently to those intuitions, and so on. Accordingly, I ascribe this attribute to man as one whereby I *cognize* him. But supposing, now that I seek to *conceive* a supersensible being (God) as Intelligence, while this is not alone allowable but unavoidable if I am to exercise certain functions of my reason, I have no right whatever to flatter myself that I am in a position to ascribe intelligence to that being and thereby to *cognize* it by one of its attributes. For in that case I must omit all the above conditions under which I know an intelligence. Consequently, the predicate that is only available for the determination of man is quite inapplicable to a supersensible object. Hence we are quite unable to cognize what God is by means of any such definite causality. And it is so with all categories. They can have no significance whatever for knowledge theoretically considered, unless they are applied to objects of possible experience. But I am able to form a notion even of a supersensible being on the analogy of an understanding—nay must do so when I look to certain other considerations—without, however, thereby desiring to cognize it theoretically. I refer to the case of this mode of its causality having to do with an effect in the world that is fraught with an end which is morally necessary but for creatures of sense unrealizable. For, in that case, a knowledge of God and His existence, that is to say a theology, is possible by means of attributes and determinations of this causality merely conceived in Him according to analogy, and this knowledge has all requisite reality in a practical relation, but also *in respect only of this relation*, that is, in relation to morality. An ethical theology is therefore quite possible. For while morality without theology may certainly carry on with its own rule, it cannot do so with the final purpose which this very rule enjoins, unless it throws reason to the winds as regards this purpose. But a theological ethics—on the part of pure reason—is impossible, seeing that laws which are not originally given by reason itself, and the observance of which it does not bring about as a practical capacity, cannot be moral. In the same way a theological physics would be a monstrosity, because it would not bring forward any laws of nature but rather ordinances of a supreme will, whereas a physical, or, properly speaking, physico-teleological, theology can at least serve as a propaedeutic to theology proper, since by means of the study of physical ends, of which it presents a rich supply, it awakens us to the idea of a final end which nature cannot exhibit. Consequently it can make us alive to the need of a theology which should define the conception of God sufficiently for the highest practical employment of reason, though it cannot produce a theology or find evidences adequate for its support.

PRINTED IN U.S.A.